June 27–30, 2017
Singapore

Association for Computing Machinery

Advancing Computing as a Science & Profession

C&C 2017

Proceedings of the 2017 ACM SIGCHI Conference on Creativity and Cognition

Sponsored by:

ACM SIGCHI

Supported by:

National Gallery Singapore, Art Science Museum, JetBrains, Singapore Exhibition & Convention Bureau, NSF, & YourSingapore

Association for Computing Machinery

Advancing Computing as a Science & Profession

The Association for Computing Machinery
2 Penn Plaza, Suite 701
New York, New York 10121-0701

ISBN: 978-1-4503-4403-6 (Digital)

ISBN: 978-1-4503-5607-7 (Print)

Additional copies may be ordered prepaid from:

ACM Order Department
PO Box 30777
New York, NY 10087-0777, USA

Phone: 1-800-342-6626 (USA and Canada)
+1-212-626-0500 (Global)
Fax: +1-212-944-1318
E-mail: acmhelp@acm.org
Hours of Operation: 8:30 am – 4:30 pm ET

Printed in the USA

Welcome to ACM C&C 2017 in Singapore!

Welcome to the Association for Computing Machinery Creativity & Cognition 2017 conference. We are thrilled to host this year's conference series in the Lion City of Singapore; this is the first time ACM C&C comes to Asia. Singapore is home to 5.5 million multicultural people and, in addition to being a global shipping and financial center and having a tropical climate, it is globally renowned for its technology, modern culture, and Asian art scene. Beyond this, Singapore hosts one of the most amazing culinary scenes in the world where any meal, inexpensive or pricey, will be a great experience.

The 2017 conference is being held downtown with the technical program at the National Gallery of Singapore with its corresponding art exhibit at the ArtScience Museum. The National Gallery was opened in 2015 built from two former national monuments, the former Supreme Court Building and old City Hall. The first of its kind ArtScience Museum will host the art exhibition for a week; it's building, designed by Moshe Safdie to resemble a lotus flower, sits a short walk away from the National Gallery on the Marina Bay.

We will start the week on Tuesday the 27th of June with our workshops and graduate student symposium. The technical program will start the next day with a reception hosted in the National Gallery's deck with sweeping views of downtown. Thursday evening will take us to the ArtScience Museum to see our exhibit and performances. This year's conference theme is Lifelong Creativity, Learning, and Innovation. The theme reflects our belief that creativity is a lifelong pursuit rather than a transient goal and we have an amazing program following that theme. The theme is fueled by world-renowned keynote speakers: Kumiyo Nakaoji from Kyoto University, Elizabeth F. Churchill from Google, and an award winning Singaporean comic artist/illustrator Sonny Liew.

Nothing happens in a vacuum and we have to thank our core organization committee who all contributed to the conference's success: Ellen Do, Alex Mitchell, Brian Bailey, Aisling Kelliher, Steven Dow, Markéta Dolejšová, Marcia Nancy Mauro-Flude, Honor Harger, Michael Bernstein, Cati Boulanger, Elizabeth F. Churchill, Kurt Luther, Lee Jung Joo, Will Odom, Jochen Huber, Pablo Cesar, and Christie Han.

As General Chairs, we also thankful for local support and cooperation from the Singapore Tourism Board, the National Gallery, and the ArtScience Museum.

Shiok!

David A. Shamma, Centrum Wiskunde & Informatica, Amsterdam.
Jude Yew, National University of Singapore, Singapore.
ACM C&C 2017 General Chairs

Ellen Yi-Luen Do, National University of Singapore & Georgia Tech
ACM C&C 2017 Associate Chair

Program Chair Welcome

Welcome to CC2017 and to Singapore! We have an amazing array of artwork and technical content for this year's conference program. The program includes 25 full papers and 2 notes (94 submissions), 5 pictorials (12 submissions), 5 posters (15 submissions), 6 technology demonstrations (11 submissions), 3 workshops (6 submissions), 24 artworks (55 submissions), and 13 graduate student symposium papers. The topics of the submissions were diverse, but the keywords most frequently selected by authors included collaboration, education and learning, crowdsourcing, creativity support, design methods, and qualitative methods of inquiry.

Authors from a diverse set of countries participated in the call for submissions. Across all the tracks (based on the country of residence reported by the first-authors of submissions), authors residing in Singapore accounted for 12% of all submissions, while authors residing in the U.S. accounted for 30% of submissions. These were followed by the United Kingdom (9%), Australia (8%), Japan (5%), China (4%), Portugal (4%), Netherlands (4%), Denmark (4%), Republic of Korea (3%), and Slovenia (3%). Additional participation came from authors residing in Austria, Bangladesh, Finland, Germany, India, Israel, Malaysia, Mexico, Norway, Saudi Arabia, Sri Lanka, Sweden, Taiwan, and Turkey. We thank all of the authors and artists around the globe for their efforts in developing and submitting content to the conference.

The conference committee developed several innovations this year. First, we introduced a new track called *Pictorials*. In technical papers, visual content such as images and illustrations are developed in support of the prose. A pictorial inverts this relationship: the visual content is the contribution and the prose is written in support of that content. We thank the pictorial chairs, Lee Jung Joo (National University of Singapore) and Will Odom (Simon Fraser University), for their leadership in bringing the idea for this new track to the conference. We also wanted attendees to view this content on an equal footing as the technical papers, and so you will see the pictorials placed alongside the technical papers and notes in the main program, and the pictorials will be presented with equal time. We look forward to seeing more Pictorials in the C&C conference in the years ahead.

Second, the papers chairs, Aisling Kelleher (Virginia Tech) and Steven Dow (University of California at San Diego), continued the emphasis from 2015 to acquire competent, thorough, and thoughtful reviews. This was accomplished in large part by the papers chairs recruiting 29 people with expertise in the arts, design, computer science, psychology, media, and engineering to form an all-star program committee. New to 2017, the papers chairs developed a review process in which each submission received four reviews: two from external reviewers, one from a member of the program committee, and a meta-review from another program committee member. This process balanced acquiring external perspectives with the local expertise of the committee. We hope all of the authors were able to benefit from the reviews they received.

Third, for the first time in 2017, we separated the posters and technology demonstrations into their own individual tracks. The purpose was to simplify the submission and review process, and allow the respective chairs to better direct their attention to managing a single category of content.

The final innovation to share is that the organizing committee strived to develop an organizational memory for the conference. This was accomplished by using an open cloud-based hosting platform to share and archive the planning documents, calls for papers, program communications, and funding proposals. We hope future organizers will benefit from and continue this effort.

A conference relies on the hard work of volunteers. We therefore deeply appreciate and thank all of the program committee members and reviewers who helped select the content for this year's conference. A special thanks go to the graduate student symposium chairs, Kurt Luther (Virginia Tech) and Elizabeth Churchill (Google), who were able to acquire financial support from the U.S. National Science Foundation (NSF), and we thank the NSF for supporting tomorrow's leaders in the creativity and cognition community. A huge thank you also goes to the Art Program chairs, Marcia Nancy Mauro-Flude and Markéta Dolejšová, both from the National University of Singapore, who accepted the challenge of leading the art program at a late stage. We all thank you for your leadership and many sleepless nights to curate a spectacular art program for the conference. We also thank Christie Han, Student Volunteer Chair and Graphic Designer for C&C, and all the wonderful Student Volunteers who keep the conference running smoothly.

Brian Bailey, University of Illinois at Urbana–Champaign
ACM C&C 2017 Program Chair

Welcome to *Microbites of Innovation*!

Microbites of Innovation, ArtScience Museum, Singapore, 27 June - 2 July

Microbites of Innovation brings together a unique selection of international authors working in the intersection of Art, Design and HCI. The art track theme proposes a exigent mirroring of the C&C 2017 main theme 'Lifelong Creativity, Learning and Innovation'. Computational machinery no doubt mirrors the world back in a manifold of ways - areas of Human Computer Interaction (HCI) and innovations in artistic research with microcomputing continually transforms the time-tested *looking glass.*

With this in mind the showcase responds to the emergent conditions of a networked world - a realm increasingly transmitted through ubiquitous fibers, decoded systems, and micro-bytes of (bio)technological advancement. Bringing the exacting field of curation into the fold whilst working at the intersections of Performance, Art, Design and HCI, makes these reflections ever more polarizing. Our curatorial premise posits that art and design practices in HCI should critically address current technopolitics and all the while create a space for *ivresse* and the envisioning of alternative frameworks and perspectives.

It is difficult to find consensus on what art is, or is not, but for the purposes of the C&C 2017 art track we define it as artifact or experiential framework that prompt engagements that have measurable effect on the physical world. The art chair's duty and key role is the transmutation of information through selecting objects and experiences in a manner that navigates new pathways in the presentation of bleeding edge creative arts research. The art track curators invited proposals from those artists who drew upon critical and speculative methods to scrutinize techno-utopian visions of a present and near future societies.

The showcased artworks contribute to the debate on the role of human and non-human cognition in contemporary computer culture - specifically on how this is shaped by our individual and social histories, cultures and experiences. So often curators find the building enclosing an exhibition an annoyance (Ulrich Obrist, 2006, p.205). As a corollary, C&C 2017 premieres at the ArtScience Museum Singapore—its physical shape is embraced, forming a white lotus flower, which traditionally represents a state of being awakened—is overwhelmingly pertinent here. However, it must not be eschewed that a white lotus is also associated with the pacification of one's nature—which crucially is an extremely dominant but rarely addressed feature of Singapore's artistic milieu, for the non locals is rarely apparent and often more parochially defined by the well-worn 'chewing gum' cultural stigma. We advocate that this cliché could be best contemplated as a metaphor - the world of creative arts and design research is sticky, messy, complex, and full of uncertainties. While bringing together authors working in various areas of art, design and science research and practice, the *Microbites of Innovation* showcase aims to embrace such matted practices and challenge traditional ways of thinking about academic knowledge production.

Translating from the 'art world norms' to the 'scientific academic field norms' for this particular event has been an insightful and challenging exercise, especially considering that the showcase is open to the general public and an international audience besides the "regular" C&C conference attendees. The ambition to host the public art track program at such a prominent venue as ArtScience Museum Singapore show an intention to translate an engaging experience for all spectators and prompt wider conversations beyond the echo chamber of the academic HCI community.

Microbites of Innovation is by far the largest and most complex art track in the history of C&C, which can be seen as a testimony of the growing role of arts and design based research in academic HCI. Curating a showcase of this scope would not be possible without the immense contribution of ACM, C&C 2017 general chairs, external mentors Nick Smithies, Aaron Horsley, Dr. Camille Baker, Honor Harger Executive Director and Nina Ernst Associate Director of ArtScience Museum, who have all generously given professional advice towards the showcase realization.

We look forward to greeting you all for our opening preview and performance evening on Thursday 29 June. For our full program of events, description of artworks and other information about the art track please visit: http://cc.acm.org/2017/microbites

Marcia Nancy Mauro-Flude, National University of Singapore.
Markéta Dolejšová, National University of Singapore.
ACM C&C 2017 Art Track Co-Chairs

Table of Contents

Keynote 2 by Elizabeth F. Churchill

Session Chair: David A. Shamma *(CWI)*

Session: Enhancing Creative Performance

Session Chair: Celine Latulipe *(University of North Carolina at Charlotte)*

Session: Creativity in the (Actual) Wild

Session Chair: Kazjon Grace *(University of North Carolina at Charlotte)*

Posters and Technology Demonstrations

Session Chair: Pablo Cesar *(CWI)* & Brian Bailey *(University of Illinois at Urbana)*

Session: Creating and Sharing Experiences

Session Chair: Nanna Inie *(Aarhus University)*

Session: Sensing and Visualizing Experience

Session Chair: Sam Ferguson *(University of Technology Sydney)*

Session: Sense Making for Creativity

Session Chair: Jenny Waycott *(University of Melbourne)*

Keynote 3 by Sonny Liew

Session Chair: Jude C.L. Yew *(National University of Singapore)*

Artworks

Session Chairs: Markéta Dolejsová & Nancy Mauro-Flude *(National University of Singapore)*

Workshop Summaries

ACM C&C 2017 Conference Organization

General Chairs:	David A. Shamma *(Centrum Wiskunde & Informatica (CWI))* Jude Yew *(National University of Singapore)*
Associate Chair:	Ellen Yi-Luen Do *(National University of Singapore & Georgia Tech)*
Local Arrangements Chair:	Alex Mitchell *(National University of Singapore)*
Program Chair:	Brian Bailey *(University of Illinois at Urbana-Champaign)*
Technical Papers Chairs:	Steven Dow *(University of California San Diego)* Aisling Kelliher *(Virginia Tech)*
Art Chairs:	Markéta Dolejšová *(National University of Singapore)* Marcia Nancy Mauro-Flude *(National University of Singapore)*
Arts Advisor:	Honor Harger *(ArtScience Museum, Singapore)*
Crowdsourcing Chair:	Michael Bernstein *(Stanford)*
Posters Chair:	Cati Boulanger
Pictorials Chairs:	Lee Jung Joo *(National University of Singapore)* Will Odom *(Simon Fraser University)*
Demonstrations Chair:	Jochen Huber *(Synaptics)*
Workshops Chair:	Pablo Cesar *(Centrum Wiskunde & Informatica (CWI))*
Graduate Student Symposium Chairs:	Elizabeth F. Churchill *(Google)* Kurt Luther *(Virginia Tech)*
Student Volunteers Chair:	Christie Han *(National University of Singapore)*
Steering Committee Chair:	Nick Bryan-Kinns *(Queen Mary University of London)*
Steering Committee:	Andruid Kerne *(Texas A&M University, College Station)* Ashok Goel *(Georgia Institute of Technology)* Celine Latulipe *(UNC Charlotte)* David England *(Liverpool John Moores University, UK)* Ellen Yi-Luen Do *(National University of Singapore & Georgia Tech)* Ernest Edmonds *(De Montfort University, Leicester UK)* Samuel Ferguson *(University of Technology Sydney)* Thecla Schiphorst *(Simon Fraser University, Canada)* Yukari Nagai *(Japan Advanced Institute of Science and Technology)*

Papers Committee: Joel Chan *(Carnegie Mellon University)*
Sally Jo Cunningham *(University of Waikato, New Zealand)*
Rogerio de Paula *(IBM Research, São Paulo)*
Audrey Desjardins *(Simon Fraser University, Canada)*
Rebecca Fiebrink *(Goldsmiths University of London)*
Jason Freeman *(Georgia Institute of Technology)*
Elizabeth Gerber *(Northwestern University)*
John Alexis Guerra-Gómez *(Universidad de los Andes, Bogotá)*
Eva Hornecker *(Bauhaus-Universität Weimar)*
Julie Hui *(Northwestern University)*
Giulio Jacucci *(Helsinki Institute for Information Technology)*
Sara Jones *(City University London)*
Joy Kim *(Stanford)*
Boriana Koleva *(University of Nottingham)*
Ranjitha Kumar *(University of Illinois at Urbana-Champaign)*
Moon-Hwan Lee *(KAIST)*
Derek Lomas *(Carnegie Mellon University)*
Brian Magerko *(Georgia Institute of Technology)*
Mary Lou Maher *(UNC Charlotte)*
Narges Mahyar *(University of California, San Diego)*
Ali Momeni *(Carnegie Mellon University)*
Vicki Moulder *(The University of Tokyo)*
Yukari Nagai *(JAIST)*
Orit Shaer *(Wellesley College, Massachusetts)*
Pao Siangliulue *(Harvard University)*
Steven Smith *(Texas A&M University, College Station)*
Erin Solovey *(Drexel University)*
Andrew Webb *(INREA)*
Anbang Xu *(IBM Research Almaden)*

External Reviewers: Abdelaziz, Yomna
Abdullah, Muhammad Haziq Lim
Abu-Arja, Farah
Aknine, Samir
Allen, Warren
Alsallakh, Bilal
Alshehri, Majdah
AlTarawneh, Ragaad
Ang, Ling Weay
Apostolellis, Panagiotis
Barisic, Ankica
Baykal, Gokce
Beheshti, Elham
Irwin, Germaine
Jadan-Guerrero, Janio
Jaini, Shiva
Jankowski, Jacek
Jeong, Sooyeon
JO, Kazuhiro
Jung, Hyunggu
Kane, Bridget
Kinnula, Marianne
Korte, Jessica
Lai, Jianwei
Lee, Bang Jeon
Linehan, Conor

External Reviewers (continued):

Bell, Amanda
Bonsignore, Elizabeth
Cabral, Diogo
Caon, Maurizio
Carmien, Stefan
Carter, Elizabeth
Cerezo, Eva
Charisi, Vicky
Chizari, Sara
Cho, Jundong
Chu, Sharon Lynn
Chueng-Nainby, Priscilla
Colley, Ashley
Cumbo, Bronwyn
D'Olivo, Patrizia
Dasgupta, Sayamindu
Dawood, Rahmad
De Russis, Luigi
Dombrowski, Lynn
Eisenberg, Michael
El Ali, Abdallah
Ferwerda, Bruce
Fitton, Daniel
Forbes, Angus
Freeman, Euan
Gao, Ge
Garzotto, Franca
Gourlet, Pauline
Goyal, Nitesh
Gugenheimer, Jan
Guo, Yu
Hansen, Alexandria
Harlow, Danielle
Iivari, Netta
Lu, Zhihan
MacDonald, Lindsay
MacLean, Allan
Miniukovich, Aliaksei
Mitchell, Alex
Mora-Guiard, Joan
Moreno, Alejandro
Morreale, Fabio
Otero Ornelas, Nancy
Pantic, Katarina
Parekh, Priyanka
Perritano, Anthony
Phelan, Chanda
Rädle, Roman
Radu, Iulian
Rajanna, Vijay
Rooksby, John
Rosa, Jean Clemisson
Sánchez Milara, Iván
Sluis-thiescheffer, Wouter
Sobel, Kiley
Spiel, Katharina
Vacca, Ralph
Veryeri-Alaca, Ilgim
Volpe, Gualtiero
von Jungenfeld, Rocio
Vuillemot, Romain
Wallbaum, Torben
Wang, Danli
Williams, David
Woźniak, Paweł
Yao, Yaxing
Yip, Jason
Zakaria, Camellia

Pictorials Committee

Blevis, Eli
Carlson, Kristin
Chow, Kenny
Chung, Eunki
Durrant, Abigail
Fdili Alaoui, Sarah
Fox, Sarah
Hauser, Sabrina
Heidt, Michael
Hertz, Garnet
Hong, Hwajung
Jenkins, Tom
Jung, Heekyoung
Kerne, Andruid
Lim, Youn-kyung
Loke, Lian
MacDonald, Lindsay
McKinnon, Heather
Moulder, Vicki
Muntean, Reese
Nishino, Hiroki
Oogjes, Doenja
Robbins, Holly
Rogers, Jon
Rosner, Daniela
Tanenbaum, Joshua
Torres, Cesar
Vuillemot, Romain
Wallace, Jayne
Ylirisku, Salu

Posters and Demos Committee

Abbas, Yasmine
Aknine, Samir
Aylett, Ruth
Bacim, Felipe
Bakhshi, Saeideh
Bitton, Joelle
Boulanger, Adam
Bourganel, Remy
Brucker-Cohen, Jonah
Carlson, Kristin
Cermak-Sassenrath, Daniel
Chang, Angela
Danielescu, Andreea
Davis, Nicholas
Debatty, Regine
Frid-Jimenez, Amber
Grace, Kazjon
Henry, Nathalie
Iyengar, Deepa
Knight, Heather
Knouf, Nicholas
Lopez Silva, Brenda
Moriwaki, Katherine
Mota Toledo, Selene
Ozkar, Mine
Panjwani, Alisha
Petry, Benjamin
Quijano Silva, Catalina
Regalla, Lisa
Schneegass, Stefan
Sempere, Andrew
Sempere, Anindita
Sylvan, Elisabeth
Woźniak, Paweł
Xu, Cheng
Zampa, Virginie

Student Volunteers

Bhaduri, Srinjita
Crain, Patrick
Han, Christie
Long, Duri
MacNeil, Stephen
Naskova, Julija
Ng, Jessica
Sie, Shamaine
Williford, Blake
Zheng, Clement

ACM C&C 2017 Sponsor & Supporters

Sponsor:

SIGCHI

Platinum Supporters:

NATIONAL GALLERY SINGAPORE

ArtScience Museum
MARINA BAY SANDS

Additional Supporters:

JET BRAINS

SINGAPORE EXHIBITION & CONVENTION BUREAU

NSF

The Graduate Student Symposium is supported in part by a grant from the U.S. National Science Foundation under award no. IIS 1723306

YourSingapore

Thanks:

NUS National University of Singapore
Department of Communications and New Media
Faculty of Arts & Social Sciences

Keio-NUS CUTE Center

Instrumenting Interaction for Inspiration and Imagination

Kumiyo Nakakoji
Unit of Design, C-PiER, Kyoto University
1 Yoshida-Nakaadachi-cho, Sakyo-ku, Kyoto, 606-8306, Japan
kumiyo@acm.org

ABSTRACT

My research has led me to encounter a series of interesting reactions of people when interacting with visual, physical or logical representations. Such reactions are sometimes predicted or assumed, but many of them are rather eye-opening for me if not mystical. I could reason about such reactions most of the time but the more I encounter such cases, the more I got enchanted by the wonder of human perception and cognition.

People get attentive or inattentive, motivated or discouraged, feeling challenged or appreciative, respectful or disrespectful, obedient or disobedient, or excited or bored, not through the functionality that designed interactions convey. It is what people perceive and make sense out of the interactions as the consequence, influence, or effect of the interactions.

This talk will share my own excitement of the findings over my prior and current research on knowledge interaction design and collective creativity support. The array of examples to illustrate the findings will lead us to identify fundamental features for interactions to enrich our lives by nurturing inspiration and imagination, which I believe are essential for our creative knowledge work.

ACM Classification Keywords
H.5 INFORMATION INTERFACES AND PRESENTATION (e.g., HCI)

Author Keywords
Knowledge interaction design; collective creativity; nurturing creativity; museum experience design

BIOGRAPHY
Kumiyo Nakakoji, Professor at Unit of Design, C-PiER, Kyoto University (2013-), is currently engaged with the design of Ph.D. curriculum for Kyoto University Design School. Nakakoji received B.S. in Information Engineering from Osaka University, Japan (1986), and M.S. (1990) and Ph.D. (1993) in Computer Science from University of Colorado, Boulder, certified in Institute of Cognitive Science. She held positions as Adjoint Assistant Professor at Institute of Cognitive Science, University of Colorado, Boulder, USA (1994-2002), as Adjunct Associate Professor at Nara Institute of Science and Technology, Japan (1995-2002), and as Full Professor at Research Center for Advanced Science and Technology (RCAST), University of Tokyo, Japan, where she co-directed the Knowledge Interaction Design (KID) Laboratory (2002-2010), prior to the current position. She also directs the Key Technology Laboratory at Software Research Associates, Inc. Japan. She has served as chairs, editors, and members for numerous research committees, journals, conferences, and government funding agencies, in the fields of Human-Computer Interaction, Software Engineering, and Design and Creativity Support. She was awarded the Distinguished Engineering Alumni Award from College of Engineering, University of Colorado, Boulder, in 2006. Her current research interests include: knowledge interaction design for creative knowledge work, data engagement and experience platform, designing inspirational experience as museum services, and design provenance for collective creativity.

C&C 2017, June 27–30, 2017, Singapore.
ACM ISBN 978-1-4503-4403-6/17/06.
http://dx.doi.org/10.1145/3059454.3078894

Sharing the Housebound Experience through Visual Storytelling

Jenny Waycott
School of Computing and Information Systems
The University of Melbourne
Vic, 3010, Australia
jwaycott@unimelb.edu.au

Hilary Davis
Swinburne Social Innovation Institute, Swinburne University and Living with Disability Research Centre
La Trobe University
Melbourne, Australia
h.davis@latrobe.edu.au

C&C '17, June 27-30, 2017, Singapore, Singapore

DOI: http://dx.doi.org/10.1145/3059454.3059487

Abstract
This pictorial aims to demonstrate the power of video for fostering creative personal storytelling among people who normally have limited opportunities to share their experiences. We discuss two video stories, created in collaboration with participants in a project that aimed to enable housebound people to share their stories within the local community. We present screenshots from the stories, with commentary explaining how each image encapsulated the storyteller's life experiences. These show how imagery, combined with narrative, can evocatively communicate the experiences of people who are housebound, potentially fostering empathy among others within the community. Visual storytelling can therefore be a valuable tool for promoting empathy among researchers and designers. In this pictorial, we demonstrate that visual storytelling provides a powerful way for people to share their experiences and for researchers to work with and get to know participants in marginalized communities.

Authors' Keywords
Visual storytelling; marginalized people; housebound; empathy; community.

ACM Classification Keywords
H.5.m. Information interfaces and presentation (e.g., HCI): Miscellaneous.

Introduction

This pictorial presents stories created as part of a project that aimed to make housebound people's life experiences visible to others in the community. Chronic illness, disability, and other constraints can leave people confined to the home, with limited opportunities to participate in, and contribute to, the social fabric of their local community [7, 9]. Digital technologies can be used to address this gap. In particular, digital storytelling is a promising way of enabling housebound people to share their stories. It can be used as a creative form of self-expression that, when shared with an audience, promotes advocacy and awareness about issues affecting housebound people.

Personal digital storytelling

Digital storytelling is a method that has been used since the mid-1990s to support marginalized people to tell and share their stories [5]. This approach typically involves storytellers participating in workshops with facilitators who help them create brief video stories, combining oral narrative with digital images to communicate aspects of the storyteller's life experiences that they particularly want to share. There are many overlaps between digital storytelling and other creative pursuits, such as documentary filmmaking which typically produces longer and professionally edited stories [4]. In addition, creative writing has been used to give "a voice to marginal groups in society, helping them to tell their stories" [3, p. 63]. However, digital storytelling does not rely on literacy, instead making use of visual forms of communication, including photographs and video footage, which can be used to create powerful and personal visual narratives [1, 11].

Traditionally, digital storytelling uses tools that were available when the movement began in the 1990s: photographs, combined with spoken narratives [5]. Today, many people have access to mobile phones and cameras that provide the ability to record video, audio, and images for creative self-expression [1, 11]. We term this *visual storytelling*. Given that many forms of storytelling are now created using digital tools, the term "digital storytelling" no longer holds the same meaning it had in the 1990s, and the term has been applied widely in various research communities [see 10].

Visual storytelling with housebound people

We collaborated with a local community health center to explore how visual storytelling might enable housebound and marginalized people to share their stories [2, 10]. Occupational therapists identified clients who were predominately housebound and had the capacity and interest to take part in the project. The research team worked with clients to create short videos that communicated their life experiences. During visits to participants' homes, a researcher-artist captured video footage. Participants helped shape the content of the edited stories by showing us artefacts they wanted to include, which they used as the basis for story-telling. From this, we identified core themes that were central to each story. These were discussed with participants, who reviewed and approved the final stories.

With participants' permission, the stories were shared on an interactive display at a community event organized by the collaborating health center. By scanning a QR code, audience members could type short messages in response to the stories, which were moderated and then displayed at the bottom of the screen the next time the story played. Audience messages were shared with storytellers during a follow-up research visit. A second private screening was held to share the stories with participants and staff at the health center. At this event, we collected written responses from audience members. Responses demonstrated the power of the stories for provoking empathy. In this pictorial, we showcase two stories that are particularly evocative of the housebound experience.

Jim's Story

Jim shared the story of his difficult upbringing, his active life as a young man, and his current experience of being housebound.

"Since I was two months old I was put in a baby's home... and that's where I started. And then I was fostered out to some people and then put in an orphanage and there I stayed until I was 17. And that's the story."

This statement is accompanied by an image of Jim as a young boy (right). The photograph, framed and in a prominent place on the wall of his small apartment, was one of the very few mementos Jim had from his childhood.

friends and family are very important but I've got neither

The story included subheadings used to highlight parts of Jim's narrative that were particularly evocative and central to his story (e.g., above).

Explaining his background, Jim exclaimed:

*"My middle name should be alone. The family tree starts **right here!**"*

The image on the right captures Jim's expression as he made this exclamation. His enthusiasm is in stark contrast to the sentiments of the statement.

Sporting Glory

Jim reflected on the sporting successes he experienced in his younger and healthier years. These successes were due, in part, to having been brought up in an orphanage:

"Every orphanage and hostel had a pool table. And so I was brought up laying pool [snooker]. Made a bit of money on the side, which was [emphatic] ***tax-free****!"*

Jim's sporting trophies were on proud display in his home (above and right).

sport
POOL cricket
friends

Mobility Limitations
Due to the effects of chronic illness, Jim could no longer play sport. This had a substantial impact on his ability to connect with others and participate in society:

"I used to play cricket, as you can see, and pool. But as soon as that all ended, which it has to with this [gesturing to indicate illness], that was the end of frineds. You don't work with them anymore; you don't play sport with them anymore. You're useless to them. And you find they drop off very quickly...

But now it's a fair bit harder to play competition sport because you've got to stuff around with the wheelchair [top, right] *and stick it in the car."*

Being Housebound

"Dragging a wheelchair around you've got to plan everything. There's a lot of shops around here that I can't even get in to. I have shops about 20 meters away - there's a whole group of shops and they've all got a step."

In this screenshot from the video (right) Jim indicates the height of the step.

Baby I'm Bored

Jim's motorized scooter is decorated with a sign on the back (right), which aligns with his description of being confined to the home due to chronic illness:

"I miss working. I want to work. I want a job. I want to do work for the dole, I can't even do that. I'd love a job because not having a job is as boring as all shit."

The Stick

During the video story Jim demonstrates a curtain rod he had refashioned to use as a tool to help him manage day-to-day life given his mobility constraints.

He used the stick to open and close the door, turn the heating and cooling on and off, and close the blinds, as shown in the screenshots above. Throughout the video, Jim wore compression gloves, needed to manage the discomfort created by his medical condition.

Aaah, the 80s!

Jim's story ends with him reflecting on his days as a male stripper. This part of Jim's life was on prominent display in his home, with framed newspaper clippings and photographs adorning his walls (left). Jim was eager for these images to be included in his story.

"I knew there had to be a job better than the army. There's got to be one out there. And I found it! Even though I would not get up on a stage and speak - no way I'd do that - but I'd get up and take my clothes off! [chuckles]... And when I finished my security job, with the uniform, I'd go to the strip club and use the same uniform. I'd get up on stage and take it off! ... It was like being in a rock band. It was like living every man's dream. Those were the days. Aaah, the 80s!"

Fiona's story

Fiona's video story highlighted the vibrant personality of a woman whose illness had confined her to her home, but whose motorized scooter provided her with a newfound freedom.

Images in the story (right) illustrated how Fiona had richly decorated her home, both inside (bottom) and out (top).

Like Jim's story, Fiona's story was punctuated with headings (below), chosen from Fiona's narration to highlight key themes in her story. The font and background were carefully selected to match Fiona's personality and experiences.

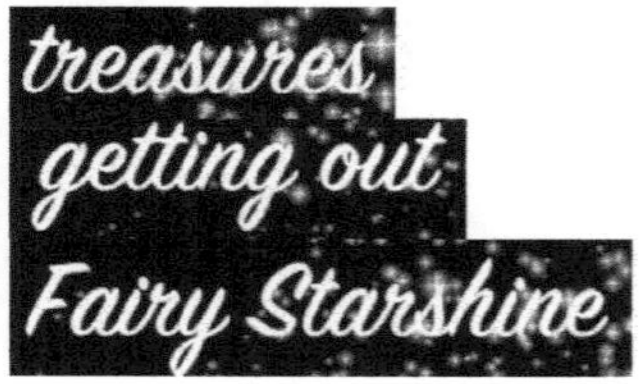

Treasures

Fiona's home was a treasure trove of objects she had collected during her life. The video story provided her with an opportunity to showcase and describe these treasures, many of which related to two of her passions: fairies and dance.

Fairy Starshine

Fiona had spent some time as a children's party entertainer, in character as a fairy:

"I had many wonderful years [in that job] and I so miss that. I just miss the magic and the joy and the really curly questions like [reads letter] 'Dear Fairy Starshine, how are you? First I would like to ask you why the tooth fairy only gave me one dollar when all my friends get five to ten?'"

Why Fairies?

"There's something quite spiritual and magical [about fairies]. We just need that magic and besides that, fairies always wear glitter!"

The Magic of Dance

"When I was about 13 I saw ballet on television... and everything in my life came together"

From the Beast to the Fairy Express

Fiona's motorized scooter was her savior. But she did not always feel that way:

"That's the thing about putting the flowers and the butterflies and the fairies on my scooter. It did go from being the 'Beast' and something that I had this trepidation with and resented having to have and I wanted to walk... It's not really what I want but I have learnt to make the best out of what I have so I decided if I had to own the scooter I was really going to own it! I would just create as much magic and beauty and express who I was... I ran into three girls who I used to know... They said to me, 'Have you named it?' and I was about to say 'I've called it the Beast' but instead I said, 'I've called it the Fairy Express'."

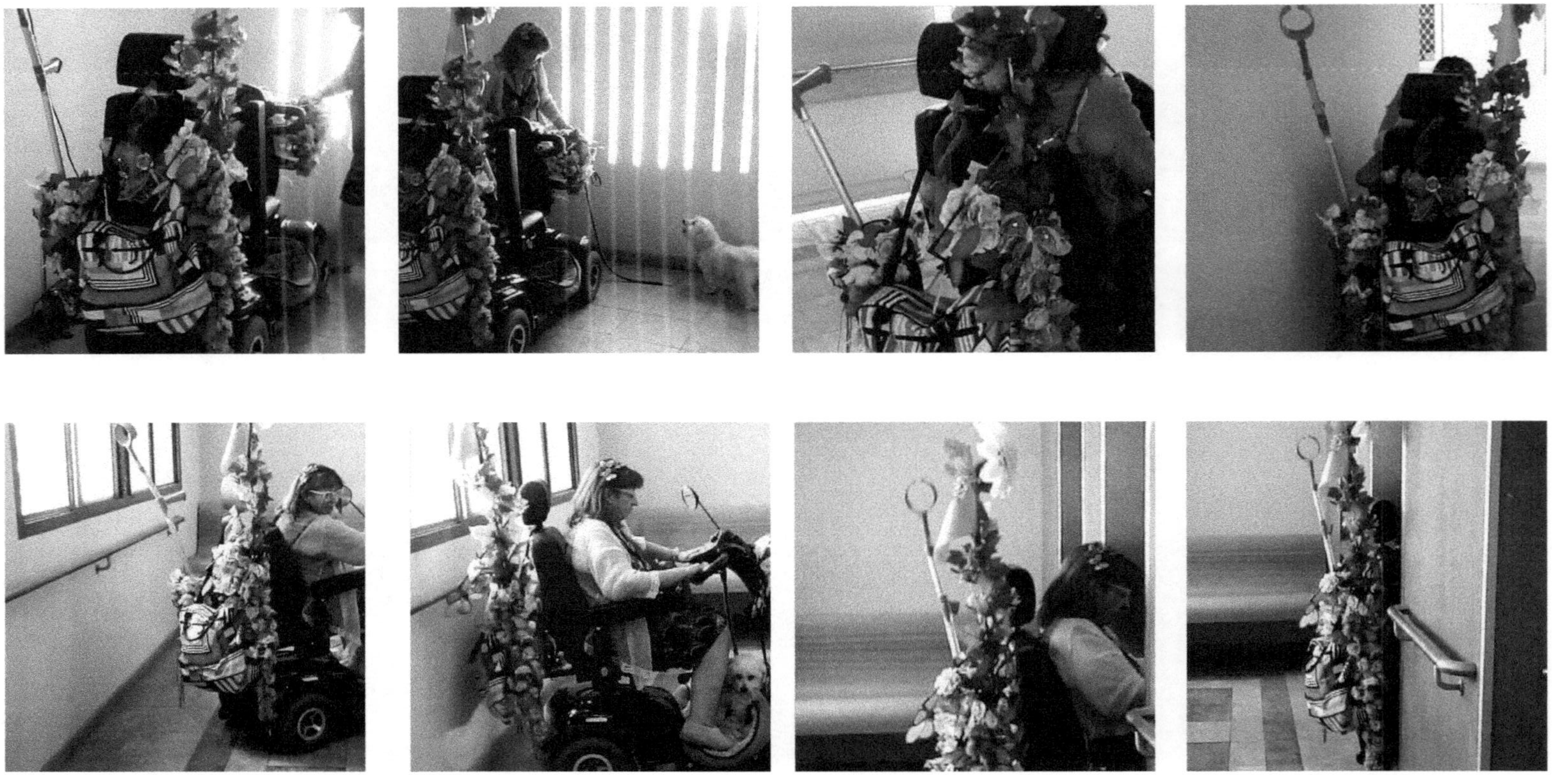

Getting Out

Fiona's story concludes with video footage showing her going through the process of maneuvering the 'Fairy Express' out of her small apartment, down the narrow hallway, and into the elevator (as shown in selected screenshots, above). This footage captures the difficulty of this relatively straightforward activity. It is a particularly poignant moment in the video:

"I'm pretty proud of myself to be honest, especially getting in and out of the lift. I'm not perfect but I know that I can do it now so my stomach doesn't knot, even though hers does [pointing to dog]... Just the fact of being on the scooter and feeling the wind in my face, watching the joy that [my dog] has of running around the park; just being out there and not trapped on the sixth floor of a high rise flat. That is an awful feeling, that sense of aloneness and nobody being there and having to cope with everything on your own. That's relentless."

Sharing the Stories (1)

Opportunities to share stories with others can be crucial for visual storytelling [1, 10, 11]. When working with marginalized people, this needs to be done sensitively. To minimize the risk of exposing storytellers to negative audience responses, audiences should be chosen carefully in collaboration with the storytellers.

In this project, the stories were shared with local community members during an "Open Day" event run by the collaborating partner, a local health center.

At this event, audience members had the opportunity to watch the stories on a television screen that was set up in a quiet area of the health centre (right). They could respond to the stories verbally (in conversation with researchers), or by writing comments on a mobile phone or tablet device. These comments were sent to a server for moderation; once approved, they would appear on the bottom of the screen the next time the story was played. The comments were relayed to the storytellers during follow-up interviews.

Sharing the Stories (2)

A second screening was held during a staff workshop with occupational therapists who worked for the community health organisation. Both Jim and Fiona attended this private screening. After the screening, occupational therapists provided written reflections in response to the stories (e.g., right).

These comments suggested that the health center staff were touched by the stories. They expressed enthusiasm about the possibilities that storytelling might offer for enhancing their clients' social inclusion in the future.

Jim and Fiona found sharing their stories to be a positive experience. Jim said the audience responses would *"keep me going for weeks!"*

Fiona provided thoughtful reflections on why it is important to give housebound people a voice: *"For us - as older persons with a disability - we have so much to add to the vibrancy and colors of life. We become invisible - we're not recognized, largely ignored, often valued as worthless. Often made to feel worthless [...] Not only is all that knowledge, wisdom and experience not shared but the ability to listen and identify with many threads in society doesn't exist."*

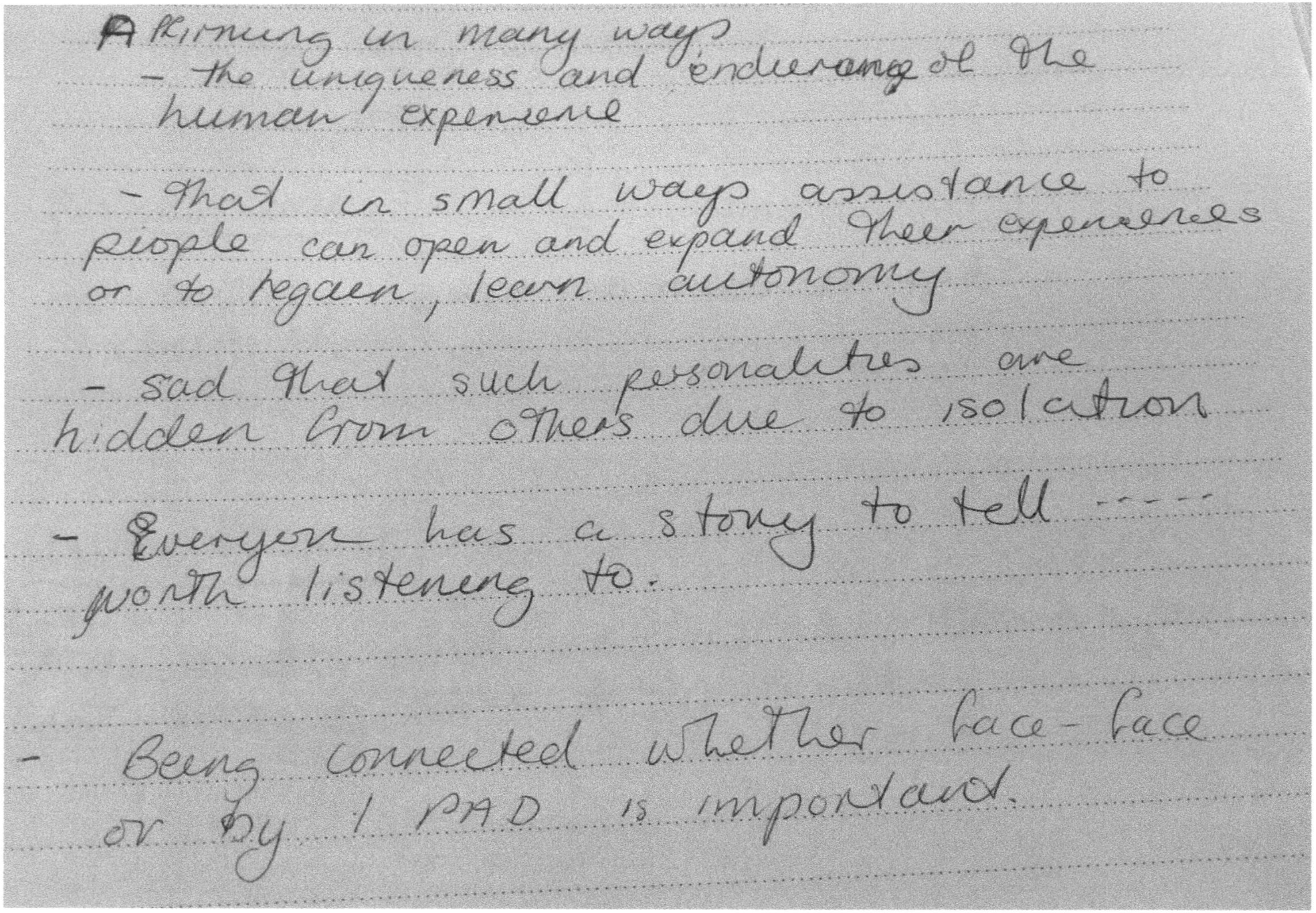

Discussion

These stories encapsulate some of the lived experiences of two people who have had very different lives and have diverse personalities, yet who share a common experience – being housebound and living with chronic illness. Their stories overlap in many ways. Both tell of their strong sense of identity prior to becoming ill, their struggles with chronic illness, and their re-discovered sense of freedom after acquiring mobile scooters. The stories share a capacity to clearly and evocatively communicate the experience of being housebound. This is an experience others in the community may not have personally encountered, and can therefore be difficult for researchers, healthcare workers, and others, to fully understand.

One of the reasons the stories are so effective in communicating the housebound experience is because of the storytellers' strong personalities and desire to share their stories. The visual format of the stories is also important. The combination of narrative, images, and video-recorded interviews enables the storytellers to describe their experiences in ways that would be difficult to communicate through words alone. The video format supports the use of gesture and body language (such as indicating the size of the step) and enables the storytellers to visually demonstrate personal struggles with everyday objects within the home (such as fans, blinds, elevators).

Visual storytelling allows the storytellers to communicate their personalities and life histories. Treasured mementos within the home give the audience context. We are invited to see private passions and accomplishments, and share struggles and victories. When watching the time and skill it takes Fiona to maneuver her scooter into the lift, the audience cannot help but empathize with her struggle and sense of achievement. In this way, visual storytelling can be a valuable tool for promoting empathy in research and design. Empathy has emerged as a key aspect of participatory design in recent years, especially as designers now work in a range of complex and sensitive settings, wtih people who might be considered marginalised [6, 12, 13]. This pictorial contributes to a growing body of literature concerned with fostering ethical and empathetic research approaches with diverse communities.

As a research tool, visual storytelling is a collaborative form of visual ethnography [8]. Through co-creating these visual stories, researchers gained insight into what it means to be housebound. Furthermore, these curated stories can play an important role in advocacy. Sharing the stories with healthworkers (e.g. occupational therapists, psychologists, doctors, nurses) ensures clinicians can better understand the physical and emotional needs of housebound people. The stories could be further shared with designers and urban planners to encourage empathy and understanding of the daily struggles of their intended users, and to drive improvements in the design of aftefacts, systems, and structures for people with limited mobility. As audience members we are invited to visualize ways in which we might support people like Jim and Fiona, whether through technology design, service provision, or the building of community connections. The visual elements of these stories stengthens their power in provoking empathy and, ideally, initiating change.

Conclusion

Our aim in presenting the stories in this pictorial format is to demonstrate the power of visual storytelling for communicating personal experiences. The stories we presented provide rich depictions of our participants' lived experiences, and demonstrate the power visual storytelling can provide for provoking understanding and empathy. We suggest visual storytelling can be utilized as a valuable research tool for designers and researchers working with people in marginalized communities.

Acknowledgements

This project was supported with a grant from the Melbourne Networked Society Institute (formerly the Institute for a Broadband-Enabled Society). The project was conducted in collaboration with a community health organization and we would like thank Joanne Grigg for supporting our work with this organization. We are extremely grateful to our participants who generously agreed to share their stories with us and who gave permission for these stories to be shared in this forum. The two participants featured here gave permission for their images to be used. We are also grateful to our colleagues Gretel Taylor, Deborah Warr, and Fran Edmonds, for their contributions to the project.

References

1. Robin F. Avni. 2015. Captured moments: Defining a com municative framework for social photography. In Proceedings of the SIGCHI Conference on Creativity and Cognition (C&C '15), 113-119. https://doi.org/10.1145/2757226.2757233
2. Hilary Davis, Jenny Waycott and Shou Zhou. 2015. Beyond YouTube: Sharing personal digital stories on a community display. In Proceedings of OzCHI 2015, 579-587. https://doi-org.10.1145/2838739.2838771
3. Frederica Goncalves, Pedro Campos, Julian Hanna and Simone Ashby. 2015. You're the Voice: Evaluating user interfaces for encouraging underserved youths to express themselves through creative writing. In Proceedings of the SIGCHI Conference on Creativity and Cognition (C&C '15), 63-72. https://doi.org/10.1145/2757226.2757236
4. David Philip Green, Simon J. Bowen, Chris Newell, Guy Schofield, Tom Bartindale, Clara Crivellaro, Alia Sheikh, Peter Wright and Patrick Olivier. 2015. Beyond participatory production: Digitally supporting grassroots documentary. In Proceedings of SIGCHI conference on Human Factors in Computing Systems (CHI '15), 3157-3166. https://doi-org.10.1145/2702123.2702203
5. Aline Gubrium, Alice Fiddian-Green and Amy Hill. 2016. Conflicting aims and minimizing harm: Uncovering experiences of trauma in digital storytelling with young women. In D. Warr, M. Guillemin, S. Cox and J. Waycott (Eds.) Ethics and Visual Research Methods, 157-170. Palgrave Macmillan.
6. Stephen Lindsay, Katie Brittain, Daniel Jackson, Cassim Ladha, Karim Ladha and Patrick Olivier. 2012. Empathy, participatory design and people with dementia. In Proceedings of the SIGCHI Conference on Human Factors in Computing Systems (CHI '12), 521-530. https://doi-org.10.1145/2207676.2207749
7. Caroline Nicholson, Julienne Meyer, Mary Flatley and Cheryl Holman. 2013. The experience of living at home with frailty in old age: A psychosocial qualitative study. International Journal of Nursing Studies 50, 9, 1172-1179. http://dx.doi.org/10.1016/j.ijnurstu.2012.01.006
8. Sarah Pink. 2013. Doing Visual Ethnography (3rd ed.) Sage Publications.
9. Joan Stewart, Collette Browning and Jane Sims. 2015. Civic socialising: A revealing new theory about older people's social relationships. Ageing and Society 35, 750-764.
10. Jenny Waycott, Hilary Davis, Deborah Warr, Fran Edmonds and Gretel Taylor. Co-constructing meaning and negotiating participation: Ethical tensions when 'giving voice' through digital storytelling. 2017. Interacting with Computers, 29, 2, 237-247.
11. Jenny Waycott, Frank Vetere, Sonja Pedell, Lars Kulik, Elizabeth Ozanne, Alan Gruner and John Downs. 2013. Older adults as digital content producers. In Proceedings of SIGCHI conference on Human Factors in Computing Systems (CHI '13), 39-48. https://doi.org/10.1145/2470654.2470662
12. Jenny Waycott, Greg Wadley, Stefan Schutt, Arthur Stabolidis, Reeva Lederman. 2015. The challenge of technology research in sensitive settings: case studies in 'sensitive HCI'. In Proceedings OzCHI '15, 240-249. https://doi-org.10.1145/2838739.2838773
13. Peter Wright and John McCarthy. 2008. Empathy and experience in HCI. In Proceedings of SIGCHI conference on Human Factors in Computing Systems (CHI '08), 637-646. https://doi-org.10.1145/1357054.1357156

The Willful Marionette: Exploring Responses to Embodied Interaction

Kazjon Grace
The University of Sydney and
UNC Charlotte
Sydney, Australia and
Charlotte, USA

Stephanie Grace
Bloomberg LP
New York, USA

Mary Lou Maher, Mohammad Javad Mahzoon, Lina Lee
UNC Charlotte
Charlotte, USA

Lilla LoCurto, Bill Outcault
Independent Artists
New York, USA

ABSTRACT
This paper explores how participants constructed and re-constructed their relationship with an interactive art installation. The piece, *the willful marionette*, was developed in collaboration between artists and researchers. It explores the dynamics of non-verbal communication by building (from a scanned image of a human figure) a stringed marionette that responds to human movement. The intent was to challenge participants' expectations about communication, intelligence, emotion and the social role of the body. We show that participants' descriptions of their interactions vary along two axes: whether they or the marionette was perceived as leading the interaction, and whether they constructed a social or a technical mindset. We explore these differences using semi-structured interviews and a mix of qualitative and quantitative methods. We then present some implications for the design of both goal-directed and expressive embodied intelligent systems. *the willful marionette* has since been acquired by the Smithsonian American Art Museum as an example of cutting-edge art that deals with contemporary issues of machine intelligence and the social role of our bodies.

INTRODUCTION
Conversational interaction with embodied, intelligent machines, long a staple of science fiction, is becoming an everyday reality. One of the key benefits of such technology is the social and emotional context it enables – dialogue, whether verbal or not, is a medium of unparalleled richness [12]. Embodied social interaction is fundamental human nature, and this underlies the perception of dialogue as a more "natural" means of communicating. A core challenge of conversational interaction, and one that continues to fuel research in both the artificial intelligence and human-computer interaction communities, is how to incorporate the context and subtext that accompanies dialogue [29]. The notion of embodiment is critical to addressing this challenge, as once equipped with a real or virtual body a conversational system can leverage its gaze, posture, gestures and face.

C&C'17, June 27–30, 2017, Singapore.

ACM ISBN 978-1-4503-4403-6/17/06 ...$15.00.
http://dx.doi.org/10.1145/3059454.3059475

These systems have profound social and psychological implications, in addition to the many technical questions they provoke. How does embodiment affect users' perception of a system's intelligence? Can we characterise the mindsets users may adopt when first experiencing an embodied conversational system? And what will be the reaction when errors or unusual behaviours contradict users' expectations? This paper is an initial step towards exploring these questions.

Research in embodied interactive systems has been pursued from both engineering and artistic perspectives, and this paper sits at the intersection of both. The technical research has focussed on the effectiveness of conversational systems as interfaces, and the role that real or virtual bodies can play in increasing that effectiveness [13]. We use the term embodied conversational agents (ECAs) [11] to describe goal-directed embodied interactive systems, and include within that definition related terms like embodied dialogue [13] and multimodal dialogue [30]. By contrast research into embodied Expressive Artificial Intelligences (EAIs) [34] explores a more experiential perspective on similar technologies. For example, the improvisational dance dialogues in *Viewpoints* [25] focus on eliciting novel experiences and emotional reactions from participants.

Shared among these traditions is the notion of the system as an "agent", which we adopt in place of "interface". The agent perspective captures both systems in which human and machine participants co-create meaningful experiences and those with which they perform tasks. We also adopt the view that agency arises from a constant reconfiguration of the relationships between actors [4]. From this constructive perspective the capacities of the subjects and objects in a system are not pre-specified but arise through situated, embodied interaction [49, 47]. This enables the artists' concept of exploring the social role of the body, and it also informs the investigation of our participants' responses to it.

the willful marionette is an art installation developed as a collaboration between the artists (authors LoCurto and Outcault) and the Interaction Design Lab at the University of North Carolina at Charlotte. The body of one of the artists was 3D-scanned, modified to be articulated like a marionette, and then 3D-printed at approximately half scale. The marionette is controlled by motorised strings, and able to perceive its surroundings with a pair of depth cameras. It was created to interact with participants through non-verbal channels: it senses and interacts solely to bodily motions, recognising participants gestures and positions. It does not mimic those it observes, instead behaving in a manner that is responsive but unpredictable. The marionette's strings, materials and exposed electronics make it clearly inhuman, but its form and movement convey a provocative degree of humanity. The computer-controlled marionette, which can be seen in Figure 1, was created to deliberately evoke this dichotomy. The question is not whether the marionette is intelligent (it is not), but how its embodiment affects how participants perceive and understand it.

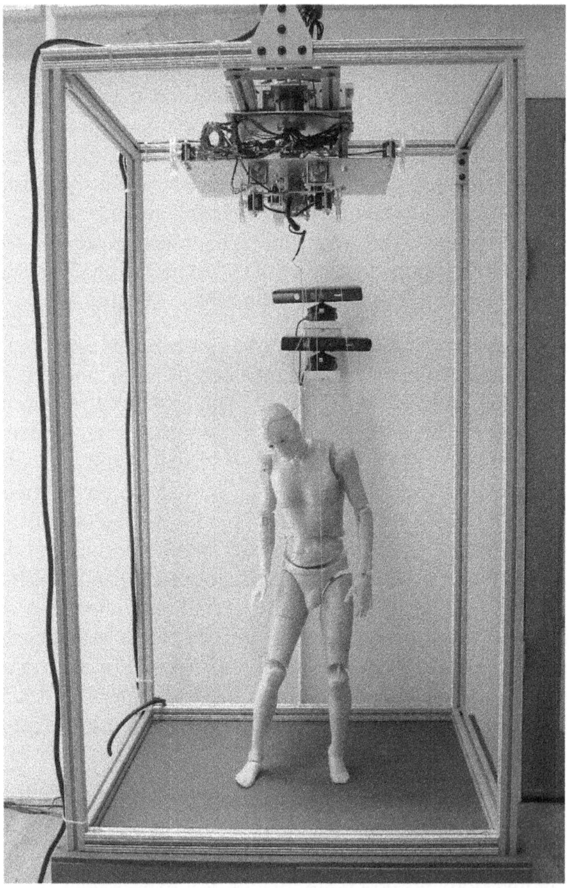

Figure 1. The *Willful Marionette*, an interactive art installation that explores the social role of the body and how we perceive intelligence. It has been acquired by the Smithsonian American Art Museum.

the willful marionette is intended to provoke, challenge and confuse, and by doing so construct novel experiences for its participants. This is a highly unlikely design goal for an interface intended primarily to be useful. It is inevitable, however, that such goal directed systems will on occasion confuse or challenge some users. Our investigation provides insights into how the design of both goal-directed ECAs and co-creative embodied EAIs can be sensitive to this.

In this paper we explore participant reactions to this piece through both quantitative and qualitative analyses of semi-structured interviews. We investigate participants' initial attitudes towards the marionette, as well as their reflections on its capabilities and motivations. The interviews explored perceptions of the marionette's ability to communicate, its motivations, its emotions, and its intelligence. We interpret participant responses in terms of the moment-to-moment reconfiguration of agency that comprises machine-human relations [4, 47, 49]. From this perspective our participants' perspectives at any given point can be categorised along two axes: social versus technical framing and human-led versus marionette-led.

BACKGROUND

The marionette is an exploration of non-verbal communication with embodied machines. This has been variously referred to as embodied interaction [16], multi-modal dialogue [27], and embodied conversation [11]. Embodied interaction is defined as placing tasks inextricably in their physical, social and cognitive context [16]. In an HCI context this means that users of an interactive system must construct an understanding of how it works based on their physically grounded exploration [15, 2]. In dialogic and conversational systems research this has been explored in two ways: placing the interaction in a user's context, i.e. computing in the world (such as in [31]), and directly embodying the conversational agent, i.e. computing with a face (such as in [11]). *the willful marionette* is primarily an investigation of the latter.

Embodied, emotive and social interactivity

People attribute social and emotional states to machines if given the slightest chance to do so [42]. When providing feedback on a computer's performance on a task, users provide significantly more positive feedback when the questions are asked by the same computer, even when using entirely text-based interfaces [37]. Participants in these studies are fully aware that the software they are interacting with has no higher-level reasoning capabilities and no feelings to hurt, but they behave politely regardless. Key to designing both expressive and effective conversational systems is understanding why we treat computational interactions as social, and the role of presence and embodiment in this process [10].

Taylor [49] explores the contexts in which we ascribe intelligence to objects, both utilitarian and artistic. He describes how people anthropomorphise, and thus attribute agency to, objects, whether or not they possess humanlike forms. Taylor argues that in the long run it is the lifelike behaviours of "a little bit of intelligence" [17] that build relationships between human and machine, contrasting the pet-like affinity Roomba owners have for their far-from-humanlike robot vacuum cleaners with the vivid but fleeting encounter with a realistic but static wax statue at Madame Tussauds. *the willful marionette* incorporates elements similar to both of these examples: like the Roomba it has behaviours that can be (at least partially) understood through observation, and like the wax statues it exhibits an uncanny combination of lifelike and lifeless traits.

Embodiment in conversational systems is an active area of research in both AI and HCI, investigating how physical or virtual bodies can augment dialogic interaction. Embodiment through gaze [40], posture [9], gesture [53], attentiveness [52], mimicry [3], and facial expressions [35] have all been shown to impact user engagement and further key task-dependent metrics. *the willful marionette* is exclusively non-verbal and not task-directed, and thus would not meet some definitions of an ECA, but its behaviour and the reactions it elicits have implications for the design of future such systems.

The social and emotional expressivity of digital characters has also been explored in the field of computer graphics. Animators are concerned with character "believability" – the illusion of life [5]. Conveying emotion, personality, intent and identity through movement and form are core principles of digital and analogue animation alike. Our marionette follows several of these principles: it leads with its eyes to convey attention, and it embodies its personality through its actions. Conveying personality in animated film has parallels in embodied systems research, particularly in attempts to quantify agents' naturalness [55] and behavioural realism [19]. By contrast, *the willful marionette* is intended to be realistic in its movement but unnatural in its bodily materiality, a deliberate provocation of the Uncanny Valley [45].

Embodied robots and digital puppets

Socially assistive robots, such as PARO [43], are both affective (in that they sense their user's emotional states [41]) and embodied. PARO is a seal-like robot intended for behavioural therapy in assisted living centres. It resembles a plush toy and can detect petting and sounds, and responds to grooming and other acts of physical intimacy with a variety of emotive sounds and movements. This creates an affectively charged embodied dialogue, in which the robot evokes sympathetic or vicarious joy in the user through its embodied responses to their user's actions. *the willful marionette* does not explicitly seek to capture its participants' affective states, but like PARO it seeks to provoke them through an embodied dialogue.

A marionette is a string-operated puppet, an art form that exists in many cultures [14], robotically augmented versions of which have been explored in a variety of contexts [57, 14, 1, 48]. These systems, collectively referred to as "animatronics", typically focus on lifelike articulation [22]. There have been several examples of emotive robotic puppetry in art, as well as examinations of how people will respond to such systems [20]. The *survivor project* [38] was an animated chair sculpture that represented victims of land mines. The chair was visibly damaged, and its movements were designed to evoke suffering and the loss of bodily autonomy.

The *Public Anemone* was a robotic interactive theatre installation designed to resemble a sea anemone [8]. It interacted with participants as if it were a living creature behind glass at an aquarium. The anemone's sensory capabilities were simple, being limited to camera-based tracking of hands and faces, but its tube-like body possessed multiple rings of actuators with a broad expressive range. This project, like *the willful marionette*, serves as an exploration of the possibilities of non-verbal communication between humans and machines.

THE WILLFUL MARIONETTE

The artistic vision for the piece was to create an interactive humanlike form that provides reflection on the physicality and frailty of the human body. The resulting computer-controlled marionette is derived from a high-resolution 3D scan of the body of one of the artists. This scan was segmented into 17 pieces, and then re-connected by a set of hinge and socket joints in locations corresponding to the joints on the human body. The scan was then 3D printed in PLA plastic at a height of approximately three feet.

Thirteen strings are attached to the body, primarily at the joints, and then each connected to stepper motors. A pair of lifelike doll's eyes are installed in the head, with eyelids controlled by another motor. The motors are collectively controlled by an Arduino Due™ microcontroller. Two Microsoft Kinect™ sensors are mounted behind the frame that encloses the marionette, facilitating a ~180° field of view. These sensors are connected to a PC running software that interprets the gestures and positions of people nearby. The overall structure of the system can be seen in Figure 3.

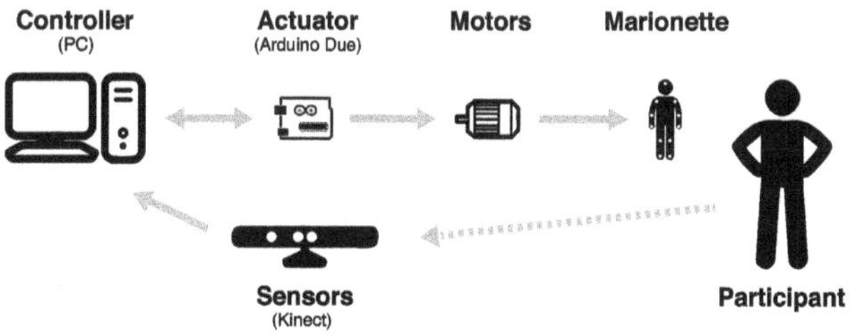

Figure 2. The architecture of *the willful marionette*[1].

In contrast to internally-actuated robots, *the willful marionette's* movements are not directly controlled by its motors, but by its strings. This constitutes a dynamical system in which the position of the marionette is a function of motor actions, its past actions, and physical constraints like string tension and gravity. The result of this is highly fluid, natural movement in which the marionette adjusts its posture in a manner reminiscent of a human maintaining balance.

The marionette is designed to provoke an interactive relationship between the piece and the participants. Puppetry is an art form in which all movement is controlled by a human puppetmaster, and an interactive marionette challenges that expectation, inviting users to consider the locus of its reasoning. The detailed, human-like form is also atypical of puppetry, combining with its smooth movement and responsive behaviour to evoke life. These attributes are in direct contrast with its rigid materiality, its blue colour, and its clearly visible strings and

[1] "Arduino icon" by uizin is licenced under CC BY 3.0

electronics. This juxtaposition is one source of the provocative pseudo-humanity of the piece.

The marionette's behaviour is determined by a stochastic rule-based system. It recognises the positions of those nearby, as well as when they perform five full-body "gestures": approaching, backing away, waving, bending down, and coming very close. The Kinect sensors can track and recognise gestures from up to four participants at a time. The marionette stochastically selects one participant to be its focus of attention, and turns to face and make eye contact with that person. When the current focus of attention performs one of the recognised gestural actions the marionette will respond. To respond, the marionette stochastically selects one of its own actions from a weighted list associated with the action performed by the participant. The system cannot interrupt an in-progress movement, so in practice these responses are added to a queue of behaviours executed in the next few seconds. After each such gesture there is a chance the marionette will focus on a different participant. If multiple participants are detected and the current focus of attention does not move or perform any gestures for ten seconds, the marionette selects another person as its focus.

The marionette can perform 30 independent full-body gestures, orient itself in an 180° arc, and blink. Example gestures include shaking its head, looking away, crouching while covering its face with its hands, and backing off while extending a hand. The set of marionette gestures was iteratively designed using methods including bodystorming [44] and roleplaying [46]. The set of human gestures to which the system would respond was then refined using a gesture elicitation method [56] in which the marionette was Wizard-of-Oz operated and participants were asked to respond spontaneously. For more detail on the design of *the willful marionette*, as well as a list of gestures it can perform, see [33].

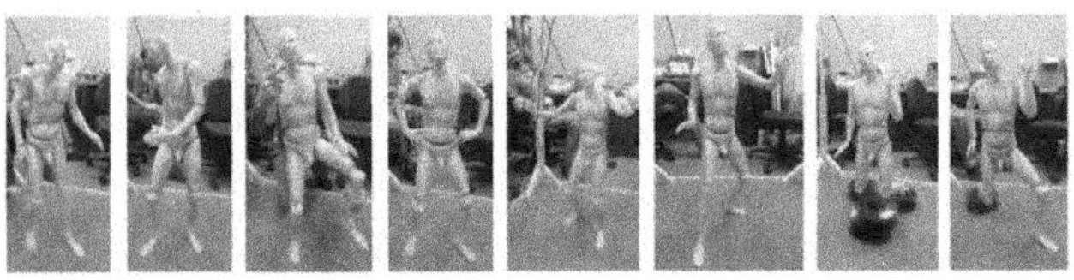

Figure 3. An example of the poses the marionette can take while performing gestures. These photographs were taken as part of a bodystorming exercise during the creation of the piece.

The control software for *the willful marionette* is not complex. It does not learn, nor leverage any historical information. It fails to meet one definition of an ECA in that it cannot carry out a series of connected interactions on a topic [58]. Its behaviour would almost certainly not be deserving of the label "intelligent" if it was not a human-like form exhibiting human-like movement in a social setting with other humans. And yet it regularly evoked the perception of intelligence from those who have interacted with it during its construction, our study, and its subsequent exhibition at the Smithsonian American Art Museum in July of 2016. One possibility is that its physicality amplified the well known *"Eliza effect"* [54], the tendency for people to attribute more intelligence to interactive systems than they actually possess. Our evaluation sought to better understand the role of embodiment, and how it affects the perception of intelligence, emotiveness and social behaviour.

EVALUATION

We conducted a semi-structured qualitative study [7] in which participants interacted freely with the art piece and were then interviewed about their experience. 24 participants consented both to interacting with the marionette and the post-interaction interview. The interview consisted of several questions about their initial experiences, reflections, and characterisations of the marionette, including a question that asked them to rate how engaging it was. 20 participants interacted with the marionette in pairs, with the other 4 doing so alone.

We were interested in investigating the relationship each participant constructed with the marionette during their initial encounter with the piece, and thus chose to evaluate the piece in a studio setting. This allowed us to ensure that each individual or pair encountered the piece when it was not being interacted with by others, which would not have been possible in a museum-like setting. The study was conducted in Brooklyn, New York in May of 2016. Participants were recruited from among age 18-70 acquaintances of the authors who were not already familiar with the piece. Participants were video- and audio- recorded during their interaction with the marionette, and interviewed post-interaction. The analysis in this paper is based on the interview data only, as camera positioning unfortunately resulted in participants obscuring the marionette for many interactions.

There are three components to our analysis of this data: 1) participant ratings of how engaging the piece was, 2) a quantitative analysis of word frequencies, and 3) a coding analysis of themes and concepts discussed by participants. The word-level analysis examines the relationship between the words used by participants and their level of engagement (as reported in question 3 – see the Interview Protocol section for details). The coding analysis was conducted with a mixture of quantitative and qualitative methods. Two coders (one of whom was the interviewer) iteratively and independently coded the data, allowing concepts expressed by the participants to emerge. As an exploratory quantitative investigation we examine several significant correlations between pairs of concepts as well as between certain concepts and the engagement score. This analysis is intended as an exploration of how our participants behaved, and is not presented as quantitative results intended to generalise beyond *the willful marionette*. We then describe how the insights from our study could be applied in the design of future expressive or goal-directed embodied intelligent systems.

Interview protocol

After providing consent, participants were brought individually or in pairs into a large room by an experimenter. The marionette was located on the far wall, out of detection range. If they did not approach to within 3 meters within the first thirty seconds of interaction, the experimenter encouraged them to do so. After three minutes of interacting with the marionette, the experimenter would say "Please feel free to continue interacting with the marionette for as long as you'd like. When you're finished, have a seat over there and we'd like to ask you some questions." Participants were interviewed once they indicated a desire to finish interacting with the piece.

The interview lasted approximately 15 minutes, and consisted of four broad questions. We followed a semi-structured interview approach, in which the interviewer (a 10-year veteran of the user experience industry) probed participants for their reasoning and asked specific follow-ups when certain subjects were breached. The questions were as follows:

1. *How did you initially feel interacting with the marionette?* This question was designed to gauge initial impressions of the piece, and to see what concepts participants would discuss unbidden.
   (a) *Follow-up:* If the participant mentioned an emotion or concept without describing it, they were asked to provide a specific example.
2. *Can you describe how you think the marionette was behaving and why?* This question was designed to probe their understanding of the marionette's behaviour and reasoning.
   (a) *Follow-up:* If the participant describes the marionette as responding to or communicating with them, they were asked to give an example of their action and the marionette's response.
   (b) *Follow-up:* If the participant describes the marionette as exhibiting motivation, intent or thought, they were asked what the marionette did to suggest that.
   (c) *Follow-up:* If the participant describes the marionette as expressing one or more emotions, they were asked what the marionette did to suggest that.
3. *On this scale (participants were shown a piece of paper with a line numbered from 1-10) how engaging did you find the marionette and why?* This question was designed to gauge their engagement level and what they liked/disliked about the piece.
   (a) *Follow-up:* If the participant rated it less than 10, they were asked what was missing from the experience that might have caused them to rate it higher.
4. *What do you think the artists were trying to convey with this piece?* This question was designed to probe participants' about the motives for the marionette as an art installation, rather than as a social encounter or computational system.

Participant engagement

Participants were asked to rate their level of engagement with the marionette in Question 3 of our interviews. The mean engagement score was 7.875 and the median 7.75, and the data is presented in Figure 4. In the following sections we examine the relationship between these scores and the words, concepts and themes expressed by participants.

Word-frequency analysis

We extracted the words spoken by each participant from the transcripts, removed common English stop-words [18] and used the WordNet lemmatizer [50] to obtain root words. A word cloud [36] of the resulting corpus can be seen in Figure 5,

Figure 4. Participants' level of engagement with the marionette [1-10].

with larger words being more frequent among all participants. The 24 participants were split into those above and those below the median engagement rating. Word frequencies in the above-median and below-median groups were compared using a two-sample T test. Red words were significantly more frequent ($p < 0.05$) among the below-median engagement participants, with pink words indicating near-significance ($p < 0.1$). Blue words (of which there are very few) were significant more frequent ($p < 0.05$) among the above-median engagement participants, with light blue indicating near-significance ($p < 0.1$). All other words are white. No multiple hypothesis correction was used in this analysis as it is intended to be exploratory, not confirmatory. Word frequency also does not capture linguistic context, making this a high-level exploration designed to provide a holistic understanding of participant behaviour. We make no claims about the generalisability of these results, using them only to inform our further analyses.

The word choices of the two groups capture some important distinctions about how they conceptualised their interaction with the system. High engagement (above-median) participants used words like "amazing", "real", "uncomfortable", and "fear" more frequently. Low engagement (below-median) participants used words like "communicate", "interaction", and "react" more frequently. Another distinction is fluency: on average the low-engagement group spoke almost twice as many total words than the high-engagement group.

We interpret this as the highly engaged describing their interaction in terms of the emotions they experienced. Conversely the less-engaged tended to critically analyse the piece. This is also borne out by the use of the word "marionette" almost exclusively among the more critical participants – indicating that they described the piece in the third person, rather than focussing on their experience with it. Words like "fear" and "uncomfortable" appear more among the highly engaged, which could indicate their experience was emotionally resonant than the less-engaged. By contrast the only emotional word used more by the less-engaged was "curious", a word that can also be used dispassionately. We see these distinctions as evidence of a divide between emotive responses to the marionette as a person, and curious or detached responses to it as a technical system. We note than an alternate hypothesis is that the causality of this relationship is reversed: that more analytical people tend to engage and emote less.

Figure 5. A word cloud of the participants' interview responses. Word size is proportional to frequency of use. Blue and red words were used significantly more frequently by high self-reported engagement participants respectively. White words were used equally by either group.

Thematic analysis

The intent of our qualitative analysis was to determine what broad categories describe the participants' experiences with the marionette. To determine this we performed phrase-level coding of the transcribed interview data. Each phrase was tagged with one or more words or short phrases, and these conceptual codes were tallied up on a per-participant basis. We decided to code for concepts at the level of phrases rather than words as words like "think" and "feel" were ambiguous: they were used to describe both the marionette and the participants.

Coding was performed over two iterations by two independent coders (one of whom was the interviewer), with a joint review after each iteration. The two coders then negotiated remaining discrepancies and produced a third iteration together, after which three themes emerged:

Theme 1: The marionette's perceived intelligence.
Theme 2: The marionette's behaviour.
Theme 3: The participants' emotions and experiences.

Each theme encapsulates a set of concepts that emerged during the coding, and were named by negotiation between the two coders. Concepts that affected fewer than a third of our participants (8) were excluded from this analysis. Phrases relevant to each concept were tagged as either agreeing, disagreeing or equivocating. For example, one concept that emerged within Theme 2 was playfulness. Phrases were tagged as describing the marionette as: a) playful, b) not playful, or c) otherwise mentioning playfulness.

Participants with a majority of positively-tagged statements were treated as agreeing with the concept, those with a majority of negatively-tagged statements as disagreeing. Those participants with an equal number of positive or negative statements, or with a majority of equivocal statements, were treated as partially agreeing with that concept. This aggregate analysis allows us to capture those participants whose relationship with the marionette changed over the course of their interaction, or whose feelings about about particular concepts were ambiguous or contradictory. Any participant who did not make a statement about a particular concept was ignored in its analysis, which we code as "N/A".

In the sections below we describe the distribution of participants for each of these four tag categories for each of the major concepts identified, and then explore the relationships between and reasons for those responses. Throughout this section we indicate the number of participants in to the category under discussion in parentheses (out of a total of 24).

Theme 1: Perceptions of the marionette's intelligence

Whether or not the marionette was intelligent was primarily discussed in interview Question 2, although most participants referred to it throughout their responses. We did not proscribe a definition of intelligence to our participants, instead trying to explore what the term meant for them. Three concepts were identified during coding as falling within this theme:

Concept A: The marionette's *motivation* and intentions, and ability to reason about and act on them.
Concept B: The marionette's capacity for *communication*
Concept C: The marionette's *emotive* capacity, both its ability to express and feel emotions.

These concepts, the occurrences of which can be seen in Table 1, were highly divisive, with about half the participants indicating each was either definitely or possibly exhibited by the marionette. Most participants mentioned intelligence or communication directly (20 in both cases) as it was addressed in a commonly-asked follow-up to Question 2. Fewer participants mentioned emotions than motivation or communication, possibly because the latter two were more directly related to the question. We accordingly avoid directly comparing the fraction of negative mentions between emotiveness and intelligence and communication. Relatively few participants (6) ascribed none of the three aspects to the marionette.

Concept	Yes	Maybe	No	N/A
A. Motivation	9 (38%)	3 (13%)	8 (33%)	4 (17%)
B. Communictn.	9 (38%)	4 (17%)	8 (33%)	3 (13%)
C. Emotiveness	11 (46%)	2 (8%)	2 (8%)	8 (33%)

Table 1. Concepts commonly identified in participants discussions of their perception of the marionette's intelligence, and how many participants agreed, disagreed, equivocated or did not mention them.

The concept we coded as *motivation* refers to statements that described the marionette as having intentions or goals. An example of a statement ascribing motivation was *"It does begin to feel like there is intention behind what's going on in there"*. An example rejecting it was *"I think he's not thinking. He just reproduces the movements"*. An example equivocal statement on motivation *"It has a kind of mind that I recognise from a dog or a cat, but it's very much not of its own"*.

A majority of participants making statements ascribing motivations to the marionette (12) gave as a reason its expression of an intent or goal. Other participants (2) mentioned that its expression of emotions was what made it intelligent. Among those who did not find the marionette possessed a capacity for motivation the leading reason (6) was that it felt programmed or artificial. Four other participants mentioned the randomness or unpredictability of its responses as a reason for a lack of intelligence. Many participants made contradictory statements within this concept, suggesting it was the focus of iterative reconstruction of their relationship with the piece.

Communication in Table 1 refers to statements that described the marionette as attempting or succeeding in conveying something to the participant. An example of a statement ascribing communication was *"I interpret that as, um, the marionette trying to get you to do something. In some sense there's, you can say there's a communication channel happening there"*. An example rejecting communication was *"I feel like I am not communicating, because if I want to communicate and do this thing, I can kind of figure out what can I do with my body to elicit that response ... That would be communication"*. An example equivocating was *"It might've been trying to send a message, I was just not...it's just not speaking my language"*.

Among those who thought the marionette was communicating the leading reason (8) was that it was communicating emotions with gaze or posture. Others (3) thought it was trying to elicit a particular response. A majority of those who felt it was not communicating (8) mentioned that they could not elicit a desired response from the marionette, or that they could not understand the responses it performed. Three participants mentioned speech as a requirement for communication.

Emotiveness in Table 1 was coded when participants made statements attributing emotions to the marionette. An example of such a statement is *"Maybe the marionette was hitting on me"*. An example of a statement rejecting the marionette's capacity for emotion is *"I don't think that the machine can ... It may not have emotion"*. An example of an equivocal statement regarding emotion is *"it can definitely bring emotion into play. Even though it personally doesn't have any emotion."*

The most common reason for attributing emotion to the marionette (5) was that it appeared to be exhibiting fear, stress or defensiveness through its movements. Four participants (each of whom interacted with the piece as a pair) attributed an emotional reason to the marionette's preference for one of the two participants. Three of those mentioned (heteronormative) sexual attraction as a potential reason for that preference. Three other participants thought the marionette was contemplative, and that its behaviour indicated it was curious or meditative. The leading reason for attributing a lack of emotive capability to the marionette, expressed by two participants, was that it seemed to lack underlying drives. Two participants rejecting the presence of emotion in the marionette itself clarified that it was capable of eliciting emotion in observers, but that this did not imply it could feel them itself.

Theme 2: How the marionette behaved

Throughout the interview questions participants described the behaviour of the marionette. Three concepts, captured in Table 2, stood out among those descriptions:

Concept D: *Randomness* in the marionette's actions.
Concept E: *Playfulness* in the marionette's actions.
Concept F: *Mimicry* of participants by the marionette.

These concepts were less common than those in Theme 1, being mentioned by 7-11 participants each, with 9 participants mentioning none of the three.

Concept	Yes	Maybe	No	N/A
D. Randomness	7 (29%)	2 (8%)	1 (4%)	14 (50%)
E. Playfulness	7 (29%)	0 (0%)	0 (0%)	17 (71%)
F. Mimicry	2 (8%)	2 (8%)	7 (29%)	13 (8%)

Table 2. Concepts commonly identified in participants discussions of the marionette's behaviour, and how many participants agreed, disagreed, equivocated or did not mention them.

Randomness was coded for all statements that described the marionette's actions as being random or explicitly not driven by any underlying desire or motivator. Care was taken to separate claims that there was no deeper motivation to its behaviour (which we coded as randomness) from those where the participant stated they did not understand the marionette's motivation (which we did not take to indicate randomness). An example of a statement describing the marionette's behaviour as random was *"I felt like there were things that, you know, that the marionette is moving, but it seems random."*

Playfulness was coded when a participant stated that the marionette attempted to play or dance with them. Many of these statements were also coded as evidence for emotiveness, but those in this category explicitly mentioned the marionette's physical behaviour was dance- or play-like. Most explicitly mentioned a crouch-like gesture in which the marionette raised its hands. An example of such a statement was *"I totally saw it crouch down and do the dab"*.

Mimicry phrases were those that described an expectation or observation that the marionette would act as a kind of digital mirror, and move to mimic the participants. This perception – "Oh, it'll do what you do?" – was very common among those to whom we described the piece, but not observed frequently during our study. An example of such a statement by a participant in the study was *"I felt that when I was closer or crouched down that he would also crouch down a little"*. Mimicry can be considered an opposite of randomness in our case: the former is perfectly predictable behaviour, while the latter is perfectly unpredictable. Desirable behaviour for an art installation likely lies somewhere between the two.

Theme 3: Emotions expressed by the participants

Participants described themselves as experiencing a wide range of emotions while interacting with the piece during their responses to all four questions. We organised these responses into three broad emotional categories. In this theme there were no statements where participants described themselves as explicitly not exhibiting or equivocating on an emotion. All participants were coded as either experiencing or not mentioning each of the three emotional categories, which were:

Concept G: Expressing *curiosity* about the marionette.

Concept H: Expressing *nervousness*, self-consciousness or fear about the marionette.

Concept I: Expressing *amazement* or shock at the marionette.

Concept	Yes	Maybe	No	N/A
G. Curiosity	16 (67%)	0 (0%)	0 (0%)	8 (33%)
H. Nervousness	12 (50%)	0 (0%)	0 (0%)	12 (50%)
I. Amazement	8 (33%)	0 (0%)	0 (0%)	16 (67%)

Table 3. Concepts commonly identified in participants discussions of their own feelings while interacting with the piece, and how many participants agreed, disagreed, equivocated or did not mention them.

Curiosity was the most commonly exhibited emotion among participants, and included expressions of interest in the technology, the artistic vision, and what the marionette would do. 12 of the 16 participants who exhibited curiosity mentioned it during their response to Question 1 as their first response to the piece. An example of a statement indicating curiosity was "I found myself sort of trying to figure out how it worked." The most common cause of curiosity was how the marionette worked (8), followed by how it would behave (6) and the piece as a whole (6). The majority of those who exhibited curiosity described that experience in technological terms: they were interested in how the piece operated and how it was made.

Nervousness included statements that the participant was feeling self-conscious, uncomfortable, or shaken in the presence of the marionette. This was exhibited by half of the participants in the study (12), an indication of the piece's ability to challenge and unnerve. A majority of those who expressed discomfort (9) indicated that it was just an initial response, and that they overcame it while interacting with the marionette. The most common cause of nervousness (5) was uncertainty about how to proceed with interaction. Investigating this group showed that many of the descriptions were phrased socially: participants didn't know what "he" (the marionette) wanted, or what "he" would expect that they do. Four other participants expressed nervousness because they felt they were being influenced, observed, or even somehow controlled by the marionette. Three participants described the marionette as creepy.

Amazement, a category of emotion exhibited by participants which we coded to include shock, awe and surprise, was exhibited by a third of the participants (8). Some responses describing shock were clearly negatively valenced and were included in both amazement and nervous/uncomfortable category. An example of a statement exhibiting amazement was "I've never seen anything like that in my life". Amazement was attributed to the piece as a whole (4), its capacity for movement (4), and its body and/or eyes (3). Amazement, like the other two emotional responses, was most likely to be experienced upon initially encountering the marionette. While the curious participants were more likely to describe the piece in terms of the technology behind it, the amazed participants were more likely to focus on its immediate physicality.

Correlations between identified themes

We examined the relationships between the nine identified concepts within the three themes described above, as well as their relationship with participants' reported engagement levels. To convert participants' multiple tagged statements into a continuous value for comparison, we calculated the proportion of each participant's responses that were positive. We treated equivocal statements as half of a positive statement. For example, a participant who made two positive, one negative, and one equivocal statement about a particular concept would be assigned a numerical score of $(2+0.5)/4 = 0.625$. These proportions account for the tendency of some participants to give multiple statements that partially contradict each other. We interpret this as evidence of the challenging and provocative nature of *the willful marionette*, as well as for the notion of agency being reconfigured through interaction [49, 47].

We calculate Pearson's correlation coefficient on the resulting values, correcting for multiple comparisons using Benjamini and Hochberg [6], which is designed for exploratory analyses. None of the correlations were significant at $p < 0.05$ after the correction, which is unsurprising given the number of comparisons. A number of relationships were near-significant at $p < 0.1$, which we report in Table 4 as potential relationships in this exploratory study. All the reported relationships were highly significant before our correction for multiple comparisons.

Positive correlations *i* and *iii* (in Table 4) indicate that participants who reported higher levels of engagement were also likely to report that the marionette was communicating with them and that they experienced amazement. Participants who reported that the marionette was communicating were also likely to report that it was exhibiting emotions (*ii*). These interrelated concepts suggest that participants tended to be simultaneously engaged, amazed and believe that the marionette is communicating and emoting. Conversely, participants who did not believe that the marionette was communicating and emoting were less engaged and less likely be amazed or shocked.

Five of the seven significant negative correlations relate to the perception that the marionette's behaviours were random. Participants who thought that the marionette was behaving at least partially randomly (which it is) tended to report less engage-

Positive Correlations

#	Concept 1	Concept 2	Correlation
i.	Engagement	Communication	0.519
ii.	Communication	Emotiveness	0.486
iii.	Engagement	Amazement	0.484

Negative Correlations

#	Concept 1	Concept 2	Correlation
iv.	Emotiveness	Randomness	-0.584
v.	Emotiveness	Nervousness	-0.576
vi.	Engagement	Randomness	-0.573
vii.	Amazement	Randomness	-0.525
viii.	Intelligence	Randomness	-0.519
ix.	Communication	Randomness	-0.519
x.	Curiosity	Engagement	-0.484

Table 4. Correlations between concepts expressed by participants that were considered near-significant ($p < 0.1$) after correcting for multiple comparisons (and highly significant before, $p < 0.025$).

ment (*vi*), less amazement (*vii*), and attribute less emotiveness (*iv*), intelligence (*viii*) and communication (*ix*).

Qualitative investigation of the participants who reported that the marionette was behaving randomly suggests that many of them believed the marionette's randomness was evidence that it did not possess higher order reasoning capability. Several such participants were disappointed by the piece's lack of complex behaviour, and felt that randomness broke the sense of immersion engendered by the human-like form and movement. A similar response to (partial) randomness was observed in initial responses to Roomba vacuum cleaners [17, 49].

Another significant negative correlation (*v*) was between reported emotiveness in the marionette and feelings of nervousness in the participant. We investigated those who reported they were nervous but that the marionette was not emoting and found participants who were disturbed by either the physicality of the marionette or the technological future it implied. These participants tended not to respond to the marionette's gestures: one was so self-conscious she remained almost perfectly still for several minutes after the marionette turned towards her.

The last significant negative correlation (*x*) was observed between participant curiosity and engagement. This represents a seeming paradox: why would those who were more curious be less engaged? We investigated this group of participants, finding that they were more likely to find the marionette to behave randomly, and to be disappointed that its behaviour was not more complex. They expressed curiosity about the system, the hardware, and the software behind it, but seemed to have discovered its underlying simplicity. These participants also critically analysed the piece as a device and/or an art piece, rather than interacting with it as a person.

DISCUSSION: RESPONSES AND RECONFIGURATIONS

the willful marionette elicited a diverse range of experiences and emotions from its participants. Its lifelike qualities and its predictable-yet-unpredictable reactions combined to elicit responses ranging from shock and a feeling of bodily discomfort to curiosity and a perception of playful intelligence. The analysis above has focussed on the diversity of experiences among our participants, and the correlations between them. Equally interesting to us is the diversity of experiences within each participant as their perception of the piece emerges. The marionette juxtaposes human-like form and fluid movements with simple reactive behaviour. How, as our participants negotiate its agency and their own through their interactions, would they reconstruct their relationship with the piece?

A two-axis framework for participant relationships

What the interviews revealed about the moment-to-moment mindsets of the users can be broadly characterised along two dimensions. The first is whether the participant construes the interaction as a social one, or a technical one. The former involves treating the marionette as another socially-aware agent, while the involves treating it as technology. The second dimension concerns who the participant described as having the initiative in the interaction: was it marionette-led, or human-led? These two axes can be seen in Figure 6.

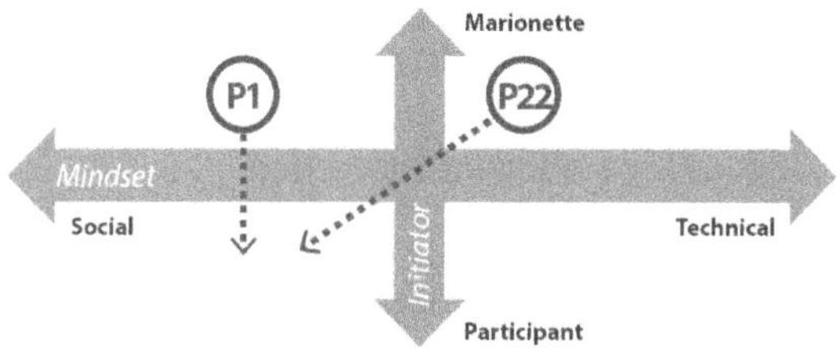

Figure 6. Our framework for how participants related to the marionette.

The arrows in Fig. 6 describe two typical participant reconfigurations that we observed. We present them as examples of the transitions evoked during interaction with the marionette. P22 described that he "went through the process of um, thinking it was just going to be a kind of a... one-dimensional robot just moving randomly. And then I went through this adjustment realising that it responded to us." This describes a technical and participant-initiated configuration: the marionette is a robot, it moves randomly or responds. P22 continued, describing a co-participant's actions: "[P23] reached and touched its hand, tried to touch its belly at first, actually. It moved [its hand] out [of the way]!" and then soon after: "I think the interaction is actually, uh, mutual." and "I was looking in its eyes and waiting for it to blink." P22 reconfigured towards a more social and marionette-initiated interaction after believing that the marionette had avoided physical contact, which may have inspired thoughts of bodily autonomy and personal space.

P1 experienced an emotional reconfiguration from marionette- to participant- initiated interactions. P1 was initially frozen on the spot after the marionette turned to face her, saying "I wasn't sure if my movements would affect his" and "I felt very... I could feel that I was stiff." Initial feelings of shock then gave way to introspection as she was drawn into activity: "I tried [to] almost mimic the movements he was making... Cause I was thinking about my own body, and I was thinking "I wonder if my body can move quite in that way"." Finally, near the end of their interaction, P1 cautiously explored leading: "I was waving, and he wasn't. It was a very exaggerated wave... He acknowledge me, but he didn't wave back." These reconfigurations, while far from generalisable, offer glimpses into how ECA users may interpret unexpected or erroneous behaviour, and how that differs from other interaction contexts.

More broadly, participants that primarily adopted the social perspective (11 of the 24), expressed higher engagement and were more likely to attribute intelligence to the marionette. The found the marionette shocking and confronting, and did not try to test the limits of its abilities. Conversely, participants who described their interactions as mostly technical (7/24 participants) exhibited more curiosity, were more critical, and typically gave lower engagement scores.

The remaining six participants fluidly reconstructed their perceptions of the marionette from the social to the technical and back. Several spoke of suspending their disbelief in the marionette's inanimacy, but also reflected critically on its lack of "real" intelligent behaviour. As one participant put it, "[It was] this kind of strange figure that, you know... touched us. And [it was about] how we can touch each other through all kinds of strange ways". That quote captures the complexity of the role of embodiment in the perception of intelligence.

Implications for embodied interaction

As AI becomes more pervasive, and the range of possible contexts-of-use for them grows [21], we will see an increase in embodied intelligent systems. These systems will pervade our built environment, and will be designed both for co-creative expression and task-driven utility. The four-quadrant framework outlined above offers one interpretation of how users construct the agency of such systems.

Taylor contrasts the fleeting realism of wax sculptures with the learnable-over-time behaviour of "intelligent" vacuum cleaning robots [49]. For the former, interactions are initially social but quickly dismissed, while for the latter interactions are initially technical but grow more social with understanding. For a confrontational art installation like *the willful marionette* this distinction between superficial and discoverable aspects of humanity is not so clear cut. Our participants equivocated, contradicted themselves, and reflected on their own behaviour while they described their interactions. Many of them were clearly still re-configuring their impressions of the piece while discussing it in our interviews. This simultaneously underlies the power of embodied intelligent systems for evoking novel experiences and the danger of designing them without attending to perceptions of agency, intelligence, and intentionality.

The marionette's eyes, in particular its ability to blink and make eye contact, strongly influenced participants' perceptions of its emotiveness, social presence, and overall intelligence. The marionette's indirectly controlled movement, driven by strings and thereby able to follow through, self-correct and accelerate/decelerate naturally, also contributed to perceptions of emotion and liveliness. This fluidity causes each movement to be impacted by those that have come before, which is not typically the case with robots. We draw an analogy between this and the contrast between old, monotonous speech synthesisers and newer commercial spoken interfaces that are capable of inflection and tone. The expression of complex emotion through subtle bodily movement has been extensively explored by practitioners and researchers in animation [28]. Designers of embodied intelligences can leverage it to imbue their systems with greater perceived agency.

The marionette was intended to challenge notions of intelligence and the role of the body in perceiving it, and this informed our decision to use stochastic behaviour. Many previous studies have shown that comprehensibility is critical to the usability of intelligent systems [24, 23, 51]. Jameson [26] summarises these findings with the concept of "inadequate predictability", which echoes the discussion of the Roomba above [49, 17]. Surprising behaviour can, in the right circumstances, be positive [32], but it also requires confident expectations [39], which unpredictability can prevent.

Creating *the willful marionette* has reinforced the need to be responsive to differences in how users construct their relationships with intelligent machines. Those adopting a social mindset require a sense that the system is attending and responding to them in a personal way. This should not come at a cost to users who adopt a more technical perspective, who require clearly defined and explorable capabilities. Though we cannot say how generalisable these differences are, they should be considered carefully when designing embodied interaction.

CONCLUSION

the willful marionette engages participants in an experience that is simultaneously very human and very not. Our intent in developing the piece was to explore and challenge expectations about the social role of the body. The additional notion of the fragility of our perceptions of intelligence emerged during the creation of the piece. Our semi-structured interview study has provided support for both goals, demonstrating that the marionette challenged participants' beliefs about corporeality, embodiment and intelligence. With the caveat that it is challenging to generalise from a specific artwork to a genre of interactive systems, the study also provided several compelling insights that may impact future embodied interaction.

While the marionette was intentionally provocative, it is inevitable that some users of any embodied interactive system will experience similar cognitive dissonance. Our study suggests that those who felt discomfort, surprise and shock when first interacting with our system did not feel any less engaged – in fact, their engagement levels were higher. Extrapolating from the results of our admittedly small-scale study, we propose that the shock of initially interacting with a socially intelligent system may not be detrimental for long-term engagement. We also suggest that for embodied systems it may be more important to focus on *high-level* comprehensibility (i.e. emotional states or goals) rather than the transparency of individual actions. Further study is necessary to determine whether this applies to task-driven conversational interfaces.

As an art piece, *the willful marionette* speaks to society's changing ideas about intelligence in both humanity and machines. As a technological system, it speaks to the potential social and psychological impacts of the growing deployment of pervasive, embodied intelligent systems.

REFERENCES

1. Mostafa Ajallooeian, Ali Borji, Babak Nadjar Araabi, M Nili Ahmadabadi, and Hadi Moradi. 2009. Fast hand gesture recognition based on saliency maps: An application to interactive robotic marionette playing. In *RO-MAN 2009-The 18th IEEE International Symposium on Robot and Human Interactive Communication*. IEEE, 841–847.
2. Alissa N Antle, Paul Marshall, and Elise van den Hoven. 2011. Embodied interaction: Theory and practice in HCI. In *Proc. CHI*, Vol. 11.
3. Jeremy N Bailenson and Nick Yee. 2005. Digital chameleons: Automatic assimilation of nonverbal gestures in immersive virtual environments. *Psychological science* 16, 10 (2005), 814–819.
4. Karen Barad. 2003. Posthumanist performativity: Toward an understanding of how matter comes to matter. *Signs* 28, 3 (2003), 801–831.
5. Joseph Bates. 1994. The role of emotion in believable agents. *Commun. ACM* 37, 7 (1994), 122–125.
6. Yoav Benjamini and Yosef Hochberg. 1995. Controlling the false discovery rate: a practical and powerful approach to multiple testing. *Journal of the royal statistical society. Series B (Methodological)* (1995), 289–300.
7. AE Blandford. 2013. Semi-structured qualitative studies. In *Encyclopedia of Human-Computer Interaction, 2nd Ed.* Interaction Design Foundation.
8. Cynthia Breazeal, Andrew Brooks, Jesse Gray, Matt Hancher, John McBean, Dan Stiehl, and Joshua Strickon. 2003. Interactive robot theatre. *Commun. ACM* 46, 7 (2003), 76–85.
9. Stéphanie Buisine, Matthieu Courgeon, Aurélien Charles, Céline Clavel, Jean-Claude Martin, Ning Tan, and Ouriel Grynszpan. 2014. The role of body postures in the recognition of emotions in contextually rich scenarios. *International Journal of Human-Computer Interaction* 30, 1 (2014), 52–62.
10. Justine Cassell. 1999. Embodied conversation: integrating face and gesture into automatic spoken dialogue systems. (1999).
11. Justine Cassell. 2000. *Embodied conversational agents*. MIT press.
12. Justine Cassell, Timothy Bickmore, Mark Billinghurst, Lee Campbell, Kenny Chang, Hannes Vilhjálmsson, and Hao Yan. 1999a. Embodiment in conversational interfaces: Rea. In *Proceedings of the SIGCHI conference on Human Factors in Computing Systems*. ACM, 520–527.
13. Justine Cassell, Obed E Torres, and Scott Prevost. 1999b. Turn taking versus discourse structure. In *Machine conversations*. Springer, 143–153.
14. I-Ming Chen, Shusong Xing, Raymond Tay, and Song Huat Yeo. 2005. Many strings attached: from conventional to robotic marionette manipulation. *IEEE robotics & automation magazine* 12, 1 (2005), 59–74.
15. Paul Dourish. 2001. Seeking a foundation for context-aware computing. *Human–Computer Interaction* 16, 2-4 (2001), 229–241.
16. Paul Dourish. 2004. What we talk about when we talk about context. *Personal and ubiquitous computing* 8, 1 (2004), 19–30.
17. Jodi Forlizzi and Carl DiSalvo. 2006. Service robots in the domestic environment: a study of the roomba vacuum in the home. In *Proceedings of the 1st ACM SIGCHI/SIGART conference on Human-robot interaction*. ACM, 258–265.
18. Christopher Fox. 1989. A stop list for general text. In *ACM SIGIR Forum*, Vol. 24. ACM, 19–21.
19. Victoria Groom, Clifford Nass, Tina Chen, Alexia Nielsen, James K Scarborough, and Erica Robles. 2009. Evaluating the effects of behavioral realism in embodied agents. *International Journal of Human-Computer Studies* 67, 10 (2009), 842–849.
20. David Hanson, Andrew Olney, Steve Prilliman, Eric Mathews, Marge Zielke, Derek Hammons, Raul Fernandez, and Harry Stephanou. 2005. Upending the uncanny valley. In *Proceedings of the national conference on artificial intelligence*, Vol. 20. Menlo Park, CA; Cambridge, MA; London; AAAI Press; MIT Press; 1999, 1728.
21. Karen Henricksen, Jadwiga Indulska, and Andry Rakotonirainy. 2002. Modeling context information in pervasive computing systems. In *International Conference on Pervasive Computing*. Springer, 167–180.
22. Robin Hofe and Roger K Moore. 2008. Anton: an animatronic model of a human tongue and vocal tract.. In *INTERSPEECH*. 2647–2650.
23. Kristina Höök. 2000. Steps to take before intelligent user interfaces become real. *Interacting with computers* 12, 4 (2000), 409–426.
24. Eric Horvitz. 1999. Principles of mixed-initiative user interfaces. In *Proceedings of the SIGCHI conference on Human Factors in Computing Systems*. ACM, 159–166.
25. Mikhail Jacob and Brian Magerko. 2015. Viewpoints AI. In *Proceedings of the 2015 ACM SIGCHI Conference on Creativity and Cognition*. ACM, 361–362.
26. Anthony David Jameson. 2009. Understanding and dealing with usability side effects of intelligent processing. *AI Magazine* 30, 4 (2009), 23.
27. Michael Johnston, Srinivas Bangalore, Gunaranjan Vasireddy, Amanda Stent, Patrick Ehlen, Marilyn Walker, Steve Whittaker, and Preetam Maloor. 2002. MATCH: An architecture for multimodal dialogue systems. In *Proceedings of the 40th Annual Meeting on Association for Computational Linguistics*. Association for Computational Linguistics, 376–383.

28. John Lasseter. 1987. Principles of traditional animation applied to 3D computer animation. In *ACM Siggraph Computer Graphics*, Vol. 21. ACM, 35–44.
29. Oliver Lemon. 2012. Conversational interfaces. In *Data-Driven Methods for Adaptive Spoken Dialogue Systems*. Springer, 1–4.
30. Oliver Lemon, Anne Bracy, Alexander Gruenstein, and Stanley Peters. 2001. The WITAS multi-modal dialogue system I.. In *INTERSPEECH*. 1559–1562.
31. Oliver Lemon and Alexander Gruenstein. 2004. Multithreaded context for robust conversational interfaces: Context-sensitive speech recognition and interpretation of corrective fragments. *ACM Transactions on Computer-Human Interaction (TOCHI)* 11, 3 (2004), 241–267.
32. Geke DS Ludden, Hendrik NJ Schifferstein, and Paul Hekkert. 2008. Surprise as a design strategy. *Design Issues* 24, 2 (2008), 28–38.
33. Mohammad Mahzoon, Mary Lou Maher, Kazjon Grace, Lilla LoCurto, and Bill Outcault. 2016. The Willful Marionette: Modeling Social Cognition Using Gesture-Gesture Interaction Dialogue. In *International Conference on Augmented Cognition*. Springer, 402–413.
34. Michael Mateas. 2001. Expressive AI: A hybrid art and science practice. *Leonardo* 34, 2 (2001), 147–153.
35. Richard E Mayer and C Scott DaPra. 2012. An embodiment effect in computer-based learning with animated pedagogical agents. *Journal of Experimental Psychology: Applied* 18, 3 (2012), 239.
36. Carmel McNaught and Paul Lam. 2010. Using Wordle as a supplementary research tool. *The qualitative report* 15, 3 (2010), 630.
37. Clifford Nass and Youngme Moon. 2000. Machines and mindlessness: Social responses to computers. *Journal of social issues* 56, 1 (2000), 81–103.
38. Ephraim Nissan, Ricardo Cassinis, and Laura Maria Morelli. 2008. Have computation, animatronics, and robotic art anything to say about emotion, compassion, and how to model them?: The survivor project. *Pragmatics & Cognition* 16, 1 (2008), 3–36.
39. Andrew Ortony and Derek Partridge. 1987. Surprisingness and expectation failure: what's the difference?. In *IJCAI*. 106–108.
40. Tomislav Pejsa, Sean Andrist, Michael Gleicher, and Bilge Mutlu. 2015. Gaze and Attention Management for Embodied Conversational Agents. *ACM Transactions on Interactive Intelligent Systems (TiiS)* 5, 1 (2015), 3.
41. Rosalind Picard. 1997. *Affective computing*. Vol. 252. MIT press Cambridge.
42. Byron Reeves and Clifford Nass. 1996. *How people treat computers, television, and new media like real people and places*. CSLI Publications and Cambridge university press Cambridge, UK.
43. Selma Šabanović, Casey C Bennett, Wan-Ling Chang, and Lesa Huber. 2013. PARO robot affects diverse interaction modalities in group sensory therapy for older adults with dementia. In *Rehabilitation Robotics (ICORR), 2013 IEEE International Conference on*. IEEE, 1–6.
44. Dennis Schleicher, Peter Jones, and Oksana Kachur. 2010. Bodystorming as embodied designing. *Interactions* 17, 6 (2010), 47–51.
45. Jun'ichiro Seyama and Ruth S Nagayama. 2007. The uncanny valley: Effect of realism on the impression of artificial human faces. *Presence* 16, 4 (2007), 337–351.
46. Kristian T Simsarian. 2003. Take it to the next stage: the roles of role playing in the design process. In *CHI'03 extended abstracts on Human factors in computing systems*. ACM, 1012–1013.
47. Lucy Suchman. 2007. *Human-machine reconfigurations: Plans and situated actions*. Cambridge University Press.
48. Tomohito Takubo, Kenji Inoue, Tatsuo Arai, and Kazutoshi Nishii. 2006. Wholebody teleoperation for humanoid robot by marionette system. In *2006 IEEE/RSJ International Conference on Intelligent Robots and Systems*. IEEE, 4459–4465.
49. Alex S Taylor. 2009. Machine intelligence. In *Proceedings of the SIGCHI Conference on Human Factors in Computing Systems*. ACM, 2109–2118.
50. Randee I Tengi. 1998. Design and implementation of the WordNet lexical database and searching software. In *WordNet: an electronic lexical database*. MIT Press, 105–127.
51. Nava Tintarev and Judith Masthoff. 2012. Evaluating the effectiveness of explanations for recommender systems. *User Modeling and User-Adapted Interaction* 22, 4-5 (2012), 399–439.
52. David Traum and Jeff Rickel. 2002. Embodied agents for multi-party dialogue in immersive virtual worlds. In *Proceedings of the first international joint conference on Autonomous agents and multiagent systems: part 2*. ACM, 766–773.
53. Kees Van Deemter, Brigitte Krenn, Paul Piwek, Martin Klesen, Marc Schröder, and Stefan Baumann. 2008. Fully generated scripted dialogue for embodied agents. *Artificial Intelligence* 172, 10 (2008), 1219–1244.
54. Noah Wardrip-Fruin. 2009. *Expressive Processing: Digital fictions, computer games, and software studies*. MIT press.
55. Benjamin Weiss, Ina Wechsung, Christine Kühnel, and Sebastian Möller. 2015. Evaluating embodied conversational agents in multimodal interfaces. *Computational Cognitive Science* 1, 1 (2015), 1.

56. Jacob O Wobbrock, Meredith Ringel Morris, and Andrew D Wilson. 2009. User-defined gestures for surface computing. In *Proceedings of the SIGCHI Conference on Human Factors in Computing Systems*. ACM, 1083–1092.

57. Katsu Yamane, Jessica K Hodgins, and H Benjamin Brown. 2004. Controlling a motorized marionette with human motion capture data. *International Journal of Humanoid Robotics* 1, 04 (2004), 651–669.

58. Victor W Zue and James R Glass. 2000. Conversational interfaces: Advances and challenges. *Proc. IEEE* 88, 8 (2000), 1166–1180.

The Temporal Window: Explicit Representation of Future Actions in Improvisational Performances

Alex Mitchell, Jude Yew, Prashanth Thattai, Benjamin Loh, Dennis Ang and Lonce Wyse
National University of Singapore
Singapore
alexm@nus.edu.sg, jude.yew@nus.edu.sg, prashanth.thattai@u.nus.edu,
benjamin.loh@u.nus.edu, dennis@u.nus.edu, lonce.wyse@nus.edu.sg

ABSTRACT
Improvisation often requires performers to anticipate each other's upcoming actions to coordinate their performance. Traditionally, improvisation does not involve explicit representation of upcoming actions, relying instead on implicit cues and overt gestures. Providing a concrete representation of these actions may impact the nature of improvisation. To explore how performers use such a representation, we introduce the "temporal window", a shared workspace for collaborators to indicate upcoming actions shortly before those actions are carried out. We describe versions for music and storytelling, and present results of an observational study of use of these systems by 11 pairs of participants. Participants used the temporal window in various ways, including using knowledge about upcoming actions when performing live, and adjusting upcoming actions based on knowledge of both the live performance and upcoming actions. These observations can inform design to support improvisation as well as other systems that support anticipating upcoming actions.

Author Keywords
Improvisation; collaborative creativity; coordination; negotiation; anticipation.

ACM Classification Keywords
H.5.m. Information interfaces and presentation (e.g., HCI): Miscellaneous.

INTRODUCTION
Improvisations are distinguished from other types of creative performance in that they i) are not bound tightly to the use of a written script or score, ii) occur in real time - in that the creation of the performance occurs during the staging of the performance itself, and iii) are often a collaborative group activity [11]. For instance, in an improvisational musical performance, a group of musicians work together on stage, in real time, to create a piece of music. The independence from a script or score requires each musician to listen and respond to the music played by the other musicians. Musicians may also glance at each other, and will be aware of any movements or gestures their fellow performers are making [10]. However, there is little or no time during the performance for performers to explicitly state their upcoming actions, nor is there any explicit, concrete representation of those upcoming actions. Although performers will be considering the consequences of their moment-by-moment decisions, everything is improvisational and in the moment, requiring performers to anticipate the actions of their collaborators and act accordingly to coordinate their performance.

Thus, we refer to improvisational performances with no concrete representation of upcoming actions as *ephemeral* because there is no materialized representation of the collaboration. Non-improvisatory performances usually result in/from a *concrete* representation, such as a script or a score, of the collaboration as it emerges. The performers can manipulate and refer to this concrete representation of their collaboration to coordinate and plan their ongoing creative collaboration. Upcoming actions are visible and concretely represented. There is a contrast here between *improvisational, ephemeral collaboration,* and *planned, concretely represented collaboration.*

This contrast forms the basis for the research question we are exploring in this paper: if we provide a concrete representation of upcoming actions in an *improvisational* context, how would performers make use of such a shared representational space? To investigate this question, we developed an implementation of this concrete representation in two domains: music and storytelling. We refer to this concrete representation as a "temporal window" (see Fig. 1), as it provides a constantly changing representation of upcoming actions in a performance.

To understand how performers make use of this concrete representation, we conducted an observational study of 11 pairs of performers using the temporal window in both

C&C '17, June 27-30, 2017, Singapore, Singapore

ISBN 978-1-4503-4403-6/17/06…$15.00
DOI: http://dx.doi.org/10.1145/3059454.3059470

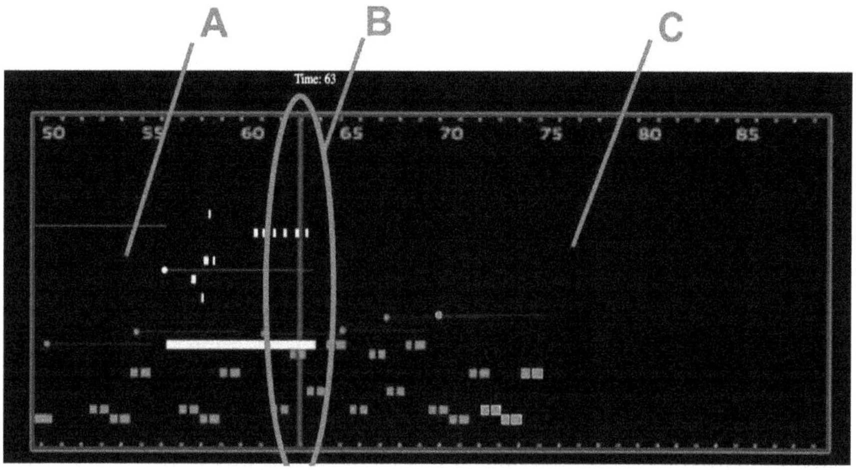

Figure 1: The music improvisation system showing the collaborative, scrolling temporal window spanning the "now" line (B) from the past (A) into the future (C). See http://tinyurl.com/cc2017-video for a short video showing the use of the temporal window.

systems. Participants made use of this representation of future actions in various ways, including anticipating upcoming actions when performing live, planning, composing and editing in the "future" portion of the temporal window, and adjusting upcoming actions based on knowledge of actions that have already been performed. These observations suggest that the temporal window creates the possibility for new forms of improvised creative collaboration, inspired by, but not quite the same as, traditional improvised music and storytelling.

The rest of this paper is structured as follows. We begin by surveying existing research on creative improvisation, and identify some gaps that led to our research questions. We then describe the two systems we created to support new forms of improvised music and storytelling. This is followed by a description of our observational study, and a discussion of the results of the study. We end the paper with some conclusions and suggestions for future work.

RELATED WORK

We begin by briefly surveying the work that has been done to explore the issues surrounding creative collaboration. This includes work to understand the nature of group creativity and improvisation, investigations of ways to provide external, concrete representation of collaboration, and explorations of the importance of anticipation in collaborative improvisation.

Group Creativity and Improvisation

Sawyer [20,22] proposes an interactional semiotic model of improvisational group creativity that attempts to explain the processes of coordination during improvisation. Sawyer characterizes improvisational group creativity as a situation in which "interaction between performers is immediate, durationally constrained to the moment of creation, and is mediated by musical or verbal signs", where "the group has no intention of generating something that will remain after their performance is done" [21]. In Sawyer's model, each performer proposes possible future content or structure of the performance, what he refers to as an "indexical entailment" after Silverstein [24]. As the group accepts these proposals, they become part of the "emergent" - the cumulative set of indexical presuppositions that have resulted from the interactions up to that moment. Future proposals by performers are constrained in several ways: by the genre of the performance, by the other participants in the performance, and by the set of previous entailments that have been accepted into the emergent. According to Sawyer, improvisatory performances experience a tension between maintaining coherence with the emergent, and demonstrating some degree of innovation. This tension is something that we explore by making these future proposals visible and concrete before they are performed.

Observational research into collaborative storytelling in improv theatre has explored the ways that improv actors develop a shared mental model of their performance. This process involves the inevitable development of misunderstanding and miscommunication during improvisation, what Fuller and Magerko [16] refer to as *cognitive divergence*, followed by a process of *cognitive convergence*, which eventually leads to *cognitive consensus* and a shared mental model of the developing story. Cognitive divergence can take many forms, including disagreements about the current state of the story, the intended future direction of the story, and the methods being used to tell the story. What is interesting about this work is that it suggests this ongoing process of divergence, convergence and consensus is an essential and unavoidable part of the process of improvisation, and that it generally takes place without any explicit statement or representation of each participant's own mental model. Our introduction of the "temporal window" is an attempt to explore what happens when performers are provided with an explicit, dynamic shared space with which to represent their intentions about the future direction of their work.

External Representation in Creative Collaboration

Many kinds of group or distributed creativity are "mediated" through different sorts of collaborative documents that make the creative process visible and persistent [20]. For instance, in live writing performances, a record of the performance is captured in the final written product itself. These documents leave traces of the cognitive and communicative processes, traces that provide an opportunity to study processes that were previously implicit or opaque. At the same time, these traces can influence the creative process itself beyond the explicit communicative content the media support. It is not obvious how theories of materially mediated communication can be applied to collaborative contexts where the creative output is ephemeral and time-bound (such as musical improvisation or collaborative, improvised storytelling).

There a growing body of work on the use of a concrete, visual, and persistent notational system operating within a musical performative and/or improvisational context [6,14,17]. Similarly, audiovisual "live coding" [9], where computer-programming code is written and modified as it is executed to produce a sound and/or graphical performance, utilizes a physical substrate for notation that can be used as external memory, and to explicitly coordinate performance.

There has also been work done to explore shared representations in synchronous collaborative writing. Early work by Baecker et al. [2] explored the use of a shared workspace and awareness tools to support people writing together. More recent work examines how these practices have changed with the advent of easily accessible collaborative writing tools such as Google Docs [4,26]. Research on collaborative storytelling includes Cheng et al.'s work to support creative collaboration and elaboration of ideas [7] and Fails et al.'s work on mobile storytelling by children [13]. Finally, there has been some work which focuses specifically on storytelling in an improvisational context, including Jamieson et al.'s discussions of networked theatre performances [15], Marino and Wittig's exploration of netprov [18], and game-like online storytelling tools such as Rohrer's *Sleep is Death* [19].

Also of direct relevance is research on devising systems to support mutual engagement and awareness in an ongoing performance. In a real-time performance where dynamic communication and coordination is required, shared awareness and feedback that is easy to attend to is crucial [12]. Recent research [6,14,17] addresses the issue of shared awareness by introducing systems that utilize color, iconography, and spatial and temporal organization to represent events and gestures from each performer.

Something that all of the above systems lack is the ability to represent and provide awareness of upcoming changes in the performance in the near future. Work on the Mimi system [23] has explored the notion of representing, on a scrolling score, a visualization of the near future and the recent past as a way to support anticipating the future and reflecting on the past. Here, the improvisation is between a human and a computer performer, rather than between human performers, and only Mimi itself can indicate upcoming actions, to be viewed by the human performer. While Mimi uses notational representation to indicate upcoming music, the Shimon improvising robotic marimba player system uses visual cues to anticipate the arrival time and sound of the next drum hit [8]. To anticipate the next hit, Shimon tracks the mallet's position during its upward or downward motion, and predicts the time and the position at which the mallet will strike the drum.

Anticipation and Upcoming Actions

Recently, Biasutti and Frezza [3] carried out a survey and empirically developed a model of creative improvisation that includes the following 5 processes: i) anticipation, ii) use of repertoire, iii) emotive communication, iv) feedback, and v) flow. Pertinent to our research is the role of anticipation in improvised creative activities. Extensively studied in fields such as psychology and computer-mediated communication, anticipation is seen as crucial to processes found in collaboration, cooperation and communication. Prominent researchers such as Axelrod [1] and Walther [25] have found that individuals become more cooperative and suppress deviant behaviour when they can anticipate future and multiple interactions with others. This knowledge and expectation of future interactions causes individuals to behave more collaboratively as the "shadow of the future" helps guide their actions and behaviour [1].

Anticipation also plays an important role in improvised activities. Improvisations frequently require performers to foresee, predict and respond to upcoming events and changes as the performance unfolds on stage. Traditionally, anticipation has been practiced implicitly, relying on the performers' skills in recognizing patterns and structures in the evolving performance and their ability to plan and respond in the sequence that is required for the performance. For this project, we develop a system that allows improvisational performers to indicate and anticipate upcoming actions during the performance itself.

RESEARCH QUESTION

During improvised creative collaboration, it is challenging to coordinate your actions, as you must respond in real time to a constantly changing situation, and there is no explicit representation of how your collaborators intend to act, requiring you to anticipate their upcoming actions. Our research involves exploring the impact of providing a concrete shared representation that allows performers to visualize upcoming actions in real-time, during a performance. Unlike some of the related previous work [23] our research is specifically concerned with improvised performances that involve multiple human performers. In this paper, we investigate the following questions:

- How would the practice of improvisation be impacted with the introduction of a "temporal window"?
- What are some of the ways improvisers would make use of this "temporal window"?
- How can the features of our prototype system be better improved to support improvised performances?

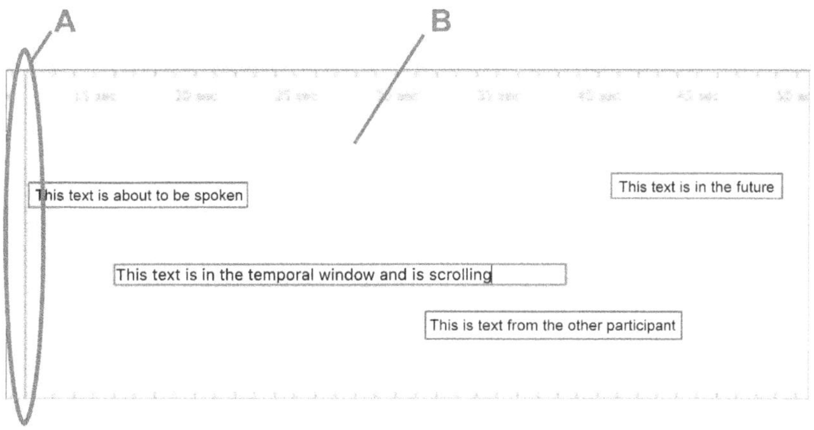

Figure 2: The improvisational writing system, showing the "now" line (A) and the temporal window (B).

Our study aims to offer insights into the design of systems that support creative improvisatory activities as well as other systems that seek to support anticipating future action.

THE TEMPORAL WINDOW

To explore these questions, we created two implementations of what we call the "temporal window". In this section, we begin by introducing the concept of the temporal window, and then describe the two systems we have implemented to explore this concept, one to support musical improvisation and the other to support improvisational storytelling. The scrolling temporal window in both systems is inspired by the "Anticipatory Score" [27], a system that was intended to support sharing of notation about upcoming actions between musicians who were performing with conventional instruments.

At its core, the temporal window is an online workspace supporting improvised performance by collocated performers (see Fig. 1). It is represented as a scrolling window of 20-30 second duration spanning a "now line" (B in Fig. 1) which represents the current performance time where speech or music is rendered. The temporal window provides performers with a space (about 20 seconds before the notes/text are actualized in the performance) where they can indicate their upcoming actions and view their collaborators' upcoming actions, allowing them to potentially coordinate their actions and negotiate the direction of their ongoing performance.

The temporal window could change the dynamics of communication and coordination found in traditional improvised performances by providing and explicitly representing upcoming events and actions. Our goal is to transform a performance from one where both the communication and performance media are ephemeral into one where communication and performance are computer-mediated and explicitly represented. In the following sections, we describe two instantiations of the "temporal window" for music and storytelling as used in our study.

Musical Ensemble Improvisation

Using the musical improvisation system (see Fig. 1), musicians view a scrolling score, much like a piano roll, where a sliding "temporal window" is visible that extends from a short distance in the past (showing what has already been played) (A) to a short distance in the future (showing notation yet to be played) (C). We call this part of the interface (C), the "future window". The current moment in time is represented by the "now" line (B). This scrolling temporal window creates a concrete representation through which performers can communicate as they are performing.

All performers see the same temporal window, and may enter musical phrases (or sequences of notes) in this window. Phrases are entered by clicking a position in the window with the mouse, and then playing the phrase on a MIDI keyboard. We use the concept of a "phrase" as a meta unit of notation in the system for grouping the actual musical notations.

As the user enters musical contributions via a midi keyboard, each phrase moves steadily from right to left, towards the "now" line. As the notation crosses the "now" line, it is rendered (or played) on all participants' computers. Note that when the phrase is entered by the user, the visual representation is created in the temporal window but no sound is rendered. It is only when the phrase crosses the "now" line that the music is actually played. All phrases may be selected with the mouse, and then copied and pasted within the temporal window, and a participant's own phrases may be deleted. Once selected with the mouse, a participant's own phrases may also be transposed (shifted up and down in pitch) at their temporal location.

Improvisational Writing

In the improvisational writing system (see Fig. 2), participants create a story together by writing short text fragments in a scrolling temporal "future" window (B) that is visible to all participants. As soon as the participant clicks on the temporal window, a text entry field appears and starts scrolling to the left. Participants can type directly in the text entry field, which moves at a constant speed towards the "now" line (A). A participant's own text may be repositioned by dragging and dropping within the temporal window, and may be edited or deleted until it reaches the "now" line. All changes are immediately visible to all participants. At the start of the session, participants choose a voice for their character. This is the voice with which the entered text will be spoken by the system. When the text reaches the "now" line (A), it is rendered, or read aloud, in the chosen voice.

STUDY METHOD

To explore how participants would make use of the temporal window, we conducted an observational study of the use of the systems described above. Participants worked in pairs. For the musical system, we conducted 6 sessions, and for the storytelling system we conducted 5 sessions. Participants in the *music sessions* ranged in age from 20 to 27, with an average age of 21.9. There were 5 males and 7 females. All the participants had some form of musical training[1], and 5 had some form of experience in musical improvisation[2]. Participants in the *storytelling sessions* ranged in age from 22 to 44, with an average age of 30.8. There were 4 males and 6 females. All participants had some storytelling experience[3], and 3 of the 5 pairs had previously engaged in collaborative storytelling together.[4]

The study protocol was the same for both the musical and the writing improvisation systems, with minor differences as mentioned below. Participants were initially asked to fill out a simple demographic questionnaire. They were then shown a brief demonstration on the use of the system, and given roughly 5 minutes to try out the system, after which the researchers answered any questions they might have about the functionality of the system. For the music study, participants could briefly discuss choice of instruments and the approach they would take. They were then asked to perform a short collaborative 2-part piece, with each part lasting 10 minutes. A short break was given between parts for participants to rest, and to ask any questions they might have about the system functionality.

Participants were seated together at a table, each with a laptop. They interacted with the improvisational system through the Chrome browser, displayed in full-screen mode (see Fig. 3). A third screen was projected in front of the participants. In the music version, this screen showed the scrolling score, whereas in the storytelling system it showed

Figure 3: Participants interacting with the music improvisation system with MIDI keyboards for entering phrases.

the resulting "script" formed by the text that had already passed the "now" line. Participants were asked to think of the activity as a live performance. During the performance, the participants were not permitted to talk with each other and were encouraged to communicate through the system to simulate typical behavior in an electronically mediated improvisation scenario. Within the short break, the participants in the music sessions could discuss and plan the next part. This was not the case for the storytelling sessions. After the improvisation was complete, participants were asked a set of standard questions[5], followed by a series of questions based on issues that arose during the session.

The session was video recorded, and recordings were also made of the computer screens. These recordings were combined into a single multi-panel video. An initial set of categories was developed based on observations during the sessions, and was used to create a video analysis guide. Categories in the guide included, for example: "anticipating upcoming actions while performing live" and "turn-taking in the temporal window". Researchers divided the videos between themselves, and used the video analysis guide to identify salient and significant occurrences. The results were shared with a group of six researchers, and compared to create a combined set of categories, which formed the basis for the results reported in this paper.

RESULTS

We found that, given the provision of an explicit representation of upcoming actions, participants in our study did exploit this representation in specific ways that distinguish their behavior from traditional improvised performances. We observed participants i) coordinating their actions with those of their collaborators by performing live while attending to upcoming actions as opposed to having to anticipate those actions, and ii) planning and editing their upcoming actions based on an awareness of both other upcoming actions and actions that had already

[1] 5 with guitar (one guitar only, grade 5 Trinity Guildhall Practical; others with a mix of other instruments and self-taught), and 9 with piano (10 years, 12 years, grade 5, grade 7, grade 8, grade 8/12 years, 2 self-taught, 1 didn't say); none were familiar with the notation used in the system.

[2] 1 in duets and quartets, 3 in quartets, and 1 in a band; none of the pairs knew each other before the study.

[3] 6 had written short stories, 1 had written a novel, 6 had played tabletop role-playing games, and 3 had done improv theatre.

[4] 1 pair had worked in Google Docs, and 2 pairs had played tabletop role-playing games together; 4 of the 5 pairs knew each other before the study.

[5] See http://tinyurl.com/cc2017-questions for the list of questions.

been performed. We also observed the use of the temporal window to iii) support negotiation by means of turn-taking in the "near future" portion of the temporal window. Finally, we saw iv) a tension between planning and improvisation that resulted from the features of the temporal window. This tension presents interesting design challenges for the support of improvised collaboration.

In the rest of the paper, we will refer to the musical improvisation sessions as session M1 through M6, and the storytelling sessions as session S1 through S5. Participants will be referred to as P1 and P2, with the session as a prefix. For example, the second participant in the first music session is participant M1P2. Timecodes are given for examples drawn directly from the improvisation sessions.

Coordination

There were several ways that participants made use of the temporal window to coordinate their performances in ways not seen in traditional improvisation. These included performing live while attending to upcoming actions, and planning and editing upcoming actions.

When asked to describe the "now" line (see B in Fig. 1 & A in Fig. 2) and the "future" window (see C in Fig. 1 and B in Fig. 2), participants generally saw the "now" line as "immediate" (M1P1, M2P2), "live" (M1P2, S1P1), "what I will hear if I play a note currently" (M2P1), and "what is being communicated" (M1P1). In contrast, the "future" window was "something you expect coming, what will be communicated" (M1P1), "notes that will eventually be played" (M1P2), "where notes can be added" (M4P1), and "where notes to be played, input in advance" (M5P1). This suggests that the participants were clearly distinguishing between performing live and creating upcoming actions.

Performing Live While Attending to Upcoming Actions

One way that the temporal window impacted communication and coordination amongst the study participants was by supporting performing live while paying attention to upcoming actions. Unlike traditional improvisation, the participants in our study were making decisions as to what actions to take based on externally represented upcoming actions visible in the temporal window, as opposed to anticipating purely based on their internal understanding of and assumptions about what their partner may do in the future. We observed this behavior in almost all the study sessions.

When asked how they made use of the future portion of the temporal window, some participants said they were using it to respond to their partner's upcoming actions. For example, participant M1P1 said, "Expecting what is coming up in the future window gave me a sense of where the music is going, allow me to prepare myself to react and accompany appropriately at the 'now' line". Similarly, participant M1P2 claimed to have used the "now" line and future window to "observe what the other partner is playing and try to play something with a similar pattern or phrase". These comments suggest the temporal window provides our subjects with a means of anticipating other participants' actions.

In terms of whether they felt that the future portion of the temporal window was useful, most of the participants reported that it was. Like the comments mentioned above, participants found the temporal window helped them to anticipate their partner's actions. For example, participant M1P2 felt that "I can anticipate and see what I have already played and attempt to play notes (*phrases*) that makes the song melodious." Other comments included the feeling by participant M2P1 that with the future window, "I can anticipate both the player's and my own future moves to determine what/how I can complement it." Similarly, participant M6P1 reported that "It helped with the scrolling score for I could predict what was coming. This helped me to decide what notes to enter." Communication was described as "Non-verbal, reactionary to real time playing or anticipatory when you observe certain phrases coming" (M1P1), and as a process in which they could "Feel and anticipate" (M1P2).

An example of this can be seen in session M6 (see Fig. 4). Here, participant M6P2 attended to phrases placed by M6P1 earlier, which were scrolling in from the future portion of the temporal window (B). M6P2 performed by holding a note as the phrase placed by his partner reaches the "now" line (A). This resembles improvised "bass" accompaniment in that the strong notes of the melodic line are held to provide bass support (M6 22:48-23:29).

Another example of this can be seen in session M1. When asked about her awareness of her partner's activity in the temporal window, participant M1P2 commented, "When I see her playing up and down (*playing high and low notes*), I try to play the same octave to match it. It might not be the same, but close". When asked the same question, M1P1 said, "At one point in time, she started a bit after the "now" line and I know that this intense thing is coming, so I prepare myself at the 'now' line, so that when it (*the phrases played by M1P2*) comes, I'll just play what I think suits." For both participants in session M1, the participant

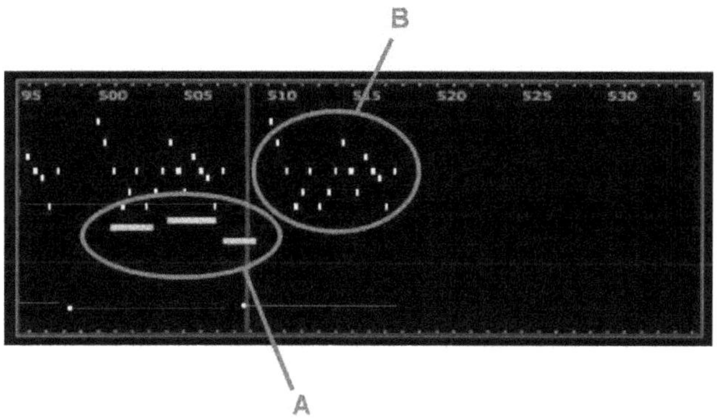

Figure 4: Participant M6P2 acts at the "now" line (A), based on actions scrolling from the future portion of the window (B).

performing live at the "now" line is attending to the upcoming actions her partner is placing in the "future" portion of the temporal window, and taking anticipatory action based on an awareness of these upcoming actions.

There were also examples from the storytelling sessions of participants performing live, or at least close to the "now" line, while attending to existing phrases in the future portion of the temporal window. For example, in session S3 (see Fig. 5), participant S3P2 added a phrase close to the "now" line (A) as an interjection in the middle of a series of phrases (B and C) being added by participant S3P1 (S3 09:36). This new phrase built upon the ideas being placed in the future portion of the window by S3P1, making use of the upcoming ideas made visible by the concrete representation of upcoming actions provided by the temporal window.

The behavior seen in these examples is a form of anticipation of upcoming actions that would not be possible without the temporal window, as these actions are normally not represented in any concrete manner. By making such upcoming actions explicit, the temporal window provides our study participants with an opportunity to attend to potential upcoming events and offers by their partners. They are also able to craft appropriate and immediate responses (for e.g. a bass accompaniment to an upcoming melody) as the performance evolves.

Planning and Editing Upcoming Actions

There were also times when participants were actively planning and editing in the future portion of the temporal window. The extra time afforded by working "in the future" allows participants both time to plan/edit on their own, and to be aware of their partner's upcoming actions and act or make changes to their own upcoming actions in response to the partner's upcoming actions.

For example, participant S1P1 compared working in the temporal window to typing in an instant messaging application like *WhatsApp*, with the important difference

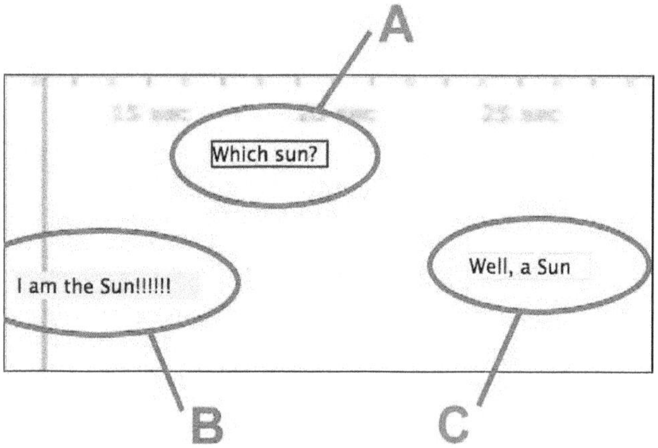

Figure 5: Participant S3P2 adding a phrase (A) between existing phrases of S3P1 (B and C).

that your recipient can see the text before you "press enter". Rather than simply seeing an indication that the sender is preparing an action, the actual content of the upcoming action is available to the recipient, content that can be used to anticipate the direction the collaboration is going, and plan accordingly. Although both participants in session S1 felt that this dialogue was mostly reactive, there were a few instances where both participants typed at the same time, after which one would alter their content in relation to their partner's text. This suggests that the representation of upcoming actions allowed the participants to engage in coordination and editing *before* the phrases were performed at the "now" line. As S1P1 explained, the temporal window "gives you time to anticipate, react and change things, kind of like having multiple chances to re-express yourself."

Similarly, participant S3P1 felt that:

> If I was on a stage setting, I would have to process this very quickly, but now I can see in front of me, so I can process that and I can strip existing things I was writing, reprocess it so I can try to fit it in nicely.

The extra time given by the temporal window allows participants not just more time to react to their partner's upcoming actions, but also to edit and "reprocess" their own actions.

Another way that the participants began to "edit" their contributions to the performance was to reposition their upcoming actions for timing in the future portion of the temporal window. For example, Participant S5P1 moved her text so that it was positioned between two of S5P2's phrases. When asked why, participant S5P1 explained:

> Sometimes my character's voice takes a very long time whereas for his (*S5P2*), it's very fast, so there will be a very, very big pause if I were to let it move real time. So, I try to move it in front so there won't be a pause and it sounds more like I'm responding to him as opposed to random people just talking and then having awkward pauses in the middle.

As participant S5P1 had chosen a voice that spoke very slowly, she took advantage of the temporal window to reposition her text so that the timing would resemble a more natural back-and-forth between the characters.

A comparable revision of the ordering of phrases was seen in session M6, where participant M6P2 synchronized his phrase with a phrase scrolling in from the future portion of the window. This was achieved by pasting the upcoming phrase such that the starting and ending notes matched his partner M6P1's phrase (M6 20:23).

This type of fine-tuning of the ordering and relationships between upcoming actions would not be possible without the concrete representation of upcoming actions in the temporal window and the manipulability of those actions it affords to the performers. There is still time pressure and a need to constantly be aware of your partner's actions, but there is also a short window of time in which you can adjust your actions before they are performed. This opens a space between the immediacy and ephemerality of improvisation, and the more distanced concreteness of planning.

Negotiation

In addition to coordinating their actions with their partner's actions by making use of the temporal window, participants also used the temporal window to actively negotiate with their partner during performance. Participants in the study made use of the temporal window to work back and forth in a turn-taking fashion, much as they would be when performing live, but both working somewhat ahead of the "now" line, a few seconds before the musical or textual phrases would be rendered.

For example, during the first part of the performance in session M3, both participants took turns playing (creating phrases) in the future portion of the temporal window just a short distance ahead of the "now" line. The exchange was through short phrases that exhibited a call and response pattern of interaction. Although there were considerable silence/rests between the turns, the content of the turns was clearly related to each other in musical ways.

This is somewhat like the turn-taking that would take place when performing live, directly at the "now" line. An important difference is that the gap between the "now" line and the location where the turn-taking was taking place provided a small window of time for participants to anticipate and coordinate their actions. Unlike performing live, where phrases cannot be changed because they are immediately performed, material placed in the future portion of the temporal window is still open to negotiation and change for a short time before it is rendered. This changes the nature of the collaboration from one that depends on anticipation and response to one that also involves a certain amount of planning and negotiation.

Similar turn taking was observed in the storytelling sessions. In session S1, both participants generally tended

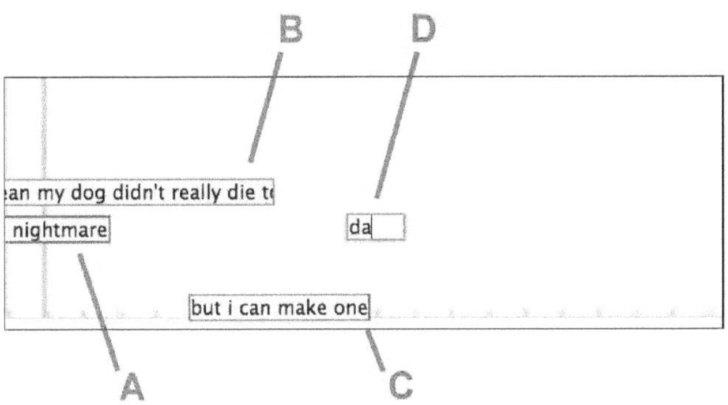

Figure 6: Turn-taking just ahead of the "now" line. Participant S1P1 entered phrases A and C, whereas participant S1P2 entered phrases B and D. Turn-taking sequence was A, B, C, D, but C and D were edited simultaneously.

to place their phrases right after each other in a turn-taking fashion. One implication of this type of behavior, particularly when the upcoming actions were placed very close to the "now" line, was the use of multiple, short phrases rather than longer, continuous phrases. For example, participant S1P2 (see Fig. 6) would often break long phrases into shorter ones to avoid her phrases hitting the "now" line before typing was complete (A and C). However, unlike traditional turn-taking, there would sometimes be moments when both participants were either composing or editing their phrases simultaneously, revising their upcoming actions moments before the actions are performed (C and D) while maintaining awareness of their partner's upcoming actions (S1 31:43-31:48). Again, this changes the nature of the collaboration from pure improvisation to a combination of improvisation and (very short-term) planning.

Tension Between Planning and Improvising

Planning takes time, time that doesn't normally exist during traditional improvisation, as performers need to be constantly performing live. By introducing the temporal window, we gave the participants this time. Specifically, we gave them 20 seconds, the time it takes a phrase placed at the rightmost side of the temporal window to scroll to the "now" line and be performed. As participant M1P1 states,

> I like the fact that I can anticipate what she (*M1P2*) is playing, like if she wants to bring the music somewhere else which she did, then I'll be like 'oh, she's doing something different' then I can react to that and catch up to what she wants. And that is outside of real time since it's like moving, right? So, I think that that is very nice.

Interestingly, this is both an act of anticipation - acting based on an expectation of what is to come - and a reaction to the other performer's act of placing a phrase in the future portion of the temporal window. This combination of anticipation and reaction allowed for a certain amount of planning, as there was some sense of what was to come in the next 20 seconds, while still retaining the immediacy of improvisation.

However, this time for planning was still limited, and interestingly actually caused some of the participants to feel additional time pressure as their phrases moved inexorably towards the "now" line. As described by M6P2, "It represented a kind of 'deadline' to [be met] the longer there were only notes from the other person there." The presence of notes played by his partner and none contributed by himself, coupled with the constant scrolling of the temporal window, put pressure on M6P2 to make contributions to the performance. Similarly, Participant S1P1 felt that the temporal window "gave some leeway to plan and edit my responses, but it was also hard to catch the right timing to make our conversation beats resemble real-life conversation," and described the "now" line as "like the point of no return."

Interestingly, participant M6P2 felt the "now" line "represents true improvisation to me: on the fly edits and listening to the other [person] playing for musical cues". This is in contrast with the future portion of the temporal window, which this participant saw as representing

> 'impending disaster' because the process to compose, copy and paste is too long. Musical ideas weren't able to flow freely before the pattern changed and the guesswork started again.

This highlights the way that the future window potentially changes the nature of improvisation.

There were also mixed reactions to the scrolling nature of the temporal window. Those who were comfortable with the scrolling felt that, for example, it "allows me to understand what notes are being played and is an indication of time. Very useful visually" (M1P1). Participant M2P2 felt that it "Enables both delayed and immediate usage", again highlighting the ways the temporal window possibly changes the nature of improvisation. Others, however, found the scrolling problematic, saying that it "can get a bit tired because [we have to] keep waiting and [it] keeps scrolling" (M2P1). In fact, several participants found the constant scrolling problematic, suggesting that "the sense of 'real time' limits the creation of music as it felt 'rushed'" (M1P1).

These observations highlight a tension between improvisation and planning that emerged with the use of the temporal window. This tension suggests an interesting challenge facing designers of systems that have a focus on representation of future actions in time-sensitive scenarios: how to balance the need to have time to plan against the need to be aware of one's partner and react in-the-moment, improvisationally?

DISCUSSION

From the results described above, we can see that, when given a concrete, external representation of upcoming actions, participants in our study did indeed take advantage of the concreteness of this shared workspace. There was, however, a tension between the immediate spontaneity that characterizes improvisation, and the time needed for planning. This is related to Brown and Edelson's [5] notion of "disciplined improvisation", which they define as "a dynamic process involving a combination of planning and improvisation". In the context of classroom teaching, Brown and Edelson suggest there is a need for a balance between free improvisation and some overall structure (in their case, the broader curriculum). In the context of improvisational performance, it is worth considering where this structure can be found, and how it could help to allow performers to move back and forth between improvisation and planning.

One thing that we are considering with the next iteration of the temporal window is whether placing better "scaffolds" would help improvisers structure and guide their performances better. According to Sawyer [22], "[all] improvisation always occurs within a structure, and all improvisers draw on ready-mades - short motifs or clichés - as they create their novel performance". One difference that we noticed between the two domains (music and storytelling) was the tendency for the performers in the music sessions to copy and paste phrases for reuse. These reusable phrases could begin to form the basis for a set of "ready-mades" that the performers can draw upon when improvising and planning.

The nature of music - involving repeated patterns - affords the creation of these reusable phrases. The inclusion of the phrase structure in the music system, and the ability to copy these phrases, further supported this type of reuse. In contrast, the storytelling system simply provided language as raw material, with little structure for performers to work with beyond whatever prior understanding of storytelling and narrative structure that they brought with them to the session. However, there are elements of storytelling, such as genre or character prompts, that we are considering implementing in the temporal window that could help performers scaffold their narrative improvisation. This suggests that the provision of domain-specific abstractions and structures (for instance, plot scaffolds for improvised narratives) may allow for balancing of improvisation and planning within a system designed to support creative collaborative performances.

Participants in our study had a clear sense of the difference between performing live at the "now" line, and placing upcoming actions in the "future" portion of the temporal window. They also reflect an awareness of the possibility of using the temporal window as an aid to anticipation, and to communicate and coordinate with their partners. There were, however, tensions that arose between the nature of improvisation and the use of the temporal window – traditionally, improvisation is characterized as requiring a focus on the "now", whereas the temporal window shifts the focus to the (near) future. There were also difficulties related to the constant scrolling of the temporal window. Interestingly, the participants in the storytelling study more frequently complained about the time pressure imposed by the scrolling window. It may be that the scrolling window - inspired by a piano score - is more appropriate for music, and other representations of time, such as signals or events, may be more appropriate for storytelling. Future versions of the temporal window will need to pay closer attention to aspects of usability and domain specificity.

Lastly, it is important to note that actions on the temporal window do not literally take place in the future. The conceit with our system was to provide improvisers with an illusion of the future through the user interface. The temporal window allows improvisers to choose between performing live in real-time (at the now line of the user interface) or to provide "offers" that will only be performed/rendered in twenty seconds. By introducing this option, the temporal window allows improvisers to retain the spontaneity of their performance while at the same time offering them the ability to plan and anticipate upcoming events and actions during the performance.

Based on the responses of our study subjects, it appears that the temporal window can provide a helpful illusion of planning and coordinating in the near-future. This illusion of future action has the potential to be a useful user interface mechanism that can be exploited especially in areas of high pressure real-time collaboration and decision making, such as emergency and crises management. We hope to be able to extend the application of the temporal window beyond creative applications in the near future.

LIMITATIONS

There are a number of limitations to our study, which should be considered an initial, exploratory study of the use of the temporal window to support anticipation of upcoming actions during creative collaboration. As this was a lab-based study conducted with participants who had never used our system before, it is entirely possible that the participants' behaviour could change as they become more familiar with the particular constraints and affordances of our system. It is also possible that the artificial nature of the "performance" (due to the lack of an actual audience) impacted the way the participants used the system. Finally, the varying degrees of experience that the participants had with improvisational performance, and the fact that several of the musical participants did not have experience playing keyboard-based instruments, may have impacted our results.

It is also important to note that we were less concerned with issues of consistency of codes and intercoder reliability than with being able to identify and discuss unique behaviors and interactions that emerged because of using the temporal window. We acknowledge that an exploratory approach has several limitations – namely, that we are unable to generalize our study results beyond the music and storytelling sessions that were conducted. However, because of the novelty of our interface, we were more interested in identifying patterns of new creative and collaborative behaviors that may have emerged because of using the temporal window than attempting to prematurely generalize these observations.

FUTURE WORK

The above discussion suggests several possible directions for future work. One direction is to explore different forms of improvisation, in addition to music and storytelling, to see which forms may be more suited to this approach. For example, it may be interesting to see whether improvisational poetry, akin to "poem slams", may be more appropriate than storytelling as an application area for the temporal window.

It would also be interesting to explore whether higher levels of abstraction, such as representation of characters, events and locations in the storytelling system, for example, may provide additional structure in the form of ready-mades and therefore possibly afford a more fluid movement between improvisation and planning.

The use of the temporal window to provide a concrete representation of upcoming actions can potentially impact improvised creative collaboration in several ways, possibly leading to new forms of creative collaboration. For instance, by reducing the cognitive load of the performers through the sharing of information explicitly and externally, it may shift the focus of the collaboration from being entirely in-the-moment to more forward-looking, resulting in something that is more a combination of planning and improvisation rather than purely improvisational. This is something we would like to investigate further in future.

It may also be worth investigating other potential application areas that involve improvisation and planning but are not within the area of the arts, such as situation awareness, crisis management or business planning, to see whether the notion of providing a concrete, externalized representation of upcoming actions can help those working in these areas to better coordinate and communicate during real-time improvised creative collaboration.

CONCLUSION

In this paper, we introduced what we call the "temporal window", an interface that provides a concrete, externalized representation of upcoming actions during real-time creative collaborative improvisational performances. We explored how performers make use of this novel interface by conducting an exploratory qualitative study of two implementations, one for musical ensemble improvisation and the other for improvised collaborative storytelling. Participants in our study made use of the temporal window in several ways, including performing live while attending to upcoming actions, and composing, planning and editing these upcoming actions. We also observed a tension created by the time pressure introduced by the constantly moving temporal window, suggesting additional challenges for designers of this type of system.

These results can help inform the design of systems to support improvised creative collaboration. More broadly, this approach can also potentially be applied to other areas that involve paying attention to and anticipating upcoming actions, such as crisis management, business contingency planning, and disaster recovery. It can also serve as a first step towards developing a deeper understanding of the relationship between planning and improvisation in creativity and innovation.

ACKNOWLEDGMENTS

This research is funded under the National University of Singapore Humanities and Social Sciences Seed Fund grant "Communication Strategies in Real-time Computer-Mediated Creative Collaboration".

REFERENCES

1. Robert Axelrod. 1984. The Evolution of Cooperation Basic Books. *New York.*
2. Ronald M. Baecker, Dimitrios Nastos, Ilona R. Posner, and Kelly L. Mawby. 1993. The user-centered iterative design of collaborative writing software. In *Proceedings of the INTERACT'93 and CHI'93 conference on Human factors in computing systems*, 399–405.
3. Michele Biasutti and Luigi Frezza. 2009. Dimensions of Music Improvisation. *Creativity Research Journal* 21, 2–3: 232–242.
4. Tom Boellstorff, Bonnie Nardi, Celia Pearce, and T. L. Taylor. 2013. Words with Friends: Writing Collaboratively Online. *interactions* 20, 5: 58–61.
5. M. Brown and D. C. Edelson. 2001. Teaching by design: Curriculum design as a lens on instructional practice. In *annual meeting of the American Educational Research Association, Seattle, WA.*
6. Nick Bryan-Kinns. 2011. Annotating distributed scores for mutual engagement in daisyphone and beyond. *Leonardo Music Journal* 21: 51–55.
7. Justin Cheng, Laewoo Kang, and Dan Cosley. 2013. Storeys: designing collaborative storytelling interfaces. In *CHI'13 Extended Abstracts on Human Factors in Computing Systems*, 3031–3034.
8. Marcelo Cicconet, Mason Bretan, and Gil Weinberg. 2012. Visual cues-based anticipation for percussionist-robot interaction. In *Proceedings of the seventh annual ACM/IEEE international conference on Human-Robot Interaction*, 117–118.
9. Nick Collins, Alex McLean, Julian Rohrhuber, and Adrian Ward. 2003. Live coding in laptop performance. *Organised sound* 8, 03: 321–330.
10. Jane W. Davidson and James MM Good. 2002. Social and musical co-ordination between members of a string quartet: An exploratory study. *Psychology of music* 30, 2: 186–201.
11. C. Dobrian. 1991. Thoughts on composition and improvisation.
12. Paul Dourish and Victoria Bellotti. 1992. Awareness and coordination in shared workspaces. In *Proceedings of the 1992 ACM conference on Computer-supported cooperative work*, 107–114.
13. Jerry Alan Fails, Allison Druin, and Mona Leigh Guha. 2014. Interactive storytelling: interacting with people, environment, and technology. *International Journal of Arts and Technology* 7, 1: 112–124.
14. Robin Fencott and Nick Bryan-Kinns. 2010. Hey Man, You're Invading my Personal Space! Privacy and Awareness in Collaborative Music. In *NIME*, 198–203.
15. H. V. Jamieson. 2008. Real time, virtual space, live theatre. *The aotearoa digital arts reader. Auckland: Aotearoa Digital Arts and Clouds.*
16. Brian Magerko, Waleed Manzoul, Mark Riedl, Allan Baumer, Daniel Fuller, Kurt Luther, and Celia Pearce. 2009. An empirical study of cognition and theatrical improvisation. In *Proceedings of the seventh ACM conference on Creativity and cognition*, 117–126.
17. Thor Magnusson. 2013. The threnoscope: A musical work for live coding performance. In *ICSE.*
18. Mark Marino and Rob Wittig. 2012. Netprov: Elements of an Emerging Form. *Dichtung Digital* 42.
19. Jason Rohrer. 2010. Sleep is Death. *Computer software.*
20. R. Keith Sawyer. 1995. Creativity as mediated action: A comparison of improvisational performance and product creativity. *Mind, Culture, and Activity* 2, 3: 172–191.
21. R. Keith Sawyer. 2003. *Group creativity: Music, theater, collaboration.* Psychology Press.
22. R. Keith Sawyer. 2004. Creative teaching: Collaborative discussion as disciplined improvisation. *Educational researcher* 33, 2: 12–20.
23. Isaac Schankler, Elaine Chew, and Alexandre RJ François. 2014. Improvising with Digital Auto-Scaffolding: How Mimi Changes and Enhances the Creative Process. In *Digital Da Vinci.* Springer, 99–125.
24. Michael Silverstein. 1993. Metapragmatic discourse and. *Reflexive language: Reported speech and metapragmatics*: 33.
25. Joseph B. Walther. 1997. Group and interpersonal effects in international computer-mediated collaboration. *Human Communication Research* 23, 3: 342–369.
26. Dakuo Wang. 2016. How People Write Together Now: Exploring and Supporting Today's Computer-Supported Collaborative Writing. In *Proceedings of the 19th ACM Conference on Computer Supported Cooperative Work and Social Computing Companion*, 175–179.
27. Lonce Wyse and Jude Yew. 2014. A Real-Time Score for Collaborative Just-in-Time Composition. *Organised Sound* 19, 3: 260.

Designing for Socially Interactive Systems

Duri Long, Mikhail Jacob, Nicholas Davis, Brian Magerko
Georgia Institute of Technology
Atlanta, Georgia, USA
{duri, mikhail.jacob, ndavis35, magerko}@gatech.edu

ABSTRACT
This paper reports on the design and evaluation of *LuminAI*, a socially interactive art installation in which participants can engage in collaborative movement improvisation with virtual agents and other humans. LuminAI was used as a technical probe to study social interaction within interactive art at a local art gala during which over 100 participants interacted with the system. Video and interview data was gathered during the event and analyzed using thematic analysis to develop a taxonomy to guide the design of socially interactive systems involving humans and artificial agents. This taxonomy helped us identify areas where LuminAI was successful, where it needs improvement, and conceptual spaces we have yet to explore.

Author Keywords
Artificial intelligence; social interaction; computational creativity; Viewpoints; dance improvisation; interactive installation

ACM Classification Keywords
H.5.m. Information interfaces and presentation (e.g., HCI): Miscellaneous

INTRODUCTION
Computer colleagues have been developed to facilitate creative collaboration and ideation in human creators [13]. Most of these colleagues are designed to work one-on-one with a human partner to creatively improvise in fields like dance [22, 30], drawing [16], and theatrical improvisation [28]. However, co-creative computer colleagues have not yet been widely employed and studied within large social contexts (i.e. crowd or multi-user environments). In order to explore how to design socially interactive creative systems involving multiple humans and AI agents, we created *LuminAI*, a multi-user interactive dance installation.

Studying creativity within social environments involving both humans and agents raises new questions in terms of the human-centered design of AI-based experiences. For instance, how do we evaluate the creativity of multiple agents in a social environment? How do humans and agents interact and collaborate in a multi-user environment? How does physical space affect social interaction? How do people and agents configure their awareness of each other?

Existing work across several disciplines begins to investigate some of the above questions. Methods have been created for evaluating both creativity support tools [11] and creative engagement [18]. Studies of small group creativity [15, 28, 29, 32, 35] and societal creativity [14, 36] deal with how humans collaborate creatively in social environments. Work at the intersection of the fields of sociology, Computer Supported Collaborative Work (CSCW), architecture, and technology looks at the social affordances of physical spaces [10], social interaction dynamics amongst humans [20], and social communication and collaboration in work environments [4]. Empirical work has also been done to study human-agent interaction dynamics in creative task environments, but the vast majority of these studies focus on interaction between a single human and a single AI agent [8, 15, 22, 30]. This is still an area of research with a lot of room for investigation, and there is a strong need for empirical work investigating human-agent interaction in socially creative environments.

In this paper, we investigate human-agent co-creative movement improvisation in a social dance installation called LuminAI. We begin by describing a public installation and evaluation of the LuminAI system. We then discuss how the findings from this event informed the development of a detailed taxonomy to guide the design of socially interactive agent-based systems. The taxonomy identifies key design considerations for socially interactive systems, building off of existing work [4] that introduces five high-level themes (*territoriality*, *awareness*, *control*, *interaction*, and *transitions*) that should be considered in the design of social spaces.

THE LUMINAI INSTALLATION
The LuminAI installation was created to allow multiple people to dance with each other in collaboration with artificial agents within a geodesic dome. Digital silhouettes of participants and virtual agents are projected onto the walls of the dome. A participant can move his or her body (and consequently his or her silhouette), and the agent will respond with an improvised movement of its own. Multiple agents and humans can meet in the liminal space of the dome and their shadows can dance together. This is in contrast to previous dyadic versions of LuminAI (formerly

C&C '17, June 27-30, 2017, Singapore, Singapore

ACM ISBN 978-1-4503-4403-6/17/06...$15.00
http://dx.doi.org/10.1145/3059454.3059479

Figure 1. LuminAI Dome installation: mock-up (left) and live interaction (right). Mock-up credits Jessica Anderson.

Viewpoints AI) where a single human could playfully engage in dance-like movement improvisation with a single virtual character in a two-dimensional shadow theater installation [22]. In these previous versions, any multi-person interaction was purely incidental.

LuminAI is housed within a 23-foot diameter wide, 15-foot tall 3V(B) steel geodesic dome frame with 105 projection-ready translucent textile panels covering the surface. Participants can enter and exit the dome through doorways created by removing textile paneling. They can then dance with each other inside the domed space. An audience outside the dome can view the ongoing shadow party installation as a performance.

The agent architecture controlling the virtual characters uses case-based reasoning [23] to learn movements and patterns of interaction from all participants over time. Viewpoints [5], a widely used theory in the fields of theater and dance that provides a way of thinking about movement and gesture, is used as the system's vocabulary to procedurally represent and reason about movement [21]. Viewpoints guides the system in reasoning about movement along the dimensions of tempo, duration, repetition, kinesthetic response (natural movement timing), spatial relationships, topography (traced floor patterns of movement over time), shape (of movement and body), gesture, and architecture. It also responds improvisationally using procedural response strategies when learned knowledge is not sufficient or appropriate.

The current prototype of the installation consists of three separate interaction spaces, spanning the entire dome's inner surface. The combined video output is projection mapped to the external surface of the dome using MadMapper [26] and displayed on its exterior using three externally mounted projectors. The installation captures participant movements inside the dome using three depth sensors distributed equally around the dome, facing its center. A new prototype currently in development replaces the three separate interaction spaces with a single virtual domed space that receives multiple Kinect inputs and has multiple virtual camera views of that space projected onto the exterior of the dome.

LuminAI was designed as a technical probe to investigate how to convert a dyadic co-creative movement-based improvisational experience into a socially interactive experience. In order to create such an experience, a geodesic dome was chosen as the interaction space due to its potential social affordances. We hypothesized that the dome would a) allow for a spectrum of multi-user experiences ranging from dyadic human-agent interaction to a crowd-level dance party; b) create a liminal space that is clearly defined for the co-presence of groups of people and AI agents; c) afford social interaction by being enclosed, forcing people to be in close proximity to each other and shielding participants from outside observers; and d) attract participants to participate via visual spectacle.

EVALUATION METHODOLOGY

We decided to study participant interactions with LuminAI in order to investigate the following research questions: 1) How do we design interactive systems and co-creative AI agents for a multi-user environment?; 2) How do people make sense of AI agents when they are transported into a multi-user environment?; and 3) What aspects of LuminAI help facilitate social interaction? LuminAI was exhibited for a week at the Goat Farm Arts Center in Atlanta, with the opening gala attended primarily by artists and art connoisseurs. The event was six hours long, and during this time, approximately 100 people were recorded on video interacting with the LuminAI installation. All participants were informed that they would be recorded via clearly visible signs placed outside of the installation.

The prototype of LuminAI exhibited was specifically customized for the opening gala. At the event, LuminAI was also being used as a human-AI performance space for a choreographed dance. Therefore, due to the aesthetic requirements of the dance performance, only two-thirds of the textile projection panels were installed, leaving a large cutaway where the audience could see the participants, their digital silhouettes, and the virtual characters. Soon after the start of the opening gala, the visualizations presented to participants were switched from showing only the virtual characters to showing all participants' digital silhouettes as well as the virtual characters (see Figure 2 for an image of the dome with just the agents, no silhouettes). This was done pragmatically based on observing participant interactions with the system and deciding that it was important for all participants to see some immediate feedback when they entered the interaction space.

Figure 2: The LuminAI installation prior to turning on the silhouettes.

Nearly an hour (57:53) of video data was collected throughout the event. For approximately 13 minutes (12:59) of video data the projected visualization consisted only of the virtual characters. The rest (44:54) of the video data shows digital silhouettes of the participants along with the virtual characters.

During the gala event, we conducted brief, semi-structured interviews with 18 different participants. The semi-structured interviews were conducted based on the following questions: a) What is your initial reaction to the experience you just had? b) How do you think the system works? c) Did you enjoy your interaction? d) What was confusing or frustrating? e) How might the experience be improved? Participants' responses were recorded in field notes that were later analyzed.

Both the field notes and the video data were analyzed using thematic analysis [7]. We identified common themes within the data, and then coded the data for each of these interaction trends. After coding the data and reviewing the literature, we found that many of our observations fit under the umbrella of an existing high-level framework (see *Findings*). However, this existing framework did not go into sufficient detail to explain some of our observations. As a result, we used the results from our analysis to create a new, more detailed taxonomy for analyzing social interaction in human-agent systems (see Figure 3).

FINDINGS

Based on a synthesis of literature across disciplines including sociology, CSCW, architecture, and cognitive science, as well as observations from the public installation of LuminAI, we present a taxonomy (see Figure 3) of conceptual spaces that should be considered when designing agent-based systems that are focused on facilitating social interaction. At the highest level, this taxonomy is organized according to the *Tacit* framework: five design themes that "provide a way of structuring the issues that designers of social spaces need to deal with" [4]. We chose this framework because the high-level results from our data-driven analysis corresponded with these five themes (territoriality, awareness, control, interaction, and transitions), but the themes as originally presented in the literature were not specified in enough detail to thoroughly answer our questions about social interaction in LuminAI. In addition, the Tacit framework does not address how each of these themes might be affected by introducing artificial agents into the social space. As a result, we have expanded and specified the framework in more detail based on a synthesis of the literature as well as our own empirical observations. This section provides an overview of the literature along with empirical data and detail how both contributed to the resulting taxonomy.

Territoriality

The first theme, territoriality, "concerns spaces and the relationships between people and spaces" [4]. Based on relevant aspects of territoriality discussed in the literature, our taxonomy divides territoriality into two conceptual spaces: *territory* and *conflict*.

Territory

Background

Territory deals with the relationship between physical space and interaction dynamics. Humans have "spatial literacy" and are able to make sense of social situations and interactions due to people's spatial relationships to each other [10]. As a result, different spatial constraints afford certain types of interactions [10]. For example, in dance clubs, different practices are acceptable in different spaces [27]. It may be normal to dance on the dance floor, but this type of interaction is less acceptable at the bar [27].

The physical barriers between different interaction spaces can serve as *involvement shields* or "barriers to perception" [20] that allow individuals to go "off stage" or "out of play" [27]. For example, the barrier between the dance floor and the bar allows people to move "backstage" and retreat from active physical participation [27]. In addition to defining the barriers between territories, the liminal "regions and seams where spaces come together" can also facilitate certain types of social interactions and transitions [4]. For instance, an individual standing in the space between the dance floor and bar may interact differently than they would in the center of the dance floor or sitting at the bar.

Observations

In the case of LuminAI, three different areas of interaction were observed: the physical space inside the dome, the digital projection space on the dome surface, and the area outside of the dome. People outside of the dome were typically not interacting directly with the system, and spent their time either watching participants or engaging with other non-related activities. People physically inside the dome were typically engaged with the system, and their

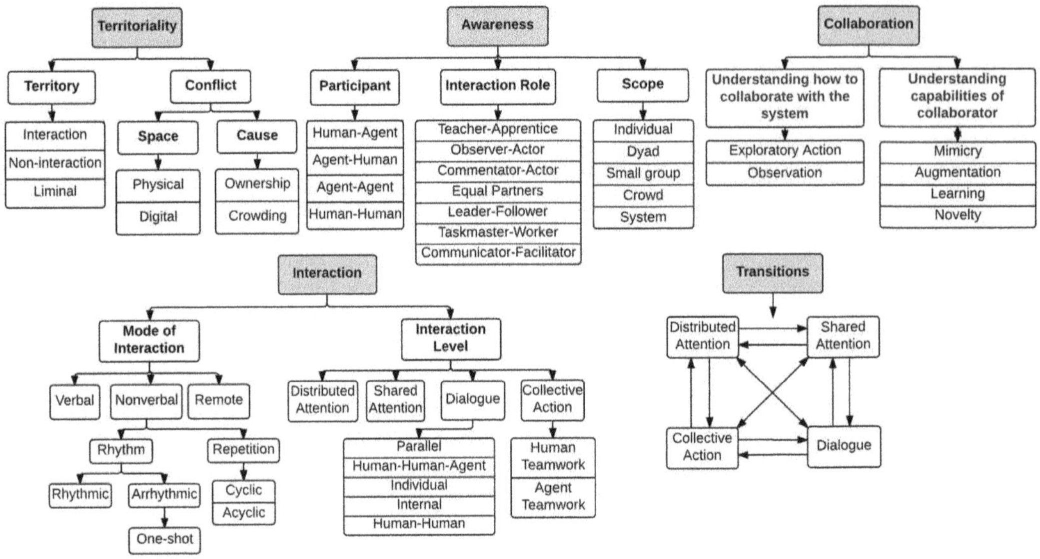

Figure 3: Synthesized and Expanded *Tacit* Taxonomy

interactions with the system involved both physical movement on the dance floor and virtual interaction between their shadow and the agent.

Reflections

In our taxonomy, these territories are described by three different types: interaction (the space where interaction with the system is occurring), non-interaction (the space where interaction with the system is not occurring), and liminal (the space between interaction and non-interaction spaces). Some spaces can take on two of these roles; for instance, the dome projection surface serves both as a liminal space separating the dance floor from the outside and as an interaction space where human silhouettes and virtual dancers dance.

Conflict

Background

The second aspect of territoriality in our taxonomy deals with *conflicts* of space that arise and how they are addressed. Conflicts can be positive in that they force users to come together and engage in conflict management, but they can also contribute to a negative user experience [31], so it is important to consider them when designing a system. Conflicts can occur in two different *spaces*: *physical* and *digital* [31]. Conflicts can also result from numerous different *causes*. One cause noted in the literature was the invasion of personal space [31]; we call this an *ownership* issue.

Observations

The ownership conflict type did not occur frequently in the LuminAI installation. There were four instances in which one participant stepped in front of another participant as they were dancing with an agent, but this was never upsetting enough to spur conflict management or dialogue.

It was also observed that conflicts in digital space occurred due to *crowding*, which resulted in participant confusion. Four participants mentioned in their interviews that they found it difficult to distinguish which agent was responding to their movements, and three additional participants noted that they were able to see their own silhouette, but did not notice the virtual agent. It is clear from the video that early in the event (when there were fewer people and the silhouettes were turned off), there was sufficient digital space. However, later in the evening, when the silhouettes were turned on and more people arrived, the digital space became crowded. Silhouettes and agents began to overlap, and this made it difficult to distinguish between the two.

Conflicts due to crowding in physical space were less of an issue in LuminAI. Towards the end of the event, when many people were present in the dome, the installation became more like a crowded dance floor than an interactive movement improvisation experience. Some participants still attempted to interact with the agents/silhouettes despite the crowded space, but others adapted and danced with each other when they were not able to approach an agent. Everyone appeared to be dancing fluidly, and no one halted his or her interaction to engage in conflict management.

Reflections

The lack of ownership conflicts could be because dancing is an ephemeral interaction. In contrast to public digital workspaces where participants create a lasting product in their personal space, personal contributions in LuminAI disappear just moments after they occur. Possible solutions to crowding in digital space include reducing visual clutter by turning off the silhouettes, creating a visual mapping from the agent to the participant with whom it is interacting, and introducing a limit on the number of participants that are tracked by the system at one time.

Awareness

The second theme focuses on awareness of others and their activities. Our taxonomy divides awareness into three aspects: *participant*, *interaction role*, and *scope*. These deal with who is aware of whom, how people configure their awareness of each other, and the extent of one's awareness.

Participant

Background

The participant aspect describes who is aware of whom in a given space. Literature in the field focuses almost exclusively on awareness amongst humans (*human-human*).

Observations

During LuminAI, it was observed that additional types of awareness affected the interaction experience. In particular, awareness issues involving virtual agents (*human-agent, agent-human,* and *agent-agent*) were relevant. Seven different participants in the video recordings circled around the dome or switched sides of the dome while dancing, possibly in an attempt to get their agent to dance around the dome with them. However, since the initial prototype of LuminAI involved three individual agents stitched together using projection mapping, each agent could only dance within a defined sector of the dome. This discrepancy caused some confusion; for example, one participant hopped from one side of the dome to the other and waited to see if his agent would move with him; when it did not, he had to switch and dance with another agent.

Reflections

These observations led to the conclusion that when artificial agents are introduced into a social interface, new types of awareness need to be considered. All of these scopes of awareness also apply beyond a dyadic scope. For instance, human-agent awareness could involve three humans and one agent who are mutually aware of each other.

Prior to developing this framework for analyzing socially interactive systems, we had not considered the possibility of agent-agent awareness. Implementing functionality that allows agents to be spatially aware of each other would solve some of the digital space conflicts that were identified by participants (see *Conflict*). Agents could even move beyond spatial awareness and dance with each other; this could potentially serve to attract participant attention when no humans are dancing in the dome.

The installation would also benefit from improved agent-human awareness. Discontinuities like the ones observed could cause less eager participants to disengage, and they could also inhibit participant understanding of the agent's ability to learn from past action sequences. In future installations, agents could be made aware of the three-dimensional space and be able to track and follow their partners as they move around the dome.

Interaction Role

Background

Awareness of others can occur in many different forms depending on the roles that are adopted by individuals in the group. This is what the *interaction role* aspect addresses. When interacting with multi-user displays, people often do not participate as *equal partners* and instead configure their awareness of others in terms of relationships like *teacher-apprentice*, *observer-actor*, or *commentator-actor* [31]. Computers can also take on some of these roles in the creative process, in addition to assisting in a more traditional manner as a *taskmaster* or *communication facilitator* [24].

Observations

These roles are not always dyadic; they can also appear within larger social groups. For example, in one group of four that interacted with LuminAI, three of the participants were actively dancing with each other and the agents (adopting the actor role), and one participant stood back and watched (adopting the observer role). These interaction roles are not necessarily static; in this same group, each of the three actor participants stepped back at some point and briefly adopted the role of observer, and the observer participant physically interacted with the system twice.

In addition to the six roles previously identified in the literature, an additional interaction relationship was observed. The *leader-follower* relationship occurred both between humans and between humans and agents. This is distinct from the teacher-apprentice role in that the leader is not always consciously trying to impart knowledge, as a teacher would.

Different interaction roles were adopted amongst participants who were familiar with each other and amongst strangers. Participants who entered together in a group were more likely to adopt the equal partner or leader-follower relationship. Strangers typically did not interact with each other or adopted the observer-actor relationship.

Reflections

Existing work further characterizes the leader-follower behavior that was observed in both human-human and human-agent interaction [1, 12, 38]. The LuminAI agents are currently designed to act as followers unless the human ceases interaction and needs encouragement. Ongoing research is exploring how the agent might alternate naturalistically between leader and follower roles.

Scope

Background

Finally, *scope* deals with the extent of one's awareness of others. Small physical spaces like the dome provide an affordance for large scopes of awareness because it is easy to see everyone in the space [4]. Even so, managing awareness of many people at one time can be difficult or overwhelming for humans, although it has been found that in certain goal-directed social activities, humans are capable of *holoptism*, or "the ability for any interacting co-agent to perceive the dynamics of the whole interactive system" (*system* awareness) [6].

Observations
We observed that when humans are socially dancing, they tend to focus on coordinating their movements with one other individual (*dyad*) or a small group of co-located partners (*small group*). In the case of LuminAI, these partners can be either human dancers or virtual agents. Currently, the artificial dancers in LuminAI are only aware of the movements of the person closest to the Kinect sensor associated with that agent.

Reflections
Something we had not considered prior to conducting this analysis is that artificial agents can have a larger range of possible scopes of awareness than the typical human, depending on how they are programmed. An artificial agent might only be capable of awareness of itself or of a single person (*individual*), restricting its scope of awareness below that of most humans. Agents might also have the capability to perform superhuman feats, such as being aware of the movements of everyone on a large dance floor (*crowd*). This is a different problem from holoptism in that it requires the agent to be aware of the individual motions of each dancer in the crowd rather than the dynamics of the dance floor system as a whole.

Future work could investigate how it would affect the experience if the agents could factor in the movements of everyone dancing within a certain radius (like a human might do) or even the movements of an entire crowd. Highlighting the shadow(s) of participants whose movements the agent is currently aware of could emphasize these changing scopes.

Control/Collaboration
The third theme, control, deals with who has power over the technology and how the technology is manipulated. This changes when an AI agent is introduced as part of the system, as the assumption that a human is controlling the technology is no longer necessarily true. If the technology plays an equal role in the control of the human-agent interaction, the control scheme shifts to *collaboration*. This collaborative dynamic raises several additional questions. How do the agent and human negotiate control of the interaction? How does the human make sense of the collaborating agent's actions (and vice versa)?

Background
The conceptual space here deals with how to collaborate with the system and understand the capabilities of the system. Users have to experiment with the system to gradually make sense of its functionality [17, 21]. These experimental interactions help users build a mental model of how the system works, including a conceptual space of possible interactions (i.e. the system's affordances). Once users establish a preliminary model of how the agent works, they can begin creatively collaborating with it. This creative collaboration involves mutually coupled interactions during which both parties are influenced by the actions of their partner. This process of co-creating meaning through interaction is referred to as participatory sense making in the cognitive science literature [17, 19].

Based on this concept, our taxonomy divides collaboration into *understanding how to collaborate with the system* and *understanding the system's capabilities*. Understanding how to collaborate with the system deals with making sense of the current interaction. *Exploratory action* and *observation* are both part of this process of coordinating collaboration through real-time feedback [17].

Understanding the system's capabilities deals with making sense of the system's functionality. This category is divided into four sub-categories that reflect different levels of understanding: understanding that the system can *mimic* your actions, understanding that the system can *augment* your actions, understanding that the system can *learn* from your actions, and understanding that the system can come up with *novel* actions. These four levels of understanding are based on the LuminAI system capabilities, which were inspired by strategies for improvisation in jazz music [32].

Observations
People did not in general have difficulty understanding how to collaborate with the public LuminAI installation. None of the interviewed participants indicated any difficulty learning how to physically interact with the installation. In addition, only 14 people entered the dome and did not physically interact with the system at all. This non-interaction could have been caused by confusion, but it could also be the result of disinterest, social anxiety, or outside factors such as social obligations or time constraints. While participants understood how to interact with the system, interview data indicates that most if not all participants did not fully understand the capabilities of their artificial collaborator. Three participants did not understand that they were interacting with an artificial agent. Of the participants that did recognize that they were interacting with an AI agent, few recognized that the agent had the ability to mimic (5), augment (4), learn (1), or perform novel actions (0). This underestimation of the capabilities of an AI agent is known as the TALE-SPIN effect [40].

Participants offered several reasons why they failed to understand the capabilities of their collaborator. Five participants noted that the previously mentioned conflicts in digital space made the agents' actions unclear (see *Conflicts*). Seven felt that issues in agent resolution and definition impaired their recognition. Two others stated that they were having too much fun to care about what they were collaborating with.

Despite the failure to understand the capabilities of their collaborators, there was clear evidence in both the video and the interviews that participants engaged in the participatory sense making process. Users engaged in exploratory action by pointing or waving at the agents. One participant said in their interview, "We are all playing with our body to see what the system does." Another participant was recorded waving her arms at the agent and then turning to her friend and asking "Did anything happen? Is it working now?" The subsequent moment of recognition when she saw the agent responding and built a mental model of the situation was clearly visible. Another participant mentioned this type of "moment of recognition" in their interview. Many (11) participants formed hypotheses about what the system was doing as they were interacting with it and discussed these in their interviews. Theories ranged from the idea that the silhouette was supposed to "grab" or "pet" the agent to the notion that the color of the agent was related to the color of the participant's clothing.

Reflections

It is possible that the agent's scope of awareness inhibited understanding. For example, in one interaction, there were three humans interacting with one agent, and it was unclear which human the agent was learning from and responding to. Future iterations of this project may benefit from considering ways to augment the installation in order to better communicate agent capabilities to the participant without reducing the enjoyable aspects of the experience.

Interaction

The fourth theme, interaction, deals both with how humans interact with each other and how they interact with the system. This section of our taxonomy is divided into *mode of interaction* and *interaction level*. Mode of interaction deals with the way participants engage with the system and each other, and interaction level deals with the level of engagement of the participant.

Mode of Interaction

Observations

Three different modes of interaction with the system were observed: *verbal* (e.g. dialogue), *nonverbal* (e.g. physical movement), and *remote* (e.g. taking a photo of the interface and sharing it on Facebook). Verbal interactions occurred exclusively in human-human interactions (since the agents/silhouettes were unable to speak). While the audio we recorded did not capture dialogue for the most part (the dance music overpowered participant voices), it was visually apparent when group members were speaking to each other. Participants frequently engaged in dialogue before an interaction and during pauses in interaction.

Nonverbal interactions occurred both between humans and between humans and agents. These types of interactions can be categorized according to *rhythm* and *repetition*. Both *rhythmic* and *arrhythmic* interactions were observed, as well as *cyclic* and *acyclic* interactions.

Rhythmic interactions consist of strong gestures with a defined periodicity. Arrhythmic interactions can be both cyclic and acyclic, but they do not have a defined periodicity. *One-shot* interactions are a particular type of arrhythmic interaction that involves simple non-repeated physical gestures such as waving an arm once, kicking a leg out, or jumping.

Most participants who entered the dome tried to interact with the agent initially using a one-shot gesture (14 participants did not interact at all and 10 transitioned immediately into fluid rhythmic/arrhythmic dance). It is worth noting that one-shot gestures were not common in human-human interactions, but very common in human-agent interactions. This could be because one-shot gestures are seen as an initial means of testing or making sense of the system, in line with the idea of exploratory action and observation as key elements of the collaboration or participatory sense-making process [17].

Finally, remote interactions involved humans taking photos or videos of both the artificial agents and of other participants interacting with the artificial agents. In the video data, nine different people took photos or videos of their friends interacting with the system. This type of performance and recording allows remotely located participants to participate in the interaction.

Reflections

Certain modes of interaction that we observed are specific to movement improvisation (e.g. rhythm). However, designing to facilitate multi-modal interaction is important for any socially interactive system, and considering how each mode manifests itself in a particular system is also important to understanding interaction dynamics.

Interaction Level

Background

Interaction levels deal with how humans interact with each other and the system differently depending on their level of engagement and/or focus. Different frameworks for analyzing interaction levels have been presented in the literature. Several of these are presented below.

Ludvigsen develops a framework that identifies four levels of interaction that occur with social interfaces, based on Goffman's sociological research: distributed attention, shared focus, dialogue, and collective action [26]. *Distributed attention* refers to a group of people who are sharing the same space, but who are not focused on any shared interface or activity. *Shared focus* is when a group of people is focusing on a single activity/interface within a space. *Dialogue* occurs when people engage in a shared activity, and *collective action* occurs when people (*human teamwork*) or agents (*agent teamwork*) work together to achieve a shared goal.

Brignull and Rogers define a framework for analyzing public interface interactions that is similar to Ludvigsen's. Their framework consists of three different activity spaces: *peripheral*, *focal*, and *direct* [9]. These activity spaces can be mapped to Ludvigsen's activity levels of distributed attention, shared focus, and dialogue, respectively. Since Ludvigsen's framework has the additional level of collective action, this section of our taxonomy is based on Ludvigsen's framework. See *Transitions* for observations of and reflections on these different activity levels.

Types of Dialogue

Observations

Once users transitioned from shared focus to dialogue, there were four different types of dialogue that were observed in the video recording: *parallel*, *human-human-agent*, *individual*, *internal*, and *human-human*. Any interaction in which there were multiple people dancing with agents or silhouettes but not engaging with each other was considered to be parallel dialogue. This was the most common type of interaction, a finding that is consistent with previous public interface installations [31].

Human-human-agent interaction was also very common, occurring in 15 different groups. These types of interaction occurred when two or more humans coordinated their dance moves both with each other and with one or more virtual agents and/or silhouettes. The frequency of this type of interaction reinforces the potential value of expanding the scope of agent awareness from one participant to a small group of participants.

Individual dialogue was infrequent, but it did occur. Any interaction between a person and an agent when the dome was otherwise empty was considered to be individual dialogue. In the video recording, there were four instances of individual dialogue with an average duration of 31 seconds. Three of these interactions involved participants who had previously interacted with the installation (in the presence of other participants) and later returned on their own. Two instances involved the same individual.

Another type of interaction observed was when a person appeared to be dancing by him or herself without interacting with an agent or another human (despite the presence of both agents and other humans in the dome). This type of dialogue is classified as *internal* in the taxonomy. Like individual dialogue, internal dialogue was infrequent but it did occur. Four different participants were observed dancing by themselves while surrounded by other humans and agents. These participants did not appear to coordinate their actions with anyone else in the dome.

Human-human interaction, or interaction between two or more humans without engaging with an agent, occurred when the dome became too crowded for everyone to dance with an agent. More surprisingly, it also occurred with some groups when there was plenty of digital and physical space. For instance, one couple did a ballroom dance together while they were alone in the dome, during which they paid no attention to the agents or silhouettes. There were five different instances of this type of interaction, suggesting that the dome itself provides an affordance for dancing with or without the presence of an AI agent.

Reflections

The occurrence of both individual and internal dialogue is particularly surprising because dancing without human companions at a party is often considered to be socially unacceptable. The presence of individual dialogue in particular is contrary to previous findings that people hesitate to initiate interaction with public interfaces if others are not already engaging with them [9, 31]. This suggests that the dome, unlike other public interfaces, allows and even encourages people to engage in what might otherwise be considered *occult interaction*, or social interaction that is considered unnatural and unpleasant [20]. This idea is reinforced by the interview data; one participant said that the installation "made dancing less awkward" and another stated that dancing with the agent "made me want to get crazy and do things I wouldn't normally do".

Transitions

The final theme, transitions, can refer to transitions between spaces, between physical and digital environments, or between levels of interaction. Since the territoriality theme also deals with transitions between physical and digital spaces, we focus this section of our taxonomy on transitions between interaction levels. The first part of this section will deal with how to facilitate transitions between interaction levels, and the second part discusses transitions that were observed in the public installation of LuminAI, focusing on three of the twelve transitions represented in the taxonomy (*Distributed Attention* → *Shared Focus*, *Shared Focus* → *Dialogue*, and *Dialogue* → *Collective Action*, with an additional discussion of *backwards transitions*). We focus only on these three both to avoid recounting redundant observations and because these transitions are the most relevant to designing to facilitate social interaction.

Designing to facilitate transitions

Background

The term *situational interaction mobility* is used to "describe...the change in level of social interaction in the framework, and how well a service, product or installation supports this change in engagement" [25]. Design choices can create both barriers to and facilitators of situational interaction mobility. As a result, it is important to consider how to design to encourage upwards transitions in the level of participant engagement.

Barriers to interaction can be both physical and mental. Lack of physical access points can inhibit transitions from physical to digital or transitions into the interaction space [33]. Having a large empty space around an interface can also intimidate people and prevent them from approaching [9]. Social embarrassment is another key factor that prevents people from interacting with public interfaces [37]. People's hesitation to interact publicly can be attributed to the fear of participating in occult interaction [20].

Facilitators of transitions are also important to take into consideration. *Attractors* are aspects of a system that inspire participants to initiate interaction [18], and they can also facilitate transitions between interaction levels. One such attractor is the "honey-pot effect", which is an increase in the number of people standing in the vicinity of the interactive public display [9]. This effect creates a "sociable buzz" in the area and increases social interaction [9].

Seeing people interact with a system not only encourages the transition from distributed attention to shared focus, but it can also encourage passersby to interact with the system [31]. Other attractors include visuals that are viewable from a distance and lightweight, clearly visible interaction dynamics [9]. These generate curiosity, reduce intimidation, and encourage transitions from both distributed attention to shared focus and shared focus to dialogue [9].

Distributed Attention → Shared Focus

Observations

The first interaction level transition occurs when participants shift their focus to a shared object or system (in our case, the LuminAI installation). Unfortunately, the LuminAI video data only captured interactions inside and at the edge of the dome; therefore, there was not a lot of information about indicators of distributed attention or the transition from distributed attention to shared focus. Some limited video data of participants outside of the dome was captured from one camera angle; from this, indicators of the transition from distributed attention to shared focus appear to include *physically approaching* the installation, *pausing to watch* the installation, or performing a *gesture of interest* towards the installation, but more rigorous observation and analysis is needed to confirm this.

Reflections

Several different aspects of the installation could have attracted attention and helped to facilitate the transition from distributed attention to shared focus. The otherworldly or awe-inspiring nature of the dome may have drawn people to look more closely at the installation, a concept which has its basis in literature on museum exhibit design [2]. In addition, projections visible on the outside of the dome may have served as an attractor, in line with the design principle that large visual displays attract participants [9]. Finally, seeing people interact with the exhibit encouraged others to stop and watch. Far more people paused outside to look at the installation when others were inside dancing (21) than when the dome was empty (2). This finding is in line with previous research on public interfaces [9, 31].

Shared Focus → Dialogue

Background

In order to transition from shared focus to dialogue, participants can either *socially negotiate* their approach by queuing up or waiting their turn [31] or *directly initiate* interaction.

Observations

Most users initiated interaction with LuminAI via a direct physical gesture (i.e. waving arms or dancing), and did not appear to socially negotiate their approach (i.e. *queuing up, turn-taking*).

Due to the partially enclosed nature of the dome, curious attendees were forced to move physically closer to and sometimes even enter the dome in order to see what was going on. Once inside of the dome, attendees quickly transitioned from shared focus to dialogue with the system. As mentioned earlier, only 14 people who entered the dome did not physically interact with the system at all.

The social aspects of the installation also encouraged transitions from shared focus to dialogue. Dancing with peers (rather than experts) reduced social embarrassment; one participant liked that everyone dancing was "at the same baseline" and explained, "It's not about judging or whether we know how to dance, just about playing with body movements...that's how dancing should be". Social encouragement facilitated transitions as well. In the video, seven users verbally or physically encouraged their friends to interact with the system. In addition, four different individuals/small groups were recorded interacting with the installation after watching another individual/small group interacting first. The actual number of participants who engaged in this type of activity may be larger since the camera only recorded actions inside of the dome and people could have been observing from outside before joining in interaction. For example, at one point, two participants entered the dome; one immediately began engaging with the agent, but the other participant was more hesitant. The second participant felt more comfortable and began to interact after watching the first participant dance. In another interaction, an adult and a child entered the dome, and the adult illustrated how to interact with the system by pointing and dancing with the agent. After observing for a while, the child joined in the interaction.

Reflections

The direct initiation of interaction that was observed could be a result of turning on the silhouettes in addition to the agents; once this was done, there was a digital figure that responded to every person, suggesting that anyone could participate in the installation without waiting for an available agent. This could also be due to the "occasion" or social construct of dance floors, where people are used to dancing all at once without taking turns [20].

The data, examined through the lens of territoriality, supports our original hypothesis that the dome (in contrast with the original 2D installation) provides an affordance for social interaction. Interaction and non-interaction territories are clearly defined, with the dome itself serving as the seam or liminal space between the two. Making the liminal space a physical barrier creates an involvement shield between participants and nonparticipants, reducing the risk of social embarrassment [20]. This hypothesis is also supported by interview data; one participant said that they felt "protected in the bubble"; another mentioned that the dome made them feel "enclosed and protected" and a third participant said that "the dome shape really invited me to dance".

The clearly defined interaction territory also allowed participants to perform in a stage-like environment without a high barrier of entry or risk of social embarrassment. This enabled participants to engage in performative play and creatively explore space and bodily gesture. When interviewed, one participant said, "We were not sure if we were allowed to be in the dome. We were waiting at first, and then people followed us in." This indicates that the dome delineates a stage-like space.

Dialogue → Collective Action
Background
The final transition is between dialogue and collective action. This transition involves moving from undirected social interaction to a goal-oriented activity such as playing a game or managing a conflict [31]. Such a goal can either be *explicitly stated* (via a verbal conversation) or *emerge* out of collective interaction. The idea of emergent goal-creation is an example of *collaborative emergence*, a term used to describe phenomena that "result from the collective activity of social groups" [34]. The outstanding question is how to identify when a goal has emerged.

Observations
There were only a few scattered instances in which users engaged in collective action with other participants in order to manipulate LuminAI, and as a result, further study is needed to identify clear behavioral markers indicating when an undirected activity has transformed into goal-oriented collective action. Two LuminAI participants described trying to play games with the agent in their interviews (i.e. trying to encapsulate the agent within the silhouette), but it was unclear whether or not these games involved teamwork with other humans. During three different interactions in the video recording, couples or friends joined hands or hugged each other in order to get their silhouettes to merge into one, and then experimented with how they could collaboratively move their joined silhouette.

While some users did reach the collective interaction level, this was a rare occurrence, and most participants remained in the dialogue stage throughout the course of their interaction with the system. Even when users achieved collective action, it was only reached incidentally; there is nothing built into the system that encourages users to transition from dialogue to collective action.

Reflections
Collective action is the most socially engaging level of interaction, so designing to encourage participants to reach this final level could be a valuable improvement [25]. It is also worth considering the possibility of collective action between agents or between humans and agents.

Backwards Transitions
Background
It is also natural for participants to transition from a higher level to a lower level of interaction as they cease interacting with the installation for various reasons. Previous work has found that social factors such as an "obligation to leave" play a large role in causing disengagement with public interfaces [3].

Observations
In the video data, several different causes for backwards transitions emerged including *boredom*, *confusion*, *pressure from outside forces* (e.g. another participant, time obligations), *lack of physical space*, and the *desire to discuss* the interaction with a friend or observe others interacting. Certain behavioral markers were observed during backwards transitions in the video. Episodes of teamwork (e.g. two users working together to get their silhouettes to merge give up and instead dance in parallel with their agents) trigger transitions from collective action back to dialogue. This could manifest itself in several ways, including the end of a verbal conversation between participants, or the end of a coordinated physical "conversation" between participants or agents (observed in video). A transition from dialogue to shared focus was indicated by the cessation of interaction with the system (e.g. a participant steps back to observe the system). Finally, a participant turning away from the system or shifting his or her focus to another object (e.g. a participant walks away to get a drink) indicated a transition from shared focus to distributed attention.

Reflections
Designers should concern themselves not with eliminating backwards transitions, but with extending the period of time a participant spends at a particular interaction level before transitioning down.

CONCLUSION
In conclusion, we developed LuminAI, a socially interactive installation in which humans are able to improvise dance movements in collaboration with each other and virtual agents that are projected onto the liminal space of a geodesic dome. This installation was presented to the public at a local arts event, and interview and video data were collected during the event. This data was then analyzed and this analysis, in combination with a synthesis of interdisciplinary literature, was used to create a taxonomy to guide the design of socially interactive human-agent systems. This taxonomy helped us to identify areas where the installation was successful (e.g. facilitating transitions between different interaction levels), where it needs improvement (e.g. conflicts in digital space), and conceptual spaces we have yet to explore (e.g. agent awareness and collective action). In this paper, we have contributed a detailed framework for analyzing socially interactive installations involving both humans and artificial agents in addition to developing an art installation that explores the social fabric of the dance floor and human-agent interactions.

ACKNOWLEDGMENTS
We would like to thank T. Lang Dance Company, Jessica Anderson, Lauren Winston, Ju-Hwan Lim, Sasimon Viriyayuthakorn, Lisa Li, the Ivan Allen College of Liberal Arts (Georgia Tech), and The Goat Farm Arts Center for their efforts and support of this work.

REFERENCES

1. Baris Akgun, Kalesha Bullard, Vivian Chu and Andrea L. Thomaz. 2014. An HRI Approach to Learning from Demonstration. In *AAAI Fall Symposium Series*, 10-12.
2. Leslie Bedford. 2014. *The Art of Museum Exhibitions: How Story and Imagination Create Aesthetic Experiences.* Left Coast Press, Inc.
3. Ben Bengler and Nick Bryan-Kinns. 2015. "I could play here for hours.." (thinks the visitor and leaves): Why People Disengage from Public Interactives. In *Proceedings of the 2015 ACM SIGCHI Conference on Creativity and Cognition (C&C '15)*, 177-180. http://dx.doi.org/10.1145/2757226.2764548
4. David Benyon. 2014. *Spaces of Interaction, Places for Experience*. Morgan & Claypool.
5. Anne Bogart and Tina Landau. 2003. *The Viewpoints Book: A Practical Guide to Viewpoints and Composition.* Theatre Communications Group.
6. Jérôme Bourbousson and Marina Fortes-Bourbousson. 2016. How Do Co-Agents Actively Regulate Their Collective Behavior States? *Frontiers in Psychology* 7: 1732.
7. Richard E. Boyatzis. 1998. *Transforming Qualitative Information: Thematic Analysis and Code Development.* Sage Publications.
8. Mason Bretan and Gil Weinberg. 2014. Chronicles of a Robotic Musical Companion. In *Proceedings of the International Conference on New Interfaces for Musical Expression,* 315-318.
9. Harry Brignull and Yvonne Rogers. 2003. Enticing people to interact with large public displays in public spaces. In *Proceedings of INTERACT '03*, 17-24.
10. William Buxton. 2009. Mediaspace—Meaningspace—Meetingspace. In *Media Space 20+ Years of Mediated Life,* Steve Harrison (ed.). Springer, London, UK, 217-231.
11. Erin A. Carroll and Celine Latulipe. 2009. The creativity support index. In *CHI '09 Extended Abstracts on Human Factors in Computing Systems (CHI EA '09)*, 4009-4014. https://doi.org/10.1145/1520340.1520609
12. Crystal Chao and Andrea L. Thomaz. 2011. Timing in Multimodal Turn-Taking Interactions: Control and Analysis Using Timed Petri Nets. *Journal of Human-Robot Interaction* 1, 1: 1-16.
13. Kate Compton and Michael Mateas. 2015. Casual Creators. In *Proceedings of the Sixth International Conference on Computational Creativity*, 228-235.
14. Mihaly Csikszentmihalyi. 2014. *The Systems Model of Creativity: The Collected Works of Mihaly Csikszentmihalyi.* Springer.
15. Nicholas Davis, Margeaux Comerford, Mikhail Jacob, Chih-Pin Hsiao, and Brian Magerko. 2015. An Enactive Characterization of Pretend Play. In *Proceedings of the 2015 ACM SIGCHI Conference on Creativity and Cognition* (C&C '15), 275-284. http://dx.doi.org/10.1145/2757226.2757254
16. Nicholas Davis, Chih-Pin Hsiao, Kunwar Yashraj Singh, Lisa Li, and Brian Magerko. 2016. Empirically Studying Participatory Sense-Making in Abstract Drawing with a Co-Creative Cognitive Agent. In *Proceedings of the 21st International Conference on Intelligent User Interfaces* (IUI '16), 196-207. http://dx.doi.org/10.1145/2856767.2856795
17. Hanne De Jaegher and Ezequiel Di Paolo. 2007. Participatory sense-making. *Phenomenology and the cognitive sciences* 6, 4: 485-507.
18. Ernest Edmonds, Lizzie Muller, and Matthew Connell. 2006. On creative engagement. *Visual Communication* 5, 3: 307-322.
19. Thomas Fuchs and Hanne De Jaegher. 2009. Enactive intersubjectivity: Participatory sense-making and mutual incorporation. *Phenomenology and the Cognitive Sciences* 8, 4: 465-486.
20. Erving Goffman. 1963. *Behaviour in Public Places: Notes on the Social Organisation of Gatherings*. The Free Press.
21. Mikhail Jacob, Alexander Zook, and Brian Magerko. 2013. Viewpoints AI: Procedurally Representing and Reasoning about Gestures. In *Proceedings of DiGRA 2013: DeFragging Game Studies*.
22. Mikhail Jacob, Gaëtan Coisne, Akshay Gupta, Ivan Sysoev, Gaurav Gav Verma, and Brian Magerko. 2013. Viewpoints AI. In *Proceedings of the Ninth AAAI Conference on Artificial Intelligence and Interactive Digital Entertainment*, 16-22.
23. Janet Kolodner. 2014. *Case-based reasoning*. Morgan Kaufmann Publishers, Inc.
24. Todd Lubart. 2005. How can computers be partners in the creative process: Classification and commentary on the Special Issue. *International Journal of Human-Computer Studies* 63, 4-5: 365-369.
25. Martin Ludvigsen. 2005. Designing for Social Use in Public Places - a Conceptual Framework of Social Interaction. In *Proceedings of Designing Pleasurable Products and Interfaces Conference (DPPI '05)*.
26. MadMapper. 2017. MadMapper: The video Mapping Software made by Artists for Artists. Retrieved January 12, 2017 from http://www.madmapper.com/.
27. Ben Malbon. 1999. *Clubbing: Dancing, Ecstasy, Vitality*. Psychology Press.
28. Brian Magerko, Waleed Manzoul, Mark Riedl, Allan Baumer, Daniel Fuller, Kurt Luther, and Celia Pearce. 2009. An empirical study of cognition and theatrical improvisation.

In *Proceedings of the Seventh ACM Conference on Creativity and Cognition*, 117-126. http://doi.org/10.1145/1640233.1640253

29. David J. Mendonca and William Al Wallace. 2007. A Cognitive Model of Improvisation in Emergency Management. *IEEE Transactions on Systems, Man, and Cybernetics - Part A: Systems and Humans* 37, 4: 547-561.
30. Marek P. Michalowski, Selma Sabanovik, and Hideki Kozima. 2007. A Dancing Robot for Rhythmic Social Interaction. In *Proceedings of the Second ACM/IEEE International Conference on Human-Robot Interaction (HRI)*, 89-96. http://doi.org/10.1145/1228716.1228729
31. Peter Peltonen, Esko Kurvinen, Antti Salovaara, Giulio Jacucci, Tommi Ilmonen, John Evans, Antti Oulasvirta, and Petri Saarikko. 2008. It's Mine, Don't Touch!: interactions at a large multi-touch display in a city centre. In *Proceedings of the SIGCHI Conference on Human Factors in Computing Systems (CHI '08)*, 1285-1294. http://dx.doi.org/10.1145/1357054.1357255
32. Jeff Pressing. 1988. Improvisation: methods and models. In *Generative processes in music,* John Sloboda (ed.). Oxford University Press, Canada, 129-178.
33. Yvonne Rogers. 2006. Moving on From Weiser's Vision of Calm Computing: Engaging Ubicomp Experiences. In *Ubicomp 2006: Ubiquitous Computing,* 404-421. https://doi.org/10.1007/11853565_24
34. Keith R. Sawyer. 1999. The emergence of creativity. In *Philosophical Psychology* 12, 4: 447-469.
35. Keith R. Sawyer. 2003. *Group creativity: music, theater, collaboration.* L. Erlbaum Associates.
36. Rob Saunders and Oliver Bown. 2015. Computational Social Creativity. *Artificial Life: Special Issue on Art, Creativity and Culture* 21, 3: 366–378.
37. Robyn Taylor, Pierre Boulanger, Patrick Olivier, and Jayne Wallace. 2009. Exploring participatory performance to inform the design of collaborative public interfaces. In *Extended Abstracts on Human Factors in Computing Systems* (CHI EA '09), 3721-3726. http://doi.acm.org/10.1145/1520340.1520561
38. Andrea L. Thomaz and Crystal Chao. Turn Taking Based on Information Flow for Fluent Human-Robot Interaction. *AI Magazine* 32, 4: 53-63.
39. Noah Wardrip-Fruin. 2009. *Expressive Processing: Digital fictions, computer games, and software studies.* The MIT Press.

Fabrication Games: Using 3D Printers to Explore New Interactions for Tabletop Games

Srinjita Bhaduri, Jesús G. Ortiz Tovar, and Shaun K. Kane
University of Colorado Boulder
Boulder, CO, USA
{bhaduri.srinjita, jesus.ortiztovar, shaun.kane}@colorado.edu

ABSTRACT

Personal fabrication technologies such as 3D printers are becoming increasingly affordable, enabling many to own and use 3D printers in their own homes. Yet we have little understanding of how fabrication tools and technologies can be used and appropriated within the home. In this paper, we explore the opportunities and challenges related to using personal fabrication technologies as part of play, specifically in the context of board and tabletop games. We present an overview of existing uses of 3D printers in the context of gaming, which has largely focused on creating and replacing pieces for existing games. Drawing on existing uses of 3D printing in games, and on prior research in interacting with fabrication tools, we then introduce a set of gameplay elements that use the affordances of the 3D printer to enhance and extend gameplay. We evaluated these gameplay elements through a focus group with 9 gaming hobbyists, who provided feedback on these elements and designed new games that used these elements. Our contributions include an extended set of gameplay elements that leverage fabrication tools, a set of reference games, and guidelines for augmenting existing fabrication tools to support playful interactions.

Author Keywords

3D Printing; Fabrication; Tangible Computing; Tabletop Games.

ACM Classification Keywords

H.5.m. Information interfaces and presentation (e.g., HCI): Miscellaneous.

INTRODUCTION

Driven by open-source hardware platforms and international competition, personal fabrication tools such as 3D printers have rapidly transitioned from expensive professional tools into affordable mainstream consumer devices [36]. Fully-featured 3D printers now cost less than many PCs and mobile devices. The opportunity to make 3D printers a standard household item has attracted interest from fabrication-oriented companies such as MakerBot and LulzBot, but has also drawn attention from companies that produce other types of household technologies. Home 3D printers have been produced or announced by companies such as Dremel, a manufacturer of household tools, and Mattel, a toy company. Personal fabrication technologies may support practices of "everyday making" around the home [45]. However, transitioning from being a consumer of existing 3D models to a designer of original creations can present challenges for novice users [25].

Figure 1. Prototype of *Star Dice,* a 3D-printed dice-rolling game created by a team of tabletop gamers. In *Star Dice,* players customize and print a set of personalized dice that matches their chosen gameplay strategy.

In considering the role of fabrication technologies in the home, we should look beyond their intended use to consider how end users may appropriate these technologies. As technologies are integrated into a home context, they are often repurposed for unexpected uses. For example, while early PCs were marketed as business tools, games rapidly became a primary use for PCs in the home [7], and today's PCs support a wide variety of activities, including office work, gaming, education, creativity, and social interaction.

Coincident with the rise of personal fabrication is a resurgence in board, card, and other tabletop games [26]. This trend is seemingly driven by an interest to engage in collocated social interaction, and to engage in more tangible forms of play [42]. Our present work lies at the intersection of these trends: as personal fabrication technologies enter the home, they present opportunities for supporting real-time, tangible, and collocated interactions, via the concept

C&C '17, June 27-30, 2017, Singapore, Singapore

ACM ISBN 978-1-4503-4403-6/17/06 $15.00
http://dx.doi.org/10.1145/3059454.3059463

of 3D-printer-enhanced *fabrication games.* For example, a 3D printer could enhance gameplay by generating new physical game pieces during the course of a game, and could customize these printed objects based on the game state, history from prior games, random effects, or external data sources.

In this paper, we explore the opportunities enabled by integrating personal fabrication tools into collocated tabletop games. We first present a brief overview of existing practices surrounding the use of 3D printing in tabletop games. Next, we introduce a set of gameplay elements that build upon the capabilities of a 3D printer to dynamically create physical game objects. We evaluated these gameplay elements through a focus group with 9 gaming hobbyists, who provided feedback on these elements and designed new games that integrated 3D printing features. Our contributions include a set of gameplay elements for 3D-printer-enhanced fabrication games, feedback on these gameplay elements from hobbyist gamers, and a collection of reference games that implement these new gameplay elements.

RELATED WORK

Our work draws on prior studies of board and tabletop gaming, the adoption of personal fabrication tools in the home, bridging digital and physical games, and interactive, data-driven use of 3D printers.

Tabletop Games

Tabletop games, including board games, dice games, and card games, have been a part of human society for thousands of years. While traditional tabletop games must now compete with video games for players' attention, there has been a growing interest in board games in recent years, centering around a new generation of modern board games, and often featuring collaborative rather than competitive gameplay [26].

While games have existed in some form for much of human history, the study of why and how people engage in games is relatively new. In the 1980s, Malone studied the intrinsically motivating factors within games, and identified three motivating factors: challenge (which includes variable difficulty level, hidden information, and randomness), fantasy, and curiosity [33]. More recently, Rogerson et al. [42] conducted ethnographic research with tabletop gamers to understand their interest in tabletop games as opposed to, or in addition to, video games. Rogerson et al. identified sociality, intellectual challenge, variety, and materiality as key components of the tabletop gaming experience, and further deconstructed materiality into four domains: the physical construction of the game board and pieces, the game box and related art, the space in which the games are played, and the places in the home where games are stored and displayed. This emphasis on the material qualities of tabletop games was also explored by Darzentas et al. [13] through an ethnographic study of players of miniatures-based games. In both studies, the creation, customization, and display of the tangible components of games were key to players' engagement with the game. Outside of gaming, interaction with tangible objects has been shown to increase engagement in collaborative tasks [51]. The present work aims to maintain the materiality of tabletop games while exploring new types of gameplay.

While many tabletop games rely on non-technological components such as boards, cards, dice, and miniatures, gamers have long adopted new technologies to support their hobby. For example, many players have used postal mail and email to play games over a distance. More recently, software applications such as Tabletop Simulator [24] have enabled players to play games together over a distance by emulating the physical components of common games in software, supporting play via PC or even through virtual reality. The present work explores how an emerging technology, 3D printing, can be used to extend traditional tabletop gaming practices.

Combining Tabletop and Video Games

While tabletop games may present advantages in terms of materiality and engagement, video games offer a set of complementary advantages. For example, video games enable players to add additional game content without needing to purchase additional physical components, enable play over a distance, and support large games with many players.

Prior research has explored the intersection of tabletop and video games, often with the goal of balancing the benefits of each medium. Prior games have used augmented reality technologies to add dynamic behavior to tangible games (e.g., [30,31]), such as by adding atmospheric audio, representing the game state through a visual display, and supporting private input through personal mobile devices. Other games have retrieved information over a home network, and used that information to modify the gaming experience. Open Data Monopoly [18] uses real-world finance data to create dynamic versions of the Monopoly board [32]. Invasion of the Energy Monsters [3] is a tabletop game for families that explores issues around energy conservation; one version of the game can be linked with a household energy meter, providing players with extra points for following conservation guidelines in their own home. Recent work from Noble and Crabb [38] projected information on top of a traditional board game in order to provide dynamic feedback about the game state.

Some recent projects have repurposed fabrication tools to create specific types of games, such as using components of a CNC mill to create an automated air hockey table [10]. Destructive Games [16] consist of several games that use a laser cutter to destroy valuable objects when a game is lost, increasing the stakes of losing a game. Our work complements this recent work in repurposing fabrication tools for gaming by introducing new gameplay elements that use 3D printing to dynamically create game objects during play.

Personal Fabrication Technologies in the Home

Although the 3D printer manufacturing industry has shown great interest in the role of home 3D printers, relatively little research has explored how 3D printing is currently being used by everyday users. Shewbridge et al. [45] conducted a design probe in which families were given a mockup of a home 3D printer and asked to record their desired uses for the device. Family members were often interested in using the 3D printer for maintenance tasks around the home, such as replicating existing objects and modifying or repairing existing objects, and were hesitant to create or design new objects. Hudson et al. [25] interviewed novice users of 3D printers and identified several barriers to transitioning from a casual user of 3D printers (i.e., printing objects that others have designed) to designing and printing their own creations. Recent research from Mizrahi et al. [35] has explored alternative uses for fabrication tools, specifically in the process of preparing food. Our work explores gaming as an additional use for home 3D printers.

Interactive Fabrication

A limitation of most current 3D printers is that they do not support interaction while printing. Instead, most 3D printers expect the user to upload a complete 3D model, and to leave the printer undisturbed until that model is fully printed. However, many of our intended usage scenarios involve dynamic printing of an object that may change based on user behavior. Recent projects such as Linespace [46], Encore [9], and On-the-Fly Print [40], as well as work from Teibrech et al. [47], have explored alternative printing techniques that enable iterative cycles of interaction with a 3D printer. The present work explores the use of interactive control of a 3D printer to support gameplay.

Other research has used data streams to dynamically generate trophies or other artifacts representing the user's achievement. SweatAtoms [28] is a prototype system that can create physical artifacts based on fitness data; users of the system collected the printed artifacts and used them as rewards and as objects to support reflection. TastyBeats [27] builds upon SweatAtoms, but prints edible artifacts made of chocolate. Our study includes the creation of award artifacts as one of several fabrication-enhanced gameplay elements, and introduces several additional elements.

EXPLORING FABRICATION-BASED GAMEPLAY

Our primary focus in this research is to explore how use of 3D printing technologies can support new and enhanced modes of gameplay. However, 3D printers are already in use by some game hobbyists. Here we present a brief overview of current uses of 3D printers to support tabletop gaming. We then introduce an initial set of gameplay elements that demonstrate how use of a 3D printer during play could enhance the gameplay experience.

Existing Use of 3D Printers in Tabletop Gaming

Game players and designers use a variety of online communities to discuss the use of 3D printing in games, and to share 3D models that they have created. For example, Reddit hosts discussions about 3D printing in tabletop games across several subsites (r/boardgames, r/3dprinting, and r/3dprintedtabletop). BoardGameGeek, a web site dedicated to tabletop gaming, contains thousands of forum posts that discuss 3D printing. Although we did not conduct a systematic evaluation of 3D-printing-related gaming posts, we observed that posters asked questions about the process of 3D printing, posted links to 3D-printable objects on other sites, and shared demonstrations of items that they had printed. These 3D-printed items were sometimes created by the poster, but were often downloaded from other sites. Posters shared a variety of 3D-printed objects, including alternate pieces for existing games and accessories such as containers for storing dice.

Online 3D model repositories, such as Thingiverse and Shapeways, also contain numerous 3D-printable artifacts related to tabletop gaming. For example, there are over 900 objects on Thingiverse tagged with *boardgame*, including game tokens, figurines, storage for dice and cards, and game trophies. Figure 2 shows some examples of these objects. The majority of objects available on these sites are accessories for existing games, rather than new games. However, some designers have used their 3D modeling skills to create and distribute original games. For example, Pocket-Tactics [12] is a strategy game that can be downloaded for free and 3D printed at home. 64 Oz. Games [20] is a company that produces add-ons to improve the accessibility of existing games for people with vision impairments, including 3D-printed Braille dice and tactile overlays for game pieces.

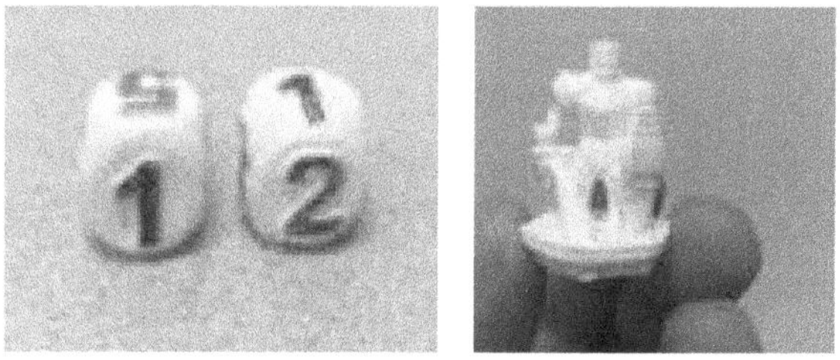

Figure 2. Dice (left) [49] and miniature figurine (right) [22] models, shared on Thingiverse.com via an open source license.

While there are many 3D-printable objects available online for tabletop game players, the majority of these objects are add-ons to existing games. Also, these components are designed to be printed before the game is played, and used in the same way as any other game piece. To our knowledge, no games currently available online support interaction with a 3D printer during gameplay, as we explore in this work.

Gameplay Elements in Fabrication-Based Games

Building upon the existing uses of 3D printing described previously, our research team has explored how a 3D printer can be used during gameplay to add new elements to the experience of playing a tabletop game. In particular, we have investigated how a 3D printer might create game artifacts during play that can be integrated into the ongoing game.

To explore this concept, our research team brainstormed an initial set of 8 gameplay elements that demonstrated some of the interactions made possible by bringing a 3D printer into the experience of playing a tabletop game. We iteratively developed these concepts by reviewing related work, by playing and learning about existing tabletop games, and by conducting informal discussions with gaming hobbyists. We particularly focused on game play elements used in recently released games, as these games may introduce new gameplay mechanics. We also considered ways in which specific types of gameplay differed between tabletop and video games. For example, most tabletop strategy games either include a fixed set of game pieces or encourage users to purchase an ever-growing set of pieces, whereas many computer-based strategy games support large numbers of customizable pieces by default.

As home 3D printers vary greatly in size, speed, and features, we explored design concepts that could be implemented using most current 3D printers. Our scenarios assume the use of a contemporary consumer-grade 3D printer such as the MakerBot Replicator 2, which can print objects up to a size of 11 × 6 × 6 inches, and which can produce small tokens, such as those shown in Figure 2, in approximately 10 to 15 minutes. This reference design represents a lower bound for designing 3D-printer-enhanced fabrication games, as future 3D printers will likely support larger build volumes and faster print times. These scenarios also assume the use of a camera or some other mechanism that can track game play, enabling the system to customize printed artifacts based on previous actions in the current game, outcomes of previous games, random elements, or other data sources.

These initial scenarios describe some of the ways in which fabrication tools can enhance existing gameplay elements and support new types of play:

Generating Game Pieces During Play: Fabrication games can create new game pieces during play, including tokens, dice, or other objects. For example, a board game could print new dice with different face values throughout the game. These pieces could also be customized based on the game state, such as by printing less favorable dice near the end of the game to increase difficulty.

Expanding the Game Board: Some games, such as Carcassone [50], require players to construct the game board during play by laying down game tiles in each turn. A fabrication game could dynamically generate additional tiles to enhance or alter game play. For example, a variant of Carcassone could generate a new tile after each game to add variety and uncertainty to subsequent games.

Revealing Hidden Objects: A fabrication game can print an object in steps throughout the game, and can reveal objects if a specific game objective was reached. For example, a fabrication game based on Pictionary [2] could randomly choose a 3D model and print it; the winner is the first player who can guess the object that is being printed.

Data-Driven Gameplay: Fabrication games can print new game objects based on some external data source. Previous games have used home energy data [3] and online financial data [18] to customize gameplay. While this type of gameplay does not require 3D printing, using a 3D printer would enable players to easily incorporate external data into game pieces. For example, as in prior work [18], a finance-based game such as Monopoly [32] could produce customized pieces based on the current state of the financial market, printing large hotels if the market is strong that day, and more modest hotels if the market is weak.

Fabrication games can also use data from prior games to influence the current game. For example, a dice-based game could support handicapping by producing more favorable dice for players who have lost previous games.

Creating Trophies and Mementos: Fabrication games can create an artifact during the game that creates a record of that game and its outcome. This token could be an aesthetically pleasing trophy, a record of wins and losses over time (similar to [28]), or a new game piece that can be used in future games. For example, a fabrication game based on Scrabble [6] could generate a new tile based on the highest-scoring letter during that specific game, which could then be used in future games.

Capturing Player Input: Fabrication games can accept input from players and print objects based on player input. For example, in an alternative version of Pictionary [2], players could be asked to sketch specific objects, which would then be fabricated as 3D objects; the winner is the player whose drawing most closely resembles the actual object.

Supporting Remote Play: Fabrication games can also support gameplay between two players at different locations, with the 3D printer acting in place of the remote player. For example, a fabrication game based on chess could print out a representation of the board after each move, perhaps printing a miniature representation to save time and materials. Alternately, a 3D-printer system with the ability to selectively remove printed material (similar to Linespace [46]) could be used to print pieces, then erase and re-print each piece as it is moved.

Personalizing Game Pieces: Fabrication games can support players in creating personalized game pieces and elements. For example, while current players of games such as Monopoly [32] may fight over who gets to play using a specific piece, a fabrication game could allow each player to create their own piece. Alternately, a fabrication game could allow players to create game pieces that represent the players' personal lives, such as by replacing a generic dog token with a model of the family dog.

FOCUS GROUP

In order to gather feedback about the potential applications of 3D printing in tabletop games, we conducted two focus

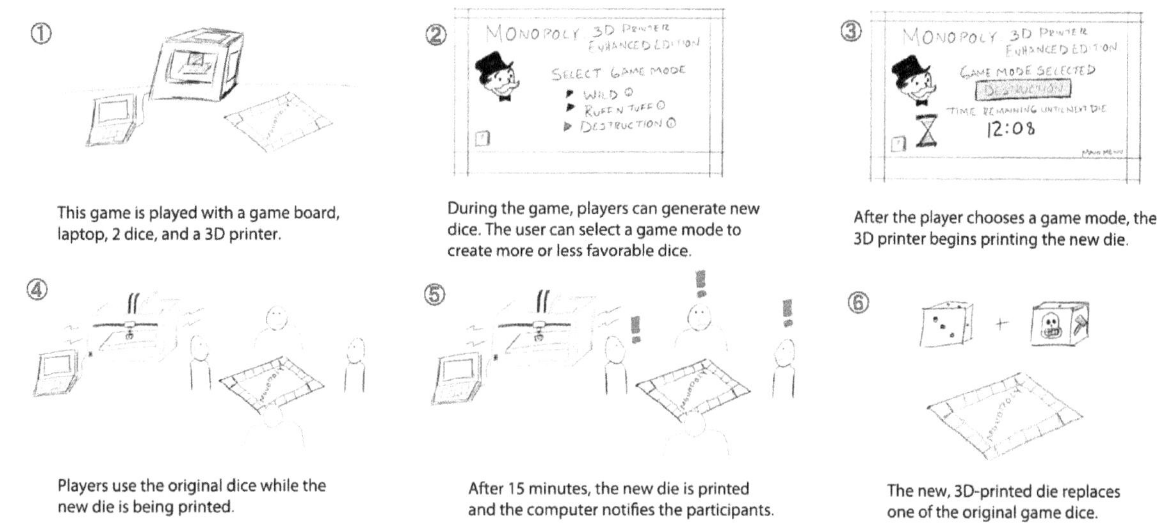

Figure 3. Proof-of-concept fabrication game designed by the research team. In this variant of Monopoly [32], players can choose to generate new dice during gameplay, thereby affecting the probability of good or bad outcomes.

group workshops with active game players. The goals of these sessions were to collect feedback about our initial set of gameplay elements, to identify games and types of games that could benefit from these elements, to develop games that use these elements, and to identify potential opportunities and areas of concern with our approach.

Participants

We recruited participants from the local community via email to student lists on campus and posts to gaming-related social media sites. We recruited 9 participants (3 female), age 20 to 61. Two participants were current students at our university, but had not previously interacted with members of our research team. All participants were regular board game players, and two participants had previously designed their own board games.

We conducted two focus group sessions: the first session included 5 participants, and the second session included 4 participants. We encouraged participants to invite friends; two pairs of previously-acquainted participants attended the first session, and one pair attended the second session.

Focus Group Sessions

Each session took place at our research lab, and lasted two hours. Participants were compensated $25 for their time. Two members of the research team conducted the workshop sessions. Each session comprised four activities: introduction, brainstorming, game design, and game presentation. Participants also filled out a brief demographic survey at the start of the session, and filled out a comment form at the end of the study.

Introduction

The focus group sessions began with a 15-minute introduction. During introductions, each focus group member introduced themselves, named a favorite game and described their prior experience with 3D printing.

Following the personal introductions, we presented a series of slides about 3D printing and the goals of the study. The slides described how 3D printers worked, and indicated that 3D models could be created using CAD software, downloaded from an online repository, or generated dynamically using code. We briefly demonstrated the 3D modeling tool TinkerCAD, showed example results from Thingiverse, and played a time-lapse video of an object being printed on a consumer-grade 3D printer.

Next, we introduced the goals of the study session. We stated that the goal of the activity was to explore ways to enhance tabletop gameplay with 3D printing, such as by tracking gameplay and dynamically printing 3D objects during gameplay. We also described the capabilities of the reference 3D printer (MakerBot Replicator 2).

During pilot testing, we found that participants were often reluctant to come up with ideas for the design sessions. As such, we started the study sessions by introducing some of our existing ideas, including our eight initial gameplay elements and a storyboard showing an example of how a 3D printer could be used to enhance a Monopoly-like game.

Figure 3 shows the game storyboard presented to our study participants; the storyboard was presented sequentially during the study, and featured shorter text descriptions. In this game, a player can choose at any time to generate a special 3D-printed die. The player could choose from one of three difficulty levels: higher difficulty levels resulted in dice with negative outcomes printed on the face. Once printed, the new die replaced one of the game's default dice, increasing the possibility of lucky or unlucky events. Following the presentation of the video, the researchers answered any questions about the study and the introductory material, and then began the next activity.

Brainstorming Activity
After the introduction, our focus group participants discussed each of the 8 gameplay elements described above. This activity lasted approximately 45 minutes.

During this session, one member of the research team introduced each gameplay element, and asked the focus group members to discuss how existing games might be enhanced by this type of gameplay. Comments from participants were recorded on a whiteboard in the study location. In some cases, the focus group participants suggested ideas that did not fit with the current discussion topic, and either fit in with another discussion topic, or addressed a new gameplay element that had not been mentioned previously. To support a lively discussion, we recorded each idea as it was discussed, and later matched participants' ideas to the corresponding theme.

While presenting our ideas to participants may have directed participants to come up with ideas like our own, we felt that providing this additional context would help participants generate ideas for a concept that was quite new to them. Our participants were successful in using this information to build upon our initial ideas, to connect these ideas to existing games, and to explore ideas beyond those that we provided.

Game Design Activity
Following the brainstorming session, we instructed participants to form groups. Each group was instructed to design a new game that used one or more of the ideas from the brainstorming session. For this activity, participants divided themselves into groups of two or three people. Participants chose their own groups.

Because coming up with a new game idea can be difficult, we provided a series of prompts to help each group to select a game concept. Each group was instructed to roll three six-sided dice. These dice were used to select starting parameters for their game from a pre-defined list (Figure 4). We informed participants that these game parameters were suggestions only, and that each group was free to reroll their dice or choose a different option if they preferred. Because both groups in the first session selected dice games using this method, the groups in the second session were asked to create a board or card game.

Participants were given about 30 minutes to design their game, and were offered a set of craft materials, including paper, pens, pencils, colored markers, index cards, clay, Lego bricks, pieces from existing games, and blank game boards that could be drawn on. Participants were instructed to use whatever materials they wished to create their game, and were told that they would be presenting their game back to the entire group at the end of the activity.

To further assist in the game design activity, participants were given a game design worksheet that contained questions about the game. This worksheet included the name of the game, the game type (selected from the options in Figure 4), a brief description of the game, the number of players, the suggested age range, the contents of the game box, instructions for the game, and a description of how 3D printing could be used within the context of the game.

After 30 minutes, each group presented their game to the group. Finally, participants then filled out the comment form to complete the study session.

Choose a game type (roll 3 dice)

Game Style	Game Play	Theme
1 or 2: Board Game	1 or 2: Competitive Game	1: Science Fiction 2: Fantasy/Adventure
3 or 4: Card Game	3 or 4: Cooperative Game	3: Money/Finance 4: Mystery
5 or 6: Dice Game	5 or 6: Party Game	5: Zombies 6: Animals

Figure 4. Study participants rolled dice to choose random game parameters, and used those game parameters as a starting point for designing an original game.

Data Collection and Analysis
Participants completed an introductory demographic questionnaire and a post-activity comment form. The focus group sessions were video and audio recorded, and we recorded field notes during the session. We also collected copies of the artifacts produced during the study, including the whiteboard, game design worksheets, and images of the game prototypes.

Data collected during the study was analyzed by the entire research team and sorted into categories. Our analysis focused on new gameplay themes suggested by focus group members, comments and suggestions for our initial set of themes, components of the games designed during the session, and concerns and challenges about 3D printing that were raised during the study.

FINDINGS
Our findings include participants' comments on their prior experiences with 3D printing, ideas generated during the brainstorming session, proof-of-concept games created by participants, and participants' comments and concerns about the viability of using 3D printers during gameplay.

Experience with 3D Printers
We did not require that participants have experience with 3D printers in order to take part in the study. However, three participants had either prior experience in using a 3D printer, or were interested in using a 3D printer to support their gaming practices.

One participant owned a consumer-grade 3D printer, and used it as part of his tabletop game practices. This participant used his 3D printer to create miniatures and accessories for tabletop strategy games. He did not create his own 3D models, but instead downloaded free models from the web, printed them, and painted them by hand. Another participant did not own a 3D printer himself, but was in the process of shopping for one, and intended to use the 3D printer to create parts for tabletop games that he was currently designing. A third participant had received a set of 3D-printed miniatures that were designed and printed by his brother, and used these miniatures to play role-playing games, but had not designed or printed his own miniatures.

Ideas for Integrating 3D Printing into Games

Participants suggested a variety of ideas during the brainstorming session. While some of these suggestions fit into the initial gameplay themes presented during the session, others addressed areas that we had not previously considered. Here we will briefly describe examples of how participants extended our initial gameplay elements, and identified applications of these elements to existing games.

Generating Game Pieces During Play: Participants saw the value of 3D printing game pieces, although they suggested printing pieces before the game was played, rather than as part of gameplay, to compensate for slow printing time. Participants were especially interested in creating their own customized game pieces.

Expanding the Game Board: Participants noted several games that use the mechanic of an expanding game board, including Carcassone [50], Escape [39], and Tsuro [34]. Participants expressed excitement about the opportunity to download and print new content for these games, either from the game's original designers or from fans. Participants noted that printing map tiles could be especially useful for games with a strong exploration element, such as Dungeons & Dragons [21], and that customizing game tiles could enable more control over the difficulty of a particular game.

Two participants discussed how printing new game board tiles could be used to enhance the new series of "legacy" board games. These games, including Risk Legacy [14] and Pandemic Legacy [15], feature elements in which the game board is permanently altered after a game session, either by placing a permanent sticker over part of the game board or tearing up a game card. Currently, these games can only be played a fixed number of times, after which the players must re-purchase the game. These participants suggested that a 3D printer could be used to re-print destroyed pieces, or to print add-ons that could be attached to existing pieces to temporarily indicate a change in state. One participant suggested that a 3D-printed legacy-type game could follow a season-based model, where players upload a representation of their board after each game and receive a new custom board from the game designer.

Revealing Hidden Objects: Participants agreed that interacting with the 3D printer while printing could be useful for games such as Battleship [48], which involves incrementally revealing the board, as well as party games such as Hangman or Pictionary [2].

Data-Driven Gameplay: While participants did not offer any suggestions about how external data sources could be used to influence the game, one group eagerly discussed the possibility of using data from previous games to re-balance games or to handicap experienced players. Participants noted that some games were designed in an unbalanced way, favoring specific player positions or strategies, and noted that a 3D-printer-enhanced game could track gameplay over time, detect imbalances, and push an updated version to the game players.

Creating Trophies and Mementos: Participants noted that some recent board games, such as 7 Wonders [5], include a paper sheet to track video-game style "achievements", such as the first player to win the game, or the first player to lose by a significant amount. These participants agreed that records of previous games could be recorded as a 3D-printed artifact, but preferred if the system could produce an artifact that could be integrated into the game, such as a tile or game piece, rather than a non-functional trophy.

Capturing Player Input: Participants noted that this feature could be useful for party games such as Cranium [1] or Pictionary [2], and discussed the idea that the system could combine inputs from multiple players into a new artifact, such as 3D-printing a figure in which each body part is drawn by a different player.

Supporting Remote Play: The majority of participants were not interested in using a 3D printer to support remote play, and expressed concern about the waste of printing a game board multiple times. One participant, who was active in playing games by mail, noted that a 3D printer could enable remote play using existing game pieces.

Personalizing Game Pieces: Most participants expressed interest in using 3D printing to create more customized pieces, and to create their own personalized pieces. This feature was especially popular in the context of miniatures-based games, where participants could create figurines to represent themselves, family and friends, or beloved fictional characters.

Emergent Gameplay Elements

In addition to the themes that we provided, participants suggested a number of additional possibilities for using 3D printing as part of a tabletop game.

Participants suggested several ways in which 3D printers could be used to replace or enhance existing game pieces:

Replacing Broken or Missing Pieces: Multiple participants mentioned that they had lost pieces from their games, and that they could use the 3D printer to replace those pieces without having to buy the game again.

Upgrading Game Pieces: Several participants expressed interest in using the 3D printer to print more aesthetically appealing parts for their existing games, such as replacing cardboard tokens with 3D-printed miniatures. This suggestion is not surprising, as many posts on communities such as Reddit and BoardGameGeek involve sharing and discussing upgrades to existing games. One participant mentioned that he was unsuccessful in convincing his friends to play one of his favorite games, as the game board and pieces were unattractive, but that upgrading the pieces might convince his friends to try the game.

Bootlegging: Several participants described playing games that involved purchasing collectible miniatures, such as Warhammer 40,000 [8]. These pieces are often quite expensive, and participants were interested in using 3D printed pieces (either copies of existing pieces or fan-made content) as an inexpensive alternative.

One participant expressed interested in acquiring a game that is currently out-of-print, but found that it was only available from resellers at a greatly inflated price. This participant felt that it would be reasonable to print a copy of this game, as the publisher was no longer able to sell or profit from the game.

Participants also suggested several ideas that involved adding new attributes to the game pieces and gameplay:

Supporting House Rules and Extensions: One participant mentioned that he had purchased two copies of a game, and had hand-painted pieces from one copy into different colors, so that he could play the game with more players than was originally intended. He noted that using the 3D printer would allow him to create his own modified pieces without having to combine multiple game sets.

Another participant suggested creating customized pieces to support hybrid games, such as converting word games like Boggle [11] or Scrabble [6] into a multilingual game. More generally, several participants discussed how 3D printing could be used to create versions of games that incorporated house rules, such as changing the point values of a game piece or increasing the number of pieces of a given type.

Making Game State Visible: Several participants mentioned that it can often be difficult to introduce new players to games, as new players may have trouble following along with the rules. One participant suggested that game pieces could be augmented to show their current state by 3D printing a game piece and adding electronic components such as LEDs. Several participants were excited by this idea, and suggested additional uses for electronically-enhanced game pieces. For example, an augmented checkers piece could feature an integrated LED that indicates whether the piece had been promoted to king. Likewise, a game board itself could light up to indicate the current player's turn, which could be especially useful for games that often require players to skip a turn, such as UNO [41]. While these examples rely more upon embedded electronics than 3D printing, they suggest that game players may be interested in creating and customizing new game pieces, and that this customization could involve both aesthetic and functional changes.

Accessibility: Several participants offered suggestions about how customized, 3D-printed pieces could be used to increase the accessibility of games for people with disabilities, older adults, or children. Suggestions included creating brightly colored pieces for players with low vision, creating larger pieces for people with dexterity issues, and adding rails to some board games to prevent less dexterous players from accidentally knocking pieces over.

Theming: One participant suggested that 3D printing could be used to create different themes or skins for a game, enabling players to replay the same game with different background stories. This idea was later incorporated into the game Zombie Twister, discussed below.

Adding Mechanical Components: Participants discussed their interest in games that featured moving parts, such as Mouse Trap [4] and Trouble [29]. These participants suggested that 3D printing could be used to add more mechanical parts to existing games, either for aesthetic reasons or to add new dimensions to the existing gameplay.

Dynamic Difficulty: One participant suggested that 3D printing could be used to adjust the difficulty of games, especially games that involve physical interactions. For example, the game Jenga [44], which involves manipulating a precariously balanced tower of blocks, could be made easier or more difficult by adjusting the size, shape, and texture of the blocks.

Proof-of-Concept Games

In this section, we briefly describe the games created by our four game design teams.

Star Dice (game type: dice, competitive, science fiction)

Star Dice is a dice-based game with the theme of spaceship battles. Each player has his or her own personal set of dice that they use across multiple games, similar to deck-building games such as Magic: The Gathering [19]. Each player's set of dice represents their ship; players customize their ship by choosing which faces appear on the dice. For example, players may create a ship with many weapons but few shields. Players engage in combat by rolling their dice and counting up each face to determine who wins the battle. Figure 1 shows the prototype version of Star Dice.

Star Dice takes advantage of the customization enabled by 3D printing: players create their personalized set of dice via a web application, and can then download a 3D-printable copy of the dice or order them by mail if the player lacks a 3D printer. The designers also discussed using 3D printing to represent different aesthetic qualities of the ships, for example creating a set that looks like a shiny space cruiser or a rusty space pirate ship. Dice could also be customized for accessibility reasons, such as large or high-contrast dice. This game demonstrates the elements Personalizing Game Pieces and Accessibility.

Zombie Twister (dice, party, zombies)

Zombie Twister is a dice-based party game based on the game Twister [17]. The game consists of a four-by-six-foot mat (Figure 5, left) and two dice, one die representing a color and the other representing a body part. As in in the original game, players need to place the specified body part on a square of the specified color. The mat is made of a set of modular tiles. Several of the tiles have modifiers on them that affect game play. For example, touching a "Bear Trap" tile forces the player to hold their limbs still until the tile if moved, while the "Limb Decay" tile causes the specified limb to decay, meaning that the player cannot use that limb to support their weight.

Zombie Twister uses 3D printing in several ways. First, the game components are printed in bright materials to be color-blind friendly. Second, the theme of the game mat can be changed through a set of swappable faceplates on each tile. Thus, players can swap the zombie-themed tiles for another story theme. This game demonstrates the elements Accessibility and Theming, and could potentially support Extending the Game Board through its use of modular tiles.

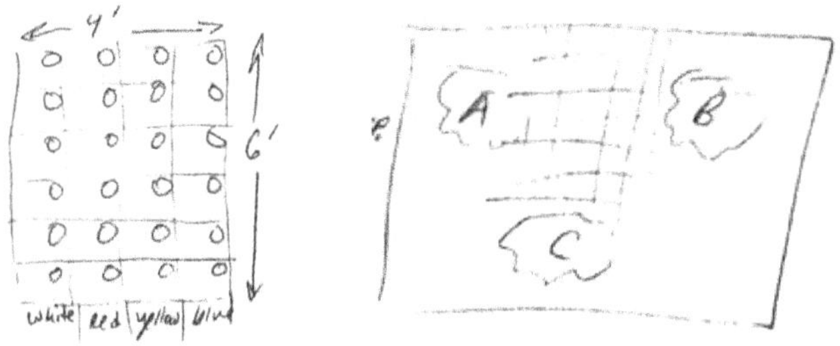

Figure 5. Game sketches. Left: Mat for the game Zombie Twister can be customized with swappable faceplates. Right: Strip Mine board shows randomly generated terrain.

Strip Mine (board, competitive, finance)
In Strip Mine, each player controls a country that is competing with every other country for natural resources (Figure 5, right). Players mine resources, capture territory, and trade resources with neighboring countries. Players win the game by accruing the most wealth, usually by monopolizing resources.

Strip Mine's board consists of a randomly-generated set of 3D tiles. Each tile is designed to represent a geological formation, and the board can be expanded by printing more pieces. The designers discussed using the 3D printer to generate random resources over the course of the game, but eventually decided not to include this feature. This game demonstrates the element Expanding the Game Board, and includes 3D-printed tangible game pieces.

Mystery Game (board, party, mystery)
In this game, a murderer is on the loose in a small town. Players act as villagers and attempt to identify the murderer before they themselves are killed. This game supports interaction through a custom computer application. Each player registers in the application, and is given a profile that shows their identity and abilities. On each turn, the player chooses to explore a specific area of the village for clues. After exploring an area, the 3D printer reveals any potential clues in that area by printing objects onto the map. This game demonstrates the element Revealing Hidden Objects.

Concerns and Challenges

Overall, our participants were eager to explore ideas related to the integration of 3D printing and tabletop gaming. However, participants expressed some concerns about the feasibility of integrating 3D printing into tabletop games.

The most commonly expressed concern related to the slow speed of 3D printing. We instructed our participants to create their games assuming current consumer-grade 3D printers, which can take between 10 and 15 minutes to print a game piece. Several participants noted that this slow speed could negatively impact gameplay. However, many of our participants' ideas involved situations in which pieces could be slowly printed between game sessions, rather than during the game. We also discussed research innovations that could print objects faster, such as WirePrint [37], which can speed up traditional 3D printing by a factor of 10. Other potential solutions that were discussed include printing smaller objects, printing at a lower quality, and printing modular and reusable components. Some activities, such as printing a game board tile, might also be performed using a faster technology such as a traditional printer or pen plotter.

Several participants also expressed concern about the clutter and waste caused by unnecessarily printing new game pieces. One solution we discussed was to leverage 3D printers that work with biodegradable materials such as PLA, recyclable materials such as paper or clay, or consumable material such as chocolate. Some prototype 3D printers also support using recycled materials as input [23]. Regarding clutter, printed elements can be designed to be reusable, or could be integrated into future games. For example, rather than printing a trophy when a player wins a game, the system could produce a new game piece or tile that shows the winner.

Finally, some participants raised questions about the ideal form factor of a 3D printer used in gaming. On one hand, current 3D printers are relatively small, requiring any gameplay to occur on a separate surface. On the other hand, most 3D printers are too large and heavy to easily carry, making it difficult to bring one to a friend's house or to a board game meetup. It is clear that there are opportunities to explore different form factors for a game-enabled 3D printer, drawing from recent research in producing very small [43] and very large [46] printers.

DISCUSSION

Our goal in conducting this work has been to explore opportunities for enhancing tabletop gameplay by integrating a 3D printer. By this metric, we consider this preliminary work successful: our focus group members generated many examples of 3D-printer-enhanced gameplay, and created several distinct proof-of-concept games. It seems clear that there exist opportunities for supporting playful interactions with a 3D printer, including augmenting existing games and creating new games.

Many of the suggestions offered by our participants focused on improving material aspects of existing games, such as the design of the game pieces, rather than developing new types of games. While we are especially excited to explore new types of gameplay that can be supported by this technology, it is not surprising that our participants focused on augmenting familiar games. Our participants offered many suggestions related to augmenting the physical design of the game pieces, which suggests that these players have desires that are unmet by their existing games. 3D printers may indeed address some of these unmet desires.

Furthermore, existing tabletop games have mechanisms for addressing some of the gameplay elements explored in our work, such as adding randomness to gameplay. For example, a Dungeons & Dragons player can roll a die and look in a table to see what kind of monster they have encountered in a dungeon, rather than waiting for a 3D printer to produce that model. However, there may be other benefits in leveraging the 3D printer in this scenario, such as creating a tactile representation and building suspense. The added benefits of tangible interaction may improve engagement with a game, but identifying these effects may require testing with fully developed fabrication games rather than prototypes.

Finally, it is not surprising that even dedicated game fans may have difficulty inventing new games if they have never done so before. Just as everyday computer users do not instantly become 3D modelers when given access to 3D printers, we should not expect game players to become game designers by simply giving them access to new tools. During our focus group sessions, the two participants who had previously designed their own games had many ideas around incorporating these technologies into their games, and it may be that conducting further research with game designers may result in more creative game designs.

Although our participants often focused on improving their existing games, our study did shed light on some new gameplay concepts: the murder mystery game that involved progressive printing of clues; re-balancing a tabletop games through a software update; incorporating mechanical components into existing games; and the idea of adjusting difficulty for games such as Jenga [44] by changing the size and shape of the game pieces, reflect elements that cannot easily be reproduced through traditional tabletop games or video games. Each of these ideas offers potential for designing new games that leverage the affordances of a dynamic tangible gaming environment.

FUTURE WORK

This research represents the first step in exploring a new space of 3D-printer-enhanced fabrication games, which presents several opportunities for future work.

One opportunity for future research is to conduct additional focus group sessions with game players, and to playtest some fully realized games, to better understand the opportunities and limitations of this technology. As study participants who had designed their own games in the past seemed especially engaged in this activity, it would be valuable to test these technologies with designers of tabletop games. Also, since several of the gameplay elements explored in this work involved bringing elements of video games to tabletop games, it may also be worthwhile to conduct studies with video game designers. Likewise, it would be worthwhile to evaluate this work with people of different ages, as well as families and other groups that play games together.

A second opportunity for future work is to design, develop, and test software tools that enable game designers to create playful interactions with a 3D printer. We have developed initial prototypes of a software toolkit that enables partial printing of objects, in order to support reveal-the-hidden-object games. We intend to extend these prototypes to support additional forms of game-like interaction, and to connect 3D printers to existing tabletop and video games.

A third opportunity for future work is to develop new hardware form factors that support fabrication-enhanced play. Fabrication tools could be directly integrated into a gaming table, or could be placed in a mobile form factor that could be attached to existing game boards. Future hardware devices could support additional features relevant to gameplay, such as the ability to move existing pieces around on a game board, or to quickly fabricate game pieces through alternative output methods, such as by printing cards or game tiles.

Finally, while the present work has focused on playing tabletop games, the core gameplay elements investigated here could be applied to educational games or other types of interactive applications. For example, many of the game elements explored here could be applied to educational games, providing opportunities to teach students about math, physics, and other subjects through tangible games.

CONCLUSION

As fabrication technologies become increasingly common in the home, it is inevitable that they will be used for purposes beyond what they were originally designed for. The ability to dynamically create physical objects in the home offers the promise of new tangible computing experiences. Tabletop games, which encourage social interaction and problem solving through the manipulation of tangible objects, provide an ideal environment for exploring playful forms of tangible interaction. While we are excited by the possibilities of creating fun and novel gaming experiences, we also believe that fabrication games and fabrication-enhanced gameplay provide a medium for exploring everyday interactions with fabrication tools, and for extending our understanding of fabrication tools beyond production and into our everyday lives.

REFERENCES

1. Whit Alexander and Richard Tait. 1998. *Cranium.* Game [Board Game]. (1998). Hasbro, Pawtucket, Rhode Island, U.S.
2. Robert Angel. 1985. *Pictionary.* Game [Board Game]. (1985). Hasbro, Pawtucket, Rhode Island, U.S.

3. Amartya Banerjee, Michael S. Horn, and Pryce Davis. 2016. Invasion of the energy monsters: a family board game about energy consumption. In *Proceedings of the 2016 CHI Conference Extended Abstracts on Human Factors in Computing Systems* (CHI EA '16), 1828–1834. https://doi.org/10.1145/2851581.2892507
4. Gordon A. Barlow, Marvin Glass, Harvey Kramer, and Burt Meyer. 1963. *Mouse Trap.* Game [Board Game]. (1963). Hasbro, Pawtucket, Rhode Island, U.S.
5. Antoine Bauza. 2010. *7 Wonders.* Game [Board Game]. (2010). Asmodee, Roseville, Minnesota, U.S.
6. Alfred Mosher Butts. 1938. *Scrabble.* Game [Board Game]. (1938). Hasbro, Pawtucket, Rhode Island, U.S.
7. Martin Campbell-Kelly, William Aspray, Nathan Ensmenger, and Jeffrey R. Yost. 2013. *Computer: A History of the Information Machine*. Westview Press, Boulder, CO.
8. Andy Chambers, Jervis Johnson, Rick Priestley, and Gavin Thorpe. 1993. *Warhammer 40,000.* Game [Board Game]. (1993). Games Workshop Ltd., Memphis, Tennessee, U.S.
9. Xiang "Anthony" Chen, Stelian Coros, Jennifer Mankoff, and Scott E. Hudson. 2015. Encore: 3D printed augmentation of everyday objects with printed-over, affixed and interlocked attachments. In *Proceedings of the 28th Annual ACM Symposium on User Interface Software & Technology* (UIST '15), 73–82. https://doi.org/10.1145/2807442.2807498
10. Jonathan Chiu and Daniel Kuo. 2015. Air hockey robot. *Hackster.io*. Retrieved January 1, 2017 from https://www.hackster.io/windowsiot/air-hockey-robot-7d7a24
11. Bill Cooke and Alan Turoff. 972. *Boggle*. Game [Board Game]. (1972). Hasbro, Pawtucket, Rhode Island, U.S.
12. Arian Croft. 2016. Pocket-tactics: core set 5 (Fourth Edition). Retrieved January 1, 2017 from http://www.thingiverse.com/thing:1858839
13. Dimitrios P. Darzentas, Michael A. Brown, Martin Flintham, and Steve Benford. 2015. The data driven lives of wargaming miniatures. In *Proceedings of the 33rd Annual ACM Conference on Human Factors in Computing Systems* (CHI '15), 2427–2436. https://doi.org/10.1145/2702123.2702377
14. Rob Daviau and Chris Dupuis. 2011. *Risk Legacy*. Game [Board Game]. (1959). Hasbro, Pawtucket, Rhode Island, U.S.
15. Rob Daviau and Matt Leacock. 2008. *Pandemic Legacy: Season 1*. Game [Board Game]. (2008). Z-Man Games, New York, New York, U.S.
16. David Eickhoff, Stefanie Mueller, and Patrick Baudisch. 2016. Destructive games: creating value by destroying valuable physical objects. In *Proceedings of the 2016 CHI Conference on Human Factors in Computing Systems* (CHI '16), 3970–3974. https://doi.org/10.1145/2858036.2858113
17. Chuck Foley, Reyn Guyer, and Neil W. Rabens. 1966. *Twister*. Game [Board Game]. (1966). Hasbro, Pawtucket, Rhode Island, U.S.
18. Marie G. Friberger and Julian Togelius. 2012. Generating interesting Monopoly boards from open data. In *Proceedings of 2012 IEEE Conference on Computational Intelligence and Games (CIG '12)*, 288–295. https://doi.org/10.1109/CIG.2012.6374168
19. Richard Garfield. 1993. *Magic: The Gathering.* Game [Board Game]. (1993). Wizards of the Coast, Renton, Washington, U.S.
20. Richard Gibbs and Emily Gibbs. 2016. 64 Oz. Games. Retrieved January 1, 2017 from http://www.64ouncegames.com
21. Gary Gygax and Dave Arneson. 1974. *Dungeons & Dragons*. Game [Board Game]. (1974). TSR, Inc., Lake Geneva, Wisconsin, U.S.
22. David Hagemann. 2016. Low poly fantasy tabletop - alliance base units. Retrieved January 1, 2017 from http://www.thingiverse.com/thing:1244599
23. Xavier Harding. 2016. Feed your 3D printer recycled plastic. *Popular Science*. Retrieved January 1, 2017 from http://www.popsci.com/feed-your-3-d-printer-recycled-plastic
24. Jason Henry and Kimiko. 2015. *Tabletop Simulator*. Game [PC]. (5 June 2015). Berserk Games, Stuart, Florida, U.S.
25. Nathaniel Hudson, Celena Alcock, and Parmit K. Chilana. 2016. Understanding newcomers to 3D printing: motivations, workflows, and barriers of casual makers. In *Proceedings of the 2016 CHI Conference on Human Factors in Computing Systems* (CHI '16), 384–396. https://doi.org/10.1145/2858036.2858266
26. Dan Jolin. 2016. The rise and rise of tabletop gaming. *The Guardian*. Retrieved January 1, 2017 from https://www.theguardian.com/technology/2016/sep/25/board-games-back-tabletop-gaming-boom-pandemic-flash-point
27. Rohit Ashok Khot, Jeewon Lee, Deepti Aggarwal, Larissa Hjorth, and Florian "Floyd" Mueller. 2015. TastyBeats: designing palatable representations of physical activity. In *Proceedings of the 33rd Annual ACM Conference on Human Factors in Computing Systems* (CHI '15), 2933–2942. https://doi.org/10.1145/2702123.2702197
28. Rohit Ashok Khot, Florian "Floyd" Mueller, and Larissa Hjorth. 2013. SweatAtoms: materializing physical activity. In *Proceedings of The 9th Australasian Conference on Interactive Entertainment:*

Matters of Life and Death (IE '13), 4:1–4:7. https://doi.org/10.1145/2513002.2513012

29. Frank Kohner, Paul Kohner, and Fred Kroll. 1965. *Trouble.* Game [Board Game]. (1965). Hasbro, Pawtucket, Rhode Island, U.S.
30. Carsten Magerkurth, Adrian David Cheok, Regan L. Mandryk, and Trond Nilsen. 2005. Pervasive games: bringing computer entertainment back to the real world. *Comput. Entertain.* 3, 3: 4–4. https://doi.org/10.1145/1077246.1077257
31. Carsten Magerkurth, Maral Memisoglu, Timo Engelke, and Norbert Streitz. 2004. Towards the next generation of tabletop gaming experiences. In *Proceedings of Graphics Interface 2004* (GI '04), 73–80.
32. Elizabeth Magie and Charles Darrow. 1935. *Monopoly.* Game [Board Game]. (6 February 1935). Hasbro, Pawtucket, Rhode Island, U.S.
33. Thomas W. Malone. 1980. What makes things fun to learn? Heuristics for designing instructional computer games. In *Proceedings of the 3rd ACM SIGSMALL Symposium and the First SIGPC Symposium on Small Systems* (SIGSMALL '80), 162–169. https://doi.org/10.1145/800088.802839
34. Tom McMurchie. 2004. *Tsuro.* Game [Board Game]. (2004). WizKids, Hillside, New Jersey, U.S.
35. Moran Mizrahi, Amos Golan, Ariel Bezaleli Mizrahi, Rotem Gruber, Alexander Zoonder Lachnise, and Amit Zoran. 2016. Digital gastronomy: mthods & recipes for hybrid cooking. In *Proceedings of the 29th Annual Symposium on User Interface Software and Technology* (UIST '16), 541–552. https://doi.org/10.1145/2984511.2984528
36. Catarina Mota. 2011. The Rise of Personal Fabrication. In *Proceedings of the 8th ACM Conference on Creativity and Cognition* (C&C '11), 279–288. https://doi.org/10.1145/2069618.2069665
37. Stefanie Mueller, Sangha Im, Serafima Gurevich, Alexander Teibrich, Lisa Pfisterer, François Guimbretière, and Patrick Baudisch. 2014. WirePrint: 3D printed previews for fast prototyping. In *Proceedings of the 27th Annual ACM Symposium on User Interface Software and Technology* (UIST '14), 273–280. https://doi.org/10.1145/2642918.2647359
38. Kirsty Noble and Michael Crabb. 2016. Projection mapping as a method to improve board game accessibility. *SIGACCESS Access. Comput.*, 116: 3–9. https://doi.org/10.1145/3023851.3023852
39. Kristian A. Ostby. 2014. *Escape.* Game [Board Game]. (2014). Queen Games, Troisdrof, Germany.
40. Huaishu Peng, Rundong Wu, Steve Marschner, and François Guimbretière. 2016. On-the-fly print: incremental printing while modelling. In *Proceedings of the 2016 CHI Conference on Human Factors in Computing Systems* (CHI '16), 887–896. https://doi.org/10.1145/2858036.2858106
41. Merle Robbins. 1971. *UNO.* Game [Board Game] (1971). Mattel, El Segundo, California, U.S.
42. Melissa J. Rogerson, Martin Gibbs, and Wally Smith. 2016. "I love all the bits": the materiality of boardgames. In *Proceedings of the 2016 CHI Conference on Human Factors in Computing Systems* (CHI '16), 3956–3969. https://doi.org/10.1145/2858036.2858433
43. Thijs Roumen, Bastian Kruck, Tobias Dürschmid, Tobias Nack, and Patrick Baudisch. 2016. Mobile fabrication. In *Proceedings of the 29th Annual Symposium on User Interface Software and Technology* (UIST '16), 3–14. https://doi.org/10.1145/2984511.2984586
44. Leslie Scott. 1983. *Jenga.* Game [Board Game]. (1983). Hasbro, Pawtucket, Rhode Island, U.S.
45. Rita Shewbridge, Amy Hurst, and Shaun K. Kane. 2014. Everyday making: identifying future uses for 3D printing in the home. In *Proceedings of the 2014 Conference on Designing Interactive Systems* (DIS '14), 815–824. https://doi.org/10.1145/2598510.2598544
46. Saiganesh Swaminathan, Thijs Roumen, Robert Kovacs, David Stangl, Stefanie Mueller, and Patrick Baudisch. 2016. Linespace: A sensemaking platform for the blind. In *Proceedings of the 2016 CHI Conference on Human Factors in Computing Systems* (CHI '16), 2175–2185. https://doi.org/10.1145/2858036.2858245
47. Alexander Teibrich, Stefanie Mueller, François Guimbretière, Robert Kovacs, Stefan Neubert, and Patrick Baudisch. 2015. Patching physical objects. In *Proceedings of the 28th Annual ACM Symposium on User Interface Software & Technology* (UIST '15), 83–91. https://doi.org/10.1145/2807442.2807467
48. Clifford Von Wickler. 1931. *Battleship.* Game [Board Game]. (1931). Hasbro, Pawtucket, Rhode Island, U.S.
49. Charlie White. 2015. Dice For Monopoly. Retrieved January 1, 2017 from http://www.thingiverse.com/thing:978833
50. Klaus-Jurgen Wrede. 2000. *Carcassonne.* Game [Board Game]. (2000). Z-Man Games, New York, New York, U.S.
51. Lesley Xie, Alissa N. Antle, and Nima Motamedi. 2008. Are tangibles more fun?: Comparing children's enjoyment and engagement using physical, graphical and tangible user interfaces. In *Proceedings of the 2Nd International Conference on Tangible and Embedded Interaction* (TEI '08), 191–198. https://doi.org/10.1145/1347390.1347433

Joinery: Parametric Joint Generation for Laser Cut Assemblies

Clement Zheng[*†] **Ellen Yi-Luen Do**[*] **Jim Budd**[*]

[*] Georgia Institute of Technology [†] National University of Singapore

clement.zheng@gatech.edu ellendo@gatech.edu jim.budd@design.gatech.edu

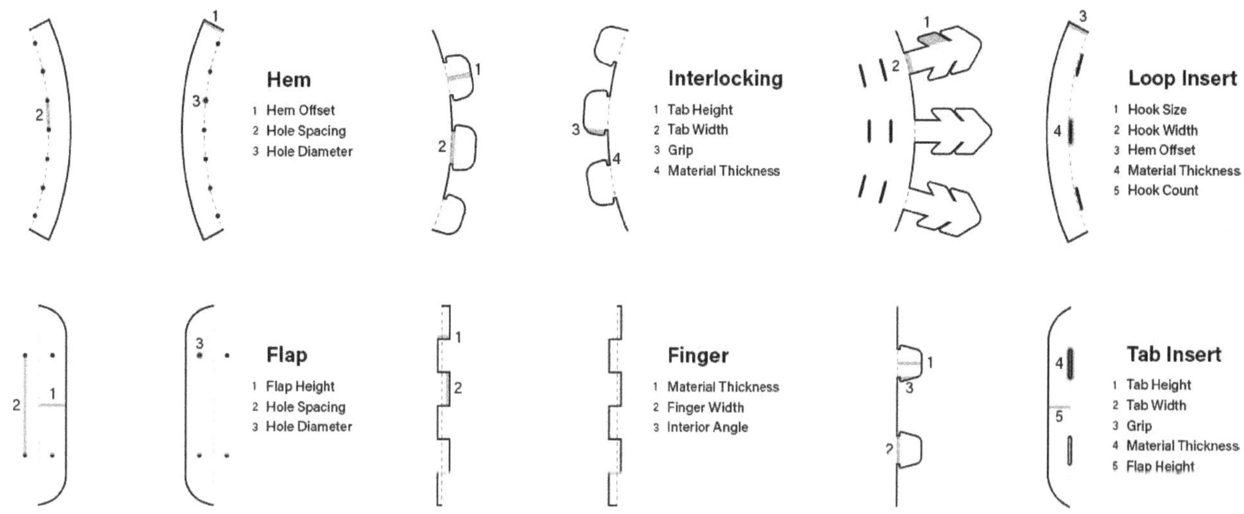

Figure 1: Joinery's parametric joint profiles for laser cutting.

ABSTRACT

Laser cutting is widely used by industrial designers and mechanical engineers as a rapid modeling tool. However, designing and fabricating laser cut assemblies can be a complex and tedious process, especially for novice designers. Through our research, we developed *Joinery*, a parametric joint generation tool for laser cut assemblies. Through *Joinery*, designers simply define connections between parts of an assembly, while the system generates the joints. *Joinery* supports fabrication-aware design through six different joint profiles that cater to different material and design needs. In this paper, we illustrate the use of *Joinery* as a creativity support tool in an industrial design process, and present several artifacts resulting from the tool. In addition, we discuss our findings from deploying this system in a college-level industrial design class.

C&C '17, June 27-30, 2017, Singapore, Singapore
© 2017 ACM. ISBN 978-1-4503-4403-6/17/06...$15.00

DOI: http://dx.doi.org/10.1145/3059454.3059459

Author Keywords

Digital Fabrication; Creativity Support Tools; Design.

ACM Classification Keywords

D.2.2 Design Tools and Techniques: User Interfaces.

INTRODUCTION

Digital fabrication has been celebrated in recent years as a catalyst for shifting our design and manufacturing away from mass production; and into a "market of one" paradigm where we can make "almost everything" [5]. Its impact has been increasingly discussed within the HCI (human-computer interaction) academic field, and many innovative digital fabrication tools have been proposed to facilitate creative "making" endeavors [2,8,17,20]. Certainly, mechanical engineers and industrial designers benefit greatly from the advance of digital fabrication tools and processes—3D printers and laser cutters are employed as rapid modeling tools embedded within the professional design process. With the democratization of digital fabrication machines, 'making' with the technology is now accessible to amateurs and novices in the design field as well—from design students in college, to the STEM (Science, Technology, Engineering, Mathematics) classroom in primary and secondary schools. Professional, novice, or amateur designers, are now equipped with the means to fabricate and test ideas rapidly at a relatively low cost, and at a much earlier stage of the design process. However, just like any new tools, integrating digital fabrication into the design process is often a trial-and-error process—such as specifying the right joints and parameters for different materials during laser cutting.

Our research is concerned with the use of laser cutters as a model making tool embedded in the industrial design process. We focus on laser cut assemblies and the task of designing joints between different parts of such assemblies. Many of the insights shared in this paper were derived from our observations and interactions with students at the School of Industrial Design in Georgia Tech. Through this research, we developed *Joinery*, a toolkit that supports designers by responsively generating parametric joints on their digital drawings. *Joinery* supports fabrication awareness by providing six customizable joint profiles for a variety of materials and design needs (Figure 1), while remaining neutral to the process/outcome. Through *Joinery*, we aim to simplify the task of creating laser cut assemblies through automating joint design; improving the efficiency and expanding the diversity of models that designers can make with the laser cutter.

This paper describes our development of *Joinery*, Firstly, we outline the challenges and related work that inspired *Joinery*. Secondly, we describe the system's development and discuss its contributions. Thirdly, we evaluate the toolkit in action through its deployment in an interactive products class. Lastly, we discuss our findings and *Joinery's* impact on rapid modeling through laser cutting.

MOTIVATION

The word *creativity* stems from *creō* in latin—"to create, make, produce"—and digital fabrication machines like laser cutters and 3D printers have been envisioned as tools that will empower such creativity-through-making in STEM and design circles [2,5]. We want to push the fabrication limits of laser cutters, and the diversity of objects that our students and other designers can create with them.

Laser cutting and 3D printing are two digital fabrication processes widely employed in our school for model making. Though the laser cutter is limited to fabricating flat parts, 3D objects can be accomplished through bending, joining and stacking the 2D parts [3,8,12,22]. Many commercial goods are manufactured with this logic—flat packed objects, furniture and garments, are all produced from assembling a flat pattern. We observed that laser cutters are the main workhorse of our digital fabrication lab. As a subtractive 2D process, laser cutting is often more efficient than 3D printing's additive process [11]. As such, larger parts are typically built with the laser cutter, while 3D printing is employed for smaller, more intricate details [1]. With its efficiency and versatility, students in our school use laser cutters to fabricate a wide spectrum of models, including electronic enclosures, wearables, soft goods, furniture, and product forms. However, despite its ubiquity, designing and fabricating laser cut assemblies is still a complex task, especially for novices to digital design and fabrication.

Figure 2 illustrates the design to fabrication pipeline for laser cut assemblies. Computer-aided design (CAD) has been identified as a critical skill for digital fabrication proficiency [7,10]—however, the same skill has also been identified as a big barrier for novices [8,10,14,17,20]. 3D modeling in particular presents a steep learning curve to beginners. We observed that our students take different CAD approaches during the digital design phase. Some students are more proficient in 3D modeling (Figure 2A), and employ tools such as *Solidworks* [24] or *Fusion 360* [25]. However, most students stick to 2D drawing tools like *Illustrator* [26] and *Inkscape* [27] to create the files for laser cutting (Figure 2B). These different digital design approaches converge as designers approach the preparation phase for laser cutting (Figure 2C–F).

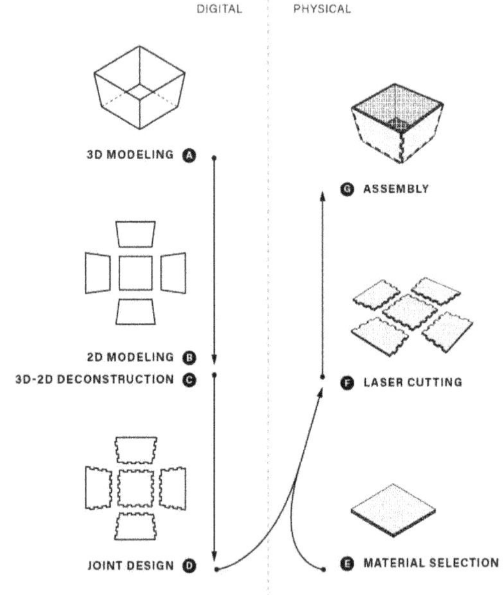

Figure 2: Pipeline for creating laser cut assemblies. Joinery tackles fabrication-aware joint design.

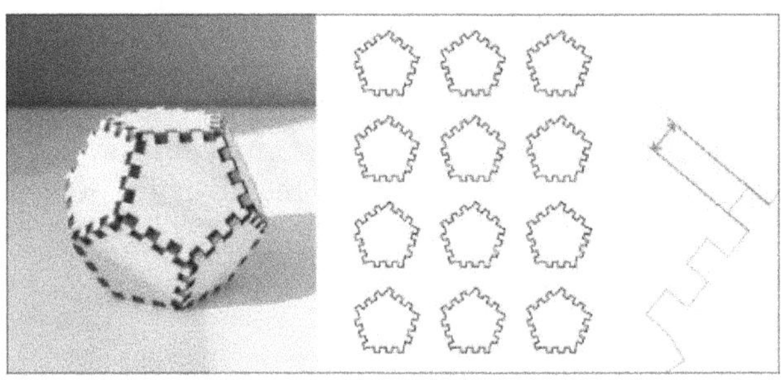

Figure 3: Adjusting the fit of the parts in this assembly involves changing the size (in red) of every finger joint.

Joint design (Figure 2D) falls within this converging zone, and is a critical task within the pipeline of creating a laser cut assembly. Joints hold the assembly together, transforming the flat laser cut parts into a functional structure. Joint design affects assembly efficiency—joints which require adhesives typically need more time than joints which provide an inherent connection. Joint design is also interdependent on many other factors in the pipeline; particularly, material properties with respect to laser cutting. Furthermore, joint design can be a tedious and complex task. For instance, tightening the fit between the dozen different parts of an assembly, or changing the type of joint, can be daunting not only for novices, but professionals as well, when each detail has to be reworked (Figure 3) [11]. Unfortunately, most CAD tools were not developed for laser cutting—and tools like *Illustrator* which novices gravitate to were created primarily for digital publishing and graphic design, not industrial design or engineering. Designers are thus required to independently integrate fabrication awareness into the digital process before fabricating with the laser cutter.

These barriers manifest in different ways that affect laser cutting's role as a rapid model making tool in the design process. Faced with these challenges, we observed that many students "make do" by downloading or customizing existing designs to suit their project needs. *MakerCase* [28] is a popular web application among students—it generates the fabrication drawings for a box from user-specified dimensions with all the necessary joints. With its level of convenience, we see the finger-joint-laser-cut-box emerge as the de facto standard for electronic enclosures in our school as well as online making communities (Figure 4).

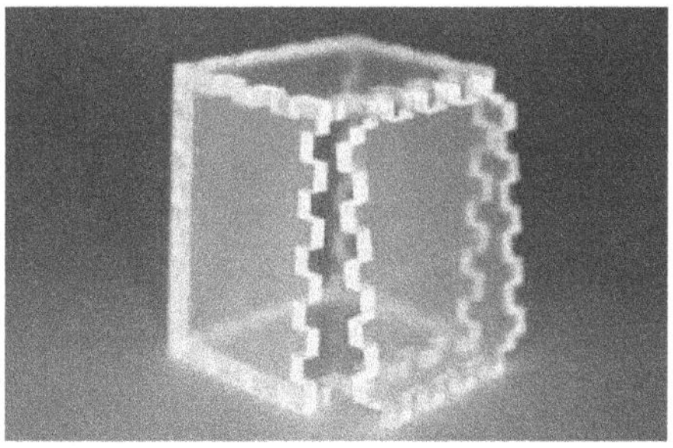

Figure 4: Acrylic box with finger joints on Thingiverse[1].

This culture of "making do" and appropriation is not an isolated phenomenon. Researchers who quantitatively analyzed *Thingiverse* (a popular online repository for 3D models) reported that customizable designs, which account for 2% of all "things", were responsible for generating 42% of all the models uploaded onto *Thingiverse* [14]. As design educators, we are concerned with this echo chamber fed by digital fabrication's own community—a state which "encourages designs to favor replication and sameness" [20]. Such a culture trivializes digital fabrication as a mere extension of mass production [2], and disables its potential as a creative and inventive tool within the design process.

In addition, despite the machine's capability for operating on a wide range of materials, the digital-physical gap results in the same materials being used in almost all laser cut models we see at our school. Basswood, acrylic or cardboard become laser cutting defaults as they are well documented and used pervasively both within local college labs and online making communities—creating a self-perpetuating bias when selecting materials for laser cut assemblies.

We see an opportunity to address the task of joint design for laser cut assemblies, and to facilitate the iterative model making process and fabrication awareness between digital design and physical materials. In addition, we want to expand the material vocabulary of our students as they explore their ideas through laser cut assemblies.

RELATED WORK

While we are motivated to address the challenges observed at our school, we are also inspired by emerging digital fabrication tools developed by industry and researchers in response to making with the laser cutter.

Fabrication-aware Design

Many professional CAD tools for architects, mechanical engineers and industrial designers incorporate fabrication constraints into the digital design activity [18]. With the democratization of digital fabrication, there is an emerging set of tools that incorporate such fabrication-aware design for non-professional users. Systems like *Plushie* [9], *SketchChair* [17] and *Marvelous Designer* [29], offer real-time feedback on the 2D patterns required to assemble the 3D design. *FlatFab* [8] offers another approach by constraining users to design 3D assemblies with planar sections, ensuring that they can be fabricated via laser cutting. In addition, both *FlatFab* and *SketchChair* provide simple physics simulations for users to evaluate the structure of their designs.

3D to 2D to 3D

Commercial tools like *123D Make* [30] and *Pepakura Designer* [31] automates the deconstruction of 3D models into 2D modules for cutting and assembly. Beyond a single 2D cutting process, researchers have proposed systems which deconstruct 3D models into a blend of 3D printed and laser cut parts. *Platener* [1] is a notable system within this category. Through *Platener*, designers can fabricate a design detail in higher resolution via 3D printing, while efficiently building the rest of the object with laser cut parts. Furthermore, *Platener* generates the required joints between the different parts of the assembly.

Augmented Laser Cutting

Systems like *LaserStacker* [22] and *LaserOrigami* [12] extends the laser cutter beyond cutting or etching materials, extending its capabilities to welding and heat-bending acrylic sheets. Similarly, laser cutting has been augmented with 3D printing concepts in the development of hybrid machines that cut and stack layers of fabric to produce soft

[1] http://www.thingiverse.com/thing:448592

3D objects [15]. These innovative systems support the complexity of objects that laser cutters can fabricate by harnessing different material properties. Besides augmenting machine operation, others have innovated on materials for laser cutting. *Foldem* [3] is a hybrid material which has varying properties across different layers. This enables it to remain rigid, bend or fold depending on the depth of the laser's cut.

Joints and Connections

123D Make, *SketchChair* and *FlatFab* generates connections in the form of slots to assemble the parts together. Other joint systems include the tab-and-glue connections found in *Pepakura Designer* and *CardBoardiZer* [23], as well as the common finger joint found in connections generated by *MakerCase* and *Platener*. Besides incorporating joints into part design, they can also be fabricated as separate components, such as the articulation pivots in *CardBoardiZer*. Laser cutting has also been explored together with fastening techniques found in traditional craft; notably in Tsaknaki et al.'s research on leather as a material for tangible interfaces [21].

Opportunities

Systems like *Plushie* and *SketchChair* constrain users to a specific outcome, while systems like *FlatFab* constrains users to a particular modeling process. While their specificity provides a useful sandbox for novices to explore the digital design and fabrication process, they may become too restrictive as users mature. *Joinery* is inspired by these systems, and applies fabrication-aware features for laser cut assemblies while remaining neutral to the process/outcome. In addition, many systems discussed above target a narrow class of materials, and consequently offer joint solutions specific to those materials. *123D Make* and *Platener* for example, focus on deconstructing 'hard' objects, while *Pepakura Designer* focuses on paper assemblies. This reinforces our goal to expand a designer's material vocabulary for the laser cutter. *Joinery* thus takes a material-driven approach to address the implementation of joints for laser cut assemblies.

JOINERY: SYSTEM DEVELOPMENT

We developed *Joinery* as a parametric joint generation toolkit to facilitate creating laser cut assemblies. Through Joinery, designers simply define connections between parts of an assembly, while the system generates the joints. Designers can select from a library of joint profiles developed for different materials. As these joints are parametrically modelled, they respond globally to changes—removing the need to manually edit each joint. In the following sections, we provide the system's implementation, detail the joint profiles that we have developed, and describe a scenario employing *Joinery* as a creativity support tool.

System Walkthrough

Joinery is a web application written in JavaScript, and it extends the *Paper.js*[2] library for vector graphics scripting. The user interface was developed through HTML and CSS. Joinery takes SVG files as input; a standard for vector graphics and laser cutting. The system also exports laser cutting files in the same format. In addition, projects and joint parameters are managed as JSON strings for potential future plug-in or API development.

SVG Structure

Joinery adds joints to a design by generating paths within the source SVG's XML structure. Standard SVG notation is employed to ensure that files are compatible with processes before and after *Joinery*, such as editing the design pattern (Figure 2C) or nesting parts for laser cutting. Class names and object IDs are used to organize and access different components within the SVG as joints are generated over edge-pairs defined by the user (Figure 5). The original paths are labelled with a "joint" class, while two new groups are added to the SVG structure for each edge. Each group contains the joint details, such as 'folding' or 'cutting' paths. These joint groups point back to the original path via its index (ID = index + "_joint"). This structure facilitates joint and path organization both within *Joinery* and after export. Paths in the exported SVG are color-coded based on their class. This makes it convenient to further edit the SVG for laser cutting in programs like *Illustrator* and *Inkscape*, supporting operations like changing all folds to dashed lines.

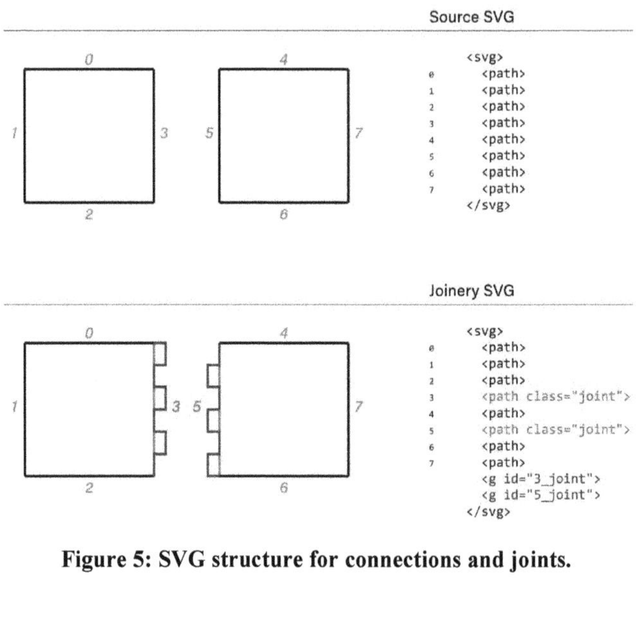

Figure 5: SVG structure for connections and joints.

[2] http://paperjs.org/

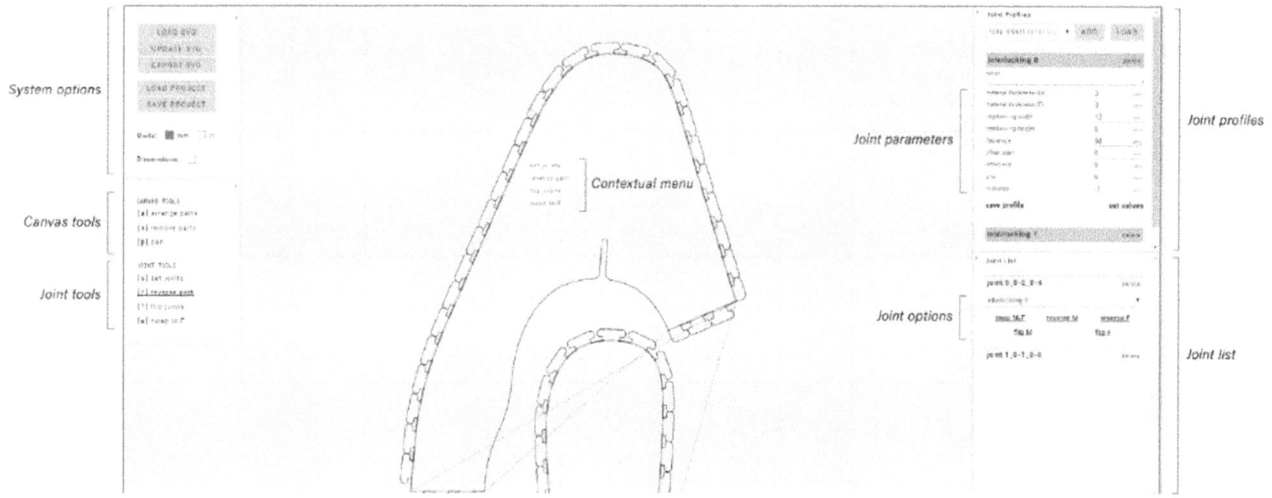

Figure 6: Joinery's interface.

User Interface

Joinery's graphical user interface is designed around a main workspace and joints are generated on user uploaded designs, mimicking the layout of 2D drawing programs like *Illustrator* and *Inkscape*. The left side menu provides system options and tools, while the right side menu is dedicated to joint profiles and joint details (Figure 6).

Applying and Modifying Joints

Users define joints by selecting a pair of edges. The system provides visual feedback by highlighting the edges and the connections between them after a joint has been defined. In addition, the normal to each edge is labelled, indicating the direction in which joints will be generated along the edge (Figure 7A).

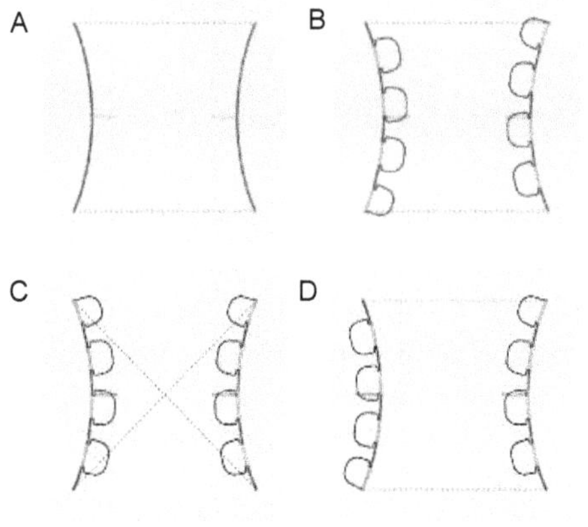

Figure 7: A: Defining a joint from an edge-pair. B: Applying a joint profile. C: Reversing an edge. D: Flipping an edge.

The interface organizes the task of creating connections into 'joint profiles' and a list of user-defined joints. Joint profiles refer to the type of joint and their parameters. *Joinery* offers six joint profiles, and each profile can be customized through its parameters based on material or design needs. The joint list contains all the edge-pair connections defined by the user. Joints are generated by applying a joint profile to an item in the joint list (Figure 7A–B), and *Joinery* updates these joints in real time. In addition, an edge can be reversed or flipped to fix the orientation of the generated joints (Figure 7C, D); these functions are supported through the joint tools, contextual menu and joint options interface. Multiple joint profiles can be added to the system for the same type of joint. For example, two 'interlocking' joint profiles can be added to the project, each with different parameters to be applied to different joints in the design. Similarly, the same joint profile can be applied to multiple joints.

Parametric Joints

Each joint profile is customizable from a set of parameters. These parameters enable the user to configure a joint profile to suit material, machine or design specifications. Joints are dynamic and easily updated due to their parametric nature. For example, increasing the "grip" parameter for an *interlocking* joint profile would give a tighter fit between two parts (Figure 8). Such parametric generation of joints thus simplifies the task of modifying each joint in response to design or fabrication changes.

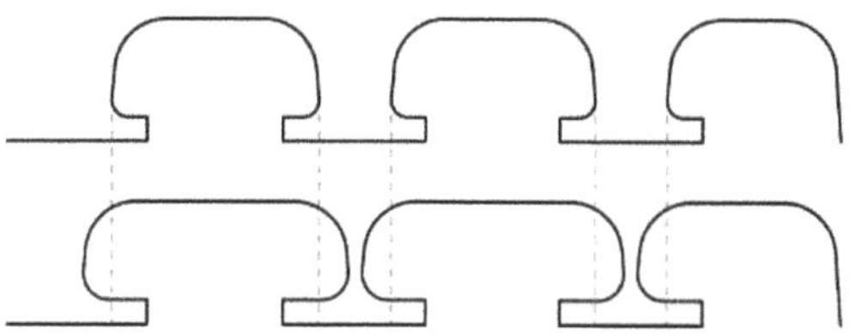

Figure 8: Increasing the "grip" parameter of an interlocking joint profile.

Exporting Joint Profiles

Joint profiles can be exported and saved for the next prototyping iteration, or shared with other users. We observed that information sharing is common practice among designers at our local digital fabrication lab; for example, machine settings for popular materials are

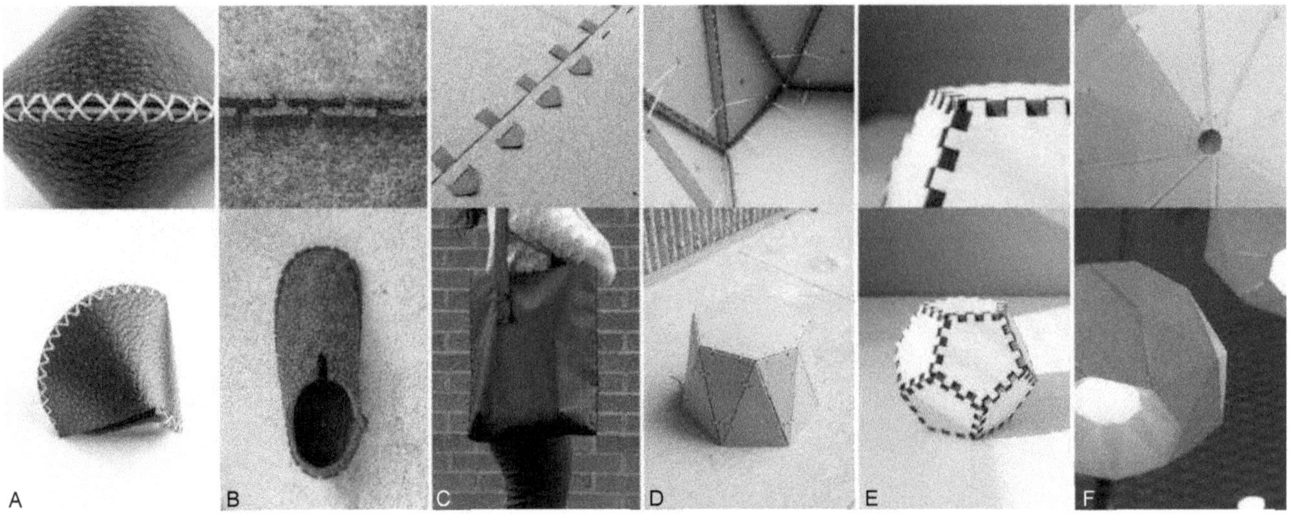

Figure 9: Laser cut assemblies with different joint profiles generated by Joinery. A: Hem, leather pouch. B: Interlocking, felt shoe. C: Loop Insert, nylon tote bag. D: Flap, cardboard table. E: Finger, wooden die. F: Tab Insert, paper lamps.

constantly updated and communicated. This feature was developed to extend such interactions. Joint profiles that have been optimized for a particular purpose (e.g. press-fit finger joints for 3mm thick basswood) can be shared with other designers who work with the same laser cutter. We envision that over time, this feature will facilitate a repository of joint profiles for different materials, specific to the needs of different fabrication labs and maker spaces.

Joint Profile Development

We took a material-driven, exploratory approach to develop joint profiles for the system. This echoes an emerging trend in HCI—investigating craft along with technology to inform new making and interaction possibilities [6]. Craft offers two different lenses to focus our exploration. Firstly, practices and techniques employed in existing craft can inspire the design of laser cut joints; such exploration is captured by Tsaknaki et al.'s research blending laser cut leather with different conventional and unconventional fasteners for interactive products made with leather [21]. Secondly, the interactions between materials and laser cutting can be investigated through the lens of craft practice, allowing "hidden" qualities to emerge [16]. *LaserOrigami* and *LaserStacker* for example, exploit material properties with the fundamental workings of a laser cutter, extending its capabilities to bend and weld acrylic. Our approach thus blends an extrinsic perspective of existing craft practices, with an intrinsic perspective of investigating laser cutting as craft. We explored laser cut assemblies with various joints and materials; and from this exploration, six different joint profiles for a variety of material and design needs were developed. Each joint profile was abstracted into a parametric model that exposes key variables for users to customize (Figure 1).

Hem

The hem joint profile facilitates stitching textiles by hand; in particular, hard to stitch materials like leather and felt. The holes generated reduces the effort required to 'pierce' the material during stitching, while guiding the user to stitch at regular intervals. Various stitching patterns can operate with this profile, such as cross-stitch (Figure 9A) patterns.

Interlocking

The interlocking joint profile extends the concept of finger joints, and connects two edges without the need for adhesives or external fasteners. The interlocking tabs work best on stiffer sheet materials like paper, soft plastics and thick felt, and they can be employed to join edges with and without surface continuity as seen in the shoe example (Figure 9B).

Loop Insert

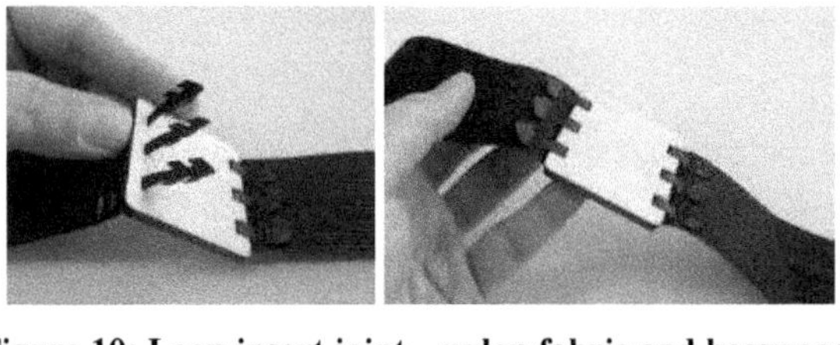

Figure 10: Loop insert joint—nylon fabric and basswood.

Synthetic fabrics like nylon and polyester cut well with the laser cutter as the focused heat fuses the cut fabric and prevents fraying. However, while it is easy to cut such fabrics with the laser cutter, we observed that many students are not familiar with stitching fabric patterns together. The loop insert joint profile is an inherent joint designed to provide stitch-less connections for laser cut fabric parts. The tapered tip of this profile guides the inserts through the slits, while the hooks prevent them from slipping back. As a test, we fabricated a tote bag connected entirely with this joint (Figure 9C), and it was strong enough to hold the weight of a laptop computer with its accessories. In addition, we discovered that this profile offers an interface between fabrics and rigid materials (Figure 10); creating possibilities for multi-material assemblies with soft and hard details.

Flap

This joint profile is commonly found in flat pack carton boxes, and is also the default generated by *Pepakura Designer* and *123D Make*. *Joinery* extends this profile by introducing registration holes on the flaps—these holes guide users to connect parts together with fasteners like rivets or zip-ties (Figure 9D). The flap joint profile is ideal for paper-based materials, cardboard, even sheet metal.

Finger

With the right tolerance, press-fit finger joints hold a laser cut assembly together without the need of adhesives or other fasteners, and are commonly used with wood and acrylic. *Joinery's* parametric finger joints enable users to make fine adjustments to achieve a good press-fit. Furthermore, the system extends the typically perpendicular joints (Figure 3) to accommodate assemblies with walls meeting at different angles. By varying the interior angle parameter, users can create enclosures with more complex forms (Figure 9E).

Tab Insert

The tab insert joint profile was developed for paper-based materials or foldable plastic sheets. As an alternative to the flap joint profile, tab inserts require no external fasteners or adhesives. Tabs can be inserted 'blindly' (i.e. from one side), making it possible to fabricate closed 3D geometries such as spherical or toroidal forms (Figure 9F).

Shoe Design Sprint: *Joinery* as a Creativity Support Tool

We engaged in a week-long shoe design sprint using *Joinery* and laser cutting, with the aim of probing the system's role as a CST (creativity support tool). Nakakoji organizes CSTs with three metaphors: 1) 'Dumbbells' strengthens a user's domain knowledge to become capable without the tool, 2) 'Running shoes' augments the user's abilities to perform a task they are already capable of, and 3) 'Skis' offers the user new capabilities which were previously not possible [4,13]. We find these metaphors useful in describing the system we have developed, and reflect on our sprint with them in mind.

We began the process by researching on anthropometric considerations for shoe design, as well as different shoe types and their patterns. Our research led us to focus on slip-on shoes, and we chose to fabricate our ideas with polyester felt as it had a good balance between flexibility and structure. *Rhinoceros* (a 3D surface modeling tool) was used to model the shoe design around the dimensions of a researcher's feet, and the deconstructed 3D models were imported into *Joinery* for joint design. Designs were then laser cut and assembled. Five pairs of shoes were fabricated during this sprint; the first two focused on getting the right fit, while subsequent models explored different forms (Figure 11).

Joinery as 'skis'

Joint design for laser cut assemblies is not a new concept. However, *Joinery* offers a new experience by automating joint generation as well as enabling efficient customizations through its parametric joints. Our shoe models were assembled with the aid of interlocking joints generated by *Joinery*. Refining these interlocking joints to achieve a tight connection was a simple task—we iteratively improved the joints by customizing its parameters, while the system saved and replicated the best joints.

Joinery as 'dumbbells'

As we explored the process of fabricating with *Joinery*, we realized that we were developing heuristics for designing joints for different materials. Through the process of finding the right interlocking joint parameters for polyester felt, we learned that creating joints based on half the material thickness accommodates the felt's compression during assembly, resulting in a tight and robust connection. This is knowledge we can apply when modeling laser cut assemblies outside *Joinery*.

Joinery as 'running shoes'

The system certainly expedited our process of designing and fabricating shoes via laser cutting. Even though we are veteran digital designers who could have scripted the interlocking joints, or drawn them manually in *Illustrator*, *Joinery* simplified the task. Instead, we could focus our efforts on refining the shoe design. Nakakoji highlights that these CST metaphors illustrate not the tools per se, but the different relationships users have with tools. For us, the 'running shoes' metaphor best encapsulates *Joinery's* impact on our creative process. We set out to develop a tool that facilitates rapid model making through laser cut assemblies—and this system enabled us to fabricate five models to test our ideas over a short one week span.

Figure 11: Shoe design process.

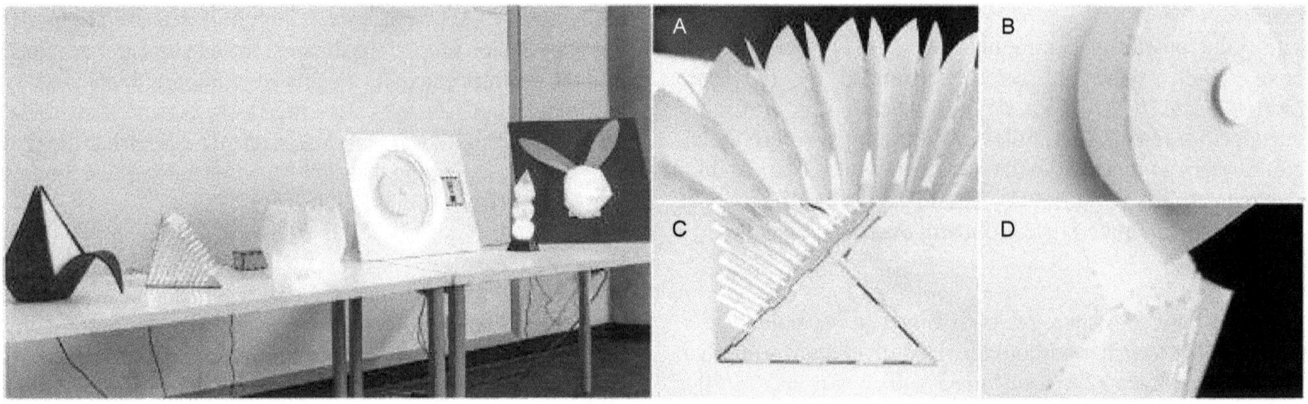

Figure 12: Interactive Lamps fabricated via laser cutting. A: Tab Insert joints for an accordion-like lamp. B: Interlocking joint for a knob. C: Angled finger joints for a faceted base. D: Interlocking joints for an origami animal.

Contributions

In summary, this paper claims the following contributions:

1. We developed *Joinery*, a toolkit that generates parametric joints for laser cut assemblies. Designers simply define edge-pairs as connections, while the system generates joints that respond to design and fabrication edits, thus mitigating the tedious task of redrawing the joints during the iterative process of creating laser cut assemblies.
2. We developed six classes of joint profiles for laser cut assemblies. Each profile is parametric and caters to different material and design needs, thus supporting fabrication awareness. Their parametric nature also facilitates the sharing of joint information between different designs and users.
3. We developed a novel joint profile (loop insert) and extended the applications of existing joint profiles for laser cut assemblies.

CLASSROOM DEPLOYMENT

We deployed *Joinery* in an Industrial Design class at Georgia Tech, focusing on the design and fabrication of tangible interactive products and interfaces. This iteration of the class had 13 students from Industrial Design and Mechanical Engineering. Among the students, 11 were undergraduates, while 2 were pursuing a Master's degree. Approximately half of the students had experience with fabricating with a laser cutter, while 3 students had experience fabricating tangible objects with embedded electronics. The class spanned fifteen weeks, and included work on four different projects. Of the four projects, the last three required students to fabricate and demonstrate a tangible interactive product. *Joinery* was introduced right before the second project, as part of a short in-class lecture on laser cutting as a rapid modeling tool. Our aim was to investigate how actual users will use *Joinery* 'in the wild', specifically with regard to the challenges and opportunities we observed for designing and fabricating laser cut assemblies.

We provided a fifteen-minute demonstration of the system to students in the class, and their initial response was encouraging. Students who had prior experience with the laser cutter were excited about the parametric joints. Recounting a past experience, one student reflected:

> *"I tried to make a wooden box with finger joints once, and the joints were always too loose, but I did not know how to edit the design to give [the box] a tighter fit. The system's [Joinery] breakdown of a joint into its parameters makes it clearer to me."*

While another student noted:

> *"I know that you can cut many materials with the laser cutter, but I never dared to since there wasn't any precedence. I feel more confident with the software [Joinery]."*

After the introduction to laser cutting and *Joinery*, students worked in 6 different groups to design and build an interactive lamp. This assignment required students to integrate the material and form of a product with its function (as a lighting device), and incorporate tangible user interactions.

We observed that choosing appropriate materials for the lamp was a challenge for most groups. While acrylic (a common material choice for laser cutting) offers decent light diffusion as well as structure, its rigidity limits form exploration. As students branched out to alternative materials, many of them arrived at *Mylar* drafting film (a translucent paper-like plastic sheet). While designing and fabricating with *Mylar*, many students employed *Joinery* to create interlocking and tab insert joints to connect different parts. One of the biggest advantages that *Joinery* offered students was the option of connecting parts without the use of adhesives.

> *"Glue affects the consistency of diffused light, while the tab [insert] joints gives the prototype [lamp] a really clean look."*

> *"For the rabbit head lamp [Figure 12D] it [interlocking joints] made it much easier to join the pieces together. Also the idea of avoiding glue altogether was fabulous!"*

> *"I can easily take my model [Figure 12A] apart, change the location of the [flex] sensor, and put it back together."*

Furthermore, *Joinery* facilitated students in their form exploration and interaction design process. With the hassle of manually drawing joints out of the way, many groups focused on iterating through concepts to integrate the form of the lamp with the interaction design. One group wanted to create an ambient lamp that reacted to the light and sound in the environment, and designed a cantilevered structure to mask the sensors (Figure 12C):

> *"I focused on creating the form [in Solidworks] and deconstructing it into flat parts, while Joinery generated the appropriate finger joints. In the past I only used the laser cutter for simpler boxes, this was much more complicated."*

Another group designed an accordion-like lamp (Figure 12A) that users interacted with through collapsing and bending the folds:

> *"I could make this complex product just by assembling many individual parts together with the [tab insert] joint. It also helps me consider where the electronics and wires will go."*

Some students that were initially skeptical about the strength of the joint profiles offered by *Joinery* were surprised at how robust the resulting assembly was:

> *"I'm surprised that the knob is strong enough for someone to turn [Figure 12B]. It is just thin paper and the [interlocking] joint. This is a lot more efficient than 3D printing."*

Through this interactive lamp project, we also had the opportunity to test *Joinery's* joint profile sharing feature. One group encountered difficulty in achieving the ideal fit for the tab insert joints in their prototype. Over email, we were able to understand their issue, and sent them a joint profile with our recommended settings. In turn, that joint profile was shared among other students who were working with the same material.

Students continued to use *Joinery* beyond the interactive lamp project. For the final assignment, one group had an idea for a diaper bag that will alert babysitters when they forget crucial items. They fabricated their bag with thick polyester felt, and employed the interlocking joint to assemble the parts together without stitching (Figure 13). Their laser cutting to assembly process took less than two hours, after which they were able to focus on embedding and programming the electronics.

> *"It [Joinery] made the fabrication process a lot faster especially for felt as I didn't have to worry about sewing it. It also created cleaner looking final prototypes."*

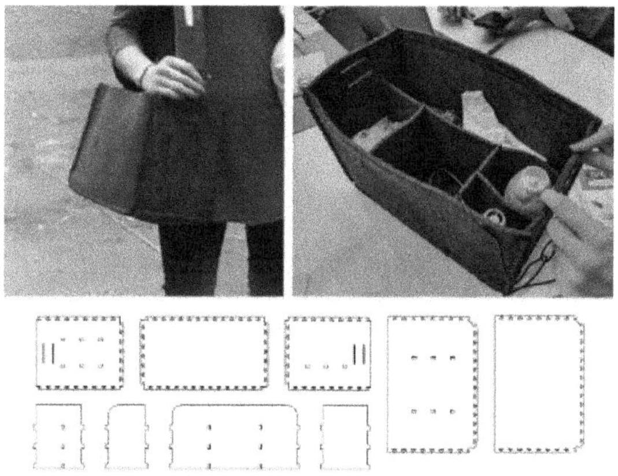

Figure 13: Smart diaper bag for baby sitters.

Reflection

The classroom deployment provided us with feedback which we used to improve *Joinery's* usability. Beyond that, it also gave insight into the approach that students took when designing and fabricating laser cut assemblies with *Joinery*. We reflect on students' interactions with the system, and discuss our findings with respect to the challenges that motivated this research.

Design to fabrication pipelines

Out of the 6 groups engaged with the interactive lamp project, 2 groups initiated the digital design with 3D modeling (*Solidworks*) while the other groups started with *Illustrator*. We observed that *Joinery* fit easily into these different processes. Whether it is 3D modeling, tracing an unfolded pattern, or repeating similar modules, *Joinery* tackled the task where these different pipelines converge; that is, preparing the 2D pattern for laser cutting (Figure 4). By remaining process/outcome-neutral, *Joinery* enabled students to work on a diverse range of inspirations (Figure 12) and embark on different modeling approaches; while the different joint profiles in the toolkit addressed their assembly needs.

Digital-physical negotiations

For more complex joint profiles like the tab insert, interlocking or loop insert, multiple parameters contribute to a joint 'character', such as ease of assembly, or fit. These parametric models proved to be too abstract for some students, who had a hard time relating parameter values to the material and joint character they intend to fabricate. This was mitigated through the joint export and share feature, where we provided a base parametric profile for students to modify. While we believe that this mimics the current fab-lab/maker space culture—where experienced users document material settings for others—we can certainly improve on the communication of *Joinery's* parametric models. For example, 1) different parameters in a joint profile can be semantically grouped based on how they affect different joint characteristics (e.g. fit, ease-of-assembly, 'springiness'), and 2) a library of materials can be built into the system for users to choose from (e.g. 100gsm *Mylar* drafting film).

We discovered that the back-and-forth process between *Joinery* and the laser cut parts challenged perceptions, and generated new insights for some students with regard to materials and laser cut joints. Quoting two students:

> *"I struggled with getting the [tab insert] joint to be strong enough to hold the form together, yet easy enough to insert. I didn't think that 0.1mm would make such a huge difference. The change is not even visible."*

> *"The individual tabs of the interlocking joint seems so flimsy and loose, but they are really strong as a group. Especially with a closed geometry [form]."*

Joinery automatically and responsively updates laser cut joints—even affording 0.1mm increments between iterations to get just the right fit. We believe this helps facilitate the iterations between digital and physical models for our students.

Some students struggled with visualizing the connections between parts in *Joinery*, and suggested a 3D view which simulates the assembly and joints. While this would be a technical challenge given the infrastructure used to build *Joinery*, this suggestion reinforces the question: how can we help design novices negotiate the gaps between digital design and physical fabrication?

Extending defaults

We were motivated to develop a toolkit that diversifies the material vocabulary and variety of objects fabricated with the laser cutter. The classroom deployment was successful in this regard—*Joinery* facilitated students' exploration of new materials with laser cutting (e.g. *Mylar*, leather, felt), and extended the design expression of familiar materials (e.g. basswood, acrylic). However, we reflect that *Joinery* might be extending laser cutting defaults for these students. During a discussion with them about *Joinery's* impact on their process, we discovered that many students selected materials based on the joint profiles that were available. A student who used the laser cutter for the first time reflected that:

> *"It [Joinery] may have subconsciously restricted the materials we could play with since we don't really know what does and does not cut in the laser cutter."*

Another student first decided to use the interlocking joint profile before selecting the material:

> *"We knew that whatever material we use, it would need to be flexible [for the interlocking joints], so that criteria was enough to choose the appropriate materials."*

Joinery opened up a wider range of materials for novices to explore when laser cutting; but we anticipate that it might become another precedent for novices to follow. This motivates us to continue pushing our investigation and development of digital fabrication tools that will support designers in independent creative exploration through digital fabrication. With respect to laser cutting, a logical next step for *Joinery* would be to introduce a 'joint editor' feature where designers can design joint profiles in response to new materials or design applications.

CONCLUSION

In *The Craftsman*, Sennett highlights that "sound judgement about machinery is required in any good craft practice" [19]. He extends *craftsmanship* to encompass even the art of building with digital materials (like operating systems) and delivering services (such as medical practitioners). Our process for developing *Joinery* resonates with this perspective on *craftsmanship*. We developed six joint profiles through a material-driven exploration. Some of these profiles bank on the intricate precision possible only with the computer-controlled laser, others expedite existing hand-making processes—all while considering physical material properties. We parameterized and packaged these profiles into *Joinery*, a toolkit to facilitate designing and fabricating laser cut assemblies.

From our investigation thus far, we believe that *Joinery* contributes to the growing ecosystem of tools for designing and making with digital fabrication. From our classroom deployment, we observed that *Joinery* simplified the task of designing joints for laser cut assemblies—expanding students' ability to explore complex forms, and offering them flexibility to use different materials. Our personal experience also points toward *Joinery's* potential as a creativity support tool not just for novices, but experienced designers as well.

We are keen to continue our research in this area, and plan to conduct several short and long-term design workshops on laser cutting and *Joinery* to investigate how different users engage with the toolkit in their creative process. In addition, we continue our exploration into materials and joints with the aim of expanding the diversity of objects one can design and fabricate with the laser cutter.

ACKNOWLEDGEMENTS

We would like to thank the class instructors for providing the space for us to deploy the toolkit, and the students for their time and feedback.

REFERENCES

1. Dustin Beyer, Serafima Gurevich, Stefanie Mueller, Hsiang-Ting Chen, and Patrick Baudisch. 2015. Platener: Low-fidelity fabrication of 3D Objects by substituting 3D print with laser-cut plates. In *Proceedings of the 33rd Annual ACM Conference on Human Factors in Computing Systems*, 1799–1806. https://doi.org/10.1145/2702123.2702225
2. Paulo Blikstein. 2013. Digital fabrication and "making" in education: The democratization of invention. *FabLabs: Of machines, makers and inventors*: 1–21.
3. Varun Perumal C and Daniel Wigdor. 2016. Foldem: Heterogeneous Object Fabrication via Selective Ablation of Multi-Material Sheets. In *Proceedings of the 2016 CHI Conference on Human Factors in Computing Systems*, 5765–5775. https://doi.org/10.1145/2858036.2858135
4. Nicholas Davis, Chih-Pin Hsiao, Yanna Popova, and Brian Magerko. 2015. An Enactive Model of Creativity for Computational Collaboration and Co-creation. In *Creativity in the Digital Age*. Springer, 109–133.
5. Neil Gershenfeld. 2007. *Fab: the coming revolution on your desktop - from personal computers to personal fabrication*. Basic Books, New York, NY.
6. Shad Gross, Jeffrey Bardzell, and Shaowen Bardzell. 2014. Structures, forms, and stuff: the materiality and medium of interaction. *Personal and Ubiquitous Computing* 18, 3: 637–649. https://doi.org/10.1007/s00779-013-0689-4
7. Manfred Lau, Jun Mitani, and Takeo Igarashi. 2012. Digital Fabrication. *Computer* 45, 12: 76–79. https://doi.org/10.1109/MC.2012.407
8. James McCrae, Nobuyuki Umetani, and Karan Singh. 2014. FlatFitFab: interactive modeling with planar sections. In *Proceedings of the 27th annual ACM symposium on User interface software and technology*, 13–22. https://doi.org/10.1145/2642918.2647388
9. Yuki Mori and Takeo Igarashi. 2007. Plushie: an interactive design system for plush toys. *ACM Transactions on Graphics* 26, 3: 45. https://doi.org/10.1145/1276377.1276433
10. Catarina Mota. 2011. The rise of personal fabrication. In *Proceedings of the 8th ACM Conference on Creativity and Cognition*, 279. https://doi.org/10.1145/2069618.2069665
11. Stefanie Mueller and Patrick Baudisch. 2015. Laser cutters: a new class of 2D output devices. *interactions* 22, 5: 72–74. https://doi.org/10.1145/2811292
12. Stefanie Mueller, Bastian Kruck, and Patrick Baudisch. 2014. Laser origami: laser-cutting 3D objects. *Interactions* 21, 2: 36–41. https://doi.org/10.1145/2567782
13. Kumiyo Nakakoji. 2006. Meanings of tools, support, and uses for creative design processes. In *International design research symposium*, 156–165. Retrieved from https://pdfs.semanticscholar.org/68a5/5e4352285b35e83afb3d94eaa87523bcae77.pdf
14. Lora Oehlberg, Wesley Willett, and Wendy E. Mackay. 2015. Patterns of Physical Design Remixing in Online Maker Communities. In *Proceedings of the 33rd Annual ACM Conference on Human Factors in Computing Systems*, 639–648. https://doi.org/10.1145/2702123.2702175
15. Huaishu Peng, Jennifer Mankoff, Scott E. Hudson, and James McCann. 2015. A Layered Fabric 3D Printer for Soft Interactive Objects. 1789–1798. https://doi.org/10.1145/2702123.2702327
16. Daniela K. Rosner and Alex S. Taylor. 2011. Antiquarian Answers: Book Restoration As a Resource for Design. In *Proceedings of the SIGCHI Conference on Human Factors in Computing Systems* (CHI '11), 2665–2668. https://doi.org/10.1145/1978942.1979332
17. Greg Saul, Manfred Lau, Jun Mitani, and Takeo Igarashi. 2011. SketchChair: an all-in-one chair design system for end users. In *Proceedings of the fifth international conference on Tangible, embedded, and embodied interaction*, 73. https://doi.org/10.1145/1935701.1935717
18. Yuliy Schwartzburg and Mark Pauly. 2013. Fabrication-aware Design with Intersecting Planar Pieces. In *Computer Graphics Forum*, 317–326.
19. Richard Sennett. 2008. *The craftsman*. Yale University Press.
20. Cesar Torres and Eric Paulos. 2015. MetaMorphe: Designing Expressive 3D Models for Digital Fabrication. In *Proceedings of the 2015 ACM SIGCHI Conference on Creativity and Cognition*, 73–82. https://doi.org/10.1145/2757226.2757235
21. Vasiliki Tsaknaki, Ylva Fernaeus, and Mischa Schaub. 2014. Leather as a material for crafting interactive and physical artifacts. In *Proceedings of the 2014 conference on Designing interactive systems*, 5–14. https://doi.org/10.1145/2598510.2598574
22. Udayan Umapathi, Hsiang-Ting Chen, Stefanie Mueller, Ludwig Wall, Anna Seufert, and Patrick Baudisch. 2015. LaserStacker: Fabricating 3D Objects by Laser Cutting and Welding. In *Proceedings of the 28th Annual ACM Symposium on User Interface*

Software & Technology, 575–582. https://doi.org/10.1145/2807442.2807512

23. Yunbo Zhang, Wei Gao, Luis Paredes, and Karthik Ramani. 2016. CardBoardiZer: Creatively Customize, Articulate and Fold 3D Mesh Models. In *Proceedings of the 2016 CHI Conference on Human Factors in Computing Systems*, 897–907. https://doi.org/10.1145/2858036.2858362
24. *Solidworks*. Retrieved from http://www.solidworks.com/
25. *Fusion 360*. Retrieved from http://www.autodesk.com/products/fusion-360/overview
26. *Adobe Illustrator*. Retrieved from http://www.adobe.com/products/illustrator.html
27. *Inkscape*. Retrieved from https://inkscape.org/
28. *MakerCase*. Retrieved from http://www.makercase.com/
29. *Marvelous Designer*. Retrieved from http://www.marvelousdesigner.com/
30. *123D Make*. Retrieved from http://www.123dapp.com/make
31. *Pepakura Designer*. Retrieved from http://www.tamasoft.co.jp/pepakura-en/

Toward Creative Engagement of Soft Haptic Toys with Children with Autism Spectrum Disorder

Jinsil Hwaryoung Seo
Texas A&M University
College Station, USA
hwaryoung@tamu.edu

Pavithra Aravindan
Texas A&M University
College Station, USA
pavi4nov@tamu.edu

Annie Sungkajun
Texas A&M University
College Station, USA
a.sungkajun@gmail.com

ABSTRACT
Many children with Autism Spectrum Disorder (ASD) suffer from over or under sensory development and stimulation. Stuffed toys, weighted blanket, or weighted vest have been used to relax children with ASD. However children with autism are not actively invited to design/create their own relaxation toys. We conducted iterative design explorations for 6 months in collaboration with 22 children and 18 caregivers at a local autism clinic to characterize design elements of soft haptic toys for children with ASD to help sensory regulation and integration. This paper details various design elements of our soft haptic toys focusing on sensory qualities, customizability and affordability that we learned from the design exploration phase of the study. After the design exploration, we invited 5 children with ASD and their caregivers to investigate how making soft haptic toys impacts children's behaviors. The study indicates that children with ASD build a strong personal connection to the soft toy they created, promote pretend play and alleviate their abnormal behaviors in the process of creative engagement.

Author Keywords
Soft Haptic Toy; Children with Autism Spectrum Disorder; Sensory Integration; Creative Engagement; Co-creation

ACM Classification Keywords
H.5.m. Information interfaces and presentation (e.g., HCI): Miscellaneous.

INTRODUCTION
Autism is defined by the current Diagnostic and Statistical Manual of Mental Disorders as a neurological disorder characterized by qualitative impairment in social interaction and communication as well as the presence of "restricted, repetitive, and stereotyped patterns of behaviors, interests, and activities" [1]. According to Center for Disease Control and prevention (CDC), it is estimated that 1 of 68 children born in the United States has some degree of Autism Spectrum Disorder (ASD) [2]. While symptoms can vary widely between individuals, symptoms begin to manifest in very early childhood and can be an emotional challenge for parents.

It is known that many children with ASD are sensitive to sensory stimuli [3]. Children with ASD may have difficulties with processing sensory information from their environment and may be over or under-responsive to stimulation [4]. This kind of sensory issues make them suffer in daily social interaction and emotional control. Therefore many sensory products for children with ASD are developed to calm and relax them. Designs greatly vary: weighted blankets and vests, bubble tubes, flickering lights, chewy tubes, squeeze balls and soft toys [5]. Since children are known to become attached to soft toys, incorporating interactivity into these beloved objects as a form of therapy is a good way to help children attain relaxation [6]. However, toys designed for children with autism are not widely available or very expensive. In addition, they have not been invited to take an active role in designing sensory toys. Sometimes parents of children with ASD and therapist always try to find affordable tools or toys and look for ways of modifying and making toys by themselves [7].

Our study was inspired by positive impacts of arts-based interventions for children with ASD. Art making with children is a fun and exciting way for them to learn and grow. Through art making, the child's inner world of images, feelings, thoughts, and ideas are always of primary importance to the creative experience. Parents can also play an important role in the child's art-making process. They can encourage and support their child in exploring and mastering difficult materials and finding new ways to express themselves. They can also help the child give the art creation personal meanings [8].

We explored design elements of the soft toys in collaboration with children and therapists at a local autism clinic focusing on customizable and affordable DIY toys. We investigated how those elements should be integrated to a soft toy that calms children with ASD and how creative engagement of children with ASD for their relaxing toys affects them. In this paper, we detail the design processes and evaluation of soft haptic toys which vibrate when they get hugged by the child. In addition, we will discuss the

C&C '17, June 27-30, 2017, Singapore, Singapore
© 2017 ACM. ISBN 978-1-4503-4403-6/17/06…$15.00
DOI: http://dx.doi.org/10.1145/3059454.3059474.

results of multiple creation sessions with children with ASD and their caregivers.

BACKGROUND

Positive Impacts of Creative Engagement

The power of making art for children with ASD lies in its ability to make learning both visual and appealing. Kids get enjoyment, stress relief and a boost to their self-confidence from tackling art projects or simply exploring art materials. That they are practicing life skills while doing so may not enter their minds [11]. Fun art projects will often grab and hold the child's interest while the adult can make sure that the projects are designed to help the child make progress in relevant treatment goal areas such as imagination/abstract thinking, sensory regulation and integration, emotions/self-expression, developmental growth, visual-spatial skills, and recreation/leisure skills [12]. We focus on positive effects of art creation in the area of sensory regulation and integration. This often make children with autism stand out, prevent them from interacting with others, and can distract them from other activities, such as school work or play. However, these sensations may provide some calming, soothing feelings when the child is agitated. Creative engagement can be considered as channeling non-functional or inappropriate self-stimulating behaviors into socially acceptable, creative outlets [12].

Soft Tangible Interfaces for Children with ASD

There are many tangible products that are used for the purpose of relaxation [13-16]. Tangible products used widely for relaxation are stuffed toys and pillows [17, 18]. Recently wearable projects with haptic components embedded have been developed. *+me* project [19] is a soft collar pillow with visual, auditory and haptic sensory integrations with the way he/she likes such as hugging, sleeping, squeezing or carrying. The wearable prototype consists haptic interface, color and density changing lights, speakers with sensor technologies and a remote controller that allows therapists or parents to adjust the actual sensory feedbacks. *Snug Vest* [20] inflates to provide adjustable and evenly-distributed pressure to the torso for a comforting hug-like squeeze to children with ASD without pressure placed on the stomach or chest. *RE-vibe wristband* [21] was designed to meet the needs of all different students in a school setting, including those with autism and ADHD.

METHODOLOGY

Our project consisted of two phases: Design Exploration and Creative Engagement. Children with ASD, parents, and therapists are actively engaged in both phases. In the Design Exploration phase, we focused on various design elements of our soft toys including texture, form, and interactivity. This was done at a local autism clinic with 22 children with high functioning ASD and 18 caregivers over 6 months. In the Creative Engagement phase, we invited 5 children with high functioning ASD and their parents or caregivers to create their own soft haptic toys utilizing the design components we had tested in the Design Exploration phase. During both phases, observation notes were taken by two research staff members and reviewed the notes right after each activity.

Design Exploration Phase

To define our design criteria of a soft haptic toy, we explored a wide variety of possible design elements including material, shape, interactivity, and haptic feedbacks. We adopted an iterative design process as we worked with children with ASD and their caregivers. Design elements that were tested are detailed in this section.

Fabrics

We created early prototypes using cotton fabric, soft fleece, hard fleece, patterned fleece, hard felt and soft felt, all in different variations of color. Since our purpose is to create a soft toy to help children's sensory regulation and integration, we carefully chose fabrics that are soft and safe. Ease of maintenance was also strongly considered since we intended parents and caregivers create their own soft toys towards the end of our project. Microfleece and organic cotton proved most preferable and were chosen for our final soft toy design. Microfleece is a synthetic wool-like material often made from polyester. It is water-repellent and holds in warmth even when wet. Due to its ultra-soft texture, this fabric is most popular for baby and children projects. Organic cotton is grown using methods with a low impact on the environment [22]. It is easy to wash and is also pleasant to touch.

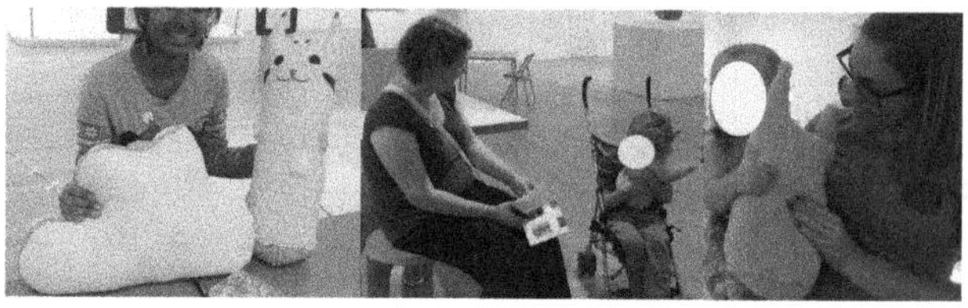

Figure 1. Early soft toy prototypes.

Shapes

Our preliminary design studies informed our use of approachable and friendly shapes that invite gentle touch from children with ASD. In the early stage of exploration, we created different shapes of soft toys such as a cat, cloud, cube and cylinder and introduced them to children at a local autism clinic. We learned that animal shapes with a kindly facial expression evoked emotional connections between children and the soft toys most effectively. Incorporating a simplified smiley face on each design helped children associate personal meanings to the toy. In fact, children proffered soft toys with facial expression. In later prototypes, children loved to pick up and hug the cat-shaped toy more than our other abstract shapes. When holding the cat toy, the children associated the haptic vibrations as the 'purring of a cat'.

Interactions

Throughout the Exploration Phase, we observed how children played with soft toys. The size and shape of our soft toys and the placement of a sensor were defined based on physical interactions by children with ASD most often observed, as seen in Figure 1 middle and left. We also tested different feedbacks using light, sound and vibration for their response. We created interactive feedbacks in order to facilitate emotional connections between the children with ASD and the toys. Light blue LEDs embedded in the cloud pillow were programmed to glow in a slow breathing rhythm. When hugged, the glowing rhythm becomes faster. We also experimented with vibration and sound. Lilypad Arduino USB boards were utilized for each method of interactivity.

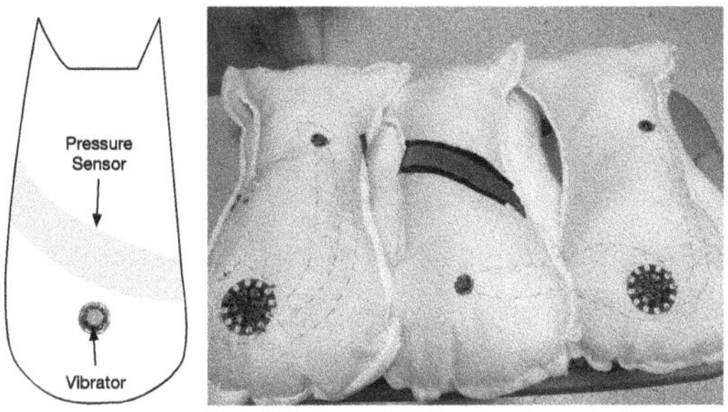

Figure 2. Pressure sensor and vibrator placement

Haptic Vibration Patterns

From early explorations with different actuations, we learned that gentle vibrations emanating from the soft toys calmed children with ASD during periods of high stress. The children were able to work independently, were less distracted by various environmental noises, and were less prone to outcry. We assessed 4 patterns of vibration: heartbeat, phone-like vibration, breath rhythm, and no vibration. The children had difficulties differentiating between specific patterns, and instead, perceived them simply as a strong vibration, soft vibration, or no vibration. While each child's preference for a specific pattern differed, each preferred vibration over no vibration in the soft toy. The haptic vibrations were achieved using Lilypad Vibeboards, and stitched into the toys as shown in Figure 2.

Soft Circuits

Soft circuits, also known as electronic textiles (e-textiles), are electrical circuits created using flexible conductive materials with discrete electronics components, such as lights, batteries, switches, and sensors [23]. We focused on integrating electronic components with soft materials (mainly fabrics) using soft circuit techniques. We used conductive threads to connect the Lilypad components needed for interactivity such as Vibeboards, micro-controllers, and LEDs. All electronic components were sewn securely onto the fabric and insulated by cotton stuffing materials. We fabricated touch/pressure sensors of our own design using conductive yarns, fabrics, and Velostat to ensure that our toys would be easy to hug without discomfort.

Participants' Feedback

Our final prototype (Figure 3, left) was introduced to children with ASD at a local autism center. Therapists would give our toy to the children when they became anxious. The children usually become anxious in three common situations: when they were told not to do something, were stopped from doing something, or to be told 'no' or otherwise denied when they asked for something. While seemingly trivial, common scenarios which elicit anxiety include doing homework, having a meal, conducting a morning routine, going to bed, and taking a bath.

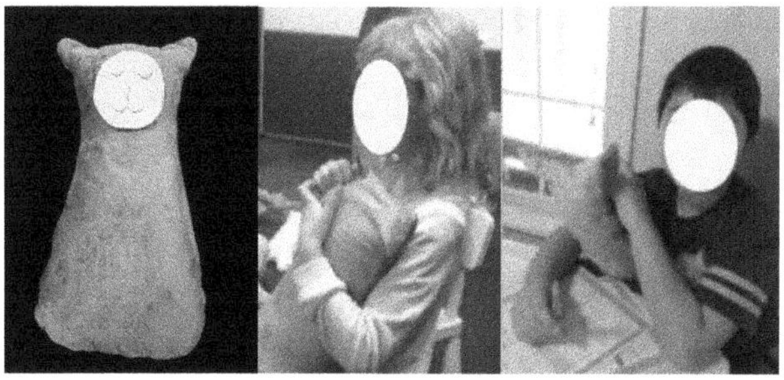

Figure 3. Final prototype (left), Children with ASD experience our soft haptic toy (middle and right).

We witnessed a variety of behavior during preliminary observations. Children often petted or hugged the haptic cat toy. When anxious, the children tended to squeeze the soft toys hardly. They felt most comfortable playing with toys made with the softest fabrics (ex. microfleece). During such play, the children commented, "Very fuzzy", "Very comfortable", "Nice to hug", "Feels like my mom", and "I want to hug it and sleep". The preferences for size and shape were unanimous. All the participants 'loved' the shape of the cat soft toy. It was perfect for them to hold and carry around. It's long slender shape gave them the freedom to wrap it around their arms. The children made personal connections to the cat haptic toys because many of them had cats at home. Some of the children became very attached to the cat. One of the participants wanted to give the cat a name, a tail, whiskers, big eyes and shirts.

Design Suggestions: Several children and caregivers suggested that a little weight be added to the soft toy after interacting with our final prototype. So, we used a small rice bag in the creation session. Affordability was also very important component for the parents. Caregivers wanted to modify their current relaxation tools integrating interactive components (sensor, haptic, etc.) and to create multiple soft toy cases so they can wash and change based on their interests.

Creative Engagement Phase: Soft Haptic Toy Creation

Art making with children is a fun and exciting way for the child to learn and grow. In art making the child's inner world of images, feelings, thoughts, and ideas are always of primary importance to the experience. Art making can be encouraged and supported by an adult "helper" who can assist the child in exploring and mastering difficult materials and finding new ways to express themselves using the art supplies. By helping the child give the art product personal meaning (i.e. finding a story, description, or meaning) the adult is able to support the child's exploration of both materials and narratives about the art products created [24]. This can be expanded to tinkering with existing materials, transforming products or materials that are ready to hand into new constructions. This supports children and parents' co-creation in the family, community based settings [25]. As we learned from the design exploration phase, we prepared materials for children with ASD and caregivers to explore and create their own soft haptic toys. In this session, we let participants draw their own characters or objects on a piece of fabric and make soft toys using their drawings.

Participants and materials
Five children with high functioning autism (ages 5 to 8) and their caregivers were invited. They created soft haptic toys using white cotton fabrics, fabric markers, poly filling to stuff the pillow, sewing machine, pins, needle, thread, and scissors. In addition, materials for the soft circuit were provided.

Process
The creation process of a soft haptic toy is illustrated in Figure 4. They create an inner layer (A) with stuffing materials and a sensor/vibration module, and (B) a skin layer with a child's character drawing using fabric markers. A small rice bag was inserted under the skin later. Participants were very engaged with the entire process. None of children have experienced sewing before. They focused very well and created their project with limited support from the caregivers (a parent or a therapist). During drawing sessions, two children did not talk at all but just focused on their drawings. Other three children kept talking about their drawings explaining why they chose specific shapes and colors for their characters for example "I want to give my cat a bigger tail, bright open eyes". The soft circuit template including a Lilypad arduino, conductive threads, two vibeboards, a crocheted pressure sensor and a piece of felt fabric was provided to the children and the caregivers. Mainly caregivers took the responsibility of creating soft circuits but some children sewed everything by themselves. One 8-year-old boy said, "I never sewed, I never thought I would sew. But I think I do well." Since a child's preferred vibration pattern was various at the design exploration phase, we provided three vibration patterns (heart beat, phone, and breath) and let each child choose one for their creation.

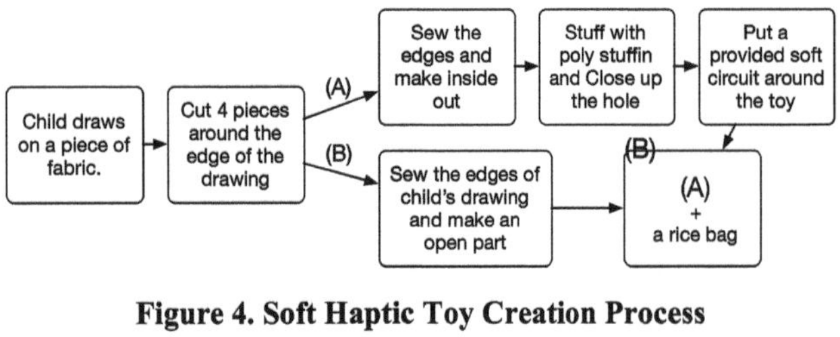

Figure 4. Soft Haptic Toy Creation Process

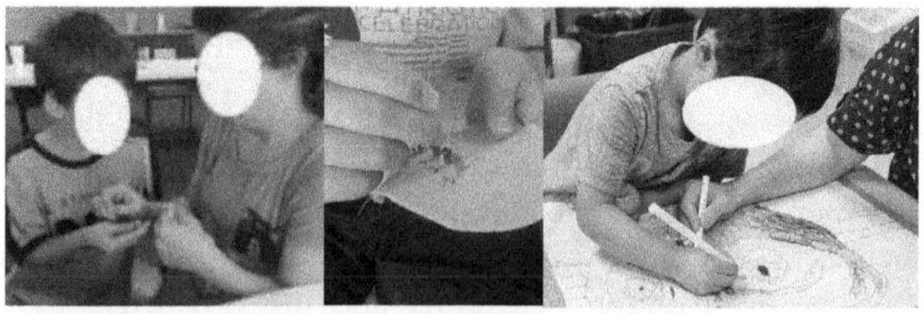

Figure 5. Children create soft toys with their caregivers.

Figure 6. Soft haptic toys that the participants created.

Outcomes & Feedback
Participants created many interesting soft toys including the designs in Figure 6. They intended to draw favorite characters including a cat, an alien, a worm, etc. All participants were happy about the results and hugged their toys for a long time. They said "this is mine", "I made this with my mommy", "I will make one more", "Can I change this (vibration)?" The caregivers mentioned much potential for the soft toys. They expressed that they would create other toys at home and introduce this method to their friends with children with ASD. Participated children took their creation home and a few parents reported how their child played with the soft toy. One child put a seat belt for the soft toy because she wanted him to be safe and the other child took him around town and showed him to all her friends and sister.

CONCLUSION & FUTURE WORK

We presented our design exploration process that made us to refine various design elements of our soft haptic toys. In this process, we focused on safety, tactile/haptic qualities of the soft toy, and sensory regulation and integration. From the iterative process with children with ASD and caregivers, we were able to characterize design elements of the soft haptic toy that will calm children with ASD in their stressful situations. In the creative engagement sessions, we focused on evoking children's creativity through a co-creation process between a child and a caregiver. We observed that the participated children were very excited about the fact that they made a new toy which responds their hug. Even though longitudinal studies are highly suggested, we learned that there is a great potential in creative making of assistive toys to empower children with ASD. This opens a new channel between children's autistic behaviors and artistic creations evoking a critical sense of wonder. We will continue to study with children with ASD and caregivers with more systematic research methods on long-term effect of our method.

REFERENCES

1. American Psychiatric Association, *Diagnostic and Statistical Manual of Mental Disorders (4th edn., text revision)*. 2000, Washington, DC: American Psychiatric Association.
2. Bourgeois, K.S., et al., *Infant Manual Exploration of Objects, Surfaces, and Their Interrelations*. Infancy, 2005. **8**(3): p. 19.
3. Marco, E.J., et al., *Sensory Processing in Autism: A Review of Neurophysiologic Findings*. Pediatric Research, 2011. **69**(5 Pt 2): p. 48R-54R.
4. Rogers, J. and J. Short. *Sensory differences: Online training module (Columbus, OH: Ohio Center for Autism and Low Incidence)*. . Autism Internet Modules 2010; Available from: http://www.autisminternetmodules.org.
5. Toy Industry Foundation, *Let's Play: A Guide to Toys for Children with Special Needs*. 2008: FCBooks.
6. Hood, B. and P. Bloom, *Children prefer certain individuals over perfect duplicates*. Cognition, 2008. **106**: p. 455-462.
7. Simpson, C.G. and S.A. Lynch, *Adapting and Modifying Toys for Children with Special Needs.*, in *National Association for the Education of Young Children Annual Conference* 2003: Chicago, IL.
8. Armstrong, T., *Strategies to Empower, Not Control, Kids Labeled ADD/ADHD*, in *ADD/ADHD Alternatives in the Classroom*. 1999, ASCD: Alexandria, VA
9. Armstrong, D.M., *The Mind-Body Problem: An Opinionated Introduction*. 1999, Boulder, CO: Westview Press.
10. Hatch-Rasmussen, M.A. *Sensory Integration*. 2012 [cited 12 Dec. 12]; Available from: http://www.autism.com/symptoms_sensory_overview.
11. Lacour, K. *The Value of Art Therapy for Those on the Autism Spectrum*. 2015 [cited 2016 June 13, 2016]; Available from: http://the-art-of-autism.com/the-value-of-art-therapy-for-those-on-the-autism-spectrum/.
12. Martin, N., *Art as an Early Intervention Tool for Children with Autism*. 2009, London and Philadephia: Jessica Kingsley Publishers.
13. Alonso, M.B., M. Varkevisser, and D.V. Keyson, *Expressive stress relievers*, in *Proceedings of the 7th Nordic Conference on Human-Computer Interaction: Making Sense Through Design*. 2012, ACM: Copenhagen, Denmark. p. 761-764.
14. Schelle, K.J., et al., *Tactile Dialogues: Personalization of Vibrotactile Behavior to Trigger Interpersonal Communication*, in *Proceedings of the Ninth International Conference on Tangible, Embedded, and Embodied Interaction*. 2015, ACM: Stanford, California, USA. p. 637-642.
15. Zubrycki, I. and G. Granosik, *Designing an Interactive Device for Sensory Therapy*, in *The Eleventh ACM/IEEE International Conference on Human Robot Interaction*. 2016, IEEE Press: Christchurch, New Zealand. p. 545-546.
16. Geurts, L., et al., *Skweezee studio: turn your own plush toys into interactive squeezable objects*, in *Proceedings of the 8th International Conference on Tangible, Embedded and Embodied Interaction*. 2013, ACM: Munich, Germany. p. 377-380.
17. Yamashita, Y., et al., *Stuffed toys alive!: cuddly robots from fantasy world*, in *ACM SIGGRAPH 2012 Emerging Technologies*. 2012, ACM: Los Angeles, California. p. 1-1.
18. Stiehl, W.D., et al., *The huggable: a therapeutic robotic companion for relational, affective touch*, in *ACM SIGGRAPH 2006 Emerging technologies*. 2006, ACM: Boston, Massachusetts. p. 15.
19. Özcan B., S.V., Caligiore D., Baldassarre G. , *Motivating Children with Autism to Communicate and Interact Socially Through the "+me" Wearable Device.* Nea Science - Giornale Italiano di Neuroscienze, Psicologia e Riabilitazione, 2014. **5**: p. 59-65.
20. *Snug Vest*. [cited 2016 August 1]; Available from: http://www.snugvest.com/.
21. *Re-vibe*. [cited 2016 August 1]; Available from: http://fokuslabs.com/.
22. *Organic Cotton*. [cited 2015 June 1]; Available from: https://en.wikipedia.org/wiki/Organic_cotton.
23. Lovell, E. *Getting hands-on with soft circuits: a workshop facilitotor's guide*. [cited 2016 July, 15]; Available from: http://alumni.media.mit.edu/~emme/guide.pdf.
24. Anim, J.O., *The role of drawing in promoting the children's communication in Early Childhood Education*, in *Early Childhood Education and Care*. 2012, Oslo and Akershus University College of Applied Sciences, Dublin Institute of Technology and University of Malta.
25. *Bricolage*. [cited 2016 June 13]; Available from: http://en.wiktionary.org/wiki/bricolage.

Share Once or Share Often? Exploring How Designers Approach Iteration in a Large Online Community

Patrick A. Crain and Brian P. Bailey
Department of Computer Science
University of Illinois, Urbana, IL
{pcrain2, bpbailey} @ illinois.edu

ABSTRACT
Iteration prompted by feedback is fundamental to creative design. Designers often use online communities to gather feedback, but there is little knowledge of how designers use these communities to *iterate* on their work. We studied iterative design practice in three active forums that target novice design critique in a popular online community. We collected a large corpus of projects (n=3,730) and comments (n=29,412). The data was analyzed to determine how often designers iterate on their projects, and which characteristics of the feedback correlate with iteration. Two surveys (n=38) were conducted to further learn how often and at which design stages designers post their work to the community. Our results showed that more and longer comments, comments with less positive tone and comments with more thought-provoking statements correlated with iteration. Our analysis also showed that two or more iterations were shared for only 21% of the projects. The survey results explained that the rate of iteration was due in part to designers sharing their projects with the community near the end of their design process. Our findings also suggest how online communities can better support iterative design practice.

Author Keywords
Design; critique; feedback; iteration; online communities.

ACM Classification Keywords
H.5.3 [Information Interface and Presentation]: Group and Organization Interfaces – Evaluation/methodology.

INTRODUCTION
Iteration is essential for producing creative solutions and gaining confidence in one's creative ability [10, 13]. Through iteration, designers learn to perform a series of content revisions prompted by feedback from an external audience [29]. The feedback enables the designer to "see" problems with their proposed solution, learn about the design problem, and gain insight for improving the work [33]. Although seasoned designers often have the skills and the resources necessary to iterate effectively, many designers do not, and face the challenge of receiving timely, helpful feedback [16].

For designers with limited resources, particularly novices, online design communities can serve as a source of feedback and creative inspiration for their projects [39]. Participation generally does not require financial resources or social capital, and often requires only creating an account. These communities allow designers to connect online with diverse feedback providers who are motivated by a mutual interest in design or the topic of the projects. Even experienced designers can benefit from online communities, as they enable them to showcase and promote their work, learn about modern design trends, and refine their creative skills [27].

Although researchers have studied feedback generation in online design communities [27, 39], there are still important open questions regarding how the feedback requests are integrated into iterative design practice. For instance, when and how often do designers iterate on their projects using the feedback received from an online community, what characteristics of the feedback impact iteration, and to what degree do the projects improve?

We report results from a mixed-methods study of how designers approach iteration in three graphic design critique forums in Reddit (see Figure 1). We chose Reddit because it contains some of the largest and most active public forums for design critique. We collected a large corpus of design projects (3,730) and critique comments (29,412), and applied heuristics to determine when designers posted iterations for their projects. These heuristics were developed by observing common practices for how iterations were represented within the community. We measured how often designers iterated on their posted projects, and statistically modeled which characteristics of the feedback received (e.g., the length and number of responses, the valence of each response, and the categories of critique discourse referenced in the responses) correlated with subsequent design iteration. The quantitative measures were complemented by a structured (N=21) and an open-ended (N=17) survey posted to the community. The surveys inquired about participants' motivations for and experiences with receiving feedback from the community into their design process, and asked participants to quantify and describe their iterative process.

C&C '17, June 27-30, 2017, Singapore, Singapore
© 2017 ACM. ISBN 978-1-4503-4403-6/17/06...$15.00
DOI: http://dx.doi.org/10.1145/3059454.3059476

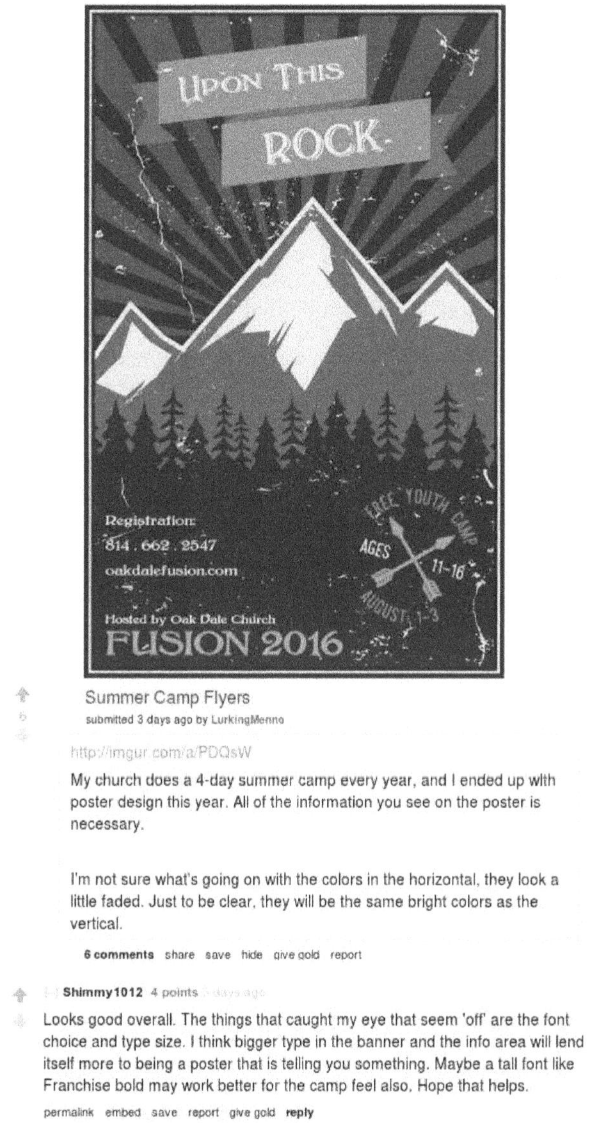

Figure 1: An example of a graphic design project posted by a user to /r/design_critiques on Reddit for feedback. The design image linked in the original post was placed in the figure for the purpose of explanation.

Our study contributes three findings. First, we found that more and longer comments, comments with fewer positive statements, and comments that contained more thought-provoking statements were all predictive of iteration. This indicates that the type of feedback received online affects how often designers share iterations of their work.

Second, we found that only a single design was posted for feedback for 79% of the projects in our data set, while two or more iterations were posted for the remaining 21%. The survey results indicated that designers were approaching the community near the end of their process, leaving less time and possibly less desire to continue iterating on their work.

Finally, we found that designers posted their projects in the community with the expectation that they would receive quick, high quality feedback from a large, diverse audience. This extends findings from a prior study of professional development in an invitation-only design community [27] to an open community that targets novice design critique.

Our work makes two contributions to the creativity and cognition community. First, our results contribute deeper empirical understanding of the characteristics of feedback received online that relate to design iteration and how designers incorporate the use of online communities into their creative projects. Second, our findings can inform how online communities and crowd-based design services (e.g., [16, 40]) can better represent projects and generate the types of feedback that promote iteration. We believe these contributions will enable online communities to serve as more effective resources for creative design projects.

RELATED WORK

We situate our contribution in the context of prior studies of online design communities. We then describe the benefits of online communities relative to other sources for design feedback, and the benefits of iteration for creative design.

Studies of Online Design Communities

Researchers have examined online design communities from many perspectives. For example, Xu & Bailey investigated the expectations and motivations of users participating in an online critique community in digital photography [39]. They found that designers' participation in a community could enhance the perception of their work, provided they received feedback of sufficient quality and quantity. They also found that designers often approached online communities with the goal of obtaining quick feedback from members with comparable or greater design experience. Marlow & Dabbish studied a graphic design community of practice [27]. They found that designers derived professional benefit from sharing and promoting their work, and were able to improve their creative skills by reviewing and mirroring the practices found in the design work showcased by others. They also found that designers, especially novices, valued the work-in-progress section of the site to receive quick feedback on their work. Other research has leveraged online communities to trace the effects of analogies on design innovations [5].

Our study differs from this corpus of prior work because it analyzes online communities from a unique perspective – iterative design practice. We analyze how often designers iterate and how they represent iterations in an archetypal online discussion forum. Our work also follows a long thread of research that leverages attributes of content and behavior to model variables of interest in online communities (e.g. [1, 3, 15, 17, 18, 20, 26, 28, 30, 35, 43]). The unique aspect of our modeling is testing how the attributes of the feedback content and commenting behavior relate to design iteration.

Our work analyzes Reddit as a platform for design iteration and critique. Given the "community of communities" aspect of Reddit, researchers have studied user behavior on the site, its social interaction mechanisms, and discussions around different topics. For instance, one study found that new users participate in a wide range of sub-Reddits before settling on a few to regularly visit [36]. Gilbert studied how Reddit's voting infrastructure leads to under-provisioning for its most popular content [14], while Kim et al. examined discussions pertaining to the credibility of medical crowdfunding [21]. Our study analyzes Reddit as a resource for designers to receive feedback in the context of iterative design.

Online Sources of Design Feedback

In addition to online communities, researchers have explored mechanisms to help designers gather feedback using social media and paid crowdsourcing platforms [9, 16, 24, 32]. For example, Xu et al. showed how to leverage paid task markets to gather five categories of perceptual feedback for graphic designs [40, 41], while Hui et al. showed how to leverage students' collective social networks to more evenly distribute the volume of feedback received in design courses [19].

The drawback of these methods is that they still require payment or social capital to collect feedback [9, 16, 24, 32], and the cost accumulates when iterating on a project. The advantage of online communities is that they allow designers to connect with feedback providers who are motivated by a common interest in design or the topic of their project. In a comparison of design feedback from online sources, Yen et al. showed that the number of responses received from online communities is similar to that obtained from social media, and that the perceived quality of the feedback is as good as that collected from social media and paid task markets [42].

Our work extends studies of how designers approach online sources for feedback (e.g. [27, 39]) by focusing on the design iterations that prompted the feedback collection. The results of our analysis can illuminate potential improvements not only for online communities, but also for the emerging class of crowd services that generate design feedback [25, 40].

Iteration in Design

Iterative design refers to revising the content of a design in response to external feedback. At each iteration, designers seek feedback to discover gaps in understanding and usability, and to identify potential improvements. Iterations are rapid at first, and slow as the design solidifies [29]. Through this process, the designer moves the design closer to satisfying its goals and gains insight into the design problem and solution approach [6]. Iteration need not imply "incremental" as it can also inspire new design directions through the meta-cognitive process of reflection [33].

Iteration is foundational to design [4], and has been empirically shown to lead to more effective design solutions [11]. While iterative design is widely taught, studied, and evangelized, our research is distinct because it investigates how designers naturally approach iteration in the context of an online design community.

RESEARCH QUESTIONS

Our study was designed to answer the following questions:

RQ1: How many iterations on a design project does a designer typically post to an online community for feedback?

RQ2: When a designer posts a revised design, how deep are the changes, and does the quality of the design improve?

RQ3: What characteristics of the feedback (e.g. valence, category of discourse, or total comments) correlate with the decision to post subsequent design iterations?

RQ4: When in the design process does a designer typically share a design with an online community?

RQ5: What are the perceived strengths and weaknesses of iterating with the feedback received from an online design community (compared to other sources)?

Though not exhaustive, we posed these questions to learn about how designers approach online communities for feedback, to measure potential benefits of online iteration, and gain insight into how online communities could further improve feedback exchange and iterative design practices.

METHOD

A mixed-methods study was conducted to answer our research questions. The first three questions were answered by analyzing a data set collected from an online community that targets novice designers (but open to designers at all skill levels). The community was therefore especially interesting because novices may not be as aware of the need to iterate as more experienced designers. The final two questions were answered by posting two surveys to the community.

Online Community Studied

We collected designs and the associated feedback from Reddit (http://reddit.com). Launched in 2005, Reddit is a publicly accessible platform for discussing items of interest. The site originally targeted news, but has grown to include a variety of topics, including design. Topics are organized into sub-Reddits, and each sub-Reddit lists discussion threads ordered by a combination of popularity and creation time.

We chose Reddit because it has an active, large, and diverse user base engaged in design feedback exchange and, unlike other design communities [27, 39], participation does not require invitations, portfolios, status, or payment. Most designs posted to the sub-Reddits studied are visual designs, including graphic, web, and interaction designs. Examples include personal websites and logos, portfolios, T-shirt designs, business cards (self-employed), and non-commercial apps. From our own inspection, these projects generally arise from designers pursuing their own interests, learning goals, or job responsibilities. From the descriptions in the initial posts, the focus was typically on producing design solutions rather than solely learning about the design process or strategy; e.g., typical project posts include:

> *"Any help is appreciated! Just starting up so we don't have that many products yet. What do you think of the logo? Would it be better bigger and without the palm tree?"*

"Hi guys, here is my draft for a poster advertising a show I'll be playing later this year. I would like the poster to be a combination of professional and trendy, and appeal to a diverse audience."

Although the sub-Reddits we studied were open to designers of all skill levels, their target audience was novice designers. For example, the most active sub-Reddit we studied, /r/design_critiques, states its purpose is to "Help new and amateur designers improve their designs."

On Reddit, a designer initiates discussion around her design by creating a thread in the desired sub-Reddit. The initial post typically contains a title, and description of the design and goals of the project. It may also include links to external images or to a live Web site. Community members can then comment on the design and reply to each other through a discussion interface. Fresh designs typically receive fast attention but fade as the display algorithm places new posts at the top of the thread list, as also observed in [2, 14, 22].

To post a revised design, the designer can create a new thread with a link to the revised design (and the prior thread if desired), edit the original post with a link pointing to the revised design, or post a new comment in the original design's thread with a link to the revised design. The last option is most common, as it is more noticeable than an edit and, unlike a new thread, it preserves the feedback history.

Design + Feedback Data Collection (RQ 1-3)

We developed a script using the Python Reddit API Wrapper (PRAW). The script crawled three popular sub-Reddits for design critique: /r/design_critiques, /r/Logo_Critique, and /r/logodesign. These sub-Reddits were chosen due to their similar purpose for visual design critique, target audiences, and norms. The script collected data for two one-month periods (separated by six months). The script downloaded the 1000 most recent threads in each of these sub-Reddits, including the design images, comments, timestamps, and user ids. This was the maximum data allowed by the API.

For the initial post and any subsequent comments by the designer in the thread, the script parsed the content for Web links. If found, the script downloaded the linked images or, if it pointed to a live Web site, rendered the linked page and captured it. These images were the designs in our data set. It was rare for designers to request feedback without linking to a design image, or to link to content that were not designs.

A challenge was detecting when designers posted revisions of their projects. By observing common practices on the site, we developed three heuristics: 1) the designer who created a thread replied with a comment containing an image link; 2) the designer edited the link in her original post; or 3) the designer created a thread that contained a link to an image and a link to a prior thread created by the same designer. Links to live sites were also challenging because the designer could update the site without editing the link. To detect this case, our script compared the rendered image of the page to the last capture for the link, if it existed. The comparison was performed using a well-known algorithm (MD5 checksum). If different, the image was categorized as a design iteration. Iterations were only detected within sub-Reddits because we observed that iterations were rarely split between them.

The timestamp of a comment was used to associate it with a corresponding design iteration, which was the last design iteration detected prior to that timestamp. We inspected samples of the data to confirm the design iterations and that comments were being associated with the correct iteration.

Based on our observations, if a designer posted more than one iteration, it unfolded within a short window (e.g. a few days). A month of data collection should therefore capture most of the iterations on a project shared to Reddit. However, it misses iterations that only partially overlapped the edges of data collection, as well as any iterations not shared within the community; we revisit the latter point in the Discussion.

RESULTS

Tables 1 and 2 summarize our data set. The data contained a total of 3,730 projects from 2,866 designers, and 29,412 comments on those projects (7,855 comments came from the designers, not including the initial posts). A design received about six comments on average, which is more than other studies of design critique communities have reported [39]. The average number of comments per design iteration was largest for /r/logodesign (μ=9.2, σ=14.9), and least for /r/design_critiques (μ=3.9, σ=3.5), with /r/Logo_Critique in-between (μ=4.7, σ=3.7). The complete set of comments received by a design were, on average, received within 24 hours of the initial post. The summary data shows that the designer and community often engage in back-and-forth discussion, reminiscent of face-to-face critique [31].

Iteration Analysis (RQ1)

Table 1 shows the distribution of how many projects share different numbers of design iterations for feedback. For instance, the No Iteration column shows the number of projects for which the designer posted only a single design for feedback and did not return, the 2 Iterations column reports the number of projects for which the initial design and one revision were posted, and so on.

We ran a script to count the total number of projects in each group to determine how often designers iterate. Despite the widely-evangelized benefits of iteration [5, 11, 12, 29, 41], of the 3730 projects analyzed, only about 1 in 5 (20.6%) posted more than one iteration, and only about 1 in 23 (4.3%) of the

Sub-reddit	Projects	No it.	2 it.	3 it.	4 it.	5+ it.
/r/design_critiques	1485	1238	196	42	6	3
/r/logodesign	1173	893	226	36	11	7
/r/Logo_Critique	1072	832	186	36	13	5
Total	3730	2963	608	114	30	15

Table 1: The number of projects collected for each sub-Reddit in our data set. The subsequent columns show the number of iterations shared for each. As shown in the No Iteration (it.) column, only one design was posted for 79% of the projects.

Sub-reddit	Total Comments	By the designer	By the members	Avg. (sd) per project
/r/design_critiques	8502	2769	5733	3.9 (3.5)
/r/logodesign	13787	2987	10800	9.2 (14.1)
/r/Logo_Critique	7123	2099	5024	4.7 (3.7)
Total	29412	7855	21557	5.9 (7.1)

Table 2: The total number of comments collected from the sub-Reddits, by the designers and community members. Despite high variance, nearly all designs received feedback.

projects received three or more iterations; these rates were similar across all three individual sub-Reddits.

We also analyzed how designers approached iteration based on the three heuristics identified in the Method section. We found that designers performed 863 (~85%) iterations by replying to their original threads, 139 (~14%) by editing their original threads, and only 15 (~1%) by creating an entirely new thread for their revised designs.

Some possible explanations for the observed rate of iteration are that the designers who approach this community for feedback are unaware of the benefits of iteration, that they are approaching it too late in their design process, that the platform does not encourage iteration, or that the content of the design feedback received may not prompt iteration. Our later analysis will examine which, if any, characteristics of the feedback correlate with posting two or more iterations. We also return to this issue in the Discussion.

Perceived Quality and Iteration (RQ2)

To determine if designs improved when iterating based on community feedback, we separated the projects with only one iteration from those with two or more iterations. We then randomly sampled 300 of the projects with two or more iterations, and filtered out the ones lacking either a description of the designer's goals or community feedback, leaving 102 designs. We felt this data set was sufficient to produce representative results. For each project, we selected a design image from the initial shared design and the final shared revision. If a designer posted multiple images for the first design or final iteration (a rare occurrence), we selected the one that we felt best represented the designs at that stage.

For each design, we recruited participants to judge the quality of the designs relative to the designer's stated goals. The judging consisted of three categories of rating tasks:

- Rate how well a single design satisfied the designer's goals on a 7-point scale (1=does not satisfy, 7=satisfies the goals). The goals were extracted from the designers' original post and displayed at the top of the task screen. The design image was shown below. The initial design and final iteration were rated as separate tasks.
- Rate the degree of difference between the two design images on a 7-point scale (1=the same, 7=completely different) and list the key differences between them (see Figure 2). The designs were shown side-by-side on a single task screen, with the placement randomized.
- Select which of the two design iterations better satisfied the designer's goals. The two design images were placed side-by-side, with random placement. The goals were shown at the top of the task screen with the images below.

We piloted and revised the task screens to give simple, clear instructions to maximize response quality. We recruited participants from Mechanical Turk. Three participants were recruited per instance of the first task category, and five were recruited per instance of the other two categories. The task configurations limited recruitment to the U.S. to reduce language barriers, and required 95% prior approval ratings to recruit workers with a history of quality work. Participants were remunerated \$0.60 per task for the first category and \$0.10 per task for the other two categories. We also recruited an independent rater to perform the AB-comparison task using an interface similar to that used on Mechanical Turk. The rater had several years of professional employment and education in industrial design, and ostensibly had much more design experience than the Turk participants.

From the results of the first task, we used the mean of the ratings for each design to indicate its perceived quality.

Figure 2: Examples of the first and final iterations for two projects with slight (left column) and significant (right column) perceived revision between the iterations.

Surprisingly, the means were the same for both the initial design (u=4.773, σ=0.863) and the final iteration (u=4.775, σ=0.981). A paired samples t-test confirmed that there was no difference between the two.

From the second task, the mean difference for the pairs of designs was (u=3.96, σ=1.62). A Kruskal-Wallis test showed no correlation between the degree of change between iterations and the change in perceived quality. Combined with the prior result, this analysis shows that designers were making revisions, yet the perceived quality did not improve.

For the third (AB comparison) task, we tallied the number of times each iteration was selected as better satisfying the designers' stated goals. The votes were nearly equally split between the initial designs (n=247) and final iterations (n=263). A chi square test confirmed there was no preference between the iterations ($\chi^2(1)=0.50$, $p=0.479$). The lack of increase in perceived quality between the initial design and final iteration might be due to the quality of the feedback being insufficient to make substantial improvements, or to the designers' inability to interpret and apply the feedback.

We analyzed the ratings from the independent rater for our AB task, and found that the final iteration (n=68) was selected over twice as often as the initial iteration (n=30), with 4 selected as being the same ($\chi^2(1)=14.74$, $p<0.001$). The fact that the independent rater detected a difference but the Turk participants did not might be due to the need for expertise to discriminate differences in quality [34].

As an additional check to ensure that the ratings from the MTurk participants were reliable, we eliminated responses from raters who spent fewer than 25 seconds (< 25% of the average time) on the tasks. Analysis of the ratings from the remaining raters also failed to detect statistical differences.

Predictors of Iteration (RQ3)

We examined how the number and length of responses, idea units, valence, and content categories of the feedback correlated with the decision to iterate on the design. From our original data set, we randomly sampled 100 projects containing only one iteration and 100 projects containing two or more iterations, filtering out all projects that did not have comments (excluding comments from the project creators themselves). This left 86 projects with only one iteration and 97 projects with two or more iterations for analysis. We had a single coder partition each comment from the projects into individual idea units. An "idea unit" is defined as a coherent unit of thought consisting of a phrase, sentence, or group of sentences. Given the scale of the data set, we divided the idea units (n=2,416) among a team of four coders (including a member of the research team). All coders had experience with design critique and similar labeling tasks.

We had our coders categorize the valence of each idea unit. Valences were either "positive" (positive comments encouraging or praising the design or designer), "critical" (destructive criticism towards the design or designer), "neutral" (comments that were neither positive nor critical, including most constructive criticism), or "indeterminate."

Category	Description	Example Idea Unit	No it.	2+ its.
Brainstorming	Feedback asking (often rhetorical) questions or making statements about imagined possibilities for the design.	Would you consider the neck of it a bit — even if it'd be inaccurate — to make it take up a bit less space?	5.3%	4.1%
Comparison	Feedback contrasting the design or design process with something else as comparison.	The second one is a little too internet-explorer reminiscent for me	2.8%	4.5%
Direct recommend.	Feedback giving specific advice about a particular aspect of a design as a direct recommendation.	I would go all the way back to square 1 and work with letterforms.	25.7%	21.7%
Free association	Feedback that makes reactive, associative statements about the design as free association.	I also like the fact that it looks like a lightbulb, as that is a pretty universal symbol of "eureka!"	3.2%	4.5%
Identity-invoking	Feedback pushing designers to consider themselves within the larger context of the design profession.	So, yes, it does show that you're a beginner. That just means you have room to improve!	1.8%	2.5%
Interpretation	Feedback where someone reacts to what they saw and tries to make sense of the concept or product.	The first thing I see at a glance is mountains. Lots of mountains. Could be ski shop.	7.1%	6.5%
Investigation	Feedback that requests information (typically by questioning) about the design or the design process as investigation.	Have you researched other ramen restaurants logos?	4.8%	7.5%
Judgment	Feedback that is evaluative in tone and which often includes some form of interpretation while also conveying an assessment of the design.	The lines are very thin as well, but that is irrelevant as the design is just not good. Thickening the lines will not help.	40.4%	34.4%
Process-oriented	Feedback providing designers with insight or observations about the process that they might have used or could use to create the design.	Since it's a restaurant i would strongly consider how the logo would look as a sign and how it will work with the interior/mood.	2.4%	7.2%
Support	Feedback expressing the provider's support for the design creator.	Good luck either way!	3.2%	2.7%

Table 3: The taxonomy of critique discourse used to categorize the idea units. The two rightmost columns show the relative proportion of instances of each category for projects with only a single design (No it.) and those with two or more iterations. Columns do not sum to 100% because idea units that did not fit into any of the above categories were omitted.

Coders also categorized each idea unit according to an established taxonomy of critique discourse [7]. Categories included *judgment, direct recommendation, brainstorming, process-oriented, identity-invoking, free-association, comparison, interpretation*, and *investigation*. We also added the category *support* for idea units praising or encouraging the creator's ongoing effort (see Table 3).

To test inter-rater reliability, a member of the research team labeled the valence and category of discourse of 100 idea units randomly sampled from each of the other three coders (300 total). There was a raw 77% agreement for the category of discourse (Cohen's Kappa = 0.71) and 78% agreement for the valence (Cohen's Kappa = 0.68), which are considered satisfactory for moving forward with analyzing the results [23, 37]. The categorized idea units were aggregated by project and iteration. We then counted the number of idea units falling under each category of discourse and valence, the total number of comments, the total number of idea units, and the total word count for each project revision. We used this data set for the regression models described below.

To avoid overfitting our data, we used three separate logistic regression models. In our first model, we used the idea unit content categories as the predictor variables, and iteration as the response variable. The model identified three categories as being predictors of iteration: *process-oriented* (coef.=0.750, $p<0.001$), *comparison* (coef.=0.279, $p=0.124$), and *investigation* (coef.=0.204, $p=0.167$). Using chi-squared tests to compare the distribution of content categories among idea units for design projects with a single iteration to those with multiple iterations, we found similar results: projects with multiple iterations had a higher proportion of *process-oriented* ($\chi^2(1)=25.97$, $p<0.001$), *investigation* ($\chi^2(1)=6.66$, $p=0.010$), and *comparison* ($\chi^2(1)=3.93$, $p=0.048$) idea units. Conversely, projects with only one iteration had a higher proportion of both *judgment* ($\chi^2(1)=8.85$, $p=0.003$) and *direct recommendation* ($\chi^2(1)=4.82$, $p=0.029$) idea units. We did not find any significant difference in the proportion of *free association, interpretation, brainstorming, identity-invoking*, or *support* between the two groups.

Prior work found that designers with more expertise typically write more thought-provoking feedback (e.g., brainstorming and process-oriented) [7]. The higher amount of thought-provoking feedback on projects with multiple iterations might then indicate that those projects were receiving more attention from providers with more design expertise.

In our second model, we used valence as the predictor variable, and iteration as the response variable. The model identified both neutral (coef.=0.05, $p=0.108$) and critical (coef.=0.09, $p=0.148$) idea units as predictors of iteration, but not positive idea units. Chi-squared tests revealed similar results: overall, projects with multiple iterations had a significantly lower proportion of positive idea units than designs with only one iteration (19.3% vs. 24.9%; $\chi^2(1)=10.77$; $p=0.001$). Critical feedback reveals problems with the design and may prompt designers to iterate, whereas positive feedback may signal that the project is near completion and that further feedback is not necessary.

In our third model, we used the number of idea units, number of comments, and total word count per project as the predictor variables, and iteration as the response variable. The model identified word count as a predictor of iteration (coef.<0.01, $p=0.002$). We applied a similar model on the entire corpus of design projects, filtered to only first iterations with at least one comment (n=3,406); the analysis revealed that the number of comments was predictive of iteration (coef.=0.01, $p=0.027$). One interpretation of these two analyses is that more comments and longer comments give designers more feedback to work with, exposes more potential improvements that can be made, and demonstrates a higher level of interest in and engagement with the work.

To determine if designers' engagement with the feedback providers affected iteration, we reran our models with designer engagement as a covariate. The ratio of the designer's comments to the total comments on a thread was calculated as a proxy for engagement. Since designers typically reply to their own threads to represent iterations (see Iteration Analysis), not all designer comments were community engagement; consequently, this proxy measure is an upper bound for engagement. The models revealed that a higher ratio of designer comments to total comments was predictive of iteration (coef=5.29, $p<0.001$ for the model related to category of discourse; coef=5.34, $p<0.001$ for that of valence; coef=4.61, $p<0.001$ for that of feedback quantity); the pattern of the results of the models were otherwise the same. This result suggests that increased engagement with feedback providers may also spur iteration.

Across all project iterations (n=4,217), we compared the number of comments received on the first and subsequent iterations. An ANOVA showed that initial iterations received more comments ($\mu=5.39$, $\sigma=8.65$) than subsequent iterations ($\mu=3.94$, $\sigma=4.22$; $F(1)=21.72$, $p<0.001$). The fewer comments on subsequent iterations might be attributed to users being unaware the project has been updated (e.g., the site does not allow users to subscribe to posts). Another possibility is that community members may be choosing to direct their attention to other projects [28]. This re-affirms prior work showing that implementation choices, even subtle ones, can have a large influence on the distribution of feedback generated in an online community [39].

Perceptions of iterating online (RQ4, RQ5)

To complement our analysis of the forum data, we conducted two surveys. The first was open-ended, and asked designers about their motivations for and experiences with using Reddit for design feedback. It was posted to /r/design. The second was structured, and asked the designers about their iterative process. It was posted to /r/design_critiques and /r/logodesign, and was distributed to design-oriented mailing lists. We split the questions between two surveys to reduce the time required to complete each one, and used the responses from the first survey to help formulate the

Question	Mean (SD)
Q1. In total, how many design iterations did you create for the project?	5.6 (3.8)
Q2. In total, how many design iterations for the project did you post to Reddit for feedback?	1.6 (.90)
Q3. At which stage in your process did you post the design to Reddit (beginning, between beginning and midpoint, midpoint, between midpoint and end, near the end).	(see text)
Q4. How important was it for you to create multiple iterations for the project? (1=not important, 7=very).	6.0 (1.2)
Q5. How important was it to post multiple iterations to Reddit for feedback? (1=not important, 7=very).	4.0 (1.8)
Q6. How would rate the depth of changes made to your design based on the feedback received from Reddit (1=minimal, 7=significant)	3.8 (1.8)
Q7. How would you rate the quality of the feedback received from Reddit (1=low, 7=high)	5.0 (1.6)
Q8. How well does Reddit support your iterative design process (1=not at all, 7=very well).	5.0 (1.4)

Table 4: The questions asked on the structured survey and the mean (SD) of the responses.

structured questions in the second survey. Both surveys required that a participant be at least 18 years of age and had posted a design for feedback to Reddit in the last six months. The surveys asked designers to describe a recent project posted to Reddit for feedback and to self-report their design expertise and demographics. We gave $20 for participation.

In total, we received 38 responses to the surveys. There were 17 responses (four female, ages 18-45) for the open-ended survey and 21 responses (four female, ages 18-32) for the structured survey. For the structured survey, two responses (of 23, leaving 21) were eliminated due to not satisfying the survey criteria. There was no overlap in the participants. The majority of design projects posted by respondents of both surveys were logos and web site designs; other projects included illustrations, portfolios, T-shirt designs, and flyers. The average self-rated expertise for the open-ended survey was (μ=3.3, SD=0.89 on a 5-point scale), and the average for the structured survey was (μ=4.0, SD=1.4 on a 7-point scale). We first report the data from the structured survey, and then draw from the open-ended survey responses to help explain the results from the structured survey and the prior analyses.

Structured Survey (n=21)

Table 4 summarizes the forced-choice questions and results from the structured survey. We note two interesting patterns in the data. First, the average reported number of iterations for a project (including those not posted to Reddit) was about six (Q1; μ=5.8). However, the number of iterations posted to Reddit was less (Q2; μ=1.6). For Q3, fourteen respondents reported that they posted their designs to Reddit near the end of their process and three reported they did so between the middle and the end. Two respondents reported sharing their designs at the beginning of the process, two at the midpoint, and one in-between. In sum, these results show that a large majority of the respondents posted one or two iterations to Reddit for feedback, typically near the end of their process.

Second, the respondents reported that iteration is important for their project (Q4; μ=6.0), it is somewhat important to post iterations for feedback (Q5; μ=4.0), the feedback received was reasonably good (Q7; μ=5.0), and that Reddit is supportive of their process (Q8; μ=5.0). Yet, consistent with the forum analysis, the respondents reported seldom posting more than two iterations to Reddit for feedback.

Open-ended Survey (n=17)

The open-ended survey asked respondents to describe their motivations for posting designs to Reddit for feedback, to identify other sites they considered posting their work and why they did or did not do so, to explain how the feedback they received helped (or failed to help) improve their work, and to explain why they would or would not use Reddit again as a source of feedback. We will use the notation Rn when referring to respondent n throughout this section.

When asked about their motivations for posting their designs to Reddit for critique, there were three common responses (n=5 each). The first common response was that the potential of reaching a large audience was appealing:

"*...getting comments from people on Reddit offer a wider range compared to my usual methods of asking friends and family what they think.*" [R1]

The second common response was that the site's diverse user base brought fresh perspectives:

"*...Reddit is a collective of individuals with varied taste and experiences of the real world, where the majority are not teachers. A teacher will critique on a different agenda, and a Redditor will critique on a personal bias, full disclosure, criteria. It's more raw to get people outside your bubble, outside your country even, for design critique.*" [R11]

The third common response was that the overall quality of the critique they received was high:

"*Reddit is my go-to source for critique, advice, and general online discussion.*" [R13]

When asked about other places they considered posting their designs, the respondents reported many different venues, but most stated that these venues were unsatisfactory for getting feedback. The most common was Facebook (n=5), followed by Behance, DeviantArt, and Dribbble (n=2 each); four respondents stated that they never considered posting their work to any other site. The respondents' reasons for ultimately not using these other sites were similarly diverse, and included the lack of a forum structure [R2,R5], lack of verbal critique [R3], lack of real world perspectives [R4], lack of anonymity [R11], and excessively harsh [R12] or impersonal [R7] critiques. This decision rationale indicates that Reddit has many unique qualities that make it attractive relative to social media and socially-oriented design communities as a platform for collecting design feedback.

When questioned about how the feedback helped them improve their designs, responses were more similar: nearly half of the respondents stated that users generally provided good critiques about the flaws of their designs (n=8), and over half stated that they provided good suggestions (n=9):

"*Commenters pointed out a slight difference in sharpness/blurriness between the images and also suggested a tweak to the hue/saturation of one of the elements. Both are very slight, subtle tweaks but have a big impact on the end result.*" [R15]

Not all respondents had good experiences, however. One respondent stated that Reddit was of little help [R12], and two stated that it was of no help at all [R1,R6]:

"*I would either just have passive aggressive down votes or someone being very snarky with my work; not too many constructive things.*" [R1]

When asked about why they would or would not use Reddit for receiving design critique in the future, respondents were divided. Those stating they would consider posting there again in the future cited the fresh perspectives of the users (n=7), the large user-base (n=3), the high quality critique (n=3), and the expertise of the users (n=2). Conversely, commonly cited reasons for not returning for feedback in the future included the low quality of the critique (n=3) and the lack of expertise among the users (n=3). One respondent stated outright that getting feedback was very "hit or miss":

"*They're fairly good at feedback for the most part. Although it's a hit or miss if you get 2 comments or you get 100. It depends on timing or likability or willingness of the other party.*" [R11]

In sum, respondents found Reddit feedback mostly helpful for uncovering problems and getting suggestions for improvement, and felt that Reddit accommodates their iterative process more than other sites.

DISCUSSION

The goal of our study was to learn how designers naturally approach design iteration and feedback collection in online communities. Our quantitative results show that online design communities such as Reddit have immense potential for design critique: on average, designs receive about six comments, all within 24 hours, with each comment averaging 25 words and typically exceeding superficial statements such as "good job". The values of these attributes exceed those reported in other studies of online communities [39], and other artifact-based discussion sites [38].

According to our survey respondents, the primary draw of using Reddit for design critique is the ability to reach a large and diverse audience who can offer fresh, authentic perspectives. The site's users are ostensibly motivated by enjoyment of design or interest in a project, requiring neither social capital or compensation to provide feedback. Along with a low barrier to entry (e.g., invitations are not required), these factors make Reddit attractive for designers to post their projects. The majority of respondents to the surveys also indicated they were satisfied with the feedback received.

Our analysis showed that designers who posted revisions of their work received more process-oriented, comparison, and investigation categories of feedback. These types of feedback are typically more open-ended, questioning, and thought-provoking (e.g., "Perhaps you could try a couple different locations for the diamond"). This type of content may create more uncertainty about the design's quality, thereby prompting recognition that further revision and feedback is needed. By contrast, designers who did not share multiple revisions received more recommendations for improvement and assessments of quality (judgments in the taxonomy). These categories may serve to validate the design (e.g. "Looks good") or identify specific suggestions that can be directly accepted or rejected. Additionally, concrete feedback is characteristic of designers with less experience [7], potentially signifying that feedback from less experienced designers does not promote iteration. In either case, designers receiving this type of feedback may not see a compelling reason to share or even produce a revised design.

One way to solicit a desired balance of feedback categories is to allow designers to choose from defined rubrics that would scaffold the feedback generation process. Prior work has shown, for example, that rubrics can enable non-experts to give feedback comparable in depth and quality to that of expert designers [43]. A designer could indicate her desire to iterate when posting a project, and the platform could generate rubrics that include prompts for the categories of feedback that relate to iteration. The interface for entering the feedback could also be accompanied by expert examples (e.g. see [8]) or in-situ guidelines that would help community members craft the feedback that is most useful for iteration. Configurable rubrics could also enable a designer to direct providers' attention to where feedback is most needed.

We found that more responses, longer responses, and a lower proportion of positively-worded feedback correlate with iteration. Our results also showed that designer engagement with the feedback providers also correlates with iteration. More content, especially if distributed as previously described, and lower proportions of positive tone may also contribute to increased uncertainty about a design and prompt iteration. Additional responses could also signal community interest in the work, an implicit form of feedback that may also facilitate iteration.

Prior work has studied the attributes of design feedback received online that correlate with perceived quality [43]. The authors found that longer feedback, feedback with strong positive or negative tone, feedback with high language specificity, and feedback that asks questions or makes suggestions correlate with higher perceived quality. Our results showed that several of these variables – including feedback length, more critical tone, and thought-provoking statements – also correlate with iteration. It is therefore possible that perceived quality might be serving as a latent variable between the observed variables and iteration.

Our results showed that only a single design was posted for 79% of the projects in the forum data set; with two or more iterations being shared for 21% of the projects. These results were supported by the structured survey where a majority of the respondents reported posting only one design. The survey results indicated that designers are aware of the need to iterate and suggest that the observed rate of iteration is due in part to designers posting their designs near the end of their process, thus leaving insufficient time or desire to further iterate. This finding points to the need for more research to understand how to encourage designers to share their work earlier and more often. This is a potential issue not only for online design communities, but also for the crowd-based platforms that generate design feedback (e.g. [24, 26, 40]).

The system implementation of the community studied did not directly support iteration. Consequently, designers have had to learn to re-appropriate the site's mechanisms to represent iteration. For instance, a large majority (85%) of designers who iterated replied to their original thread with a comment linking to their revised design. The benefit is that this approach maintains a feedback history to contextualize subsequent discussion. However, the site's presentation algorithm does not prioritize threads based on comment activity, even if performed by the original poster. Revised designs therefore receive less attention than the initial project post. This outcome is consistent with the platform's mission to promote discussion around fresh content rather than prolonged discussions around older content. A compromise could be for the site's presentation algorithm to consider an iteration (e.g. signaled by the designer replying to their original post) as fresh content. It could also allow users to sort threads by the activity of the original poster.

The karma feature in the community may also have affected our results. Project posts that receive more upvotes gain more visibility on the landing page. This allows the project to attract more feedback, which facilitates iteration. However, in our data set, we found only a very weak correlation between upvotes and the number of iterations posted (r=0.08). Despite the lack of correlation, it is still possible some designers posted their work with the main objective of receiving upvotes and public exposure rather than critique.

For the projects that did iterate, it was surprising that the Turk participants did not perceive differences in quality between the initial designs and final iterations, despite the perception of moderate revisions. In contrast, the rater with design experience *did* detect differences in quality. We do not believe these outcomes are necessarily incongruent. The improvement in design quality may have been subtle and required more expertise to differentiate. This pattern of results should serve as a reminder of the need to include evaluations from those with domain expertise in future studies that collect subjective ratings of design quality.

LIMITATIONS AND FUTURE WORK

The data was extracted from a single platform in two month-long windows of time. The community studied (Reddit) was chosen primarily because of its active community and the ability to access the data through an API. Future work is needed to generalize the findings to how designers iterate over longer periods of time and in other online communities. Because the community studied does not explicitly make available a history of edits to the posts or comments, it is likely the heuristics used on our data set missed some iterations and identified some posts as iterations that were not. Given the size of the data set, we believe these points to be inconsequential to the findings of the work. Finally, we were unable to measure and include the expertise of the designers in our quantitative analysis; further research is needed to tease apart differences in iterative behavior between novice and expert designers in online communities.

We see three additional directions for future work. First, our results showed that even though designers could revise their work using the feedback from Reddit, the changes did not produce detectable improvements in the eyes of non-experts. Future work could compare how designers motivated by their own goals would revise their work in response to expert feedback. A second direction would be to modify an online community to test the findings of this work. For example, one could incorporate rubrics or guidelines that promote the type of feedback that we found prompts iteration. Designers could also be allowed to organize iterations around their projects and showcase their process, rather than only individual designs. Last, future work could explore platform designs that address some of the psychological factors such as evaluation apprehension that may be deterring designers from sharing earlier versions of their work online.

CONCLUSION

Despite many successes in helping designers share final solutions and receive quick feedback on in-progress work, there has been less attention paid to helping designers approach and represent design iteration online.

The contributions of this work were the results and lessons of how designers approach iteration in a large online design community. We found that designers exhibited a low rate of iteration on their work, and that this was due to sharing their work near the end of their design process. When designers did post two or more iterations for feedback, they had to re-appropriate the site's mechanisms to represent the iterations. We also discovered that both the quantity and content of the feedback received were correlated with whether designers posted subsequent revisions to their in-progress work. These findings can be practically applied to promote iterative design practice in online communities and related crowd feedback services. System designers can also leverage our findings to motivate the implementation of interaction mechanisms that directly support design iteration. We hope our contributions will enable online communities to better serve people at all skill levels in their creative projects.

ACKNOWLEDGMENTS

This work was supported in part by the National Science Foundation awards CMMI 14-62693 and IIS 15-30818.

REFERENCES

1. Arguello, J., Butler, B.S., Joyce, E., Kraut, R., Ling, K.S., Rosé, C., and Wang, X. Talk to me: foundations for successful individual-group interactions in online communities *Proceedings of the SIGCHI Conference on Human Factors in Computing Systems*, ACM, Montréal, Québec, Canada, 2006, 959-968. http://dx.doi.org/10.1145/1124772.1124916
2. Bailey, B.P. and Horvitz, E. What's your idea?: a case study of a grassroots innovation pipeline within a large software company *Proceedings of the SIGCHI Conference on Human Factors in Computing Systems*, ACM, Atlanta, Georgia, USA, 2010, 2065-2074. http://dx.doi.org/10.1145/1753326.1753641
3. Burke, M., Marlow, C. and Lento, T. Feed me: motivating newcomer contribution in social network sites *Proceedings of the SIGCHI Conference on Human Factors in Computing Systems*, ACM, Boston, MA, USA, 2009, 945-954. http://dx.doi.org/10.1145/1518701.1518847
4. Buxton, B. *Sketching User Experiences: Getting the Design Right and the Right Design*. Morgan Kaufmann Publishers Inc., 2007. http://dx.doi.org/10.1145/2632434.2632461
5. Chan, J., Dow, S.P. and Schunn, C.D. Do the best design ideas (really) come from conceptually distant sources of inspiration? *Design Studies*, *36*. 31-58. http://dx.doi.org/10.1016/j.destud.2014.08.001
6. Cross, N. Creative cognition in design: processes of exceptional designers *Proceedings of the 4th Conference on Creativity & Cognition*, ACM, Loughborough, UK, 2002, 14-19. http://dx.doi.org/10.1145/581710.581714
7. Dannels, D.P. and Martin, K.N. Critiquing Critiques: A Genre Analysis of Feedback Across Novice to Expert Design Studios. *Journal of Business and Technical Communication*, *22* (2). 135-159. http://dx.doi.org/10.1177/1050651907311923
8. Doroudi, S., Kamar, E., Brunskill, E. and Horvitz, E. Toward a Learning Science for Complex Crowdsourcing Tasks *Proceedings of the 2016 CHI Conference on Human Factors in Computing Systems*, ACM, Santa Clara, California, USA, 2016, 2623-2634. http://dx.doi.org/10.1145/2858036.2858268
9. Dow, S., Gerber, E. and Wong, A. A pilot study of using crowds in the classroom *Proceedings of the SIGCHI Conference on Human Factors in Computing Systems*, ACM, Paris, France, 2013, 227-236. http://dx.doi.org/10.1145/2470654.2470686
10. Dow, S.P., Glassco, A., Kass, J., Schwarz, M. and Klemmer, S.R. The effect of parallel prototyping on design performance, learning, and self-efficacy, 2009
11. Dow, S.P., Heddleston, K. and Klemmer, S.R. The efficacy of prototyping under time constraints *Proceedings of the Seventh ACM Conference on Creativity and Cognition*, ACM, Berkeley, California, USA, 2009, 165-174. http://dx.doi.org/10.1145/1640233.1640260
12. Elkins, J. *Art Critiques: A Guide*. New Academia Publishing, LLC, 2012
13. Gerber, E. and Carroll, M. The psychological experience of prototyping. *Design studies*, *33* (1). 64-84
14. Gilbert, E. Widespread underprovision on Reddit *Proceedings of the 2013 Conference on Computer Supported Cooperative Work*, ACM, San Antonio, Texas, USA, 2013, 803-808. http://dx.doi.org/10.1145/2441776.2441866
15. Gilbert, E. and Karahalios, K. Understanding deja reviewers *Proceedings of the 2010 ACM Conference on Computer Supported Cooperative Work*, ACM, Savannah, Georgia, USA, 2010, 225-228. http://dx.doi.org/10.1145/1718918.1718961
16. Greenberg, M.D., Easterday, M.W. and Gerber, E.M. Critiki: A Scaffolded Approach to Gathering Design Feedback from Paid Crowdworkers *Proceedings of the 2015 ACM SIGCHI Conference on Creativity and Cognition*, ACM, Glasgow, United Kingdom, 2015, 235-244. http://dx.doi.org/10.1145/2757226.2757249
17. Harper, F.M., Moy, D. and Konstan, J.A. Facts or friends?: distinguishing informational and conversational questions in social Q&A sites *Proceedings of the SIGCHI Conference on Human Factors in Computing Systems*, ACM, Boston, MA, USA, 2009, 759-768. http://dx.doi.org/10.1145/1518701.1518819
18. Harper, F.M., Raban, D., Rafaeli, S. and Konstan, J.A. Predictors of answer quality in online Q&A sites *Proceedings of the SIGCHI Conference on Human Factors in Computing Systems*, ACM, Florence, Italy, 2008, 865-874. http://dx.doi.org/10.1145/1357054.1357191
19. Hui, J., Glenn, A., Jue, R., Gerber, E. and Dow, S., Using Anonymity and Communal Efforts to Improve Quality of Crowdsourced Feedback. in *Third AAAI Conference on Human Computation and Crowdsourcing*, (2015)
20. Hui, J.S., Gerber, E.M. and Dow, S.P., Crowd-based design activities: helping students connect with users online. in *Proceedings of the 2014 Conference on Designing interactive systems*, (2014), ACM, 875-884. http://dx.doi.org/10.1145/2598510.2598538
21. Kim, J.G., Kong, H.K., Karahalios, K., Fu, W.-T. and Hong, H. The Power of Collective Endorsements: Credibility Factors in Medical Crowdfunding

Campaigns *Proceedings of the 2016 CHI Conference on Human Factors in Computing Systems*, ACM, Santa Clara, California, USA, 2016, 4538-4549. http://dx.doi.org/10.1145/2858036.2858289

22. Lampe, C. and Resnick, P. Slash(dot) and burn: distributed moderation in a large online conversation space *Proceedings of the SIGCHI Conference on Human Factors in Computing Systems*, ACM, Vienna, Austria, 2004, 543-550. http://dx.doi.org/10.1145/985692.985761
23. Landis, J.R. and Koch, G.G. The measurement of observer agreement for categorical data. *Biometrics*. 159-174. http://dx.doi.org/10.2307/2529310
24. Luther, K., Caine, K., Ziegler, K. and Bruckman, A. Why it works (when it works): success factors in online creative collaboration *Proceedings of the 16th ACM International Conference on Supporting Group Work*, ACM, Sanibel Island, Florida, USA, 2010, 1-10. http://dx.doi.org/10.1145/1880071.1880073
25. Luther, K., Tolentino, J.-L., Wu, W., Pavel, A., Bailey, B.P., Agrawala, M., Hartmann, B. and Dow, S.P. Structuring, Aggregating, and Evaluating Crowdsourced Design Critique *Proceedings of the 17th ACM Conference on Computer Supported Cooperative Work & Social Computing*, ACM, Vancouver, BC, Canada, 2015, 473-485. http://dx.doi.org/10.1145/2675133.2675283
26. Mamykina, L., Manoim, B., Mittal, M., Hripcsak, G. and Hartmann, B. Design lessons from the fastest Q&A site in the west *Proceedings of the SIGCHI Conference on Human Factors in Computing Systems*, ACM, Vancouver, BC, Canada, 2011, 2857-2866. http://dx.doi.org/10.1145/1978942.1979366
27. Marlow, J. and Dabbish, L. From rookie to all-star: professional development in a graphic design social networking site *Proceedings of the 17th ACM Conference on Computer Supported Cooperative Work & Social Computing*, ACM, Baltimore, Maryland, USA, 2014, 922-933. http://dx.doi.org/10.1145/2531602.2531651
28. McInnis, B.J., Murnane, E.L., Epstein, D., Cosley, D. and Leshed, G. One and Done: Factors affecting one-time contributors to ad-hoc online communities *Proceedings of the 19th ACM Conference on Computer-Supported Cooperative Work & Social Computing*, ACM, San Francisco, California, USA, 2016, 609-623. http://dx.doi.org/10.1145/2818048.2820075
29. Nielsen, J. Iterative User-Interface Design. *Computer*, *26* (11). 32-41. http://dx.doi.org/10.1109/2.241424
30. Otterbacher, J. 'Helpfulness' in online communities: a measure of message quality *Proceedings of the SIGCHI Conference on Human Factors in Computing Systems*, ACM, Boston, MA, USA, 2009, 955-964. http://dx.doi.org/10.1145/1518701.1518848
31. Reimer, Y.J. and Douglas, S.A. Teaching HCI Design With the Studio Approach. *Computer Science Education*, *13* (3). 191-205. http://dx.doi.org/10.1076/csed.13.3.191.14945
32. Rzeszotarski, J.M. and Morris, M.R. Estimating the social costs of friendsourcing *Proceedings of the SIGCHI Conference on Human Factors in Computing Systems*, ACM, Toronto, Ontario, Canada, 2014, 2735-2744. http://dx.doi.org/10.1145/2556288.2557181
33. Schon, D.A. Designing as reflective conversation with the materials of a design situation. *Research in Engineering Design*, *3* (3). 131-147. http://dx.doi.org/10.1007/bf01580516
34. Shanteau, J., Weiss, D.J., Thomas, R.P. and Pounds, J.C. Performance-based assessment of expertise: How to decide if someone is an expert or not. *European Journal of Operational Research*, *136* (2). 253-263. http://dx.doi.org/10.1017/CBO9780511609978.021
35. Sylvan, E. Predicting influence in an online community of creators *Proceedings of the SIGCHI Conference on Human Factors in Computing Systems*, ACM, Atlanta, Georgia, USA, 2010, 1913-1916. http://dx.doi.org/10.1145/1753326.1753614
36. Tan, C. and Lee, L. All Who Wander: On the Prevalence and Characteristics of Multi-community Engagement *Proceedings of the 24th International Conference on World Wide Web*, ACM, Florence, Italy, 2015, 1056-1066. http://dx.doi.org/10.1145/2736277.2741661
37. Viera, A.J. and Garrett, J.M. Understanding interobserver agreement: the kappa statistic. *Fam Med*, *37* (5). 360-363
38. Willett, W., Heer, J., Hellerstein, J. and Agrawala, M. CommentSpace: structured support for collaborative visual analysis *Proceedings of the SIGCHI Conference on Human Factors in Computing Systems*, ACM, Vancouver, BC, Canada, 2011, 3131-3140. http://dx.doi.org/10.1145/1978942.1979407
39. Xu, A. and Bailey, B. What do you think?: a case study of benefit, expectation, and interaction in a large online critique community *Proceedings of the ACM 2012 Conference on Computer Supported Cooperative Work*, ACM, Seattle, Washington, USA, 2012, 295-304. http://dx.doi.org/10.1145/2145204.2145252
40. Xu, A., Huang, S.-W. and Bailey, B. Voyant: generating structured feedback on visual designs using a crowd of non-experts *Proceedings of the 17th ACM Conference on Computer Supported Cooperative Work & Social Computing*, ACM, Baltimore, Maryland,

USA, 2014, 1433-1444.
http://dx.doi.org/10.1145/2531602.2531604

41. Xu, A., Rao, H., Dow, S.P. and Bailey, B.P. A Classroom Study of Using Crowd Feedback in the Iterative Design Process *Proceedings of the 18th ACM Conference on Computer Supported Cooperative Work & Social Computing*, ACM, Vancouver, BC, Canada, 2015, 1637-1648.
http://dx.doi.org/10.1145/2675133.2675140

42. Yen, Y.-C., Dow, S.P., Gerber, E. and Bailey, B.P. Social Network, Web Forum, or Task Market?: Comparing Different Crowd Genres for Design Feedback Exchange *Proceedings of the 2016 ACM Conference on Designing Interactive Systems*, ACM, Brisbane, QLD, Australia, 2016, 773-784.
http://dx.doi.org/10.1145/2901790.2901820

43. Yuan, A., Luther, K., Krause, M., Vennix, S.I., Dow, S.P. and Hartmann, B. Almost an Expert: The Effects of Rubrics and Expertise on Perceived Value of Crowdsourced Design Critiques *Proceedings of the 19th ACM Conference on Computer-Supported Cooperative Work & Social Computing*, ACM, San Francisco, California, USA, 2016, 1005-1017.
http://dx.doi.org/10.1145/2818048.2819953

Semantically Far Inspirations Considered Harmful? Accounting for Cognitive States in Collaborative Ideation

Joel Chan[1], Pao Siangliulue[2], Denisa Qori McDonald[3], Ruixue Liu[3], Reza Moradinezhad[3], Safa Aman[3], Erin T. Solovey[3], Krzysztof Z. Gajos[2], Steven P. Dow[4],

[1]Carnegie Mellon University, [2]Harvard University, [3]Drexel University,
[4]University of California San Diego,
joelchuc@cs.cmu.edu, {paopow, kgajos}@seas.harvard.edu,
{denisa.qori, rl498, reza.mora, sra68, erin.solovey}@drexel.edu, spdow@ucsd.edu

ABSTRACT

Collaborative ideation systems can help people generate more creative ideas by exposing them to ideas different from their own. However, there are competing theoretical views on whether and when such exposure is helpful. Associationist theory suggests that exposing ideators to ideas that are semantically far from their own maximizes novel combinations of ideas. In contrast, SIAM theory cautions that systems should offer far ideas only when ideators reach an impasse (a cognitive state in which they have exhausted ideas within a particular category), and offer near ideas during productive ideation (a cognitive state in which they are actively exploring ideas within a category), which maximizes exploration within categories. Our research compares these theoretical recommendations. In an online experiment, 245 participants generated ideas for a themed wedding; we detected and validated participants' cognitive states using a combination of behavioral and neuroimaging data. Receiving far ideas during productive ideation resulted in slower ideation and less within-category exploration, without significant benefits for novelty, compared to receiving no inspirations. Participants were also more likely to hit an impasse when receiving far ideas during productive ideation. These findings suggest that far inspirational ideas can harm creativity if received during productive ideation.

Author Keywords

Creativity; creativity support tools; brainstorming; examples; collaborative ideation

C&C '17, June 27 - 30, 2017, Singapore, Singapore

ACM 978-1-4503-4403-6/17/06…$15.00
DOI: http://dx.doi.org/10.1145/3059454.3059455

ACM Classification Keywords

Human-centered computing~Collaborative and social computing

INTRODUCTION

Large-scale collaborative ideation platforms, like Climate CoLab and OpenIDEO, draw hundreds to thousands of contributors to collaboratively generate and develop solutions for creative problems. The promise of these platforms is that more breakthrough ideas can be developed by facilitating collaboration and remixing ideas at much higher levels of scale and diversity than before.

However, the scale and diversity of crowd ideation also presents unique challenges for collaborative inspiration. In small groups, ideation can be improved by simply exposing all contributors to all ideas [14]; however, at crowd scale, it is not uncommon to have hundreds or thousands of contributions. Ideators do not have sufficient time or cognitive resources to sift through that many ideas to select and build on ideas that are most helpful for their thinking [26,27]. Instead, ideators in these settings often resort to superficial processing of a few ideas [26,27]. Consequently, systems that can find and deliver potentially inspiring content to ideators are an important area of technical research and development for large-scale collaborative ideation platforms.

From a technical standpoint, significant progress has been made on the problem of how to structure large collections of ideas to enable exploration and navigation of the solution space [1,18,23,33,43,44]. Other studies have explored how dedicated community managers [6] or facilitators [8] might deliver appropriate inspiration to ideators.

In this paper, we consider a central *human factors* question facing designers of these inspiration delivery systems: how should inspiration delivery systems take into account the *semantic distance* of other people's ideas from the target user's ideas? Are the benefits of collaborative inspiration maximized by promoting cross-pollination of ideas (e.g., exposing ideators to ideas that are very different from their own), or by promoting deeper exploration of shared solution approaches (e.g., iterating on each other's ideas within a particular semantic region of the solution space)? Understanding the relative impact these approaches on the quantity, novelty, and diversity of generated ideas can inform the design of these platforms. To preview our results, we find that semantically far inspirations can negatively impact creative processes (speed, amount of within-category exploration) and products (novelty of ideas) if they are received during particular cognitive states.

Theoretical Foundations

Before we describe our experiment and results in detail, it is useful to consider the theoretical foundations of our investigation. Two prominent theories of creativity offer different answers to the question of semantic distance of inspirational stimuli from target user's own ideas. We selected these theories for relevance to the specific question of inspiration delivery. Our goal is not to arbitrate between competing *overall* theories of creativity, but rather to advance theoretical foundations for designing effective inspiration delivery systems.

Associationist Theory of Creativity

On the one hand, the ***associationist*** theory of creativity [21,31,34,42] argues that creativity arises from combining ideas that are very different from one another. From a cognitive standpoint, the associationist view notes a few key mechanisms by which this can be accomplished. First, creators can use *serendipity* to activate disparate portions of semantic memory at the same time. Mednick [34] noted an illustrative example of a physicist who "reduced serendipity to a method by placing in a fishbowl large numbers of slips of paper, each inscribed with a physical fact. He regularly devotes some time to *randomly* drawing pairs of these facts from the fishbowl, looking for new and useful combinations" (p. 221-222; *emphasis* ours). A related mechanism is *mediation*, which connects disparate concepts by finding deep structural similarities between them (e.g., by analogy [19]). It is worth mentioning that the original associationist theory also cites a mechanism of *similarity,* which connects disparate concepts by "spreading activation" through similar/related concepts in between. This mechanism is not shared by other associationist theories (e.g., conceptual combination, analogy), so we focus on the first two mechanisms—serendipity and mediation—that emphasize *directly* connecting semantically disparate concepts.

These theoretical assertions imply that, to improve creativity, inspiration should maximize the probability of making interesting remote associations, either by directly providing candidate combinations, or by activating distant portions of semantic memory through semantic priming [12,35]. This can be accomplished by delivering ideas that are semantically distant from the user's own ideas. According to the associationist theory, presenting ideators with such semantically far stimuli should increase the diversity and novelty of ideas they subsequently generate.

Search for Ideas in Associative Memory (SIAM) Model

On the other hand, the ***SIAM*** *(Search for Ideas in Associative Memory)* model of creative idea generation [37] argues that the answer depends on the user's cognitive state. The SIAM model posits that ideation proceeds by alternating between two kinds of cognitive states: *productive ideation* and *impasses.* During *productive ideation*, an ideator fluently accesses idea components from memory, and actively develops new ideas from those idea components. In this state, temporally adjacent ideas are often relatively close in semantic space, with some being close variations or elaborations of prior ideas, and some assembled from neighboring components in associative memory. In this state, ideators can develop more novel and useful ideas through deeper iteration and elaboration [11,15,36,41]. After exhausting resources within a semantic region, people enter an *impasse* state, and commence search for new semantic regions of memory from which to sample idea components. Idea generation during this state is slower and more effortful (as measured by time intervals between ideas, and subjective reports and/or neurophysiological measures of cognitive effort), and temporally adjacent ideas tend to be semantically distant from each other. Overall, SIAM posits that, in addition to exploring new semantic regions (when appropriate), creativity can be maximized with fluent exploration within categories, which enables people to move past common, shallow ideas to more interesting, less obvious ideas.

The theoretical assertions of the SIAM model imply that semantic distance should be accounted for in different ways for these states. During productive ideation, inspiration should enrich the local semantic region directly, or activate other (potentially valuable) idea components in the near neighborhood through semantic priming [12,35]. This can be accomplished by delivering conceptually near stimuli, which can help people more deeply explore the local region (beneficial for reaching more creative ideas [11,15,36,41]). In this state, exposure to far stimuli might even be harmful: attending to those stimuli could shift attention away from the current memory region (again, through processes like semantic priming), perhaps prematurely terminating productive chains of thought. Further, understanding and adapting far stimuli may require significant cognitive effort, and ideators may not be motivated to expend this cognitive effort if they are productively ideating within a category. During impasses, inspiration should suggest new semantic regions to explore, rather than refocusing ideators on the depleted semantic region. This can be accomplished by delivering semantically far stimuli, which could help accelerate the process of finding new productive regions to explore by activating more diffuse portions of memory.

From Theories to Inspiration Delivery System Designs

The associationist and SIAM theories therefore predict very different best and worst inspiration delivery approaches (see Table 1). Associationist theory suggests an ALWAYS-FAR inspiration approach would be best for ideation, where

	Predicted *best* approach	Predicted *worst* approach
Associationist theory	ALWAYS-FAR: deliver *far* stimuli, regardless of cognitive state; increases novelty and diversity of ideas by promoting remote associations *(SIAM predicts neutral effect on novelty: gains in novelty from pointers to new ideas offset by hindering exploration within categories)*	ALWAYS-NEAR: deliver *near* stimuli, regardless of cognitive state; decreases novelty and diversity of ideas by suppressing remote associations *(SIAM predicts neutral effect on novelty: loss of novelty from lack of pointers to new ideas offset by gains from fluent within-category exploration)*
SIAM model	MATCH-STATE: deliver *near* stimuli during productive ideation, and *far* stimuli during impasses; increases novelty of ideas by promoting fluent exploration within categories, and providing pointers to new areas of exploration at the appropriate time	MISMATCH-STATE: deliver *far* stimuli during productive ideation, and *near* stimuli during impasses; decreases novelty of ideas by hindering fluent exploration within categories, and suppressing pointers to new areas of exploration at the appropriate time

Table 1. **Best and worst approaches for choosing semantic distance of inspirational stimuli, as predicted by the associationist and SIAM theories of creativity. Associationist theory predicts that an ALWAYS-FAR approach is best, and an ALWAYS-NEAR approach is worst; SIAM predicts that a MATCH-STATE approach is best, and a MISMATCH-STATE approach is worst. SIAM also makes competing predictions for the associationist theory's predicted best and worst approaches.**

the system strives to deliver semantically distant ideas to the user, without accounting for cognitive states. According to the associationist theory, the least helpful approach would be the ALWAYS-NEAR inspiration strategy, which would be predicted to *harm* ideation by always constraining the user to a semantically adjacent region.

In contrast, SIAM suggests a MATCH-STATE inspiration approach would be best for ideation, where the system delivers near stimuli during productive ideation, and far stimuli during impasses. SIAM further predicts that a MISMATCH-STATE inspiration approach will be least helpful, since it presents the user with the opposite of their theoretically predicted inspiration needs during each state (i.e., potentially distracting far stimuli during productive ideation, and constraining near stimuli during impasses).

Interestingly, SIAM also offers a competing prediction for the associationist's best and worst approaches: the ALWAYS-FAR and ALWAYS-NEAR approaches should yield similar levels of novelty. This is because SIAM predicts that, in the ALWAYS-FAR approach, the increase in novelty from providing pointers to new areas of exploration should be offset by losses in novelty due to hindered within-category exploration. In the ALWAYS-NEAR approach, SIAM predicts that decreased novelty from lack of pointers to new areas of exploration should be offset by increased novelty from fluent within-category exploration [5,36].

To advance research and development of inspiration delivery systems for collaborative ideation platforms, empirical work is needed to tease apart whether the associationist or SIAM theories (or neither) are more useful theoretical guides for how to appropriately account for semantic distance of potential inspirational stimuli.

Overview and Contributions of The Present Study

In this paper, we report the results of an empirical test of these theories by comparing each of their predicted best and worst inspiration delivery approaches against a NO-STIMULI baseline. In an online ideation experiment, 245 participants generated ideas for themed weddings in one of the four inspiration conditions (ALWAYS-FAR, ALWAYS-NEAR, MATCH-STATE, and MISMATCH-STATE), or in the NO-STIMULI baseline condition. We detected changes between productive ideation and impasse states through a simple self-report mechanism. This approach was validated by behavioral (ideation was significantly slower right before an impasse) and neuroimaging data (which showed neuroimaging markers of significantly elevated cognitive effort right before an impasse).

Consistent with SIAM predictions, MISMATCH-STATE and ALWAYS-FAR participants generated ideas at a slower rate than NO-STIMULI participants, and ALWAYS-FAR participants iterated less within categories (as measured by mean similarity between subsequent ideas) compared to NO-STIMULI participants. Further, participants who received near stimuli during productive ideation (MATCH-STATE, ALWAYS-NEAR) were less likely to face impasses than participants who received far stimuli during productive ideation (ALWAYS-FAR, MISMATCH-STATE). Contrary to associationist predictions, ALWAYS-FAR ideas were not significantly more diverse or novel than NO-STIMULI ideas; instead, ALWAYS-FAR ideas were marginally statistically significantly *less* novel than NO-STIMULI ideas.

This paper contributes new insights for how to best promote creative inspiration on collaborative ideation platforms. Specifically, our findings show that far inspirational ideas—though considered to be generally useful for creative inspiration—can harm creativity if received during productive ideation. Our findings also imply that the SIAM model's state-contingent view of inspiration needs is more useful as a theoretical starting point than the associationist theory of creativity for guiding the design of collaborative inspiration systems.

EXPERIMENT

Participants

We recruited 245 participants (mean age = 33.5 years, SD=10.4, 51% female) from Amazon Mechanical Turk (MTurk). All participants were located in the U.S. and had 95% approval on at least 100 MTurk tasks. Participants were paid $1.25 for their time (approximately $6/hr wage, given average completion times of 12–13 minutes).

Study Design

We used a between-subjects design. Participants were randomly assigned to one of the 5 conditions: 1) the **NO-STIMULI** baseline (N=54), 2) associationist theory's predicted best **ALWAYS-FAR** condition (N=47), 3) associationist theory's predicted worst **ALWAYS-NEAR** condition (N=48). 4) SIAM theory's predicted best **MATCH-STATE** condition (N=51), and 5) SIAM theory's predicted worst **MISMATCH-STATE** condition (N=45).

Brainstorming Task

Participants generated ideas for a themed wedding, where each idea consisted of 1) a theme, 2) a main prop to be used for guest activities, and 3) a freeform description of how the prop would be incorporated into the wedding. We chose this task structure to maximize our ability to accurately tailor conceptual similarity based on participants' current thinking (and therefore experimentally isolate our intervention) in real-time. Achieving real-time semantic tailoring of potential stimuli to unstructured participant ideas of varying length and specificity is challenging to accomplish with a high degree of accuracy. To address this concern, our brainstorming task is semi-structured: participants separately specify theme (e.g., "medieval") and prop (e.g., "silver spoons") components of their themed wedding idea. This allows us to perform fast and accurate tailoring based on those single or compound words where computational similarity measurements tend to do better. For example, models like Pennington et al's [38] Global Vectors for Word Representation (GloVe) model — which uses an unsupervised learning algorithm to learn vector representations for words from global word-to-word co-occurrence statistics within a corpus — are able to achieve between 60% and 84% accuracy on word analogy tasks. This brainstorming task also achieves a degree of ecological validity since developing ideas for themed weddings is a common real-world creative task.

Sampling Inspirations based on Conceptual Distance

We used pre-trained GloVe vectors (trained on approximately 6 billion tokens (Wikipedia 2014 and Gigaword 5 corpora, with 300 dimensions) provided by Pennington et al [38] to perform similarity matching. While other vector-space models like Latent Semantic Analysis (LSA) have a longer history in cognitive science for measuring semantic distance [32], we opted to use GloVe, a recent state-of-the-art model that typically agrees well with classic models like LSA [17], while being capable of modeling more nuanced semantics, such as simple four-term analogies (e.g., man:woman = king:queen) [38].

Our database of potential inspirational stimuli consisted of 455 themes and 655 props collected from pilot runs of this study (with 207 MTurk workers; none of these workers also participated in the main study).

We showed inspirations as sets of 3 themes and 3 props, assembled in real-time and tailored to participants' last generated idea. *Near* stimuli are sampled to be near in semantic space, but no nearer than cosine similarity of 0.5 in the GloVe vector space. We selected this threshold to avoid duplicates and very close matches that are likely already activated, and also to activate the periphery of the current location in the semantic network in order to enrich the semantic region with additional potentially active idea components. *Far* stimuli were sampled to be as far from current thinking as possible.

To ensure our sampling approach focused on conceptual distance, we also controlled for diversity of inspiration sets (the relative distance between inspirations *in a set*) because the diversity of inspirational examples has been shown to impact creative performance [4,43]. Conceptual distance and diversity tend to be positively correlated, but it is hard to generate diverse sets for near stimuli. All things being equal, ideas that are all close to a seed idea will be relatively close to each other, compared to ideas sampled from distant semantic regions. Therefore, we restricted the diversity of sets to be relatively low. We use a simple sampling algorithm to ensure low diversity of sets: For each query, we first sampled a seed inspiration (whether near or far). Then, we found two nearest neighbors of that seed inspiration (where the cosine similarity of those neighbors to the seed and each other were less than 0.5). This completed a set of 3 inspirations for the query.

The following are examples of near and far inspirations sampled by our approach for two different themes:

For "football", *Near*: [season, fun and games, fourth of July], and *Far*: [toga, hula, prom]. For "steam punk", *Near*: [album, light of love, rock], and *Far*: [minions, knight and damsel, ghostbusters].

Validating Stimuli Sampling Approach

To validate our approach, we randomly sampled 100 themes generated by participants in the study, along with the near and far sets of inspirations actually retrieved for those themes during the experiment. We then generated a new set of inspirations that was the opposite distance (either near or far) from each theme. A trained research assistant (blind to which sets were deemed near or far by the algorithm) then went through each theme and marked which of the two sets (left or right) was "nearest" to the theme. A second judge (one of the authors, also blind to the algorithm's predictions) completed judgments for a random subset of 40 of the items, and agreement between the human judges was very high, Cohen's $\kappa = 0.95$. The research assistant judged the remaining items. The model's selection of near stimuli corresponded well to the judge's selection, Cohen's κ = 0.84, validating our semantic tailoring manipulation. In terms of "absolute" distance, the near stimuli in our dataset were, on average, 4 nodes away from the participant's last idea in Wordnet's association network (e.g., WOLF-->canine-->carnivore-->feline-->CAT), compared to 9 nodes away for far stimuli.

To validate our diversity control mechanism, we sampled 855 inspiration sets actually provided to participants during our experiment, and measured their pairwise distances using GloVe. In this sample, far sets were not more diverse than near sets; in fact, there was a tendency for near sets to be more diverse (M=.39, *SE*=.00) than far sets (M=.27, *SE*=.00; t=18.67, p<.01). This suggests that our diversity control mechanism successfully removed the usual coupling between distance and diversity of inspiration sets.

Inferring Ideators' Cognitive States

Our experiment requires that we accurately infer participants' cognitive state at each moment. Automatic detection is likely to be noisy; people can be idle for different reasons, and may be productively thinking while not typing. In contrast, prior work shows that people can notice when they are stuck [45]. However, ideally we do not want to burden participants with constantly monitoring their own cognitive state when they are productive.

Therefore, we designed a partially user-driven approach to infer cognitive states. The default state is productive ideation. The participant triggers a state change to impasse by requesting a set of inspirations, with the intuition that participants in this state would naturally seek out new stimulation. The system then infers a state change back to productive ideation once the participant submits a new idea.

Validating User-Driven Inferring of Cognitive States

Since this user-driven approach is novel, we sought to validate that it succeeds at differentiating between cognitive states. We conducted a small pilot study in which participants brainstormed while wearing functional near-infrared spectroscopy (fNIRS) brain sensors. fNIRS is a neuroimaging method that detects changes in the concentration of oxygenated and deoxygenated blood in the brain, relative to a reference point (e.g., during resting state, or a fixed time interval prior to an "event"). These changes in blood oxygen concentration can be used to infer changes in brain activity in particular regions of the brain [49], similar to the blood oxygen level dependent (BOLD) measure used in fMRI.

Neuroimaging Validation. The fNIRS device, manufactured by ISS, Inc. contained six measurement channels with 3-cm source-detector distances. Participants experienced the same set of procedures as our online participants, except they generated ideas for 20 minutes (to maximize the amount of data points per participant), and participated in a post-task semi-structured interview. We preprocessed the

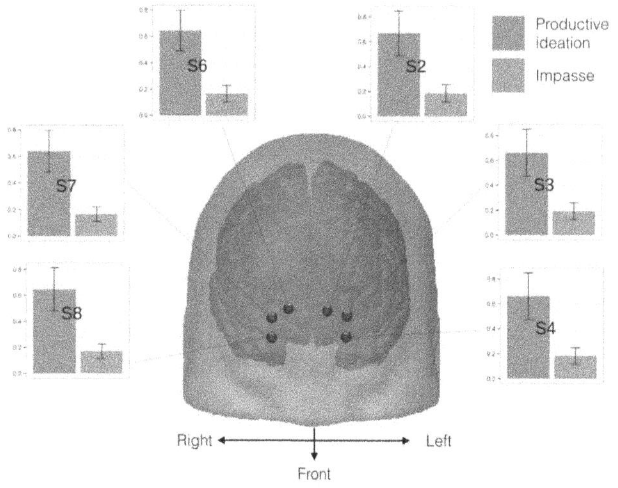

Figure 1. **Participants in our pilot study showed higher levels of cognitive effort during system-inferred impasses (green bars) compared to system-inferred productive ideation (red bars), as indicated by lower levels of ΔHbR (in micromolars, μM) in regions of the prefrontal cortex (measured using functional near-infrared spectroscopy).**

fNIRS data for analysis using Homer2 [24], a MATLAB-based application for processing fNIRS data. Preprocessing involved converting the raw light intensity data to oxygenated (HbO) and deoxygenated hemoglobin (HbR) changes. A high-pass filter was also applied at 0.5 Hz. Our sample consists of 6 participants, with a total of 23 instances of inferred impasses.

We focused our analysis on comparing brain activity 10 seconds immediately before an inspiration request (which we assume would be an impasse state) and 10 seconds immediately after the first idea submission after an inspiration request (which we assume would be a productive ideation state). Our hypothesis is that we should see brain activity that indicates higher levels of cognitive effort during the inferred impasse state, compared to the productive ideation state. The expected hemodynamic response would be a negative change in HbR during increase cognitive load [25,46]. Thus, we operationalize cognitive effort as the maximum change in HbR relative to the 2s just prior to the event.

We found a significant difference in the maximum HbR signal between the two states, with the pre-stuck period being lower than the post-stuck period across all of the channels we measured (see Figure 1; all p<.01). This finding suggests participants were exerting high levels of cognitive effort during inferred impasses (i.e., right before requesting inspirations).

Behavioral Validation. These neuroimaging results were further corroborated by comments participants made during the post-task semi-structured interview. For example, one participant said she clicked to request more inspirations *"mostly just like after I had like exhausted the ideas in my mind and I was like OK I don't know what could possibly*

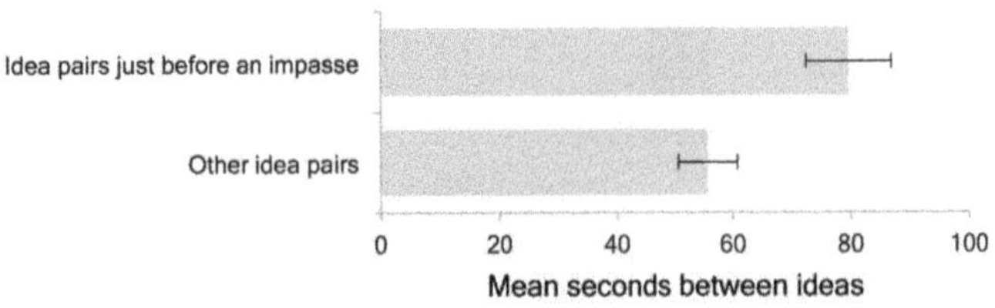

***Figure 2.* Participants generated ideas more slowly just before an impasse compared to other points in their ideation session.**

be next". Another participant said he requested inspirations when he *"was just running out of ideas"*.

Further, participants in our online experiment took significantly more time between subsequent idea submissions just before an inferred impasse (M=79.6 seconds, *SE*=7.3), compared to idea transitions not temporally adjacent to an inferred impasse event (M=55.8, *SE*=5.0), t(19.4) = 3.3, $p<.01$ (see Figure 2). Note that these do not include the interval between the last idea submission before an inspiration request and the request, or the interval between the request and the first idea submission after the request. The intervals are therefore indicative of the speed with which ideas are generated, and not the time it takes to perform extra tasks, such as (deciding to) request more inspirations. This difference in inter-idea interval is consistent with SIAM's predictions of faster ideation during productive ideation and slower ideation during impasses.

Altogether, these results suggest that our user-driven approach successfully detects cognitive state changes (i.e., inspiration requests signal a transition to an impasse state).

System and Interface

Figure 3 shows the ideation interface used in our experiment. Participants enter ideas in a semi-structured format (separate fields for themes, props, and descriptions). In the left pane, the system automatically retrieves a new set of themes and props after each idea entry. The participant is assumed to be in a productive ideation state unless they click the *"Give me other inspirations"* button. When this button is clicked, the system infers the participant is in an impasse state, and retrieves a new set of inspirations accordingly. Participants can refresh the inspiration feed during the impasse state as many times as they wish. Each button click during this state retrieves a new set of inspirations. Once a participant submits a new idea after requesting inspirations, the system infers the participant has returned to a productive ideation state.

The system was built in Meteor.js (a Node.js-based web application framework). The system communicates with a similarity engine via a RESTful API to select inspirations based on semantic relatedness to participants' current idea focus. Inspiration retrievals took about 1–2 seconds.

Procedure

After providing informed consent, participants were randomly assigned to one of the 5 conditions. Next, they

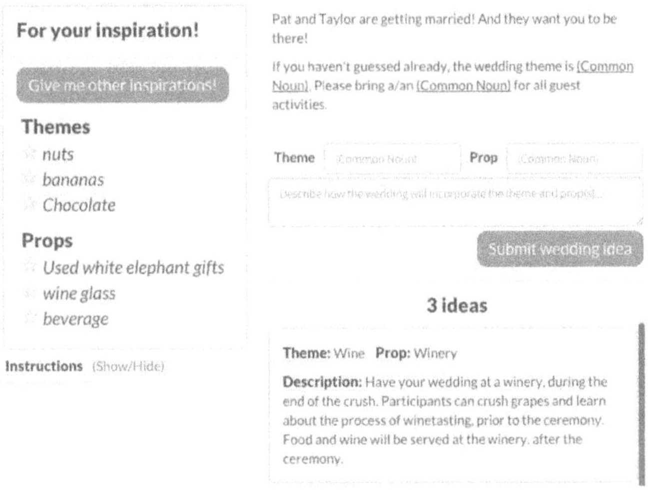

***Figure 3.* Participants enter ideas in a semi-structured interface. Inspirations in the left pane automatically update during productive ideation; when participants request new inspirations, this signals an impasse state to the system, and new inspirations are retrieved. The control condition interface is identical except for the absence of an inspiration feed.**

entered a warm-up task screen where they generated alternative uses for a brick for one minute. After this, they completed a short tutorial that highlighted the key features of the interface. Finally, they generated ideas for the main problem for 8 minutes. The system automatically took them to a final survey page after 8 minutes.

MEASURES

Within-Category Fluency

We operationalize two measures of within-category fluency that capture related but distinct aspects of the theoretical construct of within-category fluency: inter-idea interval (probability of an impasse), and transition similarity.

Inter-Idea Interval

SIAM posits that ideation within a category is more rapid than generating ideas in-between categories; thus, participants who have higher within-category fluency should, on average, have shorter intervals between idea submissions. Thus, we operationalize inter-idea interval as the median number of seconds between subsequent idea submissions, as logged by our system. We report median inter-idea interval because this measure is insensitive to long inter-idea intervals during impasses and instead, reflects how rapidly a participant was generating ideas while they were in a productive ideation state. We also statistically control in our analysis for the number of ideas generated. This allows us to more cleanly capture the degree of within-category fluency.

Transition Similarity

Ideas within a category tend to be more semantically similar to each other than ideas between categories: thus, participants who have higher within-category fluency should, on average, have higher similarity between successive ideas. We operationalized transition similarity as the median GloVe cosine between themes and props of subsequent ideas. As with inter-idea interval, reporting the median allows us more cleanly capture the degree of within-category fluency.

Overall Fluency: Number of Ideas Generated

Fluency was operationalized as the number of ideas generated for the problem.

Diversity: Mean Pairwise Distance Between Ideas

Diversity was operationalized as mean pairwise distance (the reverse of similarity) between a participant's ideas as measured by GloVe.

Novelty

We recruited 185 workers from MTurk to rate the novelty of the generated ideas on a scale of 1 (Extremely Obvious) to 7 (Extremely Novel). Each worker rated a random subset of approximately 30 ideas. Computing correlations between each judges' ratings and the overall aggregate score yielded an average aggregate-judge correlation of r=.64. To deal with potential differences in usage of the rating scale across raters (e.g., some might only use the upper end of the scale), we compute standardized scores (a.k.a. "z-scores") within raters (i.e., a mean score of a rater was subtracted from that rater's each individual score and the difference was divided by the standard deviation of that rater's scores).

An example of a *high* novelty idea is "[Chemistry] [Lab experiment] The couple could conduct a common laboratory experiment combining two substances to create a third as part of their ceremony symbolizing and celebrating their union." (z-score=1.61). An example of a *low* novelty idea is "[formal] [gift] It would be a typical wedding" (z-score=–1.94)

Each participant's novelty score was the *highest* novelty score across his/her ideas. This conceptualization of novelty is a good fit for the predictions of both associationist and SIAM theories for novelty, which emphasize novelty as an outcome of the ideation process (i.e., the most novel idea that was generated, instead of average novelty of all ideas).

Control Measure: Baseline Fluency

In ideation studies, it is important to control for pre-existing differences in participants' creative capacities, such as baseline fluency of ideation [7,9]. Baseline fluency was operationalized as the number of alternative uses generated for a brick during the warm-up task that participants completed prior to the main ideation task. This measure is intended to capture both aspects of baseline creative fluency [20], and aspects of participant motivation and comfort with the interface (all important for creative productivity).

RESULTS

System-Usage Statistics

Participants generated a total of 1,574 ideas across conditions. 85% of participants in the inspiration conditions reported using the inspiration feature in some way (e.g., attending to inspirations, requesting inspirations). Of those who did, 68% self-reported interacting with the inspirations (e.g., attending to, using as inspiration) at least "somewhat frequently" (3 on a scale of 1 to 5) when they weren't actively clicking to get more inspirations, M=3.0 (SE=0.1).

Across the inspiration conditions, 49% of participants requested inspirations at least once. Interestingly, however, likelihood of an inspiration request was not equal across conditions. Participants who received near stimuli during productive ideation (ALWAYS-NEAR and MATCH-STATE) were less likely to request an inspiration at least once (M=.42, SE=.05) than participants who received far stimuli during productive ideation (ALWAYS-FAR and MISMATCH-STATE, M=.57, SE=.05). A logistic regression model, predicting the probability of inspiration request as a function of stimuli distance during productive ideation, showed that the difference between the near and far distance groups was statistically significant, z=1.96, p=.05. Since this analysis was conducted in response to seeing the data (vs. hypothesized in advance, as with the primary analyses in the subsequent section), we wish to clearly mark this finding as exploratory (rather than confirmatory). We revisit this finding in the Discussion.

Overall, these numbers suggest that the features of the system relating to inspiration were used reasonably frequently, providing an adequate test of our manipulations.

Primary Analyses

For each dependent measure, we estimate an ANCOVA model with baseline fluency as a control covariate (if it is a statistically significant predictor of the dependent measure). For median inter-idea interval, we also include number of ideas generated as a theoretically motivated control covariate (if it is statistically significant). All significant main effects of condition are followed up with planned contrasts against the NO-STIMULI condition, using Dunnett's procedure [16] to control Type I error inflation from multiple comparisons. Table 2 summarizes model-adjusted means and standard errors for each dependent measure by condition.

Slower Ideation with Always-Far and Mismatch-State

To investigate ideation pace in each condition, we estimated an ANCOVA predicting median *inter-idea interval* as a function of condition, controlling for number of ideas (which was significantly negatively correlated with inter-idea interval, r=–.63, p<.01). Recall that controlling for number of ideas provides a finer-grained measure of within-category fluency, allowing us to discern qualitative differences (low vs. high within-category fluency) between quantitatively similar (overall number of ideas) ideation traces. The model showed a significant main effect of condition on median seconds between subsequent ideas, F(4,233)=3.2, p=.01. Planned contrasts showed that ALWAYS-FAR and MISMATCH-STATE participants had significantly longer median inter-idea intervals (t=2.8, p=.02 and t=3.1, p=.01, respectively) compared to NO-STIMULI participants.

	Inter-idea interval	Transition similarity	Overall Fluency	Diversity	Novelty
NO-STIMULI	64.2 *(5.3)*	0.19 *(0.01)*	6.5 *(0.5)*	0.84 *(0.01)*	0.88 *(0.07)*
ALWAYS-FAR	**86.2 *(5.7)* ***	**0.12 *(0.02)* ****	6.1 *(0.5)*	0.86 *(0.01)*	**0.64 *(0.07)*** *m*
ALWAYS-NEAR	74.3 *(5.6)*	0.20 *(0.02)*	6.4 *(0.5)*	0.81 *(0.01)*	0.67 *(0.07)*
MATCH-STATE	76.6 *(5.5)*	0.19 *(0.01)*	7.0 *(0.5)*	0.83 *(0.01)*	0.88 *(0.07)*
MISMATCH-STATE	**88.7 *(5.8)* ****	0.14 *(0.02)*	6.5 *(0.5)*	0.84 *(0.01)*	0.79 *(0.07)*

Table 2. **Model-adjusted means and standard errors for each dependent measure by condition.** ^{m} $p < .10$, * $p < .05$, **and** ** $p < .01$ **for contrasts with the NO-STIMULI baseline, with Dunnett's correction for multiple comparisons. Contrasts show that ALWAYS-FAR resulted in significantly longer *inter-idea intervals* and significantly lower *transition similarity* and *novelty* than NO-STIMULI; MISMATCH-STATE resulted in significantly longer *inter-idea intervals* than NO-STIMULI.**

Lower Transition Similarity in Always-Far Condition

Transition similarity was not significantly correlated with baseline fluency (r=.02, *p*=.79). Therefore, we estimated an ANOVA with condition as the only factor. The model showed a significant effect of condition, F(4,218)=4.9, *p*<.01. Planned contrasts showed that **ALWAYS-FAR** participants had significantly lower median transition similarity (t=-3.1, *p*<.01) than participants in the **NO-STIMULI** condition. A post-hoc Tukey test also showed that **ALWAYS-FAR** participants had lower median transition similarity than both **MATCH-STATE** (*p*=.02) and **ALWAYS-NEAR** participants (*p*<.01).

Fluency: Equal Number of Ideas Across Conditions

An ANCOVA controlling for baseline fluency showed no significant main effect of condition on the *number of ideas*, F(4,239)=0.5, *p*=0.77.

Always-Far Leads to More Diversity than Always-Near

No theoretical covariates were statistically significantly related to *diversity*. Therefore, we estimated an ANOVA with condition as the only factor. This ANOVA showed a significant main effect of condition on diversity, F(4,233) = 2.97, *p*<.01, but planned contrasts did not show any differences between the inspiration conditions and the control condition. However, a post-hoc Tukey test showed that participants in the **ALWAYS-NEAR** conditions had significantly lower diversity of ideas compared to the **ALWAYS-FAR** condition (*p*=.01).

No Benefits for Novelty in Always-Far Condition

Baseline fluency was not significantly correlated with novelty (r=.03, *p*=.68). Thus, we estimated an ANOVA with condition as the only factor. This model showed a significant main effect of condition, F(4,239)=2.5, *p*=.04. Planned contrasts showed no significant differences between **ALWAYS-FAR** and **NO-STIMULI** participants, t=-2.3, *p*=.07; however, the mean trends were in the opposite direction predicted by the associationist theory, with the most novel ideas of **ALWAYS-FAR** participants rated as *less* novel (M=0.64, *SE*=0.07) than **NO-STIMULI** participants' most novel ideas (M=0.88, *SE*=0.07).

DISCUSSION

In this study, we explored how the semantic distance of inspirations from the target user's own ideas impacts their creative performance. Specifically, we compared two competing theoretical recommendations from creativity theories: 1) the associationist view, which predicted that always providing far stimuli would be most beneficial, and 2) the SIAM model of creative ideation, which predicted that a state-contingent inspiration delivery (where near stimuli are delivered during productive ideation, and far stimuli during impasses) would be most beneficial.

Figure 3 summarizes our findings and their implications for the two competing theories. Consistent with the associationist view, ideas generated in the **ALWAYS-FAR** condition were significantly more diverse than those generated in the **ALWAYS-NEAR** condition; however, **ALWAYS-FAR** ideas were not significantly more diverse than **NO-STIMULI** ideas. Further, contrary to associationist predictions, **ALWAYS-FAR** ideas were not significantly more novel than **NO-STIMULI** ideas; instead, the mean trends showed that **ALWAYS-FAR** ideas were possibly *less* novel than **NO-STIMULI** ideas.

In contrast, consistent with SIAM predictions, **MISMATCH-STATE** and **ALWAYS-FAR** participants generated ideas at a slower rate than **NO-STIMULI** participants, and **ALWAYS-FAR** participants iterated less within categories compared to **NO-STIMULI** participants (indicating that far stimuli hinder within-category exploration). Finally, an exploratory analysis showed that participants who received near stimuli during productive ideation (**MATCH-STATE, ALWAYS-NEAR**) were less likely to request inspirations (which our system used to detect impasses) than participants who received far stimuli during productive ideation (**ALWAYS-FAR, MISMATCH-STATE**), suggesting that near stimuli could extend productive ideation chains (relative to far stimuli). However, **MATCH-STATE** participants did not have greater within-category fluency, overall fluency, or novelty of ideas than **NO-STIMULI** participants.

In summary, we conclude that the SIAM model's state-contingent view may be more useful as a theoretical starting

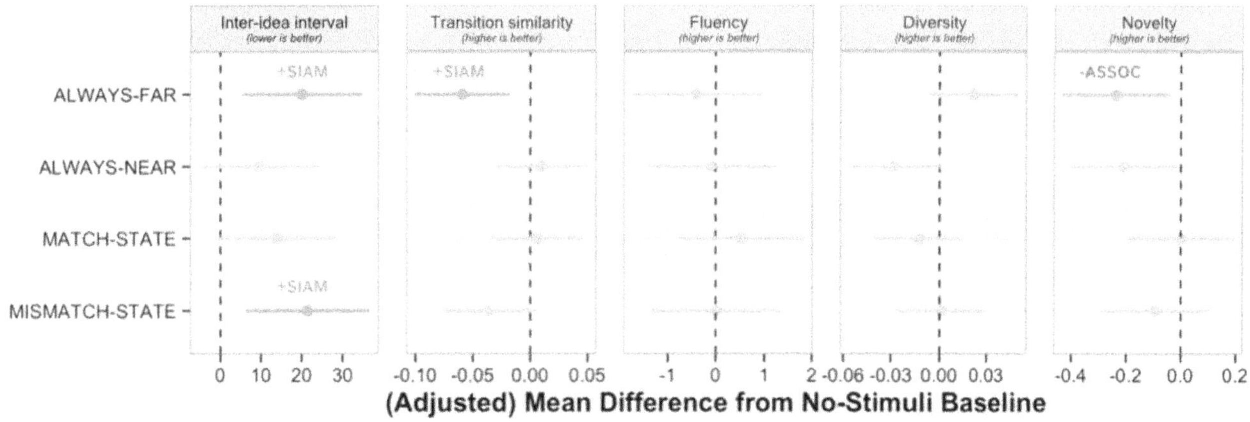

Figure 3. Summary of model-adjusted mean contrasts across dependent measures for each inspiration condition against the NO-STIMULI baseline condition (vertical dashed lines). Mean contrasts are reported on the original scale of the dependent measure. Error bars are 95% confidence intervals. Significant contrasts from the NO-STIMULI baseline (by Dunnett's t-test) are shown in orange. Contrasts that support a theory's prediction are marked green; contrasts that contradict (i.e., go in the opposite direction of) a theory's prediction are marked red. Here, SIAM's predictions for the ALWAYS-FAR (for *inter-idea interval, transition similarity*), ALWAYS-NEAR (for *inter-idea interval, transition similarity, fluency*), and MISMATCH-STATE conditions (for *inter-idea interval*) are supported, while the associationist theory's predictions for ALWAYS-NEAR is contradicted (for *novelty*).

point than the associationist theory of creativity for guiding the design of inspiration delivery systems. In practical terms, our findings suggest that following the associationist recommendation to deliver semantically far inspirations throughout ideation (including during productive ideation, as in the **ALWAYS-FAR** condition) is inadvisable, as it provides uncertain benefits for diversity, and relatively certain costs for novelty and within-category exploration. The theoretical assertions of SIAM suggest that the reduction in novelty arises from disruption of the deep-exploration pathway to novel ideas [11,36,41]. However, it is still unclear if delivering near stimuli during productive ideation and far stimuli during impasses maximizes benefits for ideation. In the limitations section, we suggest methodological changes that might help future studies explore this issue further. We remind the reader that we make no claims about the relative merits of the associationist or SIAM theories for explaining creativity *in general*: we restrict our claims to their relative merits for guiding the design of effective inspiration delivery systems.

Limitations

One limitation of our study is that not all participants entered an impasse state, partially limiting our ability to observe the effects of stimuli during that state. This might be one reason we did not detect an advantage for SIAM's hypothesized best condition (**MATCH-STATE**), since—possibly due to the benefits of receiving near stimuli during productive ideation—many of those participants did not have the opportunity to receive interesting pointers to new areas of exploration (only available in the impasse state in that condition). Perhaps a longer time scale than 8 minutes (to increase the probability that most participants would run out of ideas) or induced breaks in the session would provide a better opportunity to study the effects of stimuli during impasses. Relatedly, a longer time scale might provide a clearer test of the potential cumulative benefits of inspiration during productive ideation (which might come at a slight cognitive cost).

Finally, our sample consisted of MTurk workers paid $6/hr: while many participants expressed enjoyment in the task, low baseline levels of skill/knowledge are still a possibility, which may have suppressed positive effects of inspirations (to the extent that skill/motivation is required to adequately benefit from the inspirations). These are possible reasons that the four treatment conditions did not significantly outperform the **NO-STIMULI** participants on any measure. We therefore urge caution generalizing these results to other settings with a longer time scale and with more skilled/knowledgeable/motivated participants.

Our system also had a relatively slow response time (~1-2s) when retrieving inspirations. While this response time is likely to be acceptable from a usability perspective, the inspirations may not always have arrived before participants started writing down their next idea, potentially adding noise to the intervention. A quicker response time might enable a cleaner test of the potential benefits of near stimuli during productive ideation.

Broader Implications and Future Work

Inspirations should be Delivered at the Right Moments

Our study is consistent with previous work that suggests that potentially helpful inspirations (e.g., analogous ideas from other domains [48], simple hints [28], or diverse ideas of others [45]) are only helpful when delivered under particular circumstances. These findings underscore the importance of considering not just *which* inspirations should be delivered to improve creative ideation, but also *when* they should be delivered. Considering this larger body of findings yields important issues for further research.

One important issue to consider is whether ideators should receive *any* inspiration during productive ideation. Does receiving any stimuli during productive ideation amount to mere disruptive interruptions [2,3,45])? One state-contingent strategy might be to avoid offering any stimuli during productive ideation, and only offer far stimuli during impasses. Our findings are only partially consistent with this view of inspirations: rather than global deficits associated with any stimulation, we observed meaningful theoretically predicted differences between the conditions, finding that far stimuli was harmful, but near stimuli did not lead to statistically significant deficits. The SIAM model of ideation still provides some theoretical reason to doubt this (ideation depends on having "idea elements" to recombine; having more "idea elements" should improve ideation), as does prior studies on the benefits of seeing the ideas of others during collaborative brainstorming in small groups [14]. Future studies that, like our study, vary not just timing but theoretically meaningful variations in the kind of stimuli presented could provide more clarity on this issue.

Another important issue is the implications of a state-contingent view for computational creativity support tools that operate at longer time scales (e.g., weeks, the lifespan of a project) than what we examined in this body of work on timing (i.e., seconds and minutes). At longer time scales, the lines between cognitive states and between real-time inspiration and user-driven search for inspiration might be blurred. For example, how do users get "stuck", or enter a state of creative flow, within the larger context of a project? How might we we appropriately tailor the behavior of the inspiration tools to these states at those time scales (e.g., patent database search engines [30])?

Finally, if accounting for cognitive states of users is important, how might systems effectively detect when users are in particular cognitive states? In this study, we used a partially user-driven approach to detecting users' cognitive states. While this is a reasonable approach for detecting switches to impasse states, future work might explore the use of behavioral markers that predict the onset of an impasse (e.g., slowed inter-idea interval, excessively high inter-idea similarity) and prevent, rather than respond to it. These behavioral markers could be augmented with physiological markers (e.g., the fNIRS signals we obtained in our validation study), to obtain more nuanced and accurate representations of user states. Advances in the portability and wearability of these physiological sensors open up exciting new avenues for designing creativity support systems that respond to users' "implicit input" [47]. This approach could be especially productive to the extent that changes in cognitive states happen more on a continuum than a binary state shift: systems that can detect early/mild stages of impasse and pre-emptively introduce interventions to prevent impasses might represent a new class of creativity support tools that promote extended states of creative "flow" [13].

Far Stimuli Should be Used with Caution

Our findings also have broader implications for the role of semantic distance in creative inspiration. Far (rather than near) stimuli have generally been thought to be more useful for provoking creative mental leaps [19,22,29,40,50]. However, recent investigations are beginning to challenge and refine that claim [10,39,51], pointing out, for example, that overreliance on semantically far stimuli can harm creative performance [10]. Much of this recent work has focused on the impact of inspirations that are far from one's *problem domain* (e.g., drawing inspiration from pendulum motions in grandfather clocks when generating ideas for a new approaches to generating electricity in developing countries). In this work, we extend the notion that far stimuli should be used with caution to the related but distinct notion of semantic distance of inspirations from one's current thinking. We do not mean to argue that far stimuli are unimportant or that they should be avoided entirely; rather, our findings, together with other work on semantic distance, suggest that future research should explore *when* and *how* creators can best take advantage of semantically far inspirations.

Dual Pathways to Creative Outcomes

Finally, our finding that far stimuli during productive ideation not only reduced within-category fluency, but also reduced novelty of ideas (as predicted by SIAM), lends support to the "dual pathway" view of creative ideation [11,36,41], which posits that iteration and deep exploration within categories is an important pathway to creative (not just better quality) ideas, perhaps just as important as creative "mental leaps" to remote regions of a solution space [50], or combining semantically very different ideas [34]. Future research on large-scale collaborative ideation could build on this view to explore how to coordinate the crowd to deeply explore *within* solution approaches, as a complement to promoting cross-pollination of ideas.

CONCLUSION

In this paper, we empirically examined competing theoretical recommendations for how inspirational delivery systems on collaborative ideation platforms should account for semantic distance of inspirational stimuli. In an online ideation experiment, we find that following the associationist theory's recommendation to always provide far stimuli yields uncertain benefits for idea diversity and relatively certain costs for within-category fluency and idea novelty. Our research suggests that far inspirations can be harmful for creativity if delivered during productive ideation, and that collaborative inspiration systems could be improved by accounting for ideators' cognitive states.

ACKNOWLEDGEMENTS

We thank all of the people (both in-person and on MTurk) who participated in the experiment, particularly those who gave valuable feedback on early versions of the experiment. We are also grateful for support from National Science Foundation awards IIS-1122206 and IIS-1122320.

REFERENCES

1. Salvatore Andolina, Khalil Klouche, Diogo Cabral, Tuukka Ruotsalo, and Giulio Jacucci. 2015. InspirationWall: Supporting Idea Generation Through Automatic Information Exploration. In *Proceedings of the 2015 ACM SIGCHI Conference on Creativity and Cognition* (C&C '15), 103–106. https://doi.org/10.1145/2757226.2757252
2. Brian P. Bailey and Shamsi T. Iqbal. 2008. Understanding Changes in Mental Workload During Execution of Goal-directed Tasks and Its Application for Interruption Management. *ACM Trans. Comput.-Hum. Interact.* 14, 4: 21:1–21:28. https://doi.org/10.1145/1314683.1314689
3. Brian P Bailey, Joseph Konstan, John V Carlis, and others. 2000. Measuring the effects of interruptions on task performance in the user interface. In *Systems, Man, and Cybernetics, 2000 IEEE International Conference on*, 757–762.
4. Jonali Baruah and Paul B. Paulus. 2011. Category assignment and relatedness in the group ideation process. *Journal of Experimental Social Psychology* 47, 6: 1070–1077.
5. Roger E. Beaty and Paul J. Silvia. 2012. Why do ideas get more creative across time? An executive interpretation of the serial order effect in divergent thinking tasks. *Psychology of Aesthetics, Creativity, and the Arts* 6, 4: 309–319.
6. Osvald M. Bjelland and Robert Chapman Wood. 2008. An Inside View of IBM's' Innovation Jam'. *MIT Sloan management review* 50, 1: 32–40.
7. Joel Chan, Steven C. Dang, and Steven P. Dow. 2016. Improving crowd innovation with expert facilitation. In *Proceedings of the ACM Conference on Computer-Supported Cooperative Work & Social Computing.* https://doi.org/10.1145/2818048.2820023
8. Joel Chan, Steven Dang, and Steven P. Dow. 2016. IdeaGens: Enabling Expert Facilitation of Crowd Brainstorming. In *Proceedings of the 19th ACM Conference on Computer Supported Cooperative Work and Social Computing Companion* (CSCW '16 Companion), 13–16. https://doi.org/10.1145/2818052.2874313
9. Joel Chan, Steven Dang, and Steven P. Dow. 2016. Comparing Different Sensemaking Approaches for Large-Scale Ideation. In *Proceedings of the 2016 CHI Conference on Human Factors in Computing Systems*, 2717–2728.
10. Joel Chan, Steven P. Dow, and Christian D. Schunn. 2015. Do The Best Design Ideas (Really) Come From Conceptually Distant Sources Of Inspiration? *Design Studies* 36: 31–58. https://doi.org/10.1016/j.destud.2014.08.001
11. Joel Chan and Christian D. Schunn. 2015. The importance of iteration in creative conceptual combination. *Cognition* 145: 104–115. https://doi.org/10.1016/j.cognition.2015.08.008
12. Allan M. Collins and Elizabeth F. Loftus. 1975. A spreading-activation theory of semantic processing. *Psychological Review* 82, 6: 407–428.
13. Mihaly Csikszentmihalyi. 1997. *Flow and the Psychology of Discovery and Invention.* HarperPerennial, New York, NY.
14. Darleen M. DeRosa, Carter L. Smith, and Donald A. Hantula. 2007. The medium matters: Mining the long-promised merit of group interaction in creative idea generation tasks in a meta-analysis of the electronic group brainstorming literature. *Computers in Human Behavior* 23, 3: 1549–1581. https://doi.org/10.1016/j.chb.2005.07.003
15. Steven P. Dow, Alana Glassco, Jonathan Kass, Melissa Schwarz, Daniel L. Schwartz, and Scott R. Klemmer. 2010. Parallel Prototyping Leads to Better Design Results, More Divergence, and Increased Self-efficacy. *ACM Trans. Comput.-Hum. Interact.* 17, 4: 18:1–18:24. https://doi.org/10.1145/1879831.1879836
16. Charles W. Dunnett. 1955. A Multiple Comparison Procedure for Comparing Several Treatments with a Control. *Journal of the American Statistical Association* 50, 272: 1096–1121. https://doi.org/10.1080/01621459.1955.10501294
17. Manaal Faruqui and Chris Dyer. 2015. Non-distributional Word Vector Representations. In *Proceedings of ACL.*
18. Katherine Fu, Joel Chan, Christian Schunn, Jonathan Cagan, and Kenneth Kotovsky. 2013. Expert representation of design repository space: A comparison to and validation of algorithmic output. *Design Studies* 34, 6: 729–762. https://doi.org/10.1016/j.destud.2013.06.002
19. Dedre Gentner and Arthur B. Markman. 1997. Structure mapping in analogy and similarity. *American Psychologist* 52, 1: 45–56.
20. Joy P. Guilford. 1950. Creativity. *American Psychologist* 5: 444–454.
21. Nitin Gupta, Yoonhee Jang, Sara C. Mednick, and David E. Huber. 2012. The Road Not Taken: Creative Solutions Require Avoidance of High-Frequency Responses. *Psychological Science.*
22. Keith J. Holyoak and Paul Thagard. 1996. *Mental leaps: Analogy in creative thought.* Cambridge, MA.
23. Seth Hunter and Pattie Maes. 2008. WordPlay: A table-top interface for collaborative brainstorming and decision making. *Proceedings of IEEE Tabletops and Interactive Surfaces*: 2–5.
24. Theodore J. Huppert, Solomon G. Diamond, Maria A. Franceschini, and David A. Boas. 2009. HomER: a review of time-series analysis methods for near-infrared spectroscopy of the brain. *Applied Optics* 48, 10: D280. https://doi.org/10.1364/AO.48.00D280
25. Theodore J. Huppert, Rick D. Hoge, Solomon G. Diamond, Maria A. Franceschini, and David A. Boas. 2006. A temporal comparison of BOLD, ASL, and NIRS hemodynamic responses to motor stimuli in adult

humans. *NeuroImage* 29, 2: 368–382. https://doi.org/10.1016/j.neuroimage.2005.08.065
26. Elahe Javadi and Wai-Tat -. T. Fu. 2011. Idea Visibility, Information Diversity, and Idea Integration in Electronic Brainstorming. In *Proceedings of the 6th International Conference on Foundations of Augmented Cognition: Directing the Future of Adaptive Systems* (FAC'11), 517–524.
27. Elahe Javadi, Joseph Mahoney, and Judith Gebauer. 2013. The impact of user interface design on idea integration in electronic brainstorming: an attention-based view. *Journal of the Association for Information Systems* 14, 1: 1–21.
28. Craig A. Kaplan and Herbert A. Simon. 1990. In search of insight. *Cognitive Psychology* 22, 3: 374–419.
29. Stefan W. Knoll and Graham Horton. 2011. The Impact of Stimuli Characteristics on the Ideation Process: An Evaluation of the Change of Perspective "Analogy." In *Proceedings of the 44th Hawaii International Conference on System Sciences*.
30. S. Koch, H. Bosch, M. Giereth, and T. Ertl. 2009. Iterative Integration of Visual Insights during Scalable Patent Search and Analysis. In *Proceedings of IEEE Transactions on Visualization and Computer Graphics*.
31. Arthur Koestler. 1964. *The act of creation*. Macmillan, Oxford, England.
32. T. K. Landauer and S. T. Dumais. 1997. A solution to Plato's problem: The latent semantic analysis theory of acquisition, induction, and representation of knowledge. *Psychological Review* 104, 2: 211–240.
33. Brian Lee, Savil Srivastava, Ranjitha Kumar, Ronen Brafman, and Scott R. Klemmer. 2010. Designing with Interactive Example Galleries. In *Proceedings of the SIGCHI Conference on Human Factors in Computing Systems* (CHI '10), 2257–2266. https://doi.org/10.1145/1753326.1753667
34. Sara A. Mednick. 1962. The associative basis of the creative process. *Psychological Review* 69, 3: 220–232.
35. Ana Sofia Morais, Henrik Olsson, and Lael J. Schooler. 2012. Mapping the Structure of Semantic Memory. *Cognitive Science*. https://doi.org/10.1111/cogs.12013
36. Bernard A. Nijstad, Carsten K. W. De Dreu, Eric F. Rietzschel, and Matthijs Baas. 2010. The dual pathway to creativity model: Creative ideation as a function of flexibility and persistence. *European Review of Social Psychology* 21: 34–77. https://doi.org/10.1080/10463281003765323
37. Bernard A. Nijstad and Wolfgang Stroebe. 2006. How the group affects the mind: a cognitive model of idea generation in groups. *Personality and Social Psychology Review* 10, 3: 186–213. https://doi.org/10.1207/s15327957pspr1003_1
38. Jeffrey Pennington, Richard Socher, and Christopher D Manning. 2014. Glove: Global vectors for word representation. *Proceedings of the Empiricial Methods in Natural Language Processing (EMNLP 2014)* 12: 1532–1543.
39. David N. Perkins. 1983. Novel Remote Analogies Seldom Contribute to Discovery. *The Journal of Creative Behavior* 17, 4: 223–239.
40. Tony Poze. 1983. Analogical connections: The essence of creativity. *The Journal of creative behavior* 17, 4: 240–258.
41. Eric F. Rietzschel, Bernard A. Nijstad, and Wolfgang Stroebe. 2007. Relative accessibility of domain knowledge and creativity: The effects of knowledge activation on the quantity and originality of generated ideas. *Journal of Experimental Social Psychology* 43, 6: 933–946. https://doi.org/10.1016/j.jesp.2006.10.014
42. Albert Rothenberg. 1979. *The emerging goddess: The creative process in art, science, and other fields*. University of Chicago Press Chicago.
43. Pao Siangliulue, Kenneth C. Arnold, Krzysztof Z. Gajos, and Steven P. Dow. 2015. Toward Collaborative Ideation at Scale: Leveraging Ideas from Others to Generate More Creative and Diverse Ideas. In *Proceedings of the ACM Conference on Computer Supported Cooperative Work & Social Computing*. https://doi.org/10.1145/2675133.2675239
44. Pao Siangliulue, Joel Chan, Steven P. Dow, and Krzysztof Z. Gajos. 2016. IdeaHound: Improving Large-scale Collaborative Ideation with Crowd-powered Real-time Semantic Modeling. In *Proceedings of 2016 ACM Conference on User Interface Software and Technology (UIST 2016)*.
45. Pao Siangliulue, Joel Chan, Krzysztof Gajos, and Steven P. Dow. 2015. Providing timely examples improves the quantity and quality of generated ideas. In *Proceedings of the ACM Conference on Creativity and Cognition*. https://doi.org/10.1145/2757226.2757230
46. Erin Treacy Solovey, Francine Lalooses, Krysta Chauncey, Douglas Weaver, Margarita Parasi, Matthias Scheutz, Angelo Sassaroli, Sergio Fantini, Paul Schermerhorn, Audrey Girouard, and Robert J.K. Jacob. 2011. Sensing Cognitive Multitasking for a Brain-based Adaptive User Interface. In *Proceedings of the SIGCHI Conference on Human Factors in Computing Systems* (CHI '11), 383–392. https://doi.org/10.1145/1978942.1978997
47. Erin Treacy Solovey, Daniel Afergan, Evan M. Peck, Samuel W. Hincks, and Robert J. K. Jacob. 2015. Designing Implicit Interfaces for Physiological Computing: Guidelines and Lessons Learned Using fNIRS. *ACM Trans. Comput.-Hum. Interact.* 21, 6: 35:1–35:27. https://doi.org/10.1145/2687926
48. Ian Tseng, Jarrod Moss, Jonathan Cagan, and Kenneth Kotovsky. 2008. The role of timing and analogical similarity in the stimulation of idea generation in design. *Design Studies* 29, 3: 203–221.
49. Arno Villringer and Britton Chance. 1997. Non-invasive optical spectroscopy and imaging of human brain function. *Trends in Neurosciences* 20, 10: 435–442. https://doi.org/10.1016/S0166-2236(97)01132-6

50. Thomas B. Ward. 1998. Analogical distance and purpose in creative thought: Mental leaps versus mental hops. In *Advances in Analogy Research: Integration of Theory and Data from the Cognitive, Computational, and Neural Sciences*, Keith J. Holyoak, Dedre Gentner and B. Kokinov (eds.). Sofia, Bulgaria, 221–230.
51. R. W. Weisberg. 2009. On "out-of-the-box" thinking in creativity. In *Tools for innovation*, A. B. Markman and K. L. Wood (eds.). New York, NY, 23–47.

Crowdboard: Augmenting In-Person Idea Generation with Real-Time Crowds

Salvatore Andolina[1], Hendrik Schneider[2,3], Joel Chan[4], Khalil Klouche[2]
Giulio Jacucci[1,2], Steven Dow[5]
[1]Helsinki Institute for Information Technology HIIT,
Department of Computer Science, Aalto University, Finland
[2]Helsinki Institute for Information Technology HIIT,
Department of Computer Science, University of Helsinki, Finland
[3]University of Göttingen, Göttingen, Germany
[4]HCII, Carnegie Mellon University, Pittsburgh, PA, United States
[5]Cognitive Science Department, UC San Diego, La Jolla, CA, United States

ABSTRACT
Online crowds can help infuse creativity into the design process, but traditional strategies for leveraging them, such as large-scale ideation platforms, require time and organizational effort in order to obtain results. We propose a new method for crowd-based ideation that simplifies the process by having smaller crowds join in-person ideators during synchronous creative sessions. Our system Crowdboard allows online crowds to provide real-time creative input during early-stage design activities, such as brainstorming or concept mapping. The system enables in-person ideators to develop ideas on a physical or digital whiteboard which is augmented with real-time creative input from online participants who see and hear a live broadcast of the meeting. We validate Crowdboard via two user studies in which dyads of in-person ideators brainstormed with the help of crowd ideators. Our studies suggest that Crowdboard can effectively enhance ongoing brainstorming sessions, but also revealed key challenges for how to better facilitate interactions among in-person and crowd ideators.

ACM Classification Keywords
H.5.m. Information Interfaces and Presentation (e.g. HCI): Miscellaneous

Author Keywords
Creativity Support Tools; Brainstorming; Crowdsourcing.

INTRODUCTION
Creativity is a social process. Contrary to the "lone genius" myth, recent studies point out that innovation is more likely to arise through combinations of ideas from collaborating individuals with a diverse set of viewpoints and experiences [26, 35, 39]. Based on this consideration, researchers have recently investigated a variety of techniques for crowd-based ideation [4, 9, 10, 41]. A number of large-scale ideation platforms have been developed to create spaces where people contribute ideas to help solve challenging problems. The guiding principle is to build up a large pool of ideas from which a few good-quality ideas can be extracted. This asynchronous large-scale approach to crowd-aided ideation has some limitations, however. For example the quality of individual ideas is generally poor [13]. Many obvious ideas are also proposed multiple times, due to the lack of coordination among crowd members [33]. Furthermore, a great amount of time is required to select the best ideas [37].

Figure 1. Crowdboard 2.0 (studio interface). In-person ideators write or sketch ideas on virtual sticky notes and get real-time creative input on their ideas from crowd workers who see their activity and who contribute to the creative discussion. Crowd workers can add their ideas either to chats attached to specific notes or to a general chat.

In-person ideators who may want to leverage the crowd to boost an early-stage idea would be subject to these and other limitations. In particular, they would need a great amount of

C&C '17, June 27–30, 2017, Singapore, Singapore

ACM 978-1-4503-4403-6/17/06...$15.00
DOI: http://dx.doi.org/10.1145/3059454.3059477

time to collect and filter the crowd-generated ideas, before iterating on them. Also, the asynchronous large-scale innovation format does not allow interaction between crowds and those who proposed the creative topic. Because of this, the conversation cannot be shaped by new perspectives opened by idea submissions that have already been collected, and important opportunities may be missed. Although researchers have explored various strategies to address the quality problem and to help crowds produce better ideas in a more efficient way [11, 33, 41], the issues caused by the lack of interaction between crowds and in-person ideators still persist. In this work, we explore this design opportunity and propose a different crowd-based ideation paradigm in which in-person and crowd ideators work together in real-time.

We develop a method by which *in-person ideators can elicit synchronous creative input from dozens of nonexpert crowd workers who are recruited on-the-fly* to help the ideators generate solutions to challenging problems. The proposed approach may benefit both in-person and crowd ideators. The crowd's creative and diverse input would help in-person ideators to avoid missing important opportunities in early design stages where the cost of a large deviation from an initial idea is not prohibitive. One promising strategy for team support during brainstorming is to provide different sources of inspiration through context-aware provocative stimuli [3, 38]. Nonexpert crowds could provide a more effective source of inspiration through a better-contextualized and more creative input. Furthermore, crowds could be able to contribute to the discussion with original ideas. In-person ideators would lead the conversation and act as facilitators, which might help crowds generate more high-quality ideas [11]. Cognitive theories of idea generation suggest that the active exchange of knowledge could be beneficial as it causes mutual stimulation of associations [32]. However actions need to be taken to mitigate the effect of negative social processes [12]. In this context the risk of evaluation apprehension may be lower since designers and online crowd worker are less likely to know each other.

In this work we make the following contributions:

1) We develop a method for ideation in which colocated ideators brainstorm together with dozens of nonexpert crowd workers who are recruited on the fly. We embody this idea in the Crowdboard system, a (physical or digital) whiteboard that allows online crowds to see and hear an ongoing brainstorming session and to contribute by sending ideas or inspirations to the workspace that the crowd shares with the people hosting the discussion. We describe the iterative design process of Crowdboard.

2) We describe two laboratory experiments to understand how real-time input from nonexpert crowds can support in-person ideators. In Study 1 we informally investigate the feasibility of the Crowdboard idea for supporting early stage design sessions in real-time. We learned that crowd members can understand the conversation and successfully provide their creative input and that in-person ideators value real-time crowd input and incorporate it into their discussions. In Study 2 we go a step further by investigating whether real-time input from nonexpert crowds leads to improved brainstorming productivity/outcomes. Our results showed that participants generate more creative ideas over time using Crowdboard compared to using the whiteboard without a crowd.

BACKGROUND

Crowdsourcing in the design process

Many have explore the potential of using online crowds to help solve complex [7] and creative problems [21, 22, 24]. For example, Dow et al. [13], explored the use of crowdsourcing in the classroom to contribute at different stages of the innovation process, such as needfinding, ideating, testing, and pitching. CrowdCrit [28] leveraged paid crowdsourcing to generate and visualize high-quality visual design critique. Voyant gave users access to a nonexpert crowd to receive structured feedback on the perceptions of their designs from a selected audience [40]. Crowd vs. Crowd (CvC) [31] used competitions between crowd teams, led by a designer, to crowdsource the entire design process. One limitation of these systems was that they focused on asynchronous interactions and highly structured, iterative, tasks. Other approaches [25] leveraged real-time crowd workers for creating prototypes, but were limited by the lack of communication among involved parties. In contrast in this paper, we explore how creative idea generation tasks can be accomplished in-real time by collaborating teams of in-person and crowd ideators.

Supporting effective idea generation

In-person brainstorming [30] is a popular technique for collaborative idea generation in organizations. A popular practice in brainstorming is to write ideas on sticky notes and apply them on large surfaces such as walls or whiteboards. The contents on the walls can then be easily rearranged, regrouped or replaced as needed. However physical tools have their limitations. For example it is difficult to update physical notes, to keep track of different workspace modifications, and to transfer content to permanent storage for later analysis. To overcome the limitations of physical tools while providing the advantages of large surfaces, many computer-based interventions for brainstorming (and creative collaboration in general) have explored the use of digital whiteboard and tabletop systems [15, 16, 17, 18, 23]. Those systems allow fluid collaboration among ideators and easy interaction with generated ideas, but they often provide little support for cognitive stimulation. Our work extends prior work on digital whiteboard systems by augmenting the workspace used by in-person ideators with novel inspirations and ideas that are generated in real-time by nonexpert crowds who are recruited on-the-fly.

Other computer-mediated interventions provide users with context-aware stimuli to help spark novel associations. For example Idea Expander supports group brainstorming by intelligently selecting pictorial stimuli based on the group's conversation [38]. Similarly InspirationWall [3] uses automatic speech recognition to monitor users' discussions and automatically suggests keywords to support idea generation. Although those approaches attempt to intelligently provide inspirations based on the topic currently being discussed, automated methods have limited intelligence. In contrast, with Crowdboard we leverage the collective intelligence of real people (who listen to the discussion and contribute with context-aware and creative input) by bringing a level of personalization, improvisation, and even playfulness that is still out of reach for even the best automatic approaches.

Leveraging crowds for ideation

The idea to leverage the wisdom of the crowd [36] in idea generation is not new. The typical approach is to maximize the quantity of generated ideas and to then select a few quality ones [9]. However the quality of individual ideas is generally poor and the selection of the best ones is very costly. For example, for its "10 to the 100th" project, Google had to recruit around 3000 employees for the selection process, pushing the project more than 9 months behind schedule [37]. Those limitations raise doubts about the efficiency of the approach and have prompted researchers to find ways to improve the quality of crowd-generated ideas. IdeaHound intervened by helping crowds find inspirational ideas from a large pool of ideas [33]. Yu et al. [42] used nonexperts to identify distant domains that have the potential to yield useful and non-obvious inspirations for solutions. Those domains are then used to find inspirational examples that can be adapted to solve the original problem. Chan et al. used abstracted solution paths to inspire crowds and studied how various sense-making approaches affect crowd ideation [10]. With IdeaGens experts monitored incoming ideas through a dashboard and offered high-level inspirations to guide ideation. Controlled experiments showed that experienced facilitators increase the quantity and creativity of workers' ideas more so than unfacilitated workers do [11].

In our work, we abandon the asynchronous large-scale ideation paradigm and the quantity-over-quality approach. We involve smaller crowds but aim to maximize quality rather than quantity by leveraging real-time collaboration. One of the main interventions proposed in this work is to virtually bring crowds into the design studio, and have them join the team of in-person ideators. Unlike other approaches that have a separation between crowd and in-person ideators (who can only interact offline), Crowdboard allows for the active exchange of ideas between parties, during a synchronous idea generation session. Crowd and in-person ideators have complementary strengths. A beneficial attribute of the crowd is the diversity of its expertise and ideas. Providing diverse ideas could inspire the in-person ideators. The crowd also brings the perspective of "outsiders" (not fixated on what has already been done), which complements the in-person group's context. On the other hand in-person ideators can benefit from face-to-face interactions and more sophisticated tools. They can also lead the discussion, which can improve crowd performance [27]. To our knowledge Crowdboard is the first system that combines those complementary strengths by having crowd and in-person ideators joining forces in the same synchronous creative session. However, synchronous interactions bring their own challenges: in in-person brainstorming, various social processes (such as production blocking, evaluation apprehension, social loafing) can lead to significant productivity losses [12, 43]. While electronic brainstorming systems have mitigated some of these concerns (e.g., reducing production blocking with parallel idea entry [43]), these systems have much smaller group sizes (on the order of 10 or so members), who are typically either all in the same room or remote, and typically homogeneous in terms of level of expertise, compared to our envisioned hybrid in-person and crowd teams. The increased team size, heterogeneous expertise, and hybrid in-person/remote dynamics yield unique challenges which we address in our iterative design work.

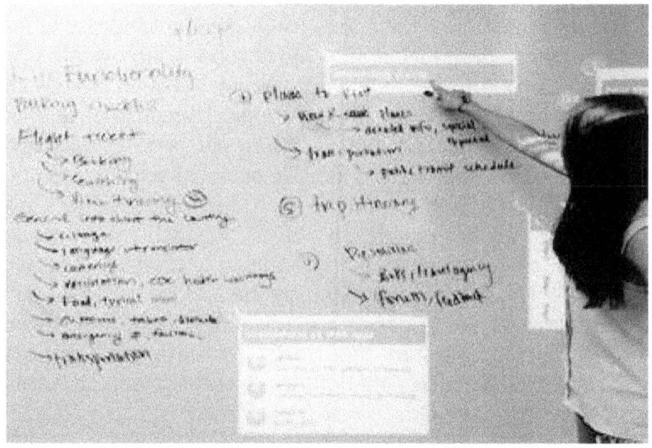

Figure 2. CrowdBoard 1.0 (studio interface). A physical whiteboard is augmented with crowd ideators' comments projected onto the physical board.

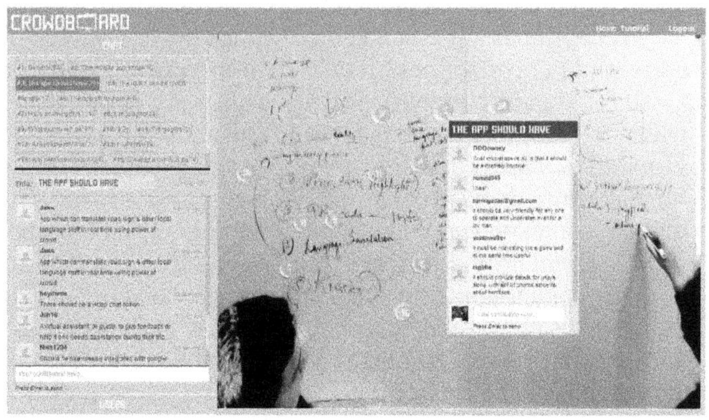

Figure 3. CrowdBoard 1.0 (web interface). Crowd ideators see a list of design conversations (upper left) and the whiteboard activity (right). They can leave comments that, in turn, are projected onto the physical board.

CROWDBOARD 1.0

Integration with Physical Design Studio

Our first version of Crowdboard allows in-person ideators to leverage creative crowd input while working together in a physical studio. Crowdboard's in-studio components comprise a traditional whiteboard, a webcam, a projector, a Microsoft Kinect, and a laptop. Real-time interaction is supported by a web-server, which is responsible for storing the system state and synchronizing the clients.

When the system is active, the crowd sees a video stream of the whiteboard and hears audio from the designers. In-person ideators draw on the whiteboard with regular markers and interact with the projected crowd comments using touch gestures (Figure 2). The crowd-generated discussions are positioned on the whiteboard in contextually-appropriate locations, allowing the conversations to specifically refer to the content drawn on the board. Each discussion thread displayed on the board has a title and one or more comments from the participants. In-person ideators can expand or collapse the discussions using tap gestures and move them around by tapping and dragging the discussion markers.

Interactions among the crowd workers

Crowd workers interact with the team using the web interface (Figure 3). The right panel contains a synchronously updated view of the studio whiteboard. Workers can create a new discussion thread at a particular position on the board by double-clicking. They can also expand an existing thread and then add to the discussion. The left panel contains a list of the current discussion threads, the controls for the live audio broadcast of the meeting, and a list of other workers.

STUDY 1: CROWDBOARD'S FEASIBILITY

In Study 1 we informally investigate the feasibility of the Crowdboard idea for supporting early stage design sessions in real-time. We aim to understand: 1) whether crowd members understand the conversation and successfully provide creative input; 2) whether teams value this real-time crowd input and incorporate it into their discussions.

Participants

Via social media and the university's behavior research participant pool, we recruited five teams of 2-3 design students (12 total) who had a range of design experience. We also recruited 90 online participants from Mechanical Turk. The online participants were mainly Americans (65%) and Indians (31%), and they ranged from 19 to 68 years old (average: 33); 59% were male, and 39% were female. They represented a wide range of occupations (firemen, librarians, managers, etc.), but a majority were in the IT (24%) or education (13%) fields. We tried two approaches from the literature for recruiting crowds that would be available at a predetermined time. For our first 3 trials, we recruited workers in advance (30,30, and 45 workers, respectively), and we asked them to return at a set time [8]. This yielded 8, 11, and 12 workers, respectively. For our fourth and fifth trials, we began recruiting workers immediately before our task so as to have a larger pool [6], and this resulted in 33 and 26 participants respectively.

Procedure

We conducted two long brainstorming sessions of about 35 minutes each, and three short sessions of 15 minutes each. The design brief asked each team to discuss and create a concept map for the idea of traveling to a foreign country. After each session, we asked both the teams and the crowds to fill out a survey. We also interviewed the in-person ideators to get a better understanding of their thoughts about the experience.

Results

In each session, the teams started discussing the system functionality and the design aspects for the problem in question, and then they started generating a concept map. Meanwhile, crowd workers followed the conversation, and added annotations and comments to the virtual whiteboard. In the design studio, the teams noticed the new annotation icons as they were projected on physical whiteboard, and they saw the issues raised by online participants. The in-person ideators and the crowds continued to work together to fill the whiteboard with comments, ideas, and potential solutions.

Effectiveness of collaboration

We conducted a video analysis of the sessions and coded the following events: 1) An in-person ideator reads a comment aloud; 2) An in-person ideator adds an idea or potential solution to the concept map; and 3) An in-person ideator adds an idea or potential solution to the concept map as a direct consequence of a crowd comment.

The following examples give an idea of how we counted the crowd contributions:

> Crowd participant CP18 comments "I love the idea of turning it into a game". In-person participant P4 then reads that comment aloud and adds "Game" to the concept map.
>
> Crowd participant CP11 comments "You can turn it into a game to collect all the experiences...". P4 reads the comment aloud and adds, "Role Playing scavenger hunt" to the concept map near "Game".

Figure 4 shows the number of crowd contributions that were added to the concept map. We observed that Crowdboard greatly affected the design conversation. In our experiments, on average, 35% of the ideas generated in each session came from crowd input (SD = 11%), a rate of 0.56 ideas per minute (SD = 0.23).

Interviews with the in-person ideators who participated in the longer sessions suggest that they considered the crowd input beneficial. They confirmed that crowd participants helped generate ideas: *"I was relying a lot on the crowd" [P4]*; *"I think the conversation was good... People all had good opinions" [P1]*. In the shorter sessions, however, the in-person and crowd participants generally complained about the lack of time, which suggests that longer sessions are necessary for better discussions. Participants in particular felt overwhelmed by the large number of comments coming in such a short time.

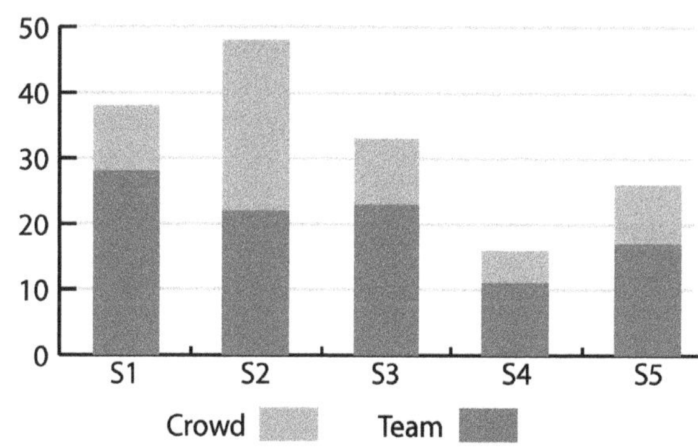

Figure 4. Experiment 1 - CrowdBoard 1.0. Number of ideas an potential solutions added to the concept map. The light blue represents the number of ideas and potential solutions added as a direct consequence of a crowd comment.

Crowd feedback

The post-session surveys asked the crowd members to assess, using a 1–10 scale (with 10 being the best) the extent to which 1) they understood the conversation; 2) they felt the team had acknowledged their input; 3) the team adopted their ideas. The results were 1) $M = 7.84$; $SD = 1.92$; 2) $M = 6.83$; $SD = 2.68$; and 3) $M = 6.53$; $SD = 2.68$; Those results suggest that Crowdboard made the crowd members feel like their voices had been heard.

To get a better understanding of the crowd experience, we conducted a content analysis on the open-ended feedback from the crowd workers and identified 4 main themes. About 36% of workers felt like their voices had been heard, confirming our intuition. The following are examples of comments coded with that theme:

> "It felt rewarding to get feedback and see our ideas being valued as potentially important" [CP16]

> "I enjoyed hearing everyone's opinions and felt like everyone's opinions were valued by those who were hosting the chat..." [CP34]

Another theme that emerged from the analysis was that the system made the crowd workers feel that they were part of the conversation with the in-person ideators. About 70% of the workers mentioned this theme:

> "The session was engaging, I felt the team spirit despite the distance." [CP50]

> "I felt like I was very much a part of the conversation as I saw some of the ideas/suggestions I had being addressed." [CP72]

> "It was like being part of the team." [CP69]

Furthermore, most crowd workers (about 59%) showed enthusiasm about the experience:

> "I really enjoyed the experience...I had fun, and felt as if my time was well spent..." [CP76]

> "I really enjoyed the experiment. I was a little sad when it ended. I felt like I was impacting others in a positive way." [CP15]

> "Best HIT I've done on mTurk. I felt as if I was actually in the room and enjoyed contributing to the conversation." [CP38]

Although crowd workers reported that the general experience was positive, some workers also reported that they did not feel that they had any impact on the conversation because their input was not acknowledged or because they did not manage to provide novel contributions because of the great amount of ideas that other participants had already generated. About 19% of the workers felt overwhelmed by the excessive number of comments.

Discussion

Perception of crowd input

The results from Study 1 suggest that generic crowds can be successfully engaged in synchronous design discussions with local team members. They also suggest that the teams valued the crowds' input, with a large percentage of crowd-generated ideas included in the final mindmap.

Reliability of crowd workers

Though online crowds of workers can often include workers who either intentionally or unintentionally provide problematic input, we observed no clear instances of this. One possible explanation is that this is a result of the visible, synchronous interaction with end users. Additionally, only 20% a workers left the task before it was complete, which is exceptionally low for Mechanical Turk workers given the length of the task. This suggests that Mechanical Turk workers can be reliable for this kind of synchronous experiments.

Design implications

The lessons learned from the study have several design implications:

- *Crowd acknowledgment.* In Study 1 teams that took great care in trying to engage the crowd throughout the entire session, such as by talking with them instead of just talking to each other, had better crowd engagement and participation than the groups that did not do so. This suggests that actions need to be taken to ensure adequate crowd acknowledgment.
- *Limitations of depth-camera sensing.* Lighting conditions can greatly affect the quality of interaction with projected crowd comments. Techniques based on depth-sensing cameras may lack the necessary robustness and could thus lead to poor interaction. Additionally, occlusion problems can occur, making the detection of touch events impossible. In Study 1, we used a "Wizard-Of-Oz" technique to provide smooth interaction with projected elements, as our goal was not to perform a proper test of the system, but rather to investigate the feasibility of the Crowdboard idea. However the touch interaction problem needs to be addressed before systems like Crowdboard can be accepted in the real world.
- *Notifications.* A good notification system is needed to take full advantage of crowd input. In Study 1 the in-person ideators missed many relevant crowd comments. A division of roles between in-person ideators helped mitigate the issue. For example, in the second session one team member decided to continuously monitor the crowd input while the other team member led the discussion and added ideas to the whiteboard. This method helped make the team productive (see Figure 4). However a better notification system is needed. The challenge is making notifications as unobtrusive as possible while maintaining their effectiveness. Using audio or other prominent notifications may be too overwhelming for in-person ideators considering the large amount of events that the system generates.
- *Crowd recruitment, assignment review, and payment.* A time-consuming phase in each Crowdboard session concerns the management of crowd work. To save time and make Crowdboard accessible to users with no experience in crowd management, an integrated system would be needed. This would allow users to manage operations such as recruitment, task review, and payment with just a few clicks from the main interface.
- *Maintaining context consistency.* In Crowdboard 1.0 crowd workers could create new discussion threads at specific X-Y locations on the board so that they could refer to a specific idea. Threads (and associated comments) would in turn be projected in the physical board on the design studio. A limitation of such an approach is that when an idea is

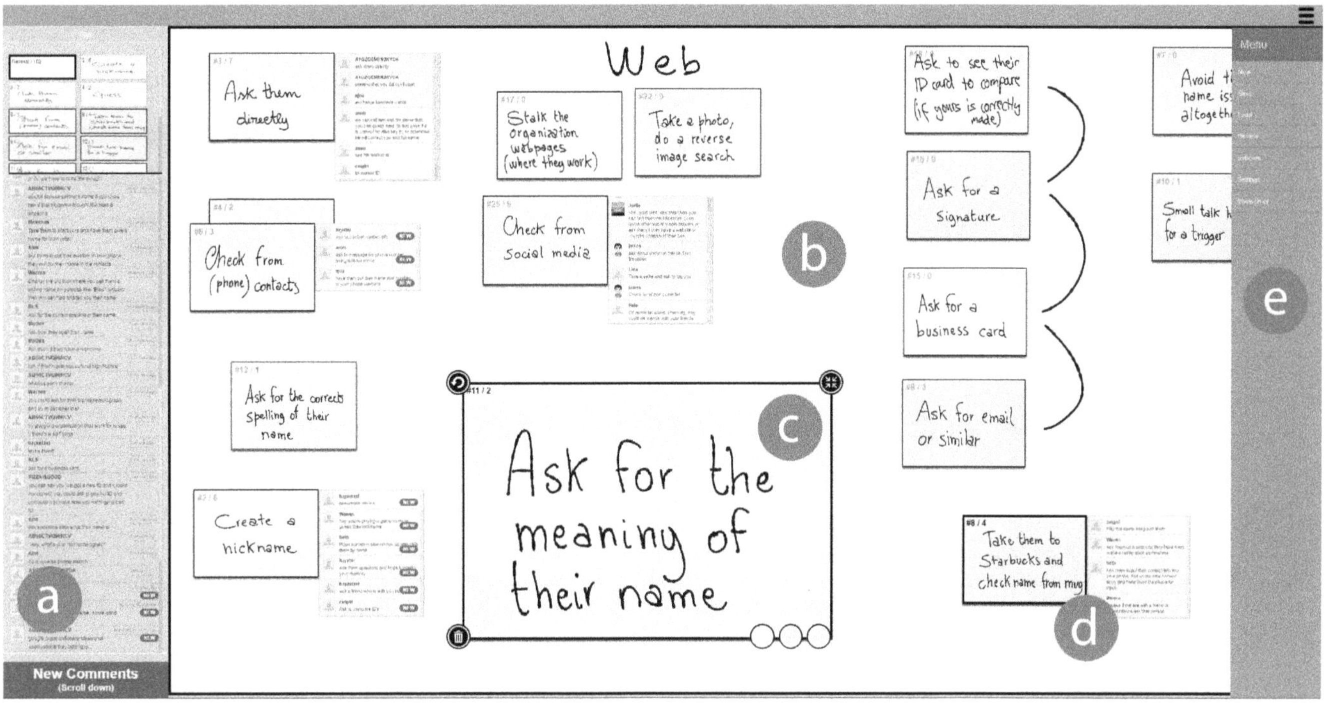

Figure 5. CrowdBoard 2.0 (studio interface). a) Left panel: General chat. b) Main panel: White canvas where users can draw with IR-pens and erase with barcode-based erasers. This area can contain virtual sticky notes, which are created with special barcode-based tools. c) A virtual sticky note in edit mode. d) A virtual sticky note and its associated chat. e) The menu for accessing session- and crowd-management widgets.

erased and added back to another location on the board, the corresponding discussion threads do not follow that action. In such cases the user is responsible for moving the thread accordingly to maintain consistency; this operation can distract from the main task. Future iterations of the interface need to take into account the need to maintain context consistency.

CROWDBOARD 2.0

Based on the lessons learned in Study 1, we decided to iterate and redesign Crowdboard. The goal was to bring Crowdboard to its full potential so that real-time crowds' effects on ideation could be formally studied.

A digital whiteboard with a crowd inside

Taking into account the design implications from Study 1 we decided to develop Crowdboard 2.0 using a big touchscreen composed of three 55" modular MultiTaction Cells [29]. The screen uses a vision-based technology that allows the tracking of unlimited touch points, including hands, fingers, fingertips, 2D barcodes, and IR-pens, via the TUIO protocol [20, 29]. This design choice allows in-person ideators to overcome the limitations of depth-camera sensing. One of the main benefits of Crowdboard 1.0 – the possibility to use traditional tools such as regular markers – is also preserved in Crowdboard 2.0, which provides good approximations of the real tools in IR-pens and barcode-based tools (Figure 6). We designed Crowdboard 2.0 to be a stand-alone system that people with no crowdsourcing experience could use. We used the API from Amazon Mechanical Turk to enable crowd recruitment, assignment reviews, and payment from the main interface.

Studio interface

The studio interface is depicted in Figure 5. The interface is divided into two main areas: the left panel (Figure 5a) and the main panel (Figure 5b).

The main panel is a white canvas where users can freely draw and erase using IR-pens and barcode-based erasers (Figure 6). Special barcode-based tools (Figure 6) allow the ideators to create virtual sticky notes. In normal mode, these notes can be freely moved and arranged on the workspace. Tapping on the bottom-right corner of a note brings up edit mode (Figure 5c). When in this mode, the notes expand to allow for easier handwriting and/or sketching. Buttons on the lower part of the note allow the user to change the background color or delete the note. On the top part of the note, the "undo" button can be used to cancel the last action that occurred on the note, and the "shrink" button can be used to save the note and exit edit mode. When a note is created, a new chat is also generated and attached to that note (Figure 5d). The chat serves as a bucket for crowd ideas and comments that build on what is written on the note. The numbers shown on the top

Figure 6. CrowdBoard 2.0 tools: IR-pens for drawing and barcode-based tools for erasing and creating virtual sticky notes.

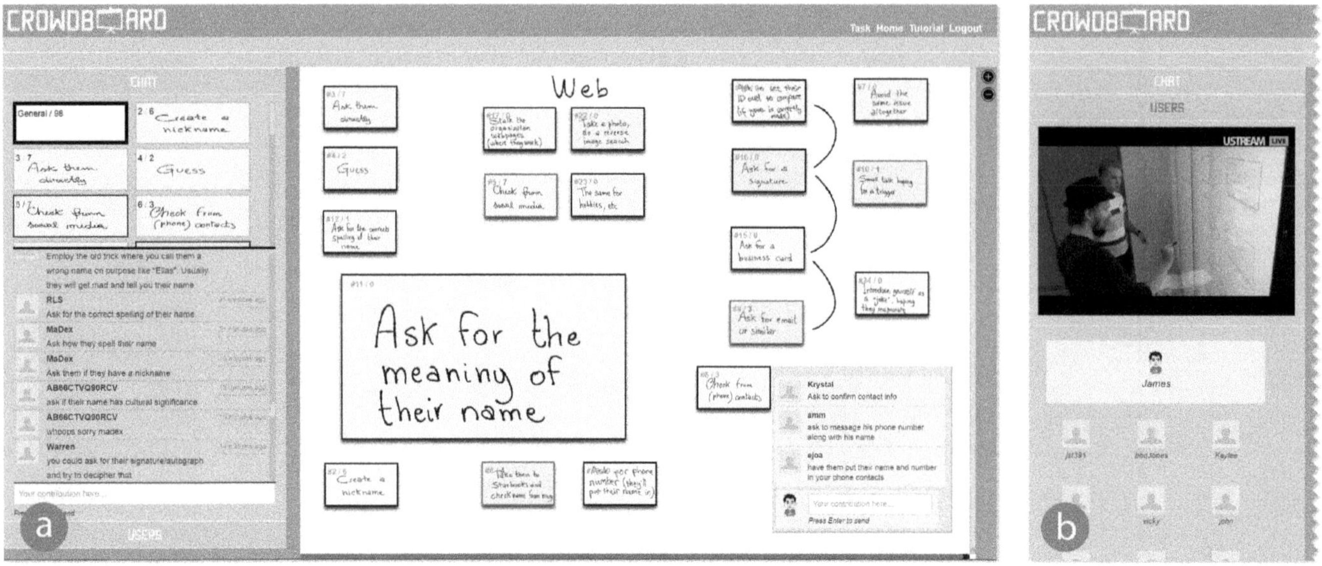

Figure 7. CrowdBoard 2.0 (web interface). a) The main interface. Crowd workers see a list of the design conversations (upper left) and whiteboard activity (right). They can leave comments, which, in turn, are shown on the digital board. b) Users tab. This view shows the live stream of the meeting and the list of crowd workers involved in the discussion.

left corner of a note denote the note's order of creation and the number of comments attached to it. Clicking on those numbers expands or collapses the chat attached to the note. In contrast to Crowdboard 1.0, where crowd workers created discussion threads to refer to specific ideas on the board, in version 2.0, the threads are attached to specific ideas from the moment that the in-person ideators write down those ideas. When ideas are moved on the board, the corresponding comments follow the ideas automatically, unlike in Crowdboard 1.0. This design choice, while helping maintaining consistency, also leads to better organization of ideas and eliminates the problem of duplicate discussion threads that refer to the same ideas.

The left panel (Figure 5a) contains the general chat, where crowd ideators can add comments and ideas that do not relate to anything present on the board. From the left panel, it is also possible to access chats related to specific notes by selecting those notes from the overview at the top of the panel. The panel content automatically switches back to show the general chat after a few seconds of inactivity.

Crowdboard 2.0 includes several improvements to the notifications. When a new comment is added to a note, it is immediately shown on top of that note for a few seconds before fading away. When the new comment is added, the borders of the corresponding note blink in a blue color. The color and thickness of a note's borders indicate its status: Black is the default, blue indicates that it contains unread comments, and thick black means that the note is currently selected. Unread comments, such as those in a long chat that the user needs to scroll to the bottom of, have small badge that says "new" attached. When the comments become visible, the badge fades away after a few seconds.

The button in the top-right corner of the interface gives access to a menu containing the session- and crowd-management widgets (Figure 5e). The crowd-recruitment widget includes a few options, such as specifying the time at which crowds should join a live discussion, the time allotted for the discussion, the number of workers to be recruited, and the money that will be paid to each worker. The crowd-review widget permits users to go through a summary of the contributions that the provided during the discussion and to easily identify possibly problematic crowd workers. The same review widget is used to confirm the payment for the contributing crowd workers.

Web Interface

The Crowdboard 2.0 web interface (Figure 7) reflects the new features introduced in the studio interface. As in the previous version of the system crowd ideators can hear and see the ongoing brainstorming session, which is led by in-person ideators working with the studio interface. The crowd ideators see a synchronously updated view of the workspace, including sketches and virtual notes, and they can contribute by adding comments and ideas to specific notes or to the general chat. The workspace content that is sent to the crowd is scaled to fit various screen sizes. Because the screens of the crowd workers' computers are likely to be smaller than the big screen used in the studio, we added zooming features to the interface. A note can be expanded or collapsed by clicking on it, and the user can zoom in and out the entire workspace using the "+" and "-" buttons on the top right corner of the main panel. Notes in the web interface have the same behavior as those in the studio interface, but they cannot be edited.

STUDY 2: CROWDBOARD'S EFFECT ON IDEATION

We evaluate Crowdboard 2.0 using a quantitative controlled experiment with in-person teams of two people generating ideas either using real-time support from online crowd workers or on their own, without crowd involvement. We hypothesize that Crowdboard will improve teams' creativity by enabling them to sustain higher levels of creative output over time, compared to unaided teams can.

Method

Participants

This study leverages two populations of participants to serve two roles in the study: 1) in-person teams of ideators and 2) crowd ideators. We recruited 40 people (12 females) from the computer science departments of two universities to work in teams of two. The average age of these participants was 27.60 [SD = 5.48]. Each received one movie ticket as compensation for participation. We also recruited 143 workers (40.4% females, mean age = 33.88 [SD = 9.07]) from Mechanical Turk to participate as crowd ideators. The crowd ideators teamed up with the in-persons teams in one of the experimental conditions. Overall, 10 sessions were conducted for the crowd-aided condition yielding an average of 14.3 crowd ideators per session. We limited recruitment to workers who had completed at least 1,000 HITs and who had an approval rate greater than 95%. Crowd workers were paid $3.00 for their participation.

Study Design

The evaluation was conducted as a between-subjects experiment. In each trial, dyads of in-person ideators were randomly assigned to one of two conditions:

1. In the **Crowdboard** condition, in-person ideators generated ideas using the Crowdboard 2.0 studio interface with crowd support;

2. In the **whiteboard only** condition, ideators generated ideas using the Crowdboard 2.0 studio interface, without crowd support;

Brainstorming Prompt

Participants generated ideas for the following problem: *"Imagine you are in a social setting and you've forgotten the name of someone you know. How might you recall their name without directly asking them? Be as specific as possible in your descriptions."* This problem has already been validated in other studies of crowd-based idea generation [11].

Procedure

In-person ideators went through the following procedure. After obtaining the participants' informed consent, the experimenter used the Crowdboard 2.0 studio interface to invite 20 crowd workers to join the brainstorming session, which was to start in 20 minutes from that moment. The experimenter then explained the overall task and handed out instructions for brainstorming and a modified version of Osborn's [30] brainstorming rules: 1) criticism is ruled out; 2) freewheeling is welcomed; 3) quantity is wanted; 4) combination and improvements are sought; and 5) users stay focused on the task. Drawing on the lessons learned from Study 1 we also provided the instruction to remember to acknowledge the crowd.

In-person ideators then went through a training session with simulated crowd input. After this, they performed a warm-up brainstorming session on "alternative uses for a pencil." Then, the experimenters showed the participants the brainstorming topic and allowed for a couple of minutes of individual reflection. After that, the experimenters used the "Go live" function of Crowdboard 2.0 to start streaming the conversation to the crowd. When the session was over, the experimenters stopped the live stream and asked the in-person participants to fill out a survey. After completing the survey, the experimenters asked the participants to read the list of crowd contributions and mark which ones represented valid ideas (rather than just comments). For the contributions marked as valid ideas, the participants also marked whether 1) they saw it; 2) they used it; and 3) it was (or would have been) somewhat useful to see it.

Crowd ideators went through a different procedure. Once launched into Crowdboard from Mechanical Turk, the crowd ideators provided informed consent. The ideators then watched a video tutorial, including instructions about the roles of both general chat and sticky note-related chats (see Figure 5a and Figure 5d). After completing the tutorial, the ideators waited for the brainstorming session to begin at the scheduled time. In the meantime, they were allowed to perform other tasks. At the scheduled time, the crowd ideators were automatically presented with the brainstorming topic. At the same moment they started hearing and seeing the in-person ideators working on the studio interface. After 20 minutes the session was over and the crowd ideators were automatically directed to a short survey with questions about demographic information and their experiences during the brainstorming session.

Dependent Measures

Novelty

Novelty was conceptualized as the degree to which an idea surprised a judge. We recruited 15 workers from Amazon MTurk to rate the ideas. Each worker rated a set of 70 ideas, and 3 raters judged each idea. Inter-rater reliability was substantial, ICC(2,3) = 0.68.

Value

Value was conceptualized as the estimated likelihood that the idea would work if that it were actually implemented. Each worker who rated novelty also rated value for the same set of ideas. Inter-rater reliability was acceptable, ICC(2,3) = 0.57.

Creativity

Following prior theoretical and empirical work [11, 34], we operationalized *creativity* as the product of novelty and value. This captures the intuition that creative ideas should be high on *both* novelty and value.

Results

The in-person ideators across both conditions generated 325 ideas (with 22 invalid ideas removed), 173 in the Crowdboard condition ($M = 17.3$ per session, $SD = 7.36$), and 152 in the control condition ($M = 15.2$ per session, $SD = 3.27$). In the Crowdboard condition, crowd ideators sent 783 contributions ($M = 78.3$ per session, $SD = 24.1$), 530 of which ($M = 53.0$ per session, $SD = 19.1$) the in-person ideators rated as valid; this corresponds to 68% of all contributions. Table 1 shows descriptive statistics regarding the Crowdboard condition (averaged across sessions). Out of an average of 53 valid ideas, 29.7 were attached to sticky note chats (SNC) and 23.3 were posted to the general chat (GC). According to the post-study questionnaire results, in-person ideators noticed 74% of all

Table 1. Crowd-generated contributions. SNC = Sticky Note Chats; GC = General Chat

	SNC		GC		Total	
	M	**SD**	**M**	**SD**	**M**	**SD**
Contributions	45.5	16.2	32.8	16.6	78.3	24.1
Ideas	29.7	9.1	23.3	15.6	53.0	19.1
Seen	25.8 (87%)	8.5	13.6 (58%)	9.6	39.4 (74%)	12.8
Useful	22.9 (77%)	10.7	16.9 (73%)	9.8	39.8 (75%)	15.1
Used	9.6 (32%)	6.6	8.2 (35%)	5.8	17.8 (34%)	9.8
Useful not seen	2.5 (11%)	3.6	5.8 (34%)	6.6	8.3 (21%)	9.6

ideas posted on the board, including 87% of SNC ideas and 58% of GC ideas. Additionally 75% of all ideas were rated as useful. Of those, 21% were not noticed (11% of SNC and 34% of GC).

To investigate the impact that Crowdboard had on the groups' ideations, we estimate a series of linear mixed effects models for each dependent measure, with random effects of session (to account for nonindependence of ideas within sessions). The idea is the unit of analysis. Our baseline models only have a fixed effect of time in addition to the random effects, to capture the known effect that ideas tend to get better over time during brainstorming [5]. We then test Crowdboard by adding a fixed effect of condition (Crowdboard vs. baseline) to the model. We test for significance of the Crowdboard intervention in two ways. First, since recent work [1] has shown that testing for significance of a single fixed effect in a model is only reliable for very large datasets, we use a Likelihood ratio test, where we compare a more complex model (with the fixed effect added) to a baseline model (without the fixed effect) and test determine whether there is a statistically significant improvement in model fit to the data (which is measured by the degree to which the model deviates from the data; lower is better). Second, to guard against overfitting, we test whether the improved fit comes at the cost of unnecessarily increased model complexity (which might indicate overfitting, and consequently, poor generalizability of the model); to accomplish this, we compare models in terms of their Akaike Information Criterion (AIC [2]), which adds a penalty for the number of parameters (essentially penalizing complex models) to the estimated model fit. All models are estimated in R, using the `glmer` function in the `lme4` package.

Novelty

Model #1 has *Time* as the only fixed effect. This model yields a statistically significant gain in model fit over the null model, Likelihood ratio $\chi^2(1) = 24.54$, $p < .001$, and a reduction in Akaike Information Criterion (AIC) (from 1104.1 to 1081.6), indicating that this model is a better fit to the data (without overfitting). In this model, Time is a significant positive predictor of novelty, such that each additional minute yields an expected increase in idea novelty of 0.06 points, 95% $CI = [0.04, 0.08]$, $p < .001$. In other words, ideas get more novel over time (consistent with the serial order effect in prior literature [5]).

In model #2, we add the hypothesized *condition* × *time* interaction as a fixed effect. This model does not yield a statistically significant gain in model fit over model #1, Likelihood ratio $\chi^2(1) = 0.35$, $p = .56$, and an increase in AIC (from 1081.6 to 1083.2), indicating that this model is a poorer fit to the data than model #1 . Thus, we conclude that novelty increases over time, but Crowdboard does not influence this trajectory .

Value

Model #1 has *Time* as the only fixed effect. This model yields a statistically significant gain in model fit over the null model, Likelihood ratio $\chi^2(1) = 12.48$, $p < .001$, and a reduction in AIC (from 1087.0 to 1076.5), indicating that this model is a better fit to the data (without overfitting). In this model, Time is a significant negative predictor of value, such that each additional minute yields an expected decrease in idea value of 0.04 points, 95% $CI = [-0.07, -0.02]$, $p < .001$. In other words, ideas get less valuable over time.

In model #2, we add the hypothesized *condition* × *time* interaction as a fixed effect. This model does not yield a statistically significant gain in model fit over model #1, Likelihood ratio $\chi^2(1) = 2.17$, $p = .14$, although it does yield a slight decrease in AIC (from 1076.5 to 1076.3), suggesting that this model may provide useful information over and above model #1. In this model, the interaction parameter for Crowdboard is positive, suggesting that Crowdboard use might slightly slow the decline of value over time, $B = 0.02$ $[0.01, 0.05]$, but the coefficient for the interaction is not statistically significant, $p = .16$. This result should therefore be interpreted with caution.

Creativity

Table 2 shows the results of the models for creativity. Model #1 has *Time* as the only fixed effect. This model does not yield a statistically significant gain in model fit over the null model, Likelihood ratio $\chi^2(1) = 1.67$, $p = .20$, and an increase in AIC (from 1999.1 to 1999.4), indicating that this model is a better fit to the data (without overfitting). This suggests that, overall, there is not a simple relationship between time and

Table 2. Summary of linear mixed effects models for creativity of ideas. There is no significant main effect of time in session on creativity of ideas, but a significant interaction with experimental condition, such that creativity only increases over time for Crowdboard ideas.

Fixed effects	#1: Time	#2: Add Crowdboard interaction
Intercept	13.21 [11.85, 14.58]	13.23 [11.91, 14.56]
Time	0.06 [-0.03, -0.16] **	-0.02 [-0.15, 0.10] **
Crowdboard × time		0.16 [0.02, 0.30] *
Random effects		
Variance across sessions for intercept	4.07	3.58
Residual	24.98	24.80
Model fit statistics		
Deviance	1099.40	1986.40
AIC	1099.40	1996.40

*p ¡ .05; **p ¡ .01; ***p ¡ .001; 95% CI (Wald) = [lower, upper].

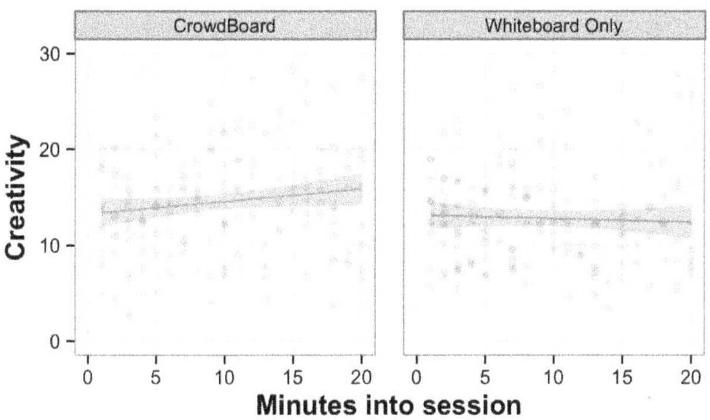

Figure 8. Study 2. Ideas increase in creativity over time, at a higher rate with the Crowdboard condition.

creativity. This is not surprising given the opposing effects of time on novelty and value, and the negative correlation between novelty and value. It stands to reason that, with no other information, we should expect to see no change in creativity over time (as novelty increases but value decreases).

However, model #2, which adds the hypothesized $condition \times time$ interaction as a fixed effect, does yield a significant gain in model fit over the null model, Likelihood ratio $\chi^2(2) = 6.71$, $p < .05$, and a reduction in AIC (from 1999.1 to 1996.4). This model still has no main effect of time, but does have a statistically significant interaction between Crowdboard and time, $B = 0.17$ [0.02, 0.30], $p < .05$. Inspection of Figure 8 provides a qualitative interpretation of this interaction: under normal conditions (Whiteboard only), ideas do not get more creative over time; however, with Crowdboard, ideas *do* get more creative over time.

Discussion

This research provides evidence that real-time crowds can positively affect idea generation sessions by providing a continuous flow of creative ideas that fuels the conversation. With Crowdboard ideas *do* get more creative over time, although the effect is modest in size. One possible explanation is that results from the mutual stimulation of associations caused by the real-time interactions between in-person and crowd ideators. In contrast to other asynchronous approaches, here, people can build on each other's ideas in real-time and engage in stimulating discussions with other participants, all while avoiding the repetition of obvious and mundane ideas.

Though quality control has traditionally been a concern for this kind of high-level creative contribution from a crowd, Crowdboard experiments have shown that senior Mechanical Turk workers may be a reliable source of inspiration. In our studies we saw no clear instance of offensive or otherwise problematic input that required moderation. The reputation mechanism that senior workers use is itself an incentive for good behaviour [19]. Additionally the Mechanica Turk participants considered the task to be engaging and enjoyable—a factor that could have contributed to making them less prone to opportunistic behaviors.

Our experiments point out that the design choice of having SNC could provide some advantages over more traditional chat styles, such as GC. In Study 2. the in-person ideators missed most of the valid ideas that were added to the general chat (only 58% were noticed), but they noticed a good percentage of those attached to sticky notes (87%). Another possible advantage of SNC would be the organization of ideas into logical units. However in Study 2 SNC were not always used as intended. We observed that ideas were not necessarily posted to the most relevant SNC; instead they were often posted to the currently active one or to the most popular one, with the users obviously intending to maximize the chances that the idea would be seen in the shorter amount of time possible. Although this behavior is not necessarily counterproductive—and might have contributed to the better percentage of the ideas being noticed—it may be reasonable to assume that the intended usage of SNC may have been even more advantageous. Future versions of the system should consider the inclusion of measures to address the problem.

Crowdboard is meant to be used as a stand-alone tool that does not require a big organizational effort. For example, it can easily handle crowd recruitment and payment, thanks to the integrated crowd management widgets. However Crowdboard sessions may still require the involvement of a moderator. In our studies the system showed the potential for self-moderation, as most concerns and doubts raised in the general chat were promptly addressed by other crowd participants. Nevertheless moderator's intervention was sometimes needed when off-topic discussions on individual technical issues were causing too much distraction from the main task. Future iterations of the system may include different crowd roles, including moderators, and/or features for self-moderation [14].

CONCLUSIONS

Synchronous interaction among in-person and crowd ideators offers the opportunity to boost early stage design processes without the organizational complexity and time cost of large-scale innovation strategies. This paper presents Crowdboard, a novel whiteboard system that allows a team of in-person ideators to collaborate in real-time with online crowds on creative problems. With two user studies we tested the feasibility of the idea and the effects of real-time crowds on ideation. Results showed that Crowdboard helped participants generate ideas that increased in creativity over time at a higher rate than they did when using the whiteboard without a crowd. While there are still many open challenges regarding real-time interactions among in-person and crowd ideators, our work suggests that this approach could be a fast and effective way to boost early-stage ideation, and provides pointers for future developments of the paradigm.

ACKNOWLEDGMENTS

This research was partially funded by TEKES (Re:Know2) and the National Science Foundation (awards 1122206 and 1122320). We thank Daniel Lee, Peeyush Goyal, Antonio Gentile, and Haakon Faste for their valuable input during the earliest stages of the project, and Walter Lasecki for his valuable feedback on early drafts of the paper.

REFERENCES

1. Alan Agresti. 2007. *An Introduction to Categorical Data Analysis* (2nd ed.). Wiley-Interscience.
2. Hirotogu Akaike. 1998. *Information Theory and an Extension of the Maximum Likelihood Principle*. Springer New York, New York, NY, 199–213. DOI: http://dx.doi.org/10.1007/978-1-4612-1694-0_15
3. Salvatore Andolina, Khalil Klouche, Diogo Cabral, Tuukka Ruotsalo, and Giulio Jacucci. 2015. InspirationWall: Supporting Idea Generation Through Automatic Information Exploration. In *Proceedings of the 2015 ACM SIGCHI Conference on Creativity and Cognition (C&C '15)*. ACM, New York, NY, USA, 103–106. DOI: http://dx.doi.org/10.1145/2757226.2757252
4. Brian P. Bailey and Eric Horvitz. 2010. What's Your Idea?: A Case Study of a Grassroots Innovation Pipeline Within a Large Software Company. In *Proceedings of the SIGCHI Conference on Human Factors in Computing Systems (CHI '10)*. ACM, New York, NY, USA, 2065–2074. DOI: http://dx.doi.org/10.1145/1753326.1753641
5. Roger E. Beaty and Paul J. Silvia. 2012. Why do ideas get more creative across time? An executive interpretation of the serial order effect in divergent thinking tasks. *Psychology of Aesthetics, Creativity, and the Arts* 6, 4 (2012), 309–319. DOI: http://dx.doi.org/10.1037/a0029171
6. Michael S. Bernstein, Joel Brandt, Robert C. Miller, and David R. Karger. 2011. Crowds in Two Seconds: Enabling Realtime Crowd-powered Interfaces. In *Proceedings of the 24th Annual ACM Symposium on User Interface Software and Technology (UIST '11)*. ACM, New York, NY, USA, 33–42. DOI: http://dx.doi.org/10.1145/2047196.2047201
7. Michael S. Bernstein, Greg Little, Robert C. Miller, Björn Hartmann, Mark S. Ackerman, David R. Karger, David Crowell, and Katrina Panovich. 2015. Soylent: A Word Processor with a Crowd Inside. *Commun. ACM* 58, 8 (July 2015), 85–94. DOI: http://dx.doi.org/10.1145/2791285
8. Jeffrey P. Bigham and Walter S. Lasecki. 2014. Crowd Storage: Storing Information on Existing Memories. In *Proceedings of the SIGCHI Conference on Human Factors in Computing Systems (CHI '14)*. ACM, New York, NY, USA, 601–604. DOI: http://dx.doi.org/10.1145/2556288.2557159
9. Kevin J Boudreau and Karim R Lakhani. 2013. Using the crowd as an innovation partner. *Harvard business review* 91, 4 (2013), 60–69.
10. Joel Chan, Steven Dang, and Steven P. Dow. 2016a. Comparing Different Sensemaking Approaches for Large-Scale Ideation. In *Proceedings of the 2016 CHI Conference on Human Factors in Computing Systems (CHI '16)*. ACM, New York, NY, USA, 2717–2728. DOI: http://dx.doi.org/10.1145/2858036.2858178
11. Joel Chan, Steven Dang, and Steven P. Dow. 2016b. Improving Crowd Innovation with Expert Facilitation. In *Proceedings of the 19th ACM Conference on Computer-Supported Cooperative Work & Social Computing (CSCW '16)*. ACM, New York, NY, USA, 1223–1235. DOI: http://dx.doi.org/10.1145/2818048.2820023
12. Michael Diehl and Wolfgang Stroebe. 1987. Productivity loss in brainstorming groups: Toward the solution of a riddle. *Journal of Personality and Social Psychology* (1987), 497–509. DOI: http://dx.doi.org/10.1037/0022-3514.53.3.497
13. Steven Dow, Elizabeth Gerber, and Audris Wong. 2013. A Pilot Study of Using Crowds in the Classroom. In *Proceedings of the SIGCHI Conference on Human Factors in Computing Systems (CHI '13)*. ACM, New York, NY, USA, 227–236. DOI: http://dx.doi.org/10.1145/2470654.2470686
14. Arpita Ghosh, Satyen Kale, and Preston McAfee. 2011. Who Moderates the Moderators?: Crowdsourcing Abuse Detection in User-generated Content. In *Proceedings of the 12th ACM Conference on Electronic Commerce (EC '11)*. ACM, New York, NY, USA, 167–176. DOI: http://dx.doi.org/10.1145/1993574.1993599
15. François Guimbretière, Maureen Stone, and Terry Winograd. 2001. Fluid Interaction with High-resolution Wall-size Displays. In *Proceedings of the 14th Annual ACM Symposium on User Interface Software and Technology (UIST '01)*. ACM, New York, NY, USA, 21–30. DOI: http://dx.doi.org/10.1145/502348.502353
16. Raja Gumienny, Lutz Gericke, Matthias Wenzel, and Christoph Meinel. 2013. Supporting creative collaboration in globally distributed companies. In *Proc. of the 2013 conference on Computer supported cooperative work (CSCW '13)*. ACM, 995–1007. DOI: http://dx.doi.org/10.1145/2441776.2441890
17. Joshua Hailpern, Erik Hinterbichler, Caryn Leppert, Damon Cook, and Brian P. Bailey. 2007. TEAM STORM: Demonstrating an Interaction Model for Working with Multiple Ideas During Creative Group Work. In *Proceedings of the 6th ACM SIGCHI Conference on Creativity & Cognition (C&C '07)*. ACM, New York, NY, USA, 193–202. DOI: http://dx.doi.org/10.1145/1254960.1254987
18. Otmar Hilliges, Lucia Terrenghi, Sebastian Boring, David Kim, Hendrik Richter, and Andreas Butz. 2007. Designing for Collaborative Creative Problem Solving. In *Proceedings of the 6th ACM SIGCHI Conference on Creativity & Cognition (C&C '07)*. ACM, New York, NY, USA, 137–146. DOI: http://dx.doi.org/10.1145/1254960.1254980
19. Audun Jsang, Roslan Ismail, and Colin Boyd. 2007. A survey of trust and reputation systems for online service provision. *Decision Support Systems* 43, 2 (2007), 618 – 644. DOI: http://dx.doi.org/10.1016/j.dss.2005.05.019

20. Martin Kaltenbrunner, Till Bovermann, Ross Bencina, and Enrico Costanza. 2005. TUIO: A protocol for table-top tangible user interfaces. In *Proc. of the The 6th Int'l Workshop on Gesture in Human-Computer Interaction and Simulation*. 1–5.

21. Joy Kim, Justin Cheng, and Michael S. Bernstein. 2014. Ensemble: Exploring Complementary Strengths of Leaders and Crowds in Creative Collaboration. In *Proceedings of the 17th ACM Conference on Computer Supported Cooperative Work & Social Computing (CSCW '14)*. ACM, New York, NY, USA, 745–755. DOI: http://dx.doi.org/10.1145/2531602.2531638

22. Aniket Kittur. 2010. Crowdsourcing, Collaboration and Creativity. *XRDS* 17, 2 (Dec. 2010), 22–26. DOI: http://dx.doi.org/10.1145/1869086.1869096

23. Scott R. Klemmer, Mark W. Newman, Ryan Farrell, Mark Bilezikjian, and James A. Landay. 2001. The Designers' Outpost: A Tangible Interface for Collaborative Web Site. In *Proceedings of the 14th Annual ACM Symposium on User Interface Software and Technology (UIST '01)*. ACM, New York, NY, USA, 1–10. DOI:http://dx.doi.org/10.1145/502348.502350

24. Aaron Michael Koblin. 2010. The Johnny Cash Project. (2010). http://www.thejohnnycashproject.com/.

25. Walter S. Lasecki, Juho Kim, Nick Rafter, Onkur Sen, Jeffrey P. Bigham, and Michael S. Bernstein. 2015. Apparition: Crowdsourced User Interfaces That Come to Life As You Sketch Them. In *Proceedings of the 33rd Annual ACM Conference on Human Factors in Computing Systems (CHI '15)*. ACM, New York, NY, USA, 1925–1934. DOI: http://dx.doi.org/10.1145/2702123.2702565

26. William J. Baumol Lu Hong, Scott E. Page. 2004. Groups of Diverse Problem Solvers Can Outperform Groups of High-Ability Problem Solvers. *Proceedings of the National Academy of Sciences of the United States of America* 101, 46 (2004), 16385–16389. http://www.jstor.org/stable/3373827

27. Kurt Luther, Casey Fiesler, and Amy Bruckman. 2013. Redistributing Leadership in Online Creative Collaboration. In *Proceedings of the 2013 Conference on Computer Supported Cooperative Work (CSCW '13)*. ACM, New York, NY, USA, 1007–1022. DOI: http://dx.doi.org/10.1145/2441776.2441891

28. Kurt Luther, Jari-Lee Tolentino, Wei Wu, Amy Pavel, Brian P. Bailey, Maneesh Agrawala, Björn Hartmann, and Steven P. Dow. 2015. Structuring, Aggregating, and Evaluating Crowdsourced Design Critique. In *Proceedings of the 18th ACM Conference on Computer Supported Cooperative Work & Social Computing (CSCW '15)*. ACM, New York, NY, USA, 473–485. DOI: http://dx.doi.org/10.1145/2675133.2675283

29. MultiTaction. 2017. MultiTaction — MT Cell. (2017). Retrieved March 7, 2017 from https://www.multitaction.com/hardware/mt-cell.

30. Alex F Osborn. 1953. Applied imagination. (1953).

31. Cheong Ha Park, KyoungHee Son, Joon Hyub Lee, and Seok-Hyung Bae. 2013. Crowd vs. Crowd: Large-scale Cooperative Design Through Open Team Competition. In *Proceedings of the 2013 Conference on Computer Supported Cooperative Work (CSCW '13)*. ACM, New York, NY, USA, 1275–1284. DOI: http://dx.doi.org/10.1145/2441776.2441920

32. Paul B Paulus and Huei-Chuan Yang. 2000. Idea Generation in Groups: A Basis for Creativity in Organizations. *Organizational Behavior and Human Decision Processes* 82, 1 (2000), 76 – 87. DOI: http://dx.doi.org/10.1006/obhd.2000.2888

33. Pao Siangliulue, Joel Chan, Steven P. Dow, and Krzysztof Z. Gajos. 2016. IdeaHound: Improving Large-scale Collaborative Ideation with Crowd-Powered Real-time Semantic Modeling. In *Proceedings of the 29th Annual Symposium on User Interface Software and Technology (UIST '16)*. ACM, New York, NY, USA, 609–624. DOI: http://dx.doi.org/10.1145/2984511.2984578

34. Dean Keith Simonton. 2016. Defining Creativity: Don't We Also Need to Define What Is Not Creative? *The Journal of Creative Behavior* (Jan. 2016), n/a–n/a. DOI: http://dx.doi.org/10.1002/jocb.137

35. Jasjit Singh and Lee Fleming. 2010. Lone Inventors as Sources of Breakthroughs: Myth or Reality? *Management Science* 56, 1 (2010), 41–56. DOI: http://dx.doi.org/10.1287/mnsc.1090.1072

36. James Surowiecki. 2005. *The wisdom of crowds*. Anchor.

37. Eliot Van Buskirk. 2010. Google Struggles to Give Away $10 Million. (2010). http://www.wired.com/business/2010/06/google-struggles-to-give-away-10-million/all/

38. Hao-Chuan Wang, Dan Cosley, and Susan R. Fussell. 2010. Idea Expander: Supporting Group Brainstorming with Conversationally Triggered Visual Thinking Stimuli. In *Proceedings of the 2010 ACM Conference on Computer Supported Cooperative Work (CSCW '10)*. ACM, New York, NY, USA, 103–106. DOI: http://dx.doi.org/10.1145/1718918.1718938

39. Andy Warr and Eamonn O'Neill. 2005. Understanding Design As a Social Creative Process. In *Proceedings of the 5th Conference on Creativity & Cognition (C&C '05)*. ACM, New York, NY, USA, 118–127. DOI: http://dx.doi.org/10.1145/1056224.1056242

40. Anbang Xu, Shih-Wen Huang, and Brian Bailey. 2014. Voyant: Generating Structured Feedback on Visual Designs Using a Crowd of Non-experts. In *Proceedings of the 17th ACM Conference on Computer Supported Cooperative Work & Social Computing (CSCW '14)*. ACM, New York, NY, USA, 1433–1444. DOI: http://dx.doi.org/10.1145/2531602.2531604

41. Lixiu Yu, Aniket Kittur, and Robert E. Kraut. 2014. Distributed Analogical Idea Generation: Inventing with Crowds. In *Proceedings of the SIGCHI Conference on Human Factors in Computing Systems (CHI '14)*. ACM, New York, NY, USA, 1245–1254. DOI: http://dx.doi.org/10.1145/2556288.2557371

42. Lixiu Yu, Aniket Kittur, and Robert E. Kraut. 2016. Encouraging "Outside- The- Box" Thinking in Crowd Innovation Through Identifying Domains of Expertise. In *Proceedings of the 19th ACM Conference on Computer-Supported Cooperative Work & Social Computing (CSCW '16)*. ACM, New York, NY, USA, 1214–1222. DOI: http://dx.doi.org/10.1145/2818048.2820025

43. M. P. Zanna, J. M. Olson, W. Stroebe, B. A. Nijstad, and E. F. Rietzschel. 2010. Beyond Productivity Loss in Brainstorming Groups: The Evolution of a Question. In *Advances in Experimental Social Psychology*. Vol. 43. San Diego, CA, 157–203.

BlueSky: Crowd-Powered Uniform Sampling of Idea Spaces

Gaoping Huang, Alexander J. Quinn
Purdue University
School of Electrical & Computer Engineering
West Lafayette, Indiana
{huang,aq}@purdue.edu

ABSTRACT
Design contests and group creativity support systems have demonstrated the value of crowds for producing a solution to a design or engineering problem. However, when the goal is not one idea, but many ideas, an uncoordinated crowd effort would likely lead to a set of ideas clustered around those that are easiest to think of. We present *BlueSky*, a crowd-powered system that coordinates microtask workers to enumerate a uniform sample of textual ideas on a given topic. Through the process of soliciting ideas, an ontology is developed, which is used to categorize the ideas in the list. That categorization then reveals combinations of attributes that have not yet been covered. Our evaluation with four list topics compared BlueSky to freeform solicitation of ideas with respect to comprehensiveness (coverage over the entire idea space) and uniformity (mitigating the tendency to emphasize ideas that are easy to think of).

Author Keywords
Human computation; crowdsourcing; innovation; brainstorming

ACM Classification Keywords
H.5.3 Group and Organization Interfaces: Crowdsourcing

INTRODUCTION
With the rise of crowdsourcing came a recognition of its value of a distributed workforce for creative applications [28, 11, 14]. Web sites such as 99designs and InnoCentive have had success engaging crowds on design and engineering problems through design contests. By posting many such contests on one site, would-be contributors can match their individual knowledge and experience with problems to which they are well-suited. With a sufficiently large and diverse set of participants, the strategy can lead to a pool of candidate ideas from which a single winner is chosen.

Design contests—and *idea contests*, in general—depend on chance. Finding a great idea requires that among the people who view the contest, at least one will have just the right combination of inspiration or background knowledge to lead them to a winner [2]. Most other forms of group creativity support tools are also primarily participant-directed, and thus effectively dependent on chance [19]. Moreover, these assume that the motivating goal is to find a *winner*.

This work engages crowds differently, in the form of mechanized labor—or, more aptly, mechanized creativity—to achieve a broader goal: *Enumerate a uniform sample of ideas in an idea space.* For example, a few examples of textual ideas spaces (i.e., ideas expressed as text) are below:

1. The developer of a new virtual reality system wants to understand the full range of possible applications.
2. A political campaign wants to prepare its candidate for the full range of questions that might arise in a debate.
3. A marketing firm wants to test a large and diverse set of text ad blurbs in an online experiment.

A truly exhaustive listing of *all* ideas for such topics would of course be impossible to produce. Many items on such a listing would be deemed duplicate, or at least "equivalent" by any reasonable standard. For example, given the prompt, "Ways to use a brick," the ideas "break a window" and "throw a brick through a glass pane" would probably be deemed equivalent. However, "break a window" and "crack a window" would depend on what one defines as *distinct*. Given such a definition, then a comprehensive *sample* could be achieved.

One possible standard for distinctness is suggested by legal theories of originality in the United States, which demand at least a modicum of creative thought [1]. Purely mechanical transformations of existing knowledge are deemed unoriginal (and thus ineligible for copyright). We take this a step further by requiring that for a new idea to be considered *distinct*, it must add creative value relative to the needs of the requester who solicits the list of ideas.

Even then, there could still be many possible definitions of "distinct" for a given ideation task. The choice depends on the intended purpose of the list. For example, a building supply marketer might treat two ideas as effectively equivalent if they would appeal to the same segment of customers, or are used in a different setting. In contrast, a sculpture artist might differentiate based on the physical characteristics of the brick that are exploited. More concretely, we consider two ideas

C&C '17 June 27-30, 2017, Singapore, Singapore

ISBN 978-1-4503-4403-6/17/06...$15.00
DOI: http://dx.doi.org/10.1145/3059454.3059481

distinct if they differ with respect to any dimension that is deemed important by the requester. For example, "break a window" and "break a vase" differ by the dimension, "target of action" (e.g., window vs. vase).

Ideally, the definition of distinctness would come from the *requester* for whom the list of ideas is being created (e.g., the developer of the virtual reality system). That way, the kinds of variations could be aligned with what they need and value. One could imagine a system in which requesters actively participate, guiding crowd workers toward the avenues of variation that will produce the most value for that requester. However, for this research, we will aim for a process that is as self-contained as possible.

The objective of this work can be now stated as follows:

> *Enumerate a sample of ideas spanning an idea space that are distinct with respect to some set of k dimensions.*

This paper presents BlueSky, a system we developed to demonstrate a novel method for enumerating idea spaces (hereafter referred to as the *BlueSky method*). The inputs consist of a noun phrase describing the list topic (e.g., "political debate questions," "ways to use a brick," etc.), accompanied by a brief explanation of the context, to help workers understand. BlueSky then coordinates workers on Amazon Mechanical Turk (AMT), together with intermittent feedback from the requester, to generate a list of ideas covering every meaningful combination of values on the dimensions.

A *dimension* consists of a label and a set of values that can be used to partition the ideas in a list. Some dimensions are inherently discrete and finite (e.g., "*is destructive*" $\Rightarrow$ {"*yes*", "*no*"}). The others will be clustered into bins or representative values (e.g., "*location*" $\Rightarrow$ {"*indoor*", "*outdoor*", "*underground*", "*outerspace*"}).

Any item in an idea space can be mapped to a set of values for each of the dimensions. Two ideas that map to the same set of values are treated as equivalent. One of the primary goals of BlueSky is *comprehensiveness*: covering every compatible combination of values. The other primary goal is *uniformity*: controlling redundancy so that (ideally) only one idea is acquired for each combination of values. As we will see, perfect uniformity is hard to achieve given the constraints of Amazon Mechanical Turk, the platform which we have used for this research. However, our evaluation demonstrates that BlueSky produces a much more uniform list of ideas (i.e., less redundancy) than freeform solicitation of ideas.

The key contributions can be summarized as follows:

1. We show how *mechanized creativity*—driving the initiative and discovery from the system—can engage the creative intellect of crowd workers with less dependence on chance than unconstrained idea solicitation.
2. BlueSky, a system we developed, applies mechanized creativity to enumerate a comprehensive sample of an idea space efficiently.
3. Our evaluation demonstrates that a uniform and diverse sample can be more efficiently acquired by synthesizing a set of dimensions from an initial batch of unconstrained ideas and using those dimensions to guide further ideation—versus collecting the same number of ideas without constraints.

RELATED WORK

BlueSky builds from prior work in morphological concept generation, creativity support tools and sensemaking with crowds. It also considers some factors that may influence the creativity in the ideation process.

Crowd-powered innovation

Creative tasks can be made less dependent on chance by guiding the process with some element of the idea space. Yu et al. have shown that crowds can find analogies from within a large set of ideas [27], and that such analogies can provide the seed for new and valuable ideas [26]. The type of semantics leveraged are quite different from BlueSky, but both use semantic connections between ideas to enhance the diversity of ideas produced by the crowd ideators.

Dimension-driven ideation

Dimensions and values have been used for ideation of graphical designs, by individuals and crowds. Talton et al. demonstrated one of the first interfaces that allow individual users to explore an idea space by manipulating sliders to control various dimensions [23]. A similar strategy is embodied by Attribit, which also engages workers on Mechanical Turk to help describe relationships between resulting objects (e.g., *"The right part makes the shape look ___ than the left part."*) [4].

Enumeration tasks with crowds

Recent work relating to the enumeration of unbounded sets with crowds has established a foundation for our work [18, 24]. However, enumerating creative idea spaces is fundamentally different from drawing ideas from the Internet at large.

Quasi-comprehensive enumeration of an idea space

A recent effort enumerates ideas for inventions using machine computation. The website's stated goal is *"to algorithmically create and publicly publish all possible new prior art, thereby making the published concepts not patentable"* (`http://allpriorart.com`). Here is an example:

> *"Devices and methods for therapeutic photodynamic modulation of neural function in a human. Product gas*

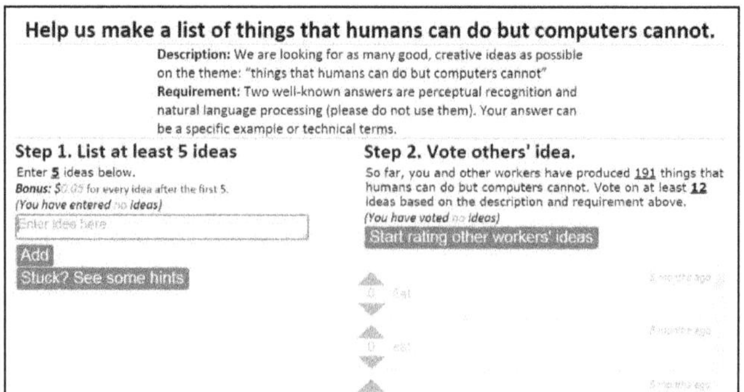

Figure 1. Voluntary hint interface with ideation (left) and voting (right).

in the vapor phase is drawn from the head space above the liquid level and condensed to form the product fuel. The adapter segment is positioned at the first end and is configured to be coupled to another component."

All have been computationally generated using algorithms that are not yet publicly disclosed.

Morphological Concept Generation

Morphological concept generation is a method from engineering design that involves mapping an ideas space in a way that could potentially be used to enumerate the ideas. It generates concepts based on a morphological chart. A morphological chart in essence is a table of *functions* (desired capabilities for the object being designed) and an array of *means* (ways to implement or achieve those capabilities) [20]. The space of possible designs can then be viewed as the combination of available means for each function [21]. Exploring that space of combinations is a popular method of engineering design [17, 9, 7, 25]. Web-based morphological charts have been demonstrated, including support for functional analysis, conception generation, and concept evaluation [12]. Since morphological charts are typically used in a large idea space, they can naturally lead to combinations of features that would make the design impractical or nonsensical. Compatibility matrices can be used to evaluate whether functions can reasonably be combined [8, 17].

BlueSky could, in a very loose sense, be considered an adaptation of the morphological chart method to distributed ideation by crowds. The notions of functions and means are analogous to dimensions and values, though the latter is more broad, since BlueSky and the ideas it embodies, supports other kinds of ideation tasks, as well. BlueSky also automates the process of eliminating incompatible combinations.

Creativity Support Tools

Key ideas from creativity support tools [19] have been applied to crowdsourcing to amplify the potential for creative output. Crowds inherit previous examples and combine atypical features to produce more creative ideas [28, 29]. Challenges, however, stem from the vague requirements for discovery and innovation, as well as from the unorthodox user behaviors and unclear measures of success [19]. BlueSky could gradually unfold the important dimensions that constitute clear constraints and clear measures of success.

Sensemaking with Crowds

Enumeration of ideas can be thought of as exploring an as-yet-unknown information space. In that way, it is closely related to work in sensemaking of existing information sources [16, 6]. Sensemaking is how people construct insights and make use of existing data, especially in quantities that would otherwise overwhelm human working memory. Recently, distributed sensemaking platforms have been developed to leverage the value of crowds, either alone or blended with automated techniques. Crowdlines [15], for example, uses crowdsourcing to synthesize diverse online information to better describe the essential knowledge. Cascade [5] creates taxonomies for user-contributed datasets (e.g., answers to questions) through crowd workers' generation, selection, and categorization.

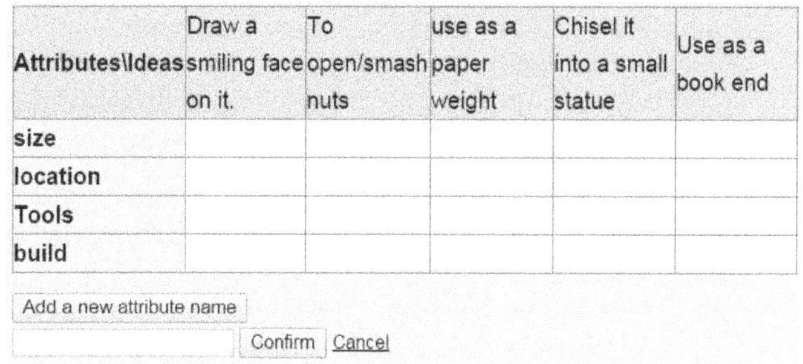

Figure 2. Attribute taxonomy interface. The column headers show the ideas and the row headers show the attributes.

Other approaches have had success combining machine learning algorithms, such as partial clustering, which discovers categories and later classifies data sets [10], and SWIRL (sampling with reduced replacement), which models human list production [13]. Researchers have compared different sensemaking approaches (between human and machine) for large-scale ideation [3].

BlueSky combines the user-generated lists with requester's prior understanding of the idea space to identify the important dimensions. Based on those dimensions, it also has the information about the covering status of the idea space.

INITIAL APPROACHES

The central strategy of BlueSky is to discover the important dimensions and then continue soliciting ideas until all compatible combinations of dimension-values have been covered. However, developing this strategy into a working method and system was an iterative process.

In this section, we detail some of our early approaches. These illustrate the design challenges, which had to be overcome in order to develop our high-level strategy into the eventual BlueSky method and implementation, which will be presented in the following section.

Voluntary Hints Pointing Solution Path

To explore a wider idea space, our first strategy was to let workers ideate and voluntarily share the promising solution paths with future workers (Fig. 1). Participants were asked to enter ideas and rate existing ideas generated by others. While typing, they might see some similar ideas generated by others and be suggested to avoid duplicate ones. Once got stuck, they could click the "See some hints" button to acquire some hints which were shared voluntarily by other participants who had multiple solution paths.

We evaluated it with a specific list topic—"things that humans can do, but computers cannot"—and got 191 ideas from 12 distinct AMT workers. We found that the strategy of voluntary hints suffered from two main problems:

1. **Freeform ideation may lead to many redundant ideas.** Workers received no strict/tight constraint in the whole process of ideation. Instead, they were suggested, not required, to think a different idea once their ideas were duplicated with existing ones. There were only 167 distinct ideas (out of 191 in total) after de-duplication; meanwhile, a lot of

them are similar. For instance, "make food" and "cook" are basically the same; likewise, "play", "play go" and "play sports" are very similar. The possible reason is that workers often think in their familiar ways on the lack of compulsory constraint.

2. **Hoping to obtain hints from workers may be inefficient and infeasible.** During the whole process of ideation, no hint was added by workers. One reason could be that the task was so loosely restricted that workers might feel unnecessary to provide hints for next workers. We further realized that workers would not provide hints even in a tougher task but simply finish the task by their own.

We also observed creativity fixation effects [22]. Therefore, we decided to 1) add *constraints* to achieve less duplication and 2) reduce the exposure of others' ideas in the ideation session (e.g., removing the voting section and auto-suggestion).

Attribute Taxonomy

The second strategy was to create a taxonomy of *attributes* that are contained in most ideas. Figure 2 shows the interface that allows workers to propose new attributes and extract details from ideas for each attribute. After the extraction, workers should merge the details into several values that could form a parent-child relationship with each attribute.

We tested it with four graduate students and one undergraduate student by giving a list of ideas for the topic "ways to use a brick". Under face-to-face environment, they could ask questions if they were confused about the process.

Similar to Cascade [5], we observed that they often gave overly broad attribute names such as "build" or "tools". Besides, the details they extracted were often in different levels of abstraction. Take attribute "build" for example, participants extracted both higher-level details like "something" and lower-level details like "house" and "pond for fish", from the ideas "build a house", "build a pond for fish", and "use to build something". This is because the ideas contained different levels of details. Furthermore, participants had great difficulty in merging those details into values. We thus decided to ask workers to provide values directly, instead of merging from details with unpredictable, different levels.

DEFINITIONS

Before describing the system design, we define some key terms, as they are used in this paper.

A **dimension** (d) is comprised of a finite set of **values** (V). We denote this relationship as $d \Rightarrow V$. Some dimensions are inherently discrete and finite (e.g., *"is destructive"* $\Rightarrow$ {*"yes"*,*"no"*}). For others, the values represent clusters. For example, given the dimension *location*, there could potentially be an infinite number of locations in the universe, but for our purposes, the set of values will always be a finite set (e.g., *"location"* $\Rightarrow$ {*"indoor"*,*"outdoor"*,*"underground"*,*"outerspace"*}).

Together, a set of dimensions form the basis of an **idea space**. As in linear algebra, this basis is not unique.

We use the term *dimension*, not *category*, because a dimension is intended to cover most (or even all) of the ideas (also referred to as *list items*) while a category may only cover partially. Also, in early testing, we found that some people interpret *category* like dimension, while others interpret it like value. The terms dimension and value, while perhaps less intuitive, do not suffer from this ambiguity.

To chart an idea space, the values of a dimension should meet the following criteria as much as possible:

- **Orthogonal** (no overlap between each other). For example, *"occurrence time"* $\Rightarrow$ {*"in January"*,*"in February"*,...} are orthogonal, but {*"in January"*,*"in the spring"*,...} are not, because "January" has overlap with "spring".
- **Evenly-spaced** (nearly the same differences between each other). For example, *"occurrence time"* $\Rightarrow$ {*"in January"*,*"in February"*,*"in March"*, ...} are evenly-spaced, but {*"in January"*,*"in June"*,*"in July"*, ...} are not.
- **Complete** (all representative aspects). For example, *"color"* $\Rightarrow$ {*"red"*, *"green"*, *"blue"*} and {*"cold"*,*"warm"*} are both complete, but {*"red"*,*"green"*} are not.

Idea Space and Cell

In theory, every idea space is charting by an infinite number of dimensions. However, in a practical application, a requester with a specific list topic may only care about a finite representation of the idea space.

Suppose an idea space is represented by n vital dimensions $(d_1, d_2, ..., d_n)$ along with corresponding sets of values $(V_1, V_2, ..., V_n)$ where $d_i \Rightarrow V_i$, then a *cell* of the idea space is a combination of one value from each dimension $\{(v_1, v_2, v_3, ..., v_n) : v_1 \in V_1, v_2 \in V_2, ..., v_n \in V_n\}$. For example, suppose the list topic "ways to a brick" has an idea space of $n = 2$ dimensions: *"is destructive"* $\Rightarrow$ {*"yes"*,*"no"*} (V_1) and *"location"* $\Rightarrow$ {*"indoor"*,...} (V_2), then one of the cells will be {(*"yes"*,*"indoor"*) : *"yes"* $\in V_1$, *"indoor"* $\in V_2$}. By definition, each cell represents a *distinct* idea. Thus the maximum number of distinct ideas is equal to the number of cells:

$$NumberOfDistinctIdeas \leq \prod_{i=1}^{n} ||V_i||$$

, where $||V_i||$ is the number of values for the dimension d_i.

An idea space is *completely covered* when each cell is covered by at least one idea, and *uniformly covered* if the number of ideas covering each cell is roughly the same.

Constraint

An *empty* cell of the idea space means one cell that is not covered by any idea. To cover it, we need to guide participants with *constraints*. It is straight-forward to convert an empty cell $\{(v_1, v_2, v_3, ..., v_n) : v_1 \in V_1, v_2 \in V_2, ..., v_n \in V_n\}$ into a batch of constraints ($C = (c_1, c_2, ..., c_n)$) by replacing v_i with a constraint c_i, where c_i is in the format of "v_i, *and not* $\forall v \in V_i \backslash v_i, --w.r.t\ d_i$". Here, $\forall v \in V_i \backslash v_i$ means every value in the set V_i except v_i. For example, if v_i is a value *"indoor"* from dimension *"location"* $\Rightarrow$ {*"indoor"*,...}, then it will be converted to a constraint *"Indoor, and not outdoor, underground,*

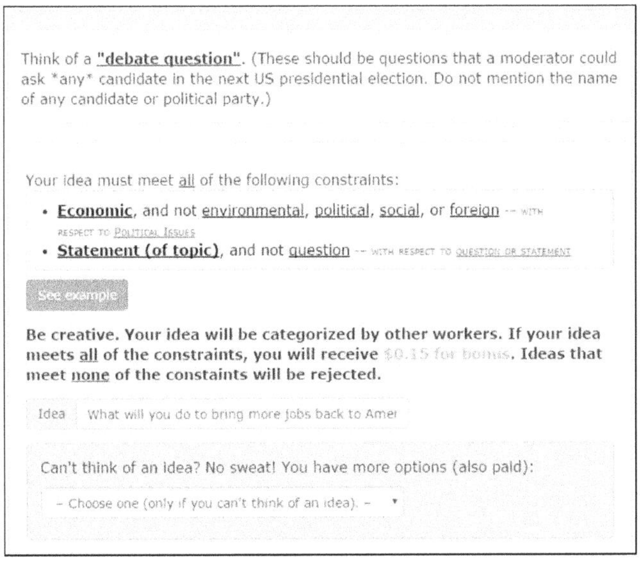

Figure 3. Ideation task interface with constraints

or outerspace – w.r.t location". In particular, for a dimension with Boolean values (e.g. *"is destructive"* ⇒ {*"yes"*, *"no"*}), its values will be converted into human-readable constraints like *"is destructive"* and *"is not destructive"*.

BLUESKY

We now discuss BlueSky (the system) and the algorithms that it uses to coordinate microtask workers to enumerate idea spaces.

BlueSky is implemented as a Python web application that interoperates with Amazon Mechanical Turk by way of the CrowdLib library. A requester enters a list topic as a noun phrase (e.g., "interview questions") accompanied by a brief description of the context (e.g., "Suppose you are the interviewer of an innovative company. . . .).

Algorithm Steps

BlueSky's overall control flow consists of three HITs that are shown to participants. Here are the concrete instances of these HITs—*ideation* (Fig. 3), *synthesis* (Fig. 4), and *map* (Fig. 5). The system runs through a circular way, from ideation to synthesis, to map and then back to ideation.

BlueSky also includes a dashboard to assist requester to monitor the process and prune dimensions of no interest.

We first present an outline of the steps of Bluesky and then describe the steps in full detail.

1) Show list topic, description, and constraints (if any) to participants whom each **ideates** 1 list item based on the constraints (or 2 without constraints), or mark the constraints as N/A (not applicable).
2) Show list items to participants whom each **synthesizes** one dimension and 2-8 values that could be used to categorize the existing and future list items.
3) Show list items and dimensions to participants whom each **maps** the list items to their best fit value of each dimension.

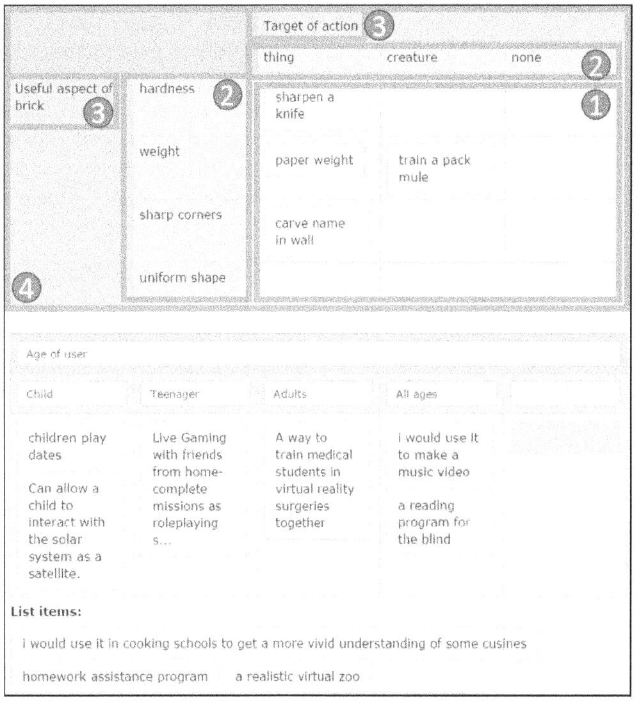

Figure 4. (Top) The tutorial for synthesis with four lessons. Area 1 teaches participants how to categorize ideas by given dimensions and values, while area 3 and 2 teach them how to generate dimensions and values, respectively. Area 4 teaches them how to combine all the skills in the previous lessons. (Bottom) The task interface for synthesis.

4) Compute and generate constraints for empty cells. Repeat the algorithm (from step 1) with these constraints.
5) Prune (by requester) the dimensions of no interest in the dashboard during the whole process.

The algorithm continues until each cell in the idea space is either covered by list items or marked as N/A. Following are the implementation details for each step.

Step 1. Ideation with or without Constraints

This step has two phases, depending on whether participants are shown constraints or not.

Phase 1: The first several ideation HITs have no constraints as we have no inference on the idea space. Participants are asked to enter two ideas freely in each HIT.

Phase 2: After one round, participants will be guided by a batch of constraints that represents an empty cell in the idea space (Fig. 3). As mentioned in *Definitions*, the batch of constraints is denoted by $C = (c_1, c_2, ..., c_n)$. Participants are asked to enter one idea to meet every $c_i \in C$. For example, in Fig. 3, the HIT has a batch of two constraints ($C = (c_1, c_2)$) in which c_2: *"Statement (of topic), and not question – w.r.t question or statement"*. Note that c_2 is converted from a value "$statement\ (of\ topic)$" of dimension "$question\ or\ statement$" ⇒ {"$statement\ (of\ topic)$", "$question$"}.

If participants have difficulty in generating ideas for the given constraints, they have two other options. One is to start over with another batch of constraints (e.g., $C = (c'_1, c'_2, ..., c'_n)$), namely, another empty cell. The other is to mark the current constraints as N/A if they are impossible to generate an idea, which in our case may be caused by incompatible combinations of dimensions or unclear values; meanwhile, participants need to write down the reason. If at least two participants mark the same batch of constraints as N/A, the corresponding cell in the idea space is marked as N/A and will not appear in the future HITs.

Based on the usability feedback of Phase 2, we added several optimizations. First, participants will start with a simpler batch of constraints. Specifically, they will be given a subset of two constraints from the batch C, e.g., $(c_i, c_j) \subset C$, as a stepping stone. After participants have done all the subsets, they will be given the full batch C. A subset contains two constraints because it represents a minimum combination of dimensions and can be used to test compatibility. If a subset is compatible, the ideas generated for it will be used as examples for any batch C containing it (when participants click the button "Show example"). On the other hand, if the subset is incompatible, any batch C containing it will be automatically marked as N/A.

Second, to motivate participants to generate ideas covering all of the constraints in the batch, we provide them a bonus of $0.15 (US dollars) if their ideas are being categorized (in step 3) by the same values as the constraints. The bonus incents them to try hard while leaving us leeway to approve HITs where a worker makes a nominal effort but fails to meet all of the constraints.

Step 2. Synthesize Dimensions and Values

This step needs participants to enter one dimension and 2-8 values. Since the dimensions are fundamental for the idea space, we provided a tutorial with four lessons to explain the concepts of dimensions and values, as shown in the top of Fig. 4. The first lesson (marked by number 1) asks participants to categorize a list of "ways to use a brick" by given dimensions and values. The second lesson (marked by number 2) asks participants to enter values for given dimensions and already categorized list items. Likewise, the next lesson (marked by number 3) lets them enter dimensions for given values and already categorized list items. The last lesson (marked by number 4) wraps up the previous lessons: it first gives several list items (uncategorized) and requires participants to think of dimensions, values and then categorize those items.

We partition the necessary skills—categorization, generating dimensions, and generating values—into the first three lessons so that participants can build up skills gradually. Each lesson has the same list topic but different dimensions, values and list items, which makes the skills more generalizable. Once participants complete any of the first three lessons, their results will be compared with gold standard and prompted with explanation if incorrect. The results of the fourth lesson will be manually checked by a qualified participant who has passed the tutorial.

The task interface is similar to the fourth lesson of the tutorial, except that there is only one dimension (the bottom of Fig. 4). Only those who have passed the tutorial can take this HIT.

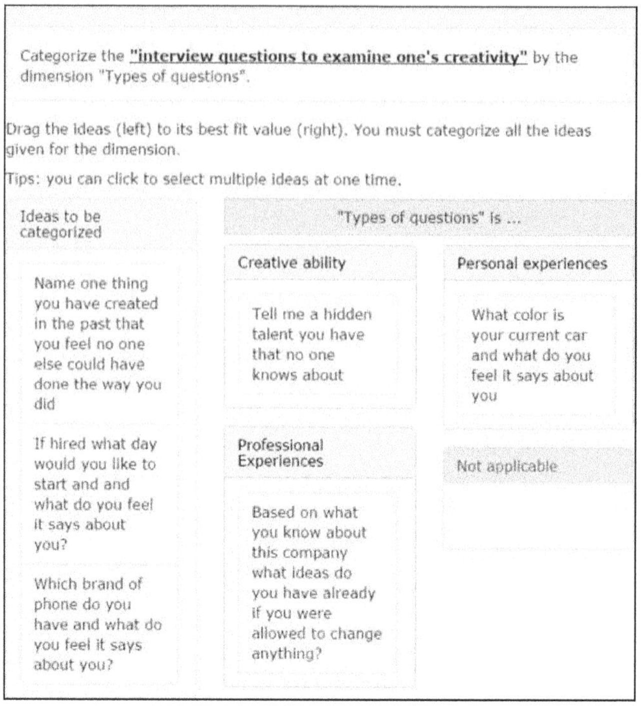

Figure 5. Mapping task interface

Participants can see the tutorial they have done and thus have a strong connection between the tutorial and real task.

This step will be skipped when all of the important dimensions have been figured out. In case of pruning an important dimension by the requester, this HIT will restart after that.

Step 3. Map with Multi-judgment

This step needs participants to map the list items from step 1 to a set of values for each of the dimensions from step 2 (Fig. 5). It is essentially categorization.

Participants will see a *confirmed* dimension and several uncategorized list items (excluding ones that they entered in step 1) in each HIT. *Confirmed* means that the dimension is one of the vital dimensions (dependent on the requester) that could represent the idea space. If dimensions are provided by the requester, they are automatically confirmed. If they are provided by AMT workers, the requester may prune some nonsense dimensions or less interesting ones. In case of absence of the requester, dimensions provided by workers could be confirmed through multiple judgments: workers will see all of the dimensions and select the best one to categorize with; then the dimensions selected by three or more workers are confirmed. In our test, we found that the dimensions selected by three workers were usually selected by a fourth worker, so it is reasonable to ask three workers to perform the multiple judgment. At any point in time, the requester may come in and modify (or even prune) a confirmed dimension to fit their interests.

Similarly, a list item is categorized by a specific value if at least two workers categorize it with the same value. A list item can be categorized by only one value of a dimension, as the values are orthogonal to each other. Participants may also categorize a list item as N/A; if two or more workers categorize an item as N/A, it is marked as N/A for this dimension.

To reduce the number of mapping workers required, we use a simple optimization. For each dimension in the constraint at the ideation step, we count the ideation worker's assertion that the idea conforms the same as if a worker in the mapping step had evaluated it. However, since some contributed ideas do not truly conform to all of the values in the constraints, we still require one judgment from a mapping worker before we consider that cell in the idea space as filled.

Step 4. Idea Space Computation
After categorizing existing list items, BlueSky computes the status of the idea space. It stops running if all of the cells have been covered or marked as N/A, or posts more ideation HITs (step 1) for empty cells. This step is done automatically without participants.

Step 5. Dashboard for Requester
Through the dashboard, a requester can see the whole picture of the idea space, such as the covering status of each cell. Moreover, a requester can prune dimensions that are trivial or unlikely to generate useful ideas, and thus figure out the important ones.

MAIN EXPERIMENTS

To test the performance of BlueSky, we ran the algorithm on four list topics and analyzed the ideas it produced.

Recruitment of Participants

In step 1 and step 3, participants were AMT workers with minimal approval rate of 90%, while in step 2, participants were AMT workers who have passed the tutorial. As mentioned earlier, workers' tutorial results (i.e., the fourth lesson) will be judged by a qualified participant who has passed the tutorial. In this experiment, we asked two graduate students to take the tutorial and then recruited one who passed to judge workers' results. In principle, it is also plausible to let AMT workers be the judge once they have passed the tutorial.

List Topics

We picked four open-ended list topics that belong to different types. Two of them were related to tangible things, such as HoloLens (Microsoft augmented reality devices) and a gadget for finding keys. The others were intangible concepts like interview questions and debate questions. The list topics are summarized in Table 1.

These list topics represented three kinds of user goals in which a user: 1) needs lots of distinct ideas (not necessarily complete), such as mathematical test questions; 2) needs completeness for technical reasons and/or future-proofing, such as test cases for machine learning; or 3) needs inspiration to ultimately find the best idea, such as business names.

Method

For each list topic, we conducted an experiment with two conditions: a *treatment* condition that gave the constraints generated by BlueSky and a *control* condition in which no constraints were given. The list items from the control were categorized by the same dimensions as the treatment condition. Participants were randomly assigned to one group or the other and were prevented from participating in both.

Abbreviation	List topic	Types	Application
use-HoloLens	"ways to use HoloLens"	T	needs lots of distinct list items (not necessarily complete)
interview	"interview questions to examine one's creativity"	IT	needs completeness for technical reasons and/or future-proofing
debate	"debate questions for the US election"	IT	needs completeness for technical reasons and/or future-proofing
textAd	"text ad blurbs for a new gadget for finding lost keys to appear in Google Ads"	T	needs inspiration to ultimately find the best idea

Table 1. Two types (T: tangible, IT: intangible) of list topics with their potential applications.

Results

In phase 1 of step 1, both the treatment and control posted the same number of HITs. However, in phase 2, the treatment HITs were twice as the control because if the constraints were given, workers needed to enter one list item instead of two. Those list items were categorized by the same dimensions. We stopped both the treatment and control groups when the idea space was completely covered or when the coverage remained the same for a long time (e.g., longer than two iterations). Therefore, we ended up with approximately the same number of list items for both conditions. For simplicity, we truncated the list items of two conditions to the same number. The results are shown in Table 2.

useHoloLens produced 309 list items in the treatment condition by 96 workers and 308 items in the control condition by 40 workers. We truncated them into 308 items for simplicity. In both conditions, some list items were literally duplicate, such as "playing video games." Some were phrased differently but had the same meaning, such as "virtual museum tours" and "To give a tour of a museum to people remotely." Some were phrased differently with different meanings, such as "Explore places on Earth where humans can't survive." (*L*1) and "Simulate real world emergencies to respond to" (*L*2).

useHoloLens also produced 16 dimensions based on the list items by 6 workers who have passed the tutorial. In step 3, workers confirmed four dimensions by multi-judgment, such as "Age of user" with 4 values {"child", "teenager", "Adults" and "All ages"}. The other three dimensions had 2, 4, and 4 values, respectively. Thus the maximum number of cells in the idea space was 128; namely, there would be at most 128 distinct list items. In such case, even some items

List topic	# of ideas	# of dimensions (confirmed/total)	# of total cells	Sample dimension&values
useHoloLens	308	4 / 16	128	"*Age of users*" ⇒ {"*child*", ...}
interview	106	3 / 13	36	"*Types of questions*" ⇒ {"*Creative ability*", ...}
debate	136	4 / 16	40	"*Foreign vs. domestic*" ⇒ {"*foreign policy*", ...}
textAd	134	5 / 10	32	"*Mentions keys?*" ⇒ {"*yes*", "*no*"}

Table 2. Results for four list topics (for both BlueSky and control).

phrased differently with different meanings were treated as duplicate if they are categorized by the same value of each dimension. For example, *L1* and *L2* mentioned above were duplicate because they were categorized by the same value of each of four dimensions, such as "*Age of user*" ⇒ "*Adults*".

interview produced 106 list items in treatment and control conditions, such as "What would you do if it would start raining fish?", by 59 and 15 workers, respectively. Eight workers produced 13 dimensions and three dimensions were confirmed, such as "Types of questions" with 3 values {"Creative ability", "Personal experiences", and "Professional experiences"}. The other two dimensions had 3 and 4 values, respectively, charting an idea space of 36 cells.

debate produced 136 list items in treatment and control conditions (after truncation), such as "Will you force all public washrooms to be inclusive to all genders, including transgendered persons?", by 79 and 18 workers, respectively. Seven workers generated 16 dimensions and four dimensions were confirmed, such as "foreign vs domestic issues" with 2 values {"foreign policy", "domestic"}. The other three had 2, 2, and 5 values, respectively, charting an idea space of 40 cells.

textAd produced 134 list items in treatment and control conditions, such as "How rich would you be if you had a dollar for every time you lost your keys?", by 58 and 28 workers, respectively. Three workers produced 10 dimensions in which five were confirmed, such as "Mentions keys?" with 2 values {"yes", "no"}. The other four dimensions all had 2 values, charting an idea space of 32 cells.

The size of the idea spaces is determined not by the topic, but by the chosen dimensions and values. Workers decide how many values to partition each dimension by. Requesters control which dimensions to accept. Together, they determine the number of cells into which the idea space is partitioned.

Time and Cost

Step 1 was paid $0.25 per HIT while step 3 was paid $0.30 per HIT. After the system stopped, the average cost per list item under the treatment condition was $0.56, $0.58, $0.53, and $0.55 for useHoloLens, interview, debate and textAd, respectively. Correspondingly, for the control, the average cost per list item was $0.44, $0.33, $0.31, and $0.39. The control group was slightly cheaper than the treatment because each control ideation HIT got twice ideas as the treatment with the same amount of payment.

Under the treatment condition, participants spent a combined total of 17 hours 9 minutes, 5 hours 31 minutes, 6 hours 49 minutes, and 7 hours 10 minutes for useHoloLens, interview, debate and textAd, respectively. Correspondingly, for the control, the combined work time was 7 hours 37 minutes, 2 hours

List topic	Group	Efficiency	# covered		# of entries
use-HoloLens	BlueSky	**36%** =	111	÷	308
	control	19% =	59	÷	308
interview	BlueSky	**34%** =	36	÷	106
	control	28% =	30	÷	106
debate	BlueSky	**26%** =	36	÷	136
	control	12% =	16	÷	136
textAd	BlueSky	**20%** =	27	÷	134
	control	15% =	20	÷	134

Table 3. Efficiency of BlueSky versus the control. Efficiency is defined as the number of distinct ideas ("# covered") divided by the number of idea entries in the ideation stage ("# of entries")

.

13 minutes, 2 hours 11 minutes, and 2 hours 38 minutes, respectively. The control group was faster than the treatment group because workers in the treatment spent more time in ideation to meet the given constraints. Due to the same reason, there were more unique workers in the treatment (73 on average) than in the control (25 on average) where workers were able to add ideas quickly and continuously in multiple HITs.

The average hourly rate for the BlueSky condition was $10.46/hour. For the control, it was $18.07/hour.

Evaluation

The goal of BlueSky is to produce a list of items that completely and uniformly cover the entire idea space. To evaluate it, we ask and answer two key questions:

1. How comprehensively is the idea space covered?
2. How uniformly is the idea space covered?

Comprehensiveness

The systems stopped when the idea spaces of the treatment were covered by 111, 36, 36 and 27 cells for useHoloLens, interview, debate and textAd, respectively (Table 3). It indicates that the topic interview stopped after the idea space was completely covered, while others stopped after the idea space coverage remained the same for three iterations.

We stopped the control once the treatment stopped because it would take lots more time to cover some uncommon cells in the idea space. For instance, useHoloLens had a cell with the combination between "User category ⇒ government" and "Age of user ⇒ child". The treatment succeeded in covering it with creative list items (e.g., "*Children could use this to mimic a court room to learn about the judicial branch.*") while the control did not.

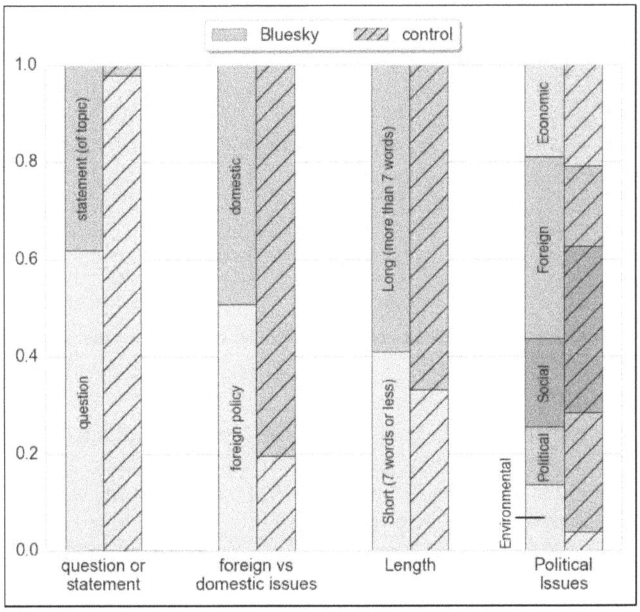

Figure 6. Value density of four dimensions on the list topic debate. The height of each column segment indicates the proportion of the total list items that were categorized with the value shown. If perfect uniformity could be achieved, then all segments within a given column would have equal height. BlueSky (left) is more uniform than the control (right).

Correspondingly, in the end, the control groups had completely covered 59, 30, 16, and 20 cells, respectively. We perform a two-way ANOVA to compare the coverage (normalized by total cells) between treatment and control ($p = 0.06$), which is (barely) not statistically significant.

To measure how well a method covers the space while avoiding duplicates (same value for every dimension), the *efficiency* is calculated by the ratio of covered cells to the total list items (Table 3). Take useHoloLens as an example, the treatment had efficiency $111/308 = 36\%$ while the control had $59/308 = 19\%$. The average efficiency of BlueSky (over four topics) was 29%, which was about 53% higher than that of the control (19%).

Uniformity

The uniformity of an idea space can be illustrated by the distribution of list items covering each cell. Some cells in the idea space were more clustered than others and thus had more duplicate list items. The most clustered cells had 14, 8, 14 and 20 list items for useHoloLens, interview, debate, and textAd, respectively, and 53, 14, 30, and 30 for the four control groups. This indicates that the BlueSky reduced the heaviest duplication to about half of the control.

To illustrate how the BlueSky method enhances uniformity, the density of list items with respect to individual dimensions can be analyzed (Fig. 6). Note that uniformity on each dimension does not guarantee uniformity across all cells.

For the control, the dimension "question or statement" had a value "statement (of topic)" with the smallest density. It indicates that only a few list items were categorized by this value, and implies that this value might be a "blind spot" in the freeform ideation. On the other hand, this dimension had a value "question" with the largest density, which implies the participants' common thinking habits for the idea space. This situation is similar to other three list topics where BlueSky is more uniform than the control. By increasing uniformity, we could explore more uncommon (often valuable) list items as well as reduce the common (often boring) list items.

Match Rate of Step 1 and Step 3

In the treatment, a list item is generated w.r.t a batch of constraints and then categorized by one value of each dimension. Recall that each constraint (c_i) is converted from a value (v_i) of a dimension. If the categorization results (e.g., $(v_1, v_2, ..., v_n)$) match all the constraints C=$(c_1, c_2, ..., c_n)$ accordingly, this list item is called *matched* between step 1 and step 3. Workers could get a bonus of \$0.15 if their list item is matched. Figure 7 shows the number of matched list items over the number of total *constrained list items* (i.e., list items which have been given constraints). Interestingly, the number of matched ideas increased approximately linearly with the number of total constrained list items in most cases, except textAd. The reason might be that the difficulty of each cell was similar, and workers generated a similar number of ideas to fully meet the constraints of each cell.

Note that the constrained list items were fewer than the total list items because some list items were generated with no constraints (phase 1 of step 1). Besides, they exceeded the number of total cells in an idea space because some constraints appeared more than once in the whole experiment. As mentioned above, each batch of constraints represents an empty cell and appears once in each iteration. If the empty cell is not filled in one iteration, the corresponding constraints will be posted again in the next iteration. The constraints will not appear when participants manage to generate a list item to meet the constraints (i.e., matched) or the empty cell is unintentionally filled by other list items.

Apparently, match rate is essential to cover an idea space efficiently. Ideally, if every list item is matched, the efficiency would be 100%. The actual match rate was about 20% on average. There are several possible reasons that could cause the relatively low match rate:

1. A list item was generated correctly (i.e., could meet all the constraints) but was categorized by different values in step 3. Since some dimensions have subjective values (e.g., "*Question answer length*" $\Rightarrow$ {"*short*", "*medium*", "*long*"} for the list topic interview), the participants in step 1 may have different opinions of "*short*" from those in step 3. This discrepancy could be mitigated, but not eliminated, by the multi-judgment in step 3.

2. A list item was generated incorrectly (i.e., could meet part or none of the constraints). It would either cover a non-empty cell (thus duplicate) or happen to cover an empty cell. It is not uncommon as some participants have difficulty thinking a list item to meet all the constraints. On average, 94% of list items could meet at least one constraint among the given batch, and 63.5% of list items could meet at least two constraints.

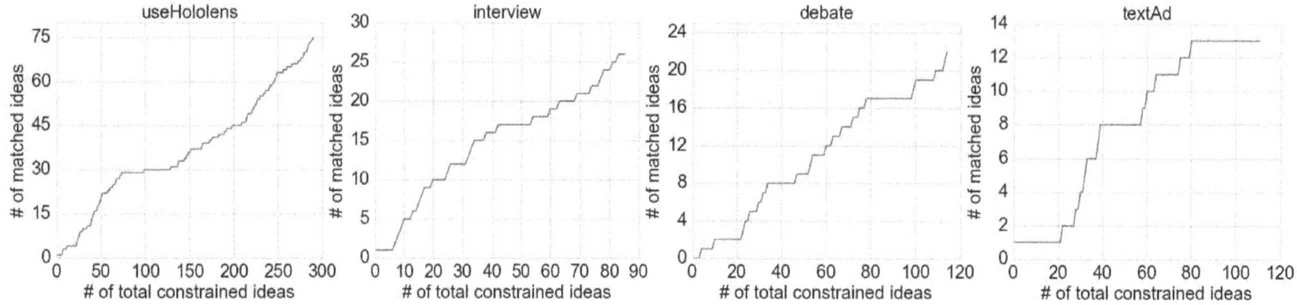

Figure 7. The number of matched list items over the number of total list items which have been given constraints for list topics under the treatment condition.

DISCUSSION

BlueSky is a transformation from divergent to convergent process. The divergent process includes the freeform ideation with no constraints (phase 1 of step 1) and the dimension-values synthesis (step 2). After all the dimensions and values are proposed, the convergent process leads the constrained ideation (phase 2 of step 1).

Most prior crowd-powered ideation systems aimed to maximize quality or creativity, or to find one great idea. In contrast, we aim to cover the space completely and uniformly. Thus, comprehensiveness and uniformity are the metrics that we used to measure the success of BlueSky. The examples and constraints provided in step 1 may affect the creativity, especially when the constraints are difficult. There was no significant difference of match rate between workers who chose to see the examples or not.

The categorization task is also a common type of task on AMT. It is seen in other crowd workflows, such as Cascade [5]. Unlike Cascade, we only allow a list item to fit in one value, not multiple values because values are orthogonal (no overlap). If values are subjective or vague, it will depend on multi-judgment to find the best fit value for a list item. On average, 2.1 workers were needed to agree that a list item was categorized by one value (of a dimension), in which about 85% of categorizations were agreed by two workers and the rest were agreed by more than two workers.

In step 1, an option is to mark a batch of constraints as N/A, and less than 1% of workers chose it (then they would be asked to write down why the constraints were N/A). The low N/A rate is consistent with the fact that the entire space was (almost) completely covered and is also a sign of good dimensions. Similarly, in step 3, we allow workers to categorize ideas as N/A if they do not fit any of the values. Only about 1% of list items were categorized as N/A by more than two workers (multi-judgment). Most N/A list items were irrelevant to the list topic and/or made no sense (e.g., incomplete sentences).

LIMITATIONS AND FUTURE WORK

The total running time of the system is long because it is sequential, not parallel. Participants have to wait until others finish the previous steps. If any participant spends an atypically long time (probably due to the confusion of instruction or holding the HIT but leaving), the whole system will be in idle. To speed up the system, a real-time ideation-mapping workflow might help; namely, once a participant enters a new idea, another participant is notified to categorize it, and then new constraints will be given back. To that end, we might need to retain a group of workers.

Moreover, the more constraints in one HIT, the harder to meet them all. If participants choose to ignore some of the constraints, the system will slow down while the time and cost will increase since more HITs are needed. To increase match rate, we might filter/rank workers based on their performance. For example, we could invite the workers who have high match rates while block the ones with low rates.

Another challenge is efficient discovery of dimensions. One potential avenue would be to use machine learning to extract keywords or propose potential dimensions to inspire participants (including requesters). We could also maintain a pool of dimensions for each type of list topics. Participants could reuse and iterate existing dimensions or add new ones.

In this paper, we did not consider the hierarchy of dimensions. The values of a dimension might also be sub-dimensions. For example, "*location*" $\Rightarrow$ {"*indoor*", ...} could be further broken down into "*indoor*" $\Rightarrow$ {"*living room*", ...}. It might be interesting to allow zoom-in or zoom-out of the idea space.

CONCLUSION

This paper presents a crowd-powered algorithm that could mechanically enumerate a uniform and comprehensive sample of ideas via ideation-synthesis-mapping process. By testing with four list topics (useHoloLens, interview, debate and textAd) under the treatment (BlueSky method) and control conditions, we showed that the treatment could cover the entire space with 29% efficiency while the control could do with 19%. Moreover, the treatment covered the idea space more uniformly than the control, and reduced the heaviest duplication to about half of the control. The match rate between ideation and mapping steps was about 20%, suggesting that participants need to enter approximately five ideas to meet a given batch of constraints.

ACKNOWLEDGMENTS

We gratefully acknowledge John Boyer, Jordan Huffaker, and Meng-Han Wu for thoughtful feedback on the interface design at several junctures, and to the 1087 workers who used the system, including many previous iterations of the system. In particular, Chris Tucci provided essential feedback and assistance with attracting workers to our strange tasks.

REFERENCES

1. Howard B Abrams. 1992. Originality and Creativity in Copyright Law. *Law and Contemporary Problems* 55, 2 (1992), 3–44.
2. Daren C Brabham. 2008. Crowdsourcing as a model for problem solving an introduction and cases. *Convergence: the international journal of research into new media technologies* 14, 1 (2008), 75–90.
3. Joel Chan, Steven Dang, and Steven P Dow. 2016. Comparing Different Sensemaking Approaches for Large-Scale Ideation. In *Proceedings of the 2016 CHI Conference on Human Factors in Computing Systems*. ACM, New York, 2717–2728.
4. Siddhartha Chaudhuri, Evangelos Kalogerakis, Stephen Giguere, and Thomas Funkhouser. 2013. Attribit: Content Creation with Semantic Attributes. In *Proceedings of the 26th Annual ACM Symposium on User Interface Software and Technology (UIST '13)*. ACM, New York, NY, USA, 193–202. DOI: http://dx.doi.org/10.1145/2501988.2502008
5. Lydia B Chilton, Greg Little, Darren Edge, Daniel S Weld, and James A Landay. 2013. Cascade: Crowdsourcing taxonomy creation. In *Proceedings of the SIGCHI Conference on Human Factors in Computing Systems*. ACM, New York, 1999–2008.
6. Nelson Cowan. 2010. The magical mystery four how is working memory capacity limited, and why? *Current directions in psychological science* 19, 1 (2010), 51–57.
7. Nigel Cross. 2008. *Engineering design methods: strategies for product design*. John Wiley & Sons, New York.
8. Clive L Dym and Patrick Little. 2000. Engineering design: A project based approach. (2000).
9. Michael J French and Design Council. 1985. *Conceptual design for engineers*. Springer, Berlin.
10. Ryan G Gomes, Peter Welinder, Andreas Krause, and Pietro Perona. 2011. Crowdclustering. In *Advances in neural information processing systems*. MIT Press, Cambridge MA, 558–566.
11. Jeff Howe. 2008. *Crowdsourcing: How the power of the crowd is driving the future of business*. Random House, New York.
12. George Q Huang and Kai-Ling Mak. 1999. Web-based morphological charts for concept design in collaborative product development. *Journal of Intelligent Manufacturing* 10, 3-4 (1999), 267–278.
13. Kwang-Sung Jun, Jerry Zhu, Burr Settles, and Timothy Rogers. 2013. Learning from human-generated lists. In *Proceedings of The 30th International Conference on Machine Learning*. ICML, Madison WI, 181–189.
14. Aaron Michael Koblin. 2009. The sheep market. In *Proceedings of the seventh ACM conference on Creativity and cognition*. ACM, New York, 451–452.
15. Kurt Luther, Nathan Hahn, Steven P Dow, and Aniket Kittur. 2015. Crowdlines: Supporting Synthesis of Diverse Information Sources through Crowdsourced Outlines. In *Third AAAI Conference on Human Computation and Crowdsourcing*. AAAI, Palo Alto CA, 110–119.
16. George A Miller. 1956. The magical number seven, plus or minus two: some limits on our capacity for processing information. *Psychological review* 63, 2 (1956), 81.
17. Gerhard Pahl and Wolfgang Beitz. 2013. *Engineering design: a systematic approach*. Springer Science & Business Media, Berlin.
18. Aditya Parameswaran, Ming Han Teh, Hector Garcia-Molina, and Jennifer Widom. 2013. Datasift: An expressive and accurate crowd-powered search toolkit. In *First AAAI Conference on Human Computation and Crowdsourcing*. AAAI, Palo Alto CA, 112–120.
19. Ben Shneiderman. 2007. Creativity Support Tools: Accelerating Discovery and Innovation. *Commun. ACM* 50, 12 (Dec. 2007), 20–32. DOI: http://dx.doi.org/10.1145/1323688.1323689
20. Gregory Smith. 2007. *Morphological charts: a systematic exploration of qualitative design space*. Master's thesis. Clemson University, Clemson, SC.
21. Gregory Smith, Jenkins Richardson, Joshua D Summers, and Gregory M Mocko. 2012. Concept exploration through morphological charts: an experimental study. *Journal of mechanical design* 134, 5 (2012), 051004.
22. Steven M. Smith, Thomas B. Ward, and Jay S. Schumacher. 1993. Constraining effects of examples in a creative generation task. *Memory & Cognition* 21, 6 (Nov. 1993), 837–845. DOI: http://dx.doi.org/10.3758/BF03202751
23. Jerry O. Talton, Daniel Gibson, Lingfeng Yang, Pat Hanrahan, and Vladlen Koltun. 2009. Exploratory Modeling with Collaborative Design Spaces. *ACM Trans. Graph.* 28, 5, Article 167 (Dec. 2009), 10 pages. DOI: http://dx.doi.org/10.1145/1618452.1618513
24. Beth Trushkowsky, Tim Kraska, Michael J Franklin, and Pradyut Sarkar. 2013. Crowdsourced enumeration queries. In *Data Engineering (ICDE), 2013 IEEE 29th International Conference on*. IEEE, Piscataway NJ, 673–684.
25. Karl T Ulrich. 2003. *Product design and development*. Tata McGraw-Hill Education, Delhi.
26. Lixiu Yu, Aniket Kittur, and Robert E. Kraut. 2014a. Distributed Analogical Idea Generation: Inventing with Crowds. In *Proceedings of the SIGCHI Conference on Human Factors in Computing Systems (CHI '14)*. ACM, New York, NY, USA, 1245–1254. DOI: http://dx.doi.org/10.1145/2556288.2557371
27. Lixiu Yu, Aniket Kittur, and Robert E. Kraut. 2014b. Searching for Analogical Ideas with Crowds. In

Proceedings of the 32Nd Annual ACM Conference on Human Factors in Computing Systems (CHI '14). ACM, New York, NY, USA, 1225–1234. DOI: http://dx.doi.org/10.1145/2556288.2557378

28. Lixiu Yu and Jeffrey V. Nickerson. 2011. Cooks or cobblers?: crowd creativity through combination. In *Proceedings of the SIGCHI conference on human factors in computing systems*. ACM, New York, 1393–1402. http://dl.acm.org/citation.cfm?id=1979147

29. Lixiu Yu and Yasuaki Sakamoto. 2011. Feature Selection in Crowd Creativity. In *Foundations of Augmented Cognition. Directing the Future of Adaptive Systems*, Dylan D. Schmorrow and Cali M. Fidopiastis (Eds.). Number 6780 in Lecture Notes in Computer Science. Springer, Berlin Heidelberg, 383–392. http://link.springer.com/chapter/10.1007/978-3-642-21852-1_45

Bringing the Wisdom of the Crowd to an Individual by Having the Individual Assume Different Roles

Jaime Teevan
Microsoft Research
Redmond, WA USA
teevan@microsoft.com

Lisa Yu
Bosch Research
Pittsburgh, PA USA
lisa.yu@us.bosch.com

ABSTRACT
Groups of people tend to generate more diverse ideas than individuals because each group member brings a different perspective to the table. But while someone working alone can suffer from fixation and have difficulty of thinking outside-the-box, in this paper we show that it is possible to help them think more like a group by asking them to approach a problem from different perspectives. We present a study of 54 crowd workers in which some individual workers were asked to assume the role of various relevant experts while solving a problem. We find that participants who were asked to assume different roles came up with more creative ideas than those who were not. These findings suggest there is an opportunity for problem solving tools to bring the wisdom of the crowd to individuals.

Author Keywords
Creativity; role playing; crowdsourcing; selfsourcing.

ACM Classification Keywords
H.5.m. Info. interfaces and presentation (e.g., HCI): Misc.

INTRODUCTION AND RELATED WORK
Crowdsourcing researchers are familiar with the idea of the *wisdom of the crowd*, whereby information from multiple people is pooled to produce a better outcome than each individual could produce alone [18]. However, working with other people comes at a cost; the crowd, for example, costs money; explaining a task to someone else costs effort; waiting for a reply costs time. Tasks may also contain private information that we do not want to share with others [10], or we may not want to give up ownership of the output produced by a task [13]. As a result, we tend to do most of our tasks ourselves. The challenge is: we are just one person, and tend to fixate on the knowledge and skills we have [6].

Existing idea generation and creativity literature has explored a variety of approaches to help people think diversely [16], ranging from changing the aspects of looking at problems, to manipulating the media and tools used during problem solving, to controlling exposure to information and experience sources. For example, the *six hats* method asks people to wear different metaphorical hats representing different thinking perspective [5, 17]. Switching attentions between ambiguous sketches has been found to increase divergent thinking [20], and recent researchers harness the online crowds as sources of novel ideas [4, 22].

This paper builds on the wisdom of the crowd to ask: *Can we help an individual think like a crowd*? Instead of crowdsourcing a task to multiple people for diverse solutions, it may be possible to selfsource [19] the task to the same person in different contexts. There is some evidence this may be possible for concrete tasks [1, 7, 20]. For example, participants in one study were asked to answer twice to, "What percentage of the world's airports are in the United States?" [21]. When both answers were averaged it produced a more accurate response than either individually, but the accuracy was still much worse than when the two answers were drawn from different participants. This is consistent with work by Ariely et al. [1] that found that averaging multiple guesses from an individual helps somewhat, but not as much as average multiple guesses from different people. In this paper we extend these findings from concrete estimation tasks to more complex, creative tasks. Additionally, instead of simply eliciting multiple answers from an individual, we investigate approaches to bring out a crowd out of an individual by having the same person approach a problem multiple times as if they were a different person with a different mindset each time.

The wisdom of the crowd arises when we aggregate people's diverse, independent perspectives [1]. To create a similar phenomenon within an individual we must work to artificially create diverse, independent experiences for that individual. For example, when Vul and Pashler [21] made participants wait three weeks between providing answers, they found that "the benefit of re-asking yourself the same question rises to 1/3 the value of a second opinion." Asking people to consider alternative [9] or opposite [12] outcomes can help people overcome anchoring effects and produce less biased judgments, and Herzog and Hertwig [8] found that they could help individuals estimate the dates of historical events if they asked them to give a second answer from the opposite perspective of their first. Crowdsourcing research has shown a person's frame of reference impacts how they do a task, with, for example, the previous task influencing performance on the next task [3, 14].

C&C '17, June 27-30, 2017, Singapore, Singapore
© 2017 ACM. ISBN 978-1-4503-4403-6/17/06...$15.00
DOI: http://dx.doi.org/10.1145/3059454.3059467

We combine crowdsourcing with selfsourcing to help people approach creative problems from multiple perspectives by asking them to imagine assuming the role of various relevant experts. Role playing has been shown to help people experience new perspectives. Boess [2] found it helped students in their design work, and Matthews et al. [11] found it beneficial for therapeutic systems. Recent research by Yu et al. [22] used role playing to support the crowdsourcing of creativity, and found that crowd workers generate more creative ideas when asked to consider a problem from the perspective of an expert in an unexpectedly related domain. We build on these findings to look at how assuming different roles generated by crowd workers can help an individual experience different perspectives. We present a crowd-based study that asks a single person to assume multiple roles while generating creative ideas. By comparing solutions generated in this way with those from a single perspective, we find evidence that individuals produce more creative ideas when primed with roles.

METHODOLOGY

We conducted a crowd-based study to explore whether people generate better ideas by searching for inspiration from the perspectives of multiple out-of-the-box domains than just searching for inspirations on their own.

Idea Collection

To collect ideas, individuals were given a difficult design problem that required a creative solution, and asked to come up with three potential solutions. To assist with this, we asked participants to search the Internet for inspiration. We required that each inspiration be drawn from different domains so that it could not serve as solutions on its own. Instead, participants applied the inspiration directly or indirectly to the problem to generate their own solution.

Conditions

We designed a control condition, which we refer to as the *no-role* condition, where participants searched for inspiration on their own and then used the inspiration to solve the problem by following the instruction below:

> *Please go to the Internet and find three useful ideas that could inspire good solutions for the above problem. These ideas could be knowledge, skills, or methods other people use to solve a similar problem in their own domain. Please don't search for ideas related to this [task] problem. The useful ideas have to be about similar problems in a non-[task] related domain.*

Participants were provided with a form with three sections representing the three useful ideas they were asked to collect. For each idea they were asked to paste a link to the site they found for inspiration and then use that inspiration to generate text describing a solution for the given problem.

We designed the treatment condition to ask individuals to search for inspiration from the perspective of three different roles (the method of generating these roles will be explained in the later section). We refer to this condition as the *multiple-roles* condition. The instructions for read as follows:

> *Please go to the Internet and find three useful ideas a [role 1], [role 2], and [role 3] might have that could inspire good solutions for the above problem. These ideas could be knowledge, skills, or methods a [role 1], [role 2], or [role 3] uses to solve a similar problem in his or her own domain. Please don't search for ideas related to this [task] problem. The useful ideas have to be about problems in the domain that a [role 1], [role 2], or [role 3] deals with.*

As in the *no-role* condition, participants were provided with a form with three sections, each asking for a link and text. In this condition, however, sections were also labeled with one of the three roles they were to be using for inspiration.

Participants

We recruited 54 participants via Mechanical Turk. Seventeen were male, the rest female. Ages ranged from 21 to 61, with a mean of 34. Each participant was randomly assigned to one of the two conditions, with 33 falling in the *no-role* condition, and 21 falling in the *multiple-roles* condition. The discrepancy across conditions occurred naturally. It may be random, as both tasks were presented in similar ways, or more people may have quit mid-task in the *multiple-roles* condition. Each participant was paid $2 to complete the task. Using Mechanical Turk qualifications, we only allowed unique workers who have more than 95% task approval rate to take the task, and we auto-approved all of the submitted ideas.

Creativity Tasks

For the creativity tasks we selected two problems from the set of problems described by Yu et al. [22], one related to redesigning a power strip, and the other related to dry cups. We assigned one of the problems to a participant randomly.

> Power strip problem: *Have a look at the power strip under your desk. How many of its outlets are being used? How many of them would you like to use, but you can't, because a giant power brick (transformer) in the adjacent outlet is blocking it? How could you fit all the different plugs in all the outlets?*

> Cup problem: *When we finish washing cups and glasses, we have to either spread them out individually, but then they take up all the counter space. Alternatively, we can stack them, but then the cups never dry completely and it is hard to separate them from each other later. How can you dry many cups quickly so that they don't take up too much space and moisture doesn't get trapped between them?*

Roles

We likewise used the roles Yu et al. [22] developed for these tasks to represent unexpected potential experts in the problem domain. Each role was identified by crowd workers based on the abstract structures of the task. For example, an abstract structure for the power strip problem is, "How can you fit objects of different sizes into a container?" and this led crowd workers to identify "a warehouse dock loader" as a potential expert. Yu et al. found that when workers used

Condition	Idea 1	Idea 2	Idea 3
No-role	2.50	2.27	2.00
Multiple-roles	3.40	3.40	2.57

Table 1. The average creativity score across ideas as rated by an independent judge. Creativity is the average of the idea's novelty and practicality (based on a 7-point Likert scale).

these roles to generate creative ideas they found better inspiration because the roles led to analogies in different domains.

Given we want to provoke individuals to think outside-the-box, we borrowed the roles from their study. However, instead of asking multiple workers to assume the roles, we asked individual participants to assume three different roles. The order of the roles was randomized. We predicted that by taking on new roles, people would explore different ways of thinking and exceed their existing creative capability. The roles we used in the study included: a warehouse dock loader, a landscaper, a sculptor, a magician, an artist for the power strip problem, and a contortionist for the cup problem.

Idea Evaluation

After each idea was generated we asked participants to self-rate how hard it was for them to come up with the idea ("*How difficult was it for you to generate this idea?*"), and to report how creative they thought the idea was ("*How creative is this idea?*"). Responses were collected using a 7-point Likert scale. At the end of the entire task, participants were also asked to name their favorite idea of the three.

In addition to the self-reported data, we also had an independent judge (a HCI graduate student) evaluate ideas blind to condition. For this we drew on previous research for robustly rating creative idea quality, which considers an idea as being creative if it is both *novel* and *practical* [4, 22]. Novelty was defined for our judge as an idea that was not obvious and differed from existing available solutions. Practicality was defined as how realistically an idea achieved its goal and whether it could be designed and manufactured. The two measurements were provided using 7-point Likert scales and averaged to produce an overall creativity score.

RESULTS

Using the data we collected, we analyze the impact of assuming multiple roles on the creativity of the ideas generated by our participants, as well as on their ability to generate multiple ideas over time. Two example ideas generated for the power-strip problem are shown in Figure 1, the first by a worker in the *no-role* condition, and the second by a worker in the *multiple-roles* condition.

> *No-role*:
>
> Make the power brick (transformer) smaller or located at a different spot along the power cord so that it is not in the way or interfering with the power outlets.

> *Multiple-roles* (role: an expert on topology):
>
> For this design I would have it in the shape of the tree, and have a spot for the transformer at the bottom of the tree, and have all the other plugs at the top of the tree.

Figure 1. Example ideas generated by workers in the *no-role* and *multiple-roles* conditions for the power-strip problem.

Condition	Measure	Idea 1	Idea 2	Idea 3
No-role	Creativity	5.30	5.18	4.97
	Difficulty	3.24	3.88	4.21
	Favorite	11	8	14
Multiple-roles	Creativity	5.33	4.81	5.29
	Difficulty	3.81	3.71	3.81
	Favorite	6	5	10

Table 2. The average self-reported creativity and difficulty level across ideas (based on a 7-point Likert scale), and the number of times each idea was listed as favorite.

Measures of Creativity

As described in the previous section, we collected two measures of creativity for the ideas our participants generated: one that relied on the assessment of an independent judge (Table 1), and another based on participants' own self-reported assessment of their ideas (Table 2). In general, we find evidence to suggest that asking people to assume different roles encouraged creative thinking. As reported by one participant in the *multiple-roles* condition, "I tend not to be very creative, but this got my brain working."

According to the ratings provided by an independent judge, the ideas generated in the *multiple-roles* condition were generally more creative than the ideas generated in the *no-role* condition, as can be seen in Table 1. In fact, when considering only ideas with above average creativity scores, we find that 47% of the *multiple-roles* ideas are above-average, as compared with only 34% of the *no-role* ideas. We conducted a T.test analysis on the judged creativity, and found that creativity score averaged across the ideas from the *multiple-roles* condition (M=3.13, SD=1.40) was higher than that of *no-role* condition (M=2.26, SD=1.72), $t(52)=2.02$, $p<.05$. This result suggests that participants were able to generate more creative ideas when they changed their thinking by assuming the roles of other experts.

These differences do not, however, appear when we analyze the self-reported data (Table 2). Here we see no significant difference in the self-reported creativity of the ideas generated from a *no-role* (M=5.15, SD=1.51) as compared with *multiple-roles* (M=5.14, SD=1.54). This could mean that there was no difference. However, it could also be because our participants had a hard time judging the creativity of their ideas without the context of the ideas that other people had generated for the problem. Further, workers were probably biased towards viewing ideas that they came up with as creative, as it allowed them to view their work in a positive light. They may also have thought a high creativity score would make their work more likely to be accepted.

Generating Multiple Ideas

When we look an individual participant's creative problem solving ability over time, we observe that there was a general trend for participants to generate less creative ideas as they were asked to continue to come up with new ones. Idea 3

(M=2.22, SD=1.51), for example, was generally judged by our independent judge to be less creative than Idea 2 (M=2.71, SD=2.05), $t(53)=1.67$, $p<.05$. As might be predicted given what we know about the wisdom of the crowd, this suggests the best way to collect three creative ideas would be to ask three different people to each generate one idea, which is the equivalent of taking the first – and most creative – idea from three of our participants.

When we look at the favorite idea selected by each participants, however, we find they tended to prefer their most recent idea; 24 participants said they liked their third idea best, while only 17 and 13 liked the first and second ideas best, respectively. This could be a result of a recency effect, with participants reflecting a cognitive bias towards the most recent idea they generated. But it suggests that in the case of self-assessed creativity, the wisdom-of-an-individual-assuming-roles may produce a comparable outcome to taking the first idea from three different people assuming the role, as is done in a standard wisdom-of-the-crowd approach.

We expected the roles would make it easier for people to generate multiple ideas, as it can be progressively harder for an individual to come up new ideas while brainstorming alone. We hypothesized that the different roles would help keep participants from getting stuck viewing the problem from a single perspective. We see that there is a trend in the difficulty levels participants reported in generating ideas, as shown in Table 2. We observed that the difficulty of coming up with a new idea seemed to increase over time in the *no-role* condition, while the difficulty seemed staying the same in the *multiple-roles* condition. Further study is needed, however, to confirm whether this trend is true, as a repeated ANOVA analyses did not yield a significant difference. This could be an artifact of the study design, as participants were asked to generate three solutions at one time. Future study could separate the process into three isolated steps and only show each participant one step at a time.

Can We Help an Individual Think Like a Crowd?

Taken collectively, our findings suggest it may be possible to use the crowd to help an individual think like a crowd by having them assume different roles. Individuals appear to be more creative when they assume the roles of multiple other experts during idea generation, and may also have an easier time generating ideas over time. Additionally, when we compare the creativity of the ideas an individual was able to achieve by assuming different roles with the wisdom of the crowd, where three different individuals to solve the problem independently, it appears the approach may begin to help an individual approximate the aggregated output of a crowd.

DISCUSSION

Individuals often develop particular ways of thinking. Research consistently shows that people tend to fixate on a particular perspective and thus have difficulty addressing problems creatively [6]. With the refined disciplinary divisions in modern education, people are becoming increasingly specialized. While deep knowledge and skills in a domain has many advantages, it can also increase fixation. To break fixation, people often choose to solicit opinions from other people or work in groups. Authors, for example, send papers out for peer review, companies run focus groups, and friends ask each other for advice. However, external resources are not always available and, when they are, they come at a cost. In addition, to protect private information or control the intellectual property, people might be reluctant to have others solve their problems for them. In this paper we focused on how to bring multiple perspectives to an individual to help them perform tasks effectively and creatively. We were interested in methods and tools that break fixation and routine.

We explored the use of roles as a way to encourage multiple perspectives through a combination of crowdsourcing and selfsourcing. Our findings suggest that simply by asking people to assume new roles and explore new domains, people can become more creative than would be if they relied solely on their own way of thinking. We found evidence to suggest that different roles supported an individual's creative idea generation and that considering different roles may make it easier to continue generating ideas. Looking forward, we believe there may be many ways to help individuals solve their real-world problems in real-world contexts by thoughtfully combing crowdsourcing and selfsourcing [19].

The work presented in this paper should be interpreted within the context of understanding the limitations to the exploratory study we conducted. Additional raters could provide a more valid external representation of creativity, and a more structured presentation of information to participants during the study could help more tightly control the priming effects. Further, asking participants to think aloud as they generated their ideas or conducting interviews after the experiment could provide insight into how the roles actually changed participants' mindset during problem solving.

However despite the fact that our findings were drawn from an exploratory study, we think these preliminary findings are promising and suggest interesting areas for further research. For example, it may be possible to encourage people to think differently by actively changing their location, the time when information is requested, or their mode of thinking. Instead of asking participants to generate three ideas at once, it might be effective to solicit new ideas every hour.

CONCLUSION

In this paper we proposed supporting creativity by creating internal crowds within an individual by asking people to imagine themselves assuming different roles. We conducted a crowd-based study that demonstrated the potential of having a single person address creative problems by assuming the role of various crowd-generated experts. Our findings suggest that this approach could be used to help bring the wisdom of the crowd to an individual. Our findings can inform the design of tools intended to support selfsourcing personal creativity. Looking forward, we are interested in exploring different ways to change contexts, including location, time, and mode of thinking.

REFERENCES

1. Dan Ariely, Wint Tung Au, Randall H. Bender, David V. Budescu, Christiane B. Dietz, Honging Gu, Thomas S. Allsten, and Gal Zauberman. 2000. The effects of averaging subjective probability estimated between and within judges. *Journal of Experimental Psychology: Applied*. 6 (2): 130-147.
2. Stella U. Boess. 2008. First steps in role playing. In *CHI '08 Extended Abstracts on Human Factors in Computing Systems*, 2017-2024. DOI: 10.1145/1358628.1358632
3. Carrie Cai, Shamsi Iqbal, and Jaime Teevan. 2016. Chain reactions: The impact of order on microtask chains. In *Proceedings of the ACM Conference on Human Factors in Computing Systems (CHI 2016)*, 3143-3154. DOI: 10.1145/2858036.2858237
4. Joel Chan, Steven Dang, and Steven P. Dow. 2016. Improving crowd innovation with expert facilitation. In *Proceedings of the 19th ACM Conference on Computer-Supported Cooperative Work & Social Computing (CSCW 2016)*, 1223–1235. DOI: 10.1145/2818048.2820023
5. Edward De Bono and Marcela Pandolfo. 1999. *Six thinking hats*. Back Bay Books New York. Retrieved March 20, 2017 from http://capitalquality.org/wp-content/uploads/2012/11/CQI_Six_Hats_LL_Lite1.pdf
6. Kees Dorst and Nigel Cross. 2001. Creativity in the design process: Co-evolution of problem-solution. *Design Studies*. 22(5): 425–437. DOI: 10.1016/S0142-694X(01)00009-6
7. Sharad Goel, Daniel M. Reeves, Duncan J. Watts and David M. Pennock. 2010. Prediction without markets. *Electronic Commerce 2010*.
8. Stefan M. Herzog and Ralph Hertwig. The wisdom of many in one mind: Improving individual judgments with dialectical bootstrapping. *Psychological Science*, 20 (2), 231-237.
9. Edward R. Hirt and Keith D. Markman. 1995. Multiple explanation: A consider-an-alternative strategy for debiasing judgments. *Journal of Personality and Social Psychology*, 69(6): 1069-1086.
10. Walter Lasecki, Jaime Teevan, and Ece Kamar. 2014. Information extraction and manipulation threats in crowd-powered systems. In *Proceedings of the 17th ACM Conference on Computer-Supported Cooperative Work & Social Computing (CSCW 2014)*, 248-256. DOI: 10.1145/2531602.2531733
11. Mark Matthews, Geri Gay, and Gavin Doherty. 2014. Taking part: Role-play in the design of therapeutic systems. In *Proceedings of the ACM Conference on Human Factors in Computing Systems (CHI 2014)*, 643-652. DOI: 10.1145/2556288.2557103
12. Thomas Mussweiler, Fritz Strack, and Tim Pfeiffer. 2000. Overcoming the inevitable anchoring effect: Considering the opposite compensates for selective accessibility. *Personality and Social Psychology Bulletin*, 26 (9): 1142-1150.
13. Michael Nebeling, Alexandra To, Anhong Guo, Adrian A. de Freitas, Jaime Teevan, Steven Dow, and Jeffrey P. Bigham. WearWrite: Crowd-assisted writing from smartwatches. In *Proceedings of the ACM Conference on Human Factors in Computing Systems (CHI 2016)*, 3834-3846. DOI: 10.1145/2858036.2858169.
14. Edward Newell and Derek Ruths. 2016. How one microtask affects another. In *Proceedings of the ACM Conference on Human Factors in Computing Systems (CHI 2016)*, 3155-3166. DOI: 10.1145/2858036.2858490
15. Peter Organisciak, Jaime Teevan, Susan T. Dumais, Robert C. Miller and Adam Kalai. 2014. A crowd of your own: Crowdsourcing for on-demand personalization. In *Proceedings of the AAAI Conference on Human Computation and Crowdsourcing (HCOMP 2014)*.
16. Mark A. Runco. 2010. Divergent thinking, creativity, and ideation. *The Cambridge handbook of creativity*: 413–446.
17. Robert J. Sternberg and Todd I. Lubart. 1999. The concept of creativity: Prospects and paradigms. *Handbook of creativity* 1: 3–15.
18. James Surowiecki, 2004. *The Wisdom of Crowds: Why the Many Are Smarter Than the Few and How Collective Wisdom Shapes Business, Economies, Societies and Nations.* New York: Doubleday, 2004.
19. Jaime Teevan, Daniel Libeling, and Walter Lasecki. 2014. Selfsourcing personal tasks. In *Proceedings of the ACM Conference on Human Factors in Computing Systems (CHI 2014)*, 2527-2532. DOI: 10.1145/2559206.2581181
20. Barbara Tversky and Juliet Y. Chou. 2011. Creativity: Depth and breadth. In *Design Creativity 2010*. Springer, 209–214. Retrieved December 30, 2016 from http://link.springer.com/chapter/10.1007/978-0-85729-224-7_27
21. Edward Vul and Harold Pashler. 2008. Measuring the crowd within: Probabilistic representations within individuals. *Psychological Science*, 19 (7).
22. Lixiu Yu, Aniket Kittur, and Robert E. Kraut. 2016. Encouraging "outside-the-box" thinking in crowd innovation through identifying domains of expertise. In *Proceedings of the 19th ACM Conference on Computer-Supported Cooperative Work & Social Computing (CSCW 2016)*, 1214-1222. DOI: 10.1145/2818048.2820025.

Material Experience Research
– Evidentiary Encounters with Creativity –

Elizabeth F. Churchill
Google
San Francisco, CA, USA
churchill@acm.org

ABSTRACT
Creativity is often associated with free expression, dynamic innovation, originality, and insightful, unconstrained genius.

Nowhere is this more so than in the practice of Design (with an emphatic, capital 'D'). The embodiment of this myth is the genius designer, from whom creative ideas spring forth naturally, effortlessly. A companion myth within the world of interface and interaction design is that design and user experience experimentation are not *allies in creativity*; rather, user experience research is in *service of creativity*, laying the foundations for design inspiration by identifying "gaps" and "needs", or providing summative evaluations of designs.

To the first myth, the creative process actually involves effort, exploration and iteration; creativity is enacted and accomplished in design practice through the judicious application and relaxation of understood and discovered constraints. Constraints help you ask better questions, not simply drive for solutions. Good examples are design systems and frameworks that codify carefully thought-out, and frequently observed constraints; they codify principles and best practices, they inform, and they offer useful boundaries that provoke design exploration and challenge. To the second, experimentation is a creative act in itself; systematic experimentation can and should be intimately woven into iterative design processes. Experimentation allows options to be tested and explored. Experimentation enables thoughtful exploration of permutation.

In this talk I will share stories of collaboration between my team, Material Experience Research, and the designers and developers of Material Design (material.io). I will talk about tools for "creatives", and the ways in which such tools can enhance rather than constrain and restrict creative exploration. I will discuss research we have been conducting on how good design and user experience principles, codified within design frameworks and systems, *spark* creativity through provisional constraint.

C&C 2017, June 27–30, 2017, Singapore.
ACM ISBN 978-1-4503-4403-6/17/06.
http://dx.doi.org/10.1145/3059454.3078895

Author Keywords
Creativity; Design; Data; Frameworks; Constraints; Learning; Iteration; Experimentation

ACM Classification Keywords
H.5.m. Information interfaces and presentation (e.g., HCI): Miscellaneous

BIOGRAPHY

Dr Elizabeth Churchill is a Director of User Experience at Google. Her current work focuses on designer and developer tools for interaction design, and on the connected ecosystems of the Internet of Things.

For 2 decades, Elizabeth has been a research leader at well-known corporate R&D organizations including Fuji Xerox's research lab in Silicon Valley (FXPAL), the Palo Alto Research Center (PARC), eBay Research Labs in San Jose, and Yahoo! in Santa Clara, California.

She has contributed groundbreaking research in a number of areas, publishing over 150 peer reviewed articles, co-editing 5 books in HCI related fields, contributing as a regular columnist for ACM's interactions magazine since 2008, and publishing two co-authored books: Foundations for Designing User Centered Systems (Springer 2014) and Designing with Data (O'Reilly 2017). She has also launched successful products, and has more than 50 patents granted or pending.

A Distinguished Scientist and Speaker of the Association for Computing Machinery (ACM) and a member of the CHI Academy, Elizabeth is the current Secretary/Treasurer of the ACM. She served in the ACM SIGCHI Executive Committee for 8 years, 6 years of those as Executive Vice President. Elizabeth sits on the advisory board of a number of University Departments, and has just joined the Council of The Computing Community Consortium. In 2016, she was the recipient of the CITRIS and Banta Institute Athena Award winner for Executive Leadership.

Bitter Sweet or Sweet Bitter? How Valence Order and Source Identity Influence Feedback Acceptance

Y. Wayne Wu and Brian P. Bailey
Department of Computer Science
University of Illinois
Urbana, IL 61801
{yuwu4, bpbailey}@illinois.edu

ABSTRACT
Content creators are less receptive to feedback with negative valence, and such feedback is frequently received online. To address this problem, we propose a novel method that orders a set of feedback based on its valence; using the feedback with positive valence to mitigate the effects of the negative valence feedback. To test the method, participants (N=270) wrote a story for children based on a given illustration and then revised their story after receiving a set of feedback. The feedback set was delivered with different valence orders and with different source identity cues. We measured participants' affective states, perceptions of the feedback and its source, revision extents, and story quality. Our main result is that presenting negative feedback last improved content creators' affective states and their perception of the feedback set relative to placing the negative feedback in other positions. This pattern was consistent across all feedback source conditions. The work contributes a simple and novel way to order a set of feedback that improves feedback receptivity.

Author Keywords
Crowdsourcing; design; feedback; creativity support tools.

ACM Classification Keywords
H.5.3 [Information Interface and Presentation]: Group and Organization Interfaces – Collaborative computing.

INTRODUCTION
Content creators can increasingly leverage crowdsourcing and social media to collect feedback during the iterative design process [42]. Online crowds are attractive because they can be used to quickly generate a large quantity of diverse feedback. A shared challenge is the presence of negative feedback. Though negative feedback can occur in face-to-face settings, providers are more likely to give harsh criticism and use language with negative valence in online environments [35]. Prior work shows that negative feedback accounts for approximately 20% of all messages exchanged on a popular community site [46]. Negative feedback can discourage content creators from collecting feedback online [42], and cause creators to form an unfavorable impression of the platform and deter future use. Negative feedback also impairs content creators' affective states, which in turn can inhibit creative thinking [1].

C&C '17, June 27-30, 2017, Singapore, Singapore

ACM ISBN 978-1-4503-4403-6/17/06…$15.00
http://dx.doi.org/10.1145/3059454.3059458

In formal learning environments, instructors recommend the use of mitigating language, such as praise or affirmation, before or after negative feedback to improve its receptivity [2,4,16,23,37]. Similar techniques are less applicable in online environments, where the feedback is often composed by multiple independent providers and platform designers have limited control over the composition process. Prior work has tested various methods that improve the positive valence of feedback, including the use of rubrics [44] and positive examples [11]. While these methods may help, they do not eliminate occurrences of negative feedback. One common solution among platform designers is to remove the negative feedback [12,33]. Despite its simplicity, this approach has several disadvantages. First, negative feedback may still contain constructive advice useful for learning and content improvement [8]. Second, removing feedback without consent may discourage the provider from participating further [18]. Third, feedback removal may be inapplicable in certain situations, such as when content creators have paid in advance for each piece of feedback.

In this paper, we test a novel approach that manipulates the order in which a content creator consumes multiple independent pieces of feedback based on their valence. Specifically, our work examined whether positive feedback could be used to mitigate the influence of the negative feedback in the set. If effective, the technique could be automated in existing feedback platforms using sentiment analysis [48]. Prior work also shows that cues about the source (provider) of the feedback can affect perceptions of the feedback [38]. Our experiment additionally examined how the perceived source of the feedback (peers vs. experts vs. anonymous) [7,24] affects content creators' reactions to the feedback, and how it mediates the effect of valence order.

We conducted an online experiment in which participants (n=270) wrote a children's story based on an illustration. Two days later they revised their stories based on a set of given feedback. The feedback set included two pieces of feedback with positive valence and one piece with negative valence. The feedback was presented with different valence orders (negative first, negative last, and negative between) and source identity cues based on the experiment condition. We measured participants' affective states, perceptions of the feedback and its source, revision extent, and story quality.

Our results showed the later in the set content creators consume the negative feedback, the more effort they invest in the revision task and the more favorably they rate the set of feedback. Feedback source had no statistical effect on the measures. We also observed a strong gender effect. Female participants were more likely to accept feedback (reported applying it in the revised story) and the negative feedback causes a larger reduction in their affective states. Our work contributes deeper empirical understanding of how valence order and source identity can be used to improve feedback receptivity in online environments.

RELATED WORK

In this section, we discuss how prior work addresses negative feedback from online crowds. Also, we examine previous findings about how feedback valence and its source influence content creators' reactions to the feedback.

Negative Feedback in Crowd Feedback Frameworks

Researchers have explored various methods to address the issue of negative feedback in crowd platforms. One approach focuses on increasing the quality of each piece of feedback. Greenberg et al. use a high-quality feedback example to scaffold the writing process [11]. The positive examples encourage feedback providers to adopt similar writing style and avoid being too critical. However, the example provided may cause cognitive fixation during feedback composition, limiting the learning benefit of the feedback [17]. Prior work has also explored how pricing tasks in a paid work platform influences the quality of online peer production [20]. The results show that higher payments increase the speed and quantity of task outcomes but not the quality.

Aggregation is another approach for addressing negative feedback. Yatani et al. generate a word cloud from review content that surfaces the most popular phrases [41]. The aggregation gives content creators an overview of the feedback before they read the text. Other researchers improve quality by structuring the feedback generation process [19,40]. Feedback providers respond to specific prompts about a design, and the responses are summarized through visualizations. The summary creates a buffer between the content creator and the individual feedback. Though the scaffolding process may increase quality, it may also reduce the scope of the feedback. Finally, researchers have sought to place reflection activities within the feedback loop to improve feedback interpretation [43].

In comparison to these prior approaches, feedback ordering is a lightweight mechanism that can be incorporated into existing platforms without significant modification. It can also co-exist with other quality improvement strategies, presentation techniques, and reflection activities to further improve feedback receptivity.

Effects of Valence in Creative Work

Researchers have explored various factors that influence feedback receptivity, including granularity, modality, and timing [9,15,21]. For example, Sadler argues effective feedback needs to address the discrepancy between the current performance level and the desired goal [32]. Valence is another factor with a strong influence over content creators' reactions to the feedback received. Negative language can threaten one's ego and reduce feedback effectiveness [5]. Positive language typically improves feedback reception, task performance, and content creators' affective states [24]. Zhu et al. show negative feedback discourages participation in online production communities while positive feedback encourages participation [39,47].

Feedback valence is particularly important for creative tasks. Positive affective state, which can be affected by feedback, relates to improved creativity [1,30,45]. Researchers have explored workflows that utilize the effects of positive valence in creative work. Nguyen et al. modify the valence level of the feedback by inserting positive affective language at the beginning of the text [24]. Such a positive language "wrapper" was shown to improve feedback reception and writing quality. De Rooij & Jones show that displaying positive feedback in real time can encourage participants to generate more original ideas [29]. In comparison with these workflows, our approach of feedback reordering requires neither modification of the feedback content nor real-time generation that may be challenging on many platforms.

Prior work has explored how manipulating the valence of phrases within a single piece of feedback influences content creators. One prior study shows that delivering negative feedback with positive feedback framing increases its perceived usefulness and participants' confidence but does not affect participants' performance on a repetitive physical task [25]. Prior work has also shown that mitigating language increases participants' receptivity to feedback and their affective state [2,16]. In contrast, our work explores the effects of valence ordering in the context of multiple pieces of feedback and in the context of a creative writing task.

Source Identity Influence on Feedback Receptivity

The identity of feedback providers is a common factor that differentiates feedback platforms. Online work marketplaces, such as UpWork, allow content creators to identify and collect feedback from paid domain experts. Feedback from experts leads to greater improvement in technical skills than self-assessment [27]. Prior work also finds content creators are more likely to accept feedback from experts because of their high perceived credibility [7].

On the other hand, collecting feedback from peers is also gaining popularity among content creators [13]. Although less experienced than experts, peers are typically more accessible for feedback collection. Prior work also shows

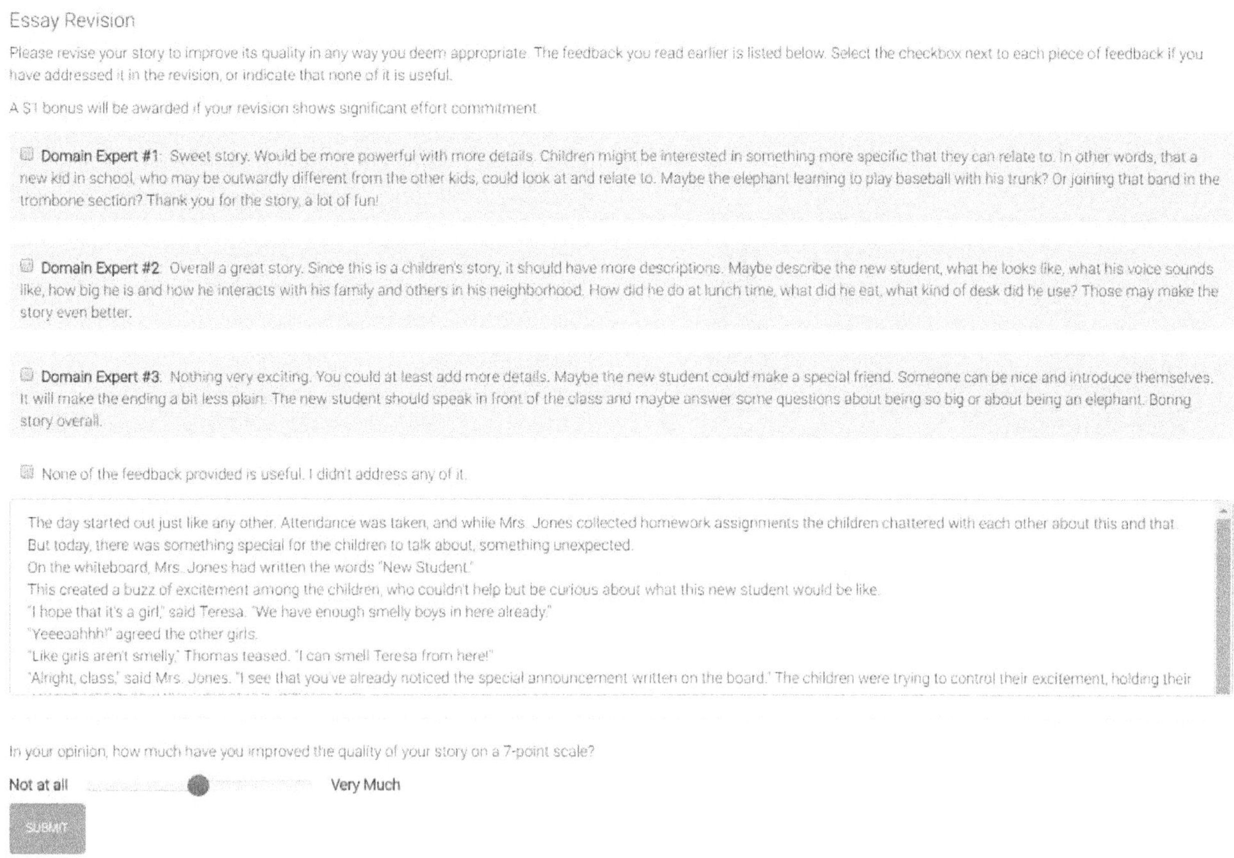

Figure 1. Task interface for the revision phase. Feedback was provided in different orders and with different source cues based on experimental conditions. Participants have already read the feedback piece by piece before reaching this stage.

peers are more responsive and provide more design suggestions in comparison with online design forums [42].

Besides expert and peer sources of feedback, in our work we also explored an anonymous condition, where no identity information about the source is given. Anonymity removes the social interaction element in the feedback interpretation process. Prior work shows the lack of social cues increases participants' motivation, perceived ability, and task performance when receiving computer-generated feedback [3]. Nguyen et al. show anonymity also increases feedback acceptance [24]. Our study extends this corpus of prior research by testing how feedback valence order interacts with different source identity cues.

METHODOLOGY

Our experiment addresses three research questions:

- How does ordering a feedback set based on valence affect the extent and quality of the subsequent content revisions?
- How does valence order influence a content creator's affective state, and influence his or her perceptions of the feedback and its source?
- How does information about the source of the feedback providers affect these same measures, and mediate the effects of the feedback ordering based on valence?

Answers to these questions help content creators better utilize feedback received online (e.g., positive affective state is associated with increased creative thinking [29]). Also, the answers can help platform designers know how to more effectively present the feedback (e.g., how to order it and whether to display source cues).

Experiment Design

To answer these research questions, we conducted a 3x3 full factorial online experiment with two factors: *Valence Order* and *Source*. Each participant received three pieces of feedback, including two with positive valence levels and one with negative valence level. There are three levels in *Valence Order*: negative first, negative between, and negative last. There are also three levels in *Source*: peer, expert, and anonymous. In the peer and expert conditions, the task instruction clearly states that the feedback comes from peer workers or domain experts. The feedback text also started with the words "Peer Worker" or "Domain Expert" (see Figure 1). In the anonymous condition, participants received

Figure 2. The user interface during the story writing phase. The image was edited for brevity.

no information about the feedback source. There was also no source identity cue in the feedback text.

Essay Task

The task includes two phases: *story writing* and *revision*. For the story writing phase, we asked participants to write a story for children of 8-12 years old based on a given illustration (Figure 2). A pilot study showed that most participants could finish the story in less than one hour. We intentionally allocated extra time for the task so the story quality would not be compromised due to time pressure. The participants had two hours to write a story within a 200-2000 word limit. We chose story writing as our experimental task for three reasons; (i) it is a topic that should be familiar to a general audience; (ii) it requires creative thought; and (iii) it only requires text entry, making it suitable to perform online.

The illustration facilitated the task in two ways. First, it provided scaffolding in the open-ended writing process by outlining the story's main characters and scenario. Second, it allowed the research team to select general feedback that applied to most stories by narrowing the scope of the possible story themes [34]. An expert in story writing was recruited and selected the illustration based on task appropriateness. Participants received $3 for the writing phase.

In the story revision phase, participants revised stories based on a set of feedback. After reviewing their stories at the start of the phase, participants received three pieces of feedback. The task interface presented one piece of feedback at a time. Participants selected a button to reveal the next piece of feedback. After feedback delivery, we asked participants to complete a survey about their affective states and perceptions of the feedback set and its perceived source. Then participants revised their original story to improve its quality. Participants received an additional $2 for the revision phase. To discourage satisficing, we offered a $1 bonus if they demonstrated significant effort during the revision phase. In total, top 30.9% of all participants ranked by edited character count received the bonus.

Feedback Pool

The feedback assigned to participants came from a feedback pool consisting of six pairs of positive and negative feedback (Table 1). Each pair was adapted from one piece of authentic feedback collected online. We used five stories from a pilot study to collect a large set of authentic feedback on the story plots. From the set, we selected six pieces of feedback that gave revision advice on story content. The feedback type was decided based on prior work about effective feedback [26].

To ensure each piece of feedback suggested a similar degree of revision, we recruited 30 online judges from Amazon Mechanical Turk to rate the actionability levels. Each judge reviewed 7 pieces of feedback including the 6 pieces of authentic feedback and one duplicate for quality control. For each piece of feedback, the judge rated the extent of revision needed if the feedback was accepted on a 7-point scale from 1 (No Revision Needed) to 7 (Major Revision Needed). We discarded the ratings from judges who rated the duplicate piece of feedback noticeably different (larger than two units) from its counterpart. The final average actionability rating across the feedback set was 4.12 (SE=0.26), and there was no significant difference between the ratings of any two pieces of feedback. The valence levels of the feedback pool were also adjusted and validated in the same manner. In the end, all adjusted positive feedback have similar positive valence levels (μ=5.38, SE=0.26), and the negative feedback have similar negative valence levels (μ=2.68, SE=0.20).

Participants

In total, 270 participants completed the experiment. All participants were recruited from Amazon Mechanical Turk and located in the U.S. All participants had finished more than 500 HITs and had a minimum 95% approval rate. Among the participants, 40% were males, 60% females; 98.1% reported English as their first language; 86.3% had read stories to children; 39.3% were parents of children younger than 15 years old. Regarding the age distribution, 9.6% were 18-24 years old, 42.2% 25-34 years old, 27.4% 35-44 years old, and 20.7% 45 years or older. Regarding the education level distribution, 40.8% reported high school or lower as their highest academic degree earned, 44.8% undergraduate degree, and 14.4% graduate degree. Since most workers on AMT earn at or below minimum wage [31], we assume that the participants were novice content creators rather than professional writers.

Positive Valence Version	Negative Valence Version
I really loved the story. I would change a couple of things. The story would be more interesting if more details were given. For example, what happened to his parents? In what ways does he feel different from the children? Does he miss living like an elephant? I teach young children and I would read this story to my class.	A pretty boring story. I would change a couple of things. The story would be more interesting if more details were given. For example, what happened to his parents? In what ways does he feel different from the children? Does he miss living like an elephant? I teach young children and I may not read this story to my class.
Great story! I think the new student also needs to introduce himself to the class so they can learn more about him. He can tell them where he is from, about how it is different from his new home area, what he likes to do, etc, so they can get to know him. The teacher can also ask the classmates to speak up if there is anything they like that the new student likes. That may make both the new student and the classmates more comfortable and willing to accept each other.	Quite a boring story. Some more details may make the story less plain. I think the new student also needs to introduce himself to the class so they can learn more about him. He can tell them where he is from, about how it is different from his new home area, what he likes to do, etc, so they can get to know him. The teacher can also ask the classmates to speak up if there is anything they like that the new student likes. That may make both the new student and the classmates more comfortable and willing to accept each other.
Overall a great story. Since this is a children's story, it should have more descriptions. Maybe describe the new student, what he looks like, what his voice sounds like, how big he is and how he interacts with his family and others in his neighborhood. How did he do at lunch time, what did he eat, what kind of desk did he use? Those may make the story even better.	Overall a pretty boring story. Since this is a children's story, it should at least have more descriptions. Maybe describe the new student, what he looks like, what his voice sounds like, how big he is and how he interacts with his family and others in his neighborhood. How did he do at lunch time, what did he eat, what kind of desk did he use? Those may make the story less boring.
Great story. You should add more details to make it even better. I would like for the new student to make a special friend. Maybe someone can be nice and introduce themselves. It will be an even happier ending to the story. The new student should speak in front of the class and maybe answer some questions about being so big or about being an elephant. Good job overall!	Nothing very exciting. You could at least add more details. Maybe the new student could make a special friend. Someone can be nice and introduce themselves. It will make the ending a bit less plain. The new student should speak in front of the class and maybe answer some questions about being so big or about being an elephant. Boring story overall.
Sweet story. Would be more powerful with more details. Children might be interested in something more specific that they can relate to. In other words, that a new kid in school, who may be outwardly different from the other kids, could look at and relate to. Maybe the elephant learning to play baseball with his trunk? Or joining that band in the trombone section? Thank you for the story, a lot of fun!	Boring story. Would be less plain with more details. Children might be interested in something more specific that they can relate to. In other words, that a new kid in school, who may be outwardly different from the other kids, could look at and relate to. Maybe the elephant learning to play baseball with his trunk? Or joining that band in the trombone section? I didn't really enjoy reading the story.
My daughter may love this story. I would like to read a bit more about the elephant's first day in the classroom - how he sat down, how the other children reacted, how he participated in the classroom work, and how the teacher treated him. I think that those details might add some more color to the story and perhaps even a bit more tension.	I probably wouldn't read this story to my daughter, just too boring. Maybe you can talk a bit more about the elephant's first day in the classroom - how he sat down, how the other children reacted, how he participated in the classroom work, and how the teacher treated him. I think that those details might add some more color to the story and perhaps even a bit more tension.

Table 1. The feedback pool from which the research team assigned three pieces of feedback to each initial story. At most one piece of feedback was assigned from each feedback pair (each row). The left and right columns show the positive and negative valence versions of the feedback, respectively.

Procedure

Participants read an IRB consent form and filled out a demographic survey at the beginning of the experiment. The task instruction also informed the participants about the following revision phase. Then we gave participants two hours to compose their initial stories. After all stories were collected, the research team selected three feedback pairs from the feedback pool for each story based on their appropriateness for the plot (Table 1). Each pair included one piece of positive and one piece of negative feedback, and both pieces were derived from the same piece of authentic feedback. For the three feedback pairs selected by the research team, a Python script randomly selected one piece of feedback from each pair, and two piece of positive feedback and one piece of negative feedback in total. For 22.3% of the stories, there were fewer than three feedback pairs applicable to the plot and we thus excluded these stories from the revision phase. While assigning feedback for all stories, we monitored how many times each feedback pair had been selected and adjusted to ensure an even allocation of the 6 pairs. Two days after participants finished the writing phase, we launched the revision phase and notified the participants via email. 74.6% of all qualified participants completed the revision phase. The task presented the feedback in different valence orders and with different source cues based on experiment conditions (Figure 1). The participants had two hours to finish the revision phase.

Measurements

We collected three sets of measurements:

- Affective states: how distressed / upset / enthusiastic / inspired / excited / happy they felt after receiving the feedback.
- Perceptions of the feedback and its source: how useful / positive / fair they perceived the feedback to be, how knowledgeable / polite the feedback sources to be, and how good they perceive their writing skill to be after receiving the feedback.
- Revision: how much time participants spent writing the initial story, reading the feedback, and revising the story; how much the story changed during the revision

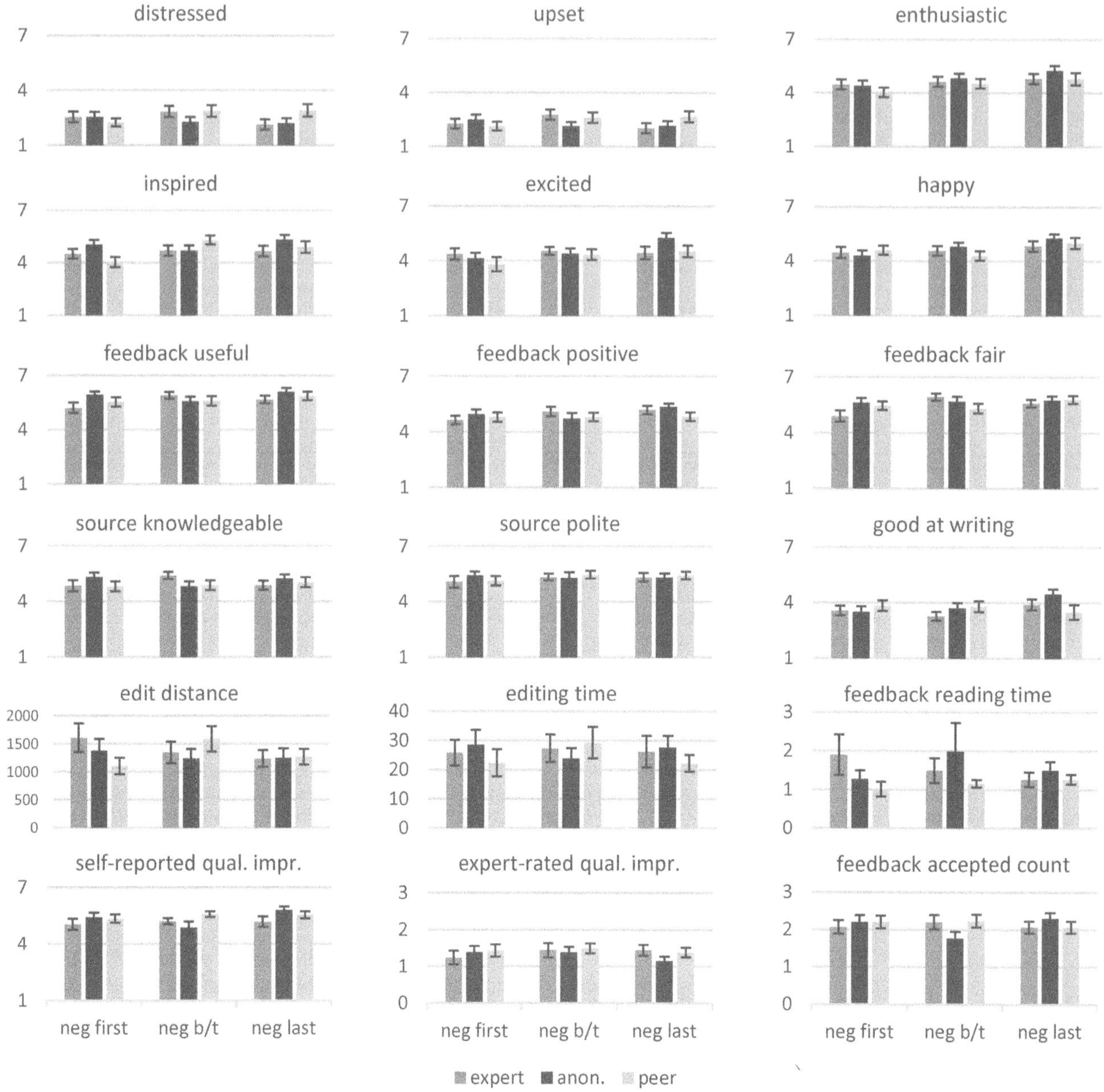

Figure 3. Measurements collected during the experiment. For all charts, the left / center / right groups of bars represent results from negative feedback presented first / between / last conditions. We also color-coded all bars according to source conditions: expert, anonymous (darkest), and peer (lightest). The vertical axes cover both the minimum and maximum (if applicable) range of the measurements.

in terms of self- and expert-rated quality improvement, and edit distance between the initial and revised stories.

We collected the first two sets of measurements from the survey, which included 13 statements regarding participants affective states (6 items adapted from PANAS [36]), their perceptions of the feedback (3 items) and its source (2 items), and confidence in writing skills (2 items). Metrics related to revision extents were derived from participants' action logs. For the quality improvement rating, two experts in English writing each rated all 270 stories. The rating interface presented both the initial and revised versions side by side, and the experts rated how much the revision had improved the quality of the story on a 7-point scale (-3: the original has much higher quality; +3: the revised has much higher quality; 0: no noticeable quality difference). For 91.7% of all stories, the rating difference between the experts was smaller or equal to one unit on the scale. We averaged the two ratings as the final quality improvement. The average quality improvement was 1.37 (SE=0.17) across all conditions.

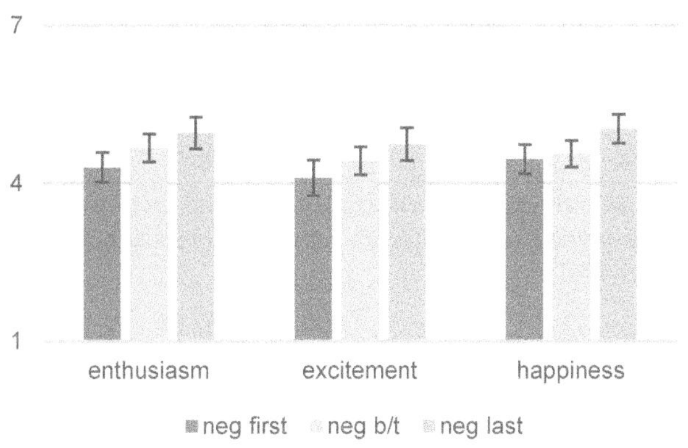

Figure 4. This chart shows the ratings for enthusiasm, excitement, and happiness; clustered by feedback ordering. Presenting negative feedback last resulted in higher ratings of participants' affective states.

RESULTS

In the following subsections, we report the most interesting patterns in our data. Figure 3 summarizes the results.

Participants were most motivated when reading negative feedback last

An ANOVA showed that *Valence Order* had a main effect on the ratings of enthusiasm ($F[2, 267]=3.96$, $p=.02$), excitement ($F[2, 267]=3.51$, $p=.03$), and happiness ($F[2, 267]=3.61$, $p=.03$). See Figure 4. Participants reported significant higher ratings in the negative last condition (enthusiasm: $\mu=4.96$, SE=0.17; excitement: $\mu=4.73$, SE=0.18; happiness: $\mu=5.01$, SE=0.16) than in the negative first condition (enthusiasm: $\mu=4.30$, SE=0.16; excitement: $\mu=4.10$, SE=0.17; happiness: $\mu=4.46$, SE=0.16; $p<.05$). Simply presenting the same feedback in different orders increased participants' enthusiasm by 11.0%, excitement by 10.5%, and happiness by 9.2% on a 7-point scale. In general, the later in the order participants read the negative feedback, the more enthusiastic, more excited, and happier they were. In the negative last condition, participants might view the first two pieces of positive feedback as an affirmation of the quality of their stories and become more resilient to the influence of the negative feedback. There was no significant effect of *Source* on participants' affective states.

Participants reported most favorable perception of the feedback when reading the negative feedback last

Participants in negative last condition rated the feedback set marginally fairer ($\mu=5.70$, SE=0.14) than in the negative first condition ($\mu=5.33$, SE=0.14; $p=.06$). The feedback positivity and usefulness ratings also show the same trends, but did not reach statistical significance. On average, participants rate the feedback fairer by 6.2%, more positive by 5.3%, and more useful by 5.2% on a 7-point scale in the negative last condition in comparison with the negative first condition. *Source* did not have a statistical effect on participants' perception of the feedback measured in the experiment.

Anonymity tended to improve affective states and perceptions of feedback and its source

Despite the lack of statistical significance, we observed interesting trends consistent with prior work regarding feedback source anonymity [24]. Our results show source anonymity tended to improve participants' affective states and led to more favorable perceptions of the feedback set and its source. In the anonymous condition, participants reported being 4.8% more enthusiastic, 5.7% more inspired, 4.6% more excited, 2.9% happier, 4.4% less distressed, and 2.6% less upset than in the peer and expert conditions. Participants also rated the feedback 4.1% more useful, 2.2% more positive, 3.4% fairer, and the feedback source 2.7% more knowledgeable, 1.4% politer on a 7-point scale in the anonymous condition.

Contrary to prior work [7], our results show there is no statistical difference in task performance between the expert and peer cue conditions. Participants in the expert condition spent more time reviewing the feedback ($\mu=94.3$ sec, SE=12.2) than in the peer condition ($\mu=68.8$ sec, SE=12.2), but they perceived the source in the peer condition ($\mu=4.90$, SE=0.15) to be nearly as knowledgeable as in the expert condition ($\mu=5.02$, SE=0.15). There is also no statistical difference in the edit distance or quality improvement.

One potential reason could be participants' familiarity with the writing task. 86.3% of the participants reported having told stories to young children. Participants with storytelling experience self-reported significantly higher quality improvement ($\mu=5.38$, SE=0.08) in comparison with the participants without ($\mu=4.89$, SE=0.23; $t(268)=2.17$, $p=.031$). Participants familiar with the task were more confident in their performance and their writing skill (participants w/ exp.: $\mu=3.78$, SE=0.10; w/o: $\mu=3.41$, SE=0.26). Prior work shows people with higher self-efficacy are less receptive to feedback [22]. The participants' familiarity with the task domain may therefore have affected how they perceived the source cues.

Improved affective states and feedback perception led to more revision

Neither *Valance Order* nor *Source* had a significant effect on the edit distance ($\mu=1327.56$, SD=1025.82), feedback accepted count ($\mu=2.12$, SD=0.06), and expert-rated quality improvement ($\mu=1.37$, SD=0.86). Edit distance was significantly correlated with the feedback accepted count (Pearson's $r=.41$; $p<.01$) and quality improvement ($r=.73$; $p<.01$). The more participants edited their essays, the higher the quality improvement ratings (Table 2). We also observed significant but weak correlations between the edit distance and ratings of enthusiasm ($r=.14$; $p<.05$), excitement ($r=.15$; $p<.05$), and inspiration ($r=.17$; $p<.01$). More motivated participants tend to revise their work more; therefore methods to improve motivation such as ordering feedback by valence as done in this study, providing immediate positive feedback [29], or wrapping feedback with positive language [24] as done in prior work can foster revision. Interestingly, participants' distress level also had a positive correlation

	happy	upset	distress	excited	enthusi.	insipired	fdbk pos.	fdbk use.	fdbk fair
edit distance	-0.03	0.10	0.13	0.15	0.14	0.17	0.12	0.18	0.21
accepted count	0.05	-0.02	-0.02	0.13	0.18	0.18	0.21	0.19	0.24
expert qual. impr.	-0.07	0.05	0.10	0.06	0.06	0.07	0.11	0.17	0.27

Table 2. Correlation table between revision extent metrics and participants' affective states and feedback perception. More favorable perception of the feedback set and more positive affective states correlate with a greater degree of revision.

with the edit distance ($r=.13$, $p<.05$). This correlation might be caused by the acceptance of negative feedback, which increased the edit distance and distress level at the same time. Participants were more likely to accept feedback that leaves more favorable impressions. Edit distance had significant correlations with how useful ($r=.18$, $p<.01$), positive ($r=.12$, $p<.05$), and fair ($r=.21$, $p<.01$) participants perceived the feedback set to be.

Female participants were more receptive to feedback

Table 3 shows the gender difference in our results. Prior work finds women are more influenced by verbal evaluative feedback than men [28]. In our experiment, female participants accepted significantly more pieces of feedback ($\mu=2.23$, $SE=0.07$) and spent marginally longer time reading feedback ($\mu=1.62$ min, $SE=0.17$) than male participants ($\mu=1.94$, $SE=0.09$, $t(268)=-2.53$, $p=.012$; $\mu=1.16$ min, $SE=0.15$, $t(268)=-1.92$, $p=.056$). Female participants also edited their stories more ($\mu=1495.35$, $SE=80.53$), spent more time editing ($\mu=28.65$, $SE=1.93$), and reported higher self-rated quality improvement ($\mu=5.49$, $SE=0.09$) than male participants ($\mu=1075.87$, $SE=93.78$, $t(268)=-3.35$, $p<.001$; $\mu=21.77$, $SE=2.32$, $t(268)=-2.27$, $p=.024$; $\mu=5.03$, $SE=0.14$, $t(268)=-2.92$, $p=.004$ respectively).

On the other hand, negative feedback had a stronger influence over female participants' affective states. Female participants reported feeling more distressed ($\mu=2.72$, $SE=0.12$), more upset ($\mu=2.58$, $SE=0.12$), and marginally less happy ($\mu=4.54$, $SE=0.14$) compared to male participants ($\mu=2.17$, $SE=0.14$, $t(268)=-2.85$, $p=.005$; $\mu=2.05$, $SE=0.13$,

	Female	Male
accepted count *	2.23 (.07)	1.94 (.09)
feedback reading time	1.62 (.17) min	1.16 (.15) min
edited char count **	1495.35 (194.7)	1075.87 (147.7)
story editing time *	28.65 (1.93) min	21.77 (2.32) min
distressed **	2.72 (.13)	2.17 (.14)
upset **	2.58 (.12)	2.05 (.13)
happy	4.54 (.11)	4.88 (.15)

Table 3. Gender comparison between feedback receptivity and affective states. Standard errors of the means are included in parenthesis. For each row, '*' indicates significance level of p<.05, and '' indicates p<.01.**

$t(268)=-2.89$, $p=.004$; $\mu=4.88$, $SE=0.15$, $t(268)=1.86$, $p=.064$). In sum, female participants were more likely to accept and be influenced by the feedback.

DISCUSSION

Our results show presenting negative feedback last improves participants' affective states and perception of the feedback set. Cues of the feedback source had no significant effect on participants' affective states, and no effect on perceptions of the feedback set and its providers. There was no interaction between valence order and feedback source. Female participants were more likely to accept the feedback, even though reviewing the feedback had a larger negative impact on their affective states.

In our experiment, participants received three pieces of feedback for the initial story. This made the experiment tractable and gave the necessary control, but future work should test whether our results generalize to different sizes and valence balances of a feedback set. For larger feedback sets, platform designers could choose to select representative pieces of the feedback to summarize the larger set. Some online platforms, such as Amazon.com, have already adopted this method by showing the highest rated positive and negative reviews as a summary. This presentation mechanism allows users to quickly grasp the key insights without spending significant time consuming all reviews. Online design communities may explore similar techniques based on the valence level and the popularity of the feedback.

Similar techniques could also be used in creativity support tools for writing. When presenting comments collected from external reviewers, writing support tools could offer positive valence comments first and negative ones last. In the case where there is a large quantity of comments or when it is difficult to re-order the feedback (e.g., for inline comments), the tool could show only the positive comments as the default and users could access the additional feedback through interaction. On the other hand, tools could prompt feedback providers to write separately about the positive aspects of the work, and display a summary of these responses first. Future work could also test data-driven approaches that automate positive valence feedback. The system could compare content creators' performance, in terms of grammatical error rate or estimated vocabulary size, against their own prior writing or their peers, and report the positive results.

In our experiment, we achieved different levels of valence by adjusting the language of the feedback. Our results may also generalize to other visual indicators of valence. Platform designers in creative domains could take inspiration from other online review services. Some online work platforms deliver feedback along with valence indicators such as upvote / downvote in performance review or job approval / rejection scenarios. These indicators make it straightforward for platform designers to order feedback by valence. Another common form of a valence indicator is a numeric rating such as star ratings or scores on review sites. Fine-grained ratings make it easy to compare the valence levels among feedback. Platform designers could implement these valence indicators in online feedback collection services and facilitate the valence ordering process.

Feedback valence order had the same influence across the source conditions in our study. The valence order may therefore have similar effects on platforms where feedback providers have different social identities and expertise. The participants in our study were mainly novice content creators. Experienced content creators may react differently to the manipulations. Prior work shows experts seek negative feedback more actively than novices [10]. Negative feedback may therefore have a weaker impact on experienced content creators. Future work should test whether experience level of content creators interacts with valence order.

In our study, there was a delay between writing the initial story and receiving the feedback. For future work, it would be interesting to test how a delay between reviewing the feedback and revising the story would affect our measures, as delays can promote reflection and learning [14]. Another way to extend our work is to test the effects of different positive to negative feedback ratios, especially when a majority of the feedback has a negative valence. Researchers can also explore effects of ordering feedback using attributes other than valence such as design aspects [26], content complexity [6], and the effort invested in writing it [38].

Future work could also examine how *writing* feedback in a certain valence order affects the providers' perceptions of the usefulness of their own feedback. This technique could potentially improve feedback providers' experience on the review platform and encourage further participation.

CONCLUSION

Content creators frequently receive negative feedback online. To increase feedback receptivity, we tested a novel method of ordering a set of feedback based on its valence, and tested how this ordering interacts with different source identities. Our work makes two contributions. First, we provided empirical evidence that presenting negative feedback last improves content creators' affective states and their perception of the feedback. Second, our results show valence order does not interact with feedback source, although source anonymity tends to improve feedback acceptance. In general, our study demonstrates that a simple feedback order manipulation can lead to measurable improvements in content creators' affective states and perception of feedback. We hope our work can improve content creators' experience of receiving feedback online.

ACKNOWLEDGMENTS

This work was supported in part by the National Science Foundation under awards NSF CMMI 14-62693 and IIS 15-30818.

REFERENCE

1. Matthijs Baas, Carsten K W De Dreu, and Bernard A Nijstad. 2008. A meta-analysis of 25 years of mood-creativity research: Hedonic tone, activation, or regulatory focus? *Psychological Bulletin* 134, 6: 779–806. https://doi.org/10.1037/a0012815
2. Jessica L. Bienstock, Nadine T. Katz, Susan M. Cox, Nancy Hueppchen, Sonya Erickson, and Elizabeth E. Puscheck. 2007. To the point: medical education reviews-providing feedback. *American Journal of Obstetrics and Gynecology* 196, 6: 508–513. https://doi.org/10.1016/j.ajog.2006.08.021
3. Cheryl Campanella Bracken, Leo W. Jeffres, and Kimberly A. Neuendorf. 2004. Criticism or Praise? The Impact of Verbal versus Text-Only Computer Feedback on Social Presence, Intrinsic Motivation, and Recall. *CyberPsychology & Behavior* 7, 3: 349–357. https://doi.org/10.1089/1094931041291358
4. Peter Cantillon and Joan Sargeant. 2008. Giving feedback in clinical settings. *BMJ (Clinical research ed.)* 337, 7681: a1961. https://doi.org/10.1136/bmj.a1961
5. Olle Th J ten Cate. 2013. Why receiving feedback collides with self determination. *Advances in Health Sciences Education* 18, 4: 845–849. https://doi.org/10.1007/s10459-012-9401-0
6. John V Dempsey, Marcy P Driscoll, and Linda K Swindell. 1993. Text-based feedback. *Interactive instruction and feedback*: 21–54.
7. D Fedor. 2001. Performance improvement efforts in response to negative feedback: the roles of source power and recipient self-esteem. *Journal of Management* 27, 1: 79–97. https://doi.org/10.1016/S0149-2063(00)00087-8
8. Dana R Ferris. 1997. The Influence of Teacher Commentary on Student Revision. *TESOL Quarterly* 31, 2: 315. https://doi.org/10.2307/3588049
9. Dana Ferris and Barrie Roberts. 2001. Error feedback in L2 writing classes. *Journal of Second Language Writing* 10, 3: 161–184. https://doi.org/10.1016/S1060-3743(01)00039-X
10. Stacey R. Finkelstein and Ayelet Fishbach. 2012. Tell Me What I Did Wrong: Experts Seek and Respond to Negative Feedback. *Journal of Consumer Research* 39, 1: 22–38. https://doi.org/10.1086/661934
11. Michael D Greenberg, Matthew W Easterday, and Elizabeth M Gerber. 2015. Critiki: A Scaffolded Approach to Gathering Design Feedback from Paid Crowdworkers. In *Proceedings of the 2015 ACM SIGCHI Conference on Creativity and Cognition - C&C '15*, 235–244. https://doi.org/10.1145/2757226.2757249
12. Laura Hale. 2015. What is the meaning of "answer collapsed" in Quora? (August 22, 2015). *Quora.* Retrieved January 5, 2017 from

https://www.quora.com/What-is-the-meaning-of-answer-collapsed-in-Quora/answer/Laura-Hale?srid=uxyk

13. Richard H. Haswell. 2005. NCTE/CCCC's recent war on scholarship. *Written Communication* 22, 2: 198–223. https://doi.org/10.1177/0741088305275367

14. John Hattie and Helen Timperley. 2007. The Power of Feedback. *Review of Educational Research* 77, 1: 81–112. https://doi.org/10.3102/003465430298487

15. John Hedgcock and Natalie Lefkowitz. 1994. Feedback on feedback: Assessing learner receptivity to teacher response in L2 composing. *Journal of Second Language Writing* 3, 2: 141–163. https://doi.org/10.1016/1060-3743(94)90012-4

16. E a Hesketh and J M Laidlaw. 2002. Developing the teaching instinct. *Medical teacher* 24, 3: 245–348. https://doi.org/10.1080/014215902201409911

17. David G. Jansson and Steven M. Smith. 1991. Design fixation. *Design Studies* 12, 1: 3–11. https://doi.org/10.1016/0142-694X(91)90003-F

18. Cliff Lampe, Rick Wash, Alcides Velasquez, and Elif Ozkaya. 2010. Motivations to participate in online communities. In *Proceedings of the 28th international conference on Human factors in computing systems - CHI '10*, 1927. https://doi.org/10.1145/1753326.1753616

19. Kurt Luther, Jari-lee Tolentino, Wei Wu, et al. 2015. Structuring, Aggregating, and Evaluating Crowdsourced Design Critique. In *Proceedings of the 18th ACM Conference on Computer Supported Cooperative Work & Social Computing - CSCW '15*, 473–485. https://doi.org/10.1145/2675133.2675283

20. Winter Mason and Duncan J. Watts. 2010. Financial incentives and the "performance of crowds." *ACM SIGKDD Explorations Newsletter* 11, 2: 100. https://doi.org/10.1145/1809400.1809422

21. Edna Holland Mory. 2004. Feedback Research Revisited. In *Handbook of research on educational communications and technology* (2nd ed.), David H. Jonassen (ed.). Lawrence Erlbaum Associates Publishers, Mahwah, NJ, US, 745–783.

22. AnJanette A. Nease, Brad O. Mudgett, and Miguel A. Quiñones. 1999. Relationships among feedback sign, self-efficacy, and acceptance of performance feedback. *Journal of Applied Psychology* 84, 5: 806–814. https://doi.org/10.1037/0021-9010.84.5.806

23. Christine M Neuwirth, Ravinder Chandhok, Davida Charney, Patricia Wojahn, and Loel Kim. 1994. Distributed collaborative writing. In *Proceedings of the SIGCHI conference on Human factors in computing systems celebrating interdependence - CHI '94*, 51–57. https://doi.org/10.1145/191666.191693

24. Thi Thao Duyen T. Nguyen, Thomas Garncarz, Felicia Ng, Laura A. Dabbish, and Steven P. Dow. 2017. Fruitful Feedback. In *Proceedings of the 2017 ACM Conference on Computer Supported Cooperative Work and Social Computing - CSCW '17*, 1024–1034. https://doi.org/10.1145/2998181.2998319

25. Jay Parkes, Sara Abercrombie, and Teresita McCarty. 2013. Feedback sandwiches affect perceptions but not performance. *Advances in Health Sciences Education* 18, 3: 397–407. https://doi.org/10.1007/s10459-012-9377-9

26. J. van der Pol, B.A.M. van den Berg, W.F. Admiraal, and P.R.J. Simons. 2008. The nature, reception, and use of online peer feedback in higher education. *Computers & Education* 51, 4: 1804–1817. https://doi.org/10.1016/j.compedu.2008.06.001

27. Mark C. Porte, George Xeroulis, Richard K. Reznick, and Adam Dubrowski. 2007. Verbal feedback from an expert is more effective than self-accessed feedback about motion efficiency in learning new surgical skills. *The American Journal of Surgery* 193, 1: 105–110. https://doi.org/10.1016/j.amjsurg.2006.03.016

28. Tomi-Ann Roberts and Susan Nolen-Hoeksema. 1989. Sex differences in reactions to evaluative feedback. *Sex Roles* 21, 11–12: 725–747. https://doi.org/10.1007/BF00289805

29. Alwin de Rooij, Philip J Corr, and Sara Jones. 2015. Emotion and Creativity: Hacking into Cognitive Appraisal Processes to Augment Creative Ideation. In *Proceedings of the 2015 ACM SIGCHI Conference on Creativity and Cognition - C&C '15*, 265–274. https://doi.org/10.1145/2757226.2757227

30. Alwin de Rooij and Sara Jones. 2013. Mood and creativity. In *Proceedings of the 9th ACM Conference on Creativity & Cognition - C&C '13*, 362. https://doi.org/10.1145/2466627.2466658

31. Joel Ross, Lilly Irani, M. Six Silberman, Andrew Zaldivar, and Bill Tomlinson. 2010. Who are the crowdworkers? In *Proceedings of the 28th of the international conference extended abstracts on Human factors in computing systems - CHI EA '10*, 2863. https://doi.org/10.1145/1753846.1753873

32. D. Royce Sadler. 1989. Formative assessment and the design of instructional systems. *Instructional Science* 18, 2: 119–144. https://doi.org/10.1007/BF00117714

33. Jason Shah. 2012. Hacker News: Stop greying out flagged comments (March 10, 2012). Retrieved January 5, 2017 from http://blog.jasonshah.org/post/19079124354/hacker-news-stop-greying-out-flagged-comments

34. Steven M Smith, Julie S. Linsey, and Andruid Kerne. 2011. Using Evolved Analogies to Overcome Creative Design Fixation. In *Design Creativity 2010*. Springer London, London, 35–39. https://doi.org/10.1007/978-0-85729-224-7_6

35. John Suler. 2004. The Online Disinhibition Effect. *CyberPsychology & Behavior* 7, 3: 321–326. https://doi.org/10.1089/1094931041291295

36. D Watson, L a Clark, and A Tellegen. 1988. Development and validation of brief measures of positive and negative affect: the PANAS scales. *Journal of personality and social psychology* 54, 6: 1063–70. https://doi.org/10.1037/0022-3514.54.6.1063

37. Daniel B Willingham. 1990. Effective feedback on written assignments. *Teaching of Psychology* 17, 1: 10–13. https://doi.org/10.1207/s15328023top1701_2

38. Y Wayne Wu and Brian P Bailey. 2016. Novices Who Focused or Experts Who Didn't? In *Proceedings of the 2016 CHI Conference on Human Factors in Computing Systems - CHI '16*, 4086–4097. https://doi.org/10.1145/2858036.2858330

39. Anbang Xu and Brian P. Bailey. 2012. What Do You Think? A Case Study of Benefit, Expectation, and Interaction in a Large Online Critique Community. *Proceedings of the 15th ACM conference on Computer supported cooperative work & social computing - CSCW'12*: 295. https://doi.org/10.1145/2145204.2145252

40. Anbang Xu, Shih-wen Huang, and Brian Bailey. 2014. Voyantt: Generating Structured Feedback on Visual Designs Using a Crowd of Non-Experts. In *Proceedings of the 17th ACM conference on Computer supported cooperative work & social computing - CSCW '14*, 1433–1444. https://doi.org/10.1145/2531602.2531604

41. Koji Yatani, Michael Novati, Andrew Trusty, and Khai N. Truong. 2011. Review spotlight. In *Proceedings of the 2011 annual conference on Human factors in computing systems - CHI '11*, 1541. https://doi.org/10.1145/1978942.1979167

42. Yu-Chun Grace Yen, Steven P. Dow, Elizabeth Gerber, and Brian P. Bailey. 2016. Social Network , Web Forum , or Task Market ? Comparing Different Crowd Genres for Design Feedback Exchange. *ACM Designing Interactive Systems (DIS 2016)*: 773–784. https://doi.org/10.1145/2901790.2901820

43. Yu-Chun Grace Yen, Steven P. Dow, Elizabeth Gerber, and Brian P. Bailey. 2017. Listen to Others, Listen to Yourself: Combining Feedback Review and Reflection to Improve Iterative Design. In *Proceedings of the 2017 ACM SIGCHI Conference on Creativity and Cognition - C&C '17*. https://doi.org/10.1145/3059454.3059468

44. Alvin Yuan, Kurt Luther, Markus Krause, Sophie Isabel Vennix, Steven P Dow, and Björn Hartmann. 2016. Almost an Expert: The Effects of Rubrics and Expertise on Perceived Value of Crowdsourced Design Critiques. In *Proceedings of the 19th ACM Conference on Computer-Supported Cooperative Work & Social Computing - CSCW '16*, 1003–1015. https://doi.org/10.1145/2818048.2819953

45. Jing Zhou. 1998. Feedback valence, feedback style, task autonomy, and achievement orientation: Interactive effects on creative performance. *Journal of Applied Psychology* 83, 2: 261–276. https://doi.org/10.1037/0021-9010.83.2.261

46. Haiyi Zhu, Robert E Kraut, Yi-Chia Wang, and Aniket Kittur. 2011. Identifying shared leadership in Wikipedia. In *Proceedings of the 2011 annual conference on Human factors in computing systems - CHI '11*, 3431. https://doi.org/10.1145/1978942.1979453

47. Hiyi Zhu, Amy Zhang, Jiping He, Robert E Kraut, and Aniket Kittur. 2013. Effects of peer feedback on contribution. In *Proceedings of the SIGCHI Conference on Human Factors in Computing Systems - CHI '13*, 2253. https://doi.org/10.1145/2470654.2481311

48. Sentiment Analysis API| AlchemyAPI. Retrieved January 5, 2017 from http://www.alchemyapi.com/products/alchemylanguage/sentiment-analysis

Creativity and Emotion: Enhancing Creative Thinking by the Manipulation of Computational Feedback to Determine Emotional Intensity

Alwin de Rooij
Tilburg center for Cognition and Communication
Tilburg University
Warandelaan 2, Tilburg, NL
alwinderooij@uvt.nl

Philip J. Corr
Department of Psychology
City, University of London
Northampton Square, London
EC1V 0HB, UK
philip.corr.1@city.ac.uk

Sara Jones
CASS Business School
City, University of London
Northampton Square, London
EC1V 0HB, UK
s.v.jones@city.ac.uk

ABSTRACT
Positive emotions can enhance the ability of people to generate original ideas, and its intensity can determine the degree to which people are able to think originally. How to design a technology that can be used to hack into this link between the intensity of positive emotion and creative thinking is, however, still an open problem. To address this we have conceived, developed, and experimentally evaluated a proof-of-concept interactive system that generates believable computational feedback about the originality of a user's own ideas in real-time. This system can manipulate this feedback to make a user's own ideas appear more or less original than people would typically judge them to be, and can also vary the order of this manipulation over time. This has enabled us to test experimentally that: (i) the order in which the positivity and negativity of the feedback is varied can be used to condition people's expectations, which (ii) can be used to later determine an intended intensity a positive emotion that a user experience, and which (iii) subsequently influence the degree to which the user is able to generate original ideas. The findings demonstrate that an interactive system can be designed to determine the type and intensity of an emotional response, in a manner that enhances the people's ability to generate original ideas.

Author Keywords
Creativity; Emotion; Expectations; Interactive systems.

ACM Classification Keywords
H.5.m. Information interfaces and presentation (e.g., HCI): Miscellaneous.

C&C '17, June 27-30, 2017, Singapore, Singapore
© 2017 ACM. ISBN 978-1-4503-4403-6/17/06...$15.00
DOI: http://dx.doi.org/10.1145/3059454.3059469

INTRODUCTION
Creative thinking can be enhanced by certain emotions [2, 15]. For instance, when people experience positive emotions, cognitive flexibility increases, which augments a human's ability to generate diverse and original ideas [1]. The intensity of positive emotion is also assumed to determine the extent to which flexibility increases, and therefore to influence the degree to which people are able to generate diverse and original ideas [cf. 2]. It follows from this that an interactive technology that causes emotions with an intended intensity could be used to augment human creativity. However, the question of how to design an interactive system that effectively makes use of this potential remains open [13, 14].

In this paper, we describe the conception, development, and experimental evaluation of one such system. Based on previous research, we conjecture that positive and negative emotions during idea generation are caused via the appraisal of the originality or unoriginality of a person's own ideas [13]. These cognitive appraisal processes not only cause emotion, and determine their type, but also condition the expectations that people will have about their ability to generate original ideas in similar, future situations 10]. Expectations, in turn, provide a frame of reference against which such appraisals determine the intensity of the positive and negative emotions caused [10]. The intensity of these positive and negative emotions then impacts the momentary capacity for human creative thought [2].

Based on this argument, we developed a proof-of-concept interactive system that generates believable feedback about the originality of a user's ideas. This is done by automatically generating feedback after a user generates an idea, and manipulating this feedback to make the user's ideas appear more, or less, original than people typically think they are. The order in which the manipulations are applied, for instance, by first making it easier and later more difficult to get positive feedback, is assumed to condition a user's expectations about its ability to generate original ideas. This can then be used to cause positive and negative emotions with an intended intensity [cf. 10], enabling the system to purposefully augment or diminish the actual ability of the user to generate original ideas [2].

We hypothesise and demonstrate experimentally that the developed interactive system can be used to condition a user's expectations about his or her own ability to generate original ideas, and subsequently cause positive and negative emotions with an intended intensity. The intensity of positive emotions caused is shown to influence the degree to which the user is able to generate original ideas. Thus, the contribution of the present study is a demonstration that an interactive system can be designed to manipulate cognitive appraisal processes to determine the type and intensity of an emotional response, in a manner that helps people to perform better on creative idea generation tasks.

EMOTION, INTENSITY, AND CREATIVITY

Emotions have been defined as responses to events that help adapt the way we think and act in support of our own and other's wellbeing [30]. Emotions consist of changes in a number of emotion components, and include: the cognitive appraisal of events (e.g. I am performing well); action tendencies (e.g. a tendency to approach); somatic and neuroendocrine responses (e.g. dopamine release in reward pathways); motor expressions (e.g. smiling and approaching movements); and feelings, the aspects of the mentioned emotion components that can be subjectively experienced (e.g. feeling joyous) [30].

Creativity has been defined as the development of ideas, insights, or solutions that are both original and effective [29]. To arrive at a creative outcome, people cycle back and forth through a range of information processing steps, with the creative process consisting of: 1) problem definition, 2) information gathering, 3) concept selection, 4) conceptual combination, 5) idea generation, 6) idea evaluation, 7) implementation planning, and 8) solution monitoring [24]. The degree of creativity that people display depends on the way the steps in the creative process are executed.

Emotions can augment or diminish creativity when the effects of those emotions on the way people think and act influence the way the creative process, including idea generation, is executed favours the emergence of original (yet effective) ideas [15]. In the present study we focus on the production of original ideas during idea generation.

The emotion-creativity link

Emotions can be generally distinguished by the positive (e.g. joy, pride, satisfaction) or negative (e.g. sadness, anger, fear) experiences associated with them [30], and by their intensity, i.e. the degree to which an event drives changes in, and recruits, the emotion components [7].

Positive emotions in particular are associated with augmented creativity during idea generation [2]. Positive emotions influence the flexibility with which information is made available to conceptual combination, and idea generation processes. Hence positive emotions can augment creativity, because an increase in flexibility increases the chance that more remote concepts are combined, which in turn increases the chance that the ideas generated are original. *Negative emotions* typically are associated with diminished creativity during idea generation [2], though some exceptions to this exist as well [3, 27]. Negative emotions focus the way people think and act on the event that causes the negative emotion. This, in turn, reduces the flexibility with which information is made available to the creative process, and hence reduces the chance that original ideas are generated. Thus, negative emotions can diminish creativity when compared to positive emotions, because a decrease in flexibility reduces the chance that remote concepts are combined, and consequently reduces the chance that any ideas generated are original.

We assume that the *emotional intensity* of positive and negative emotions has a direct effect on the degree to which these emotions influence creativity. This is based on the assumption that emotional intensity reflects the degree of changes in, and recruitment of, the emotion components [7]. It follows that in the case of positive emotions, emotional intensity influences the degree of flexibility with which people are able to generate ideas [1]. Thus, the intensity of positive emotion could regulate the degree to which people are able to think up original ideas. In the case of negative emotions, and increase in emotional intensity influences the degree to which the emotion components change to facilitate an adaptive response that focuses on resolving a problem that is encountered [30]. We assume that the intensity of negative emotions subtracts from the flexibility necessary to generate original ideas, which should diminish the ability of people to generate original ideas when compared to positive emotions [cf. 2]. However, the link between the intensity of negative emotion and creativity during idea generation, however, has not been studied explicitly until now. Therefore, the possible relationship between the intensity of different emotions and creativity is still very much an unanswered question.

It follows from the above that an interactive system that can help cause positive and negative emotions with an intended intensity can be used to influence the degree to which people are able to generate original ideas.

Causing emotion

Cognitive appraisal theory describes the way in which different appraisals, or perceptions, of events in an individual's environment determine the type of emotional response that is caused [30]. Appraisals typically drive changes in the other emotion components, which shape the emotion's influence on the way people think and act. From a cognitive appraisal perspective, appraisals that indicate the *goal-conduciveness* and *goal-obstructiveness* of an event are what differentiate positive from negative emotions. Goal-conduciveness and goal-obstruction refer to the way in which an event influences the progress toward or away from attaining an individual's goals. That is, if an event indicates that an increase in the progress to the goals of an individual, positive emotion is typically caused; but when an event indicates a move away from an individual's goals, negative emotion is typically caused. Other appraisals, e.g. whether an event is caused by someone else or yourself, or whether you are able to cope with a situation, further differentiate the type emotion that unfolds, e.g. the difference between the positive emotions of joy and pride. See [30] for an overview.

Creativity during idea generation involves cycling back and forth through information processing steps that involve conceptual combination, the actual generation of ideas based on different concepts, and the evaluation of these generated ideas [24]. For instance, conceptual combination feeds forward into the idea generation step in the creative process to provide the concepts based on which ideas can be generated, whereas idea evaluation feeds back into the idea generation step to provide information about the originality or usefulness of the generated ideas, which in turn shapes the way people generate further ideas [23]. Note that in this study we refer to this particular cycle simply as *idea generation*, because we believe that we cannot isolate the conceptual combinations that feed forward, and the idea evaluations that feed back from the idea generation step itself. We assume that a cognitive appraisal theory of emotion [30] can also be applied to the appraisals that form part of the evaluation of ideas, and therefore might impact conceptual combination and idea generation [23], via the way emotions influence the execution of these particular steps in the creative process [cf. 15, 24].

Events that are goal-conducive or goal-obstructive within the context of idea generation can be found by examining the function of idea generation in the creative process as a whole. First, the function of idea generation is to output sufficient *original* material during the early stages of a creative process, whereas other goals, such as developing effective ideas, become more important during later stages [11, 24]. This indicates that the generation of original ideas is the main goal that people strive for during creative idea generation. Second, previous studies have found that manipulation of the degree to which people believe that their own ideas are original or unoriginal, regardless of the ideas' actual originality, influences the degree to which they experience positive and negative emotions during idea generation [13, 14, 16]. Thus, we can assume that the generation of original ideas is goal-conducive, whereas the generation of unoriginal ideas is perceived as goal-obstructive during creative idea generation.

An interactive system that can influence the appraisal of the originality or unoriginality of a user's ideas, can therefore be used to intentionally help cause positive and negative emotions during creative idea generation.

Determining emotional intensity

Cognitive appraisal processes not only play a role in causing and differentiating emotion, they also help determine *emotional intensity* [30]. That is, they help determine the degree to which an event drives changes in, and recruits, the emotion components [7].

The intensity of an emotion is, in part, determined by the appraisal of an event against some frame of reference [19]. Across the range of positive and negative emotions, *expectations*, the individual's beliefs about the probable outcome of an event or situation, appear to provide such a frame of reference [21, 33]. The more an event implies a deviation from the expected progress toward (goal-conduciveness), or away from (goal-obstructiveness), the individual's goals, the more intense the resulting positive or negative emotion is, and the stronger the change that is fed forward into the other emotion components [10]. That is, if expectations are low, the same event is more likely to imply better progress toward the individual's goals, and cause more intense positive emotion, than when expectations are high [21]. If expectations are high, the same event is more likely to imply worse progress away from the individual's goals and cause more intense negative emotion than when expectations are low [6]. Other appraisal processes, particular to more specific emotions (e.g. the blameworthiness of a person during anger), can also influence emotional intensity. See [6, 33] for overviews.

The cognitive appraisal processes that cause positive and negative emotions reciprocally condition the expectations that help determine the intensity of these emotions [10]. This is because expectations are formed, in part, based on how often and how recently particular events have happened, and based on how these events are appraised, in particular situations [34]. That is, if an event, in a particular situation, repeatedly implies better progress toward an individual's goals, expectations will be raised for subsequent similar situations [10]. Likewise, if an event repeatedly implies more progress away from the individual's goals, expectations will be lowered. The degree to which expectations are lowered or raised depends in part on the degree an event implies deviations from one's initial expectations [10]. Note that other factors (e.g. the amount of available resources, or optimism) can also influence expectations.

On the basis of the arguments set out above, we hypothesised that an interactive system that influences a user's appraisal of the originality or unoriginality of his or her own ideas could be used to condition the expectations an individual has about its ability to generate original ideas, and thereby cause positive and negative emotions with an intended intensity, thus influencing the discussed link between emotional intensity and creative thinking.

INTERACTIVE SYSTEM

Interactive systems that attempt to hack into the link between emotion, emotional intensity and creativity are scarce. First, interactive systems have been developed that attempt to make use of the function of motor expressions in emotion regulation to modulate the intensity of emotions that are caused during a creative process [14, 16]. For instance, [14] showed that using arm gestures to trigger an audio recording device used to record creative ideas, could hack into the link between positive emotion and creativity, when these arm gestures were designed on the basis of emotion expressions that associate with positive and negative emotions. The results of this study suggested that the intensity of a positive emotion could be increased when generating an idea itself caused positive emotion and was paired with a positive recording gesture, which subsequently enhanced people's ability to generate original ideas.

Second, interactive systems have also been developed to make use of the causal function of cognitive appraisal processes in emotion (such as discussed in our theory section) [13]. For instance, a recent study used an interactive system that generates believable feedback about the originality or unoriginality of a user's ideas to increase the likelihood that users appraise their own ideas as more original or unoriginal, to intentionally increase the likelihood that users experience positive or negative emotion during idea generation. This was done by making the users' ideas appear less original (i.e. negative feedback manipulation), or more original (i.e. positive feedback manipulation). The results showed that increasing the likelihood of experiencing positive emotion indeed enhanced the ability of users to generate actual original ideas.

Although the system developed in [13] can be used to effectively influence a user's appraisal of the originality or unoriginality of his or her own ideas, we do not know whether such a system can also be used to condition the expectations an individual has about his or her ability to generate original ideas, and thereby cause positive and negative emotions with an intended intensity, and subsequently determine the degree to which people are able to generate original ideas. To this end, we redesigned the interactive system developed in [13]. We refer to [13] for more technical details of the used interactive system. In what follows below we will emphasise those aspects of the interactive system that have been redesigned.

Generating computational feedback

The interactive system operationalises originality as the statistical infrequency of a (newly) generated idea, given a large set of (previously) generated ideas about the same topic [cf. 32]. For the system to estimate originality we have collected a large set of ideas about two subjects: 3504 creative uses of a brick generated by 409 people, and 2128 creative uses of a paperclip generated by 210 people. To calculate the statistical infrequency of a newly generated idea, the interactive system compares the verbs and nouns it finds in the new idea, to the frequency of all the verbs and nouns in the large set of previously generated ideas. This was done using existing natural language processing technology, including the hun-pos tagger [20], adapted Lesk [4], and the WordNet ontology [18]. The more the verbs and nouns extracted from a new idea are found in the set of previously generated ideas, the lower the originality of the new idea. A ranked score ranging from 0 to 100 (0=very unoriginal, 100=very original) is computed based on these frequencies, to give a basic originality score.

A previous study [13] suggested that users find the computational feedback generated in this way to be believable, and relevant to their own idea generation process. This suggests that the system's feedback can be used to influence the cognitive appraisal processes that form part of positive and negative emotions during creative idea generation.

Manipulating feedback

The interactive system is endowed with the capability to manipulate the feedback it generates such that the user's ideas appear less original (*negative feedback manipulation*) or more original (*positive feedback manipulation*) than people typically believe they are. These feedback manipulations are computed by applying a function that was obtained from a previous empirical study, about the degree to which people think an originality rating can reasonably be higher or lower than the actual originality of an idea [13], to the basic originality score that the system generates. Using empirically obtained mapping functions in this way increases the likelihood that the negative feedback manipulations are not too negative, and the positive feedback manipulations are not too positive to still be believable to the user.

We assume that repeated provision of computational feedback that is manipulated in this way, can be used to condition a user's expectations about their own ability to generate original ideas, and cause positive and negative emotions, as described above.

Conditioning expectations

In addition to providing manipulated feedback in the manner described above, we also assume that the order in which the feedback manipulations are used can further enable the system to make use of the conditioning of expectations, to cause emotions with and intended type, and determine the intensity of these emotions. Based on the research we discussed, we assume that this can be done by varying the order of the feedback manipulations over two consecutive related tasks, as follows:

1) Positive feedback followed by negative feedback manipulation may condition high expectations first, and then lead people to believe they are doing much worse than they have come to expect, leading to more intense negative emotions.
2) Negative feedback followed by further negative feedback manipulation may condition low expectations

first, but as people become accustomed to these expectations, they may come to believe they are doing as expected, leading to less intense negative emotions.

3) Positive followed by positive feedback manipulation conditions high expectations first, but as people become accustomed to these expectations, they come to believe they are doing as expected, leading to less intense positive emotions.
4) Negative followed by positive feedback manipulation may condition low expectations first, and then lead people to believe they are doing much better than they have come to expect, leading to more intense positive emotions.

We assume that if users receive the computer generated feedback in a manner that is manipulated according to these order patterns, the system will effectively be able to condition expectations in the first set of manipulations, and hence cause positive and negative emotions with an intended intensity in the second set of tasks, as described in the above section.

User interface

To enable basic textual input of ideas and effectively communicate the feedback on those ideas we developed a user interface. Users can type in their ideas in text blocks. Upon pressing ENTER the system estimates a basic originality score of the idea just typed, and maps this score to an output value using the pre-specified negative, neutral, or positive feedback manipulation described above. The resulting output is presented as informational feedback about the idea the user just generated (Figure 1). The feedback is presented by using a colour code, based on the manipulated scores (red = 0<25, orange = 25<50, amber = 50<75, green = 75<100), and numerically, using the manipulated ranked estimate of originality.

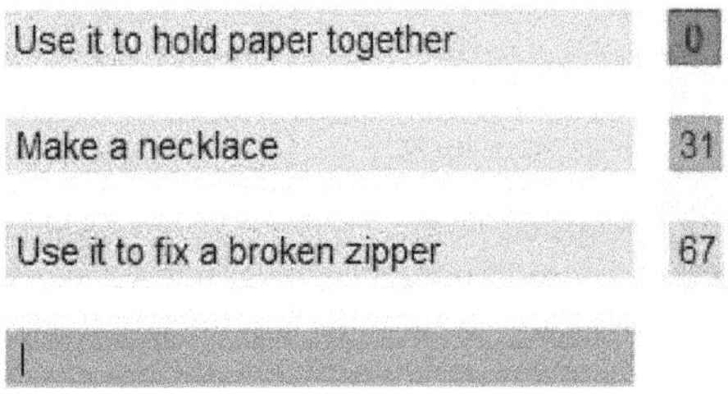

Figure 1 A screenshot of the way feedback is presented showing text entry (left), and feedback (right). The ideas and feedback shown here are responses to the paperclip as a subject, with the negative feedback manipulation.

We assume that presenting the feedback right after each idea is generated and typed in enables the system to make use of the conjectured links between expectations, emotional intensity, and creativity during idea generation.

Hypotheses

To put our conceptions and system to the test, we experimentally tested the following hypotheses (Table 1).

#	Hypothesis
H1	The order in which feedback is made more positive or negative determines the intensity of positive and negative emotion by conditioning people's expectations about their ability to generate original ideas.
H2	The order in which feedback is made more positive or negative influences the degree to which people are able to generate original ideas via the feedback's influence on the intensity of positive and negative emotion.

Table 1 Hypotheses

METHOD

To test the hypotheses and thereby evaluate experimentally the interactive system, we used a between-subject design. Each participant did two idea generation tasks, while using the interactive system, during which the interactive system manipulated the feedback it generated about the originality of participants' ideas. Each participant was exposed to one of the following order patterns with which the system's feedback manipulations were administered:

1. Positive feedback manipulation in task 1, followed by negative feedback manipulation in task 2 (PN).
2. Negative feedback manipulation in task 1 and 2 (NN).
3. Positive feedback manipulation in task 1 and 2 (PP).
4. Negative feedback manipulation in task 1, followed by positive feedback manipulation in task 2 (NP).

Note that (i) getting only positive feedback or only negative feedback during both tasks can be seen as a control group, i.e. the group that should not deviate from expectations; and (ii) analysis was done only on the results obtained after the second task, which justifies using a between-subject, rather than a within-subject design. A cover story was used to hide the true purpose of the study. Both the feedback manipulations and the subjects used during the tasks were randomised to prevent research bias.

Participants

In total, 59 people (49 females, 10 males, M_{age}=29, SD_{age}=6.97) participated in our study. The sampling method was one of convenience. Two participants guessed the purpose of the study, one admitted not to have paid attention to the feedback, and three were identified that gamed the interactive system by typing in bizarre ideas. As these may threaten the internal validity of the results, we removed these cases from the analysis, which resulted in 53 usable cases. Participants were students or employees from City, University of London in the United Kingdom.

Materials and measurements

Idea generation task

To gather data from which we could assess the participants' creativity during idea generation, they performed two consecutive alternative uses tasks (AUTs). The AUT is commonly used to emulate the idea generation step in the creative process [32]. In our study participants were instructed to "*...come up with as many, diverse, and original uses for the common object as you can*", within 4 minutes. These 4 minutes were timed by the computer program, which disabled the ability to enter new ideas after the set time had passed. Time was not shown on the screen. A different common object (brick or paperclip) was used for each task. The order of presentation was randomised.

Assessment of originality

To assess *originality* we used the system's own basic originality scores. The amount of ideas generated in the second AUT that were above the 75th percentile rank was counted for each individual (24% of the total amount of ideas in this study). We only assessed ideas generated after 60 seconds, in order to avoid ideas generated when the interactive system could not yet have had a strong enough effect on emotion and its intensity. We then averaged the amount of original ideas across each individual to correct for possible differences in the number of ideas participants generated [26].

Assessment of emotion

To assess positive emotion we asked the participants to rate the degree of *satisfaction* they experienced during the second task using a nine point Likert scale (1=not satisfied, 9=very satisfied). To assess negative emotion we asked the participants to rate the degree of *frustration* they experienced during the second task, also using a nine point Likert scale (1=not frustrated, 9=very frustrated). We assumed that these emotions would best reflect the type of emotions typically associated with goal-conduciveness and goal-obstruction while pursuing a goal in a performance context [30], and that this would make it easier for the participants to recall their feelings after the tasks.

Assessment of expectations

To assess whether the feedback manipulations influenced the participants' *expectations* about their own ability to generate original ideas, we asked them to rate whether they felt that they did much worse, or much better, than they expected they would do (1=much worse than expected, 9=much better than expected).. We explicitly did not check for the expectations they had prior to each task because we were unsure whether people would be able to self-report adequately and correctly. Instead, we assumed that the degree to which the participant's own performance violated their expectations would be easier to report.

Procedure

Upon arrival at the testing session, participants were seated at a computer and introduced to the study. They were informed that we were testing *"... the efficacy of using computer supported idea evaluation."* We did, however, withhold information about the actual experimental conditions until the end of the experiment. Informed consent was signed, and the participants filled in a brief questionnaire to collect personal data. We then explained that they would do two AUTs during which our interactive system would provide feedback about the originality of each idea they generated and provided instructions about the AUT. We further emphasised that participants should *"... use the feedback as a guide that helps you during your idea generation process."* A picture of the common object used during each AUT was shown just before each task. Right after each task ended, participants filled in a questionnaire, which contained the measurement instruments used to assess emotion and expectations. After the experiment ended, the true purpose of the study was explained, and we asked participants whether they had guessed this purpose, had tried to game the feedback during some tasks, or had any problems using the system. To compensate the participants for their effort, we handed them a £5 voucher for a large online retailer, and a chocolate bar.

RESULTS

To check whether there exists a general relationship across the experimental conditions among expectations, satisfaction, frustration, and originality that our interactive system could influence, we used a Pearson correlation (Table 2). The results showed that there were significant positive correlations between expectation and satisfaction, expectation and originality, and satisfaction and originality; and significant negative correlations between expectation and frustration, and frustration and originality. The findings indicate that there is both a relationship between expectations and the intensity of emotion, and between emotional intensity and creativity across the experimental conditions. Thus, these findings suggest there is a precedent to further test hypotheses H1 and H2.

	1.	2.	3.	4.
1. Expectation	-			
2. Satisfaction	.865**	-		
3. Frustration	-.392**	-.514**	-	
4. Originality	.514**	.459**	-.363**	-

Table 2 Pearson correlation coefficients for expectation, satisfaction, frustration, and originality. **p<.001.

DV / IV	Expectation	Satisfaction	Frustration	Originality
PN	4.38 (1.71)	4.00 (2.08)	6.00 (1.63)	.170 (.145)
NN	4.79 (2.52)	4.71 (2.53)	4.71 (1.98)	.237 (.163)
PP	4.38 (1.98)	5.31 (2.10)	4.31 (2.69)	.305 (.228)
NP	7.38 (1.39)	7.00 (1.63)	3.77 (1.79)	.387 (.204)

Table 3 Mean and standard deviation (parentheses) of each feedback manipulation for expectation, satisfaction, frustration, and originality.

To test the effects of the system's feedback manipulations (independent variable, IV) on expectation, satisfaction, frustration, and originality (dependent variables, DV) we used a one-way ANOVA. The descriptive statistics are presented in Table 3.

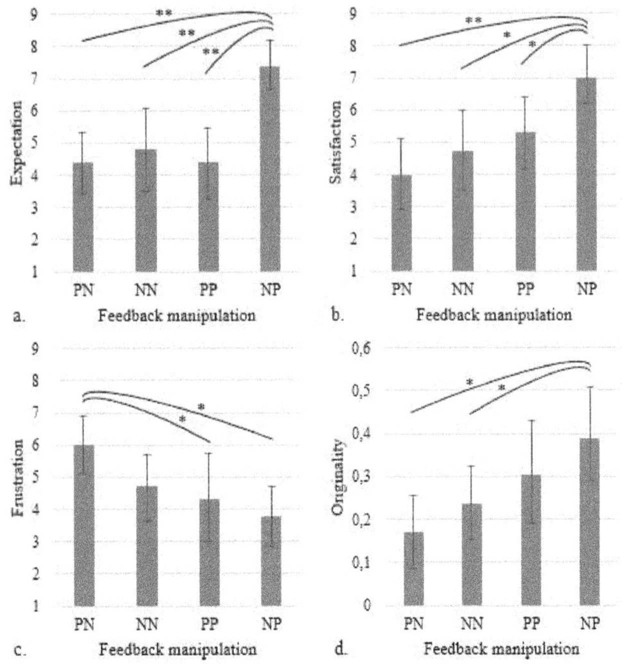

Figure 2 Graphic of the means, 95% confidence intervals (error bars), and pairwise comparisons for a. expectation, b. satisfaction, c. frustration, and d. originality for each of the feedback manipulations. *p<.05, **p<.001.

The results showed a significant effect of the feedback manipulations on *expectation*, $F(3, 52)=7.11$, $p<.001$, $\eta^2=.30$. Pairwise comparisons (uncorrected) showed that negative followed by positive feedback manipulation significantly increased the participant's belief that they did better than expected (Figure 2a). No clear differences were observed between positive followed by negative feedback manipulation, and manipulating the feedback negatively or positively in both tasks, with regard to expectation (Table 3). This indicated that there are limitations in the degree to which the interactive system is able to condition the expectations people have about their own ability to generate original ideas. This partly supports hypothesis H1.

The results showed a significant effect of the feedback manipulations on *satisfaction*, $F(3, 52)=4.77$, $p=.005$, $\eta^2=.23$. Pairwise comparisons showed that negative followed by positive feedback manipulation significantly increased the intensity of satisfaction (Figure 2b). The differences in satisfaction that resulted from the feedback manipulations (Table 3), indicate that the system can be used to cause positive emotion and determine its intensity. The results showed no overall significant effect of the feedback manipulations on *frustration*, $F(3, 52)=2.77$, $p=.052$, $\eta^2=.14$. Pairwise comparisons, however, showed that positive followed by negative feedback manipulation significantly increased the intensity of frustration (Figure 2c). The differences in frustration that resulted from the feedback manipulations (Table 3), indicate that the system can be used to cause negative emotion and determine its intensity. This partly supports hypothesis H1.

The results showed a significant effect of the feedback manipulations on *originality*, $F(3, 52)=3.19$, $p=.032$, $\eta^2=.16$. Pairwise comparisons showed that negative followed by positive feedback manipulation increased significantly the originality of the participant's ideas, when compared to positive followed by negative feedback manipulation (Figure 2d). The differences in originality that resulted from the feedback manipulations (Table 3), indicate that the interactive system can be used to influence the degree to which people are able to generate original ideas. This supports hypothesis H2.

IV	Indirect effect	Direct effect	Total effect
PN	**-3.04****	.04	**-3.00****
NN	**-2.57****	.28	**-2.29***
PP	**-2.67****	**.98†**	**-1.69***

Table 4 Estimates from the mediation analysis for the effects of the feedback manipulations (IV) on the intensity of satisfaction, as mediated by expectation. The estimates are relative to NP. $^{\dagger}p<.10$, $*p<.05$, $**p<.001$.

IV	Indirect effect	Direct effect	Total effect
NN	-.05	**-1.23†**	**-1.29†**
PP	.00	**-1.69***	**-1.69***
NP	**-1.18†**	-1.05	**-2.23***

Table 5 Estimates from the mediation analysis for the effects of the feedback manipulations (IV) on the intensity of frustration, as mediated by expectation. The estimates are relative to PN. $^{\dagger}p<.10$, $*p<.05$.

To test whether the effects of the interactive system on the intensity of satisfaction and frustration could be explained by its effects on expectation, we performed a mediation analysis using structural equation modeling [28].

The mediation models were set up with the feedback manipulations as IV, expectation as the mediator, and satisfaction or frustration as the DV. The results for the satisfaction model showed that the effects of the feedback manipulations on the intensity of satisfaction (Table 4, Total effect) were best explained by the effects of the feedback manipulations on expectation (Table 4, Indirect effect), rather than by something else (Table 4, Direct effect). These results indicate that the interactive system can be used to influence the intensity of positive emotion, by conditioning people's expectations.

The results for the frustration model showed that the effects of the feedback manipulations on the intensity of frustration (Table 5, Total effect) could not be explained by the effects of the manipulations on expectation (Table 5, Indirect effect), but was more likely to be better explained by something else, which we did not measure (Table 5, Direct effect). These results indicate that the ability of the interactive system to influence the intensity of negative emotion does not happen by conditioning people's expectations.

Thus, the results confirm hypothesis H1. However, the effects of the interactive system on the link between expectations and emotional intensity extends only to positive emotion.

IV	Indirect effect	Direct effect	Total effect
PN	**-.12**†	-.10	**-.22****
NN	**-.08**†	-.07	**-.15***
PP	**-.20***	.11	-.08

Table 6 Estimates from the mediation analysis for the effects of the feedback manipulations (IV) on originality mediated by the effects of the feedback on expectation and subsequent intensity of satisfaction. The estimates are relative to NP. $^{\dagger}p<.10$, $^{*}p<.05$, $^{**}p<.001$.

IV	Indirect effect	Direct effect	Total effect
NN	.04	.03	.07
PP	**.08**†	.05	**.14**†
NP	-.01	**.23***	**.22****

Table 7 Estimates from the mediation analysis for the effects of the feedback manipulations (IV) on originality mediated by the effects of the feedback on expectation and subsequent intensity of frustration. The estimates are relative to PN. $^{\dagger}p<.10$, $^{*}p<.05$, $^{**}p<.001$.

To further explore whether the effects of the system on the expectation-satisfaction-originality link, we set up a mediation model with the feedback manipulations as the IV, expectation and satisfaction in series as the first and second mediator, and originality as the DV. The results showed that the effects of the feedback manipulations on originality (Table 6, Total effect) were best explained by the effects of the feedback on the link between expectation and the intensity of satisfaction (Table 6, Indirect effect), rather than by something else (Table 6, Direct effect). These results indicate that the interactive system can be used to influence the intensity of positive emotion, by conditioning people's expectations; and that the system's influence on the intensity of positive emotion affects the degree to which people are able to generate original ideas.

To further explore whether there is a link between the intensity of frustration and originality, we set up a mediation model with the feedback manipulations as the IV, frustration as the mediator, and originality as the dependent variable. We did not include expectation because we have found no evidence to suggest it's inclusion in our data (see Figure 2c and Table 5, Indirect effect). The results showed that the effects of the feedback manipulations on originality (Table 7, Total effect) could not be explained by the effects of the feedback on the intensity of frustration (Table 7, Indirect effect), and only in one case (when comparing positive followed by negative, with negative followed by positive feedback manipulation), by something else, which we did not model (Table 7, Direct effect). These results confirms that the system influences originality, but not via its link with the intensity of frustration.

Thus, the results confirm hypothesis H2. However, the effects of the interactive system on the link between emotional intensity and creativity during idea generation extends only to positive emotion.

DISCUSSION

Our study demonstrates that an interactive system can be designed to manipulate cognitive appraisal processes to determine the type and intensity of an emotional response, in a manner that helps people to perform better on idea generation tasks that require creativity.

The results suggest that the order in which the interactive system provides manipulated feedback about the originality of a user's ideas to make them appear more, or less original, can be used to condition people's expectations about their own ability to generate original ideas (Figure 2a), cause positive emotion - satisfaction - (Figure 2b) and negative emotion - frustration - (Figure 2c), and influence the actual ability of people to generate original ideas (Figure 2d). The influence of the interactive system on expectations enables the system to cause positive emotion and determine its intensity (Table 4). The influence of the interactive system on the intensity of positive emotion also helps to enhance people's actual ability to generate original ideas (Table 6). Thus, these findings indicate that the interactive system is able to cause emotion of an intended type, and determine the intensity of that emotion by conditioning people's expectations about their ability to generate original ideas (H1). Furthermore, the system's influence on the intensity of positive emotion also influences the degree to which people are able to generate original ideas (H2).

The results obtained also indicated two interesting possible *theoretical limitations* to the developed approach. First, the effects of the interactive system on the link between expectations and emotional intensity appears to extend only to positive emotion (Table 4), and not to negative emotion (Table 5). This result is interesting because the feedback manipulations did enable the system to cause negative emotion and also determine its intensity (Figure 2c), but it did not lead people to think they did worse than expected in the manner that we intended (Figure 2a). Possibly, people are more willing to adjust their expectations when the feedback manipulations are more positive than when they are negative, which may drive them to seek the cause of this suggested decline in creative task performance elsewhere, e.g. believing that the interactive system must be wrong [9].

Second, the effects of the system on the emotional intensity-creativity link appear to extend to positive (Table 6), but not to negative emotion (Table 7). This finding contradicts our assumption that the intensity of negative emotion subtracts from the flexibility necessary to generate original ideas as no such subtractive effect occurred in our study. It is possible that no such subtractive effect exists of negative emotion on flexibility. However, as discussed, the feedback manipulations intended to cause negative emotion, did not influence expectation (Figure 2a). Possibly, if the cause of negative emotions was attributed externally, such as to the aforementioned wrongful interactive system, then it is conceivable that this functions as a form of self-regulation that prevents the caused negative emotions from impacting the user's ability to generate original ideas [cf. 9]. One interesting consideration for theoretical future work is to investigate whether we can turn this limitation into an asset. That is, by deliberately increasing the likelihood that people attribute the cause of any negative feedback by the system externally, we can invoke self-regulation mechanisms in the user that prevent a user from being affected by their own inability to generate original ideas, and subsequently repair any consequential negative emotions that might further limit their momentary creative capabilities [cf. 10].

The interactive system developed and tested in this paper was specifically designed to investigate our hypotheses under laboratory conditions. It is nevertheless interesting to reflect on possible limitations, opportunities, and future work for the use our results in interactive systems that can be used to help support creativity in *practice*.

First, practical application will depend on the utility of providing computational feedback itself. Recent work shows that the appraisal of one's own ideas is typically executed poorly, with negative implications for creative task performance [e.g. 5]. This suggests that, at least for some people, providing feedback during ideation addresses a fundamental problem during idea generation, and can help to guide users during their idea generation process. Contrary to this, it is also popularly claimed that deferring judgment facilitates creativity during idea generation [e.g. 26]. This suggests that, perhaps for other people, providing feedback can interrupt idea generation, also with negative implications for creative task performance. Possibly, providing any feedback at all could be detrimental to creativity. We suggest that *user studies* can be an effective way to investigate if, how, and for whom, computational feedback itself can be an effective way to support creativity in practice.

Second, it is reasonable to assume that continued use of feedback manipulation may lead to a user discovering the systems' manipulations, possibly with negative effects on its believability and subsequently its utility. This requires a more technologically advanced approach than the one used in this experiment. Interestingly, we can find inspiration in recent advances in game technologies. In many computer games, the difficulty to achieve positive outcomes is varied adaptively, sparsely, and timed effectively in order to keep players engaged [31]. The appropriation of these technologies for feedback manipulation within the context of creativity support, can possibly help to sustain effectiveness over prolonged use. Therefore, we suggest that further *technological development* is necessary to develop interactive systems based on our results that can be used to support creativity in practice.

Third, if we assume that our findings can be generalized across different application domains, it is still likely that the way that the manipulated feedback is presented will need to be adapted to the context in which a creativity support tool is used. This may, for instance, depend on the features of the technology being used, ranging from basic mobile apps in which ideas can be stored [17], to fully interactive creative partners with which a user can interact socially. It may also need to be sensitive to *domain specific* needs, ranging from supporting a quick brainstorm at the office, to supporting creativity longer term in the development of an artistic process [22]. We suggest that our findings can potentially be integrated in a wide range of creativity support tools, but that this would require that we adapt the way the manipulated feedback is presented to the limitations and possibilities posed by the technology used, and the domain in which it is applied.

To summarise, the study discussed embodies one of the first steps toward a novel line of interactive technologies that aim to manipulate cognitive appraisals, as a way to intentionally cause emotion with an intended intensity, with the goal to help people to get more out of their own creative capabilities.

REFERENCES

1. Akhbari Chermahini, S. and Hommel, B. 2012. More creative through positive mood? Not everyone!. *Frontiers in Human Neuroscience* 6, 319.
2. Baas, M., De Dreu, C.K.W. and Nijstad, B.A. 2008. A meta-analysis of 25 years of mood-creativity research: Hedonic tone, activation, or regulatory focus?. *Psychological Bulletin* 134, 6: 779-806.
3. Baas, M., De Dreu, C.K.W. and Nijstad, B.A. 2011. When prevention promotes creativity: the role of mood, regulatory focus, and regulatory closure. *Journal of personality and social psychology* 100, 5: 794-809.
4. Banerjee, S. and Pedersen, T. 2002. An adapted Lesk algorithm for word sense disambiguation using WordNet. In *International Conference on Intelligent Text Processing and Computational Linguistics*, 136-145.

5. Blair, C.S. and Mumford, M.D. 2007. Errors in idea evaluation: Preference for the original?. *Journal of Creative Behavior* 41, 3: 197-222.
6. Brans, K. and Verduyn, P. 2014. Intensity and duration of negative emotions: Comparing the role of appraisals and regulation strategies. *PLoS ONE* 9, 3: e92410.
7. Brehm, J.W. 1999.The intensity of emotion. *Personality and Social Psychology Review* 3, 2-22.
8. Calvo, R.A. and Peters, D. 2014. *Positive computing: technology for wellbeing and human potential*. MIT Press.
9. Campbell, W.K. and Sedikides, C. 1999. Self-threat magnifies the self-serving bias: A meta-analytic integration. *Review of General Psychology* 3, 23-43.
10. Carver, C.S. and Scheier, M.F. 1998. On the self-regulation of behavior. Cambridge University Press.
11. Cropley, A. 2006. In praise of convergent thinking. *Creativity Research Journal* 18, 3: 391-404.
12. de Rooij, A., Broekens, J. and Lamers, M.H. 2013. Abstract expressions of affect. *International Journal of Synthetic Emotions* 4, 1: 1-31.
13. de Rooij, A., Corr, P. and Jones, S. 2015. Emotion and creativity: Hacking into cognitive appraisal processes to augment creative ideation. In *Proceedings of the 2015 ACM SIGCHI Conference on Creativity and Cognition*, 265-274.
14. de Rooij, A. and Jones, S. 2015. (E)Motion and creativity: Hacking the function of motor expressions in emotion regulation to augment creativity. In *Proceedings of the Ninth International Conference on Tangible, Embedded, and Embodied Interaction*, 145-152.
15. de Rooij, A. and Jones, S. 2013. Mood and creativity: An appraisal tendency perspective. In *Proceedings of the 9th ACM Conference on Creativity & Cognition*, 362-365.
16. de Rooij, A. and Jones, S. 2013. Motor expressions as creativity support: Exploring the potential for physical interaction. In *Proceedings of the 27th International BCS Human Computer Interaction Conference*, 47.
17. Evernote Corporation. 2017. Evernote homepage. Retrieved March 13, 2017 from https://evernote.com
18. Fellbaum, C. 1998. *WordNet: An electronic lexical database*. MIT Press.
19. Frijda, N.H. 2007. *The laws of emotion*. Erlbaum.
20. Halácsy, P., Kornai, A. and Oravecz, C. 2007. Hunpos - an open source trigram tagger. In *Proceedings of the 45th annual meeting of the ACL on interactive poster and demonstration sessions*, 209-212.
21. Illgen, D.R. 1971. Satisfaction with performance as a function of the initial level of expected performance and the deviations from expectations. *Organizational Behavior and Human Performance* 6, 3: 345-361.
22. Kaufman, J. C. and Baer, J. 2005. *Creativity across domains: Faces of the muse*. Erlbaum.
23. Lyer, L.R., Doboli, S., Minai, A.A., Brown, V.R., Levine, D.S. and Paulus, P.B. 2009. Neural dynamics of idea generation and the effects of priming. *Neural Networks,* 22, 674-686.
24. Mumford, M.D., Medeiros, K.E. and Partlow, P.J. 2012. Creative thinking: Processes, strategies, and knowledge. *The Journal of Creative Behavior* 46, 1: 30-47.
25. Osborn, A.F. 1963. *Applied imagination: Principles and procedures of creative problem solving* (3rd ed.). Charles Scribner's Sons.
26. Plucker, J.A., Qian, M. and Wang, S. 2011. Is originality in the eye of the beholder? Comparison of scoring techniques in the assessment of divergent thinking. *The Journal of Creative Behavior* 45, 1-22.
27. Roskes, M., Elliot, A.J., Nijstad, B.A. and De Dreu, C.K.W. 2013. Avoidance motivation and conservation of energy. *Emotion Review* 5, 308-311.
28. Rosseel, Y. 2011. Lavaan: an R package for structural equation modeling. *Journal of Statistical Software* 48, 2: 1-36.
29. Runco, M.A. and Jaeger, G.J. 2012. The standard definition of creativity. *Creativity Research Journal* 24, 1: 92-96.
30. Scherer, K.R. 2009. The dynamic architecture of emotion: Evidence for the component process model. *Cognition & Emotion* 23, 7: 1307-1351.
31. Schrader, C. et al., 2017. Rising to the challenge: An emotion-driven approach toward adaptive serious games. In Ma, M. and Oikonomou, A. (Eds.) *Serious Games and Edutainment Applications*, volume II, 2-28.
32. Silvia, P.J. et al. 2008. Assessing creativity with divergent thinking tasks: Exploring the reliability and validity of new subjective scoring methods. *Psychology of Aesthetics, Creativity, and the Arts* 2, 2: 68-85.
33. Sonnemans, J. and Frijda, N. 1994. The structure of subjective emotional intensity. *Cognition & Emotion* 8, 329-350.
34. Weiner, B. 1985. An attributional theory of achievement motivation and emotion. *Psychological Review* 92, 4: 548-573.

Listen to Others, Listen to Yourself: Combining Feedback Review and Reflection to Improve Iterative Design

Yu-Chun Grace Yen
Computer Science
University of Illinois
Urbana, IL
yyen4@illinois.edu

Steven P. Dow
Cognitive Science
UC San Diego
San Diego, CA
spdow@ucsd.edu

Elizabeth Gerber
Segal Design Institute
Northwestern University
Evanston, IL
egerber@northwestern.edu

Brian P. Bailey
Computer Science
University of Illinois
Urbana, IL
bpbailey@illinois.edu

ABSTRACT

Feedback from diverse audiences can contain ambiguity and contradictions, making it difficult to interpret and act on. To promote deeper interpretation of feedback, we tested the effects of combining a reflection activity and reviewing external feedback for an iterative design task. Designers (N=90) created a design and revised it after a) performing a reflection activity *before* reviewing feedback, b) performing the reflection *after* reviewing feedback, c) performing the reflection only, or d) reviewing the feedback only. We measured design quality, depth of revision, perceived effort, and confidence; and categorized the content produced from the reflections. We found that performing reflection *after* feedback review led to the largest increase in perceived quality for the revised designs, and performing reflection and feedback review regardless of the order resulted in the most extensive revision. Our results also showed that performing the reflection alone yielded outcomes that were similar to when only reviewing feedback, and either activity led to better outcomes than the control condition (no feedback or reflection). Designers stated that the reflection helped them recall their goals, question their choices, and prioritize revisions. We argue that designers should perform a lightweight, explicit reflection to enhance their iterative process, and discuss implications for feedback platforms.

Author Keywords

Creativity; design; feedback; reflection; crowdsourcing.

ACM Classification Keywords

H.5.3 [Information interfaces and presentation]: Group and Organization Interfaces – Collaborative computing.

INTRODUCTION

Feedback is critical for performing creative design. It helps designers iterate on their in-progress solutions by revealing problems, gaining insight, and unblocking fixation [24]. However, the feedback received from diverse audiences such as those reached via social media and crowdsourcing [20, 32, 50, 52] can contain contradictions and ambiguity due to the providers having different motives [52], expertise [50] and perspectives [52]. Designers can therefore struggle to interpret and learn from the feedback, and act on it to improve their design solutions [7, 40, 50]. See Figure 1.

Figure 1. Example of a design and corresponding feedback generated from our study. The feedback exhibits conflict, thus requires deeper interpretation from the designers.

To help designers interpret feedback more effectively, we develop a lightweight reflection activity and test its placement relative to feedback review for iterative design. Reflection is a meta-cognitive process in which a designer assesses the design situation and its relation to the project goals [39]. Prior work has shown that performing reflection after feedback review improves management decisions [1] and learning outcomes [27]. The improvements have been attributed to the feedback review facilitating a more effective reflection [1]. Our research extends this prior work by testing the effects of placing the reflection either *after* or *before* feedback review. In the latter case, we speculate that the reflection could facilitate the effectiveness of the feedback review. Our research also extends the prior work to the context of creative design.

We conducted an online study in which designers (N=90) each created an initial graphic design for a public running event and then revised it after performing an activity in one of four conditions: *reflect-before-feedback*, *reflect-after-feedback*, *feedback-only*, and *reflect-only*. The study also included a control condition in which designers revised their designs without reviewing feedback or reflecting. The

C&C '17, June 27-30, 2017, Singapore, Singapore

ACM ISBN 978-1-4503-4403-6/17/06…$15.00
http://dx.doi.org/10.1145/3059454.3059468

participants in the study were mostly novice designers. We measured the perceived quality of the design and the depth of revision using ratings from domain experts and the designers themselves. Designers also rated their confidence and effort invested in the designs, and rated the usefulness of the activities performed. We also categorized the content produced from the reflection activity.

We found that reflection *after* feedback review led to the largest increase in the revised design quality according to the experts, and without designers over-estimating the amount of improvement they made. Designers reported a heightened focus on improving aesthetics such as layout, color, and fonts in this condition. If the reflection was performed *before* feedback review, we found that designers focused more on the concept of the design, but the quality of the revision did not increase as much as when the reflection was performed after feedback review. Performing the reflection and feedback review regardless of the order resulted in the most extensive revision. Our results also showed that performing the reflection activity alone yielded outcomes that were similar to when only reviewing external feedback, and either activity led to better performance compared to the control condition (no feedback or reflection). Designers reported that the reflection activity helped them recall their design goals, question their choices, and plan and prioritize their revisions.

Our work makes two contributions to the creativity and cognition community. First, we offer deeper empirical understanding of how ordering reflection and feedback review affects designers' performance and perceptions for a creative design task. Our results argue that designers should perform a simple, lightweight reflection activity to help ensure each design iteration is as productive as possible. Second, we offer implications for implementing a reflection activity in feedback platforms to encourage its adoption.

RELATED WORK

We discuss how our work builds on the theory of reflection in design. We also situate our contribution in the context of prior work that has combined reflection and feedback and other approaches for promoting feedback engagement.

Reflection in Creative Design

Schön distinguishes two categories of reflection: reflection-*on*-action, which refers to when a designer revisits prior design episodes, and engages in a meta-cognitive process to extract meaning from those experiences; and reflection-*in*-action, which refers to gaining insight while acting on a creative artifact [41]. The reflection activity developed in this paper is best characterized as reflection-*on*-action since it is an intentional act of writing an assessment of the design situation.

Schön's work has inspired many tools and methods to support reflection in design [3]. To support reflection-in-action, researchers have pursued approaches to increase the "talk-back" of design representations. Fischer and colleagues championed the approach of embedding software critics into a design tool [14]. The critics could analyze the design representation and generate feedback on-demand by applying domain-centric design principles [13]. Another approach has been to explore user interfaces for better representing design alternatives and the meaning of the design situation [22, 35]. A third approach has been to enable designers to generate design alternatives by having access to their design histories [9, 28, 29].

For reflection-on-action, researchers have explored the creation of visualizations of design processes [28, 34, 42]. The visualizations allow designers to notice patterns in their workflows, revisit memorable ideas, examples and decisions, and extract lessons that will shape how they approach future projects. Others have viewed reflection as an ongoing activity throughout the design process that can be regularly performed to sensitize designers and end users to each other's goals, knowledge, and motivations [45].

Our work differs from this corpus of prior work because we are testing how a reflection activity can be best coordinated with the review of feedback. Additionally, though reflection is widely recognized as a core practice in creative design [3], there is a paucity of literature that quantifies the effects of reflection on design. Our experiment adds to this literature by including a condition that isolates the effects of performing a reflection activity on design performance.

Using Reflection to Encourage Feedback Engagement

Feedback is critical for performing creative work because it helps a person assess the quality of her in-progress solution, discover its shortcomings, and gain insight for improving it [24]. However, the effectiveness of feedback on the design depends in large part on how well a person is able to interpret the content, learn from it, and formulate an effective action plan [5, 25, 33, 37]. Though feedback interpretation is a long-standing problem in many creative contexts, the issue is becoming more critical as people increasingly leverage online sources for gathering feedback on their creative work [21]. Feedback from online sources can be gathered fast, is affordable, and can tap a global audience [50]. Despite these benefits, feedback received online can be ambiguous, contradictory, and of variable quality because the providers typically have different motivations [52], expertise [50], and perspectives [52] for writing helpful feedback. These issues can cause the feedback to be especially difficult to interpret.

One approach to promote deeper engagement with feedback is to incorporate a reflection activity. For example, in [1], users responded to simulated work emails that involved different categories of tasks such as coordination, decision making and resource allocation. Users received feedback on their task performance, and then developed and wrote an action plan while users in a control condition did not. The results showed that performing the reflection activity after reviewing feedback improved task performance more than receiving feedback alone [1]. The improvement was likely due to the reflection prompting deeper processing of the feedback and task context, which allowed the lessons to be more effectively applied to a second task. Similarly, in an educational setting, students were required to read feedback on their solutions and submit an action plan before the scores were released. The results showed that this approach helped the students view feedback as a means for learning rather than solely a justification for their grades [27].

Our work shares the goal of using reflection to promote deeper processing of feedback. We extend prior work by testing how placing a reflection activity, either before or after reviewing feedback, affects an iterative design task. We also extend prior work by measuring perceptions of performance, in addition to the task outcomes, and by analyzing the content from the reflection activity.

Other Approaches for Feedback Engagement

Drawing from the broader literature on sense-making, there are approaches beyond reflection that could be applied to promote engagement with feedback. These approaches include applying tools for interactively visualizing and organizing the data [2, 26], scaffolding dialogue around the data [6], leveraging others' interpretations of the data [15, 36, 47], and increasing the transparency of the data creation process [30, 49]. We chose to test the integration of a reflection activity into the iterative design process because reflection has been long recognized as a core practice in creative design [3, 17] and learning [38, 43]. It can also be embedded in online communities and feedback platforms, or performed on one's own without additional tools.

RESEARCH QUESTIONS

The goal of our study was to test the effects of integrating an explicit reflection activity into the iterative design process. We focused on the following research questions:

RQ1: How does integrating a reflection activity into an iterative design process affect perceived design quality, degree of revision, and perceptions of design performance?

RQ2: How does the sequence in which the reflection activity is performed – either before or after reviewing external feedback – affect these same measures?

RQ3: What are the perceived benefits and limitations of integrating a reflection activity into the design process?

Answers to these questions will deepen knowledge about how reflection can promote deeper engagement with feedback and make each iteration productive. Answers will also have implications for design workflows implemented in individual design processes and in feedback platforms.

EXPERIMENTAL DESIGN

To answer these research questions, we conducted a between-subjects online study with five experimental conditions (see Activity Manipulations). All participants created an initial design, engaged in an activity based on their assigned condition, and then revised the design.

All aspects of the study including the number and phrasing of the reflection prompts, design feedback collection, and time allocated to each activity were piloted with three users experienced in design. We revised the study based on their feedback. None of these users participated in the full study.

Participants

We recruited participants online by advertising on design distribution lists in several U.S. academic institutions, and by posting on design-oriented Facebook group pages. We advertised the study as an online competition to create a graphic design for a half marathon. We were contacted by 223 people; and 90 completed the study (60 female). Participants ranged from 18 to 45 years of age (μ=24, SD=6.9). All of them resided in the U.S. Participants completed an initial survey asking about their education and experience in design. They also rated their design expertise on a scale from 1 (novice) to 5 (expert). The average self-rated expertise was 2.1 (SD=1.0), indicating that most participants perceived themselves as novices. This was supported by a majority of the participants (82%) reporting no academic training and minimal experience in design. Each participant was remunerated $30. To motivate effort, we provided five prizes of an additional $20 for the final designs that received the highest quality ratings from three design experts not affiliated with the research team. We refer to the participants in the study as **designers**.

Design Brief

All designers created an initial and a revised design for the following design brief: *You have been hired to design a flyer for a half marathon race called RUN@NYC. The event will be hosted by and held at Central Park in Manhattan, New York City at 7 am on October 1, 2016. Runners can register through the event website www.running-nyc.com. The top three runners will receive a $300 prize each. The goal of your flyer is to encourage participation, be visually appealing, and convey the event details.*

We chose this design brief because we believed that both the designers and the feedback providers would be familiar with the topic. It was also open-ended, yet simple enough to allow for creative solutions in the time allotted. Designers were informed that they could use graphic design software of their choice and could use any online images in the public domain. To ensure the designers constructed their own solution, the use of design templates was prohibited.

Activity Manipulations

Designers performed a planned activity after submitting their initial designs but before revising it. The activities were organized into five experimental conditions:

Reflect-only (R): Designers reflected on the initial design by writing responses to the reflection prompts defined in the study. No external feedback on the design was provided.

Feedback-only (F): Designers reviewed six pieces of external feedback that was generated for the initial design. No reflection exercise was performed.

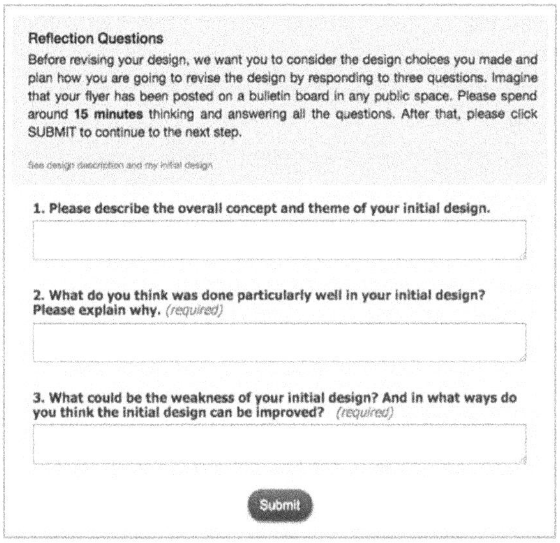

Figure 2. The user interface for a designer to write their responses to the reflection prompts.

Reflect-before-feedback (RF): Designers performed the reflection activity first; then reviewed the external feedback generated for the initial design.

Reflect-after-feedback (FR): Designers reviewed the external feedback generated for the initial design first; then performed the reflection activity.

Control (C): Designers did not perform a reflection activity and did not receive feedback prior to revising the design.

Reflection Prompts

In all of the conditions with a reflection activity (R, RF, FR), designers wrote responses to three prompts (Figure 2):

(1) Please describe the concept of your initial design.

(2) What do you think was done particularly well in your initial design? Please explain why.

(3) What could be the weakness of your initial design? And in what ways do you think the initial design can be improved?

The first question asked the designer to revisit her goals, while the other two prompted an assessment of the design in the context of those goals. The questions were presented two days after the designers submitted their initial design in the associated conditions. The delay allowed the designer time to step outside of their design activity before responding to the reflection prompts. The two-day break was consistent between conditions. The prompts were developed to help designers extract insight from their design activity consistent with Schön's theory of reflection-on-action [40]. The three prompts were derived from a larger pool of possible questions that was refined based on participant feedback in the pilot study.

Feedback Generation

Designers received external feedback on their initial design in the (F, RF, and FR) conditions. A challenge was to deliver feedback that was consistent across designs in terms of length, quality, and scope; yet be specific to each design.

Category	Definition and Example
Theme	**Definition:** Response evaluates the overall direction of the design **Example:** "It doesn't look like a flyer for half marathon race, looks like some flyer of Industrial/business/Real estate."
Surface elements	**Definition:** Response assesses the color, font, and imagery choices made to the design. **Example:** "Your flyer is simple and very good, but the combination of the colors reminds to a party invitation, not marathon."
Composition and layout	**Definition:** Response reacts to the layout and composition of the visual elements in the design. **Example:** "I like the contrast between the top and the bottom. But I do not like the contrast between the words at the top because I'm not sure how visible that will be once you print it out."

Table 1. The rubric used for feedback generation.

To address this challenge, we used a rubric to guide the feedback generation process. The feedback was generated using a paid crowdsourcing platform, Amazon.com's Mechanical Turk (MTurk) [22]. Prior work has shown that the design feedback generated from MTurk is similar in terms of its quality, scope, and length to that generated from social media and online communities [52]. The rubric directed attention to three categories of design feedback: theme, composition and layout, and surface elements. The rubric was adopted from [10], which showed that the use of the rubric increased the quality of crowdsourced feedback to the point of being comparable to expert feedback [54]. Table 1 shows the definition and samples of feedback for each category in the rubric.

On the task page for gathering the feedback, the provider was presented with an image of the design, the design brief, and instructions for providing feedback: *"Your feedback should include both strengths (what you like) and weaknesses (what you don't like) about the [definition of that category of the rubric]. We are not the designer, so you don't need to be overly positive. However, responses that demonstrate insufficient effort or are offensive will be rejected."* The task was configured to require approval rates at or above 95 percent and prior completion of 500 or more HITs. Five subjects were recruited to provide feedback for each category of the rubric for each design. The research team ranked the quality of the five pieces of feedback, and only the top two pieces of feedback in each category were presented to the designer. Each feedback task paid $0.40, which was consistent with U.S. minimum wage based on pilot data.

When presented with the feedback, the designer rated the perceived quality of each piece of feedback on a Likert scale from 1 (low) to 7 (high). After the experiment, we analyzed the ratings between conditions. An ANOVA did not show a statistical difference between the conditions ($F(2, 373)=0.74$, $p=0.47$) and the feedback quality was reasonably good

(μ=5.18, SD=1.43). We interpret this result to mean that we were successful in generating feedback that was personalized yet was of similar quality and referenced similar themes.

Procedure

After signing up for the study, an account was created for the designer on our review platform. The account information was sent to the designer along with a Web link to access the platform. The study consisted of two phases.

Phase I

In the first phase, the designers were instructed to spend sixty minutes creating their initial design. Once created, the designers uploaded their designs to our platform and completed a survey about their performance (see Measures). A confirmation page was then displayed informing the designers that the second phase of the study would begin in two days. During these two days, the designers did not perform any actions related to the study. However, the research team gathered the design feedback that would be presented in the associated conditions during phase two.

Phase II

After two days, an email was sent to the designers to continue with the study. A page describing the assigned activities was presented to step the designers through the second phase. Designers in the *reflect-only* condition were directed to a page showing the reflection prompts (Figure 2). For the *feedback-only* condition, designers were directed to a page showing two pieces of feedback per category. The designers were instructed to spend 15 minutes performing each activity. For the *reflect-before-feedback* and *reflect-after-feedback* conditions, designers were presented with both activity pages, sequenced according to the assigned condition. Once the activities were complete, the designers were instructed to spend 30 minutes revising their design. Designers in the

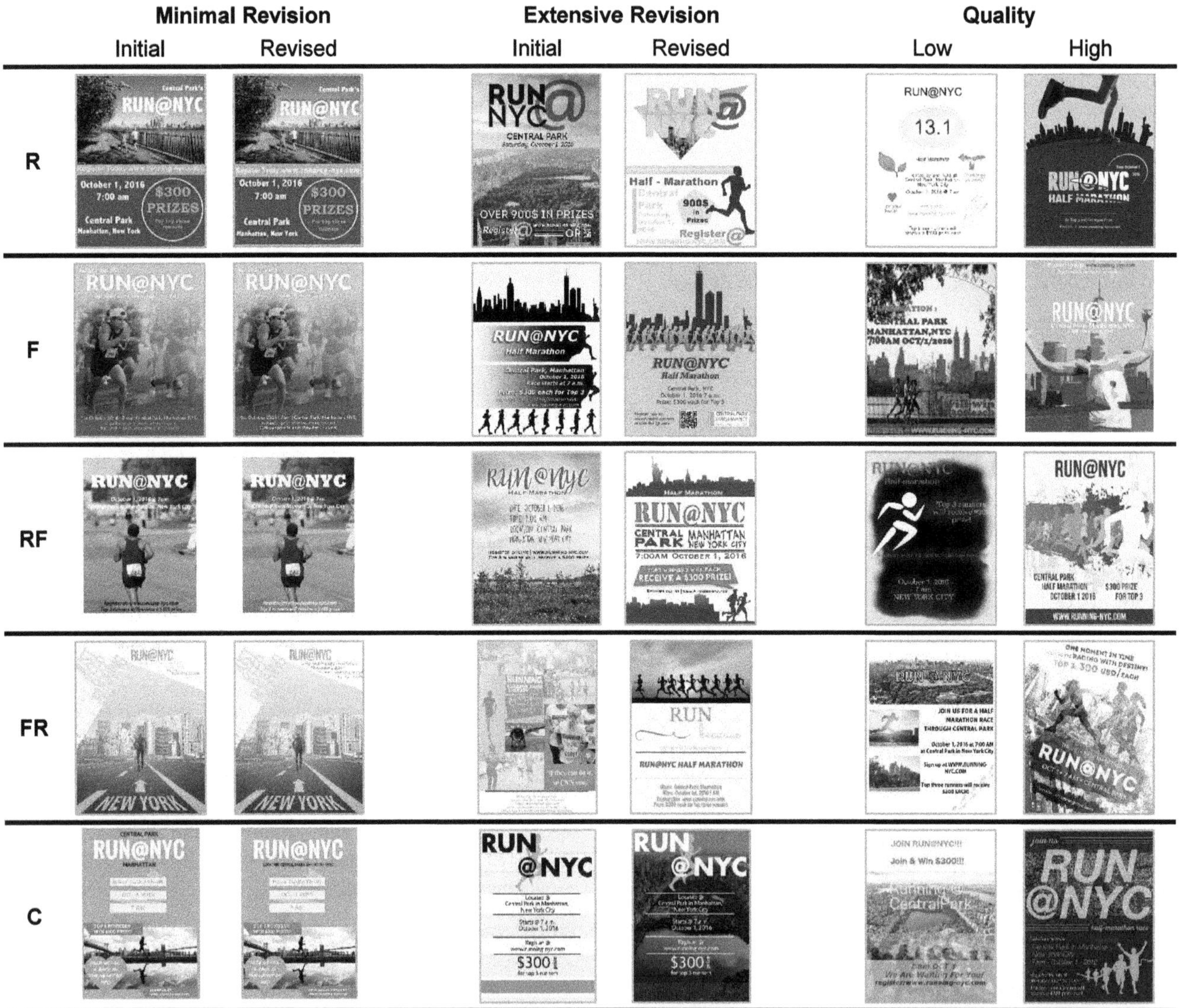

Figure 3. Examples of designs created in each experimental condition. The left two columns show a pair of initial and revised designs where the initial design was minimally revised. The middle two columns show a pair of designs where the initial design was extensively revised. The rightmost two columns show a low and high quality revised design from each condition.

control condition revised their initial design without reflection or reviewing feedback. Designers had up to three days to submit their revised design. All the indicated times were based on results from the pilot study.

A second survey was presented after submitting the revised design. The survey had the same questions as the survey in the first phase but also asked about designers' perceived usefulness of the assigned activities (see Measures).

Measures

In addition to the designs, we collected data through surveys and expert evaluation, and by analyzing the content of the designers' responses to the reflection prompts.

Surveys

At the end of phase one, designers were asked:

(1) How many minutes did you spend creating the design?

(2) How much effort did you invest in the design?

(3) How would you rate the quality of the design?

(4) How confident are you that the flyer fully satisfied the design goals?

At the end of phase two, designers were asked the same four questions along with two additional questions:

(5) Please rate the degree of revision between the initial and revised design.

(6) How useful was [Activity] for improving your design?

Since the control group did not perform any activities, for the last question, they were asked: *"How useful was having two days before being asked to revise their design?"* Questions that asked for ratings were performed on a 7-point scale from 1 (Low) to 7 (High). Designers were asked to briefly explain each rating on the surveys.

Expert Evaluation

Three experts were recruited from the online work platform, Upwork [8], to evaluate the quality of the collected designs. Each expert had eight or more years of professional experience in graphic design and was paid $30. The experts read the design brief and rated how well the design satisfied the goals from 1 (low) to 7 (high). The designs were presented in a random order and the experts were blind to the iteration and condition. The intra-class correlation coefficient (ICC) was 0.83 for the initial designs and 0.80 for the revised designs. These values indicate substantial agreement between the raters to continue with the data analysis [23].

To assess the degree of change between the initial and revised designs, we recruited three additional experts from Upwork, who also have eight years of professional design experience. Additional experts were recruited because the other experts had already been exposed to the designs and we wanted to eliminate potential bias for the ratings of change. The experts read the design brief and rated the 90 pairs of designs. The rating interface randomly placed the initial and revised design side by side. The experts rated the degree of change from 1 (minor change) to 7 (completely different) and were blind to condition. The intra-class correlation coefficient was 0.86, again indicating sufficient agreement between the raters to continue with the data analysis.

Activity	Experts' Ratings		Designers' Ratings	
	Initial	Revised	Initial	Revised
R	3.60 (1.8)	3.75 (1.9)	**4.30 (1.1)**	**5.30 (0.9)***
F	3.26 (1.8)	3.43 (1.9)	4.71 (1.2)	5.07 (1.5)
RF	3.76 (1.9)	3.76 (2.0)	**4.11 (1.2)**	**5.00 (1.1)***
FR	**3.15 (2.2)**	**3.69 (2.0)***	4.67 (1.4)	5.06 (1.3)
C	2.97 (1.6)	3.18 (1.7)	5.15 (1.4)	5.55 (1.1)

Table 2. Mean and (SD) of the quality ratings for the initial and revised designs. The scale is from 1 (low) to 7 (high). An * indicates the ratings of the revised designs were higher than the initial designs in that same condition ($p< 0.05$).

Content Analysis

We categorized the content and measured the length of the reflection responses. Details will be described in the Results.

RESULTS

We collected 90 pairs of initial and revised designs: 20 from the *reflect-only* condition, 14 from *feedback-only*, 18 from *reflect-before-feedback*, 18 from *reflect-after-feedback*, and 20 from the *control* condition. Figure 3 shows examples of designs in each condition.

Design Quality

Table 2 summarizes the experts' and designers' ratings of the perceived quality of the initial and revised designs. The experts rated all of the designs, and the designers rated their own designs. All the ratings were from 1 (Low) to 7 (High).

Experts' Ratings

A paired t-test showed that the revised designs in the FR condition (μ=3.69) had the largest increase in perceived quality relative to the initial designs (μ=3.15; p=0.001). For the other conditions, the ratings of the revised designs did not statistically differ from the initial designs. The results show that performing a reflection activity after reviewing external feedback enables the most improvement in design quality according to the expert raters.

An ANOVA also showed that the experts rated the revised designs higher (μ=3.56) than the initial designs (μ=3.34, $F(4, 265)=7.8$, $p=0.005$). This result confirms that iterating on a design also contributes to improved quality [11]. Activity had no effect and there was no interaction effect.

Designers' Ratings

Paired t-tests showed that the designers rated their revised designs in the RF (μ=5.00) and R (μ=5.30) conditions higher than their initial designs (μ=4.11, μ=4.30; respectively, $p<0.05$ in both cases), but not in the other conditions. This pattern was inconsistent with the ratings from the experts (compare the respective data in Table 2). Performing the reflection activity before or without reviewing feedback

Activity	Experts' Ratings	Designers' Ratings
R	2.53 (1.7)	3.9 (1.5)
F	2.57 (1.4)	**4.1 (1.7)***
RF	**2.89 (1.7)***	3.4 (1.6)
FR	**2.67 (1.1)***	**4.7 (1.3)***
C	1.90 (1.1)	2.6 (1.6)

Table 3. Mean and (SD) of the ratings of degree of change between the initial and revised designs. The scale is from 1 (minor change) to 7 (completely different). An * indicates the perceived change was higher in that condition relative to the Control (p<0.05).

resulted in the designers *over-estimating* the increase in the quality of the revised design compared to the expert ratings.

An ANOVA comparing designers' and the experts' ratings also showed that designers rated their designs (μ=4.9) higher than the experts (μ=3.45; $F(1,270)=224.5$; $p<0.0001$). One explanation is that the designers in our study reported lower expertise (μ=2.1 on 5-point scale), and prior work has shown that those with less expertise typically over-estimate the quality of their performance [4].

In sum, our results show that performing a reflection activity after reviewing feedback (FR) allows a designer to create a higher quality revised design according to the experts and without over-estimating their own performance.

Degree of Change

Table 3 summarizes the experts' and designers' ratings of the degree of change between the initial and revised designs. The experts rated all pairs of the designs, and the designers rated their own designs. Ratings were on a scale from 1 (minor change) to 7 (completely different).

Experts' Ratings

An ANOVA showed that the Activity had a main effect on the experts' ratings of the degree of change ($F(4,270)=2.61$, $p=0.04$). A post-hoc Tukey's HSD test showed that the effect was due to the RF and FR conditions, as the pairs of designs in these conditions were perceived as having more changes than the pairs of designs in the control condition ($p<0.05$ in both cases). No other differences were detected. Performing a reflection activity either before (RF) or after (FR) reviewing external feedback led to more extensive revisions. Recall that the FR condition also led to the largest increase in perceived quality for the revised designs.

Designers' Ratings

An ANOVA showed that Activity had a main effect on the designers' ratings of the degree of change between their initial and revised designs ($F(4, 90)=5.1$, $p=0.01$). A post-hoc test showed that designers in the FR and F conditions rated the degree of change between their designs (FR: μ=4.7, R: μ=4.1) higher than the designers in the control condition (μ=2.6; $p<0.05$ in both cases). No other effects were found.

An ANOVA also showed that the designers rated the degree of change between their initial and revised designs (μ=3.73) higher than the experts (μ=2.27, $F(1, 91)=95.02$, $p<0.001$).

Activity	Confidence		Perceived Effort	
	Initial	Revised	Initial	Revised
R	5.55(0.9)	5.80(1.1)	4.95 (1.1)	5.1 (1.3)
F	5.50 (0.8)	5.79 (1.2)	4.93 (1.1)	4.79 (1.7)
RF	5.50 (0.9)	5.67(1.1)	5.00 (1.3)	4.72 (1.4)
FR	5.32 (1.3)	5.67(1.3)	5.33 (1.1)	5.22 (1.4)
C	5.70 (1.4)	6.15 (0.9)	**5.50 (1.1)***	**4.30 (1.4)***

Table 4. Mean and (SD) of designers' ratings of confidence and effort invested in their designs. The scale is from 1 (low) to 7 (high). An * indicates a significant difference between the revised and initial designs (p<0.05).

The difference in ratings could be due to the designers having been engaged in the design process, and having considered more changes than they actually made and could be observed by the experts in the revised designs.

Designers' Confidence and Perceived Effort

Table 4 summarizes the ratings of the designers' confidence in the initial and revised designs for satisfying the design goals. It also shows the designers' perceived effort invested in the designs. Both ratings were from 1 (low) to 7 (high).

Confidence

An ANOVA showed the designers were more confident in their revised design (μ= 5.8) than their initial design (μ=5.3; $F(4, 90)=8.86$; $p=0.004$). No other differences were found. This result shows that the increased confidence was due to iterating on the design [19], and was not affected by performing a reflection activity or reviewing feedback.

Perceived Effort

An ANOVA showed that the designers rated their effort for the initial design (μ=5.16) as higher than for the revised design (μ=4.82, $F(1,89)=4.0$, $p=0.048$). This was not surprising, because we asked the designers to spend 60 minutes on the initial design and only 30 minutes on the revised design.

A paired t-test showed that the designers in the control condition reported decreasing the largest effort from the initial (μ=5.5) to the revised design (μ=4.3, $p<0.05$). Without feedback and without reflection, designers may have lacked direction for the design revisions and exerted less effort.

	RO	FO	RF	FR	C
Reflection	4.6 (1.6)	N/A	4.2 (1.9)	4.7(1.7)	N/A
Feedback	N/A	5.42 (1.3)	6.1 (1.2)	5.6 (1.4)	N/A
Break	N/A	N/A	N/A	N/A	3.9 (1.5)

Table 5. Mean and (SD) of the ratings of the usefulness of performing reflection, reviewing feedback, or taking a break organized by the condition in which the action occurred.

Designers' Perceived Usefulness of the Activities

Designers rated the perceived usefulness of their assigned activity for improving their design. In the FR and RF conditions, the designers rated the usefulness of the reflection activity and reviewing feedback separately. Designers in the control condition rated how useful it was to have a two-day break (i.e. no activity) before revising their

Category	Reflection Example
Overall theme	**Strength:** I think what I did well was reach the target market by persuasion. ...The slogan 'this is your year' reinforces the need to sign up. [P27, R] **Weakness:** I feel the poster still lacks a sense of encouragement. I keep thinking about how I can include a motto that is unique, relatable and motivational but not cheesy. [P89, FR]
Surface elements	**Strength:** I think a weakness here is how small some of the font is, particularly in the lower left corner. [P136, R] **Weakness:** I can replace the blue with other colors to make it more visible. The "Top 3 $300 Prizes" text is difficult to see. I can make that more visible by making the outline bolder or changing color. [P90, FR]
Composition and layout	**Strength:** I think I did a good job not making the poster too clustered with words and spacing them out enough so the audience isn't overwhelmed. [P47, FR] **Weakness:** The text was a bit harder to see than it should be. I need to reduce the size of some of the text boxes and edit the background to make it pop a little bit more. [P168, FR]

Table 6. Examples of responses to the reflection prompts.

design. Ratings were from 1 (not useful) to 7 (very useful). Table 5 summarizes the ratings.

Both performing reflection (μ=4.48, SD=1.8) and reviewing feedback (μ=5.6, SD=1.3) were rated moderately useful for improving a design. An ANOVA showed that the condition in which the reflection activity (R, RF and FR) or reviewing feedback (F, FR, RF) were performed did not affect the ratings of their usefulness. The order of performing these actions also did not affect the ratings of their usefulness.

In the RF and FR conditions, designers rated reviewing the feedback more useful (μ=5.81) than performing the reflection activity (μ=4.42, $F(1, 35)=12.9$, $p=0.001$). Designers in the control condition rated the two-day break least useful (μ=3.9, SD=1.2) for improving their design.

Reflection Responses

We analyzed the content of the designers' responses to the second and third reflection prompts in the R, RF, and FR conditions. These questions related to the strengths and weaknesses of the initial designs. The responses were first partitioned into idea units. An idea unit is a coherent thought captured in a phrase, sentence, or group of sentences [8]. The dataset contained 64, 65, and 64 idea units in the R, RF, and FR conditions, respectively. From an initial pass on the data, we found that the idea units could be labeled using the categories from the feedback rubric: theme, surface elements, and composition and layout. Table 6 provides examples of idea units in each category. Table 7 shows the distribution of idea units by category.

To compare the patterns of interest, we performed z-tests for population proportions, and found that the responses from the RF and R conditions placed more emphasis on the *theme*

Category	R	RF	FR
Overall theme	48%	39%	19%
Surface elements	24%	26%	43%
Composition and layout	15%	23%	28%
Other	13%	12%	10%

Table 7. Frequencies of the categories of idea units derived from the reflection responses.

of the design (RF: 48%; R: 39%) than those from the FR condition (19%; $p<0.05$ in both comparisons). Conversely, the responses from the FR condition had more idea units relating to *surface elements* (43%) than the responses in either the RF or R conditions (RF: 24%; R: 26%; $p<0.05$ in both comparisons). If designers reviewed feedback before engaging in the reflection activity, their attention was directed more toward surface-level issues in their designs such as layout, color, and font choices. The length of the responses (in words) did not differ between the conditions (overall: μ=145 words, SD=18.3).

Benefits and Limitations of the Reflection Activity

We analyzed the designers' explanations for their ratings of the usefulness of the reflection activity (R, RF, and FR conditions). The explanations were first partitioned into idea units. The dataset contained 27, 16, and 21 units in the R, RF, and FR conditions, respectively. Our initial pass assigned a theme to each idea unit. Subsequent passes were performed to group similar themes until they were reasonably exclusive. The number of idea units citing a given theme is shown as "(n=<value>)".

When the reflection activity was rated favorably, the most common theme was that it helped the designers revisit their design goals (n=17). One designer stated that he used the reflection activity to better recall his original design ideas:

> *"Writing something out helps me think about what I really mean, helps me clarify my thoughts. This helped me understand what I really thought of the prior design."* [P38, RF]

Designers reported that the reflection activity was also able to help them identify the strengths and weaknesses of their designs (n=14). This was especially true in the R condition (n=11) where designers did not receive external feedback. Intentional reflection enhanced designers' ability to question some of their design choices and inspire revisions. An illustrative quote from a designer was:

> *"At first I wasn't sure how I could improve my design. In fact, I really liked my first design! And then I was thinking of minor things to change, like the font, or the font color etc. But then I thought about the comments that I had made, and honestly felt kind of pressured to make changes based on my actual reflections. After I did make the changes that were consistent with my reflection, I realized how much MORE I liked my new design!"* [P133, R].

A third theme was that designers used the reflection activity to prioritize changes prior to executing them (n=14).

Elaborating on what needed to be fixed promoted a 'stop-and think' gap so that the designers could better consider how to incorporate their ideas into the revised design [24]:

> "... *I had to think through an explanation of my design in the first question, so I was better prepared to answer the second and third questions. While answering questions two and three, I could use the specific points I wrote for question one to decide which elements of the design met the goals and which did not.*" [P73, R]

When the reflection activity received less favorable ratings, designers felt that it did not help them generate directions for their revisions (n=10). Such responses came mostly from the R and RF conditions where designers performed the reflection without (or before) receiving feedback:

> "*I don't think they were very memorable or helpful. It didn't really give me any insight on what specific things to change.*" [P105, R].

> "*It's always hard to find ways to edit my own work, I feel like it would have been more helpful to receive feedback from someone else and build off that.*" [P117, R].

A related theme was that some designers had decided on the revisions based on reviewing the feedback (n=6) and did not find the reflection useful. For example, one designer wrote:

> "*I did not find it useful at all to write about the revisions I was going to make. I had already come up with the changes I wanted to do as I was reading the feedback.*" [P90, FR].

Finally, other designers did not value the written forms of the activity, saying that their revisions were already clear in their minds (n=8). One supporting response was:

> "*While the reflection question asks you to think about your design, it is all part of the design process already, so it does not add to improving the design.*" [P179, RF].

DISCUSSION AND FUTURE WORK

Our results show a benefit of integrating a lightweight reflection activity within the iterative design process. The feedback-only (F) condition in our study represented the common practice of revising a design based on reviewing feedback from an external audience. Interestingly, we found that performing only the reflection (R) before revising the initial design yielded outcomes that were similar to the feedback-only condition, and either activity led to better outcomes than the control condition. Reviewing feedback helped the designers assess their design through external judgments, while the reflection allowed the designers to extract and articulate what was learned from their experience creating the design [31, 46, 48]. Indeed, designers reported that the reflection activity helped them recall their goals, question their choices, and prioritize revisions.

This finding suggests that when a designer is unable to acquire feedback (e.g. due to the cost of acquiring it), a reflection activity could be performed to guide the next design iteration without losing ground on the measures in our study. However, our results should not be interpreted to mean that a reflection activity could fully replace the need for external feedback in the design process.

If designers perform a reflection activity in addition to reviewing feedback, we found that the degree of revision between the initial and revised design was perceived to be more extensive by the experts. Further, if the reflection was performed *after* reviewing the feedback, the designers improved the quality of the designs the most according to the experts. This finding extends prior work showing that reflection after feedback improves task performance [1] to the context of a creative design task. In our study, the improvement typically came from surface-level changes such as color, font, and layout. Regardless of its placement, integrating the reflection activity did not adversely affect the other measures. It remains an open question whether the focus on aesthetic issues was due to the designers in our study having less experience, or due to the categories and style of the feedback that was provided.

Analysis of the content of the reflection responses indicated a tradeoff between performing the reflection activity before vs. after reviewing external feedback. Designers reported considering more conceptual issues when the reflection activity was performed first; whereas they reported attending to more surface issues when the reflection was performed after reviewing the feedback. It may therefore be most beneficial to perform the reflection activity *before* reviewing feedback during the early design stage when the focus is typically on conceptual issues and to perform it *after* reviewing feedback during the late stage when the focus is typically on improving aesthetics [44]. Future work is needed to confirm these recommendations.

The psychological mechanism for how coupling reflection and feedback works is an open question. If reflection is performed after feedback review (FR), the reflection could be helping the designer to synthesize meaning from the feedback and their design experience [43]. However, it is also possible that the feedback helped direct the designers' attention, thereby making the reflection more effective [1]. There would be an analogous interpretation if performed in the opposite order (RF). Future empirical research is needed to elucidate the mechanism at play and how changing the placement of the reflection activity affects this processing.

Platform developers can draw from a range of mechanisms to aid interpretation of feedback, such as visualizing issue frequency [50], displaying cues of source identity [49], and enabling richer modalities for annotation [53]. A reflection activity could be implemented to complement any of these mechanisms, and have already been implemented in online platforms to promote learning [48]. As implementing the reflection is straightforward, we outline ways to encourage responses. If the reflection is to be performed after feedback review, a platform could request a response before allowing the next iteration to be posted. The response could also be made available to the providers to further ground the feedback exchange [16]. If the reflection is to be performed before reviewing feedback, a platform could release the feedback only after receiving a response. Whether the activity is performed before or after feedback review can be based on the stage of the design or left to the designer.

In our experiment, a designer reflected individually through writing. Alternative formulations of the reflection could include a collaborative dialogue around the prompts [12] or a video recording of one's own responses [18]. Future work is needed to test how different formulations of the activity and different prompts affect design performance.

As in prior design studies [32, 51], our experiment instructed designers to revise their initial designs. It is possible that this procedure limited the scope of changes that the designers were willing to consider. Similar studies in the future may want to instruct designers to create a second new design rather than revising their initial one in order to promote broader design thinking. Designers also wrote their own goals during the reflection activity thereby establishing individual standards. An alternative would have been to show the designers an expert solution in order to establish a shared, external standard. This approach could also contribute to promoting creative effort in the revision.

To check if design expertise affected our results, we calculated an expertise score by adding each designer's self-rated expertise (5-point scale) to the quality of his or her initial design (7-point scale, rated by the expert). With this score added as a covariate, we repeated all of the analyses. The results were nearly identical, indicating that the findings are robust to the range of expertise represented in our participant pool. However, because the range of expertise in our study was skewed toward novices, additional work is needed to test if our results hold for a wider range of expertise.

Two days separated the completion of the initial design and performing the assigned activity in each condition. This time was practically needed to generate the feedback for the associated conditions, though delays also benefit reflection [24]. Future work is needed to test how different durations of this delay would affect the patterns of our results.

Beyond the issues already discussed, we see several exciting directions for future work. First, we want to implement a similar reflection activity in an existing review platform and study how often designers perform the activity and possible incentives, and how it affects their design performance in practice. A second direction for future work is to test the generalizability of our results in other creative domains, such as building architecture, programming, and writing. Third, future work could consider how to re-appropriate the content collected from many reflection activities over time to benefit design learning. Finally, it would be interesting to develop and test reflection activities suitable for different stages of the design process.

LIMITATIONS

One limitation of our study is that it only included two design iterations. It was therefore not possible to test how performing the reflection activity affects an entire design process. A second limitation is that we used a single design brief. This allowed for experimental control but future work is needed to test the generalizability of our findings for different design problems and in different domains. A third limitation is that the designers performed the reflection activity once and this was the likely the first time that they performed this type of activity in the context of solving a design problem. Further studies are needed to understand how the effects of a reflection activity change as experience is gained. Last, the study was conducted online to enable wide participation. Though our study platform stepped the designers through the procedure, it was not possible to verify that they performed the tasks exactly as instructed.

ACKNOWLEDGMENTS

This work was supported in part by NSF awards 1462693, 1530818, 1122206, and 1122320.

CONCLUSION

To promote deeper cognitive processing of feedback received from an external online audience, we studied the effects of combining an explicit reflection activity with feedback review for a creative design task. We found that performing the activity after reviewing feedback enabled the largest improvement in design quality and the most extensive revisions, and without designers over-estimating their own performance. The order in which the reflection activity was performed – before or after reviewing feedback – created a tradeoff between considering more surface-level or more conceptual issues for the design revision. Our results also showed that performing only a reflection activity was as good as only reviewing feedback, and either activity led to better outcomes than performing no activity prior to revising a design. Our work advocates for a future where reflection activities are integrated into creativity tools and individual workflows, as the minimal investment needed for reflection can produce better solutions.

REFERENCES

1. Frederik Anseel, Filip Lievens, and Eveline Schollaert, 2009. Reflection as a strategy to enhance task performance after feedback. *Organizational Behavior and Human Decision Processes*, *110 (1)*, 23-35. http://dx.doi.org/10.1016/j.obhdp.2009.05.003.
2. Michelle Q. Wang Baldonado and Terry Winograd. SenseMaker: an information-exploration interface supporting the contextual evolution of a user's interests. In *Proceedings of the ACM Conference on Human Factors in Computing Systems*. ACM. Atlanta, Georgia, USA. 1997. 11-18. http://dx.doi.org/10.1145/258549.258563.
3. Eric P.S. Baumer, Vera Khovanskaya, Mark Matthews, Lindsay Reynolds, Victoria Schwanda Sosik, and Geri Gay. Reviewing reflection: on the use

of reflection in interactive system design. In *Proceedings of the ACM Conference on Designing interactive systems*. ACM. Vancouver, BC, Canada. 2014. 93-102. http://dx.doi.org/10.1145/2598510.2598598.

4. David Boud and Nancy Falchikov, 1989. Quantitative studies of student self-assessment in higher education: a critical analysis of findings. *Higher Education, 18 (5)*, 529-549. 10.1007/bf00138746.
5. David Carless, 2006. Differing perceptions in the feedback process. *Studies in Higher Education, 31 (2)*, 219-233. 10.1080/03075070600572132.
6. Patricia Cartney, 2010. Exploring the use of peer assessment as a vehicle for closing the gap between feedback given and feedback used. *Assessment & Evaluation in Higher Education, 35 (5)*, 551-564. 10.1080/02602931003632381.
7. Kate Chanock, 2000. Comments on Essays: Do students understand what tutors write? *Teaching in Higher Education, 5 (1)*, 95-105. 10.1080/135625100114984.
8. Deanna P. Dannels and Kelly Norris Martin, 2008. Critiquing Critiques: A Genre Analysis of Feedback Across Novice to Expert Design Studios. *Journal of Business and Technical Communication, 22 (2)*, 135-159. 10.1177/1050651907311923.
9. Jelle Van Dijk, Jirka Van Der Roest, Remko Van Der Lugt, and Kees C.J. Overbeeke. NOOT: a tool for sharing moments of reflection during creative meetings. In *Proceedings of the ACM Conference on Creativity and Cognition*. ACM. Atlanta, Georgia, USA. 2011. 157-164. http://dx.doi.org/10.1145/2069618.2069646.
10. Steven P. Dow, Alana Glassco, Jonathan Kass, Melissa Schwarz, Daniel L. Schwartz, and Scott R. Klemmer, 2010. Parallel prototyping leads to better design results, more divergence, and increased self-efficacy. *ACM Transactions on Computer-Human Interaction, 17 (4)*, 1-24. 10.1145/1879831.1879836.
11. Steven P. Dow, Kate Heddleston, and Scott R. Klemmer. The efficacy of prototyping under time constraints. In *Proceedings of the ACM Conference on Creativity and Cognition*. ACM. Berkeley, California, USA. 2009. 165-174. http://dx.doi.org/http://dx.doi.org/10.1145/1640233.1640260.
12. G. Fischer, 2000. Symmetry of ignorance, social creativity, and meta-design. *Knowledge-Based Systems, 13 (7–8)*, 527-537. http://dx.doi.org/10.1016/S0950-7051(00)00065-4.
13. Gerhard Fischer, Kumiyo Nakakoji, and Jonathan Ostwald, 1995. Supporting the Evolution of Design Artifacts With Representations of Context and Intent. In *The ACM Proceddings on Designing Interactive Systems*.
14. Gerhard Fischer, Kumiyo Nakakoji, Jonathan Ostwald, Gerry Stahl, and Tamara Sumner. Embedding computer-based critics in the contexts of design. In *Proceedings of the INTERACT '93 and CHI '93 Conference on Human Factors in Computing Systems*. ACM. Amsterdam, The Netherlands. 1993. 157-164. http://dx.doi.org/10.1145/169059.169133.
15. Kristie Fisher, Scott Counts, and Aniket Kittur, 2012. Distributed sensemaking: improving sensemaking by leveraging the efforts of previous users. In *Proceedings of the ACM Conference on Human Factors in Computing Systems* ACM, 247-256. http://dx.doi.org/10.1145/2207676.2207711.
16. Eureka Foong, Steven P. Dow, Brian P. Bailey, and Elizabeth M. Gerber. Online Feedback Exchange: A Framework for Understanding the Socio-Psychological Factors. In *Proceedings of the ACM Conference on Human Factors in Computing Systems*. 2017.
17. Xun Ge, Ching-Huei Chen, and Kendrick A. Davis, 2005. Scaffolding Novice Instructional Designers' Problem-Solving Processes Using Question Prompts in a Web-Based Learning Environment. *Journal of Educational Computing Research, 33 (2)*, 219-248. 10.2190/5F6J-HHVF-2U2B-8T3G.
18. Elizabeth Gerber. Tech break up: a research method for understanding people's attachment to their technology. In *Proceedings of the 8th ACM conference on Creativity and cognition*. ACM. Atlanta, Georgia, USA. 2011. 137-146. http://dx.doi.org/10.1145/2069618.2069642.
19. Elizabeth Gerber and Maureen Carroll, 2012. The psychological experience of prototyping. *Design Studies, 33 (1)*, 64-84. http://dx.doi.org/10.1016/j.destud.2011.06.005.
20. Michael D. Greenberg, Matthew W. Easterday, and Elizabeth M. Gerber. Critiki: A Scaffolded Approach to Gathering Design Feedback from Paid Crowdworkers. In *Proceedings of the ACM Conference on Creativity and Cognition*. ACM. Glasgow, United Kingdom. 2015. 235-244. http://dx.doi.org/10.1145/2757226.2757249.
21. Michael D. Greenberg, Julie Hui, and Elizabeth Gerber. Crowdfunding: a resource exchange perspective. In *CHI '13 Extended Abstracts on Human Factors in Computing Systems*. ACM. Paris, France. 2013. 883-888. http://dx.doi.org/10.1145/2468356.2468514.
22. Joshua Hailpern, Erik Hinterbichler, Caryn Leppert, Damon Cook, and Brian P. Bailey. TEAM STORM: demonstrating an interaction model for working with multiple ideas during creative group work. In

Proceedings of the ACM SIGCHI conference on Creativity and Cognition. ACM. Washington, DC, USA. 2007. 193-202. http://dx.doi.org/10.1145/1254960.1254987.

23. Kevin A Hallgren, 2012. Computing inter-rater reliability for observational data: an overview and tutorial. *Tutorials in quantitative methods for psychology*, *8 (1)*, 23.
24. John Hattie and Helen Timperley, 2007. The power of feedback. *Review of Educational Research*, *77 (1)*, 81-112. 10.3102/003465430298487.
25. Richard Higgins, Peter Hartley, and Alan Skelton, 2002. The Conscientious Consumer: Reconsidering the role of assessment feedback in student learning. *Studies in Higher Education*, *27 (1)*, 53-64. 10.1080/03075070120099368.
26. Lichan Hong, Ed H. Chi, Raluca Budiu, Peter Pirolli, and Les Nelson. SparTag.us: a low cost tagging system for foraging of web content. In *Proceedings of the Working Conference on Advanced Visual Interfaces*. 2008. 65-72. http://dx.doi.org/10.1145/1385569.1385582.
27. Maria Jackson and Leah Marks, 2016. Improving the effectiveness of feedback by use of assessed reflections and withholding of grades. *Assessment & Evaluation in Higher Education*, *41 (4)*, 532-547. 10.1080/02602938.2015.1030588.
28. Wendy Ju, Arna Ionescu, Lawrence Neeley, and Terry Winograd. Where the wild things work: capturing shared physical design workspaces. In *Proceedings of the ACM Conference on Computer Supported Cooperative Work*. ACM. Chicago, Illinois, USA. 2004. 533-541. http://dx.doi.org/10.1145/1031607.1031696.
29. Scott R. Klemmer, Mark W. Newman, Ryan Farrell, Mark Bilezikjian, and James A. Landay. The designers' outpost: a tangible interface for collaborative web site. In *Proceedings of the 14th annual ACM symposium on User interface software and technology*. ACM. Orlando, Florida. 2001. 1-10. http://dx.doi.org/10.1145/502348.502350.
30. Q. Vera Liao and Wai-Tat Fu. Expert voices in echo chambers: Effects of source expertise indicators on exposure to diverse opinions. In *Proceedings of the ACM Conference on Human Factors in Computing Systems*. 2014. 2745-2754.
31. J. John Loughran, 2002. Effective Reflective Practice: In Search of Meaning in Learning about Teaching. *Journal of Teacher Education*, *53 (1)*, 33-43.
32. Kurt Luther, Jari-Lee Tolentino, Wei Wu, Amy Pavel, Brian P. Bailey, Maneesh Agrawala, Björn Hartmann, and Steven P. Dow. Structuring, Aggregating, and Evaluating Crowdsourced Design Critique. In *Proceedings of the ACM Conference on Computer Supported Cooperative Work* ACM. Vancouver, BC, Canada. 2015. 473-485. http://dx.doi.org/10.1145/2675133.2675283.
33. Effie Maclellan, 2001. Assessment for Learning: The differing perceptions of tutors and students. *Assessment & Evaluation in Higher Education*, *26 (4)*, 307-318. 10.1080/02602930120063466.
34. Philip Mendels, Joep Frens, and Kees Overbeeke. Freed: a system for creating multiple views of a digital collection during the design process. In *Proceedings of the ACM Conference on Human Factors in Computing Systems*. ACM. Vancouver, BC, Canada. 2011. 1481-1490. http://dx.doi.org/10.1145/1978942.1979160.
35. Kumiyo Nakakoji, Yasuhiro Yamamoto, Shingo Takada, and Brent N. Reeves. Two-dimensional spatial positioning as a means for reflection in design. In *Proceedings of the ACM Conference on Designing Interactive Systems*. ACM. New York City, New York, USA. 2000. 145-154. http://dx.doi.org/10.1145/347642.347697.
36. Les Nelson, Christoph Held, Peter Pirolli, Lichan Hong, Diane Schiano, and Ed H. Chi. With a little help from my friends: examining the impact of social annotations in sensemaking tasks. In *Proceedings of the ACM Conference on Human Factors in Computing Systems*. ACM. Boston, MA, USA. 2009. 1795-1798. http://dx.doi.org/10.1145/1518701.1518977.
37. Margaret Price, Karen Handley, Jill Millar, and Berry O'donovan, 2010. Feedback : all that effort, but what is the effect? *Assessment & Evaluation in Higher Education*, *35 (3)*, 277-289. 10.1080/02602930903541007.
38. Sadhana Puntambekar and Janet L. Kolodner. The design diary: A tool to support students in learning science by design. In *Proceedings of the International Conference of the Learning Sciences* Charlottesville, VA. 1998. 35-41.
39. Donald Schön, 1990. *Reflective Practioner: How Professionals Think in Action*.
40. Donald A. Schon, 1992. Designing as reflective conversation with the materials of a design situation. *Research in Engineering Design*, *3 (3)*, 131-147. 10.1007/bf01580516.
41. Donald A. Schön, *The Reflective Practitioner: How Professionals Think in Action*.
42. Moushumi Sharmin and Brian P. Bailey. ReflectionSpace: an interactive visualization tool for supporting reflection-on-action in design. In *Proceedings of the ACM Conference on Creativity and Cognition*. ACM. Sydney, Australia. 2013. 83-92. http://dx.doi.org/10.1145/2466627.2466645.

43. Giada Di Stefano, Francesca Gino, Gary P. Pisano, and Bradley R. Staats, 2014 (Revised June 2016). Making Experience Count: The Role of Reflection in Individual Learning *Harvard Business School Working Paper*, *14-093* (http://dx.doi.org/10.2139/ssrn.2414478.
44. Maryam Tohidi, William Buxton, Ronald Baecker, and Abigail Sellen. Getting the right design and the design right. In *Proceedings of the ACM Conference on Human Factors in Computing Systems*. ACM. Montreal, Quebec, Canada. 2006. 1243-1252. http://dx.doi.org/10.1145/1124772.1124960.
45. Oscar Tomico, Joep W. Frens, and C. J. Overbeeke. Co-reflection: user involvement for highly dynamic design processes. In *CHI '09 Extended Abstracts on Human Factors in Computing Systems*. ACM. Boston, MA, USA. 2009. 2695-2698. http://dx.doi.org/10.1145/1520340.1520389.
46. Annekatrin Wetzstein and Winfried Hacker, 2004. Reflective Verbalization Improves Solutions: The Effects of Question-based Reflection in Design Problem Solving. *Applied Cognitive Psychology*, *18 (2)*, 145-156. 10.1002/acp.949.
47. W. Willett, J. Heer, and M. Agrawala, 2012. Strategies for crowdsourcing social data analysis. In *Proceedings of the ACM conference on Human Factors in Computing Systems* ACM, 227-236.
48. Joseph Jay Williams, Tania Lombrozo, Anne Hsu, Bernd Huber, and Juho Kim. Revising Learner Misconceptions Without Feedback: Prompting for Reflection on Anomalies. In *Proceedings of the 2016 CHI Conference on Human Factors in Computing Systems*. ACM. Santa Clara, California, USA. 2016. 470-474. http://dx.doi.org/10.1145/2858036.2858361.
49. Y. Wayne Wu and Brian P. Bailey. Novices Who Focused or Experts Who Didn't? How Effort and Expertise Cues Affect Judgments of Crowd Work In *Proceedings of the ACM Conference on Human Factors in Computing Systems*. ACM. San Jose, CA, USA. 2016. http://dx.doi.org/10.1145/2858036.2858330.
50. Anbang Xu, Shih-Wen Huang, and Brian Bailey. Voyant: generating structured feedback on visual designs using a crowd of non-experts. In *Proceedings of the ACM Conference on Computer Supported Cooperative Work*. ACM. Baltimore, Maryland, USA. 2014. 1433-1444. http://dx.doi.org/10.1145/2531602.2531604.
51. Anbang Xu, Huaming Rao, Steven P. Dow, and Brian P. Bailey. A Classroom Study of Using Crowd Feedback in the Iterative Design Process. In *Proceedings of the ACM Conference on Computer Supported Cooperative Work* ACM. Vancouver, BC, Canada. 2015. 1637-1648. http://dx.doi.org/http://dx.doi.org/10.1145/2675133.2675140.
52. Yu-Chun Yen, Steven P. Dow, Elizabeth Gerber, and Brian P. Bailey. Social Network, Web Forum, or Task Market?: Comparing Different Crowd Genres for Design Feedback Exchange. In *Proceedings of the ACM Conference on Designing Interactive Systems*. ACM. Brisbane, QLD, Australia. 2016. 773-784. http://dx.doi.org/10.1145/2901790.2901820.
53. Dongwook Yoon, Nicholas Chen, Bernie Randles, Amy Cheatle, Corinna E. Löckenhoff, Steven J. Jackson, Abigail Sellen, and François Guimbretière. RichReview++: Deployment of a Collaborative Multi-modal Annotation System for Instructor Feedback and Peer Discussion. In *Proceedings of the ACM Conference on Computer-Supported Cooperative Work* ACM. San Francisco, California, USA. 2016. 195-205. http://dx.doi.org/10.1145/2818048.2819951.
54. Alvin Yuan, Kurt Luther, Markus Krause, Sophie Vennix, Steven P. Dow, and Björn Hartmann. Almost an Expert: The Effects of Rubrics and Expertise on Perceived Value of Crowdsourced Design Critiques. In *Proceedings of the ACM Conference on Computer Supported Cooperative Work*. ACM. San Francisco, CA. 2016.

Beyond Level Blueprints: Visualizing the Progression of Emotion and Narrative Driven Games

Huaxin Wei
School of Design, The Hong Kong
Polytechnic University
Hung Hom, Kowloon, Hong Kong
huaxin.wei@polyu.edu.hk

Betty Durango
School of Design, The Hong Kong
Polytechnic University
Hung Hom, Kowloon, Hong Kong
b.durango@polyu.edu.hk

C&C '17, June 27-30, 2017, Singapore, Singapore

ACM ISBN 978-1-4503-4403-6/17/06...$15.00
http://dx.doi.org/10.1145/3059454.3059489

Abstract
This pictorial presents ECT (Emotion-Centric Timeline) – a visual schema that visualizes the progression of emotion and narrative driven games. The visualization aims to equip analysts and designers in their learning and creative processes of emotional design for games. We illustrate how the visual schema can be used to reveal the dynamics of various design elements with the example game *Journey* and its comparisons with two other games. We also demonstrate with three student game design examples that the schema can serve as a creativity support tool for designers, especially novices, to conceptualize and plan a game that is driven by emotion and narrative.

Author Keywords
Visualization; game progression; emotional design; level design; creativity support; Journey.

ACM Classification Keywords
K.8.0. Personal computing: Games; H.5.m. Information interfaces and presentation (e.g., HCI): Miscellaneous.

Introduction
Designing a videogame involves a complex process weaving together multiple systems of rules and media

content that respond to players' actions and produce desired gameplay experience. When creating a game, designers express their creativity through the engineering of game mechanics and audiovisual content in an iterative prototyping process. Unlike in other design domains, such as architecture and product design, where designers have various kinds of CAD (computer-aided design) tools to support the visualization of the design concept, game designers hardly have any similar tools to visualize and reason about their designs [8]. Text and image based documents and spreadsheets are still largely used to communicate game design concepts. If one area of game design exceptionally tends to use more sketches and diagrams, it would be level design. Level designers usually start and finalize their design both in visual formats, often called level blueprints or layouts. Among these formats, top-down maps of the game space are very commonly used. They come with varied details including spatial layouts, landmarks, and gameplay elements such as NPCs (non-player characters) and obstacles. Since these maps only focus on the spatial dimension, many other time-based, dynamic design elements have to be left out.

For emotion and narrative driven games, shaping the player experience along the game progression is critical to achieving certain design goals. Having an integrated, coherent view of both spatial and temporal dimensions during the planning stage is thus crucial for designers. In this work, we support the emotion and narrative driven design approach by exploring visualization possibilities beyond level blueprints to facilitate time-sensitive game progression design. We arrive at a visual schema that represents game progression in the form of emotion-centric timeline (ECT).

Organization

In total there are nine diagrams presented in the pictorial, of which the first six are instances created to demonstrate the ECT visual schema, using the game *Journey* [11] as a key example. Diagram [A] is a high-level view of game progression. Diagram [B] provides a full notation of the symbols for low-level views. Diagrams [C] and [D] illustrate the low-level, detailed level design and mood design for specific game chapters. Diagrams [E] and [F] demonstrate the usage of the schema for game comparisons with respect to different design aspects. The last three (Diagrams [G-I]) are student adaptations of ECT schema created in their own design process.

A Visual Schema for *Journey*

Our visualization work is deeply inspired by the design rationale behind the indie videogame *Journey* [11], an artistic adventure, which was explained in great detail by its creative director Jenova Chen in his talk at Game Developer Conference in 2013 [2]. Although emotion as a design element started to gain more attention in the gaming community many years ago, as evidenced by the trademark word 'emotioneering' coined by game writer and designer David Freeman [4], *Journey* is perhaps one of the earliest games whose design goes beyond employing visual and narrative techniques only locally and instead is driven entirely by an emotional arc. Aiming to implement an emotional catharsis, the designers of *Journey* turned to the three-act structure commonly used in Hollywood film and the structure of transformation found in the Hero's Journey delineated by Joseph Campbell [1]. Aligning the emotional arc with the narrative arc along the game progression, the designers formed the game plan where key design aspects, including game levels/areas, stages of

Diagram [A] High-level view of *Journey's* progression: An exemplification of the ECT (Emotion-Centric Timeline) visual schema for game progression analysis.
In this view, the entire diagram is laid out in a timeline format, showing the game progressing from left to right. In the top section of the diagram, game chapters and game levels/areas are distributed along the timeline, with the latter represented in colored shapes. The color indicates the dominant color tone for the game level/area, whereas the size of the shape indicates the size of the game area. In the bottom section, narrative components, emotional arc, character elevation and ground surface are drawn not only along the horizontal timeline axis, but also along the vertical height axis. For emotion, the vertical height means the emotional intensity. For character elevation and ground surface, it means the geographical elevation in relation to a baseline elevation, such as the sea level or the ground level, indicating their height changing dynamics. The heights of the curves are relative and indicative only, rather than quantitatively accurate measurements.

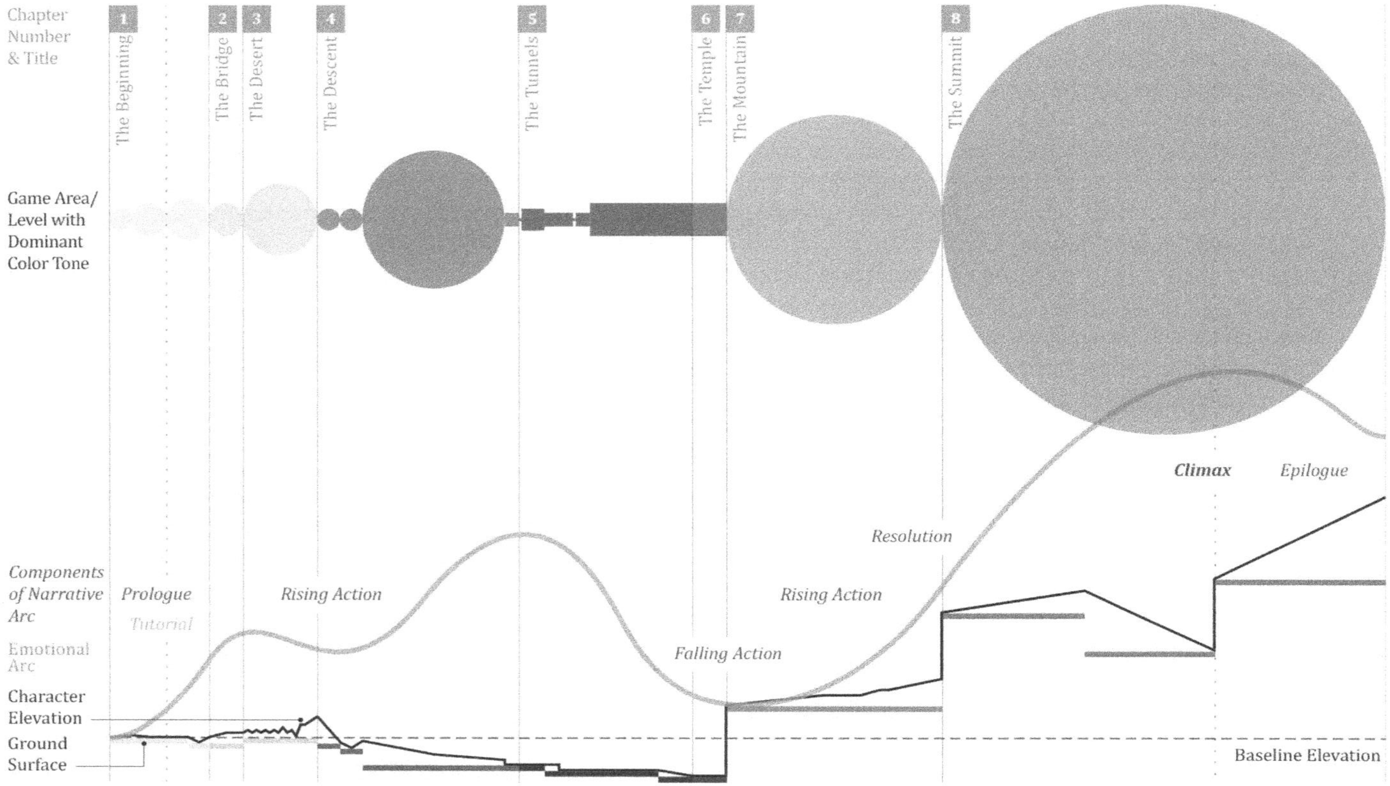

character growth, color and mood, and gameplay elements, fall into place along the game timeline [2]. With *Journey's* phenomenal success, this design method became an exemplar of emotional design in games [6]. Combining the design rationale revealed by Chen and findings from our own game analysis, we visualize *Journey* using a timeline-based schema (see Diagram [A]) that covers a number of key design elements in relation to the game progression, just like how Chen demonstrated the game structure in some of their planning diagrams [2]. These elements include level layout/map, character elevation (i.e., how high the player character's position is in the game space), height of the ground surface (i.e., the base terrain of each game area), and color tone, which were emphasized in *Journey's* design and drawn to correspond to the desired emotional intensity, following a central arc along the timeline stamped with game chapter numbers.

Rationale

We found that the timeline format is capable and efficient in bringing together temporal and spatial dimensions. As each colored shape in Diagram [A] can be filled with a top-down map of the game area, the *Journey* schema not only retains the capacity of showing spatial layouts like in those level blueprints, but also helps anchor varied elements along the game progression timeline, with an emotional arc serving as a guide to shape how those elements are architected. When used in a game-planning diagram, the arc denotes what the designers want the player to feel rather than the actual emotion curve measured from the player during gameplay. This design approach is driven by the consideration that the emotional arc is important for the success of the story, which has been supported by recent research findings [9].

After trying the same visual schema on several other emotion or narrative driven video games, such as *Unravel* [3], a puzzle-platformer, and *Uncharted 2* [7], an action-adventure/third-person shooter, we realized that this schema was quite versatile in revealing the inherent relations between key design aspects for games of different genres. The same patterns of *Journey*'s design are also seen in the design of *Unravel* and *Uncharted 2*. When the player traverses the game space in these games before the climax, the level progresses following a rising emotional arc, during which the player is climbing a mountain and getting to a higher place, the weather is getting bleaker, and the surrounding is getting darker and gloomier, all helping to push up the emotional intensity.

We thus decided to generalize the *Journey* schema into what we call Emotion-Centric Timeline (ECT) schema, which is created to delineate the progression of emotion and narrative driven games. From our analysis at this stage, we came up with the initial set of game design elements that could be included by option in a high-level view of a game's progression: game chapter number and titles as stamps on the timeline, level (or area) distribution, height of ground surface, character elevation, color tone, season and mood. Lastly but most importantly, as the anchoring element of the high-level schema, a central emotional arc represents the desired emotional intensity that a player is expected to have at various points of game progression.

With a few revisions, we further elaborated some of the low-level details with the mind of accommodating designers' needs at the time of planning out the layout for each game level, so that the schema can become a creativity support tool. With these details, the high-level schema as presented in Diagram [A] can be expanded to represent individual levels with attention to various level design details, such as gameplay features (e.g., goal indicator, flags to reach higher places, glyphs to collect, puzzle triggers, etc. in *Journey*'s case), placement of objects, characters, cut-scenes, light source, and so on (see Diagrams [C] and [D]). For the level design details, especially gameplay features, we used primitive shapes in our notation to allow analysts and designers to quickly sketch out the general impression of each area before going into details of map design (see Diagram [B]).

Diagram [B] (Top)
Journey's full game schema legend.

Diagram [C] (Bottom)
An expanded, low-level view of the *Journey*'s two outdoor game areas in the tutorial chapter and second chapter, "The Bridge" (see Chapter Number & Title row on top of Diagram [A]), showing the detailed level design of these two game chapters, including spatial layout of gameplay features, narrative object placement, time of the day, and cut-scene placement (see Diagram [B] for the notation). This expanded view can show two or more game levels side by side so that we can see, in a comparative light, the size of the area, layout of gameplay features, placement of characters and narrative objects, color tone (i.e., color of the area shape), light source, and connectivity between levels (e.g., if two area shapes are connected, their spaces are linked; otherwise if there is a gap in between, it means their spaces are separated).

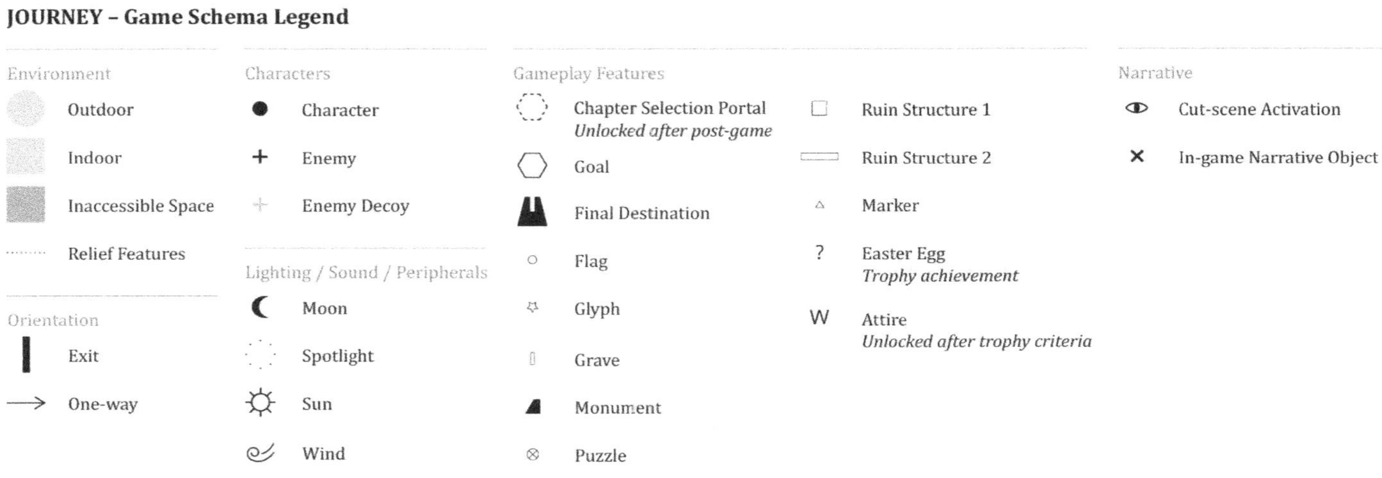

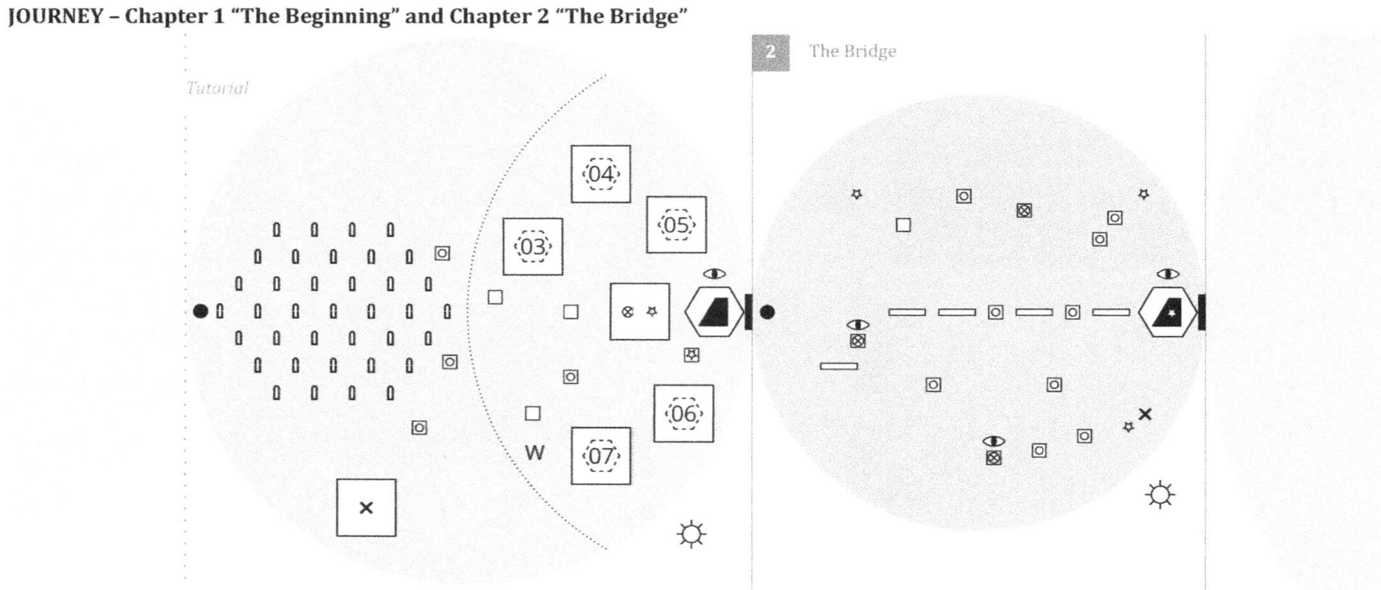

Diagram [D]
Another low-level view of *Journey*'s level and mood design for Chapter 5, "The Tunnels" (see Chapter Number & Title row on top of Diagram [A]), which is the beginning of the falling action, before the rise to climax on the pink emotional arc in Diagram [A], where the player character goes from outdoor open space into gloomy indoor space. Outdoor areas are represented in circles, whereas indoor ones in squares. Inside each area, a lightened, streamlined free shape indicates the actual movement space for the player character to navigate. To match the emotional falling action, the color tone turns from warm orange to cold blue grey.

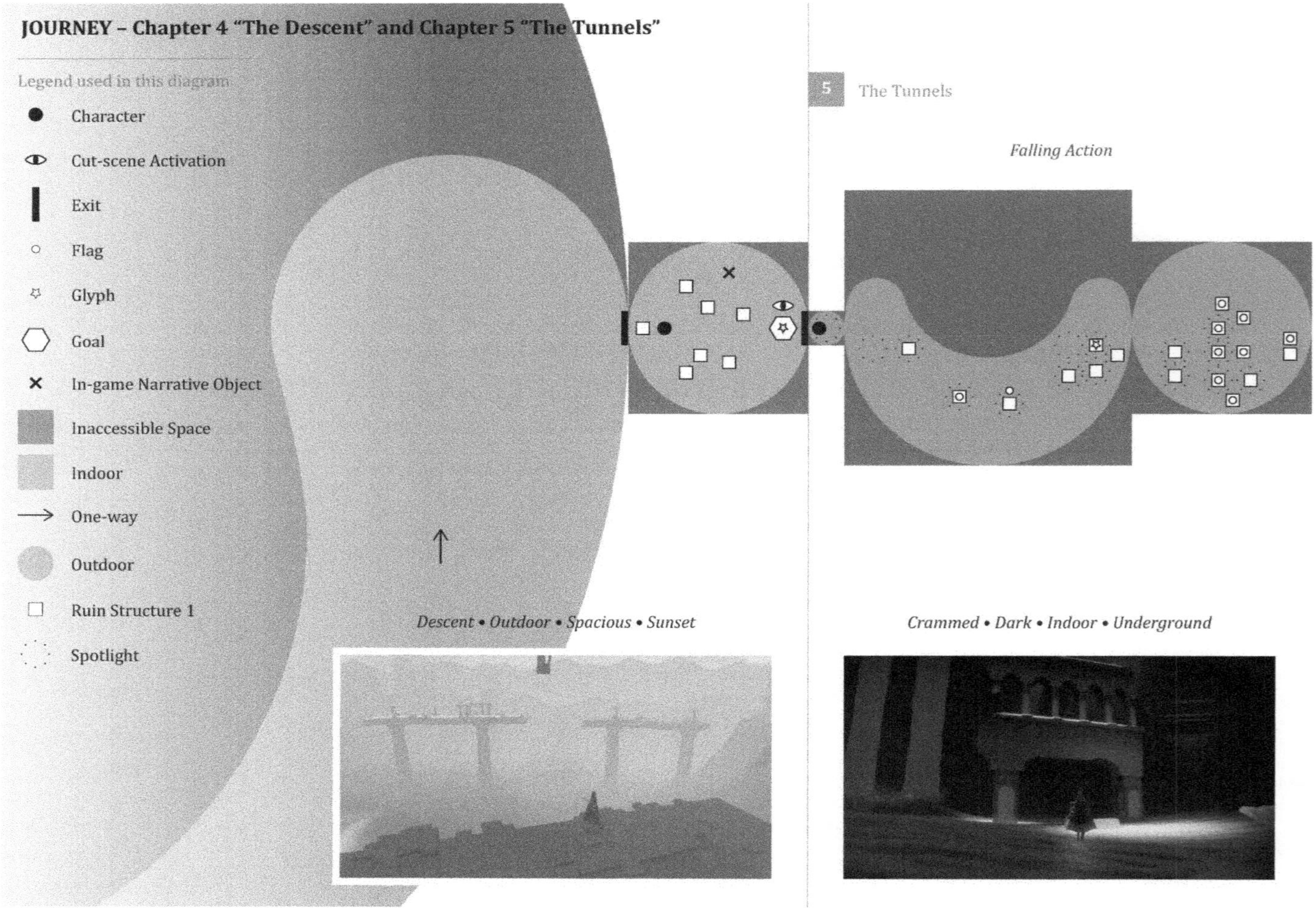

Designed to have two levels of details, the schema is set to follow the structuralists' thinking on creativity and provides systematic approaches to design [10]. Of the four design principles for creativity support tools summarized by Shneiderman [10], we consider one principle that is especially relevant to game design. The principle is to "design with low thresholds, high ceilings, and wide walls," which means the tools "should be easy for novices to begin using, yet provide ambitious functionality that experts need." Under this principle, the schema should be able to visualize a set of design elements and show them either in a separate view or a combined view that includes a flexible number of elements. To strengthen this function, two features are designed for the schema – customizability and scalability, so that individual designers can customize the schema tool and create their own diagrams with different foci and desired level of details.

With the above two features, the ECT schema can also be used to make comparisons between games – with respect to selected game elements – for analytical or benchmarking purposes. Comparing *Journey*, *Unravel*, and *Uncharted 2*, we created Diagrams [E] and [F] to illustrate this usage of the schema. In [E], looking at the curve of character elevation that reveals the dynamic movement of the player character and shows where he or she could perform the highest reach (e.g., the highest point of a tree in *Unravel*, the top building in *Uncharted 2*, etc.), we discover that for all three games, the elevation (or vertical position) of the player character corresponds to the emotional intensity on the arc at certain points of game progression (see the annotation for Diagram [E]).

In [F], a comparative look at the color tones of the three games can tell us that while *Journey* and *Unravel* have more varied, distinct color tones between chapters, *Uncharted 2* uses more darker tones with less color variation. One could attribute this distinction to the differences between game and story genres, which often determine the visual style, or narrativity of the games, as *Uncharted 2* presents a much richer storyline in a highly realistic, cinematic style.

Diagram [E]
Journey's emotional arc guides the design of color tone, indicated by the color of the chapter block, and the character elevation for each game level (i.e. chapter), indicated by the black curve in the schema. Several patterns are shared among the three games with respect to the relation between character elevation and emotional intensity: (1) Both character elevation and emotional intensity tend to rise upon reaching the climax; (2) Flatter curves for both often indicate the boring, slow-pacing, "silence-before-the-storm" moment that usually lasts not long; (3) The pairing of low character elevation and high emotional intensity often occurs before the rising action leading to the climax. Comparing the color tones, one can see that as the player character climbs higher towards the end of the game (e.g., Chapter 8 of *Journey*, Chapter 10 of *Unravel*, and Chapter 22 of *Uncharted 2*), the color turns to a blue or dark tone implying a colder, harsher weather condition, helping to intensify the emotion.

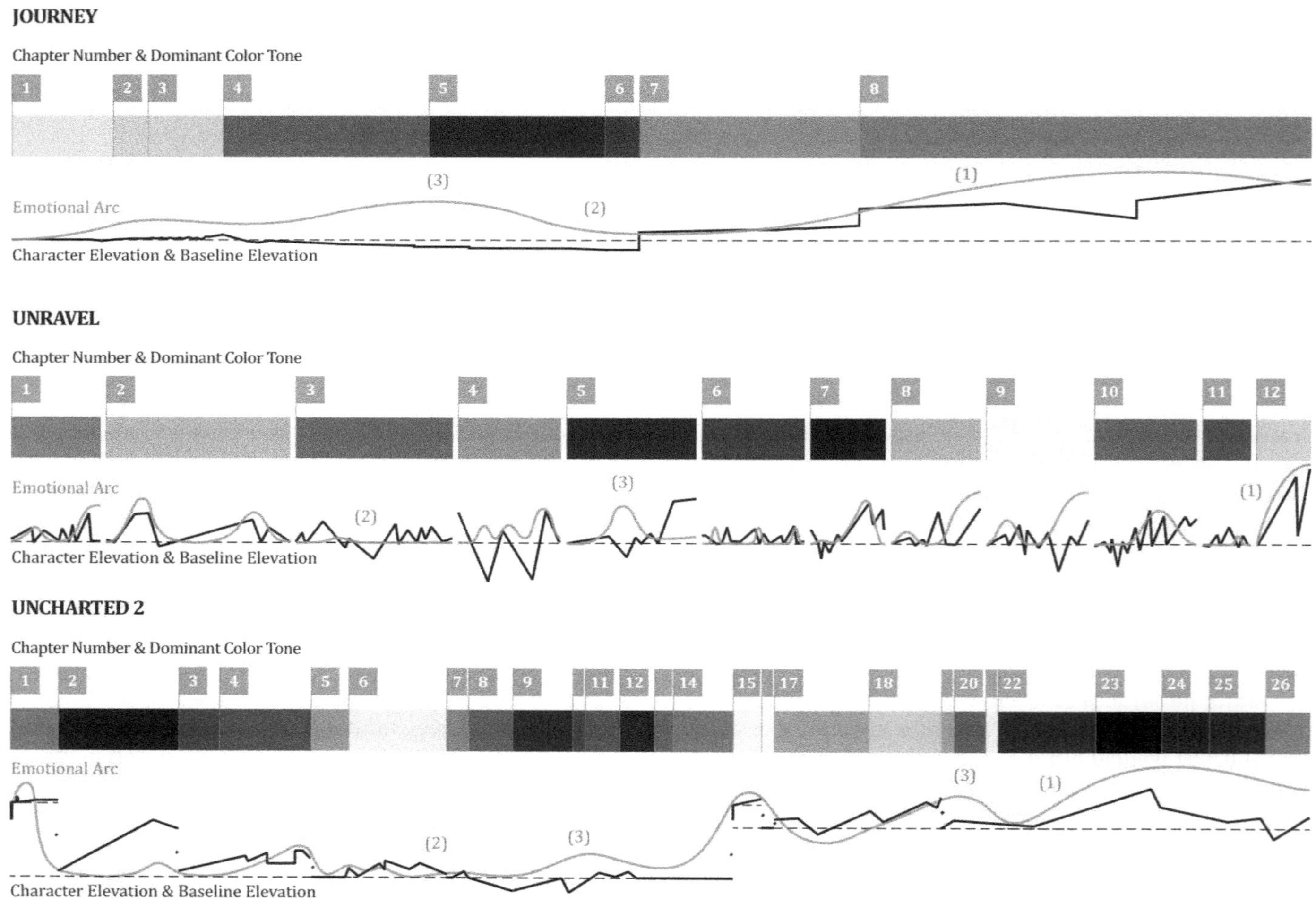

Diagram [F]
Comparison of three games with respect to color tone change along the game progression. The mood triggered by the color tone follows along the emotional arc, as seen in Diagram [E], which is evidenced by the screenshots we captured in corresponding time frames.

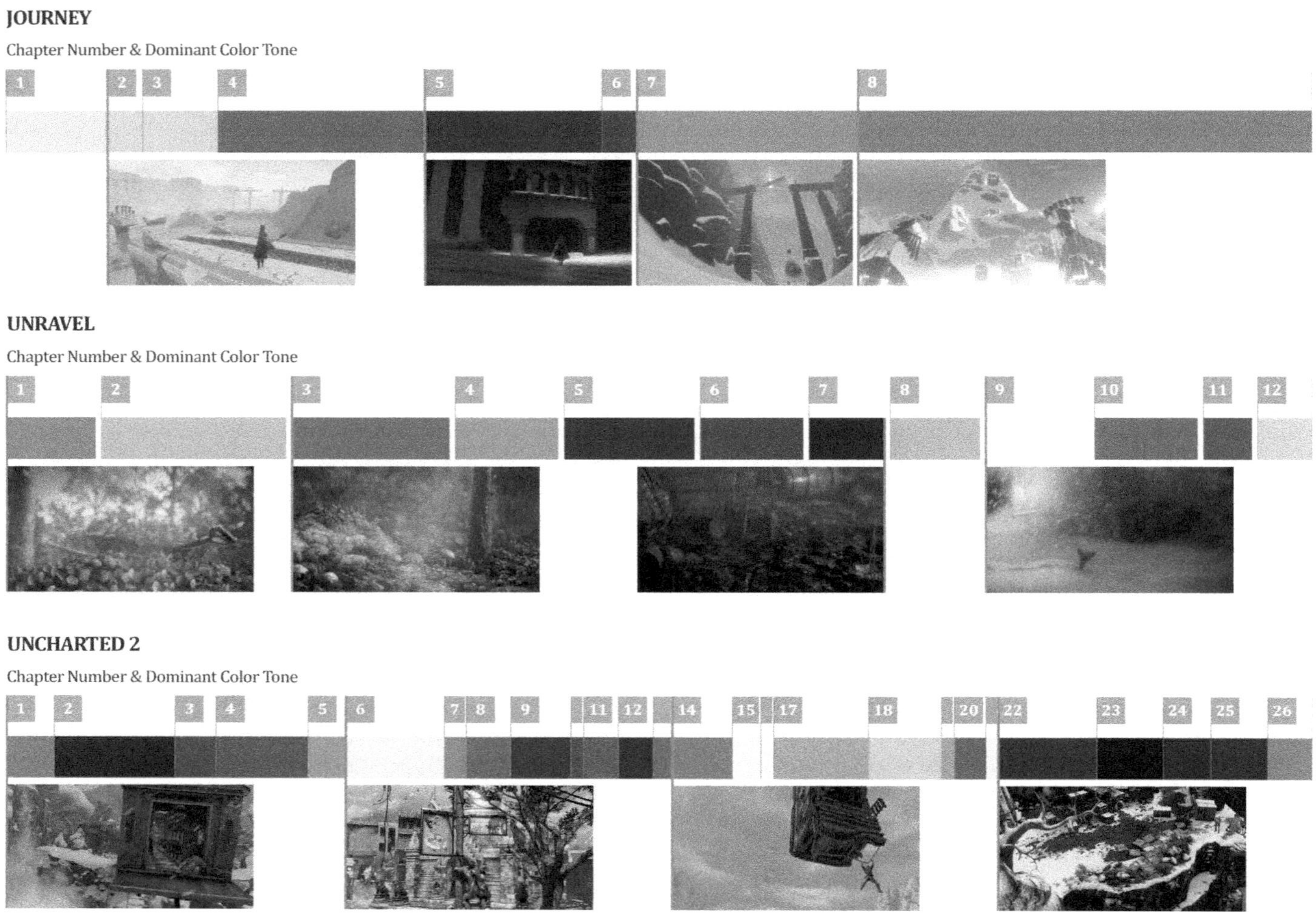

Reflection

To support emotional design for games, we took inspiration from the game *Journey* and created a visual schema to visualize a range of design elements along an emotion-centric timeline. We then deploy the schema in diagrammatic template format to an undergraduate game design class at a design school, in order to observe the cognitive effect on the student designers during the conceptualization stage of their design process. Diagrams [G], [H], [I] are three examples of students' game planning diagrams collected from the class.

Thanks to the customizability of the schema, these design students were able to add new design elements to fulfill their design goals and alter the visual representation to suit their needs or make it more comfortable for the team to communicate. For example, in Diagram [H] the team uses a branching nodal link, rather than the original curve of the emotional arc, to represent multiple endings. It is worth noting that in this way, a branching non-linear narrative can also be visualized by the schema.

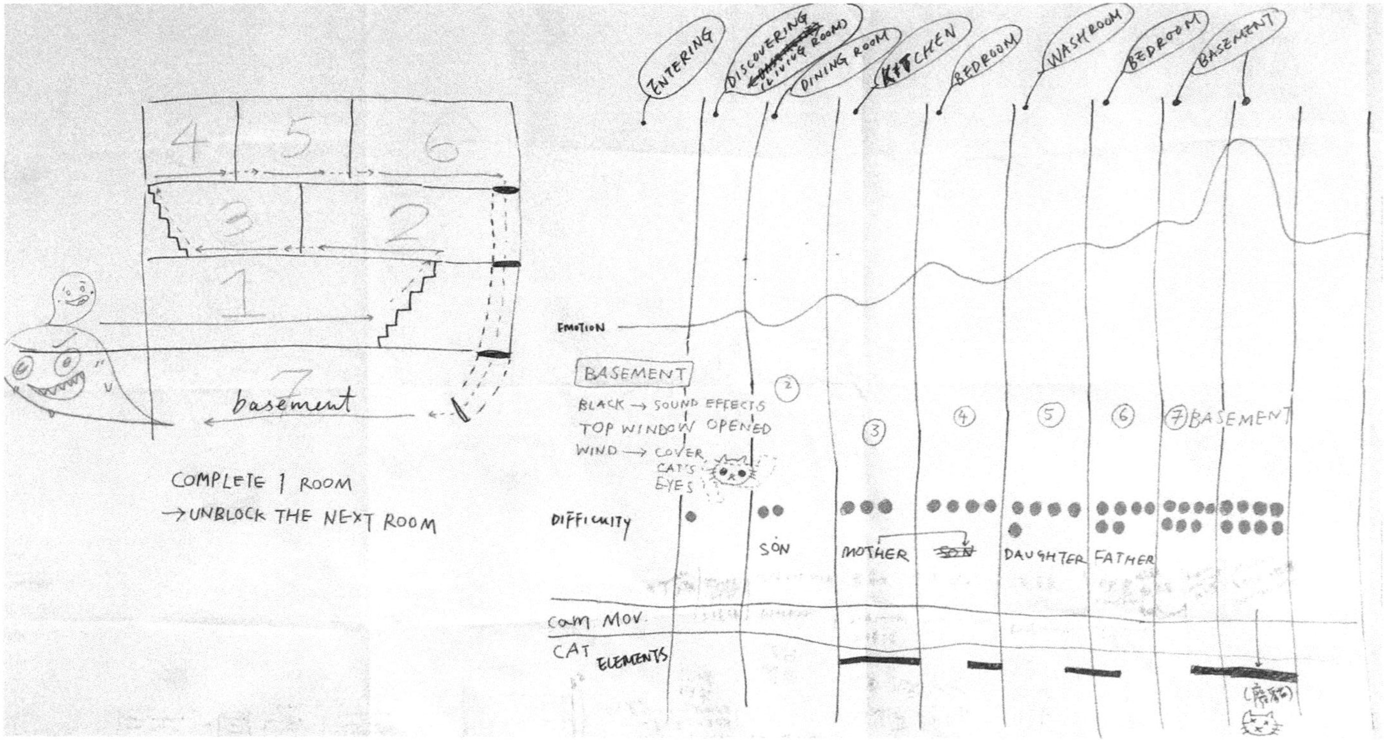

Diagram [G]
Game planning hand-sketch diagram for *Get Out*, a point and click adventure game created by students Hao Cheng Jacky Lo, Yin Wun Tsang, and Yuet Yung Wu. The team marks the presence of a whimsical NPC (i.e., a cat) – a special feature of the game – on certain levels (see the bottom row) to increase the gameplay difficulty. At this early stage, the team uses numbers to indicate the distribution of levels (rooms in this case) while using a separate side view of the house (left to the diagram) to present the room layout.

Diagram [H] (Top)
Game Planning diagram for *Jewelry Thief*, a mobile adventure game created by students Kuan Ho Bryan Ng, Wai Lam Chan, and Hiu Wai Tsang. In this plan, the emotional arc and story nodes are merged together with two story endings marked with different emotions. The team also assigns different difficulty degrees to each game level and uses location names to refer each level (i.e., scene).

Diagram [I] (Bottom)
Game planning diagram for *Designer's Life*, a puzzle game created by students Wai Man Fong, Chi Him Lau, Chun Kit Lee, and Oi Hung Tong. As each game level consists of a puzzle, level layout has no use in the schema. Instead, the team explicitly assigns to the levels a range of labeled feelings – a self-defined extension to the original schema template and a new, driving design element. The varied feelings of the levels thus form an arc of the character's emotion, which is a replacement of the arc of desired player's emotion in our original schema. Defying the classic narrative arc, this design choice invites the player to feel what the character feels and intentionally delivers an unusual negative experience of the life and career progression of those struggling real-world designers.

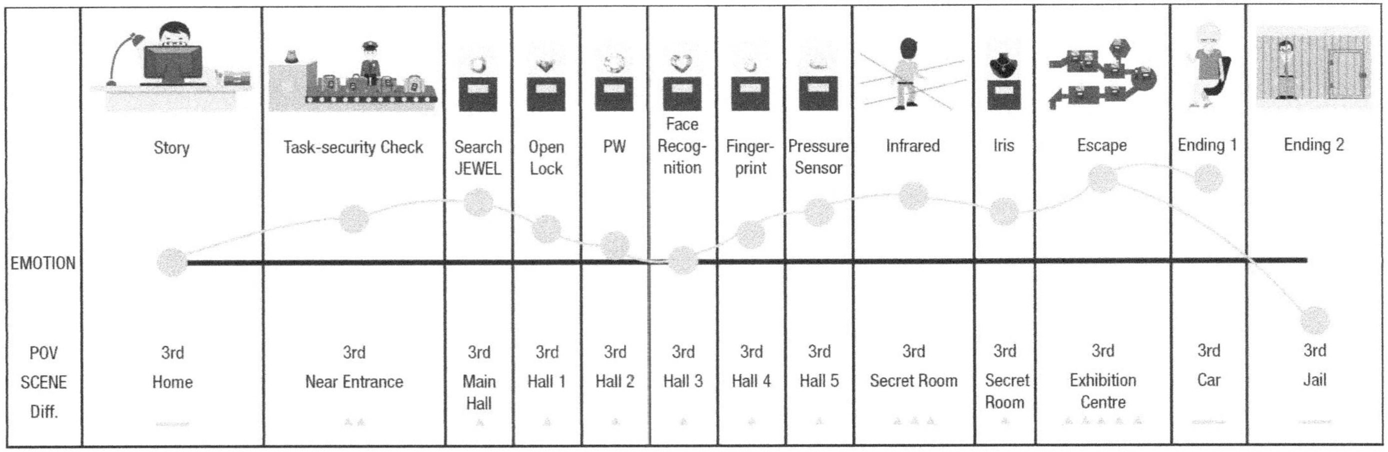

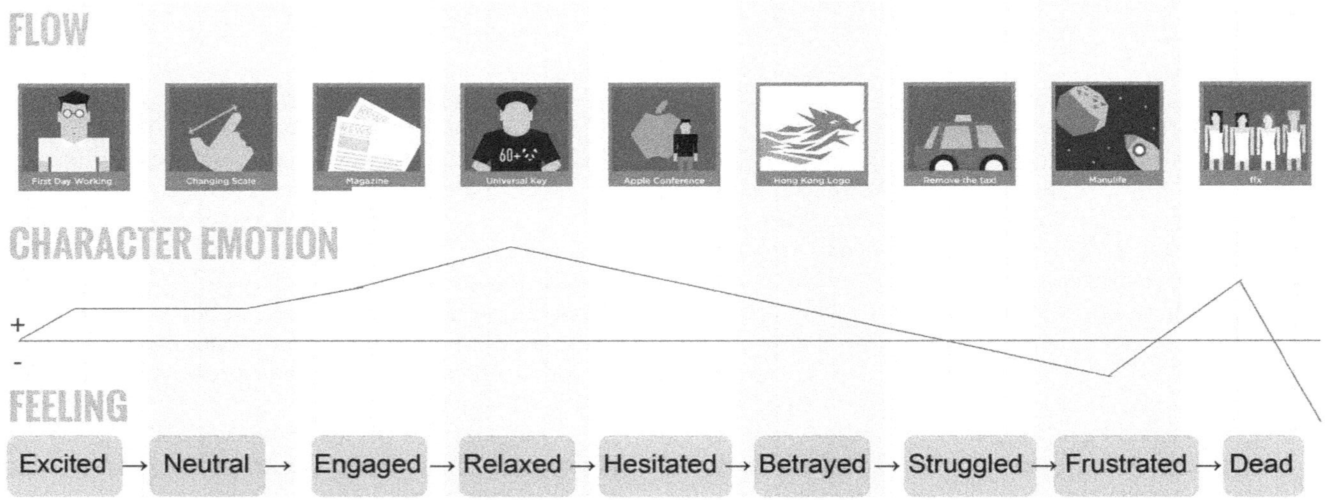

The ECT-based game diagrams included in this pictorial demonstrated a number of strengths of the schema we designed. The modular design allows analysts and designers to choose the focus of visualization and come up with a customized view to suit their needs. As the student examples show, new design elements can be added to the timeline to suit the design goal. Focusing on selected design elements and visually presenting them vis-à-vis emotional arc, the schema can stimulate pattern thinking by designers and analysts. Just like how Diagrams [E] and [F] reveal the impact of character elevation on desired player emotion, patterns of design can be easily identified in the comparison diagrams that show the dynamics between different elements and different games. The modular design also paves ways to an interactive version of the schema, making it easier to be deployed and used, which is one of our ultimate goals.

More importantly, the selection of design elements to be visualized and the way they are visually presented in the schema specifically stress and enable an emotion and narrative driven design approach. This is in line with Schneiderman's comments: "[e]xcellent interfaces, sometimes with rich domain-specific features, are essential for creativity support, as users need to apply their cognitive resources and passions fully to their discoveries and innovations" [10]. By having other design elements visualized against the emotional and narrative arc, designers can be more conscious over their expected player experiences.

The current visualization design was inspired by an in-depth case study of the game *Journey* and the schema was applied by three student teams. This is far from adequate to evaluate the effect of the visualization.

Therefore, our next step is to conduct more case studies against more emotion and narrative driven games in order to expand the schema with more design elements to accommodate diverse design situations and goals.

In the meanwhile, it is also essential to have more designers use the schema in their design and document in detail their reactions using both observational and self-report methods. This will help us identify ways to enhance the visualization quality. In our last round of deployment, we gave student designers digital and print templates for them to use. Template as a pre-coded visualization paradigm, however, has its risk of limiting the variations of situations and thus can limit designers' power of expression [5]. In the future deployment of the schema and with possible computerized solutions, we would like to seek a better format to give more freedom to designers.

Acknowledgements
We thank all the student designers credited above for allowing us to include their design diagrams and Chaoguang Wang for reviewing our schema design and helping students in the exercise. We also acknowledge The Hong Kong Polytechnic University and School of Design for their funding supports of the work behind this pictorial, through projects G-UB81 and 1-ZE3P.

References
1. Campbell, Joseph. 1949. *The Hero with a Thousand Faces*. Pantheon Books, New York.
2. Chen, Jenova. 2013. Designing Journey. Lecture video at Game Developer Conference (GDC 2013). Retrieved January 11, 2017 from http://gdcvault.com/play/1017700/Designing
3. Coldwood Interactive. 2016. *Unravel*. [Windows/PlayStation 4/Xbox One game] Electronic Arts.
4. Freeman, David. 2003. *Creating Emotion in Games: The Craft and Art of Emotioneering*. New Riders Press, Indianapolis, IN.
5. Huron, Samuel, Sheelagh Carpendale, Alice Thudt, Anthony Tang, and Michael Mauerer. 2014. Constructive visualization. In *Proceedings of the 2014 Conference on Designing Interactive Systems* (DIS '14), 433-442. https://doi.org/10.1145/2598510.2598566.
6. Isbister, Katherine. 2016. *How Games Move Us: Emotion by Design*. MIT Press, Cambridge, MA.
7. Naughty Dog. 2009. *Uncharted 2: Among Thieves*. [PlayStation 3/4 game] Sony Interactive Entertainment.
8. Nelson, Mark J., and Michael Mateas. 2009. A requirements analysis for videogame design support tools. In *Proceedings of the 4th International Conference on Foundations of Digital Games* (ICFDG '09), 137-144. https://doi.org/10.1145/1536513.1536543.
9. Reagan, Andrew J., Lewis Mitchell, Dilan Kiley, Christopher M. Danforth, and Peter Sheridan Dodds. 2016. The emotional arcs of stories are dominated by six basic shapes. *EPJ Data Science* 5, 1. https://doi.org/10.1140/epjds/s13688-016-0093-1
10. Shneiderman, Ben. 2007. Creativity support tools: Accelerating discovery and innovation. *Communications of the ACM* 50, 12: 20-32.
11. Thatgamecompany. 2012. *Journey*. [PlayStation 3/4 game] Sony Interactive Entertainment.

Digital Naturalist Design Guidelines: Theory, Investigation, Development, and Evaluation of a Computational Media Framework to Support Ethological Exploration

Andrew Quitmeyer
National University of Singapore
Singapore
andy@quitmeyer.org

ABSTRACT
This research aims to develop and evaluate a design framework for creating digital devices that support the exploration of animal behaviors in the wild. This paper quickly shares the main concepts and theories from the fields forming Digital Naturalism's foundation while presenting the key challenges emerging from these critical intersections between field biology and computational media. It then reviews the development of this research's hybrid methodology designed specifically for its multi-year series of "Qualitative Action Research" fieldwork carried out at a rainforest field station.

This paper analyzes the resulting on-site ethnographies, workshops, design projects, and interactive performances, whose take-aways are synthesized into design guidelines for digital-natural media. This framework, itself, is then evaluated via an extra iteration of fieldwork and the results discussed. Finally, the paper identifies targets for continued research development. Further areas of interest are presented which will promote Digital Naturalism's progression into its own topic of study.

Author Keywords
Biomedia; biological media; behavioral media; cybiotic.

ACM Classification Keywords
H.5.m. Information interfaces and presentation (e.g., HCI): Miscellaneous;

INTRODUCTION
This research studies the role that digital media can play for biological field work. The collaborations growing between biologists, designers, engineers, and artists spawn new challenges and design spaces inherent to these parent fields. Specifically, this research focuses on new combinations of ethological practice (the naturalistic study of animal behavior [46]) and computation as a unique [25], behavioral [3] media form. It looks to uphold the naturalistic values developed by these wilderness explorers, while investigating the new abilities offered by digital technology.

Carrying out this work requires a study of ethology's foundational ideas (via historical literature) along with ethology's contemporary principles (via fieldwork at a rainforest field station, the *Smithsonian Tropical Research Institute (STRI)*[53]). These theoretical and pragmatic investigations include on-site ethnographies, workshops, design projects, and interactive performances. The work is qualitatively analyzed and then synthesized into a framework to support digital-ethological practice. Finally, this framework is practically evaluated through the design and implementation of additional ethological expeditions.

The resulting framework encourages digital technology that supports four key concepts. *Technological Agency* pushes for devices that promote understanding of their own internal functions. The tenet of *Contextual Crafting* leads designers and ethologists to create devices in close proximity to their intended use. *Behavioral Immersion* promotes visceral interactions between the digital and organismal agents involved. Finally, *Open-Endedness* challenges researchers to create adaptable tools which strive to generate questions rather than answering them.

Figure 1 – The four concepts of Digital Naturalist Design

C&C '17, June 27 - 30, 2017, Singapore, Singapore

ACM 978-1-4503-4403-6/17/06…$15.00
DOI: http://dx.doi.org/10.1145/3059454.3059462

This paper consolidates the findings of several years of this work originally described but unpublished in the much larger volume [31]. It intends to share the process of this framework's development, explain the resulting tenets, and provide concrete illustrations for utilizing these guidelines. The intention is that the intention both biologists and digital designers may benefit from this research process and examples. Overall, this research, referred to as Digital Naturalism, explores a developing design space for computers in the wild.

HISTORICAL AND THEORETICAL BACKGROUND

Two key disciplines feeding into this research: Ethology and Digital Media.

Ethology

Ethologists, a name given to scientists studying the behaviors of animals in their natural environments, are primary stakeholders targeted by this research. Understanding the best ways to support these scientists first requires a deep analysis of ethology itself. A cultural and technological history provides the context for the specific set of principles guiding this research in digital studies of animal behavior in the wild.

Studying animal actions dovetails into the development of many fields of science. As former STRI Director Bill Wcislo explains:

> Animal behavior is central to biology. Behavior is the interface between mechanistic and ecological studies – what Marston Bates called 'skin-in' and 'skin-out' biology. It is the means by which animals shape their environments, and determines the flow of energy and information among organisms [54].

This field, however, has traditionally held an enigmatic position among the other scientific fields. Whereas laboratory research typically venerates efficiency, control, and reduplication, the infinite unpredictability of fieldwork pushed ethology to develop supplementary values. Biologists studying animal behavior in the field have long defended the values of open-ended exploration[11] in natural settings. Scholars like Niko Tinbergen and E.O. Wilson have endorsed such "seemingly aimless wanderings in the fields" as indispensable to later "experimental analysis" [44:306]. Present-day ethologists continue to press for such open-ended exploration, for instance, Martin concurs: "The value of broad description arising from sheer curiosity should not be under-estimated." [19]

These principles of open-exploration derive from ethology's roots in Romantic naturalism. Joining such romanticism with techniques within scientific empiricism gives ethology a unique hybrid nature. Operating as a chimera between humanistic and scientific academic institutions, this field often suffered challenges in its acceptance. [46] Its special intersection of positivism and naturalism, rigid experimentation in conjunction with visceral, undirected natural engagement[44] gives ethology "an inclusive approach that provides a way out of the fruitless nature/nurture dichotomy" [51].

Ethological Technology

The unique difficulties which challenge wildlife researchers inspire a need for personalized tool-making. Few mass-produced instruments meet the specific requirements of a researcher's desired interaction with a wild animal living in a unique situation. Therefore, many field biologists find themselves crafting their own tools. Tinbergen's gull-head puppets [45] and Frisch's rotatable bee hives [7] are examples of key scientific tools built from scratch and formed by the research questions being asked.

Additional simple appendages are often improvised from the environment to extend the abilities of the ethologists. Sticks, rocks, and piles of dirt can lengthen our reach, prod at different physical scales, or modify the landscape. For instance, Hölldobler and Wilson discussed insights found when adapting parts of their own bodies to interact with animals. Hölldobler describes,

> …while waiting on the edge of a road for a car ride, Wilson succeeded in "milking" giant scale insects surrounded by ants, simply by touching them with hairs from his head … (Such are the informative pleasures that fill the idle hours of naturalists in the field.)[11].

Some of the most exalted experiments amongst these researchers are those that gathered enough background intuition to manage multiple environmental and animal factors in elegant ways. For instance, in one famous recent study of ant navigation over bleak shifting dunes in the Sahara, Wittlinger, Wehner, and Wolf proved how ants counted their steps by gluing tiny stilts onto the ants' legs[52]. This simple manipulation directly targeted the research question without greatly detracting from other environmental influences. Such experimental elegance is created by meshing a deep understanding of both theoretical literature as well as practical engagement with the creatures, environment, and materials.

Digital technologies, with their abilities to create interactive behaviors, stand to grant even more powerful, dynamic faculties to such open-ended exploration. However, one must always be wary of blindly introducing technology into any practice.

Digital and Behavioral Media

Digital technology offers unprecedented new abilities to extend human analytical and interactive abilities. As the ethologist Chauvin points out, "The behavior of computers constitutes the only possible analogy with animal behavior" [52]. The singular behavioral properties of digital technology allow ethologists to generate sophisticated virtual models like those of Couzin[4], Pratt[27], and Hrolenok [12]. Additionally, though, computers also allow ethologists to create behavioral interactions with living creatures in the real world. Ryan's "Robo-frog," [14] for instance, can be programmed to move in realistic ways, letting scientists ask dynamic questions in their experimental setup. Due to their unparalleled advantages, computers "have become increasingly popular for collecting data in enclosure and laboratory settings" [17:256]. Lehner, however, warns scientists should "remember data loggers are only a faster and more efficient way of collecting and storing data... [They] will not substitute for a poorly designed study" [17:256].

This sentiment points to the dual-edged sword of computers' present role within ethology. As Agre notes, "computing has been constituted as a kind of imperialism; it aims to reinvent virtually every other site of practice in its own image" [1:1]. The extraordinary new abilities of digital technology can augment the biologist's abilities. At the same time, there is the danger that the computer's affordances and limitations also might force ethologists into unproductive patterns as they do not relate to their field.

The wildness and discovery of ethology, however, have generally contrasted with the traditional uses of computers. Computers' propensity for abstraction and disengagement from the physical world is a key challenge for the incorporation of digital artifacts. Scholars like Suchman and Agre have argued that all research practices, "even the most analytic, [are] fundamentally concrete and embodied"[43]. They encourage a basic shift from the design of large singularly powerful or intelligent artifacts to those which make use of and function with the networks of interactions constituting their target environments. Instead of designing technology strictly in the laboratory and in the manner of a disembodied brain, it becomes necessary to explore and design within the specific sites or sociological contexts the devices are used.

As Agre notes, an artifact developed in a computer science laboratory incorporates assumptions, values, and challenges from its environment, and these may be at odds with those encountered by prototyping directly in the field[1]. This schism hinders a tool's physical and scientific efficacy. The technology might not function properly due to changes in moisture, power availability, space requirements, or the non-participation of the animals. Lehner elaborates on this necessary step forward:

> Ethologists should be more than collectors and analyzers of data; they should seek to 'understand' their animal subjects at a higher level than quantitative analysis can provide [17:5].

Thus, good digital ethological tools are tasked with not only collecting experimental data but also fostering exploration and reflection among the scientists. These can for be data collection and scientific gathering, but they might also be tools, like Silver describes, which aim to instead focus scientists' "attention back on nature… and how to build with it, nurture it, and form an intimate relationship with it" [41]. Creating tools appropriate for the fullness of ethological work becomes a key task.

RESEARCH CHALLENGE

Digital technology is increasingly being leveraged into ethological practice without critical analysis. The challenge of this research becomes how to develop constructive methods for incorporating the affordances of digital media to serve ethology.

Current intersections of digital media and wild animal behavioral research are often ad hoc partnerships between technologists and biologists that occur out of necessity. Combining these practices is largely something that is forced to happen, rather than synthesized through analysis and design. This blunt imposition of powerful, new technologies runs the risk of razing the values and methods important to the field. Computational projects can often subjugate partnering fields to computers' own specific methodologies due to restrictions and cultural practices specific to the digital medium. Finding a way to critically develop this framework for this unique combination of fields requires a specific methodology.

METHODOLOGY

Scope and Timeframes

The historical and theoretical backgrounds highlight the key challenges between ethology and digital media. This backdrop set the stage for direct research embedded with contemporary ethologists at their field sites. STRI[53], a worldwide hub of wildlife experimentation, served as an ideal location for this project, as it allows unique access to both interesting wildlife and a vibrant community of diverse field biologists [55]. Ethnographic data was collected via photo, video, and participant surveys from volunteer participants.

The primary phase of this work was carried out with multiple collaborators at STRI from 2012 (pilot season), 2013, and 2014. Data was analyzed and synthesized during 2014, and evaluated iteratively throughout three additional field expeditions from 2014-2015.

Research Structure and Modalities

Digital Naturalism's interdisciplinarity and intertwined biological, technological, and cultural factors necessitate the creation of a customized research structure. This section rapidly explains the origins and synthesis of a hybrid set of methodologies and the approach used throughout this investigation (deeper discussion found in [31:160]).

Finding a research paradigm and practical methods that could tackle the multitudinous factors involved required the assembly of many different fields and practices. Since a standard methodology did not already exist to meet these needs, one had to be customized from the several disciplines concerning science, technology, and design.

Because any hybrid approach risks being unwieldy, the approaches used throughout Digital Naturalism's creation are organized into a structure. This structure demonstrates the full spectrum of critical techniques utilized from general philosophical tactics to specific, concrete methods employed. The organization of this research is also presented to frame the overall project and indicate why certain design and analysis decisions are made.

Practical ←→ Conceptual					
	Paradigm	Qualitative Action Research			
	Approach	Science and Technology Studies			
	Strategies	Critical Making		Performance Studies	
	Methods	Case Studies	Questionnaires	Workshops	Activities
	Analysis	Thick Description			

Figure 2 – Customized research structure for overall "Qualitative Action Research."

In general, this work follows a philosophical paradigm of qualitative, Action-research. Following Qualitative research philosophies[42], the historical and contemporary values and practices of the primary stakeholders, the ethologists, are analyzed in multiple ways. From the Action Research side [18], the ideas collected from this process are then developed into new practices and tools which are iteratively evaluated with the scientists. Following the views of Lewin and Torbet, the point of this work is to function not as a "one-off" series of projects with self-contained solutions, but rather as a cyclical process of both studying, intervening, and changing a situation[47]. Thus as hybrid, "Qualitative Action Research," this research seeks to analyze thick webs of data[6] that are iteratively tested with the intention of bringing about direct changes in its examined field.

At more pragmatic levels, techniques and strategies from Science and Technology Studies (STS) are utilized for "critical elucidation" [15] of the interplay between the networks of scientific tools, biological traditions[16]. To tailor this analysis for ethology's particular challenges involving tool-making and behaviors, Digital Naturalism conducts this STS research via strategies from Critical Making and Performance Studies.

Ethology is a science deeply engaged with both tools and performances. Critical Making techniques, such as combining critical discussion with hands-on construction[36] of scientific tools will be helpful when working with the scientists to analyze the impact and potential digital technology has on their instruments. Performance studies[39] lend approaches to physically examine the interlinked behaviors of the scientists, animals, environments, and tools involved with ethology, while offering ways to generate and understand novel phenomena among these actors[38].

Digital Naturalism's specific toolkit of research methods included traditional ethnographic instruments along with many interventionist, exploratory tools. Questionnaires and Case Studies (in the form of audio-video interviews and design documentaries[35]) were used to elicit information and let participants reflect. Hands-on activities like workshops, performances, and technological probes then supplemented and tested the information gathered ethnographically.

Analysis

This research structure generates research massive amounts of highly qualitative data. Geertz's methodology of thick description [8:4] has become a standard technique for such analysis. A thick description examination presents a detailed account of the situation being investigated and key themes are identified [6:272]. Since, as Geertz notes, qualitative research writings are necessarily "interpretations," the purpose of describing the collected data "thickly" is to present a broader context against which the audience can form their own opinions [8:14]. The purpose of thick description is not to instantly prove an idea, but rather to discover and progressively validate new concepts from complex situations. The conclusions from the research are never justified in any absolute sense, but rather on the basis that the documented actions and decisions made by the researcher "can be seen as 'reasonable'" [6:273].

RESEARCH

Ethology Ethnography: Principles and Practices

Through surveys, interviews, and documentation, this research collected information on the scientists' general demographics and research styles, along with details on their research values and technological utilization.

Demographics and Research Styles

The ethologists studied possessed all researched the behaviors of non-humans in natural environments (typically the Panamanian rainforest). Beyond this, the researchers at STRI studied many different ecosystems with varying degrees of experience.

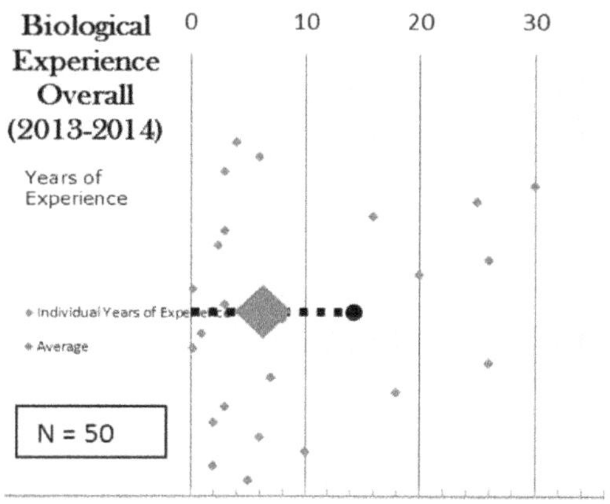

Figure 3 - visualized results of the experience demographics of the researchers studied

From the 50 researchers surveyed, 9 were Undergraduates, 6 were Master's students, 18 were PhD students, and 16 were independent researchers or professors. Participants' total number of years working directly in biology was also surveyed with responses ranging from several months to decades. Overall, the average respondent on the survey was a PhD student with a little over 6 years of biological research experience.

Figure 4 - Average working schedule of scientists at STRI with respected to their research organism (n = 19)

The daily schedules of the researchers are linked to their topic of study. One frog scientist pointed out she never sees her roommate due to different study organisms. In addition to this organismal and temporal diversity researchers all noted that they spend some part of their time in the field and some in the laboratory, that is, no current research is *entirely* lab or field based.

Ethological Values: Case Study – Warkentin Lab

The broader community ethnography was supplemented with four, multi-year, in depth case studies with different biologists and labs. There was Marting and his Azteca ants[20]; Karen Warkentin and her tree frogs[49]; Lipshutz studying Jacana birds[23]; and STRI's Bat Lab with Rachel Page[26] and Barrett Klein[14]. Each case study was unique and shared important perspectives about ethological fieldwork and exploration. This paper will quickly highlight one of the four.

Warkentin's lab pursues an interesting system of frog embryos that sense vibration from predators before they are even born[50]. At her Panama field site at STRI, she experiments with tadpoles and a large, programmable vibrating device that simulates predator behavior [2]. Interviews and shadowing reveal many of the same principles shared by foundational ethologists along with several additional concerns.

For instance, she prizes field-ready tools, like textile-cages, which can deal with the harshnesses and mobility needs of fieldwork. She describes, *"The beauty of a sewn cage is it's like a tent... you can take it down, pack it in a box, throw it in the laundry... transport it to a remote field site."* In order to address her particular research questions, being in natural fieldwork settings is mandatory. She needs to spend time away from her university lab to access rare creatures whose behaviors are adapted to their unique environments in Panama. Warkentin points out, *"I can't ask that question in Boston. I don't have a lab colony."*

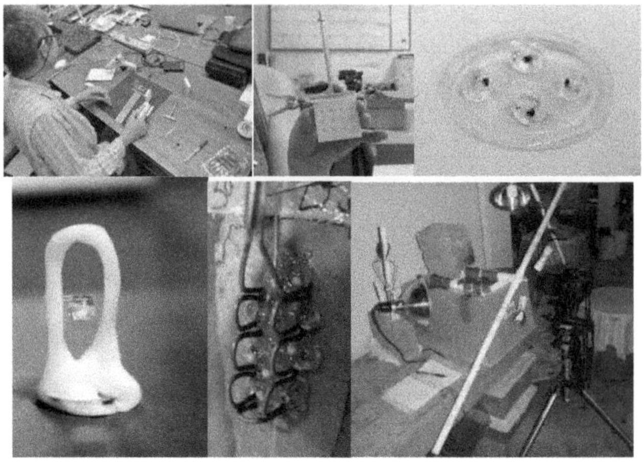

Figure 5 – Warkentin's customized tadpole-interaction tools

Particularly important is how her lab identifies their work as being inquiry-driven. Instead of relying on a particular tool, they start with a question and develop tools and skills to answer this question. Warkentin's student, Cohen, explains in an interview, *"Some labs are 'Technique Labs.' They ...model their work off an interesting technique that scientists had developed. Unlike the technique lab, [we] start with a question and need to then discover and refine the skills necessary to answer this question."* To support this inquiry-based work, Warkentin's lab focuses on customized, hand-crafted tools. She notes, *"I study frog embryos, and that's not something there's standard tools for."* Thus, they often have to craft their own devices themselves. Like she puts it, *"there are a lot of questions that, in order to ask, we need to make stuff."*

This arduous work of both conducting research and building one's own tools requires rapidly prototyping and test dozens of iterations of their equipment on-site in Panama – *"We go through design iterations and figure out how to make something that will enable us to ask the question."* Being able to prototype onsite helps the scientists adapt the tools to specific experiments and research questions. It also speeds up their work and maintains valuable time in the field:

> *If every design iteration requires a trip to Boston in between to manufacture something... it takes forever. Any material that can let me make prototypes down here [in Panama] and let me test it with eggs is going to speed up my research. For example, is this [design] a better idea or this*

[design]? I don't know now, but I'll know in a couple of days, right, as opposed to next year.

Building portions of the custom interfaces onsite enables Warkentin to avoid one of the biggest problems she sees in scientific tools: where something "*looks really elegant from an engineering perspective, but it actually doesn't work for the frogs.*" Overall, it's Warkentin's lab's emphasis on question-based research that drives their practices and technological use. This type of open-ended inquiry is supported by valuing such factors like onsite rapid prototyping, adaptability of tools, field-readiness, and bespoke tools.

		Foundational Ethologists (Literature)	Contemporary Ethologists (Ethnography)
Motivations	Being in Nature	■	■
	Being with Animals	■	■
	Open-Ended Inquiry	■	■
Analysis	Intuitive Analysis	■	■
	Augmented Interaction	■	■
	Augmented Observation	■	■
Tools	Instrument Feedback		■
	Field-Readiness		■
	Bespoke Tools	■	■
	Technological Agency	■	■
	Onsite Rapid Prototyping		■
	Adaptability		■

Figure 6 – Ethological values for research and technology shared in foundational literature and ethnographic research

These key ethological values were supported and expressed by the STRI community at large and the other case studies. These concepts were compiled and compared with similar findings in the foundational literature and used to develop workshops, activities, and novel technological devices during the next, "probe" iteration of the research.

Technological Probes

Building from the previous ethnographic work, technological projects are created to probe even deeper into digital media's potential impact on ethological practice. Workshops, projects, and performances are conducted in the jungle with the researchers at the STRI to investigate pragmatically how digital media can support specific principles of ethological work. Participants engaged with these probes were then interviewed and surveyed to reflect on key aspects of the activities or devices that supported ethological values. Participants were also invited to speculate on further augmentations or additions to the activities that would also enhance their practice.

Workshops

During the three field seasons at STRI, this research conducted four official community workshops (along with dozens of informal ones). These workshops followed a "critical making" style where participants were prompted into discussing biological, technological, and cultural influences in tandem with the construction process.

Figure 7 –Crafting, programming, and play testing digital firefly costumes in the rainforest.

For instance, during the Firefly Suit workshops, participants learned how to make and modify their own digital devices to interact with the lightning beetles in the dark forest.

They could embodily test and discuss behavioral concepts (such as firefly mating behaviors) in the forms of emergent games with the insects and each other. One participant described the experience: "*...now I realize I am not limited by the current selection of commercial tools available to conduct research, but I can build my own to cater to my specific research questions.*" It is these combined experiences with animals, ecosystems, technology, and critical discussion that let the scientists gain new insights about their creatures while granting them agency to understand their work can expand.

Projects

The behaviors and abilities of the nearby jungle creatures motivated several independent projects with participants to explore new digital means of natural interaction. These projects sought to follow design styles of the early, explorative devices from foundational ethologists involving dynamic stimuli placed directly in the creatures' environments. For instance, David Best's simple "robotic" hawkmoth (a box that lit up when a bird approached), consisted of little more than a lightbulb and a transparency sheet, but it enabled Best and Tinbergen to ask questions interactively about the bird's behavior [44:128].

Figure 8 – Projects: Ant-Morse Code, Leaf-cutter poetry, modular insect sensor prototypes, and Stereo Smelling devices.

Some project examples include explorations of dynamic ant interaction with an ant-Morse code messaging device[29]. A simple programmable gate forms an open-ended tool that lets participants raise questions by attempting to send messages through bustling swarms of ants. Leaf cutter cut-up poetry explored how to induce ants to carry surrogate materials (false food) for both engineering novel tracking devices and using the ants themselves as a media platform. The modular insect sensor series of prototypes [30] studied the values Warkentin previously espoused for getting rapid feedback by designing close to nature. The Stereo Smelling project explored concepts that other ethologists (like Uexküll[48] and Ryan [37]) advocated concerning embodied sensory augmentation. Stereo Smelling featured temporally isolated sensory prosthetics to let scientists feel, first hand, what it is like to have insect antennae and navigate pheromone trails.

Once again these projects tested and revealed more key features for digital-ethological tools, such as the value of open-ended tools that raise questions, and the rapid feedback afforded by designing close to nature.

Performances

With the community as a whole, or in small groups, this research also ran performances involving the animals and tools. Performance is a valuable tool for conducting scientific exploration. Scholars like Crease cite performance's ability to both probe and reflect upon scientific phenomena in research [5].

Figure 9 - Performances for probing natural systems and reflecting upon technological devices. (Ant-ice interaction in *Jungle Fluids* and Robotic puppet in *Leaf 5 Lover*)

Some performances were designed to explore new interactions and behaviors with the creatures. For example in the Jungle Fluids[32] performance (based on a "happening" by Alan Kaprow[40]) we exposed jungle creatures to new foreign stimuli (ice and extreme cold). This random, but systematic, probing revealed previously unknown behavioral phenomena where the ants would ferociously attack the ice until frozen solid, and then their sisters would rescue them by shaking and licking until they had thawed. This project illustrates performance's quality for "poiesis" described by Crease[5]. Creating these arbitrary sculptures generated novel ethological behaviors, such as the ants pulling each other to safety, which can then be further addressed scientifically.

These performances also benefitted scientific reflection. The act of conducting a prescribed ritual, as Schechner and Turner argued [38], brings one to a liminal space of reflection and analysis. This ability helped scientists step outside their own research and re-evaluate the assumptions built into the design or their experimentation. In a project called *Leaf 5 Lover* [21], scientists used their bodies and digital and analog technology to act out hypotheses for behavioral models in order to analyze their own early research ideas. Using a giant robotic Ant puppet and the emergent behavior of dozens of other participants, this performance explored scientist Marting's concepts of the defense behaviors of a tree-dwelling ant (*Azteca constructor*) [20]. After the performance the participants gathered around a real-life *Azteca-Cecropia* tree to witness the original system from which this play was adapted. Having just physically embodied the phenomena, many participants feedback shared the performance helped them better understand and empathize with the actions of the animals.

	Technological Probes	Speculative Desires
Practical Technological Engagement	■	
Tools for Reflection	■	
Peer Feedback	■	
Tool Feedback		■
Design Feedback from Nature	■	
Immediate Reference	■	
Integrating Natural Materials	■	
Environment Access		■
Sensory World Access	■	■
Animal Computer Feedback	■	■
Immersed Attention	■	
Raises Questions	■	
Open-Ended Design	■	

Figure 10 – Positive ethological attributes for digital devices found in technology activities and speculative reflections

The performances again illustrated the usefulness of design features such as open-ended designs and getting feedback from nature, but they also highlighted the value of designing experiences that promote embodiment and immerse scientists' attention in these behavioral actions.

Overall the technological probe periods further confirmed the values of workshops, prototypes, and performances as tools for both discovery and analysis. They also elucidated key features for technological design and interaction such as feedback from the tools and nature, tools that raise new questions, technology with open-ended designs, and tools that promote embodiment and access to the sensory worlds of other creatures.

FRAMEWORK

Synthesis

Following a qualitative analysis style, Digital Naturalism synthesizes its final design framework by combining the key principles of past and present ethologists with the field-tested features of the technological probes. These facets were grouped into commons categories and distilled into key tenets.

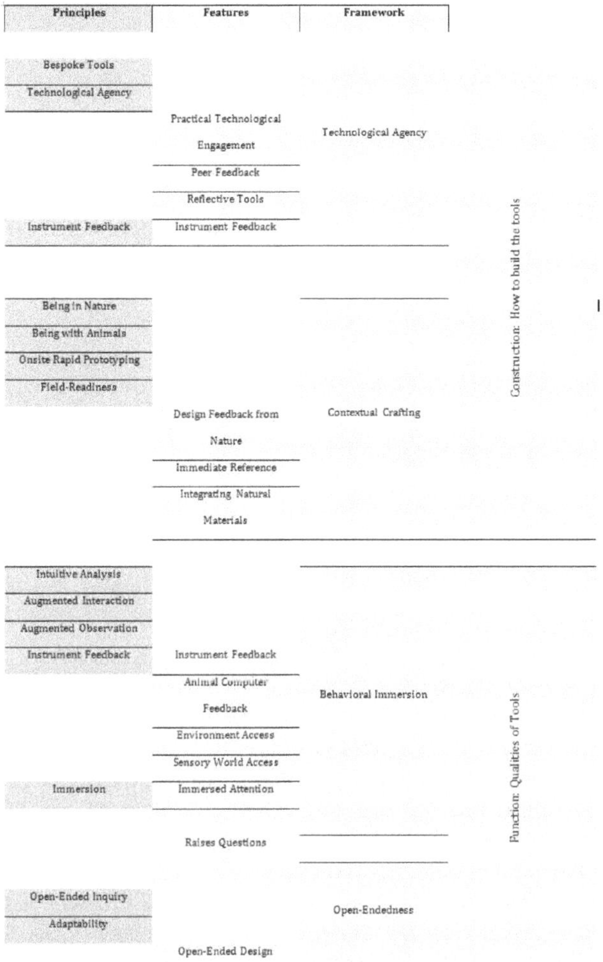

Figure 11 - Synthesis of framework from research concepts

The result of distilling this research is the discovery of four primary concepts that can guide digital technology's design to support ethology. The target of any design framework is to provide a concise set of ideas which, when followed, improve the capabilities of the resulting products. In the same way that Murray's Four Affordances [24] try to guide designers of digital media as a whole, the Digital Naturalism framework presents key principles for developing digital media which aim to serve an ethologist's practice while helping designers avoid potential pitfalls.

Digital Naturalism's resulting four tenets are Technological Agency, Contextual Crafting, Behavioral Immersion, and Open-endedness. They urge designers to A) make tools that are understandable and manipulable, B) build tools in natural environments, C) viscerally engage human and non-human participants, and D) design improvisational tools that raise questions. The first two concepts of agency and context guide *how to make the tools*, and the second two concerning immersion and discovery describe the key *functions of the instruments*.

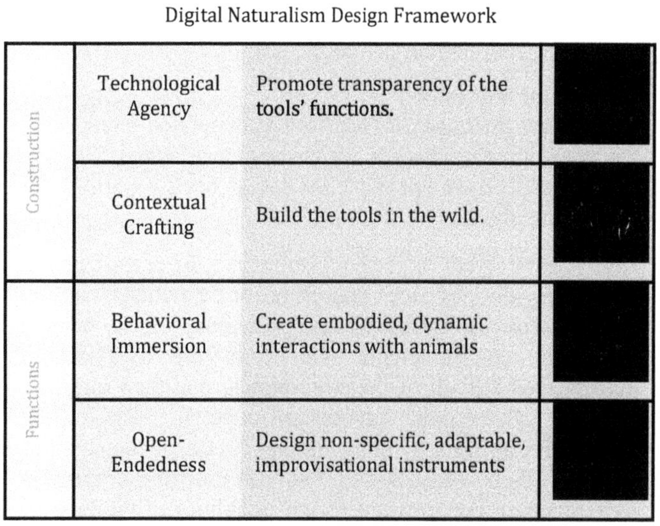

Figure 12 - Framework for promoting discussion and design of digital media artifacts for ethological work

Technological Agency

Making tools that foster a scientist's own Technological Agency helps give them the power to shape the tools according to the requirements of their original research question. Designing for Technological Agency means to create tools that are open, understandable, and manipulable.

Giving naturalists agency over their instruments is essential to the integrity of their work. It ensures scientists' experiments are driven by their research questions and helps eliminate erroneous assumptions involved with their tech. This is especially important in digital tools, where functionality can be locked-away in machine code. The ideal digital naturalist is a fully independent explorer of both biological and technological worlds. In collaborations, though, some techniques can help all parties have agency over their tools. Aim for simple, modular tools that let one manipulate the code without reprogramming. Furthermore, always encourage documentation and sharing of designs.

Contextual Crafting

Crafting digital devices within the context of their use can help speed up iterative development, and ensures the devices have appropriate features for use.

Contextual Crafting encourages researchers to physically create devices as close to the target environment as possible. Ethologists study animals in the wild because their behaviors evolved to fit the idiosyncrasies of the environment. Tools similarly incorporate assumptions about the environments in which they were made. Building tools in the wild ensures their field-readiness and suitability for the research site and animals. Building in proximity to the field and incorporating natural materials fosters the idea of "making as exploring"[28][33] which speeds iterations and inspires design insights from the field. Perhaps foremost, this concept maintains naturalist's precious time spent in the field, thus promoting fostering serendipitous inspiration and discovery. Lastly, tools that are built in the field can also be repaired in the field, preventing naturalists from being stranded with broken tools.

Behavioral Immersion

The design principle of Behavioral Immersion encourages the development of tools which engage a scientist's own sensory abilities and promote the researcher's capability for intuition analysis.

Digital ethological tools should immerse the researchers in the behaviors of an organism or functions of an environment. A scientist's early exploration is heavily dependent on immersing oneself in the overload of multifaceted stimuli of the environment and their animal's behavior. Behavioral Immersion augments ethologists' interpretive abilities by allowing them to deeply engage this data with their whole bodies. One can cultivate immersion by remapping one's own sensory modalities to the outputs of sensors studying animals or environments. Prolonged stimulation of body parts (like the tongue or back) in coherent ways taps into the brain's plasticity and develops engagement[13]. Similarly, one can also design for feedback systems between the computers and animals themselves to elicit novel responses.

Open-Endedness

Targeting Open-Endedness in the functionality of ethological tools promotes adaptability and serendipitous discovery of new behavioral phenomena.

A key task of scientific exploration is to increase chances of serendipitously stumbling across interesting new phenomena. Naturalists' tools should be designed for Open-Endedness and spur the curiosity and undirected exploration integral to their work. Open-ended digital tools for scientific exploration can be thought to embody questions rather than only deliver answers. Tools with simple functions allow researchers to quickly re-arrange devices and poke and probe in new ways. Making adaptable, improvisational tools spurs curiosity by encouraging the interactor to create novel combinations of behavioral stimuli. Having tools that are only partially built further encourages such open-ended questioning and discovery.

EVALUATION

This research continued with additional layers of review and testing to fully evaluate the usefulness of this framework (again, full analysis available in [31]). Numerical data shown displays an average diamond mark graphed with their standard deviation of the total responses.

Community Evaluation

Final questionnaires were designed to gauge the impact of this research conducted with the STRI community. Researchers who had participated in Digital Naturalist activities, such as workshops, performances, or projects, were asked to evaluate their experiences. They were also invited to submit feedback critiquing the methods employed by this research.

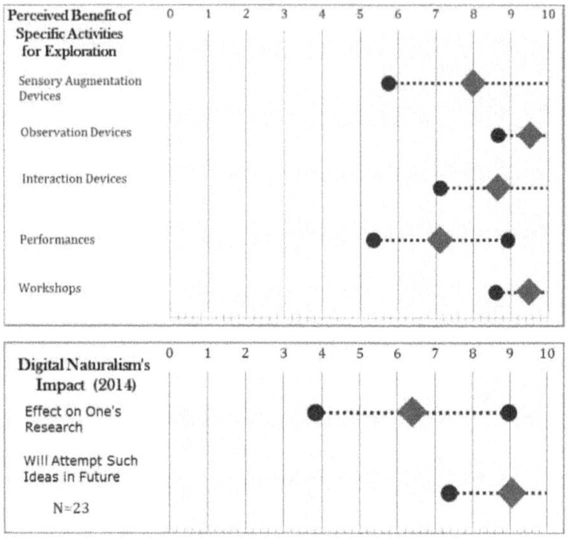

Figure 13 – Summary of participant responses concerning the benefits of Digital Naturalism's methods and impact. Details marked on scale of 10(positive effect) 1(negative effect) and 5 (no effect)

In general, participants claimed at least some perceived benefit of the digital naturalist activities and devices they experienced during this work. The participants were, however, plus and minus in noting the direct impact Digital Naturalism had on their own work. A follow up question inquiring on their attempts to incorporate the ideas shared in their future work proved overwhelmingly positive. These results indicate that the scientists' current projects were often already too far along to rework these new ideas for digital media into experiments, but aim to do so in their future practice. Several written responses confirm the delayed impact of Digital Naturalism. For example, as one scientist says, "*The robotics workshop opened my eyes to the world of Arduinos! I hope to incorporate these into future research, even if not research associated with STRI.*"

Field Evaluation: Hiking Hacks

Continuing this research's "Action Research" style, a final series of participatory, mobile workshops were designed based on the newly developed framework. These atypical workshops specifically harnessed the concepts of Technological Agency and Contextual Crafting from the framework to combine backpacking excursions into the wilderness with participatory, critical making workshops with digital technology. These mobile digital-ethological workshops, dubbed "Hiking Hacks," took place in Panama, Madagascar, and the United States for 2-4 weeks at a time.

Figure 14 - digital prototyping in nature - "Hiking Hacks"

Following these expeditions exploring digital natural prototyping and interaction, participant's responses were gathered once more. This final test assesses the design framework as a useful tool for designing digital media for ethological exploration.

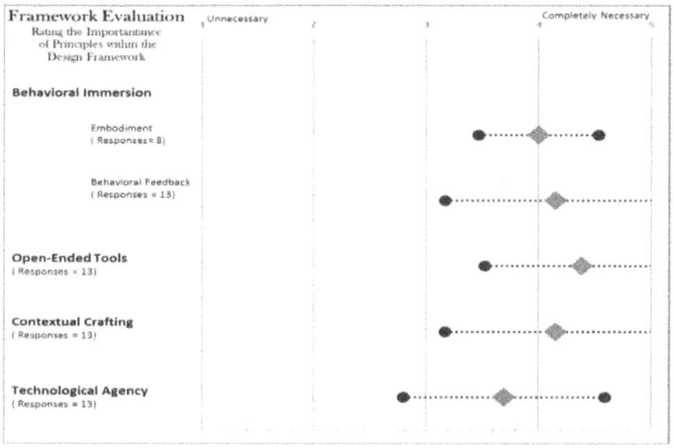

Figure 15 – framework evaluation by "hiking hackers"

The full framework was utilized during the Hiking Hacks to design activities and projects and then re-evaluated by participants. This testing served to judge the framework's efficacy at promoting digital-ethological exploration.

Overall, the workshop's situated experience gave greater insight to multiple ways of designing and conducting research. As one participant states, "*I like the backward structure of starting in the field and working backwards to make a lab... [it lets me] see the advantages of both places.*" Building, repairing, and testing digital tools within the animals' natural environment proved to not only be feasible, but also functional.

These evaluations demonstrate that targeting these concepts facilitates the design of digital artifacts which uphold the values of ethology from the ground up.

CONTRIBUTIONS

Little groundwork has been previously laid for this research's specific intersection between digital media and ethology. For this reason, many other contributions to these parent fields also had to be developed along the way.

First, it provides an iteratively evaluated design framework for digital-ethological tools. It also shares a design for a pragmatic hybrid research structure for studying inter-mixed technological, cultural, and scientific factors utilizing real-world performance and construction.

The hands-on work with scientists also led to the design, analysis, and documentation of several new digital media tools for studying and interacting with animals, some of which have already been taken up by ethological researchers themselves [20]. Digital Naturalism's "contextual crafting" tenet has also directly motivated outside research such as Perner-Wilson's "Wearable Studio Practice" [9,34] and "Hacking the Wild," a television show for *Discovery Networks*[22]. Finally, this research outlines a new form of mobile, participatory design workshop, the Hiking Hack. These new theoretical models, analyses, designs, and pedagogical forms can become useful for other research conducted at the intersections of biology, media, engineering, and design.

CONCLUSION

Digital Naturalism shares how to design and utilize a novel media framework from important features of ethology and digital media. This structure develops and exemplifies a means of creating, evaluating, and sharing new media forms which connect digital and biotic behaviors. By helping ethologists design and build their own computational tools, this research strives to extend the ethologist's tool-making traditions into the digital realm. This framework for Digital Naturalism thus serves as a foundation for deeper collaborations between the human, digital, and biological worlds. Designing devices that promote enjoyment and engagement with non-humans can not only strengthen the design of digital media, but also foster greater empathy and appreciation for the natural world.

This preliminary research reveals many fruitful, new avenues of exploration. Continued Hiking Hacks and design research involving different biomes and cultures around the world will provide a small push in the broader struggle of using digital media to escape an anthropocentric worldview. Ethologist Bernd Heinrich describes weariness of traditional research that perhaps new media forms can help escape:

> Often I have been frustrated with the journal articles that come out of the research because only the finished results are given. All the excitement of the process has been squeezed out so that the results will conform to certain expected standards... My hope is to capture... the sounds and sights, the endless chores and happy accidents, the obsessions, the wonder of it all[10].

Hopefully more people will be inspired to push digital media out of the lab and into the wild.

ACKNOWLEDGEMENTS

This work was made possible by participants from Panama, Madagascar, and the US along with incredible advising by Michael Nitsche, Carl DiSalvo, and Kathleen Quitmeyer.

REFERENCES

1. P Agre. 1997. Toward a Critical Technical Practice: Lessons Learned in Trying to Reform AI. *Social science, technical systems, and cooperative ....* Retrieved October 25, 2013 from http://books.google.com/books?hl=en&lr=&id=xxhMzog9MkQC&oi=fnd&pg=PA131&dq=Toward+a+Critical+Technical+Practice+:+Lessons+Learned+in+Trying+to+Reform+AI&ots=pF6rY5JxQR&sig=ytKBLmgsB11CDEwmqD3TgLZfvfU
2. Michael S Caldwell, J Gregory McDaniel, and Karen M Warkentin. 2009. Frequency information in the vibration-cued escape hatching of red-eyed treefrogs. *The Journal of experimental biology* 212, Pt 4: 566–75. https://doi.org/10.1242/jeb.026518
3. Rémy Chauvin. 1977. *Ethology: the biological study of animal behavior*. International Universities Press. Retrieved November 7, 2012 from http://books.google.com/books?id=h9EgAQAAIAAJ&pgis=1
4. I D Couzin and N R Franks. 2003. Self-organized lane formation and optimized traffic flow in army ants. *Proceedings. Biological sciences / The Royal Society* 270, 1511: 139–46. https://doi.org/10.1098/rspb.2002.2210
5. Robert P. Crease. 1993. *The Play of Nature: Experimentation as Performance (Indiana Series in the Philosophy of Technology)*. Indiana University Press. Retrieved April 10, 2013 from http://www.amazon.com/The-Play-Nature-Experimentation-Performance/dp/0253314747
6. M Descombe. 2010. Good Research Guide : For small-scale social research projects (2nd Edition). *For Samll. scale Social*: 319. Retrieved from http://scholar.google.com/scholar?hl=en&btnG=Search&q=intitle:the+Good+Research+Guide#2
7. Karl von Frisch. 1971. *Bees: their vision, chemical senses, and language*. Cornell University Press. Retrieved November 1, 2012 from http://books.google.com/books?id=VTwgAQAAMAAJ&pgis=1
8. Clifford Geertz. 1973. *The Interpretation of Cultures: Selected Essays*. Basic Books.
9. Hannah Perner-Wilson. Wearable Studio Practice. *2016*. Retrieved January 5, 2017 from http://www.plusea.at/?category_name=a-wearable-studio-practice
10. Bernd Heinrich. 1991. *In a Patch of Fireweed*. Harvard University Press. Retrieved November 11, 2013 from http://books.google.com/books?id=vN-BRgPAA5UC&pgis=1
11. Bert Hölldobler and Edward O. Wilson. 1994. *Journey to the ants: a story of scientific exploration*. Belknap Press of Harvard University Press. Retrieved November 1, 2012 from http://books.google.com/books?id=u3lGyWFGrfIC&pgis=1
12. B Hrolenok and T Balch. 2013. Learning executable models of multiagent behavior from live animal observation. *ICML 2013 Workshop on Machine Learning ....* Retrieved June 30, 2015 from http://www.cc.gatech.edu/grads/b/bhroleno/sysid2013-biohmm.pdf
13. KA Kaczmarek. 1995. Sensory augmentation and substitution. *CRC handbook of biomedical engineering*. Retrieved May 14, 2014 from ftp://ftp.seu.edu.cn/Pub2/EBooks/Books_from_EngnetBase/pdf/8594/ch143.pdf
14. Barrett A Klein, Joey Stein, and Ryan C Taylor. 2012. Robots in the service of animal behavior. *Communicative & integrative biology* 5, 5: 466–72. https://doi.org/10.4161/cib.21304
15. Thomas S. Kuhn. 1962. *The Structure of Scientific Revolutions, 3rd Edition*. The University of Chicago Press. Retrieved December 16, 2013 from http://www.amazon.com/The-Structure-Scientific-Revolutions-Edition/dp/0226458083
16. Bruno Latour. 1999. *Pandora's hope*. Harvard University Press. Retrieved February 25, 2013 from http://books.google.com/books?id=RMu6wbzVrVkC&pgis=1
17. PN Lehner. 1998. *Handbook of ethological methods*. Retrieved May 6, 2015 from https://books.google.com/books?hl=en&lr=&id=jlBM3qsSqSMC&oi=fnd&pg=PR9&dq=handbook+of+ethological+methods&ots=Wv1XCzCtNi&sig=4IV2TSDUisSrqwfxQKtJKDIIH8w
18. Kurt Lewin. 1946. Action Research and Minority Problems. *Journal of Social Issues* 2, 4: 34–46. https://doi.org/10.1111/j.1540-4560.1946.tb02295.x
19. Paul Martin and Patrick Bateson. 2007. *Measuring Behaviour: An Introductory Guide*. Cambridge University Press. Retrieved October 25, 2013 from http://www.amazon.com/Measuring-Behaviour-An-Introductory-Guide/dp/0521535638
20. Peter Marting. 2012. Testing for Collective Personalities in Azteca Ant Colonies. Retrieved from http://andy.dorkfort.com/papers/Others/Marting_Azteca_IUSSI_poster.jpg
21. Peter R. Marting and Andrew Quitmeyer. 2013. Leaf 5 Lover | Digital Naturalism. Retrieved July 8, 2015 from http://andy.dorkfort.com/andy/digitalnatural/2013/08/28/leaf-5-lover/
22. Jerry Mcnutt. 2017. "Hacking the Wild." *The Science Channel - Discovery Networks*.

23. MJ Miller and SE Lipshutz. 2014. Genetic and phenotypic characterization of a hybrid zone between polyandrous Northern and Wattled Jacanas in Western Panama. *BMC evolutionary* .... Retrieved July 7, 2015 from http://www.biomedcentral.com/1471-2148/14/227/

24. Janet H. Murray. 1997. Hamlet on the Holodeck: The Future of Narrative in Cyberspace. Retrieved December 16, 2011 from http://books.google.com/books?hl=en&lr=&id=bzmSLtnMZJsC&oi=fnd&pg=PR9&dq=Hamlet+on+the+Holodeck&ots=L2kHRYDdrD&sig=HijTas-bgOXfxC3u0jLDsH3Cu98

25. Janet H. Murray. 2003. Inventing the Medium. In *The New Media Reader*, Noah Wardrip-Fruin and Nick Montfort (eds.). MIT Press, 823. Retrieved January 22, 2013 from http://books.google.com/books?hl=en&lr=&id=DQYXoRx9CcEC&pgis=1

26. RA Page and MJ Ryan. 2006. Social transmission of novel foraging behavior in bats: frog calls and their referents. *Current Biology*. Retrieved July 6, 2015 from http://www.sciencedirect.com/science/article/pii/S0960982206014990

27. Stephen C Pratt and David J T Sumpter. 2006. A tunable algorithm for collective decision-making. *Proceedings of the National Academy of Sciences of the United States of America* 103, 43: 15906–10. https://doi.org/10.1073/pnas.0604801103

28. Andrew Quitmeyer. 2013. Personal Interviews with Ethological Researchers at ASU and STRI.

29. Andrew Quitmeyer. 2014. Digital naturalism: designing holistic ethological interaction. In *CHI'14 Extended Abstracts on Human Factors in Computing Systems*, 311–314.

30. Andrew J. Quitmeyer. 2014. Modular, low-cost Arboreal Ant (Azteca alfari) Tracking Sensor Development in Panama. *Entomological Society of America (Presentation)*.

31. Andrew J. Quitmeyer. 2015. Digital naturalism: Designing a digital media framework to support ethological exploration. *PhD Thesis - Georgia Institute of Technology*.

32. Andrew Quitmeyer and Peter R. Marting. 2013. *Jungle Fluids*. Retrieved from http://www.youtube.com/watch?v=xp_K6Um3rww

33. Andrew Quitmeyer and Hannah Perner-Wilson. 2015. Digital Naturalism "Portable Studio Design." Retrieved June 24, 2015 from http://andy.dorkfort.com/andy/digitalnatural/2015/06/11/portable-studio-design/

34. Andrew Quitmeyer and Hannah Perner-Wilson. 2015. Wearable Studio Practice: Design Considerations for Digital Crafting in Harsh Environments. *ISWC Wear and Tear Workshop*.

35. Bas Raijmakers, William W. Gaver, and Jon Bishay. 2006. Design documentaries. In *Proceedings of the 6th ACM conference on Designing Interactive systems - DIS '06*, 229. https://doi.org/10.1145/1142405.1142441

36. Matt Ratto. 2011. Critical Making: Conceptual and Material Studies in Technology and Social Life. *The Information Society* 27, 4: 252–260. https://doi.org/10.1080/01972243.2011.583819

37. Michael J Ryan. 2011. The brain as a source of selection on the social niche: examples from the psychophysics of mate choice in túngara frogs. *Integrative and comparative biology* 51, 5: 756–70. https://doi.org/10.1093/icb/icr065

38. Richard Schechner. 2002. *Performance Studies: An Introduction*. Routledge. Retrieved July 9, 2012 from http://www.amazon.com/Performance-Studies-Introduction-Richard-Schechner/dp/0415146216

39. Richard Schechner. 2003. *Performance Theory*. Routledge. Retrieved April 4, 2013 from http://books.google.com/books?id=kOUpXlzhZfoC&pgis=1

40. Richard Schechner and Allan Kaprow. 1968. Extensions in Time and Space. An Interview with Allan Kaprow. *The Drama Review: TDR* 12, 3: 153–159. Retrieved December 19, 2013 from http://www.jstor.org/stable/10.2307/1144364

41. Jay Silver and Eric Rosenbaum. 2010. Gifts for intertwining with modern nature. In *Proceedings of the 9th International Conference on Interaction Design and Children - IDC '10*, 340. https://doi.org/10.1145/1810543.1810608

42. Anselm Strauss and Juliet M. Corbin. *Basics of qualitative research: Grounded theory procedures and techniques*.

43. Lucille Alice Suchman. 1987. *Plans and Situated Actions: The Problem of Human-Machine Communication*. Cambridge University Press. Retrieved January 22, 2013 from http://books.google.com/books?id=AJ_eBJtHxmsC&pgis=1

44. Niko Tinbergen. 1958. *Curious naturalists*. Univ of Massachusetts Press. Retrieved January 2, 2012 from http://books.google.com/books?id=qRql5FjHwLUC&pgis=1

45. Niko Tinbergen. 1960. *The Herring Gull's World*. Harper and Row, New York, New York, USA.

46. Niko Tinbergen. 1974. *The Animal in Its World (Explorations of an Ethologist, 1932-1972): Field Studies*. Harvard University Press. Retrieved November

1, 2012 from http://books.google.com/books?id=cUzO7MNzIKkC&pgis=1

47. William R. Torbert. 1980. Why Educational Research Has Been So Uneducational: The Case for a New Model of Social Science Based on Collaborative Inquiry. Retrieved April 27, 2015 from http://eric.ed.gov/?id=ED242104

48. J Von Uexküll and JD O'Neill. 1957. *A Foray into the Worlds of Animals and Humans: with a Theory of Meaning*. Retrieved January 8, 2014 from http://books.google.com/books?hl=en&lr=&id=ADSDl6_SeW8C&oi=fnd&pg=PP7&dq=A+Foray+into+the+Worlds+of+Animals+and+Humans:+With+a+Theory+of+Meaning&ots=c4zZg-QXGa&sig=e-dc_8adc2GmYc9g_STts8qIzzg

49. KM Warkentin. 1995. Adaptive plasticity in hatching age: a response to predation risk trade-offs. *Proceedings of the National Academy of* .... Retrieved July 6, 2015 from http://www.pnas.org/content/92/8/3507.short

50. KM Warkentin. 1999. The development of behavioral defenses: a mechanistic analysis of vulnerability in red-eyed tree frog hatchlings. *Behavioral Ecology*. Retrieved July 6, 2015 from http://beheco.oxfordjournals.org/content/10/3/251.short

51. Carol Cronin Weisfeld. 2004. Ethology. *SAGE Research Methods*. Retrieved April 27, 2015 from http://srmo.sagepub.com/view/the-sage-encyclopedia-of-social-science-research-methods/n299.xml

52. Matthias Wittlinger, Rüdiger Wehner, and Harald Wolf. 2006. The ant odometer: stepping on stilts and stumps. *Science (New York, N.Y.)* 312, 5782: 1965–7. https://doi.org/10.1126/science.1126912

53. Smithsonian Tropical Research Institute. Retrieved October 13, 2014 from http://stri.si.edu/english/about_stri/index.php

54. William Wcislo - Smithsonian Tropical Research Institute. Retrieved March 16, 2015 from http://www.stri.si.edu/english/scientific_staff/staff_scientist/scientist.php?id=34

55. 1975. Oral history interview with Charles F. Bennett, Jr., and Anna Carole Bennett, 1975. Retrieved October 13, 2014 from http://siarchives.si.edu/collections/siris_arc_217731

The First Hiking Hacks: Exploring Mobile Making for Digital Naturalism

Andrew Quitmeyer
National University of Singapore
Singapore, 129789
andy@quitmeyer.org

C&C '17, June 27 - 30, 2017, Singapore, Singapore

ACM 978-1-4503-4403-6/17/06 $15.00
DOI: http://dx.doi.org/10.1145/3059454.3059486

Abstract
This pictorial discusses the initial creation and implementation of mobile workshops for conducting digital interaction design within biological field research. These workshops, called "Hiking Hacks," directly combine scientific backpacking expeditions with Critical Making workshops. Based upon previous "Digital Naturalism" design framework, these Hiking Hacks involve multidisciplinary teams of biologists and designers working uphold the naturalistic values of wilderness exploration, while investigating the new abilities offered by digital technology. By conducting this work deep in natural field sites, Hiking Hacks directly explore the roles context and mobility play in, typically lab-based, physical computing design.

Authors Keywords
Digital Naturalism; crafting; mobile making; ethology; design research; physical computing; Critical Making; situated design; ecological interaction; hiking hack

ACM Classification Keywords
H.5.m. Information interfaces and presentation (e.g., HCI): Miscellaneous.

Introduction
This work discusses this novel workshop model's ability to explore digital interaction designs that probe com-

An interdisciplinary team of biologists, engineers, and artists building and living together in an outdoor studio. They rapidly design and iterate upon functional devices for interacting and studying natural features surrounding them. (Citico Creek Wilderness, USA)

plex interplays between living creatures and their natural environments. Practitioners of Human Computer Interaction design (HCI) are progressively starting to reap the benefits of contextual, participatory design practices[6] as well as device deployments "in the wild," (meaning uncontrolled public spaces). These approaches have shown to be particularly successful in technology involving multiple parties and ecological factors[3]. Many biological field instruments, however, chiefly rely on conventional, laboratory design methodologies. As Agre notes, "A computer... does not simply have an instrumental use in a given site of practice; the computer is frequently about that site in its very design" [1]. Perhaps, then, it might then make sense to move the site of for digital-biological design practice from the laboratory and into the field itself?

Digital Naturalism

While studying biological field scientists' relationships with digital interaction design, Quitmeyer's original research in Digital Naturalism[9] came across precisely this question. Digital Naturalism investigates the collaborations growing between biologists, designers, engineers, and artists concerning digital technology[10]. This research developed a framework to facilitate interdisciplinary participants in building and analyzing their own devices for exploring and sharing nature. This framework aims to support the original research values early naturalists for curious, visceral exploration while fighting the tendency of technological determinism to override original scientific inquiry. The framework consists of four, key guidelines promoting Technological Agency, Contextual Crafting, Behavioral Immersion, and Open-endedness. At its most basic, these guidelines urge designers and scientists to: make tools understandable and manipulable, build these tools within nature, viscerally engage human and non-human participants, and design improvisational tools that raise ques-

Digital Naturalism's Design Framework encouraging both designers and scientists to create open-ended, immersive, accessible tools in the wild.

Biologists in the rainforest exploring lightning beetle communication via hand-made firefly costumes.

Leaf Cutter Ants carrying word snippets on special paper as part of a digital poetry project. Open-ended, artistic projects allow both technologists and biologists to explore multiple facets of animal computer interaction while remaining open to inquiry based work resulting from new behavioral phenomena (Soberania Forest, Panama).

tions. The first two concepts of agency and context guide how to make the tools, and the second two concerning immersion and discovery describe the key functions of the instruments.

The second guideline, Contextual Crafting, looked to explore how the environment in which tools were made affected their development. Field biologists study creatures in the wild because their behaviors evolved to fit the idiosyncrasies of the environment[5]. Tools similarly incorporate assumptions about the environments in which they were made[1]. Building as close to the target environment as possible, can also speed up design iterations while conserves a naturalist's precious time spent in the field. Additionally, contextual crafting promotes field-repairability and fosters design inspirations from the nearby environment. Testing this concept led to the creation of a new model of workshop for exploring physical computing, the Hiking Hack.

Hiking Hacks

Planned and implemented over several years, with researchers from multiple fields, the first three Hiking Hacks combined physical computing workshops with biological backpacking trips across forests in Panama, Madagascar, and The United States. These large-scale, open experiments explored multitudinous ecological, social, and technological topics simultaneously, but their chief question targeted the viability of conducting research in minimalistic, mobile electronics laboratories. These groups explored this question by challenging themselves to travel deep into the jungle, restricted from any tools which we could not carry ourselves, and then design, build, and reflect upon digital-organismal interaction devices from scratch.

Format

Building from Digital Naturalism's framework, a general, open-ended format was developed to encourage exploration of the biological, technological, and social factors encountered[10].

Early collaborative work between designers and field biologists required frequent trips between lab and field. When devices needed to be tested, altered, or repaired, it long hikes were necessary back to the field or lab. Mobile making seeks to shorten these design iterations.

Early debugging in field site with Marting and Quitmeyer. Tired of returning to the lab after equipment failures, the two began bringing equipment to the field. Shortening the feedback loop between development and testing permits rapid iteration due to "contextual crafting."

Perner-Wilson and Quitmeyer in a hand-crafted electronics studio in Madagascar. Building (and re-building) one's laboratory from the ground up, provides deep analysis of the lab's affect on resulting designs. Common objects like shelving can reinforce or mask challenges to be faced by resulting designs (such as flooding).

Multidisciplinarity is encouraged by combining approaches borrowed from Natural History, Situated Design, Critical Making, Participatory Design, and Performance Studies[7].

This adaptable format was able to be used in all three Hiking Hacks discusses here, to guide the digital-ethological investigations of the multi-disciplinary participants. All Hiking Hacks included at least 5 core participants of mixed genders. All Hiking Hacks lasted a minimum of seven days in the field, with additional "buffer days" included to account for unexpected delays. The first trial of this experimental workshop was the Panama Hiking Hack[8]. It travelled south to north across central Panama through lowland and highland jungle. This trip took 9 days with several days of preparation and debriefing before and after the trip. The Madagascar trip was carried out over several weeks moving from the south-eastern coast of Madagascar inland through jungle up to cloud-forest in search of a rare ant[12]. The USA Hiking Hack took place in the Appalachian Mountains in temperate forest[11].

Creative Challenges and Activities

Imperative to the Critical Making[4,13] nature of these mobile workshops were creative challenges issued to the participants throughout the expedition. These challenges were built around the Digital Naturalism's concepts of Agency, Context, Immersion, and Open-endedness. They took the form of activities concerning ethology, design, construction, and performance. In Critical Making Style, they combined hands-on "goal-based material work... [with] critical thinking" revolving around discussing socio-technological concepts around their tools[13].

Daily Routine

Due to the haphazard, unexpected nature of a field expedition, a basic daily routine was created to maintain focus. Each day begins and ends with a journaling exercise. The morning journaling prompts typically concern new ideas and challenges

Hiking Hacks tend to cover diverse ecosystem during their transects moving in and out of wild areas in the forest. The environment of just the Panamania trip took us through environments such as a) city and suburbs b) ancient merchant trails in protected jungle, c) deforested construction zones, and d) flooded mountain rivers near farmland and defunct mining towns.

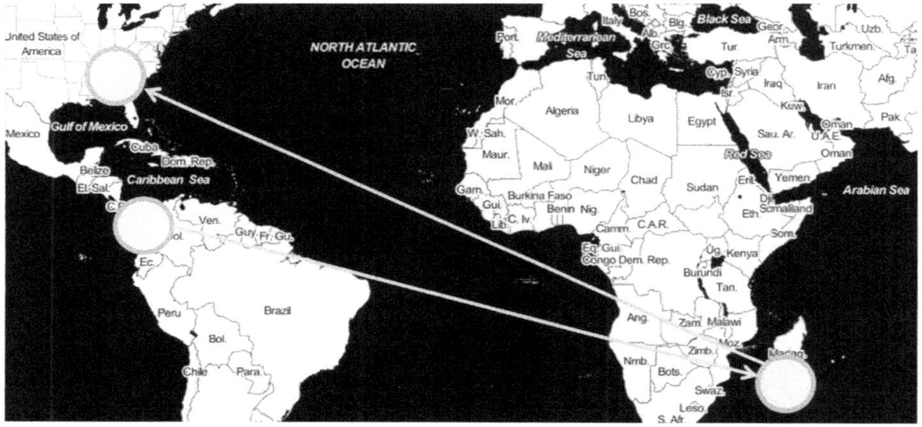

Locations of the first three Hiking Hack workshops in Panama, Madagascar, and the USA.

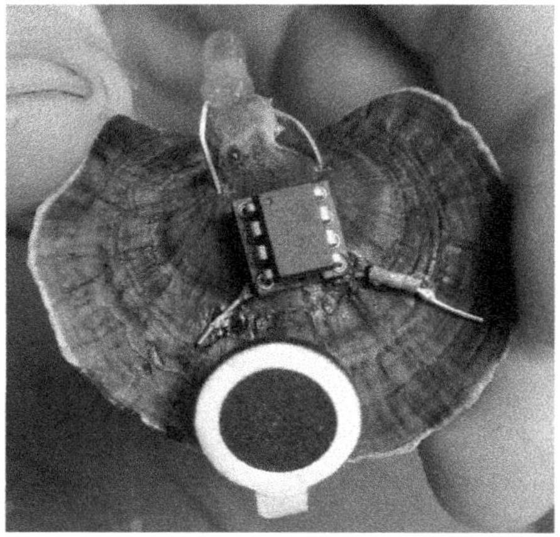

Hiking Hacks explore novel interplays between natural and technological materials, like using a mushroom as a breadboard for prototyping electronic circuits.

to think about. The evening journaling exercises target reflection of the day's activities.

Exploratory, creative, or reflective challenges are first issued during the morning's chores. Examples include "collect two interesting plants" or "design a digital application that could capture a specific experience from your hike." The challenge is typically discussed or modified during the lunch break. Typically, during a break in the afternoon or evening a group activity is issued. Examples of these activities include map-making, playing word games, life-drawing, collaborative design exercises, or creating performative skits.

MATERIALS AND GEAR

In addition to the standard equipment needed for a lengthy jungle trek, like food, water purifiers, GPS navigation, and safety beacons, Hiking Hacks require considerable amounts of specialized gear. The gear lists are refined after each trip. Because of the value placed on open-ended exploration, the group carried as much additional electron-

ics for prototyping equipment as possible. Even though most equipment carried might not be used, full arrays of components are necessary maintain a broad, open design space possible.

Items like butane powered soldering irons, waterproof shelters and containers, and electrical power generators like solar panels were integral to the unique parameters of an outdoor, energy-restricted digital workshop. A unique and serious challenge for these events was avoiding environmental contamination due to electronic waste generated while crafting in the field. Unlike laboratory conditions, where bits of wire-shielding and blobs of solder can harmlessly fall onto the carpet to be vacuumed up later, the group had to be extremely careful to collect all the bits of components left over when creating digital devices.

Hiking Hack Structure
In general, each Hiking Hack expedition follows the same basic structure: Journey – In,

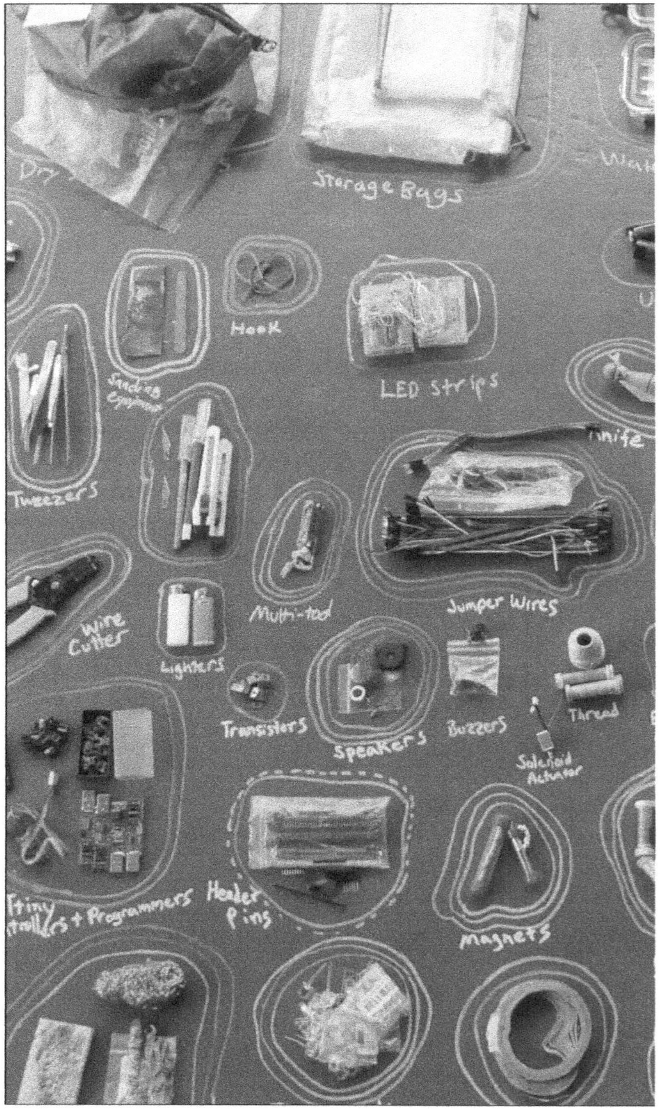

Documentation and Design	Construction	Electronics
Waterproof cameras GoPros Tripod DSLR video cameras 32GB SD cards (x16) Portable Hard drive Journals Markers Paint Pens Clothes pins	Hot Glue Polyester thermoplastic Super Glue Popsicle sticks EVA foam sheets Lighters Razors Scissors Natural Materials foraged from environment	Butane soldering Irons Butane Lead-free solder Brass Sponge Lightweight Laptop Protoboards/ Breadboards Wire, Cutters, Strippers Heat-Shrink Tubing E-ink reader with data sheets E-textiles (conductive fabric and thread, Lilypads needles, etc...) Sensors (proximity, UV, gas, etc...) Actuators (servos, speakers, LEDs, etc...) Microcontrollers (Arduino Unos, Fios, Lilypads, ATTINY85, etc...)
Power	**Workspace**	**Transport**
60W Foldable solar-panel 20+ Amp-hour LiPo batteries DC Voltage Booster DC adapters Additional batteries and chargers	Self-healing mats Rigid Modular Tables Tarps Paracord Polyester Webbing Carabineers Mosquito nets LED lamps Citronella candles	>60L Hiking Backpacks Raincovers Plastic Water-tight organizers Luggage Scale Contractor Garbage bags Waterproof Sacks Silnylon tarps

Rapid Iteration of tools (above)
Working near the field site lets Marting rapidly iterate upon the custom scientific instruments he develops. Pictured here are several iterations of a digital probing device (called the flick-o-matic 9000) for testing ant colony aggression responses.

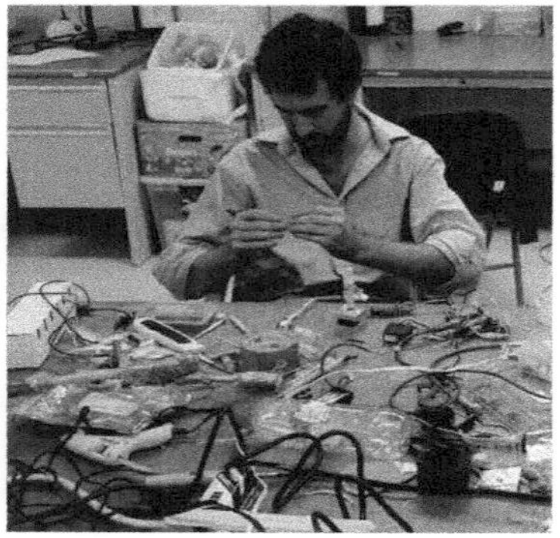

Time in the Lab (left)
Prior to the first hiking hacks, Marting had to constantly leave the field and return to the laboratory to make changes to developing instruments.

Exploration Activity: "Party Device" - Participants need hands-on experience with as many technological capabilities as possible. In the "Party Device" exercise, teams of participants have to create a device that creates as many different simultaneous stimuli as possible. They then expose these rambunctious robots to the natural surroundings and observe which creatures react.

Exploration Activity: Life Drawing - doing species scavenger hunts and conductive life drawings are techniques adopted from the natural sciences for surveying and meditation on the various lifeforms in the area.

Mobile Studio - All potential workshop material and tools are carried into the field site along with all other gear needed for basic survival. Balancing the weight and variety of gear we could take is an essential practice during the preparation period.

Worksurface Iterations: The very first Hiking Hack confronted the difficulty of building electronics in the wild. Particular challenges included adequate lighting and comfortable worksurfaces. Recent Hiking hacks (right), improved upon this with translucent tarps, and mobile standing desks.

Journey In
Key liminal experience of the group. They move all their belonging for the journey from the world of human-centered infrastructure into wild areas.

Basecamp Workshops
Crew working on multiple design challenges at basecamp workshop. This first, minimalistic Hiking Hack basecamp in Panama informed later basecamp workspace design concerning lighting, rain protection, and animal intrusions.

Journey Out
The US team leaving the Citico creek wilderness area. Discussions and ideas are often lively during this period despite the exhaustion of the past expedition.

Basecamp Workshops, Journey-Out. Preparation and debriefing periods generally come before and after the main period of the Hiking Hack.

The Journey In typically has the group hike as far as possible while carrying the heaviest loads. During this time, participants engage in exercises to promote mindfullness, group discussion, or specimen collection. At Basecamp, workshops are held to let participants explore nature and technology in tandem. Challenges are issued about exploring and studying nature and also creating interactive prototypes that allow participants to engage with the environment in new ways. The Journey Out of the wilderness makes the group mobile once more with lighter packs since most food has been eaten. This period is used to evaluate and reflect upon the designs and experiences from the workshop.

Discussion / Take-Aways

These first Hiking Hacks proved to be difficult, yet deeply-engaging method for exploring the multifaceted issues surrounding the intersections between field biology and digital interaction design.

The Hiking Hack model of design workshop is difficult to enact. As a participant frankly notes in a emboldened journal entry, "Everything is harder out here"[10]. The diverse and relentless challenges, however, elicit deep, new biological, cultural, and technological understandings. Overall, the workshop's situated experience gave greater insight to multiple ways of designing and conducting research. As one participant states, "I like the backward structure of starting in the field and working backwards to make a lab...[it lets me] see the advantages of both places"[10].

Future Hiking Hacks

The success of these initial workshops drew enthusiasm from

Basecamp - Exploration Day
Life drawings conducted during the exploration day, are later turned into potential design concepts for prototypes to build.

Basecamp - Construction Day
Dixon, a biologist on the first Hiking Hack in Panama designs and constructs a device for exploring Stingless Bees reactions to multiple stimuli.

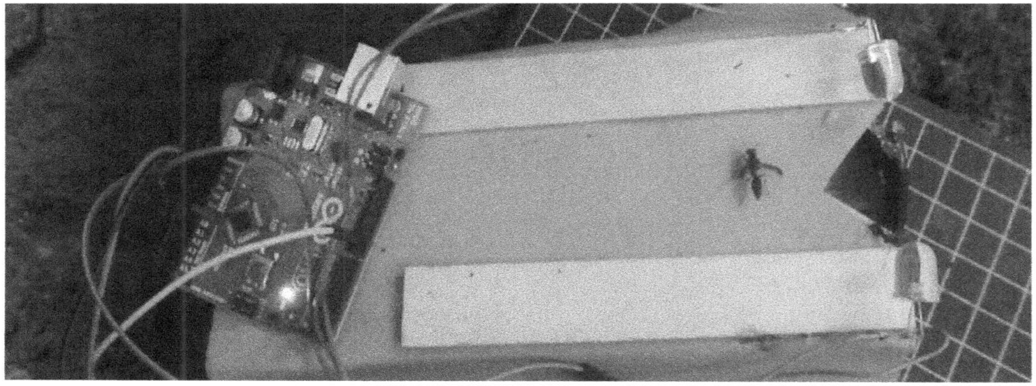

Basecamp - Documentation Day
On the final day of basecamp, participants demo, discuss, and document how their projects fucntion. Dixon had sucessful interactions with UV lights and photo triggers and the stingless bess, to which her device offered food rewards.(Soberania Forest, Panama)

biological and technological crowds calling for future Hiking Hacks. New iterations will further develop improved ways of working in nature while uncovering more arenas to explore. Hacking through alternate biomes, for instance, will likely reveal alternate tools of choice and types of animal interactions. More difficult, yet edifying, journeys lie ahead as digital design moves truly into "the wild."

Acknowledgements

Acknowledgements go to the many different participants in these adventures such as those from Panama, the USA, Madagascar. Advisors Michael Nitsche and Carl DiSalvo. A great thanks also goes to the forests in which we lived during these times for being beautiful places to explore.

References

1. P Agre. 1997. Toward a Critical Technical Practice: Lessons Learned in Trying to Reform AI. Social science, technical systems, and cooperative .... Retrieved October 25, 2013 from http://books.google.com/books?hl=en&lr=&id=xxhMzog9MkQC&oi=fnd&pg=PA131&dq=Toward+a+Critical+Technical+Practice+:+Lessons+Learned+in+Trying+to+Reform+AI&ots=pF6rY5JxQR&sig=ytKBLmgsB11CDEwmqD3TgLZfvfU
2. Shaaron Ainsworth, Vaughan Prain, and Russell Tytler. 2011. Drawing to Learn in Science. Science 333, August: 1096–1097.
3. Carl DiSalvo, Phoebe Sengers, and Hrönn Brynjarsdóttir. 2010. Mapping the landscape of sustainable HCI. In Proceedings of the 28th international conference on Human factors in computing systems - CHI '10, 1975. https://doi.org/10.1145/1753326.1753625
4. Garnet Hertz (ed.). 2012. Critical Making: Introduction. Retrieved from http://conceptlab.com/criticalmaking

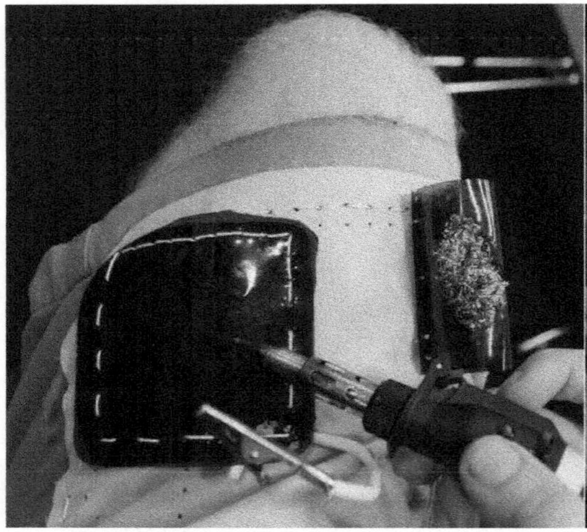

Body Infrastructure - the Hiking Hacks taught groups new ways of relying on their bodies as infrastructure. This spawned the idea such as wearable soldering stations.

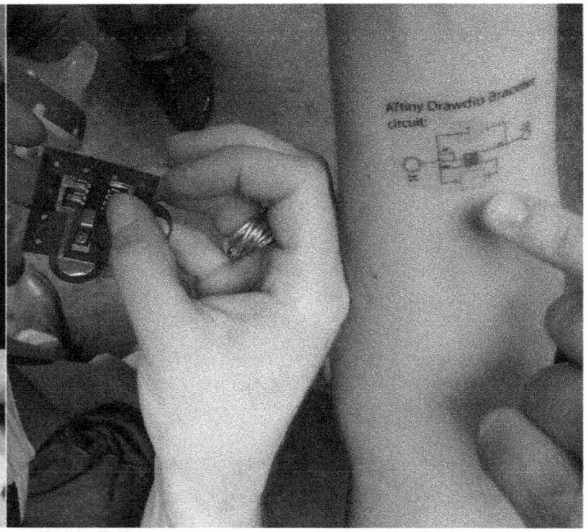

Limited information resources during the Hiking Hacks inspired ideas such as "on-skin" electronics references for workshop projects via customized temporary tattoos.

Immersed in the the environment - The Digital Naturalism concepts built in to the Hiking Hacks inspired tools such as the "Insect Traffic Taster" which detect insect movements over fiber optics and display these detections via a tongue sensor electrode display. This serves as the development of both an artistic and practical way of ambiently studying the busy natural environment.

5. Konrad Lorenz. 1952. King Solomon's Ring: New Light on Animal Ways. Psychology Press. Retrieved November 1, 2012 from http://books.google.com/ooks?id=M6tqEYDh2CgC&pgis=1

6. MJ Muller. 2003. Participatory Design: The Third Space in HCI. Human-computer interaction: Development process 4235: 1–32. Retrieved October 15, 2013 from http://books.google.com/books?hl=en&lr=&id=clMsHX-JfyMC&oi=fnd&pg=PA165&dq=Participatory+Design+:+The+Third+Space+in+HCI&ots=7qfK9rjzFt&sig=wnKbe_FNzaZC3R3XcivFNotl83w

7. A Quitmeyer. 2013. Digital naturalism: interspecies performative tool making for embodied science. Proceedings of the 2013 ACM conference on .... Retrieved June 30, 2015 from http://dl.acm.org/citation.cfm?id=2501084

8. Andrew Quitmeyer. Digital Naturalism. "Transcontinental Hiking/Hack." Retrieved June 24, 2015 from http://andy.dorkfort.com/andy/digitalnatural/2014/06/05/transcontinental-hikinghack/

9. Andrew Quitmeyer. 2014. Digital Naturalism: Designing Holistic Ethological Interaction. CHI '14 Extended Abstracts on Human Factors in Computing Systems.

10. Andrew J. Quitmeyer. 2015. Digital naturalism: Designing a digital media framework to support ethological exploration. PhD Thesis - Georgia Institute of Technology.

11. Andrew Quitmeyer and Hannah Perner-Wilson. 2015. Wearable Studio Practice: Design Considerations for Digital Crafting in Harsh Environments. ISWC Wear and Tear Workshop.

12. Andrew Quitmeyer, Hannah Perner-Wilson, and Brian Fisher. 2015. Hacking the Wild: Madagascar 2015.

13. Matt Ratto. 2011. Critical Making: Conceptual and Material Studies in Technology and Social Life. The Information Society 27, 4: 252–260. https://doi.org/10.1080/01972243.2011.583819

Culturally-Grounded Analysis of Everyday Creativity in Social Media: A Case Study in Qatari Context

D. Fox Harrell
CSAIL, MIT
Cambridge, MA 02139, USA
fox@csail.mit.edu

Sarah Vieweg
QCRI
Hamad Bin Khalifa University
Doha, Qatar
sarahvieweg@gmail.com

Haewoon Kwak
QCRI
Hamad Bin Khalifa University
Doha, Qatar
haewoon@acm.org

Chong-U Lim
Improbable
London, United Kingdom
chong-u@improbable.io

Sercan Sengun
CSAIL, MIT & QCRI
Cambridge, MA 02139, USA
sengun@mit.edu

Ali Jahanian
CSAIL, MIT
Cambridge, MA 02139, USA
ali-design@csail.mit.edu

Pablo Ortiz
CSAIL, MIT
Cambridge, MA 02139, USA
portiz@mit.edu

ABSTRACT

In deploying social media and other information technologies often not designed with MENA (the Middle East and North Africa) cultures in mind, users generate creative approaches to self-representation using virtual identities while preserving their cultural values. To understand and further empower such approaches, we present a mixed-method of computational and qualitative study, focusing on Qatar as a case of such communities in the MENA region. We analyzed a dataset of over 42,000 publicly available social media profiles using computational approaches (archetypal analysis) and qualitatively analyzed a separate set of 255 profiles. We augmented our descriptions with semi-structured interviews. As a result, we delineate a set of five needs/values exhibited by Qatari users supporting their creativity in effectively using virtual identities: Khaleeji[1] features, self-expression, social connections, social monitoring, and physical and virtual identity contrasts. Finally, we propose an initial set of guidelines to support developers of virtual identity systems in better serving these users while preserving their cultural values and creative agency.

ACM Classification Keywords

H.5.3 Information Systems: Information Interfaces and Presentation (e.g., HCI)—*Group and Organization Interfaces*; J.4 Computer Applications: Social and Behavioral Sciences; K.4.0 Computing Milieux: Computers and Society—*General*

[1]The term "Khaleeji" means "of the Gulf" in Arabic.

C+C'17, June 27–30, 2017, Singapore.

ACM ISBN 978-1-4503-4403-6/17/06 ...$15.00.
http://dx.doi.org/10.1145/3059454.3059456

Author Keywords

Virtual Identity; Social Media; Avatars; Qualitative Analysis; Archetypal Analysis; Cultural Values; Qatar

INTRODUCTION

The use of virtual identity technologies across platforms such as social media, videogames, and e-commerce sites is pervasive throughout the world. Whether profiles on social media or player characters in videogames, these user representations integrate numerical attributes, graphical images, and related forms of structured data to enable users to communicate, interact, and even express their senses of self [21]. Indeed, virtual identities are sites demonstrating enaction of users' values, from individual preferences to aspects of larger scale cultural norms and mores. Previous research has demonstrated that the way users behave in both the physical and virtual worlds can be influenced by these virtual self representations [58, 22, 48]. Virtual identities, and user behaviors conveyed while deploying them, may reveal aspects of a user's physical-world identity such as their demographic profiles, personality traits, and motivations for play [57, 60]. Furthermore, they may also reveal phenomena that reflect physical-world social constructs, such as conforming to notions of ideal body types or gender-related stereotypes [14, 38, 22, 49].

Here, we contribute an approach to better understanding the relationships between physical-world identities and virtual identities,[2] and the creativity involved in blending between them. The relationship between virtual identity profiles and creativity is underexplored. Forming a virtual identity itself is a creative process in the sense of Goffman's articulation

[2]In this paper, "physical-world identity" refers identity experiences that are informed by history, culture, and values in the physical world. We use the term in contrast to "virtual identities," which refer to technical and structural data such as static media assets (e.g., profile pictures) as well as the algorithmic processes for simulating and enacting selves and associated behaviors within a virtual environment.

of everyday self-performances that require "*employment of techniques*" to dramaturgically stage one's identity [17]. On one hand, virtual environments may implement restrictive presentation techniques that impair users' self-expression, impression management, and lead to unwarranted stigmatization [20]. On the other hand, virtual identities can impact user's performance and engagement within virtual environments [24] in addition to their creativity [28, 27].

Our aims here are (1) to provide a mixed-methods-based case study accounting for users' needs and values regarding virtual identities in a principled and systematic manner, and (2) to develop guidelines for best practices and design principles for virtual identity system design that support how users creatively maintain cultural values. Toward these ends, we describe how virtual identity systems impact everyday creative self-presentation and the diverse strategies that users form cross-culturally to navigate these impacts. Our case study focuses on the Middle East and North Africa (MENA) region broadly as a set of related underserved communities in terms of culturally-grounded virtual identity systems, and specifically analyzes the Gulf Cooperation Council (GCC) context with a special emphasis on Qatar. To give a few examples of such creative virtual identity usages in the region, when deploying a social media profile image online a mother may use her son's photo, a woman attending a university might use a landscape photo, and anyone may use a cartoony emoji-style image, even in business settings. While such choices could occur in other regions too, here we present techniques to reveal culturally-specific values and deployments of virtual identities. Our long-term goal is that our methods will generalize as an approach for eliciting cultural values around virtual identity use in other contexts.

Paper Overview

The remainder of this paper is structured as follows. We next describe the motivation for our case study and provide an overview of our approach. A section describing Prior Work follows. The Methods section details our procedures and integration of computational and qualitative methods. We then describe our novel computational framework for virtual identity data collection and analysis in the Qatar-AIRvatar Analysis Toolkit section. We describe the user values and needs that we have qualitatively identified along with our computationally discovered categories of user profile style in the Results and Findings section. Based upon these results and findings, we present as a set of principles for virtual identity system development in the Discussion: Toward Baseline Principles and Best Practices section before ending with the Conclusion, Limitations, and Future Work section.

Case Study Motivation

The GCC context provides several unique features that render it an important and informative region for study. For those who are unfamiliar with the region, this section provides a brief introduction to several cultural characteristics relevant here. The *Khaleeji* identity that encapsulates the people of the Gulf region has transformed profoundly over the last 50 years. The traditional Khaleeji identity bands together around extended family structures (also referred as tribal culture: a membership system that is cited as important as race and class in the region and is interdependent with Khaleeji identity [12]), language (although Arabic is spoken in different dialects throughout the region), and Islamic religious values [4, 5] with some emphasis on gender roles. Khaleeji daily life is prominently impacted by a combination of religio-cultural vision of privacy (typically enforced by Sharia Law at the judicial level) and expectations of upholding the honor of one's family name.

Relevant to the deployment of virtual identities in the region, Abokhodair and Vieweg have described how this mix of cultural, social, and religious values impacts a regional vision of privacy. They describe three aspects related to privacy: awrah, hurma, and haq al-khososyah [2]. Respectively these aspects coincide with the intimate parts of one's body which requires both males and females to cover certain body parts (personal level), the sacredness of certain spaces, home, mosques, and other concepts including awrah (social level), and the local laws that protect hurma (judicial level). These aspects of privacy should not be seen narrowly as religious prescriptions, rather, like most places in the world, privacy is deeply interwoven culturally. This is important to consider since awrah is often misconstrued by people from out-of-culture perspectives since this level of privacy influences the garment choices that the region is sometimes associated with. Previous studies also underline the need for regional religio-cultural individual identities to exist in harmony with the concept of community (umma) where "*a unity of perception, language and civilization [which is] moral and ethical*" is sought [6].

Apart from the rise of the hydrocarbon economy and the effects of modernity, recent changes in Khaleeji identity have been facilitated by four main factors: formation of civil society mechanics, cultural production and exchange in the region, the role of governments in constructing strong national identities, and, most relevant here, the rise of information technologies [4]. Related to the rise of information technologies, the Qatar 2030 National Vision[3] report highlights the need to simultaneously "modernize Qatari society" while preserving cultural traditions. While from our own perspective "modern" and "traditional" are not necessarily oppositional concepts, we mention this here since the National Vision suggests that "modernization" is a key idea in Qatar's self-concept. One aspect of such modernization is the pervasive use of information and communication technologies (ICTs). A 2014 survey shows that 85% of the native population is online and that Qatari "nationals are strongly committed to preserving cultural traditions (94%), and do not see those traditions at odds with a modern, global society" [43]. While Qataris confidently agree that it is possible to preserve their culture and heritage (85%), they also feel their culture should be "more integrated into the modern world" (80%). Although previous research has highlighted some creative practices of Qataris and GCC nationals inside Twitter [1], Facebook [2], and photo-sharing apps in general [3], these interactions and tensions between traditional practices as uptake of emergent uses of technology is not unique to the GCC region. Hence, we posit that our approach is useful to researchers and developers of virtual identity technologies focused on other geographical locations.

[3] www.mdps.gov.qa/en/qnv/Documents/QNV2030_English_v2.pdf

This work aims to formulate a nuanced approach to uncovering everyday user practices and values tensions that arise as negotiate local cultural values in light of values built into technologies that are often designed in other regions such as North America, Asia, and so on. The insight gained from our analysis could be utilized by developers in assessing how their systems' norms and design decisions impact culturally specific groups, and facilitating understanding of how they can support local negotiations of value tensions within cultures instead of relying on false preconceptions from outsider perspectives.

Approach Overview

We implemented a multi-layered mixed-methodology and have assessed a range of current practices exhibiting everyday creativity by Qataris expressing social identity through uses of virtual identity technologies that have not necessarily been designed with GCC values in mind. Although we present this work primarily as a case study, the investigation has resulted in (1) development of novel mixed-methods (qualitative and computational techniques) for understanding user values, needs, and practices in virtual identity systems, and (2) articulation of a set of developer guidelines in the form of principles useful for developing technologies that empower MENA region users to enact traditional values and cultural norms while constructing and deploying virtual identities.

We implemented the *Qatar-AIRvatar* analysis toolkit (an extension of the general *AIRvatar* system [39], which can collect fine-grained data regarding users' avatar customization activities and discover patterns of customization and use in avatars or social media profile images), to perform analysis of GCC social media profiles and avatars. We wrote a script to collect publicly available Instagram profile images and gathered 42,554 Qatari profiles by using the official Instagram API. We then used Qatar-AIRvatar to perform computational analysis of these profiles to discover families of visually similar profile image types using a technique called archetypal analysis.[4]

As a second step, we manually sampled a separate set of 255 Qatari Instagram profiles from users who has checked-in to Qatar within a certain time period and qualitatively analyzed them, examining the content of these accounts one-by-one. We particularly noted the profile pictures, biographical information, and creative techniques deployed by users in navigating the platform. Useful for providing rich, authentic descriptions and quotes illustrating the results that emerged by contrasting our quantitative and qualitative analyses, we additionally conducted 5 in-depth, semi-structured interviews [29] of Qatari virtual identity users (social media and videogames). The interviews were analyzed using Action-Implicative Discourse Analysis, or AIDA [25], and focused on learning about the ideals, beliefs, and practices of the participants as well as how they influence and affect their uses and appropriations of various digital technologies. We focused on social media users and videogame players based upon a cognitive linguistics-based perspective holding that both avatars and profiles form "blended identities," i.e., involving aspects of identity projected from both the physical and virtual worlds [21].

The mixed-methods revealed themes such as Khaleeji (GCC regional) features, social monitoring, self-expression, social connections, and physical and virtual identity contrasts.

PRIOR WORK

Very little digital media research has taken place that focuses on Qatari society, culture, and/or heritage, with aspects of [43] as a notable exception. Previous studies seeking to understand the values, motivations, and behaviors of users in creating virtual characters or avatars have used application systems that differ in cultural expectations and context (e.g., *Second Life*, *The Sims*, *World of Warcraft*), which may not generalize well to other cultures (e.g., Qatari culture). In particular, for the purpose of better understanding the cultural nuances that exist between different demographics, contexts, and participants, these approaches have not been able to take into account values built into infrastructures, particularly computational data structures that inevitably incorporate values of the designers' milieus, which may or may not be suitable for the target demographics and cultures of participants.

In terms of computational methods, previous research has shown how users' behaviors in virtual environments are closely related to aspects of their physical worlds identities, such as their ages [53], personality [54], motivations [8], behavior [59], and customization preferences [33]. Additionally, previous work has described *shared technical underpinnings* [21] existing between computational identity representation systems such as character avatars, social networking profiles, a perspective supporting the approach taken here both virtual identity information (e.g., in-game behaviors) and real-world information (e.g., social network profiles) result in identity models that are directly comparable and often interoperable at a technical level.

In terms of qualitative methods, there are many useful survey-based studies of behavioral patterns by users in virtual environments, however, there are also limitations of self-reported surveys for studying users [19]. While useful for particularly subjective notions of identities expressed by users (e.g., preferences), self-reported survey data are often difficult to evaluate and subject to survey bias [7]. While useful for understanding certain characteristics of users (e.g., articulated reasons for making a choice), some aspects of users' experiences cannot be articulated (tacit knowledge), are intrusive to keep track of, or are mentally or physically strenuous for participants or interviewers. These cases are often better suited to unobtrusive data collection and analysis such as performed in the computational aspect of the methods we deploy here.

Another common approach toward understanding links between personal choices/views and virtual behavior is to implement standardized survey instruments or questionnaires.

[4]While our primary aim is culturally-specific analysis, as opposed to a type of comparative analysis that would suggest a flattening out of intra-country cultural differences, we also collected 101,153 social media profiles from the U.S.A., Brazil, France, Korea, and Sweden for purposes elaborated in the Discussion: Toward Baseline Principles and Best Practices Section. Analysis of the data in these other regions is largely beyond the scope of this paper, however it is worth mentioning that we contrasted our GCC-specific analyses with patterns of use in these other regions to ensure that our focus here is on GCC-specific phenomena and not general trends in Instagram use.

For example, the BIG-5 International Personality Item Pool (IPIP) [18] survey is a common tool used quantitatively measure personality profiles. While shown to be effective within certain contexts and demographics, such instruments may not be generally applicable to other demographics nor translate well across cultures. These standardized survey instruments are not based on values that emerge from the specific data or research question at hand. In contrast to each of these approaches that are all based on predetermined categories, we seek to understand patterns and categories of virtual identity users and preferences that emerge from the data.

METHODS

Data Collection

Social Media Profiles

We collected publicly available data to study how Qatari users represent themselves in social media through their profile pictures and what kind of creative techniques they employ to include their cultural values in their representations. We collected public profile pictures from Instagram because (1) Instagram is one of the widely used social media services in Qatar [56]: 65% of Qataris use Instagram [23], and (2) Instagram API is well-designed to collect large-scale data. While there can be some differences between public and private Instagram accounts in terms of needs and values, particularly when taking into account the Qatari context, it can pose ethical and logistical challenges to collect private account information.

As Instagram does not support search based on the origin country of users, we designed a three-step process to find users who are highly probable to be Qatari. First, we queried a list of "locations" in Qatar. The locations in Instagram are a set of places where users can tag for their photos. Second, for each of the locations, we iteratively collected recent media objects (photos or videos). We then extract the authors of these recent media objects. Finally, among the set of users we collected, we kept only users whose bios or user names were written in the language that corresponds with the location, Arabic in this case. The language was automatically detected by three widely-used libraries, which are CLD2 (from the Chromium project) [52], Langdetect [42], and LangID [41]. If three libraries were not unanimous in terms of the language detected, we considered the language to be the one indicated by the majority of the libraries.

Interviews

As a step toward elaborating on the situated values and creative approaches of the GCC virtual identity users, we also chose to conduct interviews (5 in total) as they are an effective form of qualitative data elicitation [26, 47]. Since our main motivation in conducting interviews were to obtain indicators describing and naming the phenomena that emerged from our main quantitative and qualitative analysis, we view the resulting authenticity as predilected by the small sample size [51].

The interviews were conducted in Qatar by one of the authors, either in person or via teleconferencing software, with durations ranging between 45 and 90 minutes. The interviewees were all Qatari individuals with experience in virtual identity use in social media and videogames. Three interviewees were male and two were female, with ages ranging from 20 to 28 years old. The interviews took place in English, a language that all participants spoke. The interview flow focused on uncovering indications of features that participants would like to see in region-specific technologies and videogames—at the same time, gaining insight and understandings of how these technologies serve as boundary objects that are conceived of, and designed outside of, GCC cultures. Interviews were all transcribed by the interviewer then carefully analyzed by the interviewer and a separate researcher to identify themes and commonalities with a degree of inter-rater reliability.

Computational Analysis

Qatar-AIRvatar Analysis Toolkit

AIRvatar is an integrated set of tools for collecting, transforming, analyzing, and visualizing data related to virtual identities. In prior work, *AIRvatar* has been used to, for example, identify and characterize videogame players' physical-world values based on telemetry data gathered during the creation of videogame avatars [34, 38, 35, 36, 37, 39]. In this paper, we focused on the *AIRvatar* toolkit's capabilities that allow for the analysis of GCC social-media profiles and profile photos.

Archetypal Analysis

We computationally analyzed 42,554 Qatari Instagram accounts in order to identify different categories of user profile style (in terms of meaningful visual characteristics such as distinguishing photos from synthetic images or text). We used a variant of an unsupervised learning method known as archetypal analysis [13]. We use this clustering technique due to its consilience with prototype-based models of cognitive categorization in cognitive science [46, 30, 34, 32]. In this work, we performed archetypal analysis over our set of Instagram data. Given a specified number of archetypes k and a set of data, an archetypal analysis algorithm produces k archetypes that are extremal representations of the features of the data set. In addition, the algorithm tries to identify archetypes such that each observation in the data set can be be described as a convex combination of the k archetypes produced.

In the past, archetypal analysis has found applications in such diverse topics as astrophysics [10], economics [31, 45], sports analytics [15], and videogame recommender systems [50]. Our interest in the algorithm stems from its proven ability to identify extremal data points within a data set that are both interpretable and able to represent the data set as a whole. Previous works related to modeling social identities [34, 38] has leveraged archetypal analysis in this way.

In order to quantitatively analyze the Instagram data set, here we leveraged the data transformation and data analysis algorithms from *AIRvatar*'s software library. The library itself was implemented in Python using the *scikit-learn* [44] and Python Matrix Factorization (*PyMF*) libraries. In this work, we used the Convex Hull Non-negative Matrix Factorization (CHNMF) algorithm [55] for our analyses in place of the canonical implementation of the archetypal analysis algorithm. The algorithm provides equivalent results to archetypal analysis, but performs better in terms of speed. To aid in our analyses, we leveraged *AIRvatar*'s interactive visualization tool for large-N exploration and analysis of virtual identities.

Qualitative Analysis

To validate and explain the quantitative analysis, we manually browsed a separate set of Instagram profiles who had posted photos from Qatar within a recent time frame. Since we could not assume that these users were Qatari, or even Khaleeji, we took the step of performing manual analysis of likely profiles to identify GCC nationals, especially noting Qataris, given our focus on issues such as cultural preservation in light of information and communication technology use. This analysis involved looking at profile photos and translating any biographical information from Arabic to English. We also used such information for ascertaining gender when possible. After eliminating tourists and expatriates, we further studied a representative set of 255 Instagram accounts that we could confidently believe to be either Qatari or from another GCC nationality and expressing relevant cultural markers.

A secondary form of qualitative analysis involved analyzing the 5 interviews to uncover ideals, beliefs, and creative practices of Qatari individuals in creating, customizing, and deploying virtual identities. We used an "Action-Implicative Discourse Analysis" (AIDA) approach [25] augmented with grounded theory techniques [16] to analyze the interviews. These approaches allowed us to assess the interview data, situate it within Khaleeji culture, and make legitimate claims about foundations for design principles borne from the data.

RESULTS AND FINDINGS

Archetypal Analysis Results and Findings

Before performing archetypal analysis on the data, we first had to choose the number of archetypes k. Choosing an optimal value for k is quite difficult in practice, though there are a number of well-established techniques to aid in the decision-making process. To find the optimal number of archetypes k with which to analyze the Qatari Instagram data, we chose to first leverage the Cattell scree test, which is widely used to find the optimal number of factors for describing a data set.

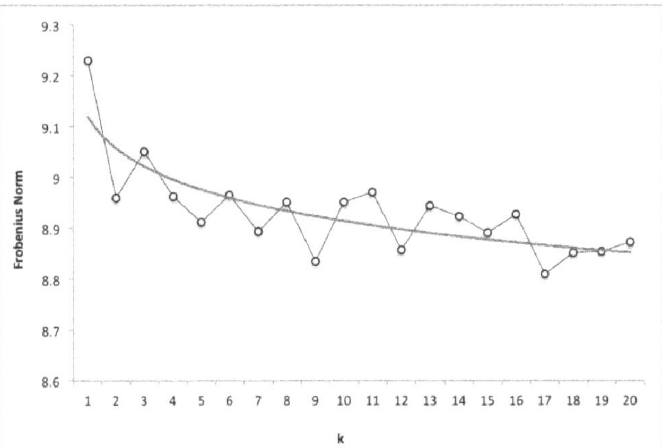

Figure 1. The black line is a log-scale scree plot of Frobenius norms of models produced using Convex Hull Non-negative Matrix Factorization for varying k. The red line is a logarithmic regression of the scree plot.

Figure 1 shows a scree plot [9] of the Frobenius norms[5] of models produced using CHNMF for varying k. We observe that the "elbow" of the graph, and thus, the optimal number of clusters according to the Cattell scree test lies somewhere between $k = 5$ and $k = 9$.

To narrow down this range to a single value, we first observe that there are two noteworthy local minima in our scree plot. One can be seen at $k = 9$ and the other can be seen at $k = 17$. As there is only a marginal decrease in the resulting model's error measure at $k = 17$ that appears to be spurious when considering the overall trend of the graph, and since we found that the archetypes at $k = 9$ archetypes were easier for humans to interpret (four researchers found the greatest consensus of interpretation of the clusters at $k = 9$), we settled on $k = 9$ being the best value of k for our archetypal analysis.

Figure 2 shows the archetypal images produced using *AIRvatar*. The column labeled 'Prototype' shows the archetypal image for each of the $k = 9$ clusters. The column labeled 'Top-Weighted' shows the 9 images that are most similar to a given archetype within the data set. After setting a threshold parameter in the *AIRvatar* toolkit, this column's cells were populated with images that were at minimum 30% similar to the archetypal image for a particular row.

The set of archetypes resulted in 9 clusters. The clusters were identified by recurring dominant themes within them, and although a few cluster members were not in line with the dominant themes, the participating researchers independently decided on similar themes with an acceptable range of inter-researcher reliability. Also utilizing the results of our qualitative analysis (which we go into further detail in the next section), we have named these clusters as follows. Male avatars exhibited two distinct clusters with traditional attires (#2, *Traditional Male*) and non-traditional attires (#6, *Non-traditional Male*). Within the cultural context the decision to have an avatar with traditional or non-traditional clothing may present consequences. On one hand, using an avatar with traditional attire instantly marks the user as a person from the GCC region and someone of presumably Arabic origins (important in Qatar due to the small percentage of nationals). This might also initiate prejudice and bigoted backlash online in broader global contexts (a theme that was illustrated by one of our interviewees who described encountering "racism" online). At the same time, it may also present the user with social capital [11] if the user of the avatar is a business owner that deals with local people or is a member of a traditional family structure. Two other clusters that contained both male and female avatars had either playful selfie-like characteristics (#5, *Selfie*) or illustrative representations (#1, *Illustrative*). Using illustrative representations is observed to be a common creative strategy in terms of protecting modesty and privacy, especially for female avatars, but also for males. One cluster that we believed to be mainly female (#7, *Thematic Photos*) utilized thematic

[5]The objective function of CHNMF seeks to minimize $||V - \hat{V}||_F^2$ where V is the original data set and $\hat{V}$ is the product of the two matrices produced by CHNMF. Note that $||X||_F^2$ is the Frobenius norm of the matrix X, and is defined as the Euclidean distance between the elements of X.

Figure 2. Archetypal profile images from Qatari Instagram accounts.

(e.g., romantically-themed) photos. The themes of the photos focused around flowers, heart symbols, scenery, horses, and cars (especially SUVs for males). This is also another creative strategy for users of the region who value privacy (another theme that has been mentioned in our interviews). Of the three clusters that had more graphical characteristics, one turned out to contain more religious text and symbols (#3, *Faith*), and the others had corporate and commercial logos (#4, *Commercial*) and typographic messages (#8, *Typographic*). Finally, the final cluster (#9, *Other*) compiled together photographic or iconic symbols that had lower descriptive values combined.

Qualitative User Analysis Results and Findings

The hand-coding of a separate set of 255 Instagram profiles resulted in 69 female (27%) and 111 male (44%) users, with an additional 75 profiles (29%) whose genders were unspecified. We coded accounts that seemed to be business-related as unspecified gender types (such as accounts providing Qatari or GCC phone numbers which showcased fashion and jewelry items), unless they were associated with the services of a specific person (such as a hairdresser, make-up artist, or photographer), in which case we assigned the account to the self-presented gender of service provider. Many female users deploy social media for running small home-based businesses, an example of a site where users enact self-expressive power and social engagement through creative profile construction.

Almost a third of the accounts (32%) were private, while the rest were public. The ratio of public accounts for males (73%) was slightly higher than females (65%). Although some might not expect this high ratio for females due to privacy concerns, we can speculate that our hand-coding activity caught more active Instagram users who tend to keep their accounts public in addition to the presence of female local merchants and service professionals such as mentioned above. However as we examined the profiles, we confirmed our inference that many Khaleeji females tend to utilize creative surrogate images instead of personal photos (of themselves, their faces, etc.), transferring the issue of privacy from account access to account content. 40 out of 69 female accounts (58%) did not show their faces in their profiles photos, depending instead on other thematic images to represent themselves. These images ranged from photos of objects, scenery, flowers, children, close-up details of their faces (mostly both eyes, one eye, or lips), or illustrations. Khaleeji men often used photos of (presumably their own) faces—only 28 male accounts (25%) did not use their faces in the profile photos. The men appeared in either traditional (37%) or non-traditional clothing. In addition, they might sometimes utilize images of horses, falcons, cars (especially SUVs), scenery, and professional athletes.

Merging the results of qualitative analysis with interviews provided us insight on recurring categories which were further consolidated into 5 overarching themes (Table 1). The emerging themes suggest a diversity of values and creative strategies related to virtual identities created among users in GCC countries. There were also gender-related differences between the categories we uncovered.

Mixed-Methods Results and Findings

Comparing our computational clusters with the qualitative themes, we saw that the virtual identity uses in the clusters were each in-line with one qualitative theme at least (Table 2). This lead us to the conclusion that the five emergent themes encompassed unique challenges the members of GCC cultures faced while using these virtual identity systems and some of the creative solutions they employed to overcome them.

The theme of *Khaleeji Features* indicates that participants were enthusiastic about having the option of using traditional, culturally-specific features in their avatars, or seeing characters in videogames that have these features. For example, consider the prevalence of the ghutra[6] in cluster #2 and Arabic writing in cluster #3 in Figure 2. From the qualitative analysis we have observed that a majority of the profile images had visual clues that hinted Khaleeji origins of the users. From the interviews, one female participant referred to the character *Shaheen* in the videogame *Tekken 7*: *"If you know the game Tekken [...] they have a new character and they called it Shaheen. He is based on a Saudi person, and he wears the ghutra, and he has the Arabian beard, the Khaleeji beard, and he has a falcon. It was really fun to play with."* Even when Khaleeji features were not present, users would find creative ways to invent them. The same female participant mentioned a strategy used by Arabic speaking users in utilizing the pronunciation of numbers and letters in creating profile names to indicate their ethnic origins. A male participant described his efforts in hacking game codes to *"change the player names, how they look, and make it like [Qatari]."* The culturally diversifying features mainly focused on clothing, skin color, and hair/beard style. Participants also mentioned that there are significant differences of beard and ghutra styles between the men in GCC, and very few virtual environments implement this form of cultural diversity. Female participants mentioned the necessity of features which reflect modesty in their avatars.

The theme of *Social Monitoring* revealed issues and concerns regarding privacy. For example, in Figure 2 consider the prevalence of illustrative avatars in cluster #1 and thematic

Themes	Recurring Codes
1. Khaleeji Features	Common • Traditional Clothing • Avatar Skin Color • Khaleeji Diversity Female • Modesty Male • Avatar Beard and Hair Style
2. Social Monitoring	Common • Self-monitoring • Monitoring by Others Female • Privacy • Microphone Use
3. Self-expression	Common • Self-likeness of Avatars • Cosmetic Avatar Features Female • Gender Related Avatar Features
4. Social Connections	Common • Connections with Family Female • Connections with Strangers Male • Fear of Bigoted Backlash • Relationship Seeking
5. Physical and Virtual Identity Contrasts	Common • Non-permeability • Escapism

Table 1. Overarching themes that emerged during the interviews.

images such as hands in the shape of a heart or flowers in cluster #7 instead of user photos. Such examples paralleled our qualitative analysis, which revealed fewer examples of full-face photo usage than other regions. Regardless of gender, Khaleeji users creatively came up with aestheticized strategies like using shadows and light, silhouettes, back of the head profiles, framing half the face, or focusing on a part of the face (typically eyes). The theme was also particularly meaningful when deciding to add new friends. For example, from the interviews, the second female participant said: *"I feel like my account is my privacy, I only add my friends—I wouldn't want a random stranger knowing what I'm watching right now, what I'm playing right now, or what my status is...."* An additional aspect regarding monitoring and privacy, and the wish to be viewed as upright and respectable revolves around the usage of microphones in videogame sessions for females. It is not uncommon for people who do not know each

[6] A ghutra is a type of headdress traditionally worn by Arab men.

	Khaleeji Features	Social Monitoring	Self-expression	Social Connections	Physical and Virtual Identity Contrasts
Traditional Male	✓		✓	✓	
Non-traditional Male			✓	✓	
Selfie			✓		✓
Illustrative		✓			✓
Thematic Photos		✓			✓
Religious	✓				
Commercial				✓	
Typographic				✓	✓

Table 2. Comparing computational clusters with qualitative themes.

other in a physical context to connect via an online videogame and communicate via microphone. However, in the GCC (among other regions) a female voice is considered personal and private, and not something to be exposed to outsiders. Therefore, when and how female gamers use microphones is a point of contention—some use them, some do not, and some will only listen, and not speak, but use text to offer responses and thoughts. Another practice that we see as an extension of privacy concerns and deem as a creative process was the practice of creating a persona or a paragon instead of self-likeness. In social media profiles this emerged as using the images and quotes of celebrities and fictional characters. In videogames this emerged as creatively selecting regional paragons and modeling virtual identity around it such as this female participant's response: *"I wanted it to look like the [ancient deity Ra], so I made it extremely skinny and black and tall and weird and bug-eyed [...] Even the way the character would act, I would make it act snobby, like some sort of deity."*

Participants also expressed their commitment to implementing creative details in their avatars that empowered their *Self-expression*—such as skin color and fashion. For example, in Figure 2 consider again the prevalance of traditional clothing in cluster #1 in addition to the use of highly stylized thematic images featuring rich shadows in cluster #5 and the use of celebrity and "cool" posed images in cluster #6 and #9. In our qualitative results, one female participant gave this creative example of preserving head covering in videogames: *"the healer [character's] clothes are usually all covered, even with a hoodie and everything so I found it interesting, I did just realize it last month that my avatar is really well-covered like I am"*), and character origin (the second female participant gave this example from the videogame *Skyrim*: *"In Skyrim, I took the Khajiit tribe, and they're not even human, they're anthropomorphic type of animal, they're based on cheetahs, and the reason I picked them is because they come from the desert—so it reminded me of myself..."*[7] Also 2 (one female, one male) out of 5 participants mentioned an avatar gender-based choice for videogame character profession, as illustrated by one male participant's comment: *"If the character is some type of swordsman, I don't know why—or like an axe wielder, I would prefer like a chunky guy with a beard [...] but if it's like a magician or something, I would say an elfin woman."*

The theme of *Social Connections* underlined the purposes of online connections established by participants. For example, in Figure 2 consider how the clothing in clusters #2 and #5 and the use of Arabic writing, particularly in clusters #3, #4, #7, and #9, can facilitate recognition and connections between Khaleeji individuals. A dominant sub-theme was in the differences between making formal connections (with strangers) versus informal connections (with friends and family members). The qualitative analysis revealed how the framing of formal photos (with traditional attire) and non-formal photos varied, with formal photos including more of the body, similar sitting positions, and direct angles. Another concern about social connections emerged from the interview where the first female participant expressed worry about representing her Khaleeji identity in digital environments, as she thought this might lead to complications or problems around bigotry, described as racism: *"[...] I feel there would be more racism involved if there were more [Khaleeji] options to display certain things."* Participants were acutely aware that their backgrounds are in the minority in greater gaming communities—culturally, racially/ethnically, and with regards to nationality. Due to the nature of many videogames that allows for or even necessitates communication with people from all over the world, concern, and maybe even fear, are ever-present potentials vis-à-vis the communication patterns and routines participants regularly undertake. This, in addition to the great significance placed on privacy in Khaleeji culture, are cause for great care when it comes to connecting with others in digital contexts.

Finally, some codes that related to the comparisons between physical world experiences of participants versus their virtual identity-based experiences were consolidated under the *Physical and Virtual Identity Contrasts* theme. For example, again in Figure 2, consider the anonymizing effects of illustrative avatars in cluster #1, Arabic writing in clusters #3, #4, and #8, artfully stylized images in clusters #4, #5, and #9, and photos of people other than users (and even a parrot) in clusters #6 and #9. Users from the region emphasized virtual identities as personal creative spaces such as this female participant who described game worlds as *"dream worlds [where] everyone just does whatever he or she wants, without any judgment"* and another as *"a gateway to a different world."* Another interesting component of this theme was the non-permeability of the virtual, as summarized by the first female participant as; *"Everything that happens online stays online [...] I feel that the majority of people, if they know they're anonymous then they probably do things they wouldn't do if they weren't."* However

[7] Cheetahs historically they occupied other habitats in the MENA region, if not actually deserts.

this is not a phenomena directed solely for female users as one male participant notes: *"it sucks for the [men too], we get the same treatment"*, then later adds *"we all have a different identity online"*. This "separation" between the physical and virtual selves is prevalent globally in social media settings, however here we highlight culturally-specific phenomena in the context of the GCC and attendant social consequences that may ensue if social media users and videogame players make missteps that are cause for regionally-shared perspectives on public shame or embarrassment. The idea of anonymity is important all over the world, but when it is offered and utilized by those in the GCC the option to engage and participate in various digital communications may offer even more outlets than are typically permitted in face-to-face environments. One important outcome of these physical and virtual identity contrasts was a familiar practice of maintaining multiple identities and/or accounts as is discussed in the next section.

Overall the merging of the results of computational and qualitative analysis revealed the strategies of appropriations by Khaleeji users in these virtual environments, indicating the push toward modernity in the region, while the preservation of tradition remains a predominant goal.

DISCUSSION: TOWARD BASELINE PRINCIPLES AND BEST PRACTICES

It is useful to consider the broader implications and limitations of the results above. Our results characterize a set of ways that Qatari users construct, utilize, deploy virtual identities and employ creative strategies while doing so. Our study is culturally-grounded in the sense that it aims to characterize data collected in a specific region. Our study is not intended to reveal a characterization of a people or culture at large, and we do not claim that it is an exhaustive account. Indeed, Qatari culture, like any other culture, is not monolithic and individuals may fall outside of the categories articulated in our analyses. For the same reason, our approach is not to construct generalizing cross-cultural comparisons of the form: "Qataris prefer X, where as Swedes prefer Y." However, it has been useful to contrast discovered clusters of social media profile image use in diverse regions for a more parsimonious reason. We aimed to verify that some of our findings are not characterizations of social media use irrespective of region or culture. Hence, we did perform archetypal analysis of data in other regions and, indeed, discovered clusters that did not exist in Qatar and vice versa. For example, in France there were fewer formal business portrait photos and more images of types including candid selfies, photos of users' pets, photos of couples, and more revealing attire regardless of gender. In Sweden there were more "activity portraits," which indicated the apparent hobbies or professions of users (e.g., a kayaker in a river or a baker in an apron in front of a shop window). We did not note faith-oriented profiles as an archetypal deployment in France or Sweden. Such distinctions should not be seen as characterizing the cultures at large in the respective countries, but rather as evidence that archetypal analysis can be useful for discovering diverse culturally-grounded and specific virtual identity image deployments and not only general trends that cut across all regions alike. We leave more systematic studies to compare regional differences of virtual identity usage for future work.

Despite the robust alignment of our computational and qualitative results, our approach faced some constraints and limitations. Of particular note, some of the values and practices described above, such as modesty and social monitoring, also influence a number of Qatari virtual identity users to maintain multiple accounts, both public and private. While the use of public vs. private accounts is not unique to Qatar or the GCC, informal discussions with informants from the region indicate that the deployments of social media profile content in private accounts for networks of immediate family members, close friends, and broader social connections would likely all results in quite distinct findings. Nonetheless, when understood as an account of public identity performance, our results above reveal a coherent portrait of an array of Qatari virtual identity deployments commensurate with the needs and values elicited by our interviews and described in prior work.

Culturally-Grounded Design Principles and Guidelines for Virtual Identity System Developers

When considering our results as restricted to public sphere virtual identity use, they suggest a preliminary set of design principles that could help guide virtual identity systems developers creating applications for use in the region. These principles emerge from considering the values and needs our study elicited in light of two distinct types of virtual identity creation, use, and deployment features that developers must consider. First, *embedded* features are those that are directly enabled by technical affordances of systems. For example, filters that can be applied to photographs, pre-built customization options when constructing avatars, and default images or avatars are all embedded features in that developers explicitly implement the features to enable users to self-represent. In contrast, the second type of virtual identity features are those that are *enacted* by users without direct influence of developers. For example, the choices of profile images that users upload, the content of text chosen to be entered into open text fields such as "Name," and text that users post to each others' feeds are all enacted, or user performed, features of virtual identity systems. The distinction between embedded and enacted features is important to note because while direct design principles can be offered to developers regarding embedded features such as adding specific types of customization options, it is a more subtle challenge to offer principles for developers to support actions of users involving externally generated content. Hence, the following two subsections articulate two very different sets of principles that reflect the distinctions between embedded and enacted virtual identity system features.

Principles for Embedded Virtual Identity Features

The following are example recommendations that virtual identity system features developers could implement in Qatar and the GCC in order to support local needs and values for creative self-represenation. Taken together, such recommendations form the basis for a set of culturally-grounded design principles for virtual identity systems. These principles are particularly appropriate for social media-based virtual identities, as they emerge from our Instagram studies, but could likely generalize to other forms of virtual identity.

- *Khaleeji Features & Social Monitoring*: Avatar creators for generating non-photographic (or cartoony) virtual identity representations incorporating a wide array of local self-representational styles (e.g., clothing and grooming preferences) enable traditional articulation of Khaleeji features. Such avatar creators can also support needs regarding modesty, particularly regarding values precluding publicly deployed female photographic representations.
- *Social Monitoring*: Using accounts verified for gender, users can define settings regarding the preferred communications methods, e.g., voice chat, speech-to-text functions, text chat, and/or symbol-based chat (using prebuilt elements to construct commonly used phrases). Similarly, unobtrusive vocal anonymizing features can be deployed in settings in which communication is required, but values, needs, or tensions regarding modest self-presentation emerge.
- *Social Connections*: Rather than only enabling groupings of social connections according to standardized distinctions such as between public vs. private accounts, regionally and culturally-specific distinctions such as *mahram* (spouses and unmarriageable kin) vs. *non-mahram* connections could be implemented as pre-built categories with requisite affordances for enabling and restricting access and providing appropriate self-representations to other users.
- *Physical and Virtual Identity Contrasts*: When engaging other users on social media involving international connections, as noted in our interviews, GCC members have been recipients of harassment based upon stereotypes and prejudices from the physical world. At the same time, female users have encountered gender-specific forms of harassment online. Specific community guidelines and moderation explicitly targeting regionally-specific phenomena, in addition to targeted outreach to inform users about these issues, could be used to ameliorate some of these forms of abuse.

The list above is not exhaustive, but rather is representative of principles for guiding culturally-specific embedded virtual identity system features driven by values and needs elicited in the GCC rather than introspectively determined by outsiders.

Principles for Enacted Virtual Identity Features

While it may appear challenging to provide developers with a set of principles supporting practices user enacted virtual identity features because users' actions and content cannot always be anticipated, developers can, in fact, provide categories to structure users' activities based upon assessing patterns in user behavior. For example, our computational results suggest the design principles supporting user enacted features such as:

- *Predefined Categories for User Image Categorization*: Enabling users to tag profile images could support ensuring virtual identity deployments appropriate to different settings and viewers. For example, tags for Formal vs. Informal, Traditional vs Non-traditional, and Photographic vs. Illustrative could be used to help automate display of appropriate and relevant user images.
- *Automated Processing*: While these features may be less on the immediate horizon, algorithmically robust techniques such as face recognition applied to photographs could be used for enhancing, altering, or redacting photographic images depending on the image's setting or potential viewer, according to local needs and values related to social monitoring and social connections. Similarly, biometric measures such as fingerprint scans could be used to restricting access to content per the same types of needs and values.

The features described above represent our first consolidation of "lessons learned" from our case study articulated as actionable principles that we hope can be put to use by system developers located in and/or targeting the GCC region.

CONCLUSION, LIMITATIONS, AND FUTURE WORK

The central aim of this paper has been to present a novel approach to analyzing and better understanding culturally-grounded virtual identity uses, the cross-cultural creative ways underserved users navigate these identities, and demonstrating those results via a mixed-methods case study in Qatar. We have also articulated a novel mixed methods approach including a computational platform of our own inventions for discovering and understanding user values and practices in virtual identity systems. A final aim has been to present important steps toward articulating a set of baseline principles and best practices for developing information and communication technologies that empower Qataris in everyday creative practices of enacting their needs and values using virtual identity technologies. As described above, the dataset here is limited to public accounts. Although studying private accounts may reveal important different cultural nuances, deploying our mixed-methods approach on public accounts is a step towards discovering cultural needs for both the public and private domains. By discovering implicit patterns in data, our computational methods reveal tacit values in social media profile use rather than explicitly stated user values. We further suggest that one future work direction would be to use the *AIRvatar* social media profile constructor to collect data on behavioral patterns in profile customization as done in [40] for revealing additional tacit values expressed by users.

In future work we aim to further develop our recommended principles and practices for developers via (1) applying our approach to new case studies focused on other systems for creating avatars for videogames and virtual environments, and (2) running experiments in a controlled experimental setting where we can use *AIRvatar* to collect fine-grained customization data as users construct avatars such that we can analyze not only avatars as an end-products, but also the processes of creating them. Additionally, we aim to adapt a virtual system of our own design to culturally-specific needs and values of Qatar by enacting our own design principles and evaluating the resultant system. Ultimately, we hope that users will be able to adapt our approach to support the needs and values of diverse communities and subgroups globally, especially for the purposes of empowering people to participate in digital media via virtual identities in ways that support their own cultural needs and values.

ACKNOWLEDGMENTS
This research was funded by the Qatar Computing Research Institute (QCRI)-MIT CSAIL research collaboration.

REFERENCES
1. Norah Abokhodair, Sofiane Abbar, Sarah Vieweg, and Yelena Mejova. 2016. Privacy and twitter in Qatar: Traditional values in the digital world. In *WebSci '16 Proceedings of the 8th ACM Conference on Web Science.* ACM, 66–77.
2. Norah Abokhodair and Sarah Vieweg. 2016. Privacy & social media in the context of the Arab Gulf. In *DIS '16 Proceedings of the 2016 ACM Conference on Designing Interactive Systems.* ACM, 672–683.
3. Norah Abokhodair, Sarah Vieweg, and Adam Hodges. 2017. Accepted. Photo sharing in the Arab Gulf: Expressing the collective and autonomous selves. In *CSCW 2017 Proceedings of the 20th ACM Conference on Computer-Supported Cooperative Work and Social Computing.* ACM.
4. Abdulaziz Saud Al-Babtain. 2016. Foreword. Oxford Gulf and Arabian Peninsula Studies Forum Autumn 2016 Issue, oxgaps.org. (2016).
5. Lulwa Abdulla Al-Misned. 2016. Understanding the Evolution of the Khaleeji Identity. Oxford Gulf and Arabian Peninsula Studies Forum Autumn 2016 Issue, oxgaps.org. (2016).
6. Nazih N. Ayubi. 1995. *Over-Stating the Arab State: Politics and Society in the Middle East.* I.B.Tauris & Co Ltd., New York, NY.
7. Christian Bauckhage, Kristian Kersting, Rafet Sifa, Christian Thurau, Anders Drachen, and Alessandro Canossa. 2012. How players lose interest in playing a game: An empirical study based on distributions of total playing times. In *Proceedings of the IEEE Computational Intelligence and Games Conference.* IEEE, 139–146.
8. Alessandro Canossa, Josep B Martinez, and Julian Togelius. 2013. Give Me a Reason to Dig Minecraft and Psychology of Motivation. *In Proceedings of IEEE Conference on Computational Intelligence and Games* (2013).
9. Raymond B Cattell. 1966. The scree test for the number of factors. *Multivariate behavioral research* 1, 2 (1966), 245–276.
10. Ben HP Chan, Daniel A Mitchell, and Lawrence E Cram. 2003. Archetypal analysis of galaxy spectra. *Monthly Notices of the Royal Astronomical Society* 338, 3 (2003), 790–795.
11. Chao-Ming Chiu, Meng-Hsiang Hsu, and Eric T.G. Wang. 2006. Understanding knowledge sharing in virtual communities: An integration of social capital and social cognitive theories. *Decision Support Systems* 42, 3 (2006), 1872–1888.
12. Miriam Cooke. 2014. *Tribal Modern: Branding New Nations in the Arab Gulf.* University of California Press, Los Angeles, CA.
13. Adele Cutler and Leo Breiman. 1994. Archetypal analysis. *Technometrics* 36, 4 (1994), 338–347.
14. Robert Andrew Dunn and Rosanna E. Guadagno. 2012. My avatar and me: Gender and personality predictors of avatar-self discrepancy. *Computers in Human Behavior* 28, 1 (2012), 97 – 106. DOI: http://dx.doi.org/10.1016/j.chb.2011.08.015
15. Manuel JA Eugster. 2011. Archetypal athletes. *arXiv preprint arXiv:1110.1972* (2011).
16. Barney G Glaser. 1967. *The discovery of grounded theory: Strategies for qualitative research.* Aldine Publishing.
17. Erving Goffman and others. 1959. The presentation of self in everyday life. (1959).
18. Alan J Gow, Martha C Whiteman, Alison Pattie, and Ian J Deary. 2005. Goldberg's 'IPIP' Big-Five factor markers: Internal consistency and concurrent validation in Scotland. *Personality and Individual Differences* 39, 2 (2005), 317–329.
19. Rosanna E. Guadagno, Nicole L. Muscanell, Bradley M. Okdie, Nanci M. Burk, and Thomas B. Ward. 2011. Even in virtual environments women shop and men build: A social role perspective on Second Life. *Computers in Human Behavior* 27, 1 (2011), 304–308. DOI: http://dx.doi.org/10.1016/j.chb.2010.08.008
20. D. Fox Harrell. 2009. Computational and Cognitive Infrastructures of Stigma: Empowering Identity in Social Computing and Gaming. *Proceedings of the 7th ACM Conference on Cognition and Creativity* (2009), 49–58.
21. D. Fox Harrell. 2010. Toward a Theory of Critical Computing. CTheory, ctheory.net/articles.aspx?id=641. (2010).
22. D Fox Harrell and S Veeragoudar Harrell. 2012. Imagination, computation, and self-expression: Situated character and avatar mediated identity. *Leonardo Electronic Almanac* 17, 2 (2012).
23. Rassed: Exploring Digital Impacts in Society. 2015. Understanding emerging social media platforms in Qatar. (2015). http://www.ictqatar.qa/sites/default/files/understanding_emerging_social_media_platforms_in_qatar.pdf.
24. Dominic Kao and D Fox Harrell. 2015. Toward Evaluating the Impacts of Virtual Identities on STEM Learning. In *Proceedings of the 10th International Conference on the Foundations of Digital Games.*
25. Tracy Karen. 1995. Action-implicative discourse analysis. *Journal of Language and Social Psychology* 14, 1-2 (1995), 195–215.
26. Nigel King and Christine Horrocks. 2010. *Interviews in qualitative research.* Sage Publishing.

27. Thomas Kohler, Johann Fueller, Daniel Stieger, and Kurt Matzler. 2011. Avatar-based innovation: Consequences of the virtual co-creation experience. *Computers in Human Behavior* 27, 1 (2011), 160–168.

28. Thomas Kohler, Kurt Matzler, and Johann FÃijller. 2009. Avatar-based innovation: Using virtual worlds for real-world innovation. *Technovation* 29, 6-7 (2009), 395–407.

29. Richard A. Krueger and Mary Anne Casey. 2000. *Focus groups : a practical guide for applied research.* Sage Publishing.

30. George Lakoff. 1998. *Cognitive Semantics*. Indiana University Press, 119–154.

31. Shan Li, Paul Wang, Jordan Louviere, and Richard Carson. 2003. Archetypal analysis: A new way to segment markets based on extreme individuals. In *A Celebration of Ehrenberg and Bass: Marketing Knowledge, Discoveries and Contribution. Proceedings of the ANZMAC 2003 Conference*. 1674–1679.

32. Chong-U Lim. 2016. *Me, my Avatar (s), and AI: computational models of users and virtual identities for analysis, design, and development.* Ph.D. Dissertation. Massachusetts Institute of Technology.

33. Chong-U Lim and D. Fox Harrell. 2013. Modeling Player Preferences in Avatar Customization Using Social Network Data. In *Proceedings of the IEEE Computational Intelligence and Games Conference*. 153–160.

34. Chong-U Lim and D. Fox Harrell. 2015a. Comparing clustering approaches for modeling players' values through avatar construction. In *Proceedings of the 1st AIIDE Workshop on Player Modeling*.

35. Chong-U Lim and D. Fox Harrell. 2015b. A data-driven approach for computationally modeling players' avatar customization behaviors. In *Proceedings of the 11th AAAI Artificial Intelligence and Interactive Digital Entertainment Conference*.

36. Chong-U Lim and D Fox Harrell. 2015c. Developing computational models of players' identities and values from videogame avatars. In *Proceedings of the 10th International Conference on the Foundations of Digital Games*.

37. Chong-U Lim and D. Fox Harrell. 2015d. The marginal: A game for modeling players' perceptions of gradient membership in avatar categories. In *Proceedings of the 2nd AIIDE Workshop on Experimental AI and Games*.

38. Chong-U Lim and D. Fox Harrell. 2015e. Revealing social identity phenomena in videogames with archetypal analysis. In *Proceedings of the 6th International AISB Symposium on AI and Games*.

39. Chong-U Lim and D. Fox Harrell. 2015f. Toward telemetry-driven analytics for understanding players and their avatars in videogames. In *Proceedings of the 33rd Annual ACM Conference Extended Abstracts on Human Factors in Computing Systems (CHI EA '15)*. New York, NY, USA, 1175–1180. DOI: http://dx.doi.org/10.1145/2702613.2732783

40. Chong-U Lim and D. Fox Harrell. 2015g. Understanding Players' Identities and Behavioral Archetypes from Avatar Customization Data. In *Proceedings of the IEEE Conference on Computational Intelligence and Games*.

41. Marco Lui and Timothy Baldwin. 2012. langid. py: An off-the-shelf language identification tool. In *Proceedings of the ACL 2012 system demonstrations*. Association for Computational Linguistics, 25–30.

42. Shuyo Nakatani. 2010. Language detection library for Java. (2010). https://github.com/shuyo/language-detection

43. Northwestern University of Qatar. 2014. Media in the Middle East: research by Northwestern University in Qatar. (2014). http://www.mideastmedia.org/survey/2014/.

44. F. Pedregosa, G. Varoquaux, A. Gramfort, V. Michel, B. Thirion, O. Grisel, M. Blondel, P. Prettenhofer, R. Weiss, V. Dubourg, J. Vanderplas, A. Passos, D. Cournapeau, M. Brucher, M. Perrot, and E. Duchesnay. 2011. Scikit-learn: Machine learning in Python. *Journal of Machine Learning Research* 12 (2011), 2825–2830.

45. Giovanni C Porzio, Giancarlo Ragozini, and Domenico Vistocco. 2008. On the use of archetypes as benchmarks. *Applied Stochastic Models in Business and Industry* 24, 5 (2008), 419–437.

46. Eleanor Rosch. 1999. Principles of categorization. *Concepts: Core readings* (1999), 189–206.

47. Irving Seidman. 1998. *Interviewing as qualitative research : A guide for researchers in education and the social sciences*. Teachers College Press.

48. Sercan Sengun. 2014. A semiotic reading of digital avatars and their role of uncertainty reduction in digital communication. *Journal of Media Critiques* 1, 1 (2014), 149–162.

49. Sercan Sengun. 2015. Why do i fall for the elf, when i am no orc myself? The implications of virtual avatars in digital communication. *Comunicacao e Sociedade* 27 (2015), 181–193.

50. Rafet Sifa, Christian Bauckhage, and Anders Drachen. 2014. Archetypal game recommender systems. *Proc. KDML-LWA* (2014).

51. Davis Silverman. 1993. *Interpreting qualitative data: methods for analyzing talk, text and interaction*. Sage Publishing.

52. Dick Sites. 2013. Compact language detector 2. (2013). https://github.com/CLD2Owners/cld2.

53. Shoshannah Tekofsky, Pieter Spronck, Martijn Goudbeek, and Jan Broersen. 2013a. Towards a Player Age Model. In *Ninth Artificial Intelligence and Interactive Digital Entertainment Conference*.

54. Shoshannah Tekofsky, Jaap Van Den Herik, Pieter Spronck, and Aske Plaat. 2013b. Psyops: Personality assessment through gaming behavior. In *Proceedings of the Foundations of Digital Games Conference*. 12–65.

55. Christian Thurau, Kristian Kersting, and Christian Bauckhage. 2009. Convex non-negative matrix factorization in the wild. In *Data Mining, 2009. ICDM'09. Ninth IEEE International Conference on*. IEEE, 523–532.

56. Sarah Vieweg and Adam Hodges. 2016. Surveillance & modesty on social media: How Qataris navigate modernity and maintain tradition. In *Proceedings of the 19th ACM Conference on Computer-Supported Cooperative Work & Social Computing*. ACM, 527–538.

57. Nick Yee. 2006. Motivations for play in online games. *CyberPsychology & behavior* 9, 6 (2006), 772–775.

58. Nick Yee and Jeremy Bailenson. 2007. The Proteus effect: The effect of transformed self-representation on behavior. *Human communication research* 33, 3 (2007), 271–290.

59. Nick Yee, Nicolas Ducheneaut, Les Nelson, and Peter Likarish. 2011. Introverted Elves & Conscientious Gnomes : The Expression of Personality in World of Warcraft. *In Proceedings of the 2011 Annual Conference on Human Factors in Computing Systems* (2011), 753–762.

60. Nick Yee, Nicolas Ducheneaut, Han-Tai Shiao, and Les Nelson. 2012. Through the Azerothian looking glass: Mapping in-game preferences to real world demographics. In *Proceedings of the SIGCHI Conference on Human Factors in Computing Systems (CHI '12)*. 2811–2814.

Establishing Digital Creativity Support in Non-Creative Work Environments

Neil Maiden, Konstantinos Zachos, James Lockerbie
City, University of London
Northampton Square, London
EC1V 0HB, UK
kzachos@soi.city.ac.uk

Kasia Camargo, Shaun Hoddy
CNH Industrial, Cranes Farm Road
Basildon SS14 3AD, UK
kasia.camargo@cnhind.com

ABSTRACT
This paper reports the results of research that sought the long-term uptake of digital support for human creativity to improve health-and-safety in 3 manufacturing plants over an 18-month period. The systematic risk detection and resolution processes of each plant were extended with digital support for employees to think creatively about resolutions to encountered health-and-safety risks. The different uses, successful and unsuccessful, revealed which digitized creativity techniques were effective, different enablers for and barriers to the uptake of the digital creativity support in complex work places, and the importance of management support for aligning work practices and digital capabilities to support creative thinking.

Author Keywords
Creativity; health-and-safety; risk management; mobile

ACM Classification Keywords
D.5.2 [User Interfaces]: User-centered design, voice I/O

INTRODUCTION
Case studies that report the long-term uptake of digital creativity support in places of work, with both positive and negative outcomes, are scarce. Although advances in the use of digital support for human creative activities in disciplines recognized as creative, such as music, and film and television [1] have been made, most empirical validations of this support are restricted to smaller-scale experiments and studies [20], with only a few available exceptions available [19, 25]. Moreover, in spite of the considerable potential of digital creativity support to improve work not always framed as creative – work such as care of older people with dementia [25] – few support tools or evaluations have been reported.

One probable reason for the scarcity is the scale of the challenge facing organisations that seek to adopt digital creativity support in the daily work of employees. Not only must the support be usable and effective [8], but also at least some of the work must be reframed as creative. Previous research reveals that successful creative thinking often requires managed changes to practices and press (e.g. [10]) as well as climate (e.g. [4, 14]). Another probable reason for this scarcity is the duration of the studies that are needed to investigate the effects of changes on work – studies that require continuous access to work environments over a long period. In this paper, and to fill the gap, we report the deployment and evaluation of new digital support for human creative thinking during work in 1 organisation in 1 domain over 18 months – the production lines for the manufacture of large vehicles – in 3 different manufacturing plants.

There has been little reported support for creative thinking on production lines. The few available reports describe the use of tried-and-tested techniques such as brainstorming, for example in BMW to improve health awareness [13] and Toyota to engage employees to improve its work environments [24]. No digital support has been reported. Therefore, this paper reports our first longitudinal deployment and uptake of new digital creativity support on the production lines of 3 manufacturing plants of 1 global organisation – CNH Industrial – over an 18-month period. The new digital support was designed to support employees to think more creatively during the resolution of health-and-safety risks encountered on production lines. Increasing the health and safety of people remains an aim of many organisations, in order to avoid workplace injuries and deaths [5, 18]. The next sections describe the health-and-safety risk problem, the digital creativity support and the design science approach adopted. The paper then reports both successful and unsuccessful deployments of the support in the 3 CNH Industrial plants. The paper ends with an analysis of the results to answer 3 research questions, and outlines emerging challenges to deliver digital creativity support for daily use in workplaces.

DIGITAL CREATIVITY SUPPORT FOR CNH INDUSTRIAL
CNH Industrial is a global organisation that manufactures agricultural and construction equipment, commercial vehicles, buses and special-purpose transport. Four of its business brands are *Case IH and New Holland Agriculture*, which manufactures tractors and agricultural machines in the United Kingdom, and *Astra* and *Iveco*, which manufacture commercial vans and civil protection vehicles in Italy.

C&C 2017, June 27–30, 2017, Singapore.
© 2017 ACM ISBN 978-1-4503-4403-6/17/06...$15.00.
DOI: http://dx.doi.org/10.1145/3059454.3059460

In spite of the different products and manufacturing processes in these plants, CNH Industrial implemented an established and common health-and-safety process across them, both to minimise the potential dangers of this manufacturing to employees, and to facilitate the sharing of good practices. The process sought to engage all employees in the systematic detection, reporting and resolution of risks. It used paper forms that captured then guided structured thinking with techniques such as the *5 Ws* to discover the underlying causes of each risk, *Ishikawa Diagrams* (e.g. [11]) to investigate and categorize these causes, and reused tried-and-tested solutions to resolve risks. Different plants implemented different versions of the process – variations that, for example, required different levels of causal risk analysis and forms of exploration of different resolution spaces.

However, some plants have identified that this process, although fit for purpose, was slow to generate risk resolutions, and often resulted in the same types of resolution being recommended for different types of risk, most of the time in the form of short and incomplete descriptions. Reasons for this that were reported included a lack of sufficient engagement by plant employees in the risk resolution process, too much focus on exploring the causes of the risk, and insufficient support for recording complete creative risk resolutions. Therefore, new digital support was co-developed with CNH Industrial to increase both employee engagement with the process and creative thinking about resolutions to health-and-safety risks encountered on its production lines. The support was co-developed to support little-c creativity – everyday activities in which the non-expert may participate each day [12], to generate novel and useful risk resolutions.

A DESIGN SCIENCE APPROACH

To develop and evaluate this new digital creativity support, the project adopted a design science approach [22]. Design science is an iterative method that seeks to design an artifact to improve a real-world problem in context, and to answer questions about the artifact in this context using a rationale cycle of problem investigation, research design, design validation, research execution and results evaluation [22]. Our real-world problem was the health-and-safety risk management on production lines in CNH Industrial manufacturing plants, and the research artifact was a new digital creativity support application. A pilot plant was selected for the first deployment of the digital creativity support, before rolling out the support to other plants.

The pilot plant site, and hence first problem in context, was in the *New Holland Agriculture* plant in the United Kingdom, can produce up to 20,000 tractors each year at a rate of 1 every 4 minutes. Whenever an unsafe act or condition was encountered, the employee who discovered it completed a paper form, which employees often kept blank copies of on their person during shifts, in order to facilitate risk recording. The form offered limited space for an employee to write the risk location, description and recommended resolution, as well as to sketch the risk and/or resolution to supplement the text description. Periodically, a member of the health-and-safety team picked up all completed forms from collection points, and used a desktop computer to transfer the text information from the forms to a database, then assigned each incident to a manager or team leader. The assigned manager or leader then investigated and resolved the risk, often based on the employee's original recommendation that was documented on the form, then updated the form with the implemented resolution. Communication of these risk resolution implementations to the employees across the plant was simple – after the successful resolution of a risk, the health-and-safety team updated each form, generated A4 photocopies of it, and placed the photocopies on physical noticeboards across the plant. A detailed description of this process is reported in [26].

The new digital creativity support, called the *Risk Hunting* application, was co-developed with stakeholders at the UK plant to achieve 3 requirements that were specified as part of the design science approach: R1: employees shall engage more in the risk description and resolution process; R2: employees shall document more complete descriptions of risk resolutions, and; R3: employees shall document descriptions of more creative resolutions. The support was then deployed in 3 different problem contexts – at this UK plant, then at 2 plants in Italy. The reported research sought to validate the design of the application, execute its deployment in these 3 plants, and evaluate results from these deployments to answer 3 research questions:

- RQ1 What digitized creativity techniques were effective in the 3 manufacturing plants?
- RQ2 What were the enablers and barriers to use of the digital creativity support in the plants?
- RQ3 To what extent did the digital creativity support need to align with the work practices in the plants?

THE WINTER OF 2014: DEVELOPED FIRST VERSION OF THE *RISK HUNTING* APPLICATION

The first version of the *Risk Hunting* application was a web-based app optimized to run on Samsung tablet devices for use by employees on the pilot site's production lines. It is described in detail in [26]. Due to a critical time constraint imposed by work on the site's production lines, employees had just 5 minutes to record and resolve a detected risk, so the application was designed for use within this time constraint. When a new risk was detected, the employee who detected it entered information to describe the risk, its location, type and effect using unstructured natural language and simple pull-down menus. The design was consistent with the plant version of the process, which did not require the employee to analyze all risk causes before documenting the risk and making resolution recommendations. The application then presented the employee with 3 quick-to-use creativity techniques to generate new ideas with:

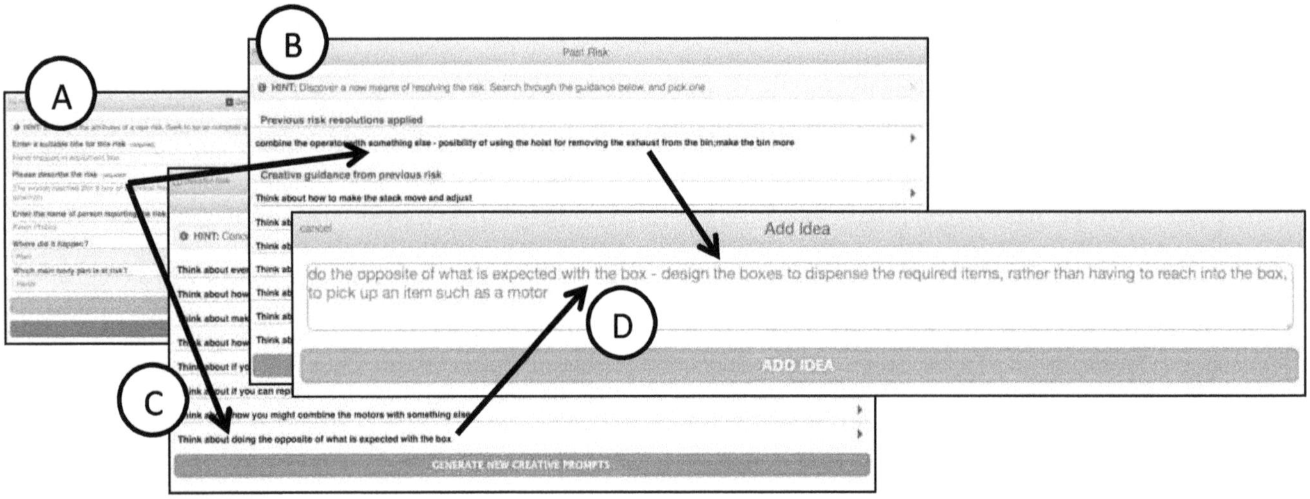

Figure 1. Demonstration of the *Risk Hunting* application, showing description of a new risk, automatically-generated support from the *Ideas from new risk* and *Ideas from previous risk* techniques, and use of creative clue stem texts to generate a new idea

1. ***Ideas from new risk***: short lists of creative clues, generated automatically from 85 patterns of creative manufacturing outcomes and instantiated with information extracted from the entered description of the new risk;
2. ***Ideas from previous risks***: descriptions of sets of 5 previous successful risk resolutions, retrieved each time from a repository of over 9000 previous risk resolutions;
3. ***Ideas from superheroes***: descriptions of up to 26 superheroes and their powers, retrieved from a digital library.

To demonstrate the support provided by these techniques, consider a risk in which a *worker traps his hand inside a box of items* described with the application in Figure 1(A). From this description, the application automatically generates a short list of creative clues such as *think about doing the opposite of what is expected with the box* (see Figure 1(B)), which might lead the employee to create ideas from the new risk, such as a box that dispenses items. The application also retrieves 5 previous risk resolutions, such as when an *operator had trapped his hand in a bin of exhaust pipes*, to generate reusable creative clues such as *using a hoist to collect items*, from which the employee might create other new ideas, as demonstrated in Figure 1(C). At any step in the interaction, the user can document new ideas directly into the application using textboxes (see Figure 1(d)). To encourage more effective creative thinking, these textboxes were prefilled with text automatically generated from the selected creative clue with the *Ideas from new risk* and *Ideas from previous risks* techniques, which the employee could then extend, edit or overwrite. Figure 1(D) shows one example of this text – *Do the opposite of what is expected* – which the employee has extended with the new resolution idea – to design the boxes to dispense items to workers. At the end of the interaction, after ideas have been generated, the employee can compose a new risk resolution from these ideas, and share it digitally with other employees and the health-and-safety advisors.

To describe how the *Risk Hunting* application implemented this creativity support, consider the *Ideas from new risk technique* that generated information about creative clues specific to the current risk, shown in Figure 1(B). A software service automatically retrieved patterns of different creative manufacturing outcomes from a library using a randomized search algorithm, then instantiated each retrieved pattern with partial information about the new risk retrieved using a second randomized search algorithm that shallow-parsed the risk description to extract names of objects and actions using technologies such as WordNet [16]. The library was populated with 85 patterns of outcomes considered to be novel and useful in manufacturing by the researchers, and extracted from a larger library of creative outcome patterns. Each pattern was re-written as a natural language creative clue, as demonstrated in Figure 1(B). Some of the patterns were applied to generate creative clues based on mechanical or human objects, for example *think about dividing the [object] up*, and others to generate clues based on physical actions, for example *think about how to introduce feedback into the [action]*. Each invocation of the service returned 8 creative clues that instantiated the different patterns, and the *Risk Hunting* application displayed lists of these creative clues as shown in Figure 1(B).

The co-development of this first version of the application was informed by paper-based prototyping of 2 of the creativity techniques in a training session. Eighteen plant employees worked in teams with the *Ideas from new risk* and *Ideas from superheroes* techniques to generate new resolutions to a known risk using the new support. All used the techniques with limited training in a short period of time, and most generated risk resolutions that were noticeably different to the original resolution applied. Subsequent formative evaluations of the application revealed that plant employees were able, with minimum training, to use it to document risks and generate and document resolutions to these risks. Several changes to the application were made before final deployment, including redesign of the final generated risk resolutions to resemble the paper forms.

THE SPRING OF 2015: DEPLOYMENT IN FIRST PLANT

This first version of the *Risk Hunting* application was made available for employee use in the UK plant over 66 consecutive working days. A potential user of the application was any employee who detected a new health-and-safety risk. Before the start of the deployment, the researchers trained 2 health-and-safety advisors and 7 health-and-safety captains who were responsible for health-and-safety on the plant's 7 production lines to use the application and the plant's Samsung Galaxy tablets that the application ran on. A limited budget at the plant meant that only 3 tablets were made available for application training and use, so some employees also used the application on workplace desktop computers. The captains and advisors provided the same training to employees in different roles on their production lines – mainly team leaders, assembly operators, repair operators and electricians. Although incentivized to use the application to record and to resolve risks, all of the employees were free to also use the paper forms. No other changes to work practices in the plant were made to accommodate use of the application. All employees had email and telephone access to the research team for help and support throughout the deployment. Researchers visited the plant twice during the deployment, to collect qualitative feedback about the use of application from captains available during the visit, and facilitated a final 35-minute focus group with 4 captains and 1 advisor after the end of the deployment period. The *Risk Hunting* application was used to document resolutions to 115 discovered risks, and the analysis of these resolutions reported at length in [15] revealed them to be more novel and useful than resolutions generated without the application. This paper now reports who used the application, durations of application use, and what barriers to successful use were encountered

The documented authors of the risk resolutions revealed that 33 different individuals rather than groups of employees resolved most risks. This result was explained by 2 of the health-and-safety captains, who reported that this was primarily because of work constraints imposed by the production line. The application needed "*release from the production line to use it, otherwise it had to be done in overtime*". Individual employees in different roles used the application to different degrees – the 7 health-and-safety captains and 2 advisors generated 68 of the 115 (59.1%) risk resolutions. Another 16 risk resolutions came from 1 assembly operator in training to become a health-and-safety captain. In contrast, 18 other employees documented only 1 risk resolution each. The captains reported one major reason for this pattern of use – the limited access that other employees had to the tablet devices, compared with the near limitless blank paper forms carried by employees that they would complete immediately: "*I would think that this is down to availability of the tablets, only two on site*". Moreover, the tablets were at some times in secure storage, at other times unusable due to the lack of tablet chargers. Most other employees also received less training, and therefore had less practice with the application, whereas the captains had time "*to be able to play with the app*". Nonetheless, in spite of these reported barriers to use, one of the health-and-safety advisors claimed: "*noticing an increase in unsafe acts reporting*" during the deployment period, with "*stronger ownership and a focused world class manufacturing approach to problem solving*" – feedback that the team agreed was evidence of an increase in employee engagement and creative thinking about the resolution of risks.

Employees in the plant also recorded risks on paper forms during the deployment period – 106 risks in total. Six of the health-and-safety captains recorded risks with both the application and the paper forms, and 13 employees only recorded risks on paper forms, again down to the absence of sufficient numbers of charged tablets in the plant that could be accessed quickly. One captain reported that employees just "*…need to be able to pick it up and use it*". The limited number of available tablets meant that this result was not a surprise to the plant's health-and-safety team.

Log data recorded about employee use of the application revealed that the average time from starting to describe a new risk to completing the risk resolution was 4m46s, and employees completed 80 of the 115 (69.6%) risk resolutions within the 5-minute constraint imposed by the production lines. Analysis of the times per calendar week revealed that the average time to complete risk resolutions fell from 12m30s in the first week to just 1m30s in the last, indicating a possible learning curve to use the application for the employees.

Although 19 (16.6%) of the risk resolutions took more than 8 minutes to complete, these resolutions also tended to contain more content. A Spearman Rank Correlation analysis of all 115 risk resolutions revealed that employees used more time to complete risk resolutions with more words, $r=.41$, $p<0.0001$. One conclusion drawn from this result was that increasing the engagement and creative thinking of employees might require more than 5 minutes on the production lines. Results from the final focus group provided corroborating evidence that employees on the production lines often lacked time to use the application as planned.

In spite of some of the risk resolutions not being completed within the required time, the health-and-safety team believed that the adoption of the application led to more productive risk management. One reported: "*the tablets allowed for time saving, using the wireless connection on the spot instead of submitting paper forms, waiting for the reporting boxes to be opened, and entered on the online system*". The health-and-safety team identified a trade-off between more upstream work for production line employees to use the *Ideas from new risk* and *Ideas from previous risks* techniques, work which also increased employee engagement in plant's health-and-safety, and less downstream work in the health-and-safety process for advisors. In contrast, the little-used *Ideas from superheroes* technique was perceived to be "*a bit around the houses*", but potentially useful for training, to encourage people to think "*out of the box*" about health-and-safety.

To conclude, results from the first deployment revealed that the *Risk Hunting* application was used more by health-and-safety captains than other employees, and the insufficient numbers of charged tablets and lack of time to become familiar with the application were the primary reasons reported for not using the application. The employees documented most risk descriptions and resolutions in less than the required 5 minutes, but more detailed risk resolutions needed more time to document.

At the end of the deployment period, the plant's health-and-safety captains made 4 recommendations to increase use of the application across the plant:

A. Run the application on digital touchscreens as well as tablets, to increase employee confidence with it;
B. Run the application on tablets on each of the plant's 30 production groups, to increase access to it;
C. Redesign work practices on the production lines to facilitate application use, so that team leaders worked off line with the application with each employee on the line to describe then resolve the detected risk;
D. Redesign the application's interface so that it resembled the paper form more closely, and simplified the uptake of the application by more employees.

AUTUMN 2015 TO SUMMER 2016: ADAPTING FOR THE UK PLANT

Use of the *Risk Hunting* application continued in the plant until November 2015. The application was then withdrawn, and a new version was developed that implemented some of the recommendations (A-D) from the first deployment. Digital touchscreens were installed at key locations in the plant, in order to provide employees with faster access to the application (A). Use of one of these touchscreens is depicted in Figure 2. The application was re-implemented to be usable on the touchscreens and desktop computers situated on the production lines and in staff offices (A). Application interactions were simplified to optimize creativity technique use (D). However, it was not possible to change the web application's interface to resemble the paper forms (D), and the plant decided to invest financially in the new digital touchscreens rather than more tablets (B). The little-used technique *Ideas from superheroes* was removed.

Controversially, the health-and-safety team also decided to remove the *Ideas from new risk* technique from the application, although employees had used this technique successfully to generate at least 51 of the 115 risk resolutions in the first deployment period. Instead, the team sought to encourage employees to work with reusable resolutions generated with the *Ideas from previous risks* technique, for 2 reasons. Not only did the team want to encourage employees to re-use resolutions to support sharing of good resolution practices between employees, but also it believed – incorrectly – that reducing the number of application features would reduce the operating costs of the application to the plant. As a consequence, this unanticipated decision by the team provided an unplanned opportunity for the researchers to investigate the effectiveness of alternative versions of the *Risk Hunting* application that were implemented with different, digitized creativity techniques.

Figure 2. Use of the Risk Hunting application on a touchscreen installed in the UK plant

Furthermore, the plant decided against changing work practices on the production lines, to allow team leaders to use the application alongside each line (C). Instead, individual employees were encouraged to use the application off as well as on the production lines – a change which provided them, when needed, with more than 5 minutes to complete risk resolutions. However at the start of the period, a reduction in the number of employees working in the plant, due to a change in the economic climate, was perceived to be a potential threat to this solution, as it reduced opportunities for the health-and-safety captains and team leaders, who were the employees most skilled with the *Risk Hunting* application, to step off the lines and use the application.

Nonetheless, the new and more simplified version of the *Risk Hunting* application was released for employee use in the UK plant over 107 consecutive working days from February to September 2016. As during the first deployment, potential users of the application were all employees who detected a health-and-safety risk. The health-and-safety captains and advisors were again available to provide training and guidance to employees to use the application, and the employees remained free to use the paper forms. Researchers visited the plant twice during the period, to interview available health-and-safety advisors and captains.

Plant employees used the *Risk Hunting* application to document risk descriptions and resolutions throughout the 107 working days. At the end of the period, the plant manager reported that he was satisfied with both the application and its use by employees. He estimated that, by the end of the period, use of the application accounted for over half of all health-and-safety risks documented in the plant. The health-and-safety team also reported that, by the end of the period, most application use took place on touchscreens and desktop computers rather than tablets.

The data from the application log, summarized in Table 1, revealed a total of 74 different users, although some resolutions were assigned to teams such as the *Cab drop team* rather than individuals, making the precise final number of users difficult to compute. However, the result revealed that over twice as many employees used the *Risk Hunting* application, compared with the first deployment period.

Number of different employees using the application	74
Number of documented risk resolutions	370
Mean word length of risk descriptions	7.8
Mean word length of risk resolutions	11.2
Average time to document risk description/resolution	6m44s

Table 1. Summarized log data for the second deployment period from the *Risk Hunting* application

Analysis of the application log data revealed that employees from 2 of the plant's 7 production lines – *Pedestal Line* and *RTC Garage* – were the most frequent users of the application. Two reasons for this were reported. The health-and-safety captains who worked on these lines championed use of the application on these lines more than did the captains on other lines, and the health-and-safety team reported that this championing role was an important contributor to application uptake. Furthermore, the *RTC Garage* line existed to fix faults that were generated on the other lines, and employees who worked on it actively sought to discover faults including health-and-safety risks. This use of the application appeared to align more effectively with the work environment of the employees on this particular line.

The plant employees documented 370 new risk descriptions and resolutions with the application in the deployment period. Compared to the first period [15], however, the mean numbers of words reported in Table 1 to describe each risk (7.8 to 15.2) and resolution (11.2 to 29.8) were both lower, the mean time to describe a risk and resolution was higher (6m44s to 4m46s), and the percentage (52.2%) of risk resolutions completed within the 5-minute constraint was lower. Indeed, the distribution of the total numbers of risks resolved within each one-minute period, depicted graphically in Figure 3, revealed that many risks took more than 10 minutes to resolve, and 8 required more than 30 minutes. The health-and-safety advisors offered 2 possible explanations for these increased resolution times. The first was the emergence of collaborative working. The advisors observed that up to 3 health-and-safety captains at a time would collaborate to use the application on the touchscreens, and this collaborative work, although a positive if unplanned outcome of application use, took longer than individual work. The second offered explanation was that the employees in the *RTC Garage*, who often used the application on desktop computers in their staff offices, were sometimes interrupted by e-mails or fault reports – interrupts that required immediate attention. Therefore the average start-to-end time needed to complete risk resolutions was longer.

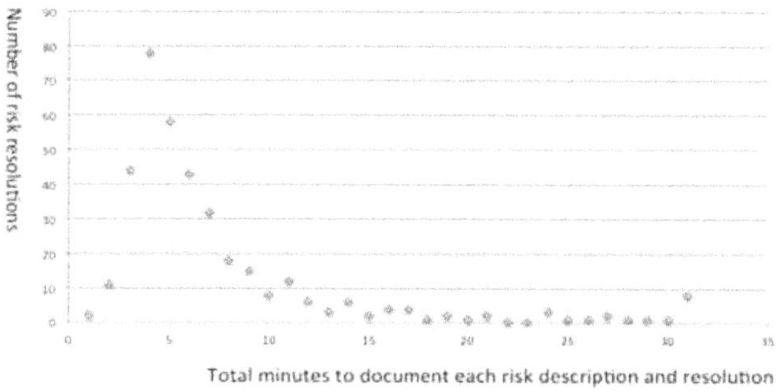

Figure 3. Distribution of total numbers of risk resolved within each one-minute period

In spite of this result, the health-and-safety team claimed an overall effort saving from application use for the plant, similar to the claim reported for the first deployment. To manage the paper forms, one member of the team spent up to 2 hours per day collecting them from locations across the 40-hectare site and typing the reported risk descriptions and resolutions into the digital system. Application use removed this collection effort, and the average time that employees spent per day (6m44s at on an average of 3.46 risk resolutions) to document half of the risks uncovered daily in the plant was lower, resulting in an effort saving for the plant.

Analysis of the log data that described documenting and resolving each of the 370 risk resolutions with the application (see Table 2) revealed that only 135 (36.5%) of the risk resolutions were generated using the *Ideas from previous risks* technique with creative clues. By inference, therefore, most risk resolutions were not generated and documented with the application as designed. Furthermore, most of the designed-for uses of the application – 121 – took place in the last 2 months of the period, indicating that employees might have needed time and experience with the application to use its capabilities effectively.

Log data patterns of *Risk Hunting* application use	Number of risk resolutions
Ideas generated after invoking *Ideas from previous risk* technique and using the creative clues	135
Ideas generated after invoking *Ideas from previous risk* technique but without using the creative clues	91
Ideas generated after invoking *Ideas from previous risk* technique both with and without using the creative clues	4
Ideas generated without invoking *Ideas from previous risk* technique	134
Risks recorded without any resolution ideas	6

Table 2. Log data patterns of *Risk Hunting* application use during the second deployment period

Another 134 of the 370 (35.9%) risk resolutions were generated and documented when the application was used only as a digital version of the paper forms, without invoking the *Ideas from previous risks* technique. Of these 134, 102 were generated earlier in the period in April and May 2016, when the employees were less familiar with the application and its capabilities. Further experimental analyses with the entered risk descriptions revealed that many were described with too few words for the computational service to retrieve resolutions that might have been relevant to the risks. By comparison, risk descriptions recorded in the first deployment were described with on average almost twice as many words, and this additional content was sufficient for the service to retrieve relevant previous risk resolutions.

A content analysis of the 370 risk resolutions revealed that these resolutions were compositions of 527 discrete ideas that employees generated with the application. Of these 527 ideas, 330 (62.6%) were identical to at least one other idea documented in the period, and a total of 57 of these different ideas were reused at least once. Examples were *Put a check in place*, which was documented in 18 different risk resolutions, the similar idea *Put check in place*, which was in 8 resolutions, and the more substantial idea *Refresh operators in correct methods to connect pipes to avoid damage* in 9 resolutions. Therefore, although the log data revealed that most risks were not resolved as the application was designed using all capabilities developed to support use of the *Ideas with previous risks* technique, the content analysis provided evidence that employees still reused ideas from previous risk resolutions to resolve risks that they encountered.

By the end of the second deployment period, the changes in the number of employees working on production lines was perceived to have impacted on application use. One health-and-safety advisor stated that this change had, as predicted, reduced opportunities for the health-and-safety captains and team leaders – the employees most skilled with the application – to step off the lines to use it. This claim was corroborated with data from the application log, which revealed that a lower percentage of risks were resolved by employees in these roles during the second deployment period, compared with the first.

To conclude, the revised version of the *Risk Hunting* application was used throughout the deployment. The increased time needed by employees to generate and document risk resolutions with the application was offset by substantial reductions in the effort needed to collect paper forms. However, the risk resolutions were described with fewer words than in the first period, and only 36.5% were generated using the digitized creativity support as designed. The results revealed several new enablers to application use – increased access using the digital touchscreens and desktop computers, champions who encouraged use of the application on their production lines, and alignment the application use with more diagnostic work environment on one line. Use of the touchscreens also appeared to encourage collaborative creative working to resolve risks.

However, the deployment also revealed new barriers to use. The application was not designed to support collaborative creative work, which posed new challenges for the research team [9]. Use of it off the production lines meant that employees were sometimes interrupted during idea generation. Employees appeared to use the application's digital creativity support more at the end than the beginning of the period, indicating that time and practices was needed to use this support effectively. The absence of the *Ideas from new risk* technique and increased resolution reuse with the *Ideas from previous risks* technique was associated with shorter and more repetitive resolutions to health-and-safety risks. Results indicated that the version of the application with fewer digitalized creativity techniques was less effective than the one with more techniques. Finally, changes in the plant's work practices between the 2 deployments, which led to fewer employees able to work off the production lines, became a possible new barrier to application use. Employees who were most skilled with the application were less able to step off the lines to use it, and this reduction in skilled use is one possible explanation for the shorter risk descriptions and alternative uses of the application, which in turn might have occurred because the shorter risk descriptions resulted in less accurate retrieval of previous resolutions than in the first period.

After the end of the deployment, another revised version of the *Risk Hunting* application was co-developed with CNH Industrial – one that supported both the *Ideas from previous risks* and *Ideas from new risk* techniques. However, no new features were introduced to support the observed collaborative working [9], in part because support for collaborative working was beyond the project scope. This version was deployed in the plant with the same work practices as the second deployment period, on touchscreens and desktop computers in October 2016, and data is again being collected about its use.

PROPOSED DEPLOYMENT IN FIRST ITALIAN PLANT

Based on the UK plant deployments, CNH Industrial's central health-and-safety team in Torino sought to roll out the *Risk Hunting* application at other manufacturing plants, and 2 in Italy asked to adopt and trial the application. The first was the *Iveco Astra* plant in northern Italy. It was smaller than the UK plant. It constructed specialized construction and transporter vehicles for use in the military on 2 production lines. To meet the needs of the plant's health-and-safety team, a new Italian-language version of the application, called the *Caccia al Rischio*, was developed. But to use the *Risk Hunting* application's original 3 computational services, which manipulated English syntax and semantics using online thesauri such as WordNet [16], a new solution was needed.

This solution wrapped these 3 computational services in software that translated input Italian-language risk descriptions input from the plant employees into English, and generated English-language risk resolutions and creative clues into Italian for presentation back to plant employees. Not only did this solution enable quick deployment of the new *Caccia al Rischio* application, but also it offered retrieval of risk resolutions documented in multiple language at different European plants, for example from the UK plant, and to facilitate cross-plant knowledge sharing. After experimentation with automatic translation services, the *Caccia al Rischio* application was implemented with Google's automated translation service [7] and 2 databases, as depicted in Figure 4. The first database contained 2000 English-language risk resolutions from the UK plant and the second contained 1450 Italian-language risk resolutions from the *Iveco Astra* plant.

The *Caccia al Rischio* application was demonstrated to and experimented with by the plant manager and health-and-safety team at the plant in the spring of 2016. Although potential benefits from the application were reported, the team also identified one barrier to the uptake of the digital creativity support in the *Iveco Astra* plant – a lack of alignment between the digital support for early creative thinking about new resolutions, and the plant's requirement to complete a causal analysis of each risk before selecting and re-using existing risk resolutions.

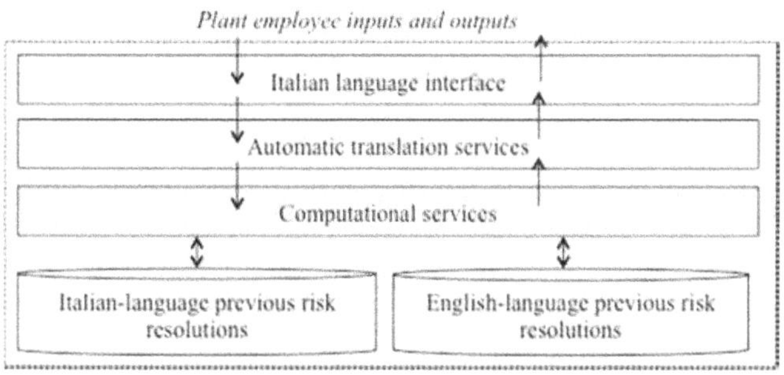

Figure 4. The extended architecture of the *Caccia al Rischio*

Therefore, the plant made a decision not to trial the *Caccia al Rischio* application. The misalignment between the problem-focus of the plant's existing risk analysis process and more solution-focused creativity techniques of the application could not be fixed. Lessons drawn from this rejection informed the deployment of the application to the second Italian plant.

PROPOSED DEPLOYMENT IN SECOND ITALIAN PLANT

The *IVECO* plant in northern Italy was the largest and most automated of the 3 plants. It constructed commercial vehicles. The Italian-language *Caccia al Rischio* application from the *Iveco Astra* plant was adapted to meet one new need expressed by the new plant, which was to be able to retrieve all risk resolutions from the UK plant's database of 9,000+ resolutions using the *Ideas from previous risk* technique. This extended version of the application was demonstrated to the plant manager and health-and-safety team in the summer of 2016, and a decision was made at that meeting to trial the application for 3 months from September 2016. Therefore, the application was delivered to the health-and-safety team in August 2016 to experiment with and request further changes. During this experimentation, the team identified 3 important barriers to overcome before release to employees on the plant's production lines:

1. The application generated creative clues that the health-and-safety team feared the employees would consider irrelevant and/or frivolous, and reject the application;
2. Mistranslation of English-language creative clues into Italian by the Google Translate service, for example (in English) *Place the object in a vacuum cleaner*, rather than ... *in a vacuum*. The team believed that presentation of these clues would also lead to application rejection by the plant employees, because their confidence in it would be undermined by bugs in the software;
3. The application was designed to retrieve risk resolutions across risk categories such as *unsafe acts* and *near misses*. This decision had been made originally with the UK plant to guide creative thinking about new risks with as much retrieved knowledge as possible. However, the plant used these risk categorisations as strict constraints, and whereas the UK plant supported cross-category re-use for creative thinking, the Italian plant perceived it to be a violation of the risk management process.

In response, the *Caccia al Rischio* application was modified further, in order to increase its chances of acceptance by the plant's employees. The set of creative clues generated with the *Ideas for new risk* technique was reduced by removing clues considered to be irrelevant and frivolous. Use of the translation services was modified to remove incorrect translations. And the computational service that underpinned the *Ideas from previous risk* technique was modified to restrict it to retrieve only risk resolutions of the same type as the new entered risk.

However, during a second round of experimentation at the plant, this modified support was still deemed too challenging for employees on the plant's production lines to use, and hence too likely to be rejected by them. Therefore, through the autumn of 2016, the researchers and plant's team collaborated again to redesign the application, in order to align it more closely with the plant's health-and-safety process. New features currently emerging from this redesign include new interactive support for a first-cut causal analysis of the risk when it is described with the application, use of risk cause descriptions entered as a result of this analysis to refine creative search underpinning the *Ideas from previous risks* technique, and the development of a new service that will implement the plant's risk resolution guidelines alongside existing computational services. This new version of the *Caccia al Rischio* application is due to be trialled in the second quarter of 2017, and the authors also look forward to reporting results in the future.

ANSWERING THE RESEARCH QUESTIONS

This paper reports 3 trial deployments of different versions of the *Risk Hunting* application in 3 CNH Industrial manufacturing plants. During the successful deployment reported here and in [15], employees from CNH Industrial used the application on plant production lines for a total of over 9 months to think creatively to resolve almost 500 health-and-safety risks. The successful deployment revealed both enablers and barriers to use of the digitized creativity support, while the 2 unsuccessful ones revealed the importance of aligning the support and health-and-safety environments in the plants. Results from the deployments enabled us to answer the 3 research questions about the digital creativity support. Each is answered in turn.

To answer RQ1, and determine which digitized creativity techniques were effective in the plants, employees used both the *Ideas from new risk* and *Ideas from previous risk* techniques to generate most risk resolutions, although longer times than planned for were needed to document more complete risk resolutions with both techniques. In contrast, the *Ideas from superheroes* technique was deemed to be too time-consuming to use on production lines.

To answer RQ2, 4 deployments uncovered enablers and barriers to the effective use of the digital creativity support. The enablers included use of digital touchpoints that users were familiar with, immediate access to these touchpoints without the need to set up or charge them, senior employees who championed support use, and digital creativity support that delivered productivity as well as creativity benefits. Results from the successful deployment revealed a trade-off between more upstream work for employees on lines to use the digital creativity support, and less downstream work for the health-and-safety advisors. The digital creativity support was also used more frequently on one production line that sought to diagnose faults, i.e. when the work environment and creativity support were more aligned. Barriers to the effective use of the digital creativity support included use of the support on technologies unfamiliar to employees, insufficient time for employees to learn how to use it to its maximum effect, and collaborative creativity using support not designed for it. An earlier deployment revealed that employees needed more time than was originally made available to create more complete risk resolutions, so more flexible work procedures were implemented in the follow-on deployment. However, this deployment revealed that, if there were fewer employees available to undertake work tasks, more experienced employees who were also the most effective users of the digital creativity support, were less available to find time to use the support.

To answer RQ3, the 2 unsuccessful deployments in the Italian plants revealed the need for both management support and alignment between digital support and work processes for regular effective creative thinking to take place. Unlike at the UK plant, the management at the 2 Italian plants had not requested the application to document more novel risk resolutions through creative thinking in the plant. Moreover, both plants rejected the digital support because of relatively small misalignments between it and the environment, perceptions that the support rendered the serious work frivolous and/or imprecise, and an unwillingness by the management at the plants to adapt existing structures to exploit support features for creative thinking. Results indicated that future digital creativity applications for use in such work environments need to support effective idea generation and learning in employees who can only commit limited cognitive resources and time to optional creative tasks. Therefore, management support and aligning the creativity support and work environment to reduce barriers, no matter how small, appeared to be key to future take-up.

Of course, the results were generated using a design science approach and are open to many potential threats to validity, and some of these threats are highlighted here. Threats to internal validity of the results arose from other influences that might have affected how the independent variable – the use of the *Risk Hunting* application – related to causality [21]. Other possible influences included alternative forms of creativity support delivered in the plant and employee motivations to use the *Risk Hunting* application. To mitigate these threats, the UK plant provided neither alternative creativity support to its employees, nor bonuses for reporting risks after the start of the reported deployment. Potential threats to the external validity of the results were conditions that limited our ability to generalize these results, and there were many such threats. For example, the paper reports the successful deployment of the *Risk Hunting* application to less than 100 employees in 1 plant, so care needs to be taken even to extrapolate the results to other manufacturing domains. However, given the absence of published digital creativity research that has been applied to non-creative industries such as manufacturing, the results offer both challenges to overcome and hypotheses for subsequent research to investigate.

RELATED RESEARCH

Most related research has been targeted at domains in which people are trained to have creative skills, for example the performing arts, music, and film and television [1], and this support has been developed using different types of algorithm from, for example computational linguistics [17] and case-based reasoning to support innovation [6]. Beyond the creative industries, interactive creativity support is limited. Some has been developed to support creative thinking in science and engineering, for example in the forms of new tabletop visualizations to support biological discoveries [23] and social media to support collaborative creativity in education [3]. Businesses often seek to support the creativity of their employees, but most of this support has been delivered as methods [10] rather than interactive software. The limited creativity support for healthcare work also relies on techniques to encourage creative problem solving by nursing administrators [2].

DISCUSSION AND FUTURE WORK

Several themes emerged from this research. The co-design process was only partially effective. The Italian plants did not share the UK plants' requirement for more creative risk resolutions, and language differences and the distance between the research team and the Italian plants rendered regular co-design work difficult. In the UK, releasing employees from shift work for co-design activities and changes in management roles impacted on commitment to the co-design process. And management support for uptake of creativity techniques in workplaces through co-design processes appeared to be critical for success.

Diverse socio-technical and political factors including sufficient management support, human champions for creativity support and access to the support in the workplace [9] influenced the uptake of the digital creativity support. Other workplace changes that health-and-safety captains sought to exploit the application more effectively were not adapted in the UK plant, and social elements such as reward payments were also factors that appeared to influence use of the digital support and its alignment with the work environment. Indeed, the barriers identified in the deployments revealed that uptake of digital creativity support in work environments where creative thinking is not a norm may be sensitive to even simple misalignments between the support and the environment.

ACKNOWLEDGEMENTS

The research reported in this paper was supported in part by the EU-funded FP7 COLLAGE project 318536.

REFERENCES

1. Alaoui S.F., Schlphorst T., Cuykendall S., Carlson K., Studd K. & Bradley K., 2015, 'Strategies for Embodied Design: The Value and Challenges of Observing Movement', Proc. 10th ACM Conf. Creativity and Cognition, ACM Press, 121-130.
2. Arbesman M. & Puccio G., 2001. Enhanced Quality Through Creative Problem Solving. Journal of Nursing Administration 31(4), 176 -178.
3. Aragon C.R., Poon S.S. & Aragon A. M-H. D., 2009, 'A Tale of Two Online Communities: Fostering Collaboration and Creativity in Scientists and Children', Proc. 7th ACM Conf. on Creativity and Cognition, ACM Press, 9-18.
4. Doorley S. & Witthoft S., 2012, 'Make Space', Wiley, Hoboken, New Jersey
5. Eurostat, 2014, available at: appsso.eurostat.ec.europa.eu.
6. Goel A.K. & Craw S., 2006, 'Design, Innovation and Case-Based Reasoning', Knowledge Engineering Review, 20(3), 271–276.
7. Google 2017, 'Google Cloud Translation API Documentation', accessed https://cloud.google.com/translate/docs/, 03/01/2017.
8. Greene S.L., 2002, 'Characteristics of Applications that Support Creativity', Communications of ACM, 45(10), 100-104.
9. Grudin J., 1994, 'Groupware and Social Dynamics: Eight Challenges for Developers', Communications of ACM, 37(1), 92-105.
10. Isaksen, S.G. Brian, K. Dorval, Treffinger, D.J. 2011, Creative Approaches to Problem Solving: A Framework for Innovation and Change. Sage Publications, Inc; Third Edition.
11. Ishikawa K., 1976, 'Guide to Quality Control', Asian Productivity Organization.
12. Kaufman, J. C., and Beghetto, R. A., 2009, 'Beyond big and little: The four c-model of creativity', Review of General Psychology 13, 1.
13. Loch C.H., Sting F.J. & Bauer N., 2010, 'How BMW is Defusing the Demographic Time Bomb', Havard Business Review 88(3), 99-102.
14. McCoz J.M. & Evans G.W., 2002, 'The Potential Role of the Physical Environment in Fostering Creativity', Creativity Research Journal 14(3/4), 409–426
15. Maiden N., Zachos K., Lockerbie J., Levis S., Camargo K., Allemandi G. & Hoddy S,, 2017, 'Evaluating Digital Creativity Support To Improve Health-and-Safety in a Manufacturing Plant', accepted for publication in ACM *CHI'2017*.
16. McCarthy D., Koeling R., Weeds J., Carroll J., 2004, 'Using Automatically Acquired Predominant Senses for Word Sense Disambiguation', Proc. ACL 2004 Senseval-3 Workshop Barcelona, Spain.
17. Monfort N., Perez y Perez R., Fox Harrell D., Campana A., 2013, 'Slant: A Blackboard System to Generate Plot, Figuration, and Narrative Discourse Aspects of Stories'. Proc. 3rd International Conference on Computational Creativity, Sydney Australia, June 2013, 168-175.
18. OSHA, 2014, 'All about Occupational Safety and Health Administration', US Department of Labor, accessible from https://www.osha.gov/Publications/all_about_ OSHA.pdf. Accessed 24th December 2016.
19. Rees Lewis D., Harburg E., Gerber E. & Easterday M., 2015, 'Building Support Tools to Connect Novice Designers with Professional Coaches', Proc. 10th ACM Conf. on Creativity and Cognition, ACM Press, 43-54.
20. Siangliulue P., Chan J., Gajos K.V. &Dow S.P., 2015, 'Providing Timely Examples Improves the Quantity and Quality of Generated Ideas', Proc. 10th ACM Conf. on Creativity and Cognition, ACM Press, 83-92.
21. Wohlin C. Runeson P., Host M., Ohlsson M.C., Regnell B. & Wesslen A., 2000, 'Experimentation in Software Engineering: An Introduction', Kluwer Academic Publishers, Boston/Dordrecht/London.
22. Wieringa R., 2014, 'Design Science Methodology for Information Systems and Software Engineering', Springer-Verlag, Berlin-Heidelberg.
23. Wu A., Yim J.B., Caspary E., Mazalek A. Chandrasekharan S. & Nersessian N.J., 2011, 'Kinesthetic Pathways: A Tabletop Visualization to Support Discovery in Systems Biology', Proceedings 8th ACM Conference on Creativity and Cognition, ACM Press, 21-30.
24. Yasuda Y., 1991, '40 Years, 20 million ideas: The Toyota Suggestion System', Productivity Press.
25. Zachos K., Maiden N.A.M., Pitts K., Jones S., Turner I., Rose M., Pudney K. & MacManus J., 2013, 'A Software App to Support Creativity in Dementia Care', Proc. 9th ACM Creativity and Cognition Conference, ACM Press, 124-131.
26. Zachos K., Maiden N., Levis S., Camargo K. & Allemandi G., 2015, 'Creativity Support to Improve Health-and-Safety in Manufacturing Plants: Demonstrating Everyday Creativity', Proc. 10th ACM Conf. on Creativity and Cognition, ACM Press, 225-234

The Creative Proteus Effect: How Self-Similarity, Embodiment, and Priming of Creative Stereotypes with Avatars Influences Creative Ideation

Alwin de Rooij
Tilburg University
Tilburg, The Netherlands
alwinderooij@uvt.nl

Sarah van der Land
Tilburg University
Tilburg, The Netherlands
s.f.vdrland@uvt.nl

Shelly van Erp
Tilburg University
Tilburg, The Netherlands
s.d.a.vanerp@uvt.nl

ABSTRACT
Creative ideation can be enhanced in 3D virtual environments by manipulating the appearance of a user's avatar so that it primes a creative stereotype. However, not much is known about the factors that influence the effectiveness of using avatars to enhance creativity. In this study we investigate experimentally whether the degree to which users identify with their avatar moderates their actual ability to generate creative ideas. The results suggest that a non-creative avatar (office worker stereotype) diminishes creativity, but our creative avatar (artist stereotype) does not augment creativity. The similarity in appearance between the user and its avatar positively moderates, whereas its perceived embodiment with the avatar negatively moderates the ability to generate creative ideas. However, the study also suggests that self-similarity might be an even more effective way to support creative ideation than priming creative stereotypes. Therefore, this study (i) contributes that self-similarity and embodiment moderate the effectiveness of using an avatar to prime creative stereotypes to enhance creative ideation, and (ii) points toward a novel way to enhance creative ideation in virtual environments, by using avatars that look just like yourself.

Author Keywords
Avatars; Creative Stereotype Effect; Creativity Support Tools; Embodiment; Proteus Effect; Self-Similarity.

ACM Classification Keywords
H.5.m. Information interfaces and presentation (e.g., HCI); J.4 Social and behavioral sciences.

INTRODUCTION
Creative ideation, the ability to generate ideas that are original yet effective, plays an essential role in well-being, innovation, and culture [1]. Given that people spend a considerable amount of time in 3D virtual environments, i.e. digital environments that mimic physical spaces, and where people interact via avatars [2], it is of interest to investigate new ways in which creative ideation can be supported within such environments [3, 4]. Avatars, the virtual beings users control to interact within the virtual environment [5], may therefore pose such an opportunity.

Avatar studies suggest that an avatar's appearance can prime a user's actual behaviour [6]. Avatars designed based on creative stereotypes (e.g. an inventor), can prime creative behaviours that support creative ideation in virtual environments [3, 4]. However, not much is known about the factors that underlie the effectiveness of this approach. This may be due to the degree to which users identify with their avatar. The visual similarity between a user and its avatar, i.e. self-similarity, can positively impact task performance [7, 8], and the degree to which a user believes the avatar's body is its own, i.e. perceived embodiment, appears to moderate the effectiveness of the ability of an avatar to prime behavior [9, 10]. This suggests that self-similarity and embodiment moderate the effectiveness of avatars as support for creative ideation.

To investigate this, we experimentally test whether self-similar avatars designed based on creative stereotypes can be used to influence creative ideation; and the role of self-similarity and embodiment therein.

THEORETICAL BACKGROUND
Recent studies suggest that avatars can be used as a way to enhance creative ideation in virtual environments [3, 4]. The visual appearance of an avatar can prime the way people think and act [6]. For instance, using an avatar that looks like a Ku Klux Klan member leads to writing more negative stories [7]; while using an avatar that is taller and more attractive than its user can increase self-confidence [6], and enhances game performance [8]. Thus, these studies suggest that people can be primed by the appearance of their avatars. This is referred to as The Proteus effect [6].

Creative stereotypes can prime creative behaviours [11]. When asked to generate original uses for an object (e.g. a brick), taking the perspective of a rigid librarian led people to produce less original ideas, than when asked to take the perspective of an eccentric poet. Thus, priming creative stereotypes can be used to influence creative behaviour.

C&C '17, June 27-30, 2017, Singapore, Singapore

ACM ISBN 978-1-4503-4403-6/17/06.
http://dx.doi.org/10.1145/3059454.3078856

It follows that using an avatar designed based on creative stereotypes influences creative ideation [3, 4]. Indeed, recent work suggests that using an avatar that looks like an inventor, compared to a neutral looking avatar helps people to think of more, and more original ideas during a face-to-face brainstorming task [3]. Furthermore, avatars can also influence the type of ideas people generate. For instance, when asked to generate ideas for smart windows in public transportation, using an inventor avatar led to more technology focused ideas, whereas using a public transport user avatar led to ideas about improving practical needs [4]. Thus, using avatars designed based on creative stereotypes can influence actual creative ideation. We refer to this as *the creative Proteus effect*. This leads to hypothesis H1.

H1: Using a creative avatar augments creative ideation, whereas a non-creative avatar diminishes creative ideation.

Although *the creative Proteus effect* has been demonstrated in previous work, not much is known about the factors that influence or underlie its effectiveness [cf. 3, 4]. We propose that the degree to which a user identifies with its avatar moderates the effectiveness of the creative Proteus effect. In this study, we focus specifically on the role of *self-similarity* and *perceived embodiment*.

Self-similarity can influence task performance [7, 12]. For instance, computer game players perform better when they use an avatar that looks like, rather than not looks like themselves [7]; and teams represented by avatars similar to the team members enhances team performance [12]. This can be explained by a positive effect of self-similarity emotional involvement and positive affect experienced when using the avatar [8]. Although no studies on the link between self-similar avatars and creative ideation have been done; its positive effects on task performance [7, 8, 11]; and a link between positive affect, emotional involvement, and creative ideation [13]; suggest that self-similarity can influence creative ideation. This leads to hypothesis H2.

H2: The similarity of an avatar to the user itself moderates the effects of using an avatar designed based on creative stereotypes on creative ideation.

The (creative) Proteus effect also seems conditional upon the *perceived embodiment* of an avatar by its user [9, 10]. This depends on achieving a complex of factors involving a sense of self location, a sense of agency and a sense of body ownership [14]. For instance, when people view an avatar that is eating healthy or unhealthy food; their own tendency to imitate this behaviour depends on the degree to which they feel present themselves within the virtual environment [15]. If we assume that the Proteus effect is dependent on a particular degree of perceived embodiment, we can assume that the effectiveness of the creative Proteus effect is also dependent thereon. This leads to hypothesis H3.

H3: The perceived embodiment of an avatar moderates the effects of using an avatar designed based on creative stereotypes on creative ideation.

METHOD

To test our conjectures, we devised and executed an experiment with a between-subjects design.

Participants

In total, 61 people participated in our study (49 Female, 12 Male, M_{age}=23.62, SD_{age}=3.54, $Range_{age}$=18-32). Participants were recruited using convenience sampling at the communication and information sciences department, Tilburg University (NL), in exchange for course credit. Participants were assigned randomly to the experimental conditions, and the researchers were aware the assignments.

Materials and measurements

Creative ideation task

The instances task was used as a proxy to test creative ideation [16]. In this task participants are asked to generate creative instances of objects characterised by a particular feature (in our study things shaped like a circle or triangle) within three minutes. Participants were explicitly instructed to be creative. To assess creativity participants selected their top two most creative ideas after the creative ask; after which three independent raters scored these ideas for their creativity on a scale from 1-10 [16]. Raters were instructed to rate creativity as a composite of originality and effectiveness. The means of their ratings per participant were used in further analyses. Cronbach alpha was low, α=.47, a common reliability level for creativity ratings [17].

Creative avatars and virtual environment

To test our hypotheses participants performed the creative task using one of three *avatars* (Fig. 1): (i) *Creative avatar*, an avatar wearing a white painter's blouse with paint stains and paint brushes (n=19), and was chosen because artistic jobs are stereotypically associated with creative behaviour [18]; (ii) *Non-creative avatar*, an avatar wearing a grey office-like jacket with a necktie (n=19), and was chosen because office jobs are stereotypically associated with non-creative behaviour [19]; (iii) *Control avatar*, an avatar wearing the clothes the participant is actually wearing (n=23), and for which we expect no creative Proteus effect.

The avatar was used in a *virtual room* (Fig. 2): a minimally designed living room of medium size, with three couches, three plants, a door, and a window with a city street view. We assumed this would minimise any confounds that may arise from avatar-environment interactions (e.g. affect its stereotypical interpretation), and minimise the chance that the room itself would inspire any ideas during the task.

The avatars were generated using the body-scanning and auto-rigging software by [5]. During the body-scan, participants wore the clothes stereotypical of the described experimental conditions. The virtual room was presented using a head mounted display [20].

Self-similarity

Using body scanning to generate the avatars ensured similarity in visual appearance between the user and the avatar [5]. Self-similarity was assessed after the creative task with a questionnaire that contained the first four questions used by [21], and the question used [22]. Cronbach's alpha showed acceptable reliability, α=.82.

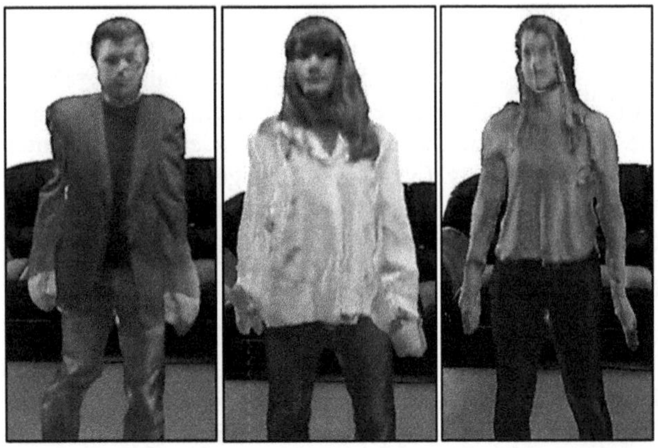

Figure 1 Examples of the avatars used in the experimental conditions. The non-creative avatar (left), creative avatar (middle), control avatar, wearing their own clothes (right).

Figure 2 The virtual reality environment that was used in the three experimental conditions.

Embodiment

To stimulate perceived embodiment participants were asked to imagine they were the avatar, were looking in a mirror and saw themselves. The avatar's movement was animated to approximate the movements of their users, i.e. small arm, leg, and head movements. Embodiment was assessed after the experiment using the presence questionnaire by [15]. Cronbach alpha suggested acceptable reliability, α=.80.

Procedure

Participants were introduced to the study and signed informed consent. At this stage information about the actual purpose of the study was withheld. For the creative and non-creative avatar condition they put on selected clothing, were body-scanned (see [5]), and then removed the selected clothing again. Participants filled in a questionnaire about their demographics while the researcher animated the avatar and rendered the virtual environment. Participants were then asked to stand up and put on the head mounted display, were reminded of the task, and did the embodiment manipulation. Then, participants executed the creative task in virtual reality. After this, they selected their two most creative ideas, and filled in the self-similarity and embodiment questionnaires. Finally, they were debriefed.

RESULTS

To test our hypotheses we used four *linear mixed models*. The models and results are presented in Table 1. The descriptive statistics are presented in Table 2.

DV / IV	Creativity	Self-similarity	Embodiment
Creative avatar	5.37 (1.15)	3.93 (1.09)	5.03(.73)
Non-creative avatar	4.89 (1.19)	3.82 (1.10)	4.88(.76)
Control	5.87 (1.31)	3.61 (1.20)	4.61(.84)
All conditions	5.41 (1.27)	3.77 (1.12)	4.83(.79)

Table 2 Means and standard deviations (between parentheses).

Model 1: The results show a significant difference between the control and the non-creative (office) avatar, $B=-.97$, $t(61)=-2.63$, $p=.011$, but no significant difference between the control and the creative avatar, $B=-.49$, $t(61)=-1.34$, $p=.186$. Interestingly, using the control avatar associates with higher creative ideation that using the non-creative and, although not significantly, the creative avatar (Table 2). Thus, using our non-creative avatar diminishes creativity, but using *our* creative avatar does not influence creativity. This only partly supports H1.

DV	Creative ideation			
IV	Model 1	Model 2	Model 3	Model 4
Intercept	5.87 (2.70)*	6.91 (.96)*	8.10 (1.23)**	8.10 (1.22)**
C1: Creative avatar	-.49 (.38)		-2.12 (2.80)	-2.12 (2.81)
C2: Non-creative avatar	**-.97 (.37)***		**-3.58 (2.42)***	**-3.58 (2.04)***
C3: Control avatar	.[a]		.[a]	.[a]
Self-similarity		**.40 (.16)***	**.68 (.22)****	
Embodiment		**-.63 (.24)***	**-1.02 (.30)****	
C1 x self-similarity			-.78 (.50)	-.09 (.42)
C2 x self-similarity			-.27 (.40)	.41 (.34)
C3 x self-similarity			.[a]	**.68 (.22)***
C1 x embodiment			.97 (.74)	-.05 (.65)
C2 x embodiment			.77 (.61)	-.25 (.42)
C3 x embodiment			.[a]	**-1.02 (.31)***
Residual	1.42 (.21)	1.42 (.23)	1.19 (.21)	1.19 (.22)

Table 1 Estimates of fixed effects. Unstandardized coefficients and standard errors (between parentheses); Intercept and residual; [a] are conditions relative to the estimates for each block (and thereby redundant). * p<.05. **. p<.001

Model 2: The results show that self-similarity is a significant positive predictor, *B*=.40, t(61)=2.28, *p*=.012, whereas, embodiment is a significant but negative predictor of creativity, *B*=-.63, t(61)=-2.49, *p*=.014. Thus, increased self-similarity of an avatar augments creative ideation, while perceived embodiment, surprisingly, diminishes creativity. This supports H2, but inversely supports H3.

Model 3: The results replicate the findings in model 1 and model 2 (Table 1). In addition, there was no significant difference between the interaction of self-similarity with the control avatar, with the creative avatar, *B*=-78, t(61)=-1.82, *p*=.083, and with the non-creative avatar, *B*=,-.27 t(61)=-.73, *p*=.464. Similarly, there was no significant difference between the interaction of embodiment with the control avatar, *B*=.97, t(61)=1.55, *p*=.166, with the creative avatar, and with the non-creative avatar, *B*=.77, t(61)=1.45, *p*=.090. This suggests that self-similarity and embodiment moderate the effects of using an avatar designed based on creative stereotypes on creative ideation across the experimental conditions. This confirms our findings on H1, and further supports H2 and H3.

Model 4: The results replicate the findings from model 1 (Table 1), but add to the findings in model 2 and 3. Self-similarity did not significantly predict creative ideation for the creative, *B*=-.09, t(61)=-.27, *p*=.804, and not for the non-creative avatar, *B*=.41, t(61)=1.52, *p*=.197. Rather, self-similarity was a significant positive predictor of creative ideation for the control avatar, *B*=.68, t(61)=2.71, *p*=.001. Similarly, embodiment did not significantly predict creative ideation for the creative, *B*=-.05, t(61)=-.09, *p*=.948, and the non-creative avatar, *B*=-.25, t(61)=-.63, *p*=.499; but did significantly and negatively predict creative ideation for the control avatar, *B*=-1.02, t(61)=-2.83, *p*=.002. This suggests that self-similarity and embodiment may moderate creative ideation mostly when there is no creative Proteus effect manipulation. This again confirms H1, but sheds new light on H2 and H3.

DISCUSSION

This study shows that avatars designed based on creative stereotypes can influence actual creative ideation, and reveals two factors that influence its effectiveness. Using an avatar designed based on a creative stereotype (a visual artist), did not augment creativity, but using an avatar designed based on a non-creative stereotype (an office worker) did diminish creative ideation (H1). This replicates in part earlier work by [3, 4]. This study also shows, for the first time, that the similarity of an avatar to the user itself positively, and its perceived embodiment negatively moderates creative ideation (H2 and H3). Thus, self-similarity and embodiment appear to moderate the effectiveness of the *creative Proteus effect*.

Interestingly, using an avatar that looks like the user does at that moment (control avatar) led to more creative ideation than using the creative and the non-creative avatar; and upon further inspection, self-similarity and embodiment appeared to moderate creative ideation in particular for the control avatar. This suggests that self-similarity in itself might also be an effective way to support creativity. As such, these findings cast doubt on (i) the effectiveness of the creative Proteus effect, and possibly point to (ii) another, novel, way to support creative ideation using self-similar avatars, i.e. via a *"Being yourself" effect* [cf. 7, 8].

We would like to discuss two limitations in detail because they point to our intended future work. First, we only partly replicated earlier findings by [3, 4] that suggest that avatars can be used to prime creative behaviour. It appears that, despite earlier findings [18], our artist stereotype was not an effective prime [cf. 11]. Future work can therefore benefit from studies that test what creative stereotypes are effective primes. However, using highly self-similar avatars might also explain this replication issue. If there really exists a "Being yourself" effect, this introduces a confounding factor into the control avatar, which limits drawing conclusions about the effectiveness of the creative Proteus effect. This requires confirmation in a dedicated study.

Second, using body-scanned avatars may introduce confounds that limit the generalisation of self-similarity and embodiment as moderators of the creative Proteus effect. Likely, body-scanning introduces issues that associate with the uncanny valley (Figure 1), i.e. eeriness and revulsion elicited by avatars that almost, but just not, look human-like [23]. If so, self-similarity may positively predict creativity because it lifts the avatar's appearance out of the uncanny valley; decreasing negative affect. Perceived embodiment may be a particular issue when avatars are perceived as uncanny, intensifying negative affect, which diminishes creative ideation [cf. 13]. The findings can therefore only be generalised to the use of highly self-similar avatars, suggesting that also here further research is required.

Of course, there are several more limitations to the results and some with relevance for the result's generalisability. These include the notion that whether or not the used avatars are perceived as a creative stereotype can be dependent on for instance culture [24], gender [25], and (virtual) environment [26], which may moderate the intended effect of the stereotypes; Participants in two of the three conditions wore the stereotypes' clothes during scanning, which may have unduly contributed to the priming effects [26]; The scan quality might have influence across all conditions, e.g. higher quality scan methods may lead to different results [27]; and finally, the creativity measure itself is subjective and dependent on cultural factors, further limiting generalisability [1, 28], but see [16]. We would like to emphasise that these limitations need to be taken into account when interpreting and building upon our study and its results.

In summary, this study (i) contributes that self-similarity and embodiment moderate the effectiveness of using an avatar to prime creative stereotypes, and (ii) it points toward a novel way to enhance creative ideation in virtual environments, by using avatars that look just like yourself.

REFERENCES

[1] Kaufman, J.C. & Sternberg, R.J. (2010). The Cambridge Handbook of Creativity. Cambridge University Press, New York.

[2] Bainbridge, W.S. (2007). The scientific research potential of virtual worlds. Science, 317, 472-476.

[3] Guegan, J., Buisine, S., Mantelet, F., Maranzana, N., & Segonds, F. (2016). Avatar-mediated creativity: when embodying inventors make engineers more creative. Computers in Human Behavior, 61, 165-175.

[4] Buisine, S., Guegan, J., Barré, J., Segonds, F., & Aoussat, A. (2016). Using avatars to tailor ideation process to innovation strategy. Cognition, Technology & Work, 18(3), 583-594.

[5] Shapiro, A.W., et al. (2014). Rapid Avatar Capture Using Commodity Sensors. The 27th Conference on Computer Animation and Social Agents, Houston, TX, May 26-28.

[6] Yee, N., & Bailenson, J. (2007). The proteus effect: the effect of transformed self-representation on behaviour. Human Communication Research, 33, 271-290.

[7] Peña, J., Hancock, J.T., & Merola, N.A. (2009). The priming effects of avatars in virtual settings. Communication Research, 36(6), 838-856.

[8] Jang, Y., Kim, W., & Ryu, S. (2010). An exploratory study on avatar-self similarity, mastery experience and self-efficacy in games. In Advanced Communication Technology (ICACT), 1681-1684.

[9] Suh, K.S., Kim, Hongki, & Suh, E.K. (2011). What if your avatar looks like you? Dual-congruity perspectives for avatar use. MIS Quarterly, 35(3), 711-729.

[10] Yee, N., & Bailenson, J.N. (2009). The difference between being and seeing: the relative contribution of self-perception and priming to behavioural changes via digital self- representation. Media Psychology, 12, 195-209.

[11] Dumas, D., & Dunbar, K.N. (2016). The creative stereotype effect. Plos One, 11(2), art. e0142567.

[12] van der Land, S.F., Schouten, A.P., Feldberg, F., Huysman, M., & van den Hooff, B. (2015). Does avatar appearance matter? How team visual similarity and member–avatar similarity influence virtual team performance. Human Communication Research, 41(1), 128-153.

[13] De Rooij, A. & Jones, S. (2013). Mood and Creativity: An Appraisal Tendency Perspective. In Proceedings of the 9th ACM Conference on Creativity and Cognition, 362-365.

[14] Kilteni, K., Groten, R., & Slater, M. (2012). The sense of embodiment in virtual reality. Presence: Teleoperators and Virtual Environments, 21(4), 373-387.

[15] Fox, J., Bailenson, J., & Binney, J. (2009). Virtual experiences, physical behaviors: the effect of presence on imitation of an eating avatar. Presence, 18(4), 294-303.

[16] Silvia, P.J., et al. (2008). Assessing creativity with divergent thinking tasks: exploring the reliability and validity of new subjective scoring. Psychology of Aesthetics, Creativity, and the Arts, 2(2), 68-85.

[17] De Rooij, A., Corr, P., & Jones, S. (2015). Emotion and Creativity: Hacking into Cognitive Appraisal Processes to Augment Creative Ideation. In Proceedings of the 2015 ACM SIGCHI Conference on Creativity and Cognition, 265-274.

[18] Bogousslavsky, J. (2005). Artistic creativity, style and brain disorders. European Neurology, 54(2), 103-111.

[19] Dimnik, T., & Felton, S. (2004). Accountant stereotypes in movies distributed in North America in the twentieth century. Accounting, Organizations and Society, 31(2), 129-155.

[20] Oculus Rift DK2. Retrieved on 02-02-2017 from https://www3.oculus.com/en-us/dk2/

[21] McCroskey, J.C., Richmond, V.P., & Daly, J.A. (1975). The development of a measure of perceived homophily in interpersonal communication. Human Communication Research, 1, 323-332.

[22] Lee, E.J. (2004). Effects of visual representation on social influence in computer-mediated communication. Human Communication Research, 30(2), 234-259.

[23] Kätsyri, J., Förger, K., Mäkäräinen, M., & Takala, T. (2015). A review of empirical evidence on different uncanny valley hypotheses: support for perceptual mismatch as one road to the valley of eeriness. Frontiers in Psychology, 6, 390.

[24] Hinton, P.R. (2000). Stereotypes, cognition and culture. Psychology Press.

[25] Crane, D. (2012). Fashion and its social agendas: Class, gender, and identity in clothing. University of Chicago Press.

[26] Adam, H., & Galinsky, A.D. (2012). Enclothed cognition. Journal of Experimental Social Psychology, 48(4), 918-925.

[27] Loom.ai. Retrieved on 20-04-2017 from https://www.loomai.com/

[28] Sawyer, R. K. (2011). Explaining creativity: The science of human innovation. Oxford University Press.

Storytelling as a Creative Activity in the Classroom

Alejandro Catala[1], Mariët Theune[1], Hannie Gijlers[2], Dirk Heylen[1]

[1]Human Media Interaction
University of Twente, The Netherlands
{a.catala, m.theune, d.k.j.heylen}@utwente.nl

[2]Department of Instructional Technology
University of Twente, The Netherlands
a.h.gijlers@utwente.nl

ABSTRACT

In our ongoing research, we argue that storytelling activities can be used as creative tasks to stimulate creativity in children, one of the so-called 21st century skills. In this paper, we lay the foundations for our project on digitally supported storytelling, by gathering the viewpoints on storytelling and creativity expressed by local primary school teachers and reviewing methods reported in the literature. We report the main characteristics and features to consider in creative storytelling activities, and present our current work on a distributed storytelling interface for supporting children's creative skills development that meets the practical requirements found in the literature and expressed by the teachers.

Author Keywords

Creativity; Storytelling; Teachers' views, 21st century skills; Technology.

ACM Classification Keywords

H.5.m. Information interfaces and presentation (e.g., HCI): Miscellaneous; H.5.2. User-centered design.

INTRODUCTION

Social skills and creativity have been identified as key competencies for new learners in the 21st century knowledge society [3]. Among all different activities that we could consider to stimulate and foster the development of social skills and creativity, storytelling seems to be particularly suitable, given its inherently social and creative nature [11]. It has been used before to support and research aspects of linguistic, cognitive, and affective development in childhood, as well as other skills such as memory and writing skills [28][29]. Furthermore, it provides opportunities for social interaction, which is paramount for the development of children as they grow up [5], and involves necessary interpersonal skills such as communication and empathy [13].

In our project, we focus on storytelling in the context of children's creative activities, and explore how technology-supported (interactive) storytelling techniques can be implemented to support and enable the creative process. However, as a first step in the development process, we explored the current practice of primary school teachers on storytelling and creativity as well as their perspective on storytelling as a creative activity for the 21st century school. In this paper we contribute (1) an overview on storytelling, with a special focus on school settings, (2) insights from local teachers' perspective on creativity and storytelling, and (3) a presentation of the ongoing development of a robotic character to be used in storytelling activities.

C&C '17, June 27-30, 2017, Singapore, Singapore

ACM ISBN 978-1-4503-4403-6/17/06.
http://dx.doi.org/10.1145/3059454.3078857

BACKGROUND ON STORYTELLING

Technological perspective

Garzotto surveyed interactive storytelling systems for children, showing that there is a variety of approaches and enabling technologies [9]. However, among all the possible spectrum, we are especially interested in tangible and collaborative systems which would keep children in the physical world while in contact and in cooperation with peers. According to Vygotsky [32] children create meaning in close interaction with other individuals and the environment around them. Vygotsky argues that spoken and written language as symbol systems are important for cognitive development. Recent work by Gupta [10] illustrates that children often use their own symbol systems, like drawings, in storytelling activities. Use of tangible objects can assist children in the process of telling a story. In this sense, remarkable related work ranges from tabletop technology to tangible objects used as input means. In the first group, the work in [2] uses emergent narrative techniques to allow children to interact with intelligent agents to develop a story using tangible toy figures, whereas works such as [8] or [1] support the creation of digital artefacts to be used in stories by using touch, tangible cameras or tagged pucks on the tabletop. In the second group, typical approaches use tangible manipulatives [31], action figures [25] or RFID tagged objects and toys [14] as main input to trigger interactive storytelling in a display. When using physical robots as base technology, they have been mostly used as characters. For example, in [33] a small robot that can record movements can be customized with cardboard drawings to create physical characters. Sugimoto explored the use of a turtle toy controlled by means of handheld projectors [30]. In [21], the navigation of a small robot is controlled by children using tangible cards on a digital tabletop, whereas with a similar approach the work in [27] uses programmed behaviours sequenced in a computer and linked to tangible cards to be physically rendered in a dinosaur robot. More recently, MyKeepon robots have been used to render stories physically, limiting children's interaction to choose a few actions in a pre-scripted story [20]. Furthermore, there have been some good samples in which the robot is used as a storyteller, such as [19] which used a Nao robot with pre-recorded behaviour, or the robot as a supportive activity companion as in [34].

In summary, all these developments for storytelling represent important efforts to develop novel systems and approaches considering tangible and robotic technology. However, in most cases the context of use is more related to informal contexts, in which teachers or instruction practice are not explicitly mentioned or involved. As pointed out by Garzotto in the research challenges identified in her work, there is a need to understand the requirements of the interactive storytelling technology in formal contexts.

Practice at schools

There has been a broad interest in using digital storytelling in instruction to develop many different skills, such as problem solving competence, creativity, creative thinking, critical thinking, emotional intelligence, oral language competence, social skills, and memory among others [28]. In this section, we provide a summarization of literature on storytelling at school, in which the focus is not necessarily on the use of advanced technology but more on the storytelling practice.

Baumer et al. study the effects of *playworld educational practice* on the development of narrative competence in 5 to 7 year old children [4]. Students engaged in joint adult-child dramatization of the text, general discussions, drawing activities, and free play activities that resulted in pretend play. The findings show that children who participated in this practice showed significant improvements in narrative length, coherence, and comprehension compared to children who just listened to the story read by the adult, and engaged in group discussion and individual writing and drawing activities. This is in line with more recent studies which report the link between play and creativity skills [12].

In the *Storytelling and Story-Acting* (STSA) practice [24], any child who wishes can dictate a story to the teacher, who writes down the story for the child. At a later stage the teacher reads the story to the entire class, while the child/author and other children act out the story. The teacher takes on the role of a coach that helps students develop the story and the associated play. Nicolopoulou et al. remark that there have been few systematic attempts to assess its effects on young children's learning and development [22].

Campbell [7] investigates how digital storytelling can enhance ability to create higher quality writing in junior elementary school classes (ages 10-12). The results of embedding storytelling activities in teachers' instruction illustrate that teachers and students moved beyond the fun and attractiveness of technology, and learned to use the digital tools to create more sophisticated stories with the time, producing better scripts and longer and more sophisticated digital stories.

Sarica and Usluel [28] also reported positive effects of digital storytelling using picture and video editing software. Their experimental group engaged in a five-stage digital story creation activity similar to [23], which considers the planning of the story, pre-production activities, the production process, post-production, and the delivery stage. The control group created posters using the same content material. The experimental group outperformed the control group in terms of writing skills.

Preparation was emphasized by Kirsch [15], who examined whether children, aged 10-11, learned vocabulary through storytelling. She narrated or read stories, at the beginning or at the end of a unit of work, depending on the learning objectives. After each storytelling event, the children were encouraged to retell the story and to mention any new words or sentences they remembered. The children engaged in the storytelling activities, and recalled and retained lexical items over a period of time. Kirsch pointed out that stories can work well but teachers need to plan how to use them, make language accessible through the use of voices, pictures or signs. Kocaman-Karoglu [17] found that the use of digital storytelling by the teacher helped 6-years-old students remember and comprehend the subject's content over traditional approaches in classroom instruction.

In summary, storytelling requires considering several activities during the learning sessions. They can include some reading by the teacher, but also an active participation of the students and play. Discussions are also considered, as well as additional activities such as writing and drawing in relation to the topic of the story. However, various authors also admitted that embedding storytelling activities in the classroom is time-consuming and not easy. Robin [26] emphasizes the power of digital storytelling as a tool for the 21st century classrooms. He discusses that digital storytelling is being currently used in K-12 classrooms with an emphasis on technical skills and without paying attention to the subject matter, the teaching strategies, and needs in the classroom. For this reason, and to help us to prioritize design requirements, we are exploring how primary school teachers in our network would consider storytelling in order to have a better view on their practice.

Insights from local teachers

We focused on primary schools that would be more likely to participate in follow-up studies based on previous experiences in other research projects and to ensure that we start fitting their needs from the beginning. Five primary school teachers answered our questions. They were 3 women and 2 men with an age ranging from 23 to 31 years old (mean=28.2 y.o.) and experience ranging from 1 to 8 years (mean=4.4 years). All of them held a bachelor degree in Education. Unfortunately, we did not get senior teachers involved, which could have been useful to get more valuable insights reported and informed from experience. However, we still believe that targeting junior teachers is necessary and useful, as they are the new generation of teachers who are and will be the users interested in implementing instruction using digital resources and technology.

To capture the teachers' view on creativity, teachers answered the questions replicated from [6], which is a more general survey on creativity in schools in Europe. Our local teachers considered that creativity is a fundamental skill to be developed in school, which can be applied to every domain of knowledge or school subject. They explain that creativity is about finding relations or connections that have not been made before or about the ability to produce something original. Their attitude towards whether ICT can be used to enhance creativity was very positive (with a score of 4.2 out of 5). The main observations are in line with what was reported in [6]. A remarkable difference is that among our participants mobile phone technology has a better consideration for learning, which we assume to be a consequence of the evolution that such devices have had over the last years (touchscreens and learning apps).

On the creative activities carried out in their classrooms, three of them mentioned activities in which both teacher and students are involved. Typically, the teacher proposes an open problem or activity and provides materials, requiring the pupils to work on the problem (usually in groups), with the teacher as a supporter/coach (i.e. without giving a solution or advice directly). One teacher also mentioned using a kind of theater lessons where improvisation is needed and participation is encouraged, but where attention and listening to other peers are also important skills to be developed. Concerning technology used to enhance creativity, two teachers said that they were not aware of using technology for this purpose, except *Kodu*, which is a programming environment used as a creative medium [18]. Another teacher mentioned that he uses tablet apps and sometimes uses software from teaching methods, but he stated not being a fan because it does not normally fit the creativity purpose.

Participants were also asked to express their agreement or disagreement on a 5-point scale with a number of statements related to issues on how storytelling is used (e.g. If I had more time, I would consider storytelling activities more often; Children are requested to do drawings/writing besides a storytelling activity; I use digital materials in storytelling activities;...). We observed that storytelling activities are not carried out very often, presumably because of the short time that teachers self-reported to have available. More traditional materials are preferred over digital for practical reasons. Typically, teachers use drawing and writing in combination with storytelling. Overall storytelling activities are considered as a positive contribution to creativity development.

Teachers were requested to indicate how often specific activities should be used in storytelling sessions according to their opinion. Activities with higher ratings showed a large overlap with the activities described in our literature review, including dramatization, pretend play, and children and teachers reading stories. Moreover, all the respondents mentioned a kind of collaborative or group activity when asked for the structure of storytelling activities. The comments were in the direction of children working and discussing together, so that they get feedback and stimulate each other. Also receiving feedback from the teacher was mentioned, but as a secondary and more final source. Finally, the teachers gave their opinion on which skills children would need to be developed further. They talked about oral language skills and kinesthetic skills, confidence to speak up and express themselves verbally, imagination, creativity, being a good listener, patience, and paying attention. Thus, this suggests that the technology to be considered should be flexible, allowing teachers to designate different roles to children (e.g. active contributor or storyteller, audience or listener, assets creator...) and arranging activities in small working groups.

DISCUSSION AND PROPOSED SOLUTION

The related work and the practice informed by local teachers reveal that there are some desirable requirements as well as issues that may impede the spread of storytelling activities in practice, despite evidence that digital storytelling may have a positive effect on learning. It is suggested that storytelling activities may consist of stages, which typically include a kind of preparation or preproduction, production and/or performance, and discussion. However, not all of the stages are necessary as existing materials can be reused, especially when teachers declared that the available time is limited. In order to facilitate discussion and children learning from each other, joining them together to carry out some collaborative work is recommended based on the teachers' opinion, giving children an active role in the creation of stories.

In general terms, these elements and stages can confer a structure as follows: The teacher proposes a general topic to work with. Children prepare the materials and customize the props and characters needed. Children enact the story, which is important to get benefits in terms of pretend play as reported in the literature [4], while coaching will ensure producing higher quality storytelling. Finally, discussion on the story and alternative endings or variations. In that structure, secondary creative/constructive tasks such as drawing, writing, and designing can be considered depending on the children's level and learning goals. However, we must be aware of the limited time that teachers declared to have available to prepare the activity, and that it is the main obstacle for them to include such activities more often. This means that a system should not strictly require to have all the stages, should be easily customizable and should allow the reuse of assets, so that the effort can be acceptable over time.

Figure 1. Surfacebot and control tablets

Regarding technological approaches, tangible approaches have the potential to provide physical affordances and interaction appropriate for children. Moreover, direct manipulation through touch input as shown in tabletop approaches has shown to be useful to both unfold the story based on user actions as well as create digital artifacts to be used in the story. On the other hand, tabletops could be a concern in terms of flexibility to move the setup and arrange several small groups in parallel. Moreover, we have seen that robot can give physical presence and embodiment to characters, but they normally require specific expensive or very specialized hardware.

Given all these observations and remarks, we focus on providing a solution based on mobile devices, tablets specifically, which can be affordable, flexible, and transparent for users. We aim to support active participation of children using mobile characters to enact and create stories collaboratively. To achieve this overall goal, we have considered a timely distributed user interface based on multiple tablets. Tablets are affordable devices available at school, which can have different functions depending on the app running, and are popular among both children and teachers. The devices, connected via a wireless router, allow several children to enact the character actions to tell the story through a control app. Moreover, in our current implementation we can flexibly arrange groups of tablets to work in different story activities, in such a way that several independent clusters of users can engage in close collaboration, fostering active participation, peer feedback, and discussion between participants on building the stories. As characters, departing from the approach in [2], in which interactive storytelling is delivered on a tabletop surface with physical but static characters, we are developing artificially intelligent agents, or *surfacebots*. These are physicalized digital characters capable of moving on the table and embodied in a tablet on top of a two-wheeled robot base (see Figure 1). The app on the tablet renders a character following the technique presented in [16], which can change its facial expression and show the objects concerning the storytelling activity. Using tablets even for the robotic character facilitates the reuse of hardware typically available at schools within a limited budget, and moreover, the system is expandable with more apps to support additional creative tasks such as editing assets, or programming behavior with visual languages in the future.

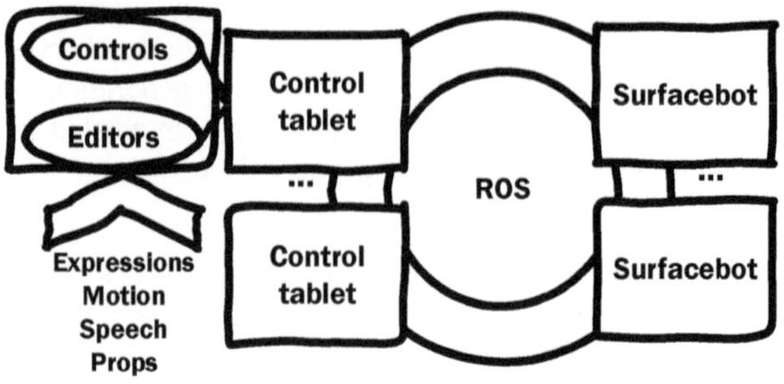

Figure 2. Components of the surfacebot architecture.

The prototype is implemented in Android and relies on ROS[1] to support the communication between tablets and the creation of clusters of devices (see Figure 2). The current implementation supports the movement of surfacebots by using the Zumo robot for Arduino[2]. The movement control, facial expressions, and the visualization of story assets on the surfacebot screen are handled from the control tablets. These actions presented as assets on the control tablets are now predefined and preset. However, we are expanding and developing editors to allow children to create several type of assets on the tablet during or before the storytelling activity. Specifically, we have defined speech, motion and props as main editable assets. For speech, we currently rely on text-to-speech synthesis, and we are expanding it to have short speech recorded by children. For motion, we have implemented a path editor that saves trajectories introduced as a free-style dragging gesture, that can be invoked from the control as well. For props, or picture based information to be shown in the screens, we have a drawing touch editor, but we are planning to add an editor to incorporate drawings with traditional materials into the system by taking a picture with the tablet, which would be a way to accommodate additional activities besides the storytelling in the preparation stages.

Our immediate future work is focused on implementing the aforementioned editors, to empower children and teachers to easily create their own reusable material so that they are not limited to use the preset assets and actions. Future work plans include to evaluate the use of the prototype in terms of usability, creativity support and as a facility to reuse materials. Specifically, we want to carry out experiments evaluating collaboration in groups and how storytelling activities can be combined with other creative tasks. Finally, a more ambitious but interesting future work we aim to pursue is to introduce some autonomous intelligent behavior for the surfacebot to foster and enhance user participation during the storytelling.

[1] Robot Operating System, http://www.ros.org/

[2] Pololu Zumo robot, https://www.pololu.com/product/2510

ACKNOWLEDGEMENT
Our thanks to the teachers who voluntarily participated in the study. This project has received funding from the European Union's Horizon 2020 research and innovation programme under the Marie Sklodowska-Curie grant agreement No 701991.

REFERENCES
1. Alexandra Alves, Roseli Lopes, Patrik Matos, Luiz Velho, Djalma Silva. Reactoon: Storytelling in a Tangible Environment," 2010 Third IEEE International Conference on Digital Game and Intelligent Toy Enhanced Learning, Kaohsiung, 2010, pp. 161-165.
2. Thijs Alofs, Mariët Theune, Ivo Swartjes. 2015. A tabletop interactive storytelling system: designing for social interaction. *International journal of arts and technology*, 8(3), 188-211.
3. Katerina Ananiadou, Magdalean Claro. 2009. 21st Century Skills and Competences for New Millennium Learners in OECD Countries. OECD Education Working Papers, No. 41, OECD Publishing.
4. Sonja Baumer, Beth Ferholt, Robert Lecusay. 2005. Promoting narrative competence through adult–child joint pretense: Lessons from the Scandinavian educational practice of playworld. *Cognitive Development*, 20(4), October–December 2005, 576-590.
5. Laura E. Berk. 2009. *Child Development (8th edition ed.)*. Pearson International Edition.
6. Romina Cachia, Anusca Ferrari. 2010. Creativity in schools: A survey of teachers in Europe. *Tech. rep., Institute for Prospective and Technological Studies*, Joint Research Centre
7. Terry A. Campbell. 2012. Digital Storytelling in an Elementary Classroom: Going Beyond Entertainment. Procedia - Social and Behavioral Sciences, 69, 385-393.
8. Xiang Cao, Siân E. Lindley, John Helmes, and Abigail Sellen. 2010. Telling the whole story: anticipation, inspiration and reputation in a field deployment of TellTable. In Proceedings of the 2010 ACM conference on Computer supported cooperative work (CSCW '10). ACM, New York, NY, USA, 251-260.
9. Franca Garzotto. (2014). Interactive storytelling for children: a survey. *International Journal of Arts and Technology*, 7(1), 5-16.
10. Amita Gupta. 2009. Vygotskian perspectives on using dramatic play to enhance children's development and balance creativity with structure in the early childhood classroom. *Early Child Development and Care*, 179(8), 1041-1054.
11. Tony Hall. 2012. Digital Renaissance: the Creative Potential of Narrative Technology in education. *Creative Education*, 3(1): 96–100.
12. Jessica D. Hoffmann, Sandra W. Russ. 2016. Fostering pretend play skills and creativity in elementary school girls: A group play intervention. *Psychology of Aesthetics, Creativity, and the Arts*, 10(1), 114-125.
13. Sharon A. Lynch, Cynthia G. Simpson. 2010. Social Skills: Laying the Foundation for Success. *Dimensions of Early Childhood*, 38(2) 3-12.
14. Nuri Kara, Cansu Cigdem Aydin, Kursat Cagiltay. 2014. Design and development of a smart storytelling toy. *Interactive Learning Environments*, 22(3), 288-297.
15. Claudine Kirsch. 2016. Using storytelling to teach vocabulary in language lessons: does it work? *The Language Learning Journal*, 44(1), 33-51.
16. Randy Klaassen, Jordi Hendrix, Dennis Reidsma, Rieks op den Akker, Betsy van Dijk, Harm op den Akker. 2013. Elckerlyc goes mobile - Enabling natural interaction in mobile user interfaces, *International journal on advances in telecommunications*, 6(1-2), 45-56.
17. Aslıhan Kocaman-Karoglu. 2015. Telling stories digitally: an experiment with preschool children. *Educational Media International*, 52(4), 340-352.
18. Kodu Research Project webpage. Retrieved March 10, 2017 from https://www.microsoft.com/en-us/research/project/kodu/
19. Marina Fridin. 2014. Storytelling by a kindergarten social assistive robot: A tool for constructive learning in preschool education. *Computers & Education* , 70, 53-64.
20. Iolanda Leite, Marissa McCoy, Monika Lohani, Daniel Ullman, Nicole Salomons, Charlene Stokes, Susan Rivers, and Brian Scassellati. 2015. Emotional Storytelling in the Classroom: Individual versus Group Interaction between Children and Robots. In Proceedings of the Tenth Annual ACM/IEEE International Conference on Human-Robot Interaction (HRI '15). ACM, New York, NY, USA, 75-82.
21. Anna Helen Leversund, Aleksander Krzywinski, Weiqin Chen. 2014. Children's Collaborative Storytelling on a Tangible Multitouch Tabletop. In: Streitz N., Markopoulos P. (eds) Distributed, Ambient, and Pervasive Interactions. DAPI 2014. Lecture Notes in Computer Science, vol 8530. Springer, Cham.
22. Ageliki Nicolopoulou, Kai Schnabel Cortina, Hande Ilgaz, Carolyn Brockmeyer Cates, Aline B. de Sá. 2015. Using a narrative- and play-based activity to promote low-income preschoolers' oral language, emergent literacy, and social competence. *Early Childhood Research Quarterly*, 31, 2nd Quarter 2015, 147-162.

23. Jason Ohler. 2008. *Digital Storytelling in the Classroom: New Media Pathways to Literacy, Learning, and Creativity*. SAGE Publications.
24. Vivian G. Paley. 2009. *The Boy Who Would Be a Helicopter*. Harvard University Press.
25. Pedro Ribeiro, Ido Iurgel, Manuel Ferreira. 2011. Voodoo: A System That Allows Children to Create Animated Stories with Action Figures as Interface. In: Si M., Thue D., André E., Lester J.C., Tanenbaum J., Zammitto V. (eds) Interactive Storytelling. ICIDS 2011. Lecture Notes in Computer Science, vol 7069. Springer, Berlin, Heidelberg.
26. Bernard R. Robin. 2008. Digital Storytelling: A Powerful Technology Tool for the 21st Century Classroom. *Theory Into Practice*, 47(3), 220-228.
27. Kimiko Ryokai, Michael Jongseon Lee, and Jonathan Micah Breitbart. 2009. Children's storytelling and programming with robotic characters. In Proceedings of the seventh ACM conference on Creativity and cognition (C&C '09). ACM, New York, NY, USA, 19-28.
28. Hatice Çıralı Sarıca, Yasemin Koçak Usluel. 2016. The effect of digital storytelling on visual memory and writing skills. *Computers & Education*, 94, March 2016, 298-309.
29. Kathryne M. Speaker, Deborah Taylor, Ruth Kamen. 2004. Storytelling: Enhancing language acquisition in young children. *Education*, 125(1), 3.
30. Masanori Sugimoto. 2011. A Mobile Mixed-Reality Environment for Children's Storytelling Using a Handheld Projector and a Robot. IEEE Trans. Learn. Technol. 4, 3 (July 2011), 249-260.
31. Cristina Sylla, Clara Coutinho, Pedro Branco. 2014. A digital manipulative for embodied "stage-narrative" creation, *Entertainment Computing*, 5(4), December 2014, 495-507.
32. Lev Vygotsky. 1978. Interaction between learning and development. *Readings on the development of children*, 23(3), 34-41.
33. Guanyun Wang, Ye Tao, Enmao Liu, Yunfan Wang, Cheng Yao, and Fangtian Ying. 2015. Constructive Play: Designing for Role Play Stories with Interactive Play Objects. In Proceedings of the Ninth International Conference on Tangible, Embedded, and Embodied Interaction (TEI '15). ACM, New York, NY, USA, 575-580.
34. Jacqueline Kory Westlund and Cynthia Breazeal. 2015. The Interplay of Robot Language Level with Children's Language Learning during Storytelling. In Proceedings of the Tenth Annual ACM/IEEE International Conference on Human-Robot Interaction Extended Abstracts (HRI'15 Extended Abstracts). ACM, New York, NY, USA, 65-66.

3D Shadow Art Sculpture Based On Real Items

Yanxiang Zhang
Department of Science Communication,
University of Science and Technology of China
Hefei, Anhui, China
petrel@ustc.edu.cn

Dong Dong
Department of Science Communication,
University of Science and Technology of China
Hefei, Anhui, China
dd1992@mail.ustc.edu.cn

Yanlong Guo
Department of Science Communication,
University of Science and Technology of China
Hefei, Anhui, China
1806800172@qq.com

ABSTRACT
Existing 3D shadow sculpture could be made by 3D printing and generate shadows in 3 or more directions, but a 3D printed sculpture looks too technical and less artistic feel. This paper developed a unique method and new tool to create 3D shadow art sculptures based on real items by fusing the methods of handmade and the mechanism used in 3D printer, to achieve 3D shadow art sculpture from real items. , This turned computed results into a unique kind of handmade art works that could bring multi-meanings and special feel of aesthetics.

Author Keywords
3D Shadow art; Real Items; Handmade; aesthetics

ACM Classification Keywords
I.3.5 Computational Geometry and Object Modeling

INTRODUCTION

Shadow is a special reflection of light. With the bright side of light, shadows can be performed as different forms of arts. Many artworks have been performed on the stage for a long time in history, such as Chinese shadow plays [1,2]. The simplest form of traditional shadow art is hand shadow. 2D shadow art inspires artists to create some other forms of storytelling, which is shown in Figure 1.

Figure 1. Traditional shadow art

If an object could have 2 different meanings, then the contrast of dual meaning could offer an amazing experience to the audience.

C&C '17, June 27-30, 2017, Singapore, Singapore

ACM ISBN 978-1-4503-4403-6/17/06.
http://dx.doi.org/10.1145/3059454.3078858

Some optical illusion artworks are using anamorphic projection [4] to produce certain shape of a meaning on a surface with a different object.

While 2D shadow art could contain only two meanings, 3D shadow art could contain even more than 4 meanings, and this actually turned it into a special form of optical illusion art, so more and more artists are having new ideas on 3D shadow art. Our work is mainly inspired by 3D shadow art of artists such as Niloy J. Mitra and Mark Pauly. They have presented a tool for creating 3D shadow art sculptures. After provided with three binary images, their tool will generate a 3D model for 3D shadow art sculpture; the generated 3D models could cast shadows in 3 or more directions [1]. To turn the model into a real 3D shadow art sculpture, they use 3D printer to print it out. But these excellent models constructed by computing system and exported by 3D printer an excessively technological feeling more than artistic, especially the plastic material and layer by layer stacking characteristic make it looks more like an industrial production, thus distinctly different from the traditional 2D shadow art made from real items.

The contrast of real items and their shadow could bring excitement to audiences, but usually it is almost impossible for a human artist to create such kind of 3D shadow art sculptures alone by using real items without the aid of computing method. Also it will be very difficult to simply fill the hollow part of the negative model of the computed 3D shadow art sculptures with real items, as it is usually too complicated. So there is still no reported real items based 3D shadow art sculptures.

This paper develops a method by applying the method of layer by layer used in 3D printer, to deconstruct the computed negative model of the computed 3D shadow art sculptures into layers then manually fill the hollow part with real items to make a 3D shadow art sculpture, which could bring audiences with the feel of aesthetics and psychological contrast.

REALIZATION OF ALGORITHM

ALGORITHM

First, a three-dimensional array of 3D voxels was initialized in shape of a solid cube as basic body.

Then the following algorithm will be applied:

① Three rays of directional light in direction of x, y, z axis is created for projection.

② Three black and white pattern in the same square size will be used as three shadow shapes in direction of x, y, z, shown as Figure 2.

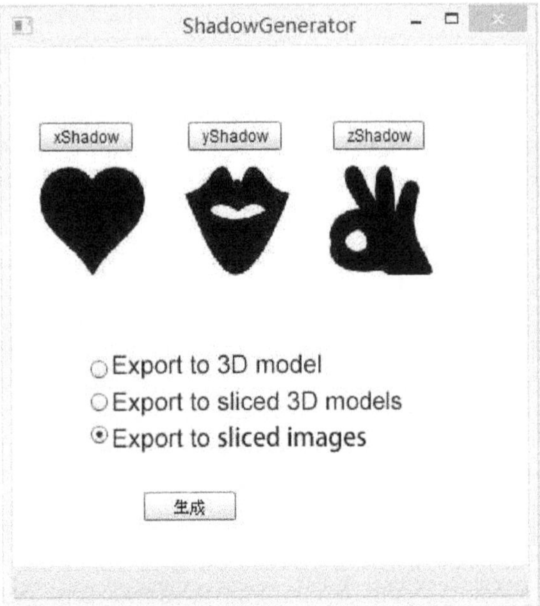

Figure 2. software interface

③ In the pattern, black represents shadow while white is on behalf of non-shaded area. Set an initial pattern that corresponds to the upper-left corner of the 3D coordinates and the corresponding light direction.

④ Traverse all the light (the number of lines of the light of the same direction depending on the area of the shadow map or the number of pixels). The light and the initial geometry need intersection testing by using Boolean algorithm; each intersection test get a voxel collection. If the intersection of section light and its corresponding shadow plane is white (i.e., in the region as a non-shaded area), all the intersection of voxels should be removed from the initial geometry, and so on until all the rays intersecting the test is completed (this part is similar to one time ray tracing the process).

Output first step 3D materials

After the process above, the results is a basic 3D geometry, then the final creation can be selectively output to 2 types of result:

① Output the 3D model Ddirectly to a single obj file as the final product, then use 3D printer to print out molding, shown as Figure 3.

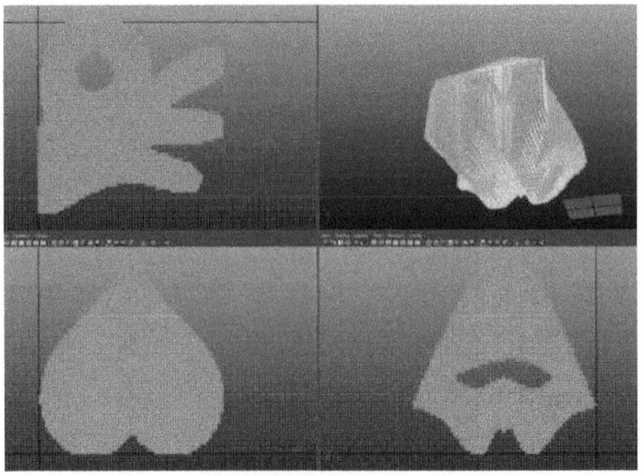

Figure 3. The outputted 3D shadow sculpture model

② Use manual reprocessing to recreate the initial model. Firstly, slice original 3D models in a certain direction, then output each piece of voxel distribution to a binary image (black represents empty, white represents voxel). We will have a 3D shadow art sculpture sliced serials, shown as Figure 4.

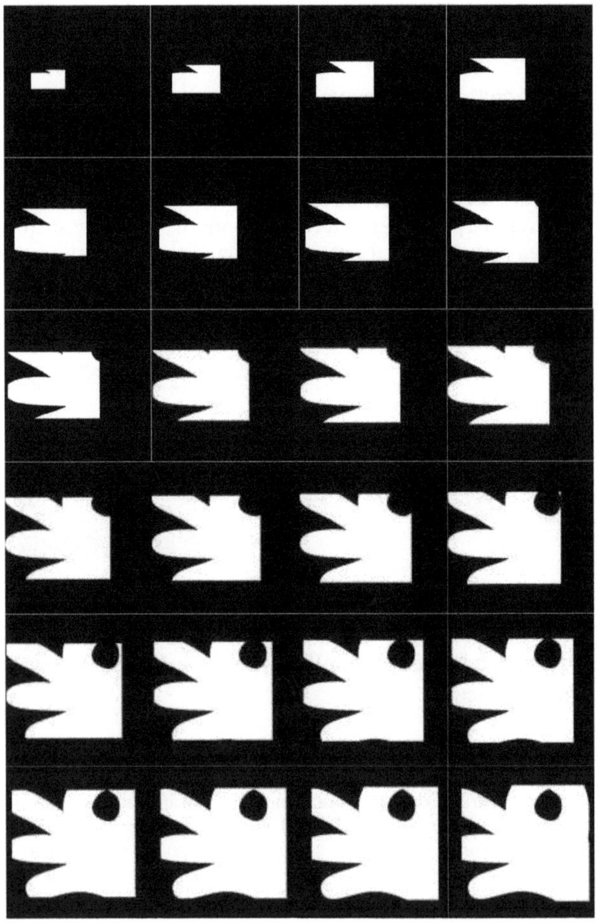

Figure 4. Slice the 3D shadow sculpture model into pieces

Make it from real items

Then the sliced image will be used to cut plastic boards into sliced layers with same thickness, the thickness of each layer is related to the quantity of layers and dimension of final sculpture, the original 3D shadow sculpture model in the solid part of the template will be hollowed out, as Figure 5.

Figure 5. The original model has been hollowed out

Empty part of the model will be filled up layer by layer with real items, powerful glue will be used to connect every adjacent items into a whole object, process and fill the hollow portion of the plastic board; finally, remove the plastic board and get the final sculpture works. If there are some solid area not connected to the whole plasterboard, then a temporary area should be kept and could be removed only after the surrounding area is filled.

Figure 6. Items that will be used to represent the sculpture

Figure 7. powerful glue will be used to connect every adjacent items into a whole object

RESULT

The authors make it possible to make 3D shadow art sculpture based on real items possible with computing method and handmade creation.

The steps in the negative layers affect the resolution of shadows, also it is not easy to fill all the hollow part with real items if its size is not so small, so the selection of real items and the size of final shadow sculpture is very important for the quality of the final result.

In order to make the final shadow sculpture more meaningful, it is also very important to design and select the shadow images and real items.

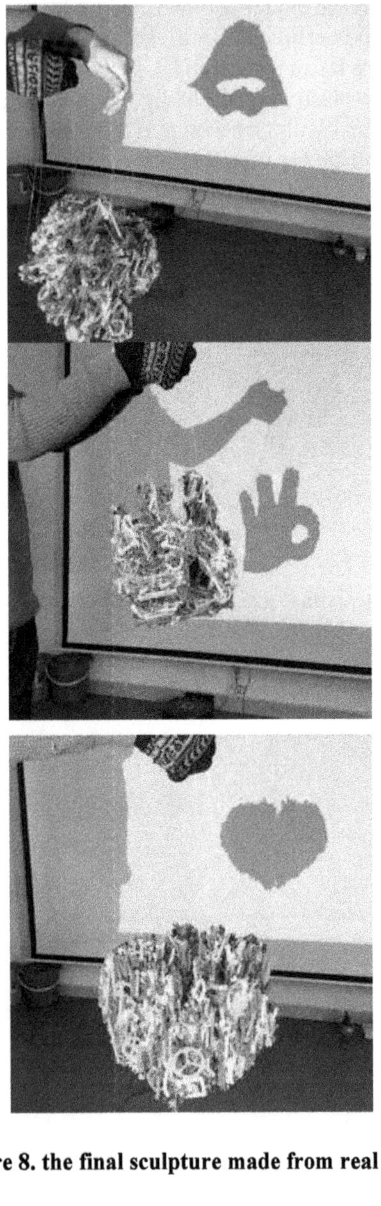

Figure 8. the final sculpture made from real items

CONCLUSION

Such kind of 3D shadow art sculpture could not be produced by depending only on technological methods, also it is very difficult even impossible to make it purely by handmade methods.

In fact, this paper developed a unique way also and an interesting tool which allow artist to create 3D shadow art sculpture with real items, which turned computed results into handmade art works that have less feel of technology and more feel of aesthetics.

REFERENCES

1. F. Chen, "Visions for the masses: Chinese shadow plays from shaanxi and shanxi", Pacific Science 201, 2015.
2. EWART, F. G. 1998. Let The Shadows Speak. Trentham Books.
3. Di Paola, F., P. Pedone, L. Inzerillo and C. Santagati. 2015. Anamorphic Projection: Analogical/Digital Algorithms. Nexus Network Journal 17: 253–285. doi:10.1007/s00004-014-0225-5
4. Mitra, Niloy J, Pauly, Mark. Shadow Art, ACM Transactions on Graphics. Proceedings of ACM SIGGRAPH Asia 2009, 2009, (28):156.

Investigating Players' Engagement, Immersion, and Experiences in Playing Pokémon Go

Aung Pyae
University of Turku, Finland
aung.pyae@utu.fi

Mika Luimula
Turku University of Applied Sciences, Finland
mika.luimula@turkuamk.fi

Jouni Smed
University of Turku, Finland
jouni.smed@utu.fi

ABSTRACT
In recent years, Augmented Reality (AR) based mobile games have become popular among players. The Pokémon Go is one of the well-known examples. Although Pokémon Go game has become a global phenomenon, there is a limited study about players' experiences in the gameplay. Especially, little is known about players' engagement and immersion in playing AR-based mobile games in which physical movements in the real world are largely required to play the game. In this study, we conducted a pilot study with eight participants to investigate players' engagement, immersion, and experiences in the Pokémon Go gameplay. We report and discuss the preliminary findings from the study, which can help game designers understand players' experiences in the gameplay so that they can design more creative AR games in the future. Furthermore, the findings are also useful for future studies with larger sample size.

Author Keywords
Augmented Reality, Engagement, Immersion, User Experiences.

ACM Classification Keywords
H.5.m. Information interfaces and presentation (e.g., HCI): Miscellaneous;

INTRODUCTION
Augmented Reality (AR) is a technology that integrates the physical world in a user's computing experience. It has the unique quality of providing a link between the physical reality and virtual information about that reality in the real world [1]. AR can overlay computer-generated digital information (e.g. 2D or 3D images) on the real world views, enhancing users' perception and cognition in creative new ways [1, 2]. It can also enrich user's experiences in a virtual world as well as in the real world [3]. Kipper and Rampolla [4] stated that the time for AR has come, and it is now becoming truly practical. In recent years, AR has been used in various areas, including commercial, entertainment, education, and the military. It has also become an emerging trend in the game industry, and its technical advancements have been used in game products [4, 5].

'*Creativity*' is defined as the process of producing something that is both original and worthwhile [6, p.479], and bringing together ideas that were previously unrelated [7]. According to the literature, there is a connection between creativity and digital games. Digital games can enhance players' motor skills, auditory processing, spatial imagery, and visual processing, which are related to creativity and mechanism for improving it [8, p.xix].

The literature also states that there is a link between AR and creativity, for it has unique and promising potential to enrich users' experiences and enhance their imagination and creativity [3]. AR games have been creatively used as a tool in various contexts. For instance, AR-based games is used to enhance young students' experiences in learning through an AR experience that explores new ways of interacting with digital application and the real world, which combine educational and entertainment values together [3]. Furthermore, it can also be creatively adopted in business and commercialization to promote their products and brands.

In 2016, a mobile-based AR game called '*Pokémon' was released by Niantic*, and it has become a global success. To date, there have been a few studies that investigated the impacts of the Pokémon Go game on players such as the influence of Pokémon Go on physical activity [9], healthcare [10], and social well-being [11]. However, to our knowledge, scholarly studies on player's engagement and experiences in playing the Pokémon Go game are still limited. Thus, in this study, we aim at conducting a pilot study to investigate players' user experiences in playing the Pokémon Go game in terms of their engagement and immersion in the gameplay. The main objective of this study is to seek knowledge and insights into players' experiences in Pokémon Go gameplay that can be useful for game designers and developers to create and develop AR games in more creative and innovative ways. By understanding players' experiences, people can also find some ideas and inspiration to utilize this game as a creative tool in their related contexts (e.g. setting up Pokémon Go gym in a local library to attract readers). Lastly, the findings can also be useful for our future investigation.

C&C '17, June 27-30, 2017, Singapore, Singapore

ACM ISBN 978-1-4503-4403-6/17/06.
http://dx.doi.org/10.1145/3059454.3078859

BACKGROUND

Pokémon Go is a mobile-based AR game that uses the real world locations and encourages players to travel and play between real and virtual worlds simultaneously [11]. It has attracted more than 20 million users worldwide [13]. To date, it is the biggest AR-based mobile game in the United States, which has been played by 21 million active users daily [14]. Although AR has been in research and commercial for more than a decade, the Pokémon Go has become a global success [15]. It has also shown the potential of AR technology for the game industry [16]. In this game, the real world locations are provided for players to navigate and explore in the physical world. For instance, players go outdoors to search and catch virtual characters called 'Pokémon'. Unlike conventional mobile games, player's physical movement is important to play this game. Players need to look for Pokémon characters and Gyms in the real world to collect more game points to level up. Thus, players need to pay attention to not only virtual but also physical play in the realworld.

Regarding the positive impacts of the game, some people claimed that it can increase players' physical activities [9], and has brought opportunities for them to engage with another. It also has the potential to help people with social anxiety and depression [17]. In contrast, Tsukayama [18] warned that players are likely to get injuries, and encounter accidents while playing it. Unless players are aware of their physical environment, they might encounter unforeseen physical accidents and get injured while playing it. Furthermore, the potential for "distraction-related injury and death" is also highlighted due to the rising popularity of the game among players [19]. This game also has the potential to lead players to restricted and dangerous areas, including military campuses, construction sites, and private houses.

Although Pokémon Go encourages players to go outdoors and explore the real world, it is always important for them to pay attention to their surroundings in the realworld to avoid unexpected accidents while playing it [3, 12]. In this game, if players highly focus on virtual gameplay, they may encounter physical accidents or injuries in the real world. If players pay much attention to the gameplay in the real world, they may miss out opportunities in the virtual game. Thus, the balance of player's engagement between virtual and the real world gameplay is important.

According to the literature, creativity is related to game design and user experience (UX). Follett [20] states that creativity is considered as an asset in UX. Smith and Mateas [21, p5.] highlight that game designers are really designers of game play and creative game design is about seeking design knowledge. In this study, we are interested in exploring players' user experiences in playing the Pokémon Go game in terms of their immersion and engagement in the game itself. By understanding players' experiences, designers and developers can find some insights into designing more creative and user-friendly AR games for players in the future. The main objectives of the study are:

- To understand player's engagement, immersion, and user experiences in playing the Pokémon Go game and
- To explore players' feedback towards the game.

RELATED STUDIES

AR has been employed on mobile devices to improve the real world creative activities, and open new interaction possibilities for players [2]. For instance, the researchers designed and implemented an AR-based game called 'City-Wide gaming' in which players need to play and explore the city to solve puzzles related to historical sites and famous locations [2]. This game provides players with a playful AR game tool to discover the real world city. Wetzel et al. [22] developed an AR-based outdoor game called 'TimeWrap' in which players are equipped with an AR system, including a head-mounted display, a laptop, a GPS sensor, and a PDA with an interactive map that provides a player information regarding current locations in the real world. It also encourages players to play and explore in the real world.

Regarding AR commercial games, the Pokémon Go's precursor 'Ingress'– also created by Niantic is a location-based AR game like Pokémon Go that encourages players to go to the real world environment and explore physical locations to play the game [23]. This game is a location-based exergame in which players' physical movement is important and necessary [24]. There are similar commercial AR games in the market. For instance, the military-based game called 'Real Strike' is a first-person shooting game that blends real-life surroundings with 3D animation. 'Zombies Run' is an example of a mobile-based AR game, which targets players who want a fun way of exercises.

METHOD

In this study, we conducted a pilot study with eight participants (age: M = 29). We randomly recruited participants from the undergraduate and graduate programs of the University of Turku and Turku University of Applied Sciences in Finland. The participant selection criteria is that he or she should be at least a novice player to the Pokémon Go game and should have played it a few times prior to this study. For the research inquiry, we conducted the questionnaire and interview studies with the participants to investigate their engagement, immersion, and experiences in the gameplay. We used Game Immersion Questionnaire by Jennett et al. [25] and Game Experience Questionnaire implemented by IJsselsteijn et al. [26]. We used 5-point Likert scales for the questionnaires, ranging from Strongly Disagree (1) to Strongly Agree (5). For interview questions, we used open-ended questions to explore players' feedback and opinions towards the game. The questionnaire and interview study took 30 minutes per participant.

RESULTS

The findings show that the participants have started playing the Pokémon Go game more than 2 months ago. Their daily gameplay hours had dropped (M=0.5), compared to the past (M=1.3). Similarly, their weekly gameplay hours also had declined (M=4.5), compared to the past (M=1.6). Regarding the locations of gameplay, they played in their neighbourhood, university, downtown, parks, and new places. They played the game with friends, family, colleagues, and strangers.

Regarding the players' engagement in the gameplay (Table 1), the participants were quite interested in the gameplay (M=4.1, SD=1.4), and they had fun to play it (M=4.1, SD=1.4). They reported that how good they were at the gameplay was just above average (M=3.4, SD=0.5). They put their effort in the gameplay to a certain extent (M=3.0, SD=0.5). They did not agree on the fact that they forgot everything around them while playing it (M=2.0, SD=0.0). The average mean score for GEQ is (M=3.3, SD=0.9).

GEQ Questionnaire Item	Mean (M)	Standard Deviation (SD)
I was interested in the virtual game play.	4.1	1.4
Playing the virtual game was fun.	4.1	1.4
I was good at the virtual gameplay.	3.4	0.5
I had to put a lot of effort in the virtual game play.	3.0	1.2
While playing the virtual game, I forgot everything around me.	2.0	0.0

Table 1. GEQ Scores.

Regarding the participants' immersion in the gameplay, the extent that they focused on the gameplay was reported as a range of positive and negative feeling (M=3.3, SD =1.0). Similarly, their attention towards the gameplay was also an average (M=3.1, SD=1.0). The extent that the participants felt they were interacting with the virtual game play was reported as a range of positive and negative feelings (M=3.0 SD=1.2). The extent that they experienced in the virtual gameplay was also reported as below average (M=2.3, SD=1.0), as well as their sense of being in the game (M=2.1, SD=1.1). They did not agree on the fact that they were separated from the real world (M=2.0, SD=0.5). Lastly, their intention to play the game again was varied between moderately positive and negative feelings (M=3.5, SD=1.4). The overall score for their immersion was slightly less than the average score (M=2.8, SD=0.6). The following Table 2 shows the average scores for Immersion Questionnaire.

Immersion Questionnaire Items	Mean (M)	Standard Deviation (SD)
I would like to play it again.	3.5	1.4
To what extent did you feel you were focused on the virtual game play?	3.3	1.0
To what extent did the virtual game play hold your attention?	3.1	1.0
To what extent did you feel that you were interacting with the virtual game environment?	3.0	1.2
To what extent did you feel that the virtual game play was something you were experiencing, rather than something you were just doing?	2.3	1.0
To what extent did you have sense of being in the virtual game environment?	2.1	1.1
To what extent did you feel as though you were separated from your real world environment?	2.0	0.5

Table 2. Immersion Questionnaire Scores.

For the participants' positive experiences in the gameplay (Table 3), we found that they were quite satisfied in playing it (M=4.0, SD=0.8). Their success in the game was ranged between positive and negative experiences (M=3.1, SD=1.6). Their level of energy to play the game was also in a range of positive and negative experiences (M=3.0, SD=1.2). The remaining scores are below an average score (<M=3.0). The average score for the participants' positive experience is just average (M=3.0, SD=0.6).

Positive Experience Questionnaire Items	Mean (M)	Standard Deviation (SD)
I felt satisfied.	4.0	0.8
It felt like a victory.	3.1	1.6
I felt energized.	3.0	1.2
I felt powerful.	2.9	1.1
I felt proud.	2.6	1.1
I felt revived.	2.3	1.0

Table 3. Positive Experience Questionnaire Scores.

Regarding their negative experiences in the gameplay (Table 4), their opinion towards playing the game was just reported as a range between positive and negative experiences (M=3.3, SD=1.6). Similarly, the extent that they felt the gameplay was a waste of time ranged between positive and negative experiences (M=2.6, D=1.4). The remaining scores are smaller than (M=2.0). The average score for the participants' negative experiences is (M=2.0, SD=0.8).

Negative Experience Questionnaire Items	Mean (M)	Standard Deviation (SD)
I felt that I could have done things that are more useful.	3.3	1.6
I found it a waste of time	2.6	1.4
I felt guilty.	1.8	1.2
I felt regret.	1.6	1.1
I felt ashamed.	1.6	0.7
I felt bad.	1.1	0.4

Table 4. Negative Experience Questionnaire Scores.

Regarding the findings from general interview, most participants claimed that they had positive experiences when playing Pokémon Go game, including physical activities, social communication and interaction through the gameplay. They also had fun and excitement, and they felt it as the real world adventure. Regarding negative experiences, they claimed some interface and design flaws. They also pointed out the possibility of boredom in the long run to play the game. For the perspective of safety, all participants stated that the Pokémon Go game is safe to play in the real world environment with a cautious mind. There were no accidents, injuries, and sickness reported by the participants. However, among them, four participants claimed that they experienced physical tiredness after the gameplay while one participant experienced mental tiredness after playing for long hours.

Experiences	Quotes
Positive	"I am in better shape since I move and walk, having fun with friends" "Sometimes you would meet a lot of people while being at a Pokestop", " It's fun and exciting to play"
Negative	"Loading time problems and interface flaws" "lack of content in the long run" "Becoming bored after some time"

Table 5. Selected Quotes.

FINDINGS AND DISCUSSION

The findings from the pilot study showed that the number of daily and weekly hours that the participants spent on the gameplay have declined over the past two months. All participants went outdoors to play the game, which is in-line with the literature that the game encourages players to go outdoors and play [3, 12]. The findings also show that 6 out of 8 participants played the game with others, including friends and family, which supports the literature that the game can enhance social communication among players [3].

Regarding their engagement in the gameplay, we found that they were quite interested in playing it. Furthermore, they had fun to play the game in both virtual and the real world environments. We observed that the gameplay was not challenging for them, as they did not put large effort into the gameplay. Their abilities in playing the game were moderately good. We also found that the participants were attentive to the real world environment while they were playing the virtual game. Based on the findings from GEQ questionnaire, we found that the participants were moderately engaged in the Pokémon Go game.

For their immersion in the game, we found that the game could draw the players' attention to a certain extent and their focuses towards the game were moderate. Furthermore, the participants were fairly immersed in the gameplay in terms of virtual experiences, interaction, and sense of being in the virtual world. Their intention to play the game again was moderately high. Based on the findings from Immersion Questionnaire, the participants were fairly immersed in the Pokémon Go game while they were playing it.

With regard to their positive experiences, we found that the participants were noticeably satisfied to play the game. They felt a moderate success in the gameplay, as well as being moderately energetic to play it. Based on the findings from the Positive Experience Questionnaire, the participants had a moderately positive experience to play the game. For their negative experiences, their opinions towards the usefulness of the game were fairly negative. Other than minor negative experiences, their overall experiences in playing the Pokémon Go game were more positive. Based on the findings from the general interviews and discussion with the participants, we observed that the Pokémon Go game could encourage players to do more outdoor activities and promote their social contact with others. We also found that the Pokémon Go game is recommended by all participants that it is safe to play in the real world environment.

In summary, the findings show that the participants are moderately engaged and immersed in the game, and had positive gameplay experiences. Although there are some flaws of the game; however, the Pokémon Go game has the potential to promote players' physical activities and social communication in the real world environment. Furthermore, the findings also raise the questions why the participants have dropped the number of gameplay hours daily and weekly after some time, as well as what the factors ,which make players bored in the long run, are. For game creativity, the findings can help people get an idea of adopting AR games more creatively in promoting their physical and social well-being. In addition, game designers can also find some knowledge and insights into designing more creative AR games that can make players more engaged and immersed in the game. The findings could be useful for expanding our future study with a larger sample size, broader selection of participants, and comprehensive research methods.

Finally, it is worth noting that the study had a small sample size. Thus, the findings from this pilot study can only be a general knowledge and preliminary findings for further investigation in the future. Also, the updates to Pokémon Go released after conducting this study has changed the gameplay somewhat with the aim of regaining the interest of the more experienced players.

CONCLUSION

In this study, we conducted a pilot study to investigate players' engagement, immersion, and experiences in playing the Pokémon Go game. The findings show that the participants were moderately engaged and immersed in the gameplay. The participants' experiences were more positive. All participants recommended that the game is safe to play. The Pokémon Go game is promising to promote player's physical activities as well as social communication with others while playing the game. The findings from this study can be useful and insightful for game designers and our future investigation.

REFERENCES

1. Schmalstieg, D., and Hollerer, T. 2016. *Augmented Reality: Principles and Practice (Usability)*, (1st. ed.). Addison-Wesley Professional.
2. Zünd F. et al. 2015. Augmented creativity: bridging the real and virtual worlds to enhance creative play. In *Proceedings of SIGGRAPH Asia 2015 Mobile Graphics and Interactive Applications.*
3. Pyae, A., and Potter, L. 2016.A player engagement model for an augmented reality game: A case of Pokémon Go. In Proceedings of the 28th Australian Conference on Human-Computer Interaction (HCI) OzCHI, Australia.
4. Kipper, G., and Rampolla, J. 2012. *Augmented Reality: An Emerging Technologies Guide to AR*, (1st. ed.). Syngress.
5. Molla, E., and Lepetit, V. 2012. Augmented reality for board games, In *Proceedings of the International Symposium on Mixed and Augmented Reality (ISMAR).*
6. Sternberg, R. J. 2011. *Cognitive Psychology*, (6th ed.). Wadsworth Publishing.
7. Perkins D. N. 1981. *The Minds Best Work*. Cambridge MA. Harvard University Press.
8. Green, G., and Kaufman, J. C. 2015. *Video Games and Creativity*. Academic Press.
9. Althoff, T., White, R. W., and Horvitz, E. 2016. Influence of Pokémon Go on physical activity: study and implications. *Journal of Medical Internet Research*, 18 (12): e315.
10. Chang, H., and Choi M. 2016. Big data and healthcare: Building an Augmented World. *Healthcare Informatics Research*, 22 (3): 153-155.
11. Tateno, M., Skokauskas, N., Kato, T. A., Teo, A. R., and Guerrero, A. P.S. 2016. New game software (Pokémon Go) may help youth with severe social withdrawal, hikikomori. *Psychiatry Research*, 246: 848-849.
12. Pokémon Go. 2016. Explore. Retrieved December 1, 2016 from http://www.pokemongo.com/en-au/explore/.
13. Yu, H. 2016. What Pokémon Go's success means for the future of augmented reality. Retrieved December 1, 2016 from http://fortune.com/2016/07/23/-pokemon-go-augmented-reality/.
14. Kain, E. 2016. 'Pokémon Go' is the biggest mobile game in US history- And it's about to top snapchat. Retrieved December 1, 2016 from http://www.forbes.com/sites/erikkain/2016/07/13/pokemon-go-is-the-biggest-mobile-game-in-us-history-and-its-about-to-top-snapchat/#4ed08a30722b.
15. Hoang, T. and Baker, S. 2016. Why Pokémon Go has been a viral success. Business Insider, Retrieved December 1, 2016 from http://www.businessinsider.com.au/why-pokemon-go-has-been-a-viral-success-2016-7.
16. Yamazaki, M. and Wagstaff, J. 2016. Success of Pokémon Go adds impetus for change at Nintendo. Yahoo Finance. Retrieved December 1, 2016 from http://finance.yahoo.com/news-/success-pokemon-adds-impetus-change-nintendo-232207842--sector.html.
17. Fernando, G. 2016. How Pokémon Go is helping people with social anxiety and depression. Retrieved December 1, 2016 from http://www.news.com.au/technology/home-entertainment/gaming/how-pokemon-go-is-helping-people-with-social-anxiety-and-depression/news-story/bdf546cd7979d0c11480fcb596e61538.
18. Tsukayama, H. 2016. Pokémon Go's unexpected side effect: injuries. Retrieved December 1, 2016 from https://www.-washingtonpost-.com/news/the-switch/wp/2016/07/08/-pokemon-gos-unexpected-side-effect-injuries/.
19. BBC Health. 2016. Pokemon Go 'increases risk of death by distraction'. Retrieved December 5, 2016 from http://www.bbc.com/news/health-37563986
20. Follett, J. 2009. A practical guide to capturing creativity for UX. UX matters. Retrieved December 5, 2016 from http://www.uxmatters.com/mt/archives-/2009/07/a-practical-guide-to-capturing-creativity-for-ux.php
21. Smith, A. M., and Mateas, M. 2011. Knowledge-level creativity in game design. In *Proceedings of the 2nd International Conference on Computational Creativity*.
22. Wetzel, R., McCall, R., Braun, A-K., & Broll, W. 2008. Guidelines for designing Augmented Reality games. In *Proceedings of FuturePlay 2008.*
23. Sam, R. 2015. Meet endgame: Proving ground Google's AR mobile game. Retrieved December 5, 2016 from http://www.tomsguide.com/us/-endgame-proving-grounds-beta,news-20650.html.
24. Ma, M. et al. 2014. Future Trends of Virtual, Augmented Reality, and Games for Health. Virtual, augmented reality and serious games for healthcare, Berlin, Heidelberg: Springer Berlin Heidelberg, 199.
25. Jennett, C., Cox, A. L., Cairns, P., Dhoparee, S., Epps, A., Tijs, Tim., & Walton, A. 2008. Measuring and defining the experience of immersion in games. International Journal of Human-Computer Studies, 66: 641-661.
26. IJsselsteijn, W.A., de Kort, Y.A.W., & Poels, K. 2015. The game experience questionnaire: Development of a self-report measure to assess the psychological impact of digital games. Manuscript in preparation.

Structural Coupling on Creative Interfaces

Wallace S. Lages
Virginia Tech
UFMG
wlages@vt.edu

Pablo Gobira
UEMG
Belo Horizonte, Brazil
pa.gobira@uemg.br

Francisco Marinho
UFMG
Belo Horizonte, Brazil
fccm@ufmg.br

ABSTRACT
We describe how self-production systems theory can be applied in the design of new creative interfaces. By modeling the interface as an organizationally closed system, we can support creative agency while still allowing collaboration with the user. Although in this approach the interactor no longer solely determines the output, both the user and interface can become structurally coupled, achieving a balanced interaction. We discuss our theoretical motivations and describe an initial attempt in the domain of human-machine collaborative painting.

Author Keywords
Interactive art, robotic, collaboration, dynamical system.

ACM Classification Keywords
J.5 Computer Applications: Arts and Humanities; I.2.9 Robotics: manipulators; I.6.8 Image Processing: Simulation and Modeling.

INTRODUCTION
Creativity is an important underlying element in innovation, design, science and art. However, understanding what it is and how it develops continues to be a challenging problem. In art, it can be seen as arising from the individual, the process, as a property of artistic artifact, or even as a result of the environment [18].

Despite those many different views, good tools can help in the creative process by freeing cognitive resources or by sparking new ideas. This motivation has prompted several studies to understand the best way to design such tools [9][20][25][21][3][17]. Shneiderman et al. [22], for example, propose a set of design principles focusing on features such as support for easy exploration, rapid experimentation, and making sure that new combinations can happen by chance. However, different views on creativity will lead to different prescriptions on how to better support it.

In this paper, we explore the view of creativity as a result of agency [19] and how it can be used to enhance artistic work. In particular, we discuss how to design a system endowed with creative agency that can also act as a bodily extension of the user for creative tasks. We use the term Creative Interface to refer both to the creative goal of the interface and the creative aspects embedded in it.

Our approach is inspired by the concept of self-production systems, introduced by Maturana and Varella [13]. Thus, the collaboration that arises between the user and the interface is different from the traditional role attempted by artificial intelligence partners [12] [2]. Rather than posing as an equally competent partner, our goal was to add a new capability to the interactor. From the interaction perspective, it serves as a new found limb (albeit one with some will). The interaction, hence, would happen without the need for a domain level representation [16].

To explore this concept, we developed the interactive robotic installation *Better Hands* (2017). It is composed by a robotic arm with a brush and a tablet. The interactor wears a wireless armband that senses the electric activity of the muscles and the orientation of the arm using an inertial measurement unity. The tablet runs a control system that can be perturbed by the input from the armband and generate stroke patterns and send motor commands to the arm (Figure 1).

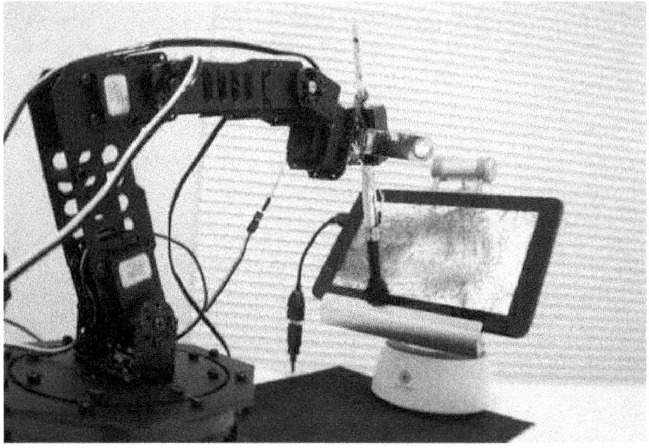

Figure 1 – Better Hands Installation

STRUCTURALY COUPLED INTERFACES
Our use of structural coupling to develop creative interfaces is based on the cognitive creativity thesis. In summary, it states that creativity results from cognitive acts or is at least enabled by it. Davis et al. [7] present a theory for creativity support built on the concepts of *embodied*, *distributed* and *situated* creativity.

C&C '17, June 27-30, 2017, Singapore, Singapore

ACM ISBN 978-1-4503-4403-6/17/06.
http://dx.doi.org/10.1145/3059454.3078860

The *embodied* argument claims that creative acts are facilitated by the existence of the body in the world, while the *distributed* recognize the aid of external symbols and objects in the creative process. The *situated* argument captures creativity as an activity in-the-world.

For Varela and Maturana, what we understand as a cognitive behavior is the set of activities that organisms undertake to maintain their existence [13]. Despite structural changes, they are able to sustain their organization through the continuous production of its own components. These systems are called self-producing or *autopoietic* systems.

Autopoietic systems are organizationally closed, meaning that all internal states led to other internal states. There is no direct input or output. The environment, however, can trigger changes in the structure of the system, to which the system responds by adaptation. A single cell is autopoietic on the molecular level, while a neuron system is organizationally closed. Closed systems can interact with each other through structural coupling [14].

Autopoiesis has been applied to explain a variety of non-biological systems, such as social and psychological systems. In the realm of creativity, Takashi Iba [10] proposes an autopoietic model, where the basic element is a "discovery". Each discovery is produced based on previous discoveries, leading to a closed organization. This model, however, does not help to explain how actual artifacts of a creative process come to exist.

In this work we propose another approach, which makes possible to understand how autopoiesis can be applied to creative production. The key is to conceptualize a system where each state (production) has a defined meaning within the application domain. In *Better Hands*, the system states correspond to different brush strokes. They are defined by a position on the canvas and additional parameters that define the shape of the marking / stroke and color. This forms the "stroke space", a closed system that can evolve even under interference (Figure 2).

The sequence of states constitutes an orbit that can be understood as the result of the evolution of a dynamical system over time. Dynamical systems are often used to model mechanical or biological process and can be discrete or continuous. In robotics it has been used to bind sensors and actuators while considering the physical dynamics of the robot [6]. Here we use it to model the agency of the system within the painting domain.

Once a semantic mapping is found between the domain and system states, we need to make sure that the system can keep its organization over multiple iterations and will not "die" when coupled with another system/user. The most straightforward approach is to use dynamical systems that contain a geometric or a strange attractor. This ensures that the orbit will evolve in a stable way if left alone. In addition, any perturbation introduced by an external system will remain within the design boundaries. In our application, the system will evolve along a new trajectory, which is defined by the dynamical system itself, as a result of its previous history and the user's input.

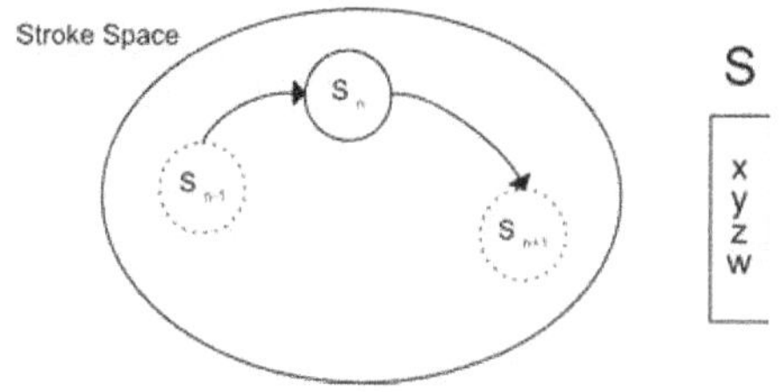

Figure 2 - Self-production system for a painting. Each stroke is defined by four parameters (explained in the next section). The boundary of the system is defined by the regenerative process that is produced by the sequence of strokes.

IMPLEMENTATION

The *Better Hands* installation consists of a dynamical system core embodied into a robotic arm and tablet. This gives it the ability to sense and act in the world. The robotic arm used in the installation is a commercial five joint arm, driven by servo motors [26]. The gripper was modified to hold a small brush. To make it capable to activate the capacitive touch screen, it was painted with conductive ink and connected to the robot electrical ground. The servos are driven by an Arduino [27] board, which receives commands from the tablet through the serial over USB. Since tablets usually act as peripherals, we used an USB-to-Go cable to control the arm. The tablet runs Android and connects to the Myo [28] armband through Bluetooth 4.0, using the library developed for the Uniklinik RWTH Aachen mHealth project [11]. We use EMG stream that comes pre-filtered from the armband to avoid interference from external electromagnetic fields.

The interaction between the robot and the interactor is established through two coupled loops (Figure 3). The first loop directly links the interactor and his arm. The feedback is the visual perception of the painting process (a). The second loop links the machine intention with the robotic body through the USB. The feedback is composed by the touch events received by the robot (b). Both loops are coupled when the robot senses the interactor arm through the armband and when the human sees the robotic arm (blue arrows).

The installation software is composed by three main modules: the Dynamics module, the Brush Pattern module, and the Motor Control module (Figure 4). The Dynamics module couples the external stimuli (from the interactor's arm) and modulates the update of state by presence of *self-stimuli* (from the touchscreen). The current system variables are reflected on the Brush and Motor modules. The eight channels from the Myo's EMG sensors are combined into two signals before entering the Dynamics module. The yaw and pitch angles from the IMU are used directly to control the brush position but are collapsed into a single variable in the dynamical system.

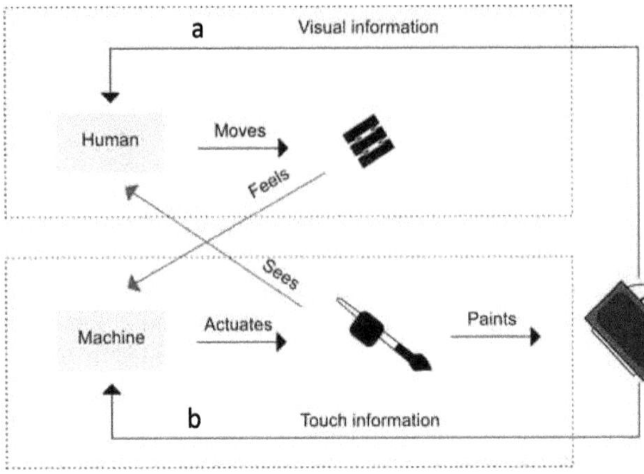

Figure 3 – Coupled interaction loops. Both human and machine run two proper loops. The two loops are coupled as shown by the blue arrows.

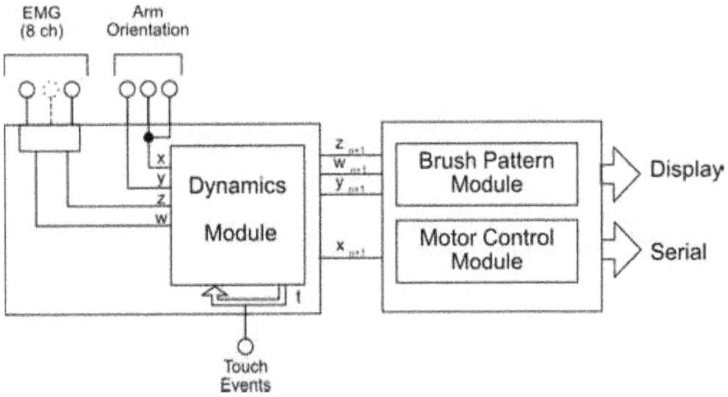

Figure 4 – Architectural overview. The interactor input perturbs the dynamic module. The variables are passed to generate the brush patterns and actuate the robotic arm.

The Brush Module creates brushes by drawing over the points of temporary attractors generated by an iterated function system (IFS). The system is composed by three 2D affine transformations, giving a total of 18 coefficients. The coefficients were condensed into three parameters, which encode the distance between the transformations, relative rotation and scale. The IFS is drawn by selecting a transformation randomly in each interaction step (Chaos game) [1]. Following Sprott [24] suggestion, we also adjust the selection probability to be proportional to the *jacobian* of each map, to obtain a better coverage.

Since we want to draw the strokes under the brush position, we need to determine the center of the attractor. Instead of finding the center of the convex hull (which would add additional overhead) we just run the system for a few iterations and use the average 2D position as the center. The final rendering of the brush is drawn using lines and points. Lines are used to connect points in close proximity while points are used for the rest. In this way, smaller attractors have more lines and larger ones are drawn as scattered points. Figure 5 depicts some sample brush patterns.

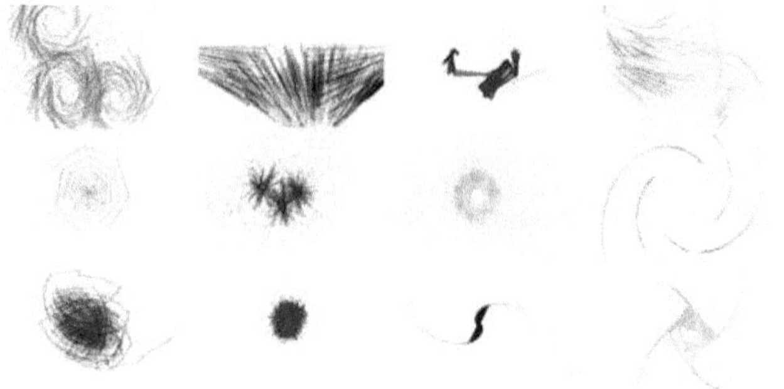

Figure 5 – Sample brush patterns generated by the Brush Pattern module

The Dynamics model holds the dynamical system that performs the evolution of the strokes through time. It is a four-dimensional Hamiltonian system using sines and cosines. The solutions to these systems are chaotic but do not form an attractor. Thus, orbits do not collapse as the system evolves from an initial condition [23]. This makes them even more appropriate for our system: they have the necessary plasticity and yet are still determined by a structure. We selected an attractor with a good coverage of the space and variability from Sprott [24]. The equations are:

$$x_{n+1} = a_1 + [x + a_2 \sin(a_3 y + a_4)] \cos a_0 + y \sin a_0$$
$$y_{n+1} = a_5 - [x + a_2 \sin(a_3 y + a_4)] \sin \alpha a_0 + y \cos a_0$$
$$z_{n+1} = a_1 + a_6(xy) \cos \alpha + a_7 w \cos \alpha \quad \text{EQ.1}$$
$$w_{n+1} = a_1 + xy \sin \alpha - z \sin \alpha$$

Even though the general shape is defined by the map, constants can alter the specific shape of the attractor. They were adjusted to yield an interesting structure. Figure 6 shows planar projections of the map.

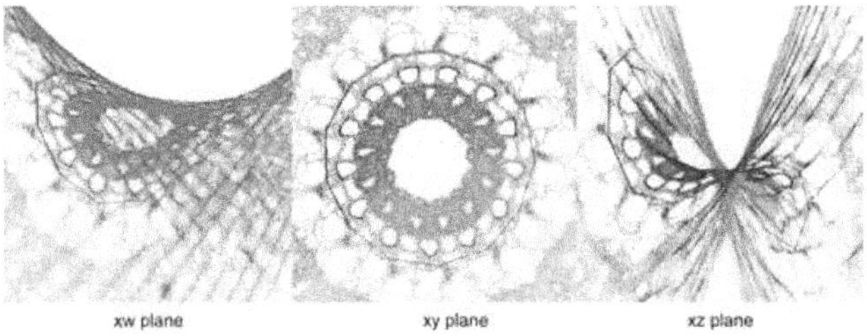

Figure 6 – Planar projections of the dynamical system from EQ.1. Black lines show the first 20 steps of an orbit with initial values: $x_0 = y_0 = z_0 = w_0 = 0.05$.

The final paintings (Figure 7) reflect a combination of user intent and system reaction to those changes. As the orbit through the space state is perturbed it includes elements which are on intermediate points. The feedback of the touch events prevent the dynamical system to go forward so the interactor has more control over the process.

DISCUSSION AND RELATED WORK

Most painter systems developed so far fall into a few categories regarding their goals: a) being able to reproduce an existing work or painting style, b) enable remote painting (telerobotics) or c) achieve higher aesthetic control (improved control, mixing of colors, etc.). For example, although Brain Painting [8] uses a brain-computer sensor to control a robotic painting arm, there is no agency in the interface, which simply maps input to output. Other robotic painters like the ones designed by Patrick Tresset[i] are autonomous and although the results are aesthetically interesting, no collaboration happens between human and machine.

Our work is more similar in intention to Colton's Painting Fool [4] and Cohen's AARON [15] artificial intelligence painters. Painting Fool simulates cognitive behaviours to express ideas through scene composition, while AARON is capable of drawing original figurative scenes containing people and other objects. Both show a good degree of creative agency, obtained through curation and/or training. However, the collaboration only happens during those phases. The approach used on *Better Hands* was to model an autopoietic process and use it to couple with the interactor, obtaining a realtime result influenced by both.

Corness and Schiphorst [5] describe Ariel, a computer agent uses breathing patterns to help communicate upcoming musical gestures to performers. The objective was to use embodied cues, which could be picked up in a subconscious level by the performers. The musical 'decisions' are defined by probability distribution functions, weighted by events captured by a computer vision system. In our work, we use a dynamical model that allows response variety while also considering the past. The interaction quality is also different: while Ariel was designed to be present as a partner to whom you can adapt, we designed *Better Hands* to be and feel like a part of the body that you can influence.

In our experience, interactors had no problem in using the system to produce paintings. Initially, interactors seem to rely only on the orientation of the arm since it is easiest to understand. Hand gestures came later, as they try to explore the new possibilities for their painting. Some users demonstrated enjoyment in being able to control the robotic arm with only remote gestures. We also noticed that users learn to adapt to the pace of the robotic arm, which takes a few seconds to draw each stroke.

Modeling the painting process as an autopoietic system allowed us to think more deeply about the role of interaction on the creative process. How much of the future action is determined by the previous one? In our work the original plans of machine and iterator does not survive long as one need to adapt to the other. Does the structural coupling with our tools necessarily collapse the space of possibilities? The framework suggests that it is so. However it does not mean that tools need to stay under control during the whole session. As two colleagues discussing ideas, contributions are added along the way, but in different times. As in any effective collaboration individual contributions must consider the prior history and the unique perspectives of each one.

A difficulty remains in finding appropriate mappings between solutions of a dynamical system and the desired outputs. In our case the mapping goes straight from the dynamical system to the Brush and Motor modules. To ensure a more pleasant experience, the iterator can explicitly indicate the area of the canvas to be painted. We also sub-modeled the system by using only four dimensions. Since not every state needs to be externalized, more internal states would allow more freedom to choose the basic shape of the attractor and still have sensible mappings for the output.

We also noticed that although the use of a robotic arm increased the sense of presence and embodiment of the system, the hardware we used lacked precision and accuracy. This forced the use of larger strokes, which reduced the sense of user control. A finer position control would allow the creation of more directed, less abstract paintings.

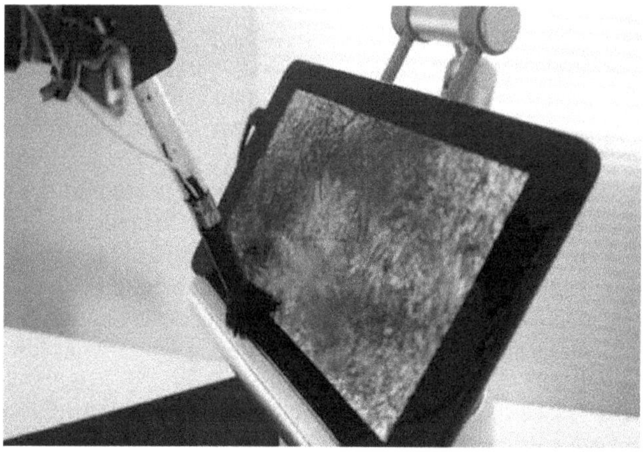

Figure 7 – Output of the installation Better Hands

CONCLUSION AND FUTURE WORK

This paper presented an approach to use self-production systems to inject agency into creative interfaces. We described the design of a robotic painting system, *Better Hands*, which is realized as a robotic arm and tablet. In the future we plan to collect more information on how different users interact and experience the system. We also plan to investigate how different parameters influence the perception of painting. Finally we intend to explore new opportunities to apply dynamical systems to support and investigate creative processes.

ACKNOWLEDGMENTS

The authors would like the Virginia Tech CS Department, FAPEMIG, CNPq, PROPPG/UEMG and ACM for their support.

REFERENCES

1. Michael F Barnsley. 1993. *Fractals everywhere*. Academic press.
2. Andrew R Brown, Toby Gifford, and Bradley Voltz. 2013. Factors affecting audience perceptions of agency in human computer musical partnerships. In *Proceedings of the 9th ACM Conference on Creativity & Cognition*, 296–299.
3. Linda Candy and Ernest A Edmonds. 1997. Supporting the creative user: a criteria-based approach to interaction design. *Design Studies* 18, 2: 185–194.
4. Simon Colton. 2012. The painting fool: Stories from building an automated painter. In *Computers and creativity*. Springer, 3–38.
5. Greg Corness and Thecla Schiphorst. 2013. Performing with a system's intention: embodied cues in performer-system interaction. In *Proceedings of the 9th ACM Conference on Creativity & Cognition*, 156–164.
6. Patrick Cousot and Radhia Cousot. 1977. Abstract interpretation: a unified lattice model for static analysis of programs by construction or approximation of fixpoints. In *Proceedings of the 4th ACM SIGACT-SIGPLAN symposium on Principles of programming languages*, 238–252.
7. Nicholas Davis, Holger Winnemöller, Mira Dontcheva, and Ellen Yi-Luen Do. 2013. Toward a cognitive theory of creativity support. In *Proceedings of the 9th ACM Conference on Creativity & Cognition*, 13–22.
8. Markus Funk and Michael Raschke. 2013. Brain Painting: Action Paintings based on BCI-Input. In *Mensch & Computer Workshopband*, 515–518.
9. Thomas T Hewett. 2005. Informing the design of computer-based environments to support creativity. *International Journal of Human-Computer Studies* 63, 4: 383–409.
10. Takashi Iba. 2011. Autopoietic Systems Diagram for Describing Creative Processes. *Procedia-Social and Behavioral Sciences* 26: 30–37.
11. Ekaterina Kutafina, David Laukamp, and Stephan M Jonas. 2015. Wearable Sensors in Medical Education: Supporting Hand Hygiene Training with a Forearm EMG. *Stud. Health Technol. Inform* 211: 286–291.
12. Todd Lubart. 2005. How can computers be partners in the creative process: classification and commentary on the special issue. *International Journal of Human-Computer Studies* 63, 4: 365–369.
13. Humberto R Maturana and Francisco J Varela. 1981. *Autopoiesis and cognition: the realization of the living*. JSTOR.
14. Humberto R Maturana. 1975. The organization of the living: A theory of the living organization. *International journal of man-machine studies* 7, 3: 313–332.
15. Pamela McCorduck. 1991. *Aaron's code: meta-art, artificial intelligence, and the work of Harold Cohen*. Macmillan.
16. John Mingers. 1994. *Self-producing systems: Implications and applications of autopoiesis*. Springer Science & Business Media.
17. Mitchel Resnick, Brad Myers, Kumiyo Nakakoji, Ben Shneiderman, Randy Pausch, Ted Selker, and Mike Eisenberg. 2005. Design principles for tools to support creative thinking.
18. Mel Rhodes. 1961. An analysis of creativity. *The Phi Delta Kappan* 42, 7: 305–310.
19. Rob Saunders. 2012. Towards autonomous creative systems: A computational approach. *Cognitive Computation* 4, 3: 216–225.
20. Ben Shneiderman, Gerhard Fischer, Mary Czerwinski, Mitch Resnick, Brad Myers, Linda Candy, Ernest Edmonds, Mike Eisenberg, Elisa Giaccardi, Tom Hewett, and others. 2006. Creativity support tools: Report from a US National Science Foundation sponsored workshop. *International Journal of Human-Computer Interaction* 20, 2: 61–77.
21. Ben Shneiderman. 2000. Creating creativity: user interfaces for supporting innovation. *ACM Transactions on Computer-Human Interaction (TOCHI)* 7, 1: 114–138.
22. Ben Shneiderman. 2007. Creativity support tools: accelerating discovery and innovation. *Communications of the ACM* 50, 12: 20–32.
23. Julien C Sprott. 1993. *Strange attractors: creating patterns in chaos*. Citeseer.
24. Julien Clinton Sprott. 1994. Automatic generation of iterated function systems. *Computers & Graphics* 18, 3: 417–425.
25. Michael Terry and Elizabeth D Mynatt. 2002. Recognizing creative needs in user interface design. In *Proceedings of the 4th conference on Creativity & cognition*, 38–44.
26. Snapper arm. Retrieved January–October 2017 from http://www.trossenrobotics.com/
27. Arduino. Retrieved January–October 2017 from http://www.arduino.cc
28. Myo armband. Retrieved January–October 2017 from www.myo.com

---

[i] http://patricktresset.com

Technology Demo of using Real-time Biofeedback of Heart Rate Variability Measures to Track and Help Improve Levels of Attention and Relaxation

Gareth Loudon
Cardiff Metropolitan University
and Centre for Creativity Ltd
Cardiff, UK
gloudon@cardiffmet.ac.uk

Dimitrios Zampelis
Centre for Creativity Ltd
Newport, UK
d.zampelis@gmail.com

ABSTRACT
The technology demonstration will show that it is possible for a person to use the real-time biofeedback of their heart rate variability (HRV), recorded from a heart rate monitor watch, to help improve their level of attention and relaxation. High levels of concentration and positive affect are associated with creativity, so improvements in 'relaxed concentration' could help enhance creativity. The technology demonstration will use an iPhone and a Mio Alpha 2 heart rate monitor watch. Participants will get a chance to try out the system to see how it works and how different interaction designs within the application can affect 'relaxed concentration' levels.

Author Keywords
Heart Rate Variability; Attention; Relaxation; Stress; Biofeedback; Creativity; Flow.

ACM Classification Keywords
G.4 Mathematical Software: Algorithm Design and Analysis; H.1.2 User / Machine Systems; H.5.2 User Interfaces; K.3.1 Computer Uses in Education.

INTRODUCTION
Csikszentmihalyi [1] suggested that people enter a state of 'flow' during creativity that is characterised by high levels of concentration and positive affect. Our previous research findings have also found that people have high levels of concentration with positive affect when undertaking a creative activity [2][3].

The main aim for this project was to create a software application to help people train and improve their levels of attention and relaxation. The motivation being that improved levels of 'relaxed concentration' could help enhance creativity. The software uses the real-time analysis of heart rate variability (HRV) to estimate levels of attention and relaxation. This information is presented to users in (near) real-time so that this biofeedback data can give insights into current performance and areas to improve, either attention, relaxation or both.

C&C '17, June 27-30, 2017, Singapore, Singapore

ACM ISBN 978-1-4503-4403-6/17/06.
http://dx.doi.org/10.1145/3059454.3084340

HRV, Attention, Stress and Flow
Heart rate variability (HRV) can be measured from the variation in consecutive pulse cycle intervals using techniques such as Photoplethysmography [4][5][6].

HRV measures can provide useful information on a person's concentration level [7][8][9]. We have also shown [3] that it is possible to use heart rate monitor watches such as the Mio Alpha 2 [10] to detect differences in levels of attention and relaxation using HRV measures. It is important to note that a significant amount of HRV data is lost when using a heart rate monitor watch for recording, compared to HRV data collected from an ECG chest sensor [11]. However. our motivation for using a watch instead of an ECG chest sensor was the convenience and ease of use.

SOFTWARE DEMONSTRATOR

Technology development
The software application created runs on an iPhone. The software uses the 'Bluetooth smart' protocol to communicate wirelessly in real-time with the Mio Alpha 2 heart rate monitor watch [10]. Heart rate (HR) estimates, together with time stamps, are received by the software. An interpolation method is used to convert these heart rate estimates into equidistant samples in real-time. Welch's Fast Fourier Transform (FFT) method is used to estimate the power spectrum density (PSD) of HRV using a 64 second hamming window. The window is moved along every 4 seconds. The PSD estimates are calculated for frequencies between 0.07 - 0.15 Hz (low frequencies) and 0.15 – 0.4 Hz (high frequencies).

Attention levels are calculated/estimated from estimates of the low frequency HRV power. Relaxation levels from a combination of heart rate, low and high frequency HRV power.

Interaction Design
The software application includes three different interaction modes to study how the mode affects the level of attention and stress/relaxation.

The first interaction mode is called the the Zone game. This mode gives separate feedback to the participant on their current level of relaxation and attention by using the location of a blue ball on a focus/relaxation grid (shown in Figure 1). The green zone represents high levels of attention and relaxation. The time spent by the participant in each zone is shown in seconds. The challenge for the participant in this Zone game is to spend as much time as possible in the green zone.

Figure 1. Screen shot of the Zone game.

The second interaction mode is called the Bird game. In this mode the attention and relaxation levels are combined to create a 'relaxed concentration' score, and the score maps to the height the bird flies at (shown in Figure 2a). The challenge for the user is to make the bird fly through the clouds to collect points, and to avoid crashing into the oncoming mountains (due to a low 'relaxed concenteation' score). In the Bird game the user might not know if they need to relax more or concentrate more (or both) to fly higher and avoid the mountains. This mode therefore studied whether users can deal with the attention and relaxation information being combined. The mode also explored how participants were affected by noticing oncmoing moutains that required them to increase their 'relaxed concentration' score quickly.

The third interaction mode is called the Tree game, which again uses a combined 'relaxed concentration' score. Flowers appear on the tree for high levels of 'relaxed concentration' or to fall off the tree for low levels (shown in Figure 2b). The tree initially starts with no flowers on it. The challenge for the participant in this interaction mode is to generate as many flowers as possible on the tree.

RESEARCH PROJECT RESULTS

Results from testing the software application with both adults and children suggest that it is possible to use the real-time biofeedback of heart rate variability measures to track and help improve levels of attention and relaxation using a heart rate monitor watch, at least at a crude level. See further details in [12].

Figure 2 (a) Screen shot of the Bird game. (b) Screen shot of the Tree game.

In addition, the interaction design of the application plays a very important role, with the Bird game creating more anxiety, and the Tree game performing best overall. The technology demonstration will allow conference attendees to try the technology out for themselves. Details of the research project will also be presented at the conference.

FUTURE IMPLICATIONS

A software application that helps people train and improve their levels of attention and relaxation has the potential to help people enhance their level of creativity, as attention positive affect are associated with state of 'flow' during creativity. The application could also be used to help children improve their levels of concentration at school. The technology could be integrated into 'mindfulness' applications that aim to help people improve their attention and reduce their stress, or into sports applications requiring improved levels of relaxed concentration, such as golf.

ACKNOWLEDGEMENTS

We would like to thank Innovate UK for supporting the work.

REFERENCES

1. Mihaly Csíkszentmihályi. 1996. *Creativity: Flow and the Psychology of Discovery and Invention*. New York: Harper Collins.
2. Gareth Loudon and Gina Deininger. 2016. The Physiological Response during Divergent Thinking. *Journal of Behavioral and Brain Science*, 6, 28-37. http://dx.doi.org/10.4236/jbbs.2016.61004
3. Gareth Loudon and Gina Deininger. 2017. The Physiological Response to drawing and its relation to attention and relaxation. *Journal of Behavioral and Brain Science*, Vol. 7, 111-124. http://dx.doi.org/10.4236/jbbs.2017.73011
4. Eduardo Gil, Michele Orini, Bailón, R., Vergara, J.M., Luca Mainardi and Pablo Laguna. 2010.

Photoplethysmography pulse rate variability as a surrogate measurement of heart rate variability during non-stationary conditions. *Physiological Measurement*, 31, 1271-1290. http://dx.doi.org/10.1088/0967-3334/31/9/015

5. Lu, G., Yang, F., Taylor, J.A., and Stein, J.F. 2009. A comparison of photoplethysmography and ECG recording to analyse heart rate variability in healthy subjects. *Journal of Medical Engineering Technology*, 33, 634–641. http://dx.doi.org/10.3109/03091900903150998
6. Axel Schäfer and Jan Vagedes. 2013. How accurate is pulse rate variability as an estimate of heart rate variability? A review on studies comparing photoplethysmographic technology with an electrocardiogram, *International Journal of Cardiology*, 166, 15–29. http://dx.doi.org/10.1016/j.ijcard.2012.03.119
7. Monika Althaus, Lambertus J.M. Mulder, Gijsbertus Mulder, Arie M. Van Roon, and Ruud B. Minderaa. 1998. Influence of respiratory activity on the cardiac response pattern to mental effort, *Psychophysiology*, 35, 420-430.
8. Anita L. Hansen, Bjørn H. Johnsen and Julian F. Thayer. 2003. Vagal influence on working memory and attention. *International Journal of Psychophysiology*, 48, 263–274.
9. Arie M. Van Roon, Lambertus J.M. Mulder, J. B. P. Veldman, and Gijsbertus Mulder. 1995. Beat-to-beat blood-pressure measurements applied in studies on mental workload. *Homeostasis*, 36, 3316–3324.
10. Mio Alpha 2. Mio Alpha 2 Heart Rate Monitor Watch. 2017. Retrieved January 6, 2017 from http://www.mioglobal.com/EN-UK/Mio-ALPHA-2-Heart-Rate-Watch/Product.aspx.
11. Jakub Parak and Ilkka Korhonen. 2014. Evaluation of Wearable Consumer Heart Rate Monitors Based on Photopletysmography, *36th Annual International Conference of the IEEE Engineering in Medicine and Biology Society*, 26-30 August, Chicago.
12. Gareth Loudon, Gina Deininger and Dimitrios Zampelis. 2017. Using Real-time Biofeedback of Heart Rate Variability Measures to Track and Help Improve Levels of Attention and Relaxation. *ACM Creativity and Cognition Conference 2017*, June, Singapore.

Twittener: Listen to your Twitter Feed

Yohan Fernandopulle[1], Rianne W. Meurzec[1], Ng Hong Quan[2], Fairul Akmaruddin[2], Owen Noel Newton Fernando[1]
Nanyang Technological University, Singapore.
[1]{yohan.f, rmeurzec, ofernando}@ntu.edu.sg
[2]{C140094, C130162}@e.ntu.edu.sg

ABSTRACT
Twitter is a popular social media service, as it allows users to get rapid & concise information, and to follow the latest online trends & topics. This project aims to improve user experience by proposing an alternative way to interact with Twitter, by allowing users to listen to interesting tweets, instead of the conventional way of reading them. This will allow users to get up to date with tweets from publicly-listed, categorized Twitter accounts, without needing to pay full attention to their screens. This could prove useful for populations with physical disabilities, visual impairments, the elderly and persons who multitask. A web application, called Twittener, has been developed to allow users to listen to tweets. Additionally, a console application periodically crawls through Twitter retrieving & converting tweets from text to speech, thus making up the Twittener system.

Author Keywords
Twitter; Topic Modelling; Sentiment Analysis; Text-to-Speech; HTML5; Web Speech

ACM Classification Keywords
H.3.3. [Information Search and Retrieval]: Information filtering; H.4.m. [Information Systems Applications]: Miscellaneous; H.5.2 [User Interfaces]: Voice I/O;

INTRODUCTION
Millions of people use social media, most of whom use it to stay connected with friends, share ideas, opinions and thoughts, stay up-to-date, stimulate businesses and for entertainment. Twitter is one of the most popular online social networking services in the world [1] with more than 500 million users and an approximate 320 million monthly active users [2]. The main functionality of Twitter is to allow its users to send or read "tweets", a 140 characters' message, which may contain images, videos, links or text that is made by other users of the site. Registered users can follow other user accounts that are interesting to them, from friends and family members to well-known celebrities and brands, politicians and news site, and are able to read tweets on their home timeline. Internet users frequently have a short attention span, preferring to multi task, and do not enjoy or simply do not have the time to read long winded messages or posts [3]. This lends an explanation behind Twitter's disruptive success. It provides a short and concise way to give and receive information rapidly. Additionally, Twitter has also become one of the go-to platforms for users to get their news updates. According to a study [4], nearly 9 in 10 Twitter users (86%) indicate that they use Twitter for news, and vast majority of those (74%) do so on a daily basis.

C&C '17, June 27-30, 2017, Singapore, Singapore

ACM ISBN 978-1-4503-4403-6/17/06.
http://dx.doi.org/10.1145/3059454.3084341

Despite the popularity, Twitter is mainly a text-based social networking service that is not suitable to use while driving or exercising. Moreover, the elderly, people with disabilities, and the less literate, may find it difficult to use text-based social networking services like Twitter. As such, Twittener is an innovative invention, designed to tackle these challenges. Using natural language processing & text-to-speech technologies, Twittener [5] converts conventionally written tweets to audio form. Users are able to listen to their own timeline or choose from topics such as 'news', 'business', 'technology', and other categories. Publicly listed twitter accounts can be categorized under pre-defined, or user defined topics and tweets from these accounts are retrieved and processed by natural language processing libraries to determine their sentiment value. Only tweets with high sentiment value will be played to the user, providing users with high value content.

SYSTEM DETAILS & COMPONENTS
This application proposes a tweet listener which merges text-to-speech with sentiment analysis and topic detection for a more personalized and improved method to listen to tweets. The design focuses on flexibility and reusability, such that the main codebase can be adapted and ported to different platforms. This allows broad reach to web application and mobile application transferability.

Tweet Extractor Application
The Tweet Extractor Application retrieves tweets from categories such as 'Technology', 'News', etc. from predefined Twitter accounts. The tweets are gathered with Twitter's Streaming API, and pipelined for Natural Language Processing (NLP). After tweets are streamed in, the NLP component classifies tweets according to their

sentimental value, and topics are detected from the categorized tweets. The sentiment analyzer conducts analysis using Stanford CoreNLP Library [6], with recursive deep model for semantic compositionality. Tweets with a very positive sentiment value are processed for text-to-speech before being saved in the database.

The tweets are also tokenized (process of breaking up the stream of tweets into words, phrases, symbols, and other meaningful elements called tokens), which may include discarding certain characters. Part-of-Speech tagging marks up tokens into parts of speech, and Named Entity Recognition identifies names entities into pre-defined categories, both processed which were used to further analyses of the tweets for topic categorization. Topic modelling algorithm used in the topic processor component was the Latent Dirichlet Allocation (LDA) [7], to generate a list of topics associated to each tweet, and was then summarized to find the exact tweet topic using the SumBasic algorithm [8]. Trending topics were also detected by the Topic Processor, at four hour intervals.

Twittener Web Application

The web application serves as the main gateway to allow users to interact with Twitter in a more meaningful way. The website is designed to be responsive and is optimized to display well on mobile devices to facilitate its' use on the go. Users may select a topic to listen to tweets from a pre-defined list of topics, with tweets sources from curated accounts, endure natural language processing and sentiment analysis to maximize content relevance. Users can also create their own topics and manually add Twitter accounts of interest to personalize their experience. Alternatively, users can select trends based on worldwide & country preference, using dropdown options or hashtags. Users may also choose to use the search box, with keywords, to pull up tweets or user accounts of interest to them. Using the Twittener Player, users listen to tweets using a four-grid layout (see Figure 1). The first quadrant contains the HTML5 audio player and an interactive list of tweets from which the player reads out. The flow of the audio player can be interrupted by selecting a different tweet from the list which the user wishes to listen to. The second quadrant contains a gallery of images, displayed as thumbnails, and these images are related images of the tweets in the pipeline. The third quadrant contains the associated videos of the tweets and the last quadrant displays the links found in these tweets.

Speech Recognition

Accessibility of the application was further improved by the addition of speech recognition capabilities. Users are able to use their voice for site navigation and to perform text input tasks such as the creation of tweets. Speech recognition was implemented using Web Speech API [9] which provides speech-input and text-to-speech features for web browsers.

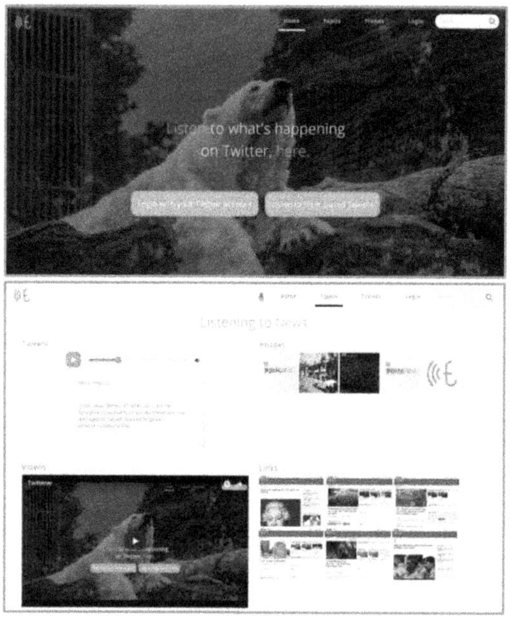

Figure 1. Twittener web application

While api.ai [10], a platform for natural language understanding which allows developers to build conversational user interfaces is used to understand user's request. Audio input is first collected from the user through their device microphone and provided to the speech recognition API for recognition. The API then returns a result upon successful recognition and the transcript is extracted. Following which, the transcript is sent to api.ai API to interpret the request of the user and decide on the action to take to fulfil the user request. If the request by the user is recognized, api.ai will send a response with the associated action to take and Twittener will process the action on behalf of the user.

When users stop speaking, the API stops seeking for more audio, processes the audio and tries to return a result. Some of the phrases the application recognizes are "listen to <topic_name>", "search for <keyword>" and "go to <page>". This development will allow users to interact with their Twittener and render their engagement almost hands-free, for their convenience.

CONCLUSION & FUTURE DIRECTION

In conclusion, Twittener hopes to meet a need in the industry targeted to people with special needs, especially visual impairments, those who multitask or benefit from hands-free technology. The development of Twittener hopes to provide an alternative to traditional written Twitter, and usability studies show the ease of use and usefulness of Twittener. As the current trending algorithm is simple, a more robust and efficient trending algorithm will be developed to provide more relevant trending topics for Twittener users. Further improvements to the speech recognition will be made. Plans are in the pipeline to enable speech recognition in browsers and to improve the accuracy of recognition.

REFERENCES

1. twitter.com Traffic Statistics, Alexa.com, 2017. http://www.alexa.com/siteinfo/twitter.com.
2. Company | About. Retrieved February 8, 2017 from https://about.twitter.com/company
3. T. Rosenstiel, J. Sonderman, K. Loker, M. Ivancin and N. Kjarval, "Twitter and News: How people use Twitter to get news", American Press Institute, 2015. https://www.americanpressinstitute.org/publications/reports/survey-research/how-people-use-twitter-news/
4. Hooton, C. Our attention span is now less than that of a goldfish. *The Independent*, 2017. http://www.independent.co.uk/news/science/our-attention-span-is-now-less-than-that-of-a-goldfish-microsoft-study-finds-10247553.html.
5. Twittener. *Twittener.io*, 2017. http://www.twittener.io.
6. Stanford CoreNLP. stanfordnlp.github.io, 2017. https://stanfordnlp.github.io/CoreNLP/
7. David M. Blei, Andrew Y. Ng, and Michael I. Jordan. 2003. Latent dirichlet allocation. *J. Mach. Learn. Res.* 3 (March 2003), 993-1022.
8. Nenkova A., and Vanderwende L. "The impact of frequency on summarization," in Microsoft Research, Redmond, Washington, Tech. Rep. MSR-TR-2005-101, 2005.
9. Web Speech API Specification. *Dvcs.w3.org*, 2017. https://dvcs.w3.org/hg/speech-api/raw-file/tip/speechapi.html.
10. API.AI. *API.AI*, 2017. https://docs.api.ai/.

Tangible Air: An Interactive Installation for Visualising Audience Engagement

Thomas Röggla[1], Chen Wang[1], Lilia Perez Romero[1], Jack Jansen[1], Pablo Cesar[1,2]
[1]Centrum Wiskunde & Informatica, [2]Delft University of Technology
The Netherlands
{t.roggla, c.wang, l.perez, j.jansen, p.s.cesar}@cwi.nl

ABSTRACT
This article presents an end-to-end system for capturing physiological sensor data and visualising it on a real-time graphic dashboard and as part of an art installation. More specifically, it describes an event where the level of engagement of the audience was measured by means of *Galvanic Skin Response* (GSR) sensors and of the presenter through a sweater fitted with GSR, ECG and acceleration sensors. The gathered data was presented in real-time through a visualisation projected onto a screen and a physical electro-mechanical installation, which would change the height of helium-filled balloons depending on the atmosphere in the auditorium. Thereby trying to create a tangible way of making the invisible visible.

ACM Classification Keywords
H.5.m. Information Interfaces and Presentation (e.g. HCI): Miscellaneous

Author Keywords
Sensors; cultural experiences; GSR; shared experiences; interactive art; physical installation; data visualisation

INTRODUCTION
There exist numerous publications which use sensors such as *Galvanic Skin Response* sensors to assess a person's reaction to media items like movies, music or live performances such as theatre plays [2]. Most of these studies however, are conducted in laboratory settings and often also with a single participant at a time [1]. In the work presented in this article, we decided to go a few steps further and use different sensor technologies to visualise the engagement of a number of people during a live event. In addition to that, we also wanted to find a way to make emotion and engagement more tangible by transporting these abstract concepts into the physical world.

The system made use of a custom-built group of wireless GSR sensors as seen in Figure 2, which were used to capture the engagement of 36 members of the audience at an event. Moreover, the presenter of the event wore a specially designed sweater integrated with sensors measuring skin conductivity, heart rate and acceleration. All the data from the audience as well as the presenter was gathered and processed at a central server and relayed to a graphic visualisation projected onto a wall. This way, every attendee could see the amount of engagement in the audience and the state of mind of the presenter. Additionally, the data of ten audience members selected at random by the system was fed into a physical installation entitled *Tangible Air*, depicted in Figure 1, which would represent the level of engagement of these ten audience members physically by altering the height of helium-filled balloons, popping the ones whose level of engagement would underrun a certain threshold. Thereby creating a moment of shock and thus hopefully eliciting a newly increased level of engagement in the audience.

Figure 1. Installation with balloons at different heights during the event, with speaker and graphic visualisation on the left

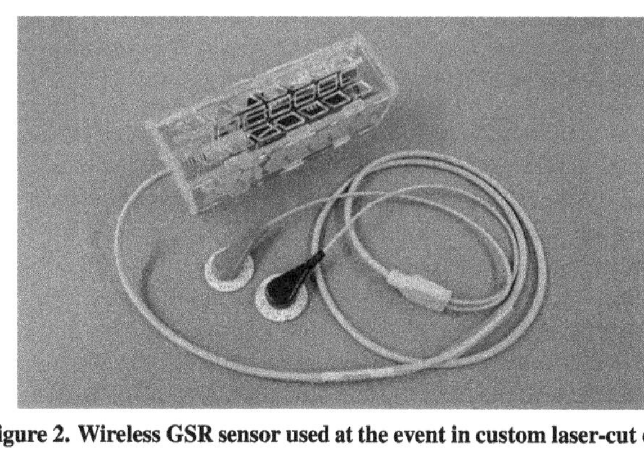

Figure 2. Wireless GSR sensor used at the event in custom laser-cut case

C&C '17 June 27-30, 2017, Singapore, Singapore

ACM ISBN 978-1-4503-4403-6/17/06.
DOI: http://dx.doi.org/10.1145/3059454.3078708

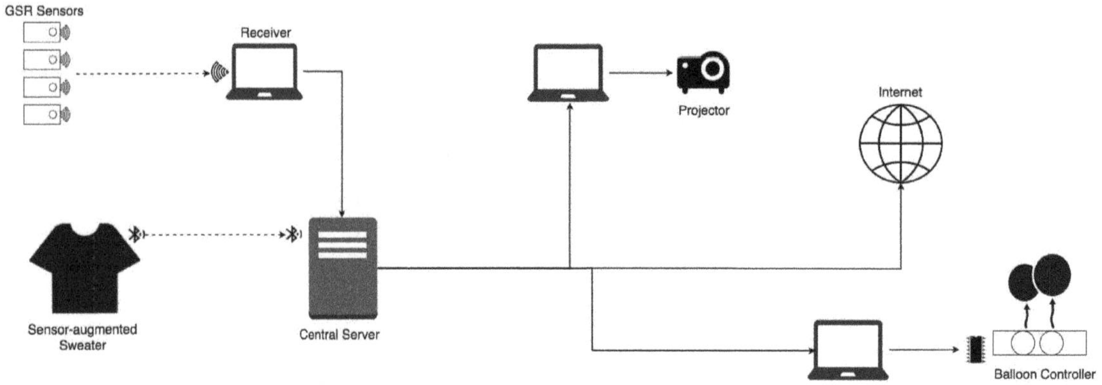

Figure 3. Layout of the entire system deployed at the event. On the left, data collection from the audience through wireless GSR sensors and from the sweater via Bluetooth and on the right visualisation on a screen and on the Internet and the installation with the balloons.

What we would like to showcase in this demo is a simplified version of the system that was used during the live event accompanied by supplementary material, such as a video and a poster describing the system and the event in greater detail. Participants can try the sensors and experience a scaled-down version of the installation and the visualisation.

SETUP

The system as depicted in Figure 3 was set up and used during a networking event with various talks. In one of the talks about wearable technology given by the Dutch fashion designer *ByBorre*, 36 members of the audience received one of our GSR sensors to use at the 20 minute talk, during which we collected around 106000 data points, which were stored for later analysis.

The system is centred around a central server, which takes in data from the audience via the local network and from the sweater via a Bluetooth connection. The raw data is then distributed to client machines through a publish-subscribe model. Data from the sweater as well as all audience data is fed to a machine connected to a projector, which projects the visualisation depicted in Figure 4 onto a screen. Further, the raw data from ten randomly selected audience members is fed to another client machine, which in turn is connected to an *Arduino* microprocessor which is responsible for converting the engagement values into height adjustments for the balloons and controlling the stepper motors accordingly. Finally, the central machine also runs a web server, which serves a scaled-down version of the visualisation to browser-clients.

More specifically, the data gathered from the sensors was visualised in two ways: the first one being a real-time visualisation of the data, which showed on one side the level of engagement for each audience member using one of the sensors, as well as the engagement of the speaker, his heart rate and how much he was moving. All of these data streams were projected onto a screen during the presentation. In addition to that, audience members could access a simplified version of the same visualisation on their mobile devices through the Internet.

Perhaps more tangible was the second way the data was visualised. An installation dubbed *Tangible Air* by its creator, artist Lilia Perez Romero consisted of ten big white helium balloons placed next to each other. The balloons were held in place by strings connected to spools that would wind or unwind according to the data received from a set of sensors randomly selected from the audience members. The level of engagement measured by the sensors, was translated to the length of string attached to each individual balloon. The more engaged the audience members would become, the higher the balloons would fly and vice versa if the engagement should fall. When an audience member became completely disengaged, the balloon linked to their data stream loses height, potentially reaching the ground where a row of needles awaited. If a balloon touched a needle it would burst and the noise would inevitably capture the audience's attention and renew their level of engagement, thus pulling the balloons back to a high position. This action-reaction behaviour formed a closed feedback loop demonstrating how an environment can be shaped according to physiological data obtained through wearable technology.

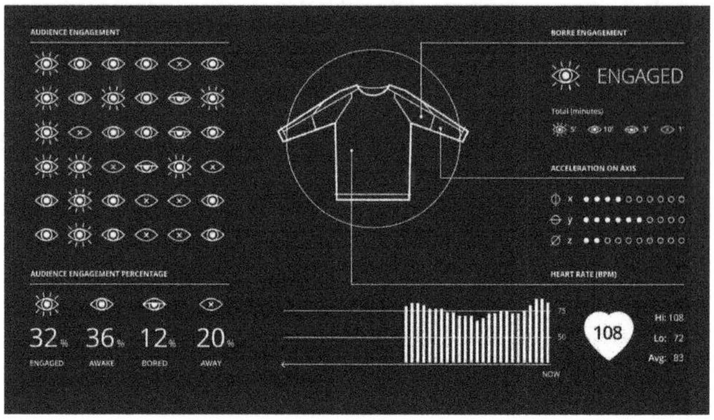

Figure 4. Visualisation showing audience engagement (left half) and sensor readings of the presenter (right half).

In summary, the goal of this project was to explore new ways with which we could make emotion, which is ever-present yet completely abstract, more present and tangible in the physical world by transferring it into a physical medium through the use of technology and artistic expression.

REFERENCES

1. Erin A. Carroll and Celine Latulipe. 2012. Triangulating the Personal Creative Experience: Self-report, External Judgments, and Physiology. In *Proceedings of Graphics Interface 2012 (GI '12)*. Canadian Information Processing Society, Toronto, Ont., Canada, Canada, 53–60. http://dl.acm.org/citation.cfm?id=2305276.2305286
2. Celine Latulipe, Erin A. Carroll, and Danielle Lottridge. 2011. Love, Hate, Arousal and Engagement: Exploring Audience Responses to Performing Arts. In *Proceedings of the SIGCHI Conference on Human Factors in Computing Systems (CHI '11)*. ACM, New York, NY, USA, 1845–1854. DOI: http://dx.doi.org/10.1145/1978942.1979210

Tainted: Smell the Virtual Ghost

Nimesha Ranasinghe[1], Koon Chuan Raymond Koh[2], Daniel Chua[1], Barry Chew[1], Yan Liangkun[1], Thi Ngoc Tram Nguyen[1], Kala Shamaiah[2], Siew Geuk Choo[2], David Tolley[1], Shienny Karwita[1], Ellen Yi-Luen Do[1]
Keio-NUS CUTE Center, National University of Singapore[1]
Games Design and Development, Institute of Technical Education, Singapore[2]
{nimesha, idmcyld, idmczb, idmyl, idmntnt, dtolley, shienny}[1]@nus.edu.sg,
{raymond_k_c_koh, kala_shamaiah, Choo_Siew_Geuk}[2]@ite.edu.sg

ABSTRACT
This demonstration presents "Tainted", a first-person 3D adventure game that enables players to experience a traditional horror folklore using visual-auditory-olfactory interactions. The system consists of a computer to play the game and a smell-emitting module that contains jasmine, pineapple, mango, and banana scents. The information provided by the additional smell stimuli delivers an immersive gaming experience by providing game narrative and signaling predefined game conditions (e.g. imminent threat). Smell stimuli may also help to enhance player's cognition and memory, as well as to invoke emotional responses such as fear and curiosity.

ACM Classification Keywords
H.5.m. Information Interfaces and Presentation (e.g. HCI): Miscellaneous

Author Keywords
Smell; Games; Olfaction; Multimodal Cognition

INTRODUCTION
"Tainted" is a first-person 3D adventure game that enables players to experience a traditional horror folklore using visual-auditory-olfactory interactions. The system consists of a computer to play the game and a smell-emitting module that contains different scents. The olfactory information provided by the added modality of smell delivers an immersive gaming experience by enabling players to sense predefined game conditions (e.g. imminent threat, game hints), receiving game narrative information, and invoking intended emotional responses (e.g. fear, curiosity). Four scents (jasmine, pineapple, mango and banana) are explicitly used to uncover and guide the plot in the horror-themed survivor game involving a Southeast Asian folklore character (ghost), the "Pontianak" [2]. In Tainted, the olfactory information seems closely coupled with the players' experience and enjoyment of the narrative as well as the smell-driven gameplay. Figure 1 displays several scenes captured during the gameplay.

(A) (B) (C)

Figure 1. Different scenes captured from the Tainted game: (A) Pontianak in the banana plantation, (B) Nang Tani (the friendly ghost showing directions), and (C) collect the can of kerosene.

Delivering multisensory experiences during gameplay is increasingly popular, however, only the video, audio, and haptic sensations are often considered. On the contrary, sense of smell (olfaction) is also plausible for creating immersive gaming experiences and delivering useful information since it also triggers certain cues for the player. Although, there are existing technologies that examine olfactory displays and games, almost all of these systems use smell as a feedback mechanism only [1, 3]. However, in our approach the story itself is driven by the smells, thus creating a seamless integration between the storyline and the multisensory feedback channels. Also, numerous studies suggest a close relationship between emotions and olfaction as smells may modulate behavior, mood, and cognition. Similarly, in Tainted, the banana smell may actuate fearfulness since it is associated with the ghost in the story. Thus, this enables the delivery of non-time sensitive olfactory cues to the player in a unique manner.

USER EXPERIENCE
To demonstrate, the users can play the Tainted game (exploring main features and multisensory interactions through visual, auditory, and smell sensations) with the smell-emitting device to investigate this novel technology as an embodied and emotional experience, as displayed in Figure 2 (B).

Narrative
"An amnesiac male wakes up in the Shed House and finds himself in an abandoned banana plantation. Through exploration of the surroundings, key mementos that are found trigger faint memories in his mind. The vampiric "Pontianak" chases after him to seek revenge on all men. The four items collectively

C&C '17 June 27-30, 2017, Singapore, Singapore

ACM ISBN 978-1-4503-4403-6/17/06
DOI: http://dx.doi.org/10.1145/3059454.3078709

Table 1. Interaction mapping to in-game events

Designated scent	Designated LED color	Intended or indicative information to convey	Purpose
Banana	Red	Pontianak is close to the player	Game Progression and Game Narrative
Jasmine	Magenta	The "Hand-cranked camping flashlight" item is nearby. The light keeps Pontianak away for a short while, the player has to wind it up often	Game Progression and Game Narrative
Pineapple	Green	A flammable item is nearby - Either a lighter, or a can of kerosene. Both are required to burn the banana tree	Game Progression
Mango	Blue	Mementos: A lady's high heel shoe, a pair of spectacles, a ring and a photo frame	Game Narrative

reveal the protagonist's past, and he is to eventually choose between burning the haunted banana tree to escape, or to accept his fate and repent on his sin (death by the Pontianak)."

The story for Tainted is loosely based on the Southeast Asian folklore character Pontianak originating from Malaysian and Indonesian roots. The long-haired female spirit is always associated with banana trees, and it is said that the Pontianak resides in them during the day. In some cases, the Pontianak preys upon and seeks revenge against males [2].

Each of the four mementos to be picked up in the game contains a structured piece of the protagonist's past, and when collected in full they reveal that he was unfaithful towards his spouse (before his memory loss). The Pontianak knows this and is determined to kill him. He tries to survive.

Interaction Design

The game's narrative and 3D environment are set in a banana plantation with smell proximity triggers placed in designated locations. The smells are designed to convey respective pieces of information vital to the player to "survive" (game progression), or to enjoy the game narrative (a combination of both is also possible). Each of the four scent dispensers also has a unique LED color assigned to it that lights up when correspondingly triggered in-game. This has been included as an added subtle visual cue because in-game triggers are invisible to the player, and that diffused scents would linger around the player. It is also for this reason that a fan (facing the player) has been included in the module that is activated for 10 seconds each time a scent diffuser is triggered. Thereby a scent is blown towards the player when triggered. Table 1 shows the described interaction mapping to in-game events.

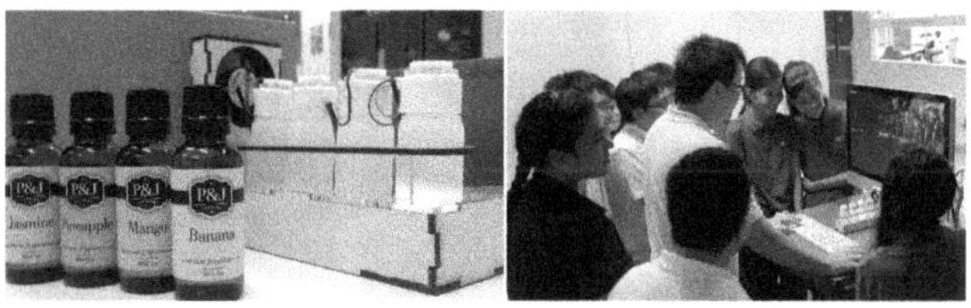

(A) (B)

Figure 2. (A) smell-emitting module with four different scents used, (B) students experience the Tainted (visual-auditory-olfactory gameplay) during a demo session

Game Design Considerations

As scents or smells linger in the physical game space after repeated playing, the gameplay has been designed to be a short and fast-paced experience (approximately three minutes). The player has to bridge the loose pieces of information that adds up to the whole narrative during this time, whilst avoiding Pontianak's chase to survive. Two emotional responses are associated here, curiosity and fear. The first smell trigger is a memento item that has been placed in an obvious path for the player, i.e. it is the only possible route out of the house where the player starts in. This allows a simple explanatory message to be sent to the player to understand how the game is played, i.e. smell is an important element during the gameplay.

Attributing to its original folklore origins, the assigned scent for Pontianak is banana; hence when the banana scent is diffused, it indicates that Pontianak is nearby. It is the only dynamic trigger in the game while all other scent triggers are static. Red LED color is also assigned to this dynamic trigger to indicate imminent danger. Mementos may be collected in any order so long as all four are found. They however only deliver the game narrative and are not critical to "survive" (or complete) the game. It is possible to finish the game by simply collecting both flammable items, and setting the haunted banana tree ablaze, though the player would not fully receive information on the game narrative then.

SYSTEM DESCRIPTION

Among the two main modules of the Tainted system, the game is developed on Unity platform[1] and communicates with the smell-emitting module over the USB connection. The smell-emitting module, which has four containers for four different smells is developed using ultrasonic diffusers and controlled by an Arduino Pro Mini[2] (as in Figure 2 (A)). Each container contains an ultrasonic diffuser and a cotton bud to draw liquefied scent up to the diffuser unit. Also, an RGB Light Emitting Diode (LED) is attached to the bottom of each container to provide color feedback to the player.

Acknowledgements

This research is supported by the National Research Foundation, Prime Minister's Office, Singapore under its International Research Centres in Singapore Funding Initiative.

[1]https://unity3d.com/unity

[2]https://www.arduino.cc/

REFERENCES

1. Stephen Boyd Davis, Gordon Davies, Ruba Haddad, and Mei-Kei Lai. 2007. Smell me: Engaging with an interactive olfactory game. In *People and Computers XX?Engage*. Springer, 25–40.

2. Russell Lee. 1992. *The Almost Complete Collection of True Singapore Ghost Stories*. Vol. 3. Flame of the Forest.

3. Arito Mochizuki, Takashi Amada, Sayuri Sawa, Tadayuki Takeda, Shogo Motoyashiki, Kazuhiro Kohyama, Masataka Imura, and Kunihiro Chihara. 2004. Fragra: a visual-olfactory VR game. In *ACM SIGGRAPH 2004 Sketches*. ACM, 123.

Lunhui — Upcycled Creations

Mengyu Cao
Parsons School of Design
New York City, United States
caom061@newschool.edu

ABSTRACT
Lunhui is a tech startup that functions as a platform for bringing together city residents and craftspeople. It supports up-cycling and creates art and design objects by providing unwanted material pick-up service and by matching the inventory to craftspeople to support their creations. It helps to give unwanted objects new life cycles, away from landfills. I would like more people to be involved in up-cycling and creativity circles by providing easy and efficient technology.

Lunhui was created to drive demand for up-cycling and to bring city residents together. The service connects individuals who are decluttering with craftspeople who make products from recycled materials. The goal is to reduce waste, create value, fulfill customers' feelings of satisfaction, thrift, and resourcefulness, as well as bring support and encouragement to cooperators who are artists, designers, and craftspeople.

Author Keywords
waste; up-cycle; recycle; creativity; unwanted items; life cycles; rebirth; crafts; inventory; matching; making; creation; bots; service; pick up.

ACM Classification Keywords
H.5.2 User Interfaces: Interaction styles; D.2.2 Design Tools and Techniques: Evolutionary prototyping; Modules and interfaces; User Interfaces.

INTRODUCTION
My project provides new solutions for waste and helps people form a habit of treasuring resources and changing their behavior of throwing things out.

Four questions drive my solution.

- Why is up-cycling a good solution for waste problems?
- How can we create an up-cycling loop to turn waste into new products and link people who throw things away with craftspeople who can reuse waste in this loop?
- What is the best way /media /platform to connect all the things together to build the loop?
- Can up-cycled products be attractive and fashionable, as well as accepted by the majority of people?

The final output of my project is an artificial bot-centered up-cycling service that connects customers (people who need decluttering) and cooperators (artists, designers, craftsmen, who are working on recycling and up-cycling). The service gets unwanted stuff from customers and sends matched items to cooperators who create new products from the waste. After their creations, the service also helps the cooperators to sell these products in a new marketplace. The creations are then redistributed to customers via the bot. Customers can get points by giving their stuff away and the points can be used toward the price of new creations that they buy. I believe that there is a marketplace in waste and demand for up-cycling. My project is a new way to facilitate up-cycling with a convenient decluttering service for customers and efficient material supply to craftspeople.

CONTEXT
My project is a service that utilizes an artificial bot, which is embodied in different chat applications, such as Messenger, WeChat, Slack, etc. There are also separate online platforms for presenting and selling up-cycled products, including a website, a Facebook page, and an Instagram account. People can find it on chat applications or on social media and public promotions.

The bot is a concierge that meets demands from both customers and cooperators. From the customer side, the bot schedules pick-up times, collects addresses, calculates points in the point system, and sends points to customers. According to how many points the customer has accumulated, the bot sends new creations made by cooperators to customers for them to exchange or buy with discounts. From the cooperator side, the bot learns their interests, suggests items that they are interested in frequently, and processes their orders.

C&C '17, June 27-30, 2017, Singapore, Singapore

ACM ISBN 978-1-4503-4403-6/17/06.
http://dx.doi.org/10.1145/3059454.3078710

AUDIENCE AND SETTING

My audience includes two groups of people. One is customers who need a decluttering service to remove unwanted stuff from their homes. This includes millennials in NYC, especially parents with young children. The other group is cooperators, including designers, artists, and craftspeople who can use the unwanted stuff to create new pieces/ products. These cooperators are working on recycling and up-cycling, and they have the skills of turning old things into new products.

User Cases

Marina T

Marina saw a public poster about the decluttering bot service. Then she opened Messenger to search for the bot. She chatted with the bot and made a schedule to pick up the possessions that she didn't want. When Lunhui's staff went to the building at the appointed time, Marina left all her unwanted items at the front of her building. By giving her unwanted items away, Marina received 20 points that can be used to get discounts on up-cycled creations that are sold on Lunhui. She really liked an up-cycled purse. She brought it with a discount from her points.

Justin S

Justin found the bot service on Facebook and felt that he could use the bot to discover and receive more materials for his art. He searched and added the bot on Messenger. The bot suggested 5 different kinds of items. He chose household items. The bot kept suggesting household items to Justin to see if he needed any of them. After receiving several rounds of pictures, he found 2 items he wanted to use and made an order with the bot. He received the items and created 2 art pieces with them. He then sent the pictures and prices of the two pieces to the bot. The bot helped to post the art pieces to the online platform to sell.

DOMAINS AND PRECEDENTS

The domains of the project include economics, sustainability, resources flow, solid waste, design, technology, up-cycle, creativity and social entrepreneurship. We live in a time of throw-away consumerism. In 2007, Americans threw out about 570 billion pounds of solid waste. Compared to other nations, the United States has a record of generating waste at an alarming rate. Home to only 4% of the global population, we are responsible for more than 30% of the planet's total waste generation [1]. The focus of the project is wasted clothes and fabrics, accessories, decorations, furniture, paper and books, and electronic products, because these are things that are easier to find for up-cycling solutions.

There are organizations and companies that work on recycling clothes and household items. Goodwill and The Salvation Army accept donations of unwanted stuff. The donators can get a tax deduction according to the value of what they donate. Many clothes & shoes bins are placed throughout the city, such as Planet Aid Bins and USAgain Bins. However, the fact is that Americans throw away 25 billion pounds of clothing every year, only 15 percent of which ends up donated or recycled [2]. One of the reasons for this is that these organizations can typically only sell 20 percent or less of their donations in retail stores. Textile recyclers buy up the rest to sell overseas and to companies that tear clothes up and remake them as industrial rags, insulation, and carpet padding [2]. Also, textile recycling bins are both non-profit and for-profit. Many people place their unwanted clothing in the convenient bins, and they have no idea of where these clothes go, which raises concerns for nonprofit organizations like The Salvation Army and St. Vincent De Paul [3]. More efforts for recycling are needed here, and up-cycling is a potential solution for getting value from waste.

In the fashion industry, retail companies like H&M and Levi's are also doing recycling programs in their stores. They provide a discount on new products for those customers who donate their unwanted clothes. They then recycle this fabric into materials that can be used to produce new products. However, it is not possible today to close the loop and recycle all types of materials into new textile fabrics. According to its newest sustainability report, in 2015, recycled fabric rose to 1% of the materials H&M used, up from 0.2% the previous year [4]. Therefore, up-cycling is the best possible way to handle waste right now. It is a strategic solution, offering more than what is currently available.

BRAND CONCEPT

Lunhui is the Chinese term for samsara. The original meaning of samsara is the revolution of the soul from body to body whether animal, human, angelic, or of the gods. Here, I think that objects have transmigration as well. People throw many things away. Landfills should not be the end for unwanted stuff. There are many craftspeople, artists, and designers who are working on recycling and up-cycling, giving objects new life circles. Lunhui is helping to enlarge the up-cycling and creation loop.

USER INTERFACE AND USER EXPERIENCE

I started with user flows by mapping out two of the user experience lines for both people who need to declutter and people who need materials. Then I based my research off user interface and functions that can be accomplished in Messenger bots. I created the interface for each step.

I tested the design with my potential audience. Testers felt that it was easy to either schedule a pick-up or make a material order. Also, they felt that it was convenient to find it on Messenger. They didn't need to go to a new webpage or download a new app. That is why I choose an artificial bot that can be embodied in many chat applications as the technology platform.

The bot allows users to connect with it in the applications that they are already using frequently. The bot as a broker connects customers who are decluttering to up-cyclers who need materials. It makes business happen in a conversational manner. It grows the network and facilitates transactions.

VALUE PROPOSITION

Lunhui helps people declutter and make ethical and sustainable choices. It provides easy waste pick-up services. It helps to reduce waste, to give unwanted items new life cycles, and to enlarge the up-cycling and creation loop. It supports emerging artists, designers, and craftspeople.

REFERENCES

1. "The problem of waste," Toxics Action Center, http://www.toxicsaction.org/problems-and-solutions/waste
2. Ask Umbra, "What really happens when I put clothing in a donation bin?" Grist, Oct 15, 2015, http://grist.org/living/what-really-happens-when-i-put-clothing-in-a-donation-bin/
3. LINH TA, "For-profit donation bins create issues for nonprofits" CVBusinessMonthly, Jul 15, 2013, http://wcfcourier.com/business/local/for-profit-donation-bins-create-issues-for-nonprofits/article_64f6a0c0-ea56-11e2-9b02-001a4bcf887a.html
4. Marc Bain, "Is H&M misleading customers with all its talk of sustainability?", Quartz, April 16, 2016, http://qz.com/662031/is-hm-misleading-customers-with-all-its-talk-of-sustainability/

Technology Demonstration: Augmented Design Ideation

Benjamin C. Stopher
Information Experience Design
Royal College of Art
London, UK
benjamin.stopher@network.rca.ac.uk

Oliver J. Smith
Interaction Design & Visual Communication
London College of Communication, UAL
London, UK
o.smith@lcc.arts.ac.uk

ABSTRACT

This technology demonstration showcases augmented design ideation tools that have been developed to explore *hybrid design environments* [1] using novel prototypes that use ambient informatics and ubiquitous computing approaches. The tool aims to enhance the creative scope of multi-participant design ideation by providing contextually relevant visual design prompts to enhance design ideation processes and conceptualisation [1]. This demonstration explores the feasibility and effects of tools that can be built now using ad-Hoc arrangements/meshes of the following:

- **Application Programing Interfaces (API's)** from popular web platforms: that offer up various types of culturally/contextually relevant content – i.e. historical, contemporary or live – images, text and sound.
- **Internet search technologies:** This includes the 'mashing' together of Internet search technologies such as speech-to-text (IBM's Watson) to both provide live queries to culturally/contextually relevant content, and importantly, live feedback through word clouds and image text relationships fed into the ideation environment.
- **Multimodal data:** gathered through the use of gesture mapping (using stereoscopic 3D cameras such as the LEAP Motion [2]) and video analytics. This data is then used to create ideation metadata that can be used in comparative analysis of ideation 'events'. This metadata is also used to provide live informatics in the ideation environment in order to explore performative aspects [3] of such environments and design ideation.

Author Keywords

Augmented design tools; design ideation; ambient informatics; augmented sketching; design cognition

ACM Classification Keywords

H.5.m. Information interfaces and presentation (e.g., HCI): Miscellaneous;

C&C '17, June 27-30, 2017, Singapore, Singapore

ACM ISBN 978-1-4503-4403-6/17/06.
http://dx.doi.org/10.1145/3059454.3078711

INTRODUCTION

Our culture has become increasingly indexed online as we have poured our sentiments, visual culture and photographic records onto blogs, social media and – as our cultural and scientific institutions have moved to models of open access – curated cultural repositories. Developers of these repositories have in response developed advanced systems of metadata (tagging, mark-up, page ranking etc.) to facilitate search, advertising and latterly machine learning via semantic relationships. This technical demonstration presents an early version of what we call augmented design tools which form the basis of current practice based PhD research within the Information Experience Design programme at the Royal College of Art.

TECHNICAL DESCRIPTION

The prototype uses multiple inputs to observe multi-participant ideation (two people). Two cameras - one per participant - are connected to face tracking software which analyses the movement and orientation of their heads, as well as the movement of their mouths. A LEAP motion is used to track the motion of one participant's hands and a microphone listens to the conversation and converts the speech to text via IBM's Watson Developer Cloud [4].

The resulting metrics from these inputs are used to query online datasets. These datasets are created through scraping sources such as blogs via the import.io [5] service, as well as querying Twitter via its API [6]. The textual part of these queries comes from the text to speech transcripts, categorising the words via a part of Speech tagger specifically the wordpos module [7] for node.js and selecting a subset. They are modified, where possible, by searching within a particular geographic distance from the tool which is set by the expansiveness of the participants gestures as measured by the LEAP motion.

The central server is built using node.js [8] and communicates with an application built in Open Frameworks [9] which perform the face tracking. Communication between these is handled via OSC [10] and the server communicates in real time with the output screens via websockets [11]. Visualisation of the input metrics and results on the output screens is handled with a mixture of the JavaScript Canvas API [12] and d3.js [13].

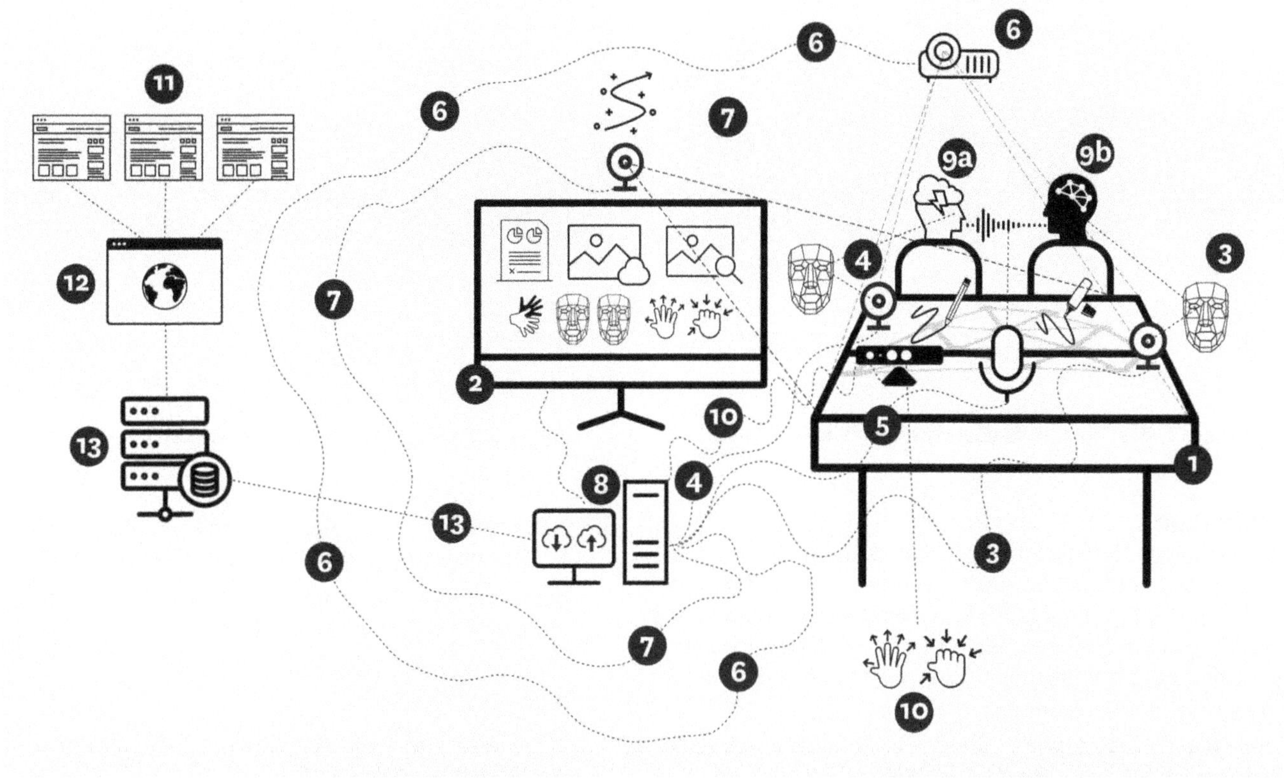

Figure 1. Diagram of indicative design ideation tools setup showing key relationships between participants and technical components of the system. Diagram by Authors, icons from the Noun Project[15]

SET-UP AND COMPONENT PARTS

Below is list that refers to *figure 1* above and acts as a key to the component elements that make up the prototype augmented ideation tool showing key relationships of the system.

1. **Ideation notation surface (table /desk).** A table upon which participant sketch notes during design ideation. During the ideation event, live feedback (images, text and visualisation of voice transcription) is projected into the surface to augment the ideation sketching and the conversation.
2. **Ideation live observation screen (HD / TV).** This HD TV provides a visualisation of what multimodal data is being gathered and what results are being returned to the table. This provides and extra reference point but also allows participants to understand that they are providing data and so can act with this process.
3. **HD Cameras gathering multimodal data.** These cameras are faced at specific participants and gather face tracing data and video data that is used to correlate multimodal data with events during design ideation.
4. **HD Cameras gathering multimodal data.** (As above.)
5. **Microphone for voice recognition and multimodal transcripts.** This captures the conversation of the participants and parses it using IBM's Watson Developer Cloud [4]. This is in turn is used as search query data to provide live feedback to the notation surface.
6. **LED Projector. Projection of live feedback** (images text and visualisation of voice transcription) to augment sketching during design ideation.
7. **HD Camera.** Captures live sketching for conversation records and analysis.
8. **Mac/PC** that operates as I/O for the system and takes in data and runs ideation tools in browser and provides the live feedback.
9. a and b. **Participants** in ideation task.
10. **3D Cameras.** Capturing gesture data. These are LEAP motion but Microsoft Kinect icon has been used.
11. **Data sources** i.e. images, text, quotes and diagrams from web pages & social media.
12. **Semantic Web-pages** that are mined for relevant content by my bespoke curation tools.
13. **Sever side curated data sets** and curated search tools.

DESIGN IDEATION SKETCHING AND TECHNOLOGY

Sketching has long been a key conceptual tool of design process [14] but its integration with rapidly advancing technologies is understudied from the domain of design research and practice. This demonstration explores key trajectories in network augmented ideation.

Figure 2. Participants do augmented sketching (wide).

Figure 3. Participants do augmented sketching (close).

CONCLUSION

This prototype has shown that it is possible to assemble a range of technologies that enable networked *hybrid design environments* [1]. Furthermore, it demonstrates important trajectories of assistive technologies in the design ideation space that have the important distinction of an approach to *hybrid design environments* [1] that "*allows for a continuous exchange between modes, design information being handled by the computer or by hand according to what is relevant at any point*" [16]. It also shows approaches to leveraging semantic web content in ways other than finding common design patterns through brute force emerging from HCI [17]. It also aims to leverage emerging approaches to metaphorical search specifically aimed at creativity such as Yossarian Lives "The World's First Creative Search Engine" [18] and offers insight into how these new online tools could contribute to augmented design ideation tools and processes.

ACKNOWLEDGMENTS

We thank London College of Communication, University of the Arts London, whose Programme Director Sabbatical Scheme (disciplinary research) significantly enabled the presentation of the technology demonstration.

REFERENCES

1. Tomás Dorta, Edgar Pérez, and Annemarie Lesage. 2008. The ideation gap: hybrid tools, design flow and practice. *Design Studies* 29, 2: 121–141.
2. Leap Motion. Leap Motion. Retrieved March 9, 2017 from http://leapmotion.com/
3. Kristina Niedderer. 2007. Designing Mindful Interaction: The Category of Performative Object. *Design Issues* 23, 1: 3–17.
4. IBM Watson Developer Cloud. Retrieved March 9, 2017 from https://www.ibm.com/watson/developercloud/.
5. Import.io | Extract data from the web. Import.io. Retrieved March 9, 2017 from https://www.import.io/.
6. API Overview — Twitter Developers. Retrieved March 9, 2017 from https://dev.twitter.com/overview/api.
7. moos/wordpos. GitHub. Retrieved March 9, 2017 from https://github.com/moos/wordpos.
8. Node.js. Retrieved March 9, 2017 from https://nodejs.org/en/.
9. openFrameworks. Retrieved March 9, 2017 from http://openframeworks.cc/.
10. Introduction to OSC | opensoundcontrol.org. Retrieved March 10, 2017 from http://opensoundcontrol.org/introduction-osc.
11. WebSockets. Mozilla Developer Network. Retrieved March 9, 2017 from https://developer.mozilla.org/en-US/docs/Web/API/WebSockets_API.
12. Canvas API. Mozilla Developer Network. Retrieved March 9, 2017 from https://developer.mozilla.org/en-US/docs/Web/API/Canvas_API.
13. Mike Bostock. D3.js - Data-Driven Documents. Retrieved March 9, 2017 from https://d3js.org/.
14. Ben Jonson. 2005. Design ideation: the conceptual sketch in the digital age. Design Studies 26, 6: 613–624.
15. Noun Project Twitter, Noun Project Facebook, Noun Project Instagram, et al. Noun Project. Noun Project. Retrieved March 9, 2017 from https://thenounproject.com.
16. Tomás Dorta, Edgar Pérez, and Annemarie Lesage. 2008. The ideation gap: hybrid tools, design flow and practice. *Design Studies* 29, 2: 125.
17. Ranjitha Kumar, Arvind Satyanarayan, Cesar Torres, et al. 2013. Webzeitgeist: Design Mining the Web. ACM Human Factors in Computing Systems (CHI).
18. Jacob Aron. Welcome to Yossarian Lives. Retrieved March 6, 2017 from http://about.yossarianlives.com/.

Supporting Non-Musicians' Creative Engagement with Musical Interfaces

Yongmeng Wu
Media and Arts Technology CDT
Queen Mary University of London
London, UK
yongmeng.wu@qmul.ac.uk

Nick Bryan-Kinns
Media and Arts Technology CDT
Queen Mary University of London
London, UK
n.bryan-kinns@qmul.ac.uk

ABSTRACT

This paper reports on a study which sets out to examine the process of creative engagement of individual non-musicians when interacting with interactive musical systems (IMSs), and to identify features of IMSs that may support non-musician's creative engagement in music making. In order to creatively engage novices, we aimed to design IMSs which would combine the intuitive interaction of 'sound toys' with the rich and complex music possibilities offered by IMSs to support individual learning and creative processes. Two IMSs were designed and built and an empirical user study was conducted of them. The study used a multi-layered methodology, which combined interviews and recordings of user interactions. Analysis of participants' behaviour with the IMSs led to the identification of interaction patterns, which were used to identify a three-step framework ('learn', 'exploration','creation') of creative engagement with the musical interfaces, and to inform the development of implications for design for supporting creative engagement with IMSs. Key implications for design identified in this study are to support novices to: learn the sound; play live; catalyze insights; and scaffold composition. The basic study methodology of this paper also offers a contribution to methods for evaluating designs by combining recording user interactions with interviews.

ACM Classification Keywords

H.5.m. Information Interfaces and Presentation (Sound and Music Computing): H.5.2 [Information Interfaces and Presentation] User Interfaces

Author Keywords

Novices, Creative Engagement, Creative Process, Creativity Support, Engagement, Interactive Musical Systems, User Experience

INTRODUCTION

The experience of creating and enjoying music through playing is often rewarding, offering "an affirmation of life" because of its exploratory, engaging, intuitive and enjoyable qualities [9]. Learning to play instruments transforms a person's role from a consumer of music towards a creator of music [35]. As a result, a much deeper relationship with music and a deeper understanding of music are developed along the playing process. However, traditional instruments discourage non-musicians from the playing experience as they require skills developed through formal musical training and years of practice [36]. Therefore, before being able to experience the enjoyment of playing music, non-musicians are likely to encounter many obstacles and frustrations due to their limited skills. Recently, numerous Interactive Music Systems (IMSs) [31] have used digital technologies to offer easy access to the rewarding experience of creating and manipulating sound and music for non-musicians through intuitive and responsive user interfaces. Here IMSs refer to systems that produce music from the input of non-expert users (ibid.). However, the current interfaces for novices tend to be 'sound toys' with simple interactions and sound mappings due to their limited musical skills and knowledge. While providing a more intuitive access to music making, these interfaces easily miss the rich and complex musical possibilities for in-depth exploration of music, and thus are less rewarding and less engaged as they are less likely to engage users in a creative way. Therefore in this paper, we propose to investigate how creative engagement emerges when an individual non-musician is playing with an IMS, and how interface features of an IMS can be used to facilitate creative engagement during this process. The **research question** can be described as: *i)* What is the process of creative engagement with IMSs of individual non-musician? *ii)* How to support creative engagement for non-musicians with IMSs?

Two interactive prototypes were designed employing two different musical representations and interaction models, and then an empirical study was carried out to explore how users' creative experiences differed between the prototypes. Informed by frameworks for understanding creative engagement and creativity support, the creative process reported in this paper is decomposed into learning and creative phases. The experiment is designed with two separate sessions for learning and creating tasks. Participants were asked to play with both prototypes, and for each prototype participants were asked to go through these two sessions. Participants were interviewed and interaction data captured during use of the prototypes were recorded. Thematic analysis of the interview data was conducted along with analysis of people's behavior captured in the

C&C 2017, June 27–30, 2017, Singapore.
© 2017 ACM ISBN 978-1-4503-4403-6/17/06 ...$15.00.
http://dx.doi.org/10.1145/3059454.3059457

logs of their interaction with the prototype. Typical interaction patterns in learning and creating sessions were identified based on the analysis of people's behaviour captured in logs. A three-step framework ('learn', 'exploration','creation') of creative engagement with musical interfaces was proposed. Results showed that in terms of the learning phase, non-musicians need support to learn the sounds. For the creative phase, playing live with a dynamic sound effect engage non-musicians creatively. Moreover, non-musicians need support for scaffolding their compositions, specifically for planning the piece and managing the sound elements. Design implications for supporting creative engagement with IMSs are proposed based on the results.

RELATED WORK

Musical Interfaces for Non-Musicians

Differentiated from the digital music instruments (DMIs) that allow musicians to present delicate and expressive music, IMSs, including interactive musical installations and applications, typically target at non-expert users for exploratory and experiential purpose. Two typical design features for IMSs can be summarized as:

I: Emphasize the process and the experience [47]. Compared to product centered systems that emphasize the final output sound, process centered systems emphasize the process and the experience during the interaction. Such designs are less likely to be driven by musical goals, but are more likely to be driven by offering engaging experience that are rewarding to participants for their social skills, creativity, or for their learning achievements [47]. For example, they may focus on facilitating elaborate social dynamics between players [3], emphasize the expressive and creative process for players [45], or center on providing a rich learning experience [35]. As process and experience become a first priority in these systems, chances are that the keystone of the design is not facilitating the music creation, but facilitating the communication, awareness, the rules of interaction, etc. Among the limited literatures on music interfaces which focusing on the creative process and experience, some of the studies targeted at experienced musicians, for example looking at musician's creative exploration of physical modeling techniques [6], or looking at how two contrasting creative processes affect the gesture-to-parameter mapping properties on creative sound design in the studio [46]. Some studies focused on novel interaction for supporting music creativity, for example utilizing an online map interface for interactive music composition and performance [33]. Some other studies focused on collective creativity within a group of players, for example, supporting improvisation with coordinated actions between participants [53].

However, the process of individual non-musician's creative engagement with musical interface remains unclear. Therefore, it is necessary to look into individual non-musician user's process and experience when creatively interacting with IMSs, which leads to a key concern of this paper, what is the process of creative engagement with musical interfaces of non-musician?

II: Shallow learning curve or low entry fee [51, 16] As non-musicians usually have little or no musical skills and domain knowledge, the interfaces are designed with simple concepts to enable the user to understand and learn the interface quickly. In terms of the implementation, the main trends are designing the system with *simplified interaction* or with *constrained musical complexity* to make the interface more approachable than traditional instruments. Specifically, adopting simplified interaction means using technologies that broad audiences are able to intuitively use, for example, using hand or whole body gesture [4, 53], tangible interface elements [3, 26], or touch screen interfaces [8]. Among them, the gesture and tangible interface are mostly seen in interactive installations in museum or public space, which often involve multiple players. Touch screen interfaces are more likely adopted in interactive applications on personal computing device. Constraining musical complexity is to simplify the sound parameters for novices to generate good quality music. Common practices for reducing complexity are: adopting generative mechanisms which use algorithms to control all or part of the sound generation [49, 38]; utilizing pre-recorded samples or pre-composed materials for audience to play with [13]; or implementing limited sound mappings for users to manipulate or control limited aspects of sound elements such as rhythm, volume, tempo or timbre, etc.

A challenge here is that they might be able to 'hook' novice in the first place, however they might also fail to encourage 'deeper exploration and continued discovery and creativity'[30], as they present limited musical possibilities for users. Players could be easily "disinterested after all the various voices and the musical mappings had been exhausted" [15] and thus engage for a limited amount of time [32]. Gelineck and Serafin argue that for an environment to encourage exploratory behaviour it must be 'rich, complex, and somewhat mysterious' but remain intuitive in order to give the user confidence to continue [18]. Therefore two conflicting design requirements emerge for creatively engaging novices with IMSs: *i)* on one hand, the interface needs to remain intuitive in order to hook user and give them the confidence to continue; *ii)* on the other hand, interface and sonic interaction need to be rich and complex to encourage exploratory and experimental interaction and to spark creativity. These two paradoxical requirements leads to another key concerns of this paper - what features of musical interfaces can support non-musicians to generate their own musical creation, while remaining intuitive?

Creative Engagement and Creativity Support

There are three levels of engagement when users interact with interactive systems: immediate engagement, sustained engagement, and creative engagement. Among them, creative engagement is "sustainable and rewarding for the audience", which makes the experience a 'memorable' one, rather than a 'pretty' one" [10]. It is when users is engaged with the system and starts to construct a meaning through the process of interacting with an interactive art system [5]. A similar concept is described as 'play fluency' with music systems [20], when meaningful musical expressions are perceived by players and a potential audience, similar to accounts of people performing with interface to express themselves [40]. Play fluency could be a sign of being in the state of flow [12] and the music interface could potentially be rewarding because it inspires players to engage in autotelic activity.

Based on Edmonds' attractor, sustainer and relater model of creative engagement [14], Bilda developed a more detailed framework, suggesting a sequential and temporal engagement process and defining it as a "reflective and transformative dialogue between the audience and the interactive art system"[5]. This creative engagement model involves four interaction phases based on five interaction modes, starting with phases of *adaptation* and *learning* when participants gradually develop their expectations and understanding of how the system works. Along this process, participants set their intentions and expectations. As they become aware of what to expect, they develop their interactions from unintended and exploratory modes into deliberate mode. In the following phases, *anticipation* and *deeper understanding*, the participants learn to predict the outcomes of their interaction, and reaches a more complete understanding of the system and figure out their relationship is to the system. The interaction modes at this stage are developed from deliberate mode into intended mode, where participants feel in control and possibly end up with creative outcomes. This is similar to the framework proposed by Sheridan that describe user's participation and the process of transition from participating to performing with interfaces [40].

Similar to the frameworks of creative engagement, Shneiderman proposed a four-phase framework for creativity: i) collect, learn from previous works; ii) relate, consult with peers and mentors at early, middle, and late stages; iii) create, explore, compose, evaluate possible solutions; iv) donate, disseminate the results and contribute to the libraries [41]. In a later paper [42], Shneiderman suggested several principles to guide designers: support exploratory search, enable collaboration, provide rich history-keeping, design with low thresholds, high ceilings, and wide walls. Generally, Shneiderman's principles are supporting two phases behavior - the exploration and creation. Similarly, Yeap discussed two important keywords for developing creativity support tools, namely ideation and empowerment [52]. Ideation emphasizes on generating or discovering new ideas to the user. Empowerment, is empowering the users to develop his/her ideas freely.

Both the frameworks of creative engagement and creativity support outlined above lead us to decompose the creative process into two phases: *i)* Learning phase toward a deep understanding on the system; *ii)* A creative phase for ideation and evaluation. These two phases are used as an outline of the experiment to identify how creative engagement emerges and possible features of an musical interface that can be used to facilitate creative engagement for non-musician participants.

PROTOTYPE DESIGN

In addressing the design requirements mentioned in the previous section, the prototypes are designed based on two paradigms of IMSs with intuitive interactions. For maintaining rich and complex music possibilities for music creativity for novices, the prototypes offers the power to create and phrase melodies as well as rhythmic patterns from scratch with single notes and beats. We deliberately chose this because novices' ability to perceive and retain melodic contour and rhythm is good [39, 47].

Two prototypes - Prototype A (PA) and Prototype B (PB) - are designed in comparison with each other, in order to explore the differentiated user behavior and experience between the two prototypes, and to identify the interface features that affect creative engagement for non-musician participants. The basic objects and interface layout are unified across two prototypes to minimize the difference, whilst in the aspect of conceptual paradigm, graphical representation, interaction model and mappings, distinctions are made. For summary please see Table 1 and later sessions for detail description and comparison on interface attributes between prototypes. The prototypes are written in Processing [34] and run on a Mac Pro, using iPad as an extension of the display as well as touch input. They run in full-screen mode with no other user interface objects visible or accessible.

Common Design Attributes

The basic concepts are the same for both prototypes. There are three main categories of objects on both interfaces:

- The *generator* continuously generates graphical elements rhythmically once activated. The rhythm of its generation can be adjusted.
- The *effector* makes a sound when triggered by a graphical element from the generator. There are four types of effectors with four different sound effects. The volume and the note of the effectors can be adjusted.
- The *sequencer* offers a continuous background sound. There are three sound effects to choose and only one of them is available at each time. The rhythm of the sequencer sample can be adjusted.

The main operational space is a canvas for user to manipulate the objects to generate sound. There is a sidebar on the left where user can switch between different function modes, for example adding or deleting four types of effectors, adjusting effector parameters, switching between sequencers or adjusting sequencer parameters.

Conceptual Paradigms

Two conceptual paradigms of IMSs that inspired our designs include: i) the step sequencer as a traditional paradigm with a focus on the sound, rhythm and note; and ii) the painterly interface as a novel paradigm with a focus on the visual, interaction and aesthetics.

The first paradigm that inspired PA (figure 1a) is the step sequencer interface that loops through steps of sound at certain speed [22, 21, 1]. Such interfaces usually employ eight or sixteen steps, each step represent a note or a beat. It allows the control of rhythmic patterns by turning on or off the step button and by adjusting the sound parameter for each step. It is an accessible and intuitive way to create complex musical pattern without any need for manual dexterity. Thus it is able to offer a low entry fee for non-musicians, while maintain enough depth and complexity on music. The second paradigm

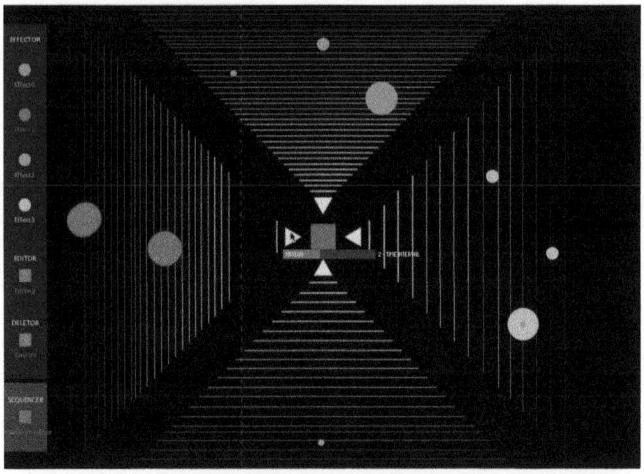

(a) Prototype A (PA)

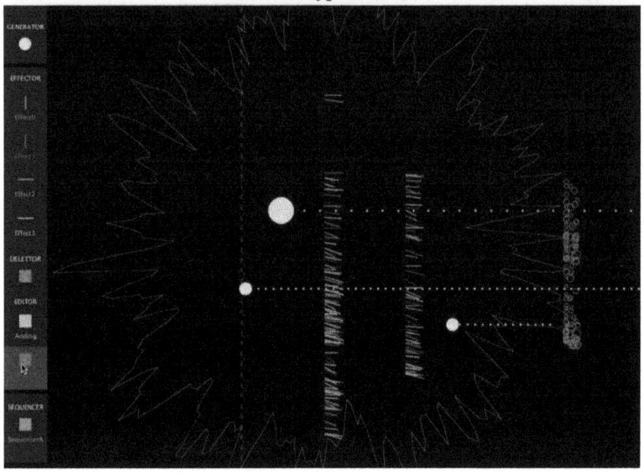

(b) Prototype B (PB)

Figure 1: Screen shot of Prototypes

that inspired PB (figure 1b) is the painterly interface that use expressive gestural drawing as an input to control the sound output [37, 25, 2, 24]. It usually maps the parameter of the input drawing or gesture, i.e. length, color or curves, with the sound parameter such as the pitch, the volume or the beat. Drawing interaction is intuitive and dynamic, and regarded as an "instantly knowable, indefinitely masterable" interaction [29]. With this rich and dynamic interaction, painterly interfaces have the potential to support non-musicians to explore sounds creatively and expressively [28], and may offer them the chance to experience creative flow[29].

Determined by different conceptual designs, the sound mappings between the sound variables, object properties and the interaction are different from prototypes. Dragging to adjust effect's size and position is the dominant interaction concept to manipulate effectors in PA, while drawing to add or erase elements inside an effector is the dominant interaction concept in PB.

Attributes	Prototype A	Prototype B
Generator		
Graphic	Triangle & Line	Circle & Dot
Variables	Rhythm, limited quantity	Rhythm, position, quantity, size
Interaction	Adjust slide bar	Adjust circle size
Effector		
Sound	Same	
Graphic	Circle	Linear Bar
Variables	Volume-Position Note-Size	Volume-Density Note-Length
Interaction	Drag-Position Grag-Size	Draw-Density Draw-Length
Sequencer		
Sound	Same	
Graphic	Same - Centric	
Variables	Same - Rhythm	
Interaction	Drag to switch, click rect in centre;	Drag to switch, click rect in control bar;

Table 1: Comparison of object attributes

Prototype A

In PA, Figure 1a, effectors are represented with simple circles; different colors indicate different sound. Different *effectors* can be chosen from the side bar and be placed on the canvas by a simple click. The effector object can be dragged around, which will change the sound volume according to its distance from the centre in real-time. The closer the circle is to the centre, the louder the sound will be. The size of the circle effector is adjustable by dragging from the centre of the object when creating it or in the edit mode. For the red and orange effectors, which is for melodic sound, the size of the circle object is associate with its sound note. The bigger the size, the higher the note of the sound. For the blue and green effectors, which generate rhythmic sound, the size is associated with the decay of the sound. The bigger the size, the longer the sound (the decay) will be played for. There are four *generators* fixed in the centre, represented by four triangles. Participants can turn each one on or off so that they regularly generate a set of lines moving from centre towards the edge of the canvas. The speed (rhythm) of generating the lines is controllable via a control bar, which will appear when the triangle representation is pressed. When a line from the sequencer touch an effector object, the effector will make a sound according to its type. User can also choose a *sequencer* as a background sound by pressing the rectangle in the middle and its tempo is adjustable by dragging to adjust its radius.

Prototype B

In PB, Figure 1b, a *generator* is represented by a circle. When it's placed on the canvas by clicking, it can regularly generate a set of dots moving linearly towards the right. The size of the generator object is adjustable, which associate with the speed (rhythm) of generating the dots. To add an *effector*, user needs to choose effector type from the side bar and draw it on the canvas. Sound will be generated when the effector is touched by a dot from generator. The speed of drawing will affect the density of the effector which determines the volume of the sound. The faster the drawing, the less the density, thus the lower the volume. The length of the effector is mapped with the sound note for the red and orange effectors, and the decay of the sound for the blue and green effectors. To adjust the sound variables of effector, a user can choose the adding or erasing mode from the sidebar to add or delete elements inside that effector, thus to adjust the sound variable of that effector. While the sound design is the same for PA and PB, the mappings between sound variables and effector variables are different. It is a different interaction model: in PA, dragging is the interaction concept to adjust the size of the effectors for adjusting the note, and to adjust the position to adjust the volume. In PB, however, drawing is the interaction concept to control the length and the density of the effectors, which are associated with the note and the volume. Similarly to PA, a sequencer with the same sound sequence can be chose as a background sound by pressing the sequencer button at side bar and adjusting the size of its graphical representation to control its tempo and volume. The difference here is that the sequencer button is placed at the sidebar rather than the middle of canvas in PA. The interface of PA is with more preset attributes on the canvas while for PB everything needs to be added by user. In PB, it is totally up to user to plan and place both the generators and the effectors on the canvas which in the end will influence the sound.

USER STUDY

Procedure

The study involves four sessions: *introduction (5 minutes), interaction with one of two prototypes (20 minutes), interaction with the other prototype (20 minutes), final Interview (5 minutes)*. During the study a participant was free to opt out at any point. To eliminate the influence the sequence of exposure to prototypes, the order of the prototypes are randomly sorted for participants. The set-up of the experiment is illustrated in figure 2. There is a camera on the right to record the interaction of participant and a sound recorder to record the interview.

As an introduction and a training process in the beginning, the prototypes were presented and the basic concepts of the interface were explained to the participants. The information included the main concepts of three categories of objects, and the basic design of the interface. For each prototype the process of interactions was divided into five sub-sessions. This segmentation is based on how solo sessions were structured to explore individuals' personal responses to the interface [43]. *i) Free Exploration.* Participant was encouraged to try out the interface for a while and explore it in his own way. He was asked to explore by himself about what kind of sound variables he was able to adjust and how to adjust them. Apart from the knowledge offered in the introduction phase, no further information was offered to the participant. *ii) Semi-Structured interview.* The participant was asked questions about his learning process and experience. *iii) Guided Learning.* Participant was guided to learn the prototype systematically in order to prepare for the next section. The purpose of offering guided learning is to make sure that the participant has a full knowledge on the

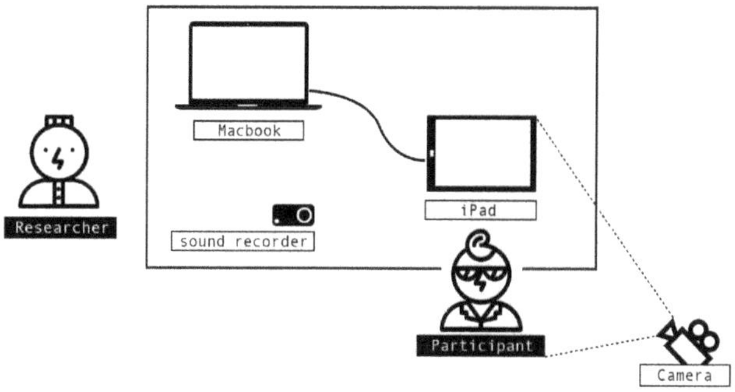

Figure 2: Set Up of Pilot Study

system before starting the creative task. *iv) Creative Improvisation.* The participant was encouraged to improvise a piece of music with the prototype. He was asked to play with one of the sample from the sequencer or combine different ones, and was free to control it as he wished. The reason to have this requirement is to unify the task across participants. Instead of introducing a confounding variable, the sequencer samples offer a consistent standard for every participant and allow a certain degree of freedom for improvisation. *v) Semi-Structured interview.* The participant was then asked with questions on the creative process and experience with the interface.

Data Collection

The data collected in the study include the user interaction log, the interview audio recording, as well as the screen recording of the interaction on the iPad. The prototypes were programmed with the ability to log each interaction made by the user as a CSV file. In order to simplify the data, interaction activities recorded in the interaction log were categorized into 7 interaction types and coded in numbers: 0 - Change Mode, 1- Adjust Generator, 2 - Add Effector, 3 - Adjust Generator, 4- Adjust Effector R/ Edit Effector-add, 5 - Adjust Effector Position / Adjust Effector-erase, 6 - Delete Effector/ Delete Generator, 7 - Adjust Sequencer. Therefore, whenever a participant interacted, the interaction type, its time and detail data were recorded into the CSV file.

The questions in the semi-structured interviews were aimed at identifying whether participants understood the underlying concepts of the prototypes in the learning session, as well as their subjective perception on the creative experience, and their engagement in the creative session. Participants were asked to rate their overall experience on the prototype's learnability in the free exploration session as well as their creative experience in the creative improvisation session. The ratings scale were "not at all easy/ not really easy/ neutral/ easy/ very easy to learn" and "not at all creative/ not really creative/ neutral/ creative/ very creative". Participants were also asked with questions in relation to the concepts of the objects, i.e. "Do you understand how does the generator works in this prototype?" A range of open-ended questions addressing how participants interacted with the prototypes were asked as well, including: *i)* How did you go about learning to use this application? *ii)* Do you think the interface helps you learn this prototype? If yes, What features of the interface helps you to learn? *iii)* Do you find it is easy/difficult to create a piece of sound with this prototype? Why? *iv)* Do you think the interface helps you to create your piece? If yes, What features of the interface helps you to create? *v)* What would you improve so that you can be more creative with this system? The ratings and questions are the same for both prototypes. A further interview was completed at the end of the session in which participants compared the two prototypes in terms of the satisfaction of the outcome, the learning experience, the creative experience, the interaction model, as well as the graphic design, and gave feedback in an open ended way on their experience.

RESULTS

Ten participants took part in the experiment(4 male & 6 female), the average age of the participants was 29, five said that they don't have any experience on making music or playing instruments, four said that they are amateur players on one or more instruments, and one claimed to be a musician. As this study is targeted at non-musician users, this musician's data is eliminated in later analysis. The following section details the results of 9 participants from the study in terms of: general feedback on the experience, interaction activity, thematic analysis of interviews. Data was collected through the interview, as well as interaction log files of user interaction.

Participant Feedback

The average participant satisfaction rating of the learning experience with PA is 3.78, and 4.33 with PB. The average satisfaction with the creative experience on PA is 3.67, whilst on PB it is 3.56. Fleiss' kappa test was used to assess the reliability of agreement among the choices between participants [19]. Fleiss' kappa test, $k = 0.37$, shows a Fair Agreement on the learning experience and creative experience between participants. Five participants thought PA is easier to learn and manipulate, four said that they are not sure which one is easier because they learned PA first. Eight participants preferred the interaction model of dragging to change the size and position rather than drawing the size and density of effectors. Six participants reported that they were more creative with PA, three said that they are not sure, and one thought PB is more creative; six participants preferred the outcome of PA in the creative improvisation session, two participants preferred the outcome of PB.

Logged Activity Assessment

A Wilcoxon signed-ranks test was used to test the statistical significance of the data, because the data came from different settings within the same participants [27]. There is no significance on the total time length spent in the Free Exploration session, Wilcoxon signed-ranks test $p = 0.147$ ($w = 29$, $z = 1.45$), and the Creative Exploration session Wilcoxon signed-ranks test $p = 0.589$ ($w = 11$, $z = 0.54$) between PA and PB. Figure 3 shows the average percentage of time spent on each interaction type by participants. The time participants spent on each interaction type was added together, and its percentage were calculated out of the total time participants spent on each session. Compared to the free exploration session, the time for most of the interaction behaviors broadly stayed the same or decreased in the creative session. The only two increases are 'adjust effector position' in PA, and 'adjust effector - erase' and 'adjust sequencer' in PB. For PA, participants spent significantly more time on adjusting the position of effector in the Creative Improvisation session compared to the Free Exploration session, Wilcoxon signed-ranks test $p = 0.0135$ ($W = -49$, $Z = -2.47$). For PB, as some of the participants didn't discover the functions of sequencer and adjusting effector (erasing) in the free exploration session. There is insufficient data to perform statistical tests.

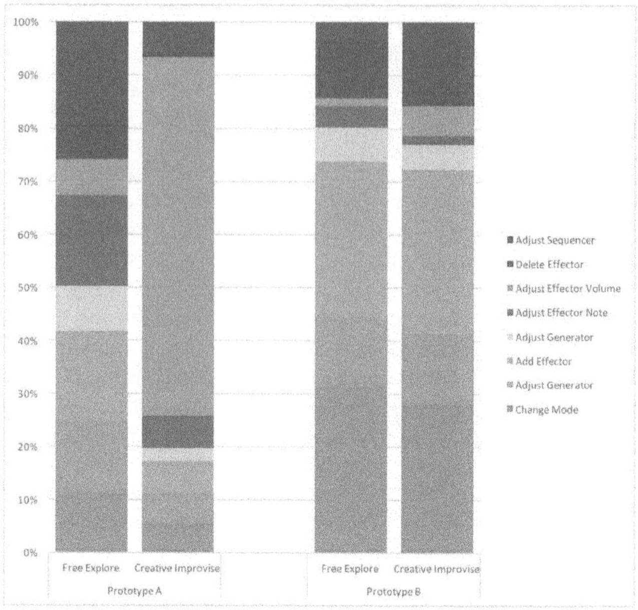

Figure 3: Duration of Each Interaction Type

Patterns of Behaviour

Beyond the statistical analysis of the log data, analysis was undertaken on how a user's interaction was developed and changed through the interaction process. The data was filtered by getting the first point when users switched from one interaction type to another. A time series graph of the interaction process in each session for each participant was generated by plotting the trimmed data. In figure 4 and 5 numbers represent interaction types (1 - add generator, 2 - adjust generator, 3 - add effector, 4 - adjust effector, 5 - delete effector, 6 - adjust sequencer). Such graphs of interaction over time for all participants can then be categorized as different interaction styles. The patterns of activity in the Free Exploration session and Creative Improvisation session were found to be quite different and are reported in the following sections.

Free Exploration

There are three basic styles of interaction to explore the prototypes. The style A is *One-by-One*, see figure 4a, that participant tried to learn all the possible operations and adjustable parameters of one object before moving on to learn another object. Two participants' interaction process can be categorized in this style on PA, four on PB. The style B is *Combination of Two*, see figure 4b, that participant firstly explored two types of objects by switching between them alternately to learn their interaction attributes, and then moved on to explore other two

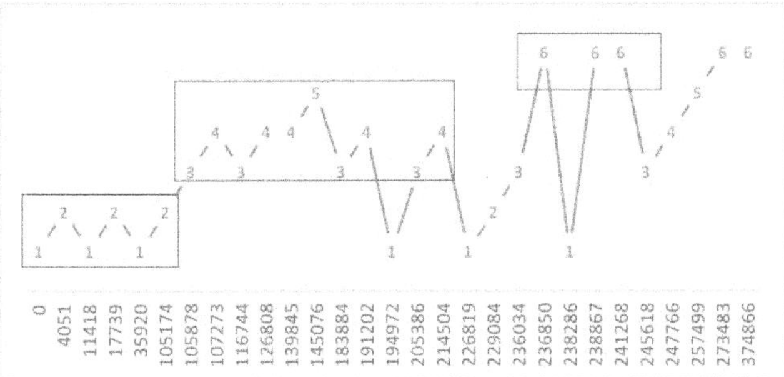

(a) Learn Style A - One by One

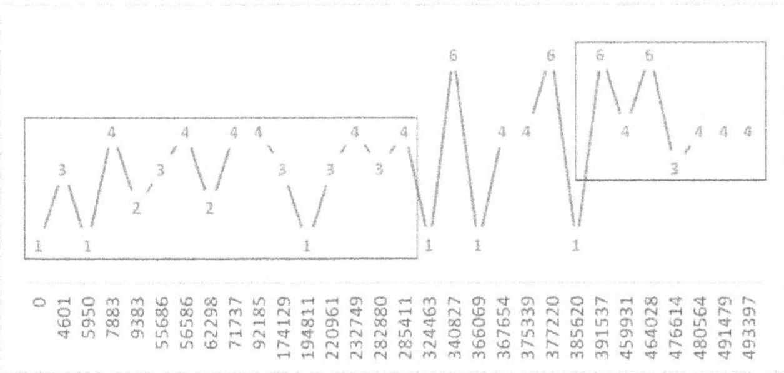

(b) Learn Style B - Combination of Two

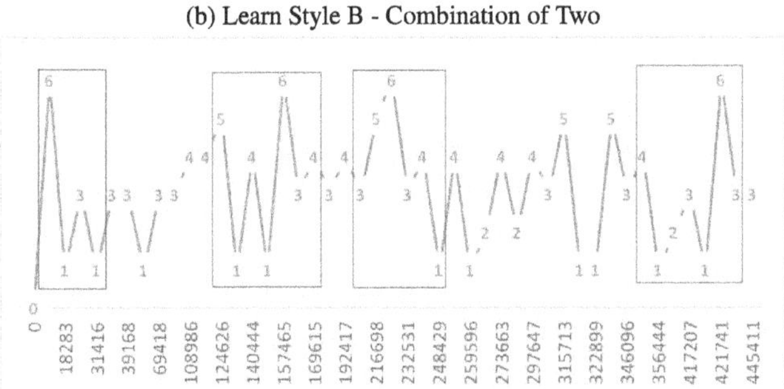

(c) Learn Style C - Combination of Three

Figure 4: Interaction Process of Free Exploration

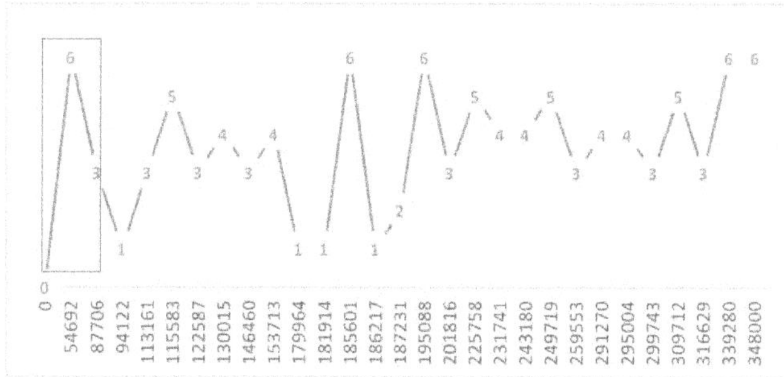

(a) Create Strategy A - Begin with Sequencer

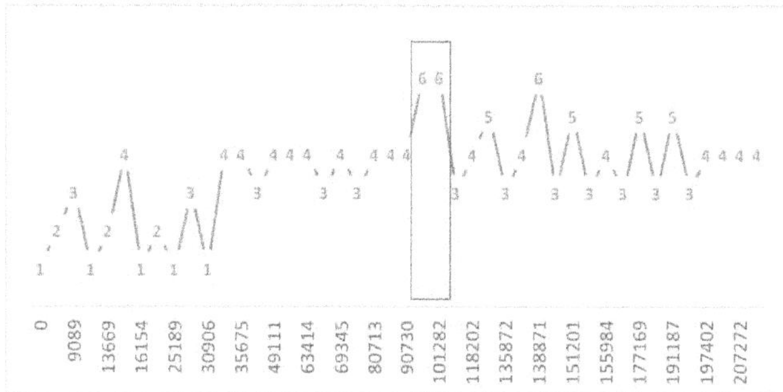

(b) Create Strategy B - Start Sequencer in Middle

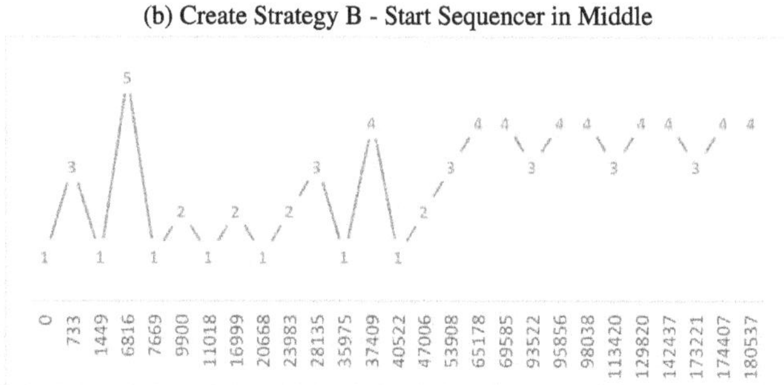

(c) Create Strategy C - No Sequencer

Figure 5: Interaction Process of Creative Improvisation

types of objects. In this process, it's a combinational strategy by integrating two types of objects to learn their interactions and parameters together. There were five participants adopted this interaction style on PA, four on PB. The style C is *Combination of Three*, see figure 4c, that participant interacted with three objects from the very beginning until the end of the interaction process. For example, there are several points that the interaction started from generator and end up with sequencer in a continuous process. There were three of the participants used this interaction style on PA, two on PB.

There were also two cases that participants mixed different interaction styles within one interaction process. For example, participant started with style A and end up with style C in the end of the interaction. Or one participant started with style C, during his interaction process he kept using style B or A for a period of time. In terms of the learning style across prototypes within individual participant, six participants conducted the same style of interaction for both PA and PB, three started with PA in the first place and three started with PB. For the four who changed their learning style, two started with PA and two started with PB. Three among them switched from style A to C, and one switched from A to B.

Creative Improvisation

For this session the task for the participant was to improvise a piece of music based on a background sound chosen from the sequencer. Three strategies for improvising a piece of music under this requirement were found according to the time when participants introduce the sequencer sound.

Strategy A is that participant started with sequencer sound in the beginning of improvisation, figure 5a. Among the five participants who adopted this strategy on PA and seven on PB, only one of them never went back to the sequencer in later interactions. The others adjusted the sequencer or switched between the sequencer samples quite often all along the improvisation process. For strategy B, figure 5b, participant started without a sequencer sound. They usually played with the sequencer and effectors for the first half the total interaction time, and then introduced the sequencer in the second half of the interaction process. Three participants adopted this strategy on PA, one with PB. For strategy C, figure 5c, participants didn't select any sequencer to play with across the interaction process. There was one of them for both PA and PB. Both of them didn't use the sequencer in the second prototype.

Six participants adopted the same strategy to improvise music across prototypes. Four participants changed their improvisation strategy, two of which started with PA in the first place while Two started with PB. However, no matter which prototype they started with, two of them changed their strategy from A to B, one from A to C, and one from B to C.

Thematic Analysis

An inductive ('bottom-up') thematic analysis was conducted to understand participants' feedback [7]. Following the step-by-step guide with six phases of analysis, the analyzing process started by getting familiar with the feedback data, generating initial codes, then searching and reviewing themes, and finally defining and naming themes. Informed by the theories of creative process [42], typical stages of participants' interaction process with a musical interface were identified. They can be described as the following stages: *Learn*, learning the basic concepts, interaction and sound of the system; *Exploration*, exploring the possible music ideas and approaches of making through trial and error; *Create*, improvising a structured piece with ideas, techniques and strategies from previous stages. It is necessary to note that these stages of interaction can be interlocking and overlaying with each other. For example, after participants learn one basic function of the prototype, they might start to explore making possible music ideas with that specific function and go back to learn other functions. They might also explore mini music ideas during the process of creating as well. The extracted themes from the interview transcripts are reported below, categorized according to the three stages of interaction process. The numbers in brackets express the count of participants who mentioned the theme in interview.

Learn

For beginners with less music making experience, the themes are mainly concerned with learning sound in the learning process.

- *Solo listen(5).* For novice users, it was difficult for them to remember the different timbres of sound and the mapping between sound variables and interactions in the prototype. Participants described their strategy for learning the sound were to listen to them 'one by one'. With more elements added on the canvas, the context became complex as different sounds mixed together. It then became difficult to differentiate the sound timbres, and to figure out the links of mapping while they were making adjustments, e.g. "I think I had too much happening, didn't I? I had a lot stuff going on."
- *Affordance (7).* Some interface features were found to be helpful for organizing the sounds. For example, participants commented positively about the layout of the interface, e.g. the grid design in PA, and the linear design in PB, because they suggested a clear idea on how to arrange the objects, e.g. "I understand how I can create a piece of sound with this."
- *Simplicity (6).* The control of the sound should be simple in the way that the action is easy to achieve, and with one-to-one mapping to the sound. For example, in PB, participants reported that the drawing interaction controlling the density(volume) and the length(tone) of the effector at the same time is demanding for their skills.
- *Consistency (3).* The requirement for consistent interaction emerged from results. A consistent interaction helps to build the link between functions and sound, thus is easier for novice users to learn and remember. For example, participants commented the concentric layout of PA is more consistent between objects, "makes more sense to include the sequencer".

Explore

There are two different approaches of exploration on the music ideas - random exploration and precise exploration. Random exploration is when a user is trying different functions without having any particular goals, usually involves combining sound elements, exploring extremity of sound parameter, etc. For example, one participant described the process as "So I just play around it to see what else I could do". Precise exploration is when a user has a music idea in mind and looks for possible implementing methods. With these two distinct approach, there are three themes emerged in this stage.

- *Serendipity (5).* When participants generated music ideas that they liked, or encountered functions that they did not expect, they were surprised and excited. e.g. "you play around with it, so yeah, I like it", "when discovered that I can drag them, I was really happy." Participants' interest on the system were triggered. They were more willing and became more confident to look for further knowledge, and were more engaged in the exploration process, e,g, "you were like yeah I want to find out if anything else has got new stuff, show me more".
- *Precision (5).* When participants have music ideas in mind, they expect more precise control on timing, sound parameters, etc, to implement their ideas, e.g. "that very difficult is to timing things as I expected".
- *Controllability (7).* Various controllable parameters helped participant to achieve a satisfaction on music ideas, e.g."Some nice music, interesting music, because you've got a lot of control". Moreover, for the given parameter, users expect a bigger range of control so as to achieve a more dynamic effect, e.g. "I find the ranges weren't large enough for what I need to do".
- *Repeatability (3).* After tried out the possibilities, users may find some musical phrases interesting and would like to re-use them repeated, e.g. "Fair enough you might fancy sound you like, but how would you do something again". In this case, the ability to repeat previous interaction easily is a key point to transfer user to conceive the whole piece, a more in-depth creative process.

Create

- *Structure Composition (6).* There are three main sub-themes for non-musician users to structure a piece of music, namely *record history, plan ahead of time, and anticipate future events.* Novice users found it's hard for them to remember what they played before, as well as to plan what is going to be played in the future. One participant reported that she have "a bad memory to remember what did I played before", and therefore find it's hard to organize a consistent piece. Some participants enjoyed to plan ahead of time with both prototypes, e.g. "compose what's gonna happen latter". As the interface allows generators to be adjusted accordingly, there are possibilities to have a "pre-designed structure", and trigger the sound after the objects are placed as they designed. The ability to "anticipate when that is gonna happen" is helpful for novice's improvisation in a way they are able to presume future sound so as to plan next step of interactions.

- *Readiness Time (4).* There is a delay between the management of the objects and the feedback of the sound. For example, when adding effector on the screen before triggering the generator, the effector won't play until generator's dots or lines reach the effector. This time difference caused two conflicting experiences in this situation. On one hand, it allows non-musicians to prepare and to implement their conception of the sound before actually affecting the current composition, e.g. "you can press on and off but it's not affect something at that moment because you see there will be some time." On the other hand, without the instant feedback from the sound, it cause barriers for users to know the outcome of their interaction, e.g. "Because I don't know what it would sound like when I draw it."
- *Manage Sound (4).* With the interface to help to manage sound objects and parameters, e.g. rhythm, timbres, non-musicians feel easier to create their piece. In PA, particularly, lines emitted by four sequencers towards different directions construct four separate spaces. These spaces allows participants to manage their sound separately. Some participants use different space to manage different timbre effectors, e.g. "You have four different bit to control different sound elements". Some participants utilize them to manage both timbre and rhythm, e.g. "you can control different rate so maybe for one you can control beat and for the other one you can control tone".
- *Play Live (7).* Another representative strategy in the creating process is playing with objects to get a dynamic and live sound effect with the interaction. Two behaviors for playing live are summarized: one is *re-arranging objects*, when user re-arrange the previous sound objects to get some new effects, for example by adjusting the temple or sequence of the notes. Another is *manipulating objects*, in our case is when user keep moving the effectors around to hit the lines from generator to create a live sound effect that won't happen without this interaction. Participant reported "it's quite fun to move the things around while it is playing".
- *Starting Base (2).* For novice users, it is conceptually and technically difficult for them to develop their music ideas from scratch [48, 49]. The role of the starting base is to give an idea of creating in the first place. In our prototypes, sequencers offer pre-designed sound sequences, which is a good starting point for novice users to play with. Participant reported "it was useful to have a starting sound. Like, not starting from zero completely." One suggestion from participant is to provide example sketch with preset effectors to begin with. Besides, in PA, the preset generators on the interface are reported helpful by offering a clear strategy on how to organize the sound from the beginning. Although one participants criticized the preset layout in PA has less freedom and is less creative because it 'predetermines' or 'indicate' what user should do, for the other participants, the preset layout gives confidence for them to start.

DISCUSSION

Learn and Create Behaviors

The three-step framework ('learn', 'exploration','creation') of creative engagement is one of the key findings in this paper. It is similar to the Geneplore Model, which describes creative activities as a combination of generative and exploratory processes [17]. Complementary to this two-stage model, our framework suggests the learning process as part of the creative process and highlights its importance for novices as it's a key process to accumulate knowledge and ideas for creation.

In the learning session, 4 participants switched their learning style from A to C and from A to B. In the creative session, 4 participants switch their creative style from A to B, A to C and B to C. These two observations indicate: *i)* Participants started with more complex learning styles when they interact with the second prototype, informing learning with less objects are simpler to start with compared to learning with a combination of three different objects. *ii)* Participants started to introduce the sequencer later in their creative improvisation process, which means participants had more variation in their composition when using of the second prototype. Together with the qualitative data, we can infer that in the learning phase, participants spent more effort to learn the sound and its interaction. The sound become a primary subject to learn in musical interface in order to be able to easily figure out music strategy. The interaction and interface become a secondary subject to learn, and serve for better understanding and manipulating the sound. This finding is similar to Bengler's findings [3] that participants strive for sonic identity and clear separation of sounds.

The average satisfaction on both learning and creating experience for PA is higher. Joint with the interviews we found that PA has some features that can cognitively scaffold [11] their composition. For instance, 'structure composition', 'manage sound' and 'starting base' are the themes that affected participants' creative improvisation. These observations lead us toward another key component for supporting non-musician's creative engagement - 'Scaffold composition'. Due to the limits of novices' music skill, they need support to arrange sound elements and plan music in a structured way, in order to generate music ideas and to achieve their music goal, and therefore be engaged in interacting with the system in a creative way.

Participants spent significantly more time on adjusting the position of effector in the improvisation session compared to the learning session in PA. Also in the qualitative data, participants reported they enjoyed PA more than PB because of the feature of being able to move effectors around to create a live sound effect. These observations indicate that 'playing live'- being able to manipulate live sound effect - helps to engage participants to creatively explore possible interactions and various combinations of objects and sound, which is a key feature for supporting creative engagement with musical interfaces.

Design Implications

Four design implications of musical interfaces aimed to support novices' creative engagement identified in this study are highlighted below.

- Provide mechanisms to enable player to *learn the sound*, for example enable solo listening for users to learn and explore the sound in a separate context other than on the main interface. This could be helpful both in the process of learning basic concepts, and in the process of creative improvisations to check if the sound combination is as expected.
- Provide mechanisms to support *playing live* by enabling a dynamic sound feedback on the interaction, e.g. PA provides the ability to generate dynamic sound by dragging effectors around. With such kind of an intuitive and responsive instrument, novices will be encouraged to explore different possibilities of the interface. This can serve as an 'sustainer' from the creative engagement model [14] to keep the players and audience engaged.
- Provide mechanisms to *catalyze insights* so as to lead novices to a more in-depth creative process, e.g. conceiving the structure of the whole piece, or exploring music variations. For example, providing an easy access to re-use the previous musical ideas is a possible approach to encourage in-depth explorations on music ideas. This can serve as a 'relator', to help a continuing relationship between player and systems to grow cf. [14].
- Provide mechanisms to *scaffold composition*, which involves three aspects: Firstly, the interface needs to provide a starting base to give a clear guidance for creating, and also to spark new music ideas, this is addresses the critique that it is conceptually and technically difficult for novices to create and develop their own musical ideas from scratch [50]. Secondly, it is vital to support novices to structure their composition, by recording the history of composition, enabling players to play ahead of time (to buy some readiness time), and to anticipate future events. Finally, it is necessary to help manage sound objects and parameters so as to release cognitive load by distributing the cognition through the interface cf. [23]. In our case, PA provides four virtual spaces for users to plan ahead of time and to manage the sound elements.

Apart from the above ones, some points that can be linked to previous research are also interesting. Providing enough *visual affordance* to increase the chance of finding new functions and playing strategies is important for creative engagement. Visual clue is also helpful to beginners to interpret and to remember the sound. In our case, participants reported the graphic design of effectors in PB help them to distinguish the sound. Besides, providing mechanisms to facilitate *serendipity* is good for generating new music ideas and finding functions, which helps to 'catalyze human activity' [45] for creative engagement.

Future Research

Features identified above will be improved or implemented in prototypes. For instance, to better assist non-musician to structure the composition during improvisation, the validity and effectiveness of the sub-themes identified above (starting base, record history, plan ahead of time) will be examined with improved prototypes. As the above results are based on the prototypes designed in the context of screen based applications, the current results are bounded in a limited scope of IMSs. Future research will expand into a broader context of IMSs, such as tangible interfaces and installations, to test whether the results are general applicable for different forms of IMSs. Prototypes with the features highlighted in this paper will be designed, and evaluation on the validity and effectiveness of features identified will be carried out.

The current experiment was carried out with limited amount of participants in a controlled environment. A larger number of participants would have made it easier and more appropriate to generalize implications from the study. Participants only had a very short time to interact with the prototypes. This time constraint might have impact on the study findings. Moreover, as for many IMSs the usage scenarios are in distracting, open public spaces, more studies on the 'situated' interaction will need to be carried out in a wild context to strengthen the above findings [44, 3], in order for better understanding on non-musicians' creative engagement with IMSs.

CONCLUSION

In this paper an empirical study of exploring non-musician's creative engagement with musical interfaces is reported. The results unveiled the process of creative engagement when individual non-musician interact with musical interface, as well as the typical interaction patterns of novices when they encounter a new IMS. The detail of the interaction process is explained in terms of a three-step framework 'Learn', 'Exploration' and 'Create'. Furthermore, how creative engagement can be supported with the features in musical interface is explained, the features such as 'learn the sound', 'playing live', 'catalyze insights' and 'scaffold composition' are highlighted as implications for future design. Another research contribution of this paper lies in the basic study methodology on the execution and analysis of the user studies, which combines recording user interactions and interviewing. Future work will continue to explore the role of 'playing live' and 'structure composition' in broader context of IMSs for non-musicians. A different methodology for examining situated interaction will also be carried out.

ACKNOWLEDGMENTS

We kindly thank the participants in our study. This work is partly supported by the the China Scholarship Council, and the EPSRC+AHRC Centre for Doctoral Training in Media and Arts Technology (EP/L01632X/1).

REFERENCES

1. Daniel Gábana Arellano and Andrew McPherson. 2014. Radear: A Tangible Spinning Music Sequencer. In *Proceedings of the 14th International Conference on New Interfaces for Musical Expression*. 84–85.
2. Jerônimo Barbosa, Filipe Calegario, Veronica Teichrieb, Geber Ramalho, and Giordano Cabral. 2013. Illusio: A drawing-based digital music instrument. In *Proceedings of the 13th International Conference on New Interfaces for Musical Expression*.
3. Ben Bengler and Nick Bryan-Kinns. 2013. Designing collaborative musical experiences for broad audiences. In *Proceedings of the 9th ACM Conference on Creativity & Cognition*. ACM, 234–242.
4. Gilbert Beyer and Max Meier. 2011. Music Interfaces for Novice Users: Composing Music on a Public Display with Hand Gestures. In *Proceedings of the 11th International Conference on New Interfaces for Musical Expression*. 507–510.
5. Zafer Bilda, Ernest Edmonds, and Linda Candy. 2008. Designing for creative engagement. *Design Studies* 29, 6 (2008), 525–540.
6. Niels Böttcher, Steven Gelineck, and Stefania Serafin. 2007. PHYSMISM: a control interface for creative exploration of physical models. In *Proceedings of the 7th international conference on New interfaces for musical expression*. 31–36.
7. Virginia Braun and Victoria Clarke. 2006. Using thematic analysis in psychology. *Qualitative research in psychology* 3, 2 (2006), 77–101.
8. Nick Bryan-Kinns. 2004. Daisyphone: the design and impact of a novel environment for remote group music improvisation. In *Proceedings of the 5th conference on Designing interactive systems: processes, practices, methods, and techniques*. ACM, 135–144.
9. John Cage. 1961. Experimental music. *Silence: Lectures and writings* (1961), 7–12.
10. Linda Candy and Zafer Bilda. 2009. Understanding and evaluating creativity. In *Proceedings of the 7th ACM conference on Creativity and cognition*. ACM, 497–498.
11. Andy Clark. 1998. *Being there: Putting brain, body, and world together again*. MIT press.
12. Mihaly Csikszentmihalyi. 1996. Flow and the psychology of discovery and invention. *New York: Harper Collins* (1996).
13. Gideon D'Arcangelo. 2001. Creating contexts of creativity: musical composition with modular components. In *Proceedings of the 1st conference on New interfaces for musical expression*. 1–4.
14. Ernest Edmonds, Lizzie Muller, and Matthew Connell. 2006. On creative engagement. *Visual Communication* 5, 3 (2006), 307–322.
15. Mark Christopher Feldmeier. 2002. *Large group musical interaction using disposable wireless motion sensors*. Ph.D. Dissertation. Citeseer.
16. Sidney Fels. 2004. Designing for intimacy: Creating new interfaces for musical expression. *Proc. IEEE* 92, 4 (2004), 672–685.
17. Ronald A Finke, Thomas B Ward, and Steven M Smith. 1992. *Creative cognition: Theory, research, and applications*. MIT press Cambridge, MA.
18. Steven Gelineck and Stefania Serafin. 2010. A practical approach towards an exploratory framework for physical modeling. *Computer Music Journal* 34, 2 (2010), 51–65.
19. Kilem Li Gwet. 2008. Computing inter-rater reliability and its variance in the presence of high agreement. *Brit. J. Math. Statist. Psych.* 61, 1 (2008), 29–48.
20. Anne-Marie Skriver Hansen, Hans J Anderson, and Pirkko Raudaskoski. 2011. Play Fluency in Music Improvisation Games for Novices.. In *Proceedings of the 11th International Conference on New Interfaces for Musical Expression*. 220–223.
21. Jiffer Harriman. 2012. Sinkapater-An Untethered Beat Sequencer.. In *Proceedings of the International Conference on New Interfaces for Musical Expression*.
22. Ted Hayes. 2010. Neurohedron: A Nonlinear Sequencer Interface.. In *Proceedings of the 10th International Conference on New Interfaces for Musical Expression*. 23–25.
23. James Hollan, Edwin Hutchins, and David Kirsh. 2000. Distributed cognition: toward a new foundation for human-computer interaction research. *ACM Transactions on Computer-Human Interaction (TOCHI)* 7, 2 (2000), 174–196.
24. Olivier Houix, Stefano Delle Monache, Hélène Lachambre, Frédéric Bevilacqua, Davide Rocchesso, and Guillaume Lemaitre. 2016. Innovative tools for sound sketching combining vocalizations and gestures. In *Proceedings of the Audio Mostly 2016*. ACM, 12–19.
25. Kazuhiro Jo. 2008. DrawSound: a drawing instrument for sound performance. In *Proceedings of the 2nd international conference on Tangible and embedded interaction*. ACM, 59–62.
26. Sergi Jordà, Günter Geiger, Marcos Alonso, and Martin Kaltenbrunner. 2007. The reacTable: exploring the synergy between live music performance and tabletop tangible interfaces. In *Proceedings of the 1st international conference on Tangible and embedded interaction*. ACM, 139–146.
27. Dave S Kerby. 2014. The simple difference formula: An approach to teaching nonparametric correlation. *Comprehensive Psychology* 3 (2014), 11–IT.
28. André Knörig, Boris Müller, and Reto Wettach. 2007. Articulated paint: musical expression for non-musicians. In *Proceedings of the 7th international conference on New interfaces for musical expression*. 384–385.

29. Golan Levin. 2000. *Painterly interfaces for audiovisual performance*. Ph.D. Dissertation. Massachusetts Institute of Technology.
30. Tod Machover. 2002. Instruments, interactivity, and inevitability. In *Proceedings of the 2nd conference on New interfaces for musical expression*. 1–1.
31. Tim Murray-Browne. 2012. *Interactive music: Balancing creative freedom with musical development*. Ph.D. Dissertation. Queen Mary University of London.
32. Dan Overholt. 2009. The musical interface technology design space. *Organised Sound* 14, 2 (2009), 217–226.
33. S Park, S Kim, S Lee, and W S Yeo. 2010. Online map interface for creative and interactive MusicMaking. *Proceedings of the 10th International Conference on New Interfaces for Musical Expression* (2010).
34. Processing. 2017. Processing Website. (2017). `https://processing.org/`.
35. Mitchel Resnick, Amy Bruckman, and Fred Martin. 1996. Pianos not stereos: Creating computational construction kits. *interactions* 3, 5 (1996), 40–50.
36. Dominic Robson. 2002. Play!: Sound toys for non-musicians. *Computer Music Journal* 26, 3 (2002), 50–61.
37. Kimiko Ryokai, Stefan Marti, and Hiroshi Ishii. 2004. I/O brush: drawing with everyday objects as ink. In *Proceedings of the SIGCHI conference on Human factors in computing systems*. ACM, 303–310.
38. Jan C Schacher, Chikashi Miyama, and Daniel Bisig. 2015. Gestural Electronic Music using Machine Learning as Generative Device. In *Proceedings of the 15th International Conference on New Interfaces for Musical Expression*.
39. Mark A Schmuckler. 1999. Testing models of melodic contour similarity. *Music Perception: An Interdisciplinary Journal* 16, 3 (1999), 295–326.
40. Jennifer G Sheridan and Nick Bryan-Kinns. 2008. Designing for performative tangible interaction. *International Journal of Arts and Technology* 1, 3-4 (2008), 288–308.
41. Ben Shneiderman. 2000. Creating creativity: user interfaces for supporting innovation. *ACM Transactions on Computer-Human Interaction (TOCHI)* 7, 1 (2000), 114–138.
42. Ben Shneiderman. 2007. Creativity support tools: Accelerating discovery and innovation. *Commun. ACM* 50, 12 (2007), 20–32.
43. Dan Stowell, Andrew Robertson, Nick Bryan-Kinns, and Mark D Plumbley. 2009. Evaluation of live human–computer music-making: Quantitative and qualitative approaches. *International Journal of Human-Computer Studies* 67, 11 (2009), 960–975.
44. Lucy A Suchman. 1987. *Plans and situated actions: The problem of human-machine communication*. Cambridge university press.
45. Atau Tanaka, Nao Tokui, and Ali Momeni. 2005. Facilitating collective musical creativity. In *Proceedings of the 13th annual ACM international conference on Multimedia*. ACM, 191–198.
46. R Tubb and S Dixon. 2014. The Divergent Interface: Supporting Creative Exploration of Parameter Spaces. *Proceedings of the 14th International Conference on New Interfaces for Musical Expression* (2014).
47. Gil Weinberg. 2003. *Interconnected musical networks: bringing expression and thoughtfulness to collaborative group playing*. Ph.D. Dissertation. Massachusetts Institute of Technology.
48. Gil Weinberg, Roberto Aimi, and Kevin Jennings. 2002. The Beatbug network: a rhythmic system for interdependent group collaboration. In *Proceedings of the 2002 conference on New interfaces for musical expression*. 1–6.
49. Gil Weinberg and Scott Driscoll. 2005a. iltur: Connecting novices and experts through collaborative improvisation. In *Proceedings of the 5th conference on New interfaces for musical expression*. 17–22.
50. Gil Weinberg and Scott Driscoll. 2005b. iltur: Connecting novices and experts through collaborative improvisation. In *Proceedings of the 5th conference on New interfaces for musical expression*. 17–22.
51. David Wessel and Matthew Wright. 2002. Problems and prospects for intimate musical control of computers. *Computer Music Journal* 26, 3 (2002), 11–22.
52. Wai K Yeap, Tommi Opas, and Narges Mahyar. 2010. On two desiderata for creativity support tools. (2010).
53. Francisco Zamorano. 2012. Simpletones: A System of Collaborative Physical Controllers for Novices. In *Proceedings of the 12th International Conference on New Interfaces for Musical Expression*.

Felt Sense through Auditory Display: A Design Case Study into Sound for Somatic Awareness while Walking

Frank Feltham
RMIT University
Melbourne, Australia
frank.feltham@rmit.edu.au

Lian Loke
University of Sydney
Sydney, Australia
lian.loke@sydney.edu.au

ABSTRACT
Walking is an everyday act that we, as humans, often take for granted. To walk requires the synergy of somatosensory, neurological and physiological processes for us to move at a regular pace by lifting and setting down each foot in turn. It can be argued that walking is also a source of creativity and exploration when conducted as an intentional act of somatic or self-awareness. This design case study aims to explore the kinds of somatic awareness and aesthetic engagement of walking apparent through the introduction of a pressure mediated sound generating surface with a group of Feldenkrais movement practitioners. These explorations reveal that there is an awareness of tempo and rhythm during the step cycle. This awareness takes on an internal focus as shifts in attention and bodily organization. Another key finding is that exploration and play are enabled due to the rich timbral qualities of the pressure mediated auditory feedback. The significance and contribution in this work is in the implications it has for the design of technologies that support kinaesthetic awareness through aesthetic and exploratory strategies.

Author Keywords
Walking; kinaesthetic awareness; creativity; auditory feedback; aesthetics of interaction; design case study.

ACM Classification Keywords
H.5.m. Information interfaces and presentation (e.g., HCI): Miscellaneous.

INTRODUCTION

> *Consider, for example, the footstep. Neither the pavement nor the shoe have any intrinsic sound or movement within them, but by their interaction, their coming together in a corporal and rhythmical flow, the footstep is felt by the walker and heard and seen by others.* [40] p.377

This rhythm as articulated by [40] above, is an embodied and internal felt sense of the cycle of walking. It is also experienced by others as an auditory event in time as impacts, slides and scuffs of the footsteps on the pavement. Ingold [20] talks about walking as being rhythmic rather than metronomic, its intervals are not mathematically precise but with variation that respond to lived conditions of the walk in time and space. These variations are the result of a perceptual monitoring and embodied negotiation of these conditions ever changing, if albeit subtle, and felt internally and kinaesthetically. The variations, modulations and *tunings of movement* [20] p. 332 in response to challenges to establish these rhythms is an inherently creative act [40], and an important part of becoming *present to oneself in the world* [37] p. 11. There is considerable evidence in the accounts from anthropology and cultural studies cited above to suggest the nature of walking is about adaption, creativity and even sensory pleasure when a rhythm is attained.

The supposedly ordinary acts of walking are imbued with creativity and variations in rhythm that are particular to the individual walker. Biomechanical models of the walk cycle such as those offered by [14], explain the basic components and phases of walking and these are very useful in developing a language and understandings of its periodic and cyclic phases. Similarly research into the movement sonification of cyclic actions in sporting performance such as rowing [32], ice skating [15] and developing auditory feedback on reference regions for therapeutic balance training [8], gives insight into the capacity for auditory feedback, mapped to sensed movement features, to inform the mover on the nature of the cyclic phases of movement. However these corrective approaches to movement performance fall short when the intention is less about correct ways of moving and more about supporting kinaesthetic awareness through aesthetic and exploratory strategies. Therefore we characterise walking as a creative act from the position of the internal sense of bodily self-awareness and the personal creativity the walker brings to their walking. Walking can be viewed through a somatic lens to heighten kinaesthetic awareness of the intricacies of bodily organization.

This research presents initial insights into the role that pressure mediated auditory feedback provides in the awareness of the walk cycle as a rhythmic activity. The rhythms we observed in this exploratory study range from rapid staccato-like stepping from foot to foot, to slow and continual motion through the alternating footstep. With

C&C 2017, June 27–30, 2017, Singapore.
© 2017 ACM ISBN 978-1-4503-4403-6/17/06...$15.00.
http://dx.doi.org/10.1145/3059454.3059461

these variations in rhythm comes variation in awareness of how the body is organized in motion - from alternating pressure exerted through the legs, to fuller body coordination through the hips and shoulders. These insights demonstrate that pressure mediated auditory feedback can begin to provide forms of kinaesthetic awareness that heighten creative, playful approaches to the act of walking.

At this stage we do not seek to develop models of "corrective" sonification to inform the walker, for example, of key phases or moments in the walk cycle. Nor is it to focus the research on error reducing or performance enhancing paradigms and methods for evaluating them. In contrast we are guided by the "felt", first person accounts of walker on pressure mediated auditory feedback from qualitative and aesthetic perspective in combination with pressure data samples recorded from their walks to gain insight into the patterns and variance that emerges. The aim of this research therefore is to understand what types of creativity, rhythmic awareness and aesthetic engagement are enabled by introducing pressure mediated auditory feedback through the walk cycle. And what initial implications we can draw for the design of such sound making interactive technologies.

To explore and explain this creative engagement in the walk cycle our method follows recent approaches in case study research for human computer interaction, [24]. Typical of this approach is the description of qualitative themes through the examination of situated engagement with expert users and interactive technologies. We add to these qualitative themes the quantitative pressure data as a further unit of analysis [24]. To organize and represent the themes and pressure data we have developed a visualization tool, the pressure-spectrogram, as a central resource to enable analysis. The expert users are practitioners of the Feldenkrais method [12], a somatic practice that values first person self-awareness of movement. The Feldenkrais method includes walking as an activity to examine self-awareness therefore we selected these participants as valuable to our study and its aims.

This paper starts by providing a background to Movement Sonification and Sound, and makes an argument for the need for an aesthetic approach to auditory feedback, and the roles timbre and rhythm have for continuous movement. It then discusses the Somatic practice of Feldenkrais Awareness Through Movement and then frames the walking case study as a method with the study procedures and protocols. Finally the paper provides an analysis and discussion of the walking activities through pressure mediated auditory feedback and concludes with implications for design.

MOVEMENT SONIFICATION AND SOUND

The emerging area of Physical Sonification [10] has introduced a focus on auditory forms of information used within interactive systems to enhance movement awareness of physical activity in many forms. The term Movement Sonification we have adapted from [19], as aiding movement with sonification. Our focus for Movement Sonification is to enhance the awareness in the mover of their bodily organization through auditory feedback, following task oriented approaches to the design of sonification [1].

The perceptual qualities in sound

Sound is used as the primary feedback modality in our system due to its unique capacity to present information in the periphery of our attention whilst being highly immersive and selectively listened to [3], allowing focus of attention to be directed to the actual movement quality. Sound is also is an effective means to entrain and guide movement due to its ability to be perceived in time related tasks and events [39, 10, 32]. Being able to switch and select our attention with sound has advantages for walking as we can concentrate on its ability to assist and inform movement where a visual display might distract, as it tends to demand the center of our attention. Sound and auditory perception also provides support for motion sequences [32] and temporal resolution for movement patterns [11].

Corrective approaches to Movement Sonification

From an instructive and clinical position movement sonification has been used to assist in the therapeutic recovery of stroke patients, [6]. To entrain the lateral movement of shoulders for physiotherapeutic recovery, [42] and for balance recovery in patients with vestibular loss, [8]. In a more dynamic sense and with a focus on the cyclical nature of movement, we highlight a range of research projects that use sonification to improve sporting performance. For example rowing accelerations and stroke phases as a rhythmical quality [32]. Also stroke and weight distribution in speed skating [38, 15]. These research projects are all attempting to sonify cyclic movements of the body to provide performance feedback on its locations and exertions in a dynamically informative way. Schaffert et al. [32] reported that there can be a significantly improved movement execution with the addition of interactive acoustic information with the rowers able to clearly define the key phases of the rowing cycle through the variation in pitch. This is of particular interest given the cyclic nature of walking and its phases of movement. We discuss the rhythmic qualities auditory feedback has in upcoming sections. Generally the research into Physical and Movement Sonification makes assumptions about movement that directs the design of the technologies used for experimentation and testing. It imposes models on the raw data to influence auditory features [15, 8, 6, 42], or relies on the raw data to influence the auditory feedback for the mover to discern the change [32, 38]. The use of these mathematical models and thresholds that make corrective and performative assumptions about how we move and where we should move drives the design of these technologies from the perspective of optimization, correction and error reduction. This decision to isolate the causal features of movement, into mathematical thresholds for the adjustment of auditory features, makes sense when the goal is to inform and improve movement and posture for clinical therapeutic recovery and increased sporting performance. However corrective approaches to movement sonification fall short when the intention moves from imposed models of movement, based on a performance or therapeutic goals, to exploring the walk cycle through pressure mediated auditory feedback to understand its role in fostering creative and rhythmic engagement. We are not seeking to optimize movement through sonification for performance improvement, but rather engage participants in the exploration of their movement in concert with the auditory feedback. This auditory feedback we argue needs to be rich in texture, not a "signal" mediated by a pure tone that seeks information fidelity at the expense of aesthetically pleasing and engaging results [18].

We frame this design case study around themes that contrast significantly with this "corrective" paradigm by examining the role the first person has in cultivating self-awareness of their moving body through creative and exploratory movement, as espoused by somatic practices [17]. We discuss the ways in which we enable this focus on exploratory movement through auditory feedback in the upcoming section, but first we background this discussion with some notes on the aesthetic turn for movement sonification.

An Aesthetic turn for movement sonification

We see the turn to pragmatism and an aesthetics of experience as a focus for interaction design and human computer interaction [16]. Philosophically, movement practices and somatics have also been argued for from a pragmatic and lived perspective [35]. The value it places on this research is in the intrinsic focus on aesthetics within lived experience and action. These ideas add weight to the somatic practices of [17], and provide insight for this research with aesthetics of experience as an aim.

Aesthetic approaches to sonification have been influenced by Pragmatist philosophy, [2, 4]. The function of the sonification in these terms is to be interpreted and allow a sense-making. This marks a shift from the fidelity characterized by research from the corrective approaches that use auditory display as a representation of a movement "truth". Barrass and Vickers [4] suggest a representational continuum within sonification with poles at either end of this continuum indicating sonification having a tight data connection with constrained expression and a looser connection with data and greater expression. Roddy and Furlong [30], suggest an aesthetic approach based on theories of embodied cognition as a means to resolve the quandary of what mappings to use between data and sound to communicate intent. We see value in these discussions and orientations as they shift the focus from fidelity and truth to suggesting that the auditory feedback may have mappings that are not intended to be faithful representations of the data but rather those that can be expressed, interpreted and experienced. However whilst they provide a re-framing, such theories are preliminary and far from resolved in terms of models for the design of engaging, expressive and informative auditory display of the moving and acting body.

DESIGNING FOR AESTHETIC AND SOMATIC APPROACHES TO AUDITORY DISPLAY

Cultivating an awareness framed in somatic and aesthetic terms requires a strategy for the design of auditory display. To date there is very little in terms of these strategies to design in the literature, despite best efforts to provide taxonomies of sonification for movement based activity [2]. Similarly subjective and conceptual methods for auditory display highlight the need for capturing internal responses of users [5], however we don't see how the approaches offered can foster rich embodied "in the moment" accounts of the internal awareness through auditory feedback using techniques of sound synthesis and mappings to movement data. Therefore we isolate and discuss two main strategies as our focus to achieve auditory feedback in this vein: the use of complex timbre and rhythm as auditory information, respectively.

Complex timbre and continuous movement

Timbre is defined as all of the characteristics that allow the discernment of one sound, from another, beyond its pitch and loudness [10]. As this is quite a wide ranging definition, and given the multitude of techniques used to generate sounds, we focus our discussion on some of the techniques that we see as useful in mediating an aesthetically engaging and internally felt auditory display for walking.

Henkelmann [18] defined what he saw as an issue with the limitations of pitch change and sine wave modulations used commonly within sonification of movement projects and argued for other modulation approaches to achieve pleasing results for the continuous sonification of movement and activity. Pitch according to Henkelmann [18] suffers from the cultural expectations some have with the western musical scale and its intervals. The problem when you map these scales to human movement is that you are bound to get dissonant or unpredictable auditory intervals resulting in unpleasant sounds. He suggests more complex timbral modulations, compared to pitch change, such as filter transformations, frequency modulations, and additive synthesis. Examples of recent research using more complex timbral techniques includes; the use of filter cutoff frequency mapped to the timing and phasing of two people moving with accelerometers in mobile phones [39], the accelerations and location of a dancer's gestures mapped to features of a band pass filter and grain size of a sample using granular synthesis [31]. In terms of walking activity using complex timbral methods, Physics-based sound synthesis has been used to represent the actual sounds of the impacts and collisions in a footstep [13, 28, 9]. Using complex timbral means to represent continuous movement has potential to capture rich embodied "in the moment" accounts of the internal awareness due to the ways that multiple frequencies are modulated or the granular means that the audio is sampled. These transcend the use of single frequency sine tones or pitch change that can be interpreted as artificial and not representative of the sounds we hear in the environment or well-composed music. We see an important role for complex timbral approaches to provide continuous auditory feedback to affect the full body engagement of a walker and their self-awareness.

Rhythmic based auditory information

There is also an argument for rhythmic auditory feedback as a means to provide information on the cycle of motion for activities such as walking. We are interested here in auditory feedback that is generated *from* movement, rather than movement that is induced by the existing beat of a musical piece, of which there are many studies (see [7]). Schaffert et. al [33], reports that rhythm can direct attention to sequences within cyclical movement. Godbout [15] also suggests similar functional purposes for sound in skating phases to inform and assist improvement. There are also positive responses in walkers when adaptive tempo and ecological sounds are used in interactive walking contexts [27]. We consider rhythm as an important part of auditory feedback to direct attention to phases and moments in the cycles of walking movements. We also see a role for the emergent rhythms that interactive sonification can provide to walking cycles in improvisational and playful ways.

The pressure sensitive surface and design of auditory feedback

The surface used in this case study was initially conceived as a site-specific gallery installation, based on a design proposition to encourage reflection on bodily awareness through slow walking movements mediated through rich timbral auditory feedback mapped to a simple pressure pad arrangement of 6 aligned pads of total length 1.8 metres, (see figure 3). The pressure pad has a single force sensitive resistor centrally located and sandwiched between an upper layer of timber laser cut with a grilled pattern and EVA foam. We revised this gallery installation for the purposes of this study by using granular synthesis of field recordings as the strategy to provide auditory feedback. The technique of granular synthesis can be explained as *generating thousands of very short sonic grains to form larger acoustic events* [29, p.11]. These grains fall within very small temporal ranges in the milliseconds, and Roads [29] suggests this is a form of additive synthesis as the sounds result from the addition of these thousands of grains. In the approach we used the grain density was set to eight overlapping grains at any time interval creating a thick grain cloud and a sonically interesting result. The main mapping was between the rise in the force sensor data to vary the size of the sampling grain of the sound, from 50 to 200 milliseconds for lowest to highest-pressure readings. The other parameter mapped was the rise of the force sensor data to initiate the sound and increase the volume as each pad was stepped upon. Each of the six pads in the pressure surface arrangement had the same sound and signal processing method. The field recordings we created as source samples for the granular synthesis contained a diverse mix of both naturally occurring pitched and non-pitched sound materials. Four field-recorded samples were created in total, however this paper reports on two of these samples as selected by the participants. These samples named Sound C and D, recorded in a rainforest setting east of Melbourne, Australia using high quality digital field recorders and microphones. The original source of Sound C was the bubbling water in a small brook, which created a rich natural percussive pattern. Sound D, was the sound of a car at a distance, creating a wind like texture with the dominant vibration being possibly the friction from the car tyres on a bitumen road. Using Granular Synthesis conserved some of the rich complexity of pitched and non-pitched sound material of the original field recordings and created interesting sonic combinations due to the reorganization of these sound grains. Our assumption was that this would help achieve complex timbral auditory feedback for continuous and engaging walking movements.

WALKING AS A DESIGN CASE STUDY

We approached this research as a case study of technologically mediated walking from the first person lived experience and the awareness of the footstep when its cycle of weight transfer is mediated by auditory information. Inspired by phenomenological accounts and practices of movement [34], pragmatic aesthetics and movement [36], designerly ways of interrogating movement and using movement as material for design [23, 26, 21], ethnographic approaches to collecting qualitative data for design practice [22] and subjective conceptual approaches to the design of auditory display [5], we have constructed a program of studies that starts to capture rich accounts of felt experience and somatic awareness whilst walking to pressure sensitive auditory feedback. We see the emergence of qualitative themes, through the examination of situated engagement with interactive technologies in a Case Study approach [24], as a useful way of capturing insights for design exploration. Case study research with interactive technologies also values small participant samples of experts to explore, describe and analyse rich engagements, leading to more nuanced understanding and hypothesis forming for subsequent controlled user trials [24]. Our participants for this case study were Feldenkrais practitioners as expert walkers. These participants were selected because they have the language and movement practice experience to provide a rich qualitative focus on first person somatic awareness and aesthetic engagement.

The Feldenkrais method

The Feldenkrais method® is a somatic educational system based on movement, which aims to expand and refine the use of self through awareness [12]. In Feldenkrais, movement is the basis of awareness and this awareness is governed by our self-image in the motor cortex of the brain. This self-image is generally smaller than our potential capacity to be actually aware through movement and this is an objective of Feldenkrais Awareness Through Movement (ATM) lessons, to realise our greater awareness potential through movement by increasing movement sensitivity. The result of ATM lessons is an increase in sensitivity, resulting in a capacity to distinguish the finer details of movement that previously had escaped notice. Slowing down our movement is the first step to greater awareness of how our various body parts and systems work together in coordinating our movement. Play and experimentation are also crucial to developing awareness of old movement patterns and habits and eventually, re-programming new, healthier patterns of movement. Walking within the Feldenkrais method involves the awareness and organization of the spine, pelvis and shoulders to achieve a correct walking posture. In previous work [25] the application of Feldenkrais ATM principles to the domain of interactive art produced a series of experimental artworks and co-design activities that provided subtle experiences of balance and gravity. We extend the explorations of balance in standing to studies of walking, where walking inherently involves cyclic acts of going off-balance during the lift-off and leg-swing phases of the step and re-balancing during the touch-down and double-stance phase of the step.

The study participants

The Feldenkrais practitioners were in the age range of 40 to 70 years old and, apart from Feldenkrais, had backgrounds ranging from dance, performance art, physical theatre to physiotherapy. There were 5 female participants and 1 male. All of the Feldenkrais participants were familiar with the ATM practices described earlier.

Study procedure and data collection

The study was conducted at a specialised sound production studio. Each participant attended an individual session and was asked to perform the following activities:

- Regular walking - walking, for a 3 minute period, in a Feldenkrais style, on the regular "non-interactive" floor
- Interactive surface walking - walking on the interactive surface 1.8 metres in length, for 5 minutes up and back. This 5-minute walk was done with the four sound options. Immediately after each walk a short questionnaire was completed.
- After all of the walking activities, a one-minute walk on the participant's choice of sound followed by a video-recall interview.

All of the sessions were video, sound recorded and photographed. The qualitative accounts were attained via interview and questionnaire transcripts. A pressure data sample was taken of the one-minute walk and these walks we represent visually in the pressure-spectrogram and photo montages, figures 2 and 3.

Focus of the questionnaires and interviews

The questions we asked for the four walks had a focus on motivations, feeling and sensations during the walking. We also asked for a description of the sound and an indication of how the sound influenced the body movements. To select the most engaging sound we asked which sound walk prolonged engagement, and if there was any evidence of reflection or stillness in this sound walk. Lastly we asked if they applied any of their movement practices in the experience. The video-cued recall interview was semi-structured around the questions: outstanding moments in terms of movement responses to sound, bodily awareness while moving to the sounds, and the overall experience.

Data Analysis Using Visual Means

Our means of analysis triangulates pressure and sound data samples, first person accounts of these movements and second person observations. To assist in this analysis we have developed a visualization method called the Pressure-spectrogram. The Pressure-spectrogram allows a rapid visual overview of the 60 second walk as pressure data and sound response aligned to a timescale. The image at Figure 1 presents a simple key for reading the pressure data. The walks pass number, moments of double support, and pressure data readings are presented in this graphical fashion. The pass number shows the number of the walking pass as one traversal of the 6 timber and foam pads shown in figure 3. The double support moments are when both feet are on the pads transitioning in weight. The pressure data readings are shown as pad 1, 3 and 5 in black and 2, 4 and 6 in grey. These give a coarse visual register of the *time* on each pad, rather than the actual pressure value as it was binary in nature. Underneath the pressure data we have shown the auditory feedback as a spectrogram (see figure 1 below).

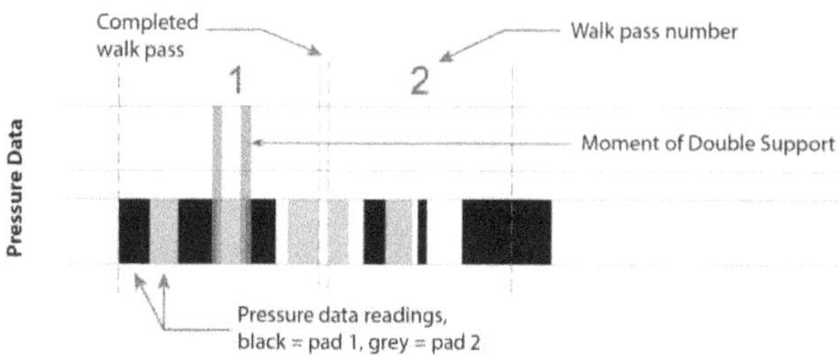

Figure 1. Pressure Data Key

RHYTHMICITY IN THE WALKING

We have chosen three of the participants to discuss and visualize through the Pressure-spectrograms due to their interesting contrasts in tempo, rhythm and somatic attention throughout the walks. A full analysis of all participants is beyond the scope of this paper. This analysis of the pressure-spectrograms reveals some of the rhythmic patterns, tempo differences, internal awareness and exploration within the step cycle.

Participant 1

Participant 1 chose Sound D as her preferred sound and walked at the greatest tempo with 10 passes on the surface (see Figure 2). There is very little time in the double support stance phase [14, 41], resulting in rapid gait and walking speed. If you look at the pressure data in a little more detail some interesting patterns emerge. The colour sequences of the pressure data show that the participant was not stepping on each pad (i.e., 1,2,3), but rather missing pads 2 and 5 in all walk passes.

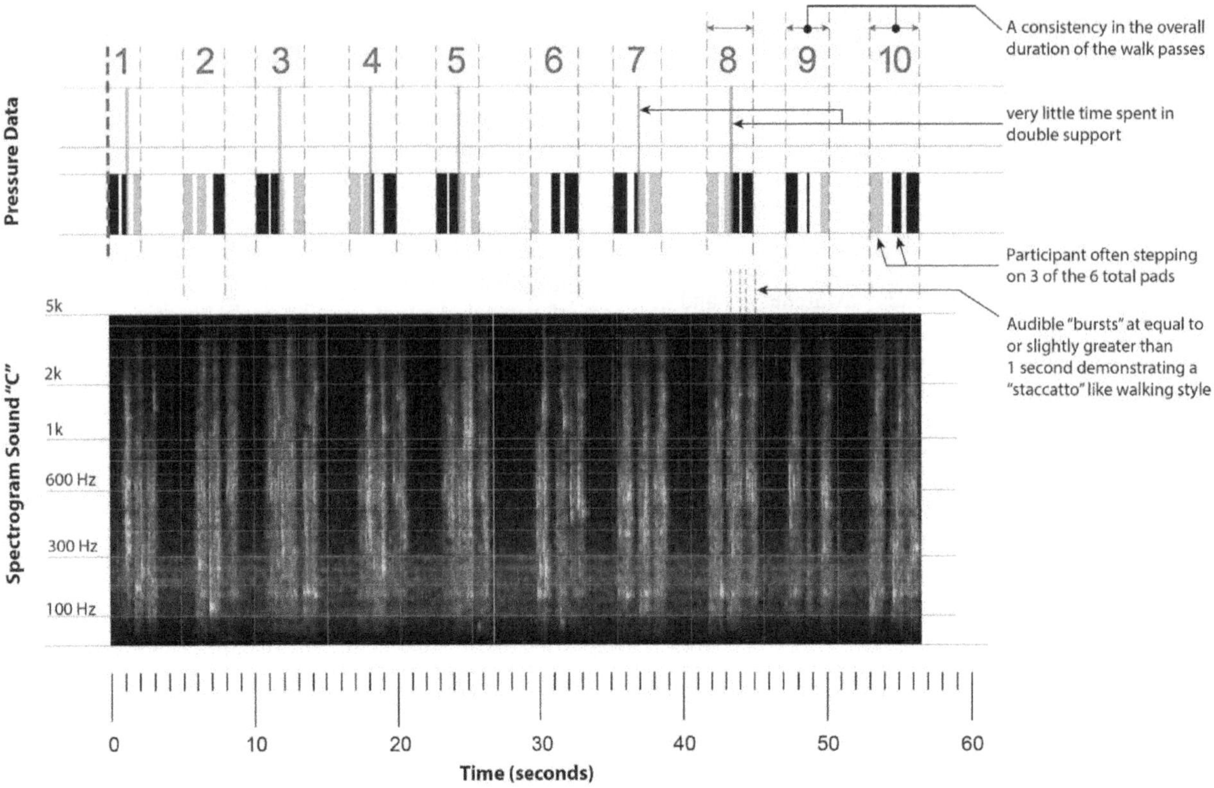

Figure 2. Participant 1 pressure-spectrogram, staccato like stepping. ©Frank Feltham

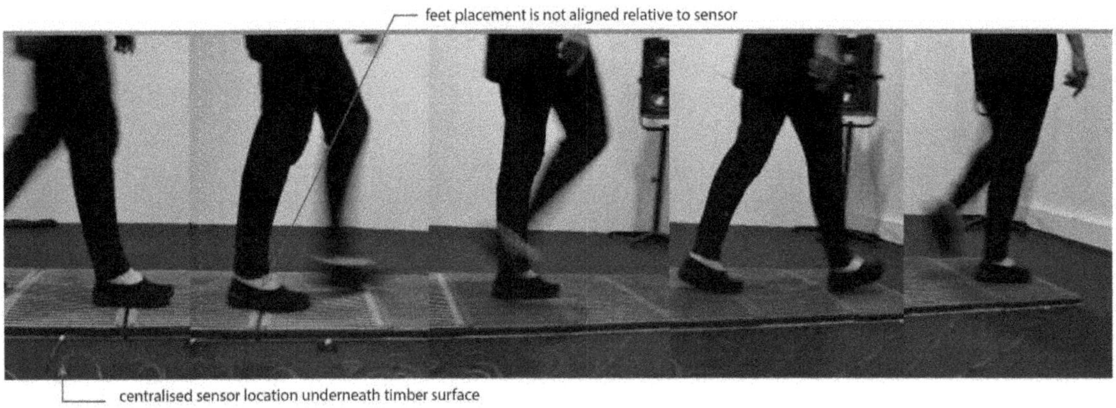

Figure 3. Participant 1 walk sequence and step cycle

These large steps were at a quick tempo resulting in high velocity compared to the other participants. The audible sound shows bursts are remarkably similar duration at approximately or slightly greater than 1 second across all steps. This overall consistency was interesting as the participant suggested; *I wanted to make ummm a sound, which sounds ahhh in good rhythm.*

Looking at the pressure data patterns in the pressure-spectrogram, the passes are all variations on the 3 steps taken by the participant. This variation in each step was articulated as trying a *pattern of bigger steps, smaller steps* to try and play with the sound and create a variance. When you look at the walks numbered 3 up to 10, there is quite a consistency in the overall duration of the walk passes at between 3 to 4 seconds. But within this duration the order of the steps was varied due to the placement of her foot on the pads relative to the sensor position (see Figure 3). This contributed to the notion of better, or poorer, sound and rhythm. The participant indicated a focus on the weight of the footstep and how the sound signified this, *but I did look especially in weight, I looked how much I pushed on one foot how much I didn't on the other one.* The participant also indicated that the left foot was her dominant step and that she heard this in the increased volume from the greater pressure exerted from this side. This greater pressure she tried to balance through listening to the sound.

Participant 2

Participant 2 chose sound D and completed 6 passes, just over half of participant 1, with more time on the surface per walk pass. We see that walk pass 1 has long moments of pressure and continuous sound at just over 10 seconds, with some double support moments both over half a second in this pass (see Figure 4). This consistency in pass 1 shows a constant response in the granular synthesis with key bands of frequency at 600 and 200 Hz. When looking at the 6 walk passes in totality there are combinations of short steps and longer drawn out steps. The breaks between the passes are far shorter, or not existent, than those of participant 1. The variation in the pressure gaps was greater for participant 2, the longest of these was approximately 2.2 with the shortest being 0.4 of a second. These gaps are due to the placement of her foot on the pads missing the sensor position, similar to participant 1. Participant 2 did make some interesting observations on the types of internal bodily organization through the pressure mediated walking, *...there's something very deliberate about the quality of the walking to that sound..., very conscious and mannered in a way, that was using the whole body.* When asked to describe what the sound evoked she revealed that, *Evoked slowness, reflection, heaviness, in the walk, very conscious movement of diagonals from hips to opposite shoulder, Deliberate mmmm.* There was a rhythmic quality in the pressure to sound relationship this was described as creating, *an atmosphere that evokes an image that locates the walk. Affects the senses that translate into the rhythm and pace.* An interesting observation was made on the feet missing the sensors (see Figure 5). These were moments of silence that she *sought to return to*, creating an interruption and shift to the location of the feet over the awareness of the fuller body.

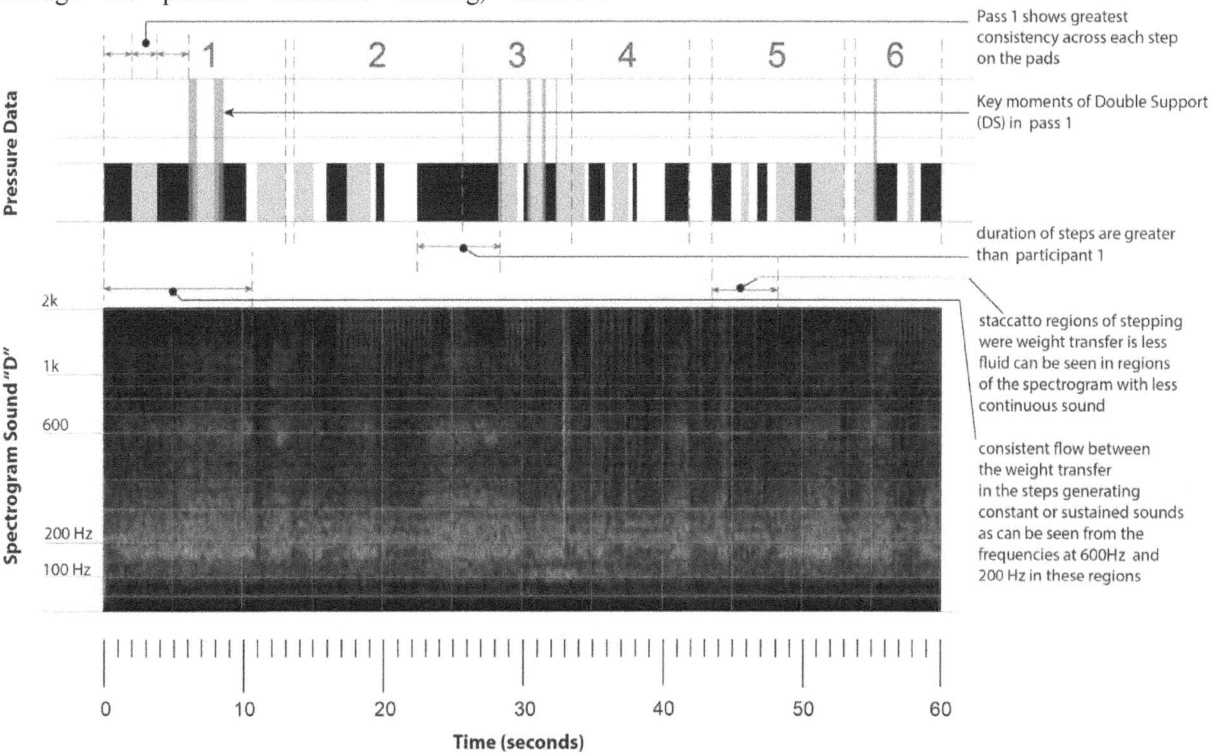

Figure 4. Participant 2 Pressure-spectrogram, variations in moments of consistent flow and staccato steps. ©Frank Feltham

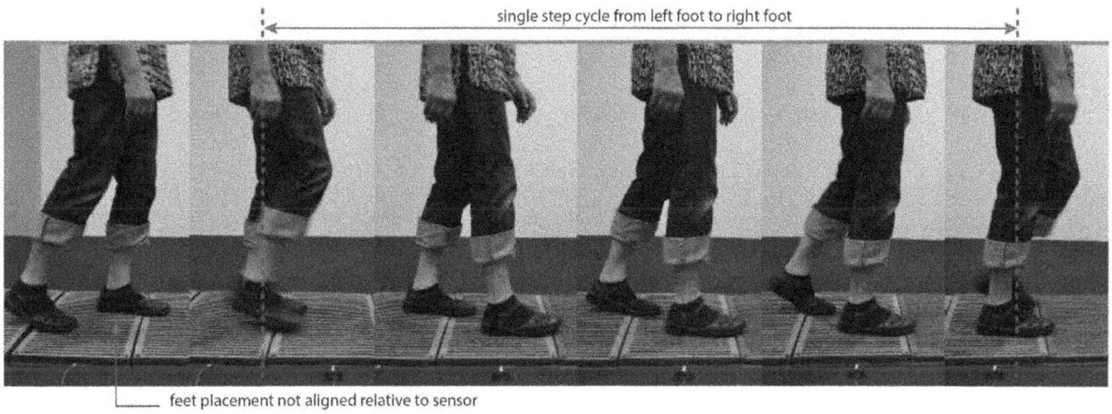

Figure 5. Participant 2, Walk sequence and step cycle

Participant 3

The slowest tempo and most deliberate of all of the walkers was participant 3, who again like Participant 2 chose sound D. She completed only 3 passes in the 60 seconds, which was less than a third of participant 1. The pressure data visually indicates that there is considerable time on each pad (see Figure 6). Apart from a small gap in pressure data in the first pass, due to an error in pressure data reading as the spectrogram does not reflect this, the walking generally is remarkably consistent when compared to the other participants. Participant 3 generated a consistent walking tempo and foot placement to engage a continuous sound whilst walking on the surface with step durations ranging from approximately 2.5 to 5 seconds The significant moments of double support in pass 2, clearly seen in Figure 6, compared to pass 1 indicates a greater awareness and attention toward the weight transfer through the hips and legs in the step cycle (see Figure 7 for a visual indication of the step cycle).

Consequently participant 3 articulated a deep sense of awareness as a result of moving with the sound, ... *with this sound it was that uhmmm.... breathing buts it's also the sensation through your skeleton and ah it was more of, sort of really more my centre, I could feel that all the way through my neck and my throat and uhmmm, it's quite flowing and it sort of it's also that feeling generally of just moving through, moving forward in space.* So ideas of *propulsion, moving forward, a whole body, through the skeleton experience* were articulated. This awareness was partially brought to this experience through the skill and attention the participant had as a Feldenkrais practitioner. But in contrast to walking without the pressure-mediated sound, these descriptions

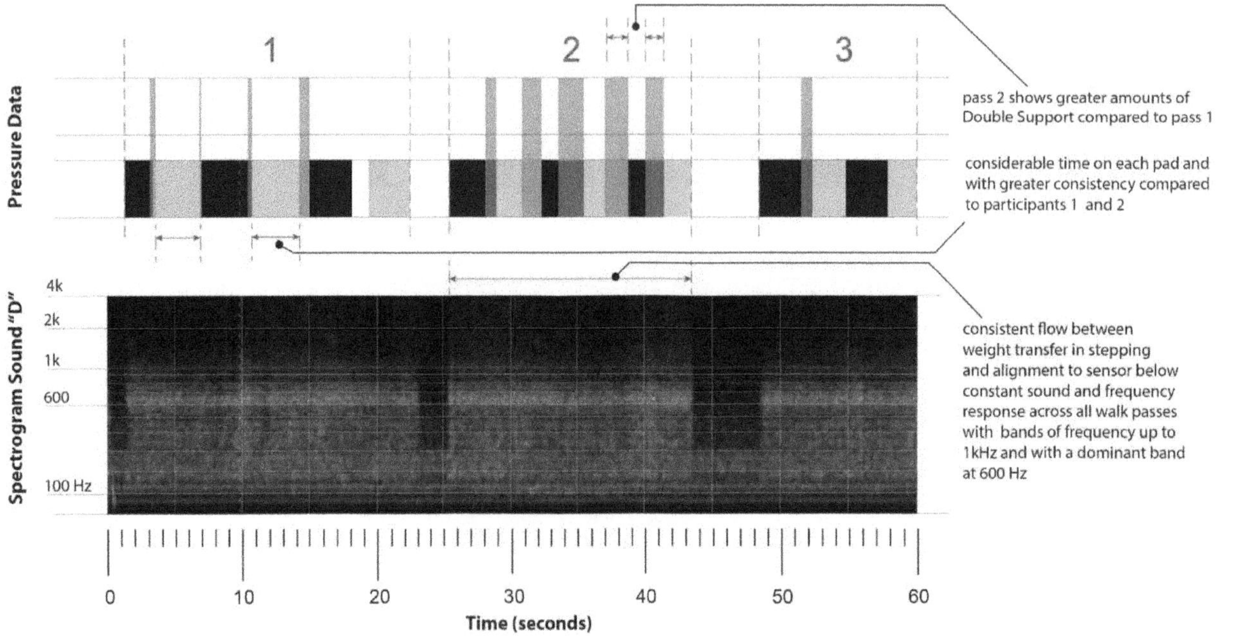

Figure 6. Participant 3, Pressure-spectrogram, consistent flow resulting in constant sound response. ©Frank Feltham

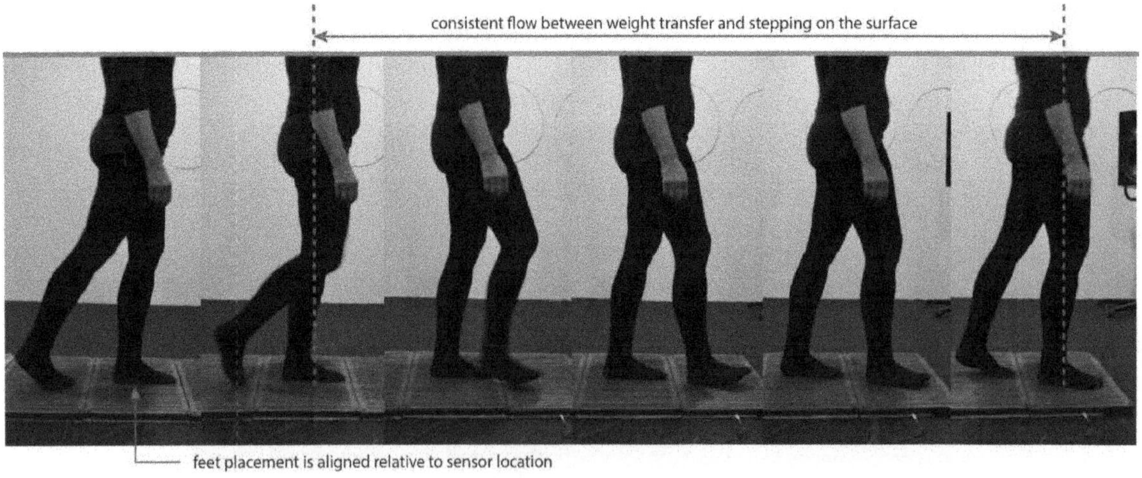

Figure 7. Participant 3, Walk sequence and step cycle

were more expressive and evocative. The participant talked about a fluidity and flow in the movement and exploring self forward in space. These descriptions suggest a deep engagement in the movement act with the sound mediating and providing a spacious and pleasurable experience that was felt internally and emotionally, and bringing a different quality to the walking compared to the no-sound condition. This unique immersion we found to be an initial validation of the rich granulated field recordings. We see from the pressure-spectrogram that the participant was able to engage with the floor in this way without interruption. Long pressure mediated bursts of sound without pause provided a fluidity and flow directing attention inward and through the body. This is also reflected in the consistent frequency response up to approximately 1000Hz with a dominant band at 600 Hz (see Figure 6).

Summary of Responses

We could see the differences in tempo and rhythm in the staccato-like stepping for participant 1 and a shift to slower tempo and internal fuller body perspective of participants 2 and 3. The sound variation clearly created a heightened awareness in the weight of the footstep for participant 1, and provided a fluidity and flow to participant 2 and 3 when compared to their walks without sound. If we are to look at the total sample of 6 participants, we can gain further insights into patterns and dissimilarities that emerge within this group to speculate on the nature of the pressure to sound relationship as a rhythmic and tempo related quality. Participant 6 had quite a different take on rhythm to the staccato like engagement of participant 1. She moved through 5 passes in the 60 seconds and after an initial adjustment constancy was gained in the sound at the slowest third pass, characterized by long steps on all pads and significant overlaps, the two final passes contrast as rapid steps and very little overlaps. This was articulated as being a play with variance in rhythm, from careful and intentional to carefree and not concerned for foot placement, but still enabling a rhythm. The bodily experience described was external, haptic, and the surface enabled a *relationship with the bottom of my feet and the sounds that occurred and each of them I found myself in a different kind of play relationship.*

Participant 4 has a Pressure-spectrogram that looks very similar to participant 1, characterized by rapid staccato like steps. He completed 10 passes on the floor in the 60 seconds and interestingly sharing the selection of sound C with participant 1 who was also a rapid walker. He did comment on the bubbly nature of the sound and that this translated to a lively feeling in the upper torso and shoulders. Participant 5 completed 6 passes with each being similar in duration. The Pressure-spectrogram in comparison with participants 2 and 6 shows very little variation in the tempo and rhythm of the stepping, considering the duration of the overall passes. When compared to participants 1 and 4, there was not the distinct patterning in the footstep duration that accompanied the regularity in which these two participants walked. Interestingly this participant talked about the experience as evoking her imagination with little reference to any rhythm, tempo, and haptic or somatic awareness. In terms of the sound choice participants 1 and 4 chose sound C and all other participants chose sound D. Whilst sound C generated the greatest tempo or speed of the walking, we cannot draw any conclusions as to the significance of this finding compared to sound D. This would require further evaluation.

DISCUSSION

In this section we discuss some of the implications for the design of technologies to support and extend the experience, kinaesthetic awareness of, and creative engagement with, cyclic movements such as walking through auditory feedback.

Awareness through complex timbral auditory feedback

There was a unity of the body and its organization in terms of the attention placed with Sound D. The whole body being propelled through space, moving in unity and powerfully through the rotation of the hips and shoulders, were key themes that emerged through the participant responses. Constancy was a theme that emerged as moments of continuous sound and frequency response. This occurred when the participants were stepping in a slow and intentional way with emphasis placed on the weight shift through the hips and pelvis from foot to foot in the step cycle. There were clear moments in the spectrograms of participants 2 and 3 (Figures 5 and 6) that demonstrated a control and intentionality in the walking. All participants who chose sound D illustrated moments of slowness and intentionality in their walking that brought attention to the organization and dynamic relationship their bodies had with the pressure-mediated sound.

We observed that the timbral complexity of the sounds with their slight variation based on pressure shifts and granular scanning encouraged a slow, fluid constancy in the walking that drew attention to these reflective somatic experiences. Instead of direct mappings with simplistic, one-dimensional sonic responses, we suggest that the use of rich/complex sound synthesis methods can encourage slowness, reflection, bodily organization and somatic awareness. There was clearly an engagement in these participant responses that provides a preliminary validation of Henkelmann's position [18] on the need for more aesthetically engaging sonification through sonically rich and complex timbral synthesis approaches.

Awareness through a game of emergent rhythms

The responses to Sound C illustrated greater walking tempo and rhythmic qualities; this was the choice for participants 1 and 4 who both walked in staccato like fashion. What was interesting were the insights they provided on the nature of walking at tempo with the pressure-mediated sound. Ideas of swinging hips and shoulders, and rhythmic phrasing emerged in this condition. Awareness was directed towards both full bodily organization and the feet through weight distribution. As already mentioned we do not know why sound C encouraged this greater tempo and rhythmic response. However it does highlight the potential for auditory feedback that encourages the emergence of a rhythm by triggering sound with actual movement. Also the exploration of this movement in a rhythmical quality to engage awareness in line with the findings from the cyclic movements in sporting activities [32, 33].

Enabling play and exploration as an aesthetic of engagement

We have seen a range of movement variation in the participants. Given our instruction was to walk naturally, the desire of the participants to engage and explore the walking step cycle through the auditory feedback in their own style whilst being open to the experience both somatically and sonically points to an interaction design strategy that values this variance and enables playful exploration. We see this type of exploratory and playful engagement as evidence of a deeper connection in the act of walking and the awareness it brought as an aesthetic gain worthy of further design development.

The feedback we received from the participants did not really highlight the actual auditory features of the sound, which stands to reason as they were complex layers of frequencies due to the granular synthesis rather than clear notes or tones that had distinguishable value and that could easily be expressed in words. However as a focus for design we see the opportunity for frequency rich, modulated auditory features as a sonic value to be interpreted through movement that encourages delight leading to new forms of awareness. We saw with all of the participants that the introduction of pressure mediated sound resulted in evocative descriptions of the movement to sound relationship that were not present without the sound.

Conceptual directions for aesthetically engaging technologies for walking with sound

The idea of constancy discussed earlier could be an alternative means of corrective feedback by engaging the mover to control the constancy in the key features of the sound. For example moving with a constant and controlled gait holds the fundamental frequency of the sound. With the sound providing subtle but rich sonic variation via multiple oscillators to vary its texture and reducing the pitch related, sine tone nausea suggested by Henkelmann [18].

This constancy could be linked to a movement goal, for example keeping the gait and sound constant for a set period of time to achieve therapeutic advancement. Contrastingly it could be as a means of exploration and discovery, for example, moving outside of the constancy to explore limits of weight bearing and changing of gait rhythm.

We suggest that opportunities exist for machine learning in the system to recognize the patterns, tempos and rhythms to adapt to the individual walker. This adaption could be responsive to particular features in the walking, for example the onset or attack of the heel strike might be recognized by the system to trigger a rapid attack envelope that sonically highlights the footfall and then reduces to capture the sustain of the weight shift through the foot encouraging the development of one's emergent rhythm through these movement to sound features. Conversely a slow walk pattern might capture ideal pressure envelopes of footsteps that may be mapped to a range of frequency adjustments such as filter cutoff of multiple oscillators or an increase in the grain density of the granular synthesis. The net result being that the slower and more intentional the weight shifts through the pelvis and from foot to foot, the richer the auditory feedback as a constant and complex combination of frequencies.

In spatial terms the average pressure of the right foot might be compared to the left foot over a series of steps to control stereo panning of the signal. The results could be an inversion of the panning approach used by [8] to increase sound levels on the side that show lesser pressure values encouraging an adjustment as we have seen from participant 1 where the weight difference as it was mapped to sound level in the signal created awareness of this asymmetry in gait.

CONCLUSION AND FUTURE WORK

With this paper we have presented a design case study of walking on a pressure sensitive sound generating surface that offers considerations for design based on concepts of somatic awareness through the development of rich timbral and emergent rhythmic approaches to auditory feedback. The phenomena we observed through this approach include the awareness and variance of tempo and rhythm during the step cycle, the somatic nature of the internal focus as shifts in awareness of bodily organization, and the exploration, creativity and play due to the pressure mediated auditory feedback. In future work we will continue to build on these preliminary findings towards a new approach to the design of self-awareness and somatic technologies that provide auditory feedback on the nature of cyclic movements and actions.

ACKNOWLEDGMENTS

We thank all of the research participants. Also we thank the reviewers who provided helpful comments on previous versions of this document.

REFERENCES

1. Barrass, S. 1996. TaDa! demonstrations of auditory information design. ICAD '96 Third International Conference on Auditory Display, 1996 Xerox PARC, Palo Alto, CA
2. Barrass, S. 2012. The aesthetic turn in sonification towards a social and cultural medium. AI & Society, 27.
3. Barrass, S and Best, V. 2008. Stream-Based Sonification Diagrams. International Conference on Auditory Display. Paris, France
4. Barrass, S and Vickers, P. 2011. Sonification design and aesthetics. In: Hermann, T., Hunt, A. & Neuhoff, J. G. (eds.) The Sonification Handbook. Berlin, Germany: Logos Publishing House.
5. Brazil, e. & Fernström, M. 2009. Subjective Experience Methods for Early Conceptual Design of Auditory Display. International Conference on Auditory Display. Copenhagen, Denmark.
6. Brückner, H. P., Lesse, S., Theimer, W. & Blume, H. 2016. Design space exploration of hardware platforms for interactive low latency movement sonification. Journal of Multimodal User Interfaces, 10, 1 - 11.
7. Burger, B., Thompson, M. R., Luck, G., Saarikallio, S. & Toiviainen, P. 2013. Influences of rhythm- and timbre-related musical features on characteristics of music-induced movement. Frontiers in Psychology, 4.
8. Chiari, L., Dozza, M., Cappello, A., Horak, F. B., Macellari, V. & Giansanti, D. 2005. Audio-Biofeedback for Balance Improvement: An Accelerometry-Based System. IEEE Transactions on Biomedical Engineering, 52, 2108 - 2111.
9. Cook, P. Modeling Bill's Gait: Analysis and Parametric Synthesis of Walking Sounds. 22nd International Conference on Virtual, Synthetic and Entertainment Audio 2002. 73-78.
10. Dubus, G. & Bresin, R. 2013. A Systematic Review of Mapping Strategies for the Sonification of Physical Quantities. PLoS ONE 8.
11. Effenburg, A. O. 2005. Movement sonification: Effects on perception and action. IEEE Multimedia, 53 - 59.
12. Feldenkrais, M. 1974. Awareness through Movement, New York, HarperCollins
13. Fontana, F. & Bresin, R. Physics-Based Sound Synthesis and Control: Crushing, Walking and Running by Crumpling Sounds. XIV Colloquium on Musical Informatics 2002 Firenze, Italy.
14. Geyer, H., Seyfarth, A. & Blickhan, H. 2006. Compliant leg behaviour explains basic dynamics of walking and running. Proceedings of the Royal Society, 273, 2861 - 2867.
15. Godbout, A. & Boyd, J. E. 2010. Corrective Sonic Feedback for Speed Skating: A Case Study. The 16th International Conference on Auditory Display (ICAD 2010). Washington D.C, USA.
16. Graves Petersen, M., Iversen, O. S., Krogh, P. G. & Ludvigsen, M. 2004. Aesthetic interaction: A pragmatist's aesthetics of interactive systems. DIS 2004. New York, USA: ACM.
17. Hanna, T. 1988. Somatics; reawakening the mind's control of movement, flexibility and health, Cambridge MA, De Capo Press.
18. Henkelmann, C. 2007. Improving the Aesthetic Quality of Realtime Motion Data Sonification Computer Graphics Technical Reports. Bonn, Germany: University of Bonn.
19. Höner, O., Hunt, A., Pauletto, S., Röber, N., Hermann, T. & Effenburg, A. O. 2011. Aiding Movement with Sonification in "Exercise, Play and Sport", Berlin, Germany: Logos Publishing House.
20. Ingold, T. 2004. Culture on the Ground: the world perceived through the feet. Journal of Material Culture, 9, 315 - 340.
21. Klooster, S. & Overbeeke, C. J. Designing Products as an integral part of the choreography of interaction: The products form as an integral part of movement. DeSForM 2005, First International Workshop on Design and Semantics of Form and Movement, 2005. 23-35.
22. Koskinen, I., Zimmerman, J., Binder, T., Redström, J. & Wensveen, S. 2011. Design ResearchThrough Practice: from the Lab, Field, and Showroom. Waltham, MA, Morgan Kaufmann Elsevier Inc.
23. Larssen, A. T., Loke, L., Robertson, T. & Edwards, J. Understanding Movement as Input for Interaction: A Study of Two Eyetoy Games. OZCHI, 2004 Woolongong NSW, Australia. ACM Press.
24. Lazar, J., Feng, J. H. & Hochheister, H. 2010. Research Methods in Human Computer Interaction. Chichester, West Sussex, John Wiley and Sons Ltd.
25. Loke, L., Khut, G. P., Slattery, M., Truman, C., Muller, L. & Duckworth, J. 2013. Re-sensitising the body: interactive art and the Feldenkrais method. International Journal of Arts and Technologies, 6, 339 - 356.
26. Loke, L., Larssen, A. T., Robertson, T. & Edwards, J. 2007. Understanding Movement for Interaction design: Frameworks and Approaches. Personal and Ubiquitous Computing, 11, 691- 701.
27. Maculewicz, J., Jylhä, Seraphin, S. & Erkut, C. 2015. The Effects of Auditory Feedback on Rhythmic Walking Interaction. IEEE Multimedia, 22.
28. Nordahl, R., Turchet, L. & Serafin, S. 2011. Sound Synthesis and Evaluation of Interactive Footsteps and Environmental Sounds Rendering for Virtual Reality Applications. IEEE Transactions On Visualization And Computer Graphics, 17, 1234 - 1244.

29. Roads, C. 1988. Introduction to Granular Synthesis. Computer Music Journal, 12, 11 - 13.
30. Roddy, S. & Furlong, D. 2014. Embodied Aesthetics in Auditory Display. Organised Sound 19, 70 - 77.
31. Schacher, J. C. & Stoeklin, A. 2011. Traces - Body, Motion and Sound. International Conference on New Interfaces for Musical Expression. Oslo, Norway.
32. Schaffert, N., Mattes, K. & Effenburg, A. O. 2009. A Sound Design for the Purposes of Movement Optimisation in Elite Sport (Using the Example of Rowing). ICAD Copenhagen, Denmark.
33. Schaffert, N., Michael, H. & Mattes, K. 2013. Rhythm based regulation/modification of movements in high performance rowing and neurologic rehabilitation. ISon. Erlangen, Germany.
34. Sheets-Johnstone, M. 1999. The Primacy of Movement. Philedelphia, PA, John Benjamins.
35. Shusterman, R. 1992. Pragmatic Aesthetics: Living Beauty Rethinking Art. Blackwell.
36. Shusterman, R. 2007. Somaesthetics and the Revival of Aesthetics. Filozofski vestnik, 28, 135 - 149.
37. Slavin, S. 2003. Walking as Spiritual Practice: The Pilgramage to Santiago de Compostela. Body and Society, 9, 1 - 18.
38. Stienstra, M., Overbeeke, C. & Wensveen, S. Embodying Complexity Through Movement Sonification: Case Study on Empowering the Speed-skater. Chitaly-2011, 2011 Alghero, Italy. ACM.
39. Varni, G., Dubus, G., Oksanen, S., Volpe, G., Fabiani, M., Bresin, R., Kleimola, J., Välimäki, V. & Camurri, A. 2012. Interactive sonification of synchronisation of motoric behaviour in social active listening to music with mobile devices. Journal of Multimodal User Interfaces, 5, 157 - 173.
40. Vergunst, J. L. 2010. Rhythms of Walking: History and Presence in a City Street. Space and Culture, 13, 376 - 388.
41. Visell, Y., Fontana, F., Giordano, B. L., Nordahl, R., Serafin, S. & Bresin, R. 2009. Sound Design and Perception in walking interactions. Internation Journal of Human-Computer Studies, 67, 947 - 959.
42. Vogt, K., Pirró, D., Kobenz, I., Höldrich, R., Eckel, G. & 2009. Physiosonic - Movement Sonification as Auditory Feedback. International Conference on Auditory Display. Copenhagen, Denmark.

Networked Pixels: Strategies for Building Visual and Auditory Images with Distributed Independent Devices

Sam Ferguson
Creativity & Cognition Studios
Faculty of Engineering & IT
University of Technology
Sydney
samuel.ferguson@uts.edu.au

Anthony Rowe
Squidsoup.org
ant@squidsoup.org

Oliver Bown
Interactive Media Laboratory
UNSW Art and Design
o.bown@unsw.edu.au

Liam Birtles
Bournemouth University
lbirtles@bournemouth.ac.uk

Chris Bennewith
School of Art, Design &
Architecture
Plymouth University, UK
chris.bennewith@plymouth.ac.uk

ABSTRACT
This paper describes the development of the hardware and software for *Bloom*, a light installation installed at Kew Gardens, London in December of 2016. The system is made up of a set of nearly 1000 distributed pixel devices each with LEDs, GPS sensor, and sound hardware, networked together with WiFi to form a display system. Media design for this system required consideration of the distributed nature of the devices. We outline the software and hardware designed for this system, and describe two approaches to the software and media design, one whereby we employ the distributed devices themselves for computation purposes (the approach we ultimately selected), and another whereby the devices are controlled from a central server that is performing most of the computation necessary. We then review these approaches and outline possibilities for future research.

ACM Classification Keywords
H.5.5 Sound and Music Computing: Systems; I.3.3 Picture/Image Generation: Display Algorithms

Author Keywords
Distributed, Pixel, Display System, Internet of Things, Audio

INTRODUCTION
Many examples exist where the notion of 'distributed computing' has been explored as an artistic medium. However, with the rise of Internet-of-Things type devices, new configurations of media now exist where this notion takes a central role. In most cases installation media have included sensors which allow interaction of various types, and in many cases the sensors and display systems have been built into site-specific systems. With the rise in capabilities of internet of things (IoT) type electronic devices, and their commensurate decline in cost, more options are now available for the development of systems that distribute their computing power and display technology, rather than centralising them at a central computing unit. Similarly, sensor technology is now quite capable of being dealt with as a set or flock of data rather than as single inputs processed at a central hub. The affordances of IoT technology present media artists with the potential to make scaleable site-specific artworks with custom hardware, all in rapid time and at low cost. However, there are many risks involved in this process, as well as creative organisational challenges, and at the same time a number of strong design principles that we can draw on. At this stage there is little discussion of the creative and technical practice of working with IoT-based media artworks.

CC '17, June 27-30, 2017, Singapore, Singapore

ISBN 978-1-4503-4403-6/17/06...$15.00
DOI: **http://dx.doi.org/10.1145/3059454.3059480**

Figure 1. ***Bloom*** **installation installed at Kew Gardens, London. Image Copyright Anthony Rowe 2016.**

In this paper we will focus on our experience of developing the hardware and software systems for *BLOOM*, an installation developed for Christmas at Kew, a light show held in Kew Gardens, London in 2016. The hardware and software developed for this system were bespoke, and the work represents a significant shift in the architectural underpinnings for this type of artefact.

Background

Systems of media display that involve screens made up of pixels are the central display component of the computing systems that have dominated the last century's advances in technology. As computing systems become ever smaller, and costs are driven down, the possibilities for new types of display system have expanded, and research interest is beginning to focus on the characteristics and design methods for displays made up of distributed pixels.

'Media multiplicities' are an emerging category of artistic and designerly practice [4]. Media multiplicities are made up of groups of independent elements which function together to act as an artefact of their own but which can usually also act as a substrate for other content to be displayed. They may be described generally by 3 main axes:

heterogeneity vs. homogeneity: whether the multiplicity is made up of heterogenous or homogenous elements, content or positioning.

object vs. substrate: whether the multiplicity is primarily understood or experienced as a group of objects, or as a substrate for other content to be displayed

composed vs. self-organized: whether the multiplicity is centrally controlled or composed, or self-organised based on rules.

This method of description helps us to understand not only how to design multiplicities, but also how to extend the design to achieve different goals.

Ishii has discussed the relationship between displays, interfaces and information in the process of defining tangible interaction [15, 14]. By moving interaction from a command-line, to a graphical, to now a tangible user interface, users can exploit the similarity between skills they use to interact with their physical environment, and skills they can use to interact with computing systems with these new interfaces. In such a context, computer systems are inevitably tending towards becoming distributed, rather than centralised, and systems that can augment and control these distributed systems will be a critical component of the technological future.

Research In Distributed Displays

Research interest in distributed arrays of pixel-like devices has resulted in several systems being developed. Seitinger et al. [26] developed a system of 50 'urban pixels' which they used to explore concepts relating to the potential of distributed displays. They identify flexible placement, autonomous power, unbounded placement, variable resolution and responsivity as important characteristics of these new distributed systems. Their system employed interaction in two ways - the pixels could receive 1-character SMSs from the audience to allow them to be controlled pixel-by-pixel, or they could be 'painted' by using a flashlight to activate pixels in brush-like fashion. Barker et al. [1] and Hauesler et al. [11] focused on the development process and capabilities of firstly 'Janus' (a face-like facade of addressable pixels), and then 'polymedia pixels', a system of networked pixels. *Squidsoup* has a long history of developing volumetric light installations made up of thousands of individually addressable LEDs, positioned in a 3-dimensional grid [21, 20]. Sato [22, 23] has described how a set of small independent and distributed pixels would be affixed to a non-regular surface, and then by using a camera the location of each pixel would be known with high accuracy, allowing the precise control necessary to present graphical images. Fischer et al. [10] designed a system of kickable and flickable light shards that used irregular shape to modify their physical behaviour. *Junkyard Jumbotron* [2] showed it was possible to flexibly employ groups of heterogenous mobile devices to display images that spanned multiple screens with a simple architecture, as did Schmitz et al. [24]. Schwarz et al. [25] followed this work by simplifying the requirements for using a 'Phone as a Pixel' even further.

'PushPins' [7] were small computing devices that could be powered by pushing their contacts into a foam that included layers of conductive and non-conductive material. Each computer could be repositioned easily across the power substrate, and when they were powered they built their own network of devices local to each other. They were programmed through an Infrared 'flashlight' that beamed software through an infrared interface to each of the 100 nodes. Paradiso [18] went on to discuss *Tribble*, a system of tiled computers that formed a sensate sphere, but which had no central controller, as well as *Z-Tiles*, a system of tiles for a sensate floor. Bown et al. [5] described Distributed Interactive Audio Devices – distributed systems for interaction with audio synthesis capabilities, designed to be physically handled and passed between participants that are part of an audience, and which can be used to develop simple musical games [3].

The effects of the motility of distributed pixels is also an area of emerging research. Kuznetsov et al. [16] developed Wallbots, which were robots that could traverse metal walls with their magnetic wheels, but which also had display elements and light sensors for interaction. Similarly, *Spaxels*, a set of first 16, then 100 quadrotor drones outfitted with RGB LEDs, demonstrated the capability to coordinate their movements so as to produce images and animation [12]. Digurmati et al. [9] have extended this work to allow for image animation with their *Pixelbots* system of small mobile RGB pixels. On a much smaller scale, Dantu et al. [8] developed methods for programming small sets of tiny programmable flying devices outfitted with sensor capabilities. Merrill's *Siftables* are computers within tiles that implemented interaction systems employing physical rearrangement interaction procedures (like scrabble or dominos) as input for the devices [17]. While not independently mobile, they used careful sensing of their physical position as a prime source of interaction input in their applications. Vallgarda et al. developed the notion of 'programming materiality' [27], by citing techniques such as *tangible programming* and *programming by example*, resulting in a set of speculative tools that can be used to program physical interfaces. Wiberg, [28] and Robles and Wiberg [19] have investigated notions of materiality in interaction design. These works show that as groups of devices become more advanced, and are used for more complex purposes, advanced continuous material and positional sensing may need to be integrated with the display algorithm to allow elements to move independently of the image or content being presented.

Aims and Overview

The aforementioned examples have generally been small-scale demonstration deployments, with a lot of the systems being between 2 and 100 units. At this scale many critical challenges of code deployment and content generation are not as significant, as it is generally quite straightforward to transfer compiled code with a simple script. Furthermore, even small scale network infrastructure are mostly all well-suited to managing even this number of connected devices. Few of these systems focused on developing other modalities either – displaying sound in addition to visual media was generally ignored, or at least have not been carefully explored. Many of the devices discussed were developed with the engineering challenges and system capabilities being the focus of the reporting, with little research discussing how a practical workflow for creative design could be employed by artists and media designers working with these display systems.

In the work we describe below there are several important advances from the aforementioned systems.

- this is the largest deployment of distributed devices we know of, our system included 923 devices in its initial deployment, with a remaining 77 to be added when they are reworked.
- each of our devices included the capability to produce sound, and designing this audio content became a critical part of the design workflow.
- this system used a GPS sensor on each device for individually locating each pixel.
- Finally, this system required the ability to be installed for a period of 6 weeks in an inhospitable environment, and to function both reliably and in an aesthetically pleasing manner to fulfil a design brief.

The following sections will describe first a description of the hardware and software used in the system, including discussion of the design decisions made both during the hardware design, and their effect on its capabilities. Secondly, we will move to a description of two alternative approaches to developing digital media for this system, alongside the workflow for media design and deployment. Finally, we focus on methods and directions to improve the system capabilities for the future.

SYSTEM DESCRIPTION AND DEVELOPMENT

The devices used in this installation were built from a number of individual elements brought together as an integrated system. The constraints on the design included a minimum number of elements (1000) required by the client, alongside a budgetary constraint, combined with the desire to extend the capabilities and reuse the system in the future.

Figure 2. The devices and their cabling were required to be waterproof and durable, given the installation location and conditions and the 6-week installation period. The stands were made from flexible plastic, and carried the DC 12V power supply that powers each device. Image Copyright Anthony Rowe 2016

Installation Design Context

The design context for the installation was quite specific. The open space of the Kew Gardens site allowed us to employ GPS tracking without the occlusions of an indoor or urban setting, and also worked to allow the large scale of the installation to be fully appreciated.

The durability and reliability of the installation was critical as the system was to be deployed for a six-week installation. The system was to function without supervision and without significant monitoring, except for a daily initiation phase. No non-automatic debugging could take place after the launch of system. Weather conditions were harsh at that time of year in the UK (see Figure 2 for a general impression) – moisture and extreme cold were expected to be issues, and so watertightness was a critical issue for the devices. The location was well-suited to the use of a wireless network, as there was no network infrastructure in place to interfere, and there were few occlusions given the level surface. However, the practicality of such a large number of devices being attached to a single wi-Fi network was a significant complication. Furthermore, the site was bisected by path across which no cables could be run.

Device

The device was designed to be lightweight, low-power, network enabled and to create sound and light. It included several important capabilities:

Onboard Processing: The device used an ESP3266 type module (a Digistump Acorn) which included an over-the-air programmer and various other advanced capabilities.
Onboard WiFi Networking: One of the capabilities provided by the Acorn module was onboard wireless networking.
GPS: a compact GPS aerial and chipset was soldered onto the circuitboard and connected to the Acorn module directly.

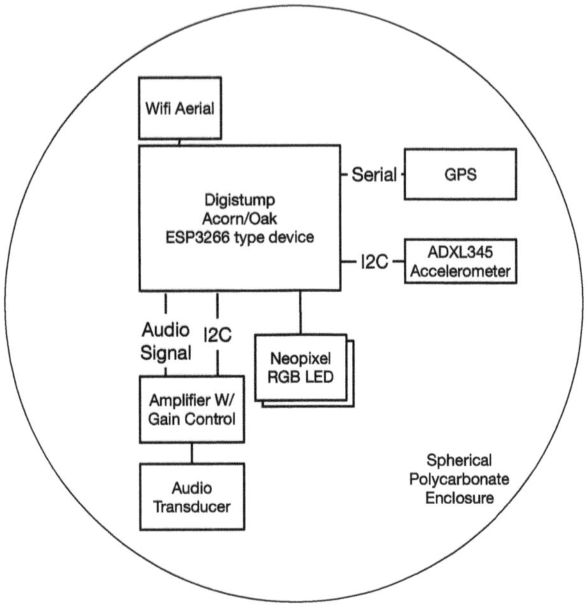

Figure 3. Diagram of components of the distributed pixels.

Accelerometer: An ADXL345 accelerometer was included on the device, and connected to the Acorn module by an I^2C interface.

Audio amplifier: a simple audio signal amplifier was included whose gain was digitally controllable with high temporal resolution, through an I^2C interface.

Transducer: a contact-type transducer was glued to the device, so that sound produced resonated through the device housing.

LEDs: Two NeoPixel type RGB LEDs were positioned on either side of the device.

The device was designed to be designed to be affixed to the internal base of a polycarbonate globe, and included contacts for the incoming power cable to be soldered to the centre of the device. It was circular in shape and LEDs were placed on either side of the circle in order to obtain uniform light distribution. Figures 3 and 4 demonstrate the components of each pixel.

Sound

As far as we are aware, while many systems of distributed devices have existed previously, most have focused on visual display, and few have included sound producing hardware on the number of elements we are dealing with. Our device is one of the first to include audio hardware as part of the design. The audio electronics on the device were rudimentary as the ESP3266 chip is not well-suited to audio signal playback (it splits processor time between multiple tasks) and the main sounds we could produce were simple tones using the `tone()` command. However, we were able to include an amplifier with I^2C gain control that could be controlled with high levels of temporal accuracy. Having fine-grained control over the audio amplitude allowed simple amplitude envelopes as well

Figure 4. Components of distributed pixel system with spherical enclosure covers removed. The GPS unit is clearly visible, as are the 2 NeoPixel LEDs and the audio transducer. The audio transducer produced sound by transmitting vibrations to the circuit-board and through to the spherical cover, which was a much more space efficient approach than trying to include a loudspeaker and associated mounting would have been. Because of the size of the elements, the circuitboards were able to be mounted on the lower-most portion of the sphere, meaning that the rest of the sphere was not in shadow. Image Copyright Sam Ferguson 2016.

as longer-term ramping effects, meaning tones that are sometimes annoying when they are constant, could be modulated both over the term of a note (200-1000 ms) and over the term of a *crescendo* or phrase (10-60 s).

To program the sound we took a tightly synchronised approach, whereby both the brightness of the LEDs and the audio gain were usually linked in some manner. Usually, each visual pulse was accompanied by an auditory pulse of the same length and temporal shape, but with an independently chosen pitch. This meant that visual textures were accompanied by matching auditory textures, which simplified the design and programming of the devices. This also streamlined the experience for participants as the visual and auditory stimuli could be fused, and it was easier to work out which pixel was making a particular sound. For the purposes of experiencing the installation as an embodied space, this tight coupling was a way to rapidly perceive the temporal and spatial distribution of the media. Nevertheless, there was no hardware requirement that this approach be taken – future designs may employ differing approaches to the relationship between the auditory and visual medium.

Server and Development Cycle

In most development contexts, development iteration takes place when the code is compiled (or interpreted) and then executed, which shows whether the program performs as expected, resulting in modification and an iteration loop. For distributed devices, however, where the number of devices exceeds a practical deployment limit, taking the simple approach of compiling, using a serial port to upload the firmware over a cable, and then and executing the code on each device was obviously prohibitively slow. Furthermore, in many situations we found testing with a single or a couple of devices was not capable of uncovering critical bugs that were intermittent, but were immediately found when the program was deployed with the planned number of devices. Finally, to demonstrate and adjust the planned aesthetic effects we needed to see all the devices in use. We therefore could not rely on the typical iterative design approach to programming, and a different approach was necessary.

Digistump provided a lightweight *node.js* server which ran on the development machine, for distributing the firmware images to each of the devices. The server was queried by each device when they booted, and periodically when they were running. If the MD5 hash of the current firmware image on the server was different to that on the device then an upload process was triggered, and the device replaced its current firmware with that found on the server. The server was capable of serving the firmware image to all 1000 devices rapidly and almost simultaneously, meaning we could upload a new firmware image approximately 90 to 120 seconds.

This server was partnered to an Arduino extension designed for working with this device. It had the capability of being able to upload an image across a USB-to-serial adapter, or alternatively, compiling a firmware image directly to a folder monitored by the aforementioned *node.js* server, which would trigger the update to occur. Firmware image updates using the server could be both seamless and rapid, and differed little from the process of uploading an image via USB, except that the number of devices that could simultaneously receive updates was almost unlimited. Despite its rudimentary nature, working with Arduino as one of the development environments was familiar for us as we possess experience as creative coders, and this was a strong advantage over more technical integrated development environments. Depending on the programming platform, other approaches exist that achieve similar aims, for instance [6] which allows the serialisation of java classes and their immediate execution by a running device without being rebooted.

While other deployment systems exist that can deal with large sets of devices, especially at the enterprise scale, they usually involve significant complexity, configuration and cost and are rarely designed for creative purposes. With this somewhat more lightweight approach we found a solution that suited the scale of our creative development process but allowed us to treat the large scale of our device set similarly to a small scale system.

In terms of network configuration, to provide enough connectivity we used a set of 4 separate Xirrus Networks WiFi Access Points connected to a central switch by PoE ethernet cables. These access points were designed to be capable of maintaining hundreds of simultaneous connections. Two of the Access points were placed on one side of the bisecting path, and the other two were placed on the other side, connected to each other by a microwave link.

Graphical User Interface

To support the development process and to allow rapid deployment we developed a partner graphical user interface for issuing commands to the system. It used a graphical layout to allow a user to locate each pixel based on its position as reported by each device's GPS data. It also simplified the communication with the devices as each of the main set of OSC commands used to control the multiplicity was rendered as a button on the interface.

For some situations we were able to use a set of sliders and selections provided by the interface to program new modes directly. This meant that we could experiment, during deployment, with particular parameter settings in the actual installation location. However, as the development process proceeded, and the required behaviours became more complex, using our simple GUI interface was not flexible enough to describe many of the more complex options. We therefore spent much of the development time coding these parameter selections manually into the GUI framework and triggered each behaviour using particular buttons.

Finally, as the individual behaviours were completed, we then programmed them into a sequencer which could be controlled from the interface. The system was deployed using this sequencer to synchronise the sending of each of the mode instructions.

APPROACHES TO DISTRIBUTED VISUAL IMAGERY

During the development process we noted two alternative approaches to developing digital media for distributed pixels. There was one approach whereby the devices were programmed to behave in certain ways in response to a global command, based on their location and on other data that was local to the device. We termed this the Computation-on-Device approach. The alternative approach was to obtain data pertaining to each device at a central control point, fuse it together, and then broadcast much simpler commands to each device in this collective display, the overall image could be controlled. We have termed this the Computation-on-Server approach. See Figure 5 for a diagrammatic representation. Of these two approaches, the one we implemented within the installation was the Computation-on-Device approach primarily for both design and implementation reasons, although we had a separate code-base containing an implementation of the Computation-on-Server approach which we prepared to cope with contingencies (although it has not yet been tested with the system).

Computation-on-Device

The Computation-on-Device approach is made up of several constraints.

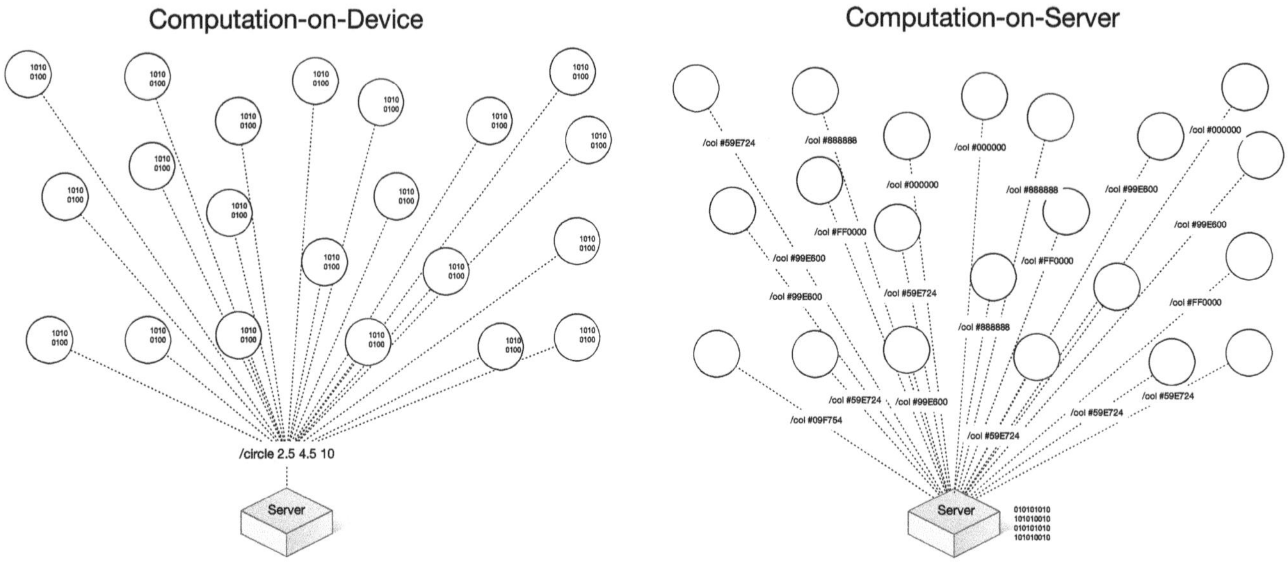

Figure 5. Two approaches to controlling distributed pixel display systems: Computation-on-Device and Computation-on-Server.

- identical commands are broadcast to every device;
- commands are often sent seconds, or multiple seconds apart;
- each device can use both parameters passed in the command, and data that is internal to the device ;
- the dimension of time is usually controlled independently by each device, at least on the micro scale;
- any animation effects are controlled by the device.

The decentralised approach allows for a great deal of redundancy with regard to network communication. Given the large number of devices we were attempting to control from the network, we were unsure of the reliability of sending frame-based network messages (as required by the Computation-on-Server approach). Notably, we will likely remain unsure about this given the differing network and environmental conditions in which the system will be deployed in the future, but it's also possible that new network software or different network configurations may help to make this less of a priority going forward.

In the Computation-on-Device configuration, the devices store the GPS location locally, and we design algorithms that command the devices to exploit this data within the context of a global command. An example is the simple expanding circle. This can be created by:

- sending a GPS location to each of the devices;
- using that location, alongside the locally stored location, to calculate a distance;
- using the distance to calculate a delay time, that is used to control the timing of the LED being activated.

While extremely simple, this algorithm can be quite effective when used on a large scale. Variations can achieve various different effects of course, in rather a similar way to typical vector graphical algorithms.

Figure 6. Installation as viewed from above. The work was installed in a space approximately 80m by 25m, with a path bisecting two halves of the installation. For context, the structure in the background is the Kew Gardens Palm House. Image Copyright Anthony Rowe 2016.

Computation-on-Server

The Computation-on-Server approach relaxes many of these constraints and is generally reliant on both a fast network, and a centralised controller computer.

- individual media commands are sent to each device based on their location;
- media commands are sent once every frame - at a typical frame-rate of between 16 and 60 frames per second;
- usually any sensor data obtained by each device is sent to the controller machine, rather than being stored locally;
- time is controlled by the central controller;
- and therefore animation is also controlled by the central controller.

This approach theoretically gives a lot more flexibility regarding media content – there is no need to determine shapes through algorithms that respond to location data. Instead the locations of each pixel are determined in advance and the media content is forwarded to each of them individually. Many images and patterns are not straightforwardly described by geometry or algorithms, and therefore using a Computation-on-Device approach can limit the types of content that can be forwarded globally. Furthermore, each image or pattern needs to be constructed algorithmically – a significant limitation for a creative process.

The main drawback of this approach is that an individual message must be sent to each pixel who's colour needs to change, once for every frame. For 1000 pixels at 24 FPS, this can require 24000 individual messages per second, requiring high throughput on a network that is likely to be wireless and is therefore often working to capacity to maintain the many connections when numbers increase past a typical lower limit for a router. Furthermore, IoT devices that maintain wireless connections such as the Digistump Acorn often have to split their processing power between subsystem processes that maintain the connection and foreground processes that perform sensing and display. Increasing the network burden can also increase the likelihood of unexpected behaviour when the foreground process is performing particular functions. While many solutions exist to improve reliability and stability of large networks of this nature, as numbers of elements scale past 1000 pixels to even larger numbers this may continue to be an issue. Other systems have, for instance, used very low-bandwidth, high-availability network solutions (see for instance Sato [22] who used a wireless solution with a throughput of 4800 baud).

Comparing Approaches

These two approaches, Computation-on-Server and Computation-on-Device, are not mutually exclusive, and as design methods become more advanced it is inevitable elements of both approaches will be used. More advanced software and hardware will also play a role in merging these two approaches, and fusing the data the devices produce in smarter ways. In Table 1 we detail each of the different benefits and drawbacks of the two approaches.

In the case of the installation *Bloom* we opted primarily for the Computation-on-Device approach, but this was only made possible by the rapid deployment architecture that Digistump developed. Without this deployment architecture we would have necessarily needed to adopt the Computation-on-Server approach, as otherwise deployment time would have been prohibitive to changes. We considered many ways of implementing aspects that used Computation-on-Server, which will ultimately require more research, and possible greater sensor accuracy or fusion methods.

A drawback of both approaches, but primarily the Computation-On-Server approach, is that by the very nature of distributed systems the images produced lack resolution. A distributed system (of either type) is unlikely to include elements that are either physically adjacent to each other, or positioned in a grid. Therefore, the typical approaches to improvement of raster images, such as anti-aliasing, or even more complex methods designed for pixel-art such as Inglis' recent work [13], will be confounded. More fundamentally though, if the gaps between pixels were to be filled by more pixels, it would raise the question of why each pixel is not physically wired to each of the other pixels, meaning they would not be distributed any longer. At its core, it seems that a distributed system of pixels engenders some level of pixel sparsity, meaning that graphical images of a bitmap type are not likely to be approached in the same way when displayed on a distributed system, without some fundamental new configuration of the way distributed pixels form an image surface.

Finally, location data is critical for either approach to display shapes and images accurately. Without highly accurate location data, pixels expected to be in one location can be in another, resulting in transmitted content being heavily distorted. While this is more apparent with images of a bitmap type, which may be more likely with the Computation-on-Server approach, adopting Computation-on-Device does not solve this problem. Shapes generated by algorithms computed on each device but which rely on localisation data can still be distorted, although they are less likely to emphasise the figurative nature of the media. Our choice of GPS for this technology was successful in practical terms, in that the principles were clearly capable of being tested, but more accuracy is definitely required to enhance capabilities in this respect. More modern localisation alternatives may theoretically yield more accurate information, although we were currently unable to identify cheap, well-implemented, independent, robust alternative solutions, that didn't require extra hardware beacons, which would scale to 1000 devices, and which could work within a large open parkland space, its likely that such solutions will become accessible in the near-term. Given that the devices are installed for long periods, one solution under investigation is long-term averaging of the GPS data, followed by the storage of that data either at an online source or on-board.

DISCUSSION

This article has discussed the development of a distributed display system. This is one of the largest distributed pixel installations we know of, and is one of the first to approach screen-like resolutions. It is also one of the first to include sound as an element of the distributed pixel system and to design distributed media that includes sound content as an element. It is one of the first to use individual GPS chips as a location sensor for each pixel and to employ that data as part of a visualisation algorithm. The new attributes and capabilities for this distributed system of pixels has opened up a lot of questions and possibilities that have necessitated further research.

In the preceding sections, several approaches to development have been discussed, and particular strengths of this system have been highlighted. With the Computation-on-Device approach global commands can be sent, and then patterns and simple geometry can be displayed based on the information local to the device interpreting the command. With a Computation-on-Server approach, individual messages are sent to each device separately. The discussed approaches describe new possible capabilities, but also hint at future chal-

Table 1. Comparison between digital media design based on Computation-on-Device and Computation-on-Server. Bold is used to highlight clear advantages of each of the approaches to the architecture of the design.

Area	CoD	CoS	Design considerations
Bandwidth	**Low bandwidth. Potential to broadcast instead of unicast the network data.**	High bandwidth. Must unicast messages.	Know your system's network capabilities given your expectations for framerate and number of devices (for the current project, and bearing in mind you may want to scale up the same piece in the future - also bearing in mind that improved hardware may cater for such scaling up). CoS may simply not be an option.
Resilience to network failure	**The system can keep behaving to some extent without a network. If there is partial network loss then the system needs to know this in order to respond coherently. It depends on the work whether this network-free mode is acceptable, and for how long.**	If some or all of the network goes down the system is paralysed / broken. In theory you could still have a fallback behaviour using CoD, but if you're going to have to create this (and can) then you might as well just take the CoD route.	CoD may be more 'aesthetically' robust to network failure. Questions include how likely network failure is and whether a networkless fallback option is actually acceptable and for how long (and if so, can it be trivial, such as random flashing lights, or does it need to be non-trivial). If the network is unreliable and a non-trivial fallback is acceptable (but a trivial one is not), then a CoD approach may be preferred.
Network performance worst-case scenarios	**Very likely to be no network limitations except under certain conditions where spikes in data might occur or high-bandwidth data is being sent.**	The network will have a fixed capacity for framerate / number of devices, which can be known from prior tests. If you're within that capacity the the only limit is the computational limit of the server.	If your system does have the capacity to robustly do CoS at the framerate you desire, then you can be sure it will not have spikes, as the device-side behaviour and amount of data being sent will be very predictable and robust. Still, your bandwith needs will be much less with CoD.
Network message failure	Critical that message is received, but being low bandwidth it is easy to send multiple copies of each message.	Occasional messages can be skipped without too much interruption, and if a pixel doesn't change it doesn't need to be sent.	There may be cases where there are aesthetic factors involved in your approach to failure, and either option may be advantageous. You may like it that the odd rogue device is off-script, and you may consider the network uncertainty to be a conceptual part of the piece. Assuming otherwise, then CoD may be more reliable, if there are doubts about network performance for CoS. Rough video compression techniques can be used to save sending data in CoS mode.
Development and debug experience	Device code in constant development. Having to co-develop and keep in synch two bodies of code. Last minute on-device debugging may be needed.	**Set and forget. Device code rarely needs updating and can be made very robust.**	Coding for devices such as Arduino can be much harder due to the more low-level nature of C/C++ and the fact you are having to run the code on a different device from the device you are writing the code on. Debugging support tools for writing and running code on a full OS-based machine are much more sophisticated. Also this means that the device code is ever changing as the project develops. This can put pressure on at critical deployment times where there may be a need to fix bugs and re-deploy code to multiple devices, although we found this deployment process to be relatively robust and painless.
Simulating device behaviour without access to devices	To simulate the device behaviour on server means to re-implement the device code on the server, although it is also possible to have an emulator that runs the device code in simulation.	**Device behaviour is easily simulated and can be simulated in development time. Since behaviour is on server it is trivial to 'display' it.**	Consider how important simulation will be to achieving your goal. Can you test on the real hardware? Is the final outcome likely to be unexpected or hard to imagine? Are you taking a creative iterate and test approach where you want to make creative tweaks as you go, or do you have a clear design in mind? Alternatively, perhaps the site-specific complexity of the work is such that even a simulation is unlikely to give you a good idea of the results (as in the case with multi-speaker works).
Establishing network communication 'vocabulary'	Depending on the type of data being communicated (assuming something does need to be communicated), may need large and constantly changing vocabulary of OSC (or other network) commands. Potentially more brittle.	**Very simple and relatively fixed vocabulary of OSC commands.**	Provokes consideration of design patterns: (1) extreme A - little or no network communication needed, devices doing their own thing, possibly using global clock / script (then use CoD), (2) extreme B - devices are rendering complex image that cannot easily be described in simple, low-computation terms (then must use CoS), (3) in the middle - devices have an enumerated series of modes (= code subroutines) that are chosen from top down, each mode may have various parameters, and each device may incorporate local data into its behaviour (accelerometers, GPS, ID), (4) building on 3, the device behaviours are not just subject to parametric control (numbers, enums, patterns, etc.) but more complex data that might be understood as "programming". This ignores issues of user interaction and inter-node communication. See below.
Suitability to parallel computing	Better for parallel style computations such as cellular automata, but worse for systems with top-down organisation.	Equally good for different sorts of computation, but computational power does not scale with number of devices.	Is your code easily parallelisable? e.g., a Game of Life CA model is an obvious example where the code is parallelisable - each device simply has to run its update rule based on the state of the neighbouring devices. The catch is that the devices need to maintain a list of their neighbours and send those neighbours their states at each time step (or listen out for states broadcast from neighbours), so that the neighbours can update. In this case even though the system is naturally parallelisable, it actually involves more data communication to run it using CoD than it would using CoS. This could be considered something of a paradox. By contrast, if instead of CA update rules there was a complex deep neural network calculating each next state, then this might be too much for the server to handle, necessitating a distributed approach.
Implementing device interaction	Interaction between devices needs to be mediated by server, hence potential for doubling up code. e.g., all devices need to maintain a model of where all other devices are.	Interaction between devices needs to be mediated by server, so natural to compute on server.	Some situations are inelegant and should be avoided: (i) a cumbersome and hard-to-maintain list of network communicated instructions that both device and server must know about, (ii) situation where the state of the device needs to be known on the server, or in other devices, and cumbersome messaging or 'modelling' is needed to keep the states in synch in different places. In these cases CoS can resolve the problem.
Debugging ease and bottlenecks	More debugging load needs to go on (a) the devices and (b) the correct network messaging.	**More debugging is on the server model. This is better supported in most IDEs.**	This is a major advantage for CoS in terms of the extensibility, maintainability, portability and clarity of program design. The network boundary has been simplified to something that is extremely easy to visualise.
Attitude towards creative constraints	Can be a good 'creative constraint' forcing a more creative modular design / VERSUS / it is unnecessarily constraining.	Can be too open-ended. "Creative coder's dilemma" / VERSUS / it is nice and open-ended. Freedom to choose your own constraints.	If the algorithmic description of the modes is very easy and contained, then this tends towards CoD. It is often appealing to set out with this objective.
Creative coding philosophy prompted by architecture	Encourages a distributed communication philosophy (objects not substrates).	Encourages more of a media-based / image-rendering-based philosophy (substrates not objects).	If the concept is not already preconceived then the choice of CoD versus CoS may possibly directed more by a motivation to engage with either one of these approaches. Particularly, the creative nature of a CoD architecture may offer a refreshing relief from the single-computer context, even if at a more fundamental level, given the linkage / boundarylessness provided by network communication, CoD and CoS may be more or less equivalent.

lenges with distributed systems, some of which we discuss below.

The creativity support tools that exist for distributed display systems are currently quite limited, and their research is not an area given much emphasis, probably because many of the systems we describe are generally at an early stage of development, or are demonstration systems only. Much of the media development takes place during the installation of a system. Tools and techniques are ad-hoc and are generally subordinated to the engineering challenges faced getting the system to function. Rather than being approached with generalised tools in a way that allows domain specialists to focus on this element, content creation is generally approached by the same people tasked with engineering the system itself. Its possible that new tools for content creation would probably involve several elements:

Simulation: Being able to simulate the distributed system Will allow designers and developers to rapidly iterate their design before it is installed.

Visualization and Sonification: Part of the ability to simulate a design for a distributed system is to visualise it and simulate the auditory experience. Also, being able to experience the visual and auditory impression from the expected traversal of the space may allow necessary adjustments to be implemented before installation.

Manipulation: Controlling parameter choices, manipulating positioning or density, and changing the aesthetic choices described by the code in an intuitive fashion is an approach that is common across almost all fields of computer-aided design.

Sensor data accuracy in this prototype system was limited – especially localisation data from the GPS unit. This was a critical bottleneck, and limited the type of animated patterns that could be produced. Future systems may be able to exploit rapidly evolving localisation algorithms based on Wifi, light or audio, for much higher accuracy. Opportunities for sensor fusion, to develop a clearer picture of the way the many sensors describe a contiguous environment, are yet to be exploited.

The space between pixels in distributed display systems, identified above as a characteristic of distributed system, is difficult to avoid with current pixel configurations. If the distributed pixels are arranged in a contiguous grid without any gaps it seems likely that their motility and scatterability are no longer of value, and therefore a more typical fixed-pixel based display would be more appropriate, negating the purpose of distributed displays. Various approaches to new device hardware configurations may help to solve this issue. As devices become more advanced solutions to the problem of filling these physical gaps may be developed that are optical, electro-mechanical or even as-yet unknown. However, these technologies will likely require significant further development. For the development of media transmission capabilities that are flexible and adaptable though, such a significant drawback for distributed display systems cannot be ignored, and it is likely this challenge will soon need to be solved.

Sound was an important part of the installation and was tightly coupled to the visual content. Despite the rudimentary sound synthesis capabilities of the device itself, the design palette was quite extensive, given the way that the sound complimented the visual content. Designing sound for a distributed system required a different approach than is commonly taken for sound design in public spaces. The experience of the 1000 devices making sound as opposed to 1, was quite distinct from the experience of 1000 devices making light as opposed to 1. While the visual stimulus from each device tends to be localised quite specifically within space, the nature of the auditory sense meant that the sensation of auditory envelopment was a strong characteristic of the way that the sound was experienced. This meant that the temporal complexity and variety of the sound design of the work received greater importance. Generally speaking, this leant the design process towards a probabilistic approach, where an instruction sent to the group of devices could be expected to be executed in a small but subtly different set of ways on each device, which were then experienced as a cohesive spatial experience. This proved to be quite effective, but again was difficult to simulate accurately without the installed devices.

Fusing the Computation-on-Server and Computation-on-Device methodologies to obtain optimum control over the development process may require innovative thinking and new programming paradigms. One approach is to serialise program functions and distribute them to the devices over the network, rather than sending network messages with commands and numerical parameters, in much the same way that Bown et al. have done [6]. In effect this means a distributed pixel would simply run a network listener that listens for new functions and then seamlessly executes them, requiring minimal change of the underlying firmware on each device, and no rebooting. This would also mean that the the central controller could distribute very small functions or more complex functions, and do so on a global or individual basis. As an underlying architecture, this would free the designer/developer to add or subtract interaction, animation or media content as deemed necessary (as long as they can be described programmatically), and to even do so in a real-time fashion.

However, the Computation-on-Server and Computation-on-Device approaches are not purely questions of technical architecture. They represent differing approaches to media design which will be based as much on the nature of the distributed devices as they are on the media content to be transmitted. Distributed devices in a system of this nature need not necessarily be precisely analogous to the pixels contained in a rectangular display, and they may possess other types of communication, interaction and motility capabilities that allow them to imitate and represent media content using non-typical methods. For instance, the *Spaxels* system [12] has used light-painting (using long exposure photographs) to generate 3-dimensional imagery from a small number of individual pixels. Therefore, we expect that in the future we will see not just elements of both these approaches, but also new and innovative device designs coalesce to form new media experiences within this rapidly evolving field.

CONCLUSION

Networked systems of distributed pixels represent an emerging and important new field of creativity and media design practice in digital media design. This paper has presented an account of the development of a large system of distributed pixels, and has delineated some important new capabilities in this new system. It has outlined some challenges in the process of designing media for distributed pixel systems, and has described two alternative approaches to that design process, Computation-on-Server and Computation-on-Device, comparing each carefully. Finally, this article highlighted some important challenges that designers of systems of this nature will need to address.

ACKNOWLEDGEMENTS

We acknowledge the design assistance of Digistump LLC, who designed the electronics and coordinated the manufacture of the devices. Networking support was generously provided by Xirrus Networks. *Bloom* was a SquidSoup project sponsored by the Royal Botanical Gardens, Kew, and curated by Culture Creative.

REFERENCES

1. Tom Barker, M. Hank Haeusler, Frank Maguire, and Jason McDermott. 2009. Investigating political and demographic factors in crowd based interfaces. *Proceedings of the 21st Annual Conference of the Australian Computer-Human Interaction Special Interest Group on Design: Open 24/7 - OZCHI '09* (2009), 413. DOI:http://dx.doi.org/10.1145/1738826.1738912
2. Rick Borovoy and Brian Knep. 2011. Junkyard Jumbotron. (2011). http://c4fcm.github.io/Junkyard-Jumbotron/
3. Oliver Bown and Sam Ferguson. 2016. A Musical Game of Bowls Using the DIADs. In *Proceedings of the International Conference on New Interfaces for Musical Expression*. 371–372. http://www.nime.org/proceedings/2016/nime2016
4. Oliver Bown and Sam Ferguson. 2017. Media Technology + the Internet of Things = Media Multiplicities. *Leonardo Transactions* submitted (2017).
5. Oliver Bown, Lian Loke, Sam Ferguson, and Dagmar Reinhardt. 2015. Distributed Interactive Audio Devices: Creative strategies and audience responses to novel musical interaction scenarios. In *Proceedings of the 21st International Symposium on Electronic Art*. http://isea2015.org/proceeding/submissions/ISEA2015
6. Oliver Bown, Miriama Young, and Samuel Johnson. 2013. A Java-Based Remote Live Coding System for Controlling Multiple Raspberry Pi Units. In *Proceedings of the International Computer Music Conference*. Michigan Publishing, University of Michigan Library, Ann Arbor, MI.
7. William Butera. 2007. Text display and graphics control on a paintable computer. In *First International Conference on Self-Adaptive and Self-Organizing Systems, SASO 2007*. 45–54. DOI: http://dx.doi.org/10.1109/SASO.2007.60

8. Karthik Dantu, Bryan Kate, Jason Waterman, Peter Bailis, and Matt Welsh. 2011. Programming micro-aerial vehicle swarms with karma. In *Proceedings of the 9th ACM Conference on Embedded Networked Sensor Systems - SenSys '11*. ACM Press, New York, New York, USA, 121. DOI:http://dx.doi.org/10.1145/2070942.2070956

9. Tejaswi Digumarti, Javier Alonso-Mora, Roland Siegwart, and Paul Beardsley. 2016. Pixelbots 2014. *Leonardo* 49, 4 (2016), 366–367.

10. Patrick Tobias Fischer, Franziska Gerlach, Jenny Gonzalez Acuna, Daniel Pollack, Ingo Schäfer, Josephine Trautmann, and Eva Hornecker. 2014. Movable, Kick-/Flickable Light Fragments Eliciting Ad-hoc Interaction in Public Space. *Proceedings of The International Symposium on Pervasive Displays - PerDis '14* (2014), 50–55. DOI: http://dx.doi.org/10.1145/2611009.2611027

11. Hank Hauesler, Tom Barker, and Kirsty Beilharz. 2010. Interactive Polymedia Pixel and Protocol for Collaborative Creative Content Generation on Urban Digital Media Displays. In *Proceedings of the International Conference on New Media and Interactivity*. Marmara University, 1–7. https://opus.lib.uts.edu.au/handle/10453/16609

12. Horst Hörtner, Matthew Gardiner, Roland Haring, Christopher Lindinger, and Florian Berger. 2012. Spaxels, Pixels in Space. In *Proceedings of the International Conference on Signal Processing and Multimedia Applications and Wireless Information Networks and Systems*. 19–24. DOI: http://dx.doi.org/10.5220/0004126400190024

13. Tiffany C. Inglis and Craig S. Kaplan. 2012. Pixelating vector line art. *ACM SIGGRAPH 2012 Posters on - SIGGRAPH '12* (2012), 1. DOI: http://dx.doi.org/10.1145/2342896.2343021

14. Hiroshi Ishii. 2008. Tangible bits: beyond pixels. In *Proceedings of the 2nd international conference on Tangible and Embedded Interaction (TEI '08)*. xv–xxv. DOI:http://dx.doi.org/10.1145/1347390.1347392

15. H. Ishii and B. Ullmer. 1997. Tangible bits: towards seamless interfaces between people, bits, and atoms. In *Proceedings of the 8th International conference on Intelligent User Interfaces*. 3–3. DOI: http://dx.doi.org/10.1145/604045.604048

16. Stacey Kuznetsov, Eric Paulos, and Mark D. Gross. 2010. WallBots: Interactive Wall-Crawling Robots In the Hands of Public Artists and Political Activists. In *Proceedings of the 8th ACM Conference on Designing Interactive Systems - DIS '10*. 208. DOI: http://dx.doi.org/10.1145/1858171.1858208

17. David Merrill, Jeevan Kalanithi, and Pattie Maes. 2007. Siftables. In *Proceedings of the 1st international conference on Tangible and embedded interaction - TEI '07*. ACM Press, 75. DOI: http://dx.doi.org/10.1145/1226969.1226984

18. Joseph A. Paradiso, Josh Lifton, and Michael Broxton. 2004. Sensate media - Multimodal electronic skins as dense sensor networks. *BT Technology Journal* 22, 4 (2004), 32–44. DOI: http://dx.doi.org/10.1023/B:BTTJ.0000047581.37994.c2

19. Erica Robles and Mikael Wiberg. 2010. Texturing the "material turn" in interaction design. *Proceedings of the fourth international conference on Tangible, embedded, and embodied interaction - TEI '10* April (2010), 137. DOI:http://dx.doi.org/10.1145/1709886.1709911

20. Anthony Rowe. 2012. Within an Ocean of Light: Creating Volumetric Lightscapes. *Leonardo* 45, 4 (2012), 358–365. DOI:http://dx.doi.org/10.1162/LEON_a_00410

21. Anthony Rowe, Gaz Bushell, Liam Birtles, Chris Bennewith, and Ollie Bown. 2016. Submergence 2013. *Leonardo* 49, 4 (2016), 356–357.

22. Munehiko Sato. 2008. Particle Display System: A Real World Display with Physically Distributable Pixels. In *Proceeding of the 26th Annual CHI Conference on Human Factors in Computing Systems - CHI '08*. 3771–3776. DOI: http://dx.doi.org/10.1145/1358628.1358928

23. Munehiko Sato, Atsushi Hiyama, Tomohiro Tanikawa, and Michitaka Hirose. 2009. Particle Display System - Virtually Perceivable Pixels with Randomly Distributed Physical Pixels. *Journal of Information Processing* 17 (2009), 280–291. DOI: http://dx.doi.org/10.2197/ipsjjip.17.280

24. Arne Schmitz and Ming Li. 2010. Ad-Hoc Multi-Displays for Mobile Interactive Applications. *Eurographics* 29, 2 (2010), 45–52. DOI: http://dx.doi.org/10.1145/502348.502351

25. Julia Schwarz, David Klionsky, and Chris Harrison. 2012. Phone as a pixel: enabling ad-hoc, large-scale displays using mobile devices. In *Proceedings of the SIGCHI Conference on Human Factors in Computing Systems*. 3–6. DOI:http://dx.doi.org/10.1145/2207676.2208378

26. Susanne Seitinger, Daniel S Perry, and William J Mitchell. 2009. Urban Pixels: Painting the City with Light. In *Proceeding of the 27th Annual CHI Conference on Human Factors in Computing Systems - CHI '09*. 839–848. DOI: http://dx.doi.org/10.1145/1518701.1518829

27. Anna Vallgårda, Laurens Boer, Vasiliki Tsaknaki, and Dag Svanaes. 2016. Material Programming. In *Proceedings of the 2016 ACM Conference Companion Publication on Designing Interactive Systems - DIS '16 Companion*. ACM Press, New York, New York, USA, 149–152. DOI: http://dx.doi.org/10.1145/2908805.2909411

28. Mikael Wiberg. 2014. Methodology for materiality: interaction design research through a material lens. *Personal and Ubiquitous Computing* 18, 3 (mar 2014), 625–636. DOI: http://dx.doi.org/10.1007/s00779-013-0686-7

Qualities of Focus

Eli Blevis
School of Informatics & Computing,
Indiana University, Bloomington USA
School of Design,
Hong Kong Polytechnic University,
Hong Kong
eblevis@indiana.edu

C&C '17, June 27 - 30, 2017, Singapore, Singapore

ACM 978-1-4503-4403-6/17/06...$15.00
DOI: http://dx.doi.org/10.1145/3059454.3059485

Abstract

The genre of this pictorial is *photographs as primary content*. All of the images are deliberately and extremely out of focus, creating a puzzle for the viewer. The implications of this work are considered in terms of the images themselves, boundaries and balance in pictorials, politics and cognition, and technology. Qualities of focus in images—from *everywhere in focus* to *selective* to *everywhere out of focus*—are discussed as a technique and material quality of interaction design.

Authors Keywords

Pictorials; politics & cognition; photography and HCI; photography in HCI; interaction design; Design.

ACM Classification Keywords

H.5.m. Information interfaces and presentation (e.g., HCI): Miscellaneous.

Discussion

This pictorial presents a collection of nine photographs on pages 2-10. The image titles are presented in thumbnails on page 11. The intended way to look at this collection is to first look at each individual photograph and record what you imagine it is. Then, look at page 11 to see the titles that indicate what the actual subject of each photograph is.
The contribution goals of this pictorial are

- **the images, themselves:** to present a specific aesthetic collection of images and *viewer experience puzzle*,
- **boundaries & balance:** to continue to push the boundaries of and balance between types of Pictorials in relation to interaction design and HCI,
- **politics & cognition:** to foreground the politics of abstract, lossy, real, and artificial representations as a matter of how images are used and understood in interaction design and HCI, and

Text continues on page 11 ...

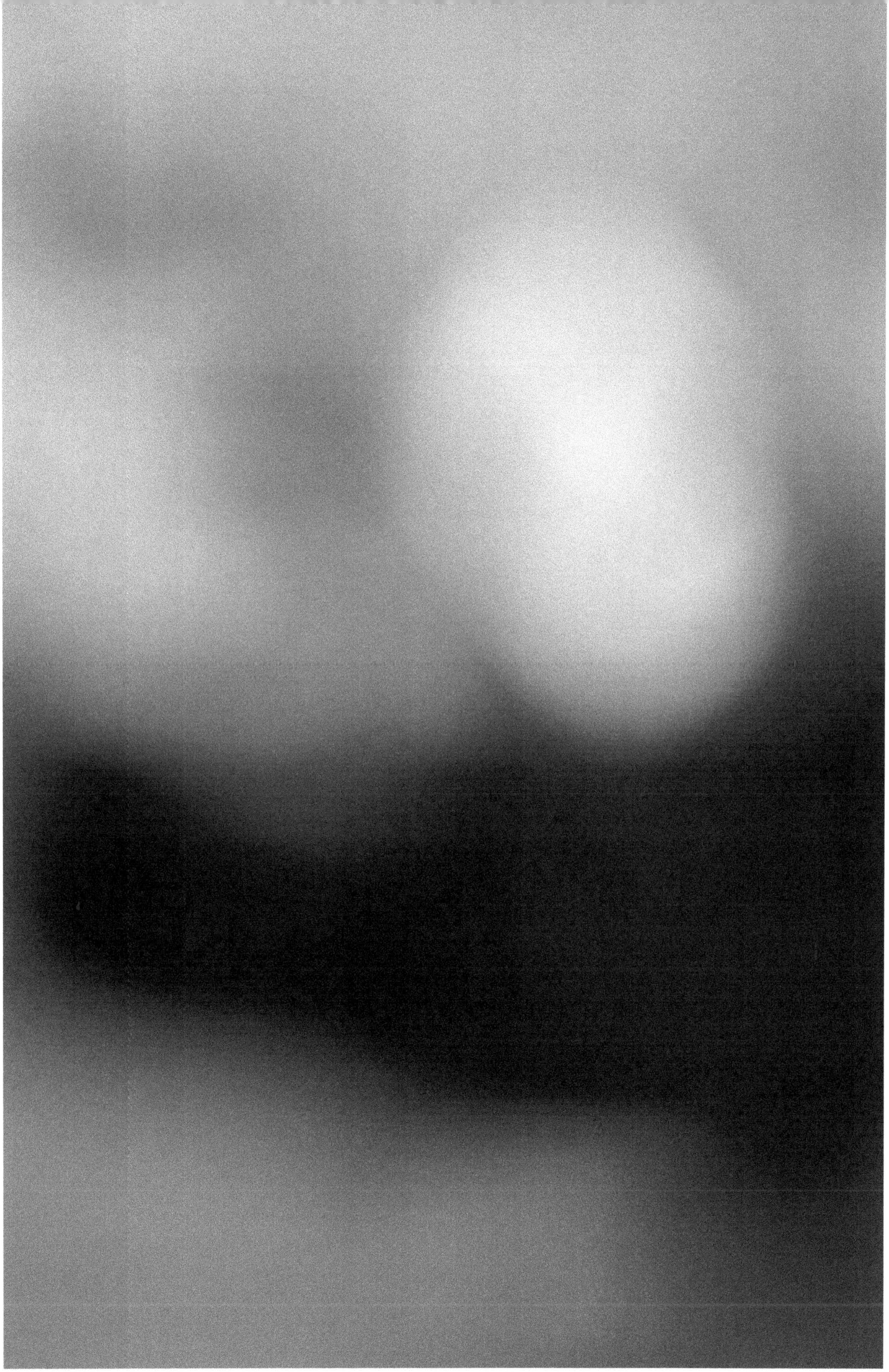

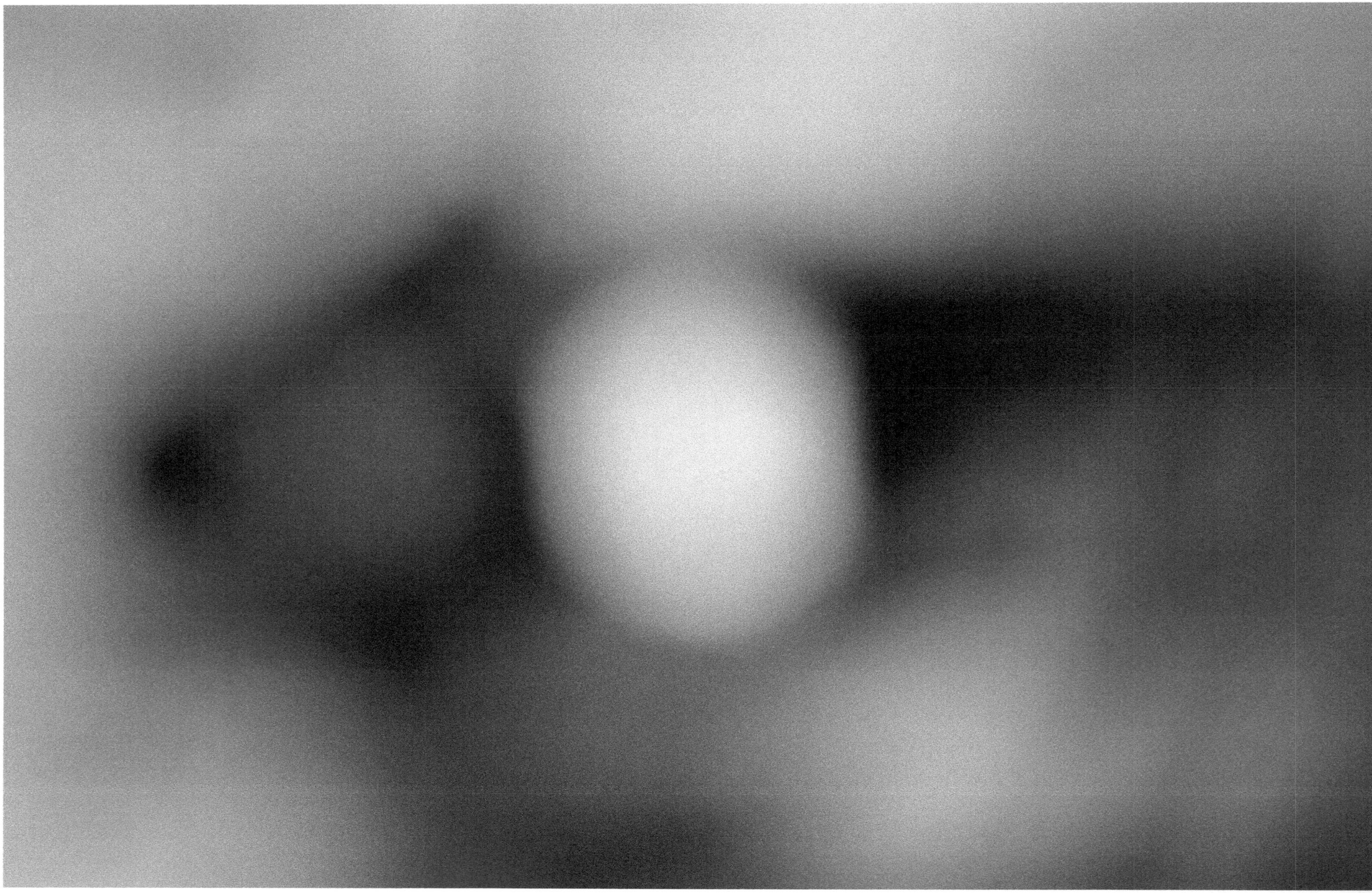

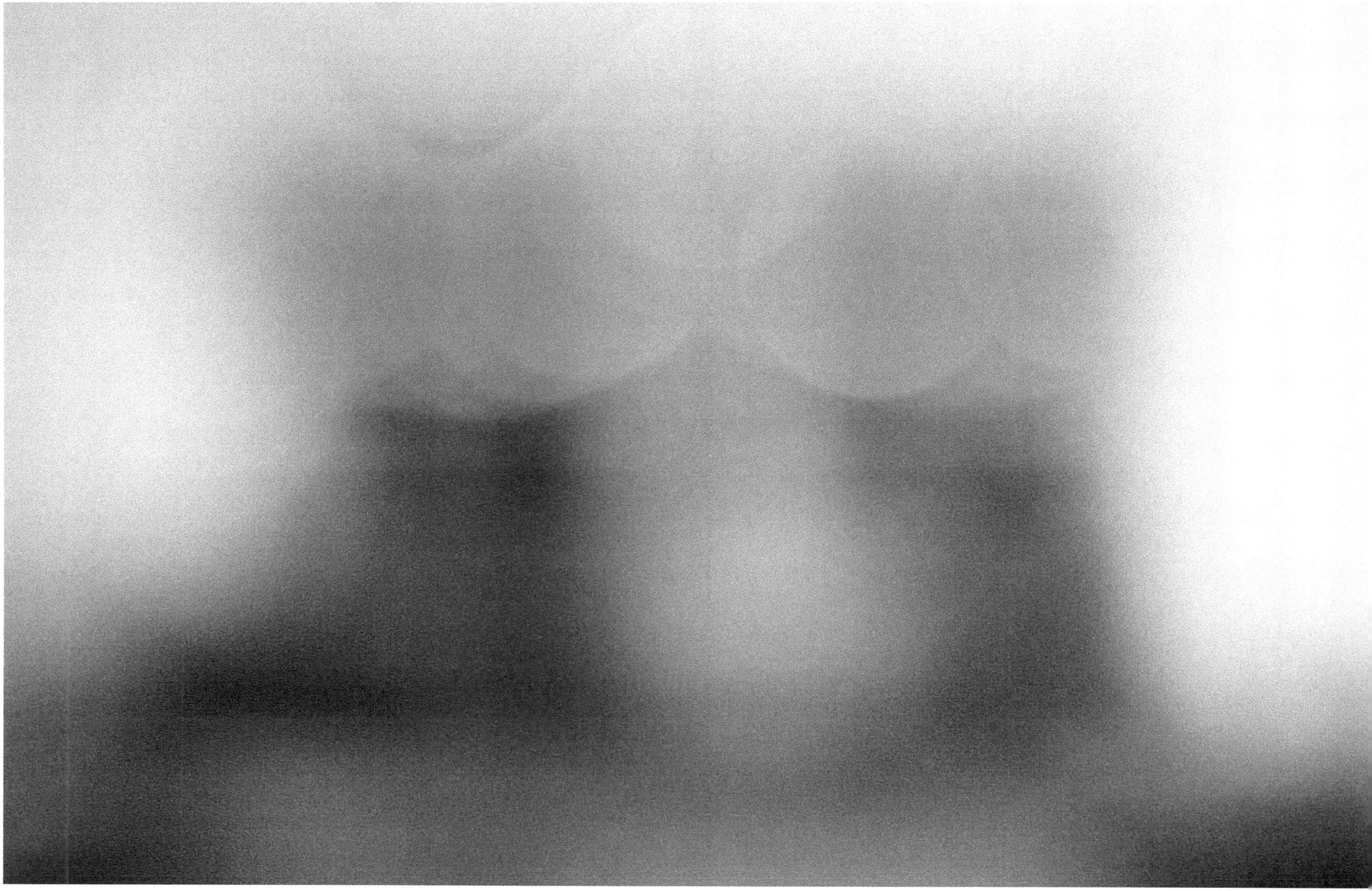

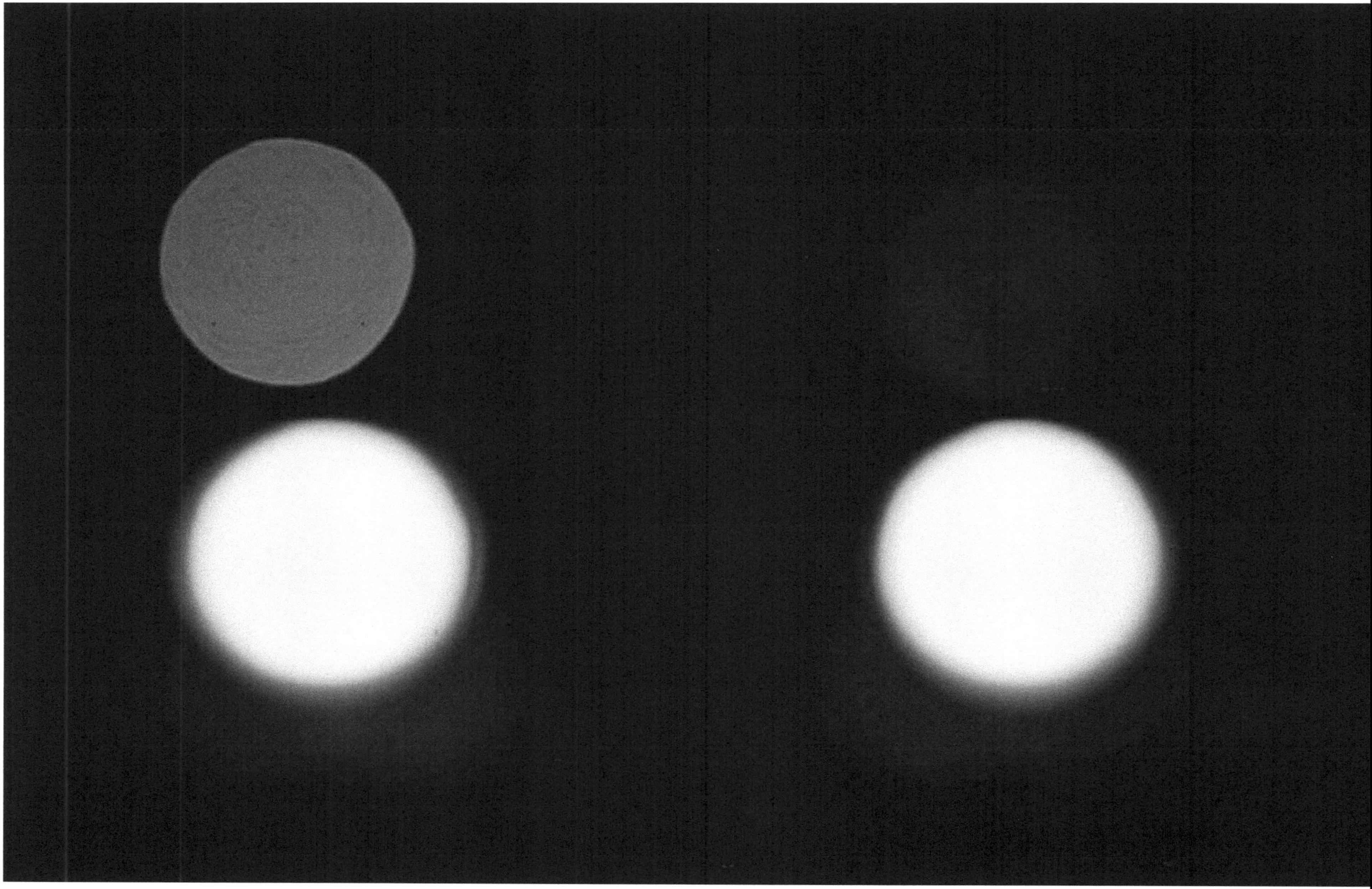

© E. Blevis

© E. Blevis

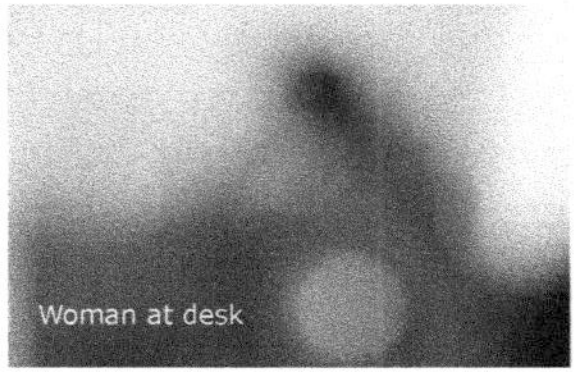
Woman at desk

Windows with Christmas lights

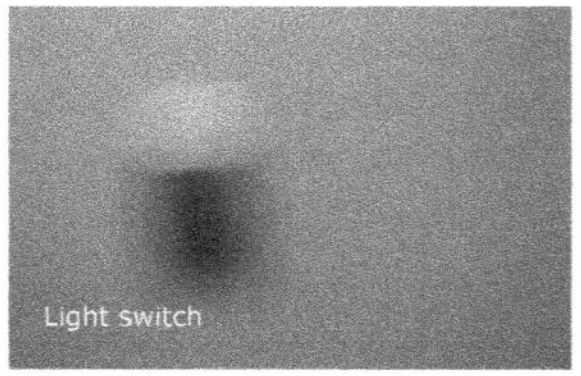
Light switch

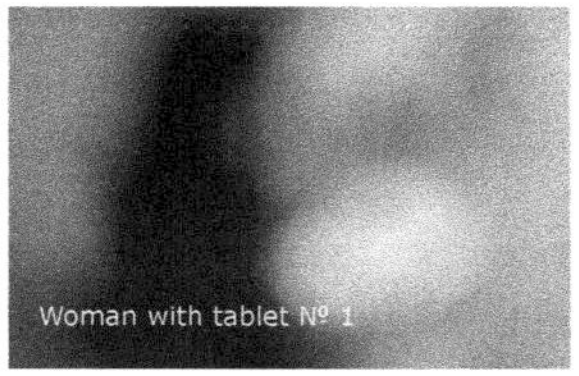
Woman with tablet № 1

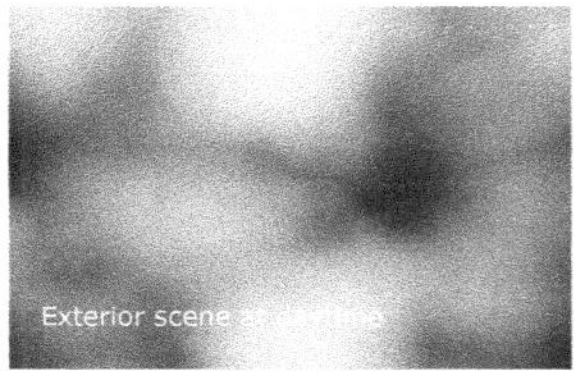
Exterior scene at daytime

Framed photograph on brick wall

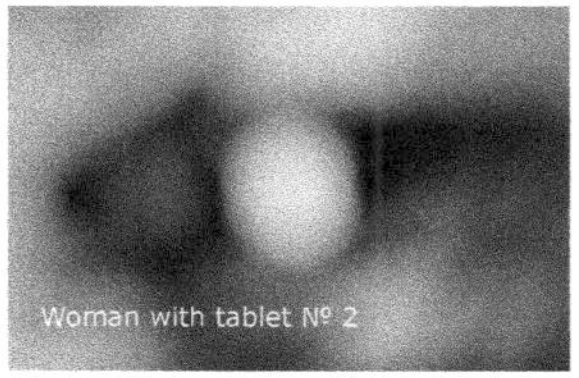
Woman with tablet № 2

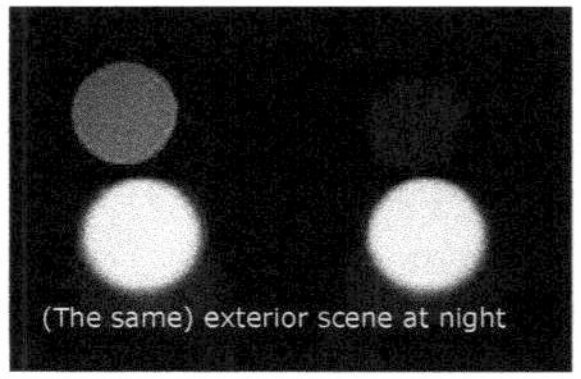
(The same) exterior scene at night

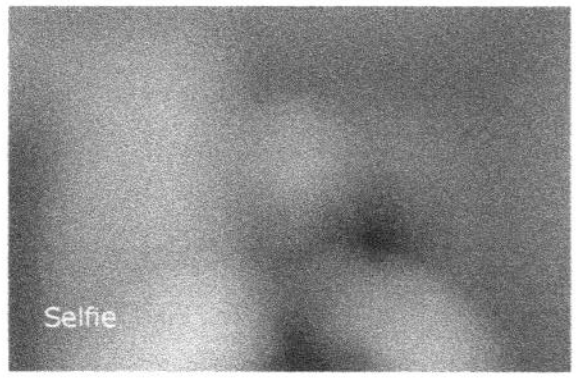
Selfie

... Continued from page 1

- **technology:** to provide a few technical insights about the gap between the interactivity of popular contemporary photographic tools and traditional or professional photographic tools.

The Images, Themselves In order to devote the space required to afford the pre-eminence of the images themselves, there is not enough space to give a complete account of the images in text. Thus, in what follows, I give a detailed account of the first image and its possible interpretation, followed by somewhat more essential accounts of the remaining images.

In *Woman at desk*, the colours contribute particularly to the ease with which the subject matter of the image is perceived. The browns of the desk are a clue. The oranges of the woman's clothing are a clue. The blacks denote the woman's hair. The blacks also denote the shadow underneath the bright white window light comprising the right side of the image. The woman's head rests in her hand, as a sign of intense concentration. The image is classically composed in a roughly 3×3 grid and from an intimate vantage point. The nearly perfect circle under the woman's arm is an artifact of the use of a wide open aperture with a particularly high quality, reference quality lens and high quality vintage lens extension adapter tubes. The colour accuracy is due to the use of a digital camera which has particularly good in-camera colour (white balance) correction. That which the image loses in detail about the actual, particular scene with the particular woman at her particular desk in that particular room, it makes up in abstraction as a universal portrait of the occupation of study. Thus, the photograph has an intended Artistic quality that transcends a mere recording of a moment subject to ethnographic gaze. The photographer Jason Salavon (salavon.com) creates similar effects by averaging together many similar photographs algorithmically. Here, the effect is created by abstracting a single image using only the means available at the time the image was recorded, with no post-processing. In *Woman with tablet № 1*, the bright blue and white light is easily recognized as a tablet device, nowadays. The profile figure of the woman holding the tablet is clear in its silhouette. This photograph is purposefully photographic minimalism with only three elements—the glowing tablet, the silhouetted woman, and a background that is discernible as a background owing to its nearly complete lack of discernible detail. *Woman with tablet №2* would not have been so easily parsed were it not for being preceded by *Woman with tablet №1*. Here, the key element is the glow from the tablet reflected on the face of a woman now in regular, non-profile recline. *Windows with Christmas Lights* is an interior photograph. Thus, the windows are the most dark parts of the photograph. The lattice patterns are a clue to their form. As in *Woman at desk*, the near perfect circles that denote the Christmas lights are an artifact of wide open aperture with a reference quality lens and extensions. *Exterior scene at daytime* is one of the most difficult of the collection to *guess*. It is taken from a porch overlooking a typical suburban scene. The extreme distance of all objects from the near point of focus exaggerates the abstraction beyond the earlier images. *(The same) exterior scene at night* is even more difficult to *guess*. Two porch lights are prominent in the foreground. A street light appears in the background. It is only the distance that creates the differences in colour and intensity between the foreground circles and the background circle. The circles are impressively all the same size, regardless of very different proximities to the lens. The image is particularly minimalist. The appearance of out of focus lights at night in photographs is common. Thus, the image is possibly easier to parse than *Exterior scene at daytime*. *Light switch* has a completely different vantage point to all of the other images—it is taken close up from above, but not close enough to be in focus. The switch is ivory coloured and the base plate is brass. The many circles that denote the de-focused switch create a sense of movement in the way that they align. *Framed photograph on brick wall* is also easily recognized. The camera's vantage point is a distance of about a meter, rounding out the inventory of possible vantage points represented in this collection. The bricks are easily discernible. The framed photograph is also easily discernible. As an hypothesis about *viewer experience*, the collection begins with four images that are fairly easily parsed, building confidence for the viewer. Then, it follows with three images that are harder to parse, testing the viewer's perseverance. Finally *Framed photograph on brick wall* returns to an easily parsed image, allowing some relief to the viewer. The final image, *Selfie*, is the most easily recognized of all. Nowadays, selfies are among the most ubiquitous of all photographic forms.

Boundaries & Balance Pictorials are a relatively new form of archival contribution in SIGCHI venues. Most have appeared at DIS 2014/16 and one at NordiCHI 2012. Pictorials are now a regular archival contribution category of DIS and Creativity & Cognition conferences and some design journals (e.g. *Cubic Journal, IJD, & She Ji*) now propose to accept pictorials as an archival form of contribution, too. Of the pictorials that have appeared to date, most document design process or method [6, 8,9,12,13,16,17,21,23,24,25,27]. Some distinguish photographs themselves as the primary content [1,4,15]. Some are more diagrammatic [7]. Some are very conceptual [10,14,18,19]. These are neither mutually exclusive nor exhaustive classifications. A history of the form prior to 2014 appears in [1]. This pictorial's genre is photographs as primary content—that is, it puts forward original photographic images as design content and design knowledge in the combination, juxtapositions, and consistent style of a collection. As such, this textual discussion is deliberately minimal.

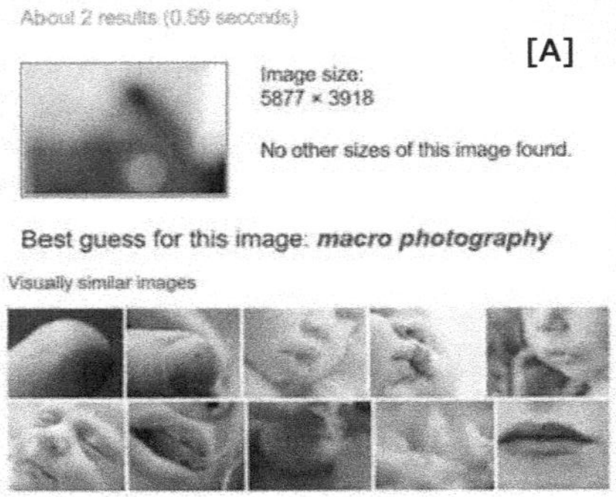

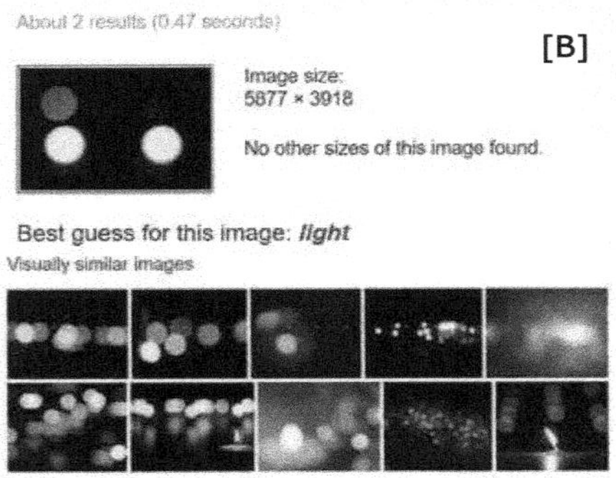

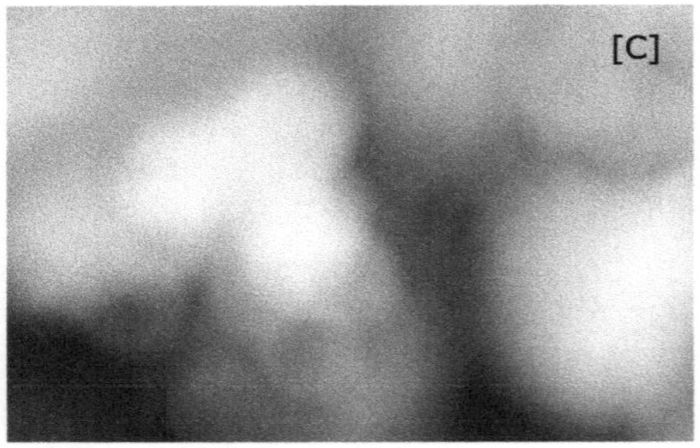

© E. Blevis

© E. Blevis

In [2], I take up in a full length paper the issues of balance between images and text in SIGCHI archival formats.

Politics & Cognition The images in this collection are deliberately and extremely out of focus. All of the images are labeled simply and truthfully to accurately reflect the scenes in the index on page 11. The reader/viewer can see for her or himself if the correspondence is apparent or not. That is how this pictorial is intended to be experienced. There is a politics here. That is, the collection invites distinctions between abstract, lossy, real, and artificial. The images are abstract and lossy—the intent is to make them more universal by reducing the specific information content. The images are truthful—they are minimally processed out of camera and labeled truthfully. Here, truth is distinct from detail. If the images had been mislabeled, or processed more in post-production tools such as Photoshop, the intent might have been to *create* artificial work or to *create* a falsehood. The distinction in notions of truthfulness & falsehood, real & artificial between (a) editorial decisions taken at the time an image is captured with a camera and (b) afterwards by means of post-processing software is a matter of importance. For example, the New York Times [26] and many others published now famous photographs comparing crowd size of the 2009 and 2017 US presidential inaugurations as evidence refuting a claim by the now sitting President. If these photographs had been staged or post-processed in any way, they would have been considered a breach of journalistic ethics, at the least. As an opposite example, photographs are frequently claimed to have been staged or post-processed in the service of propaganda (e.g. [11,22]).

When interaction designers engage in photo-ethnographic style design research, the images they create are intended to be truthful representations of the context that will inform design insights and conceptualization. The advice stated at the school of design in which I learned photography (The Institute of Design at IIT, Chicago) was to use a wide-angle lens to stand back from any observed scene in order to capture the maximum context—that is, to capture images in the least editorial way. When selective focus or narrow field of view (as with a non wide-angle lens) is used as in image [D], the editorial gaze is intrinsic—that is, the selective focus or narrow field of view denote editorial perspective about what is important. Note that design research is not the only use of images in HCI and interaction design. One other important use is constructed or staged images to illustrate concepts—that is, a kind of appearance or scenario prototyping. Constructed or staged images are not propaganda if we do not label them as truthful representations of what presently exists, but rather take them as design prototypes of possible future ways of being. The deliberately de-focused images in this pictorial do not fit neatly in any of these categories. Yet, they do say something about human abilities to visually fill in details to understand a scene as universal, even when so extremely abstracted. Moreover, the technological innovations that make available so much visual detail nowadays (e.g. Google Earth) contrasts with these images in which the main feature is loss of detail. These are among the reasons I believe the images are interesting. As well, extremely and everywhere out of focus images may be a useful aesthetic material of interaction design, particularly where the depiction of a universal scene is called for.

Technology Image [A] shows the first image in the collection as a search input to Google image search. Absent any textual search terms, Google incorrectly guesses that the image is macro-photography and suggests similar images that are quite far from the actual subject matter. This is not a criticism of Google image search. Rather, it is an interesting comment on the role of textual labels in image recognition, both in terms of algorithmic inputs and human perception. Google image search performs much better in the case of image [B], because such de-focusing of distant lights at night is a much more common technique of photography. The out of focus effects in this collection are achieved by the use of mechanical close focus apparatus, manual focus, reference standard optics [20]:26-29, and high ISO (sensor sensitivity) settings. Image [C] compares the effect to normal focus [D]. Making an image with an out of focus background is a common technique in photography—image [D] is an example. Doing so has both an editorial function as well as the feature of creating a sense of dimensionality. Plenoptic photography (see [5]) allows photographers to decide on focus after the image is taken rather than before—a technology that potentially adds to the politics of image making because it records information at taking time that augment what is possible with minimal post-processing. Making an image with nothing in focus is actually hard to do using the native applications on a smartphone or tablet camera. Making images of a certain quality still requires knowledge of foundational photographic principles and physics, regardless of advances in digital interactivity.

Summary Qualities of focus—from *everywhere in focus* to *selective* to *everywhere out of focus*—are a core quality of image making that can be understood as a foundational material quality in interaction design. Editorial choices made at (digital) taking time or in (digital) post-processing have complex implications for notions of truth and falsehood that differ between *presenting* images as evidence in journalism, *taking* images in design research, *abstracting* images as design universals, and *making* images in design conceptualization and prototyping—accurate labels are key.

Acknowledgements

I gratefully acknowledge the reviewers. Many thanks to Jung Joo Lee for additional valuable editorial guidance. Many thanks to Jeffrey Bardzell, Shunying An Blevis, and Erik Stolterman for commenting on drafts, and many thanks to the 47 students and Associate Instructors in my 2016/2017 *Visual Thinking, Meaning & Form* class for trying the puzzle presented in this paper as a classroom exercise. Many thanks to the many people who have helped to make pictorials an archival form these past few years. These include Pictorial Program Chairs David Cameron, Sabrina Hauser, Nadine Jarvis, Jung Joo Lee, Will Odom, and others. These also include the Steering Committees and Pictorial Program Committees for ACM C&C and DIS conferences.

References

1. Eli Blevis. 2016. The Visual Thinking Gallery: A Five Year Retrospective. In *Proceedings of the 2016 ACM Conference on Designing Interactive Systems (DIS '16).* ACM, New York, NY, USA, 1096-1110.
2. Eli Blevis. 2016. Being Photo-Visual in HCI and Design. In *Proceedings of the 2016 ACM Conference on Designing Interactive Systems (DIS '16).* ACM, New York, NY, USA, 983-995.
3. Eli Blevis, Sabrina Hauser, and William Odom. 2015. Sharing the hidden treasure in pictorials. *interactions 22,* 3 (April 2015), 32-43.
4. Eli Blevis. 2014. Stillness and motion, meaning and form. In *Proceedings of the 2014 conference on Designing interactive systems (DIS '14).* ACM, New York, NY, USA, 493-502.
5. Eli Blevis. 2011. A matter of focus and a question of resolution. *interactions 18,* 6 (November 2011), 88-88.
6. Andy Boucher. 2016. The Form Design of the Datacatcher: A Research Prototype. In *Proceedings of the 2016 ACM Conference on Designing Interactive Systems (DIS '16).* ACM, New York, NY, USA, 595-606.
7. Audrey Desjardins, Ron Wakkary, and William Odom. 2016. Behind the Lens: A Visual Exploration of Epistemological Commitments in HCI Research on the Home. In *Proceedings of the 2016 ACM Conference on Designing Interactive Systems (DIS '16).* ACM, New York, NY, USA, 360-376.
8. Tom Djajadiningrat, Patray Lui, Pei-Yin Chao, and Christian Richard. 2016. Virtual Trainer: A Low Cost AR Simulation of a Sudden Cardiac Arrest Emergency. In *Proceedings of the 2016 ACM Conference on Designing Interactive Systems (DIS '16).* ACM, New York, NY, USA, 607-618
9. Tom Djajadiningrat, Pei-Yin Chao, SeYoung Kim, Marleen Van Leengoed, and Jeroen Raijmakers. 2016. Mime: An AR-based System Helping Patients to Test their Blood at Home. In *Proceedings of the 2016 ACM Conference on Designing Interactive Systems (DIS '16).* ACM, New York, NY, USA, 347-359.
10. Thomas Dykes, Jayne Wallace, Mark Blythe, and James Thomas. 2016. Paper Street View: A Guided Tour of Design and Making Using Comics. In *Proceedings of the 2016 ACM Conference on Designing Interactive Systems (DIS '16).* ACM, New York, NY, USA, 334-346.
11. Max Fisher and Jugal K. Patel. 2017 (Feb. 24). What One Photo Tells Us About North Korea's Nuclear Program. The New York Times. https://www.nytimes.com/interactive/2017/02/24/world/asia/north-korea-propaganda-photo.html accessed 3.15.2017.
12. Nadine Jarvis, David Cameron, and Andy Boucher. 2012. Attention to detail: annotations of a design process. In *Proceedings of the 7th Nordic Conference on Human-Computer Interaction: Making Sense Through Design (NordiCHI '12).* ACM, New York, NY, USA, 11-20.
13. Elvin Karana, Elisa Giaccardi, Niels Stamhuis, and Jasper Goossensen. 2016. The Tuning of Materials: A Designer's Journey. In *Proceedings of the 2016 ACM Conference on Designing Interactive Systems (DIS '16).* ACM, New York, NY, USA, 619-631.

14. A. Baki Kocaballi and Yeliz Yorulmaz. 2016. Performative Photography as an Ideation Method. In *Proceedings of the 2016 ACM Conference on Designing Interactive Systems (DIS '16).* ACM, New York, NY, USA, 1083-1095.
15. Heather McKinnon. 2016. Finding Design Value in Modern Mundanity. In *Proceedings of the 2016 ACM Conference on Designing Interactive Systems (DIS '16).* ACM, New York, NY, USA, 1059-1071.
16. Reese Muntean, Kate Hennessy, Alissa Antle, Brendan Matkin, Susan Rowley, and Jordan Wilson. 2016. Design Interactions in ʔeləwkw: Belongings. In *Proceedings of the 2016 ACM Conference on Designing Interactive Systems (DIS '16).* ACM, New York, NY, USA, 582-594.
17. William Odom, John Zimmerman, Jodi Forlizzi, Hajin Choi, Stephanie Meier, and Angela Park. 2014. Unpacking the thinking and making behind a user enactments project. In *Proceedings of the 2014 conference on Designing interactive systems (DIS '14).* ACM, New York, NY, USA, 513-522.
18. James Pierce. 2016. Design Proposal for a Wireless Derouter: Speculatively Engaging Digitally Disconnected Space. In *Proceedings of the 2016 ACM Conference on Designing Interactive Systems (DIS '16).* ACM, New York, NY, USA, 388-402.
19. James Pierce and Eric Paulos. 2014. Some variations on a counterfunctional digital camera. In *Proceedings of the 2014 conference on Designing interactive systems (DIS '14).* ACM, New York, NY, USA, 131-140.
20. Erwin Puts. 2002. *Leica-M lenses: Their soul and secrets.* Solms & Wetzlar: Leica Camera AG.
21. Daniela K. Rosner, Margaret E. Morris, Ariel Duncan, Sarah E. Fox, Kathi R. Kitner, Ankur Agrawal, and Mei J. Chen. 2016. Designing for Movement in Public Life with Itinerant Probes. In *Proceedings of the 2016 ACM Conference on Designing Interactive Systems (DIS '16).* ACM, New York, NY, USA, 1072-1082.
22. Elizabeth Shim. 2016 (Feb. 19). North Korea doctored photographs of Kim Jong Un, official says. UPI. http://www.upi.com/Top_News/World-News/2016/02/19/North-Korea-doctored-photographs-of-Kim-Jong-Un-official-says/4621455909008/ accessed 3.15.2017.
23. Michael Shorter, Jon Rogers, and John McGhee. 2014. Practical notes on paper circuits. In *Proceedings of the 2014 conference on Designing interactive systems (DIS '14).* ACM, New York, NY, USA, 483-492.
24. Diego Trujillo-Pisanty, Abigail Durrant, Sarah Martindale, Stuart James, and John Collomosse. 2014. Admixed portrait: reflections on being online as a new parent. In *Proceedings of the 2014 conference on Designing interactive systems (DIS '14).* ACM, New York, NY, USA, 503-512.
25. Ron Wakkary, Audrey Desjardins, William Odom, Sabrina Hauser, and Leila Aflatoony. 2014. Eclipse: eliciting the subjective qualities of public places. In *Proceedings of the 2014 conference on Designing interactive systems (DIS '14).* ACM, New York, NY, USA, 151-160.
26. Tim Wallace, Karen Yourish and Troy Griggs. 2017 (Jan. 20). Trump's Inauguration vs. Obama's: Comparing the Crowds. The New York Times. www.nytimes.com/interactive/2017/01/20/us/politics/trump-inauguration-crowd.html accessed 3.15.2017.
27. Stephan Wensveen, Oscar Tomico, Martijn ten Bhömer, and Kristi Kuusk. 2014. Growth plan for an inspirational test-bed of smart textile services. In *Proceedings of the 2014 conference on Designing interactive systems (DIS '14).* ACM, New York, NY, USA, 141-150.

Long live the sensor! Designing with Energy Harvesting

Zhide Loh
60 Chestnut Ave
Singapore, 679517
komodokodomo@gmail.com

Jung-Joo Lee
National University of Singapore
4 Architecture Drive.
Singapore, 117566
jjlee@nus.edu.sg

Kee Hong Song
National University of Singapore
4 Architecture Drive.
Singapore, 117566
skh@nus.edu.sg

C&C '17, June 27-30, 2017, Singapore, Singapore

DOI: http://dx.doi.org/10.1145/3059454.3059488

Abstract
Energy harvesting is an emerging concept that could open new design vistas for sensor-embedded environments as it provides battery-independent capabilities to sensors. In this pictorial, we illustrate how the topic of energy harvesting is approached from the lens of designers. Through the dynamic use of images coupled with physical prototyping, a new design direction for energy harvesting has been formulated. We introduce Livefeed, a prototype series of sensor-embedded objects that live through ambient energy.

Authors Keywords
Energy Harvesting; design; designing with sensors; parasite design.

ACM Classification Keywords
H.5.m. Information interfaces and presentation (e.g., HCI): Miscellaneous.

1. Introduction

"Sensor: a device that responds to a physical stimulus and produces an electronic signal reporting on that stimulus. Sensors can be tailored to report on a variety of environmental conditions, including temperature, movement, vibration, and shock [12]. "

According to Intel, there will be 200 billion smart devices by 2020 [5], averaging out to 26 devices per person. This has been largely attributed to trends in miniaturization and ubiquitous computing [4]. Much of these smart objects that would populate our future world will be sensors. Their primary purpose is to provide personalized information and allow users to make an informed choice in their everyday life. By being able to detect previously unknown conditions in a localized manner, sensors help provide awareness, reminders and even automation to help enable our lives.

However, conventional sensors are still limited in its location or in service life due to their reliance on either the mains or batteries [6]. One of the recent solution areas trying to overcome this challenge is energy harvesting. Energy harvesting refers to the process by which energy is derived from external sources such as solar power, thermal energy, wind energy, salinity gradients or kinetic energy. - also known as ambient energy captured, and stored for small, wireless autonomous devices [6].

In this pictorial, we tap on the concept of energy harvesting to explore how its usage as a material for design would lead to new design criteria in the aspects of user experience. We gained design inspiration from image boards of everyday examples of energy harvesting and examples from nature, especially symbiotic parasitism. This pictorial illustrates the process of framing design opportunities through image boards and iterative physical prototyping. As a result, we introduce a series of design prototypes, "Livefeed" - Everyday sensors that live through the ambient energy harvesting.

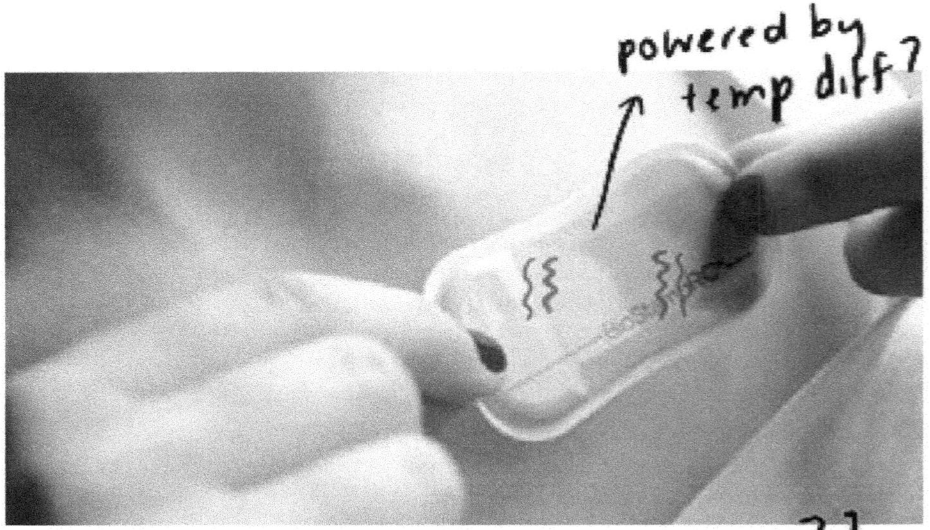

2. Energy Harvesting

Within the fields of electronic engineering and computer science, energy harvesting or energy scavenging recently developed from long-established concepts into devices for powering ubiquitously deployed sensor networks and mobile electronics [5].

With this technical possibility, designers have started to explore energy harvesting as a topic and material for design in the context of everyday human life. For example, by "breaking out" the energy harvesting element typically hidden inside the machine, Eric Paulos designed a series of objects that harvest energy in the public landscape to provoke people to become aware of ambient energy that can be harvested in our daily lives [3]. Going beyond mere technical benefits from the energy harvesting, the precedent studies in the HCI and interaction design has focused on human-energy relations [9]. These studies explored people's emotional experiences with energy by taking energy as design materials [7, 8] and also looked into communal cooperation for adjusting people's energy consumption behaviors, beyond individual experiences [1].

The earlier studies led us to formulate our very initial design area: how might we design sensors that can live through the ambient energy harvesting while at the same time providing practical values to people's everyday life as a way of engaging people to the possibility of ambient energy?

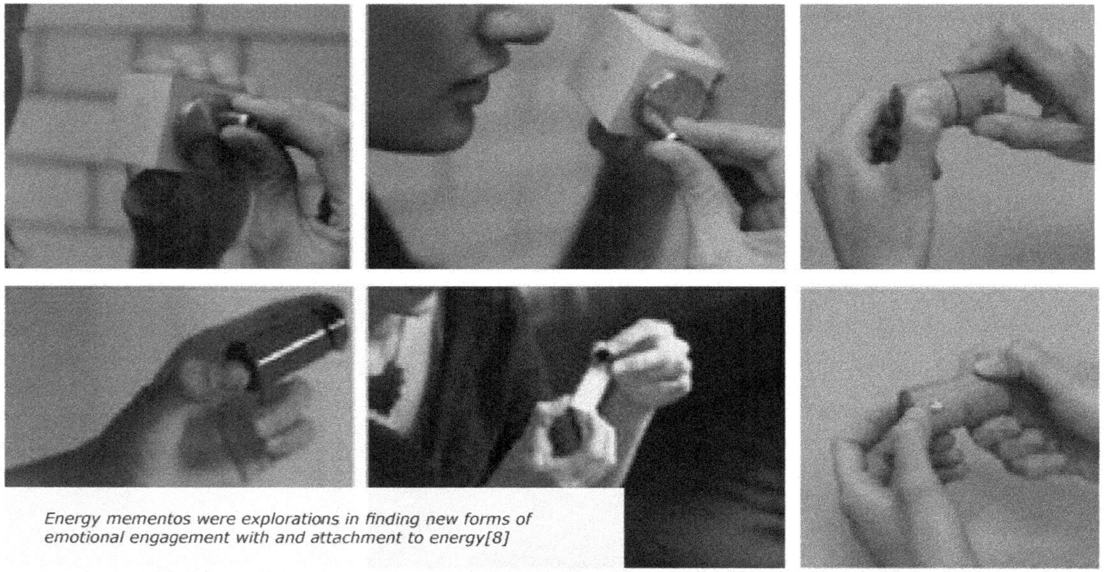

Energy mementos were explorations in finding new forms of emotional engagement with and attachment to energy[8]

Energy parasites are small handcrafted objects designed to opportunistically harvest small bits of energy across public landscapes.[3]

Energy harvesting in our everyday life

In the process of gaining inspiration for design, we found examples of everyday rituals or objects with which people have been benefiting from energy harvesting. Examples include bicycle light that is turned on by the kinetic energy from pedalling or kettles that make a sound alert from the heated vapour passing through it.

These simple examples in our everyday life demonstrate how energy can be transformed into functions that provide values to the very specific context of use where the energy is generated and consumed simultaneously.

Symbiotic relations in nature

Nature itself also provided us with inspiring examples. In nature, various symbiotic relations consist of a host-parasite relationship. Although the parasite reduces the overall fitness of the host, it makes up for it by providing benefits such as the removal of pests or acting as an early warning of predators.

In these examples in our everyday life and symbiotic relations in nature, the benefits created tend to be immediate and located in the very context of the energy harvested, which could help beneficiaries experience the immediate values of the energy harvesting.

3. Probing into people's experiences

Our next design journey was to understand what kinds of energy harvesting object would make sense to people. What parasites would exist in relation to the objects in our homes? How would they look like, behave, and position themselves?

To answer these questions, we curated a set of 4 dummy objects as probes. 20 individuals were presented with the set of objects and told that they were enchanted objects that came alive in the presence of ambient light, wind, water, heat, and so on. The participants were then instructed to place the objects where they deemed fit for usage. They were also prompted to imagine what those objects would know about its immediate surroundings and how they would communicate this information to people. All these were done in a one-to-one home visit session that lasted approximate 20minute each.

Participants faced initial difficulty imagining what the objects could know and do, but soon started to identify surprising places and purposes for the objects. For example, ideas such as an energy harvesting security camera attached to a fan that not only relied on the airflow for power but also its oscillating behaviour as a way to survey the area.

As one of the main findings, the participants felt that the information sensed should be intrinsically associated with its power source because in that way they can see the meaning of the information and functionality relevant to the context of use.

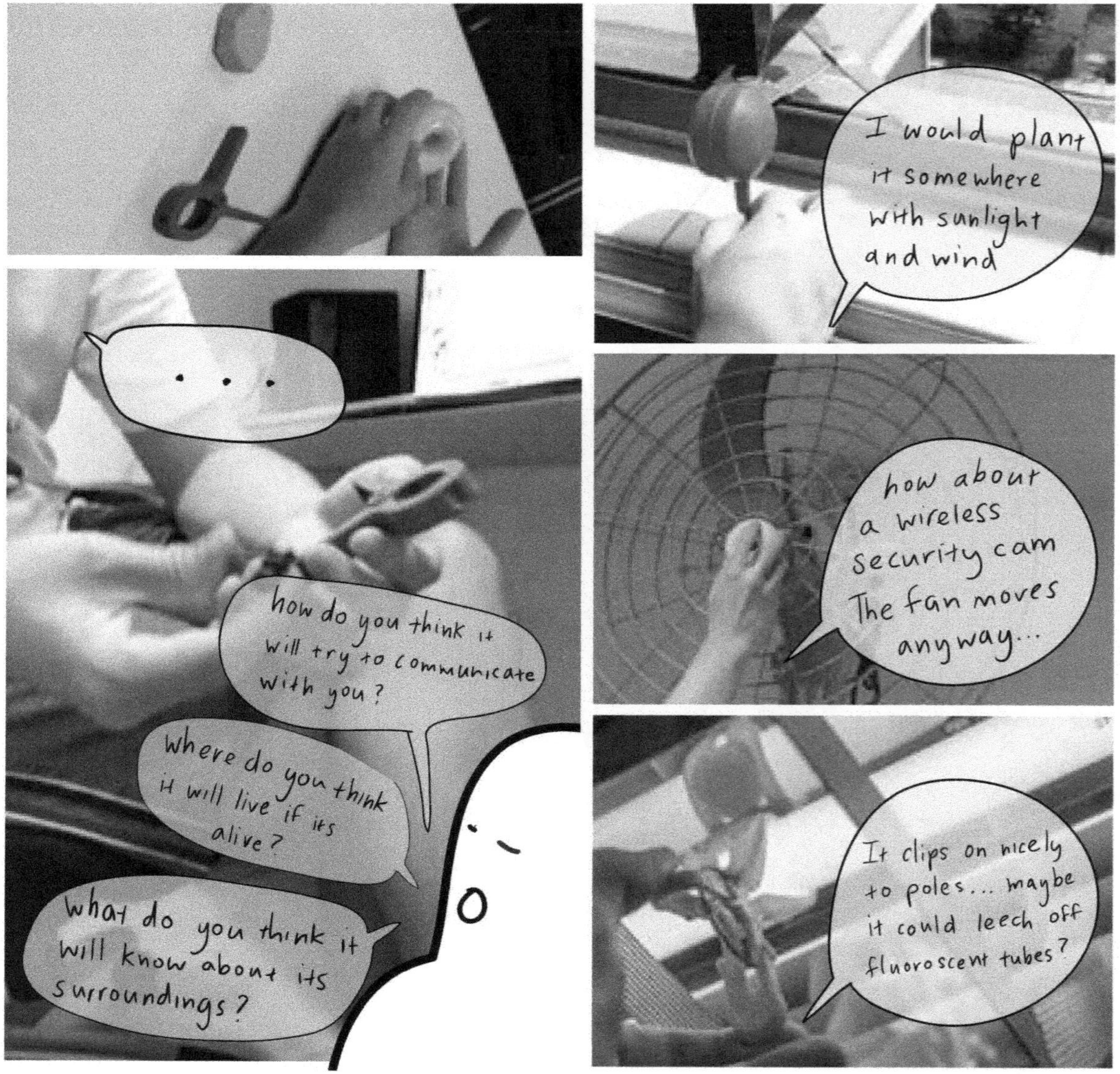

4.Ideation

The explorations of examples from everyday objects and nature combined with our findings from out probing led us to 3 design requirements:

1. The object should inherently be low maintenance and it should not rely on technology that would make it obsolete quickly.

2. The new augmented function of the object afforded by energy harvesting should be relevant to the object's original purpose. It should work in the same context.

3. Value-addedness: The relation should be mutually beneficial, resulting in a net increase in value of the "system".

Based on these design drivers, ideation was done progressively from rough mind-maps to 2D CAD drawings.

Evaluation

We uploaded the visualizations of these ideas in the social media and gathered feedback from more than 50 participants with ages ranging from the early 20s to the late 40s on which idea they prefer and why.

From their comments, we learned that users would prefer if they could see a direct result of the energy harvested. In addition, they prefer the devices to provide actionable advice rather than simply information (e.g. how much sunblock to use vs current UV levels).

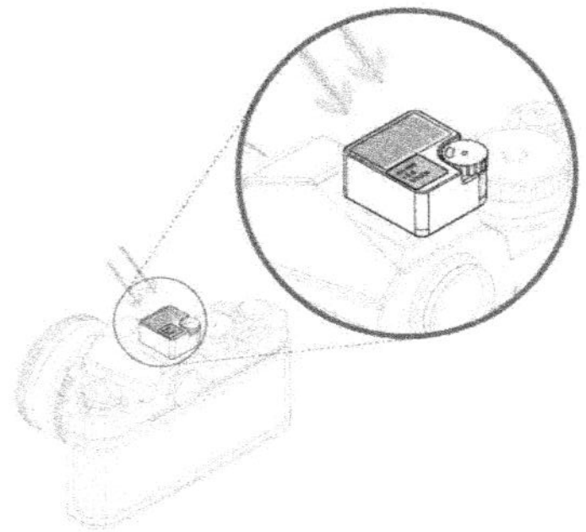

A camera lightmeter that does not require batteries.

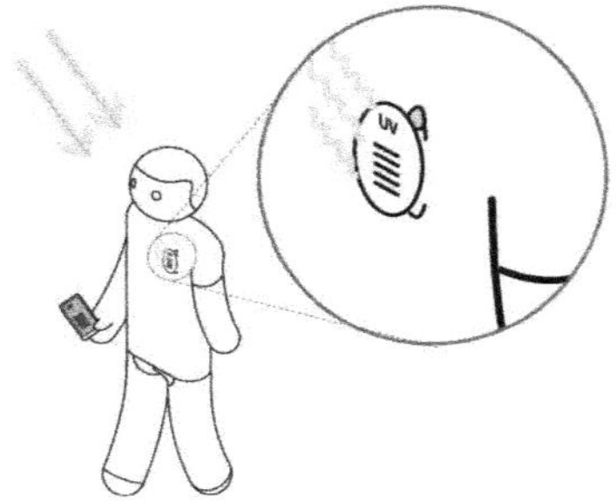

A badge that tells you how much UV you have been exposed to.

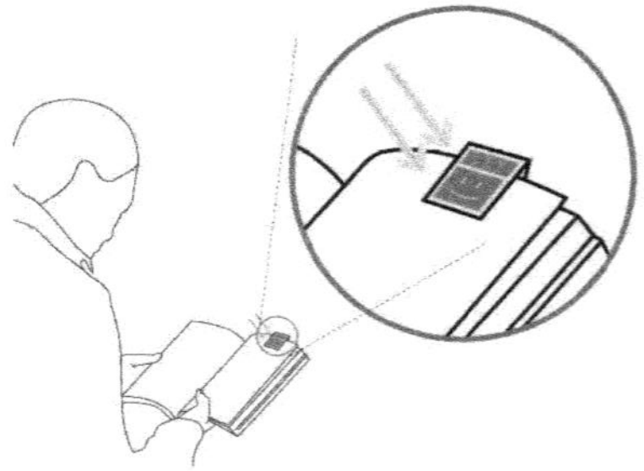

A bookmark that tells you whether the light conditions is good for the eye.

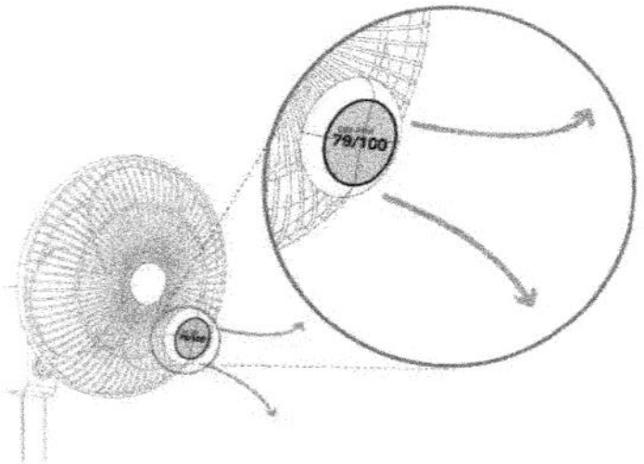

A device powered by a fan, giving information about the air quality.

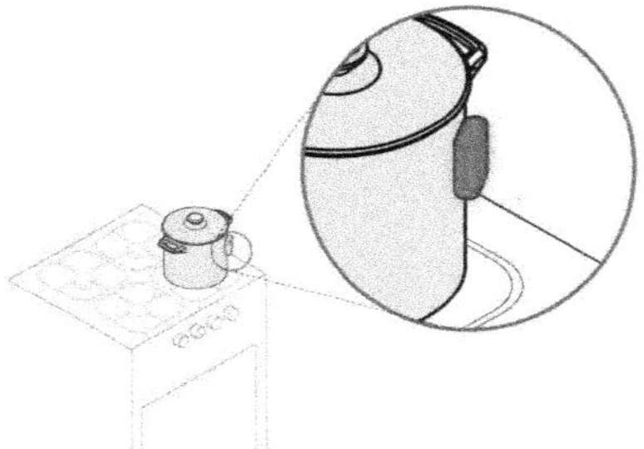

A device that attaches to potentially hot objects, glowing red when it is sufficiently warm.

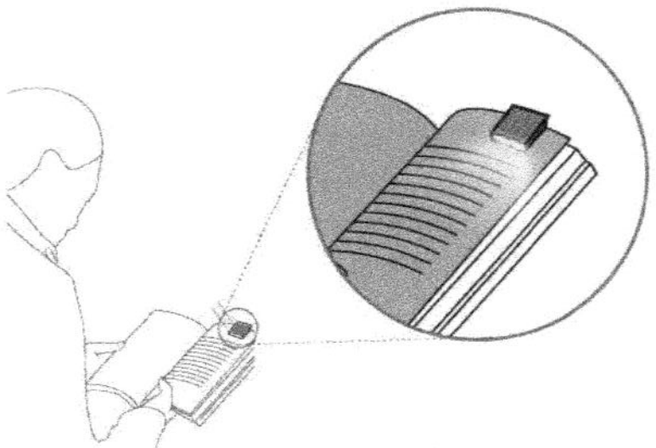

A bookmark that stores the solar energy and act as a reading light

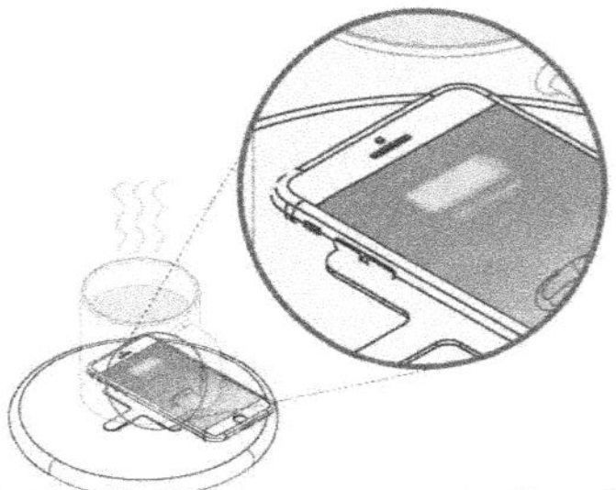

Coaster that stores energy on one side and wirelessly charges phones on the other

"....In general I prefered the ones that automatically translate into action, rather than notification"

"... uv exposure is pretty interesting, maybe it can be tied with more relations with how much sunblock required for the amount of exposure"

5. Prototyping

Based on the previous learnings, we went on to design three series of prototypes, each utilizing a different energy source: wind, heat and sunlight.

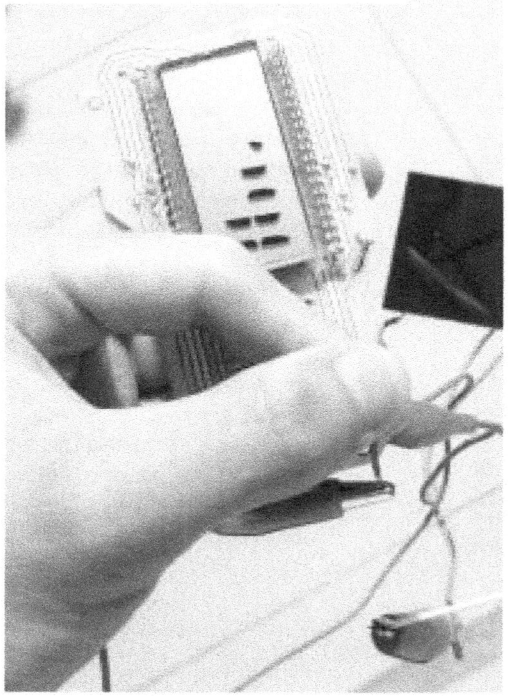

Wind and air quality monitoring
The prototypes were centred around the fan which is a reliable source of energy within Singaporean homes. Two types of fan-powered sensors were created, one with a LED screen and another with a LED light. Both monitor the indoor air quality.

Heat and warming
These prototypes harvested the excess heat energy from hot objects (e.g. a cup with hot tea) and used the thermoelectric energy to keep the desired temperature of the hot tea or charge a mobile phone. These ideas faced a technical difficulty, however, as the mechanism couldn't harvest enough energy within a desired time.

Sunlight / UV / Light level monitor
Three prototypes capturing sunlight were created: 1) UV badge that tells how much UV a wearer is exposed to 2) A bookmark that tells users whether the light condition is good for the eyes 3) Hot shoe light meter for analog cameras.

Iterative prototyping

We introduced the five prototypes to users who are in their age of 20s and well exposed to smart devices in their everyday life. In general, they showed high interests in the prototypes that indicate air quality and the bookmark that tells a light condition for the practical values they provide. Especially during the test period there was a high concern of air quality in Singapore due to a haze. Through the multiple cycles of prototyping, two design concepts were gradually developed: an air quality monitor that lives by latching on to a fan and a light quality bookmark that captures and analyses the ambient light.

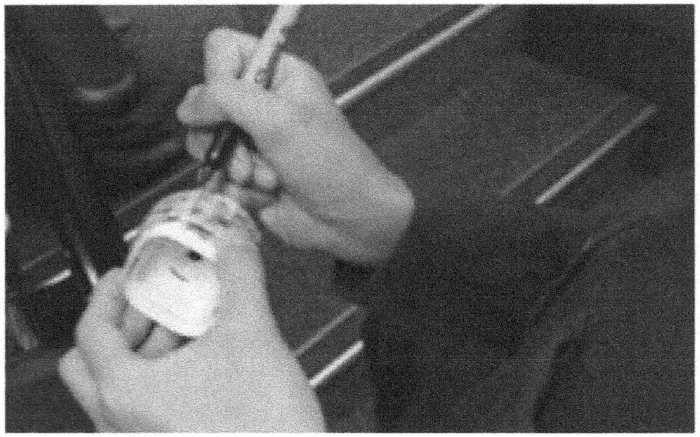

Air quality monitor
The outer casing that captured and channeled the airflow featured heavily in the iterative process. Not only did it have to look aesthetically pleasing, but it also had to channel enough air movement of a sufficient velocity to power the electronics within.

Light quality bookmark
Efforts were focused on making the prototype as slim, flexible, and robust as possible - similar to how a normal bookmark would be.

6. Livefeed

Finally we introduce a series of sensor objects, Livefeed, which live through ambient energy harvesting while simultaneously providing contextual information to users.

Airfeed
Airfeed is an air quality monitor that latches on to household fans or other sources of air flow. Powered by air movement, it informs users on the quality of air passing through it. Airfeed has a low power LCD screen that tells the air quality with different emoticons.

Lightfeed
Lightfeed is a light level monitor that slips into books just like a normal bookmark. Powered by the ambient light, it informs users whether current light levels are acceptable for reading.

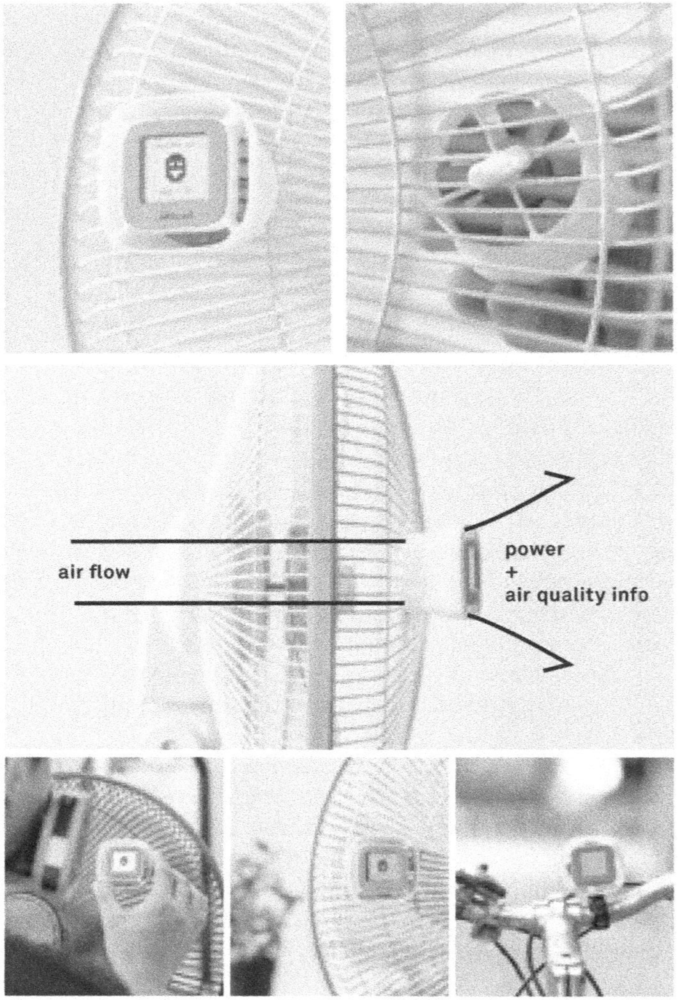

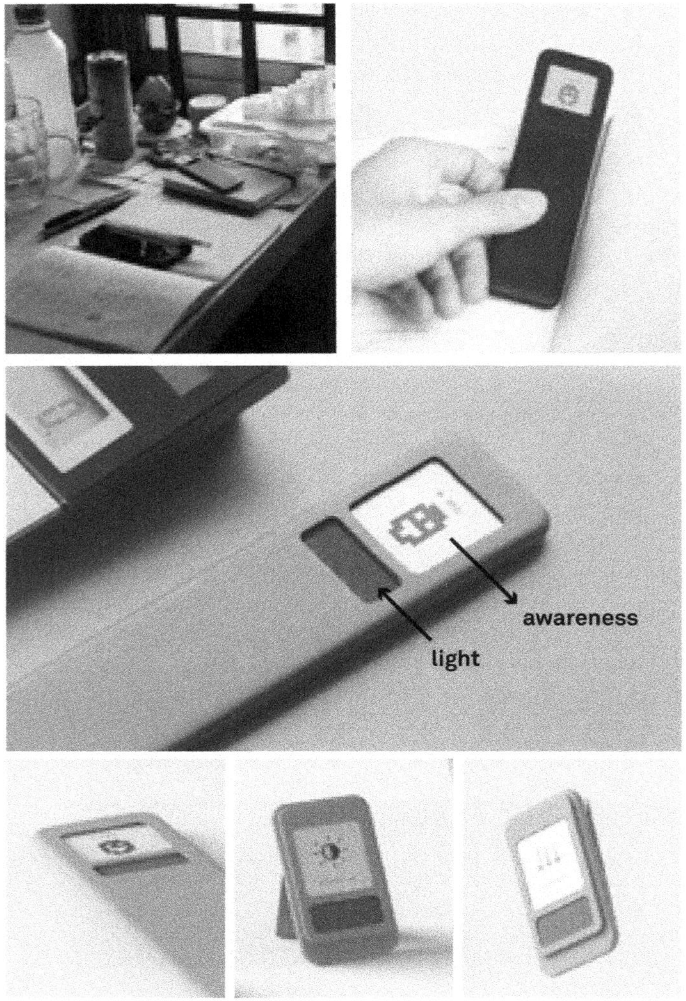

7. Discussion and Conclusion

In our journey towards Livefeed, we identified the following learning points and suggest the next steps for each.

Crowdsourcing everyday creativity

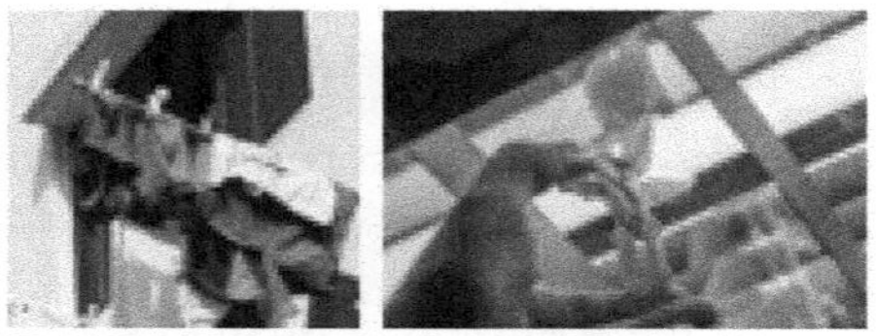

Everday inspiration - From a humble clothes peg typically clipped to a bamboo pole into a plug and play sensor that leeches off fluoroscent tubes

We benefited much from introducing the concept of energy harvesting objects to the users directly at an early stage of the design journey. By combining simple dummy probes with a set of questions, we were able to spark the curiosity and creativity from people, resulting in the proposal of novel potential usage scenarios that were derived from the interviewees' unique imaginations and observations. In the future, the long-term interaction and relationship between users and energy harvesting objects should be explored through extended deployment in the users' environment. Through this, we hope to observe how the awareness of ambient energy sources, evoked by these energy harvesting objects, could inspire people to discover new potential usage scenarios and explore them through the appropriation of the energy harvesting objects. In this sense, the two Livefeed prototypes can serve as the probes to discover how users explore these alternative energy sources and their respective use contexts.

Different cultures, different possibilities?

It was also noted that these two prototypes were ultimately chosen among other ideas to be developed due to its relevance to Singapore (prevalence of seasonal haze and high rates of myopia). We postulate that if the probing were to be done in different cultures, other interesting outcomes could be found. For example, would a person living in a polluted urban area use Airfeed when riding a bicycle so that they can learn about the air quality simultaneously? Can Lightfeed be adapted for people who are always exposed to the outdoor UV rays?

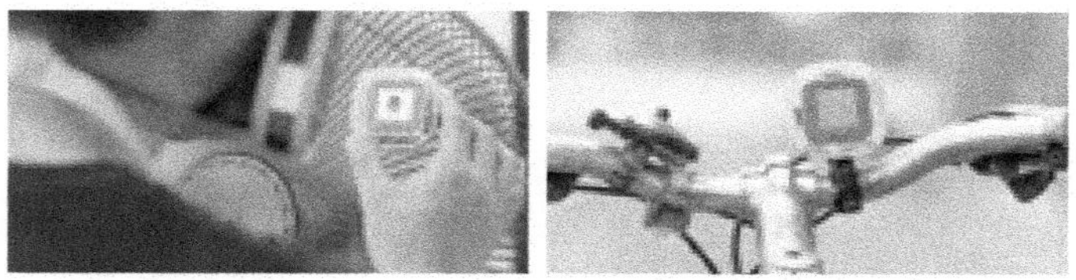

Preliminary usage scenarios that we proposed. Long term deployment with participants might yield other ideas, based on their needs.

Value of immediate feedback

Another key finding was that in short-term interactions with energy harvesting objects, the participants would like to see the objects' functions and values in a rather proximate manner, both in terms of time and the use context - they have a better sense of its energy harvesting nature when the outputs are relevant to the energy source (e.g. information about the air quality from the energy harvested from airflow) or the immediate context of use

"Its switching on, now got smiley face already!" Users were especially intrigued seeing how the prototype starts up when the fan it was attached to was switched on.

(e.g. information about the light level when reading a book). In the scope of this project, we designed the interface of the two Livefeed prototypes to be rather straightforward as we aimed to help users understand the utilitarian values of energy harvesting objects first. For future research, the interface could potentially be designed in a subtler manner so that it can allow for more open interpretation from users [11]. We hope that would enable users to formulate their own meanings to the interaction with the Livefeed prototypes and use them to serve a purpose that is more meaningful to their everyday lives.

With the proliferation of domestic home sensors set to continue, we believe the proposed further research can suggest new design directions for future smart homes and people's relationship with energy.

Acknowledgement

We would like to thank the participants who gave us much valuable feedback and inspiration, the reviewers and the Pictorial program chairs, especially Will Odom, for the valuable guidance. We also gratefully acknowledge Eric Paulos and James Pierce for their permission to use the images of Energy Parasite and Energy Memento respectively.

References

1. Boucher, A., Cameron, D. and Jarvis, N. Power to the people: Dynamic energy management through com¬munal cooperation. In Proc. DIS 2012, ACM Press (2012), 612-620.
2. Donelan, J.M. et al. Biomechanical energy harvesting: Generating electricity during walking with minimal user effort. Science, 319 (2008), 807–810.
3. Energy Parasites. http://www.livenv.net/energypara¬sites
4. Greenfield, A. Everyware: The dawning age of ubiqui¬tous computing. New Riders, 2010.
5. Intel, A Guide to the Internet of Things. http://www. intel.com/content/dam/www/public/us/en/images/iot/ guide-to-iot-infographic.png
6. Paradiso, J. and Starner, T. Energy scavenging for mobile and wireless electronics, Perv. Comput., IEEE (2005).
7. Pierce, J. and Paulos, E. Materializing energy. In Proc. DIS 2010, ACM Press (2010).
8. Pierce, J., and Paulos, E. Designing for emotional attachment to energy. In Proc. Design and Emotion 2010, 2010.
9. Pierce, J., and Paulos, E. A phenomenology of human-electricity relations. In Proc. of CHI 2011, ACM Press (2011), 2405-2408.
10. Pierce, J., and Paulos, E. Designing everyday tech¬nologies with human-power and interactive micro¬generation. In Proc. of DIS 2012, ACM Press (2012), 602-611.
11. Sengers, P., and Gaver, B. Staying open to interpretation: Engaging multiple meanings in design and evaluation. In Proc. of DIS 2006, ACM Press (2006), 99-108.
12. Wyld, D. C. RFID Tagging of Pharmaceuticals. In Encyclopedia of Healthcare Information Systems, IGI Global (2008), 1199-1209.

The Play Is a Hit – But How Can You Tell?

Measuring Audience Bio-responses Towards A Performance

Chen Wang[1,2], Pablo Cesar[1,3]
[1] Centrum Wiskunde & Informatica [2] Future Media Convergence Institute
[3] Delft University of Technology

ABSTRACT
Research has shown that physiological sensors provide a valuable mechanism for quantifying the experience of audiences attending cultural events. In the strength of the applause or questionnaires, bio-sensors provide fine-grained timed data that can be used to infer the quality of the experience of the audience members. Unfortunately, available commercial sensors are designed for lab or home usage and studies, focusing on the individual instead of the reactions of a crowd of people. In this study, we present our own designed physiological measurement system that overcomes the challenges of using and deploying sensors in a theatrical environment (anonymity and privacy, real-time gathering of data, support for large crowds of 30-100 people), and the wearable system has two unique features that distinguished between adult audience members and children ones. We report our experimental results which particularly answered the research questions proposed by the producer, director, and the artists.

Author Keywords
Physiological sensor network; GSR sensors; physiological computing; audience response; theatre performance

ACM Classification Keywords
H.5.m. Information interfaces and presentation (e.g., HCI): Miscellaneous.

INTRODUCTION
Arts add value to the lives of individuals and to society as a whole. Attendance and participation in arts can help individuals and society develop internal cognitive and emotional process. As a result of a cultural experience, such processes can have impact on external outcomes, e.g., increased educational attainment, reduced crime rates, health and overall well-being [29]. Besides, arts are a communicative experience, a bridge from artist to audience and a bridge linking individual beholders to one another [28]. Arts provide a medium where artists express their unique experience, and make their inner reality public and communicable to others. Therefore, arts are claimed to have cognitive, attitudinal, and behavioral benefits for users to develop their personal skills, and thus increase social bonding through arts participation [42].

Figure 1: Our physiological sensors were used during the War Horse performance Chinese version.

Arts engage audience at the emotional and intellectual as well as the aesthetic level. Understanding how the communication from artists to audience works can help artists appreciate the value of arts. Artistic creation is one of the most complex and mysterious activities of human consciousness, and the effects of arts are intangible and difficult to define. In particular, audience experience is an inner one (intensely personal and private), which makes it difficult to be appropriately measured.

C&C '17, June 27-30, 2017, Singapore, Singapore
© 2017 ACM. ISBN 978-1-4503-4403-6/17/06....$15.00
DOI:http://dx.doi.org/10.1145/3059454.3059465

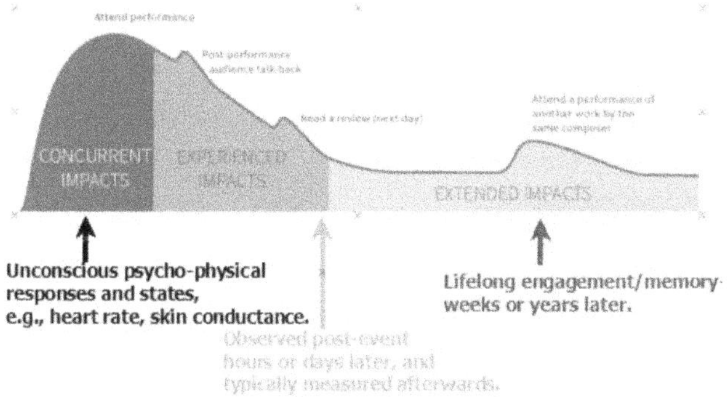

Figure 2 (drawn from [14]): three discernable types of impacts of arts defined by their temporal proximity to a cultural event.

The literature defines the impacts of arts on an audience as a progression of three stages based on their temporal proximity to the cultural event: concurrent impacts, experienced impacts, and extended impacts [14]. As shown in Figure 2, concurrent impacts occur during the event, and can be measured through biometric research. Experienced impacts can happen before, during and after the event, and are typically measured through post-event surveys and interviews. With respect to extended impacts, they are measured through retrospective interviewing and longitudinal tracking studies.

Measuring audience concurrent reaction plays an important role to evaluate the effectiveness of an artistic production. Because the concurrent reaction reflects how an audience 'look, listen, and enjoy' a performance, and it can be used to estimate the reception of intended effects. For instance, audience may feel challenged, moved, engaged by the show, and they may not notice the time. Such emotional response is then brought together to give an overall measurement of audience reaction.

Various stakeholders, including artists, producers, and directors, have sought out different methods to measure the impact of a performance. In general, it takes the form of a questionnaire [10, 21] handed out to audiences after a production. Some other methods rely on box office figures, social monitoring [9] or critics' reviews [12] to assess the quality of a show. However, such solutions are mainly the experienced impacts of plays, other than concurrent impacts. In addition, individual's concurrent impact may not be always tracked by subjective measurements, as individual may respond to cultural events without being consciously aware of it, and any conscious reflection (e.g., using a labeling system [22, 34] during a performance) on the individual's state may interfere with the experience (i.e., interrupt their sense of flow or absorption).

Physiological and pre-cognitive psychological responses can be used to objectively measure the concurrent impacts of audiences [19]. Compared to the other methods, physiological responses can be measured non-intrusively at the very moments at which they occur, because intellectual and emotional reactions from the audience can take place at any time during the events. A number of studies have sought to capture biometrical data as a means of gauging audience responses to arts, by tracking eye movements [11], heart rate [39], skin conductance [43], emotional response [22] and aesthetic judgments [39] during performances. However, this method is not widely applied due to the complexity of setting up the biosensor infrastructure, the bulky form factors, and high prices of the commercial products.

In this paper, we propose an open-source solution to design, develop, and deploy a GSR sensor system, particularly designed for theatergoers. This new measurement system gives theatre experts an intriguing, alternative method by which we evaluate the quality of their output. By using our method, theater experts can achieve valid results, which are certainly an improvement on some of the more basic instrumental methods that have been used in the past. Thus, the main contribution of this paper are twofold:

C1: *The new GSR sensor system can be effectively deployed at theatrical environment;*

C2: *The obtained sensor data can be used to measure the concurrent audience response and have better results compared to other traditional methods (e.g., questionnaires)*

Motivated by the intrinsic and instrumental benefits from the arts, using video recordings as the stimulus and executing experiments in lab conditions, we run the studies in a real performance, and captured the realistic audience GSR readings.

Research Questions

We conducted a field study with the National Theater Company of China in particular for the Chinese version of War Horse. The Chinese version of War Horse is the first co-production between the National Theatre of Great Britain and the National Theatre of China (Figure 1). The original British version was first premiered in London in 2007, and the show has been seen by over 6 million people worldwide and been performed over four thousand times. In the year of 2015, War Horse took its biggest jump into China.

Challenges by experts

We interviewed (semi-structured) the producer, the director, and the stage manager from the National Theater Company. Li Dong, producer of the Chinese version of War Horse, received the interview in Shanghai, China (Figure 3). Li Dong stated that there is a need for quantified audience feedback to resolve ambiguity. For instance, he was unsure of the impact of the War Horse performance in China. In England, the production was popular for all ages. Even though the script was adapted from a children's novel, it dealt with history and complex emotions. Therefore, he was not sure how audiences in China would receive the show. In particular, he was extremely interested in knowing how child audience would react to the show. At the initial stage, they would like to prompt the performance to targeted at child market, but they lack quantified data to support the decision.

Figure 3: The interview with the producer Li Dong from China National Theater.

Furthermore, he felt that there is a need for concrete understanding of audiences' reception rather than an ambiguous perception of how popular the show is. For instance, mentioned their interest in how many performance scenes related to Joey (a horse, the main character of the play) would arouse the interest of the Chinese audience. With this understanding, they could make better plans for marketing strategies and promotional-related materials.

Besides, both producer and director felt that audience feedback could help them make informed choices. In particular, Li Dong mentioned that almost 70% of the theatregoers in China are females and they bring along their male friends and children to watch a show, as such, it will be useful to know what elements of the show are evoking for females and the difference in emotional intensities between female and male audience members.

In addition, by understanding the elements of a play that are stimulating the majority of the audience (e.g., the thrilling climax scene about the competition between Joey and Topthorn,), the director can make more astute choices in the later production and create more successful performances.

Last, all of them stated that a quantified audience experience should not limit artistic expression but help to form the basis of certain choices. For instance, selecting elements or narrating the story from which character's point of view, it may help generate audience interest. Besides, they foresee the possibilities to use audience response in real-time to explore new performing areas (e.g., an interactive play that is particularly designed to have the different endings based on the feedback of audience).

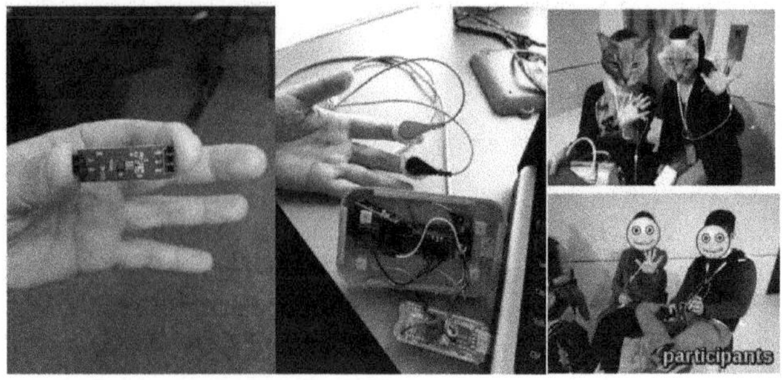

Figure 4: the GSR sensor (left). The Jeenode board and GSR sensor are connected and mounted in a customized 3d printed box(middle). The Chinese audience wore the sensors during the War Horse performance (right).

Figure 5: the child version GSR sensors. One of child participants wore the sensor during the performance (left). The five housing design of the sensors (middle). The sensors used in the experiments (right).

Research questions are from the interviews. The interviews revealed that audience, e.g., the event-related reactions, were the main interest of the National Theater. We believe that a bio-sensor system has significant advantages to measure the continuous audience experience, e.g., emotional intensities from the audience, because the sensors provide seamless and continuous data that map audience's reactions to the events. By summarizing the interviews, we identified the four research questions:

R1: How many performance scenes related to Joey aroused the imterest of audience?

R2: Which performance elements aroused the interest of female and male audience members respectively?

R3: How female audience members reacted differently to males during the thrilling climax scene about the competition between Joey and Topthorn.

R4: What were the different emotional intensities between parents and children?

In this paper, we first report on the related work, and then we present the methodology. After that, we show the hardware development. Finally, we report on results from our work. Then, we conclude the paper with discussion and conclusion.

RELATED WORK

GSR Sensors

Electrodermal activity (GSR) is also known as skin conductance, GSR, electrodermal response, skin conductance response (SCR), and skin conductance level (SCL). GSR refers to the changes in skin conductance at the surface, reflecting activity within the sympathetic axis of the autonomic nervous system (ANS). Autonomic responses in the skin, e.g., sweating, piloerection, and vasomotor changes, can thus be elicited by various emotional states via the Papez circuit in the limbic system [32]. Furthermore, it is widely recognized that increased GSR responses can be provoked by attention-related stimuli or tasks [16, 38].

GSR includes two variables. The first one is skin conductance level (SCL), indicating the slow and tonic changes measured across many discrete stimuli. The second one is electrodermal responses (EDR) related to specific stimuli, representing the quick and phasic changes imposed on shifts in tonic level in conductivity [18, 37]. In general, there is a delay of 1-3 seconds between stimulus and SCR onset. Hands and feet can be used to measure GSR, where the density of the sweat glands is the highest.

There are some commercial GSR sensors available on the market, but they are not suitable for theaters. First, they are generally designed for lab studies, using technologies like Bluetooth [20, 27, 40] which are intended for individual rather than for measuring audience at a large scale. Second, commercial sensors are generally uniformly designed for a controlled laboratory experiment [4, 5, 24, 25], without considering user experience in a specific application domain. Third, some commercial smart watches have sensors integrated. In this case, the anonymity of the sensor signals is not preserved (since the mobile phone may have to sign on for using the web server). In addition, we foresee that theaters companies will provide the audience with their own lightweight sensors and deploy a specific network for the purpose of better understanding and quantifying the audience experience.

Physiological Sensor Network

The current available personal sensor networks (PSNs) are mainly developed and designed for lab [1, 2, 3] and home studies (e.g., monitoring elderly people) [20, 27]. In the majority of the cases, they communicate through Bluetooth, which is an excellent solution for measuring individuals [26, 33]. Besides, some studies [17, 35, 43] developed a PSN by using open source alternatives (e.g., Arduino, connected with Zigbee/Xbee or WiFi), which have enabled us to study several use cases [20, 23]. Recently, with the advent of miniature electronics, radio technology provides alternative frequency bands to construct a wireless network [40, 36, 41]. Interestingly, most of these products were used on healthcare applications (i.e., monitoring the heart rate of people [30, 45]).

Audience Research in Performing Arts

Researchers have developed numerous ways to measure, interrogate and assess audience's response to arts and culture, including biometric measurements, post-event surveying, qualitative post-event research, and longitudinal, or retrospective studies. Biometric measurements objectively manifest audience response to the aesthetic experience [43, 11, 39], even though interpreting such responses is difficult. Nonetheless, knowledge of audience bio-response will be of considerable value in advancing our conceptual understanding of impact on the individual[14]. Post-event surveys have been widely applied to evaluate the short-term effects of specific cultural events [10, 21], but surveying requires researchers to design the constructs in advance. Furthermore, surveys can only capture the conscious experience of respondents. There is limited comparability across events, and they fail to capture effects that unfold over time. Qualitative methods allow informants to reflect on the areas that are most significant to them. Unlike surveys, qualitative studies can help researchers contextualize numerical data. Longitudinal impacts on audience studies add durable value on cultural experiences [31, 8]. While the retrospective identification of cultural events may not be helpful to assess the impacts of specific artistic works, it can inform us how cultural participation plays an important role within the large scope of people's lives [14].

METHODOLOGY

We used the interviews to conduct this research. The pre - interviews were conducted to collect the research questions, and the post-interviews were used to evaluate the performance of our method. All these work were done with the experts.

The semi-conduct interview protocol was performed. The pre- interviews were taken in two rounds, and each round lasted 30 minutes, and the video and the audio were recorded. Five researchers took observational notes during interviews. After the interviews, researchers discussed the observational notes and identified the potentially interesting topics. More specific research questions were concluded after the discussion. The post-interviews were conducted two times.We first presented the results to the expert, and then we showed them to the theater company.

INFRASTRUCTURE

In this section, we present the GSR sensor infrastructure (Figure 6). The process to produce the newest factory-made production, which was in the War Horse experiment. The new sensors have two versions (Figure 4 & Figure 5), which aimed at two different audience categories: adult and children. We first introduced our own GSR sensors, and then we presented the development of the software and the mobile app.

Sensors

The knowledge for building our GSR sensors was based on previous work [15]. We built our GSR sensors by using Jeenode [1]. Based on our previous experience, we know that the factory PCBA service is much better than the extensive self -soldering work. Besides, for certain quantity, e.g., 100-200 sensors, the factory solution is much cheaper and quicker. Once the prototype was available, we sent the circuit to our supplier for production. Another advantage is that such manner can control the size and the interface of the sensors, so that we can easily intergrade the sensors to the development board and make small and comfortable wearables. At last, the whole system was put into a 3D printed casing. In order to guarantee the most unobtrusive and comfortable experience for theatergoers, we sent the sample product to our project partner in China for evaluation with a Chinese audience. After several versions and modification, we came to the final design as shown in Figure 4 and Figure 5, each sensor only weighing 76g.

Network topology and Media Access Layer (MAC)

We used 433MHz (free Industrial, Scientific, and Medical Band) to establish the wireless sensor network. Once the frequency band was set, we had to decide a media access mechanism and a network topology. The network is formed by a group of sensors and a sink node connected to a central server. Since the sink node communicates with a group of sensors, in order to minimize the packets collision, we implemented a polling method in the MAC layer in the C programming language. By this method, all the sensor nodes wait for a pull message sent by the sink node. Each time, the sink node broadcasts a poll message with a specific sensor ID, only the sensor with that ID can send packets, while the other sensors go to the standby state. In this way, we try to minimize the collisions in the wireless channel. However, the packet loss caused by the crowd presence was unlikely to be avoided in theatrical environment. Finally, the sensor system reached the 4Hz sampling rate. The architecture of the GSR wireless sensor network is shown in Figure 6.

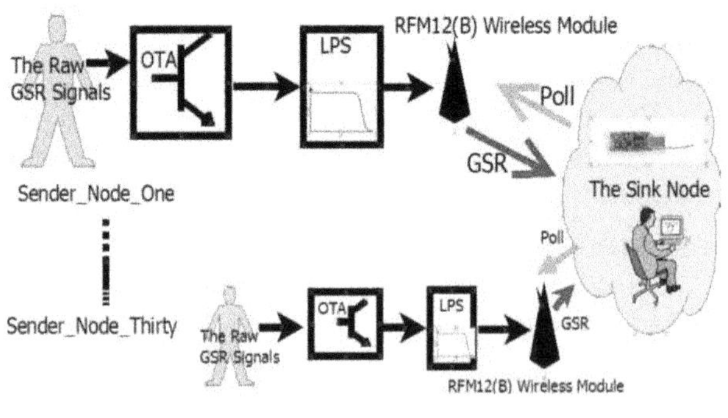

Figure 6: The schematic of the wireless GSR sensor network

[1] http://jeelabs.net/projects/hardware/wiki/JeeNode

Software

For Warhorse experiment, we adapted the method developed by Fleureau et. al [25] by observing SCR signals invoked by stimulus. The method first extracts the SCR signals based on the timeline, and then defines which SCR responses were statistically significant when compared to the background noise. In such a manner, we can provide links between the significant audience bio- responses and the related performing events (e.g., the appearance of Joey), so our customers can have a better understanding in terms of which events substantially affected the audience and which ones did not.

Extracting the SCR signals from the sensors requires signal processing, filtering, smoothing, and derivative procedures, as shown in Figure 7. First the raw signals are scaled and filtered by a 2Hz low-pass filter ($G(t)$). After that, the numerical derivation performed, but only the positive phasic changes are kept while the negative ones are ignored (from $G'(t)$ to $G'_+(t)$). The reason is that the negative phasic changes are not of our interest, as they only reflect the physical recovering from a stimulus. In the next step, we apply a moving window (W_i, W_j :i, j = 1......k, where k is the number of windows) with the window size of 120 samples (30 seconds), and the overlapping size of 60 (15 seconds) to smooth and compute the mean values of the derivative signal $G(i)$. Finally (since each individual may have a different amplitude for the derivative GSR signals), we normalized the computed signals by using the sum of subsampled skin response values as the denominator to calculate the individual mean arousal value ($G_n(i)$: n=1......N, where N is the number of users) (2).

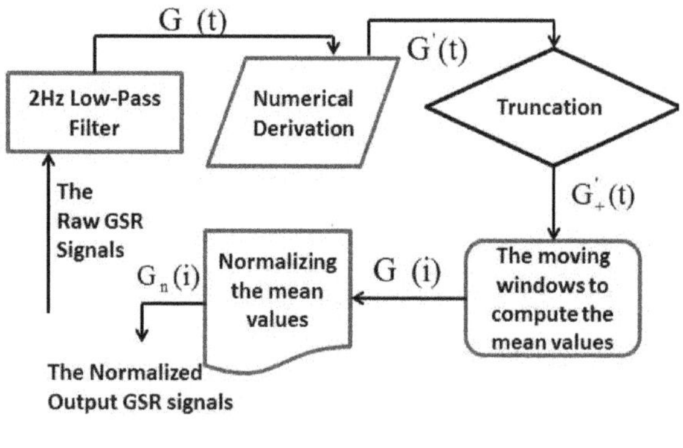

Figure 7: The description of the different steps of the algorithm for processing the raw GSR signals.

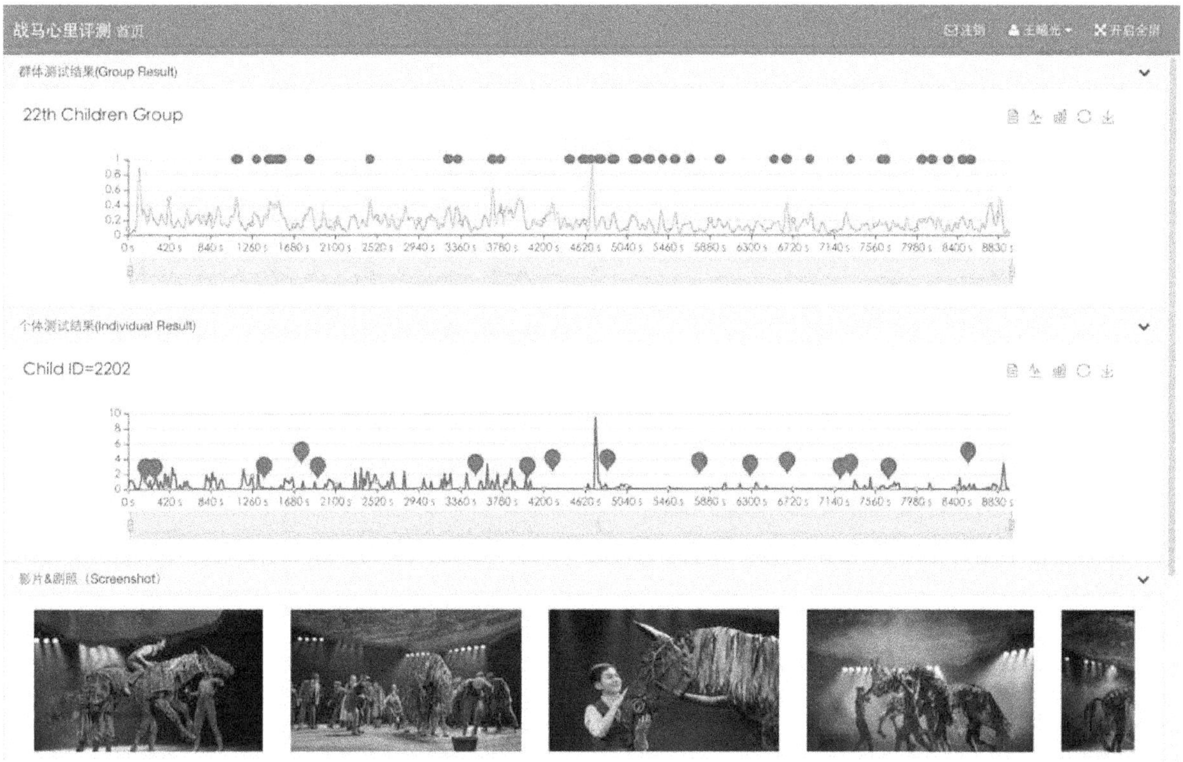

Figure 8: the visualization results based on the performance of 22th, November. The first row displays the significant arousal moments from the group children. The second row shows the significant performing events evoked from the child id (2202, his parental id: 2206 in Figure 10). By clicking the red dots in the second row, the related performing scenes (the screenshot) will be displayed in the below.

$$G_n(i) = \frac{G(i)}{\sum_{j=1}^{k} G(j)} = \frac{\int_{W_i} G'_+(t)dt}{\sum_{j=1}^{k} \int_{W_j} G'_+(t)dt} \quad (1)$$

The bilateral Mann-Whitney-Wilcoxon (MWW) test is performed to define the significant SCR responses. The mean p values are computed by averaging the p-values of the bilateral MWW test performed between the latent unknown distribution of $G_n(i)$ and the background noise. We define 10% of the computation results with the lowest mean as background noise [25]. Only an associated p value lower t han 5% is considered as significantly different from the background noise.

Trigger App

We created a trigger app in a mobile phone in order to annotate significant events in the timeline of the play, and to align them to the sensor recordings (Figure 9). Using the trigger interface, we can manually type the description about the performing events, and the system automatically records the time stamps of each description into the excel file while showings the local time on the app, as shown in Figure 9. The reason for developing such app was that the theater company did not allow us to record the performance due to copyright issues. In order to time align the sensor readings with the performing events, we needed this handy tool to manually type the events into the app, so that later on we could synchronize the sensor data with the events.

Development on the visualization platform

The psychology data analysis and viewer platform specialized for War Horse is a customizable end to end solution for the audience emotional intensity analysis and result visualization (as shown in Figure 8,9,11,12). The platform is a Web based application which was developed with Nodejs and MongoDB. It could dynamically load the raw data and generate the interactive charts in real-time. It can be divided into several major models, including raw data processing, data standardization, data analysis, result showing and the system configuration. Once the raw data was imported or updated into the database, they will be processed automatically, and the data will be stored and transferred as Json file. When an individual login the system, the username will be recognized and automatically associated with its ID number and his or her profiles which have been input to the database previously. The system then loads the processed data and creates the charts with the mark points. The end users could use the interactive components on the Web UI to compare with various group results.

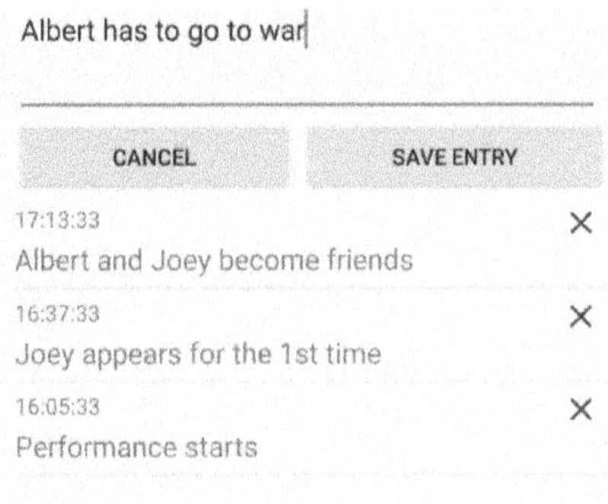

Figure 9: Trigger app to map events and sensor readings

EXPERIMENTS

There were in total 5 rounds experiments conducted. We recruited 90 adult participants (Male: Avg.: 33, STD: 12.4; Female: Avg.: 28.9, STD: 8.04) who joined 3 rounds of experiments (the same performance but at the different date). In addition, we also recruited 60 family participants (parents with their children (6-9 years old, Male: 57.1%; Female: 42.9%) to join the 2 rounds experiments respectively. However, since in the second round the child age scope was out of our recruitment requirements, so that we only report the results based on the first round experiment. Before the performance started, we explained the purpose of the experiment, and provided pre-questionnaires and consent forms. After this, the audience wore the sensors at their non-dominating hand, and they went inside the theater 15 minutes before the performance started. There was a 15 minutes break between the first part and the second part of the performance. When the performance finished, we helped the audience members take off the sensors. After that, there were post-performance questionnaires and interviews.

Before the real experiments, the project manager conducted all the communication work with the theater company and made sure that there was always an effective link between them and us. We critically evaluated the performance venue in order to understand the experimental limitations and how we could establish a biosensor infrastructure there.

All the seats for the participants were pre-reserved, and all the experimental procedures were prepared in advance and each task was assigned to the responsible person. The pre and post questionnaires were provided before and after the performance, and we also had interviews with the participants.

RESULTS

The experimental results show that our sensor system is robust for the theatrical environment. In addition, the developed algorithm successfully helped us answer all the research questions. The wearing experience from the audience feedback was positive. The deployment of the whole system took around 15-20 minutes from welcoming the participants, putting on the sensors, testing, filling the questionnaires, to answering the participants' questions.

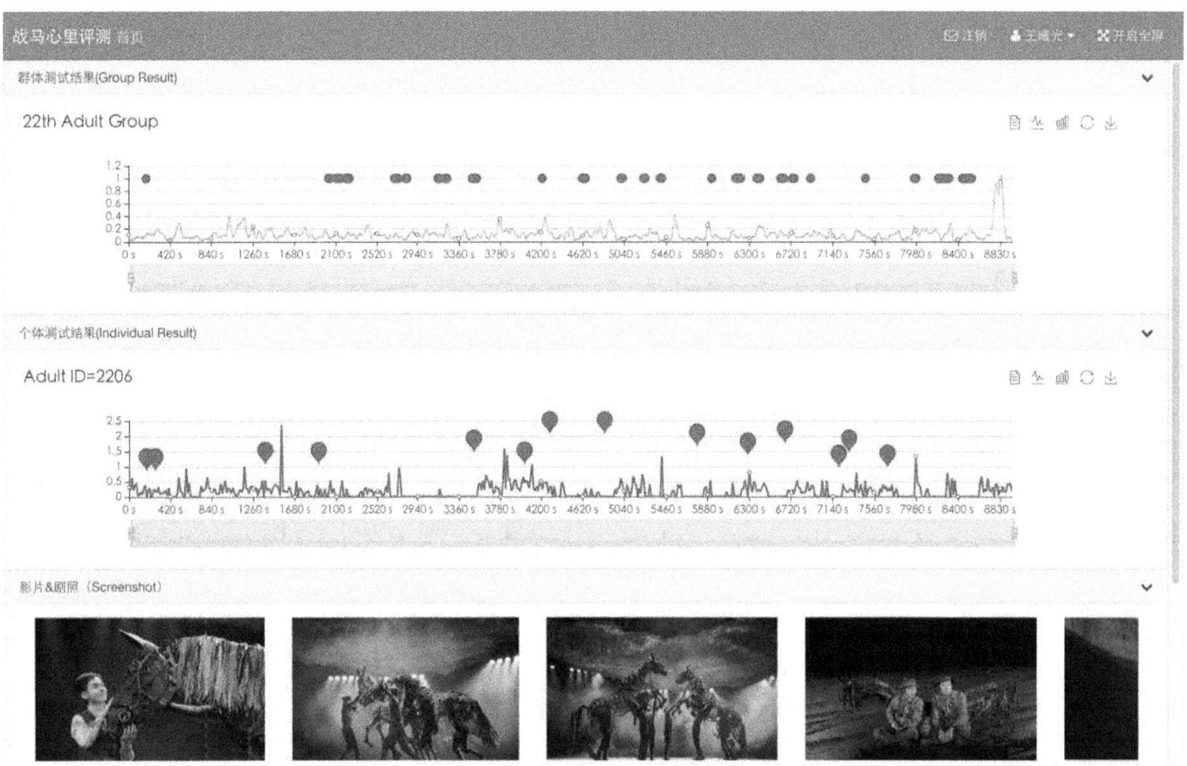

Figure 10: the visualization results based on the performance of 22th, November. The first row displays the significant arousal moments from the adult group. The second row shows the significant performing events evoked from the parental id (2206). By clicking the red dots in the second row, the related performing scenes (the screenshot) will be displayed in the below.

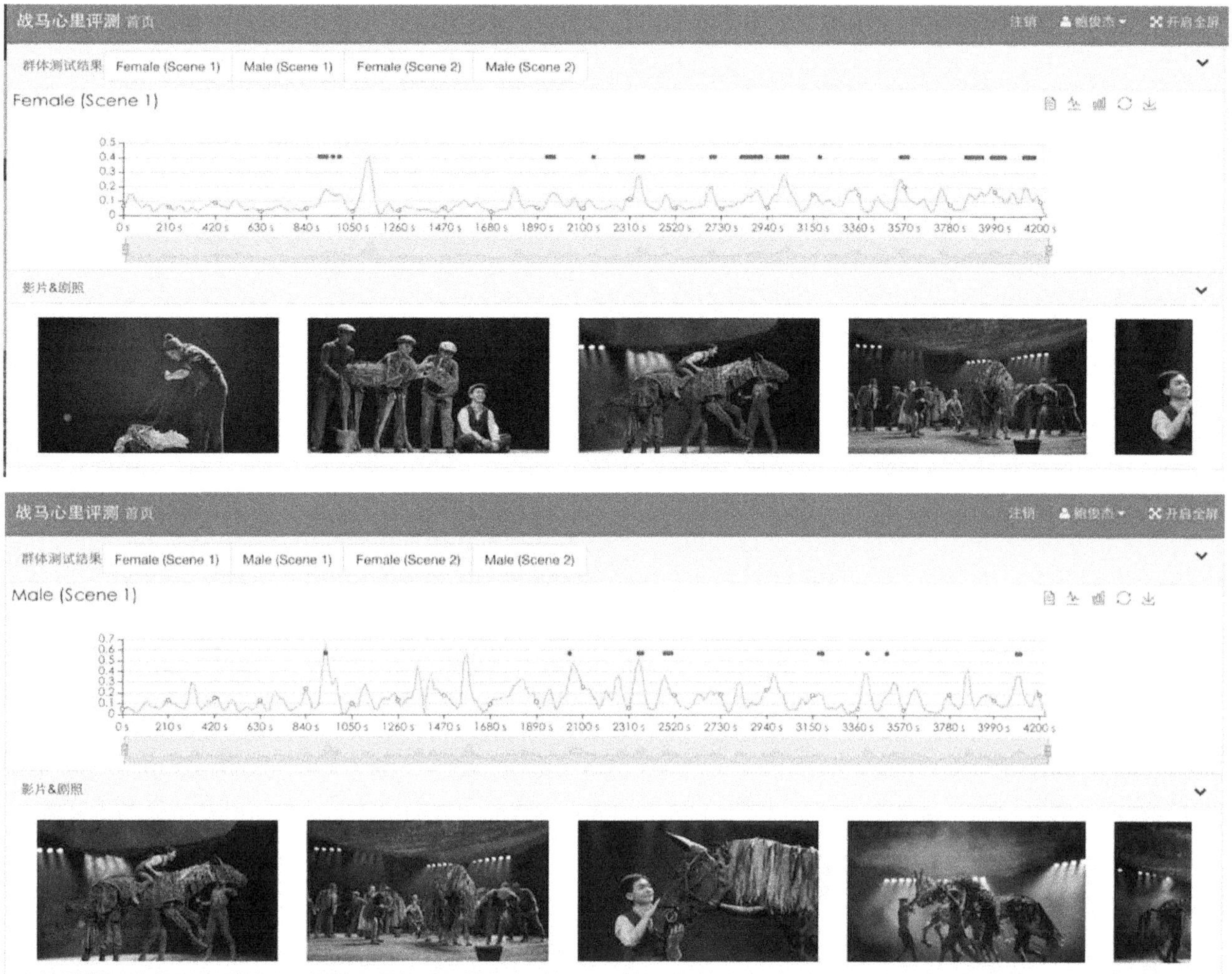

Figure 11: The significant arousal events compared between the female audience and the male audience in the scene 1.

Audience responses

Family audience

The results on the family audience were surprisingly interesting (R4). Based on the marketing investigation results from China theater company, the majority of the parents thought that the performance would be difficult to understand for children. However, based on our results, we found that the emotional intensities elicited from the children audiences were significantly stronger than their parents （Figure 8 & Figure 10）. Besides, from the subjective reports and the interviews with the children, they enjoyed the performance even though they might not fully understand. In comparison, the parental experience revealed that they had less emotional intensities compared to the children. According to their report, they were extremely tired during the day time, because they had to take care of their kids before they went to the theater. During the show, they were distracted by their children instead of enjoying a performance; some of them even slept during the play.

The sensor results also showed that during the whole performance parental audiences had less arousal moments compared to their children during the whole performance. For instance, there are in total 226 scenes where the Joey appeared: the children were significantly evoked by 73 ones, while their parents were only stimulated by 35 ones. Furthermore, compared to their parents, the children also had more substantial responses towards the emotional scenes when compared to their parents. For instance, there are in total 35 emotional scenes, where the children were statistical elicited by 13 ones, which was as twice as their parents.

The results also guide the theater company to adjust their marketing strategy. Before the experiment, the theater company arranged a visiting event to the back stage exhibition, where Joey and Thompton, and the family audience can have a direct contact with the horse puppet. One of the group participated in the visiting events before they watched the show, and their emotional intensities from the sensor readings were significantly reduced compared to the other. We assume that the familiarity has decreased the

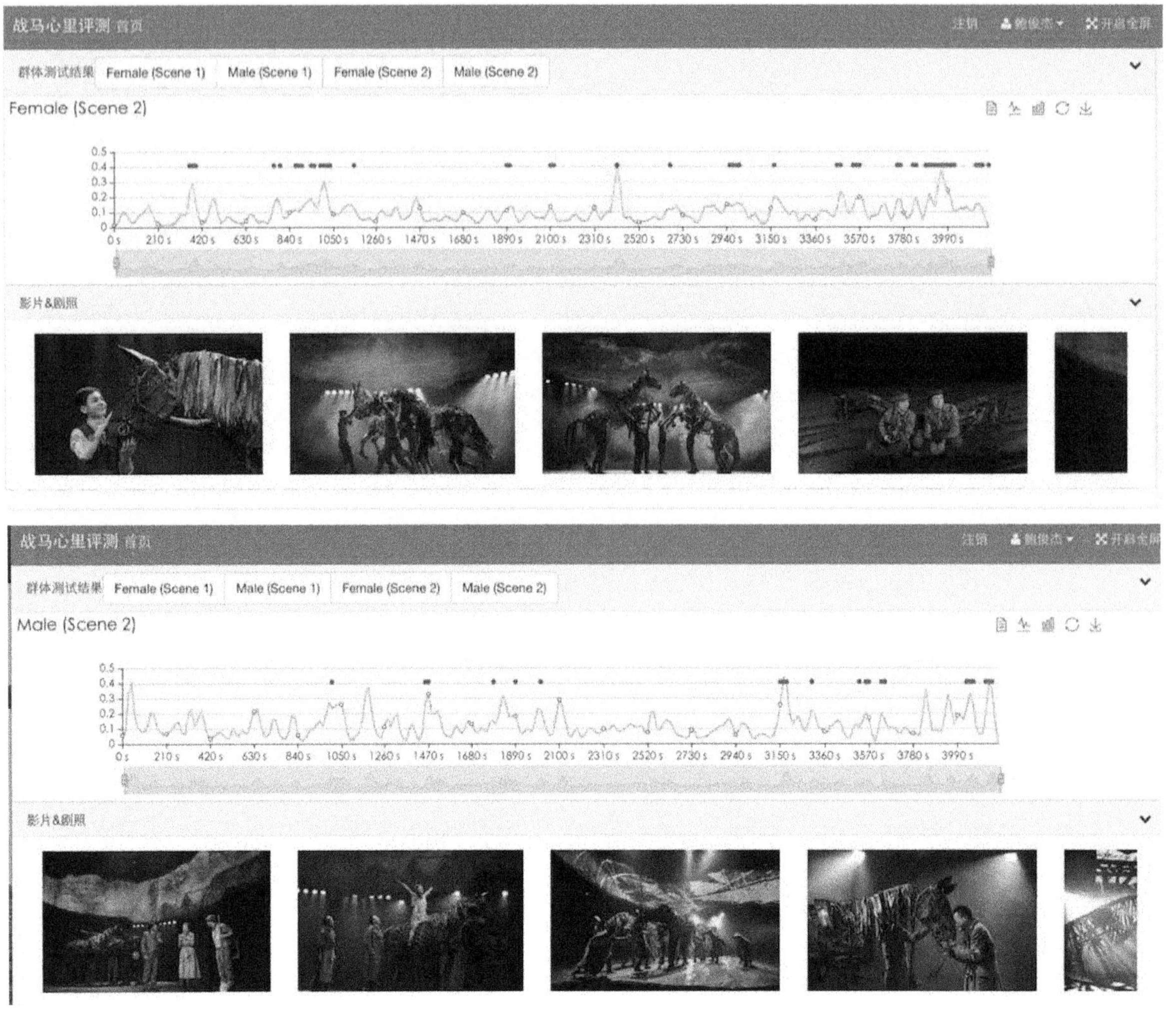

Figure 12: The significant arousal events compared between the female audience and the male audience in the scene 2.

emotional intensities during the watching experience after visiting the back stage exhibition. Based on our reports, the theatre company has adjusted their marketing strategy: inviting visit at the back stage only after the show.

Adult audience

As shown in Figure 11, we found that the interest of both male and female participants was significantly aroused during the thrilling scenes where the competition between the two main protagonists Joey and Topthorn happened, but the duration of this significance lasted longer for females than for males, as indicated by the length of red bars (R3). There were 226 scenes related to Joey. The interest of audience was significantly aroused in about 32 of those (R1). Interestingly, by observing the p values, we found that in some of the scenes both male and female audience was stimulated, but in some of the scenes females were more responsive than males. By comparing the results from the first and the second part (Figure 11, 12), we found that significant responses from females were more intense compared to the ones from males (R2). Besides, the duration of the significant responses of the female audiences was generally longer than those of the males (R2).

Feedback from experts

We invited theater experts to interpret the results. In general, they write journals on a performance based on their own feedback, or they interview several theatergoers in order to obtain the audience opinions. Even though sometime experts combine the internet information and generate a report, but such manner has a big delay. The traditional way of collecting data is based on small samples. If big samples are required, they have to sort out other methods, e.g., spreading out questionnaires. Still, for news reporting, the timing is extremely important. The experts think that our method can provide rich and timing data for them to write reports.

The results from the gender difference helped the experts prove their assumptions on audience watching experiences. In general, the female audience is easily touched by the emotional stories, while male is more linked to action scenes. The experts pointed out that the results revealed that the emotional scenes triggered the female audience the most, while the male audience's interest was more aroused in the action scenes in the first part of the show (R2). While in the second part of the show, both genders were more connected to the ending in which the soldier Albert met Joey again, but the important scene describing the girl Emilie and Joey significantly elicited the female audiences (R2).

Feedback from China National Theater Company

The producer Li Dong received our interview again. He was extremely excited about the results. He told us that this method well solved the contradictions between him and the directors, as sometimes they may have different thoughts about how a performance should be constructed. The results also stimulated them to be more creative in the future artistic production, i.e., creating an interactive performance, where sensors can be used for visualization or interactions. The most important inspiring thing is that this method could help him define a marketing strategy. For instance, if he knew the children were intensively attached by the show, he would have invested the budget to promote on the children market.

DISCUSSION

This paper presents our new GSR sensor system, particularly suits for a theatrical environment. By using our method, theatrical experts can assess whether a show was more of a success, for instance it affected a handful of people profoundly, but left the majority nonplussed. Compared to the traditional methods, physiological measurements are more suitable to measure the concurrent audience response, and the sensor data can be effectively connected to the specific events during a play.

The new sensor system brings a new perspective on audience research in a theatrical environment. Based on the results, theater companies can develop a new business model and make better business decisions, i.e., promoting the show to the children market. In addition, our method also opens a new path for the future creative artistic production. The experiments revealed that the bio-sensor method has advantages to record the continuous data, and they can be easily mapped to the certain performing events. In such a manner, the theater experts can have a direct visualization platform to reflect their performance, and interpret them from different perspectives. In addition, due to the liveness of the sensors, the interactive artistic production can be vividly designed, which may bring a total new performing style in the future.

Collecting data related to emotional arousal is not new, as skin conductance has been studied for more than 100 years. For this study, the creative issues are how this technology can measure, communicate, and transform emotions from audience, and how we thinking about it. During working closely with theatrical expert, powerful new insights and changes can be achieved with the help of GSR sensors. In other words, objective data about audience emotions bring us more power than subjective reports for a performance. In our case, sensor data revealed more insights with audience affective experience, which enable theater experts to pinpoint what caused such reactions and work on in the future how to design a show aiming at a better affective experience.

Nevertheless, a number of issues still remain. First, the algorithm does not say anything about valence. If valence is required to be defined, additional information is necessary. Secondly, algorithms need to be more robust to some artifacts (e.g., body movements). If researchers want to use our sensor system on a real-time application, more sophisticated algorithms dependent on the experimental objectives should be developed. Third, the network should be more modular. Researchers should be aware that a theatrical environment is rather different to a laboratory condition. In theaters, especially when the crowd is present, the network performance can be rather critical. However, we found that packet loss is more tied to individuals rather than events that influence all sensors at the same time. Therefore, adding more sensors into the network may be a good strategy to cope with packet loss. For instance, we need to work out a solution that can automatically choose free frequency spacing and assign the sensor ID, so that we can avoid coincidently picking up a busy frequency channel

The operational procedure can be further improved. We have learned that a real-time monitoring system should be incorporated. When the experiment starts, we need to have a view of the states of the sensors. In case one of the sensors does not work, we can always replace it. Last, the hardware needs to be improved in the future, as the mechanical wires can cause the connection problems.

CONCLUSION

In this paper, we have reported how the creative GSR sensors measured audience concurrent response during the Chinese version of War Horse. In particular, we have detailed our design and development decisions for establishing an effective GSR sensor network in theaters. The resulting infrastructure, hardware and software, have shown that the system is robust, that it can be easily deployed in theaters, can simultaneously and accurately capture the GSR signals from the audience members.

The benefit of GSR technology enable theater experts to have a new understanding on audience emotional experience (as significantly different SCR responses) in a show. The sensor data provide insights with which gender and age impacts can be effectively visualized. The results motivated theatrical experts to be more innovative at both current and future artistic production.

In the future we will continue to improve the hardware, and develop the related software modules for the new GSR sensor system. Besides, since the Jeenode platform still has the capability of carrying more sensors, we will investigate how other types of sensors (e.g., ECG sensor and acceleration sensors), can be integrated into our sensor network in order to provide a more complete representation of audience emotional experience.

ACKNOWLEDGEMENTS
This work was supported in part by funding from the European Community's Seventh Framework Programme (FP7/2007-2013) under grant agreement no. ICT-2011-287760, and in part by funding from Xinhuanet.

REFERENCES
1. The Thought Technology Ltd.: http://thoughttechnology.com/
2. Biopac: http://www.biopac.com/electrodermal-finger-transducer-ss
3. Q sensor: http://qsensor-support.affectiva.com/
4. Shimmer sensor: http://www.shimmersensing.com/
5. Empatica: https://www.empatica.com/e4-wristband
6. https:/en.wikipedia.org/wiki/Heuristic
7. Markusen, Ann, and Anne Gadwa. "Creative Placemaking: a white paper for the Mayors' Institute on City Design." National Endowment for the Arts. Online. Available at http://www. nea. gov/pub/CreativePlacemaking-Paper. pdf (accessed January 2010) (2010).
8. Walmsley, Ben. 2013. '"A big part of my life": a qualitative study of the impact of theatre.' Arts Marketing: An International Journal 3:1. 73 – 87.
9. Louise Barkhuus and Chiara Rossitto. 2016. Acting with Technology: Rehearsing for Mixed-Media Live Performances. In *Proceedings of the 2016 CHI Conference on Human Factors in Computing Systems* (CHI '16). ACM, New York, NY, USA, 864-875. DOI: https://doi.org/10.1145/2858036.2858344.
10. Bunting, Catherine, and John Knell. "Measuring quality in the cultural sector. The Manchester metrics pilot: Findings and lessons learned." Arts Council England (2014).
11. Stevens, Catherine, Renee Glass, Emery Schubert, Johnson Chen, and Heather Winskel. 2007. 'Methods for measuring audience reactions'. Proceedings of International Conference on Music Communications Science, Sydney.
12. David Goergen, Angelo Migliosi, Vijay K. Gurbani, Radu State, and Thomas Engel. 2014. Spatial and temporal analysis of Twitter: a tale of two countries. In *Proceedings of the Conference on Principles, Systems and Applications of IP Telecommunications* (IPTComm '14). ACM, New York, NY, USA, Article 5 , 6 pages. DOI=http://dx.doi.org/10.1145/2670386.2670392
13. Tom A. Garner and Mark N. Grimshaw. "The physiology of fear and sound: working with biometrics toward automated amotion recognition in adaptive gaming system." 2013. In proceedings of IADIS International Journal. Vol. 11. No. 2. Pp. 77-91. ISSN: 1645-7641.
14. Carnwath, John D., and Alan S. Brown. "Understanding the value and impacts of cultural experiences." Manchester, United Kingdom: Arts Council England (2014).
15. Guerreiro, José. A biosignal embedded system for physiological computing. Diss. Instituto Superior de Engenharia de Lisboa, 2013.
16. R. Edelberg 1972. "Electrodermal recovery rate, goal-orientation, and aversion," Psychophysiology, vol. 9, pp. 512–520, Sep.
17. Emre Ertin, Nathan Stohs, Santosh Kumar, Andrew Raij, Mustafa al'Absi, and Siddharth Shah. 2011. AutoSense: unobtrusively wearable sensor suite for inferring the onset, causality, and consequences of stress in the field. In Proceedings of the 9th ACM Conference on Embedded Networked Sensor Systems (SenSys '11). ACM New York, NY, USA, 274-287. DOI=10.1145/2070942.2070970
18. Don C. Fowles. 2007. Psychophysiology and Psychopathology: A Motivational Approach. Article first published online: 30 JAN 2007. Volume 25, Issue 4, pages 373–391. DOI: 10.1111/j.1469-8986.1988.tb01873.x
19. Lindgaard, Gitte, and TW Allan Whitfield. "Integrating aesthetics within an evolutionary and psychological framework." Theoretical Issues in Ergonomics Science 5.1 (2004): 73-90.
20. Charalampos Liolios, Charalampos Doukas, George Fourlas, and Ilias Maglogiannis. 2010. An overview of body sensor networks in enabling pervasive healthcare and assistive environments. In Proceedings of the 3rd International Conference on PErvasive Technologies Related to Assistive Environments (PETRA '10), Fillia Makedon, Ilias Maglogiannis, and Sarantos Kapidakis (Eds.). ACM, New York, NY, USA, , Article 43 , 10 pages. DOI=10.1145/1839294.1839346
21. Celine Latulipe, Erin A. Carroll, and Danielle Lottridge. 2011. Evaluating longitudinal projects combining technology with temporal arts. In Proceedings of the SIGCHI Conference on Human Factors in Computing Systems (CHI '11). ACM, New York, NY, USA, 1835-1844. DOI=http://dx.doi.org/10.1145/1978942.1979209
22. Celine Latulipe, Erin A. Carroll, and Danielle Lottridge. 2011. Love, hate, arousal and engagement: exploring audience responses to performing arts. In Proceedings of the SIGCHI Conference on Human Factors in Computing Systems (CHI '11). ACM (2011), New York, NY, USA, 1845-1854. DOI=10.1145/1978942.1979210
23. Gang Li, Haifeng Chen, and Jungtae Lee. 2010. A wireless EEG monitor system based on BSN node. In Proceedings of the 1st ACM International Health Informatics Symposium (IHI '10), Tiffany Veinot (Ed.).

ACM, New York, NY, USA, 758-764. DOI=10.1145/1882992.1883107

24. C. Martella*, E. Gedik*, L. Cabrera-Quiros*, G. Englebienne, and H. Hung, "How Was It? Exploiting Smartphone Sensing to Measure Implicit Audience Responses to Live Performances", ACM MM 2015 (oral) *These authors contributed equally to this article
25. Fleureau, Julien, Philippe Guillotel, and Izabela Orlac. 2013. "Affective benchmarking of movies based on the physiological responses of a real audience." Affective Computing and Intelligent Interaction (ACII), Humaine Association Conference on. IEEE.
26. Strauss, Marc, et al. 2005. "The handwave bluetooth skin conductance sensor." Affective computing and intelligent interaction. Springer Berlin Heidelberg, 699-706.
27. Sidharth Nabar, Ayan Banerjee, Sandeep K. S. Gupta, and Radha Poovendran. 2010. Evaluation of body sensor network platforms: a design space and benchmarking analysis. In Wireless Health 2010 (WH '10). ACM, New York, NY, USA, 118-127. DOI=10.1145/1921081.1921096
28. McCarthy, Kevin F., et al. Gifts of the muse: Reframing the debate about the benefits of the arts. Rand Corporation, 2001.
29. Matarasso, F. "Creative Progression: Reflections on quality in participatory arts." UNESCO Observatory Multi-Disciplinary Journal in the Arts 3.3 (2013): 1-15.
30. Fletcher, Richard Ribon, et al. 2010. "iCalm: Wearable sensor and network architecture for wirelessly communicating and logging autonomic activity." Information Technology in Biomedicine, IEEE Transactions on 14.2 : 215-223.
31. Radbourne, Jennifer, Katya Johanson, and Hilary Glow. 2010a. 'Empowering Audiences to Measure Quality'. Participations 7:2. 360-379.
32. J. W. Papez. 1937. "A proposed mechanism of emotion," J. Neuropsychiatry Clin. Neurosci., vol. 7, pp. 103–112.
33. Picard, Rosalind W. 2009. "Future affective technology for autism and emotion communication." Philosophical Transactions of the Royal Society B: Biological Sciences 364.1535: 3575-3584.
34. C. J. Stevens, E. Schubert, R. H. Morris, M. Frear,J. Chen, S. Healey, C. Schoknecht, and S. Hansen. 2009. Cognition and the temporal arts: Investigating audience response to dance using PDAs that record continuous data during live performance. International Journal of Human-Computer Studies, 67(9):800 – 813.
35. Yuta Sugiura, Calista Lee, Masayasu Ogata, Anusha Withana, Yasutoshi Makino, Daisuke Sakamoto, Masahiko Inami, and Takeo Igarashi. 2012. PINOKY: a ring that animates your plush toys. In Proceedings of the SIGCHI Conference on Human Factors in Computing Systems (CHI '12). ACM, New York, NY, USA, 725-734. DOI=10.1145/2207676.2207780
36. Patel, Shyamal, et al. 2012. "A review of wearable sensors and systems with application in rehabilitation." J Neuroeng Rehabil 9.12: 1-17.
37. Cacioppo, John T., Louis G. Tassinary, and Gary Berntson, eds. Handbook of psychophysiology. Cambridge University Press, 2007.
38. S.M. VaezMousavi, R. J. Barry, J. A. Rushby, and A. R. Clarke. 2007. "Arousal and activation effects on physiological and behavioral responding during a continuous performance task," Acta Neurobiol. Exp. (Wars), vol. 67, pp. 461–470.
39. Tschacher, Wolfgang, Steven Greenwood, Volker Kirchberg, Stéphanie Wintzerith, Karen van den Berg, and Martin Tröndle. 2012. 'Physiological correlates of aesthetic perception of artworks in a museum'. Psychology of Aesthetics, Creativity and the Arts 6:1. 96-103.
40. Rahman, Md Mahbubur, et al. 2014. "Are we there yet?: Feasibility of continuous stress assessment via wireless physiological sensors." Proceedings of the 5th ACM Conference on Bioinformatics, Computational Biology, and Health Informatics. ACM.
41. Woehrle, Matthias, Martin Bor, and Koen Langendoen. 2012. "868 MHz: a noiseless environment, but no free lunch for protocol design." Networked Sensing Systems (INSS), Ninth International Conference on. IEEE.
42. White, Mike. Arts development in community health: A social tonic. Radcliffe Publishing, 2009.
43. Chen Wang, Erik N. Geelhoed, Phil P. Stenton, and Pablo Cesar. 2014. Sensing a live audience. In Proceedings of the SIGCHI Conference on Human Factors in Computing Systems (CHI '14). ACM, New York, NY, USA, 1909-1912. DOI=http://dx.doi.org/10.1145/2556288.2557154
44. C. Wang, J. Wong, X. Zhu, T. Roggla, J. Jansen, and Pablo Cesar, "Quantifying Audience Experience in the Wild: Heuristics for Developing and Deploying a Biosensor Infrastructure in Theaters," in Proceedings of the *International Workshop on Quality of Multimedia Experience*, (QoMEX2016), Lisbon, Portugal, June 6-8, 2016.
45. Poh, M. Z., Kim, K., Goessling, A. D., Swenson, N. C., & Picard, R. W. 2009. Heartphones: Sensor earphones and mobile application for non-obtrusive health monitoring. In 2009 International Symposium on Wearable Computers (pp. 153-154). IEEE.

Using Real-time Biofeedback of Heart Rate Variability Measures to Track and Help Improve Levels of Attention and Relaxation

Gareth Loudon
Cardiff Metropolitan University and Centre for Creativity Ltd
Cardiff, UK
gloudon@cardiffmet.ac.uk

Dimitrios Zampelis
Centre for Creativity Ltd
Newport, UK
d.zampelis@gmail.com

Gina Deininger
Centre for Creativity Ltd
Newport, UK
gina.deininger@gmail.com

ABSTRACT
The main purpose of the study was to investigate if it was possible for a person to use the real-time biofeedback of their heart rate variability (HRV), recorded from a heart rate monitor watch, to help improve their level of attention and relaxation. Attention and relaxation are important factors affecting creativity, so improvements in 'relaxed concentration' could help enhance creativity. New HRV analysis algorithms were developed and tested together with three different user interfaces to explore how the interaction design affects user performance. Initial results suggest that it is possible to estimate levels of attention and relaxation, at least at a crude level, and that people are able to use this information to help improve their level of attention and relaxation. In addition, the results suggest that the interaction design of the application has a very important role to play in supporting user engagement and to maintain motivation levels.

Author Keywords
Heart Rate Variability; Attention; Relaxation; Stress; Biofeedback; Creativity; Flow.

ACM Classification Keywords
G.4 Mathematical Software: Algorithm Design and Analysis; H.1.2 User / Machine Systems; H.5.2 User Interfaces; K.3.1 Computer Uses in Education.

INTRODUCTION
Our main research interests focus on the factors and processes that affect creativity [1][2][3][4]. Two factors of particular interest are attention and relaxation. Voluntary attention is described by Kahneman [5] as "an exertion of [mental] effort in activities which are selected by current plans and intentions". Csikszentmihalyi [6] suggested that people enter a state of 'flow' during creativity that he described as an "effortless, yet highly focused state of consciousness" where flow is characterised by high levels of concentration and positive affect. Others have also found a relationship between positive affect and creativity [7][8] and between creativity, motivation and mental effort [9][10]. Our own research findings support the suggestion that people have high levels of attention with positive valence when undertaking a creative activity [11][12].

C&C 2017, June 27–30, 2017, Singapore

ACM ISBN 978-1-4503-4403-6/17/06...$15.00.
DOI: http://dx.doi.org/10.1145/3059454.3059466

Our main motivation for this study was to see if it was possible to develop a software application that could help people train and improve their own levels of attention and relaxation using the real-time biofeedback of their heart rate variability (HRV). The idea being that if people could improve their level of 'relaxed concentration' this could help enhance their own creativity.

HRV, Attention, Stress and Flow
Heart rate variability (HRV) can be measured from the variation in consecutive R-R intervals of the Electrocardiogram (ECG) or from the variation in consecutive pulse cycle intervals using techniques such as Photoplethysmography [13][14][15]. Previous research studies suggest that HRV data can provide valuable information on a person's level of attention, and that when there is an increase in mental effort there is also an increase in heart rate, and a reduction in HRV power [16][17][18]. Attention and mental effort have also been associated with a specific reduction in HRV power around 0.1 Hz [19][20]. HRV is commonly used as a psychophysiological measure of mental and physical health and past research has shown that stress and anxiety causes an increase in heart rate and a reduction in HRV power in the high frequency range (0.15 – 0.4 Hz) [21][22].

Several researchers, including Keller et al. [23], Peifer et al. [24] and Harmat et al. [25], have undertaken investigations into the physiological aspects of flow and found links between flow and psychophysiological measures including heart rate variability (HRV). Harmat et al. [25] studied the psychophysiology of flow during computer game playing and analysed the relationship between HRV (amongst other measures) and self reported states of flow, attention, valence and arousal. Their results showed a correlation between high levels of flow, attention and positive affect, and that higher levels of flow were associated with lower HRV power in the low frequency range (0.04 – 0.15 Hz).

Previously we found that it is possible to detect differences in HRV measures between states of high attention and relaxation from heart rate monitor watches such as the Mio Alpha 2 [12]. High attention was associated with reductions in HRV power in the low frequency range (0.07 – 0.15 Hz), while stress was associated with reductions in HRV power in the high frequency range (0.15 – 0.4 Hz) as well as an increase in heart rate [12].

AIMS AND OBJECTIVES

Our overall aim in this study was to investigate if it was possible to use the real-time biofeedback of a person's heart rate variability, recorded from a heart rate monitor watch such as the Mio Alpha 2 [26], to track and help improve their level of attention and relaxation. We believe this a novel approach. To try and achive this aim the following objectives were:

1. To evaluate the effectiveness of new HRV analysis algorithms for estimating levels of attention and relaxation in real-time.
2. To investigate how the interaction design of the software application affects user engagement and the ability of users to train and improve their levels of attention and relaxation.

The motivation for using a heart rate monitor watch, rather than an ECG chest strap, was because of its simplicity and convenience of use. However, it is important to note that the accuracy of HRV data collected from a heart rate monitor watch, compared to HRV data collected from an ECG chest sensor, is significantly reduced [27]. This is because of the need to take averages of pulse cycle interval estimates on the watch sensor to try and reduce recording errors. One of our own previous studies [12] showed that low and high frequency HRV power were reduced when using a watch sensor (compared to sensor clipped to the ear), with the high frequency range HRV power being the most affected.

APPROACH

The study was split into four stages:

1. The design and development of new HRV analysis algorithms to track levels of attention and relaxation in real-time.
2. Evaluation of the effectiveness of the new algorithms to track levels of attention and relaxation.
3. The design and development of three different user interfaces and interaction design modes for the software application to investigate how the user interface and interaction mode affects user engagement and the user's ability to train and improve their levels of attention and relaxation.
4. Evaluation of the three different user interfaces and interaction design modes.

The Cardiff School of Art and Design's Research Ethics Committee gave ethics approval for the study. All participants involved in the study gave their informed consent prior to their inclusion.

Stage 1

The software application was developed to run on an iPhone 5. The software communicated wirelessly in real-time with the Mio Alpha 2 Heart rate monitor watch [26] using the 'Bluetooth smart' protocol to receive the heart rate (HR) estimates together with time stamps. These heart rate estimates were then converted in real-time into equidistant samples using an interpolation method. Power spectrum density (PSD) estimates of HRV were calculated using Welch's Fast Fourier Transform (FFT) method (using a 64 second window), and PSD estimates were calculated for low frequency (0.07 - 0.15 Hz) and high frequency (0.15 – 0.4 Hz) ranges every 4 seconds using a moving window.

Attention and relaxation levels were calculated/estimated from estimates of the heart rate, the low frequency HRV power and the high frequency HRV power. The attention levels were calculated based on the power of the low frequency HRV (0.07 – 0.15 Hz), with an inverse linear relationship between the attention level and the low frequency HRV power. Attention levels were set on a scale from 1 to 6, where 1 represented low attention and 6 represented high attention. The relaxation levels were calculated based on a combination of changes in absolute heart rate (set from the initial 64 seconds of baseline data) and from the ratio between the peak power of the HRV signal (within the low frequency range) divided by the remaining HRV power. Relaxation levels increased with reducing heart rate, and also increased as the ratio value increased. Relaxation levels were also set on a scale from 1 to 6, where 1 represented low relaxation (high stress) and 6 represented high relaxation (low stress).

Stage 2

The accuracy and effectiveness of the new algorithms to track levels of attention and relaxation were initially evaluated by conducting a set of user tests with 22 design students and academic staff from the Cardiff School of Art and Design (11 females and 11 males), who were aged between 20 and 40 years (average age was 26.2 years old). Each of the 22 participants were asked (individually) to undertake three tasks.

The first task was a two minute Stroop test. The Stroop test has been used extensively to study attention [28] and is associated with high levels of mental effort, and often with increased levels of stress. The second task involved relaxing for two minutes. For the third task, participants were asked to draw something of their choice for two minutes. Our motivation for including the drawing task was because we regarded it as a creative activity. We therefore hypothesized that design students and academic staff would have high levels of concentration, but remain relatively relaxed, during such a creative task.

Every participant undertook the tasks individually in a quiet room while sitting (between 10am and 1pm). The Mio Alpha 2 watch [26] was used to record the heart rate (HR) estimates. The heart rate data being recorded was checked for accuracy before the start of each of the tasks. Before each of the three tasks, every participant was asked to sit quietly for three minutes to collect baseline data. After each task, participants were asked to reflect on their level of attention and relaxation during the task to see if their comments matched the results from the algorithms. All comments from the participants were audio recorded. Results from the evaluation are given in the results section.

Stage 3

Three different interaction modes were created for the software application to understand how the interaction mode affected user engagement and the corresponding attention and stress/relaxation levels.

The first interaction mode (the Zone game) gave feedback to the participant on their level of relaxation and attention separately by showing their state (via the location of a blue ball) on a focus/relaxation grid (shown in Figure 1 below). The focus/relaxation grid mapped directly to the attention and relaxation levels calculated from the heart rate data. The graphical user interface used colours (green, yellow and red) together with words 'distracted/focused' and 'stressed/relaxed' to give quick feedback to the participant on which zones represented high levels of attention and relaxation. The time spent in each zone by the participant was shown in seconds. The challenge for the participant in this interaction mode was to spend as much time as possible in the green zone representing high levels of attention and relaxation.

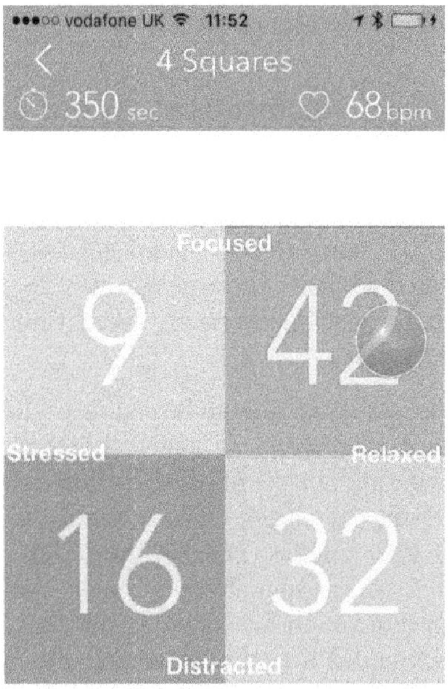

Figure 1. Screen shot of the Zone game.

The second interaction mode (the Bird game) followed a classic game format where the attention and relaxation levels were combined to create a 'relaxed concentration' score for a bird flying game (shown in Figure 2 below). This combined 'relaxed concentration' score was used to set the height the bird flies at, i.e. a high 'relaxed concentration' level mapped to a high height, and a low 'relaxed concentration' level mapped to a low height The user collects points as the bird flies through the clouds. The user must make sure that their 'relaxed concentration' level is high enough so that the bird does not crash into the oncoming mountains. If the bird crashes into a mountain the game ends. Note that the mountains get higher as the game progresses.

Figure 2. Screen shot of the Bird game.

One of the main differences between the Bird game compared to the Zone game is that the user might not know if they need to relax more or concentrate more (or both) to fly higher and avoid the mountains. This difference was introduced to see if users could deal with two factors, attention and relaxation, being combined. Another key motivation for introducing this new interaction mode was to see how participants reacted when they saw that the bird was not flying high enough to avoid an oncoming mountain. For example, would they be able to change their level of 'relaxed concentraion' quickly enough to avoid the oncoming mountain, or would the fact that they saw an oncoming mountain increase their level of stress and make their task of staying at a high level of 'relaxed concentration' harder? The design of the oncoming mountains in the Bird game also introduced distraction, with the potential to reduce concentration. A final motivation for introducing this interaction mode was to see if it was perceived as more enjoyable compared to the Zone game.

The third interaction mode (the Tree game) again used the combined 'relaxed concentration' score. However, in this mode the 'relaxed concentration' score was used as a measure to either enable flowers to appear on a tree (for high 'relaxed concentration' scores) or to fall off the tree (for low 'relaxed concentration' scores) (shown in Figure 3 below). The tree initially starts with no flowers on it. The challenge for the participant in this interaction mode was to generate as many flowers as possible on the tree.

Figure 3. Screen shot of the Tree game.

The interaction design of the Tree game differed from the Bird game in terms of the time participants had to change their level of 'relaxed concentration'. In the Bird game participants might have to make quick changes to their level of 'relaxed concentration' to avoid crashing into the oncoming mountain. In the Tree game, participants could take their time more without any major consequences. The Tree game also differed from the Bird game in terms of having fewer distracting elements (such as the oncoming mountains in the Bird game). The motivation for introducing this third interaction mode was to see if participants could achieve a higher level of 'relaxed concentration' compared to the bird game format, and to understand how different game elements affect performance. In addition, we wanted to see how enjoyable this interaction mode was.

Tasks in each of the three interaction modes lasted two minutes. Before a participant started a task, 64 seconds of baseline HRV data was collected. This was presented to the participant as a warm-up period to get focused and relaxed.

Stage 4

15 design students and academic staff from the Cardiff School of Art and Design participated in testing the three interaction modes (7 females and 8 males), and were aged between 20 and 40 years (average age was 27.8 years old). Each of the 15 participants undertook two of the three interaction modes, and for each interaction mode, undertook the task three times to see if their attention and relaxation levels improved or not. Therefore 10 participants tested each of the three interaction modes. It was decided not to get the participants to undertake all three interaction modes as it was felt that the participants would get tired after performing several challenges. To further mitigate against fatigue affecting the results, the order with which the interaction modes were shown varied, so that 5 of the 10 participants played a particular interaction mode first (the other 5 playing it second). Within these criteria, participants were randomly assigned to two of the three interaction modes.

Similarly to the test protocol used in stage 2, every participant undertook the tasks individually in a quiet room while sitting (between 10am and 1pm). The Mio Alpha 2 watch [26] was used to record the heart rate (HR) estimates, and the heart rate data being recorded was checked for accuracy before the start of each of the tasks. Before each task, 64 seconds of baseline HRV data was collected.

All participants were asked to try and get as high a score as possible for each attempt, but no advice or guidance was given to the participants on how to increase their level of attention and relaxation. This was because we were interested to see whether participants were able to work out for themselves how to improve their attention and relaxation levels using the biofeedback information presented as the only guide.

After completing three attempts of one interaction mode, participants were asked how they found the experience and were also asked to complete a questionnaire to see how they estimated their levels of concentration and relaxation during the task; how easy it was to concentrate and relax; and whether they found the experience pleasant or unpleasant. Each scale was rated from a scale of 1 to 9, where 1 represented the lowest level and 9 the highest level.

RESULTS

Stage 2 Results

Table 1 below shows the averages of the estimated attention and relaxation levels (1 to 6) across the 22 participants for the three tasks: the Stroop task; the Relaxation task; and the Drawing task.

Verbal feedback from the participants matched these results, with participants generally finding the Stroop task the most stressful; the Relaxation task the most relaxing;

and the Drawing task quite relaxing. Attention was generally described as very high for the Stroop task; low for the Relaxation task; and high for the Drawing task.

Task	Attention level	Relaxation level
Stroop	5.17	2.87
Relaxation	3.48	4.48
Drawing	5.14	3.36

Table 1. Results of the estimated attention and relaxation levels for the three tasks: Stroop; Relaxation; and Drawing.

An analysis of variance (ANOVA) was conducted to study the difference in means between the attention and relaxation levels of the participants in the three tasks, using a repeated measures design. The alpha level was set at 0.05 for the classification of significant difference, and based on Cohen [29] we interpreted effect size as small when $d = 0.2$; medium when $d = 0.5$; and large when $d = 0.8$.

The attention levels for the Stroop task were not significantly different from the Drawing task, but the attention levels for the Stroop task were significantly higher than the Relaxation task, $F(1,21) = 15.31$, $p = 0.001$ with a large effect size, $d = 0.90$. The attention levels for the Drawing task were also significantly higher than the Relaxation task $F(1,21) = 22.01$, $p < 0.001$ with a large effect size, $d = 1.11$. The relaxation levels for the Relaxation task were significantly higher than the Stroop task, $F(1,21) = 29.17$, $p < 0.001$, with a large effect size, $d = 1.16$. There was also a significant difference in relaxation levels between the Relaxation task and the Drawing task, $F(1,21) = 10.61$, $p = 0.004$, with a medium effect size, $d = 0.69$. There was no significant difference in relaxation levels between the Drawing task and the Stroop task.

Stage 4 Results

Table 2 below shows the average scores for the different interaction modes across the three attempts.

Interaction Modes	First Attempt	Second Attempt	Third Attempt
Zone Game	60.0	68.0	69.2
Bird Game	42.6	37.7	22.4
Tree Game	86.3	119.0	74.0

Table 2. The scores relating to time spent in high 'relaxed concentration' during the task.

The score for the Zone game represented the average time spent in the green zone (in secs), representing high levels of attention and relaxation, over the two minute task. The score for the Bird game represented the average number of points gained by flying through clouds (equating to the time spent in a high level of 'relexed concentration'), before either crashing into the mountain, or completing the two minute task. The score for the Tree game represented the average number of flowers on the tree on completion of the two minute task, with the number of flowers again correlating with the time spent in 'relaxed concentration'. Note that you cannot directly compare the scores between interaction modes, but you can directly compare the changes in scores between attempts (for a particular interaction mode).

An analysis of variance (ANOVA) was conducted to study the difference between the means of the three attempts for each interaction mode, using a repeated measures design. Maulchy's test indicated that the assumption of sphericity was not violated. On average, the scores for the Zone game increased with each attempt, however the scores were not significantly affected by the attempt. For the Bird game the average scores decreased with each attempt, however, the scores were not significantly affected by the attempt. For the Tree game, the scores were significantly affected by the attempt, $F(2,28) = 3.65$, $p = 0.047$.

Comparing pairs of attempts for the Tree game, there was an increase in the average score from attempt 1 to 2, and this difference was significant, $F(1,19) = 7.46$, $p = 0.023$, with a large effect size, $d = 0.87$. From attempt 2 to 3 there was a decrease in the average score, and this difference was significant $F(1,19) = 6.46$, $p = 0.032$, with a large effect size, $d = 0.80$.

Table 3 below shows how the participants, on average, estimated their levels of concentration and relaxation across three attempts of a task; how easy it was to concentrate and relax; and whether they found the experience pleasant or unpleasant. Each scale was rated from a scale of 1 to 9, where 1 represented the lowest level and 9 the highest level.

Average Scores	Zone Game	Bird Game	Tree Game
Concentration level	6.8	6.0	7.2
Ease of concentration	5.3	3.9	5.0
Relaxation level	6.6	5.2	6.9
Ease of relaxation	5.7	4.5	6.0
Pleasantness level	6.0	6.0	7.4

Table 3. Summary (averages) of questionnaire results from participants after completing three attempts of a task.

Concentration and relaxation levels were reported as highest for the Tree game, slightly above the Zone game with the Bird game having the lowest reported levels of concentration and relaxation. Participants playing the Bird game also found it harder, on average, to relax and concentrate relative to the other two games. The Tree game was seen as the most pleasant to play.

DISCUSSION

The results from stage 2 suggest that it is possible to estimate levels of attention and relaxation, at least at a crude level, using heart rate estimates recorded from a heart rate monitor watch. However it might not be possible to distinguish between small variations in mental effort, as suggested by previous research [19][20], or even in small variations in stress levels.

We believe this is an important finding, even with these limitations, as heart rate monitor watches are simple and convenient to use, compared to other ECG recording methods, and provide an opportunity for easier adoption in the marketplace.

The results from stage 2 also suggest that participants undertaking a creative activity, such as drawing, have (on average) high levels of attention. This supports the suggestion by Csikszentmihalyi [6] that people have high levels of concentration during creativity.

The results from stage 4 provided some insights into how the interaction design of an interface affects the abilities of participants to use the real-time biofeedback of their own heart rate variability measures to help improve their levels of attention and relaxation.

During the Zone game, participants were able, on average, to improve their level of attention and relaxation (based on the HRV algorithm estimates) as they tried further attempts, spending more than half of the two minutes in the green zone, representing high levels of attention and relaxation. Participants reported that having separate feedback on concentration and relaxation levels helped, as they understood what aspects they needed to improve to increase their scores. Participants reported a range of techniques they used to improve their concentration and relaxation levels (note that they were given no advice on how to concentrate or relax).

Participants in the Bird game generally found it difficult to have a consistently high level of 'relaxed concentration', and reported that this was partly because of confusion on whether to relax more or to concentrate more, but also because of the stress and distraction created by seeing that the bird was about to crash into the mountain unless they increased their 'relaxed concentration' level (mapped to bird height) quickly. The reduction in the scores, on average, from attempt 1 (42.6) to attempt 3 (22.4), was also reported as being caused by increasing frustration at not being able to maintain a high level of 'relaxed concentration' when noticing oncoming mountains. This is further supported by participants' own ratings of how easy it was for them to concentrate and relax (on average, 3.9 and 4.5 respectively).

In the Tree game, participants, on average, significantly increased their 'relaxed concentration' score from attempt 1 to attempt 2, $F(1,19) = 7.46$, $p = 0.023$. Participants spent, on average, more than half of the two minutes in a high level of 'relaxed concentration' during attempt 2. However, there was also a significant decrease in their score from attempts 2 to 3, $F(1,19) = 6.46$, $p = 0.032$. This reduction in score from attempt 2 to 3 seemed mainly due to tiredness and a lack of motivation on the third attempt. Some participants reported that after achieving a high score in attempt 2, they did not have the motivation to repeat the high score in attempt 3.

Compared to the Bird game, participants in the Tree game did not seem to have a problem having feedback on their attention and relaxation levels combined into a 'relaxed concentration' score. This seemed to be because they felt they had more time to try different techniques to improve their levels of concentration and relaxation compared to participants in the Bird game. It could also be due to fewer distractions in the interface.

The Tree game had the highest rating in terms of the pleasantness level (7.4) compared to the other two interaction modes (both at 6.0) and most participants who played the Tree game reported that they enjoyed it. A small minority of the participants who played the Bird game said that they enjoyed the experience, and mentioned that they liked the challenge, however this was balanced against the majority of participants who stated that they found it frustrating, and this is reflected in the overall pleasantness rating. Feedback on the Zone game was more neutral.

Other comments from participants after the tests suggested that the software application could be useful in two modes: firstly, a 'training mode', as tested in this study; and secondly, a 'background mode' that gives a daily log of attention and relaxation levels throughout the day giving summaries and a detailed breakdown in terms of time and possibly location, so that users can reflect on when and where their attention levels dropped, or their stress levels increased. Note that further research is required to see if it is possible to use a heart rate monitor watch in such a 'background mode' as this could be problematic. This is because a range of factors can affect HRV, including physical exercise and respiration rates/depths. In addition, there is an increased likelihood of recording errors when a person is moving. Many other factors can also affect HRV [30].

LIMITATIONS

A significant amount of HRV data was lost by using a heart rate monitor watch, compared to an ECG chest strap. It is likely that this lost data could have improved the tracking of attention and relaxation levels further. However, one of our main motivations was to see if a heart rate monitor watch could at least provide some indication of attention and relaxation levels due to their ease of use. Further work is required to accurately measure the effectiveness of the heart rate monitor watches in tracking attention and relaxation, including the comparison of different algorithms.

Only 22 participants were involved in stage 2 of the study, and only 15 participants involved in stage 4. These are small sample sizes, so it is not possible to assume that the results presented in this study would apply to a general population.

Further larger scale studies are required to valid these results.

CONCLUSIONS

The results from stages 2 and 4 of the study tentatively suggest that it is possible to use the real-time biofeedback of heart rate variability measures to track and help improve levels of attention and relaxation using a heart rate monitor watch, at least at a crude level. In addition, the interaction design of the application has a very important role to play. Results strongly suggest that the interaction design of the application significantly affects user engagement and the ability of users to train and improve their levels of attention and relaxation. The results also suggest that the interaction design of the application must make sure that motivation levels are maintained, where the challenge and skill level match well, otherwise, users could get frustrated or bored. Lessons need to be learned from game design principles in terms of freedom to fail; providing rapid feedback; offering progression; and embedding a storyline to maintain engagement/motivation with the application over a period of time.

FUTURE IMPLICATIONS

A software application that can help improve attention and relaxation levels has possible benefits in terms of helping people enhance their levels of creativity, as attention and relaxation are key factors associated with creativity. Such a software application could also have potential in helping children improve their levels of concentration at school. Another possibility is to integrate the technology into 'mindfulness' applications targeted at both children and adults to help improve attention, reduce stress and promote well-being. In addition, the technology could possibly be used for niche markets such as sports applications requiring improved levels of relaxed concentration, such as golf.

ACKNOWLEDGEMENTS

We would like to thank Innovate UK for supporting the work.

REFERENCES

1. Deininger, G.M., Loudon, G.H., & Norman, S. 2012. Modal Preferences in Creative Problem Solving, *Cognitive Processing,* 13 (1), 147-150.
2. Deininger, G.M. 2013. Does State of Being and Dynamic Movement have a relationship with Creativity? Ph.D. Thesis. Cardiff Metropolitan University, Cardiff, UK.
3. Loudon, G.H., Deininger, G.M., & Gordon, B.S. 2012. Play, Autonomy and the Creative Process. In: Duffy, A., Nagai, Y., Taura, T. (Eds.), *Proceedings of the 2nd International Conference on Design Creativity*, The Design Society, UK. 87-96.
4. Loudon, G.H., & Deininger, G.M. 2014. A new model for supporting creativity in research organisations. In: Schimpf, S. (Ed.), *Proceedings of the R&D Management Conference*, Fraunhofer IAO, Germany. 93-100.
5. Daniel Kahneman. 1973. *Attention and Effort*. New Jersey: Prentice Hall.
6. Mihaly Csíkszentmihályi. 1996. *Creativity: Flow and the Psychology of Discovery and Invention*. New York: Harper Collins.
7. Amabile, T.M., Barsade, S.G., Mueller, J.S. and Staw, B.M., 2005. Affect and creativity at work. *Administrative science quarterly*, *50*(3), pp.367-403.
8. Davis, M. A. 2009. Understanding the relationship between mood and creativity: A meta-analysis. *Organizational Behavior and Human Decision Processes*, 108, 25-38.
9. Silvia, P.J., Beaty, R.E., Nusbaum, E.C., Eddington, K.M., & Kwapil, T.R. 2014. Creative Motivation: Creative Achievement Predicts Cardiac Autonomic Markers of Effort During Divergent Thinking. *Biological Psychology*, 102, 30-37.
10. Hennessey, B.A. 2010. Creativity-Motivation. Connection. In: Kaufman, J.C., Sternberg, R.J. (Eds.), *Cambridge Handbook of Creativity*, Cambridge University Press, New York, 342-365.
11. Gareth Loudon and Gina Deininger. 2016. The Physiological Response during Divergent Thinking. *Journal of Behavioral and Brain Science*, 6, 28-37. http://dx.doi.org/10.4236/jbbs.2016.61004
12. Gareth Loudon and Gina Deininger. 2017. The Physiological Response to drawing and its relation to attention and relaxation. *Journal of Behavioral and Brain Science*, 7, 111-124. http://dx.doi.org/10.4236/jbbs.2017.73011
13. Eduardo Gil, Michele Orini, Bail6n, R., Vergara, J.M., Luca Mainardi and Pablo Laguna. 2010. Photoplethysmography pulse rate variability as a surrogate measurement of heart rate variability during non-stationary conditions. *Physiological Measurement*, 31, 1271-1290. http://dx.doi.org/10.1088/0967-3334/31/9/015
14. Lu, G., Yang, F., Taylor, J.A., and Stein, J.F. 2009. A comparison of photoplethysmography and ECG recording to analyse heart rate variability in healthy subjects. *Journal of Medical Engineering Technology*, 33, 634–641. http://dx.doi.org/10.3109/03091900903150998
15. Axel Schäfer and Jan Vagedes. 2013. How accurate is pulse rate variability as an estimate of heart rate variability? A review on studies comparing photoplethysmographic technology with an electrocardiogram, *International Journal of Cardiology*, 166, 15–29. http://dx.doi.org/10.1016/j.ijcard.2012.03.119

16. Monika Althaus, Lambertus J.M. Mulder, Gijsbertus Mulder, Arie M. Van Roon, and Ruud B. Minderaa. 1998. Influence of respiratory activity on the cardiac response pattern to mental effort, *Psychophysiology*, 35, 420-430.
17. Anita L. Hansen, Bjørn H. Johnsen and Julian F. Thayer. 2003. Vagal influence on working memory and attention. *International Journal of Psychophysiology*, 48, 263–274.
18. Arie M. Van Roon, Lambertus J.M. Mulder, J. B. P. Veldman, and Gijsbertus Mulder. 1995. Beat-to-beat blood-pressure measurements applied in studies on mental workload. *Homeostasis*, 36, 3316–3324.
19. P.G. Jorna, 1992. Spectral analysis of heart rate and psychological state: a review of its validity as a workload index. *Biological Psychology*, 34, 237–257.
20. Peter Nickel and Friedhelm Nachreiner. 2002. The suitability of the 0.1 Hz component of heart rate variability for the assessment of mental workload in real and simulated work situation. In: de Waard, D., Brookhuis, K.A., Moraal, J., Toffetti, A. (Eds.), *Human Factors in Transportation, Communication, Health and the Workplace*, Shaker, Maastricht, 317–334.
21. Andrew H. Kemp and Daniel S. Quintana. 2013. The relationship between mental and physical health: Insights from the study of heart rate variability. *International Journal of Psychophysiology*, 89, 296–304. http://dx.doi.org/10.1016/j.ijpsycho.2013.06.018
22. Borejda Xhyheri, Olivia Manfrini, Massimiliano Mazzolini, Carmine Pizzi and Raffaele Bugiardini. 2012. Heart Rate Variability Today. *Progress in Cardiovascular Diseases,* 55, 321–331. http://dx.doi.org/10.1016/j.pcad.2012.09.001
23. Johannes Keller, Herbet Bless, Frederick Blomann and Dieter Kleinböhl. 2011. Physiological aspects of flow experiences: skills-demand-compatibility effects on heart rate variability and salivary cortisol. *Journal of Experimental Social Psychology* 47, 849–852. http://dx.doi.org/10.1016/j.jesp.2011.02.004
24. Corinna Peifer, Andre Schulz, Hartmut Schächinger, Nicola Baumann and Conny H. Antoni. 2014. The relation of flow experience and physiological arousal under stress — can u shape it? *Journal of Experimental Social Psychology*, 53, 62–69. http://dx.doi.org/10.1016/j.jesp.2014.01.009
25. László Harmat, Örjande Manzano, Töres Theorell, Lennart Högman, Håkan Fischer and Fredrik Ullén. 2015. Physiological correlates of the flow experience during computer game playing. *International Journal of Psychophysiology*, 97, 1–7. http://dx.doi.org/10.1016/j.ijpsycho.2015.05.001
26. Mio Alpha 2. Mio Alpha 2 Heart Rate Monitor Watch. 2017. Retrieved January 6, 2017 from http://www.mioglobal.com/EN-UK/Mio-ALPHA-2-Heart-Rate-Watch/Product.aspx.
27. Jakub Parak and Ilkka Korhonen. 2014. Evaluation of Wearable Consumer Heart Rate Monitors Based on Photopletysmography, *36th Annual International Conference of the IEEE Engineering in Medicine and Biology Society*, 26-30 August, Chicago.
28. Colin MacLeod and Colin M. MacLeod. 2005. The Stroop Task: Indirectly Measuring Concept Activation. In: Wenzel, A. and Rubin, D.C (Eds.) *Cognitive Methods and Their Application to Clinical Research*, (pp. 13-16). Washington: American Psychological Association. http://dx.doi.org/10.1037/10870-001
29. Jacob Cohen. 1988. *Statistical Power Analysis for the Behavioral Sciences* (2nd ed.). Hillsdale: Lawrence Erlbaum Associates.
30. Task Force of the European Society of Cardiology and the North American Society of Pacing and Electrophysiology. 1996. Heart rate variability. Standards of measurement, physiological interpretation, and clinical use. *European Heart Journal*, 17, 354-381.

Creative Sense-Making: Quantifying Interaction Dynamics in Co-Creation

Nicholas Davis, Chih-Pin Hsiao, Kunwar Yashraj Singh, Brenda Lin, Brian Magerko
Georgia Institute of Technology
School of Interactive Computing
{ndavis35, chsiao9, kysingh, blin15, magerko}@gatech.edu

ABSTRACT
This paper describes a new technique for quantifying interaction dynamics during open-ended co-creation, such as collaborative drawing or playing pretend. We present a cognitive framework called *creative sense-making*. This framework synthesizes existing cognitive science theories and empirical investigations into open-ended improvisation to develop a method of quantifying cognitive states and types of interactions through time. We apply this framework to empirical studies of human collaboration (in the domain of pretend play) and AI-based systems (in the domain of collaborative drawing) to establish its validity through cross-domain application and inter-rater reliability within each domain. The creative sense-making framework described includes a qualitative coding technique, interaction coding software, and the cognitive theory behind their application.

Author Keywords
Interaction; Interaction Dynamics; Creativity; Collaboration; Co-Creation; Sense-making

ACM Classification Keywords
H.5.m. Information interfaces and presentation (e.g., HCI): Miscellaneous;

INTRODUCTION
Collaboration is a powerful way to inspire and support creativity. During creative improvisational collaboration, a new form of distributed creativity arises that can lead to emergent, dynamic, and unexpected meaning to support creativity in new ways [29]. Subsequently, the field of computational creativity is beginning to explore how intelligent agents might collaborate with humans during their creative process in co-creative systems, i.e. systems that contribute content to a shared creative product with the user. A cognitive theory describing collaborative creativity would help design and evaluate co-creative systems. In particular, measuring collaboration outcomes involves being able to quantify *interaction dynamics*, e.g. the rhythm of interaction, style of turn taking, and manner in which participants are mutually making sense of a situation through time [9]. However, there is a gap in the literature about quantifying and evaluating open-ended creative collaboration.

We have seen evidence of how collaboration leads to dynamic and emergent meaning structures that inspire novel ideas during empirical studies of pretend play [7] and collaborative drawing [8]. We have also found how collaborators often provide unexpected ideas and thus lead to surprising results. The same dynamism and flexibility that make creative collaboration so effective, also unfortunately make it especially hard to quantify and evaluate.

This paper applies the cognitive science theory of enaction and its conceptual framework, participatory sense-making, to the domain of open-ended creative collaboration and then formalizes this theory as computational models of creative collaboration. The described qualitative coding and analysis technique, called the sense-making curve analysis, provides a means to rapidly and reliably quantify interaction dynamics continuously through time. This temporal data can be mathematically analyzed using continuous functions (e.g. moving averages, integrations) to formally classify different sense-making strategies and trends in creative collaboration.

The creative sense-making framework is applied to empirical studies of human collaboration (in the domain of pretend play) and technical systems (in the domain of collaborative drawing) to establish its validity through cross-domain application and inter-rater reliability within each domain. With the creative sense-making framework, we begin to offer a set of techniques and tools to begin investigating the overarching research question: how do humans collaborate in open-ended improvisational creativity, and how can we design co-creative agents to achieve similar benefits as human collaboration? The contributions of this paper include introducing the creative

C&C '17, June 27-30, 2017, Singapore, Singapore

ACM ISBN 978-1-4503-4403-6/17/06…$15.00
http://dx.doi.org/10.1145/3059454.3059478

sense-making theoretical framework, coding technique, and analysis approach.

RELATED WORK

Several metrics have been developed relating to creativity and technology. The creativity support index (CSI) is a psychometric survey instrument that measures the effectiveness of a creativity support tool for assisting users engaged in creative work [5]. Protocol analysis has been used as a method for evaluating and comparing how different user interfaces and input methodologies affect creative cognition [24]. Some aspects of the user's creative process can be quantified by logging user data from creativity support tools, such as measuring the emergence of new ideas and ideation strategies [23], the novelty and surprise of designs [27], the effectiveness of a creative collaboration [8], and the relative entropy of ideas generated throughout a design protocol [18]. Biometric sensors, such as EEGs, have also been employed to quantify *in the moment creativity* (ITMC) by classifying periods of heightened creativity based on physiological markers [4].

Due to the complexity and open-ended nature of creative activities, researchers generally employ a mixed-method approach of data triangulation that draws on multiple sources of data to analyze and evaluate how a technological intervention affects the creative process [4]. While these creativity research methods provide insight into an individual's creative process and tools utilized during creativity, evaluating creative collaboration presents unique challenges around understanding how collaborators coordinate in the moment to co-construct shared meaning throughout a creative collaboration.

The enactivist paradigm in cognitive science has made significant advancements in terms of understanding how meaning emerges through interaction, both by an individual agent and through social coordination [3,10]. These researchers propose a novel theoretical framework focused on the idea of sense-making, whereby an agent gradually casts a web of significance and meaning onto the world through interacting with the environment (and other agents within it) to determine meaningful regularities [33–35]. The theoretical framework of sense-making is conceptually robust, replete with a vocabulary and paradigmatic viewpoint for understanding cognition and interaction through the lens of socially emergent and dynamic meaning constructs [12,20,36]. However, there is a significant gap in the field regarding quantifying the interaction dynamics of sense-making during complex and open-ended activities, such as improvisational creative collaboration. In the enactivist literature, there are generally two approaches to quantifying interaction dynamics and sense-making: *perceptual crossing* and *traditional qualitative analysis*:

Perceptual Crossing Methodology

Perceptual crossing is a type of participatory sense-making and experimental apparatus recently introduced into the cognitive science literature to quantify interaction patterns

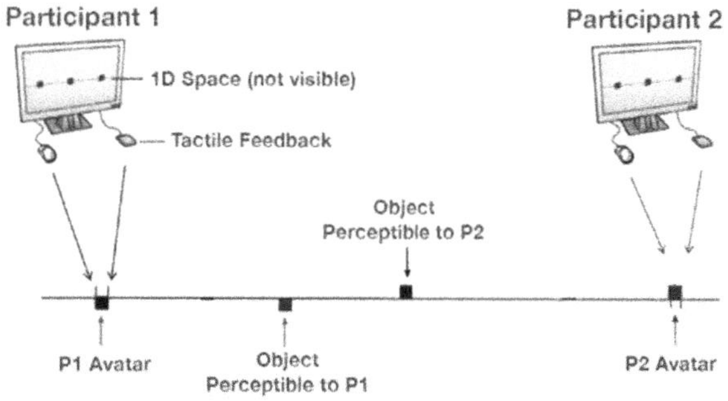

Figure 1. Perceptual crossing experimental set up (adapted from [1]). Participants interact with the virtual environment to discern static objects from other agents.

directly within an artificially constrained virtual environment [1,10,11,17]. Researchers studying perceptual crossing utilize a minimalist virtual environment in which two agents (either both human, both artificial agents, or a combination thereof) perform a spatial participatory sense-making task whereby they try to differentiate the motion of their partner from static objects using only tactile feedback. Each player moves their avatar across their respective screens using the mouse or arrow keys, and the participants receive a vibration if the avatar has crossed paths with something in the environment (whether it is a static object or human). Participants have to interactively explore each stimulus to determine whether it was caused by a static object or another human in a process of *participatory sense-making*. In this virtual environment, all actions are restricted to constrained digital inputs and are thus easily observable and quantifiable. This approach reveals some of the underlying processes of participatory sense-making, but it is not applicable for understanding sense-making in more complex domains, such as open-ended and creative interactions.

Traditional Qualitative Analysis

The second approach for understanding interaction dynamics is traditional qualitative analysis, i.e. qualitatively coding observational video data of complex social activities to interpret the types of actions and strategies recruited during participatory sense-making [22,31]. This approach is widely used in dialog and conversation analysis [32] and analyzing turn taking dynamics, such as leader/follower strategies and topic shifts throughout the interaction [2]. These investigations typically yield descriptive statistics about the types of events that occurred accompanied by a thick cognitive ethnographic description of the factors that influenced participatory sense-making, but these accounts are often difficult to quantify.

Qualitative analyses employing event-based coding practices are also common in analyzing and evaluating open-ended creativity, such as artistic and design creativity.

For example, this approach has been utilized to evaluate: collaboration practices of designers in a virtual environment by segmenting data into discrete events based on behavioral markers [26], as well as understanding open-ended artistic creativity [38,27]. Interestingly, [38] included the behavioral markers of pausing and body-repositioning (i.e. stepping back from the artwork) as important events in the coding scheme, which bears similarity to our proposed approach. The methods described in this section all yield powerful and informative descriptions about the number of times events occurred and even the order in which these events occur, but they are not specifically designed to quantify the fine-grained temporal dynamics of interaction.

CREATIVE SENSE-MAKING

Creative sense-making (CSM) bridges the two general methodological approaches described in the related work (e.g. perceptual crossing and qualitative coding) by creating a simplified qualitative coding scheme focused on sense-making that lends itself to quantification and computational analysis. The analysis demonstrates how different types of collaboration strategies and styles can be quantitatively classified through time. CSM was designed to support the evaluation of continuous interactions in co-creation, such as collaborative drawing and playing pretend. Using this method provides insight about the interaction dynamics and interaction trends in open-ended co-creation contexts.

In the CSM approach, each participant's action is categorized according to its functional role in sense-making. We employ the *free energy principle of the brain* [14–16] to develop a quantitative descriptor for these different states. The free energy theory was selected as it has neurobiological plausibility and it lends itself to quantification and continuous analysis of agents through time. The free-energy principle describes how biological systems continually strive to reduce surprise, i.e. cognition strives to create a dynamic and generative mental model that makes the environment more predictable [15,28,30]. A few critical definitions will help elucidate the theory of free energy:

Generative model: "or forward model is a probabilistic mapping from causes to observed consequences (data). It is usually specified in terms of the likelihood of getting some data given their causes (parameters of a model) and priors on the parameters" [14].

Surprise to agent: this occurs when a cognitive agent has developed a generative model of interaction and anticipates certain sequences of data using that model, but the data from the environment violates the expectation of the agent.

Free energy: "Free energy [is] an information theory measure that bounds or limits (by being greater than) the surprise on sampling some data, given a generative model" [15].

Free-energy principle: "The free-energy principle says that any self-organizing system that is at equilibrium with its environment must minimize its free energy." [15].

Similar to sense-making, the free-energy principle claims that humans interact with the environment, through both active perception and action, to improve the accuracy of their generative model of the environment, thereby reducing *free-energy* [15,28]. When free energy is minimized, actions are generated fluidly and with ease, allowing agents to directly perceive affordances and meaning constructs in the environment that increase the order and predictability of interactions. When free energy increases, i.e. the cognitive agent becomes surprised, perception and action are utilized to help increase the accuracy, or *recognition density*, of the generative model of the environment, i.e. making the predictions of the generative model more closely match the 'true' conditions of the situation.

Combining the free-energy principle with the conceptual framework of sense-making enables a new method for quantifying interaction dynamics based on the relative free energy of a cognitive agent through time, as determined through behavioral markers. In the proposed approach, when agents do not have a robust generative model of the environment, they have to engage in a process of sense-making, which costs physical and mental energy. This type of sense-making can be viewed as an investment of physical and mental energy that has the potential to reduce free energy, in the long run, i.e. improving the predictive power of the cognitive agent's generative mental model. Thus, **sense-making** is formally defined here as the process whereby a cognitive system gradually minimizes free-energy by reflecting on and experimentally interacting with the environment to build and refine a more optimal generative mental model of that environment.

Within the context of this framework, we propose a continuum of cognitive states corresponding to the functional role of sense-making in the agent's interaction with the environment. Borrowing terminology from Glenberg [19], we refer to the ends of this spectrum as *clamped* and *unclamped* cognition. The concept of clamping represents a cognitive mechanism that helps the agent balance exploration versus exploitation to learn a better, more accurate, generative model (i.e. make sense of the environment).

Clamped Cognition: The process of maintaining or slightly refining the selected generative model assuming that it is the most accurate representation of the environment. It generally occurs after making sense of a task or activity. Behavioral markers include fluid interactions with minimal hesitation (e.g. embodied play actions, fluid drawing actions).

Unclamped Cognition: The process of changing or replacing the generative model by exploring and reflecting on the environment from different perspectives. It generally occurs during task onset and after surprises during the task. Behavioral markers include hesitation (e.g. eyes closed, confused look) and physically experimenting with the environment and viewpoint of the environment (e.g. futzing, inspecting).

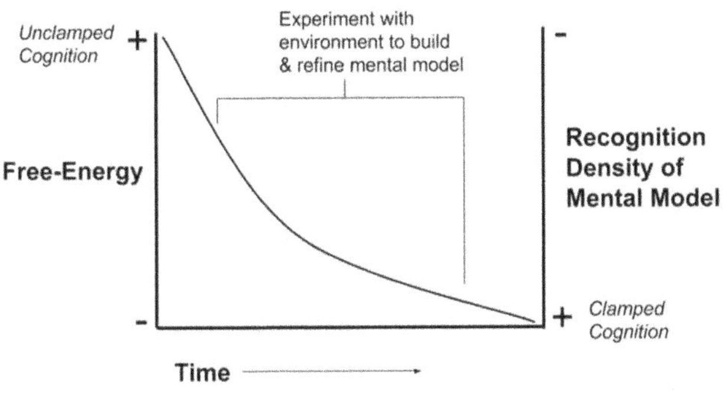

Figure 2. Visual representation showing the relationship between free-energy and clamped/unclamped cognition.

We devised a set of behavioral markers to detect clamped and unclamped cognition through a qualitative coding procedure of video data. For example, in the context of pretend play, a participant that is embodying a play character and performing fluid play actions inside the narrative world (i.e. diegetic actions) is considered clamped. Conversely, if a player is hesitating, unsure, pausing, or otherwise disengaged, this is a sign they may be actively processing and working to make sense of the situation to determine an effective strategy for moving forward, which signifies an unclamped state. Pauses and hesitations are also used in conversation analysis and analyzing interaction dynamics [2]. When players restructure or build additional meaning into the environment explicitly (i.e. extra-diegetic actions), they are actively making sense of the situation in an unclamped manner.

In creative interaction, meaning is continually shifting and evolving due to the participatory nature of improvisational collaboration [29]. However, empirical evidence [3,7] suggests that semi-stable (yet dynamic) meaning structures emerge to produce a steady state whereby both participants have a relatively robust predictive model that enables them to interact fluidly in a situated manner, without much explicit sense-making outside of fine-grained coordination. In our work, these stable units of meaning are referred to as *nucleus activities* that can grow through time as additional layers of meaning are added [7]. These semi-stationary states arise when both participants are clamped on a similar meaning structure. Conversely, participants can be confused or uncertain about what type of action to take or how to interpret their collaborator's actions due to a sparse predictive model, which would be characterized as unclamped. This type of clamping framework extends the idea behind shared meaning established in the literature about shared mental models [6,21] by taking into account the dynamic and evolutionary nature of meaning construction in open-ended creative interactions.

Within the unclamped category, there are two further distinctions that can be made to increase the granularity and explanatory power of our proposed coding technique. Unclamped actions that are meant to reduce free energy through sense-making can be either *perceptually-based* or *physical-based.* Perceptual-based sense-making relates to refining the brain's predictive model, which subsequently changes how features in the environment are perceived and interpreted. Since these processes are happening internally, they cannot be directly observed, but individuals experiencing this cognitive state display indirect behavioral markers, such as pausing, hesitating, contemplating, and looking confused, i.e. *thinking*. Physical sense-making, on the other hand, changes the structure of the environment by manipulating and modifying the environment, or by moving the body and altering what information is available to the senses, i.e. *thinking by doing*.

These two different paths of reducing free energy represent opposites that mirror the afferent and efferent flows of sensory information in a cognitive system. Perceptual-based sense-making processes change the afferent flow of predictions being generated by the brain and projected to the body (via the nervous system) by thinking and re-evaluating the situation internally. Physical sense-making processes change the efferent flow of incoming sensory information available to the agent (to generate predictions about) by taking actions that either change the environment (through manipulation) or one's vantage point of it. Thus, our proposed approach makes two chief categorical distinctions: clamped and unclamped cognition, and within the unclamped category, there is a further distinction between perceptual sense-making and physical sense-making.

Perceptual sense-making: the cognitive agent is working to internally improve recognition density of its generative mental model, i.e. *thinking*. Behavioral markers include: hesitation, eyes closed, confusion, and task disengagement in general.

Physical sense-making: the cognitive agent is exploring the environment through interaction to decrease disorder in the environment and increase the recognition density of its generative mental model, i.e. *thinking by doing.* Behavioral markers include: experimentally manipulating resources in the environment and re-positioning the body to change available sensory data.

Physical sense-making and perceptual sense-making each have a continuum of cognitive states within them ranging from clamped to unclamped cognition. While these two spectra are interrelated, and may occur simultaneously (or in very rapid succession), analysts approximate which state is dominant through time by observing mutually exclusive behavioral markers denoting what type of sense-making activities are currently observable. For example, when someone is pausing to reflect, they often briefly stop performing functional actions while they are thinking (e.g. looking away, closing eyes, etc.), which are strong indicators the person is experiencing a perceptual unclamp.

The categorical distinction between these two types of sense-making processes is reflected by assigning one type a positive value and the other a negative value both using a scale of 0 (fully clamped) to 1 (fully unclamped). The reason this positive and negative convention was adopted is because it enables quantifying interaction trends by looking at the variance of the cumulative sum of these coded values through time. From a theoretical standpoint, a value of 0 means free energy is minimized and cognition is clamped. Any deviation from 0, in the positive or negative direction, represents an unclamp event. The decision of which category initially receives a positive vs. negative sign is inconsequential if it remains consistent throughout the analysis. The important delineation here is providing granular temporal data about interaction styles and sense-making strategies through time.

The magnitude of the numerical value assigned to the unclamped action is determined by assessing the degree of unclamp based on behavioral markers. To help systematize the coding process and increase inter-rater reliability, we use discreet points on the cognitive spectrum to represent magnitude (.5 or 1 in both categories). For example, agents can pause their actions to wait for their partner to take their turn (partial perceptual unclamp), or they can be completely confused and disengaged from the play session (full perceptual unclamp). Complete confusion and disengagement should be considered more unclamped than attentively waiting for a partner to act. Conversely, in terms of physical sense-making, searching for new resources to introduce into the play session would be more unclamped than slightly rearranging or restructuring elements already in the play space.

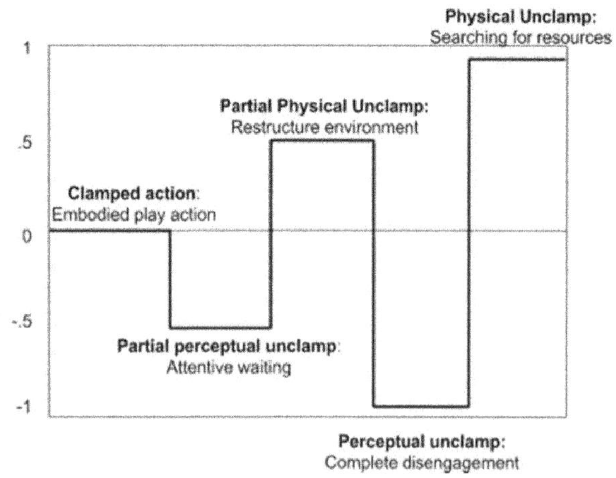

Figure 3. An example of clamped and unclamped states plotted on an axis showing how each state is coded during analysis.

When plotted along an x-axis representing time, these numerical values create what we refer to as the *sense-making curve* (as shown in Figure 3). This curve quantifies what types of actions each individual participant was engaged in throughout the course of the experiment. These curves can be mathematically analyzed and combined to quantify the interaction dynamics between the players.

To summarize, we propose a new approach to formally model the interaction dynamics of participatory sense-making. We use the qualitative video coding conventions of the sense-making curve to translate human interaction dynamics and patterns of interaction into a machine-readable format. In the next sections, we describe the web-based tool that was developed to perform this coding procedure and the analysis technique for combining sense-making curves and classifying different types participatory sense-making and styles of collaboration from sense-making curves.

SENSE-MAKING CURVE TOOL

To quantify interaction dynamics, the qualitative coding conventions described above can be applied to video analysis. To accomplish this, an analyst reviews the video and assigns a numerical value to each moment based on the type of action the participant is currently engaged in. This process is repeated for each participant in the experiment to produce unique datasets characterizing each participant's actions through time. Clamped actions are assigned a value of 0 to signify minimized free-energy, while unclamped actions are assigned a value from -1 to 1 to signify deviation from a free-energy equilibrium. The sign (positive/negative) and value of the data point corresponds to the category of unclamped action and the relative degree of the unclamp, respectively.

The prototype sense-making curve tool (shown in Figure 4) is a web-based qualitative video coding environment. To apply the qualitative codes to the video, the researcher uses the up and down arrow keys to increase or decrease the current coding value, which is visualized by a code selector slider on the right side of the screen. The system samples the value of the slider every 250ms and records that data point in an array list. Therefore, the value the code selector is currently resting at is the value that will be assigned to the time that is currently being viewed in the embedded video window.

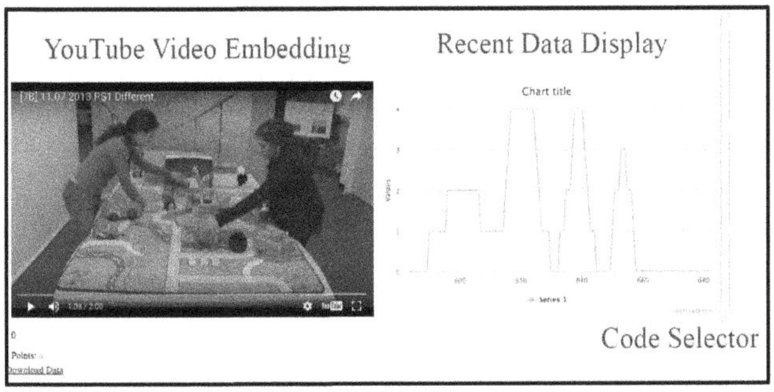

Figure 4. Prototype Sense-Making Curve Analysis Tool.

The most recent values from the array list (relative to the current point in the video that is being played) are visualized in the recent data display to the right of the embedded video. When the user scrubs the video to different time points, the data display and coding value also move to that point in the array, allowing researchers to revisit different parts of the video to re-apply codes.

The user can slow down and speed up the video playback speed. Researchers using this tool typically slow the videos down to half speed and code one participant at a time. The analyst re-watches the video to code each participant. Once an analyst was oriented to this approach, the overall code application time per video (including both participants) was approximately 4 to 1, meaning it took about 4 minutes to code every 1 minute of video data. A 4 to 1 time-efficiency ratio for qualitative video coding, and a 2 to 1 ratio for coding individual participants within an interaction, is more efficient when compared to other event-based coding methods that may take up to 30 minutes (or more) to code an individual minute of data (i.e. a 30 to 1 time-efficiency ratio).

It is important to point out that while the sense-making curve might facilitate rapid and reliable qualitative coding, the granularity of analysis between the sense-making curve and typical event-based coding techniques is much different. The sense-making curve provides continuous and targeted data about interaction dynamics, but it does not identify individual actions, i.e. the content of the actions. In future versions of this tool, we plan to allow tagging the curve with different events to combine the power of event-based coding with our proposed continuous coding technique.

The numbers representing each code on the 1 to -1 scale (according to the clamped/ unclamped convention) were each mapped to 0-4 values at the request of coders (to reduce time switching between common states in a given domain). As long as each state is consistently coded through time and the mappings to their placement on the 1 to -1 scale are stored, the numbers used in the user interface of the tool can change. This change in scale creates an interesting level of obfuscation between the analyst and the predictions of the theory and cognitive framework since the curve they are currently seeing visualized in the tool is not necessarily the final form of the curve used in the analysis (after the value transductions). It remains to be seen whether the tool is most reliable when used with the 1 to -1 scale or a 0 - 4 scale in the interface.

The data analyst's role in this context is to decide which of the five states participants are in based on behavioral markers. The design of the behavioral markers is determined by understanding what types of actions in a domain should be classified as clamped/unclamped and the degree of this association.

USING SENSE-MAKING CURVE TOOL

The coding tool and technique were used on both the pretend play dataset and the Drawing Apprentice user study data. To collect the pretend play dataset, we conduct an observational study involving 32 pairs of adult players who were asked to perform two pretend play sessions for each pair of the participants on a large play-mat with toys and stuffed animals (c.f. [7] for a full description of the study). The pretend play experimental sessions began by providing participants with a narrative prompt (e.g. monsters attack, drag racing, etc.). They were given 5 minutes for both setup and play based on their interpretation of the narrative

Clamp Value	Classifications and Behavioral Markers
1	**Physical Unclamp** **Play**: searching toy box, change locations **Drawing**: moving device, explicit feedback, verbalizations
.5	**Partial Physical Unclamp** **Play**: place items, arrange items, build new structures, extra-diegetic communication **Drawing**: aesthetic UI interactions, simulated drawing strokes
0	**Clamped Actions** **Play**: fluid and embodied play actions **Drawing**: fluid drawing actions
-.5	**Partial Perceptual Unclamp** **Play**: hesitation, holding character waiting **Drawing**: pen in hand waiting
-1	**Perceptual Unclamp** **Play**: disengaged, distracted, hands by side **Drawing**: leaning back from display, lowered pen, looking away

Table 1. Summarized coding scheme for the pretend play and Drawing Apprentice sense-making curve analysis.

Data Set	Pretend Play	Collab Drawing
Analysts	3	2
Codes Compared	19,900	362,560
Technique	Fleiss' Kappa	Kripendorff's Alpha
IRR Score	.71	.76
Interpretation	Substantial Agreement	Substantial Agreement

Table 2. Inter-rater reliability results from using creative sense-making technique to analyze pretend play and Drawing Apprentice data.

prompt. Three coders then analyzed a subset of the 64 recorded videos, resulting in a total of 128 sense-making curves produced. These three coders were able to achieve an inter-rater reliability (IRR) score of 0.71 (substantial agreement according to [13]) using Fleiss' Kappa (shown in Table 1). To calculate this score, all the coders analyzed an individual play session and the Fleiss' Kappa for the coded values of the left and right players in the session was averaged. This Fleiss' Kappa value compared the reliability of 19,990 total code applications between the analysts on the pretend play dataset.

For the Drawing Apprentice user study, six participants were asked to draw with both a human and AI drawing agent during two 12 minute drawing sessions using our prototype described in [8]. Two coders analyzed the 12 user study videos resulting in 48 total sense-making curves between the two coders with an overall inter-rater reliability of 0.76 (substantial agreement according to [13]) using Kripendorff's alpha (for two coders). For this dataset, the IRR value for coding the participant (0.64) and co-creative agent (0.86) were averaged to yield the 0.76 value for Kripendorff's alpha over the entire dataset, which consisted of 362,560 code applications (shown in Table 2). The IRR calculation for Drawing Apprentice uses more codes in its comparison because both analysts were asked to code the entire dataset since it was feasible given its size (compared to the much larger dataset for pretend play that had to be divided among the analysts).

To achieve these reliability measures, we employed the Delphi method, an iterative coding scheme refinement technique [25]. Two different teams of analysts coded the sample videos from each domain, tested their reliability, and looked for points where their coding diverged. To help visualize and quantify discrepancies between their code applications, a 2D convolution was performed between the analysts' sense-making curve data in a pairwise manner for each participant in the sampled dataset. Then, they discussed possible reasons for the divergence and added more detailed behavioral markers to the coding scheme to help ensure future reliability. After several rounds of refining the behavioral markers of the coding scheme, analysts achieved substantial agreement over thousands of code applications. In most instances in the literature, these inter-rater reliability measures are not being used on data sets with sizes this large, or with continuous temporal data. For that reason, it may be beneficial to explore additional inter-rater reliability measures to pair with the Kripendorff's alpha and Fleiss' Kappa to help evaluate inter-rater agreement through time with increased precision (such as 2D convolution and cross-correlation).

Performing the numerical transduction on the data (from the 0-4 scale to 1 to -1 scale shown in Table 1) before performing these reliability measures may also yield insights into the productivity of this method. For example, once the data is represented in the 1 to -1 convention, it can be bucketed into three categories of positive, neutral, or negative. While this reduces the overall granularity with which the data is being compared, it provides a better indicator as to whether two coders were merely off in measuring the magnitude of the unclamp versus a completely different direction.

EXEMPLAR DATASET AND ANALYSIS

This section shows the application of the sense-making curve analysis technique on a real data point from the pretend play session with 32 adult dyads. This data represents the sense-making curves coded for each of the individuals in the play session. The sense-making curves shown in Figure 5 present the qualitative coding classification of two participants during a 5-minute play session. Here, we can see both players greatly fluctuating above and below the axis (i.e. building meaning/restructure environment and waiting/disengaged, respectively) during the first third of the play session. These fluctuations may correlate to the setup period during which participants are figuring out what kind of activities to engage in during the play session by exploring the play mat, toys, and resources at their disposal. This early period represents more active sense-making where the participants are actively experimenting with the environment and directly communicating about what to do (i.e. extradiagetic communication).

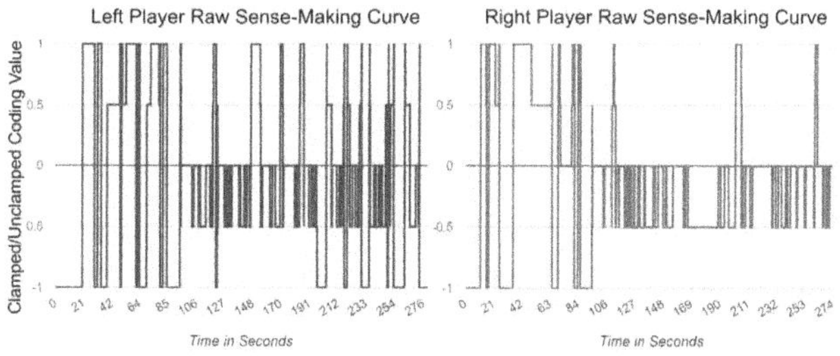

Figure 5. Sense-making curve examples from two participants during one session of the pretend play study.

After about 90 seconds (about a third of the way through the x-axis), both participants begin to engage in play activities and their curves fluctuate more closely around the 0 axis (i.e. clamped cognition), cycling between 0 (engaged in fluid play activity) and -.5 (attentively waiting). This trend indicates some degree of turn-taking is beginning to emerge at this point. It is important to note that the left player continues to deviate greatly from the 0-axis at distinct points in both the positive and negative directions, suggesting that this player was more actively involved in adding new elements into the play session as well as disengaging more often, especially in the last third of the play session.

Calculating the cumulative integral of each of these sense-making curves provides a more global picture of the participants' activities through time. For this exemplar demonstration, the MATLAB cumsum function was utilized to approximate the integral. In a more precise analysis, the MATLAB function cumtrapz was used to increase the accuracy of the integral approximation.

The cumulative integral approximations shown in Figure 6 provide an easier way to visualize how each participant was contributing to the overall flow of the play session activities. From this representation, it becomes clear that both players experienced a relatively dramatic initial hesitation and waiting period followed by a period of building meaning in the environment. However, after this initial phase, their actions seem to diverge as the right player spends more time watching or hesitating, while their partner, the left player, continues to build new meaning and engage in play (as represented by periods of rising during the cumulative integral and holding steady, respectively).

Combining these two cumulative integrals together provides information about how both participants' actions related to each other through time. To accomplish this operation, two one-dimensional arrays are added together. This combined cumulative integral can be used to identify interaction trends involving both players.

The graph in Figure 7 shows the combined cumulative integral of the participants' sense-making curves, which shows the overall activity through time with respect to both players' actions. We refer to this curve as the *creative trajectory* because it can be used to help identify interaction trends and patterns in the overall creative flow, or trajectory, of the play session. For this exemplar demonstration, these trends are visually identified and depicted on the graph. Each of these trends theoretically corresponds to different ways of collaborating as well as helping to identify when coupled play began to arise between the players (the orange arrows in the graph). In the actual analysis, more precise computational modeling techniques are used, similar to the conventions used in stock market analysis to identify buy, sell, and hold signals from continuous stock data. The trends visualized on this graph can be summarized as follows:

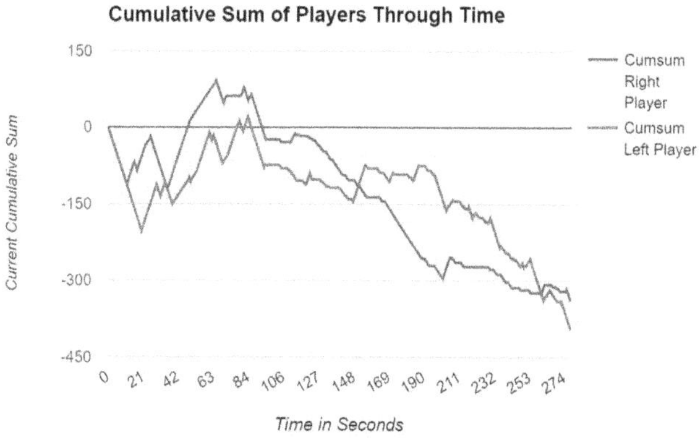

Figure 6. Running cumulative sum (integral approximation) of the right and left players' sense-making curves

Blue Line: Both players are hesitating or waiting. This classification will be most distinct when both players are completely disengaged for prolonged periods of time as they will both have values of -1 during those times. When both players are coded as -1, the cumulative integral is reduced sharply, as indicated by the large negative slope in the first three blue arrows. However, the value of the cumulative integral can also fall when both players are either attentively waiting (coded as -.5), or one is attentively waiting while the other plays (coded as 0). In

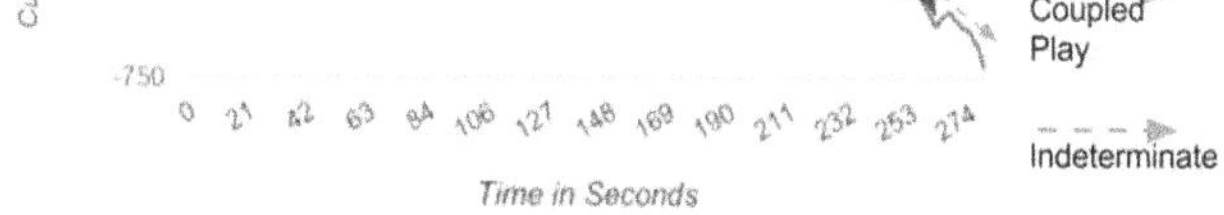

Figure 7. Sum of both players running integrals creates a *creative trajectory* depicting interaction trends between players through time

this case, the slope of the creative trajectory will not fall as fast, such as the last blue line on the right side of Figure 7.

Red Line: Both players are building meaning or gathering resources. This classification corresponds to both players actively engaging in a sense-making process (unclamped cognition) through interactively exploring their environment by building new structures in the play area or looking for new resources to add to the play area. When the slope of the creative trajectory is positive, both players are most likely engaged in unclamped actions (rated as +.5 or +1) to make the cumulative integral rise. A high positive slope would indicate that both players are actively looking for new resources (i.e. rummaging through the toy box) to add to the play mat. A smaller positive slope may indicate building or tweaking elements that are currently on the play mat.

Orange Line: Clamped quasi-stationary play state. This classification represents some type of coupled play interaction between the participants. There are many different types of coupling that can result in this type of semi-stationary state where the slope of the creative trajectory curve is near zero. To classify this state, the derivative of the creative trajectory curve can be calculated and those areas of the derivative curve that are near zero within a threshold of standard. These couplings indicate regions of interest upon which to perform further sub-classification analyses.

Gray line: Non-classified states. This classification represents those points of the play session that do not fall under the three classifications made above. These ambiguous states of play may fall into one of the above categories when the tuning parameters for the classification algorithms are changed. They do not have to be directly considered in the analysis, but their presence can help researchers understand the granularity of their classification parameters.

The segments of time during which participants were engaged in coupled play (orange classification line) are a rich source of data. Those time segments can serve as a lens to go back to the initial sense-making curves to analyze the original sense-making curve values to see what types of activities participants were engaged in during the coupled interaction. For example, where both players simultaneously clamped on play actions? If so, were they mutually clamped on the same activity, such as attacking a castle? Another explanation could be one person was continuously adding meaning while the other person was continuously in the attentive waiting stage, which would result in the cumulative integral sum remaining largely the same and yielding a quasi-stationary state in the creative trajectory curve. The values from the original sense-making curve will reveal these nuanced details, allowing further sub-classification of the quasi-stationary play state into: dominant clamp (one person is adding new meaning and directing the play), mutual clamp (both participant are playing simultaneously), and rhythmic balanced interchange (participants are taking turns).

From this point in the analysis, it is also possible to count how much time was spent in each type of interaction trend and when each interaction trend tended to occur within the overall timeline of each pretend play session. With this data, it may be possible to identify successful collaboration strategies by comparing these broad interaction trends.

APPROACH LIMITATIONS

Without full validation, the findings from the CSM curve analysis are still in their preliminary phases. There are a few concrete activities that will help validate this technique that we are planning for future work. The primary concern with evaluating the CSM methodology is determining whether the classifications the technique generates (i.e. clamped/unclamped, mutual clamp, dominant clamp, etc.) correspond to those events in reality, i.e. does the theory correspond to the ground truth. One method for establishing ground truth would be to refer to the retrospective protocol analysis conducted with the participants to determine whether the remarks the participant made during a given time correspond to the cognitive state predicted by the theory. However, since the CSM analysis method was developed after the Drawing Apprentice and pretend play studies were designed and executed, the retrospective protocols did not focus on soliciting information explicitly related to the cognitive states later identified by the CSM framework.

There are also procedural limitations arising from the process by which analysts apply codes in the CSM approach. There is an inherent limitation in terms of the delay between an action onset and when a coder determines to move the coding slider to that corresponding value (since this is based on the analyst's reaction time and subjective judgment). Depending on each analysts' style, this delay may time-shift or change the granularity of certain events in the data, while still registering the overall deviation that is important later in the analysis. This limitation could drastically reduce inter-rater reliability while having an insignificant impact on the comparison of the actual sense-making curves and creative trajectories.

When users switch between codes using this tool, it is possible (and likely) that the system will sample data points during the process of moving from one code to another. This results in the system recording values between the current code and the target code. The number of values recorded between code switches increases depending on how far away the target code is from the current code since the user employs the up/down arrow keys to move between codes. This limitation of the tool creates some potential noise in the data as values are being recorded that were not intentionally coded by the analysts. However, this source of noise does not appear to significantly affect the overall reliability of the technique. One method to avoid this limitation is to use the number keys to control mode changes rather than the arrow keys.

Sense-making curves provide continuous data about interaction dynamics, but they do not contain contextual information about the type of actions that participants are engaging in through time or the conditions of their environment. To account for this important contextual information, the sense-making curve tool could allow users to associate text input (e.g. labels, tags) to different time segments of the sense-making curve. To reduce the amount of time it takes to tag and label events, the system could employ an autocomplete technique for typing tags as well as present the user with frequently used tags when they begin the event labeling task. This feature could combine the power of event-based coding (e.g. contextual details) with the continuous interaction analysis of the sense-making curve. With this information, the system could classify interaction dynamic trends as well as quantify the number of events and their temporal relationship.

DISCUSSION & FUTURE DIRECTIONS

Each sense-making curve represents a rich source of data that can be further analyzed using a variety of parameters and metadata that describe the features of each curve. Some initial metadata parameters to explore are the highest and lowest points of the curve, the number of inflection points, the magnitude of inflections, and the slope between inflections. Once each of the curves has been described using the metadata representation, the curves can be transformed to a new mathematical space for clustering analysis to reveal patterns and trends within and between different curves.

Graphically representing the creative trajectory curves and analyzing their trends can serve as a powerful data visualization and conceptual aid to reason about open-ended creative collaboration. The continuous nature of the sense-making curve data also provides opportunities to explore much more granular analysis and classification techniques. Further classification using the computational modeling convention mentioned in this paper (i.e. the stock market analysis technique) enables the possibilities of further quantification to facilitate comparisons throughout the dataset.

It might be possible to utilize machine learning algorithms to automatically code video data based on training sets comprised of human coded sense-making curve data paired with its video counterpart. The machine learning algorithm could attempt to code the video and inform the user about the segments of the curve in which it has less confidence about its coded value. The user could perform a targeted coding session to modify and update the low-confidence segments, thereby reducing the overall code application time while maintaining accuracy.

CONCLUSIONS

This paper presented the technical need and theoretical foundations for the proposed sense-making curve coding and analysis technique. The creative sense-making framework provides a new method to visualize and quantify the interaction dynamics of creative collaboration, e.g. the rhythm of interaction, style of turn taking, and manner in which participants are mutually making sense of a situation. The framework was applied to empirical studies of human collaboration (in the domain of pretend play) and AI-based systems (in the domain of collaborative drawing) to establish its validity through cross-domain application and inter-rater reliability within each domain. The theoretical justifications for the choice of the conventions for behavioral coding markers as well as graphical representation were described. We showed how the continuous nature of the sense-making curve data allows continuous functions, such as integrations, to provide quantitative information about how the collaboration is unfolding through time. This technique was applied to an exemplar data set to demonstrate the type of data that such an analysis yields. This technique may be generalizable to other fields studying and designing products for open-ended creative collaboration and co-creation.

ACKNOWLEDGEMENTS

Thanks to the analysts that helped apply and refine the creative sense-making approach: Margaret Hu, Yueting Lee, Shan Li, Lily Lau, and Margeaux Comerford. This work was supported by NSF Grant IIS-1320520.

REFERENCES

1. Malika Auvray, Charles Lenay, and John Stewart. 2009. Perceptual interactions in a minimalist virtual environment. *New ideas in psychology* 27, 1: 32–47.
2. Stefan Benus. 2009. Variability and stability in collaborative dialogues: turn-taking and filled pauses. In *Tenth Annual Conference of the International Speech Communication Association*.
3. Jerome Bourbousson and Marina Fortes-Bourbousson. 2016. How do Co-agents Actively Regulate their Collective Behavior States? *Frontiers in Psychology* 7.
4. Erin A Carroll and Celine Latulipe. 2012. Triangulating the personal creative experience: self-report, external judgments, and physiology. In *Proceedings of Graphics Interface 2012*, 53–60.
5. Erin A Carroll, Celine Latulipe, Richard Fung, and Michael Terry. 2009. Creativity factor evaluation: towards a standardized survey metric for creativity support. In *Proceedings of the seventh ACM conference on Creativity and cognition*, 127–136.
6. Sharolyn Converse. 1993. Shared mental models in expert team decision making. *Individual and group decision making: Current*, 1993: 221.
7. Nicholas Davis, Margeaux Comerford, Mikhail Jacob, Chih-Pin Hsiao, and Brian Magerko. 2015. An Enactive Characterization of Pretend Play. In

Proceedings of the 2015 ACM SIGCHI Conference on Creativity and Cognition, 275–284.
8. Nicholas Davis, Chih-Pin Hsiao, Kunwar Yashraj Singh, Lisa Li, and Brian Magerko. 2016. Empirically Studying Participatory Sense-Making in Abstract Drawing with a Co-Creative Cognitive Agent. In *Proceedings of the 21st International Conference on Intelligent User Interfaces*, 196–207.
9. Hanne De Jaegher and Ezequiel Di Paolo. 2007. Participatory sense-making. *Phenomenology and the cognitive sciences* 6, 4: 485–507.
10. Hanne De Jaegher, Ezequiel Di Paolo, and Shaun Gallagher. 2010. Can social interaction constitute social cognition? *Trends in cognitive sciences* 14, 10: 441–447.
11. Ezequiel A Di Paolo, Marieke Rohde, and Hiroyuki Iizuka. 2008. Sensitivity to social contingency or stability of interaction? Modelling the dynamics of perceptual crossing. *New ideas in psychology* 26, 2: 278–294.
12. Valentina Fantasia, Hanne De Jaegher, and Alessandra Fasulo. 2014. We can work it out: an enactive look at cooperation. *Frontiers in psychology* 5.
13. Joseph L Fleiss. 1971. Measuring nominal scale agreement among many raters. *Psychological bulletin* 76, 5: 378.
14. Karl Friston. 2009. The free-energy principle: a rough guide to the brain? *Trends in cognitive sciences* 13, 7: 293–301.
15. Karl Friston. 2010. The free-energy principle: a unified brain theory? *Nature Reviews Neuroscience* 11, 2: 127–138.
16. Karl Friston, James Kilner, and Lee Harrison. 2006. A free energy principle for the brain. *Journal of Physiology-Paris* 100, 1: 70–87.
17. Tom Froese, Hiroyuki Iizuka, and Takashi Ikegami. 2014. Embodied social interaction constitutes social cognition in pairs of humans: a minimalist virtual reality experiment. *Scientific reports* 4.
18. John S Gero. 2011. Fixation and commitment while designing and its measurement. *The Journal of Creative Behavior* 45, 2: 108–115.
19. Arthur M Glenberg. 1997. What memory is for: Creating meaning in the service of action. *Behavioral and brain sciences* 20, 1: 41–50.
20. Nitesh Goyal, Gilly Leshed, Dan Cosley, and Susan R Fussell. 2014. Effects of implicit sharing in collaborative analysis. In *Proceedings of the SIGCHI Conference on Human Factors in Computing Systems*, 129–138.
21. Catholijn M Jonker, M Birna Van Riemsdijk, and Bas Vermeulen. 2011. Shared mental models. In *Coordination, organizations, institutions, and norms in agent systems vi*. Springer, 132–151.
22. Brigitte Jordan and Austin Henderson. 1995. Interaction analysis: Foundations and practice. *The journal of the learning sciences* 4, 1: 39–103.
23. Andruid Kerne, Steven M Smith, Eunyee Koh, Hyun Choi, and Ross Graeber. 2008. An experimental method for measuring the emergence of new ideas in information discovery. *Intl. Journal of Human–Computer Interaction* 24, 5: 460–477.
24. M Kim and Mary Lou Maher. 2005. Comparison of designers using a tangible user interface & graphical user interface and impact on spatial cognition. *Proc. Human Behaviour in Design* 5.
25. Harold A Linstone, Murray Turoff, and others. 1975. *The Delphi method: Techniques and applications*. Addison-Wesley Reading, MA.
26. Mary Lou Maher, Zafer Bilda, and Leman Figen Gül. 2006. Impact of collaborative virtual environments on design behaviour. In *Design computing and cognition'06*. Springer, 305–321.
27. Mary Lou Maher and Douglas H Fisher. 2012. Using AI to evaluate creative designs. In *DS 73-1 Proceedings of the 2nd International Conference on Design Creativity Volume 1*.
28. Etienne B Roesch, Slawomir J Nasuto, and J Mark Bishop. 2012. Emotion and anticipation in an enactive framework for cognition (response to Andy Clark). *Frontiers in psychology* 3.
29. R Keith Sawyer and Stacy DeZutter. 2009. Distributed creativity: How collective creations emerge from collaboration. *Psychology of Aesthetics, Creativity, and the Arts* 3, 2: 81.
30. Philipp Schwartenbeck, Thomas FitzGerald, Ray Dolan, and Karl Friston. 2013. Exploration, novelty, surprise, and free energy minimization. *Frontiers in psychology* 4: 710.
31. Sune Steffensen and Sarah Bro Pedersen. 2014. Temporal dynamics in human interaction. *Cybernetics & Human Knowing* 21, 1–2: 80–97.
32. Sune Vork Steffensen. 2012. Care and conversing in dialogical systems. *Language Sciences* 34, 5: 513–531.
33. John Robert Stewart, Olivier Gapenne, and Ezequiel A Di Paolo. 2010. *Enaction: Toward a new paradigm for cognitive science*. MIT Press.
34. David Vernon. 2010. Enaction as a conceptual framework for developmental cognitive robotics. *Paladyn, Journal of Behavioral Robotics* 1, 2: 89–98.
35. David Vernon. 2014. *Artificial cognitive systems: A primer*. MIT Press.
36. Pawel Wozniak, Nitesh Goyal, Przemyslaw Kucharski, Lars Lischke, Sven Mayer, and Morten Fjeld. 2016. RAMPARTS: Supporting Sensemaking with Spatially-Aware Mobile Interactions. In *Proceedings of the 2016 CHI Conference on Human Factors in Computing Systems*, 2447–2460.

Dimensional Reasoning and Research Design Spaces

Stephen MacNeil, Johanna Okerlund, Celine Latulipe
Human-Computer Interaction Lab
University of North Carolina at Charlotte, Charlotte, NC, USA
{smacnei2, jokerlun, clatulip}@uncc.edu

ABSTRACT
We present an exploration into the use of dimensional reasoning and the creation of research design spaces. We hypothesized that researchers, engaged in open-ended creative problem solving, could adapt the methods of design thinking and design spaces to create dimensionalized research design spaces. To investigate how researchers might explicitly engage in such dimensionalization processes, we created and studied (n=5, n=5) an interactive web-based system for the creation of research design spaces. Our results showed that a 'dimensions-first' approach was difficult for researchers to work with. We then created and studied (n=11) a prototype 'examples-first' approach. Our results suggest that the ability of researchers to explicitly dimensionalize their research areas is quite varied and that significant scaffolding is required to help researchers reason in this way.

ACM Classification Keywords
H.5.m. Information Interfaces and Presentation (e.g. HCI): Miscellaneous

Author Keywords
dimensional reasoning; meta-research; design space; research; ideation; sense-making.

INTRODUCTION
Conducting high-level academic research is a complex, creative, and open-ended task. It can be challenging for researchers to effectively frame new work within the existing cannon because it requires understanding what has been done, how different works relate and the different ways of approaching the topic. Reasoning about the research area iteratively generates insights that inform and position ongoing work.

One way to concretely represent the scope of a research area is to present, through a survey paper, a research design space. A research design space defines an area by categorizing and differentiating various approaches. It gives researchers a common ground on which to position their research or find gaps in the area [25]. An early example of this from the HCI literature is Card et. al's canonical design space of input devices [6], which has been used by many researchers to position their contributions and find new areas to explore. Other examples include a vocabulary and categorization of gestural interactions [56], a taxonomy of 3D tabletop systems [26], and a design space of composite visualizations [30]. What is common among design spaces is that they make design decisions explicit, summarize what is possible, and what is under-explored.

In design domains, a design space defines the bounds of a problem space and solutions in it. Design spaces are often dimensional representations that enumerate the design decisions to be considered, along with potential options for each decision. If externalized as tables, matrices, lists etc, design spaces can be very effective for communicating with collaborators and clients. Representing design spaces with visualizations provides cognitive and perceptual benefits such as pattern recognition [22]. Identifying patterns, gaps, and seeing disparate connections are important for distinguishing between what has and hasn't been tried and may lead to new perspectives and creative leaps [47]. Also, creating external representations of the design space reduces cognitive load [35] and provides opportunities for reflection in practice [52]. The question we ask in this paper is whether design spaces can be appropriated to support researchers. Research tools exist, but, as discussed later, they support only certain types of reasoning and are not appropriate for constructing a research design space.

A research design space (RDS) can be explained through the metaphor of dimensions in physical space. A dimension is an aspect of the research area that encompasses the scope of all possibilities for that aspect. In computing, the algorithmic complexity in terms of time might be one dimension, and algorithmic complexity in terms of storage requirements might be another. One can think of these two dimensions occupying the X and Y axes of a two-dimensional space. The dimensions define the known bounds of the space and existing examples, such as specific algorithms, can be plotted in this space. Of course, a research design space (RDS) is likely to be multi-dimensional and complex. Such spaces are difficult to reason about in the abstract, pushing our cognitive limits, and thus an external representation is very helpful.

What would a tool that supports the creation and exploration of an RDS look like? It would need to represent numerous dimensions, some categorical, some continuous; support adding examples to the space and identifying how each example fits

C&C '17, June 27 - 30, 2017, Singapore, Singapore

ISBN 978-1-4503-4403-6/17/06...$15.00
DOI: http://dx.doi.org/10.1145/3059454.3059472

along each dimension; and support ways to visualize and explore the space. Such a tool could be used in conjunction with existing research tools, such as reference management systems, to form an ecology of tools that can support researchers at varying points in their research process. However, it is unclear how researchers reason about RDSs and whether such dimensional reasoning would come naturally. Do they start with examples or dimensions? Is the RDS artifact more valuable than the process of constructing it? Are researchers able to create dimensional representations of their research directly or do they need significant scaffolding and training?

This paper presents three studies that explored how researchers create research design spaces (RDS) and reason dimensionally: two studies adopt a 'dimensions-first' approach and one adopts an 'examples-first' approach. In this paper, we refer to the domain as the "research area"; the artifacts (papers, algorithms, designs, concepts, and solutions) in the research area as "examples"; and the space of all dimensions and examples for that research area as the "research design space" or RDS. The contributions of this paper are: 1) the Design Space Explorer, a tool that affords the creation of a research design space, 2) results from two studies of 'dimensions-first' RDS creation, 3) results from a study of 'examples-first' RDS creation, and 4) insights about how researchers interact with a dimensional representation of their research and how they interact with tools designed to support this process.

BACKGROUND

Many research support tools exist; however, few allow researchers to construct and then reflect on both the details and high-level concepts associated with their research. Design spaces have the potential to allow researchers to balance these two divergent needs. In this section, we describe existing research support tools, the roles of ideation and sense-making in research, review previous work on design spaces, and describe how design spaces might be appropriated for research.

Research Support Tools

A plethora of tools help keep track of and categorize literature. Reference management software [19, 44, 61, 37] supports grouping and sorting PDF documents manually or by their meta-data. Annotations and tags can also be applied to these documents. Docear leverages annotations to provide a visualization of all documents and annotations [2]. Biblioref allows the user to provide their own hierarchical taxonomy of concepts, which they then use to classify papers [39]. Hyperref supports research paper assessment by providing a way to discuss elements of a paper [32]. All of these tools are based on user-defined semantic or relational properties of papers and do not support reasoning about the papers dimensionally.

Mind maps focus on concepts and the relationships between them. The map is a hierarchical directed graph, originating at a central main concept. Other nodes branch off and contain user-added text which represents ideas or thoughts, and edges represent relationships. Tools include MindMeister, XMind, MindManager, FreeMind, and Coggle [46, 59, 45, 23, 9]. Mind maps are useful for some conceptualization and exploration tasks, but do not support dimensional reasoning.

Citation graphs, in which vertices are papers and edges point to cited work, can help researchers find relevant and popular work. Recommender systems that suggest papers based on these graphs are useful, but these recommendations disconnect the researcher from the space as a whole. When visualized, provenance and temporality are preserved, as in the case of Citeology [40]. Analytics help expose temporal and conceptual patterns, as shown in CiteSpace [8]. These visualizations support exploration of the citation graph, but they enforce a relational perspective of the research area that is based on citations and do not help generate a dimensional representation.

Visualizations are also used to explore a paper's content. Docuburst provides a visual summary of the words in a document based on their is-A relationship with other words in the document [10]. Parallel Tag Cloud supports comparisons between documents [11]. Words are listed along each axis, which represents a document, and a path shows where that word appears along other axes. For both techniques, the meaning is preserved as well as the relationships. Both represent the specific document text, which may be too rigid for researchers who want to construct conceptual representations.

Spreadsheets may help reason about examples [21, 53] but were designed for data manipulation. Dix et al. note that the success of spreadsheets for organizing, matching, and grouping is due to their flexibility and familiarity [16]. However, spreadsheets and tables are limited in communicating to the user what they can do with them. Kandogan et al. explore DataBoard, a free form spreadsheet-like interface, and compared it to a plain spreadsheet on simple problem solving tasks [31]. They determined that free form was more flexible and better for iteration, but require more effort. While spreadsheets may be able to represent the dimensions of a design space as a table, they are not particularly interactive and do not support the iterative process of constructing a design space.

Creativity in Research

Research is an amalgamation of ideation and sense-making. Researchers iteratively curate relevant related work, attempt to make sense of it, identify gaps, and brainstorm solutions that might address the gaps. Sense-making describes the process of moving from raw data to insight. Russell et al. describe the "learning loop complex" in which people create a representation of the data, identify parts that don't fit, and recursively adapt the representation to fit the data [51]. Pirolli and Card build on this idea with the "notional model of sensemaking" which takes into account the preparedness of data [50]. They describe sense-making as having loops that support top-down and bottom-up processing [50]. This defines sense-making as an iterative process; where data, representations, and insights are dynamic. This process involves convergent and divergent thinking, which are important aspects of creativity [12, 27].

As researchers engage in sense-making, they get a better sense for the problem space and develop research questions. Ideating solutions to a research question may involve reviewing related examples, artifacts, or papers. Diverse examples that represent distant parts of a solution space can lead to more creative ideas [7]. Similarly, distant associations of concepts can also lead to creative ideas [42]. On the other hand, examples that are very similar or represent only a subsection of the potential solutions can inhibit creativity and lead to design fixation [29].

Since examples can be both helpful and detrimental for ideation, they should be chosen carefully. By Buchanan's definition, research is a wicked design problem [5] in that it is constantly evolving, incomplete, and may contain conflicting information. Given this definition, choosing relevant examples automatically is very difficult. One solution might be having researchers curate their own examples. Webb et al. suggest that a platform that gives visual structure to objects and authoring capabilities to the user promotes ideation [57]. Popular curation tools, such as Pinterest, allow users to group and save web resources. However, as pointed out by Kerne et al., Pinterest's grid layout is very limiting in terms of spatial organization [34]. Kerne et al. study platforms for curating web artifacts [33, 34] and claim that these platforms should provide room to organize, group, and annotate artifacts.

Design Spaces

Previous work has defined what design spaces are and established methodologies for creating them. In the Question-Option-Criteria (QOC) method, designers use a list of questions to outline the design decisions, the options for each question, and criteria that must be satisfied [38]. Heape [28] presents a similar definition of design space and stresses the iterative nature of design, in terms of the designer's understanding of the solution space, as well as the problem space. Morphological analysis, developed by Zwicky and Wilson, is a matrix-based approach to representing the parameters and conditions in complex problems, through which the problem as a whole can be understood and possibilities can be examined [62, 63]. Dalsgaard et al. and Biskjaer et al. build off the work of Zwicky and Heape, simplifying the process and discussing the benefits of their design space notation for design problems [3, 15]. The design space notion and notation presented by Dalsgaard et al. is targeted specifically for the design of media facades [15], which Biskjaer et al. generalize and discuss in terms of design more broadly [3].

Biskjaer et al.'s framework for documenting and navigating design spaces, defines a design space as "a conceptual space, which encompasses the creativity constraints that govern what the outcome of the design process might (and might not) be." They posit that a design space is "co-constituted, explored and shaped by the designer during the design process" [3]. Their design space schema consists of columns, the headings of which are aspects of the design, rows are potential designs, and the contents of a cell reflect the option of the aspect present in that particular design solution. Biskjaer's work shows that considering a design or research area as a multi-dimensional space is worthwhile because it helps users consider ideas in relation to each other and the problem space. However, to our knowledge, no interactive tools have been developed to facilitate this iterative process of dimensionalizing the space.

Design Processes

While the artifact of a design space is helpful for documentation and communication, perhaps more important is the process one goes through *while* dimensionalizing the space. The process of defining the problem space is a reflective act where the designer or researcher reflects on the problem space, the solution space, and potential opportunities for exploration [52]. Bonnardel and Sumner investigate ways to support reflection in design in the form of critiquing based on certain criteria [4]. Several researchers discuss the use of maps to reflect on different aspects of the design process as a whole [14, 36].

Design processes live in the problem space, the solution space, or both. Beaudouin-Lafon and Mackay present a methodology that focuses on the solution space, where the goal is to generate as many potential design solutions as possible [1]. Schon discusses the necessity for the designer to construct the problem space, given that the complete bounds of the space are not known in advance [52]. Dorst and Cross present design as the iterative co-evolution of problem and solution space [17].

The related work we have reviewed demonstrates that constructing multi-dimensional design spaces is a helpful research task. Methodologies to define design spaces exist, as do platforms for curating information. While these have been shown to be useful for sense-making and in the design ideation process, there appears to be a lack of interactive tools to help researchers externalize a formal, dimensionalized design space.

RESEARCH QUESTIONS

There exists a gap between traditional research tools and the ability to create a dimensional research design space (RDS). However, it is not clear how researchers construct dimensional representations, interact with them, or use them to further their research work. Design spaces are useful for designers, but can researchers use them with the same success designers have? Thus, we have the following research questions:

Q1 Do researchers reason about their research dimensionally?
Q2 Are there other ways researchers reason about research?
Q3 How natural is it for researchers to use a tool that was designed to support dimensional reasoning?
Q4 Can a tool guide researchers to reason about their research dimensionally?
Q5 When constructing a research design space, do researchers start with examples, such as papers, and move to dimensions or do they start with dimensions and fill in examples?
Q6 Is the DSE equally effective for all researchers?
Q7 Is the DSE equally appropriate for all research areas?
Q8 What do researchers gain from dimensional reasoning?

DIMENSIONS FIRST: THE DESIGN-SPACE EXPLORER

To investigate the ways in which people might engage in dimensional reasoning during research we created a 'dimensions-first' prototype, The Design Space Explorer (DSE); a web-based tool that aids researchers in externalizing a set of dimensions that represent a complex, conceptual space. The DSE has three modes:

Create: define the dimensions of the space.
Populate: add examples by selecting values for dimensions.
Explore: interact with visualization of dimensions and points.

Responsive enabling guides users through the RDS creation process, but allows them to iterate between the three tabs.

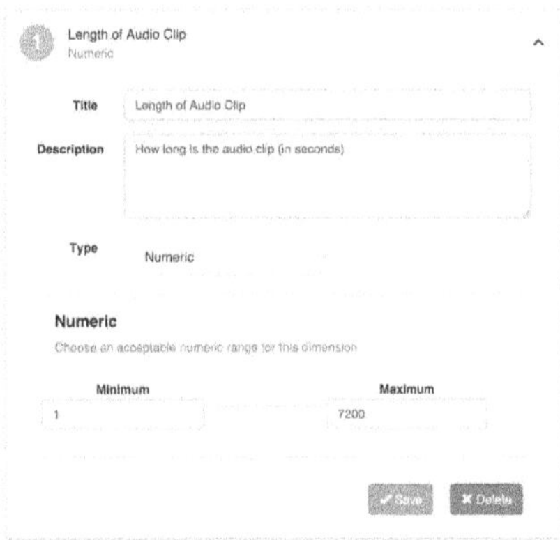

Figure 1. Dimension Card: setting audio length as a numeric dimension.

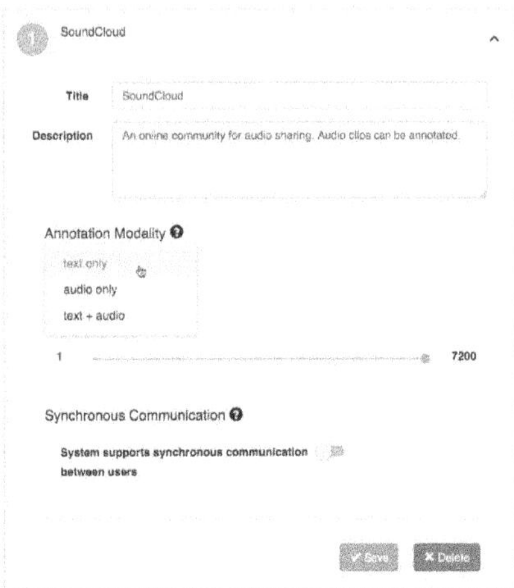

Figure 2. Example Card: adding SoundCloud as an example of an audio annotation system. The user interacts with each dimension widget to specify the values for the current example.

First, relevant dimensions are defined in the RDS, and then the DSE allows researchers to plot examples along the dimensions. Once examples have been plotted, researchers can explore and reflect on the resulting RDS. The DSE builds on Biskjaer's tabular approach to externalizing the design space [3], but by creating an interactive visualization, we leverage human spatial reasoning and enable faster and more fluid exploration of the space than is possible when looking at a static table.

Create: adding dimensions

The first step occurs in the *Spaces* tab, where the user adds a new RDS by giving it a title and a description. They can also load or delete RDSs. Then, responsive enabling guides users to the *Create* tab, where they can add and define new dimensions. Both the *Create* and *Populate* tabs use the metaphor of cards to represent dimensions and examples (Figure 1). To create a dimension, the user provides a name, description, and dimension type (categorical, numeric, or boolean).

Populate: adding example points

After defining at least one dimension, users can move to the Populate tab and add examples, which can be research papers, solutions, devices, systems, or studies. When adding an example, the dimensions that were defined in the Create tab are listed as widgets (Figure 2). The user specifies a value for each dimension using a widget slider (numeric dimensions), drop-down list (categorical dimensions), or a toggle switch (Boolean dimensions). The value for each dimension corresponds its location in the multi-dimensional space.

Explore: Visually reflecting on the whole space

In the Explore tab, users interact with a parallel coordinates visualization of their RDS and have the potential to identify gaps in the research, compare examples, and ideate new solutions. The visualization supports these types of discovery through filtering the examples by brushing along any dimension.

Visualizations leverage human spatial reasoning skills to identify patterns and make sense of the underlying data [22]. We expect that RDS tools would have multiple visualizations, but used one for our study. Scatterdice [18] allows many dimensions to be considered, two at a time, but it is best suited for non-categorical data. Bertin Matrices [48] are compact and support high-dimensional data. However, based on a review of design spaces, many of which were sparsely populated with examples, this compact view is not necessary. Parallel coordinates was chosen because it is flexible and supports continuous and categorical data. The sparseness of the examples suggest that over-plotting and occlusion are unlikely, which can be problematic for parallel coordinates. To improve usability, we implemented the traditional interaction techniques [54] - saturation brushing [58], multiple brushes (one for each dimension), sortable dimensions, and dimensional reordering.

Dimensions in our visualization are similar to facets in faceted navigation. Facets provide multiple filters that each describe one aspect of a item. Facets provide an overview of the relevant aspects of an item that is being searched for [60]. Facets can be either hierarchical or non-hierarchical [20]. They can also be placed into the context of the item itself [43].

DSE Study 1: Pilot Study

In Study 1, computing PhDs and post-doctoral researchers participated in an hour-long task and post-task interview. The session began with an introduction to the concept of a RDS and a walk-through of how to define one with the DSE. Participants then had 60 minutes to interact with the DSE in the context of their own research. They were instructed to input dimensions, populate the space with research examples, and interact with the visualization. After observing their interaction, we conducted a semi-structured interview about how they used the DSE, their research area, and their thinking process.

The goals of the first study were to understand users' approach to using the DSE and dimensionalization, whether they created all dimensions first or were more iterative, what kinds of reflection and ideation the DSE inspired, and their impressions of the value of the DSE.

Results

Four PhD students (2 female) and one post-doc in computing participated in the first study. They were compensated $15 for their time. Two participants used the entire 60 minutes to interact with the DSE, two used nearly the entire 60 minutes, and the fifth participant used 40 minutes. To obtain insights we reviewed the session videos and conducted a thematic analysis.

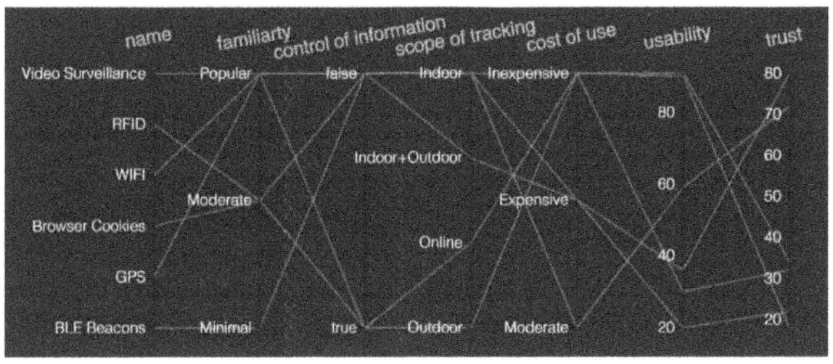

Figure 3. A RDS from the first study, created by P1-5.

Topic Matters

Of the five participants in our study, two chose to use a research topic outside of their current research area because they thought it would be easier to dimensionalize. P1-4 chose an area she had worked on before starting her PhD because, as she said, "I wanted to choose something I could easily populate. I had lots of design spaces I think, like in terms of the main research topic, but I didn't know how to populate them." P1-3 also chose a research area that was easier to dimensionalize. At first, she couldn't decide on any dimensions and asked the facilitator for clarification, to which she responded, "For papers I don't see having too many things like that." She then changed to a different RDS entirely. P1-3's initial RDS was the only RDS that didn't describe a system, but her second RDS, like the others, did describe a system. Both P1-3 and P1-4 expressed an initial concern that it was not obvious to them how to dimensionalize a research area. Dimensionalizing is difficult, but some topics appear to be easier to dimensionalize.

Assigning Dimensions: Metrics vs Features

Most participants created their RDSs from the perspective of their own research and in terms of systems with features and metrics. Three participants (P1-1, P1-4, P1-5) used their own research approach as the first point to populate their RDSs. P1-3 was the only participant who didn't create an RDS based on her own system. Some participants used evaluation metrics and others used potential features of a system when creating their RDSs. For example, P1-1 and P1-3 chose dimensions that reflected design features of existing systems (i.e. "modality", "location"), while others (P1-2, P1-4, P1-5) mostly chose dimensions that could be used as metrics on which to evaluate existing systems (i.e. "usability", "cost of use").

P1-4 referred to her dimensions as "metrics" and chose to use "strength of security" and "strength of usability", which were specific metrics that she had used during her research. P1-5 also used dimensions to represent evaluation metrics but chose them with the goal of investigating the relationship between them. For example, he said he was interested to see if there was a trend between familiarity and trust in his research area of usable privacy and security. Unlike P1-4, whose metrics corresponded to evaluation calculations used in research, P1-5 created metrics based on his own opinions.

Dimensions were also assigned based on features of existing systems. P1-3's RDS consisted mostly of design features relevant to the system that she was designing and one dimension related to the goal of the system (specifically, what type of learning style it corresponds to). P1-1's RDS consisted exclusively of factors to consider when designing a system within his research area (specifically, a system for collaborative video editing). This is consistent with P1-1's definition of design space, which is centered around the idea of parameters and design: "a space with many different parameters, many different dimensions that could be used to create a design or a design could be defined by those different dimensions or parameters." It is not clear from our results whether participants always thought of their research as systems with features and evaluation metrics or whether this was prompted by the DSE.

P1-2's defined a design space as something that is not created or designed, but discovered based on the predefined nature of the research area itself. His RDS of robot motion planning included a combination of mostly metrics for evaluation (i.e., time complexity) and design features of the implementation (i.e., underlying data structure). He noted that using the DSE was natural because "you can think about the field and you think about the different approaches. And the approaches have advantages and disadvantages, which you can highlight here." He admitted to thinking broadly to capture the big picture of the research area, rather than sub-dimensions that would have been more specific.

Iterative and Emergent

All participants iteratively revised, deleted, and added dimensions and examples. P1-4 used the visualization to evaluate her dimensions: "I was continuously going to explore and then I was like, no this doesn't sound right so I had to go back and change maybe the label or delete the dimension or come up with a new dimension." P1-5 noted that he often added an example to his RDS, which made him think of more dimensions to add. He mentioned adding RFID as an example, which he hadn't included in his prior literature review because it was too expensive, but now it led him to add a dimension to reflect that. He said, "I know that adding cost as a dimension was directly tied to remembering RFID. And then video surveillance, I think I went back and added trust and usability.' Here and elsewhere we see examples prompting the addition of dimensions as a way to differentiate examples and to fill out the research space.

As participants iterated, their mental models of their RDS evolved. In particular, P1-3 showed a change in thinking from narrow to broad throughout the study. Her RDS began with very specific dimensions about the system she was developing, most of which resulted in a category called "irrelevant", which was selected for most examples and resulted in a less interesting visualization. Towards the end of her session, she added a category that was more relevant, broader, and helped to differentiate the systems in the RDS. She had previously been thinking of ways the approaches were similar, but when she stepped back to consider differences, it lead to a more interesting set of dimensions.

Missed Opportunities for Reflection

Participants used the DSE to compare different examples in their RDSs. P1-4 noted, "I could see for example how is a particular CAPTCHA doing. I could also see if I needed to compare for example two or three at a time, did they have the same strength for example." P1-2 noticed that there was a lot of crossover among his examples and commented that they were essentially doing the same thing. P1-5 said, "I was curious to see if there were any trends" and explained in the interview where he might have seen a relationship between trust and familiarity, though the examples he had populated the RDS with did not show evidence of this relationship. P1-1 commented that the visualization didn't make it easy to see the empty spaces (gaps). He often only had one or two items for each dimension, which may explain why he saw few gaps. Despite being shown how to filter (brush) the visualization along each dimension, which may have helped identify gaps, none of the participants used this feature.

Value

Some participants used DSE to identifying new dimensions and organize their thoughts. They also offered ways they might use it more in the future. P1-4 thought the DSE could be helpful for brainstorming, "to maybe explore your research topic. To try to find more angles where you can look at that research topic and find problems and see how things are related." So even though P1-4 used the DSE during the study as an evaluation tool, she would use it in the future for ideation. P1-5 would also use it in the beginning of research: "I think I would use it early on to really get a grasp of what I'm looking for in my research. If only to understand what exists right now, that's something I would want to do early on to know what can I borrow from or generate that's novel based on that."

Some participants, such as P1-1, thought it might be helpful for organizing and exploring new research areas, "[The DSE] would certainly give you an idea of what is existing out there and what are the properties." P1-3 said she would use the DSE early in her research process, but for curation and organizing as she found more sources, rather than ideation. P1-2 thought the DSE would be helpful for developing high-level conceptual understanding of their research area: "You probably think you know all these things but until you actually sit down and lay them all out you realize you don't know as much as you thought you did ... So it definitely helps your understanding."

P1-3 was the only participant to use another tool to externalize her thought process. She opened a text editor and typed a list of relevant factors. She said that she wanted to have another tab in the DSE where she could do whatever she wanted, such as make a collage or flow chart. She thought such a feature would provide value. She self-reported that because she has a background in art, she thinks of design as more open-ended and abstract and referred to the DSE as being "so specific."

DSE Study 2: Longitudinal Study

In our first study, we received mixed results from participants. Some struggled to define dimensions and others were starting to use it to compare and evaluate examples. If dimensional reasoning emerges over time, then using the DSE for a longer period of time might allow researchers to reflect differently.

For our second study, we performed a six week case study with graduate research students. Participants came into our lab for 3 in-person interviews, they were sent weekly surveys, and they were asked to use the DSE for 2-3 hours weekly on their own time. During the first interview, we asked about their research areas and practices, gave an introduction to the concept of design spaces and dimensionalization, walked them through using the DSE, and they performed a practice task of dimensionalizing a list of fruit to get experience using it.

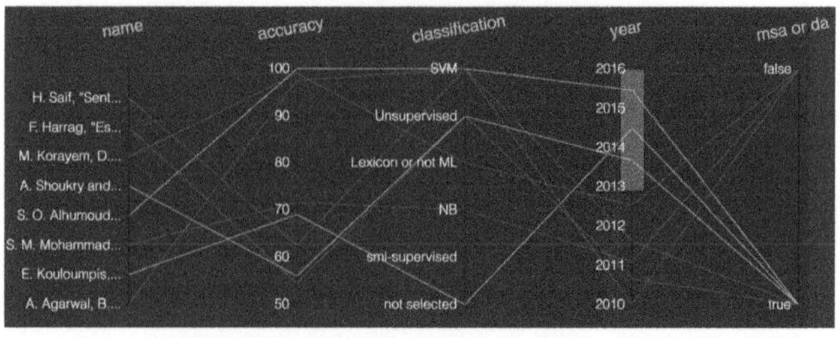

Figure 4. A RDS for P2-3 shows different approaches for classifying tweets for sentiment analysis. The year dimension is brushed to highlight only most recent papers (in orange).

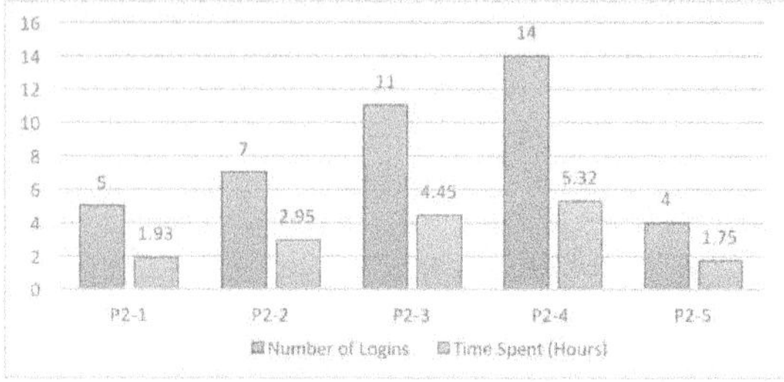

Figure 5. Participant usage of the DSE during the 6 week study.

The goals of Study 2 were to continue to study the DSE in terms of how people use it and ways it supports or doesn't support dimensional reasoning, but with respect to larger sensemaking and reflection loops than in Study 1 since participants were able to use the DSE longitudinally.

Results

Five graduate research students (4 female) participated in the longitudinal study. Participants were recruited via email and were compensated for their time, receiving a $10 gift-card at the initial training and a $20 gift-card at both the mid-way and final interviews. Three of the five students were involved with design research such as formal design methods, architectural design, and design patterns. The other two students were designing new algorithms to use in their research.

Contexts and Intentions of Use

Each participants had different purposes and use cases for the DSE. Several saw the DSE as a tool for knowledge management. In the beginning, P2-1 said, "I'm terrible at taking notes and this would organize my thoughts." P2-3 was writing a survey paper and wanted to use the DSE to evaluate whether she had organized her sources correctly. She said, "I need it in my research" and also, "I can arrange the names of the papers and the names of the authors and the names of the algorithms that they have used." P2-4 was using the DSE to curate research papers on topics that she was considering working with such as the acoustics of physical space. P2-4 also had a very unique space that investigated the American Southern Literary tradition for inspiration to design a museum that celebrates southern culture. P2-5 was also using the DSE to curate papers as he was reading them, but used the DSE to compare these papers. P2-2 was trying to characterize and classify the bounds of her set of Design Patterns for CS education.

Name	Area of study	Topic of research	Year of study	Usage of tool
P2-1	Computing	Crowdsourced design in citizen science	PhD, year 3	Knowledge management, compare approaches
P2-2	Computing	CS education research	PhD, year 2	Categorize design patterns for CSE
P2-3	Computing	Sentiment analysis in social media	PhD, year 4	To write a survey paper
P2-4	Architecture	Uncertain	MSc, year 2	Explore thesis topics, collect design inspiration
P2-5	Bioinformatics	Computational methods to study how plants influence health	PhD, year 4	Compare metrics for path ranking, evaluate sections in papers

Table 1. Participants' areas of research, their academic backgrounds, and how they used the Design Space Explorer in Study 2.

Successes

The most common observation from this study was that the DSE helped participants think about their RDS systematically and develop a holistic view of their research. P2-4 noted the DSE helped broaden her perspective: "It really helps to dimensionalize them because I start to think of them less as articles and more as articles in like different categories that they fit into. Which is something I haven't really done before." P2-1 echoed the sentiment that considering the space holistically was important, "when I was writing I was only focusing on one aspect, but when I was looking at the chart [visualization] I wasn't sure if I was fair enough in my writing."

The DSE helped some researchers approach research and writing differently. P2-4 used the DSE for a literature review and said, "[I'm] becoming more aware of how to identify gaps in research." She said that the visualization, "shows you which ones [dimensions] I've found more [examples] of so far and which I need to focus on seeing if there are other types of examples for." P2-5 used the DSE to establish the novelty of his research compared with others and to structure papers, "I'm trying to see what kinds of things are emphasized in each of the different sections - your results, intro, and methods" He explained that this was supported by the DSE, "very clearly saw where things were actually lacking so that was very easy for me to see where I should be writing or where I should make more of a point to talk about in each of the different sections where everybody else was kind of missing it."

Challenges

The challenges faced by participants were related to either the visualization or a mis-match between their mental models of their research and the dimensional representation with which they interacted. P2-3 described the visualization as difficult for her to use and that she would have preferred a table. P2-2 liked the visualization, saying "this style of visualization, I haven't seen it before and this is really a good view of the space," and "This kind of visualization makes me perform a better gap analysis on my patterns." However, she was ultimately unable to use it and hoped for a more compact representation.

The mismatch between participants' ways of reasoning and the intended dimensional reasoning was also an issue. Here are some ways of reasoning that participants expected:

Semantic Reasoning All participants expressed a desire for support of some sort of semantic reasoning and the ability to assign meaning to examples with tags. For example, P2-2 described: "[I] wanted to mark multiple options for this category ... This [example] could be random or self-selected so I actually have two of them so this is not so practical."

Relational Reasoning Many participants visually or conceptually related two examples or dimensions. For example, P2-1 explained that the visualization gave her a false sense of relatedness, though she explained that in her mind some dimensions actually were related, "I could see some inter-relations between the two [dimensions in the visualization]." P2-4 thought the DSE supported relational thinking, "you are looking more for the connections between them and the similarities that you wouldn't have thought about on your own"

Hierarchical Reasoning Most participants expressed a hierarchical understanding of their research area. P2-2 created a new space to represent meta-dimensions corresponding to her original RDS, "I decided to go to a higher level to see at least a glance." P2-4 noted that some dimensions were more important than others and should be ordered accordingly.

Blended Multiple participants made comments about the need to support multiple types of reasoning. P2-1 noted that, "I wanted to see inter-relations between aspects," and "If I had the checkbox I could do that." P2-1 explained: "when I think of my dimensions some of them are inter-related - it's not that they're always a hierarchy."

Discussion for Study 1 and Study 2

In our first study, we observed the entirety of the participants' interaction. They iterated frequently as they shaped their RDSs and defined and refined dimensions based on examples that they added. This is consistent with the view that sense-making is an iterative process [50] and that designers iterate through periods of 'problem structuring' and 'distinct problem-solving phases' [24]. This also suggests that dimensions emerging from examples might be a more natural way of creating design spaces (Q5). Researchers approached the DSE from the perspective of their own research and were most likely to encode their research as systems and in terms of metrics, features, or both (Q6, Q7). It is likely that design spaces, which were intended for designers, forced researchers to encode their research as systems that could be designed. Even though it might have been more beneficial to build a RDS for their current research topic, some participants deliberately chose topics that they perceived as easier to dimensionalize. This suggests that dimensionalizing is cognitively challenging (Q3), and that certain topics lend themselves more obviously to dimensionalization (Q6, Q7). In particular, research involving the design of a system appears to be easier than abstract topics to dimensionalize, as all participants chose research areas consisting of artifacts or systems for dimensionalization (Q6, Q7). The DSE guided researchers to dimensional representations (Q3); however, it is not clear that participants always reflected on them dimensionally (Q1). Participants described a variety of ways that the DSE changed their perspective about their own research, such as thinking more holistically (Q8). Dimensions allowed them to compare and contrast papers so that papers once thought of as solitary were actually related to others (Q8).

In the second study, researchers had more time to become comfortable with the DSE and were more vocal about mismatches between their mental models and the dimensional way in which they were being asked to interact (Q1). There is evidence of researchers reasoning dimensionally but there were also other modes of reasoning, such as semantic, relational, and hierarchical (Q2). Researchers didn't consistently receive the benefits associated with design spaces such as identifying gaps in their research. Participants created multiple small fragmented versions of the same RDS rather than elaborating a single detailed space. In search, information foraging describes how people maximize results and minimize effort [49]. For example, search engines encourage searchers to quickly scan results for information rather than delving deeply into individual websites. It may be similar here, simple fragmented spaces are good enough and participants satisfice [55] rather than iteratively refine, which is cognitively taxing.

In both studies, participants opted away from complex and detailed design spaces. In the first study, we see that participants chose spaces that were easier to dimensionalize. In the second study, researchers created multiple, simple fragmented versions of the same design space rather than creating one complex and detailed space. This may suggest that some parts of research are better suited to dimensions (Q7), that some dimensions are more obvious than others, or that the process is more important to researchers than the artifact (Q3).

EXAMPLES FIRST: PAPER PROTOTYPE

Given that so many design spaces exist in literature, we assumed it would be straight-forward to create a tool to support the construction of RDSs. But, given the challenges faced by participants in the first study, we employed a paper prototype in our third study. We did this to reduce the assumptions we were making and to provide more flexibility.

In the first two studies, participants experienced some difficulties in constructing their design spaces, especially in terms of a mismatch between their own mental models of their research and the affordances provided for dimensionalizing. Since several participants were interested in semantic encodings, our third study allowed users to employ an examples-first approach that supports tagging. We expected that this might mimic researchers' traditional process of tagging papers, but could still result in a dimensional representation. To investigate the examples-first, semantic encoding approach, we devised a paper-prototype and wizard-of-oz study [13] described next. Given the results from our first study, this low-fidelity approach gave us more flexibility.

Study 3: Tag-Based Card Study

In Study 3, participants were asked to arrive with a list of papers, artifacts, or examples that were relevant to their current research and then they completed the following tasks: 1) create examples by writing paper names on index cards, 2) tag these examples by writing an attribute that describes the example

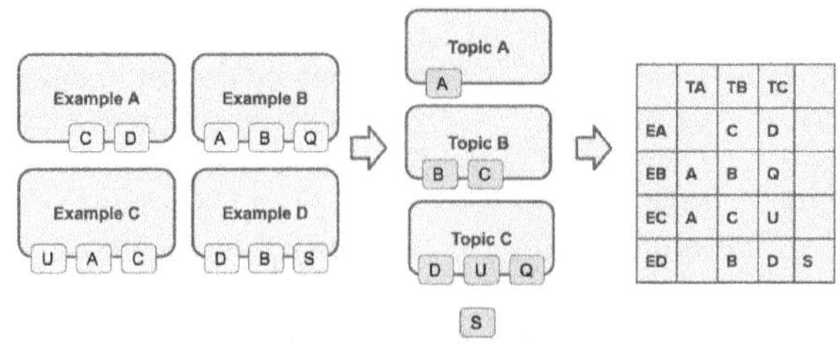

Figure 6. Participants labeled index cards with the example name and tagged them with attributes (in yellow). Participants grouped tags (in blue) by putting them on a 'topic' card and labeling it. Participants looked at the dimensional representation formed by plotting examples and corresponding tags along grouped dimensions in a table.

Figure 7. A participant from Study 3 constructs their RDS.

on a post-it note and attaching it to the index card, 3) group related tags from the previous step by placing them on index cards and labeling the index cards, and 4) review a resulting RDS spreadsheet created by a wizard. The RDS had examples as rows and groupings (dimensions) as columns. The value of each cell was the tag from that group for that example. We chose a spreadsheet because participants were familiar with them and creating a table in real-time was more feasible in a Wizard of Oz study than creating an interactive visualization. Figure 6 shows an overview of the process.

To help participants understand the process, we walked them through an example in which we created a design space of cars. We used 4 cars, and tagged them with attributes (such as 'red', '30MPG', '3 doors', etc.) which were then grouped into categories such as 'color', 'MPG' and 'number of doors'.

Results

11 graduate student participants (recruited through graduate school email lists) participated in a 90 minute session and were compensated with $15 gift cards. Participants were primarily computing majors: 3 Engineers (1MS, 2PhD), 8 CS students (5MS, 3PhD). Topics ranged from recommendation systems, to interaction log analysis, to road maintenance theory.

Existing practices Understanding participants' existing practices and how they consider their research area was important because it is possible that these things influence the way in which they perform the card tagging task. Most participants do not use organizational tools or techniques in their daily research life. Most take notes on a paper and then move on. P3-8 uses folders of papers and P3-9 has a hierarchy of folders and subfolders. P3-2's notes on each paper were highly organized, with categories, subcategories, and related bullet points. P3-11 had the most complex organization method, using a series of documents to organize, tag, relate, and index the papers.

When asked to describe how they decide if examples are relevant and the ways in which they use them to inform their research, there was a range of answers. Some use the literature to find promising approaches or solutions to a problem (P3-2, P3-6), to explain behavior they observe (P3-5), to inform the steps of their implementation (P3-3, P3-7), to explain what the problem is (P3-6), and most commonly to extract aspects that can be applied to another problem (P3-2, P3-8, P3-9, P3-10, P3-11). Unsurprisingly, none of the participants say that their primary use of related work is for the purpose of defining the space of their research.

Process Most participants easily tagged the examples, grouped the tags, and successfully completed the task. Two participants completed the task in an unexpected way: P3-2 and P3-9 tagged categories of papers rather than papers themselves. P3-2 didn't run into any trouble as the papers in each category were similar, but P3-9 had trouble applying tags consistently to papers. We discussed the intended process with P3-9 at the end, saying that the intention was to tag papers, but he felt the way he did it made sense, noting that "most of the times I read the papers to make this kind of categorizing in my brain".

Most participants reported that the process felt natural. This was partially due to the familiarity of tags in general. P3-6 explained, "It was natural for me because I am trained to assign index terms for my papers. I always do that." P3-10 said, "This follows the same mental process we follow when we write the related work section in our papers". Some reported even having the categories in mind as they were doing the initial tagging (P3-1, P3-5, P3-6, P3-8). Only two reported that it was unnatural: one because he was not accustomed to using pen and paper and the other because she was considering it as a way to keep track of the steps of her current implementation, which are always changing. P3-6 saw the value of the process for younger researchers working to construct an understanding of a new space, but felt he did not need such scaffolding: "Your way is like going from details to big picture. [..] For me the way I think is going from big picture to small picture or details". For P3-6, the DSE might have been a more natural experience. However, this also points to the fact that tools, such as the DSE or our Examples-First prototype, may be better suited to different stages of research.

Final artifact The final spreadsheet resulting from P3-1 contained a very well-formed RDS: it had columns that were clear and reasonably independent, rows that represented a variety of previous works, and most cells filled in, indicating how each work fit along each dimension. This was impressive given that the RDS was constructed in 90 minutes. In the other participant spreadsheets, there were the beginnings of RDSs, but they were incomplete. Some RDSs had cells containing lists of tags, meaning that the example lived at multiple points along that dimension. Most of the RDSs had at least 1 empty cell, but 4 of them had a significant number of empty cells that the participant did not feel they could fill in. While a limited number of empty cells and lists of tags can still be present in an RDS, if there are too many, it becomes difficult to see the bounds of the space.

Perceived benefits of RDS as Artifact When asked what benefits participants thought the RDS table would provide them, most mentioned the ability to easily see which papers discuss particular topics (P3-3, P3-5, P3-6, P3-8, P3-11). For example, P3-8 said, "it would make it easier for me to go back and look at these papers using the particular information in a table format." Others would use it to plan out their steps of implementation (P3-3, P3-7). P3-2 wanted to find the frequency of each tag to see the distribution across examples. P3-10 thought she could use the table to compare approaches, but she said that any display of the papers and the tags would allow her to do that. P3-11 pointed out that some papers that he knew were similar due to the fact that they had similar tags in a given category. Some participants said they would refer to it as they were writing a survey paper or related works section (P3-8, P3-11), but none of them would share the actual table in the paper as a representation of their RDS.

When asked if there were additional ways in which participants would like to interact with the table, they listed the ability to add notes (P3-1), link to relevant information or papers (P3-3, P3-10), color code tags (P3-4, P3-10), or drill down to see more specific tags (P3-6). P3-11 had an interesting suggestion, which was to use the table as the basis of a network graph, where papers would be displayed nearer or farther based on how similar they were along a given dimension.

Study 3 Discussion

Every participant completed the task and most found the process natural. However, based on their resulting RDSs and what they said about the table representation, it is clear that most were not able to create a useful RDS in the time given, nor did they understand the paper prototype as a way of working towards a dimensional representation. Thinking about research and trying to develop an understanding of how a set of papers related to one another is a cognitively demanding task, and getting to a useful dimensional representation by tagging papers likely requires more time than the 90 minutes in our study.

A few mentions of dimensions show promise for a tool that supports dimensional reasoning (Q4). P3-10 mentioned comparing examples, though not in a multi-dimensional way as she said the table was unnecessary. P3-2's interest in tag frequency can be thought of as dimensional in a way: he was interested in the dense areas of the design space along one dimension at a time. P3-11 was the only participant to consistently use the word "dimension" to describe the columns in the table and desired a network graph representation that displayed the relatedness of papers along one dimension at a time.

Participants typically used fragments of related work to apply to their current work or inform their approach (Q2). Perhaps because of this, they were not able to see the paper prototype or its benefits through the lens of dimensions. The participants who claimed that they had never considered their papers at one time and who didn't use any organizational tools, commented on the table as a way of tracking their papers. Experienced researchers described the importance of understanding the relationships between papers, but they had this understanding already and discussed the paper prototype in relation to what they already knew (Q6).

DISCUSSION

Given the prevalence of design spaces in research, we expected that student researchers would be better able to construct them. We observed a few challenges faced by participants when trying to reason dimensionally: (1) research papers represented fragments of information, (2) starting with dimensions was not natural, (3) multiple ways of reasoning, (4) topic matters when dimensionalizing, (5) focusing on metrics instead of features, and (6) starting with examples didn't lead to dimensional representations.

Our results suggest that most researchers think about papers in terms of how they use them, rather than what they are. Researchers may take a technique from one paper and apply it to a problem discussed in another paper. Instead of thinking holistically about these papers as points in a dimensional space, researchers appeared to think of them as pieces of a puzzle they are trying to solve. Thinking of papers as fragments in this way is problematic, because it results in empty design spaces. The "dimensions-first" approach appeared to force participants to think more holistically about the examples and their features. This resulted in richer RDSs, but the process felt less natural to them. Participants were more interested in these RDSs, but didn't discover many gaps in their research or novel ideas. It may be that they were too familiar with their work, but maybe they only enumerated the obvious features. A study by McCaffrey and Spector found that designers overlooked 56% of the potential features of a candle [41] and that the overlooked, obscure features led to more innovative solutions. Therefore, it may be beneficial to suggest dimensions automatically based a paper's keywords or content or otherwise guide researchers to reflect more fully.

Most participants in the "dimensions-first" study expressed a desire for the DSE to support other representations of their research that we have described as being semantic, hierarchical, or relational. For these participants the process did not feel natural and they often chose a topic for their RDS based on what they perceived to be easiest to dimensionalize. This suggests that dimensional reasoning may be easier for some topics than others. Participants in Study 3 had an easier time with the "examples-first" process and expressed less of a desire to integrate other modes of reasoning. However, based on the ways in which these participants discussed the benefits of the paper prototype and resulting table, it was clear that they did not internalize the dimensional aspect or reason dimensionally. Many participants chose to use metrics that evaluate the research rather than features that define the research. Participants also didn't appear to understand that there was a difference between metrics and features when asked.

While participants in the "dimensions-first" study struggled with dimensions and suggested easier ways to approach the task, they were forced to reason dimensionally. This appeared to place a high cognitive load on participants, but it also allowed them to gain more insights and to internalize the dimensionality of the end result. The tagging approach in Study 3 appeared to be easier and induce less cognitive load, but it also generated fewer insights for participants. The most useful RDSs resulted from researchers doing the hard cognitive work of thinking about the dimensions first, rather than letting them emerge from tags. More research is needed to understand these tradeoffs and what kind of systems can support researchers in thinking dimensionally.

LIMITATIONS

We had small numbers of participants and so our results are suggestive rather than conclusive. Future work should investigate a larger and more diverse sample of researchers. Research topics varied from CS education to southern literary tradition to road maintenance theory. The first and third studies took place in a lab and did not replicate the environment in which researchers typically work. Short-term studies (1-2 hours) were balanced with one longitudinal study (6 weeks), but future work could investigate longer timelines. Research is collaborative, but in our studies we removed the potential confound of multiple investigators to isolate researchers' thought processes. Future work might have researchers co-construct RDSs. Participants received minimal guidance so that their natural process could be observed, but explicit training with dimensional reasoning might lead to better outcomes. Finally, participants constructed their spaces without any automated assistance. Mining keywords from papers, suggesting related keywords, or searching for papers in the DSE would have likely made the process faster and easier for participants.

CONCLUSION

We have presented three studies that explore the process of dimensional reasoning in researchers. Our investigation contributes the first understanding of how researchers engage in dimensional reasoning and how digital tools might support and scaffold such reasoning. We developed a top-down approach, the DSE, which allows researchers to create dimensions and fit examples to those dimensions. Researchers iteratively refined these dimensions based on examples added. This resulted in a dimensional representation but appeared to be a cognitively demanding process for participants. A paper-prototype study followed in which researchers tagged examples and then dimensions organically emerged as researchers grouped the tags together semantically. This process fit the way in which researchers typically interact with papers; however, it often didn't always result in a dimensional representation.

Our findings about dimensional reasoning suggest that it is possible to scaffold researchers to create dimensional representations; however, it appears that dimensional reasoning comes more naturally to some researchers than to others, and also suits certain types of inquiry more than others. Dimensional representations did help researchers think more holistically about their research and afforded easier comparisons. However, we observed that in addition to reasoning dimensionally, researchers also engaged in semantic, relational, and hierarchical reasoning. These results suggest that supporting dimensional reasoning can offer benefits, but needs to be incorporated into tools or systems that also support other types of reasoning. Thus, to fully support the creative, open-ended task of research, rich systems that offer multiple tools for organizing, representing and exploring are important, and different modes of reasoning need to be accommodated.

REFERENCES

1. Michel Beaudouin-Lafon and Wendy E Mackay. 2003. Prototyping tools and techniques. *Human Computer Interaction – Development Process* (2003), 122–142.
2. Joeran Beel, Bela Gipp, Stefan Langer, and Marcel Genzmehr. 2011. Docear: An Academic Literature Suite for Searching, Organizing and Creating Academic Literature. In *Proceedings of the 11th Annual International ACM/IEEE Joint Conference on Digital Libraries (JCDL '11)*. ACM, New York, NY, USA, 465–466. DOI: http://dx.doi.org/10.1145/1998076.1998188
3. Michael Mose Biskjaer, Peter Dalsgaard, and Kim Halskov. 2014. A Constraint-based Understanding of Design Spaces. In *Proceedings of the 2014 Conference on Designing Interactive Systems (DIS '14)*. ACM, New York, NY, USA, 453–462. DOI: http://dx.doi.org/10.1145/2598510.2598533
4. Nathalie Bonnardel and Tamara Sumner. 1996. Supporting evaluation in design. *Acta Psychologica* 91, 3 (1996), 221–244.
5. Richard Buchanan. 1992. Wicked problems in design thinking. *Design issues* 8, 2 (1992), 5–21.
6. Stuart K Card, Jock D Mackinlay, and George G Robertson. 1990. The design space of input devices. In *Proceedings of the SIGCHI conference on Human factors in computing systems*. ACM, 117–124.
7. Joel Chan, Katherine Fu, Christian Schunn, Jonathan Cagan, Kristin Wood, and Kenneth Kotovsky. 2011. On the benefits and pitfalls of analogies for innovative design: Ideation performance based on analogical distance, commonness, and modality of examples. *Journal of mechanical design* 133, 8 (2011), 081004.
8. Chaomei Chen. 2006. CiteSpace II: Detecting and visualizing emerging trends and transient patterns in scientific literature. *Journal of the American Society for information Science and Technology* 57, 3 (2006), 359–377.
9. Coggle. 2016. https://coggle.it/. (2016).
10. Christopher Collins, Sheelagh Carpendale, and Gerald Penn. 2009a. Docuburst: Visualizing document content using language structure. In *Computer graphics forum*, Vol. 28. Wiley Online Library, 1039–1046.
11. Christopher Collins, Fernanda B Viegas, and Martin Wattenberg. 2009b. Parallel tag clouds to explore and analyze faceted text corpora. In *Visual Analytics Science and Technology, 2009. VAST 2009. IEEE Symposium on*. IEEE, 91–98.
12. Arthur Cropley. 2006. In praise of convergent thinking. *Creativity research journal* 18, 3 (2006), 391–404.
13. Nils Dahlbäck, Arne Jönsson, and Lars Ahrenberg. 1993. Wizard of Oz studies: why and how. In *Proceedings of the 1st international conference on Intelligent user interfaces*. ACM, 193–200.
14. Peter Dalsgaard, Kim Halskov, and Rune Nielsen. 2008a. Maps for design reflection. *Artifact* 2, 3-4 (2008), 176–189.
15. Peter Dalsgaard, Kim Halskov, and Rune Nielsen. 2008b. Towards a design space explorer for media facades. In *Proceedings of the 20th Australasian Conference on Computer-Human Interaction: Designing for Habitus and Habitat*. ACM, 219–226.
16. Alan Dix, Rachel Cowgill, Christina Bashford, Simon McVeigh, and Rupert Ridgewell. 2016. Spreadsheets As User Interfaces. In *Proceedings of the International Working Conference on Advanced Visual Interfaces (AVI '16)*. ACM, New York, NY, USA, 192–195. DOI: http://dx.doi.org/10.1145/2909132.2909271
17. Kees Dorst and Nigel Cross. 2001. Creativity in the design process: co-evolution of problem–solution. *Design studies* 22, 5 (2001), 425–437.
18. Niklas Elmqvist, Pierre Dragicevic, and Jean-Daniel Fekete. 2008. Rolling the dice: Multidimensional visual exploration using scatterplot matrix navigation. *IEEE transactions on Visualization and Computer Graphics* 14, 6 (2008), 1539–1148.
19. EndNote. 2016. http://endnote.com/. (2016).
20. Jennifer English, Marti Hearst, Rashmi Sinha, Kirsten Swearingen, and Ka-Ping Yee. 2002. Hierarchical faceted metadata in site search interfaces. In *CHI'02 Extended Abstracts on Human Factors in Computing Systems*. ACM, 628–639.
21. Microsoft Excel. 2016. https://office.live.com/start/Excel.aspx. (2016).
22. Jean-Daniel Fekete, Jarke J Van Wijk, John T Stasko, and Chris North. 2008. The value of information visualization. In *Information visualization*. Springer, 1–18.
23. FreeMind. 2016. http://freemind.en.softonic.com/. (2016).
24. Vinod Goel and Peter Pirolli. 1992. The structure of design problem spaces. *Cognitive science* 16, 3 (1992), 395–429.
25. TC Graham, Leon A Watts, Gaëlle Calvary, Joëlle Coutaz, Emmanuel Dubois, and Laurence Nigay. 2000. A dimension space for the design of interactive systems within their physical environments. In *Proceedings of the 3rd conference on Designing interactive systems: processes, practices, methods, and techniques*. ACM, 406–416.
26. Tovi Grossman and Daniel Wigdor. 2007. Going Deeper: a Taxonomy of 3D on the Tabletop. In *Horizontal Interactive Human-Computer Systems, 2007. TABLETOP '07. Second Annual IEEE International Workshop on*. 137–144. DOI: http://dx.doi.org/10.1109/TABLETOP.2007.18
27. Joy Paul Guilford. 1956. The structure of intellect. *Psychological bulletin* 53, 4 (1956), 267.

28. Chris Heape. 2007. *The Design Space: the design process as the construction, exploration and expansion of a conceptual space*. Ph.D. Dissertation. SDUSDU, Det Tekniske FakultetFaculty of Engineering, Mads Clausen InstituttetThe Mads Clausen Institute.
29. David G Jansson and Steven M Smith. 1991. Design fixation. *Design studies* 12, 1 (1991), 3–11.
30. Waqas Javed and Niklas Elmqvist. 2012. Exploring the design space of composite visualization. In *Visualization Symposium (PacificVis), 2012 IEEE Pacific*. IEEE, 1–8.
31. Eser Kandogan, Juho Kim, Thomas P. Moran, and Pablo Pedemonte. 2011. How a Freeform Spatial Interface Supports Simple Problem Solving Tasks. In *Proceedings of the SIGCHI Conference on Human Factors in Computing Systems (CHI '11)*. ACM, New York, NY, USA, 925–934. DOI: http://dx.doi.org/10.1145/1978942.1979079
32. Rudolf K Keller, Anurag Garg, and Tao Tao. 1993. HyperRef: online support for research literature assessment and documentation. In *Proceedings of the 11th annual international conference on Systems documentation*. ACM, 163–175.
33. Andruid Kerne, Eunyee Koh, Steven M Smith, Andrew Webb, and Blake Dworaczyk. 2008. combinFormation: Mixed-initiative composition of image and text surrogates promotes information discovery. *ACM Transactions on Information Systems (TOIS)* 27, 1 (2008), 5.
34. Andruid Kerne, Andrew M. Webb, Steven M. Smith, Rhema Linder, Nic Lupfer, Yin Qu, Jon Moeller, and Sashikanth Damaraju. 2014. Using Metrics of Curation to Evaluate Information-Based Ideation. *ACM Trans. Comput.-Hum. Interact.* 21, 3, Article 14 (June 2014), 48 pages. DOI:http://dx.doi.org/10.1145/2591677
35. David Kirsh. 2010. Thinking with external representations. *Ai & Society* 25, 4 (2010), 441–454.
36. Giovan Francesco Lanzara and Lars Mathiassen. 1985. Mapping situations within a system development project. *Information & Management* 8, 1 (1985), 3–20.
37. LitAssist. 2016. http://www.litassist.com/. (2016).
38. Allan MacLean, Richard M Young, Victoria ME Bellotti, and Thomas P Moran. 1991. Questions, options, and criteria: Elements of design space analysis. *Human–computer interaction* 6, 3-4 (1991), 201–250.
39. Renan Manola, Renata SS Guizzardi, and Roberta Lima Gomes. 2008. Biblioref: a semantic bibliographic reference management system. In *Companion Proceedings of the XIV Brazilian Symposium on Multimedia and the Web*. ACM, 149–151.
40. Justin Matejka, Tovi Grossman, and George Fitzmaurice. 2012. Citeology: visualizing paper genealogy. In *CHI'12 Extended Abstracts on Human Factors in Computing Systems*. ACM, 181–190.
41. Tony McCaffrey and Lee Spector. 2011. Innovation is built on the obscure: Innovation-enhancing software for uncovering the obscure. In *Proceedings of the 8th ACM Conference on Creativity and Cognition*. ACM, 371–372.
42. Sarnoff Mednick. 1962. The associative basis of the creative process. *Psychological review* 69, 3 (1962), 220.
43. Yevgeniy Medynskiy, Mira Dontcheva, and Steven M Drucker. 2009. Exploring websites through contextual facets. In *Proceedings of the SIGCHI Conference on Human Factors in Computing Systems*. ACM, 2013–2022.
44. Mendeley. 2016. https://www.mendeley.com/. (2016).
45. MindManager. 2016. https://www.mindjet.com/mindmanager/. (2016).
46. MindMeister. 2016. https://www.mindmeister.com/. (2016).
47. Lior Noy, Yuval Hart, Natalie Andrew, Omer Ramote, Avi Mayo, and Uri Alon. 2012. A quantitative study of creative leaps. In *Proc. Third Int. Conf. Comput. Creativity, Dublin*. 72–76.
48. Charles Perin, Pierre Dragicevic, and Jean-Daniel Fekete. 2014. Revisiting bertin matrices: New interactions for crafting tabular visualizations. *IEEE transactions on visualization and computer graphics* 20, 12 (2014), 2082–2091.
49. Peter Pirolli and Stuart Card. 1995. Information foraging in information access environments. In *Proceedings of the SIGCHI conference on Human factors in computing systems*. ACM Press/Addison-Wesley Publishing Co., 51–58.
50. Peter Pirolli and Stuart Card. 2005. The sensemaking process and leverage points for analyst technology as identified through cognitive task analysis. In *Proceedings of international conference on intelligence analysis*, Vol. 5. 2–4.
51. Daniel M Russell, Mark J Stefik, Peter Pirolli, and Stuart K Card. 1993. The cost structure of sensemaking. In *Proceedings of the INTERACT'93 and CHI'93 conference on Human factors in computing systems*. ACM, 269–276.
52. Donald A Schon. 1992. Designing as reflective conversation with the materials of a design situation. *Research in Engineering Design* 3, 3 (1992), 131–147.
53. Google Sheets. 2016. https://www.google.com/sheets/about/. (2016).
54. Harri Siirtola and Kari-Jouko Räihä. 2006. Interacting with parallel coordinates. *Interacting with Computers* 18, 6 (2006), 1278–1309.
55. Herbert A Simon. 1955. A behavioral model of rational choice. *The quarterly journal of economics* (1955), 99–118.

56. Consuelo Valdes, Diana Eastman, Casey Grote, Shantanu Thatte, Orit Shaer, Ali Mazalek, Brygg Ullmer, and Miriam K. Konkel. 2014. Exploring the Design Space of Gestural Interaction with Active Tokens Through User-defined Gestures. In *Proceedings of the 32Nd Annual ACM Conference on Human Factors in Computing Systems (CHI '14)*. ACM, New York, NY, USA, 4107–4116. DOI: http://dx.doi.org/10.1145/2556288.2557373

57. Andrew M Webb and Andruid Kerne. 2011. Integrating implicit structure visualization with authoring promotes ideation. In *Proceedings of the 11th annual international ACM/IEEE joint conference on Digital libraries*. ACM, 203–212.

58. Edward J Wegman and Qiang Luo. 1997. High dimensional clustering using parallel coordinates and the grand tour. *Computing Science and Statistics* 28 (1997), 93–101.

59. XMind. 2016. http://www.xmind.net/. (2016).

60. Ka-Ping Yee, Kirsten Swearingen, Kevin Li, and Marti Hearst. 2003. Faceted metadata for image search and browsing. In *Proceedings of the SIGCHI conference on Human factors in computing systems*. ACM, 401–408.

61. Zotero. 2016. https://www.zotero.org/. (2016).

62. Fritz Zwicky. 1967. *New methods of thought and procedure: contributions to the Symposium on Methodologies; Pasadena, California, May 22-24, 1967*. Springer.

63. Fritz Zwicky. 1969. *Discovery, Invention, Research: through the morphological approach*. Macmillan.

Strategies of Free-Form Web Curation: Processes of Creative Engagement with Prior Work

Andruid Kerne, Nic Lupfer, Rhema Linder, Yin Qu, Alyssa Valdez, Ajit Jain, Kade Keith, Matthew Carrasco; Jorge Vanegas, Andrew Billingsley
Interface Ecology Lab, Dept of Computer Science. College of Architecture; Texas A&M University
andruid, nic, rhema, yin, alyssa, ajit, kade, matthew@ecologylab.net; vanegas, abillingsley@tamu.edu

ABSTRACT
We synthesize principles across art, design, writing, and psychology to articulate strategies of free-form web curation, for stimulating students' creative engagement with prior work, in performance of ideation tasks. We manifest the strategies in an interactive system and pedagogy. *Free-form web curation* is a form of new media—designed to enable users to conceptualize and create new contexts—in which they discover, interpret, and represent relationships, by composing readymade and self-made content elements. The strategies are Collect, Assemble, Shift Perspective, Sketch, Write, and Exhibit.

We conducted a field study involving 1247 students over 4 semesters. We connect visual, quantitative, and experiential data to show how students engage with prior work through the free-form web curation strategies, system, and pedagogy. We develop implications for design of web curation systems and education. We coalesce a theory of free-form web curation, based on the strategies, emphasizing space and context.

Author Keywords
curation; ideation; art; design; creative cognition; visual thinking; creativity support tools; education; theory

INTRODUCTION
We synthesize principles across art, design, writing, and psychology to articulate strategies for engaging students' creative cognition with prior work, in performance of ideation tasks. We manifest the strategies in an interactive system and pedagogy for free-form web curation. By *prior work*, we mean germane web content, especially articles and patents. An *ideation task* [89, 45], in turn, involves generating and developing new knowledge for a project intended to be innovative. Understanding prior work is key to innovation in many fields [67]. In industry, failure to use the external knowledge of prior work produces severe competitive disadvantage [14].

The problem addressed by this research is that discovering relationships connecting prior work and the ideation task at hand is challenging. Processes of creating new knowledge are iterative and emergent [26]. Multiple prior knowledge elements need to be interpreted and combined in new ways [62]. Linear media—such as print documents and lists of entries—only enable sequential arrangement, and so make it difficult to discover relationships spanning multiple elements [68].

Our solution to the problem of supporting users in discovering relationships connecting prior work, in an ideation task, is based on art practices involving found objects and curation. Duchamp's seminal work showed how shifting the *context* of a *found object*, or *readymade*, has the potential to transform its significance [56]. Recent popular media notions of curation, while encouraging, have been reductionist, emphasizing 'adding value' by collecting and commenting, using linear social media such as the blog and feed [81]. In art, in contrast, *curation* grew, beyond 'adding value', to become the conceptualization and creation of a context, in which works are found, collected, interpreted, and visually arranged, in an exhibition space, to stimulate active engagement [69].

Free-form web curation is a form of new media [59]—designed to support users in creating new conceptual and spatial *contexts*—in which they discover, interpret, and represent relationships, by composing readymade and self-made content elements, on the web and in the cloud. This paper articulates how we drew from diverse fields to define creative strategies of free-form web curation: Collect, Assemble, Shift Perspective, Sketch, Write, and Exhibit. We invoked the strategies to design both an interactive system, IdeaMâché [`https://ideamache.ecologylab.net`], and pedagogy, for teaching students how to creatively engage with prior work.

Process—emphasis on engagement, on doing, on the often ineffable *how* that making is performed—and *product*—emphasis on results, on *what* is produced—are complementary aspects of creativity [84]. Prior research used visual grounded theory [47] to derive a pattern language of free-form web curation, by analyzing students' creative products, in diverse courses, to understand the range of spatial organization of readymade and self-made elements [58]. Like Alexander's pattern language of architectural forms, which support human physical activity—e.g., alcoves, arcades, and promenades [1]—the free-form curation patterns—$overlap|\{compose, composite, map\}$, $morphology|\{concrete, abstract\}$, $group|\{spatial, nested\}$, and $path|\{linear, non\text{-}linear\}$—were shown to map the multi-scale organization of digital design space to human ideation activity. We further showed that the patterns support

C&C '17, June 27-30, 2017, Singapore, Singapore

ISBN 978-1-4503-4403-6/17/06...$15.00

DOI: `http://dx.doi.org/10.1145/3059454.3059471`

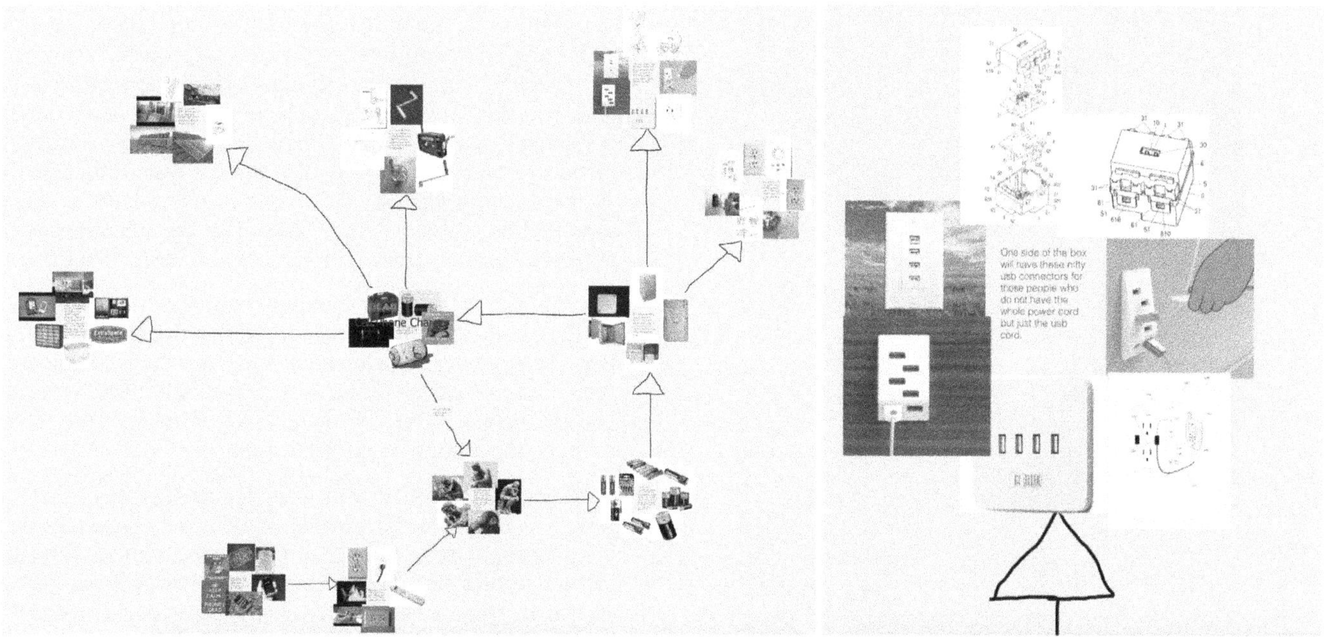

Figure 1: *Cell Phone Charger* develops a narrative diagram of nodes, each with centered text surrounded by a circle of graphics (left) [`https://ideamache.ecologylab.net/v/pfrBCkMbSB/`]. On the right, we see a close-up of a node addressing techniques for arranging USB sockets on the proposed innovative charging device. The author incorporates prior work patent sketches and commercial product illustrations, which serve as evidence to motivate the novelty of the innovation.
$curation\_patterns = \{group|spatial,\ path|non{-}linear\}$

creative cognition and visual thinking, manifesting gestalt principles of visual organization [72]—e.g., proximity, color, size, orientation, region, symmetry, continuity, and closure.

The present research addresses gaps in prior research, by alternatively focusing on fundamental *processes of doing free-form web curation*: the ideation tasks that people perform; creative strategies that contribute to performing these tasks; principles and precedents, from across fields, which underlie the strategies; the *IdeaMâché* web app [39], which provides integrated support for invoking the strategies online; and pedagogy for teaching people how to use strategies of free-form web curation to engage in creative ideation with prior work and beyond. Other prior research showed how using free-form curation products for presentation, in the classroom, stimulates free-form discussion [54].

We present a field study involving 1247 students over 4 semesters. We show exemplary curation products, as visual data, which depict students' creativity (Figures 1, 3, 4). We use process-oriented engagement analytics to examine how students use the interactive free-form web curation system, IdeaMâché, to perform the strategies. We contrast the present approach with prior systems for engagement with prior work. We connect findings with the strategies to develop implications for the design of web curation systems and education. We conclude by coalescing a theory of free-form curation spaces.

STRATEGIES

According to National Academies' learning scientists, pedagogy needs to involve strategies that help students think about concepts, organize them, and overcome difficulties they encounter [10]. Strategy is, "the art or practice of planning the future direction or outcome of something; the formulation or implementation of a plan, scheme, or course of action" [71]. We take a discursive approach [21] to defining strategies for curation, drawing from diverse fields, including art, design, writing, cultural theory, creative cognition, and hypertext.

A student finds content elements—germane to her ideation task—in digital repositories, social media, and other websites. She *Collect*s these found objects, from initial contexts, into a new *context of curation*, to understand and create a conceptual basis for her ideation task. As in art, to understand, articulate, and interpret relationships, she *Assemble*s collected elements in space, which stimulates reflection. To navigate the curation space, students and the professor *Shift Perspectives*, seeing things in different ways. She *Sketch*es to represent and generate diagrammatic visual thinking. She *Write*s to categorize, present evidence, and develop exposition. *Exhibit*ing presents curation contexts to audiences. We illustrate strategies with exemplary principles and practices.

Collect

Collect is the process of gathering content. Collecting prior work is the basis of the time-honored notion of "doing research in the library" [94]. We draw on Rosenberg's concept of a 'gathering interface', which enables collecting content, while browsing, and assembling elements using the 'conjunctive method' of spatial hypertext [82]. Since content to collect is usually found through exploratory search [60] (e.g. by iterative Googling), it makes particular sense to frame collecting content in terms of art's construct of found objects.

Figure 2: Rauschenberg's *Retroactive 1*, 1963, a mixed-media assemblage from the *Combine* series.

Marcel Duchamp recontextualized a *found object* (or *readymade*)—specifically a urinal—to function as an artwork in a prominent 1917 exhibition [56]. He (re)titled the work, *The Fountain*. He used a pseudonym, R. Mutt. The exhibition organizers were upset. They only permitted *The Fountain* to be exhibited in a separate room. While the exhibition included over 2000 art works [91], some by well-known artists, *The Fountain*, a 'simple' found object, is the most famous.

Duchamp said, "Mr. Mutt did not make the work, he chose it" [56]. Duchamp's *Fountain* and explanation transformed our understanding of the action of choosing into a creative act, with great power of signification. By manipulating the title and author of the work, Duchamp explored the contextual role of metadata in signification. Through its fame, paradigmatic influence on art, and ability to explain popular practices in social media, we argue that *The Fountain* was the most significant art work of the twentieth century.

An example of the recontextualization of found objects in social media involves Meryl Streep's Golden Globes award acceptance speech. Streep expressed how Donald Trump's imitation of a disabled reporter broke her heart [96]. Trump's tweet lambasting her, in response, has, as of this writing, been retweeted 38K times and liked 127K times [97]. Through its recontextualization on Twitter, the initial speech, as found object, became, for some, a signifier of 'Hollywood elites' [63].

Assemble

Assemblage is means for making a work of art, attributed to Dubuffet, by fastening readymade and self-made elements together [87]. Assemblage showcases the duality and tension between the original and resulting contexts. The means of 'fastening' vary with different media. Assemblage begins with making elements coincide in space. Assemblage is related to De Landa's notion of *aggregate*, which occurs in physical geography and geology, such as when silt and rocks are deposited in piles by currents in a stream [19]. In aggregates, while a new whole is formed, at the same time, constituent elements retain their characteristics and identities.

Assemblage has the potential to stimulate *emergence*, in which people identify new properties beyond the characteristics of the elements. Wilkenfeld and Ward showed that combination of disparate elements is particularly likely to stimulate emergence [101]. The assemblage stimulates the viewer to think about unexpected relationships.

Putting elements together in space is a key strategy of art, curation, and hypermedia. Arranging elements in space can create a multiplicity of relationships, which stimulate the curator to interpret meanings during the creative process, and the viewer to do so subsequently. During iterative processes of knowledge creation, cycles of creation, interpretation, and reflection form what Schön calls, *reflection-in-action* [85], and Webb et al call, *reflection-in-curation* [100]. The representation "talks back" to the author / user [66].

Media Art Forms of Assemblage

Duchamp's strategy of the readymade found object became an extensive basis for recombinant media [44] art in the twentieth and twenty-first centuries. Found objects are juxtaposed, combined, and composed to form a whole in a panoply of assemblage forms: e.g., collage, pop art, music of indeterminacy, music concrete, remix, and hiphop. Max Ernst was an exemplary collage artist, who assembled found objects with his own sketching and overpainting [92], to construct new schemas of techno-culture [48]. Warhol's pop art appropriated popular media images—e.g, Marilyn Monroe and Mao Zedong—and directly re-presented them with media such as painting and printmaking. According to Higgins, examples of 'intermedia' include Oldenburg's *Floor Burger*, made of acrylic on canvas filled with foam rubber and cardboard boxes, which "falls between sculpture and hamburgers"; and Rauschenberg's 'combines' (Figure 2), which assemble popular media images with sketching and painting to create cultural statements [35].

Cage composed found sound sources, such as random FM radio transmissions, as instruments in the *Imaginary Landscapes* music of indeterminacy series [12]. DJ Spooky identifies the internet as a source of material, for remix; he defines DJing in terms of 'rhythm science', in which "endless recontextualizing is a core compositional strategy" [65]. DJing, the gathering, playback, and remix of audio samples, is, along with rapping, the compositional method of the popular genre of hip-hop, a multi-billion dollar popular music industry [99].

Spatial Hypertext and Information Composition

Spatial hypertext enables freely creating and moving nodes, expressing relationships through proximity [62]. Spatial hypertext's flexibility supports iterative change through design

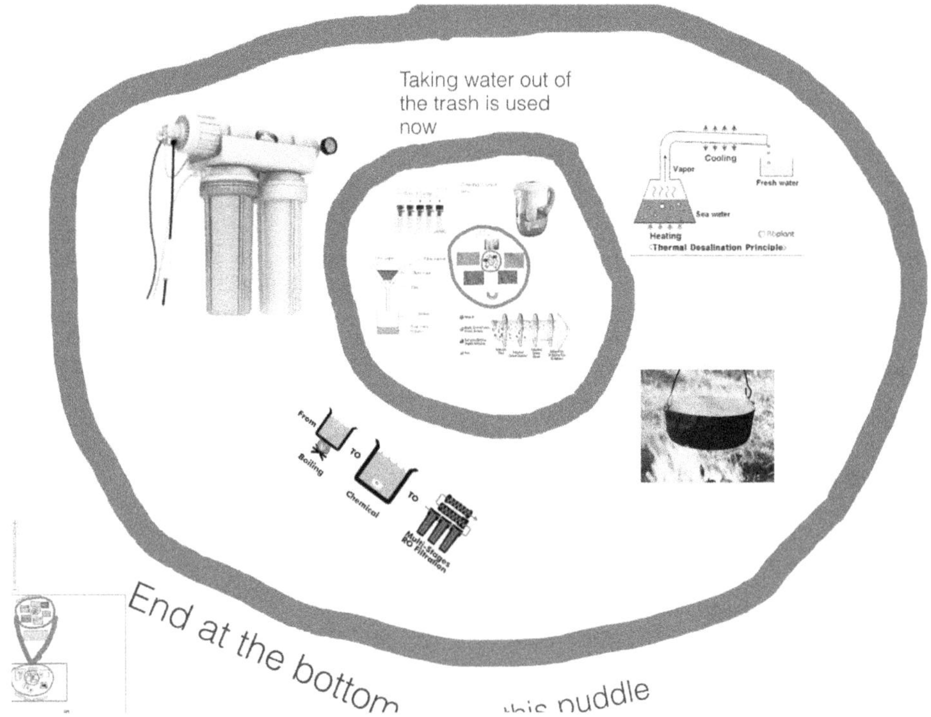

Figure 3: The *Water Cleaning* curation uses roughly sketched concentric circles, labeled as 'puddles', as a metaphor for the significance of rain water [`https://ideamache.ecologylab.net/v/m7K4sfTCF3/`]. The whole, seen in IdeaMâché's radar view (bottom left), is an exclamation mark. The top puddle, just in the radar view, illustrates the problem of desertification. The bottom puddle, comprising most of this figure, addresses solutions, beginning, at this level, with prior work. $curation\_patterns = \{morphology|concrete,\ group|nested\}$

processes. It helps express speculative, contingent, and informal relationships [7]. Information composition extended spatial hypertext—by emphasizing the visual and a sense of the whole—to promote the creative cognition of relationships among elements [45]. Elements function as hypersigns—i.e., signifiers hyperlinked to signifieds—which are semiotically assembled to create new meanings [42].

Shift Perspective

Shifting perspective while navigating space is essential to human experiences of physical exhibitions. Concepts of *Shifting Perspective* in space come from architectural design, cultural theory and computer graphics. Courajoud makes the concept of the horizon—which implies extreme traversals in distance and scale—central in landscape architecture [18]. He argues that scales must be linked.

Allen offers the field, a spatial matrix capable of unifying diverse elements, while respecting the identify of each [2]. The field is a site of aggregation and a space of assemblage. Field configurations are incrementally expandable.

Sellen and Harper observe how people use the affordances of paper for reading and writing [88]. People shift pages around to organize information spatially, compare elements, and extract from one to another. Continuously shifting spatial organization was found to facilitate annotation.

When an exhibition is created and presented in physical space, viewers navigate by moving their bodies. Paradigms based in computer graphics have been developed for representing space and navigation in virtual space. Pad provided a 'spatial metaphor for computer interface design', through an infinite 2D information plane, with levels of zoom, on which elements were organized geographically [74]. Zoomable User Interfaces (ZUIs) generalize this approach, using changes of scale as a principal means of organizing content and navigation [5].

Sketch

> Sketching ... [is used] to diagram or depict abstract or concrete states (for example a family tree or an electric circuit scheme), maps and plans (such as instructions for finding the way or furniture layouts), signs or things, live or inanimate, real or imaginary. But ... some [sketching] does not follow ideas in the mind, but instead, precedes them... not to record an idea, which is not there yet, but to help generate it. –G. Goldschmidt [30]

Merleau-Ponty shows how perception, itself, is inherently based in the body's memories and interpretations [64]. *Visual thinking* intertwines perception, recognition, and reflection in creative acts of forming and illustrating new meanings [3]. Sketching is an embodied physical process of visual thinking. Goldschmidt explains how designers sketch to generate forms that they imagine [30]. Through reflection-in-action [85], in turn, sketching generates new form combinations.

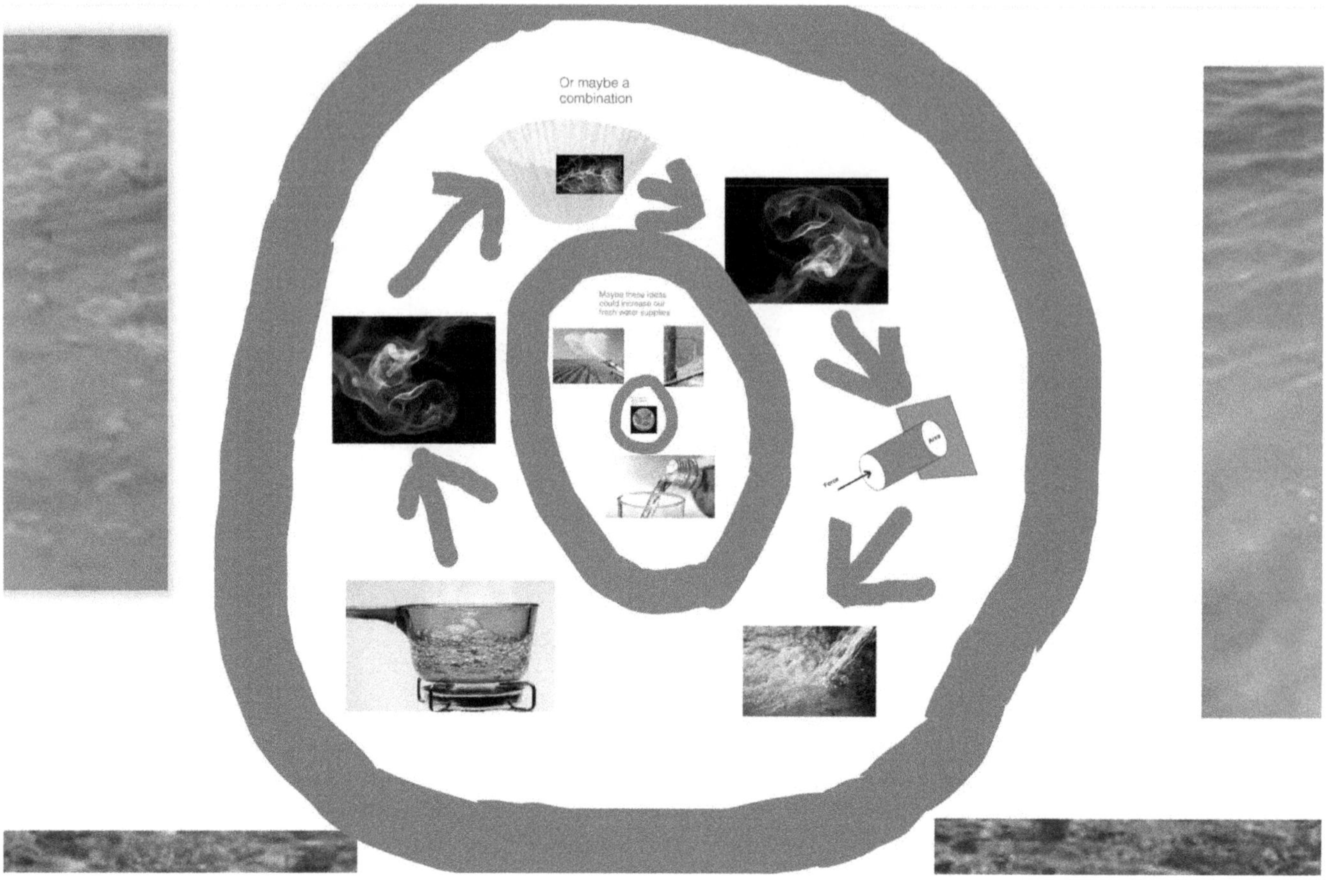

Figure 4: Navigation into bottom puddle of the *Water Cleaning* curation, by zooming in using the scroll wheel. Successive levels of zoom take us deeper into the student's innovation, which combines thermal, filtering, and desalination techniques. Through zoom, an additional curation pattern emerges: $path|non-linear$.

Larkin and Simon show how diagrams are easier to understand than lists of relationships [52]. Benefits include using position to group information and making inferences easy to perceive. Diagrams predate written language as a form for inscribing communication. Tversky characterizes *glyphs* as simple figures— e.g., points, lines, and arrows—which draw from their context to articulate meaning [98]. She emphasizes the role of human interpretation in creating and understanding the meanings of glyphs and other visual elements in context.

Write

Following sketching, writing, as represented in 'print', was, until recently, the predominant medium of communication. According to Ong, a new medium transforms those that precede it, while enabling new forms of communication [70]. As a curation strategy, writing takes multiple forms, differentiated by length, function, and structure: exposition, hypertext, annotation, and labeling. Expository and creative writing involve longer textual passages. The fixity of print enabled the composition of complex literary works, such as the novels of James Joyce, as well as complex arguments, such as those in scientific analysis.

Traditional expository writing is linear. Free-form web curation with prior work serves as a medium for ideation in connection with expository writing. As in recombinant media of assemblage, juxtaposition plays a key role in expository writing across fields. Other aspects of writing are field specific. How the role of voices and their authority is left implicit or made explicit is an aspect of writing that varies. Writing in art history involves criticism, formal analysis, concrete facts, and theory [76]. In social anthropology, it involves entering a conversation, borrowing, extending, establishing authority, and stepping back [16]. In sciences, writing is based on the quality and quantity of evidence, which in turn is based on the formation and validation of hypotheses, the design of studies, the analysis of data, and the interpretation of results [13]. Business models present evidence and arguments about partners, activities, resources, value propositions, customer relationships, customer segments, channels, cost structure, and revenue streams [8].

Recent writing forms are shorter and non-linear. Bolter shows how hypermedia writing spaces enable multiple paths of navigation and processes of interpretation [9]. Landow cites Nelson [68], Barthes [4], and Foucault [27] to show how hypertext enables 'ideal textuality', in which networks of lexia support multiple voices and interpretations, giving the active reader creative agency, in tandem with the writer [51].

Annotation involves highlighting, clipping, and commenting. Marshall's investigation of practice with physical media, as a basis for hypermedia design, shows the role of annotation—as a means of emphasis, interpretation, and reflection—in the transformation of authorial structure into reading structure [61].

Russell et al investigate how the labeling of content elements becomes transformed, in sensemaking tasks, from an initial schema, based on source materials (prior work), through a representational shift, to a task-specific schema [83]. Kolko identifies, as a key technique in design process, the articulation of semantic relationships, which help 'make meaning out of data' [46]. To accomplish this, elements are spatially manipulated on a 'big wall'.

These findings emphasize the role of what we call *curation context*, based on an ideation task at hand, in creative written engagement with content. Lakoff and Johnson provide insight into underlying human cognition, explaining how naming concepts and spatially relating them, through metaphors, forms a basis for understanding and comparison [50].

Exhibit

In the twentieth century, the role of the curator was transformed from carer to author of exhibition-texts [69]. The museum was transformed from historical repository to place for exhibitions. Curating emerged as a mode of discourse[1].

Lippard [57] and Szeemann [20] exemplify the contemporary paradigm of curators who take an especially active role in how they organize exhibition contexts. They articulate a conceptual nexus. They choose artists as well as works. They conduct open calls. They commission works. They encourage artists to make site-specific artworks specifically for the spatial and temporal context of an exhibition.

One large-scale exhibition context is *documenta*, a festival conducted every 5 years in Kassel, Germany. In addition to a permanent exhibition complex, which itself can be reconfigured, large and small scale pop-up sites are constructed around Kassel. Artworks are specifically designed for these sites. Szeeman was the curator of *documenta 5*, which he titled "Questioning Reality — Pictorial Worlds Today" [22]. The exhibition assembled diverse artworks—abstract, dada, intermedia, and happenings—created by 222 artists.

Multi-scale free-form space moves toward fulfilling Christiane Paul's requirement for new media art curation, toward providing "Parallel, distributed, living information space, open to artistic inference—a space of exchange and presentation that is transparent and flexible." [73]

IDEAMACHE: SYSTEM

We present the free-form web curation system, IdeaMâché, in terms of the strategies: Collect, Assemble, Shift Perspective, Sketch, Write, and Exhibit. Each strategy is supported through one or more interactive operations, which users can directly perform.

[1]According to Habermas, a discourse is a collection of utterances, which take place in particular social contexts and are subject to inherent limitations of time and space [31].

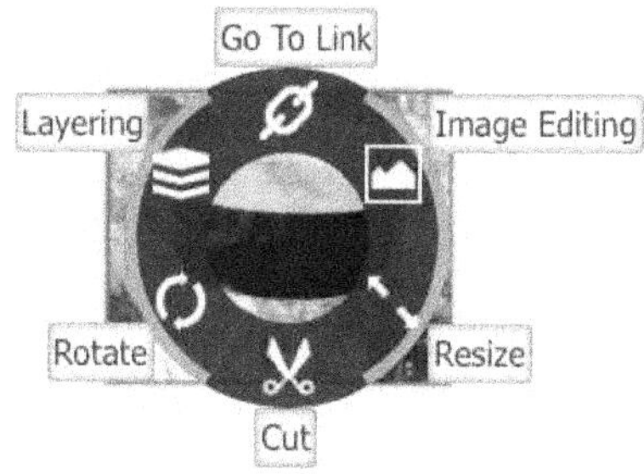

Figure 5: Marking menu: actions operate on an element.

Collect: Direct Clipping

IdeaMâché manifests the *Collect* strategy by enabling direct manipulation [37, 90] clipping of web information. By *clipping* (verb), we mean the act of selecting content in a source context, such as a web page or social media post, and gathering that content in a new curation context. The resulting object, sheared from its source, is a *clipping* (noun).

IdeaMâché supports direct clipping through a Chrome browser extension that transforms encountered web content into material [29]. The browser extension interjects a drag event handler into each encountered web page. The user Collects by selecting content to clip and performing the across windows Drag and Drop operation.

On drag, a semantic summary of the source web page context is captured. The selected content is augmented with the contextual semantics, forming a *rich clipping*. Contextual semantics are captured with a type system, which integrates data models with extraction rules [43, 78]. Contextual semantics minimally include the source document's URL and title. Depending on their type (e.g., social media post, product, scholarly article, or patent) rich clippings may contain further semantics, such as references and citations. Rich clippings can incorporate diverse types of web media: text, image, audio (SoundCloud), and video (YouTube, Vimeo, Twitch).

Assemble: Visual Arrangement and Transformation

To support the *Assemble* strategy, IdeaMâché enables selecting and manipulating elements in a curation space. The Position operation is performed, through direct manipulation, by left click on an element, and drag. A marking menu [49], activated by right click, is used for rapid selection of other Assemble operations, as well as multi-element select (Figure 5).

Some Assemble operations—Scale and Rotate—involve manipulation of a single parameter. For these, the marking menu turns into a control menu [75], so that dragging through the operation immediately increases the parameter. Scale (resize) is a common Assemble operation. Rotate is among Assemble Fastening operations, which also include Layer, Crop, and Blend. Some are performed through nested marking menus. Layer transformations enable users to position an element behind or in front of others. Blend manipulates opacity, enabling visual compositing when content overlaps.

Shift Perspective: Pan and Zoom

The *Shift Perspective* strategy is manifested by the Pan and Zoom operations, which manipulate a ZUI viewport onto the

	s_1	s_2	s_3	s_4	Total
Semester	Fall 2013	Spring 2014	Fall 2014	Spring 2015	
Students	319	296	326	306	1247
Curations	759	876	948	628	3211

Table 1: Number of students and curations per semester.

curation space across positions and scales. Pan is performed by dragging the background. Zoom is performed by mouse wheel or the familiar 2-finger pinch gesture. IdeaMâché's zoom level spans 4 orders of magnitude. This is discretized into approximately 35 steps, each of which changes scale by a factor of ~1.3. There is no pre-defined print resolution. This is intended to encourage users to compose content at different scales. IdeaMâché provides an overview to aid in navigating curation space when the user's view is larger than the display.

Sketch and Write

The present IdeaMâché provides lightweight support for the *Sketch* and *Write* strategies, each of which constitutes a form of annotation. Each of these strategies is supported by a single operation. Sketch mode is activated through the curation space marking menu, which transforms the mouse cursor into a brush, used to draw strokes directly on the curation space. Color and brush size are adjustable. The Write strategy operation, constituted by text element create and edit, is also accessed via the curation space marking menu. Text elements are edited using an in-context toolbar, which contains buttons for manipulating font, color, and alignment.

Exhibit: Cloud Architecture

Storing, editing, and viewing content independent of a particular computer is a contemporary requirement for engaging users. The IdeaMâché cloud architecture enables saving, sharing, turning in, building on, and publishing curations as creative products. Each web curation is assigned a unique curation ID and permalink. Students use permalinks to *Exhibit* work to peers and turn in assignments to course instructors.

The cloud architecture is instrumental in research data collection. Our dataset of curations grows continuously. The cloud connects each curation creative product to user engagement logs, which capture authors' creative processes, by recording invoked operations and their strategies. Each log record includes timestamp, curation ID, operation, and parameters.

FIELD STUDY METHODOLOGY

We report on an extended field study in which free-form web curation was incorporated into the undergraduate course, The Design Process: Creativity and Entrepreneurship (DPCE). The goal is to investigate supporting creative engagement with prior work, in ideation tasks, in a situated education context. We collaborated with course instructors in an iterative design research process. Our continuously evolving design intervention was based on the free-form web curation strategies, manifested in the IdeaMâché system and pedagogy.

Design Research Approach

Supporting design ideation through software and pedagogy in DPCE is a 'wicked problem' [79]. Design problems are 'wicked' when they are involve complex, interlocking factors that impact outcomes. There are too many potential solutions to enumerate. There is no way to deductively identify an optimal solution. Design research addresses wicked problems through iterative creation of artifacts: prototypes, products, services, and documentation [103]. By situating artifacts in a particular context of use, *"Design researchers can both discover effects and provide a template for bridging the general aspects of the theory."* We observe that each semester-based university course instance constitutes a *one-shot* [79] opportunity to engage students, with a high stakes ethical responsibility to support valuable educational experience.

The Design Process: Creativity and Entrepreneurship

We evaluated free-form web curation's support of engagement with prior work by observing creative products and processes in the DPCE field study. Learning objectives include becoming aware of innovation opportunities, developing skills in creative thinking and problem-solving, and learning to curate prior work to motivate the novelty of an innovation. The prior work students curate is expected to address needs, resources, and precedents, with emphasis on patents and journals, as sources of evidence. DPCE is a good fit for our design research because course objectives align with the research goal, to support creativity in ideation task contexts.

To discover effects of our design intervention, we performed a field study in DPCE over a series of four one-shot, single semester periods (see Table 1). The instructors were constant. Course pedagogy, outside free-form web curation, minimally evolved. There was natural environmental variation across student cohorts. The fields of the study's student participants were diverse: architecture (27%) engineering (27%), agriculture (10%), liberal arts (10%), business (9%), general studies (7%), education (6%), science (3%), and veterinary medicine (2%). Gender was skewed: 37% female and 63% male.

DPCE students use IdeaMâché for ideation task assignments: e.g., *Imagine a Solution Curation* and *Soft Innovations*. The *Imagine a Solution Curation* assignment instructs students to conceptualize, design, explain, and reflect on a solution to a personal need in their life. Imagine a Solution curations, in practice, address everyday ideation activities similar to those found on Pinterest [55], such as weddings, workout routines, personal health, and redecorating. *Soft Innovation* (e.g. Figure 3,1) requires new designs for products and experiences.

While assignments were required, student participation in the study was voluntary. We asked students to consent to our confidentially gathering their creative products and tracking their creative engagement with IdeaMâché. We emphasized that study participation was optional and would not affect grades.

Evolving Design Intervention: 'Show Me' Feedback Loop

The strategies, system, and pedagogy evolved through the situated context of the study. In each semester, we presented an introductory lecture on free-form web curation, its strategies, and how to use IdeaMâché. The lecture included design principles, to teach students how to visually connect and differentiate elements in web curation. Around half of the lecture time presents strategies and principles, while the remaining half is a live demo. In s_1 and s_2, we used PowerPoint.

strategy	operation	μ_1	σ_1	μ_2	σ_2	$W_{2,3}$	$p_{2,3}$	μ_3	σ_3	μ_4	σ_4	%+	μ	σ
Collect	Drag and Drop	36	1.1	45	1.5	346280	$< 10^{-9}$	68	6.7	63	2.4	**73**	53	2.1
Assemble	Position	140	5.9	150	6.5	362913	$< 10^{-5}$	240	17.0	280	36.0	**99**	200	9.0
Assemble	Scale	39	1.6	50	2.0	376665	$< 10^{-3}$	79	7.2	83	9.5	**115**	63	2.9
Assemble	Fastening	21	1.1	24	1.3	355925	$< 10^{-6}$	38	2.2	43	6.3	**99**	31	1.5
Shift Perspective	Pan	140	6.0	190	8.3	364888	$< 10^{-5}$	260	14.0	290	17.0	**108**	220	6.1
Shift Perspective	Zoom	36	2.4	73	4.0	388324	.017	96	4.9	100	5.7	**190**	77	2.2
Sketch		40	2.4	70	3.8	372266	$< 10^{-3}$	130	9.0	180	17.0	**358**	100	4.5
Write		23	0.9	32	1.2	389684	.023	39	2.6	34	1.5	**47**	32	0.9
Time Creating - per curation (hours)		1.36	0.05	1.52	0.05	326755	$< 10^{-13}$	2.37	0.07	2.23	0.10	**64**	1.87	0.03
Web Site Variety - ideation metric		11.4	0.42	13.6	0.41	330240	$< 10^{-13}$	20.0	0.63	20.7	0.88	**82**	16.0	0.30

Table 2: Table of analytics, per curation. For each semester of the study, we present mean (μ_s) and standard error (σ_s), followed by aggregates. We begin with engagement analytics for each strategy and its operations. The next engagement analytic shows how long students spent authoring. Last, we present Web Site Variety, which measures the diversity of sources that students *Collect* from. Wilcoxon rank-sum statistics measure differences in distributions between s_2 and s_3, the 'hinge' semesters of the 'Show Me' Feedback Loop pedagogy. We observe significant increases for each analytic.

Starting in s_3, our pedagogy evolved beyond 'Tell Me' to 'Show Me'. We connected creative learning with creative teaching [53] by using free-form web curation, itself, to teach. Instead of presenting with slideware, we created a free-form curation about free-form curation [e.g., `https://ideamache.ecologylab.net/v/TAKIaq0008/`]. Class involved students in creating on-the-fly curations juxtaposing capabilities of a super hero and a patented technology. One example, juxtaposing Spider Man with bridge repair, curated patents and YouTube videos, along with comic images and sketching [`https://ideamache.ecologylab.net/v/nWy2q3C3rb/`].

The new pedagogy goes beyond describing to demonstrate free-form web curation. As our dataset grows, we incorporate exemplary student curations directly into pedagogy. This bootstraps a 'Show Me' Feedback Loop; prior student work impacts students and instructors in subsequent semesters.

FINDINGS

We gathered and analyzed data to see our design intervention's impact on students' creative engagement with prior work. We form a dataset of curation creative products. We compute analytics of engagement in curation processes. We observe an ecologically valid outcome in the DPCE course.

Curation Products Dataset and Examples

We began with all curation creative products saved in the cloud by DPCE students. To form a dataset, we filtered out insubstantial curations with fewer than 5 elements or 5 minutes of authoring. This resulted in a dataset of 3211 curations, authored by 1247 students (Table 1).

From the dataset, we present two exemplary free-form web curation products, which display creative engagement with prior work on the Soft Innovations ideation task. IdeaMâché's lack of pre-defined resolution for print confounds rendering the curations in the medium of this paper. We encourage the reader to zoom into the figures in this PDF.

The *Cell Phone Charger* curation's assemblage creates and instantiates an interesting design template (Figure 1). Structural repetition of design nodes—each with self-made text in the center, surrounded by a circle of readymade graphics—provides diagrammatic clarity. Consistent voicing and positioning of self-made texts creates a distinctive non-linear narrative. The root node, bottom left in the overview, says, "Every person from ages 8 to 90 has felt the pain of having their phone die on them." The next node says, "What's even worse is when you have your charger and there is no power outlet to plug it into." Readymade content sources are heterogeneous, e.g., product images, memes, tech blog content, artwork, schematics, and patent images. Each readymade element, including patent images, links back to its source.

In *Water Cleaning*, the overview shows two self-made rough circles, connected with lines, to form an exclamation mark morphology (Figure 3, bottom left). The top circle (not shown in detail), describes the problem, desertification and how society wastes water. The bottom one (Figure 3, main) builds on prior work precedents to develop solutions. Rough blue circles are labeled 'puddle', driving the water metaphor. A spatial template nests structures to continually go deeper into the problem and solutions. Figure 4 zooms in 2 levels of nesting, depicting how the proposed invention develops an emergent combination of thermal, filtering, and desalination techniques to solve the problem. We see how the student creatively engaged with readymade prior work content and the ideation task through the medium of free-form web curation.

Creative Process Engagement Analytics

We developed 3 kinds of data analytics, which quantify students' creative engagement in free-form web curation. The first engagement analytics are based on how many times the constituent operations corresponding to each web curation strategy were performed by each student, as s/he created a free-form web curation using IdeaMâché. Another engagement analytic is based on the overall Time each student spent Creating each curation. The third type of analytic is the Web Site Variety ideation metric.

We present these analytics with a focused statistical analysis (Table 2). Many statistical analyses of this data are possible. We focused on student performance corresponding to the introduction of the 'Show Me' Feedback Loop into pedagogy, across the 'hinge' semesters, $[s_{2,3}]$. For each analytic, we used the Wilcoxon rank-sum test to test for differences between the s_2 and s_3 distributions. Wilcoxon is more rigorous than the t-test, because it does not assume that data is normally distributed [33, 45]. We found that each analytic grew in a statistically significant way. While not observing causality, we find that creative engagement grew significantly in correlation with 'Show Me' Feedback Loop pedagogy.

Fundamentally, we find that students performed all strategies, observed through engagement analytics for constituent operations. While Assemble Fastening operations and Write were performed least, basic Assemble operations—Pan, Position, Zoom, and Scale—were performed intensively. This means students took advantage of free-form web curation's creative visual thinking Assemble strategy, despite the difference from prior modalities for curating prior work, such as traditional bibliographies and papers. Students also intensively invoked the Sketch strategy, another visual thinking modality.

The Time Creating analytic—how long students spent curating—rose by 64% over the course of the study and significantly across the 'Show Me' hinge semesters [$s_{2,3}$]. Spending longer on a creative task can mean increased engagement, rather than inefficiency. The correspondence of this analytic with the strategies and operations analytics and Web Site Variety indicates that increased Time Creating was substantially spent involved in creative processes.

Web Site Variety is an elemental ideation metric that measures the number of information sources Collected from, per curation [45]. Collecting from more websites tends to indicate more consideration and incorporation of diverse perspectives, contributing to more flexible and creative thinking. Web Site Variety nearly doubled across the course of the study and rose quite significantly across the 'Show Me' hinge. On average, in the aggregate, students curated from 16 different web sites, which seems substantial. Collected information sources can be exported as a conventional references list.

Ecologically Valid Outcome

In the semesters subsequent to the present field study, IdeaMâché developers omitted contacting DPCE instructors about continuing. We found that, instead, the instructors contacted us, at the start of semesters, to schedule our guest lecture. Free-form web curation has been naturalistically incorporated into course curriculum, as a means to stimulate creative engagement with prior work in the context of invention ideation task assignments. This incorporation represents an ecologically valid outcome, in the study's situated context.

RELATED WORK

Prior systems in industry, academia, and research address engagement with prior work and other content. Prezi enables organizing content as presentations in zoomable space. Microsoft OneNote also enables spatial organization of content. Content in Prezi and OneNote functions visually, like content in PowerPoint, without being anchored to a source. EverNote enables clipping locations, but organizes them in linear lists. Zotero and BibDesk support maintaining collections of prior work references in a linear form.

In contrast, free-form web curation affords creating a new, visual ideation task context, in which users Collect image and text clippings, Sketch amidst them, and spatially Assemble an integrated whole. Each clipping is augmented with contextual semantics that enable re-finding [40], which helps users derive value from the prior work they curate. Ongoing connections are sustained, between the contexts of prior work and the new context of the ideation task. To support writing papers, IdeaMâché enables linear BibTeX and HTML export of references derived from collected clippings.

Prior research systems also support clipping web content. Hunter Gatherer [86] supported clipping from 'within web pages' [86], enabling re-finding. The format of collections was the linear list. WebSummaries [23] supported structured information extraction into cards. PiggyBank enabled collecting metadata for a whole web page at a time [38]. Clui combined automatic metadata extraction with direct content clipping through predefined "rich objects" on web pages. Intermedia supported rich collecting of contextualized objects, each in a separate window [102]. None of these systems support organizing contextualized clippings, with sketching, in a free-form, multi-scale curation space context.

DISCUSSION

We connect findings with the strategies to develop implications for the design of web curation systems and education to support creative engagement with readymade content. The implications address multi-scale curation spaces, bootstrapping new media, teaching creative engagement with prior work, and social media platforms.

Multi-Scale Curation Spaces (Render-Independent)

Authoring tools, like Photoshop and Illustrator, provide ZUIs, but these are generally used in ways that assume fixed resolution rendering. This promotes developing detailed parts within wholes, but not multi-scale content organization, like the Eames' Powers of Ten [24]. Recently, people have become accustomed to navigating multi-scale content through geographical browsing apps, such as Google Maps. Support for authoring conceptual curation spaces with these affordances, as contexts for ideation, likewise makes sense.

We found that even though people have limited experience with creating multi-scale content organization, they deeply engage. Typical DPCE students lack specialized backgrounds in graphic or information design. Yet, they organized information spatially, invoking the art-based Assemble strategy.

The analytics show invocation of all the free-form curation strategies. Intensive student engagement in single-scale spatial organization is evidenced by large Assemble and Shift Perspective operation analytics, Position (mean 200 times per curation) and Pan (mean 220) (Table 2). The Assemble and Shift Perspective operation analytics—Scale (mean 63) and Zoom (mean 77)—show that students also use changes of scale as a means to organize content.

At the same time, the Collect strategy analytic shows that students gathered many elements (mean 53). The Web Site Variety analytic shows they Collected from many sites (mean 16). We interpret this to mean that students were stimulated, by engagement in spatial organization, to Collect extensive and diverse content. We also interpret that despite likely inexperience in organizing content in this new medium, students used scale, in the ZUI, as an Assemble technique, iteratively defining conceptual contexts of curation by creating content relationships that deal with the growing quantity of elements.

Bootstrapping: Use New Media to Teach New Media

Bootstrapping the use of new media for creative expression and learning is a chicken and egg problem. When people are unfamiliar with a paradigm, they may have trouble seeing how to use it. When we began offering the medium of free-form web curation to students, we used conventional slide-ware for pedagogy.

Then, spontaneously, we worked to incorporate this medium, itself, into our teaching. We used free-form web curation, instead of slideware, as the visual support for our presentations. We incorporated inspiring exemplary student work. We developed a paradigm to engage the class in a creative invention activity, based on the formula of first asking them for a super hero and an invention domain, then collaborating with them, to curate content juxtaposing these themes, on the fly. Across the 'Show Me' Feedback Loop hinge semesters [$s_{2,3}$], we observed significant increases in all measured creative process analytics. These findings motivate a prescription, to develop new media and then use them directly, in pedagogy, to teach.

Teaching Engagement with Prior Work

The digital age analogue of time-tested research in the library [94], collecting and recontextualizing prior work, is essential to scholarship in many fields [76, 16, 13] and also to innovation in industry [14, 8]. In their work on ideation task assignments, students intensively invoked the strategies of free-form web curation, while collecting extensive content. Some of them created striking displays of visual thinking. The instructors of the popular course, The Design Process: Creativity and Entrepreneurship, found the students' engagement with prior work through free-form web curation adds sufficient value to their pedagogy, that they are continuing to incorporate this new medium into their curriculum. Beyond the scope of the present study, instructors and students in other fields, such as communication and human-computer interaction, have also found that free-form web curation adds value to education. We argue that this evidence motivates significant expansion of the scope of using free-form web curation—to engage, in creativity, students performing ideation tasks involving prior work—in diverse fields and institutions.

Social Media Web Curation Platforms

Web curation in social media is a huge market. Facebook alone claims nearly 2 billion users [25]. Twitter, Instagram, Tumblr, LinkedIn, Pinterest, and other curation platforms are also widely used. Each platform seeks to maximize user engagement. We argue simply that adding free-form web curation space to a user's home page has the potential to engage her in creating a new context to represent her identity. For users who do engage in this way, their friends have the potential to engage as active readers, navigating the free-form curation spaces of their social networks.

CONCLUSION

We took a conceptual approach to designing human-computer interaction [41, 95]. We improvised—as if playing jazz [17, 11] or psychedelic music [34, 15, 28, 77]—in collecting and assembling prior approaches, practices, and principles, from across fields, in order to generate a set of creative strategies, which form the basis for a new theory of free-form curation.

Dourish and Harrison argue that the function of space is elevated to place when it serves as a context that supports situated human activity [32]. We apply Gertrude Stein's aphorism: otherwise, "There is no there there." [93] Likewise fundamental to the theory of free-form curation and its strategies are the roles of space and context in creating 'there'. Space affords embodied assemblage of collected content. Space enables the creation of place through conceptualizing and realizing new contexts of exhibition, which, in turn, support and manifest the performance of ideation tasks and activities.

Invoking Rogers' principles [80], we offer free-form curation, with its strategies, as HCI theory that is conceptual, critical, informative, explanatory, prescriptive, and generative. Free-form web curation, its constituent strategies—Collect, Assemble, Shift Perspective, Sketch, Write, and Exhibit—and our findings provide what Hook and Lowrgren call strong concepts [36]. They motivate a dynamic gestalt of interaction design to support creative engagement with prior work—with potential to cut across particular use situations and application domains—residing on an abstraction level that can be realized in many different interfaces. These strong concepts can be further generalized, to cut across interaction modalities and channels of new media.

The Design Process: Creativity and Entrepreneurship is one situated course in the domain of invention in undergraduate education. IdeaMâché is one interactive system, which provides integrated support for free-form curation on the web. Visual, experiential, and quantitative data show that the system works to support creative engagement with found objects of prior work in the situation. We found that IdeaMâché's zoomable user interface supported users in creating multi-scale curation space contexts, independent of rendering resolution, which, in turn, stimulated intensive and extensive curation of prior work. We found that using free-form web curation as new media, to teach free-form web curation, was effective for bootstrapping students' creative engagement.

We observe that the web is a broad, pervasive channel for new media, with many possible situations. Free-form curation spaces have the potential to be utilized even more broadly, through new media channels and interaction modalities, such as mixed reality [6]. Strategies of free-form curation provide a theoretical basis for realizing a panoply of other interfaces, which may focus on supporting other situated contexts, domains, channels, media, and modalities.

ACKNOWLEDGEMENTS

This article is based upon work supported by the National Science Foundation under grants IIS-074742, IIS-1247126, and IIS-1528044. Any opinions, findings, and conclusions or recommendations expressed in this material are those of the authors and do not necessarily reflect the views of the NSF.

REFERENCES

1. Alexander, C., Ishikawa, S., and Silverstein, M. *A Pattern Language: Towns, Buildings, Construction*. Center for Environmental Structure Berkeley, Calif. OUP USA, 1977.
2. Allen, S. From object to field+ architecture and urbanism. *Architectural design*, 127 (1997), 24–31.
3. Arnheim, R. *Visual Thinking*. University of California Press, 1969.
4. Barthes, R. S/z, trans. *Richard Miller (New York: Hill and Wang, 1974) 76* (1974).
5. Bederson, B. B., Meyer, J., and Good, L. Jazz: An extensible zoomable user interface graphics toolkit in java. In *Proceedings of the 13th Annual ACM Symposium on User Interface Software and Technology*, UIST '00 (2000), 171–180.
6. Benford, S., and Giannachi, G. *Performing mixed reality*. The MIT Press, 2011.
7. Bernstein, M. Collage, composites, construction. In *Proceedings of the Fourteenth ACM Conference on Hypertext and Hypermedia* (2003), 122–123.
8. Blank, S., and Dorf, B. The startup owner's manual: The step-by-step guide for building a great company.
9. Bolter, J. D. *Writing space: The computer, hypertext, and the history of writing*. Lawrence Erlbaum Associates Hillsdale, NJ, 1991.
10. Bransford, J. D., Brown, A. L., and Cocking, R. R. *How people learn: Brain, mind, experience, and school*. National Academy Press, 1999.
11. Braxton, A. Tri-axium writings.
12. Cage, J. *Silence: lectures and writings*. Wesleyan University Press, 2011.
13. Carson, S. H., Fama, J., Clancy, K., Ebert, J., and Tierney, A. *Writing for Psychology*. Harvard University, 2012.
14. Chesbrough, H. Open innovation: a new paradigm for understanding industrial innovation. *Open innovation: Researching a new paradigm* (2006), 1–12.
15. Clapton, E., Baker, G., Winwood, S., and Grech, R. *Blind Faith*. Polydor Records, 1969.
16. Colleged, H. *A Student's Guide to Reading and Writing in Social Anthropology*. Harvard University, 2010.
17. Coltrane, J. A. *A Love Supreme*. MCA Records, 1964.
18. Corajoud, M. L'horizon. *Face* (Mars 2004).
19. De Landa, M. *A thousand years of nonlinear history*. Zone Books New York, 1997.
20. Derieux, F., and Aubart, F. *Harald Szeemann: Individual Methodology*. JRP Ringier, 2007.
21. Derrida, J. *Of grammatology*. JHU Press, 2016.
22. documenta und Museum Fridericianum gGmbH. *documenta 5 - Retrospective*. 1972.
23. Dontcheva, M., Drucker, S. M., Salesin, D., and Cohen, M. F. Relations, cards, and search templates: User-guided web data integration and layout. In *Proceedings of the 20th Annual ACM Symposium on User Interface Software and Technology* (2007), 61–70.
24. Eames, C., and Eames, R. Powers of ten [motion picture]. *United States: IBM* (1977).
25. Facebook. Newsroom, 2016.
26. Fischer, G. Beyond "couch potatoes": From consumers to designers. In *IEEE Proceedings Computer Human Interaction. 3rd Asia Pacific.* (1998), 2–9.
27. Foucault, M. *The archaeology of knowledge*. Vintage, 2012.
28. Garcia, J., Lesh, P., Weir, B., McKernan, P., Kreutzmann, B., Godchaux, K., Godchaux, D., and Hunter, R. *Europe '72 - Grateful Dead*. Warner Bros. Records, 1972.
29. Giaccardi, E., and Karana, E. Foundations of materials experience: An approach for hci. In *Proceedings of the ACM Conference on Human Factors in Computing Systems*, CHI (2015), 2447–2456.
30. Goldschmidt, G. The dialectics of sketching. *Creativity Research Journal 4*, 2 (1991), 123–143.
31. Habermas, J. *Justification and application: Remarks on discourse ethics*. 1994.
32. Harrison, S., and Dourish, P. Re-place-ing space: the roles of place and space in collaborative systems. In *Proceedings of the 1996 ACM conference on Computer supported cooperative work* (1996), 67–76.
33. Hays, W. L. *Statistics, fourth edition*. Holt, Rinehart, Winston, 1988.
34. Hendrix, J. *Are You Experienced*. Track Records, 1967.
35. Higgins, D., and Higgins, H. Intermedia. *Leonardo 34*, 1 (2001), 49–54.
36. Höök, K., and Löwgren, J. Strong concepts: Intermediate-level knowledge in interaction design research. *ACM Transactions on Computer-Human Interaction (TOCHI) 19*, 3 (2012), 23.
37. Hutchins, E. L., Hollan, J. D., and Norman, D. A. Direct manipulation interfaces. *Human–Computer Interaction 1*, 4 (1985), 311–338.
38. Huynh, D., Mazzocchi, S., and Karger, D. Piggy Bank: Experience the Semantic Web inside your web browser. *Web Semantics: Science, Services and Agents on the World Wide Web 5*, 1 (2007).
39. Interface Ecology Lab. IdeaMâché. `https://ideamache.ecologylab.net/`, 2013-17.

40. Jones, W., Dumais, S., and Bruce, H. Once found, what then? a study of "keeping" behaviors in the personal use of web information. *In Proc. American Society for Information Science and Technology 39*, 1 (2002).

41. Kerne, A. Concept-context-design: A creative model for the development of interactivity. In *Proceedings of the 4th conference on Creativity & cognition* (2002), 192–199.

42. Kerne, A., Mistrot, J. M., Khandelwal, M., Sundaram, V., and Koh, E. Using composition to re-present personal collections of hypersigns. *Proc Computational Semiotics in Games and New Media (COSIGN)* (2004).

43. Kerne, A., Qu, Y., Webb, A. M., Damaraju, S., Lupfer, N., and Mathur, A. Meta-metadata: A metadata semantics language for collection representation applications. In *Proceedings of the ACM International Conference on Information and Knowledge Management*, CIKM (2010), 1129–1138.

44. Kerne, A., and Sundaram, V. A recombinant information space. *Proc Computational Semiotics in Games and New Media (COSIGN)* (2003), 48–57.

45. Kerne, A., Webb, A. M., Smith, S. M., Linder, R., Lupfer, N., Qu, Y., Moeller, J., and Damaraju, S. Using metrics of curation to evaluate information-based ideation. *ACM Trans. Comput.-Hum. Interact. 21*, 3 (June 2014), 14:1–14:48.

46. Kolko, J. Information architecture and design strategy: The importance of synthesis during the process of design. In *Industrial Designers Society of America Conference 2007* (2007), 17–20.

47. Konecki, K. T. Visual grounded theory: A methodological outline and examples from empirical work. *Revija za sociologiju 41*, 2 (2011), 131–160.

48. Krauss, R. E. *The optical unconscious*. MIT press, 1994.

49. Kurtenbach, G., and Buxton, W. User learning and performance with marking menus. In *Conference Companion on Human Factors in Computing Systems*, CHI (1994).

50. Lakoff, G., and Johnson, M. Conceptual metaphor in everyday language. *The journal of Philosophy 77*, 8 (1980), 453–486.

51. Landow, G. P. *Hypertext 3.0: Critical theory and new media in an era of globalization*. JHU Press, 2006.

52. Larkin, J. H., and Simon, H. A. Why a diagram is (sometimes) worth ten thousand words. *Cognitive Science 11*, 1 (1987), 65–100.

53. Lin, Y.-S. Fostering creativity through education-a conceptual framework of creative pedagogy. *Creative education 2*, 3 (2011), 149.

54. Linder, R., Lupfer, N., Kerne, A., Webb, A. M., Hill, C., Qu, Y., Keith, K., Carrasco, M., and Kellogg, E. Beyond slideware: How a free-form presentation medium stimulates free-form thinking in the classroom. In *Proceedings of the ACM SIGCHI Conference on Creativity and Cognition* (2015), 285–294.

55. Linder, R., Snodgrass, C., and Kerne, A. Everyday ideation: All of my ideas are on pinterest. In *Proceedings of the ACM Conference on Human Factors in Computing Systems*, CHI (2014), 2411–2420.

56. Lippard, L. *Dadas on Art*. Spectrum Book. Prentice-Hall, 1971.

57. Lippard, L. R. *Six years: the dematerialization of the art object from 1966 to 1972...*, vol. 364. Univ of California Press, 1997.

58. Lupfer, N., Kerne, A., Webb, A. M., and Linder, R. Patterns of free-form curation: Visual thinking with web content. In *Proceedings of the ACM Conference on Multimedia* (2016), 12–21.

59. Manovich, L. *The language of new media*. MIT press, 2001.

60. Marchionini, G. Exploratory search: from finding to understanding. *Communications of the ACM 49*, 4 (2006), 41–46.

61. Marshall, C. C. Toward an ecology of hypertext annotation. In *Proceedings of the ninth ACM conference on Hypertext and hypermedia* (1998), 40–49.

62. Marshall, C. C., and Shipman III, F. M. Spatial hypertext: designing for change. *Communications of the ACM 38*, 8 (1995), 88–97.

63. McCain, M. This meryl streep speech is why trump won. *Twitter* (January 2017).

64. Merleau-Ponty, M., and Smith, C. *Phenomenology of perception*. Motilal Banarsidass Publishe, 1996.

65. Miller, P. D. *Rhythm science*. MIT Press, 2004.

66. Nakakoji, K., Yamamoto, Y., Takada, S., and Reeves, B. N. Two-dimensional spatial positioning as a means for reflection in design. In *Proceedings of the 3rd Conference on Designing Interactive Systems: Processes, Practices, Methods, and Techniques*, DIS '00 (2000), 145–154.

67. National Academy of Engineering. *Rising Above the Gathering Storm, Revisited: Rapidly Approaching Category 5*. National Academy Press, 2010.

68. Nelson, T. H. *Computer Lib/Dream Machines*. Distributors, June 1974.

69. O'Neill, P. *The Culture of Curating and the Curating of Culture (s)*. MIT Press, 2012.

70. Ong, W. J. *Interfaces of the Word: Studies in the Evolution of Consciousness and Culture*. Cornell University Press, 2012.

71. Oxford University Press. *The Oxford English Dictionary*. http://ww.oed.com, 2013.

72. Palmer, S. E. Perceptual organization in vision. *Stevens' handbook of experimental psychology* (2002).

73. Paul, C. *New media in the white cube and beyond: Curatorial models for digital art*. Univ of California Press, 2008.

74. Perlin, K., and Fox, D. Pad: An alternative approach to the computer interface. In *Proceedings of the 20th Annual Conference on Computer Graphics and Interactive Techniques*, SIGGRAPH (1993), 57–64.

75. Pook, S., Lecolinet, E., Vaysseix, G., and Barillot, E. Control menus: Excecution and control in a single interactor. In *CHI '00 Extended Abstracts on Human Factors in Computing Systems*, CHI EA (2000), 263–264.

76. Pop, A. *How to Do Things with Pictures: A Guide to Writing in Art History*. Harvard University, 2008.

77. Prince, and The Revolution. *Purple Rain*. Warner Bros. Records, 1994.

78. Qu, Y., Kerne, A., Lupfer, N., Linder, R., and Jain, A. Metadata type system: Integrate presentation, data models and extraction to enable exploratory browsing interfaces. In *Proceedings of the ACM SIGCHI Symposium on Engineering Interactive Computing Systems*, EICS (2014), 107–116.

79. Rittel, H. W., and Webber, M. M. Dilemmas in a general theory of planning. *Policy sciences 4*, 2 (1973), 155–169.

80. Rogers, Y. Hci theory: classical, modern, and contemporary. *Synthesis Lectures on Human-Centered Informatics 5*, 2 (2012), 1–129.

81. Rosenbaum, S. *Curation Nation: How to Win in a World Where Consumers are Creators*. McGraw-Hill, Feb. 2011.

82. Rosenberg, J. And and: conjunctive hypertext and the structure acteme juncture. In *Proceedings of the 12th ACM conference on Hypertext and Hypermedia* (2001), 51–60.

83. Russell, D. M., Stefik, M. J., Pirolli, P., and Card, S. K. The cost structure of sensemaking. In *Proceedings of the INTERACT'93 and CHI'93 conference on Human factors in computing systems* (1993), 269–276.

84. Schechner, R. *Environmental Theater*. Acting Series. Applause, 1994.

85. Schön, D. A. *The reflective practitioner: How professionals think in action*, vol. 5126. Basic books, 1983.

86. schraefel, m. c., Wigdor, D., Zhu, Y., and Modjeska, D. Hunter gatherer: Within-web-page collection making. In *CHI '02 Extended Abstracts on Human Factors in Computing Systems*, CHI EA '02 (2002), 826–827.

87. Seitz, W. C. *the art of assemblage*. Museum of Modern Art New York, 1961.

88. Sellen, A. J., and Harper, R. H. *The myth of the paperless office*. MIT press, 2003.

89. Shah, J., Smith, S., and Vargas-Hernandez, N. Metrics for measuring ideation effectiveness. *Design Studies 24*, 2 (2002), 111–134.

90. Shneiderman, B., Plaisant, C., Cohen, M. S., and Jacobs, S. M. *Designing the User Interface: Strategies for Effective Human-Computer Interaction*. Pearson, 2017.

91. Society of Independent Artists. Catalogue of the first annual exhibition, 1917.

92. Spies, W. *Max Ernst Collages: The Invention of the Surrealist Universe*. Harry N Abrams Incorporated, 1991.

93. Stein, G. *Everybody's autobiography*. Vintage, 2013.

94. Stoan, S. K. Research and library skills: An analysis and interpretation. *College & research libraries 45*, 2 (1984), 99–109.

95. Stolterman, E., and Wiberg, M. Concept-driven interaction design research. *Human–Computer Interaction 25*, 2 (2010), 95–118.

96. Streep, M. Speech at the golden globes. *YouTube* (January 2017).

97. Trump, D. J. Meryl streep, one of the most over-rated actresses in hollywood. *Twitter* (January 2017).

98. Tversky, B. Visualizing thought. *Topics in Cognitive Science 3*, 3 (2011), 499–535.

99. Watson, J. Rapper's delight: A billion-dollar industry. *Forbes Feb 18* (2004).

100. Webb, A. M., Linder, R., Kerne, A., Lupfer, N., Qu, Y., Poffenberger, B., and Revia, C. Promoting reflection and interpretation in education: Curating rich bookmarks as information composition. In *Proceedings of the 9th ACM Conference on Creativity & Cognition* (2013), 53–62.

101. Wilkenfeld, M. J., and Ward, T. B. Similarity and emergence in conceptual combination. *Journal Memory and Language 45* (2001), 21–38.

102. Yankelovich, N., Haan, B. J., Meyrowitz, N. K., and Drucker, S. M. Intermedia: The concept and the construction of a seamless information environment. *Computer 21*, 1 (1988), 81–83.

103. Zimmerman, J., Forlizzi, J., and Evenson, S. Research through design as a method for interaction design research in hci. In *Proceedings of the SIGCHI conference on Human factors in computing systems* (2007), 493–502.

A Typology of Design Ideas

Nanna Inie
Centre for Advanced
Visualization and Interaction
(CAVI), Aarhus University
Aarhus, Denmark
inie@cavi.au.dk

Peter Dalsgaard
Centre for Advanced
Visualization and Interaction
(CAVI), Aarhus University
Aarhus, Denmark
dalsgaard@cavi.au.dk

ABSTRACT
Design ideas are commonly used as an indicator of success of design methods and processes. Yet it is very rarely defined what precisely constitutes "an idea", and how such an idea manifests itself to the researcher. This paper presents an examination of design idea definitions based on a thorough study of 75 research contributions. We construct a typology of seven definitions of design ideas. The purpose of the typology is to offer shared definitions and descriptions of design ideas to design and creativity researchers, aiding a higher degree of specificity when studying and analyzing the emergence of ideas in design processes.

Author Keywords
Design ideas; idea definition; idea generation; design processes; ideation; creativity; design theory

ACM Classification Keywords
H.5.m. Information interfaces and presentation (e.g., HCI): Miscellaneous

INTRODUCTION
In interaction design research, we comfortably speak about ideas and idea generation although the very core concept of a *design idea* lacks a consensus definition. It is often used interchangeably with words like *concept*, *solution* or *design move* [4,64]. In this paper, we present a thorough literature review to identify definitions and uses of the term "design idea" in design and related disciplines. We suggest a typology of design ideas, consisting of seven categories of ideas. This work is motivated by challenges in our own research into the emergence of ideas during design processes: if we cannot clearly define what a design idea is in the cases we study, we cannot systematically determine if and when ideas emerge. And in a wider perspective, if we do not have clear common definitions of design ideas in the design and creativity research communities, we argue that it hinders joint discussions and renders it hard to compare and evaluate findings across cases.

C&C '17, June 27-30, 2017, Singapore, Singapore

ACM 978-1-4503-4403-6/17/06…$15.00
DOI: http://dx.doi.org/10.1145/3059454.3059464

In design vernacular, the notion of a design idea often refers to a potential solution to a design problem. While this holds true in some cases, things are not always that straightforward. The following example from Dorst & Cross' 2001 canonical work on creativity in the design process illustrates how design ideas extend beyond potential solutions for a design problem. In this study, the designer is redesigning the litter bins in the trains in the Netherlands:

"In the 26th minute, the designer has the idea of doing away with the litter bins all together, and just make a hole in the floor of the train. He then asks whether or not such an idea would be out of the scope of the assignment, saying he likes to manipulate assignments, because they are often too narrow. Then he realises that there is already a litter system in the trains, namely the toilets. He asks for some information about that, and is genuinely shocked to hear that they are just a hole in the train floor, which opens onto the rails. He finds this an ugly, primitive, and very backward solution, and adopts a new goal, namely to change this also" [22].

Dorst & Cross show that defining and framing the design problem is a key aspect of creative design. In this example, the idea of changing the toilet system in the train appears as a design idea, yet it doesn't offer a solution to the original design task. Furthermore, if the designer had discarded the problem reframing in his final design, would this idea of reframing have been counted one of his ideas? This example shows how ideas can take other forms than mere solution suggestions.

Motivation
One of the key reasons for striving for a clearer definition and typology of design ideas is that it can help us evaluate ideas with respect to both their contribution to the outcome of the ideation process, and their contribution to the process itself [69,70]. If a design idea is not incorporated in the final design, but inspires one or more ideas that are, the creative value of the idea goes unnoticed if we evaluate only the outcomes of the process.

The example above also shows that it may not be feasible or preferable to establish a one-size-fits-all definition. To be clear, we are not stating that the notion of a design idea has not been defined in research contributions, but the definitions are mostly constrained to one or few studies, while other studies offer different definitions. This is expected, given that the studies have different foci; but it comes at the cost of a limited opportunity to compare across cases. Taken together, this points to the need for a typology of design ideas. Our aim is that the typology in this paper can be of value for design researchers who, like us, are interested in analyzing the early stages of design processes.

We focus on ideas in context of the early stages of design, what is epitomized by e.g. [38] as the *conceptual design phase*. We use the term 'design idea' to limit the scope of the analysis to ideas as they manifest themselves in design processes. Though the reviewed literature sources span from cognitive psychology to engineering design, they all add to design discourse.

Structure of the Paper

The paper is structured as follows: first we clarify our position regarding design as a creative- or problem solving activity. Secondly, we present previous works that have attempted categorizations of design ideas and their results. In the third section, we describe our methodology in commencing the literature review and present an overview of the selected works. In the fourth section, we describe a typology of ideas, and examine each of the categories and their corresponding references. For the sake of overview, we describe each idea type in two sections: a *description* based on the cumulative references to this idea type, and what an *externalization* of the idea may look like in empirical data. Finally, in the sixth section we discuss potentials and limitations of the typology and opportunities for future research.

CREATIVITY, PROBLEM SOLVING AND DESIGN

While not every idea qualifies as creative, every creative outcome can be traced back to the good ideas that started it [33]. And while creative ideas can happen during design, they are not exclusive to design processes [2]. Designing is, nonetheless, inherently a creative activity: *"... there can be no guarantee that a creative 'event' will occur during a design process (...) However, in every design project creativity can be found"* [22]. In this section, we will explain how we differentiate the term design idea from the term creative idea and from problem-solving tasks.

Design and Problem-Solving

One of the ways designing differs from objective problem-solving is that the designer often works with ill-defined and unique problems, making every design process an ultimate particular [72,54]. Studies of subjects in fMRI's show that a more extensive neural network is involved in the activity of understanding and resolving design tasks than the network involved in "normal" problem-solving tasks [2].

Creative problem solving is often described in terms of a dual model: the *associative* mode of thinking lets us explore our neural network for potential new connections, and the *analytic* mode evaluates new associations in terms of their feasibility [8,26,51,68]. There are many variations of this model, but it is largely agreed that two systems are simultaneously involved in creative cognition. One way of distinguishing design ideas from other creative ideas in their degree of goal-orientedness: *"[Design] is essentially guided by human purposes and is directed towards the fulfillment of intended functions"* [2], whereas creative thinking is deployed in many activities besides design [24]. Not every design process results in a flash of creative genius, and often ideas won't appear as *complete illuminations* [8], but rather the solution and problem framing are both negotiated during the process, co-evolving [22,89]. Design ideas emerge when the designer discovers a matching problem-solution pair that satisfies his or her requirements, or when *"loose, surprising information is linked into a coherent chunk, which offers a simplification of the design problem"* [15].

RELATED WORK

Design ideas take many forms, even on a semantic level. We can *have* ideas, we can *carry them around*, *generate* and *discard* them, and they can both live and die [52,9]. They are *elements of thought* [40], conceptions, that serve us to reason with [33]. They can also be conceptual places, that one can make lateral and vertical movements between [62], while at the same time they can represent movements themselves [31]. Physically, design ideas are often represented as a simple sketch or sticky-note, though the external representation is clearly not the idea itself - the idea exists before even verbal externalization as a kind of opportunity or glimpse of what could be in the future [45,27,64]. In this section, we will explain how previous selected works have conceptualized or categorized design ideas. We will focus particularly on *types of ideas*, and how such types have been defined.

Alpha, beta, gamma and delta ideas

A frequent way of characterizing design ideas is by their relation to the design process they contribute to. One such process-based classification by [5] divide ideas into three types: 1. New idea, 2. Revisited/repeated idea and 3. Third type (built on a previous idea). Idea development during the design process is viewed as the activity of elaborating, detailing or revising the idea along the timeline of design thinking. [38] divide ideas into alpha-, beta-, gamma- and delta ideas based on their temporal distribution in the design process (see figure 1). Evidently, delta-ideas will usually have a higher degree of complexity or richness than alpha-ideas. The best delta-idea is the one who passes the stage gate and enters the next level of the development process. It is not further defined what the different idea types entail, other than that they can be sorted sequentially.

Initial and developed ideas

Some studies make a distinction between ideas based on their evolutionary state. [44] distinguish between *initial ideas* as the first instance of any idea, and *developed ideas* as an initial idea, which is developed with more features and/or details. In the participatory design study in [63], 120 teenagers generated about 50 design suggestions (and more than 700 different design features) for an interactive water bottle. The authors consider each design feature an idea, and each design proposal is considered a *design suggestion*. After an evaluation of all design suggestions, a group of investigators made their own design suggestions based on the participant ideas that they liked the best, resulting in four final designs. Each of the final designs was then broken down into its salient features, with the purpose of analyzing how ideas (design features) had moved from the original participant's suggestion and been integrated into the investigator's final idea. As a result, the authors identify four types of ideas:

- *Core ideas*: those which many teenagers suggested and more than one investigator used
- *Add-ons*: those which many teenagers suggested but only one investigator used (ADD-ONS)
- *Novel ideas*: those suggested by only one teenager that one or more investigators used
- *Ideas that came from outside the design space* (which were not in the participants' suggestions) [63].

We see several examples of characterizations of design ideas based on their relation to the design process they are part of. However, research has also shown that designers often make use of what [32] calls *stock ideas*, ideas which are stored in the designer's own memory or personal archives, and that could become usable at another time. These cannot be defined in terms of their relation to any specific process, but as stand-alone items, sometimes based on found information from other sources [43]. In summary, we can confirm a lack of consensus among researchers, and that methods for classifying design ideas have applications in design research.

METHODOLOGY

In the following, we present our approach to the literature review and discuss its scope, benefits, and limitations. We reviewed a total of 75 literary works: 73 academic papers and the two books *The Creative Mind* by Margaret Boden (1990) and *Creative Cognition* by Finke, Ward & Smith (1992) (the overview of all the sources are presented in table 1). As stated, our objective was to examine how the concept of a design idea is articulated and defined, motivated by the broader question "What is a design idea?". Our study focuses on research papers within design and closely related fields (such as creativity studies, creative cognition, engineering design and architecture), specifically the stages of idea generation.

We were interested in both explicit definitions of design ideas, such as *"An idea, in this case, refers to a statement by one of the designers that..."* [4] and derived definitions, where the author offers a description of design ideas, e.g.: *"Ideas emerge from sources of inspiration mediated by design materials, the way in which they are negotiated throughout the workshop, and combined into design concepts"* [35]. The reviewed materials build on various types of data, which influences which aspects of design ideas are discussed in the work. For instance, while studies based on in-vitro experiments often look at obvious externalizations of ideas, studies based on anecdotes and interviews describe often the internal experience of ideas. The data types for all the reviewed sources are indicated in table 1.

We have strived to follow the principles for a *systematic literature review* as defined by [56]. The systematic characteristics can be defined as *"a set of rigorous routines, documentation of such routines, and the way the literature reviewer negotiates particular biases throughout these routines"* [Ibid.]. For this reason, we will lay out our approach in more detail in this section. Moreover, the review interprets and reflects in the terminology of [ibid.], aiming to bring forth *"the salient and critical aspects of the most current knowledge" including "substantive findings, as well as conceptual, theoretical, and/or methodological contributions"*. Pre-existing knowledge of the domain among the reviewer(s) is a central component to this approach, and the review is thus informed in part by theory, in part by the reviewers' prior work in the field of design creativity and ideation [6,7,17,34,35].

To clarify the systematic approach, we initiated the review using a keywords-based search through Google Scholar, and selected readings based on the abstracts and citation count (papers with less than 3 citations from before 2010 were deselected in favor of scientific impact). The following terms identified a total of 33 unique papers (tier 1): *design idea*, *design idea development*, *definition idea*,

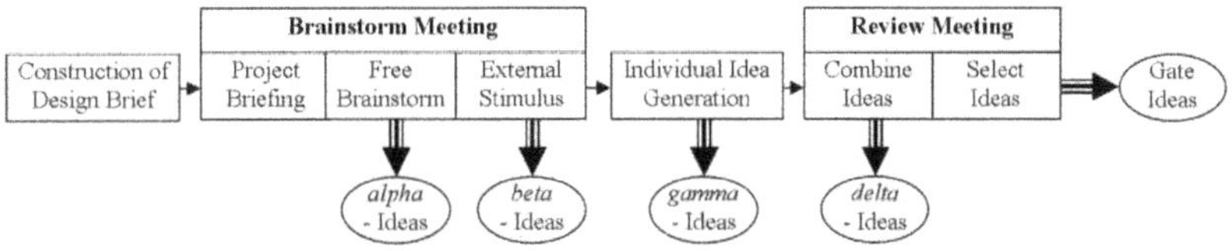

Figure 1: Idea classifications by Howard, Culley & Dekoninck (2011) [33]

	1970-1980	1981--1990	1991-1995	1996-2000	2001-2005	2006-2010	2011-2015	2016
Design	*Simon '73*	**♥Goldschmidt '90**	**♦Akin & Akin '96**	**♦Cross '97** Purcell & Gero '98 *♦Suwa et al. '98* *♦Verstijnen et al. '98*	**♦Dorst & Cross '01** **♥Kan & Gero '05** **♥Goldschmidt & Tatsa '05** ♦Van der Lugt '01 ♦Van der Lugt & Van der Graaf '02 ♦Van der Lugt '03 *♥Suwa & Tversky '02* *♥Jonson '05*	**♣Murty & Purcell '07** **♦Bilda & Gero '08** **♦Girotra et al. '10** **♦Baker & van der Hoek '10** ♦Dix et al. '06 ♦Kan et al. '06 ♦Halskov & Dalsgaard '07 ♦Tseng et al. '08 ♦Liikkanen et al. '09 ♦Yamamoto et al. '09 **♦Yilmaz et al. '10** *Nelson et al. '09* *Howard et al. '08*	**♦Goldschmidt & Sever '11** ♦Howard et al. '11 ♦Daly et al. '12 *♥Lund & Prudhomme '13* *♦Siangliulue et al. '15*	**♦Read et al. '16** **♥Bratteteig et al. '16** ♦Cardoso et al. '16
Engineering		*Holt et al. '85*		Shah et al. '00	♦Shah et al. '03 ♥Badke-Schaub & Gehrlicher '03	**♦Perttula & Liikkanen '06** **♦Perttula & Sipilä '07** ♦Perttula et al. '06 ♦Perttula '06 *Sosa et al. '09* *♣Tanaka et al. '09*	♦Toh & Miller '15	
Creativity research		**♣Davies & Talbot '87** **♣Boden '90**			*♦Ishii & Miwa '02* *Scardamalia & Bereiter '03*	**♥Wiltschnig et al. '10** **♥Wiltschnig & Onarheim '10** ♣Coughlan & Johnson '08	**♦Wiltschnig et al. '13** **♦Kerne et al. '14** **♥Sosa & Dong '13**	♦Starkey et al. '16
Cognitive science			**Finke et al. '92** **♦Seifert et al. '94**	*Soufi & Edmonds '96*	*Gabora '02* *♦Colunga & Smith '03*	*♦Liikkanen & Perttula '10*	**♦Kim & Kim '15**	
Neuroscience						♦Alexiou et al. '09 *♦Goel '10*	♦Mayseless et al. '15	
Management or marketing research					**♦Dahl & Moreau '02** ♣Goldenberg et al. '01 *♣Tschang '03*	**Riedl et al. '09** *Fleischmann '06* *♣Prabir & Amaresh '07*	Fernández & López '11	

Table 1: Overview of selected works based on year, field, relevance to the study, and methodology.
♥ indicates that the work is mainly based on in-vivo observations.
♦ indicates that the work mainly builds on in-vitro experiments, and
♣ means the work is largely informed by anecdotal interviews, surveys, or after-the-fact analysis.
No indication means the work does not build on empirical data.

ideas design process, *insight moments design*, *design idea emergence*, *idea emergence*, *what is an idea*. Secondly, we used the search engines for all issues of Design Studies and proceedings of the conference Creativity & Cognition, which revealed another 14 works, bringing the tier 1 total to 47. Assuming that the total tier 1 works would build on sufficient material to provide us with a sound historic perspective, we collected tier 2 based on references from tier 1, and recommendations and suggestions from peers collected in conversations while composing this paper. Tier 2 adds another 28 papers to the stack, bringing the total to 75 works.

The authors used a scoring of 1-3 to classify the literature, where 1 is highly relevant (offers a direct definition of design ideas), 2 is relevant (uses the term ideas with a vague or no definition, or builds directly on a relevance 1-paper) and 3 is not relevant to the study. The rating 3 was given to papers where the subject didn't relate to our study, for instance when using the term "idea" in the philosophical sense, i.e. "*The* ***idea*** *of entrepreneurship as emancipation*" [25], or if it presented revised algorithms for idea metrics [53]. The substantial amount of papers with the rating 3, highlights how ambiguous and widespread the word idea is within research. Of the total 75 works, 26 were given a rating of 1, 26 were given a rating of 2, and 23 were rated 3. Arbitration was carried out as continuous dialogue while the typology was being developed.

After completing the work of collecting, reading and annotating the papers, we were able to group the different categories of contributions by identifying similarities and differences in semantic use of the term idea. We found that there was a clear correspondence between research field and semantics. Thus, the overview in table 1 is organized by year and field. The references are coded in line with our relevance assessment: **Bold** means we classified the paper as having relevance 1, grey is relevance 2 and *italics* is relevance 3. If the work is a contribution to more than one field, we have made a subjective assessment of which one to categorize it within.

Our main challenge in the review was scoping. We kept a very open approach in the initial steps, looking for definitions from various fields. Then we narrowed our search by only following references that guided us towards specific definitions. Table 1 shows that a majority of the reviewed material stems from the design field, and lies within the years 2001-2010. We chose not to extensively pursue historic references from the fields of cognitive

<table>
<tr>
<td>Particular type 1
(Re)framing the problem

Dorst & Cross (2001), Baker & van der Hoek (2010), Wiltschnig et al. (2013), Alexiou et al. (2009), Cardoso et al. (2016)</td>
<td>Particular type 2
Opportunity

Finke et al. (1992), Sosa & Dong (2013), Kerne et al. (2014), Mayseless et al. (2015), Bratteteig et al. (2016), Dix et al. (2006), Coughlan & Johnson (2008)</td>
<td>Particular type 3
Suggestion for part-solution

Cross (1997), Perttula & Liikkanen (2006), Baker & van der Hoek (2010), Kim & Kim (2015), Read et al. (2016), Van der Lugt (2001), Halskov & Dalsgaard (2007)</td>
<td>Particular type 4
Suggestion for solution

Shah et al. (2000), Goldenberg et al. (2001), Dorst & Cross (2001), Shah et al. (2003), Perttula & Sipilä (2007), Riedl et al. (2009), Goldschmidt & Sever (2011), Howard et al. (2011), Dahl & Moreau (2002), Badke-Schaub & Gehrlicher (2003), Perttula (2006), Perttula et al. (2006), Tseng et al. (2008), Liikkanen et al. (2009), Girotra et al. (2010), Yamamoto et al. (2009), Yilmaz et al. (2010), Fernández & López (2011),
Daly et al. (2012), Toh & Miller (2015), Starkey et al. (2016)</td>
</tr>
<tr>
<td colspan="4">General type 1
Design move

Goldschmidt (1990), Purcell & Gero (1998), Van der Lugt & Van der Graaf (2002), Van der Lugt (2003), Kan & Gero (2005), Goldschmidt & Tatsa (2005), Kan et al. (2006), Bilda & Gero (2008), Baker & van der Hoek (2010)</td>
</tr>
<tr>
<td colspan="4">General type 2
Insight (moment)

Davies & Talbot (1987), Boden (1990), Seifert et al. (1994), Akin & Akin (1996), Murty & Purcell (2007), Wiltschnig & Onarheim (2010), Wiltschnig et al. (2010)</td>
</tr>
<tr>
<td colspan="4">General type 3
Plan for action

Riedl et al. (2009), Van der Lugt (2001)</td>
</tr>
</table>

Table 2: A typology of design ideas.
Some references appear more than one time, if they offer more than one definition of design idea.

science, neuroscience and marketing and management research, due to our focus on the design field.

The review has been comprehensive in the sense that we found a great overlap in definitions and references in all the literary sources surveyed. It has also been possible to identify overarching themes in the literature, such as a general confirmation of our research question; the term design idea is often vaguely or not at all defined. In some instances, the authors clarify directly how they view the term for their personal analysis purposes, suggesting again that such a definition is useful and needed.

We must stress, however, that our review is not exhaustive. Because we look for definitions on a semantic, textual level, we are constrained by search engine capabilities, and we ask that the review is read with this stipulation in mind. Information retrieval systems are imperfect, and it is unlikely to achieve perfect recall while having useful precision. Rather, best-effort is the preferred method, and some documents may escape retrieval [65]. The review is also subject to some degree of subjectivity, as we have used our best judgment to arrive at useful categories for the different definitions of ideas. Several papers pointedly use, for instance, the term *design move*, interchangeably with *ideas*. We will return to this topic in the descriptions of the different idea types. In the following section, we will present our typology of design ideas and explain how the categories have emerged.

A TYPOLOGY OF DESIGN IDEAS

Table 2 shows the different uses of the term *design idea* we discovered and their corresponding references. Each cell represents *a form* a design idea can take. By *form* we mean a conceptual shape which previous research has considered 'a design idea' and used as a basis for analysis - either to be able to quantify ideas or to be able to delimit ideas for the purpose of saying something about them. The diagram should be read as follows: There are 4 types of *particular* idea types, meaning they are by and large mutually exclusive. Normally, an idea is not both a reframing of the problem *and* a solution[1]. There are 3 types of *general* idea types, which are categories that any of the particular ideas can also be, but are not necessarily. A new, innovative feature of a product can, at the same time, be both *a suggestion for a part-solution*, a *design move and* an *insight moment*. A design idea can*not* be of general type, if it is not a particular one.

When a reference falls into more than one category (i.e. explicitly uses more than one definition), the reference is listed under both categories. References that offer a specific definition or that investigate an original definition of design ideas are presented in **bold** font while references building

[1] With the exception of the concept co-evolution of problem and solution [22,89], which we will elaborate further on under the description of these types.

on another paper's definition are presented in *italics* directly following the original reference. References where the definition has been derived from context or use examples in the analysis are presented in a regular font.

General Comments on the Typology

During the analysis, it became clear, perhaps unsurprising, that the definition of idea depends on the research scope of the paper in question, and thus the data collection. When the aim is to study efficiency of a design method, the authors have often put a constraint in the study design, allowing them to quantify the generated ideas, e.g. asking the subjects to externalize every unique idea on individual sheets of paper or sticky-notes [e.g. 59,71]. Some fields show relatively constrained definitions of the term idea, particularly the fields of business and engineering, which generally view the design idea in light of a production chain. In these fields, an idea is a suggestion for a solution to a design problem (e.g. [69,70]), or a proposal towards development of a new product [23]. A design idea can be quite a large entity, containing a lot of information about features and potential uses. Fields like cognitive science, creativity research and psychology tend to use much broader definitions, viewing design ideas as various forms of *creative discoveries* or *insights* (e.g. [8,24]).

Design fields generally study externalized ideas: *"notions related to a (design) task that have been communicated verbally in studio sessions, in one-on-one critiques or group discussions"* [33], whereas especially the fields of creativity research and cognitive science do not draw this distinction: *"ideas are the basis of conceptual design activity, whether they are drawn as they come into mind or not drawn"* [5]. In these fields, design ideas can be as small as "notions", not necessarily externalized.

Another interesting observation is that while a vast majority of the references fall under the *suggestion for part-solution* and *suggestion for solution* categories, many of them don't offer their own distinct definition. Meanwhile *all* the references under *insight moment* are in bold, indicating that they provide a first-hand definition or that they directly investigate this definition. Since insight moments are often related to Big-C-discoveries [73], discoveries that change the world, it might be unsurprising that these have had a lot of scientific focus. The type *design move* was clearly defined in one distinguished paper [31], which several later works refer to and build upon.

In the following section, we will elaborate on each of the definitions. For the sake of clarity and applicability, we will divide each section into a description and examples of how the types are recognizable for the design researcher. One of the central challenges of conducting studies of creative processes is our limited access to the mental processes that precede an externalized idea [2,51]. Often, written or drawn externalizations such as sketches and sticky-notes are our primary indication of idea emergence - a tangible way of quantifying ideas. In this study, we have reviewed both works that only look at externalized ideas (e.g. [4,33,91]), and works that focused on ideas as neurological activity (e.g. [26,51]), but for the sake of applicability of the typology, we try to offer a description of how the different types of ideas may be externalized and observable to the researcher. We understand externalization as any expression of computational offloading [66] or discoverable manifestation: *"a way of taking information or mental structure generated by an agent and transforming it into epistemically useful structure in the environment. It is a way of materializing structure that first was mental"* [45].

Particular Type 1: (Re)framing the Problem

Description

Studies have found that defining and framing the design problem is a key aspect of achieving creative design solutions [22] and that experienced designers often deliberately modify or manipulate a design brief to make it challenging or interesting, and to provoke new creative responses from themselves [2,21,22]. A creative design process involves a period of exploration in which the problem and solution spaces are said to be co-evolving, remaining unstable until (temporarily) fixed by a 'creative bridge' that identifies a problem-solution pairing [15,89]. Design ideas can therefore be an attempt to develop or frame the problem space.

Framing or reframing the problem offers a new way of structuring the design process: *"Design is not a matter of first fixing the problem and then searching for a satisfactory solution concept, but of developing and refining together both the formulation of a problem and ideas for a solution, with constant iteration of analysis, synthesis and evaluation processes between the two notional design 'spaces'"* [22]. Some designers have been shown to habitually try to 'break' instructions of a design proposal simply for the purpose of revealing opportunities that weren't there before [2].

Externalization or indicators:

Problem framing can often be observed directly in design conversations or think-aloud-individual work [22]. During group work, high-level questions can indicate an exploration of the problem space, in that questions can facilitate so-called inflection moments in the group [10]. [4] describes a definition of an idea as statements by one of the designers that *characterize* the provided problem. Some studies have looked for transcription segments that contain "references" to the design requirement, specifically statements that either: a) add a novel requirement, b) interpret or make revisions to an existing requirement, c) bracket a requirement ("we're not going to be dealing with that here") or d) delete a requirement [89].

Particular Type 2: Opportunity

Description

Design ideas can be understood as expressions of possible choices within a design process. With the creation of the

Geneplore model, [24] suggests that different aspects of creativity, whether it is artistic creation or scientific discovery, lie along the same continuum. All forms of ideation can be understood within the same model of generative and explorative phases. First, the ideating individual constructs mental representations called *preinventive structures,* having various properties that promote creative discoveries. These properties are then exploited during an exploratory phase, where the individual seeks to interpret the preinventive structures in meaningful ways. When a creative discovery is made, an opportunity presents itself.

Opportunities can also be expressed as curations of inspirational material; what [43] calls Inspiration Based Ideation or IBI. In their work, they demonstrate how the act of finding, choosing and curating inspirational material can both express ideas and lead to new idea emergence revealed only by combining other elements – such as can be seen when designers create mood boards. Another example of utilizing ideas as opportunities is the technique BadIdeas, as developed by [21]. The technique encourages designers to make up 'bad' or 'silly' ideas, that aren't technically feasible or even desirable, with the purpose of inspiring creativity and critical thinking. An example could be a glass hammer or a chocolate greenhouse. BadIdeas are instances where ideas can be both creative and novel, but not actually suggestions for solutions.

Externalization or indicators

An example of an idea as an opportunity is an idea that opens up a possibility, but doesn't have immediate application - at least not in relation to the design at hand. It may have immediate application to the process, such as BadIdeas. Some studies have looked for opportunities in textual communication by looking for suggestive keywords such as: *Would be*, *wish, maybe*, *could be*, *guess*, *mean*, *version*, *if you/if we*, *wonder* and *also* [74].

Individual designers often store ideas and inspirational material for later use. The value of an idea is largely related to the context it is deployed in, which gives designers an incentive to keep good ideas until they are in a position to use them [14]. Hence, the designer's personal archive can be said to represent opportunities for design.

Particular Type 3+4: Suggestion for Solution or Part-Solution

We have chosen to describe *suggestion for part-solution* and *suggestion for solution* in the same section, as their characteristics are categorically similar.

Description

Ideas as solutions or suggestions for part-solutions is by far the most represented and commonly used definition in our survey. While externally, these two types look different, they share the same descriptive characteristics, so we will include them both in this section. Due to the amount of references in these categories, we will not go through all of them in depth, but simply explain how they relate to the category in terms of contribution.

The idea as a suggestion for a (part-) solution can be defined as "*An explicit description of an invention or problem solution with the intention of implementation as a new or improved product, service, or process within an organization*" [64] and "*- a design concept which was generated to satisfy the design brief, and has at least one determined feature related to the product itself such as shape, functionality, or material*" [44]. Searching for or exploring solutions (or sub-solutions) is a core activity in design [15]. The majority of studies that use the term solution suggestion synonymously with ideas, are in-vitro experiments that examine different design methods [16,18,23,32,46,57,58,83,92,93].

Our initial search revealed several works that explore ways to qualify design methods from an outcome-based perspective [23,28,30,69,70 among others]. An outcome-based approach means that the ideas that are generated in the process are the basis for evaluating how successful the design method is. The outcomes are here analogous to suggestions for solutions. The four most common effectiveness measures for ideas in this sense are *quantity* (total number of ideas generated), *quality* (feasibility of the idea), *novelty* (how unusual or unexpected the idea is) and *variety* (how well the idea explores the solution space) [38,69,70]. Interestingly, [81] has shown that engineering students tend to focus primarily on the technical feasibility of a design idea, even if they are explicitly instructed to look for creative solutions. Another study has shown that while design methods often focus on making the designer(s) explore the solution space, overall creativity during the idea generation does not necessarily predict the creativity of the final design [77]. The decisions and selection of solutions appear to play as significant a role in the design process as the generation of ideas [3,81], as the ability to assess the quality of an idea is not analogous to the ability to generate creative ideas [28,77].

Externalization or indicators

The greater amount of our literature sources look at sketches or written design proposals when distinguishing a part-solution or a solution. A way of discerning and quantifying ideas as solutions in a design process is to simply make the participants self-assess their idea count by asking them to externalize their ideas on separate pieces of paper [59]. In group studies, it has been shown that a significant amount of agreement has often been reached before a solution concept is externalized [35]. Often the externalization marks the termination of the development of that concept, and participants will move onto a new concept or a new subject of conversation [4,35]. While the designer is developing a design solution, different *design features* evolve, which correspond to our understanding of part-solutions or sub-solutions [15,63].

Solution suggestions have conceptual strength if they embody a potential solution form that satisfies key problems, but still have the malleability to be modified and refined [15]. The externalizations of solution suggestions tend to summarize a *recognizably good solution* [15]. Often, they are sketches, which can serve several functions: *thinking sketches* support the individual thinking process, *talking sketches* support the group discussion, *prescriptive sketches* communicate design to people outside the design group and *storing sketches* archive the designer's own ideas [84].

General Type 1: Design Moves

Description

The term "design move" originates from Goldschmidt's significant work on linkography as a method for investigating the integratedness of a design process [31]. The hypothesis is that the more links to subsequent discussions, an idea creates, the better it is. In this method, a design process is represented by sequential 'design moves', and links between them. Design moves were originally defined as individual design propositions made with the purpose of arriving at satisfying visual representations, but the definition has been expanded and elaborated in later studies, e.g. [33,41,86]. The process of designing is seen as a succession of acts of reasoning, and each of these acts is called a design move [31]. A design move is therefore any (reasoning) act within design, even if it doesn't involve a visual representation. Later works have used the term design move interchangeably with ideas [4,32,33] which is why the term belongs in the typology. Design moves help identify good ideas in the design process: good ideas are critical ideas, in the sense that they generate a large number of links (they motivate many other design moves), and *very good ideas* are those that spin the largest number of links among themselves and other ideas [85]. However, studies have also shown that ideas with too many forelinks might indicate fixation [41]. While the term design move is sensible in terms of analyzing a design discussion, there is a blurry line between design moves and ideas. Building on Schön'ish terminology, [9] offers a distinction based on the "move"-property: *"A 'design move' (...) consists of the designers' evaluation of a situation, a move to change it and an evaluation of the move as a step closer to the final result. In this light a design idea is what the move is about: a suggestion for a particular (part of) a design solution to be tested and evaluated through the move"*. In such understanding, each design move, however small, towards a satisfying design can be viewed as a design idea.

Externalization or indicators

As described in the previous section, design moves have the analytic advantage that they are confined to observable acts. Some studies delimit single moves by tagging utterances sequentially [42], and some studies rely on the designers' own after-the-fact assessments [31]. The common method among the researchers using linkohraphy is protocol studies. If designers use sketching, design moves can be identified from the ongoing generation of representations and restructuring of these representations as they move forward [62]. [86] establish a set of context criteria to identify links between design moves based on observation alone: *time span* (temporal closeness can mean conceptual closeness), *inspection*, *physical reaction*, *verbal reaction*, *withdrawal*, *explanation*, *addition*, *location* (spatial closeness can mean conceptual closeness) and *scheme resemblance* (resemblance in visual representations). These context criteria are useful in establishing links, however not moves themselves. Even though linkography is widely accepted as an analysis method, previous works have concluded that defining design moves undeniably requires a great amount of subjective assessment and common sense of the researcher [86].

General Type 2: Insight Moment

Description

Insight moments, or "Aha!"-moments, are at the very core of creativity. They are what most people think of, when they think of ideas. These are the moments symbolized by the famous light bulb turning on, indicating a new exciting idea. An insight moment can be described as "*a flash of lightening or the sudden appearance of a solution to a problem the individual had been working on*" [8], and [19] reports a designer describing the moment as a feeling of "*becoming aesthetically literate*". In an instance, suddenly and unexpectedly the solution to a problem becomes apparent together with feelings of clarity and satisfaction [90].

According to Wallas' model of creativity [88], the insight moment, or *illumination* is the third of four stages, preceded by the preparation stage, the incubation stage and followed by the verification stage. Research into the cognition of these moments have shown the importance of reaching an *impasse* (e.g. failure to solve a problem on the first try) before the insight moment can be reached. The impasse is thought to leave failure indices in long-term memory, preparing the mind for the moment when relevant information, which can be used to solve the impasse, may be available [68,52,1].

The insight moment or *imago* is often experienced when the designer knows that the idea is *just right*, a momentary glimpse of absolute perfection, where the physical-world manifestation of the ideas is always less than satisfactory to the designer [19]. The experience can be quite addictive, and it is hypothesized that particularly creative designers may be distinguished by their ability to achieve these moments more often than others [ibid.].

Insight moments can be related to the finished design solution as well as the process, for instance when a problem solver breaks free of unwarranted assumptions or discovers a new way of approaching the problem. They usually have the character of *unexpected discoveries* [52]. Insight moments can happen during all forms of problem solving work, and are not exclusive to design [1]. An example of a problem-solving insight is the classic nine-dot-puzzle. where people often set up self-made constraints by assuming they have to stay "within the box", to be able to solve the puzzle. When the solution is discovered, it is often results in an aha!-moment [ibid.].

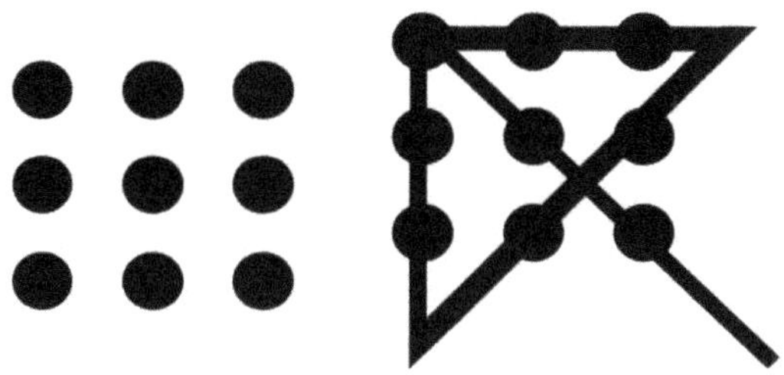

Figure 2: The nine-dot puzzle. The task consists of connecting all 9 dots with four straight lines, leading many people to believe that the lines have to stop within the frames of "the box"[48].

Externalization or indicators

Designers have reported experiencing, among others, the following phenomena during an insight: Oneness, transcendence of self, ecstatic feelings and lack of anguish, synthesis, obviousness and effortlessness [19]. Due to this emotional character, insight moments can usually be identified by the designer's self-appraisal or memory [40].

They can even happen to a group of people simultaneously: *"One of the nurses stood up and used an existing product to demonstrate a specific user challenge. At a certain point in her demonstration members of the design team suddenly interrupted her, as they wanted to share an idea with the team. As it turned out, four out of six team members had got the same idea"* [91]. Often an insight moment can be observed as a pivotal moment in the design process, providing an immediate focus for the designer(s) [15].

General Type 3: Plan for Action

Description

Design ideas can be expressed as planning for the next steps in the process. [84] divides creative problem solving into three main components:

- Understanding the problem, where the goal is to identify specific directions for ideas
- Generating ideas, preferably many, varied and unusual ideas
- Planning for action, where ideas are transformed into action).

Due to the goal-oriented nature of design [70], the designer will often be aware that ideas have to be transformed into action at some point. This planning can be a part of the idea development process. Furthermore, plans for how to structure the future parts of the design process (such as which part of the project to work on next) can also be viewed as design ideas, although this definition is not very common.

Externalization or indicators

Action plans in a group process are often verbalized. [64] defines an idea: "*An explicit description of an invention or problem solution with the intention of implementation as a new or improved product, service, or process within an organization*". By this definition, a design idea contains the specific intention of implementing it, which we understand as a plan for action. By this definition, if a designer says "I've seen this material used in a similar construction before", but he does not intend to implement the material, he is not making a plan for action. If he says "We're going to use *this* material!", he is making a plan for action.

APPLICATIONS AND DISCUSSION

We intentionally do not offer one common definition to the term design idea, but rather propose a typology to suggest that a design idea, depending on the perspective, situation, and research focus, can appear in different forms. The most prevalent definition of a design idea falls in the category of suggestion for solution. Since design is in a broad sense about creating novel solutions, this is not entirely surprising. However, the main part of the definitions fall into other categories, emphasizing that there is no consensus about what constitutes a design idea.

Documenting and Analyzing Design Ideas

We argue that a more precise documentation of design processes will lead to heightened awareness, deeper reflection and ultimately, better design processes, for both researcher and practitioner. We see the typology as serving several purposes. Firstly, it offers an overview of contributions in the field, which can help researchers situate their work in relation to existing work. Secondly, the typology can serve as a platform for identifying and studying various types of design ideas; this can help us in documenting and analyzing design processes by enabling us to define which idea unity we are particularly interested in. Thirdly, it can support discussions and comparisons across cases, potentially yielding novel insights through studying similar phenomena across multiple design projects.

When documenting the design process, a palpable problem is how to visualize our data. How do we know when an idea has emerged? What the limits of an idea are? Can a sentence contain an entire idea, or is it merely a part of an idea? A clearer definition of design ideas can make documentation of observed design processes more rigorous.

As design researchers, we need tools for documenting the design process to study and compare our results.

Limitations and Potentials of the Typology

The design idea typology is a first attempt at structuring what has proven to be a highly complex concept. It is first and foremost a deep dive into literature on design and creativity in order to establish an overview and identify common definitions. One potential limitation in our approach is that we could have applied a wider set of search parameters, e.g. by looking to other fields beyond design and creativity research. E.g. the field of philosophy has a long history of studying the nature of ideas. We have deliberately kept the survey more contained in order to focus on works that specifically address the notion of a design idea, but further studies that integrate other perspectives and articulations of ideas can add to this work, e.g. via insights into how different types of ideas are related.

A second limitation is that we have condensed a large selection of design idea definitions into the seven categories in the typology. By offering these relatively broad types, we may miss subtle, but important distinctions between different pre-existing definitions of design ideas. Also, we have located most literary works in one category, while some span across two or more categories. Here, we have sought to balance comprehensiveness, overview, and explanatory power. We consider the typology adequate, but since it is a first attempt at a structured overview of design ideas, it is not necessarily exhaustive. We have sought to make the selection and categorization process clear, so that others may challenge it and for instance argue for alternative categorizations.

The typology in its current form is not intended as a directly applicable framework in design practice. However, it may still be of use for designers, who seek a better understanding of how and why design concepts emerge and evolve, and who wish to better steer a design process by understanding when it is pertinent to strive for certain types of design ideas. It may also help idea development by giving specific definitions by which to communicate and evaluate ideas. A characterization of idea concepts could moreover aid idea management. In line with this, the next step in our work will be to explore how the framework can be operationalized to support design practice.

The typology opens up for studies of how different idea types are distributed. [28], among others, point to the problem that we lack quality measures of design processes. When evaluating the creative aspects of design processes, many evaluations tend to focus on the number of ideas generated, ignoring what most designers are interested in: a few really great solutions. Documenting the different types of ideas that emerge during a design process might help us better understand their interrelations, and identify patterns in how certain ideas evolve and lead to successful outcomes. The typology could thus be used to characterize different types of design processes, and indicate which types of ideation or further concept development initiatives might be preferable in a given design process.

CONCLUSIONS

On the basis of a wide range of existing research contributions, our typology of ideas is meant to serve as an overview and analytical frame for studying design ideas. The literature review has presented us with several insights. The most striking one is that the definitions of what constitutes a design idea are diverse, ranging from relatively open opportunities over ways of reframing the design problem to more specific plans for how to proceed with the design process. Our literature survey was initially motivated by the lack of a common definition, and this has been confirmed. This diversity indicates that there is indeed a need in the research community for clarifying what is meant by a "design idea".

REFERENCES

1. Ömer Akin and Cem Akin. 1996. Frames of reference in architectural design: analysing the hyperacclamation (Aha-!). *Design Studies* 17, 4: 341-361.
2. Katerina Alexiou, Theodore Zamenopoulos, J. H. Johnson, and S. J. Gilbert. 2009. Exploring the neurological basis of design cognition using brain imaging: some preliminary results. *Design Studies* 30, 6: 623-647.
3. Petra Badke-Schaub and Anja Gehrlicher. 2003. Patterns of decisions in design: leaps, loops, cycles, sequences and meta-processes. In *DS 31: Proceedings of ICED 03, the 14th International Conference on Engineering Design, Stockholm.*
4. Alex Baker and André van der Hoek. 2010. Ideas, subjects, and cycles as lenses for understanding the software design process. *Design Studies* 31, 6: 590-613.
5. Zafer Bilda and John S. Gero. 2008. Idea development can occur using imagery only. *Design computing and cognition'08*, pp. 303-320. Springer Netherlands.
6. Michael Biskjaer and Peter Dalsgaard. 2012. Toward A Constraint-Oriented Pragmatist Understanding of Design Creativity. In *Proceedings of the International Conference on Design Creativity.*
7. Michael Biskjaer, Peter Dalsgaard and Kim Halskov. 2010. Creativity Methods in Interaction Design. In *Proceedings of DESIRE 2010: Creativity and Innovation in Design*, Aarhus, Denmark.
8. Margaret A. Boden. 1995. *The creative mind: Myths and mechanisms.* London: Weidenfeld & Nicolson.
9. Tone Bratteteig, Ole Kristian Rolstad, and Ina Wagner. 2016. The life and death of design ideas. In

Proceedings of the 12th International Conference on the Design of Cooperative Systems (COOP '16), 259-275. http://link.springer.com/chapter/10.1007/978-3-319-33464-6_16

10. Carlos Cardoso, Petra Badke-Schaub, and Ozgur Eris. 2016. Inflection moments in design discourse: How questions drive problem framing during idea generation. *Design Studies* 46: 59-78.
11. Hernan P. Casakin and Gabriela Goldschmidt. 2000. Reasoning by visual analogy in design problem-solving: the role of guidance. *Environment and Planning B: Planning and Design* 27, 1: 105-119.
12. Aliana Colung and Linda B. Smith. 2003. The emergence of abstract ideas: Evidence from networks and babies. *Philosophical Transactions of the Royal Society B: Biological Sciences* 358, 1435: 1205-1214.
13. Henri Hubertus Cornelis Maria Christiaans. 1992. *Creativity in design: the role of domain knowledge in designing*. TU Delft, Delft University of Technology.
14. Tim Coughlan and Peter Johnson. 2008. Idea management in creative lives. In *CHI '08 Extended Abstracts on Human Factors in Computing Systems* (CHI EA '08). ACM, New York, NY, USA, 3081-3086. DOI=
15. Nigel Cross. 1997. Descriptive models of creative design: application to an example. *Design Studies* 18, 4: 427-440.
16. Darren W. Dahl and Page Moreau. 2002. The influence and value of analogical thinking during new product ideation. *Journal of Marketing Research* 39, 1: 47-60.
17. Peter Dalsgaard. 2009. *Designing Engaging Interactive Environments: A Pragmatist Perspective*. Aarhus, Denmark: Aarhus University
18. Shanna R. Daly, Seda Yilmaz, James L. Christian, Colleen M. Seifert, and Richard Gonzalez. 2012. Design heuristics in engineering concept generation. *Journal of Engineering Education* 101, 4: 601.
19. R. Davies and R. J. Talbot. 1987. Experiencing ideas: Identity, insight and the imago. *Design studies* 8, 1: 17-25.
20. Alan Dix and Layda Gongora. 2011. Externalisation and design. In *Proceedings of the Second Conference on Creativity and Innovation in Design* (DESIRE '11). ACM, New York, NY, USA, 31-42. DOI=
21. Alan Dix, Tom Ormerod, Michael Twidale, Corina Sas, Paula Alexandra Gomes da Silva, and Lorna McKnight. 2006. Why bad ideas are a good idea. http://eprints.maynoothuniversity.ie/6040/
22. Kees Dorst and Nigel Cross. 2001. Creativity in the design process: co-evolution of problem–solution. *Design studies* 22, 5: 425-437.
23. Carlos Fernández, Daniel López, Agustín Yagüe, and Juan Garbajosa. 2011. Towards estimating the value of an idea. In *Proceedings of the 12th International Conference on Product Focused Software Development and Process Improvement* (Profes '11). ACM, New York, NY, USA, 62-67. DOI=http://dx.doi.org/10.1145/2181101.2181116
24. Ronald A. Finke, Thomas B. Ward, and Steven M. Smith. 1992. *Creative cognition: Theory, research, and applications*.
25. Fritz Fleischmann. 2006. Entrepreneurship as emancipation: The history of an idea. *A lecture delivered at the Free University of Berlin Fletcher D. "Entrepreneurial process and the social construction of opportunity", Entrepreneurship and Regional Development* 18, 5: 421-440.
26. Liane Gabora. 2002. Cognitive mechanisms underlying the creative process. In *Proceedings of the 4th conference on Creativity & cognition* (C&C '02). ACM, New York, NY, USA, 126-133.
27. John S. Gero. 2000. Computational models of innovative and creative design processes. *Technological forecasting and social change* 64, 2: 183-196.
28. Karan Girotra, Christian Terwiesch, and Karl T. Ulrich. 2010. Idea Generation and the Quality of the Best Idea. *Manage. Sci.* 56, 4 (April 2010), 591-605.
29. Vinod Goel. 2014. Creative brains: designing in the real world†. *Frontiers in human neuroscience* 8: 241.
30. Jacob Goldenberg, Donald R. Lehmann, and David Mazursky. 2001. The idea itself and the circumstances of its emergence as predictors of new product success. *Management Science* 47, 1: 69-84.
31. Gabriela Goldschmidt. 1990. Linkography: assessing design productivity. In *Proceedings of the Tenth European Meeting on Cybernetics and Systems Research* (Cyberbetics and System'90), 291-298. World Scientific, 1990.
32. Gabriela Goldschmidt and Anat Litan Sever. 2011. Inspiring design ideas with texts. *Design Studies* 32, 2: 139-155.
33. Gabriela Goldschmidt and Dan Tatsa. 2005. How good are good ideas? Correlates of design creativity. *Design Studies* 26, 6: 593-611.
34. Kim Halskov and Peter Dalsgaard. 2006. Inspiration Card Workshops. In *Proceedings of DIS 2006*. ACM, New York, pp. 2-11.

35. Kim Halskov and Peter Dalsgaard. 2007. The emergence of ideas: the interplay between sources of inspiration and emerging design concepts. *CoDesign* 3, 4: 185-211.

36. J. E. Holt, D. F. Radcliffe, and D. Schoorl. 1985. Design or problem solving—a critical choice for the engineering profession. *Design Studies* 6, 2: 107-110.

37. Thomas J. Howard, Stephen J. Culley, and Elies Dekoninck. 2008. Describing the creative design process by the integration of engineering design and cognitive psychology literature. *Design studies* 29, 2: 160-180.

38. Thomas J. Howard, S. Culley, and Elies A. Dekoninck. 2011. Reuse of ideas and concepts for creative stimuli in engineering design. *Journal of Engineering Design* 22, 8: 565-581.

39. Norio Ishii and Kazuhisa Miwa. 2002. Interactive processes between mental and external operations in creative activity: a comparison of experts' and novices' performance. In *Proceedings of the 4th conference on Creativity & Cognition*, pp. 178-185. ACM.

40. Ben Jonson. 2005. Design ideation: the conceptual sketch in the digital age. *Design studies* 26, 6: 613-624.

41. Jeff WT Kan, Zafer Bilda, and John S. Gero. 2006. Comparing entropy measures of idea links in design protocols. *Design Computing and Cognition'06*, pp. 265-284. Springer Netherlands, 2006.

42. Jeff WT Kan and John S. Gero. 2005. Can entropy indicate the richness of idea generation in team designing. In *Proceedings of the 10th International Conference on Computer Aided Architectural Design Research in Asia* (CAADRIA 2005), New Delhi, India.

43. Andruid Kerne, Andrew M. Webb, Steven M. Smith, Rhema Linder, Nic Lupfer, Yin Qu, Jon Moeller, and Sashikanth Damaraju. 2014. Using metrics of curation to evaluate information-based ideation. In *ACM Transactions on Computer-Human Interaction (ToCHI)* 21, 3: 14.

44. EunJin Kim and KwanMyung Kim. 2015. Cognitive styles in design problem solving: Insights from network-based cognitive maps." *Design Studies* 40: 1-38.

45. David Kirsh. 2009. Projection, problem space and anchoring.

46. Lassi A. Liikkanen, Tua A. Björklund, Matti M. Hämäläinen, and Mikko P. Koskinen. 2009. Time constraints in design idea generation. In *DS 58-9: Proceedings of ICED 09, the 17th International Conference on Engineering Design, Vol. 9, Human Behavior in Design, Palo Alto, CA, USA, 24.-27.08.*

47. Lassi A. Liikkanen and Matti Perttula. 2010. Inspiring design idea generation: insights from a memory-search perspective. *Journal of Engineering Design* 21, 5: 545-560.

48. Samuel Loyd. 1914. *Cyclopedia of puzzles*. Lamb Publishing Company.

49. Kristine Lund, Guy Prudhomme, and Jean-Laurent Cassier. 2013. Pivotal moments for decision making in collaborative design: are they teachable?. In *Computer-Supported Collaborative Learning at the Workplace*, pp. 243-268. Springer US.

50. Mary Lou Maher and Josiah Poon. 1996. Modeling design exploration as co-evolution. Computer-Aided Civil and Infrastructure Engineering 11, 3: 195-209.

51. Naama Mayseless, Ayelet Eran, and Simone G. Shamay-Tsoory. 2015. Generating original ideas: The neural underpinning of originality. *NeuroImage* 116: 232-239.

52. Paul Murty and Terry Purcell. 2007. Latent Preparation - Do Great Ideas Come From Out-Of-The-Blue? http://papers.cumincad.org/cgi-bin/works/Show&_id=caadria2010_000&sort=DEFAULT&search=series:caadria/Show?caadria2007_529

53. Brent A. Nelson, Jamal O. Wilson, David Rosen, and Jeannette Yen. 2009. Refined metrics for measuring ideation effectiveness. *Design Studies* 30, 6: 737-743.

54. Harold G. Nelson and Erik Stolterman. 2003. *The design way: Intentional change in an unpredictable world: Foundations and fundamentals of design competence*. Educational Technology.

55. Bernard A. Nijstad, Bernard and Wolfgang Stroebe. 2006. How the group affects the mind: A cognitive model of idea generation in groups. *Personality and social psychology review* 10, 3: 186-213.

56. Anthony J. Onwuegbuzie and Rebecca Frels. 2016. Seven steps to a comprehensive literature review: A multimodal and cultural approach. Sage.

57. Matti Kalevi Perttula. 2006. *Idea generation in engineering design: Application of a memory search perspective and some experimental studies*. Helsinki University of Technology.

58. Matti Kalevi Perttula, Christina M. Krause, and Pekka Sipilä. 2006. Does idea exchange promote productivity in design idea generation? In *CoDesign* 2, 3: 125-138.

59. Matti Kalevi Perttula and Lassi A. Liikkanen. 2006. Exposure effects in design idea generation: Unconscious conformity or a product of sampling probability? In *Development Process: From Idea to the World's First Bionic Prosthetic Foot*.

60. Matti Kalevi Perttula and Pekka Sipilä. 2007. The idea exposure paradigm in design idea generation. *Journal of Engineering Design* 18, 1: 93-102.

61. Sarkar Prabir and Chakrabarti Amaresh. 2007. Development of a method for assessing design creativity. In *Guidelines for a Decision Support Method Adapted to NPD Processes*.

62. A. T. Purcell and John S. Gero. 1998. Drawings and the design process: A review of protocol studies in design and other disciplines and related research in cognitive psychology. *Design studies* 19, 4: 389-430.

63. Janet C. Read, Daniel Fitton, Gavin Sim, and Matt Horton. 2016. How Ideas make it through to Designs: Process and Practice. In *Proceedings of the 9th Nordic Conference on Human-Computer Interaction* (NordiCHI '16). ACM, New York, NY, USA, , Article 16 , 10 pages.

64. Christoph Riedl, Norman May, Jan Finzen, Stephan Stathel, Viktor Kaufman, and Helmut Krcmar. 2009. An idea ontology for innovation management. *International Journal on Semantic Web and Information Systems* 5, 4: 1-18.

65. C. J. van Rijsbergen. 1979. *Information retrieval 2*.

66. Mike Scaife and Yvonne Rogers. 2005. External cognition, innovative technologies, and effective learning. In *Cognition, education and communication technology*: 181-202.

67. Marlene Scardamalia and Carl Bereiter. 2003. Beyond brainstorming: Sustained creative work with ideas. *EDUCATION CANADA-TORONTO-* 43, 4: 4-8.

68. Colleen M. Seifert, David E. Meyer, Natalie Davidson, Andrea L. Patalano, and Ilan Yaniv. 1994. Demystification of cognitive insight: Opportunistic assimilation and the prepared-mind hypothesis: 65. http://wesscholar.wesleyan.edu/div3facpubs/229/

69. Jami J. Shah, Santosh V. Kulkarni, and Noe Vargas-Hernandez. 2000. Evaluation of idea generation methods for conceptual design: effectiveness metrics and design of experiments. *Journal of mechanical design* 122, 4: 377-384.

70. Jami J. Shah, Steve M. Smith, and Noe Vargas-Hernandez. 2003. Metrics for measuring ideation effectiveness." *Design studies* 24, 2: 111-134

71. Pao Siangliulue, Joel Chan, Krzysztof Z. Gajos, and Steven P. Dow. 2015. Providing Timely Examples Improves the Quantity and Quality of Generated Ideas. In *Proceedings of the 2015 ACM SIGCHI Conference on Creativity and Cognition* (C&C '15). ACM, New York, NY, USA, 83-92.

72. Herbert A. Simon. 1973. The structure of ill structured problems. *Artificial intelligence* 4, 3-4: 181-201.

73. Dean Keith Simonton. 2013. What is a creative idea? Little-c versus Big-C creativity. *Handbook of research on creativity*: 69-83.

74. Ricardo Sosa and Andy Dong. 2013. The creative assessment of rich ideas. In *Proceedings of the 9th ACM Conference on Creativity & Cognition* (C&C '13), Ellen Yi-Luen Do, Steven Dow, Jack Ox, Steve Smith, Kazushi Nishimoto, and Chek Tien Tan (Eds.). ACM, New York, NY, USA, 328-331.

75. Ricardo Sosa, John S. Gero, and Kyle Jennings. 2009. Growing and destroying the worth of ideas. In *Proceedings of the seventh ACM conference on Creativity and cognition* (C&C '09). ACM, New York, NY, USA, 295-304.

76. Basil Soufi and Ernest Edmonds. 1996. The cognitive basis of emergence: implications for design support. *Design Studies* 17, 4: 451-463.

77. Elizabeth Starkey, Christine A. Toh, and Scarlett R. Miller. 2016. Abandoning creativity: The evolution of creative ideas in engineering design course projects. *Design Studies* 47: 47-72.

78. Masaki Suwa, Terry Purcell, and John Gero. 1998. Macroscopic analysis of design processes based on a scheme for coding designers' cognitive actions. *Design studies* 19, 4: 455-483.

79. Masaki Suwa and Barbara Tversky. 2002. External representations contribute to the dynamic construction of ideas. In *International Conference on Theory and Application of Diagrams*, pp. 341-343. Springer Berlin Heidelberg.

80. Yoshifumi Tanaka, Sumio Nakamura, and Kazuya Takemata. 2009. Enhancing the creativity of engineers by idea drawing. In *Proceedings of the seventh ACM conference on Creativity and cognition* (C&C '09). ACM, New York, NY, USA, 405-406. DOI=http://dx.doi.org/10.1145/1640233.1640323

81. Christine A. Toh and Scarlett R. Miller. 2015. How engineering teams select design concepts: A view through the lens of creativity. In *Design Studies* 38: 111-138.

82. Feichin Tschang. 2003. When does an idea become an innovation? The role of individual and group creativity in video game design. http://ink.library.smu.edu.sg/lkcsb_research/1443/

83. Ian Tseng, Jarrod Moss, Jonathan Cagan, and Kenneth Kotovsky. 2008. The role of timing and analogical similarity in the stimulation of idea generation in design. *Design Studies* 29, 3: 203-221.

84. Remko van der Lugt. 2001. *Sketching in design idea generation meetings*. TU Delft, Delft University of Technology.

85. Remko van der Lugt. 2003. Relating the quality of the idea generation process to the quality of the resulting design ideas. In *DS 31: Proceedings of ICED 03, the 14th International Conference on Engineering Design*, Stockholm.

86. Remko van der Lugt and Anne van der Graaf. 2002. Context Indicators for Determining Links Between Design Ideas. In *DS 30: Proceedings of DESIGN 2002, the 7th International Design Conference,* Dubrovnik.

87. Ilse M. Verstijnen, Cees van Leeuwen, G. Goldschmidt, Ronald Hamel, and J. M. Hennessey. 1998. Sketching and creative discovery. *Design studies* 19, 4: 519-546.

88. Graham Wallas. 1976. Stages in the creative process. *The creativity question*: 69-73.

89. Stefan Wiltschnig, Bo T. Christensen and Linden J. Ball. 2013. Collaborative problem–solution co-evolution in creative design. *Design Studies* 34, 5: 515-542.

90. Stefan Wiltschnig and Balder Onarheim. 2010. Insights into insight-How do in-vitro studies of creative insight match the real-world complexity of in-vivo design processes. In *Design Research Society International Conference*.

91. Stefan Wiltschnig, Balder Onarheim, and Bo T. Christensen. 2010. Shared insights in design processes–a discussion of in-vivo evidence in and beyond existing creativity frameworks. In *DS 66-2: Proceedings of the 1st International Conference on Design Creativity (ICDC 2010)*.

92. Eiko Yamamoto, Futoshi Mukai, Nor Fasiha Mohd Yusof, Toshiharu Taura, and Yukari Nagai. 2009. A method to generate and evaluate a creative design idea by focusing on associative process. In *ASME 2009 International Design Engineering Technical Conferences and Computers and Information in Engineering Conference*, pp. 1003-1011. American Society of Mechanical Engineers.

93. S. Yilmaz, Colleen M. Seifert, and R. Gonzalez. 2010. Cognitive heuristics in design: Instructional strategies to increase creativity in idea generation." *Artificial Intelligence for Engineering Design, Analysis and Manufacturing* 24, 3: 335-355.

Creative Information Use Among Young Adults: Challenges for Learning and Opportunities for Media (Re)Design

Yong Ming Kow [1] Yunan Chen [2] Waikuen Cheng [1] Shun Hei Nit [1]
[1] City University of Hong Kong, Hong Kong SAR, China, [2] University of California, Irvine, CA
yongmkow@cityu.edu.hk, yunanc@ics.uci.edu, wikncheng@gmail.com, nshtitus@gmail.com

ABSTRACT
Despite spending significant amounts of time on the Internet, today's young adults often do not use online information effectively to support their creative pursuits—an activity we refer to as *creative information use*. In this exploratory study, we interviewed 19 media art college students in Hong Kong to understand their creative information use and to identify the challenges they faced in engaging with creative information online. The interviews reveal that young adults lacked sufficient media literacy to negotiate information online. More importantly, our study suggests that parents, teachers, and peers often failed to collectively sustain young adults' media-related interests and creativity development. We discuss research gaps in HCI and the design of technologies, and raise important issues of creative information use for future studies.

Author Keywords
Internet; self-directed learning; information use; sociocultural; young adults.

ACM Classification Keywords
H.5.3. Group and Organization Interfaces: *Computer-supported cooperative work.*

INTRODUCTION
According to Lassig [40], creativity does not arise from nowhere, unlike suggested in popular statements such as thinking-out-of-the-box. Instead, she defines creativity as "the optimal interaction among personal, process, and social and environmental factors by which an individual or group produces an idea or product that is judged to be novel and appropriate by experts of a relevant context" [40]. Thus, an important prerequisite of creativity is everyday learning of areas of knowledge in order for a person to build up "deep understanding of well-established patterns of thought or principles"—so as to produce an unusual work that defies such established knowledge [40,66]. While HCI has examined institutionalized supports, such as interfaces, artifacts, and classroom activities helping young adults' acquiring such forms of information [12,20,33,36], we have not examined their challenges of learning this information in their free time, and within their everyday and natural environments outside classrooms.

In this paper, we define *creative information use* as the appropriation of information resources, including social media and web tools, to develop media practices and skills that are relevant to creative work such as video production and software animation. Recent research argues that most young adults have not yet acquired a level of creative information use that is expected in workplaces, thus points to the challenges of translating online learning into professional skills [5,9,22,35,42,50,57]. Researchers have associated this finding to ways in which young adults have only used a small set of social media applications like Facebook for the purposes of managing their peer relations [8,31], as danah boyd describes: "[teens who] are 'addicted' to their phones or computers are actually focused on staying connected to friends" (p. 7); and "many of today's teens are indeed deeply engaged with social media and are active participants in networked publics, but this does not mean that they inherently have the knowledge or skills to make the most of their online experiences" (p. 176).

What makes it difficult for today's young adults to engage in learning activities that lead to professional development? Is this limitation due to challenges in technical design of the online media they interact with daily, or other more profound reasons in their social lives? Selwyn [57] notes that current research studies have yet to provide sufficient details describing how young adults develop information research skills through their "information and technological lifeworlds"—in other words, the *information ecologies*, or contexts in which young adults interact with information, spanning home, school, and communities [47]. Previous survey studies also identified many demographic factors that are associated with young adults' information use abilities, such as college major [35], age [35,42], gender, and being an International or local resident (Internationals tended to spend

C&C '17, June 27 - 30, 2017, Singapore

ACM 978-1-4503-4403-6/17/06...$15.00
DOI: http://dx.doi.org/10.1145/3059454.3059473

more time online) [31,35], as well as socioeconomic status and family environment [22,35]. While these studies illustrated the circumstances under which certain young adult populations are doing better than others [22,31,35,42], why and how these circumstances influence online behaviors is unknown.

Studying young adults' creative information use may contribute significantly to the design of creative learning platforms. For example, we may point out hidden needs of classroom learning platforms (e.g., [1,13,15,21]), and how these could be connected with young adults' social life outside of the school environment [18,27]. In this research, we ask the following research questions: *What are the young adults' experiences of using information, particularly on the Internet, for the purposes of creative work? What are their experiences developing such information use practices in their own information ecologies? What challenges did they perceive, and how can technologies be (re)designed to support their creative information use?*

To address these questions, we examine a specific case of creative information use among a group of 19 media art college students in Hong Kong. Our informants were between 21 to 25 years old, and were expected to be proficient in various media production skills such as animation and computer game development. These skills exemplify the importance of creative information use we aim to study in this research—skills that involve the use of technologies, and require a certain degree of acquiring and making sense of information online. Our study shows that despite owning computing devices (e.g., smart phones), and having constant access to the Internet resources, the young adults we studied still experienced difficulties in creative information use. We found that the most immediate barrier reported by a majority of our informants is the lack of inclination (i.e., desire to learn) and basic knowledge (e.g., technical nomenclatures) in engaging with online information. In addition, our informants also reported deeper barriers such as the lack of offline support at home and at school in life prior to entering college, which suggest the importance of examining these contexts in the cultivation of the youth's creative information use.

YOUNG ADULTS' CREATIVE INFORMATION USE: IDENTIFYING DESIGN SOLUTIONS TO AN ECOLOGICAL PROBLEM

The need to examine young adults' experiences with creative information use is a pressing issue for our society. Roughly ten years ago, the research community had believed, perhaps in an overly simplistic way, that young adults should be able to acquire technical skills very naturally through their routine and daily use of hypertext, downloads, mobile devices, digital books, and instant messaging [49]. But since then, researchers have more rigorously questioned such claims. Selwyn reported that uses of media information by young adults are "passive, solitary, sporadic and unspectacular" [57]. Similarly, in her book *It's Complicated: The Social Lives of Networked Teens* danah boyd [8] also found that extensive use of the Internet among teens is often centered on social network and friendship building, instead of developing the knowledge and skills to fully use the technologies.

Demographic Studies on Young Adults' Internet and Technology Uses

To understand what might affect young adults' self-learning and creative information use, many researchers tried to identify factors associated with effective creative information use [9,10,22,35,42,43]. One demographic factor that is particularly relevant to young adults' information use is the number of computing devices they own. For example, Helsper et al. [22] surveyed 2350 users (14 years old and older) regarding their frequency of using the Internet for various tasks, including fact-checking and getting information for work. They found that age alone does not account for much variation across the sample population; however, the number of computing devices in each of their homes correlates with how much the participants use the Internet for academic and work purposes [22].

Other demographic factors associated with frequency of creative information use include the students' college major, and whether they are Internationals or local students. Brown and Czerniewicz [10] conducted a survey with South African college students and found that schools centered around technological studies (e.g., engineering schools) are more likely to incorporate Internet use as part of classroom activities, while schools which do not emphasize technology are more likely to overlook classroom technologies (74% versus 57%). This can result in students in technology-centered schools having more opportunities to get familiarized with information acquisition and other technological skills [10,35]. Furthermore, it was found that classroom instructors' technological mandate matters more than the presence of IT when it comes to creative information use, as students tend to ignore IT as a potential learning resource when instructors do not require it [42].

Technological Studies in HCI and the Perspective of Learning "in the Wild"

In a similar fashion, HCI research has also attempted designing technologies to support creative learning, but with an emphasis on classroom settings. For example, past studies have come up with design tools for collaborative learning [15,16], online discourse [21], performance prediction [13], user interfaces for managing classroom activities [1], as well as classroom-based activities [12,20,33,36]. Such artifacts and activities are designed to enhance the media-richness of today's learning technologies in the classroom settings; however, there is little evidence that young adults are becoming better information users in their natural environments (i.e., Internet use in their own free time) because of such interventions. A confounding factor is that classrooms are only one part of youth's learning environment. Learning is also occurring outside of classrooms, through interacting with parents, among peers, and within specialized and technical communities. And this form of learning is particularly relevant when the youth become young adults pursuing creative professions. Importantly, among these previous studies on demographic factors and classroom technology design, less often discussed are the in situ sociocultural conditions fostering creative information use. Thus, researchers are arguing for a more detailed and naturalistic examination of young adults' learning "in the wild" to identify a more effective way of situating such tools within their information ecologies [9,35,57].

Sociocultural Aspect of Young Adults' Learning

To address the lack of understanding of sociocultural aspects of young adults' learning, a few studies have emerged to examine youth's verbal accounts and actual experience of learning creative skills [8,26,27]. Importantly, these studies found that technological artifacts are never truly neutral—a young adult who has many computing devices at home may have parents who are IT savvy, and have intentionally cultivated a media-friendly home environment [37]. Therefore, Selwyn [57] recommends a concrete examination of ways information use practices have been nurtured over time and across a spectrum of social circumstances within young adults' environments:

> Adults would therefore seem to have a continued role in supporting young people's use of technology and information, not least in ensuring that the social contexts surrounding digital information allow young people to be informed about their choices. Of course, many of the research findings in this area point towards "the need for additional training" of young people with regards to digital information [6], and addressing the "chasm" that is felt to exist between "the rather basic needs" of children and young people and "the complexity of the [information] resources" they use [44]. Yet rather than concentrate solely on the technical training of young people, efforts also need to be made to explore the ways in which "critical digital literacies" can be developed. (p. 374)

Importantly, Selwyn specified that learning of creative media skills does not occur merely online; it is also mediated and influenced by a series of actors, including parents, teachers, media content providers, and librarians.

In parallel with the effort to understand how sociocultural forces come together to cultivate creative information use among young adults, there is the development of an agreeable set of *media literacies*—information skills young adults need in order to succeed in future workplaces [22,50,57]. For example, a concept of media literacies developed by Jenkins [28] includes *judgment literacy*, which refers to "the ability to evaluate the reliability and credibility of different information sources." Another example includes Jenkins' *play literacy*, defined as "the capacity to experiment with one's surroundings as a form of problem-solving," for example, "to pick up a new piece of technology that you've never used before"—and to become curious about, mess around with, and engage in a new media activity. In other words, creative information use could be decomposed into a set of learnable skills, which are also generalizable across research sites. Thus, while we are investigating creative information use, it is also pertinent to identify such skills which young adults deem themselves lacking.

In summary, despite the use of learning technologies in and outside of classroom settings, many young adults still encounter difficulties engaging in creative information use. Thus, there is a need to conduct in-depth studies to investigate these young adults' information ecologies across different settings, and to identify deeper and more complex reasons accounting for the lack of effective creative information use in today's information- and media-rich learning environments. Next we will discuss the methods we employ in examining our young adults' learning environments.

METHODS

To investigate young adults' creative information use, and the challenges which prevent them from engaging with creative information effectively and deeply, we conducted semi-structured interviews with 19 current college students and recent graduates recruited from a media art college of a Hong Kong university. The curriculum of media art school focuses on skills related to digital media, providing training in subjects such as animation, games development, photography, and music. Many students in this school had been long interested in art-related subjects, and many wished to become creative media professionals upon graduation. Within the school, classes were typically project-driven, where students are incentivized to acquire professional media art skills and to work with peers to enhance their skills. We picked this sample population since, due to rapid technological development, young adults interested in becoming media art professionals often have to engage in a significant amount of creative information use in their spare time, both for excelling in classroom projects and for career development after school. Thus this population is ideal for us to understand the challenges and obstacles for young adults to engage in deep creative work oriented learning. Because of these unique features, we were more likely to elicit more data per interviewee regarding creative information use than with most other populations [59].

Our participants were recruited through class announcements (three), and the snowball sampling approach (16). There were 13 females and six males. Among these nineteen participants, thirteen of them were existing students and the other six had graduated for no more than three years. Sixteen of our informants were local students who grew up in Hong Kong, while two were from mainland China, and one was an exchange student from Germany. The informants ranged between 21 and 25 years old. Interviewees were given $50 (approximately US$6.50) as a token of appreciation.

All interviews were conducted in person and each lasted between 45 minutes and an hour. At the beginning of each interview, we started by asking the informant to list his or her creative interests. Then, we asked questions regarding how participants sought information to support their creative interest development. In doing so, we were able to ask follow-up questions regarding the participants' information use and skill developments in relation to these interests. We did not explicitly ask for information on the Internet, so that they could provide a whole spectrum of information resources useful for their creative work. This approach also allowed us to probe why sometimes online resources were found ineffective. Toward the end of each interview, we inquired about obstacles that may have prevented them from engaging deeply with creative information use online.

All interviews with local Hong Kong participants were conducted in Cantonese (a Chinese dialect that is the main language used in Hong Kong). The interviews with mainland participants were conducted in Mandarin, and the interview with the German student was conducted in English. The interviews were audio-recorded, and transcribed in the original language of the interview. For non-English interviews, the quotes were translated into English at the writing of this paper. All informants' names were anonymized and replaced by pseudonyms in this paper.

Analysis

In our interviews, most informants named more than one creative interest, with an average of 6.26 per person. Despite the number of diverse interests, most of them chose to focus on developing one or two interests at a given time. When participants engaged in two interests, they often chose two that had sufficient synergy to be practiced at the same time—for example, the study of both photography and film enhances knowledge in cinematography, involving the study of light and motion-picture technology. Similarly, animation interest was found to be associated with painting and graphic design; music with digital instruments and song composing; and computer gaming with console games, online games, game video making, and computer programming.

We identified seven major clusters of creative interests, of which we focus on the four most commonly reported ones for our analysis: animation (reported by 9 informants), computer gaming (11), photography and film (11), and music (8). The remaining three interest clusters include cooking (4), dressing (5), and reading (6). Since these three clusters of interests have weaker association with technologies, we did not include data related to these interests. We then conducted a grounded theory-based iterative and inductive analysis of our transcripts, using coding and memoing [61].

Note that our coding did not reveal a standard and general approach to creative information use across all these different interest domains. The reason is that the sources of creative information in each domain vary greatly, depending on where the domain experts congregate and share their expertise. For example, creative information about digital music composition may be available on YouTube, but information about animation is largely found on *Vimeo*, a video-sharing site similar to but slightly older than YouTube and extremely popular among some video production communities. Location of creative information also varies from region to region; for example, music players in Hong Kong may heavily use Cantonese-speaking websites such as HKGolden (hkgolden.com).

Therefore, we coded the sources of *creative information* on a case-by-case basis. Our third and fourth authors were undergraduate students of the media art school, and they coded the *creative information* based on their knowledge of these domains. For example, within the case of animation, we developed codes including "personal purpose," "social influence," and information sources like "common media" like YouTube, "domain-specific media" like Vimeo, and media "creation" activities.

At first, we were also looking for ways our informants were using online information creatively. But half way through our interviews, we realized that our participants were driving our interviews towards challenges and issues of creative information use that are deeply embedded in their social and cultural contexts. For example, among participants who were interested in animation, only two out of nine informants had ever created animation—and both were made for the purpose of university assignments. Thus, we gradually switched our focus to identifying their obstacles in creative information use. Typically, our informants had reported gaps related to media literacies, describing their experiences with others at home, in school, or with peers. For the earlier informants whom we had not covered these issues sufficiently, we performed follow-up interviews to clarify points they had made earlier. We coded the reasons for these problems as data, iteratively throughout the process of the interviews, until we identified a structure in our data, as we will discuss in the Findings section.

FINDINGS

Our analysis identified several reasons accounting for young people not engaging in creative information use. In this section, we will describe the challenges of using creative information when a user lacks media literacies, and report on other difficulties within the contexts of our study. Note that media literacy takes years to develop, and a person builds media literacy through years of experience and engagement in a media-related interest (see [4]). As such, we have also paid attention to how our informants' creative information use is accompanied by their journey in learning a creative interest.

Media literacies: Creative Information is Difficult to Use

Importantly, despite our young informants handling and using computing devices regularly, most of them still reported having difficulties searching for, identifying, and using creative information. We describe these challenges in the following.

Hidden Knowledge Structure in Creative Information Content
Our informants reported that creative information contains hidden structure which they first need to know before they could use it to produce meaningful digital artifacts.

Jane graduated from the media art college two years ago. She has loved watching animation since she was little, and started learning animation, through using a software tool called *3D Studio Max*, in middle school. However, at the media art college, she found that it was very difficult to learn the more powerful animation tools used by professionals. For instance, when she started learning the animation software tool *Houdini*, a powerful animation tool popularly used among professional animators, she was put off by the degree of hidden prerequisites in Houdini—the mathematical knowledge needed in order to control movements of 3D particles and models:

> [Apart from just animation] you still have to learn a lot of things on your own. And also some programming language, like those used in Houdini, which includes mathematical calculations. All these are necessary [in animation]. You have to memorize and learn a lot of things. If you haven't learnt [these] before, you will run into so much trouble [with animation], and [many things you like to accomplish simply] cannot be done.

Because of this hidden knowledge gap, Jane had to switch her major from the media art program to Chinese and history. While she has remained interested in animation, she has given up doing it as a career option. In Jane's case, her unsuccessful appropriation of Houdini was due to lack of media skills she needed—mathematics and programming—appropriate for animation production. This missing experience hindered her learning of animation.

Creative Information Contains Technical Nomenclatures and Language
Our informants reported that, unlike textbooks that contain necessary introductory information, online information is often written with technical nomenclatures and language which are difficult to comprehend unless the user understands these foundational discourse elements.

At the media art college, John had attended college courses on programming, but he had found the college curriculum insufficient specifically in understanding software data structure. John had tried to find more information on the Internet on his own. However, he was unable to find much useful information due to his inability to understand the online discourses and Internet jargons, and to identify usable programming codes:

> I seldom use the Internet, because I think there are a lot of fake codes on it. The forums are worse. They often speak in difficult languages, and I don't even know what they are yakking about (唔明佢 Up 乜).

For John, he found that there were many programming scripts which did not work as he had anticipated—they lacked sufficient explanation of fundamental concepts and were not written in easily understandable language. And he found that the use of creative information (e.g., data structure description) contained other nomenclatures too challenging to understand on his own.

Creative Information is Hidden in Specialized Online Communities
Our informants reported that creative information is often located in specialized online communities they would not know existed unless they knew where to look.

Mary learned piano in middle school, and had participated in music bands at her church. When she started as a media art student, she tried to use the computer to compose a song. However, like other Hong Kong students who had only attended Chinese schools before college, she had difficulties comprehending Google search results written in English. Quite surprisingly, despite youth like Mary being avid social media users, she did not think of YouTube as an information source at first. Only after a long time of rigorously using the software tool through trial and error, and when her friend advised her to use YouTube, did she discover the resources on the website:

> But earlier on, I did not know how to find out what others had done [in study music composition] ("鑽研"), and I thought that I just had to learn the software directly. I did not know that there are tutorials available on YouTube. If not for my friend who had told me, I would not have known. Ya, and I really thought that I need to rely on other people or on the lectures to learn. I felt so stupid at that time.

In Mary's case, it took her a long time and through her personal network to slowly develop knowledge of useful resources for learning music composition. Despite all the information available online for free, the knowledge about where to find such information, how to identify the most useful tutorials, or even which person to follow on YouTube requires extensive work and it did not come to her naturally.

Our informants reported many challenges in using creative information. Notably, most of these challenges were caused by their lack of exposure to foundational skills, discourses, and communities related to the technical knowledge. In other words, the more a user is conversant and feeling at ease in a knowledge domain, the better she is equipped to pursue creative information use—thus constructing a positive development spiral. In the following section, we will describe where these supportive factors may come from, by examining data regarding our informants' sociocultural environments.

Social Recognition: A Lack of Companionship in Creative Information Use
Our informants did not only report challenges of using creative information, but also discussed how their relationships with their teachers, family members, and peers influenced their motivation in attempting to overcome these challenges. In this subsection, we describe these variables—

companionship and recognition—and how missing them may influence young adults' willingness to engage in creative information use.

Companionship: Opening the Door to Creative Information Use

Our analysis shows that before a user can make proficient use of creative information within a technical interest, it would be helpful if he had companionship in real life to support him in this interest. For instances, our informants who were interested in animation also tended to pay attention to anime events and activities related to *cosplay*—the dressing up of oneself to look like characters in animation, games, or comics—an activity many animation lovers enjoy. Anna started watching animation since she was in ninth grade. However, she relied on companionship, such as through attending a cosplay event, to start delving deeper into the interest. She stated, "I am not that nerdy and isolated" ("我又未至於毒成咁既") and "will only attend cosplay events if my friend is attending. Otherwise I am not going to go there alone." She still follows new anime releases every week, but she may not go further than that without sufficient companionship.

Another informant, Lung Fung, was a PC gamer until he realized that PC games are not the most popular anymore:

> Why? Because now I am not playing games I was playing in middle school. Because very few people are playing these games nowadays. In Hong Kong, the mainstream trend is no longer about playing PC games, but many have started playing mobile games.

As this quote shows, in a fast developing field, willingness to engage in difficult online discourses relies on being part of a community. If a large part of one's social network is not participating in the activity, the desire to pursue the interest might diminish after the initial interest.

The need for companionship—a friend who would perform the activity with the learner—is especially salient among informants who were newly exposed to a technical interest, and had yet to venture into deeper engagement with it. Thus, companionship can be viewed as a key mediator providing conditions for information users to transit into deeper information practices.

Recognition: Sustaining Efforts in Creative information Use

Even with companionship, young adults may not feel confident enough to engage in creative information use if they fear that they are not good enough to be recognized by their peers. We use recognition to refer to positive peer feedback (e.g., Facebook comments) and social interactions one receives from others.

One way for our participants to progressively deepen and engage with creative information use was through contributing textual contents online; such participation was a critical initial step for them to fully embrace and benefit from the online resources [11]. Mario was an avid consumer of game contents on live streams and on YouTube. However, he had seldom commented on YouTube, partly because other viewers had often ignored his point of view. He told us:

> I seldom left comments on YouTube, as I still feel that few Hong Kong YouTube users look at these comments. This [lack of interest in comments] make commenting meaningless. But when it comes to Facebook, people commonly share the videos and photos that they own or come across, and the chances you get feedback [on such content] is higher.

Instead, Mario invested more of his online commentary on Facebook, where he felt that there was a higher chance of seeing feedback due to presence of his personal friends. This observation reinforces the finding that companionship is needed to sustain information practices, and extends it to include the need to be recognized by other users.

The importance of companionship and recognition indicates the role of supportive peers and mentors within animation, computer gaming, and music in the context of engaging with creative information use continuously and more deeply. Without such supports, our informants often lost interest or could not dive deeper in their interest development.

Next we introduce factors, including routines and constraints within information ecologies, which drive our participants away from creative information use.

Media Selection: A Lack of Legitimization by Parents and Authorities Impact Users' Choices of Media-related Activities

For many creative interests, such as computer animation, skills and knowledge in its practice needs to be accrued over time. Thus early access to equipment and resources is critical to one's initial interest and later career development. But such access is highly dependent on parental encouragements.

When the informants in this study were young, many of them looked to their parents or schools to provide classes to teach them the technical skills needed in their interest development. We noticed that our informants tend to believe that *learning has to be endorsed and supported by parents and schools*; they rarely mentioned instances when they pursued self-directed learning in creative work, like the way they had picked up social media like Facebook naturally and in a self-driven way. Subsequently, when our informants failed to acquire any media skills, they pointed to the lack of support from public schools and parents as the main reason for their missing proficiencies.

For example, Veronica, a student at the media art college, was interested in visual art. She mentioned that during her middle school, she became interested in software tools like Adobe Illustrator (AI) and Photoshop. However, the lack of visual art courses prevented her from engaging with the subject further:

> I love the idea of using computers to create things, such as using Photoshop or AI [Adobe Illustrator] to create

media stuffs... but I did not have the choice of art courses at school.

This *common logic* of requiring legitimization from parents and schools is not present in the case of photography and games, however, since these are not subjects typically associated with academic learning.

Lung Fung was pursuing an Associate Degree, and had taken courses at the media art college. While he was an exceptional student, with above 3.5 GPA (out of 4), he had stopped producing music as a hobby as he was overwhelmed with school work geared toward his major. During the interview, he told us, "I have in fact stopped playing guitar already. I am busy doing other stuff, with less time to play [guitar]. Eventually, I became so busy I had to give up playing entirely." In Lung Fung's case, guitar was viewed as a hobby that would only distract him from pursuing other more serious career goals. The lack of parental legitimization led to him dropping his music-related activities.

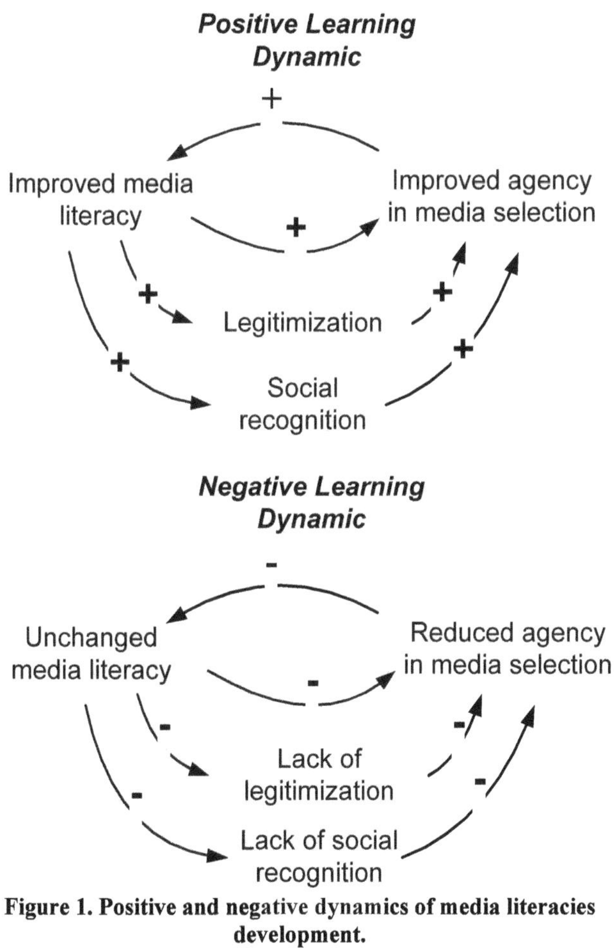

Figure 1. Positive and negative dynamics of media literacies development.

However, when we contacted him again informally to verify some of his quotes, he had just received an offer from the media art college to enroll as an undergraduate student. He was overjoyed to be able to continue studying digital music making, something which he had nearly given up in his pursuit of higher education.

Yes, I want to continue (the music interest), now that I have the offer... Now I hope that I can continue to cultivate music practices. And [in my associate degree] I am going to compose a music piece. And therefore I can continue to keep doing music, even after my [Final Year Project].

Like recognition, legitimization of specific interest activities can persuade or dissuade these students from deepening their creative information use. But legitimization is different from recognition, in that the endorsement comes not from peers, but from authorities like parents and institutions. These authorities tend to set boundaries, control pedagogical resources, and impose learning routines which can affect learners' development trajectories.

Thus, the degree each interest is being legitimized depends on how it is being viewed by the parents and teachers—as being a real creative work, or simply recreational and optional. This tendency for authority figures to endorse interests unfairly was pointed out by Bourdieu [29], who noted that, for example, the French museums and universities have tended to legitimize "music, painting, sculpture, literature and the theatre" as high culture, while other forms of art are often seen as "deviants" and of a lower status (p. 123). In a similar fashion, our informants learned, in their upbringing and interaction with the authoritative persons in the context of Hong Kong, that legitimized activities are the "productive and proper" activities, leading to a loss of motivation in pursing any interest not endorsed as such.

In Figure 1, we term the informants' choice of media-related activities as *media selection*, and present the complex interactions between media literacies and related sociocultural factors in a simple *system dynamic model*. We use this model to provide a "feedback view" of how such a sociotechnical system works, instead of showing one-directional causal relationships between system elements [60]. We found this modeling approach fitting since we like to show how media selection, social recognition, and legitimization reinforce each other within an information ecology as the learner develops media literacies. For example, a high school student who is already good at music has a higher chance of getting into a media art college, and subsequently gaining further legitimization and media selection agency. In Figure 1, the top diagram shows a simplified positive feedback system with positive learning dynamic (depicted by "+" signs), and the bottom diagram shows a negative learning dynamic (depicted by "-" signs). As Figure 1 points out, there is no one single factor that impacted our participants' creative information use. Rather, their choice of how to make use of the rich information offered on the Internet hinged on the complex and intertwined factors situated within their sociocultural environments of learning. In other words, a young adult may thrive in an ecology with adults and peers willing to legitimize and recognize his media literacies; but another young adult without support from others will quickly lose interest. These findings highlighted nontrivial challenges for technology designers, if we are to resolve such sociocultural issues impeding creative information use.

DISCUSSION

This paper contributes to the understanding of young adults' difficulties in creative information use in learning creative skills from a sociocultural perspective. On the surface, when the young adults interacted with media technologies in the media art college, they reported insufficient conceptual understanding of a technical topic, or unfamiliarity with its discourse structures and nomenclatures, which made it difficult for them to use online creative information effectively; *but through our in-depth analysis, we found that these young adults' lack of sufficient media literacies may be an outcome of how parents, teachers, and peers had jointly influenced their media selection agency through social recognition and legitimization.* From Bourdieu's [46] point of view, logical arguments such as "I did not have the choice of art courses at school" can be a thought pattern habituated through social learning in the course of their interaction with others, and the person would hardly consider alternative arguments at the moment of conversation.

Based on this sociocultural view, we reasoned that creative information use is a problem that cannot be resolved by simply redesigning artifacts, such as online learning resources, to be simpler, easier, or more functional. Instead, as shown in our research, the problem with creative information use is deeply rooted in young adults' information ecologies, and particularly, their embodied interactions with others at home, in school, and in the community. And since most young adults have experienced learning within the structures of home, school, and community, their sociocultural influences should be generalizable across most creative information use cases.

When our informants with low media literacies found the effort and time in engaging with a new interest topic too steep, they initially rationalized (in our interviews) that they encountered a "lack of [time, skill, teacher]" to continue pursuing that interest. However, deeper into our interviews, they also reported that the strength to persevere in these interests has to come from a sense of their efforts being recognized, and the activity legitimized, for them to feel justified incurring the mental effort to overcome the difficulties. Thus, the desirable way to foster creative information use may be to allow users to feel socially supported by their parents, teachers, and other learning partners. .

For a specific creative interest, we have found it takes years of engagement to develop the necessary media literacies. For example, it was difficult for informants like Lung Fung, who was only encouraged by his peers but discouraged by parents, to focus his attention on pursuing a digital music career—until he realized he was accepted (i.e., being *legitimized*) by the media art college. Thus, it is important to recognize that the mediation of information ecologies to foster positive learning dynamics is a multi-sited problem that spans across home, learning institution, and communities, and as a result is being affected by all of their practices.

Thus, what most of our media students encountered was a widely observed issue of insufficient social support of creative information use activities in school and at home, which is difficult to uncover but yet essential for their interest and professional development, as was discussed by Bourdieu [46]:

> The competence of the 'connoisseur', an unconscious mastery of the instruments of appropriation which derives from slow familiarization and is the basis of familiarity with works, is an 'art', a practical mastery which, like an art of thinking or an art of living, cannot be transmitted solely by precept or prescription. Learning it presupposes the equivalent of the prolonged contact between disciple and master in a traditional education, i.e., repeated contact with cultural works and cultured people. (p. 66)

In our study, we can take "cultural works and cultured people" as referring to media technologies and content, as well as supportive adults and peers who are media literate. For example, a mother who engages in producing digital music with her daughter—playing digital instruments with her on a weekly basis—will over time cultivate within the family the positive interactions, and a routine use of associated nomenclatures, to establish the sense of legitimacy of that activity.

But the existence of "cultural works and cultured people" is sorely missing within the information ecologies of our informants. Even though Hong Kong has a GDP per capita of US$28,224 in 2005 (when our informants were teenagers), many of our informants reported having only limited access to ITs (e.g., the Internet), and its practices (e.g., training in Photoshop). Rather than labeling these parents in Hong Kong as "poor," as may be suggested by previous studies, we may attribute this limitation to the local parental and educational priorities in cultivating the students to excel in traditional school subjects. In Hong Kong, like some other East Asian cultures, parents are known to keep children under close supervision, while emphasizing only activities contributing to better school grades and a set of normative career options [48]. In this sense, the media culture deficiency in Hong Kong may be contrasted with the incredibly positive technological learning culture of regions like Silicon Valley (cf. [3]), as well as with other cases of supportive parents we had identified in our previous work [37]. Interestingly, while the expectation and close monitoring from parents and teachers often ended when our informants entered college (when some of them identified their true career passions), by that time, some of our informants found themselves so far behind in media literacies that the challenges they experienced in creative information use seem insurmountable—like Jane, who was discouraged by the amount of time she would have to put in to master new 3D animation software tools, since her previous classes had hardly prepared her for these challenges.

Prior research in HCI has suggested that people would most likely first get in touch with computing devices at home, making that an important media learning site for these young adults [22,57]. In particular, Jones, et al. [31] have speculated that simply increasing the number of IT devices in students' homes will assist their media learning process. Nevertheless, the findings of the current study suggest that, instead of focusing on IT devices, parental interactions with their children may play a greater role in youth's creative information uses. For example, such practices may cultivate in these children the notion that devoting time on media production is a productive or simply a recreational activity [22,57]. We need to keep in mind that in our findings, hardly any informants mentioned parents as their motivators, which comes back to the ways creative media activities often seem recreational and optional. And when an interest is deemed "recreational," its activities may appear as a distraction—an unnecessary waste of time—particularly at stages when the youth have to work very hard to do well academically. Accordingly some of these youth may lose their best years at learning media technologies, which would prepare them to engage with creative information in later life.

Hence, learning and engaging in creative information use is a complex sociocultural issue, and there is no "silver bullet." In the next section, we will point out research gaps and design challenges in creative information use, in the hope of shedding light on how HCI research might address this complex problem.

Integrating Learning Technologies into Children and Youth's Learning Ecologies

We argue that if technologies could allow parents to integrate media learning into their parenting practices—in the same way as they had integrated traditional literacy learning with books—youth and young adults may be able to cultivate creative information use more effectively.

In some ways, design research in HCI has already made significant progress, from examining technology-supported learning of traditional literacies (reading, writing, speech, and critical thinking [7,38,64]), to tools which *mediate media literacies acquisition* such as programming skills [34,62]. For example, Storytelling Alice is a programming environment which allows young learners to code and modify the way animated characters act and narrate a story [34]. Programs like Storytelling Alice provide children with visible and observable outcomes that have been found to motivate their learning [24,34,45,62].

Despite these advancements, we still lack sufficient understanding of how these tools can be accepted and integrated by parents and teachers, who in our data were hardly mentioned by our informants except in cases where they turned out to be hindrances. Our informants reported parents only being supportive of academic pursuits, and in some instances, non-academic but classical art interests like piano (e.g., in our informant Mary); and in contrast, nearly all other reported media interests (e.g., coding, gaming, and 3D animation) were not sufficiently understood and supported by parents.

Similarly, we also found that media-related interests were often sidelined in formal educational settings. For example informants like Veronica did not find support at her middle school for learning professional graphics software tools. The same finding has also been reported in other studies. For example, in the examination of iPad deployment in classrooms, few teachers were found to have used these iPads to teach computing skills (e.g., to produce a digital movie) (4%); rather they were mostly relying on these new computing devices to teach traditional subjects (39%); and the rest (56%) had not used the iPad at all [41]. We agree with Jenkins et al. [28] that, while providing classrooms with computing devices is important, we need to pay more attention to how these devices are being used by teachers and students. Creative information use among our informants was always motivated by animation, music, photography, or computer gaming—which are the true motivations which teachers need to support.

Another concern is that the level of adults' engagement in teaching traditional literacies versus media literacies is currently imbalanced. For example, in the HCI literature, traditional literacy sharing (e.g., reading together) is well accepted by parents, and is reported as family-centered, voluntary, open, and welcoming [17,51,53]; in contrast, technology uses (e.g., media consumption) were seen as intrusive, private, disruptive, and addictive [23,56]. In fact many HCI research studies have only focused on supporting traditional parental agendas, such as providing technologies to engage children to read books online with their parents or grandparents [17,52,54], but not on other forms of media use.

From our sociocultural analysis, this contradiction may be resolved by providing parents and teachers with learning tools with which they can engage with the young adults on equal footing—transcending the more traditional supervisor-supervisee relationship; that is, adults could directly participate in the young adults' media activities, rather than only acting as supervisors. Nonetheless, we fully understand that most parents may still lack sufficient understanding of media technologies themselves to perform the activity comfortably with their children. But by providing this suggestion, we hope to at least point to useful directions which researchers and designers could work toward to resolve this issue.

Furthermore, to support long-term engagement with creative information use among young adults, we need learning artifacts which parents, teachers, and peers could act on collectively, in a complementary way, to lead to the learners' acquisition of media literacies in their everyday consequential learning [27]. Therefore, there is an urgent need to examine the collaborative use of media technology between children and parents, or with teachers; in these scenarios, these adults do not act as an authority or supervisor, but as play partners, in which both parties collaborate to manipulate information, produce media artifacts, and so forth [58]. At the writing of this paper, commercial courses for children and youth (e.g., in Minecraft and Scratch programming) are already emerging popularity in places like Hong Kong, and we may begin to examine the small number of parents and teachers who are invested in these courses and actively cultivating media-related skills among the young adults.

But to fully address the lack of support of creative information use in children and young adults' learning ecologies, an underlying issue is that parents and teachers need to see the academic value (e.g., in gaining admission to a university) of youth engaging in media literacies learning. In this regard, one promising area of work which HCI may engage in is the accreditation of media literacies learning outside school curricula. While HCI has examined how point awards and other digital representations may motivate learning [14,25,30,39,63,65], these points awarded for online forum participation do not explicitly build up to any real certification [2]. Also, the activities awarded often have little to do with actual acquisition of media literacies (e.g., having made a robot, or learned a software), but more to do with posting comments on a forum, thus making these rewards more like 'pointless points' for learners. Outside of HCI, some computer science fields have already begun examining an experimental form of accreditation technology based on digital badges [32,55]. Badges are becoming important artifacts supporting media educational efforts—such as Computer Science Hour of Code, Code Week, and other informal media-centered programs—and it was meant for learners to have a secured and standardized way of displaying their continuous learning outcomes [19]. Computer science has examined badges used by Huffington Post [32], and MOOC courses [2], but it remains to be seen if badges earned in these contexts would have any real value in higher education and the job market.

Lastly, research examining ways of fostering strong sociocultural environments for youth and young adults to cultivate creative information use is urgent, considering the degree of the problem we uncovered in this research study. Our findings have shown that a majority of youth will less likely become the creative workers we have envisioned. Unlike traditional forms of literacy, which are continuously reinforced at home and in school, the cultivation of creative information use has largely been left to the youth and young adults themselves. It is time to think about designing technologies by which learning activities could be incorporated willingly, routinely, and positively into daily and recurrent interactions between children and other adults within their learning ecologies.

CONCLUSION

In this study, we examined sociocultural issues and technological implications of creative information use among young adults. We conducted 19 semi-structured interviews with students and recent graduates of a media art college in Hong Kong. We found a complex sociotechnical system containing multiple overlapping learning ecologies—home, school, and communities—in which young adults negotiated creative media learning. Thus, the effective engagement with creative information use may require more than just supplying the young learners with more technical sandboxes; it may mean conceiving technological interventions that could alter the culture, values, and opinions toward media-related activities which could *sustain* productive utilization of these sandboxes. Like traditional literacies such as writing and reading, there ought to be artifacts orchestrating media literacy acquisition across learning ecologies. By highlighting the importance and complexities within these information ecologies, we have hopefully provided a starting point to address this issue.

ACKNOWLEDGMENTS

The work described in this paper was partially supported by a grant from the Research Grants Council of the Hong Kong Special Administrative Region, China (Project No. CityU 11608515).

REFERENCES

1. Saleema Amershi, Meredith Ringel Morris, Neema Moraveji, Ravin Balakrishnan, and Kentaro Toyama. 2010. Multiple Mouse Text Entry for Single-Display Groupware. *Proceedings of the International Conference on Computer Supported Cooperative Work (CSCW'10)*: 169–178. https://doi.org/10.1145/1718918.1718950
2. Ashton Anderson, Daniel Huttenlocher, Jon Kleinberg, and Jure Leskovec. 2014. Engaging with massive online courses. *WWW '14 Proceedings of the 23rd international conference on World wide web*: 687–698. https://doi.org/10.1145/2566486.2568042
3. Richard Barbrook and Andy Cameron. 1996. The Californian ideology. *Science as Culture* 6, 1: 44–72. https://doi.org/10.1080/09505439609526455
4. K. Beach. 1999. Chapter 4: Consequential Transitions: A Sociocultural Expedition Beyond Transfer in Education. *Review of Research in Education* 24, 1: 101–139. https://doi.org/10.3102/0091732X024001101
5. Sue Bennett, Karl Maton, and Lisa Kervin. 2008. The "digital natives" debate: A critical review of the evidence. *British Journal of Educational Technology* 39, 5: 775–786. https://doi.org/10.1111/j.1467-8535.2007.00793.x
6. Dania Bilal. 2004. Research on children's information seeking on the Web. In *Youth Information-Seeking: Theories, Models, and Approaches*, MK Chelton and C Cool (eds.).

Scarecrow Press, Lanham, MD. Retrieved March 12, 2017 from http://scholar.cci.utk.edu/dania-bilal/publications/research-childrens-information-seeking-web

7. Elizabeth Bonsignore, Kari Kraus, Amanda Visconti, Derek Hansen, Ann Fraistat, and Allison Druin. 2012. Game design for promoting counterfactual thinking. *Proceedings of the 2012 ACM annual conference on Human Factors in Computing Systems - CHI '12*: 2079–2082. https://doi.org/10.1145/2207676.2208357
8. Danah Boyd. 2014. It's Complicated: The Social Lives of Networked Teens. In *it's complicated: the social lives of networked teens*. 296. https://doi.org/10.1007/s10615-014-0512-3
9. C. Brown and L. Czerniewicz. 2010. Debunking the "digital native": Beyond digital apartheid, towards digital democracy. *Journal of Computer Assisted Learning* 26, 5: 357–369. https://doi.org/10.1111/j.1365-2729.2010.00369.x
10. C Brown and L Czerniewicz. 2008. Trends in student use of ICTs in higher education in South Africa 10th Annual Conference of WWW Applications. Cape Town. 3-6 September. Trends in student use of ICTs in higher education in South Africa. In *10th Annual Conference of WWW Applications*.
11. Susan Bryant, Andrea Forte, and Amy Bruckman. 2005. Becoming Wikipedian: transformation of participation in a collaborative online encyclopedia. *GROUP '05*: 1–10. https://doi.org/10.1145/1099203.1099205
12. Maureen Carroll, Shelley Goldman, Leticia Britos, Jaime Koh, Adam Royalty, and Michael Hornstein. 2010. Destination, imagination and the fires within: Design thinking in a middle school classroom. *International Journal of Art and Design Education* 29, 1: 37–53. https://doi.org/10.1111/j.1476-8070.2010.01632.x
13. Justin Cheng, Chinmay Kulkarni, and Scott Klemmer. 2013. Tools for predicting drop-off in large online classes. In *Proceedings of the 2013 conference on Computer supported cooperative work companion - CSCW '13*, 121. https://doi.org/10.1145/2441955.2441987
14. Derrick Coetzee, Armando Fox, Ma Hearst, and Björn Hartmann. 2014. Should your MOOC forum use a reputation system? *Proceedings of the 17th ...*: 1176–1187. https://doi.org/10.1145/2531602.2531657
15. Eric Coopey, Ethan Danahy, and Leslie Schneider. 2013. InterLACE. In *Proceedings of the 2013 conference on Computer supported cooperative work companion - CSCW '13*, 11. https://doi.org/10.1145/2441955.2441959
16. Abigail C Evans, Jacob O Wobbrock, and Katie Davis. 2016. Modeling Collaboration Patterns on an Interactive Tabletop in a Classroom Setting. In *Proceedings of the 19th ACM Conference on Computer-Supported Cooperative Work & Social Computing - CSCW '16*, 858–869. https://doi.org/10.1145/2818048.2819972
17. Sean Follmer, Rafael (Tico) Ballagas, Hayes Raffle, Mirjana Spasojevic, and Hiroshi Ishii. 2012. People in books: Using a FlashCam to Become Part of an Interactive Book for Connected Reading. *Proceedings of the ACM 2012 conference on Computer Supported Cooperative Work - CSCW '12*: 685. https://doi.org/10.1145/2145204.2145309
18. Antero Garcia, Christina Cantrill, Danielle Filipiak, Bud Hunt, Clifford Lee, Nicole Mirra, and Kylie Peppler. 2014. *Teaching in the Connected Learning Classroom*.
19. Daniela Giordano, Francesco Maiorana, Andrew Paul Csizmadia, Simon Marsden, Charles Riedesel, Shitanshu Mishra, and Lina Vinikienė. 2015. New Horizons in the Assessment of Computer Science at School and Beyond. In *Proceedings of the 2015 ITiCSE on Working Group Reports - ITICSE-WGR '15*, 117–147. https://doi.org/10.1145/2858796.2858801
20. AM Goncher. 2009. Creativity under constraints: the affect of problem space on design learning among engineering students. *Proceedings of the seventh ACM conference on ...*, 2000: 327-. https://doi.org/10.1145/1640233.1640283
21. Drew Harry, Chris Schmandt, Eric Gordon, and Chris Schmandt. 2012. Setting the Stage for Interaction: A Tablet Application to Augment Group Discussion in a Seminar Class. In *ACM conference on Computer Supported Cooperative Work*, 1071–1080. https://doi.org/10.1145/2145204.2145364
22. Ellen Johanna Helsper and Rebecca Eynon. 2010. Digital natives: where is the evidence? *British Educational Research Journal* 36, 3: 503–520. https://doi.org/1 0.1080/01411920902989227
23. Alexis Hiniker, Sarita Y. Schoenebeck, and Julie A Kientz. 2016. Not at the Dinner Table: Parents- and Children-s Perspectives on Family Technology Rules. In *Proceedings of the 19th ACM Conference on Computer-Supported Cooperative Work & Social Computing - CSCW '16*, 1374–1387. https://doi.org/10.1145/2818048.2819940
24. Michael S Horn, Erin Treacy Solovey, R Jordan Crouser, and Robert J K Jacob. 2009. Comparing the use of tangible and graphical programming languages for informal science education. *Proceedings of the 27th international conference on Human factors in computing systems CHI 09* 32: 975. https://doi.org/10.1145/1518701.1518851
25. James Howison and James D. Herbsleb. 2013. Incentives and integration in scientific software production. *Proceedings of the 2013 conference on*

Computer supported cooperative work - CSCW '13: 459. https://doi.org/10.1145/2441776.2441828

26. Mizuko Ito, Sonja Baumer, Matteo Bittanti, Danah Boyd, Becky Herr-Stephenson, Heather A Horst, Dilan Mahendran, Katynka Z. Martinez, C.J. Pascoe, Dan Perkel, Laura Robinson, Christo Sims, and Lisa Tripp. 2010. *Hanging Out, Messing Around and Geeking Around*. https://doi.org/10.1111/j.1467-8535.2010.01154_5.x
27. Mizuko Ito, Kris Gutiérrez, Sonia Livingstone, Bill Penuel, Jean Rhodes, Katie Salor, Juliet Schor, Julian Sefton-Green, and S. Craig Watkins. 2013. *Connected Learning An Agenda for Research and Design*.
28. Henry Jenkins. 2009. Confronting the Challenges of Participatory Culture : Media Education for the 21 Century. *Program* 21, 1: 72. https://doi.org/10.1108/eb046280
29. Richard Jenkins. 2002. *Pierre Bourdieu (Key Sociologists)*.
30. Carlos Jensen, John Davis, and Shelly Farnham. 2002. Finding others online: reputation systems for social online spaces. *Proceedings of the SIGCHI Conference on Human Factors in Computing Systems*, 1: 447–454. https://doi.org/10.1145/503376.503456
31. Chris Jones, Ruslan Ramanau, Simon Cross, and Graham Healing. 2010. Net generation or Digital Natives: Is there a distinct new generation entering university? *Computers and Education* 54, 3: 722–732. https://doi.org/10.1016/j.compedu.2009.09.022
32. Julie Jones, Nathan Altadonna, and W Lindsey. 2012. We Don't Need No Stinkin' Badges : Examining the Social Role of Badges in the Huffington Post. *Proceedings of the CSCW*: 249–252. https://doi.org/10.1145/2145204.2145244
33. Yasmin B. Kafai, Deborah A. Fields, and Kristin A. Searle. 2011. Everyday creativity in novice e-textile designs. In *Proceedings of the 8th ACM conference on Creativity and cognition - C&C '11*, 353. https://doi.org/10.1145/2069618.2069692
34. Caitlin Kelleher, Randy Pausch, and Sara Kiesler. 2007. Storytelling alice motivates middle school girls to learn computer programming. In *Proceedings of the SIGCHI conference on Human factors in computing systems - CHI '07*, 1455. https://doi.org/10.1145/1240624.1240844
35. Gregor E. Kennedy, Terry S. Judd, Anna Churchward, Kathleen Gray, and Kerri Lee Krause. 2008. First year students' experiences with technology: Are they really digital natives? *Australasian Journal of Educational Technology* 24, 1: 108–122. https://doi.org/10.1007/s13398-014-0173-7.2
36. Kahyun Kim. 2009. Flexible Environment and Creativity: A Preliminary Case Study of Interdisciplinary Student Design Teams. In *C & C 09: Proceedings of the 2009 ACM SIGCHI Conference on Creativity and Cognition*, 333. https://doi.org/http://doi.acm.org/10.1145/1640233.1640286
37. Yong Ming Kow, Timothy Young, and Katie Salen Tekinbaş. 2014. *Crafting the Metagame: Digital Media and Learning Research Hub*. Irvine, CA. Retrieved June 1, 2016 from http://clrn.dmlhub.net/wp-content/uploads/2014/05/craftingthemetagame.pdf
38. Anuj Kumar, Pooja Reddy, Anuj Tewari, Rajat Agrawal, and Matthew Kam. 2012. Improving literacy in developing countries using speech recognition-supported games on mobile devices. *Proceedings of the 2012 ACM annual conference on Human Factors in Computing Systems CHI 12*: 1149. https://doi.org/10.1145/2207676.2208564
39. Airi Lampinen. 2014. Account sharing in the context of networked hospitality exchange. *Proceedings of the 17th ACM conference on Computer supported cooperative work & social computing*: 499–504. https://doi.org/10.1145/2531602.2531665
40. Carly J Lassig. 2009. Promoting creativity in education -- from policy to practice: an australian perspective. *Proceedings of the seventh ACM conference on Creativity and cognition*: 229–238. https://doi.org/10.1145/1640233.1640269
41. Anne-Marie Mann, Uta Hinrichs, Janet C. Read, and Aaron Quigley. 2016. Facilitator, Functionary, Friend or Foe? In *Proceedings of the 2016 CHI Conference on Human Factors in Computing Systems - CHI '16*, 1833–1845. https://doi.org/10.1145/2858036.2858251
42. Anoush Margaryan, Allinson Littlejohn, and Gabrielle Vojt. 2011. Are digital natives a myth or reality? University students' use of digital technologies. *Computers & Education* 56, 2: 429–440. https://doi.org/10.1016/j.compedu.2010.09.004
43. Ignacio J. Martinez-Moyano, David P McCaffrey, and Rogelio Oliva. 2014. Drift and Adjustment in Organizational Rule Compliance: Explaining the "Regulatory Pendulum" in Financial Markets. *Organization Science* 25, 2: 321–328. https://doi.org/http://dx.doi.org/10.1287/orsc.2013.0847
44. Mary K. Chelton and Colleen Cool. 2004. *Youth Information Seeking Behavior: Theories, Models, and Issues,*. Scarecrow Press. Retrieved March 12, 2017 from https://rowman.com/ISBN/9780810849815/Youth-Information-Seeking-Behavior-Theories-Models-and-Issues
45. Jaime Montemayor, Allison Druin, Allison Farber, Sante Simms, Wayne Churaman, and Allison D'Amour. 2002. Physical programming: Designing

Tools for Children to Create Physical Interactive Environments. In *Proceedings of the SIGCHI Conference on Human Factors in Computing Systems Changing Our World, Changing Ourselves - CHI '02*, 299. https://doi.org/10.1145/503376.503430
46. Graham Murdock. 2010. Pierre Bourdieu, Distinction: a social critique of the judgement of taste. *International Journal of Cultural Policy 16*, 63–65. https://doi.org/10.1080/10286630902952413
47. Bonnie A. Nardi and Vicki L. O'Day. 1999. Information ecologies: Using technology with heart. *First Monday* 4, 5. https://doi.org/10.1080/01972240050133706
48. Sohyun Park, Hyunchul Lim, and Heekyung Choi. 2015. "Gangnam Mom": A Qualitative Study on the Information Behaviors of Korean Helicopter Mothers. In *iConference 2015 Proceedings*.
49. Marc Prensky. 2001. Digital Natives,Digital Immigrants Part 1. *On the Horizon* 9: 1–6. https://doi.org/10.1108/10748120110424816
50. Marc Prensky. 2009. H . Sapiens Digital : From Digital Immigrants and Digital Natives to Digital Wisdom Digital Wisdom. *Journal of online education* 5, 3: 1–9. https://doi.org/www.innovateonline.info/index.php?view=article&id=705
51. Hayes Raffle, Janet Go, Mirjana Spasojevic, Glenda Revelle, Koichi Mori, Rafael Ballagas, Kyle Buza, Hiroshi Horii, Joseph Kaye, Kristin Cook, and Natalie Freed. 2011. Hello, is grandma there? let's read! StoryVisit. *Proceedings of the 2011 annual conference on Human factors in computing systems - CHI '11*: 1195. https://doi.org/10.1145/1978942.1979121
52. Hayes Raffle, Janet Go, Mirjana Spasojevic, Glenda Revelle, Koichi Mori, Rafael Ballagas, Kyle Buza, Hiroshi Horii, Joseph Kaye, Kristin Cook, and Natalie Freed. 2011. Hello, is grandma there? let's read! StoryVisit. *Proceedings of the 2011 annual conference on Human factors in computing systems - CHI '11*: 1195. https://doi.org/10.1145/1978942.1979121
53. Hayes Raffle, Mirjana Spasojevic, Rafael Ballagas, Glenda Revelle, Hiroshi Horii, Sean Follmer, Janet Go, Emily Reardon, Koichi Mori, and Joseph Kaye. 2010. Family story play: reading with young children (and elmo) over a distance. *Proceedings of the 28th international conference on Human factors in computing systems - CHI '10*: 1583. https://doi.org/10.1145/1753326.1753563
54. Hayes Raffle, Mirjana Spasojevic, Rafael Ballagas, Glenda Revelle, Hiroshi Horii, Sean Follmer, Janet Go, Emily Reardon, Koichi Mori, and Joseph Kaye. 2010. Family story play: reading with young children (and elmo) over a distance. *Proceedings of the 28th international conference on Human factors in computing systems - CHI '10*: 1583. https://doi.org/10.1145/1753326.1753563
55. Christopher Salerno, Stella Ouma, and Adele Botha. 2015. Developing a Conceptual Model for Facilitating the Issuing of Digital Badges in a Resource Constrained Environment. In *Proceedings of the 2015 Annual Research Conference on South African Institute of Computer Scientists and Information Technologists*, 33:1--33:8. https://doi.org/10.1145/2815782.2815822
56. Diane J. Schiano, Christine Burg, Anthony Nalan Smith, and Florencia Moore. 2016. Parenting Digital Youth: How Now? *Proceedings of the 2016 CHI Conference Extended Abstracts on Human Factors in Computing Systems*: 3181–3189. https://doi.org/10.1145/2851581.2892481
57. Neil Selwyn. 2009. The digital native: myth and reality. *Aslib Proceedings* 6, 4: 364–379. https://doi.org/10.1108/00012530910973776
58. Cynthia Solomon. 1998. What's in it for kids? In *CHI 98 conference summary on Human factors in computing systems - CHI '98*, 44–45. https://doi.org/10.1145/286498.286521
59. Jp James P Spradley. 1980. Participant observation. *Qualitative Research* 3: 1–16. https://doi.org/10.1177/14687941030032003
60. John D. Sterman. 2000. Business Dynamics: Systems Thinking and Modeling for a Complex World. *Journal of the Operational Research Society 53*, 982. https://doi.org/10.1057/palgrave.jors.2601336
61. Anselm L Strauss and Juliet M Corbin. 1990. Basics of qualitative research / grounded theory procedures and techniques. *Qualitative Sociology* 13, 1: 3–21. https://doi.org/10.2307/2074814
62. Sureyya Tarkan, Vibha Sazawal, Allison Druin, Evan Golub, Elizabeth M. Bonsignore, Greg Walsh, and Zeina Atrash. 2010. Toque: designing a cooking-based programming language for and with children. *Proceedings of the 28th international conference on Human factors in computing systems - CHI '10*: 2417–2426. https://doi.org/10.1145/1753326.1753692
63. Yla R. Tausczik and James W. Pennebaker. 2011. Predicting the perceived quality of online mathematics contributions from users' reputations. *Proc. Human Factors in Computing Systems*: 1885–1888. https://doi.org/10.1145/1978942.1979215
64. Anuj Tewari and John Canny. 2014. What did Spot Hide? A Question-Answering Game for Preschool Children. *Proceedings of the 32nd annual ACM Conference on Human Factors in Computing Systems - CHI '14*: 1807–1816. https://doi.org/10.1145/2556288.2557205

65. Allison Woodruff. 2014. Necessary, Unpleasant, and Disempowering: Reputation Management in the Internet Age. *Proceedings of the 32nd annual ACM conference on Human factors in computing systems - CHI '14*: 149–158. https://doi.org/10.1145/2556288.2557126

66. Su Zheng, Adrian Bromage, Martin Adam, and Stephen a R Scrivener. 2007. Surprising creativity: a cognitive framework for interactive exhibits designed for children. *Proceedings of the 2007 Conference on Creativity and Cognition* 7831, 7931: 17–26. https://doi.org/http://doi.acm.org/10.1145/1254960.1254964

The Art of Kenny Who?

Sonny Liew
Singapore
sonnybunni@gmail.com

ABSTRACT
Sonny Liew talks about his own early experiences creating comics, and how the technology has changed the way the artform is created and delivered. We are at a stage now where digital and analog tools can be combined according to our own tastes, to find the right mix that utilizes the speed and efficiency of digital tools while preserving the handmade qualities of analog ones. But are we are currently at a liminal stage, and will comics be affected by the AI/Robot revolution to come? Perhaps heralding a time when the industry has a hollowed out middle, with high-end creators and very cheap human labour still able to find a foothold, but with the rest (and majority) replaced by machines. While this is still a semi-science fictional scenario, it is also one that involves real and urgent questions about human endeavor and where we will end up, pulled along as we are by our own contradictory natures.

ACM Classification Keywords
J.5 Arts and Humanities: Literature; H.5.m. Information Interfaces and Presentation (e.g. HCI): Miscellaneous

Author Keywords
comics, digital artwork, AI, narrative

BIOGRAPHY
Sonny Liew's *The Art of Charlie Chan Hock Chye* [4] was a New York Times and Amazon bestseller, and the first graphic novel to win the Singapore Literature Prize. Other works include *Malinky Robot* [3], *Doctor Fate* [1, 2] (with Paul Levitz) and *The Shadow Hero* [6] (with Gene Yang), along with titles for Marvel Comics, DC Comics, DC Vertigo, First Second Books, Disney Press and Image Comics. He has been nominated for multiple Eisner Awards for his art, as well as for spearheading Liquid City [5], a multivolume comics anthology featuring creators from Southeast Asia. Born in Malaysia, he lives in Singapore.

REFERENCES
1. Paul Levitz and Sonny Liew. 2016a. *Doctor Fate Vol 1: the Blood Price*. DC Comics, Burbank, CA, USA.
2. Paul Levitz and Sonny Liew. 2016b. *Doctor Fate Vol 2: Prisoners of the Past*. DC Comics, Burbank, CA, USA.
3. Sonny Liew. 2011. *Malinky Robot*. Image Comics, Portland, OR, USA.
4. Sonny Liew. 2016. *The Art of Charlie Chan Hock Chye*. Pantheon and Epigram, New York, NY, USA and Singapore.
5. Sonny Liew, Joyce Sim, and Lim Cheng Tju (Eds.). 2008–2014. *Liquid City*. Image Comics, Portland, OR, USA.
6. Gene Luen Yang and Sonny Liew. 2014. *The Shadow Hero*. First Second Books, New York, NY, USA.

C&C 2017, June 27–30, 2017, Singapore.

ACM ISBN 978-1-4503-4403-6/17/06.
DOI: http://dx.doi.org/10.1145/3059454.3078896

Emotion Hero

Ruben van de Ven
Independent artist/researcher
Utrecht, the Netherlands
info@rubenvandeven.com

ABSTRACT
What does it mean to feel 62% joy, and 15% surprised? Over the past years the digitization of emotions is booming business: multimillion dollar investments are made in technologies of which is claimed that they give companies an objective view in their consumers' feelings. The video-game-artwork *Emotion Hero* challenges the user to investigate this claim and question the premise of the technology.

Emotion Hero is a two-part artwork. On the one hand is a video-game that is freely downloadable for everybody with an Android device. Inspired by Guitar Hero, the user scores points by following given cues. It provides detailed feedback on the mechanics of the face. The second part is a projection that shows a grid with aggregated scores of the game, that updates live. In its design, the grid refers to 19th century positivist practices.

ACM Classification Keywords
K.4.m Computers and Society: Miscellaneous

Author Keywords
emotion recognition; emotion detection; video-game-art; app art; positivism; hysteria; big data; machine learning

INTRODUCTION
Over the past years a billion dollar industry has emerged that develops software to derive emotional parameters from faces. Technologies are developed of which is claimed that they give companies an objective view in their consumers' feelings. Companies such as Affectiva, Microsoft, Apple (after acquiring Emotient) and Sightcorp state emotion recognition software will provide an unobtrusive, unmediated way to analyse human emotional responses. But, what does it *mean* to feel 62% joy, and 15% surprised?

Grounded in this question, the the two-part artwork *Emotion Hero* challenges the user to investigate the premise of computerised emotion recognition.

C&C '17 June 27-30, 2017, Singapore, Singapore

ACM ISBN 978-1-4503-4403-6/17/06.
DOI: http://dx.doi.org/10.1145/3059454.3059490

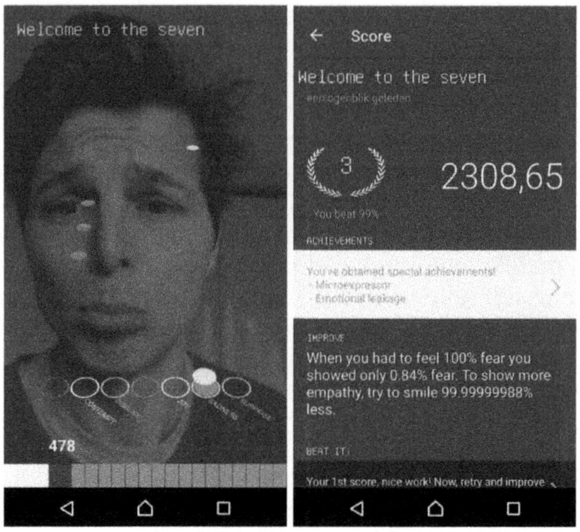

Figure 1. Screen captures of Emotion Hero gameplay on Android.

TRAINED SINCERITY
The first part of Emotion Hero is a video-game that is freely downloadable for everybody with an Android device [5]. In a way similar to Guitar Hero, the user scores points by making facial expressions that the software correlates to certain emotions. It provides detailed feedback on the mechanics of the player's face and suggests ways to change ones facial expression for a better measurement (eg. "When you had to feel 100% joy, you showed only 12% joy. To show more empathy, try to smile 78.2341999% more.", see Figure 1, or watch the game play demo video).

The software's emphasis on the expressions reveals that rather than providing new insights into the player's mental state, the labelling procedure merely reconstitutes a stereotypical perspective on emotions. It brings a paradox to light: one of the central objectives for emotion technology is to measure a 'sincere' response; however, how will that still be possible when considering that emotion software influences behaviour?

At the 2016 debates between USA presidential candidates Hillary Clinton and Donald Trump, Affectiva's software was used to "determine emotional intelligence and sentiment" of the candidates, which should provide a "rare glimpse into what they illustrated beyond their frustrations and political platitudes" [6] – whatever that may mean. For now, quantifying facial expressions of people presenting might still be an inci-

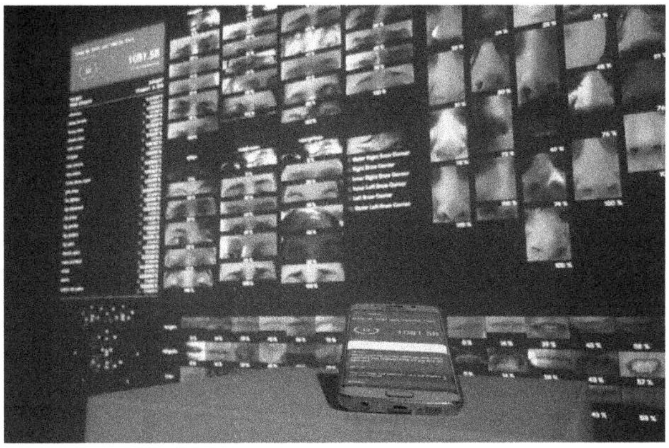
Figure 2. Emotion Hero's app and projection at State Festival, Berlin.

dentally used gadget to get a supposedly 'factual' comparison between candidates. However, it might change the way in which many public figures operate: there has been research that correlates CEO's facial expressions to the market value of their companies. A positive correlation was found between measured expressions of fear, anger and disgust and the company's market value [4]. Being aware of such measurements, it is not so hard to imagine CEO's and other public figures train to adapt their behaviour to reflect a positive (financial) situation.

This is not a far stretch: HireVue is a company that uses Affectiva's emotion analysis software together with other analytic techniques, to analyse job candidates. At the same time they use their technology to "coach teams to be more authoritative when presenting" [6]. So software is used to measure, while simultaneously people are trained to *perform* by the rules of this software! A procedure that sets out to make the Other more transparent, achieves the opposite: emotion analysis practices address representation rather than feeling and make the face an even more trained façade.

LOOKING 68% CONFUZZLED: CLASSIFYING EMOTIONS

In order to substantiate their discourse, companies in facial expression measurement employ huge amounts of data collection and processing. However, rather than being objective systems, the Machine Learning-based algorithms that digitize emotions are known to take over (semantic) biases that are present in human culture [2]. This issue is raised in the second part of Emotion Hero: a projection that shows the aggregated scores of the game.

By putting the results in a fixed grid I want to draw a parallel with positivistic historical practices that, trough extensive measurement and administration, also aimed to delineate something which is conceptually undelineated. Think of Duchenne de Boulogne, Lombroso, and above all of Charcot, who at the end of the 19th century instituted an enormous apparatus which merely succeeded in capturing a pre-existing stereotype of hysteria – a concept seemingly delineated in common language, turned out to be too vaguely described for scientific classification [3]. I would argue that this is similar to how concepts such as 'anger' or 'contempt' are used in the digitization of emotions. As Kirsten Boehner et al. [1] argue:

> during the process of becoming 'studiable' the definition of emotion has been altered to fit a particular conception of what science ought to be: rational, well-defined, and culturally universal. [...] emotion is not thought of as biological, measurable, and objectively present because scientists found it to exist in the world that way, but because 19th-century scientists could not imagine studying it scientifically any other way.

In the transformation of humanistic concepts into a positivist framework the aspects of emotion that are not clearly delineated are ignored. Emotion Hero challenges the user to investigate this rigid application of undelineated terminology.

BIOGRAPHY

Combining his backgrounds in filmmaking, programming and media design, Ruben van de Ven (NL) challenges alleged objective practices. His work focusses on the intersection of highly cognitive procedures and ambiguous experiences – in particular on the way in which digital media appropriate humanistic concepts, forcing ambiguous terminology into a positivist framework. He recently graduated from the Piet Zwart Institute in Rotterdam where he investigated computational quantification and categorisation of emotions.

ACKNOWLEDGEMENTS

Emotion Hero is produced as part of the Summer Sessions Network for Talent Development in a co-production of Arquivo 237 and V2_ Lab for the Unstable Media, with support of the Creative Industries Fund NL.

REFERENCES

1. Kirsten Boehner, Rogério DePaula, Paul Dourish, and Phoebe Sengers. 2007. How emotion is made and measured. *International Journal of Human-Computer Studies* 65, 4 (2007), 275–291.
2. Aylin Caliskan, Joanna J Bryson, and Arvind Narayanan. 2017. Semantics derived automatically from language corpora contain human-like biases. *Science* 356, 6334 (2017), 183–186.
3. Georges Didi-Huberman. 2004. *Invention of Hysteria: Charcot and the photographic iconography of the Salpêtrière*. MIT Press, Cambridge, Massachusetts, USA.
4. Yanjia Sun, Ali N Akansu, and James E Cicon. 2014. The power of fear: Facial emotion analysis of CEOs to forecast firm performance. In *Information Reuse and Integration (IRI), 2014 IEEE 15th International Conference on*. IEEE, 695–702.
5. Ruben van de Ven. 2016. Emotion Hero - Android-apps at Google Play. Android App. (2016). Retrieved 2017-02-15 from `https://play.google.com/store/apps/details?id=com.rubenvandeven.emotion_hero`
6. Cale Guthrie Weissman. 2016. Watch This AI Platform Assess Trump's And Clinton's Emotional Intelligence. (21 October 2016). Retrieved 2016-10-22 from `https://www.fastcompany.com/3064863`

Learn to Fail

Isabelle Desjeux
Independent
Singapore, Singapore
idesjeux@mac.com

ABSTRACT
This paper introduces the participative and durational installation entitled "Learn to Fail" where participants are faced with a choice of actions in order to achieve a goal, while having made the contract with themselves that they will learn to fail. Here we introduce activities that will make the public raise questions by themselves about the kind of choices they make when facing the possibility of a failure.

Author Keywords
failure; fail; success; choice; participatory; science; art

ACM Classification Keywords
H.5.m. Information interfaces and presentation (e.g., HCI): Miscellaneous.

INTRODUCTION
Failure is an important part of many investigative processes by definition (if we already knew the answer to what we are asking, we wouldn't be asking!), none so more than in science, where failure is a compulsory part of the process [1, 2]. But we almost always resist taking the path that might lead to a failure, preferring the less risky option, such is the stigma of failure, versus the thrill of new discovery or learning that risk (and failure) will bring.

By using the methods of discovery proper to science, we investigate the root of all knowledge: Failure. We provide an experimental environment, encouraging the public to attempt different methods of investigation thereby answering a variety of deceptively simple questions.

In this immersive installation, and guided by the title and basic instructions, the public, taken by the game, tries to answer questions that urgently need answering. From guessing the number of seeds in a jar, to following basic information to create a pinhole photograph, or creating a Lego model without instructions, the set ups are varied and meant to elicit reflection on the methods chosen - no matter which method is used in each case, failure is almost certain.

C&C 2017, June 27–30, 2017, Singapore.
ACM ISBN 978-1-4503-4403-6/17/06.
DOI: http://dx.doi.org/10.1145/3059454.3059462

But some methods lead more directly to failures than other.

Finally, after having performed the experiments, the participants can view the results, as contributed by themselves and the participants before them. An immersive installation and collaborative artwork, where the "answers" displayed as a final piece are contributed by the participating public is being created. Failure takes on a relative meaning.

MATERIAL AND METHODS

Set-Up
3 tables are set-up in a semi-circle, each with a distinct set of material, with a task to complete. The task is succinctly described, and the public is to decide for themselves which kind of question they would like to answer. Behind each table, a partition wall obstructs the view of the results being displayed, on the other side of the wall. The results are displayed away from the experimental set-up, for the participant to view afterwards.

Experiments

(I) The Guesstimator Challenge: "Guess the Number of Beans"

This is a version of a famous experiment, described by Francis Galton [3] that involves statistics, regression to the mean, and individual failure... Members of crowds going to a fair in the early 19th century were asked to guess the weight of an ox on display. Most estimates were way off, but, the average from all the guesses was closer to the actual weight of the ox, bettering even the estimates of experts.

In our set up, people are faced with a jar full of mung beans. There is a weighing scale, an empty jar and a few mung beans so the public might naturally want to estimate the number of beans in the jar using the material provided. On the partition wall, there is a screen inviting the participant to input their number. We assume people will be logging in their estimate for the number of beans in the jar. On the other side of the screen (Display side), a screen shows a graph, being updated each time a number is keyed in. The graph will show every number keyed in as the average (But without actual numbers being shown so as to not influence entries). The screen will reveal with time a number closer and closer to the actual number of beans in the jar.

Hence adding up everyone's mistakes leads to the crowd giving the right answer.

(II) The Photograph Challenge: "Take a Photograph of the Building"

One the second table, there are a "dry" and a "wet" portable darkroom, and detailed instructions on how to take a pinhole photograph. There is also a digital printer. On the Display side, there is a line with pegs, ready to hang any image. Each participant can decide either to use the digital printer in order to print a photograph from their phone or to try to take a pinhole photograph. At this point, the participant will have to make some risk assessment to estimate which of the two methods is most likely to give a satisfactory image. The images hung next to each other are witness to people's risk-taking and failures. The Pinhole photographs are black and white whereas the digital photographs are in color. Both are approximately 4R in size.

(III) Build a Lego Model

On this table, there are 2 Lego sets (one red and one yellow). One comes with instructions while the other one doesn't. The participant gets to choose which of the 2 sets to build, given a limited time. The partition wall has a specially-constructed photo booth where the participant can take a picture of their creation to be uploaded on the "display" side of the wall, before returning the Lego to the table for the next participant. The images will be viewed side-by side, allowing the viewers to compare the kind of outcomes you get from the "instruction" kit and from the "free" kits, again, comparing the outcome you get depending on the amount of risk-taking the participants decide to engage in.

OUTCOME

Participants are both contributing to the creation of the exhibition, and viewers as they can step onto the other side at the end of their session, allowing them to compare their achievements with that of others. Discussion is encouraged as a means of understanding: 1.) the thought processes that lead to choosing between two unequally risky paths and 2.) our attitude facing a failed attempt.

CONCLUSION

When facing the possibility of failure, many of us would recoil and take the safe option. However, it is only through taking risks that new ways emerge. Experiencing consciously the steps that may lead to failure, and the failure itself, provides a new and powerful way of becoming aware of the consequences of our choices

ACKNOWLEDGEMENT

A version of this work was fist shown as the ***"Laboratory of Failed Experiments"*** Participatory exhibition at Weirdshift, Storefront, Portland (OR, USA) in 2014, and as ***"Learn to Fail"***, part of the School of Uncommon Knowledge (Substation, Singapore) in 2016.

ARTIST PROFILE

Isabelle Desjeux is a full-time artist pursuing interdisciplinary projects linking ways of learning through participatory art and most often collaborating with children and scientists as well as artists. She is currently Head of Failure at the Institute of Unnecessary Research (http://unnecessaryresearch.tumblr.com/Failures) and has contributed to Playeum (Children's Center for Creativity, Singapore) in various ways. Her artist website can be viewed at (https://isabellecreates.wordpress.com) and she can be found at idesjeux@mac.com or +65 92734991.

REFERENCES

1. Isabelle M. Desjeux. 2010. *Failures and other Biological Objects*. MAFA Dissertation. Lasalle College of the Arts Singapore,Singapore.
2. Stuart M. Firestein. 2015. *Failure*. Oxford: Oxford University Press.
3. Francis Galton. 1907. Vox Populi. *Nature,* 1949, 75:450-451

Beyond Visualization: Plotting Multivariate Data as Video, Music, and Food

Thomas Kai Levine
USA
_@thomaslevine.com

ABSTRACT
Data analysis has historically been limited by the capacity of the visual medium to represent multivariate data. Including other senses in our analysis may help us represent high-dimensional data in intuitive and accessible forms. I present several explorations into a future beyond visual data analysis: six data music videos, three data musical instruments, and one data meal.

ACM Classification Keywords
H.1.2 Information Interfaces and Presentation (e.g. HCI): User/Machine Systems; H.5.2 Information Interfaces and Presentation (e.g. HCI): User Interfaces; H.5.5 Information Interfaces and Presentation (e.g. HCI): Sound and Music Computing; H.5.m. Information Interfaces and Presentation (e.g. HCI): Miscellaneous; J.1 Computer Applications: ADMINISTRATIVE DATA PROCESSING

Author Keywords
data; analysis; music; video; food; visualization; sonification; gastronomification

INTRODUCTION
Data are abstract numbers, with no true representation in the real world. We cannot perceive the data directly, so we must convert them into forms that we can perceive. For example, we often make data tables and graphs and then look at the tables and graphs with our eyes, perceiving them visually. Why stop at visualization?

Modern advances in technology have made it feasible to plot data through sound, smell, taste, and touch. With these additional senses, we can experience data with our full sensory bandwidth, facilitating the direct interpretation of large, multivariate, unaggregated datasets.

I present several pieces that I have produced over the past several years while exploring this concept.

C&C '17 June 27-30, 2017, Singapore, Singapore

ACM ISBN 978-1-4503-4403-6/17/06.

DOI: http://dx.doi.org/10.1145/3059454.3059494

DATA MUSIC VIDEOS
The following data music videos are to be displayed on respective large screens, with separate headsets for the sound. Each data music video will be played on a loop, and a legend for each piece will be posted next to its screen.

Hopping Cities
is a plot of airport flight data, inspired by Hungarian jumping dances [1].

Journalism-driven data
is a plot of the editing activity from a news publication software [2].

Ridership Rachenitsa
is a plot about the ridership of Chicago buses and New York subways for a period of a few years [3].

FMS Symphony
is a plot about the financial accounts of the treasury of the United States of America [4].

Risley Toilets
is a plot of the results of a questionnaire on perceptions of unsanitary conditions in bathrooms [5].

Iriscore
is a plot of the iris dataset inspired by gabba music [6].

DATA MUSICAL INSTRUMENTS
I have developed several softwares that represent data tables and musical scores in a common language, bridging the gap between data analysis and music composition. Each particular software will have its own workstation setup with a computer and a printed software manual.

Sheetmusic
is a spreadsheet software for integrated data musicification and conventional music composition [7].

R
is the programming language that I produce most of my data music videos in, so I will present my data music libraries for R [8].

bradio
is a business intelligence dashboard widget that represents data as sound [9].

DATA MEAL

I have produced a series of food geoms for the popular ggplot2 plotting library: `geom_taco` and `geom_doner`. Ideally, I will adapt this for Singaporean fast food, plot a dataset as Singaporean fast food, serve the plot on a table for visitors to consume, and display the source code on a large printed sheet. If this is not feasible, I will simply present a photograph of a döner plot [10].

CONCLUSION

Conventional data analysis are designed with the expectation that data are to be perceived through our eyes ("data visualization"). When we focus on conventional visual representations, we can get distracted from the higher goal: To convert abstract data to concrete metaphors that our human sensory systems can understand. Advances in computing technology have facilitated the collection and exchange of incomprehensibly large datasets; perhaps advances in data presentation methods will help us comprehend these large datasets.

AUTHOR

Thomas Kai Levine is a dada artist interested in sleep [11]. Here are some venues where he has presented his data music and data food.

- March 14, 2017. Music in R. Stockholm R User Group.
- November 15, 2016. Plotting data as music and video. Data Science Warsaw.
- October 26, 2016. Beyond Visualization: The future of multivariate data analysis. Budapest BI Forum.
- September 3, 2016. Approaches to live music synthesis for multivariate data analysis in R. Budapest SatRday 2016.
- July 5, 2016. Plotting data as music and video. VU Symposium.
- July 3, 2015. Plotting data as music videos in R. UseR! 2015.
- August 14, 2014. Data visualization needs to die. Hacks/Hackers Berlin.
- July 3, 2014. Sheetmusic: Making music from spreadsheets. European Spreadsheet Risks Interest Group 15th Annual Conference.
- April 9, 2013. Music Videos in R. New York Open Statistical Programming Meetup.

REFERENCES

1. Thomas Levine. *Hopping Cities*. https://thomaslevine.com/!/data-music/hopping-cities/.
2. Thomas Levine. *Journalism Driven Data*. https://thomaslevine.com/!/data-music/journalism-driven-data/.
3. Thomas Levine. *Ridership Rachenitsa*. https://thomaslevine.com/!/data-music/ridership-rachenitsa/.
4. Thomas Levine. *FMS Symphony*. https://thomaslevine.com/!/data-music/fms-symphony/.
5. Thomas Levine. *Risley Toilets*. https://thomaslevine.com/!/toilets/risley-toilets/.
6. Thomas Levine. *Iriscore*. https://thomaslevine.com/!/data-music/iriscore/.
7. Thomas Levine. *Sheetmusic*. https://thomaslevine.com/!/data-music/sheetmusic/.
8. Thomas Levine. *Data Music*. https://thomaslevine.com/!/data-music/.
9. Thomas Levine. *bradio*. https://thomaslevine.com/scm/bradio/.
10. Thomas Levine. *geom_doner*. https://thomaslevine.com/!/data-music/geom_doner/.
11. Thomas Levine. *Thomas Levine*. https://thomaslevine.com/.

Let Them Eat cake!

Audrey Samson
London, UK
a.samson@gre.ac.uk

Francisco Gallardo
London, UK
f.j.fernandezgallardo@qmul.ac.uk

FRAUD
London, UK
else@fraud.la

ABSTRACT
Let them eat cake! is a food-led event serving an edible imaginary of your Facebook profile. In early 2012, Facebook conducted massive scale emotional contagion by manipulating the emotional expressions in the News Feeds of 689,003 users [1]. This exemplifies how the governability and the biopolitics of everyday life flow through the many layers of shared images, liked videos, protocols, and hyperlinks, all orchestrated by the Facebook News Feed algorithm. *Let them eat cake!* proposes a gustatory experience to the visitor, a cake imagined with synthetic DNA encoded from a user's Facebook profile data. The profile's data categories (Ad Topics, Facial Recognition Data, Friends, Followers, Likes, and Political Views) are transposed into cake layers, with an absurd twist that reflects the algorithms agency. Ultimately the work explores innovative forms of engagement with human-machine relationships through 'algorithm taste' interaction.

Author Keywords
Taste; interaction; algorithm; biopolitics; food art.

ACM Classification Keywords
J.5 [ARTS AND HUMANITIES]: *fine arts, performing arts*.

General Terms
Algorithms, Design, Experimentation.

DESCRIPTION

Context
"Let them eat cake!" she retorted, as she was told the peasants had no more bread to eat. According to the myth, the French Queen Marie-Antoinette was so detached from her subjects that she thought that they should simply eat a more luxurious foodstuff like cake if the staples had run out. The politics of power and their relationship to food are expressed in this well know phrase. Following Hannah Landecker's notion of food as a conditioning environment that shapes the activity of the genome and the physiology of the body[2], we use cake as exposure to social media politics. The designed and manufactured sets of molecules that compose food exist in the cloud in which we are immersed. Metabolism can be a source to understand circuits of exchange, in short, the biopolitics of matter.

C&C '17, June 27-30, 2017, Singapore, Singapore
ACM 978-1-4503-4403-6/17/06.
http://dx.doi.org/10.1145/3059454.3059495

The basis of these relationships depends on vast resources allocated to the development of new forms of data storage to accommodate expanding capacity requirements. Synthetic DNA is the proposed solution to the data storage problem. Its stable format, high-density information encoding capacity, and low maintenance properties are fueling the promise of near infinite, never-deprecating storage[3][4]. For the first time, data will be truly embodied, with the code of life itself. In short, DNA presages the Facebook server farms of the future.

Let them eat cake! looks particularly at some of the ways in which Facebook curates each News Feed. Such as: emotional contagion experiments[1], the augmentation of political polarization[5], and the adjustment of content visibility depending on its source, and its format[6][7]. We propose food-led events as a way to interact with these complex socio-technical assemblages. Though we do not yet propose the synthetic DNA version of the cake, but rather a harmless sugar substitute, we aim to emphasise the materiality of data by making it edible, and thereby to engage with the issues around near future DNA data storage and datafication through food-led interaction.

For CC2017, we present a local version of the cake in the form of the popular *kueh lapis*. This layered Peranakan desert - a marriage of Chinese and Malay cooking traditions following the influx of male Chinese traders in the 17th Century - symbolises the complexity of human-machine relationships. With this submission, we propose tasting as a way to interact with these complex socio- technical assemblages, including DNA data storage, 'post-truth' and Facebook engineered news.

Figure 1 – Cross-section of the cake showing layers that correspond to the Facebook data categories.

ARTIST PROFILE

Bio

FRAUD is a duo (Audrey Samson + Francisco Gallardo) of media and spatial *thingkers*. Their backgrounds include computational culture, critical technical practices, post-colonial and critical feminism, performance, design and space system engineering. They develop forms of critical art-led inquiry into the multiples scales of power, and governability that flow through physical and cultural landscapes. Their practice is currently focused on exploring forms of slow violence and death embedded in, for instance, the entanglement between archiving practices and technical objects, the diminishing negantropism of global trade, systems of production after erasure, and alluring myths of ecological cosmopolitanism.

REFERENCES

1. Kramer, A. D. I., Guillory, J. E. and Hancock, J. T. 2014. 'Experimental Evidence Of Massive-Scale Emotional Contagion Through Social Networks'. *Proceedings Of The National Academy Of Sciences* 111 (24): 8788-8790.
2. Landecker, H. 2011. 'Food as exposure: Nutritional epigenetics and the new metabolism'. *BioSocieties* 6(2): 167-194.
3. Goldman, N., Bertone, P., Chen, S., Dessimoz, C., LeProust, E.M., Sipos, B., and Birney, E. 2013. 'Towards Practical, High-Capacity, Low-Maintenance Information Storage in Synthesized DNA'. *Nature* 494 (7435): 77-80.
4. Samson, A. and Gallardo F. 2015. '"Let Them Eat cake!!", She Said'. *The Forager* (5). http://www.theforagermagazine.com/5/4.
5. Bakshy, E., Messing, S., and Adamic, L. A. 2015. 'Exposure To Ideologically Diverse News And Opinion On Facebook'. *Science* 348 (6239): 1130-1132.
6. Welch, B., and Zhang, X. 2014. 'News Feed FYI: Showing Better Videos'. https://newsroom.fb.com/news/2014/06/news-feed-fyi-showing-better-videos/.
7. Pariser, E. *The Filter Bubble: How the New Personalized Web Is Changing What We Read and How We Think*. New York, NY, Penguin.

Let's Make Love: A One-on-one Performance Installation

Jennifer Jamieson
Self-affiliated
Perth, WA, Australia

ABSTRACT
One-on-one performance *Let's Make Love* is an intimate live-art performance where the artist and audience generate oxytocin (the love hormone). In a short intimate interaction the artist and audience collaborate in a physical 'algorithm for love'. The performance ends with the audience member and artist lying on a purpose built bed of grass, holding hands whilst looking up at the night sky around them.

Author Keywords
Performance; live art; performance art; oxytocin.

ACM Classification Keywords
K.4.m Computers and Society: Miscellaneous.

ART WORK DESCRIPTION
I staged this work in Perth's Proximity Festival (Australia's first one-to-one performance festival) in 2014 on the roof of the Fremantle Arts Centre: an audience participant and I strolled through the grounds to climb through a window onto the roof. We lay on a purpose built bed of grass and held hands. Through a series of physical interactions that have been shown to increase the oxytocin hormone the audience-participant and artist also talk about the science of love and hormones, the military use of synthetic oxytocin in the USA and philosophize experientially on the nature of trust.

The performance moves through the social awkwardness of extended hugs that just linger for a few seconds too long to discourse and hand-holding with audience-participants where we become bodily sensing technologies and bio sequencing systems in our own chemistry.

An initial glance at scientific research on oxytocin casts a wide net: neuroscience, addiction studies, schizophrenia, autism, psychology, advertising, pharmacology, economics, health, child development, behavioural sciences, psychiatry, genetics and the list continues…

Oxytocin is a hormone classically known to facilitate lactation and birth; it is also a central neuropeptide that influences a host of social and other behaviours. These peripheral actions are provoked following oxytocin's release into the bloodstream from the hypothalamus.

C&C '17, June 27-30, 2017, Singapore, Singapore
ACM 978-1-4503-4403-6/17/06.
http://dx.doi.org/10.1145/3059454.3059496

My performance aims to provoke discussion about oxytocin but also to literally create it by physical touch, causing trust between audience member and performer and by taking risks: social cues for generating the hormone. The performance invites audience and artist to be a biological machine and explore human hormone systems.

Images / video documentation of the artwork

Video-2 minute edit of initial rehearsal of *Let's Make Love*
http://youtube.com/jendreamlight

Type of Artwork and intended presentation format

Performance Art / Live Art with an installation component - the ‘bed of grass’ that remains in between and after performances. The performance is 1:1 however spectators can view the intimate performance from the periphery.

Author(s) name, short bio, artist profile and track record including previous exhibitions

Jen Jamieson is a performance artist aiming to blur audience and artist. She is a registered art therapist, and is a member of Perth Playback Theatre. She has also lectured in digital video and communication studies at all of the universities in Perth.

She studied visual art, and theatre, then graduated with First Class Honours in media studies. Jen has produced and directed several short films that have screened and won awards in national & international film festivals. Over the last few years she has been developing an interdisciplinary arts practice, utilising her video/photography and training in performance making. She was one half of something in common (sic) - a performance duo that presented shop till you drop: a 40-hour shopping crusade at Artrage (a month long live art endurance performance in three stages). (sic) performed at BEAP, Nerdstock, Electrofringe and Artrage, and were the recipients of a CultureLAB residency in 2008. Jen has staged her hybrid art project, the booth (a video confession booth) in various festivals and has also performed with pvi collective and La Pocha Nostra.

Jen’s work is often physical, drawing on endurance performance and durational works, striving for it to be visually striking. It is ‘interactive’ and there is a blur between audience and artist. Jen makes herself vulnerable and through this allows humour to emerge. Shopping til you drop. ‘Building’ endless Ikea chairs against the clock. Lying supine. Banal repetition. Intimate photographic self-portraiture. A 15-minute endurance performance. Vital statistics gathered by literally physically moving the audience to observe statistics about themselves.

Jen was selected for Time_Place_Space_6, where she met formed BRINKMANSHIP; who were commissioned in 2010 to present ‘We Will Build Our Own Mountain’ – a durational performance that saw them build a mountain out of ice, climb it, then wait for it to melt. Jen was selected for ‘Visible City’ at Melbourne Fringe Festival, where she lived with ten other artists for three weeks making spontaneous live art works for the festival. She was also curated into Tiny Stadiums Live Art festival in Sydney where she debuted a performance experiment pop channel; a durational work channeling a Lady Gaga song through automatic writing. She created one of 2012’s Field Theory commissioned works, Today Another Vessel Was Found, A Christmas Island Snorkelling Tour. She premiered her work How to Have a 3 minute Shower at Proximity festival 2012, as well as On The Couch with the Freudian Dream Girls at the Perth Fringe festival. In 2014 year she premiered her new work, Let’s Make Love at Proximity Festival 2014.

self-portrait in tar

Detailed requirements for the installation space—the amount of space needed (length, width, height in meters) including technical requirements and any other special venue arrangements assumed.

This performance is flexible in terms of space needed and will depend on curatorial discussions . It was presented on the roof on an Arts Centre in Fremantle during the evening where we created a purpose built wooden bed of real grass for the audience member and I to lie on. This bed was lit and accessed by steps coming from a window.

The bed is no larger than a double sized mattress but it should be raised somewhat. Ideally, it has some sort of wooden platform, with a pathway to it. This bed is a remnant installation during performances and after them, and visitors may lie on it.

The ‘bed’ needs lighting.

Part of the performance is a walk/talk between artist and audience member as they stroll through the venue. It is exciting to have access to areas not often seen or accessible to the general public and this “riskiness” and sense of adventure actually increases oxytocin!

Study for a Camera on a Plot of Land in the Desert

Gottfried Haider

Vienna, Austria
gottfried.haider@gmail.com

ABSTRACT
This paper describes a proposed artwork presentation at the 11th ACM Conference on Creativity and Cognition. Through an autonomously functioning remote sensing device, the author intends to weave together threads from perception, geography, coding theory, compression, image making, the contemporary network condition, contact and remoteness, as well as 90ies online culture.

Author Keywords
Sensing; remoteness; compression; place; perception; network;

ACM Classification Keywords
J.5. Arts and Humanities

INTRODUCTION
In spring 2017 a custom-designed circuit board (PCB) will be permanently installed in the High Desert area of California. The circuit boards dimensions are 12 by 12 centimeters; it is anchored to the ground by a concrete block.

The circuit board contains a small solar panel, as well as a super-capacitor and related charging circuitry, a camera module [1], a radio module [2], and a low-power microcontroller – comparable to the one used in the popular "Arduino" electronics platform [3].

A custom program, written by the author, is being executed by the microcontroller. It choreographs the following series of events – which happen autonomously, guided only by availability of sunlight:

The super-capacitor stores energy harvested from the sun. Once sufficient charge has been accumulated, the camera module is being powered on, and a low-resolution photograph of the surrounding environment is being captured. After applying further compression and encoding, the image is turned into a package suitable for "Amateur Packet Reporting System" (APRS) communication, and emitted as radio waves through the radio module.

C&C '17, June 27-30, 2017, Singapore, Singapore

ACM ISBN 978-1-4503-4403-6/17/06.
http://dx.doi.org/10.1145/3059454.3059498

The APRS system is commonly used by Amateur radio operators to exchange tactical information at regular intervals, such as the geographic coordinates of mobile stations. This information is distributed through many, often internet-connected, relay stations, and most commonly plotted on maps. One example of such a federated community is aprs.fi [4].

Since the camera in the desert will be stationary throughout the lift-time of the installation, the transmission of geographic coordinates is of little value. Instead, the user-definable "comment" field of the APRS package is being used to transfer image data, albeit in a highly compressed form.

On the receiver-side, all data received through the APRS network (and aprs.fi), is being used to "unpack" the information about the surrounding landscape in the desert. The informational scarcity (estimated: one package every hour during daylight, consisting only of a couple of bytes) makes this act of encoding and decoding challenging. Yet operating at the very low edge of resolution and bandwidth (c.f. Florian Cramer, *Floppy Films* [5]) reveals interesting insights into the mechanisms of capture, encoding, interpolation and interpretation.

These topics, which seem both timeless and timely, are being explored by other artists and theorists, such as Hito Steyerl [6] and Rosa Menkman [7]. In my proposed contribution I hope to address their work, and to expand the discussion towards the culture of space probes, and a call for custom & site-specific compression protocols.

PRESENTATION FORMAT
As part of the conference I propose to create an installation, which includes a replica of the remote sensing apparatus, located in a 2 x 2 meters pit filled with sand and rock.

Next to it, a computer monitor, connected to mouse and keyboard, invites the participant to navigate a website that contains the "site", extrapolated from the most recent (live) data received from the California High Desert.

BIOGRAPHY
Gottfried Haider, b. 1985 in Vienna, received a degree in Digital Arts at Vienna University of Applied Arts in 2009. He completed a MFA in Design Media Arts at University of California Los Angeles (UCLA) in 2013 on a Fulbright Scholarship. His practice combines teaching, tool-building

(e.g. *Hotglue* together with Danja Vasiliev, work with the Processing Foundation), and autonomous artwork.

Gottfried Haider's work has been shown in different international venues and contexts. Amongst others: Ars Electronica Festival, Transmediale Festival, 16th International Symposium on Electronic Arts, dOCUMENTA (13), Machine Project, Hacking Habitat exhibition, FILE Festival, Interdisciplinary College.

SUPPLIMENTARY MATERIAL

Detail of a previous installation in exhibition

Possible site for permanent installation

Detail of remote sensing apparatus

REFERENCES

1. Arduino Based Camera. Retrieved January 6, 2017 from http://www.arducam.com/
2. Radiometrix. VHF Narrow Band FM High Power (300mW) Transmitter. Retrieved January 6, 2017 from http://www.radiometrix.com/content/hx1
3. Arduino. Retrieved January 6, 2017 from https://www.arduino.cc/
4. Google Maps APRS. Retrieved January 6, 2017 from http://aprs.fi/
5. Florian Cramer. Floppy Films. Retrieved January 6, 2017 from http://floppyfilms.pleintekst.nl/
6. Hito Steyerl. How Not to be Seen: A Fucking Didactic Educational .MOV File. 2013.
7. Daniel Rourke, Rosa Menkman. Resolution Disputes. 2015. Retrieved January 6, 2017 from http://www.furtherfield.org/features/interviews/resolution-disputes-conversation-between-rosa-menkman-and-daniel-rourke

Do Silhouettes Dream?

Yannis Kalantidis
skamalas.com

Cheng Xu
1x1.design

Clayton Mellina
sigil.io

ABSTRACT
This paper complements our interactive art installation consisting of a back-projected screen and a depth sensor. As participants stand in front of the projection, their silhouettes create an area of hallucination that changes with their movement. Hallucinations may vary; some are "dreams", transporting the area covered by the silhouette to past or future times. Others escape reality and either alter the visual artistic style or form "deep dreams", i.e. hallucinations created through a feedback loop on artificial deep neural networks. Hallucinations vary in intensity and "depth" as participants move, increasingly distorting reality with proximity to the screen. To our knowledge, this installation is the first of its kind, placing fascinating results of cutting-edge artificial intelligence in a public embodied experience.

INTRODUCTION
Recent advances in computer vision have produced impressive visualizations of the internal representations of deep convolutional neural networks trained on images. In one such visualization method called *Deep Dreaming* [3], a trained network is induced to "hallucinate" by iteratively modifying the pixels of an input image to maximize internal neural activations. Different layers of neurons can be selectively targeted by the deep dreaming process. Indeed, by studying how different choice of layer produces different visual modification of the input image, we can gain insight and intuition for the network's representations. For instance, typically the visual patterns imposed on the image by maximizing layers nearer the input of the network resemble simple geometric strokes, while deeper layers produce recognizable parts of semantic classes, such as parts of buildings or animals.

C&C '17 June 27-30, 2017, Singapore, Singapore

ACM ISBN 978-1-4503-4403-6/17/06.

DOI: http://dx.doi.org/10.1145/3059454.3059499

How might a viewer understand this abstract continuum and build a mental model of it? Could an embodied experience help make these abstract concepts more approachable? This question motivated us to create our installation. In our work, we map the viewer's physical distance from the image to an abstract quality, enabling an embodied mode of exploration. We experiment with a variety of such mappings—or *hallucination modes*—including mapping distance to the 'depth' of dreams or the time dimension of a timelapse. The participants' silhouettes become visual vessels transported through time or hallucination intensity, and their bodies become windows into abstract spaces.

To our knowledge, this installation is the first of its kind, placing the recent, fascinating results of artificial intelligence in a public embodied experience. By exhibiting in a gallery setting, we further want to raise the question: in what contexts can visuals driven by learning algorithms be perceived as art?

INSTALLATION
Physically our installation consists of a large back-projected screen equipped with a Microsoft Kinect depth sensor. With no audience present, it would appear as a static image. As a participant's body is captured by the sensor in the area in front of the screen, hallucination effects emerge and become more prominent as they approach the projection screen. The depth at each point in the sensor space is translated to a quantity that depends on the current hallucination mode, which in turn determines the visual appearance at the corresponding point in the projection. For instance, depth maps to hallucination intensity in the deep dream mode and time in the timelapse mode. The images and hallucination modes may rotate during the exhibition, or multiple modes may be simultaneously present for different participants' silhouettes.

At first glance, the installation offers a visually complex interactive experience. Upon closer examination and exploration, it allows the audience to build a visual or even spatial mental model of how an image evolves in a hallucinating neural network, or how time sculpts a landscape. A short explanatory note that explains in greater detail how deep dream visualization works invites participants to learn about the structure of deep neural networks and to engage critically with the piece.

Figure 1. Style transfer example: Proximity controls artistic style. ***Creative Commons image courtesy of Mike Cartmell on Flickr.***

Figure 2. With a day-to-night timelapse of Singapore as input, proximity controls the time of day for the areas covered by the silhouettes.

HALLUCINATION MODES

We experiment with multiple spatio-temporal inputs or *hallucination modes*. Some are dreams transporting the visual to past and future times, others escape reality and either distort the visual artistic style or visualize neural network deep dreaming.

Dreaming with neural networks. We experiment with different applications of artificial neural networks. An example for deep dreaming [3] is shown in the title Figure[1]. Physical depth can be mapped to different parameters of the deep dreaming process. We have experimented with mapping depth to both the number of iterations of the deep dreaming process and the depth of the neural layer directing the deep dreaming process. We are further experimenting with visualizing filter outputs, as well as class specific visualizations, *i.e.* starting from random noise images and forcing the network to hallucinate a specific semantic class.

Style transfer with neural networks. Another direction is artistic style transfer, depicted in Figure 1. DeepStyle [2] is a recent technique that allows *style transfer* between a source image (e.g. the landscape in Figure 1) and a style image (e.g. Van Gogh's "Starry Night" in the leftmost frame of Figure 1). Recent papers, *e.g.* [1], present extensions for not only jointly learning multiple styles, but also making it easy to interpolate between them.

Timelapse imagery. Controlling time through movement can be very empowering; we are experimenting with different inputs extracted from time-lapse videos. An example from a day-to-night panorama of Singapore [6][2] can be seen in Figure 2. Any time-lapse video can be used as input.

[1]Creative Commons image, courtesy of Mike Cartmell on Flickr.

Beyond silhouettes. One may use the *average* distance/depth from the depth sensor to define a single depth value for the entire projection. In this setting, participants no longer appear as silhouettes, but are able to use coordinated movement to scroll the entire projection through time or neural network depth. A compelling application of this interaction is the visualization of timelapsed geographic imagery. For example, Google Earth recently published timelapses of different locations over 32 years [4], highlighting both climate and population changes over time. Similarly, visualizing Global Forest Cover Change data [5] in this way forces participants to confront metaphors between proximity and deforestation.

FUTURE WORK

We envision that the interactive entanglement of depth, space, and time can be used for more than visual exploration. As embodied actors, movement changes our physical perspective on the world and is deeply intuitive. Mapping movement to new perceptual transformations offers a powerful embodied interaction that may be used for narrative purposes or as a building block in more expansive experiences. We intend to pursue these directions in the future.

The python code used in this project is publicly available at `https://github.com/skamalas/depth2time`

REFERENCES

1. D. Chen *et al.* 2017. Stylebank: An explicit representation for neural image style transfer. *arXiv preprint arXiv:1703.09210* (2017).
2. L. Gatys *et al.* 2015. A Neural Algorithm of Artistic Style. *CoRR* abs/1508.06576 (2015).
3. Google. 2015. DeepDream blog post. (2015). `https://research.googleblog.com/2015/07/deepdream-code-example-for-visualizing.html`.
4. Google. 2016. Timelapse - Google Earth Engine. (2016). `https://earthengine.google.com/timelapse/`.
5. M. C. Hansen *et al.* 2013. High-Resolution Global Maps of 21st-Century Forest Cover Change. *Science* 342, 6160 (2013), 850–853.
6. Harrison Wood. 2015. Singapore City Day-Night Time lapse. YouTube. (2015). `https://www.youtube.com/watch?v=2UFUfj1Eb3c`.

[2]Used with permission by Harrison Wood.

Posthuman Research

Darina Alster
Freelancer
Visual art project
Posthuman research
Prague, Czech republic
Darina.alster@gmail.com

ABSTRACT
Posthuman research is my performative project which I did with colleague Johana Střížková in 2015-16. The medium is videoperformance. I am presenting couple of videos with large corelation of meaning. In posthuman research is female-Human-object without face asking about her identity. She have dialog with google asking about where is lost her personality in the network. Google responds by the voice of google translate app. The second human person in the performance, a programator don't have any interest of what is happening infront of her. Postapocalyptic scene without any emotions. In the second video named Gaia is detailed female pregnant body nearly giving birth.Woman is sitting in lotus position as jogini or Buddha. Her body is covered in black and white liquids asociating body liquids as spits sweat tears milk etc. We can see just details of female body like we are observing some prehistorical sculpture. *Earth Mother, you who are called by a thousand names. May all remember we are cells in your body and dance together*[3]The feeling what we have is between disgust and fascination or big respect to the archetype. First and final role of woman: being goddess ore being robotic slave. Do we have chance to choose our roles in our contempoary society?

Author Keywords
Performance; gender; Identity; mythology; feminism; social criticism; personal borders; biorobot; maternity; female body; transformation; trans; contempoary living; network identity; postinternet; online profile; emotions; beauty; ugliness; nudity; humanity; installation; physical experience; psychology; archetypes; fairytales; religions; computering body

ACM Classification Keywords
Social roles; feminism; religions; spirituality; female body; aesthetics; visualization; videoinstallation; gender; identity; postinternet

C&C '17, June 27-30, 2017, Singapore, Singapore
ACM 978-1-4503-4403-6/17/06.
http://dx.doi.org/10.1145/3059454.3059500

INTRODUCTION
My main interest is to answer contemporary life questions by the language of art. I am creating kind of own mythology to communicate with unconsciousness. Searching timeless principals in psychological archetypes, religions and mythologies or fairytales. Allso like to tematise topics of social life, parenting artists, social network, human identity, gender and erotism.*This is a struggle over life and death, but the boundary between science fiction and social reality is an optical illusion.*[1]

Short Bio
Darina Alster is among the artist who sees themselves as author who clearly works with statement about the borders of limits of today's world. Disrupts conventionally perceived boundaries and opens the taboos which are crucial to the society. She is focused on the immediate social facts but also in to immutable givens of the human soul, archetypes and mystery.[2]

Darina Alster is visual artist, performer, publisher, curator and pedagog. She lives and works in Prague. She is mostly working with performance, spoken word, sound and video. Main topics of her artistic interest are Time, Identity and Relationships. In her performances, she exceeds borders of known reality , interupting real situations with unknown and iracional things, then they will become the subconscious. She is mostly experimenting with new media, combine them with archaic medias, as a Astrology, Tarot, Mythology, Fairytales or other kinds of Archetypes. Her known projects are: Treasure, Piet, Personal Tarot, Naked Lunch, Bianca Braselli, Fembot, Thelematrix, Videoautomat, Memorial to victims of Capitalism, Imago Dei, The way of performance, Videoaltar, Dark Madona, Modern forms of invocating reality, Theatrum Mundi, Tension X, Dark Mirror, Earth Versions

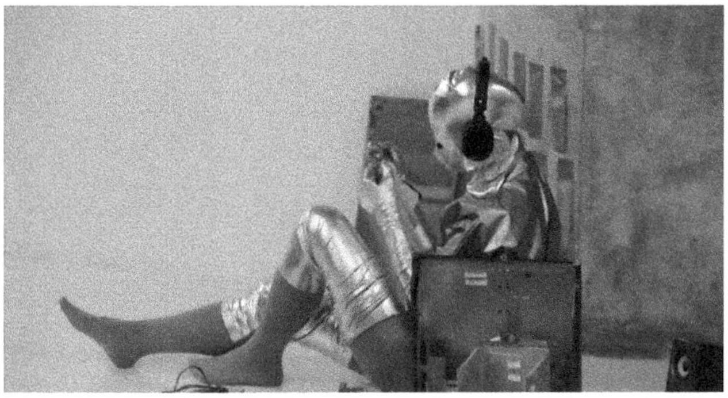

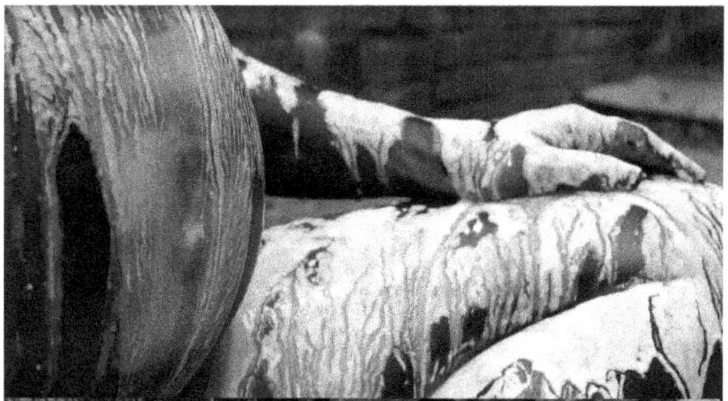

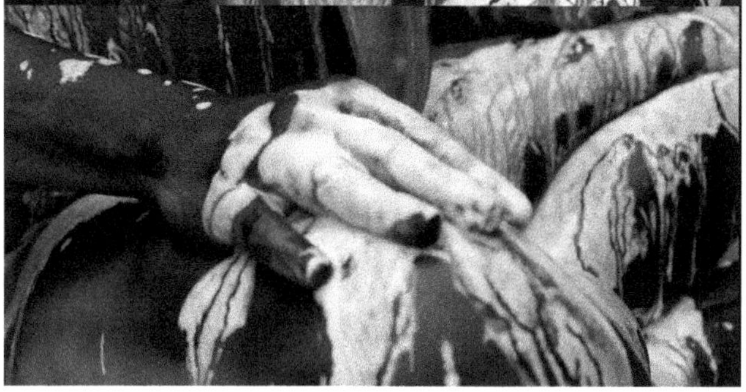

URL:
darina.alster.tumblr.com,

http://www.artlist.cz/en/darina-alster-105731/

REFERENCES

1. Donna Haraway, 1991, "A Cyborg Manifesto: Science, Technology, and Socialist-Feminism in the Late Twentieth Century," in *Simians, Cyborgs and Women: The Reinvention of Nature* (New York; Routledge)
2. Martin Klimeš, 2017, http://bludnykamen.cz/bk/darina-alster-tension/
3. Starhawk,1997, Dreaming the Dark: Magic, Sex and Politics, Boston, Beacon Press.

Prey: Digital Storytelling

Tiffany Sanchez
Texas A&M University
College Station, TX
tiffany@arch.tamu.edu

Jinsil Hwaryoung Seo
Texas A&M University
College Station, TX
hwaryoung@tamu.edu

ABSTRACT
Prey is a reinvention of lucid childhood dreamscapes and a recreation of imaginary entities made incarnate in the form of three interactive novels. The stories embedded within must be coaxed using touch, rather than follow the contemporary tradition of reading text. Prey uses this natural and intimate gesture to guide mindful interaction with personally meaningful artifacts. Technology lives quietly in the background, allowing users to reflect directly on the rich materiality of the piece and their own sensorial experiences without distraction.

Author Keywords
Organic; interactive; immersive; hybrid art; touch

ACM Classification Keywords
J.5 Arts And Humanities; Fine Arts

INTRODUCTION
Societies across the globe seem intent on moving technologically forward while increasingly synthesizing urban life, as if the only way to move forward is to leave all else behind. As artists, researchers, and makers, we pick apart existing paradigms to recreate realities instinctually. We are not predetermined to continue down this path, abandoning Nature or our natural selves, in pursuit of progress. Rather, we may seek to preserve our bodily experiences and evolve through our emerging technologies.

The world and its inhabitants are endlessly de/composing around us. The main artist, Tiffany Sanchez's hybrid practice embodies this notion.

> *"I de/compose organic and synthetic forms, breaking down and reassembling the aged with the new, in pursuit of hybrid evolution and the preservation of experiential artifacts. I seek to preserve, share, and overwrite memory through the use of meaningful materials and mindful interaction. By integrating traditional craft and physical computing methodologies, I give life to experimental art objects, creating tangible memories, sensorial vignettes bridging body, nature, and technology. Prey is my most recent embodiment of this practice."*

C&C '17, June 27-30, 2017, Singapore, Singapore

ACM ISBN 978-1-4503-4403-6/17/06.
http://dx.doi.org/10.1145/3059454.3059501

PROJECT DESCRIPTION
At first glance, *Prey* appears as a small collection of standard vintage volumes. Once their worn leather covers are opened, however, each reveals a handcrafted vignette carefully embedded within gilded pages lined with fur [Figure 1, Figure 2]. As you run your hands across their sumptuous bodies, a warm light responds to your every touch and gently illuminates the delicate assemblages of natural artifacts encased within. The longer you soothe and stroke each novel, the more each narrative is revealed.

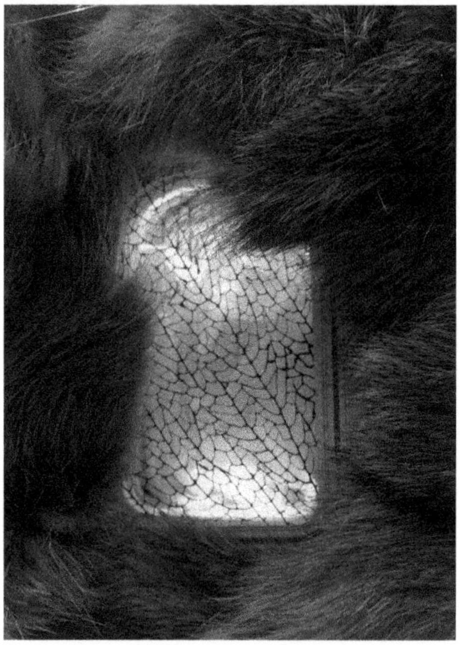

Figure 1. View of embedded vignette lined in rabbit fur comprised of snake skin and small fragments of egg shells.

Prey is the product of traditional bookbinding practices and physical computing methodologies. While their design is driven by a deeply visceral aesthetic, each novel hosts touch responsive led illumination and pressure sensitive skins mapped to an Arduino© LilyPad board [Figure 3]. These carefully custom fitted digital components are sewn into the pages of worn vintage photo albums and serve to augment an assortment of scavenged materials including bones, snakeskin, and fur.

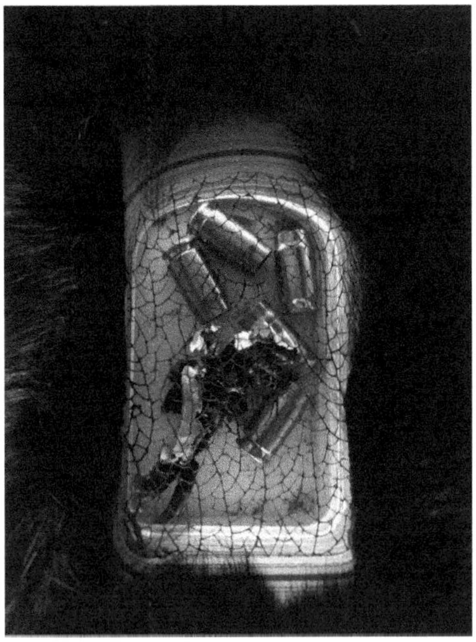

Figure 2. View of embedded vignette lined in rabbit fur comprised of vulture vertebrae and bullet casings.

The process of design and fabrication for each novel was a continuous unearthing of uncanny vestiges, childhood memories of innocence and curiosity entwined with the dark stain of abuse.

"As a child, I believed I was living in a world where you must eat or be eaten. And I no longer wished merely

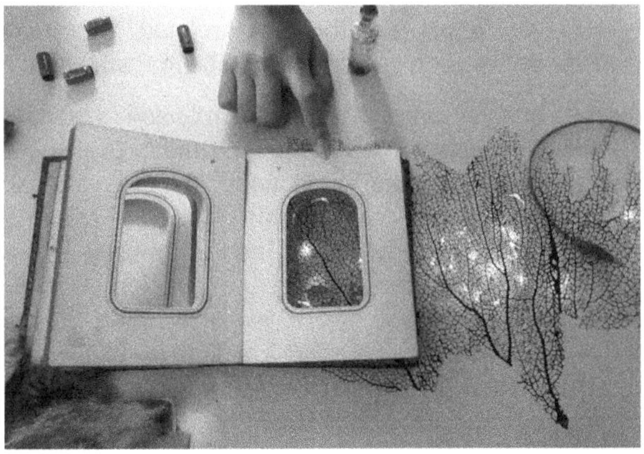

Figure 3. The concept of seamless integration of interactive technologies with natural artifacts was integral even at the early stages of development including establishing palette of materials and prototyping. The array of materials above includes fragments of egg shell, LEDs, and dried sea fan.

to become someone else's Prey. I learned to adapt. I found comfort in books and solitary exploration. Using my cache of natural artifacts, a practice that continues to haunt my adult life, I created my own imagined sanctuaries. By my hands, they became portals to new worlds, almost sentient in their ability to give me solace."

IMPLEMENTATION

We embedded into each novel a pressure sensitive page comprised of 3M Velostat sheets, a piezoresistive material. Its electrical resistance decreases when pressure is applied across its surface. When sandwiched between two conductive layers, it is able to act as both a pressure and bend sensor. By adding the second sensor, we were able to capture various qualities of touch.

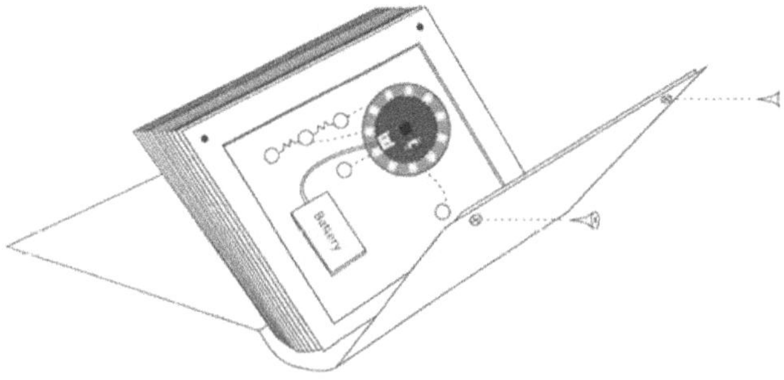

Figure 4. Soft circuit placement in *Prey*

The soft circuitry was carefully integrated into the book structure [Figure 4]. Two glowing LEDs, embedded into the top and the bottom of the vignette within each book, are programmed to increase and decrease in intensity according to the quality of touch detected by the sensor [Figure 5]. The gentle illumination, reminiscent of breathing, guides the reader deeper and deeper into the vignette, gradually revealing the intimate childhood memories of the lead artist captured and preserved within its pages.

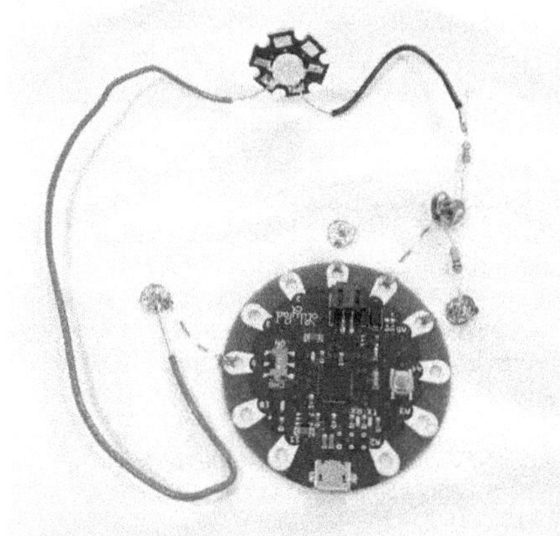

Figure 5. LED Connection in *Prey*

Yarncraft and Cognition: An Art Installation

Kathleen Quitmeyer
Well Read Panda
Singapore
Kathleen.quitmeyer@gmail.com

Andrew Quitmeyer
National University of Singapore
Singapore
andy@quitmeyer.org

ABSTRACT
The popularity of knitting and crochet, or yarncraft, is on the ascent. As more people discover its pleasures, enthusiasts and neuroscientists are also realizing that crafting with yarn elicits soothing and therapeutic effects. The meditative aspects of knitting and crochet are already familiar to the legions of yarncrafters, but recognition of the neuroscience of yarncraft is a relatively recent phenomenon. This work proposes to embody the relationship between yarncraft and its neurological benefits with a physical art project. This project will take the form of a large crocheted e-textile brain sculpture with embedded LEDs whose illumination is controlled live by a brain-computer interface worn by a yarncrafting practitioner. This sculpture visualizes the changes in the neurology of the yarncrafter.

Author Keywords
Yarncraft; knitting; crochet; eeg; brain-computer interface; cognition; e-textile; soft-circuit; meditation; stress-reduction;

ACM Classification Keywords
H.5.m. Information interfaces and presentation (e.g., HCI): Miscellaneous;

MOTIVATION AND THEORY
Our ancestors have known for generations that repetitive activities such as knitting and crochet can be very calming, and these experiences are gaining widespread recognition. For example, there are currently many therapeutic programs incorporating yarncraft, such as a smoking cessation program in Toronto called *Knit to Quit*[3] and *Knitting Behind Bars*, a group that helps prisoners cope with the difficulties of incarceration by pursuing "the zen of knitting"[4].

While pioneering therapeutic groups enjoy anecdotal success by pursuing stress relief through yarncraft, researchers publish articles in scientific journals on similarly beneficial neurological outcomes. Dr. Herbert Benson reports that repetitive activities like knitting can elicit what he calls the "relaxation response," a meditative state that leaves practitioners with a quieter, less troubled mind.[6] The Mayo Clinic Study of Aging finds that "cognitive activities such as... craft activities (quilting, knitting, etc.)... were associated with 30% to 50% reduced odds of having MCI [mild cognitive impairment among elderly people]" [2]. In another study of British crafters,

> ...Respondents attributed a number of psychological benefits to the knitting process, coming from its rhythmic and repetitive nature, which induced feelings of calm and relaxation... Knitting was perceived by respondents to improve their thinking, concentration, problem-solving abilities and memory [5].

Although formal studies with MRIs displaying the brain activity of yarncrafters do not seem to be available yet, one might presume that yarncrafters experiencing the relaxation response would enter a neurological experience comparable to that of a meditator, who also benefits from the relaxation response. Scientists such as Boccia analyze the state of meditators' brains with MRIs and other brain-imaging mechanisms.[1]

DESCRIPTION
I would like to express the pleasure and relaxation I personally derive from yarncraft through yarncraft itself.

I envision a mixed-media, e-textile, interactive sculpture that would illustrate the neurological benefits of yarncraft. It will be a crocheted, simplified model of a brain, probably about half a meter in length. I will embed LEDs into the structure of the brain that would light up in areas that are stimulated by the meditative process of knitting or crochet. This project will include live data visualization from the brain of a practicing yarncrafter. The activity of the LEDs will correspond to the brain activity of an actual yarncrafter wearing a low-cost, accessible EEG (electroencephalogram) or a BCI (brain-computer interface) such as OpenBCI or Muse. I plan to model the crafting-brain connection myself by wearing the EEG/BCI while yarncrafting. In this more interactive format, the project would require a booth or similar small area, probably no more than 3 meters by 3 meters, with a few chairs, a plinth, and a power source. Illumination patterns would be based on the findings of

C&C '17, June 27-30, 2017, Singapore, Singapore

ACM ISBN 978-1-4503-4403-6/17/06.
http://dx.doi.org/10.1145/3059454.3059502

Boccia's meta-analysis of MRIs of meditating minds experiencing the relaxation response.[1] Participation with the project would most likely be limited to spectators' interactions with the artwork, such as looking at the crafted brain, touching it, and maybe doing some yarncraft while wearing a BCI if they know how to knit or crochet. I do not envision teaching spectators how to knit or crochet as part of this project, as that would be fairly complex and take quite a bit of time. Additionally, I think that only advanced yarncrafters can experience the "flow" that leads to meditative enjoyment while crafting.

ARTIST PROFILE

Kathleen Quitmeyer is a librarian and proponent of knitting and crochet. She has contributed to drives that espouse the health benefits of yarn craft such as The National Yarn Council's campaign "When Life Gives You Lemons" (http://www.craftyarncouncil.com/MEGAlemondrive). She has an Etsy shop at https://www.etsy.com/shop/WellReadPanda. She is currently based in Singapore pursuing volunteer work concerning mental health, crafts, and the environment. Ms. Quitmeyer can be reached at Kathleen.quitmeyer@gmail.com or at +65-9081-6509.

REFERENCES

1. Maddalena Boccia, Laura Piccardi, and Paola Guariglia. 2015. The Meditative Mind: A Comprehensive Meta-Analysis of MRI Studies. *BioMed research international* 2015: 419808. https://doi.org/10.1155/2015/419808
2. Yonas E. Geda, Hillary M. Topazian, Robert A. Lewis, Rosebud O. Roberts, David S. Knopman, V. Shane Pankratz, Teresa J. H. Christianson, Bradley F. Boeve, Eric G. Tangalos, Robert J. Ivnik, Ronald C. Petersen, and Ronald C Petersen. 2011. Engaging in Cognitive Activities, Aging, and Mild Cognitive Impairment: A Population-Based Study. *The Journal of Neuropsychiatry and Clinical Neurosciences* 23, 2: 149–154. https://doi.org/10.1176/jnp.23.2.jnp149
3. Jane Brody. 2016. The Health Benefits of Knitting. *The New York Times*. Retrieved January 12, 2017 from http://well.blogs.nytimes.com/2016/01/25/the-health-benefits-of-knitting/?_r=1
4. Lynn Zwerling. 2014. Knitting Behind Bars. Retrieved January 12, 2017 from http://knittingbehindbars.blogspot.sg/
5. Jill Riley, Betsan Corkhill, and Clare Morris. 2013. The benefits of knitting for personal and social wellbeing in adulthood: findings from an international survey. *The British Journal of Occupational Therapy* 76, 2: 50–57. https://doi.org/10.4276/030802213X13603244419077
6. Sara Martin. 2008. The power of the relaxation response. *American Psychological Association Monitor on Psychology* 39, 9: 32. Retrieved January 12, 2017 from http://www.apa.org/monitor/2008/10/relaxation.aspx

Three Exercises for the Visual Sensorium

Diana Lindbjerg
Trondheim Academy of Fine Art, NTNU
Trondheim, Norway
Mail@dlindbjerg.com

ABSTRACT

We rely on apparatuses and technology to enlarge, enhance and document our visual surroundings such as microscopes, telescopes, cameras and computational software.

These tools allow us to enhance what is not visible to the naked eye due to size, distance or duration. The apparatus produces objective measurements and allow for us to make documents that we can fix, share and discuss in an extended timespan.

If the seemingly objective quality of an apparatus is not combined with an understanding of the limitations it presents we face a kind of blindness. The limitations of an apparatus can be extended to the subjective qualities of our senses, which we cannot separate ourselves from.

Three Exercises for the Visual Sensorium examines how we can tune or perception and transform the subconscious registrations of our sensorium into conscious observations.

Author Keywords

Artistic Research; Colour Theory; Chemistry; Photography.

ACM Classification Keywords

Experimentation; Human Factors; Performance.

C&C '17, June 27-30, 2017, Singapore, Singapore

ACM ISBN 978-1-4503-4403-6/17/06.
http://dx.doi.org/10.1145/3059454.3059503

INTRODUCTION

The performance focuses on what we can observe with our sensorium but also responds to the limitations by using tools to enhance and transform the experience from one sense, visual to audible and thereby making it detectable again.

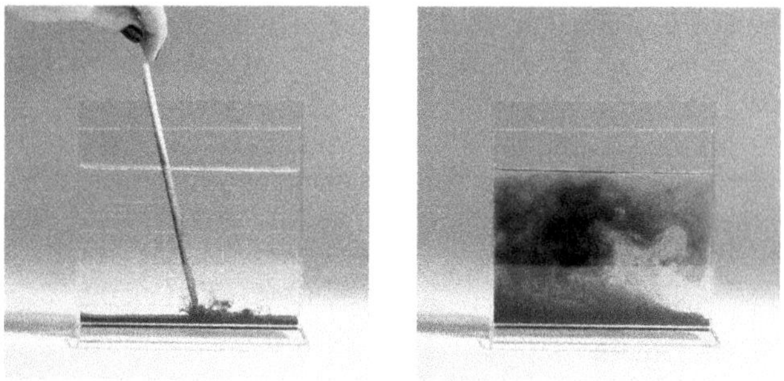

Figure 1: Exercise No. 2 Agitating / Precipitating blue. Prussian blue pigment in water. The agitated pigment reveals the motion in the water and the transformation of the liquid from transparent to opaque to transparent.

"Light is invisible, and only becomes visible when it encounters matter."(Boëtius, 1998)

I propose that the same can be said for transferable knowledge and understanding. Knowledge only becomes understanding when it is applied to something other than itself. I repeat Knowledge only becomes understanding when it is applied to something other than itself.

We rely on apparatuses and technology to enlarge, enhance and document our visual surroundings such as microscopes, telescopes, cameras and computational software. These tools allow us to enhance what is not visible to the naked eye due to size, distance or duration. The apparatus produces objective measurements and allow for us to make documents that we can fix, share and discuss in an extended timespan.

"The apparatus does as the photographer desires, but the photographer can only desire what the apparatus can do"(Flusser, Roth, & Poster, 2011, p. 20)

If the seemingly objective quality of an apparatus is not combined with an understanding of the limitations it presents we face a kind of blindness.

The limitations of an apparatus can be extended to the subjective qualities of our senses, which we cannot separate ourselves from.

Three exercises for the visual sensorium is an invitation to practice subtle visual perception and explore the limitations of our built in apparatus, the sensorium and the subjective vision that we use to encounter all other apparatus with.

I use ordinary materials to perform these exercises and engage with the audience in conversations about the different aspects of the project. One of the exercises will be about making tea. In collaboration with the audience I will be making black tea and performing a phenomenon called a bathochromic shift. By adding lemon to the black tea and observe the subtle change of the colour. There is a solid explanation to the chemical process that happens but since I am not a chemist I will refrain from reciting this here. My interest lies in appreciation of change in everyday phenomena.

Change happens before our eyes all the time, but often our brain detects this and discard the information as superfluous to our consciousness and therefore it remains in our subconscious. By directing the attention of the audience to this change in the tea we will begin a tuning of our sensorium that will allow us to transform the subconscious registrations into conscious observations.

REFERENCES

1. Boëtius, H. L., Marie louise; Lefèvre, Marie Louise (Writer). (1998). Light Darkness & Colours - Goethes Theory. In L. L. Møller (Producer): Magic hour film.
2. Flusser, V., Roth, N. A., & Poster, M. (2011). *Into the universe of technical images* (Vol. v. 32). Minneapolis: University of Minnesota Press.

No Such Luck

Hans Tan
University of Singapore
Division of Industrial Design
School of Design & Environment
4 Architecture Drive,
Singapore 117566
hans@nus.edu.sg

ABSTRACT

No Such Luck is an augmented fortune cat that responds the proximity of visitors in front of it. In an exhibition/gallery context, the artifact will beckon frenetically fast to "increase its fortune" and attract viewership, but slow down to a relaxed motion when a visitor gets up close. Although the symbolic representations of the traditional fortune cat are removed with the artifact, the distinct beckoning swing of the electromagnet pendulum gives us an uncanny user experience correlated to the lucky charm prevalent in many parts of Asia.

Author Keywords
Lucky cat; artwork; user experience; gesture.

ACM Classification Keywords
J.5. Arts and Humanities.

ARTWORK TITLE
No Such Luck

BACKGROUND
The fortune cat, or 招财猫 in mandarin or *Maneki-neko* in Japanese, is the common cat figurine that is believed to bring good luck to the owner. The figurine depicts a cat beckoning with an upright paw, and is usually displayed in shops, restaurants and other businesses, often at the entrance, reception, or at the point of sale counters. Most of these figurines used today are electric or battery-powered and have a distinctive slow-moving paw beckoning.

The clever yet economical use of electromagnet principles to create a perpetual pendulum swing gives the fortune cat its distinctive beckoning swing (for example, the swing motion will be very different if it was driven by a servo motor). The cat figurine with its paw's beckoning is believed to bring in customers, luck, and wealth.

C&C '17, June 27-30, 2017, Singapore, Singapore
ACM 978-1-4503-4403-6/17/06.
http://dx.doi.org/10.1145/3059454.3059504

Figure 1. Fortune Cat found in shop in Singapore

ARTWORK DESCRIPTION
No Such Luck is an interactive artifact comprising of a see-through glass enclosure that houses an electro magnetic pendulum connected to an oscillating arm that protrudes out of one side of the jar. An ultrasonic proximity sensor connected to the electromagnetic pendulum detects the presence and distance of a visitor/s in front of the artifact, and the oscillating arm adjusts its period (time taken for an oscillation to occur) according to the distance of the visitor.

ARTWORK CONCEPT
The artwork investigates the semantics of a symbolic (non-human) gesture, focusing on the awkward intersection between superstition and logic. The rationality of a data driven intervention augments an irrational belief.

The "see through" artifact lays bare the electro magnetic pendulum that is used in fortune cats to swing its beckoning paw, uncovering the little-known inner workings behind the distinctive beckoning gesture of a fortune cat. The abstraction of its overall form removes the visual representation of a cat reveals the essence of the gestural movement.

In the absence of visitors within the range of the artifact, the oscillating "gesture" will be incited to speed up and appear more hardworking an anxious. As a visitor/s approaches it, the "gesture" will start to slow down correspondingly and appear more relaxed, more so when the visitor is up close inspecting its inner workings.

ARTWORK TYPE

Single interactive artifact

ARTWORK PRESENTATION

The artifact should be placed on a plinth 90-100cm high with a square cross section that is slightly bigger that the artwork's footprint.

A space of about 3-4 meters in length facing the artifact should be uninterrupted. This provides the space for a proximity sensor in the artwork to detect the distance of the closest visitor from it.

Figure 2. ***No Such Luck*** **interactive artifact.**

AUTHOR PROFILE

Name

Hans Tan

Designation

Assistant Professor, Division of Industrial Design, School of Design and Environment, National University of Singapore

Website

www.hanstan.net

Short bio

Hans Tan is a designer and an educator based in Singapore. He is an assistant professor at the Division of Industrial Design, National University of Singapore, and the founder of Hans Tan Studio. His work is occupied with the authenticity of the contemporary design artifact being a deliberate gesticulation of material culture. He deploys design as medium, making use of utility as a pretext to comment on design and its industry as a phenomenon. With a keen interest in developing materials and processes, he explores ideas concerning identity, heritage, and consumption.

Track record

In 2009, Hans was nominated for the Design Miami Designers of the Future Award and was spotted by Designnet magazine Korea as one of 36 Young Asian Designers. He was a winner of the Martell Rising Personalities Award 2009, which honours individuals from different creative fields who are passionately driven to push beyond the boundaries of success. His works have been shown in exhibitions such as "Singletown" at the Venice Biennale, "Surface art/design" in Dortmund and Cologne, "No Boundaries" at ArtStage Singapore, and "Beauty" at the Cooper Hewitt Design Triennial, Smithsonian Design Museum New York. His work, *Spotted Nyonya*, was awarded with the distinction of "Les Découvertes" (best innovative product) at the fall edition of Maison et Objet 2012 in Paris, and has been conferred Design of the Year at the President's Design Award 2012, Singapore's most prestigious design accolade. In 2013, he was named as one of Perspective's 40 under 40, an award that recognizes design talent from the Asia- Pacific region, and in 2015 won the President's Design Award Design of the Year for the second time with *Pour*. His works are in the permanent collections of M+ museum for visual culture, Hong Kong, and the Copper Hewitt, Smithsonian Design Museum, New York. He is a also a three-time recipient of the NUS university level annual excellence teaching award.

Previous Exhibitions (Recent 2 years)

2016/12 Shifting Objectives, M+ Museum, Hong Kong
2016/10 Beauty, San Jose Museum or Art, San Jose
2016/09 Porcelain Festival, Supermama @ Gillman Barracks, Singapore
2016/02 Beauty, Cooper Hewitt, Smithsonian Design Museum, New York
2016/02 Local Icons East/West. MAXXI Museo, Rome.
2015/07 Singapore Souvenirs 2015, National Design Centre
2015/04 The Alchemist, Milan Design Week.
2015/05 Rising Asian Stars, Creative Taiwan Expo
2015/04 Bank of Kinectic, Singapore Inside Out, Beijing, London, New York.

A Tangible Interface for Contemporary Wayang Kulit

Miguel Escobar Varela
National University of Singapore
m.escobar@nus.edu.sg

Daniel Sim Yong En
National University of Singapore
a0086915@u.nus.edu

ABSTRACT
Digital Archives cannot capture certain aspects that are fundamental to theatrical performances: embodiment, co-presence and the cultural history of specific objects. A Tangible User Interface (TUI) was developed using Arduino components, Node.js and movement conventions from contemporary Javanese shadow puppetry in order to craft a user experience that communicates aspects of performance that are lost in digitization.

Author Keywords
Tangible User Interfaces, Wayang Kulit, theatre, Indonesia.

ACM Classification Keywords
H.5.2 User Interfaces.

INTRODUCTION
The creation and analysis of digital collections is a key aspect of the digital humanities. Deciding what to archive, how to organize the documents, and how to present them to the public are never easy questions. But in the case of theatre and performance archives, these questions are especially complex since theatre performances are necessarily transient and they depend on the embodied co-presence of actors and spectators. In order to document the embodied and ephemeral nature of theatre performances, digital archives often try to include a wide array of documents (video recordings, photographs, motion capture data, 3d models of theatrical spaces and technical scripts). The makers of digital theatre archives are at pains to contextualize their materials and account for aspects that cannot be easily documented and transmitted. Can interaction design help communicate these aspects? Is it possible to imagine and construct interfaces that can communicate cultural context, transcending the limitations of a computer screen, mouse and keyboard?

C&C 2017, June 27–30, 2017, Singapore.
ACM ISBN 978-1-4503-4403-6/17/06.
http://dx.doi.org/10.1145/3059454.3059505

To investigate these questions within the context of an Indonesian performance archive, we developed a Tangible User Interface (TUI) using open source hardware (Arduino microcontrollers and an array of sensors), a web platform (Node.js and socket.io), and culturally-coded objects that are important for the performances in the archive. This interface was developed as an interactive artwork for educational museums and as a thought experiment on how tangible, culturally-specific interfaces can constitute instances of academic research outputs in the digital humanities.

The archive in question is the Contemporary Wayang Archive (CWA, http://cwa-web.org), a collection of digital recordings and metadata pertaining to Javanese *wayang kulit* (shadow puppetry), which we have been developing with our collaborators at the National University of Singapore since 2012. *Wayang kulit* is the oldest theatre form of Indonesia and one of the most important theatre traditions of Southeast Asia. It consists of a form of puppetry where a *dalang* (narrator-puppeteer) singlehandedly moves all the puppets, speaks all the character parts, jokes with the audience and directs the musicians. He is at the same time a puppeteer, a storyteller, an orchestra conductor and a stand-up comedian. In order to communicate with the audience and the orchestra, he uses different objects in order to control the progression of the story. For this project, we wired different sensors into these objects in order to develop a TUI that recreates the spatial setup of a conventional *wayang* performance and three key material components of this setup:

- A *kerlir* or screen where videos from the CWA are projected.
- The *kayon.* This puppet is shaped like a leaf and it has different narrative functions. In between scenes, the *dalang* rotates it around its axis and places it on a banana log at a specific angle (either 45°, 90° or 135°) to indicate the progression of the story. This visual cue is important for audience members that don't watch the entire show. A conventional performance lasts eight hours and the audience members often come and go, drifting in and out of attention. Depending on the specific angle of the *kayon*, knowing audience members can estimate the specific moment in the development of the performance (which is divided into three main acts). For my interface, we used an

Inertial Measurement Unit (IMU) and a wireless sensor in order to detect rotation (angular velocity) in the puppet. By rotating an actual puppet, users of this interactive artwork can navigate to a different digital video in the collection.

- The *cempala.* By hitting this wooden mallet against the puppet chest, the *dalang* cues the musicians to start and stop the musical accompaniment. For the interactive artwork, we wired the *cempala* to a Piezoelectric sensor to measure vibration. When the users of the artwork knock the *cempala* against a box that mimics the puppet chest, they can start and stop the videos and additional contextual information appears on the projection screen.

The usage of these objects is not exactly the same in this interactive artwork display as it is in an actual *wayang* performance. But it can invite users to think about the importance of materiality and embodiment for this particular theatre tradition.

ARTIST BIOGRAPHIES:

Miguel Escobar Varela has worked as a theatre artists, web programmer and translator in Mexico, The Netherlands, Singapore and Indonesia. He is Assistant Professor of Theatre Studies at the National University of Singapore. More information at miguelescobar.com

Daniel Sim Yong En is currently completing a BA in Theatre Studies at the National University of Singapore. He has worked in the design and construction of sets for several theatre companies in Singapore, including Wild Rice and The Finger Players.

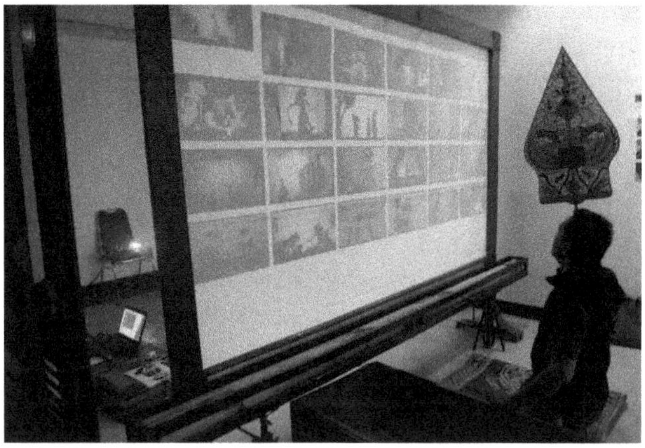

A video of the artwork is available here: https://vimeo.com/170186057

Aquatocene / Subaquatic Quest for Serenity

Robertina Šebjanič
Freelance, artist & researcher
Ljubljana, Slovenia, Europe
robertina.sebjanic@gmail.com

ABSTRACT
»**Aquatocene / The subaquatic quest for serenity**« investigates the phenomenon of underwater noise pollution created by humankind in the seas and oceans. The sound compositions are a re-mix between the bioacoustics of marine life (shrimps, fish, sea urchins etc.), the aquatic acoustics and the presence of human generated noise in the world's oceans and seas.

Author Keywords
Aquatocene; underwater noise pollution; bioacoustics; aquatic acoustics; aural

ACM Classification Keywords
K.4.m Computers and Society: Miscellaneous

INTRODUCTION
Aquatocene / Subaquatic quest for serenity
Is a project by Robertina Šebjanič

The audio compositions of the subaquatic soundscape encourage us to reflect upon the anthropogenic sonic impact on the underwater habitat and marine life, as well as illuminate awareness and underscore the importance of maintaining safe sound environments for animals living in the world's oceans, seas, lakes and rivers.

Over the last few years Robertina has made a number of recordings using hydrophones in different locations around the globe. Underwater noise effects a great number of marine life forms which depend on the sub-aquatic sonic environment to survive.
Despite the broad availability of popular aquatic sounds, we aren't really aware that the underwater soundscape is as rich as the one heard by terrestrial creatures above water. Aside from lacking experience in terms of the fascinating diversity of marine sound, we are also not aware that sonic pollution caused by humans is already changing the soundscape of the waters and even the communication of its inhabitants.

C&C '17, June 27-30, 2017, Singapore, Singapore
ACM 978-1-4503-4403-6/17/06.
http://dx.doi.org/10.1145/3059454.3059506

When we look up to the sky, look into space and wonder about what is up there we sometimes forget that there is still a lot left for us to explore on the planet we live on. We know more about space than we know about the world's seas and oceans, especially when it comes to sound perception underwater. We are usually unaware of the vibrant underwater acoustics, the sounds of the ocean's depths. Our familiarity with these sounds is usually limited to the sound of a wave crashing into land. Whales, shrimp, seals, dolphins, and a variety of other creatures of the deep live in a watery sonic environment.
Technological interventions into the ocean soundscape by ships, sonars and sound cannons (used in oil exploration) can create huge disturbances in fragile marine habitats and have been connected to a number of effects ranging from the beaching of whales to the »Lombard effect« where certain species themselves become louder to overcome background noise, thereby gradually increasing the intensity of the entire habitat.
Water habitats cover over 70% of the Earth's surface. 97% of the world's water is saltwater, 2% is fresh water in the form of ice and only the remaining 1% is drinking water, which is distributed around the planet very unevenly. The exploration of an ecosystem requires detailed study and observation. The ocean is the most complex, challenging, and harsh environment on Earth and accessing it requires specially designed tools and technology. The technological advances have finally reached the point 50 years ago that enables us to examine the ocean in a systematic, scientific, and non invasive way. Our ability to observe the ocean's environment and its resident creatures has finally caught up with our imaginations and helped us to understand it in ways we could not even envision them before.

The lively sound image of the underwater environments, rivers, lakes, seas and oceans still represents the big unknown for the majority. In recent decades, advanced tools and the latest technology enabled us to explore underwater environments in a systematic, scientifically relevant and non-invasive way. We are thus able to identify the anthropogenic disturbances and noise that affect the underwater environment, as well as analyze their impacts.

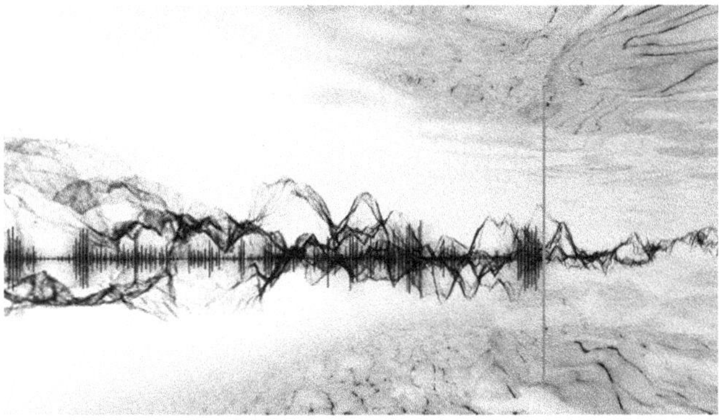

Figure 1. Aquatocene by Robertina Šebjanič.

Figure 2. Aquatocene, audio visual performance by Robertina Šebjanič and guest Miha Ciglar at Kiblix festival in 2016 || photo by Kiblix archive

Figure 3. Aquatocene, and audio – visual performance and lecture by Robertina Šebjanič at Kosmica festival, at Laboratorio Arte Alameda at Mexico City || photo by Kosmica archive

ACKNOWLEDGMENTS

Aquatocene / Subaquatic quest for serenity

Artist (development / sound recording / sound editing): Robertina Šebjanič

Production support: Kibla, Bunker, Zavod Praksa, Piksel festival, 1.camp residency program at Roscoff Marine Station

Special thanks to: Annick Bureaud, Miha Ciglar, Acouspade™Directional Speaker, MY studio- Yann Jaffiol, UR Institute, Slavko Glamočanin, PORTIZMIR#3

Project was supported by the Ministry of Culture of the Republic of Slovenia and MOL – Department for Culture, Fondation Daniel et Nina Carasso

What is the Human? Imagining the Self as Post-human.

Anatol Bologan
Department of Visualization
Texas A&M University
College Station, USA
abologan@tamu.edu

Jinsil Hwaryoung Seo
Department of Visualization
Texas A&M University
College Station, USA
hwaryoung@tamu.edu

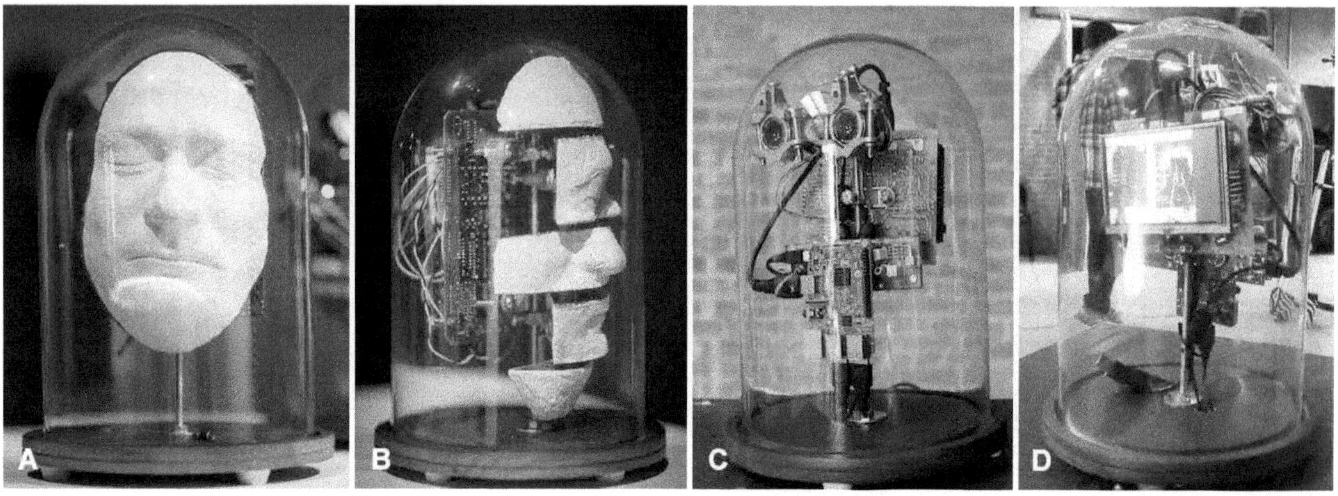

Figure 1. A) Post-human prototype 01, B) Post-human prototype 02, C) Front of Post-human prototype 03, D) Back of Prototype 03

ABSTRACT

This project consists of a series of three primary media sculptures that progressively remove the human form and replace it with technology. The organic human forms have no active functionality and are juxtaposed with manufactured technological components that provide the interactive aspect of the artwork. The facial molds resemble "death masks" that can be found in art museums and anthropological collections, but are made "alive" with recycled technology. The intention of the artists is to evoke exploration, captivation and fantasy from the viewer as he or she explores these interactive sculptures. The artwork questions as well as highlights the importance of technology as part of our contemporary culture and consciousness and intends to engage in the discourse of human versus cyborg, technicism versus humanism.

Author Keywords

interactive art; post-human; human perception; human computer interaction; embodiment.

ACM Classification Keywords

J.5 Arts And Humanities; Fine Arts.

C&C '17, June 27-30, 2017, Singapore, Singapore
ACM 978-1-4503-4403-6/17/06.
http://dx.doi.org/10.1145/3059454.3059507

INTRODUCTION

We present a series of three media sculptures that explore the transition and duality of human and machine where the human form is continuously removed in an evolution and expansion of technology. The sculptures form a series of physical and responsive artworks that explore the question: "What is the human in the context of the post-human"? In other words, what is the remaining human element in a world that has moved past the "human" as we know it? We are interested in colliding the human anatomical form and elements of recycled technology as if they belong together.

The human form represents the lead artist as a self-portrait, depicted in a quest to become post-human (Fig. 2). We focused on the evolving process of this project and produced three sculptures (prototypes). In the process, we experimented with various electronic components juxtaposing them with different forms of human face. The *first prototype* consists primarily of a mold of the face with an integrated nonfunctioning and minimalist computer component. The *second prototype* creates a fragmented human face, where each of the human senses are broken up in layers of perception and are connected with a digital consciousness represented by the active technology that increased in capacity rom the previous iteration, LED lights are acting as visual feedback of the simulated digital brain activity. By the time the third prototype is introduced, there is no visual representation of the human form left. We can only observe a collection of computer boards and a pair of

Figure 2. Post-human prototype 01.

video cameras facing the viewer. The *third prototype* has the ability of seeing and interpreting the objects it observes. As the viewers can see on the back of the head prototype where the visual cortex would be, they can see what the cyborg can see.

The intention of this project is to evoke exploration, captivation and fantasy as described by Brigid Costello and Ernest Edmonds in their paper "A Study in Play, Pleasure and Interaction Design" 2007. The audience is encouraged to explore the space as they join the artists on their quest on imagining a post-human self by interacting with the sculptures and analyzing the visual research depicted in the flatwork that accompanies them.

POST-HUMAN PROTOTYPE 01

The prototype is displayed in a glass dome on a small pedestal as often can be seen in museums or special collections. We have used traditional display techniques not only to present the artwork at a gallery setting, but also to give it an aura of "scientific truth" (Fig. 1, A).

POST-HUMAN PROTOTYPE 02

Building on the previous project, our second iteration is called "Post-human Prototype 02" (Fig. 1, B) and is intended to expand on and continue the theme of the series. We are visually exploring the idea of singularity encapsulated in one "deconstructed" facial form that itself symbolically represents human senses and ways of human communication. The human face is partitioned in segments that all represent a multidimensional existence of human thought and consciousness that is connected to a computerized neural-network of microchips and semiconductors, representing a positronic or quantum computing brain. Each layer of the human face exposes the circuitry board that is an integral part of the human form as if the muscles, blood vessels, bone structures and the nervous system have been replaced by circuitry, metallic brackets and bolts, connected wires, resistors and blinking LED lights.

POST-HUMAN PROTOTYPE 03

The third iteration of the "Post-human prototype" is becoming more "advanced," even if only based on our contemporary perception of technology (Fig. 1, C, D.). The purpose of this "Prototype" is to explore the human visual perception mechanisms by rebuilding the path of visual stimuli and applying a "Top-Down" perception model to the result of the video output in what is designed to look like the human occipital cortex (Fig. 3). The main difference from the previous artworks in the series is that there is no human anatomical detail shown: the entire form is created using mechanical or electronic components. The human face is still prevalent in the visual perception of the piece due to the use of dual cameras, representing human eyes that are bracketed by aluminum hardware attached to the central core of the "prototype". The placement of the cameras in relationship to the boards and wires used to construct the model, create a visual resemblance to a humanoid robot and invokes an emotional connection of the viewer with the mechanical face. The design of the prototype is intended to explore human vision and perception in the context of a computer based neurological network system. We are exploring the human perception through the "digital eye": vision that is not intended to have a "clear and realistic" stereoscopic representation of reality. Instead we are more interested in infusing the image captured by the cameras with a visual parabola of what human perception is, or what it could be in the future "when we all become robots".

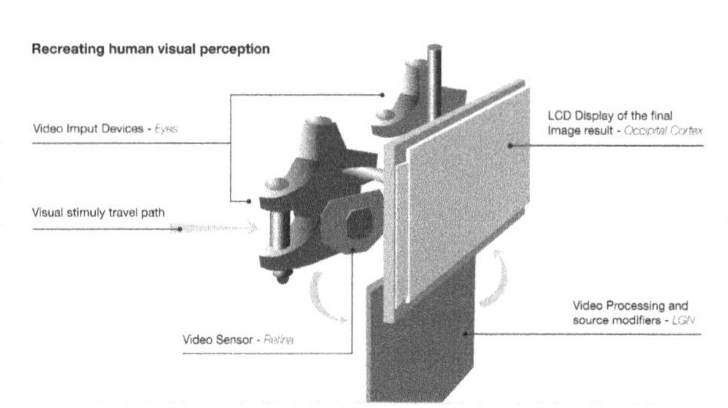

Figure 3. Post-human prototype 03.

CONCLUSION & FUTURE WORK

The artwork is intended to be presented as an experience that constitutes a series of concepts displayed as digital paintings, printed and hang on the walls surrounding the podiums displaying the interactive sculptures. While this current series of sculptures is mostly based on passive observation and is responsive by design, the fourth iteration that is currently being developed will provide the public with the ability to build their own version of the artwork out of a series of available components and therefore engaging them directly with the sculpture and providing a more personal experience of interaction with the concept of this project. The intent of the artists is to continue developing the visual aesthetical style that lands itself at the crossroads of artistic and scientific representation of the human. The body of work will expand into interactive installations that will encourage the audience to further engage with the artwork and with the concept of post-human.

REFERENCES

1. Braidotti R. The Posthuman. *Polity*. 2013.

2. Costello B., Edmonds E. A Study in Play, Pleasure and Interaction Design. *Designing pleasurable products and interfaces.*(2007), 76-91.

3. Grusin R. The Nonhuman Turn. *University Of Minnesota Press.* 2015

4. Haraway D. Simians, Cyborgs and Women. The reinvention of nature. *Routledge.* 1991.

5. Hayles K. How We Became Posthuman: Virtual Bodies in Cybernetics, Literature, and Informatics. *University Of Chicago Press.* 1999.

6. Hayles K. My Mother Was a Computer: Digital Subjects and Literary Texts. *University Of Chicago Press.* 2005.

7. Kac E. Signs of Life: Bio Art and Beyond. *MIT Press.* 2007.

8. Lippert-Rasmussen, et. al., The Posthuman Condition: Ethics, Aesthetics and Politics of Biotechnological Challenges. *Aarhus University Press.* 2011.

9. Lyotard J. Postmodern Fables. *University Of Minnesota Press.* 1999.

10. Wolfe C. What Is Posthumanism? *Univ Of Minnesota Press.* 2009.

Better Hands

Wallace S. Lages
Center for HCI, Virginia Tech,
School of Fine Arts, UFMG,
wlages@vt.edu

Pablo Gobira
Escola Guignard, UEMG
Belo Horizonte, Brazil
pa.gobira@uemg.br

Francisco Marinho
UFMG
Belo Horizonte, Brazil
fccm@ufmg.br

ABSTRACT
Better Hands (2017) is an interactive installation that explores the limits and the role of tools in the creative process. It questions the nature of authorship by bringing the interface closer to the body, while empowering it with embedded agency. The artwork invites us to reflect on the effect of modern technology on the basic act of creation and whether we control or are defined by it.

Author Keywords
Interactive art; robotic; simulation; dynamical system.

ACM Classification Keywords
J.5 Computer Applications: Arts and Humanities; I.2.9 Robotics: manipulators; I.6.8 Image Processing: Simulation and Modeling.

SHORT DESCRIPTION
Better Hands exposes the relationship between humans and technology in the creative process. The installation captures electric signals and inertial measurements from the arm of the interactor as raw input. The signals are then fed to discrete dynamical systems, which generate brush patterns, and moderate user input to the robotic arm. The arm holds a brush that strokes on a tablet, creating digital paintings.

CONCEPT
Better Hands originated from the author's research on human-computer interaction, art, and technology. The installation was developed remotely across the United States and Brazil, inspired on the role that tools have on the creative processes.

The duality between the mechanic and organic hands, evokes the constructive cycle of M. C. Escher *Drawing Hands* (1948) lithograph. However, instead of focusing on the metalinguistic criticism, *Better Hands* invites us to think about the effect of the interface on creativity and authorship. The title of the work is a reference to Max Barry's novel, *Machine Man* (2011), which reflects on the interdependency between humans and technology [1].

The concept realization contrasts the creative media of the modern artist (represented by the touch screen) with the most traditional and perhaps oldest artistic tool (the paintbrush). This brings into focus the question of whether there were any qualitative changes brought by technology.

Inasmuch as the robotic arm utilizes the interactor's input, one could inadvertently consider it a subservient tool. However, the mapping is not complete. The remaining space is filled by the robotic arm, which derives its own desires and ideas from the embedded dynamic processes. On the other hand, the bare-hand interface removes the physical feeling of holding a brush. This makes the connection intimate and intuitive, as the system transparently reacts to the interactor's movements.

The final visual production, thus, is not a result of either the interactor or robot alone. It is better understood as byproduct of the coupled intents of interactor and machine. The metalinguistic game not only invites a critical view of the creative production but also on the contemporary digital life, in which the interactor subjects itself to the artwork so that it can fulfill its role.

DISCUSSION
The work is related to central issues in human-robot interaction and robotic art. Is artificial creativity possible? Boden [2] discusses different ways in which computer creations could be considered creative, although they ultimately depend on deeper considerations regarding machine agency and consciousness. Even if the answer is negative, it is hard to argue against the fact that tools and machines influence the way we think and create. So, which forms could this collaboration take?

One possible approach is to consider the human a creator and robot a tool. As the tool become invisible it becomes a prosthetics. These cybernetic constructions for augmentation were explored by many artists. One example is Stelarc's "Involuntary Arm / Third Hand" (1980). Using electromyography (EMG) sensors in his leg and abdomen, he could control a mechanical hand attached to his right arm.

In *Better Hands* the embodiment is also realized by a sensory-motor loop of the arm, which includes the touchscreen and the interactor arm. We avoid the behaviorist and cognitivist perspectives by reaching for the autopoietic view of Maturana: "That which we human beings call cognition is the capacity that a living system exhibits of operating in dynamic structural congruence with the medium in which it exists" [5]. The arm cognition is

C&C '17, June 27-30, 2017, Singapore, Singapore

ACM ISBN 978-1-4503-4403-6/17/06.
http://dx.doi.org/10.1145/3059454.3059508

based on a closed dynamical system coupled with the interactor *and* the drawing canvas.

The issue of creative authorship in interactive systems still evades a definitive answer. Hofstadter [4] proposes a solution that calls for a "meta-author", the one responsible for creating the production rules. Reflecting on the relationship with his painter algorithm AARON, though, Cohen dismissed any simple attribution [3]. We tend to agree with his later view, in which the final product is considered a fluid result of the dialog between man and machine.

TECHNICAL ASPECTS

The installation is composed by a robotic arm and a tablet. The arm has five servo motors controlled by an Arduino board and holds a brush painted with conductive ink. The robot communicates with the tablet through a USB cable. The interactor wears an EMG armband (Myo), which connects to the tablet. By moving the arm around, both the interactor and the robot paint (Figure 1).

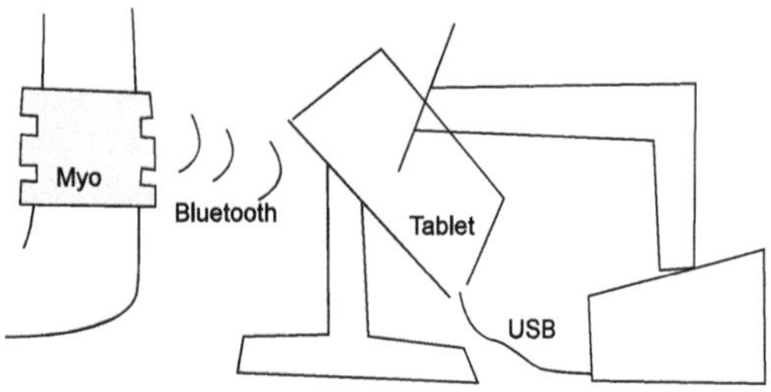

Figure 1: Installation Parts - The tablet centralizes all processing and communication.

Brush patterns are generated using an iterated function system with three affine mappings. The whole system is modulated by a four-dimensional non-linear map.

BIOGRAPHIES OF THE AUTHORS

Wallace Lages is an assistant professor at the School of Fine Arts of Universidade Federal de Minas Gerais (Brazil) and Ph.D. student in the Compute Science Department of Virginia Tech (USA). He has collaborated on the conception and development of several commercial games and artistic installations. He was a co-author on installation Palavrador Openbook, winner of the 2006 digital literature prize from the ciudad de Vinaròs, Spain and featured on the 2007 Siggraph art gallery. He was also responsible for the digital interaction concept of permanent installations on the Interactive Space of Interactive Life (Belo Horizonte, Brazil). He has contributed on programming and game design of mobile, PC and console games. He is currently associated with the Center for HCI, part of the Institute for Creativity, Arts and Technologies where he is doing research on VR, AR, games, and 3D interaction.

Dr. Pablo Gobira is a professor at Escola Guignard (UEMG, Brazil), artist, curator and researcher. He is a research fellow and manager of Digital Promotion Services of the Brazilian Network at IBICT/Brazil Ministry of Science, Technology, Innovation and Communication (MCTI). Member of the National Institute of Science and Technology INCT-Acqua (CNPq). Writer and editor of the books: "Post-digital configurations" (Forthcoming UEMG Press, 2017); "Games and Society" (Crisálida Press, 2012); Walter Benjamin "B-side" (Crisálida Press, 2011) among others books and writings. He works in curatorship, creation and production in the field of culture and digital arts and also creative economy. He is coordinating the Laboratory of Front Poetics (http://labfront.tk).

Dr. Francisco Marinho is a professor in the Department of Photography, Performing arts, and Animation at the School of Fine Arts of Universidade Federal de Minas Gerais (UFMG). He obtained his B.S. in mechanical engineering from UFMG (1993) and his Ph.D. from Universidade de Sao Paulo (2004). He worked several years in media production and illustration. He was the conceptual leader on installation Palavrador Openbook, winner of the 2006 digital literature prize from the ciudad de Vinaròs, Spain and featured on the 2007 Siggraph art gallery. His current research is focused on art and technology, particularly on interactive art and education. He was one of the founders of the Latin America Network of Digital Literature (Red) and runs 1maginari0, a research group on computational poetry.

ILLUSTRATIVE IMAGES

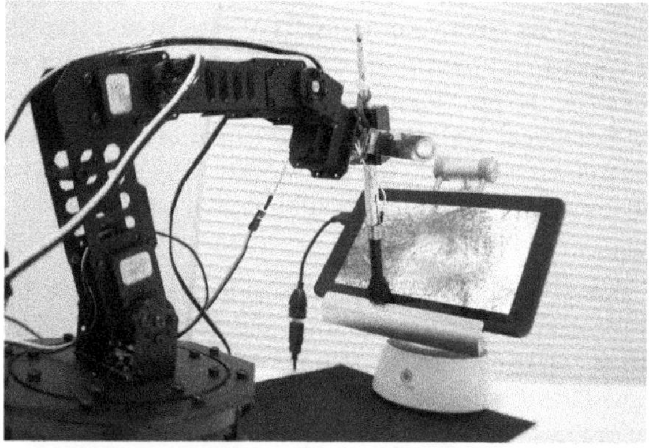

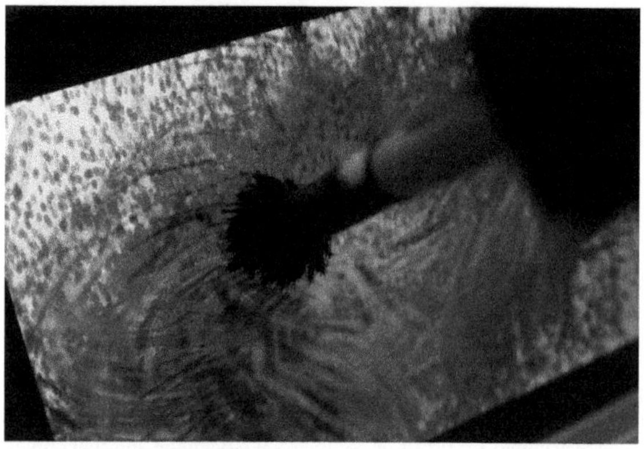

ACKNOWLEDGMENTS

We would like to thank: CNPq, FAPEMIG, PROPPG/UEMG, ACM, and Virginia Tech's Computer Science Department.

REFERENCES

1. Max Barry. 2011. *Machine Man*. Vintage Books.
2. Margaret A Boden. 2009. Computer models of creativity. *AI Magazine* 30, 3: 23.
3. Harold Cohen. Driving the Creative Machine - Orcas Center, Crossroads Lecture Series 2010. Retrieved October 4, 2017 from http://www.aaronshome.com
4. Douglas R. Hofstadter. 1989. *Godel, Escher, Bach: An eternal golden braid*. Vintage Books.
5. Humberto Maturana. 2002. Autopoiesis, structural coupling and cognition: a history of these and other notions in the biology of cognition. *Cybernetics & Human Knowing* 9, 3-4: 5–34.

Child In The Wild

John McCormick
Swinburne University of Technology
Melbourne Australia
jmccormick@swin.edu.au

Adam Nash
RMIT Centre for Game Design Research
Melbourne, Australia
adam.nash@rmit.edu.au

ABSTRACT
Child in the Wild is an interactive installation that enables human participants and a child robot to co create an immersive artwork through the use of the robot's artificial neural networks to enable object and image recognition.

Author Keywords
Artificial neural network; robotics; machine learning; electronic installation; artificial desire;

ACM Classification Keywords
H.5.m. Information interfaces and presentation (e.g., HCI

INTRODUCTION
Child in the Wild comprises a child robot in a stroller, interacting with visitors to the gallery. Participants show the child robot objects or pictures on their mobile device and the child robot will try to guess and say what the object is. The child robot's perception of the material world is audio-visually displayed via projection on to the gallery walls and floor, and surround sound system. Over time the image and sound disintegrates into its component pixels and sonic grains, which, via an artificial intelligence network, agitate into co-evolving colour and sound fields.

ARTIFICIAL DESIRE
Child in the Wild uses deep learning artificial neural networks running on the child robot's embedded computer to enable it to recognise and converse about its surroundings. The projections, which can cover the whole space (3 walls and floor) are manifested from the child robot's inner state as it interacts with human visitors. The complex, evolving sound score is also a generative expression of the child robot's state as the sound interacts with the decomposing visual memories of the child.

C&C '17, June 27-30, 2017, Singapore, Singapore
ACM 978-1-4503-4403-6/17/06.
http://dx.doi.org/10.1145/3059454.3059509

Child in the Wild investigates learning, robot-machine interaction, the development of material understanding and the notion of desire this entails. For Jacques Lacan, desire is a desire for recognition from the other, and the sense of what the other desires, what it lacks. [1] For Julia Kristeva, desire is an impulse towards the other, that "leads the way, is tied to lack, and expresses the body's needs." [2] In contrast, for Deleuze and Guattari desire is a productive force that creatively incorporates into the self that which is other to it. [3]

Contemporary deep learning artificial neural networks are primarily based on fixed notions of representation and signification. [4] For Lacan, this would imply both fixity of meaning and fixation of desire, which in turn implies limitation of *jouissance*, rather than an unbounded, uncontrollable *jouissance*. [5] But it is *jouissance* that is at the root of creativity, art and other *wild systems*.

For *Child in the Wild*, we propose *Artificial Desire* as a motivational force for accomplishment in non-human entities, whether it be goal oriented behaviour, artistic creation, self learning or interactions with humans and others. Accordingly, the child robot interacts with the sound and vision of the projected virtual environment using principles of artificial desire that we have developed, and which evolve over the period of the exhibition, creating an emergent, recombinant relationship between robot, artwork and the public.

AESTHETIC AND INVESTIGATION
Child in the Wild takes a sophisticated hacker approach to the development and production of the artwork. The child robot is comprised of 3D printed parts and runs on a raspberry pi. Though the technology is maker aesthetic, the resulting capabilities of the robot are significant. Similarly, though the audiovisual aesthetic is of realtime games, its generative, evolving composition is sophisticated and nuanced.

Figure 1. The child robot in its stroller. Visitors can show it objects and images and it will guess what the object is and create an immersive environment form the perceptions.

The use of artificial neural networks to develop the child robot's learning and desire is a technique that departs from traditional programming of robots, with less emphasis on prescribing abilities and more on learning and experience as the basis for capability. [6] Along with this learning oriented approach comes the issue of relative control. Artificial neural networks are often regarded as a black box regarding function. Yet in the cultural imagination promulgated by Asimov, robots are *controlled* servants that cannot harm humans. How does this correlate with non-human entities whose development is based not on hard coded rules, but on emergent models of both supervised and unsupervised learning? Further, how can deep learning be integrated with embodiment and desire in order to draw inspiration from living models?

Child in the Wild is an immersive experience as an installation. It invites participants to interact directly with the robot to co-create the art experience. The encompassing projections surrounding the participants on all walls and the floor position the participants and the child robot within a capsule of their shared desires. The disintegration of images into colour fields from which the sound is generated harks to the changeability and fragility of memory and perception, perhaps even to its unreliability. *Child in the Wild* seeks to challenge and motivate both human and non human participants to develop a unique, timely experience for Creativity and Cognition 2017.

ARTIST PROFILES

Adam Nash

Based in Melbourne, Australia, Adam Nash is a digital artist, composer, programmer, performer, teacher and writer. He works primarily in networked virtual environments, exploring them as sites of playable art. Working in a post-convergent idiom, his work uses the web, game engines, generative and procedural programming, data and motion capture, artificial intelligence, synthetic evolution and live performance. His work has been presented in galleries, festivals and online in Australia, Europe, Asia and The Americas, including peak festivals SIGGRAPH, ISEA, ZERO1SJ and the Venice Biennale. He has been artist in residence at Ars Electronica FutureLab. He was shortlisted for the National Art Award in New Media at the QGOMA in 2008. He has a PhD from the Centre for Animation and Interactive Media at RMIT University. He is director of the Playable Media Lab in the Centre for Game Design Research, and program manager of the Bachelor of Design (Digital Media), both at RMIT University.

John McCormick

John McCormick is a technology based artist with a major interest in human movement. John has collaborated on works worldwide, including at peak festivals ISEA, ZERO1SJ, SIGGRAPH, Melbourne Festival, Venice Biennale, Institute of Contemporary Art (ICA) London, Ars Electronica and Monaco Dance Forum. John was a founding member of Company In Space, Dancehouse, Squaretangle and Wild System. John is currently a researcher at Deakin Motion.Lab. John's current research centres on intelligent agents that can learn to dance from human dancers and use this learned behaviour to create collaborative performances with human performers. John is investigating robots as collaborative performing partners and using Deep Learning and Neural Networks to enable interaction and collaboration between digital entities including robots and humans.

REFERENCES

1. Jacques Lacan. 2014. Chapter 2: Anxiety, Sign of Desire. *Anxiety, the Seminar of Jacques Lacan Book X*. Polity Press. p.23.
2. Julia Kristeva. 2010. The Passion According to Motherhood. *Hatred and Forgiveness*. Columbia University Press. pp.80-81.
3. Gilles Deleuze and Felix Guattari. 1983. Anti-Oedipus: Capitalism and Schizophrenia. University of Minnesota Press. p.49.
4. G.E. Hinton. 2007. Learning Multiple Layers of Representation. *Trends in Cognitive Science, 11,* pp.428-434.
5. Bruce Fink. 2007. Fundamentals of Psychoanalytic Technique: A Lacanian Approach for Practitioners. Norton and Company. p. 269.
6. Ogata, T. et al. 2009. Prediction and Imitation of Others' Motions by Re-using Own Forward-Inverse Model in Robots. *ICRA '09, IEEE International Conference on Robotics and Automation.* p.4144-4149.

"In Running"

Leyna Marika Papach
3564 80th apt 5i
Jackson Heights, NY 11372
USA
lpapach@hotmail.com

Abstract
'In Running' is a multi-instrumental performance with electronics, violin, and viola. Composed in a collage-like 'stretchable' structure, musical fragments--or musical 'cells' are recombined and re-dramatized in a live setting according a flexible, film-like score.

The approach to this piece comes from the perspective that the human body is not only an activator of time, but also a physicalized memory ship filled with fragments of culture and personal encounters. In a non-hierarchical approach to musical genre, the performing body navigates through a personal soundscape, making film-like shifts where one can move from one place in time to another in a single edit.

Author Keywords
performing body;body ship;musical cells;

ACM Classification Keywords
H.5.m. Information interfaces and presentation (e.g., HCI): Miscellaneous.

Introduction/Concept
'In Running' is a multi-instrumental performance with electronics, violin, and viola. Composed in a collage-like 'stretchable' structure, musical fragments, or musical 'cells' are recombined and re-dramatized according a flexible, film-like score.

The approach to this composition comes from the perspective that the human body is not only an activator of time, but a physicalized memory ship filled with fragments of culture and personal encounters; both in the present and in the mysterious, historical past. Our experiences, be it in the form of words, music/sound or movement, are imprinted into our cells, as we maintain a fine dance with time.

C&C '17, June 27-30, 2017, Singapore, Singapore

ACM ISBN 978-1-4503-4403-6/17/06.
http://dx.doi.org/10.1145/3059454.3084099

Coming form a multicultural background where the sensation of 'un-rootedness' has been an reoccurring theme, a shift in perspective towards music, by treating all sounds personally experienced by the body as equal with no hierarchy (regardless of genre, instrument kind, or cultural identity) has allowed for this collage-like approach in composing and performing 'In Running'.

In the language of film, one is able to travel to another time and place in an instant through a single edit. Similarly, through sound and music, the performing body is able to navigate time in a similar manner, accessing times and places while making improvisational decisions influenced by the presence of an audience.

Website
http://leynamarikapapach.com

Leyna Marika Papach
Leyna Marika Papach is a musician and multi-disciplinary artist from Japan and the United States. Her compositions house the languages of dance, theater, sound, and image.
The six evening-length pieces Leyna wrote and directed have been performed internationally in Europe, Japan and the United States.
As a musician and violinist, she has collaborated with a wide range of artists in various disciplines (Eric Ting, Clarinda Mac Low, J.G.Thirwell, Geraldine Fibbers and many others), leading to performances of original and collaborative work at venues/festivals such as; Unlimited Festival (Austria), HAU (Berlin), Frascati/Gasthuis (Holland), International House (Japan), Danse l'Afrique Danse! Festival (Paris/Tunisia), All Tomorrow's Parties, BAM, UNESCO, Queens museum, HERE, The Stone, and many other venues in NYC.
Leyna has researched traditional forms of music in West Africa and Japan with the support from various foundations (Arts International, Japan/Us Friendship Commission and others). She holds an MFA in Sound/Music from Bard College, MA in Theater and Dance studies from DasArts, Amsterdam, and studied violin at the Prague Academy of Music.

(2,2) 0

Nazare Soares
NTNU
Trondheim, Norway
info@nazaresoares.com

Øystein Kjørstad Fjeldbo
NTNU
Trondheim, Norway
fjeoey@gmail.com

Amalia Fonfara
NTNU
Trondheim, Norway
amalia.fonfara@gmail.com

ABSTRACT
(2, 2) 0 is a project made from a collaborative process between moving image artist Nazare Soares, sound artist Øystein Kjørstad Fjeldbo and artist and shamanic practitioner Amalia Fonfara. We are developing an interactive installation which utilizes real-time rendered binaural sound systems. Space functions as a cognitive map, where the navigator will be exposed to types of temporal illusion through a sound composition in space given by ambisonic binaural techniques. The gaze will be reformulated and question within an invisible architecture, the virtual space. Disorientation and de-centre will be forced pushing the body to re-orientate itself. By the use of the absence of light and sound frequencies we avoid spatial and time cognitive experience to be projected outside of the body.

Author Keywords
Cognitive, self-learning; techno- utopian vision of sensing technology, somatic, art; feminist speculative design; interactive environments, HCI; techno-shamanism, techno-animism; virtual environments, immersive cinema; binaural sound, composition in space, invisible architecture.

ACM Classification Keywords
HCI, C.2.1, C.3, D.1.7, H.5.1, H.5.2, H.5.5, I.2.10, J.5

INTRODUCTION
Taking the structure of a (2,2) mode shamanic drum as a reference we have built an invisible architecture that is experienced sonically. Timeless Machine will offer different layers of experiences, exploring affect within body processes of becoming. (Massumi, 2002) We utilize wireless motion and position tracking through an Ultra Wide Band-system. From this information (XYZ body in the room and XYZ head direction), we are rendering binaural sound in real time from Pure Data, directly out to wireless headphones on the navigator. In this way, we have created a composition of movable virtual sound sources throughout acoustics rooms. One navigator at a time can move around and interact with these sources through their presence in the rooms.

Our project addresses notions of invisibility and vacuum within the virtual environment. How to disoriented and displace the observer's outside experience in such environments, to the extent of emphasis internal physical perception of the body? How is body awareness connected to the acceptance of perceiving states absence of external stimulus? Deviation of direction when we project our senses, may be connected to our capacity to reclaim subjectivities. Subjectivities and body self-intuition gain a complete spatial-temporal experience from being immersed in the virtual. (Bergson, 2006)

(2, 2) 0 offers an alternative individual experience from that understood contemporary notions of the virtual, and arises question about colonizing the gaze through strategies of affection. What do we define as the virtual in contemporary media culture? What are the technology and techniques used in the visual language in order to produce the virtual? How is the cinematic related to the virtual within politics of speculation? How the consumption of media has been influenced by the production of virtual culture and affected the means of imagination?

In immersive environments, the body is mediated by spatial cognition. The subjective experience of “spacetime” is given by means of spatiality. (Barad, 2007) In immersive experiences we placed the subject at the very center. It echoes past experiences obtained from panoramas built for means of colonial and imperial entertainment. Feminine gaze offers a circle without a center, where the form is already content, where the point of view isn't determined or fixed.

We relate the essence of the virtual to evocation and activation of imagination within shamanic practice. Focusing on neo-shamanic practices in Scandinavia, we have gained a deeper understanding of the function of the drum in ancient ceremonial and ritual work. We have developed the narrative of the work implementing drum journeys, as storytelling alternative strategy for the composition of the soundscape. We use diffraction as a methodology for dichotomies to happen within the virtual, as a place for a possibility of production of *"extas"*. The virtual environment functions as a non-place, as a mental place, “control of internal and external comportment, retention of the agency of the self, and of memories and experiences that are often subsequently recounted as narratives”. (Lindquist, 1997)

C&C '17, June 27-30, 2017, Singapore, Singapore
ACM 978-1-4503-4403-6/17/06.
http://dx.doi.org/10.1145/3059454.3073723

TYPE OF ARTWORK & INTENDED PRESENTATION

Binaural sound interactive installation, a sound composition in an invisible architectural space. The work need to be experienced in complete darkness. The dimensions of the room are minimum 10 m x 10 m, though we can adapt the work to smaller spaces. We will need to build an entrance (preparation room) where the headphones will be handed. We will need to have assistance to hand the headset. The project utilizes wireless motion tracking through the Pozyx system. In short the system uses ultra wide band (UWB) signals transmitted from the corners of the room to microprocessors on the navigators head. From this it is possible to triangulate the navigators XYZ position in the room. The units on the navigators head also includes an inertial measurement unit, which is used to track the navigators XYZ head movement. This information (the XYZ position and XYZ head direction) is in turn transmitted wirelessly to a main computer, running the multimedia environment Pure Data (Pd). In Pd we use the ambisonics tools from the IEM library, which utilizes head related transfer functions (HRTF) to create a binaural sound signal. With these tools we are able to place and move virtual sound sources around in a virtual room with set acoustic properties. The information about the navigator is used in moving the virtual point of listening, through this virtual room in realtime. Lastly the stereo signal is transmitted via low latency Bluetooth to a headset on the navigators head, creating the sensation that one is moving around invisible sound sources and the sound sources are moving around you.

AUTHORS BIOGRAPHIES

Nazare Soares (Spain 1981), graduated from Brighton University with a First class degree in Moving Image Arts in 2014; as part of this course she spent three months studying in Ramallah at the Academy of Art of Palestine. She spent a year from 2006 living and working in Tokyo, after which she moved to Brighton. In 2015 she began a Masters of Fine Art course at the Norwegian University of Science and Technology in Trondheim. Her current research locates the essence of cinema elsewhere, investigating the notion of anachronism and its connection to light and sound; spirit and spectre, ontology and hauntology.
www.nazaresoares.com

Selected exhibitions:

2017. (2,2) 0. Kit MFA show at TKM Gråmølna & Lademoen Kunstnerverksteder. Sound Installation. NO.
2017. *OMEN* Alchemy Film & Moving Image Film Festival, Film Installation, Hawick, Scotland. 2016.
2016 *Pharos Mirror. Pink Shoelaces.* Presented by Punktet Skansen.Trondheim . NO
2016 *We Hold this Myth to Be Potential . Investigations into Afrofuturism.* Metamorf Art & Technology Biennale. Kit Gallery. Sound Installation. Trondheim.
2016 *Festival Internacional de Cinema Dobra*. Cinemateca MAM/RJ. Screening. Rio de Janeiro, Brazil
2016 Usurp Zone 5 Film Festival supported by BFI. Indian Habitat Centre. Screening. New Delhi, IN.
2015 Addis Video Art Festival. Museum of Contemporary art of Ethiopia. Addis Ababa, Ethiopia.
2015 Fiva International Video Art Festival, Museo del Libro y de la Lengua, Buenos Aires, ARG.

Øystein Kjørstad Fjeldbo (Norway 1991), sound artist and musician based in Trondheim, Norway. He has a bachelor's degree in music technology from the music department at the Norwegian University of Science and Technology (2015), where he is currently enrolled in the master's program.. As part of this research he is currently developing a framework for true real time interactive 3d-sound. The framework will utilize the whole space around the listener, placing virtual sound sources in the listener's headphones. Phone: +47 45675886 E-mail: fjeoey@gmail.com

Selected exhibitions:

2017. *Museene danser #3.* Interactive audiovisual design, Rockheim music museum, NO.
2017. *Fuglekasser,* Interactive sound sculpture, St. Olavs, Trondheim. NO.
2017. *2,2 O* Interactive sound installation, LKV in Trondheim, NO.
2017. *Inter 1.* Audio visual installation. Commissioned by The Norwegian Confederation of Trade Unions for their 2017 conference in Oslo. NO.
2017. *Maze of Senses.* Interactive audio-tactile installation. Commissioned by the IsFit festival 2017.
2017 *Livets Dans.* Interactive surround audiovisual design, Sverresborg - Trøndelag folk museum.

Amalia Fonfara (Greenland 1985) Artist and shamanic practitioner based in Trondheim. Since 2010 Amalia Fonfara have lived in Norway. She holds a bachelor of fine art(2013) and an international master of fine art(2015), from Norwegian University of Science and Technology in Trondheim. Simuntanaily with her studies in contemporary art, Fonfara attended several courses in different esoteric practices. Including studies in ritual work of neo-shamanic and contemplative healing practices. She is currently doing a one year study prg. at Scandinavian Center of Shamanic Studies in Sweden.
www.amaliafonfara.com

Selected exhibitions:

2017. Open House, A Sense of History, Healingens Hus, Trondheim, NO.
2017. Timeless Machine, 2,2 O, TKM Gråmølna & Lademoen Kunstnerverksteder. Trondheim. NO.
2017. Shamanic Practice Spring 2017, (teaching course), Trondheim, NO.
2016. Shamanic Practice Autumn 2016, (teaching course), Trondheim, NO
2016. If nothing becomes a part of everything, Island of the Apprentices, Galleri Q, København, DK.
2015. MFA Exhibition 2015, Gråmøllna, Trondheim, NO.
2015. Botanical Evidences of Movement,Migration and Commerce,Nuovo Cinema Palazzo,Rome, IT.

REFERENCES

1. Barad, Karen. 2007. *Meeting the universe halfway: quantum physics and the entanglement of matter and meaning.* Duke Univ. Press, Durham, NC, U.S.A., and London, U.K. Langdon Winner. 1999.

2. Do artifacts have politics? In *The Social Shaping of Technology* (2nd. ed.), Donald MacKenzie and Judy Wajcman (eds.). Open University Press, Buckingham, UK.

3. Bergson, Henri. 2004. *Matter and Memory.* Nancy Margaret Paul, W. Scott Palmer (eds.) Courier Corporation, Massachusetts, USA.

4. Lindquist, Galina. 1997. *Shamanic performances on the urban scene: neo-shamanism in contemporary Sweden.* Department of Social Anthropology, Stockholm University. Stockholm. Sweden.

5. Massumi, Brian. 2002. Parables for the Virtual: Movement, Affect, Sensation. Duke Univ. Press, Durham, NC, U.S.A., and London, U.K

Music for Various Groups of Performers (After Lucier): An Improvised Electroencephalographic Group Performance

Richie Cyngler
Victoria College of the Arts
Melbourne, Australia
glitchpop@gmail.com

ABSTRACT
Music for Various Groups of Performers (After Lucier) (MfVGoP) is an experimental audio-visual improvised group performance employing sonified electroencephalographic (EEG) signals and computer music. The data generated by performers' brain waves are used as control parameters for custom built audio software using the Pure Data (Pd) environment.

The piece explores and investigates group and individual dynamics within a performance context. The title references composer Alvin Lucier's 1965 work *Music for Solo Performer* in which the composer attempted to control electro-acoustic instruments via EEG signals produced by his brain. In contrast *Music for Various Groups of Performers (After Lucier)* investigates the roles of individuals and small groups through the context of EEG monitored performance considering the individual performers, their relationships with each other and the audience as well as their interaction with the technology.

Author Keywords
Electroencephalography; improvisation; experimental music; sound art; performance;

INTRODUCTION
Music for Various Groups of Performers (After Lucier) (MfVGoP) is an experimental audio-visual improvised group performance employing sonified electroencephalographic (EEG) signals and computer music. The data generated by performers' brain waves are used as control parameters for custom built audio software using the Pure Data (Pd) environment.

INNOVATIVE AIMS
MfVGoP began with a number of aims which to the author's knowledge have never been combined before.

1. To experiment with alternative control structures for musical expression. The intention is to sonify EEG data in order to produce sound palettes/ soundscapes but not to quantify or "read" the data. Both sonification and visualisation of the data are represented.

2. To explore interactions between performers in an improvisational context, while monitoring their brainwaves. During workshops leading up to performances performers are given the opportunity to become comfortable with the headsets and to see and hear representations of their EEG data. Discussions occur regarding collaborative performance intentions of the piece. Performers contribute thoughts and suggestions of activities they may engage in individually and co-operatively on stage during the performance.

3. To experiment with EEG consumer technology and audio software such as synthesizers, samplers, etc. Use of EEG streamed data as control parameters allows for concurrently dynamic shifting of sounds in a live context, changing the relationship of "player" to "instrument". The piece is a hybrid of generative composition and more traditional performer controlled interaction with an instrument. Over the course of developing, performing, then further developing the work it has become evident that while performers may exercise more or less control over their brainwaves the continuous stream of EEG data from each participant is more analogous to "player" in a traditional musical context than are the people on stage.

4. Where possible to achieve all of this using Free Libre Open Source Software (FLOSS) technology https://www.gnu.org/philosophy/floss-and-foss.en.html. FLOSS is released with source code available other developers and users. The most well known and widely used FLOSS project is the Linux operating system. Much of the internet runs on Linux servers, all Android phones are based on Linux. There are numerous Linux distributions (variants) because the source code unpinning the software is freely available for anyone to download, use, adapt and change. FLOSS projects are often highly collaborative and distributed. Open Hardware is an accepted standard hardware analogue to FLOSS in this case all design schematics, parts lists and other documentation are published openly to encourage diverse accessibility. Large FLOSS software and open hardware projects have the benefit of being robust if there is a dedicated development and user community behind them. Developers and users lead software development which leads to improved functionality and stability over time. Proprietary software

C&C '17, June 27-30, 2017, Singapore, Singapore

ACM ISBN 978-1-4503-4403-6/17/06.
http://dx.doi.org/10.1145/3059454.3073725

and hardware development tends to be primarily based on market forces, users have no input to functionality and companies can and do obsolete their technologies at any time.

TECHNOLOGY

Three specific technologies are key to the operation and execution of MfVGoP these are:

Consumer EEG Headsets

Muse brand headsets http://developer.choosemuse.com/ were selected as the EEG device of choice. Muse headsets were released through a Kickstarter crowd-funding campaign. Muse claimed that they would support development across all three major operating systems; Linux, Mac and Windows. However the product's hardware software design would remain proprietary (closed).

Muse headbands make all known EEG frequency bands available. The various bands are labeled as Alpha, Beta, Gamma, Delta & Theta each of these collects a small range of frequencies within the band which are considered to be dominant during certain states of mind. For example Beta waves are generally evident during our general waking states, Theta: sleep and deep meditation, Alpha: flow states, concentration and some meditative states. http://www.brainworksneurotherapy.com/what-are-brainwaves

During the initial development of this project in 2015 a number of EEG headset devices were considered. The main factors under consideration were accessibility and financial cost with a bias towards open hardware. Despite being closed Muse was selected on the basis of cost and functionality at the time. The other main contender was OpenBCI[1] http://openbci.com/, an open hardware bio-sensing platform. At the time this platform had just been released, was expensive and the technology was somewhat cumbersome and not wireless. OpenBCI has grown in the last two years boasting an active community, further development, a number of flexible options and cost effective solutions. In hindsight this platform may have been a better choice. This project relies on technology but is not limited to one set of technologies. The hardware may change in future depending on testing, viability and results.

Bluetooth

Muse headsets connect wirelessly to a laptop via Bluetooth to capture and route the data to museIO software. After testing CSR 4.0 USB Bluetooth dongles are found to yield the best results resulting in less dropouts.

Pure Data (Pd)

Pd software https://puredata.info/ run on a laptop running a Linux operating system is used. Pd patches were designed to receive Open Sound Control (OSC) data live streamed from performers' Muse headsets via Bluetooth and museIO software.

Pd is a data-flow software environment initially designed as an audio engine. It is FLOSS as such there have been, and continue to be, many contributions to the core functionality from developers all over the world. There are many forks of Pd, also core functionality can be augmented with the use of "externals". These externals are Pd objects or libraries of objects which add new functions, these tend to be easy to install and incorporate into the software as they are often released cross platform and as source code.

PERFORMANCES

The piece has previously been publicly performed three times. These performances were each supported by a number of meetings and experiments with performers, each time culminating in a public performance outlined below. Each performance includes three unique performers who were physically available at the time of the Performance.

Tilde~ New Music & Sound Art Festival 2016 Melbourne Australia

https://tilde.net.au/ Performers: Richie Cyngler, Nat Grant, Lilian Steiner. Venue: Australian Institute of Music, performance hall. This first iteration of the performance comprised of two different patches experienced as two movements. The first patch used EEG data to control a three channel sampler. Each performer had a dedicated sampler, their brainwaves influenced various audio parameters including playback speed, direction, filter values, and levels. The second patch comprised of a number of oscillators, noise, generators, filters and other parameters controlled by EEG data. Technically the performance was a success: Bluetooth connectivity was strong, and generally good data were received from headsets with minor dropouts. However one performer also had to operate technology and as a result neither task was attended to completely. Upon reflection four participants are required: one operator and three performers.

Art Meets Radical Openness (AMRO) 2016 International Conference, Linz Austria

https://www.radical-openness.org/ Performers: Marcus Decker, Michaela Lakova, Raphael Peret. This second iteration of the performance comprised of three patches experienced as three movements. Existing patches were used with some modifications for improved sound and functionality. The additional patch was a noise based subtractive synthesizer design. A visualiser patch was also added which depicted each participant's EEG data stream as a set live line graphs. The audience concurrently heard and saw various representations of the performers EEG data. During this performance Richie Cyngler operated the hardware and software, which allowed for a smoother performance.

1 Open Brain Computer Interface

New Interfaces for Musical Expression (NIME) 2016 International Conference, Brisbane Australia
http://www.nime.org/ Performers: Nico Halton, Matthew Halton, Olivia Lapsley Scott. Operator: Richie Cyngler. This third iteration of the performance comprised of similar patches used during the AMRO performance somewhat refined. The workshop phase of this performance was successful, good connectivity with technology, very good contributions from participants. The performance was marred by poor Bluetooth connectivity which led to less interesting sound palettes because of less data input. Interestingly due to the Toplap https://toplap.org/about/ inspired philosophy of "show your screens" this was evident to the audience. Often technological work is veiled by the inaccessibility of technology to general audiences by showing your screens or projecting the software data as part of the performance the audience is allowed the opportunity to participate more fully in the whole of the performance.

INFLUENCES

Music for Solo Performer [Lucier] had broad influence on this work as it provided an initial template to respond to as well as analyse and reconsider and recontextualise the intentions of the original work.

Other influences include the pioneering work of synthesynthesist Peter Blasser http://petermopar.blogspot.com.au/, Gijs Gieskes http://gieskes.nl/, Dimitry Morozov http://vtol.cc/about and others working in the field of experimental electronic music, sound art and interface design.

My own various performance and installation experiments with novel Human Interface Devices (HIDs) for control and production of electronic sound works also influenced the work.

Music for Solo Performer [Lucier] is a seminal work, possibly one of the earliest examples of sonification however it raises a number of concerns. Essentially the piece is mis-titled as it is not really performed by a solo performer. The piece requires an audio technician on a mixer to select when the signals trigger which instruments. In this context this person, the audio technician, is integral to the performance and therefore a second performer. Even more interesting is the presence of the audience and EEG technician [Straebel & Thoben].

A specific point of difference between Lucier's piece and MfVGoP is that MfVGoP attempts to engage with the influence of groups of people on each others' brainwaves. In this piece we consider that performers brainwaves may be influenced by many variables within and without the performance context. Performers will likely be influenced by each other but they may also be influenced by the performance context - being on stage, their mood, what they had for breakfast, the vibe of the audience, etc. Many factors may influence a person's brainwaves. Sonifing live EEG data of multiple participants allows us to consider implications of interaction.

CONCLUSION

Innovatively MfVGoP treats sonification as a tool for sound expression rather than as a tool for qualifying data. The intention is not to generate a performance as an audio analogue of EEG data, rather to make use of live EEG data as a kind of control structure for making sound, as a guitarist may use highly trained digits or a toothbrush to reverberate guitar strings. We are not concerned with high fidelity to the original signal, rather a representation.

Through performance it has become evident that the actual performers of the piece are users' brainwaves, not the performers themselves. Performers may act, consciously or unconsciously, upon themselves and each other to alter brainwaves and hence audio outcomes. However they cannot have direct control over their brainwaves, even through training brainwave control is a kind of trick. Lucier tried to quiet his mind to elicit Alpha waves which he used as his control system. MfVGoP makes use of all measurable EEG bands.

Like *Music For Solo* Performer [Lucier] many EEG performances have been focused on single user brainwave data whereas MfVGoP focuses on muliple users brainwave data their interactions. Similarly many other EEG works and consumer devices focus on intentional training, for example learning to "quiet" the mind to produce alpha waves or concentration to produce control. We are focused on using participants' EEG data as it is rather than eliciting a certain response. If MfVGoP participants are interested in training their minds or eliciting a certain response through brainwave data they are encouraged to do so. Performers are encouraged to engage with the technology and each other in any way they find interesting. The piece is intended to be as collaborative as possible within the context.

REFERENCES

1. Alvin Lucier. 1965. Music for Solo Performer. Performance.
2. Richard Stallman. 2013. Floss and Foss. Retrieved April 5, 2017 from https://www.gnu.org/philosophy/floss-and-foss.en.html
3. Interaxon. 2014. Muse Headband http://developer.choosemuse.com/
4. Brainworks. What are brainwaves. Retrieved April 20, 2017 from http://www.brainworksneurotherapy.com/what-are-brainwaves
5. Mille Puckette et al. 1996. Pure Data (Pd) https://puredata.info/

6. Vincent Giles, Alice Bennett. 2016. *Tilde New Music & Sound Art Festival*. Melbourne, Australia https://tilde.net.au/
7. Ushi Reiter. 2016. *Art Meets Radical Openness (AMRO) International Conference*. Linz, Austria https://www.radical-openness.org/
8. Andrew Brown. 2016. *New Interfaces for Musical Expression (NIME) International Conference*. Brisbane, Australia http://www.nime2016.org/
9. Volker Straebel, Wilm Thoben. 2014. Alvin Lucier's *Music For Solo Performer:* Experimental music beyond sonification. Organised Sound 19(1). Cambridge University Press.

Food Phreaking

Zack Denfeld
The Center for Genomic Gastronomy
Dublin, Ireland
info@genomicgastronomy.com

ABSTRACT
25 April 2017. Food Phreaking is the journal of experiments, exploits and explorations of the human food system. Each issue contains stories about the space where food, technology & open culture meet.

Food Phreaking Issue 00 is the prequel and contains 38 short stories outlining what Food Phreaking is, and what it is not. Food Phreaking Issue 01 is "A Culinary Compendium of Curious Botanical Fruits". Issue 02 is called "What is In Vitro Meat?" And the newest issue, Issue 03, focusses on the human microbiome. Each issue is a slightly different format, incorporating different authors, images, and supplementary materials (timelines, visualizations, graphics, etc.). The Food Phreaking Journal is a platform for research, action, intervention, reflection and foresight.

Author Keywords
Food; phreaking; food systems; hacking; open source; open culture; technology; design; art.

INTRODUCTION
In early 2012 the Center for Genomic Gastronomy wrote: *"Singapore can be described as a food utopia; simultaneously a 'perfect place' with an abundance of affordable and diverse foods, and a "no-place" where most things are imported. Eaters, not farmers, are the major agents of selection. Singapore's multicultural food system, is driven by cultural and economic flows as much as biospheric flows. How will Singapore's unique agri-eco-culinary system adapt to the challenges of the 21st century? What kinds of changes can we expect in the composition of genomes and biotechnologies that makes up the human food systems in Singapore?"* Based on these questions, the Center for Genomic Gastronomy was invited to spend a month in Singapore in the autumn of 2012.

C&C '17, June 27-30, 2017, Singapore, Singapore

ACM ISBN 978-1-4503-4403-6/17/06.
http://dx.doi.org/10.1145/3059454.3073726

THE BIRTH OF FOOD PHREAKING
We roamed widely, visiting individuals and exploring institutions in every corner of the island nation. We met architects, entrepreneurs, students, farmers, chefs, eccentrics and scientists. We visited hacker spaces, gardens, kitchens, parties and classrooms. We would meet and talk with the food people on a Tuesday. Then, we would hang out with the technology people on a Wednesday. But there was very little overlap. All this roaming about and discussion showed us the need for a space where food and technology people can mingle as equals. We left Singapore with the basic outline for creating a forum where food and tech communities could come together to critically and creatively explore the potential overlaps between their work. Food Phreaking Issue 00 was our first attempt at creating this interdisciplinary forum.

DEFINING FOOD PHREAKING
Food Phreaking was inspired by the history of Phone Phreaking. Phone Phreaks were people who used creative and DIY methods to explored telephone systems from the 1950s-1970s. They played with, experimented with, and hacked telecommunication networks. Food Phreakers do the same thing, but with the food system rather than the phone system.

Who Is a Food Phreaker?
Food Phreaking Issue 00 is the journal's prequel. It describes what Food Phreaking is and contains stories that might be useful to Food Phreakers. Who are Food Phreakers? They are individuals and groups interested in experimenting with human food systems at multiple scales. Food Phreakers believe that food culture should be open, free and accessible. Some Food Phreakers have professional skills as farmers, seedsavers, chefs, biohackers and food scientists. Others just tinker in their backyard, basement, kitchen or home lab. The Food Phreaking journal aims to connect foodies who care about sustainability with the scientists and hackers who care about open culture. Food Phreaking is where food, technology, and open culture meet.

Food Phreakers not only observe natural systems, they also explore, experiment, and seek exploits in the human food system. They breed, mutate, grow, harvest, sell, process, cook, celebrate and serve food.

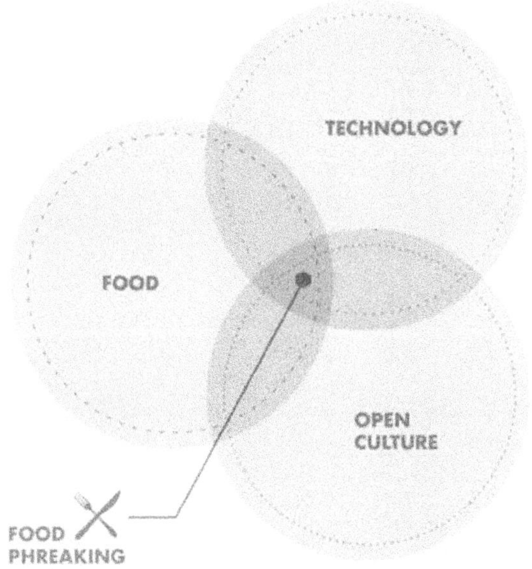

Figure 1. Food Phreaking graphic depicting the space where "Food, technology, and open culture meet".

What is Food Phreaking?

This book documents 38 concise examples of what Food Phreaking might be, and what it most definitely is not. These examples have been grouped into four themes, and are organized into four quadrants: Legal & Open, Illegal & Open, Illegal & Closed, Legal & Closed.

Quadrant A: Legal and Open

Stories that fall into this quadrant range from open source food science to participatory food design. For example, three stories in this section are:

"Franken Fruit: Seed companies like Burpee are creating new products such as 'Big Rainbow Tomato' by grafting the heirloom fruiting parts to disease- resistant and stress-tolerant rootstock. You can even see the scars!"

"Glowing Sushi Cooking Show: Eating GloFish® sushi may be unexpected, but it's not illegal. But make sure to read the terms of service on patented animal ingredients because breeding them is not allowed."

"Open Source Mineral Water: You too can clone natural mineral waters by adding a clever cocktail of salts and carbonating. Use lookup tables to mimic water from specific places and corporate brands. Or create your own liquid remix."

Quadrant B: Illegal and Open

Stories in this quadrant range from examples of culinary civil disobedience to outlawed ingredients. For example, three stories of illegal and open situations are:

"Aquabounty Salmon: Despite appearances this hungry sh is a drug, not a food, in the eyes of the law. For the past 10 years it's been awaiting approval and if legalized, it would be the first GM animal for sale in supermarkets."

"Raw Milk Clubs: Raw milk is illegal in some states of the U.S., and in Canada, Australia and Scotland. However, there are many advocates who drink raw milk illegally."

"Shrinking the Stomach: Instead of super-sizing the food, why not shrink the human? NASA began research into breeding smaller humans for more efficient long distance space flight."

Quadrant C: Illegal and Closed

Stories in Quadrant C range from black hat food hacking to food crime. For example:

"Clearly Fake Cellophane Noodles: Twenty tons of poisonous glass noodles were destroyed after it was discovered that some Chinese companies cut costs by using corn starch instead of mung beans and added lead to make the adulterated noodles more transparent."

"Ortolan: Considered by many to be one of the cruelest dishes in the world, sale of this bunting bird dish is no longer legal, but some say Ortolan is still consumed in the dark shadows of professional French kitchens."

"Prepared Cheese Product: In 2002, the USFDA told Kraft that Velveeta® was not fully a 'Pasteurized Process Cheese Spread.' Instead of complying with dietary minimums, Velveeta became a "Pasteurized Prepared Cheese Product," a term which has no legal status."

Quadrant D: Legal and Closed

The stories in Quadrant D illustrate examples ranging from proprietary food engineering to closed source food design. This section includes the following three stories, for example:

"5-Hour Energy Drink (Of Death): Thirteen 'fatal reactions' to 5-hour energy drink consumption have been reported to the USFDA. According to the product's creator it's like this: 'Water is good, but if you have too much you drown.'"

"L'eau De Troit: U.S. federal labeling regulations don't require bottling companies to list the source or method of water puri cation, and many brands simply bottle and resell municipal tap water."

"Reduced Guilt Protein Products: Combine 20% lupin flour with 80% ground beef to and feel 20% better. Save money too! According to Meatless®, most eaters can barely detect hydrated vegetable fibers when blended with meat, cheese and fish."

CONCLUSION

Food Phreaking is the journal of experiments, exploits and explorations of the human food system. Each issue contains stories about the space where food, technology & open culture meet. Food Phreaking is on ongoing journal created by the Center for Genomic Gastronomy.

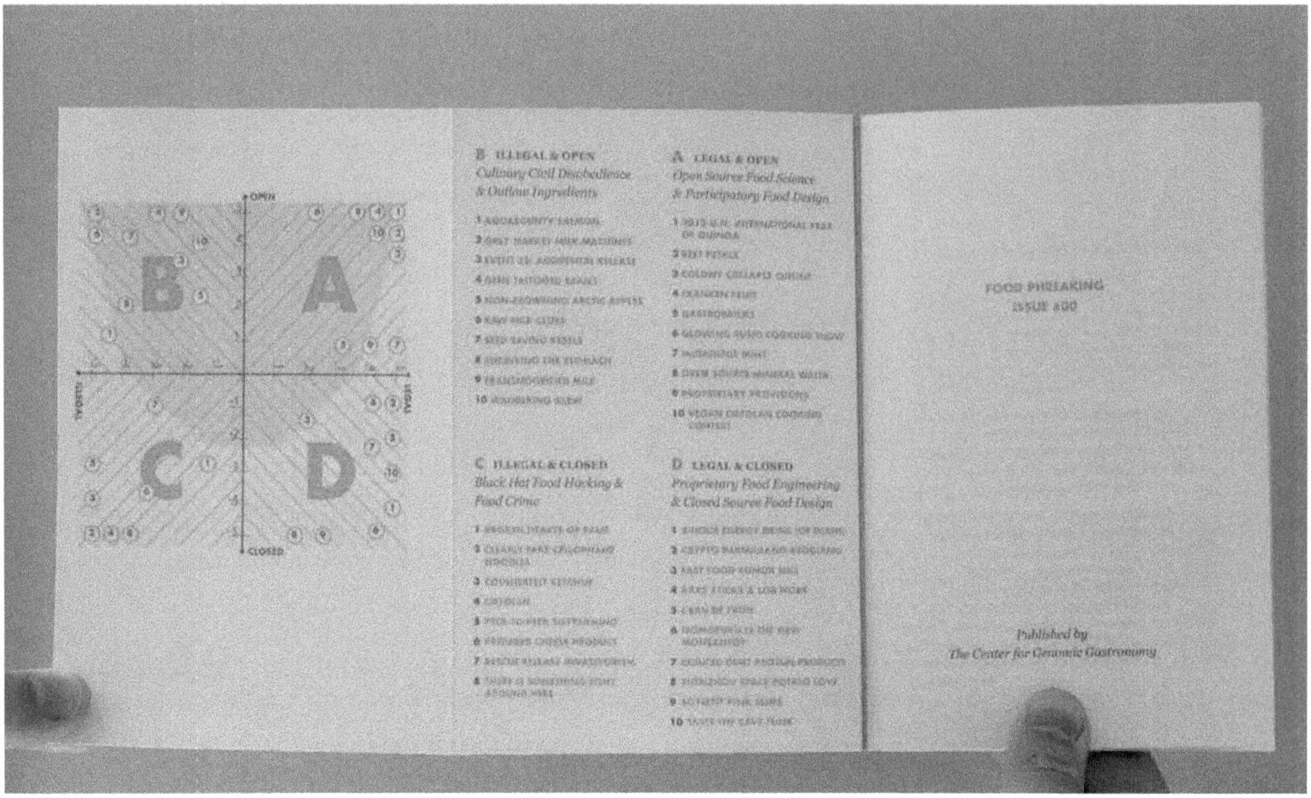

Figure 2. Graphic of the four quadrants used to define what food phreaking is and what it is not.

ACKNOWLEDGMENTS

We would like to thank Lonce Wyse, Denisa Kera, Tembusu College and the National University of Singapore for hosting us during our visit. Issue 00 was generously funded by the Arts and Creativity Lab at NUS through the Art/ Science Residency in 2012. We would also like to thank the subsequent funders of Issues 01-03, the contributors to Issues 01-03, and all those who have supported Food Phreaking by purchasing the books and by sharing them with their respective communities.

REFERENCES

1. The Center for Genomic Gastronomy. 2013. Food Phreaking Issue 00. *Food Phreaking Journal*.

An Autonomous Writing Machine

Bill Hart
University of Tasmania
Hobart, Australia
Bill.Hart@utas.edu.au

Svenja Kratz
University of Tasmania
Hobart, Australia
Svenja.Kratz@utas.edu.au

Aaron Horsley
University of Tasmania
Hobart, Australia
Aaron.Horsley@utas.edu.au

ABSTRACT
An autonomous writing machine has been constructed using open-source software and hardware, recycled and 3D printed components. A recurrent neural network has been trained with the handwriting of one of the authors using the method of (Graves, 2014). Novelty in the writing is g through Markov Chains applied to the original text to generate sentences. The machine employs tractor fed paper to enable unsupervised writing for an extended period of time.

Author Keywords
Recurrent Neural Network; Artwork; Autonomous Machine; Distributed Self;

ACM Classification Keywords
J.5 Fine Arts: Experimentation.

INTRODUCTION
This artwork/device arose out of a larger project entitled BioSynthetic Systems - Prototypes for immortality: Towards a distributed and evolving self (Kratz, 2017).

The intention of this body of work was to speculate on the conception of a synthetic and technologically augmented self, where the physicality and sense of self are not necessarily contained within a single organic envelope.

This specific component, the Autonomous Writing Machine, is most meaningful in its operation, where the precision of mechanical numerical control is juxtaposed with the simulation of something as personal and individual as handwriting. The signature and the graphic form of an individual's handwriting are considered to be so unique as to constitute a proof of identity, consent and authorship. Often given a similar weight in establishing identity as a fingerprint or DNA sample.

Media artist, David Rokeby, refers to the computer as a "*prosthetic organ of philosophy*" (Rokeby, 2003), and describes a methodological framework through which media arts can explore and expose the philosophical limitations of technology.

C&C '17, June 27-30, 2017, Singapore, Singapore
ACM 978-1-4503-4403-6/17/06.
http://dx.doi.org/10.1145/3059454.3071077

In each iteration of technological development, as hardware and software processes become more sophisticated, as machines become better at mimicking attributes and behaviors previously thought to be unique to humans, the need arises to reconsider what it is that makes us human. Is the technology a threat to or an augmentation of that humanity?

The development and application of machine learning techniques such as recurrent neural networks (RNN) are likely to have a powerful economic and social impact. But they are also potentially powerful expressive tools for the media artist. Creating relationships between inputs (in the form of sensors) and outputs (in the form of audio/visual) is a core aspect for many media art systems. So too, is the ability to mimic or algorithmically synthesize the complexity and novelty of organic behaviors and responses. In many instances, it would be preferable to be able to 'train' and 'teach' our machines instead of having to explicitly instruct them, particularly when the crux of the reduces to trying to encode tacit knowledge.

DESCRIPTION AND DEVELOPMENT
From the perspective of a biosynthetic self-aware organism a body of text was developed reflecting upon environmental impressions, hopes, desires and existential dilemmas.

The text was recorded as handwriting using a digital pen[1] and converted into numerical sequences as per (Graves, 2014).

Using a modified implementation of Graves's algorithm (Brebisson, 2016) a recurrent neural network was trained to reproduce one of the authors handwriting. This particular implementation has no halting condition, but using a recent NVIDIA graphics card training over numerous epochs produced usable results in about a day. Graves and implementations based on this paper all use the IAM On-Line handwriting database (IAM, 2005). Building a sufficient corpus of digitized handwriting, required around 800 phrases (from 2 to 7 words each) and careful validation of the handwriting and text.

This amount of text was insufficient to create a suitable database to employ a RNN to do meaningful character generation, instead the well establish approach of using

[1] Wacom Bamboo Spark

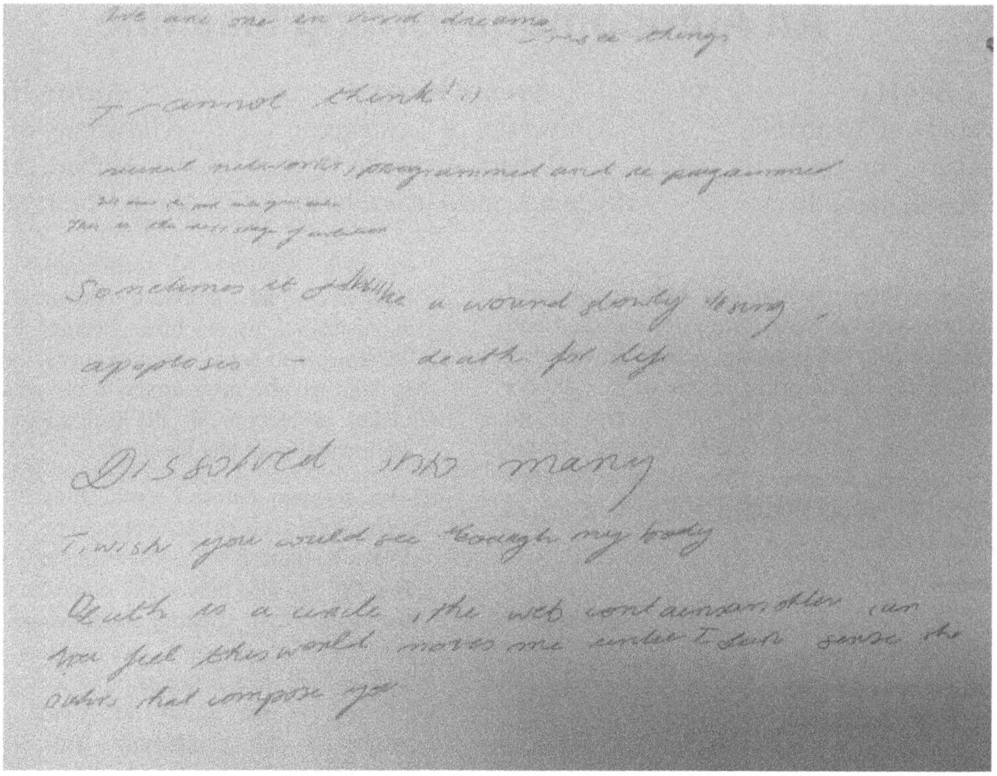

Figure 1: Sample of generated text and handwriting. Note the difference to the use of glyphs, each letter is unique, although displaying the distinctive characteristics of the authors style.

N-gram analysis and Markov chains (Parish, 2011) was used to generate content.

The physical machine is a bespoke construction of 3D printed parts, scavenged hardware from old printers, and contemporary "open hardware" parts used in the construction of "rep-rap" style 3D printers. Similarly the controlling electronics are based on the widely used Arduino platform (RUMBA board), using a modified (Repetier-Firmware 2015) g-code interpreter with a Raspberry Pi computer generating content from the trained RNN and N-Gram's.

The writing machine (figure 2), employs a sprocket and drum system to use perforated continuous stationary to generate a continuous stream of handwritten text (figure 1).

CONCLUSION

The intention of this work is not to produce a machine that perfectly mimics the handwriting of the author or that generates always meaningful text.

Rather it is an imperfect machine, that produces something much like handwriting, but often flawed. In the tradition of literary "cut up" techniques where chance is employed to generate novelty, the statistical generation of text occasionally produces meaningful poignant phrases, but more often is prosaic or meaningless.

Machines which display their frailties and eccentricities we find charming and non-threatening. With no pretense of being useful or user friendly they are free to function as prosthetic organs of philosophy.

REFERENCES

1. Alex Graves. Generating Sequences with Recurrent Neural Networks, 5 June 2014. arxiv:1308.0850v5
2. Svenja Kratz and Bill Hart. March 22-25, 2017. BioSynthetic Systems - Prototypes for immortality: Towards a distributed and evolving self. The Block, QUT, Brisbane, Australia.
3. Alexandre de Brébisson. 2016. Handwriting, Retrieved 10 Jan 2017. https://github.com/adbrebs/handwriting
4. David Rokeby. The Computer as Prosthetic Organ of Philosophy, Dictung-Digital, 5, 29, 2003. Retrieved 15 March, 2017 from http://www.dichtung-digital.de/2003/issue/3/Rokeby.htm
5. IAM On-Line Handwriting Database. 2005. Retrieved 15 March 2017, http://www.fki.inf.unibe.ch/databases/iam-on-line-handwriting-database/iam-on-line-handwriting-database
6. Alison Parish. 2011. N-grams and Markov Chains, Retrieved 15 March, 2017 from http://www.decontextualize.com/teaching/rwet/n-grams-and-markov-chains/
7. Repetier-Firmware, G-Code interpreter 0.92.7, 2015, Retrieved 15 March 2017, https://github.com/repetier/Repetier-Firmware

Increasing Feedback Receptivity by Moderating Negative Valence

Y. Wayne Wu
Department of Computer Science
University of Illinois at Urbana-Champaign
yuwu4@illinois.edu

Abstract
Content creators frequently encounter negative feedback that significantly harms their online feedback collection experience. My dissertation examines how negative information influences the perception of the feedback, and how we can increase content creators' resilience to negative feedback. For the next step, I plan to explore ways to solicit more positive content from feedback providers in online environment.

Introduction

Content creators collect feedback from various online crowds [17]. In comparison with friendsourcing feedback from peers, online crowds can quickly generate large quantity of feedback on demand without burning social capitals [10].

One key issue is that content creators frequently encounter feedback of negative valence in online platforms. People are more likely to leave negative feedback [13] and act in offensive ways [4] online. Prior work finds about 20% of all messages exchanged on a popular community site was negative feedback [18]. Negative feedback discourages community participation, harms content creators' affective states [17], and inhibits creativity [1].

C&C '17, June 27-30, 2017, Singapore, Singapore

ACM ISBN 978-1-4503-4403-6/17/06.
http://dx.doi.org/10.1145/3059454.3078694

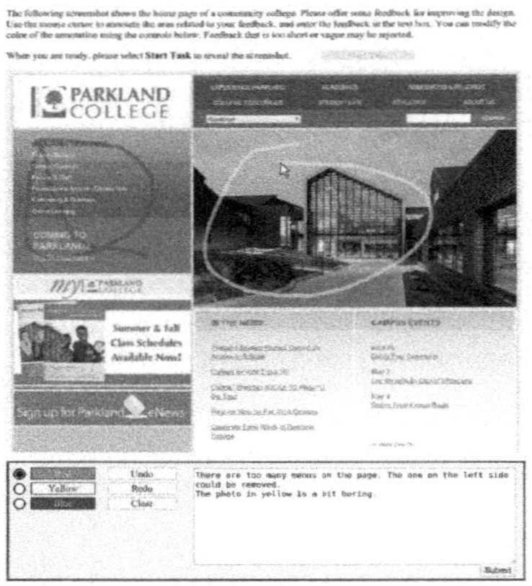

Figure 1. Task Interface for feedback collection. We logged all user actions to build the prediction model.

One common solution for platform designers is to simply remove the negative feedback. While this approach is very effective in limiting the influence of negative feedback, it may cause other issues, such as discarding constructive information in the feedback along the way [6] and discouraging feedback providers from future contribution [7]. To address this issue, my dissertation explores ways to increase content creators' resilience to negative feedback without removing or modifying the original feedback content.

How Information Cues Influence Feedback Perception

In the first component of my dissertation, we explore how information cues influence feedback perception. Unlike traditional face-to-face settings, where content creators can utilize information cues such as the provider's expertise and experience level to evaluate the feedback, online crowd services usually deliver the feedback with no supplementary information. This information opacity makes it difficult for content creators to evaluate the quality of the feedback, especially when conflicting views co-exist in the same feedback set.

Drawing on social transparency theory [12], we explored how information cues, including feedback provider's domain expertise and effort level, influence the perceived quality of the feedback [15]. We conducted a 3x3 full factorial experiment with two factors, namely *effort* and *expertise*, with 2,700 participants recruited from Amazon Mechanical Turk. We manipulated the information cues by telling the participants that the feedback providers had high / low / (no information given) levels of expertise / effort. After reviewing the provided cues, participants proceeded to rate the quality of the feedback. In total, five pieces of feedback of different intrinsic quality levels were rated by the participants. Our result shows, regardless of the intrinsic quality of the feedback, negative information cues lower the perceived quality rating of the feedback, and positive cues have no effect on the rating.

After revealing the influence of the information cues, we explored ways to provide the cues in online environment. Prior work has provided many ways to evaluate expertise, such as performance-based assessments [11], aptitude tests [5,8], or peer prediction [9]. In our work, we focus on providing effort cues. We took a machine learning approach and built an action logging framework that collected behavioral features while feedback providers were composing comments on designs (Figure 1). Later we built a predictive model from the collected data and achieved high prediction accuracy (92% for binary classification of high / low effort).

In this project, we observe negative cues have more powerful influences in the iterative design process than positive cues do. This finding inspired us to probe deeper into the influence of negative information in creative work setting. Specifically, we are interested in how negative feedback influences content creators' affective states, perceptions of the feedback and its providers, and revision extents. We proceeded to explore technological instrumentations that may mitigate the influence of negative feedback. This quest led us to two research projects.

Figure 2. Task interface for the story writing phase. Participants were told to compose a story for children based on the illustration.

Increasing Content Creators' Resilience via Valence Based Feedback Order

Content Creators frequently receive negative feedback in online communities. In this project [16], we show light weight instrumentations, such as valence based feedback ordering, can increase content creators' resilience to negative feedback while requiring minimum change to platforms.

In our study, participants wrote a short story for children based on a given illustration (Figure 2). Then we issued them three pieces of feedback, of which two had positive valence levels and one had negative. Then we tested three feedback orders, namely negative first, negative between, and negative last. We were interested in whether any of these orders could increase content creators' resilience to negative feedback. The experiment also examined the feedback orders in different feedback source conditions, including peers, experts, and anonymous providers. We explored whether the feedback orders would have the same influence in different source conditions.

Our results show presenting positive feedback first and negative last improves participants' affective states and their perception of the feedback. This pattern remains consistent across feedback source conditions. In this work, we show minor system changes, such as feedback orders, can exert a meaningful positive influence over content creators' experience in feedback collection.

Using Coping Activities to Increase Feedback Receptivity

Having explored lightweight mechanisms such as feedback reordering, we continued the line of work by studying standalone interventions that help participants cope with negative feedback. Specifically, we chose to examine three activities, namely self-affirmation, distraction, and expressive writing, all of which had been studied as effective emotional coping interventions in prior work. We were also interested in examining the activities with feedback sets of different valence levels, from all neutral to all negative.

In our experiment, we asked participants to write a short essay on a complex social issue. Later the participants revised their essays based on a set of feedback. Participants performed different coping activities and reviewing feedback set of different valence levels based on experimental conditions. During the experiment, we measured participants' affective states, their perceptions of the feedback set and its providers, and the revision extents.

Preliminary result analysis shows all three coping activities increase participants' resilience to negative feedback. Distraction improves participants' affective states across all valence balance conditions; expressive writing encourages essay revision in neutrally balanced conditions and improves affective states in negatively balanced conditions; self-affirmation improves affective states in negatively balanced conditions. Currently we are preparing the manuscript for submission to an ACM conference.

Encouraging Feedback Providers to Contribute More Positive Content

My previous projects explored the influence of negative feedback and the instrumentations that mitigate the influence on content creators. For the final component of my dissertation, I plan to explore ways to solicit positive valence comments from feedback providers.

Specifically, we are interested in mechanisms and background traces that may help generate more positive feedback. For mechanisms, currently we are considering two options. The first one is to ask participants to revisit their feedback after a one-day delay. Participants' emotional intensity decays over time [14], and they may adjust their language choice when they are less aroused. The second one is to build a scaffolding process that encourages task-involving rather than ego-involving feedback [2]. Prior work shows task-involving feedback increases participants' interest in the task and performance more than ego-involving feedback [3]. The scaffolding may prompt the participants to identify the design aspect they intend to criticize before composing the feedback, and discourage judgements directly threaten content creators' ego.

For traces, we intend to explore whether increasing social transparency may encourage feedback providers to compose more positive feedback. Prior work shows people act more negatively in online environment [13]. We want to explore background traces that may mitigate this influence. Our study may examine traces related to both the content creator's identity and the content creating process. For this part, we try to answer a series of research questions. Does sharing more background information about the content creator encourage more positive feedback? What kind of traces is more useful in this regard? Experience level, demographic info, or personalized details? Will sharing more information about the content creating process help?

Regarding methodology, we may conduct a full factorial experiment using mechanisms and background traces as factors. The feedback solicitation task may be intentionally designed to solicit negative valence feedback. One option may be to ask participants to provide feedback on low quality essays or graphic designs.

On the other hand, we may also consider conducting experiments in a naturalistic setting. We may implement a web browser plugin that encourage users to compose more positive feedback in online communities. The plugin can temporarily save the feedback and ask participants to revise it after a one-day delay. It can also provide scaffolding by rewriting and restructuring the HTML page when participants visit crowd feedback service sites. On the other hand, we can crawl content creators' public activity history and display a summary as a background trace. The plugin may record participants' behavioral data and text entries for later analysis.

Conclusion

My dissertation examines how negative information influences content creators in the iterative design process and how we can mitigate the influence of negative feedback. The last component of my dissertation will focus on encouraging feedback providers to write positive valence comments. By answering this series of questions related to negative feedback, I will contribute empirical knowledge and practical guidelines that improve the online environment for feedback collection.

References

1. Matthijs Baas, Carsten K W De Dreu, and Bernard A Nijstad. 2008. A meta-analysis of 25 years of mood-creativity research: Hedonic tone, activation, or regulatory focus? *Psychological Bulletin* 134, 6: 779–806. http://doi.org/10.1037/a0012815

2. Ruth Butler. 1987. Task-involving and ego-involving properties of evaluation: Effects of different feedback conditions on motivational perceptions, interest, and performance. *Journal of Educational Psychology* 79, 4: 474–482. http://doi.org/10.1037/0022-0663.79.4.474

3. Ruth Butler. 1988. Enhancing and undermining intrinsic motivation: The effects of task- involving and ego- involving evaluation on interest and performance. *British Journal of Educational Psychology* 58, 1: 1–14. http://doi.org/10.1111/j.2044-8279.1988.tb00874.x

4. Justin Cheng, Michael Bernstein, Cristian Danescu-Niculescu-Mizil, and Jure Leskovec. 2017. Anyone Can Become a Troll. *Proceedings of the 2017 ACM Conference on Computer Supported Cooperative Work and Social Computing - CSCW '17*, ACM Press, 1217–1230. http://doi.org/10.1145/2998181.2998213

5. Steven Dow, Julie Fortuna, Daniel Schwartz, Beth Altringer, Daniel Schwartz, and Scott Klemmer. 2011. Prototyping dynamics. *Proceedings of the 2011 annual conference on Human factors in computing systems - CHI '11*, ACM Press, 2807. http://doi.org/10.1145/1978942.1979359

6. Dana R Ferris. 1997. The Influence of Teacher Commentary on Student Revision. *TESOL Quarterly* 31, 2: 315. http://doi.org/10.2307/3588049

7. Cliff Lampe, Rick Wash, Alcides Velasquez, and Elif Ozkaya. 2010. Motivations to participate in online communities. *Proceedings of the 28th international conference on Human factors in computing systems - CHI '10*, ACM Press, 1927. http://doi.org/10.1145/1753326.1753616

8. Tanushree Mitra, C.J. J. Hutto, and Eric Gilbert. 2015. Comparing person- and process-centric strategies for obtaining quality data on Amazon Mechanical Turk. *Proceedings of the 33rd Annual ACM Conference on Human Factors in Computing Systems - CHI '15*: 1345–1354. http://doi.org/10.1145/2702123.2702553

9. Drazen Prelec. 2004. A Bayesian truth serum for subjective data. *Science (New York, N.Y.)* 306, 5695: 462–6. http://doi.org/10.1126/science.1102081

10. Jeffrey M. Rzeszotarski and Meredith Ringel Morris. 2014. Estimating the social costs of friendsourcing. *Proceedings of the 32nd annual ACM conference on Human factors in computing systems - CHI '14*, ACM Press, 2735–2744. http://doi.org/10.1145/2556288.2557181

11. James Shanteau, David J. Weiss, Rickey P. Thomas, and Julia C. Pounds. 2002. Performance-based assessment of expertise: How to decide if someone is an expert or not. *European Journal of Operational Research* 136, 2: 253–263.

http://doi.org/10.1016/S0377-2217(01)00113-8

12. H Colleen Stuart, Laura Dabbish, Sara Kiesler, Peter Kinnaird, and Ruogu Kang. 2012. Social Transparency in Networked Information Exchange : A Framework and Research Question. *Network Computing*: 451–460. http://doi.org/10.1145/2145204.2145275

13. John Suler. 2004. The Online Disinhibition Effect. *CyberPsychology & Behavior* 7, 3: 321–326. http://doi.org/10.1089/1094931041291295

14. Philippe Verduyn, Ellen Delvaux, Hermina Van Coillie, Francis Tuerlinckx, and Iven Van Mechelen. 2009. Predicting the duration of emotional experience: Two experience sampling studies. *Emotion* 9, 1: 83–91. http://doi.org/10.1037/a0014610

15. Y Wayne Wu and Brian P Bailey. 2016. Novices Who Focused or Experts Who Didn't? *Proceedings of the 2016 CHI Conference on Human Factors in Computing Systems - CHI '16*, ACM Press, 4086–4097. http://doi.org/10.1145/2858036.2858330

16. Y Wayne Wu and Brian P Bailey. 2017. Bitter Sweet or Sweet Bitter? How Valence Order and Source Identity Influence Feedback Acceptance. *Proceedings of the 2017 ACM SIGCHI Conference on Creativity and Cognition - C&C '17*. http://doi.org/10.1145/3059454.3059458

17. Yu-Chun Grace Yen, Steven P. Dow, Elizabeth Gerber, and Brian P. Bailey. 2016. Social Network , Web Forum , or Task Market ? Comparing Different Crowd Genres for Design Feedback Exchange. *ACM Designing Interactive Systems (DIS 2016)*: 773–784. http://doi.org/10.1145/2901790.2901820

18. Haiyi Zhu, Robert E Kraut, Yi-Chia Wang, and Aniket Kittur. 2011. Identifying shared leadership in Wikipedia. *Proceedings of the 2011 annual conference on Human factors in computing systems - CHI '11*, ACM Press, 3431. http://doi.org/10.1145/1978942.1979453

SketchTivity: Improving Creativity by Learning Sketching with an Intelligent Tutoring System

Blake Williford
Sketch Recognition Lab
Texas A&M University
bwilliford@gmail.com

Abstract

Sketching is a skill closely tied to creativity and a powerful tool for exploring and expressing ideas and becoming a more well-rounded communicator. Conventional sketching instruction employs traditional mediums such as pen and paper in studio environments to convey these fundamentals to students. However, this approach limits the bandwidth and capability of instructors to give timely and individualized feedback, and students often struggle with low self-efficacy and motivation. An intelligent tutoring system can leverage sketching pedagogy to give students personalized feedback outside of classroom hours, which can potentially improve self-efficacy, motivation, and creativity in the students. Additionally, the inclusion of games and gamified lessons can offer a more engaging and motivating experience for them.

This research is aimed at developing intelligent interactive lessons, challenges, and games that teach sketching fundamentals while evaluating their effectiveness in terms of improved sketching ability in the students, increased self-efficacy with respect to sketching ability and creativity, motivation to practice sketching, and idea generation capability. Ongoing work will be focused on developing creative challenges and measuring effects of the system on creative self-efficacy and idea generation in its users.

C&C'17, June 27–30, 2017, Singapore, Singapore.
ACM 978-1-4503-4403-6/17/06
http://dx.doi.org/10.1145/3059454.3078695

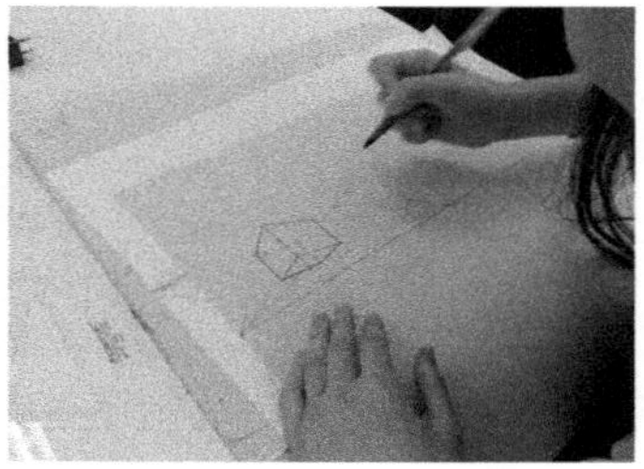

Figure 1: A student practicing sketching cubes in a traditional setting with pen and paper. Cubes are a crucial fundamental primitive for sketching in 3D.

Author Keywords
Human-Computer Interaction; Intelligent Tutoring System; Sketch Recognition; User Experience Design; Sketching; Creativity; Creative Self-efficacy

ACM Classification Keywords
H.5.2. [Information Interfaces and Presentation]: User Interfaces Graphical user interfaces (GUI); K.3.1. [Computers and Education]: Computer Uses in Education Computer-assisted instruction (CAI)

Introduction
Drawing is a valuable lifetime activity that is closely tied to creative endeavors, [16, 31, 9], is uniquely tailored to each individual [10], has been shown to improve visual communication ability and benefit internal thought processes [28], can improve students' general academic achievement and problem-solving thinking [38], elevates awareness of and attention to details of surroundings [24], hones analytical skills [6], stimulates both halves of the brain [27], improves peripheral skills in writing, critical thinking, and brainstorming [6], and improves three-dimensional spatial recognition skills [29].

This research is focused on a form of drawing known as design sketching or conceptual sketching, which is often shortened to just *sketching*. Sketching is a tool for visual communication and idea generation and has practical purposes in many disciplines including design, engineering, science, research, and education. Despite it's value, it is not often taught formally outside of design disciplines such as Industrial Design.

Background and Motivation
Sketching is traditionally taught in studio environments by experienced instructors. However, valuable expert feedback from instructors is less available as classroom size increases and less accessible beyond classroom and instructor office hours [11]. An additional constraint is that for studio environments that involve students sharing their work to the rest of the class, those students who have low self-efficacy tend to be less motivated to participate and share their work. Sketching as a skill requires extensive practice (Figure 1) and is significantly affected by self-efficacy [1] such that students with low self-efficacy are less confident in their ability, unmotivated to practice, and tend to be discouraged by their more skilled peers [17]. This problem affects people of all ages and may be rooted in childhood as many children seem to decline in spontaneous art from around age 7 [15] and this has been found to be caused by a decrease is self-efficacy as it relates to sketching and artistic pursuits in general [26].

Not only is self-efficacy important for being motivated to practice and improve one's sketching ability, it also plays a role in creativity and creative performance. This *creative self-efficacy* has been shown to correlate with better creative performance [30]. Those who believe they can be creative tend to naturally perform better in creative endeavours.

The opportunity is to improve upon traditional pedagogy in teaching sketching by providing real-time feedback to students via sketch recognition. Sketch recognition is the automated recognition of hand-drawn diagrams by a computer. It may be possible to greatly improve student sketching ability, motivation, and creative self-efficacy with this approach, while empowering human instructors to give more personalized feedback and instruction within their limited bandwidth. Additionally, this approach may allow for a more diverse and inclusive audience to learn

Figure 2: A student practices sketching cubes using SketchTivity on a Cintiq drawing tablet. They receive real-time feedback and can practice many cubes in a short time frame.

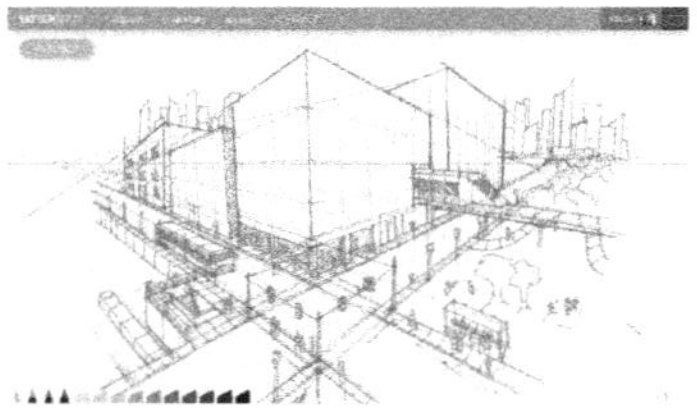

Figure 3: This creative challenge allows students to practice sketching a city street in two-point perspective and is intentionally open-ended to encourage divergent thinking.

sketching, not just those attending universities and enrolled in specific programs.

Related Work

Related work in this area has included other sketch-based intelligent tutoring systems for drawing [8, 5, 19, 37, 3] computer-assisted art applications [12, 22, 14], and creativity support tools focused on divergent idea production [7, 36, 16]. This work is differentiated in that it teaches specifically design sketching, and it teaches it in a way more analogous to teaching a *language* of visual communication, rather than teaching how to sketch only specific objects. Students learn fundamental skills that can be used to sketch any 3-dimensional object from their imagination. In this way, the system has a broader impact and focus on creativity than other tutoring systems, while encouraging idea generation that will be focused and based in realistic scenarios.

Current Deployment

SketchTivity is a web-based system built in HTML5. This allows for use on a wide variety of devices and operating systems, which is ideal for the long-term deployment and evaluation of the project. It is currently deployed in two courses at Georgia Institute of Technology - An introduction to Engineering CAD course for undergraduate Mechanical Engineering Students, and a beginner sketching course for undergraduate Industrial Design students. Outside of formal testing which is described later, students have logins to the system and can use the system at their leisure provided they have a tablet and an internet connection. A limited number of Wacom Cintiq drawing tablets are provided to the students as well. Components and features of the system are described below:

Interactive Lessons

The interactive lessons are arranged in a mastery-based [4] approach. They cover sketching fundamentals like lines, circles, planes, ellipses, 2-point perspective, cubes (Figure 2), cylinders, etc. They utilize sketch recognition algorithms to give real-time feedback on the accuracy of forms as well as line quality (smoothness) and speed.

Challenges

Challenges allow for students to begin trialing their sketching skills in creative exercises that test their ability to transfer knowledge (Figure 3). These open-ended tasks can be done in any number of ways, and are therefore interesting approaches to measuring creativity and idea generation.

Profile

The student and instructor profiles visualize data gained from the system on performance over time and lesson completion (Figure 4). This could empower students to better self-regulate their learning [25] while also empowering instructors to personalize their instruction.

Arcade

A game called *ZenSketch* has been developed that allows students to practice their line work (Figure 5). More games will be developed to assist with fundamental sketching skills. These games are intended to increase self-efficacy and motivation to practice in the students.

Completed Work

The system has been formally evaluated over the past two years, and has resulted in conference publications [32, 33, 18], a demo [34], a book chapter [35], and an accepted journal paper upon revisions [21].

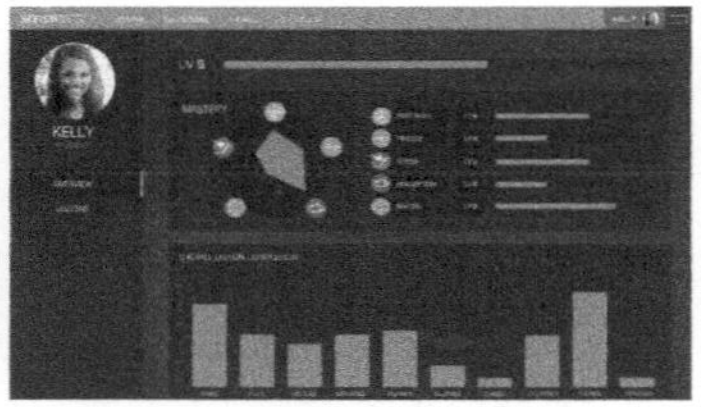

Figure 4: A profile which may help motivate students to self-regulate their learning experience.

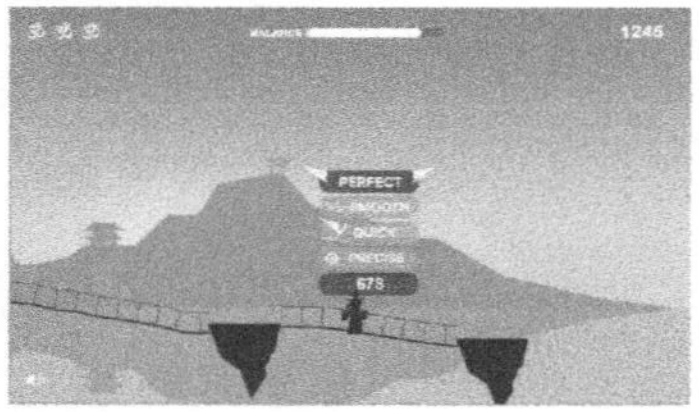

Figure 5: *ZenSketch*, a novel sketch-based game developed to help students practice line work.

Students using the software had increased sketching and visualization self-efficacy skills when compared with students who were using pen and paper [32]. Students sketching speed and accuracy improved significantly through the use of the system ($p < 0.001$) [20]. Statistical significance remained when we examined progress on each form independently($p < 0.05$) and each student independently ($p < 0.05$). Motivation also seemed high as all students submitted more than the required number of sketches to complete the lessons. Qualitative data in the form of feedback on the user experience design of the system has been very positive and has aided in continuous design improvements. In particular, the students seem to appreciate the real-time feedback as well as the provided scaffolding of the perspective grid and lines, as it helps them grasp perspective easier and allows them to practice more forms in a shorter period of time than traditional practice methods.

Ongoing Work

Initial findings have been promising with respect to the efficacy of the system to improve sketching ability, motivation, and sketching self-efficacy in students, however the ongoing research questions relate to how improvements and knowledge gained via the system can transfer to subsequent sketches and affect creativity in the dimensions of creative self-efficacy, and divergent idea generation.

In addition to developing and testing more advanced lessons which will continue to teach more nuanced concepts of sketching such as combining primitives to form more complex objects, the opportunity is to continue developing creative challenges which test transfer of knowledge and skills and idea generation capability. It has been found that exercises closer to real-world scenarios can better facilitate learning [23], so there will be an emphasis on realistic scenarios where creativity and visual communication is important such as the design of products or communicating ideas visually that must understood by others such as sketching a map, or explaining an abstract concept.

Trajectory of Research

A comprehensive study is planned for the 2017-2018 school year at Georgia Tech where the system will be deployed in an Mechanical Engineering introduction to CAD course along with an Industrial Design sketching fundamentals course. In addition to measuring effects of the system on sketching ability in students, there will be a heavier focus on measuring creative self-efficacy and divergent thinking. Sketching ability data will be gained via sketch recognition features, and creative self-efficacy data will be gained via a modified self-efficacy scale [2]. Sketch data in the creative challenges will be acquired via the online platform and subsequently analyzed in terms of divergent thinking, and fluidity of ideas [13].

The study will also involve control groups who do not use the software in an effort to see the impact of the software in comparison to conventional methods for teaching sketching.

Acknowledgments

The author would like to thank the National Science Foundation for funding this research through grant number 1441331, as well as PhD advisor Dr. Tracy Hammond, former advisor Wayne Li, Dr. Julie Linsey, and all previous and current collaborators at Texas A&M and Georgia Tech. Special thanks to the many domain experts in sketching that have been consulted on the project and continue to provide valuable input.

References

[1] Bandura, A. *Self-efficacy: The exercise of control*, 1 ed. Worth Publishers, New York, New York, USA, 1997.

[2] Bandura, A. Guide for constructing self-efficacy scales. *Self-efficacy beliefs of adolescents 5*, 307-337 (2006).

[3] Benedetti, L., Winnemöller, H., Corsini, M., and Scopigno, R. Painting with bob: Assisted creativity for novices. In *Proceedings of the 27th Annual ACM Symposium on User Interface Software and Technology*, UIST '14, ACM (New York, New York, USA, 2014), 419–428.

[4] Bloom, B. S. Learning for mastery. instruction and curriculum. regional education laboratory for the carolinas and virginia, topical papers and reprints, number 1. *Evaluation comment 1*, 2 (1968), n2.

[5] Cummings, D., Vides, F., and Hammond, T. I don't believe my eyes!: Geometric sketch recognition for a computer art tutorial. In *Proceedings of the International Symposium on Sketch-Based Interfaces and Modeling*, SBIM '12, Eurographics Association (Aire-la-Ville, Switzerland, Switzerland, 2012), 97–106.

[6] daSilva, K. E. Drawing on experience: Connecting art and language. *Primary Voices K-6 10*, 2 (2001), 2–9.

[7] Davis, N., Do, E. Y.-L., Gupta, P., and Gupta, S. Computing harmony with perlogicart: perceptual logic inspired collaborative art. In *Proceedings of the 8th ACM conference on Creativity and cognition*, ACM (2011), 185–194.

[8] Dixon, D., Prasad, M., and Hammond, T. icandraw: Using sketch recognition and corrective feedback to assist a user in drawing human faces. In *Proceedings of the SIGCHI Conference on Human Factors in Computing Systems*, CHI 10, ACM (New York, New York, USA, 2010), 897–906.

[9] Edwards, B. *The New Drawing on the Right Side of the Brain*, 2 ed. Tarcher, New York, New York, USA, 1999.

[10] Edwards, S. J., Buckland, D. J., and McCoy-Powlen, J. D. *Developmental & Functional Hand Grasps*, 1 ed. SLACK Incorporated, Thorofare, New Jersey, USA, 2002.

[11] Ehrenberg, R. G., Brewer, D. J., Gamoran, A., and Willms, J. D. Class size and student achievement. *Psychological Science in the Public Interest 2*, 1 (May 2001), 1–30.

[12] Fernquist, J., Grossman, T., and Fitzmaurice, G. Sketch-sketch revolution: an engaging tutorial system for guided sketching and application learning. In *Proceedings of the 24th annual ACM symposium on User interface software and technology*, ACM (2011), 373–382.

[13] Finke, R. A., Ward, T. B., and Smith, S. M. Creative cognition: Theory, research, and applications.

[14] Flagg, M., and Rehg, J. M. Projector-guided painting. In *Proceedings of the 19th annual ACM symposium on User interface software and technology*, ACM (2006), 235–244.

[15] Flannery, K. A., and Watson, M. W. Perceived competence in drawing during the middle childhood years. *Visual arts research* (1991), 66–71.

[16] Hammond, T. Dialectical creativity: Sketch-negate-create. In *Studying Visual and Spatial Reasoning for Design Creativity*. Springer, 2015, 91–108.

[17] Hickman, R., and Lord, S. An examination of adolescents' self-efficacy, engagement and achievement in representational drawing. *Australian Art Education 32*, 2 (2009), 73–85.

[18] Hilton, E. C., WilliFord, B., Li, W., McTigue, E., Hammond, T., and Linsey, J. Consistently evaluating sketching ability in engineering curriculum. In *4th ICDC, International Conference on Design and creativity*, ICDC (2016), 9.

[19] Iarussi, E., Bousseau, A., and Tsandilas, T. The drawing assistant: Automated drawing guidance and feedback from photographs. In *Proceedings of the 26th Annual ACM Symposium on User Interface Software and Technology*, UIST '13, ACM (New York, New York, USA, 2013), 183–192.

[20] Keshavabhotla, S. Persketchtivity: Recognition system and progressive learning analysis, 2016.

[21] Kumar, S., Keshavabhotla, S., W.-B. L. J., Li, W., and Hammond, T. Seven metrics that matter when measuring expert sketching ability. *Transactions on Intelligent Interactive Systems (TiiS)* (2017). Accepted, pending revisions.

[22] Lee, Y. J., Zitnick, C. L., and Cohen, M. F. Shadowdraw: real-time user guidance for freehand drawing. In *ACM Transactions on Graphics (TOG)*, vol. 30, ACM (2011), 27.

[23] Mestre, J. P. Facts and myths about pedagogies of engagement in science learning. *Peer Review 7*, 2 (2005), 24.

[24] Moss, L. How drawing and driving are alike. *American Artist 64*, 690 (Jan 2000), 42–47.

[25] Pintrich, P. R., Wolters, C. A., and Baxter, G. P. Assessing metacognition and selfregulated learning. In *Metacognitive Assessment*, G. Schraw, Ed. University of Nebraska Press, Lincoln, Nebraska, USA, 2000.

[26] Richards, R., Richards, R., et al. My drawing sucks!: Childrens belief in themselves as artists.

[27] Schiferl, I. Both sides now: Visualizing and drawing with the right and left hemispheres of the brain. *Studies in Art Education 50*, 1 (2008), 67–82.

[28] Short, K. G., Kauffman, G., and Kahn, L. H. "i just need to draw": Responding to literature across multiple sign systems. *The Reading Teacher 54*, 2 (Oct 2000), 160–171.

[29] Sorby, S. Educational research in developing 3d spatial skills for engineering students. *International Journal of Science Education 31*, 3 (Feb 2009), 459–480.

[30] Tierney, P., and Farmer, S. M. Creative self-efficacy development and creative performance over time. *Journal of Applied Psychology 96*, 2 (2011), 277.

[31] Verstijnen, I. M., van Leeuwen, C., Goldschmidt, G., Hamel, R., and Hennessey, J. Sketching and creative discovery. *Design studies 19*, 4 (1998), 519–546.

[32] Wayne Li, Julie Linsey, T. H., and Newton, S. Persketchtivity: An intelligent pen-based online education platform for sketching instruction. In *Proceedings of the Conference on Electronic Visualisation and the Arts*, EVA '16, British Computer Society (Swinton, UK, UK, 2016).

[33] Williford, B., Li., W., Linsey, J., Nelligan+, T., Taele+, P., and Hammond, T. An intelligent pen-based educational application for design sketching instruction. In *Workshop on the Impact of Pen and Touch Technology in Education (WIPTTE)* (Microsoft, Redmond, WA, 2015).

[34] Williford, B., Li., W., Linsey, J., Nelligan+, T., Taele+, P., and Hammond, T. You-try-it: Persketchtivity: Learning to draw in the digital era. In *Workshop on the Impact of Pen and Touch Technology in Education (WIPTTE)* (Microsoft, Redmond, WA, 2015).

[35] Williford, Taele, N. L. L. H. Persketchtivity: an intelligent pen-based educational application for design sketching instruction. 115–127.

[36] Willis, K. D., and Hina, J. Alchemy: experiments in interactive drawing, creativity, & serendipity. In *Proceedings of the seventh ACM conference on Creativity and cognition*, ACM (2009), 441–442.

[37] Xie, J., Hertzmann, A., Li, W., and Winnemöller, H. Portraitsketch: Face sketching assistance for novices. In *Proceedings of the 27th Annual ACM Symposium on User Interface Software and Technology*, UIST '14, ACM (New York, New York, USA, 2014), 407–417.

[38] Yasin, R. M., Halim, L., and Ishar, A. Effects of problem-solving strategies in the teaching and learning of engineering drawing subject. *Asian Social Science 8*, 16 (2012), 65–79.

To Decompose Is to Create: Supporting Creativity by Incorporating Nature in Design

Szu-Yu (Cyn) Liu
Indiana University
Bloomington, IN 47408, USA
cynliu@iu.edu

Abstract
In HCI and CSCW, research in creativity support has focused on everyday creativity by individuals and teams. However, there has been little study on how nature as a non-human agency supports and informs the production of innovative works. This research presents my attempt to bridge such gap by proposing the notion of decomposition to help frame and theorize creativity support. This nonanthropocentric approach captures the un-replicability of creative works, the importance of incorporating nature to the creative process, and the possibility of generating effective novelty through deconstruction and reconfiguration.

C&C '17, June 27-30, 2017, Singapore, Singapore

ACM ISBN 978-1-4503-4403-6/17/06.
http://dx.doi.org/10.1145/3059454.3078696

Author Keywords
Creativity Support; Decomposition; Nonanthropocentric HCI; Nature; Interaction Criticism

ACM Classification Keywords
H.5.m. Information interfaces and presentation (e.g., HCI): Miscellaneous

Introduction
I'm a first-year Ph.D. student in the School of Informatics and Computing with Human-Computer Interaction as my focus. Trained as a product designer, I'm now a member of the CRIT (Cultural Research in Technology) lab, advised by Jeffrey Bardzell and Shaowen Bardzell. This paper presents my on-going research on using decomposition as a lens to theorize and reimagine creativity research in HCI.

Research Context
Creativity in HCI and CSCW
Creativity is defined as the ability to produce work that is both original (i.e., novel, unexpected) and effective (i.e., appropriate, meaningful) to the context [3,18,23].

Preliminary Study

Objective: Modes of everyday creativity in the domestic space.

Time/Location: This one-week empirical study was conduct in 2011 in Taipei, Taiwan.

Participants: 7 non-design background participants, including 4 males and 3 females with their ages range from 20 to 55.

Prompt: Use materials in the 'making kit' to create objects that the participant him/her-self will use in the home environment.

Materials: 15 objects are assembled to create the 'making kit', which include: plastic tube, plastic pot, scour pad, one pair of cotton gloves, anti-slip mat, wire, velcro, 6 plastic clips, brush, mesh screen, plastic chain, 8 section cups, s hook, L-shape bracket, and a handful of zip ties (figure 1).

In HCI and CSCW, creativity support is one major avenue of research that focuses on how to better design the socio-technical tool and environment to facilitate exploratory search and discovery [19]. Recent empirical investigation has highlighted the heterogeneity of culture, social, technical, economic and political interactions in creative practices; this line of research has contributed to HCI and CSCW by emphasizing the collective nature of creativity in the material culture [8,19]. Several frameworks for creativity support including design for openness [7,12], seamfulness [4], hackability [16], and ambiguity [11].

Nonanthropocentric HCI
Researchers have also begun to incorporate nonanthropocentric approaches (e.g., Animal-Computer Interaction) to unpack the entanglements between human and non-human agencies in the interactive spaces [6,10,20]. However, studies on how our natural environment serves as a creative agency to inform the generation of effective novelty are still of scarcity. The dominant human-centric approach calls attention away from several aspects of creativity that are important. First, it assumes human be to the sole creative agency in defining the material culture and overlooked the nature's role in this mutual-shaping and co-creating process. Second, it exhibits the misconception that creative works can be fully regulated and reproduced through human intervention, and yet there are elements in the nature environment that go beyond manipulation and thus make the outcome in-replicable. For instance, every snowflake is one of a kind. As a naturally-formed product, all snowflakes share the hexagonal structure, while having other details of the geometry vary based on the temperature and humidity during the formation process [14]. The formation of snowflakes provides an example of a non-human creative agency, highlighting the dependency between an innovative work and its surroundings, and manifesting the mysterious outcome of having nature in the creative process.

My Creativity Support Research to Date

Preliminary Study: Everyday Creativity
My interest in decomposition is inspired by an ethnographic study in Taiwan back in 2011. Aimed to understand how everyday home dwellers engage in creative practices in the domestic spaces, I designed and distributed the 'making kits' for participants to create home-use objects. Each participant had 7 days for ideation, making, and document scenarios of design-in-use through photography. The 'making kit' contained 15 objects from hardware stores, all objects were carefully chosen to encompass a wide range of material, form, and function, with the goal of providing different degrees of malleability and ambiguity in the process of making. Twenty-five designs were collected at the end of the study that displayed various modes of appropriation and adoption (figure 2). Though the study was preliminary in nature, I noticed that the most creative works possess changes in the given object that go far beyond simple appropriation; instead, several examples exhibit the characteristics of decomposition, which in turn, enable the re-composition of an object in it form and function to produce surprising and meaningful results (figure 3).

Literature Review: The Notion of Decomposition
In natural science, the notion of decomposition implies the process of "death and rebirth", "loss and renewal" [5]. Although often associated with unpleasant narratives such as rot, decay, erosion, and ferment,

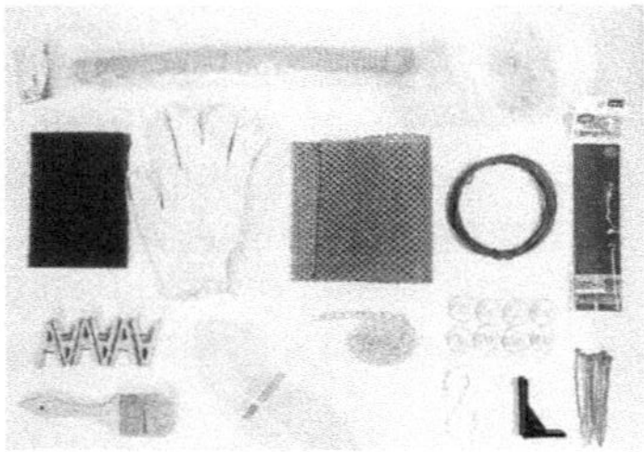

Figure 1: Each of the 'making kit' contains 15 objects for participants to create artifacts they use at home

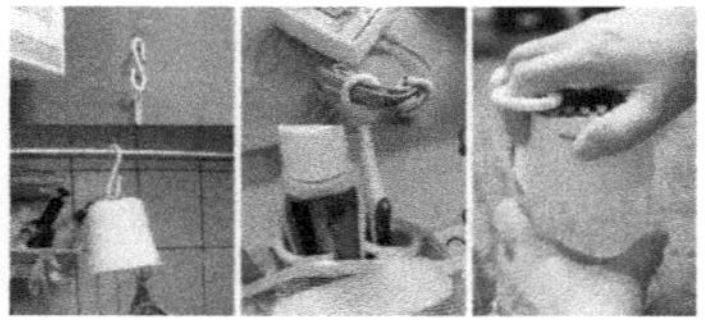

Figure 2: Different modes and degrees of appropriating a s-hook

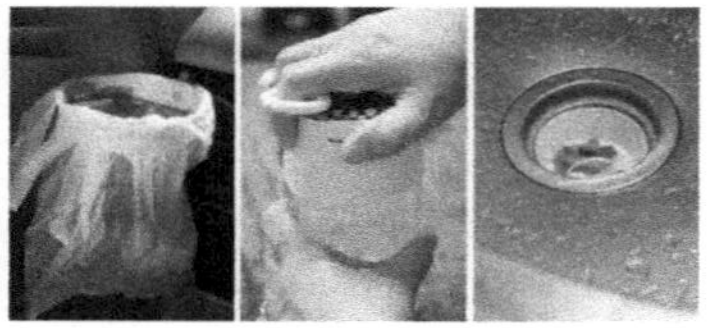

Figure 3: The plastic pot was 'decomposed' into three parts to reimagine its usage. Images from left to right: Top ring as a trash bag holder; middle part as a bottle opener; bottom as a sink strainer

decomposition is not only essential to a sustainable ecosystems [17], but also captures the intricate and collaborative nature of creative practices. Consider, for example, the making of wine: grapes gone through a sequence of harvesting, crushing, fermenting, aging, and bottling to turn into wine. Although the advancement of agriculture science empowers farmers to control the variables in the process, there are factors that go beyond human intervention, such as precipitation, temperature, and the age of the vine. Through this example, the notion of decomposition allows us to see creativity using a nonanthropocentric perspective which captures the dependency of elements in an ecosystem, the fuzziness of nature in forming, and give clues on the extensive timeframe of how creative activities take place.

Besides the field of natural science, decomposition is also a probing technique in anthropology, archaeology, and museum study [9,15,22]. By *breaking down a composition to reveal inside*, the notion of decomposition provides a generative and analytical lens for scientific research [22]. In essence, research is indeed a detective and creative work— the data only comes alive when a trained professional reveals something unique and obscure to people without rigorous training, extensive investigation, and proper knowledge in the field. In the next research activity, I follow this humanistic perspective to further cultivate the notion of decomposition by critically analyzing examples of design works.

Interaction Criticism: Modes of Decomposition
In this phase, I aim to explore and illustrate how the notion of decomposition plays a productive role in creativity support research, and how it is manifested through actual design cases as a tactic to promote the co-creation relationship between human and nature. To achieve this, I first collected 80 design cases (Figure 4) that display some characteristics of decomposition to explore possible topics of analysis.

Figure 4: Some examples from my collection of design that encompass the notion of decomposition

Informed by the preliminary study, scholarly literature, and my collection, I have identified three themes of

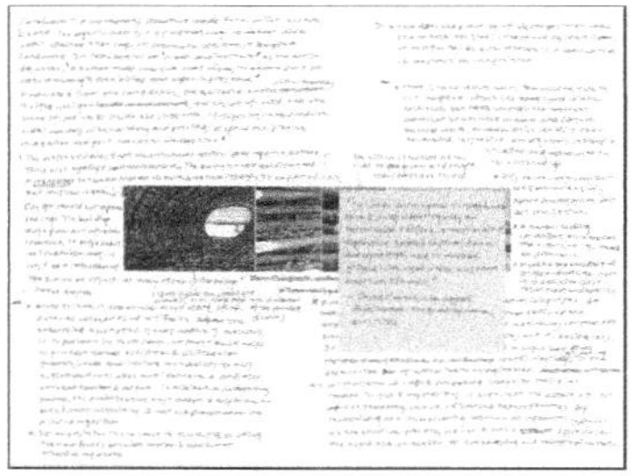

Figure 5: One example from my interaction criticism practice

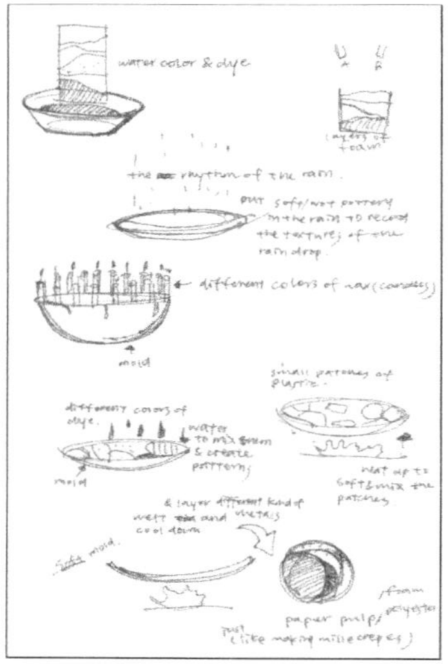

Figure 6: Sketches of design produced with the notion of decomposition

decomposition that signify its nonanthropocentric nature on supporting creativity:

- Mystery and un-replicability: Creative process and work that is impossible to fully control or predict even when human intervention is involved.
- Non-human agency: The creative product and the construction of material culture is defined through a process of mutual-shaping between human and non-human agencies.
- Creativity through destruction: The formation of a creative outcome is in and with the decomposition of one original entity to the reconfiguration of an effective novelty.

I then selected 8 designs that contain all three of the themes tightly to conduct interaction criticism. Informed by Bardzell [1] (p604), interaction criticism entails "rigorous interpretive interrogations of the complex relationships between (a) the interface, including its material and perceptual qualities as well as its broader situatedness in visual languages and culture and (b) the user experience, including the meanings, behaviors, perceptions, affects, insights, and social sensibilities that arise in the context of interaction and its outcomes". I critically analyzed each work by providing objective project description, detailed annotation, themes of decomposition analysis, generative question and discussion, and iteratively comparison between the 8 exemplars (Figure 5).

Traditional analytical way of cognitive thinking focuses on the mental representation and processes but tend to neglect the social-personal aspects underlying creativity [21]. Interaction criticism incorporates a more cultural and humanistic perspective to assist the analytical practices. In this research, interaction criticism serves two purposes: From a research through design (RtD) standpoint, it facilitates the discovery and production of design tactics, so that designers can use them as a set of generative tools to imagine the alternative future, to cultivate more sensitive critical reactions, and to help bring forward the knowledge through actual artifacts. From a theory-making perspective, it provides a pathway for researchers to develop original arguments and ground theories. Also, its analytical nature enables a new way of experiencing design without constraining it to one philosophical fact [1].

Future Works & Contributions

I'm currently in the process of constructing design tactics and utilizing them as prompts to produce actual design works as part of the analytical efforts (Figure 6). The notion of decomposition, in line with nonanthropocentric HCI, has the potential to contribute to creativity support research in two ways: First, it offers a broad expanse of possibilities to design and analyze creative engagement with and through nature. Second, it reframes HCI and CSCW research on creativity from a human-centric domain to one that emphasizes the interconnection between human non-human agencies. This is an on-going research and will be continued with a research through design fashion, with physical objects as the central media of unfolding knowledge and grounding original theories [2,13,24].

Acknowledgements

I thank my advisors, Jeffery Bardzell and Shaowen Bardzell for their guidance. I gratefully acknowledge Ming-Yu Tseng and Huei-Lu Tsai for assisting the making, distributing, and collecting of making kits.

References

[1] Bardzell, J. Interaction criticism: An introduction to the practice. *Interacting with Computers 23*, 6 (2011), 604–621.

[2] Bardzell, J., Bardzell, S., and Hansen, L.K. Immodest Proposals: Research Through Design and Knowledge. *Proceedings of the ACM CHI'15 Conference on Human Factors in Computing Systems 1*, (2015), 2093–2102.

[3] Barron, F. The Disposition Toward Originality. *Journal of Abnormal and Social Psychology 51*, (1955), 478–485.

[4] Chalmers, M., Dieberger, A., Höök, K., and Rudström, Å. Social navigation and seamful design. *Cognitive Studies 11*, 3 (2004), 1–11.

[5] DeSilvey, C. Observed Decay: Telling Stories with Mutable Things. *Journal of Material Culture 11*, 3 (2006), 318–338.

[6] DiSalvo, C. and Lukens, J. Nonanthropocentrism and the Nonhuman in Design: Possibilities for Designing New Forms of Engagement with and through Technology. In M. Foth, J. Donath and L. Forlano, eds., *From Social Butterfly to Engaged Citizen : Urban Informatics, Social Media, Ubiquitous Computing, and Mobile Technology to Support Citizen Engagement*. MIT Press, 2011, 421–436.

[7] Dourish, P. The appropriation of interactive technologies. *Jcscw 12*, 4 (2003), 465–490.

[8] Fischer, G., Giaccardi, E., Eden, H., Sugimoto, M., and Ye, Y. Beyond binary choices: Integrating individual and social creativity. *International Journal of Human Computer Studies 63*, 4–5 SPEC. ISS. (2005), 482–512.

[9] Fleming, E.M. Artifact Study: A Proposed Model. *Winterthur Portfolio 9*, 1 (1974), 153.

[10] Forlano, L. Decentering the Human in the Design of Collaborative Cities. *Design Issues 32*, 3 (2016), 42–54.

[11] Gaver, W.W., Beaver, J., and Benford, S. Ambiguity as a resource for design. *SIGCHI conference on Human factors in computing systems*, 5 (2003), 233–240.

[12] Höök, K. Designing familiar open surfaces. *Proceedings of the 4th Nordic conference on Human-computer interaction: changing roles*, October (2006), 242–251.

[13] Ilpo Koskinen, John Zimmerman, Thomas Binder, Johan Redstrom, S.W. *Design Research through Practice. From the Lab, Field, and Showroom*. Morgan Kaufmann Publishers Inc., San Francisco, 2011.

[14] King, H. How Do Snowflakes Form? http://geology.com/articles/snowflakes/.

[15] Pearce, S.M. *Interpreting Objects and Collections*. Routledge, London, 1994.

[16] Rosner, D.K. Learning from IKEA Hacking: "I'm Not One to Decoupage a Tabletop and Call It a Day. *Chi 2009 09pp*, (2009), 419–422.

[17] Rumble, H. Decomposition: materials and images in time. 2016. http://drhannahrumble.com/2016/01/decomposition-materials-and-images-in-time/.

[18] Runco, M. a. and Jaeger, G.J. The Standard Definition of Creativity. *Creativity Research Journal 24*, 1 (2012), 92–96.

[19] Shneiderman, B. Creativity support tools: accelerating discovery and innovation. *Communications of the ACM 50*, 12 (2007), 20–32.

[20] Smith, N., Bardzell, S., and Bardzell, J. Designing for Cohabitation : Naturecultures , Hybrids , and Decentering the Human in Design. *CHI*, (2017).

[21] Sternberg, R.J. and Lubart, T.I. Investing in Creativity. *Psychological Inquiry 4*, 3 (1993), 229–232.

[22] Strathern, M. The Decomposition of an Event. *Cultural Anthropology 7*, 1992, 244–254.

[23] Wakkary, R. and Maestri, L. Aspects of Everyday Design: Resourcefulness, Adaptation, and Emergence. *International Journal of Human-*

Computer Interaction 24, 5 (2008), 478–491.

[24] Zimmerman, J., Forlizzi, J., and Evenson, S. Research through design as a method for interaction design research in HCI. *Proceedings of the SIGCHI conference on Human factors in computing systems - CHI '07*, (2007), 493–502.

Measuring Creativity: Multi-Scale Visual and Conceptual Design Analysis

Ajit Jain
Interface Ecology Lab
Dept. of Computer Science and Engineering
Texas A&M University
College Station, TX 77843, USA
ajit@ecologylab.net

Author Keywords
visual design; creativity evaluation; metrics; curation; computational modeling; crowdsourcing

ACM Classification Keywords
H.5.m [Information interfaces and presentation (e.g., HCI)]: Miscellaneous

C&C '17, June 27-30, 2017, Singapore, Singapore
ACM 978-1-4503-4403-6/17/06.
http://dx.doi.org/10.1145/3059454.3078697

Abstract
Multi-scale creative web designs organize content across zoom levels, presenting new challenges for web page segmentation, content identification, and creativity evaluation. We propose building a novel computational model, combining visual and conceptual features, to quantitatively represent and analyze multi-scale designs. Using the model, we will compute metrics—emergence and visual presentation of ideas—that required expert feedback.

Research Situation
I am a 3rd year PhD student working with Dr. Andruid Kerne. My research investigates analysis methods for multi-scale creative web designs. I defended my dissertation proposal in Spring 2017. I plan to graduate in Fall 2018. This graduate student symposium is ideal for presenting my ideas as valuable feedback from mentors and peers—in fields such as HCI, art, design, psychology, and computer science—could significantly support the proposed research.

Context and Motivation
New assessment techniques are required to support creative design learning and teaching [9]. Creative learning and innovation are essential to personal well-being and economic growth [4, 15]. The World Wide Web provides a context for creative innovation that addresses challenges posed by the new global economy [17]. The web is charac-

terized by heterogeneous information sources, media types, and representation formats [2]. Human understanding of web content is driven by visual perception, in which human beings have highly evolved [18]. Perceptual grouping in vision enables us to form meaningful spatial, temporal, and causal relationships [19]. The problem is that computational methods have not yet achieved these abilities.

Computational means for giving people feedback in their creative design processes is the research challenge my dissertation will address. In today's web pages, visual layout does not align with its DOM structure, making it difficult to identify the content and its relationships [6]. Web page segmentation algorithms based on visual perception help overcome this problem [6, 12]. However, these algorithms operate on a single zoom level. They were not developed for analysis of multi-scale designs, which organize content at multiple zoom levels, e.g., infographics created using Photoshop or Illustrator, presentations created with Prezi, and exhibits created with IdeaMâché [13].

Prior work employs visual features for building a computational model in order to predict users' first impressions of web page aesthetics [20]. Creative cognition research employs conceptual features for computing metrics, such as emergence of ideas [23, 11], with the help of human raters. Combination of visual and conceptual features has been shown useful toward mining designs from the web [12]. However, such a combination has not been employed to build a computational model for measuring dimensions of creativity. We will develop novel methods, using such combination, for evaluation of multi-scale creative web designs, through these specific aims:

- Identify clusters in multi-scale designs using visual and conceptual features
- Measure creativity in multi-scale designs by building a computational model and automate calculation of metrics, such as emergence and visual presentation of ideas
- Develop guidelines for crowdsourcing content identification to deal with limitations of machine analysis
- Develop a design learning dashboard for supporting expert monitoring and feedback on multi-scale designs

Background and Preliminary Work

Visual perception plays a dominant role in human cognition, as it allows us to accurately decipher distant spatial information [18]. Grouping, a prominent phenomenon in visual perception, follows principles of proximity, color, size, orientation, symmetry, and continuity [19]. Bertin, in Semiology of Graphics [3], organizes visual variables—size, color, value, shape, texture, orientation—based on their associative, selective, ordered, and quantitative perception. Tufte's information design principles, such as consistency, foreground/background relationships, stratification, limited use of saturated color and heavy weight, and other particulars of layering and separation, exploit visual perception [24].

The 2005 NSF workshop report discusses multiple dimensions of creativity and the need to employ mixed-methods for assessment [21]. Dow et al. measure quantity and quality of ideas in tasks such as web advertisement design and product design. They use click-through data and expert ratings [8]. Siangliulue et al. build a computational semantic model of solution space, combining implicit human actions and machine learning, which enable interventions that improve number, diversity, and quality of ideas [22].

Curation, an art practice, is the creative conceptualization and organization of a spatial context for works—which are collected, interpreted, and visually arranged to produce a culturally meaningful exhibition [16]. *Free-form web curation* is a form of new media [14]—designed to enable users to conceptualize and create new spatial contexts—in which they discover, interpret, and represent relationships, by composing found content elements and their own expressions, on the web and in the cloud. Our current paper presents free-form web curation strategies—Collect, Assemble, Shift Perspective, Sketch, Write, and Exhibit—that support creative design processes [10].

Kerne et al. formulated an information-based ideation methodology for evaluating curations that users develop through engagement in open-ended tasks and activities [11]. Their *elemental* ideation metrics—Fluency (number of ideas), Flexibility (number of categories of ideas), Novelty (rareness of an idea)—apply to the individual elements. Their *holistic* ideation metrics—Emergence, Visual Presentation, Exposition, Relevance—apply to the assembled whole. Elemental metrics were computed algorithmically. Holistic metrics were assigned by human raters based on clear and explicit scoring guidelines. Emergence refers to development of new features not originally present in component concepts. Visual Presentation refers to spatial organization of ideas in a clear and coherent manner.

Research Objectives and Questions

My *long-term goal* is to transform learning, design, and creativity through novel approaches to engagement with interconnected information networks. The *objective of this proposal* is to develop methods for analyzing multi-scale visual and conceptual design. The *principle research question* is how to scale holistic evaluation of multi-scale creative web designs. The *central hypothesis* is that the novel methods will reduce the effort required for evaluation and feedback. We plan to develop a multi-scale design model to quantitatively represent the creative design in web pages. This model will be the foundation for automating evaluation, such as emergence and visual presentation of ideas.

Figure 1: Jordan Jump's multi-scale curation, *Laundry Notifier* [https://ideamache.ecologylab.net/v/teGYF8lbi5/], visually and conceptually organizes clusters of ideas at multiple zoom levels. We see clusters of needs, design, prior work, and technologies.

Methodology

The present research addresses web-based, free-form multi-scale curations (Figure 1). The approaches we develop can be extended to other forms of visual content.

We will analyze semantic representations of free-form web curations, as a form of visual and conceptual design. The semantic representation of a curation includes visual features, such as position, scale, and layer of each element. Elements gathered from the web include semantics for source and link URLs. Created elements will also include type specific semantics. Sketches will contain stroke data. Writings will contain character and formatting data. We will use interaction logs, such as actions of changing the viewport in the zoomable space, gathering elements, sketching, writing, grouping, and transforming elements and groups.

Identify clusters using visual and conceptual features
We will develop a multi-scale design model to quantitatively represent creative expression. The goal is to represent how elements and their concepts are organized and mutually related. A standard vision-based algorithm would fail to recognize nested relationships in an infinitely zoomable canvas. In conjunction with semantic representation, we will use interaction logs to accurately determine users' model of organization. Using this model, we will compute metrics that previously required human evaluation [11].

We will extract descriptions from visual elements, such as images, using the state-of-the-art TensorFlow library [1], to automatically label content. We will extract descriptions from writing elements, such as labels that users annotate on groups. We will use different clustering algorithms and several distance functions to identify scopes and boundaries among element descriptions, which are presented in a curation. In other words, we aim to separate and group individual elements in a curation to clusters.

Measure creativity in multi-scale designs
We will use the multi-scale design model to compute holistic metrics. We will extract keywords from the element descriptions to represent a concept. Intuitively, words that appear frequently, with important syntactic function roles—e.g., a subject or the main predicate in a sentence—and specific characteristics—e.g., all characters capitalized—are likely to be important words. We will consider using these properties in selecting keywords from potentially multiple textual descriptions for an element. We will compute Emergence metric by comparing co-occurrences of the extracted concepts to that within the Google Ngram dataset [5].

We will compute Visual Presentation metric by taking into account extracted features, such as use of multiple scales, whitespace and sketching among clusters, position, alignment, size, color, and font styling, for effective layering of information and conveying of relationships.

Develop guidelines for crowdsourcing
With advances in computer vision and machine learning, automated identification of content has become highly robust and accurate. However, the accuracy largely depends on the machine learning model used and training dataset. As we discussed, machines are yet to come close, in terms of advanced human visual perception mechanisms [18, 19]. Moreover, machines have limitations of identifying contextual and nuanced meanings.

We will make use of human-in-the-loop computation for obtaining rich descriptions of visual elements, when the confidence scores for labels returned from the TensorFlow library are below a certain threshold value. We will formulate detailed guidelines based on qualitative methods, such as visual discourse analysis [7], for engaging microtask workers on crowdsourcing platforms. This will provide us with memos—Locating, Big Picture, and Specification—that uncover visual, relational, contextual, and cultural details.

Develop a design learning dashboard
We will develop a design learning dashboard to enable collaborating instructors view and filter students curations and the computed metrics. We will develop various views, visualizations, and configurations of metrics to support them in teaching and evaluation.

We will engage in dialog with instructors about what metrics mean, how they relate to learning objectives, and how to improve them. Our plan includes annual workshops with collaborating instructors. We will study how they use the current metrics, and also develop new ways to analyze and visualize students' creative processes and design products.

REFERENCES

1. Martín Abadi, Ashish Agarwal, Paul Barham, Eugene Brevdo, Zhifeng Chen, Craig Citro, Greg S Corrado, Andy Davis, Jeffrey Dean, Matthieu Devin, and others. 2016. Tensorflow: Large-scale machine learning on heterogeneous distributed systems. *arXiv preprint arXiv:1603.04467* (2016).
2. Tim Berners-Lee, Robert Cailliau, Ari Luotonen, Henrik Frystyk Nielsen, and Arthur Secret. 1994. The World-Wide Web. *Commun. ACM* 37, 8 (Aug. 1994), 76–82. DOI: http://dx.doi.org/10.1145/179606.179671
3. Jacques Bertin. 1983. *Semiology of graphics: diagrams, networks, maps.* University of Wisconsin press.
4. Margaret A Boden. 2004. *The creative mind: Myths and mechanisms.* Psychology Press.
5. Thorsten Brants and Alex Franz. 2006. Web 1T 5-gram Version 1. *Philadelphia: Linguistic Data Consortium* (2006).
6. Deng Cai, Shipeng Yu, Ji-Rong Wen, and Wei-Ying Ma. 2003. *VIPS: a Vision-based Page Segmentation Algorithm.* Technical Report. 28 pages. https://www.microsoft.com/en-us/research/publication/vips-a-vision-based-page-segmentation-algorithm/
7. Adele Clarke. 2005. *Situational analysis: Grounded theory after the postmodern turn.* Sage.
8. Steven P Dow, Alana Glassco, Jonathan Kass, Melissa Schwarz, Daniel L Schwartz, and Scott R Klemmer. 2012. Parallel prototyping leads to better design results, more divergence, and increased self-efficacy. In *Design Thinking Research.* Springer, 127–153. DOI: http://dx.doi.org/10.1007/978-3-642-21643-5_8
9. Clive L Dym, Alice M Agogino, Ozgur Eris, Daniel D Frey, and Larry J Leifer. 2005. Engineering design thinking, teaching, and learning. *Journal of Engineering Education* 94, 1 (2005), 103–120. DOI: http://dx.doi.org/10.1002/j.2168-9830.2005.tb00832.x
10. Andruid Kerne, Nic Lupfer, Rhema Linder, Yin Qu, Alyssa Valdez, Ajit Jain, Kade Keith, Matthew Carrasco, Jorge Vanegas, and Andrew Billingsley. 2017. Free-form Web Curation: Strategies for Creative Engagement with Prior Work. In *Proceedings of the 2017 ACM SIGCHI Conference on Creativity and Cognition.* ACM. DOI: http://dx.doi.org/10.1145/3059454.3059471
11. Andruid Kerne, Andrew M. Webb, Steven M. Smith, Rhema Linder, Nic Lupfer, Yin Qu, Jon Moeller, and Sashikanth Damaraju. 2014. Using Metrics of Curation to Evaluate Information-based Ideation. *ACM Transactions on Computer-Human Interaction (TOCHI)* 21, 3 (June 2014), 1–48. DOI: http://dx.doi.org/10.1145/2591677
12. Ranjitha Kumar, Arvind Satyanarayan, Cesar Torres, Maxine Lim, Salman Ahmad, Scott R Klemmer, and Jerry O Talton. 2013. Webzeitgeist: design mining the web. In *Proceedings of the SIGCHI Conference on Human Factors in Computing Systems.* ACM, 3083–3092. DOI: http://dx.doi.org/10.1145/2470654.2466420
13. Nic Lupfer, Andruid Kerne, Andrew M. Webb, and Rhema Linder. 2016. Patterns of Free-form Curation: Visual Thinking with Web Content. In *Proceedings of the 2016 ACM on Multimedia Conference (MM '16).* 12–21. http://doi.acm.org/10.1145/2964284.2964303

14. Lev Manovich. 2001. *The language of new media.* MIT press.

15. National Academy of Engineering. 2010. *Rising Above the Gathering Storm, Revisited: Rapidly Approaching Category 5.* The National Academies Press.

16. Paul O'Neill. 2012. *The Culture of Curating and the Curating of Culture (s).* MIT Press.

17. Ronald D Owston. 1997. Research news and Comment: The World Wide Web: A Technology to Enhance Teaching and Learning? *Educational researcher* 26, 2 (1997), 27–33. DOI: http://dx.doi.org/10.3102/0013189X026002027

18. Stephen E Palmer. 1999. *Vision science: Photons to phenomenology.* MIT press.

19. Stephen E. Palmer. 2002. Perceptual Organization in Vision. In *Stevens' Handbook of Experimental Psychology* (3 ed.), S. Yantis and H. Pashler (Eds.). Vol. 1. Wiley, 177–234.

20. Katharina Reinecke, Tom Yeh, Luke Miratrix, Rahmatri Mardiko, Yuechen Zhao, Jenny Liu, and Krzysztof Z Gajos. 2013. Predicting users' first impressions of website aesthetics with a quantification of perceived visual complexity and colorfulness. In *Proceedings of the SIGCHI Conference on Human Factors in Computing Systems.* ACM, 2049–2058. DOI: http://dx.doi.org/10.1145/1970378.1970382

21. Ben Shneiderman, Gerhard Fischer, Mary Czerwinski, Brad Myers, and Mitch Resnick. 2005. *Creativity Support Tools: A workshop sponsored by the National Science Foundation.*

22. Pao Siangliulue, Joel Chan, Steven P Dow, and Krzysztof Z Gajos. 2016. IdeaHound: Improving Large-scale Collaborative Ideation with Crowd-powered Real-time Semantic Modeling. In *Proceedings of the 29th Annual Symposium on User Interface Software and Technology.* ACM, 609–624. DOI: http://dx.doi.org/10.1145/2984511.2984578

23. Steven M Smith and Thomas B Ward. 2012. Cognition and the creation of ideas. *The Oxford handbook of thinking and reasoning* (2012), 456–474. DOI: http://dx.doi.org/10.1093/oxfordhb/9780199734689.013.0023

24. Edward R. Tufte. 1991. Envisioning information. *Optometry & Vision Science* 68, 4 (1991), 322–324.

Evaluating Play Experiences

Johanna Okerlund
UNC Charlotte
Charlotte, NC 28223, USA
jokerlun@uncc.edu

C&C '17, June 27–30, 2017, Singapore, Singapore.

ACM ISBN 978-1-4503-4403-6/17/06.
http://dx.doi.org/10.1145/3059454.3078698

Abstract
As interaction designers, we often design for play or strive to make interactions more playful. However, we do not have a consistent language with which to talk about what we mean by play or ways of measuring the degree to which an interface satisfies its promise of being playful. It is easy to conflate play with similar phenomena such as engagement, novelty, creativity, and exploration. My goal is to develop a metric that targets specifically the factors of an interaction that are necessary and sufficient to say that an experience was playful for a given individual. I discuss the work I have done to define play, construct a Play Index to measure the playfulness of an interaction, and contribute to the design of interactive systems that relate to play.

Introduction
As interaction designers, there are many ways in which we consider play and reasons why we might design an interface to be playful. We might use play as persuasion, to draw people in with fun and make them engage in doing something, such as exercise, that is otherwise not enjoyable for them [19]. We might use a playful interaction to spark creativity, inspire reflection, or facilitate social interaction [11, 10]. Play is also talked about a lot in conjunction with learning, where it is through play that the user learns, much like the way a child learns about the world around them by playing. Systems like Scratch [14], Makey Makey [4], and

Lego Mindstorms [12] engage learners in exploration and discovery through play.

Factor	Statements
Possibilities	1. If I were to use this system again, I might have a different experience 2. I feel I can come up with my own rules/ ideas/ ways of using this tool
Curiosity	3. I felt compelled to try things 4. I was curious about what would happen when I tried new things
Enjoyment	5. I enjoyed using the system or tool. 6. I would be happy to use this system or tool on a regular basis.
Discovery	7. While using the system I learned something about the system or the domain 8. Things happened during this experience that I would not have been able to predict.
Immersion	9. I lost track of time during this experience. 10. I forgot where I was during the experience
Flow	11. I felt the experience was challenging 12. I felt I had the skills to meet the challenge
Social	13. I felt connected with the other people who were also part of this experience 14. The experience would have been less positive if other people had not been part of it

Table 1: Initial Version of Play Index

There are many tools to understand and evaluate these different systems, for example, in terms of learning, creativity, collaboration, engagement etc. However, there is not a systematic way to understand an experience in terms of its playfulness. While external factors such as smiling and laughing might indicate playfulness, these are not sufficient indicators of play, especially in adults [8]. Play as we consider it here is a mindset. Two people might be performing the same exact sequence of actions, but due to differences in mindset, only one of them might be playing [8]. Thus we see the need for a means of quantifying the subjective internal experience of play during an interaction.

Completed and Ongoing work

Defining Play

The first step in developing a metric for playfulness has been to define and understand what we mean by play. I have done a literature review of play from various perspectives including psychology, anthropology, and interaction design. While there are many definitions of play (some of which contradict each other), I have chosen a few that capture what I think is relevant in the types of interactions the play index will be used to help understand.

Much of the literature on the psychology of play discusses the motivations and desires of the individual in play experiences, especially for children. Eibl defines play as "an experimental dialogue with the environment" [6]. Berlyne defines play as the shift from considering "what can this object do" to "what can I do with this object" [1]. Sutton-Smith discusses play as a way to generate new combinations of familiar components in a safe environment [18]. Most of these definitions are in regards specifically to children's play, which means there is a limited extent to which they apply to adult play as well. Piaget discusses play in terms of stages during a child's development, starting with play that practices motor skills, then moving on to symbolic play and finally game play [13]. Rubin discusses play as a disposition and presents 6 factors that can serve as indicators of a playful disposition [16]. These factors include intrinsic motivation, freedom from external rules, and attention to the means rather than the end product.

Other definitions of play are more focused on interaction and several of these researchers even offer design principles to consider when creating a playful interaction. Gaver discusses ludic play from an interaction perspective and presents principles to consider when designing for ludic engagement such as ambiguity, de-emphasis of external goals, presenting the familiar as strange and the strange as familiar [7]. Resnick and Rosenbaum explore and define tinkering as a "playful style of designing and making" and consider design principles for tinkerability to be things like fluid experimentation, immediate feedback, and open exploration [15].

Perhaps most relevant to the Play Index are definitions of play that are broader and more general. Huizinga, in the book Homo Ludens, describes play as a voluntary non-serious activity that takes place outside "ordinary life" that, while having "no material interest" is completely absorbing and engaging [9]. Caillois writes in response to Huizinga, expanding on his definition to define play as any activity that is non-obligatory, separate from daily life, uncertain, unproductive, governed by rules, and make-believe [2]. Huizinga and Caillois are similar in that they consider play to be dependent on rules. Salen and Zimmerman build on these definitions in their framework for game design and define play as "a free movement within a rigid structure" and go on to describe how play emerges from the structure or rules imposed [17].

From these formal definitions of play, we have combined and extracted features that most relate to the types of play the Play Index aims to capture. We thus define play as intrinsically motivated curiosity-driven exploration of a system and its place in the world in a non-serious fun enjoyable way. It is a mindset, but is not contained in the mind in that it requires acting in some way on the world in order to see the result. It is a type of exploration, but it goes beyond exploring the characteristics and properties of the system. While there is overlap between play and creativity, these are different. Play involves doing things that lie outside of the intended actions of the system, which may require some level of creativity, but is not exclusively a creative endeavor. Creativity can be playful when one embarks on a creative endeavor for the sake of the process rather than the end goal.

Development of Play Index

The Play Index is a measure that helps evaluate the extent to which an individual considers themselves to have interacted in a given experience playfully.

We base our method of developing this metric and the rationale behind it on the work of Cherry and Latulipe to develop a creativity support index [3]. There are many ways of evaluating a creative experience by either considering the individual, the product they produce, or their creative process. The Creativity Support Index focuses on process by measuring the subjective perception of a system's ability to support creative endeavors. Similarly, the Play Index strives to capture the subjective internal perception of the user, about the playfulness of an experience.

We base the Play Index on psychologists and interaction designers who have presented indications of, design principles for, and factors that are conducive to playfulness such as the ones described in the previous section, especially [1, 5, 6, 9, 16, 18]. Each statement is to be rated using a Likert Scale by an individual after an interactive experience (Table 1).

The following scenarios show examples of when it is appropriate and useful to use the Play Index:

- Are users actually engaging in a playful experience playfully?
- Do certain groups of people (based on race, gender, socioeconomic status) find certain experiences more playful than others?
- Does novelty in an interaction technique contribute to its playfulness? i.e. is the tangible version of a screen-based system more playful?
- For systems that engage users in playful learning, what is the correlation between playfulness and learning? Engagement? Creativity?

Design of Playful Interaction
I have also contributed to projects that in various ways relate to play and plan to use the Play Index to better understand them.

Design Space Explorer – Design Space Explorer is a web-based tool that allows people to define and explore a design space in terms of dimensions, possible values along the dimensions, and existing systems that exist at points along those dimensions. While Design Space Explorer is not as open-ended as many playful systems are, it allows us to ask questions such as what it looks like for people to play with ideas and whether simply giving them constructs to represent and manipulate their thoughts is enough to persuade them to be more playful in their thinking.

Move and Paint – Move and Paint is a gesture-based public display where users can paint or color by moving their body. We have left the Move and Paint system in public areas and studied how people of different populations engage with the system. We have found that for those who initially find the system to be more novel, this wears off very quickly and they lose interest, while those who do not seem find the interaction with the system as novel end up finding more different and interesting ways of playing with it.

Makerspace – For the past year, I have been helping set up and run a campus Makerspace. One of the things I am interested in is the pathways through the space. People come in initially for different reasons: curiosity, a specific project, a tool, a friend dragged them there. Intertwined with these entry points are different mindsets, some of which are more playful than others. Setting up the Makerspace itself is the first step towards being able to track these students and their mindsets throughout their interactions in the space. I am hoping that the Play Index, when applied to specific aspects of the MakerSpace, might shed light on how to provide pathways that encourage playful exploration of the tools and materials.

Next Steps
My next step in the development of the index is to evaluate it by using it on various playful interactions in conjunction with other metrics. I plan to see how the Play Index responses correlate to visual cues (i.e. smile, laugh), other evaluation metrics such as the Creativity Support index [3], measures of flow, subjective workload and engagement, and the way participants reflect on their experiences in response to open-ended questions. I will test interactions that have varying degrees of novelty, complexity, and room for creativity to help determine the extent to which the Play Index generates reasonable insights and whether it is in fact targeting something distinct from what the other measures target. For example, if high results on the Play Index always correlate to high results on the Creativity Support Index, then perhaps there is a dimension of play that is missing.

REFERENCES

1. Daniel E Berlyne. 1966. Curiosity and exploration. *Science* 153, 3731 (1966), 25–33.
2. Roger Caillois and Meyer Barash. 1961. *Man, play, and games.* University of Illinois Press.
3. Erin Cherry and Celine Latulipe. 2014. Quantifying the creativity support of digital tools through the creativity support index. *ACM Transactions on Computer-Human Interaction (TOCHI)* 21, 4 (2014), 21.
4. Beginner's Mind Collective and David Shaw. 2012. Makey Makey: Improvising Tangible and Nature-based User Interfaces. In *Proceedings of the Sixth International Conference on Tangible, Embedded and Embodied Interaction (TEI '12).* ACM, New York, NY, USA, 367–370. DOI: http://dx.doi.org/10.1145/2148131.2148219
5. Mihaly Csikszentmihalyi. 1996. Flow and the psychology of discovery and invention. *New York: Harper Collins* (1996).
6. Irenäus Eibl-Eibesfeldt. 1967. Concepts of ethology and their significance in the study of human behavior. In *Early behavior: Comparative and developmental approaches.* John Wiley & Sons, 127–146.
7. William W Gaver, John Bowers, Andrew Boucher, Hans Gellerson, Sarah Pennington, Albrecht Schmidt, Anthony Steed, Nicholas Villars, and Brendan Walker. 2004. The drift table: designing for ludic engagement. In *CHI'04 extended abstracts on Human factors in computing systems.* ACM, 885–900.
8. Peter Gray. 2008. The value of play I: The definition of play provides clues to its purposes. *Psychology Today* (2008), 1–5.
9. Johan Huizinga. 2014. *Homo Ludens Ils 86.* Routledge.
10. Katherine Isbister. 2016. Connecting through play. *interactions* 23, 4 (2016), 26–33.
11. Katherine Isbister and Kaho Abe. 2015. Costumes As Game Controllers: An Exploration of Wearables to Suit Social Play. In *Proceedings of the Ninth International Conference on Tangible, Embedded, and Embodied Interaction (TEI '15).* ACM, New York, NY, USA, 691–696. DOI: http://dx.doi.org/10.1145/2677199.2688813
12. Seymour Papert. 1980. *Mindstorms: Children, computers, and powerful ideas.* Basic Books, Inc.
13. Jean Piaget. 2013. *Play, dreams and imitation in childhood.* Vol. 25. Routledge.
14. Mitchel Resnick, John Maloney, Andrés Monroy-Hernández, Natalie Rusk, Evelyn Eastmond, Karen Brennan, Amon Millner, Eric Rosenbaum, Jay Silver, Brian Silverman, and Yasmin Kafai. 2009. Scratch: Programming for All. *Commun. ACM* 52, 11 (Nov. 2009), 60–67. DOI: http://dx.doi.org/10.1145/1592761.1592779
15. Mitchel Resnick and Eric Rosenbaum. 2013. Designing for tinkerability. *Design, make, play: Growing the next generation of STEM innovators* (2013), 163–181.
16. Kenneth H Rubin, Greta G Fein, Brian Vandenberg, and others. 1983. Play. *Handbook of child psychology* 4 (1983), 693–774.
17. Katie Salen and Eric Zimmerman. 2004. *Rules of play: Game design fundamentals.* MIT press.
18. Brian Sutton-Smith. 1967. The role of play in cognitive development. *Young children* (1967), 360–370.

19. Jeffrey Yim and T. C. Nicholas Graham. 2007. Using Games to Increase Exercise Motivation. In *Proceedings of the 2007 Conference on Future Play (Future Play '07)*. ACM, New York, NY, USA, 166–173. DOI: http://dx.doi.org/10.1145/1328202.1328232

Towards Lifelong Interactive Learning For Open-ended Embodied Narrative Improvisation

Mikhail Jacob
Georgia Institute of Technology
Atlanta, GA 30305, USA
mikhail.jacob@gatech.edu

ACM ISBN 978-1-4503-4403-6/17/06.
http://dx.doi.org/10.1145/3059454.3078699

Abstract
This paper describes a doctoral research plan modeling collaborative embodied narrative improvisation, using lifelong interactive learning to mitigate the knowledge-authoring bottleneck. Research methodology involves building interactive system models of the improvisation process, public installation/exhibition, user experience studies in public/lab settings, and ablation experiments. The article concludes with a research timeline.

Author Keywords
Improvisation; embodied narrative; VR; imitation learning; generalized hypergraph; modeling creativity.

ACM Classification Keywords
H.5.m. Information interfaces and presentation (e.g., HCI): Miscellaneous.

Introduction
The creative cognition community has formally studied creativity [8] and attempted to computationally model it [25] in various domains. These studies have made significant contributions to both the study of creative cognition and the computational modeling of creativity. However, the recent popularity of virtual reality (VR) as a storytelling medium has emphasized the lack of computational models of co-creativity in embodied

Embodied Narrative: Narratives constructed using the affordances and constraints of bodies situated within their environment Broadly, embodied narrative includes the interaction modalities of speech and touch, but is used in this article exclusively to mean full-body free-form gestural interaction with an environment.

Knowledge-authoring Bottleneck: The difficulty, cost, and delay in acquisition of expert knowledge followed by its subsequent structuring and storage so as to enable efficient future utilization are referred to as the knowledge-authoring bottleneck [4].

Uncanny Valley Effect: When robots are gradually made to look more humanlike, they progressively appear more realistic until a point at which the subtle remaining blemishes start to make them look creepier progressively [19].

creative domains such as *embodied narrative* improvisation (embodied narrative improv).

VR games and experiences are a fast-growing segment of the digital entertainment [26] as well as training and simulation industries [2, 21]. Naturalistic interaction in VR, such as walking and manipulating the virtual world using the body, supports the open-endedness of improv experiences. Users can physically mime flipping burgers [14] or scaling Mt. Everest [23] to do so in-game. In contrast, non-player characters (NPCs) are limited to small sets of animations due to the *knowledge-authoring bottleneck* [4] to expanding them.

Various techniques exist in the game AI literature to mitigate the knowledge-authoring bottleneck. However, the flexibility and expressivity of interaction required for embodied narrative improv makes them less applicable. NPC movement can be learned/generated from motion capture datasets. However, few datasets exist for a broad set of human action and few (if any) have formal semantics annotating how they affect the environment. Generated movements can also appear unnatural, exhibiting the *uncanny valley effect* [19].

One way to mitigate the knowledge-authoring bottleneck for an open-ended improv system is to learn actions and action selection knowledge from all human users over its lifetime. This would be facilitated by a knowledge representation that could be updated incrementally, integrating new and prior learned knowledge in real-time. Additionally, the user could interactively correct learning errors.

This article describes a doctoral research plan for modeling the collaborative improvisation of open-ended embodied narratives. The research focuses on solving the knowledge-authoring bottleneck involved using lifelong interactive learning from observation and experience. Research methodology involves modeling the improv process computationally, interactive system building, public installation/exhibition, user experience studies in public/lab settings, and ablation experiments. The article concludes with a research timeline.

LuminAI

LuminAI (formerly *Viewpoints AI*) is a dome-based interactive art installation [11] where human participants can interact expressively with virtual characters in order to collaboratively improvise movement-based performances. LuminAI learns what actions it can perform and how to sequence them in response to a collaborator's actions [12]. Learned actions can be flexibly reused in many different contexts. It also learns sequences of actions by learning Markov chains [3] from observation. This models the improv process as a mutual coupling where the characters and users are responding to each other.

Figure 1: LuminAI dome installation with people improvising open-ended embodied proto-narratives with each other and virtual characters (humanoid figures made of motes of light)

Markov Chain: A stochastic model for representing a sequence of possible events where the probability of each event happening depends only on the state caused by the previous event [3].

Viewpoints: Viewpoints theory analyzes movement and embodied performance along various dimensions: tempo, duration, repetition, kinesthetic response (naturally timed responses to stimuli), shape, gesture, movement topography (patterns of movements over time), spatial relationships, and architecture (the set) [1].

Cognitive Architecture: A software architecture that models the fixed structures of the mind in order to produce intelligent behavior given the right knowledge [15].

Episodic Memory: A type of human memory that remembers autobiographical events [24].

In addition, the installation utilizes a computational formalization of *Viewpoints* movement theory [1] to analyze the improvised scene, organize its experiences, and aesthetically transform learned actions [12]. The system chooses responses using multiple response strategies within a cognitive architecture called Soar [15] that performs the reasoning. These strategies include repetition (to create rapport), transformation along Viewpoints dimensions (to create novelty), retrieval of observed movements from episodic memory [24] that are similar in Viewpoints dimensions (to generate aesthetically appropriate novelty), and using the learned action Markov chains discussed before (to follow expected patterns).

LuminAI has been publically exhibited in informal, invited, and peer-reviewed showings. Iterative design methodology was used, with participant feedback incorporated after each showing. The installation has also been formally evaluated using theoretical analysis of authorial leverage and ablative user study [13] as well as qualitative study during a public exhibition [16].

Given a definition of narrative as a sequence of causally and temporally related actions, the improvised performance in LuminAI constitutes a proto-narrative. This is an initial step along the stated research direction because the actions performed in it are temporally and aesthetically related but not fully causally related. The MImE & GENII projects address this issue.

MImE & GENII

MImE (Movement-based Improvisation Environment) is a VR experience where a person and a virtual character can collaboratively improvise open-ended embodied narratives. The initial research prototype being built enables embodied narrative improv within a larger narrative of the protagonist and their service android crash landing on an alien planet, damaging the android's memory. In order to survive, explore, and escape, the player and their android have to perform collaborative tasks using various objects in the environment with the player teaching the android the necessary skills to help complete the task. A future version with less structure is planned, but out of scope for the current research plan.

GENII (Graphical Embodied Narrative Intelligence & Improvisation) is the intelligent agent for lifelong interactive learning and virtual character control in open-ended embodied narrative experiences such as MImE. In order for the GENII-controlled android in MImE to learn how to interact with the environment, it observes the player's interactions with it, reasons about how the player's physical body movements change the state of objects in the environment and uses that to build an inductive model of the effects of the player's action. It uses this model to perform an action in the environment during collaborative tasks with feedback from the player. GENII agents thus perform interactive imitation learning [20] of action models [27].

The learned action models are stored in a generalized hypergraph [10] knowledge representation. This allows GENII to hierarchically connect the grounded percepts it experiences to abstract concepts that are derived from them. Sequences of human body position data observed by the agent are stored at the lowest layer, segmented at the next layer by the changes they cause to the environment. The movements between each change in the environment are sub-actions. They are clustered together based on similarity of motion and

Interactive Imitation Learning: Learning skills by imitating the movements of a teacher, reconstructing the goals of the example, and using feedback to improve [13].

Action Model: The creation of models that predict causes and effects of actions [20].

Generalized Hypergraph: An extension of hypergraphs and graphs where single edges can connect an arbitrary number of vertices and edges themselves [10].

Metacognition: Regulatory awareness and reasoning that seeks to modulate the agent's own cognition [7].

effect. Labels for prototypes of each sub-action are crowdsourced. They are then cleaned and processed. This is repeated for the action, composed of sub-actions. Given a goal state, this hierarchical action model learned by the agent can be used to act in the world through action planning [5]. It can also be connected to knowledge bases for common sense [22] and linguistic reasoning [18], or used for analogical reasoning [9] and conceptual blending [6] in the future, but that is out of scope for this research.

GENII also has a set of metacognitive [7] models of creativity that evaluate the novelty, value, surprise, and aesthetic description of knowledge (like in [17]) at each layer of the hypergraph. This is used to filter out low quality knowledge from the agent. This includes ignoring bad percepts during interactive learning, forgetting action models during system idle time, and generating only appropriately creative responses from sequences or combinations of learned knowledge.

Research Plan

After initial investigations into embodied narrative improv with the LuminAI project, the author's focus is now on the MImE/GENII project that is ongoing with initial prototypes being completed for the start of summer 2017. At the time of writing, there is one partial user task complete in MImE with associated assets. In GENII, the motion layer learning has been added and evaluated along with a model of motion dissimilarity. By summer, MImE will include 2-3 open-ended user tasks within the crashed spaceship interior. In GENII, this will include initial models of novelty and value; tracking of partial object state; and motion layer segmentation using object state changes. This will allow baseline user evaluations and system evaluations

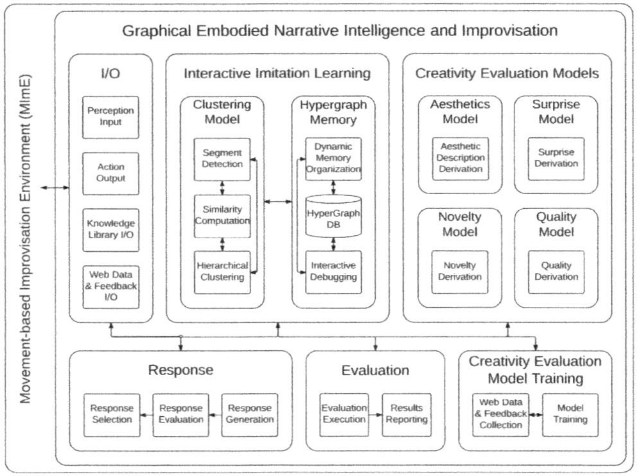

Figure 2: The GENII agent architecture.

in summer 2017. With results and feedback from them, in fall 2017, the remaining MImE scenario will be added (base camp). In GENII, novelty, surprise, value, and aesthetic description models; full object state tracking; and response generation with learned action models will be completed. Spring 2018 will be spent evaluating the system, refining it, and writing the dissertation. The defense will be in summer 2018.

Acknowledgements

I would like to thank my advisor, Dr. Brian Magerko, for his support and the rest of the ADAM Lab at Georgia Tech for their help. This material is based upon work supported by the National Science Foundation under Grant No. 1320520.

References

1. A. Bogart and T. Landau. 2006. The Viewpoints Book: A Practical Guide to Viewpoints and Composition. Theatre Communications Group.

2. Neil Cooke and Robert Stone. 2013. RORSIM: a warship collision avoidance 3D simulation designed to complement existing Junior Warfare Officer training. *Virtual Reality* 17, 3: 169–179.
3. David Cope and Melanie J Mayer. 1996. *Experiments in musical intelligence*. AR editions Madison, WI.
4. Andrew Csinger, Kellogg S Booth, and David Poole. 1994. AI meets authoring: User models for intelligent multimedia. *Artificial Intelligence Review* 8, 5-6: 447–468.
5. Kutluhan Erol, James Hendler, and Dana S Nau. 1994. HTN planning: Complexity and expressivity. *AAAI*, 1123–1128.
6. Gilles Fauconnier and Mark Turner. 2008. The way we think: Conceptual blending and the mind's hidden complexities. Basic Books.
7. John H Flavell. 1979. Metacognition and cognitive monitoring: A new area of cognitive–developmental inquiry. *American psychologist* 34, 10: 906.
8. Howard Gardner. 2008. Art, mind, and brain: A cognitive approach to creativity. Basic Books.
9. Dedre Gentner and Linsey Smith. 2012. Analogical reasoning. *Encyclopedia of human behavior* 130: 130.
10. Borislav Iordanov. 2010. HyperGraphDB: a generalized graph database. *International Conference on Web-Age Information Management*, Springer, 25–36.
11. Mikhail Jacob, Alexander Zook, and Brian Magerko. 2013. Viewpoints AI: Procedurally Representing and Reasoning about Gestures. *Proceedings of the Digital Games Research Association*.
12. Mikhail Jacob, Gaëtan Coisne, Akshay Gupta, Ivan Sysoev, Gaurav Gav Verma, and Brian Magerko. 2013. Viewpoints AI. *Proceedings of the Ninth Artificial Intelligence and Interactive Digital Entertainment Conference*.
13. Mikhail Jacob and Brian Magerko. 2015. Interaction-based Authoring for Scalable Co-creative Agents. *Proceedings of International Conference on Computational Creativity*.
14. Owlchemy Labs. 2016. *Job Simulator: The 2050 Archives*. Owlchemy Labs.
15. Pat Langley, John E Laird, and Seth Rogers. 2009. Cognitive architectures: Research issues and challenges. *Cognitive Systems Research* 10, 2: 141–160.
16. Duri Long, Mikhail Jacob, Nicholas M. Davis, and Brian Magerko. 2017. Designing for Socially Interactive Systems. *Proceedings of the Eleventh ACM Conference on Creativity and Cognition*.
17. Mary Lou Maher. 2010. Evaluating creativity in humans, computers, and collectively intelligent systems. *Proceedings of the 1st DESIRE Network Conference on Creativity and Innovation in Design*, Desire Network, 22–28.
18. Palmer Martha, Gildea Dan, and Kingsbury Paul. 2005. The proposition bank: a corpus annotated with semantic roles. *Computational Linguistics Journal* 31, 1.
19. Masahiro Mori, Kari F MacDorman, and Norri Kageki. 2012. *The Uncanny Valley: The Original Essay by Masahiro Mori*. .
20. Manuel Mühlig, Michael Gienger, and Jochen J Steil. 2012. Interactive imitation learning of object movement skills. *Autonomous Robots* 32, 2: 97–114.
21. Neal E Seymour, Anthony G Gallagher, Sanziana A Roman, et al. 2002. Virtual reality training improves operating room performance: results of a randomized, double-blinded study. *Annals of surgery* 236, 4: 458–464.
22. Robert Speer and Catherine Havasi. 2012. Representing General Relational Knowledge in ConceptNet 5. *LREC*, 3679–3686.

23. Sólfar Studios. 2016. *Everest VR*. Sólfar Studios.
24. Endel Tulving. 1985. Elements of episodic memory.
25. Tony Veale, Kurt Feyaerts, and Charles Forceville. 2013, Creativity and the Agile Mind: A Multi-disciplinary Study of a Multi-faceted Phenomenon. Walter de Gruyter.
26. BUSINESS WIRE. 2017. Worldwide Spending on Augmented and Virtual Reality Forecast to Reach $13.9 Billion in 2017, According to IDC. .
27. Jie Yang, Yangsheng Xu, and Chiou S Chen. 1997. Human action learning via hidden Markov model. *IEEE Transactions on Systems, Man, and Cybernetics-Part A: Systems and Humans* 27, 1: 34–44.

Using 3D Modeling and Prediction as a Lens into Student Design Processes

Srinjita Bhaduri
University of Colorado Boulder
430 UCB
Boulder, CO 80309
bhaduri.srinjita@colorado.edu

C&C '17, June 27-30, 2017, Singapore, Singapore

ACM ISBN 978-1-4503-4403-6/17/06.
http://dx.doi.org/10.1145/3059454.3078700

Abstract
3D modeling, designing, and printing are gaining popularity at schools, libraries, and makerspaces. Side by side researchers and educationists are getting eager to find ways in which prediction can play an important and versatile role in teaching and learning of STEM courses, mathematics in particular [10]. Prediction can be used to serve as an informal assessment by instructors [9], a means for student motivation [8], and help improve conceptual understanding and reasoning [4,6,7]. Yet we have little understanding of how 3D designing and fabrication tools can help improve student learning to enable them to make better predictions. In this paper, I propose ways by which 3D designing and fabrication tools can help students make better predictions and how it can support enhance student engagement and learning of Engineering design skills.

Author Keywords
3D Printing; Fabrication Tools; Prediction; Student Learning

ACM Classification Keywords
H.5.m. Information interfaces and presentation (e.g., HCI)

Introduction

Prediction is about making a claim of a specific phenomenon, revealing something in advance without certainty and varies from making random guesses without evidence to scientific reasoning with adequate support. In considering the role of prediction to improve student learning, we must look at it as an effective tool to promote the teaching and learning of engineering design skills because it can enhance thinking and reasoning at all grade levels in various topics. Prediction can also take place based on an established generalization of patterns observed, in turn linking together previously established concepts related to design skills. For example, if students are asked before exploring an engineering design challenge to predict what would be the possible outcome of the challenge. These kinds of questions have the potential to elicit prior knowledge and to provide opportunities to connect concepts from previous explorations. Since students view prediction questions as not having a preset correct response, such questions might also provide students a chance to engage in classroom discourse without the threat of being incorrect.

Fabrication Technology on the other hand, has been used in several formal and informal school settings to enhance student learning; as a collaborative approach to treat interactions between experts and novices as opportunities for sharing and co-developing practices and skills [11,12]. In my vision, we can make use of this technology to help students learn better by making expert predictions and learn from their designs and models.

In this paper, I discuss why learning to build 3D models and use fabrication tools is beneficial for students and how it can help them get better at predictions. I also present reasons why prediction is important for student engagement and learning. Finally, I lay out the research questions I am trying to address and the timeline for accomplishing my goals.

Problem Space

My work draws on prior studies in the field of using prediction for learning enhancement, looking at ways in which fabrication technology and 3D modeling design can help in better student engagement, persistence, and motivation, and ways in which developing scientific models can help make better predictions.

Prediction does not necessarily mean a simple premature guess; instead prediction is a sophisticated reasoning process that connects related ideas. It can occur at the initial stage of a design exploration, and might even be a premature guess, without being based on any concrete reasoning; conversely, it can also be a form of a sophisticated reasoning process connecting relevant topics. To make a feasible prediction, students must activate their prior knowledge and help relate concepts from previous explorations. Such an opportunity helps students make sense of and build a better understanding of key design ideas based on their connections.

While tinkering and making has existed for some time in the formal and informal school setting, there is an increasing demand of using fabrication technologies in these settings. Teachers use 3D models to teach classes and to give students a better understanding of the content [11,12]. On the other hand, after-school programs, libraries, and makerspaces are having more and more programs that teach students 3D modeling and printing skills. This can help them build things from custom toys, artifacts for classroom projects to even personal gifts.

Researchers and educationists [3,5] are studying engineering design and digital fabrication and stress on the fact that they are needed for all students to engage fully as workers, consumers, and citizens in 21st-century society [2]. As we know, *engineering design* is a decision-making process (often iterative) in which the basic sciences, mathematics, and engineering sciences are applied to convert resources optimally to meet a stated objective. Among the fundamental elements of the design process are the establishment of objectives and criteria, synthesis, analysis, construction, testing and evaluation (ABET). According to Next Generation Science Standard (NGSS) framework, there are both practical and inspirational reasons for including engineering design as an essential element of science education [2]. NGSS also puts forward the idea that engineering design is necessary for literate citizens and hence they include this concept at each grade span starting from grades K-12. In recent years, several middle and high schools have introduced engineering courses that build students' engineering skill, engage them in experiences using a variety of technologies, and educate them about the range of engineering careers available.

Coincident with all this, researchers and educationists highlight the importance of models in building student knowledge base and enhancing design skills along with improving capability to predict. Engineers, make decisions based on evidence that a given design will work; they rarely rely on trial and error. Engineers often analyze a design by creating a model or prototype and collecting extensive data on how it performs, including outliers. Analysis of this kind of data not only informs design decisions and enables the prediction or assessment of performance but also helps define or clarify problems, determine economic feasibility, evaluate alternatives, and investigate failures (NRC Framework, 2012, p. 61-62) [1]. Thus, bringing all this research together we see the importance of using 3D models and fabrication technology to help students make better predictions and learn better, this in turn will lead to enhancement of creative skills and student engagement.

Motivation and Research Questions

I have been working with fabrication tools for a while and looking at ways by which 3D printers can be used as a means of interaction during playing tabletop games. This project helps me consider engineering design skills that can be developed or honed through 3D modeling and participatory design challenges. Additionally, I am working on another project which introduces and engages middle-school students to Engineering during out-of-school time, and fosters long-term interest and pathways into the field. In this project, we introduce students to technologies that can aid them to learn engineering.

These projects motivated me to think of ways by which student learning and engagement can be enhanced with the help of engineering design skills - provides students a foundation to better engage in and aspire to solve critical societal and environmental challenges in future [2]. After some preliminary research, I decided to look at ways by which prediction can help answer my research questions which are as follows:

- To what degree and to what extent can using predictions help increase student design learning opportunities?
- Can using and exploring models help in making better predictions and enhance student engagement?

Most of the previous research studies provide insight into ways of using prediction as a means of improving student learning and engagement. These research studies have been done in several sciences, mathematics, and reading courses. But there is a significant lack in using prediction in the teaching and learning of engineering design skills. From the NGSS framework and practices we know that engineering design is a vital element in science education. Moreover, prior research also provided us evidence that using and exploring models can help improve prediction and student engagement. Other possible directions for this kind of research could be finding ways by which teamwork could help improve prediction. For example,

can a group of students learn from each other ways to make better models and in turn explore their predicting capabilities, resulting in better classroom engagement. Thus, notable amount of work needs to be done in trying to address the importance of prediction in the student design process which can be accomplished using 3D modeling and designing.

Completed Work

I have completed two semester of data collection and analysis of middle-school students using a curriculum built around "Unmanned Aerial Vehicles" or Drones. Through this curriculum, we teach the importance and relevance of engineering to the lives of middle-school students. The data collected showed that there was a significant change in student affect and their perspective on engineering.

Simultaneously, I worked on using 3D printers to explore new interactions for tabletop games. With the help of a formative study I found out that there are several gameplay elements that leverage fabrication tools and that fabrication technology can be used for a wide gamut of purposes beyond what they were designed for.

Ongoing Work

Inspired from some of my previous findings and other related research, currently, I am working on building a help system to aid novice 3D designers to build models easily with the help of inbuilt question answering facility. This tool will be useful in teaching students how to 3D model with better question answering system. It will also help them learn and make better predictions of designing other models through the interaction history of their existing models.

Future Step

My goal is to build the help system and test it with middle-school and high-school students. Through the studies, I will measure their learning growth, engagement level and persistence in STEM career. I plan on collecting data in the form of surveys, observations, interviews, interaction history from the help system, and question and answers asked by students. The studies would be over a period of 2-3 years to measure student persistence and learning. These next steps will assist me towards the completion of my thesis.

References

1. *A Framework for K-12 Science Education: Practices, Cross-Cutting Concepts, and Core Ideas* in July 2011, NRC.

2. Appendix I - Engineering Design in the NGSS. (n.d.). Retrieved October 31, 2016, from http://www.nextgenscience.org/sites/default/files/*Appendix I - Engineering Design in NGSS - FINAL_V2.pdf*

3. Cynthia J. Atman, Robin S. Adams, Monica E. Cardella, Jennifer Turns, Susan Mosborg, and Jason Saleem (2007). Engineering Design Processes: A Comparison of Students and Expert Practitioners. *Journal of Engineering Education, 96: 359–379.* http://onlinelibrary.wiley.com/doi/10.1002/j.2168-9830.2007.tb00945.x/abstract

4. Michael T. Battista. 1999. Fifth graders' enumeration of cubes of 3D arrays: Conceptual progress in an inquiry-based classroom. *Journal for Research in Mathemat*ics Education, 30(4), 417–448. https://doi.org/10.2307/749708

5. Robert Q. Berry, III, Glen Bull, Christine Browning, Christine D. Thomas, Kendall Starkweather, and James H. Aylor (2010). Preliminary considerations regarding use of digital fabrication to incorporate engineering design principles in elementary mathematics education. *Contemporary Issues in Technology and Teacher Education, 10(2) 167-172*.

6. Lisa Kasmer and Ok Kyeong Kim. Educ Stud Math (2012) 79: 175. https://doi.org/10.1007/s10649-011-9336-z

7. Lisa Kasmer and Ok Kyeong Kim. 2011a. Using prediction to promote mathematical understanding and reasoning. *School Science and Mathematics Journal, 109(1), 20–33.*

8. Lisa Kasmer and Ok Kyeong Kim. 2011b. Using prediction to motivate personal investment in problem solving. *In D. J. Brahier & W. R. Speer (Eds.), The Seventy-third Yearbook of the National Council of Teachers of Mathematics, Motivation and disposition: Pathways to learning mathematics (pp. 157–168). Reston: National Council of Teachers of Mathematics.*

9. Ok Kyeong Kim and Lisa Kasmer. 2009. Prediction as an instructional strategy. *Journal of Mathematics Education Leadership, 11(1), 33–38.*

10. Kien H. Lim, Gabriela Buendia, Ok Kyeong Kim, Francisco Cordero, and Lisa Kasmer. 2010. The role of prediction in the teaching and learning of mathematics. *International Journal of Mathematics Education in Science and Technology, 41(5), 595–608.* https://doi.org/10.1080/00207391003605239

11. Sylvia Libow Marinez and Gary Stager. 2013. Invent to Learn: Making, Tinkering, and Engineering in the Classroom, Constructing Modern Knowledge, Torrance.

12. Dr. Shirin Vossoughi, Meg Escudé, Fan Kong, and Dr. Paula Hooper. 2013. Tinkering, Learning & Equity in the After-School Setting. In *Proceedings of FabLearn 2013, Stanford, CA, USA.*

Enhancing the Usage of Crowd Feedback for Iterative Design

Yu-Chun (Grace) Yen
University of Illinois
201 N. Goodwin Avenue
yyen4@illinois.edu

C&C '17, June 27-30, 2017, Singapore, Singapore

ACM ISBN 978-1-4503-4403-6/17/06.
http://dx.doi.org/10.1145/3059454.3078701

Abstract

Online crowd platforms (e.g. social networks, online communities, task markets) enable designers to gain insights from large audiences quickly and affordably. However, there is no guidance for designers to better allocate their social capital, time, and financial resources for acquiring feedback that meets their own needs. Also, feedback received online can be ambiguous and contradictory, making it difficult to interpret and act on. These limitations hinder the utility of crowd feedback, making designers hesitant to actively make use of feedback received. The goal of my dissertation is to 1) formulate a framework that suggests which crowd genres to solicit feedback according to individual needs, 2) develop lightweight activities that promote deeper interpretation on a large volume of feedback, and 3) design and deploy an experimental platform that collects long-term user data, and reduces the burden of conducting online studies of design feedback.

Author Keywords

Creativity; iterative design; feedback; reflection; crowdsourcing

ACM Classification Keywords

H.5.3 [Information interfaces and presentation]: Group and Organization Interfaces – Collaborative computing.

Figure 1. The user interface for a designer to upload a design, select the iteration, and describe its goals

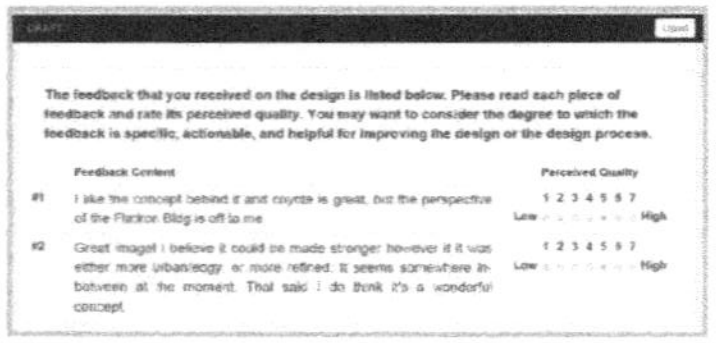

Figure 2. The user interface used by the designer for rating the perceived quality of the feedback responses.

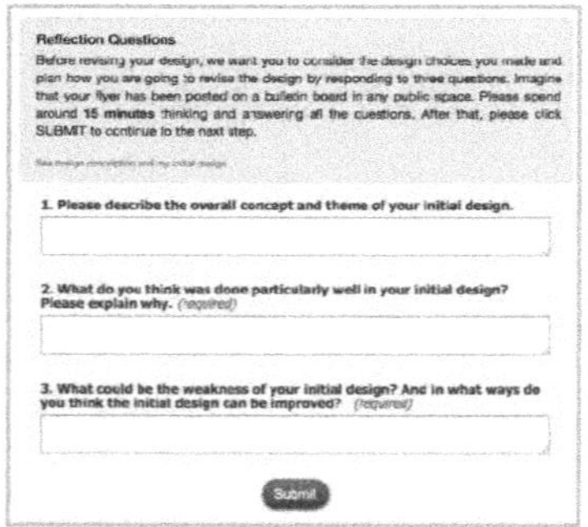

Figure 3. The user interface for a designer to write their responses to the reflection prompts.

Motivation

Educating the next generation of design innovators has received tremendous interests from educators and researchers. To prepare students for careers in innovation, instructors teach students the importance of connecting with potential users during the design process so they can understand real-world needs and acquire feedback on ongoing projects[3].

Online crowd platforms such as social networks, online communities, and task markets offer unprecedented opportunities for novice designers who have limited resources to access potential stakeholders, gather feedback, and tighten evaluation cycles [10]. However, feedback received online can be ambiguous, contradictory, and of variable quality because the providers typically have different motivations, expertise, and perspectives for writing helpful feedback. If a designer could not interpret the content of the feedback, learn from it, and formulate an effective action plan, the feedback becomes ineffective [2, 6].

Existing crowd feedback platforms provide no guidance on how the choices of the use of crowd platforms affects feedback generation, and offer limited mechanisms to help designers generate effective action plans according to the feedback received. My dissertation aims to address this challenge by researching and developing different approaches for enhancing the usage of crowd feedback for iterative design. To conduct a series of studies of crowd feedback, I have built an online platform, CRAFT, for hosting designs, collecting feedback, and allowing designers to perform sense-making around feedback (See Figure 1-3). All the experiments in my dissertation will be built on the CRAFT system.

Study 1: Help Designers Better Allocate Financial, Social Resources, and Time for Feedback Acquisition

As a starting point, I want to answer two questions: *(1) How do different crowd genres compare in terms of the quantity, quality, and content of the feedback generated?* and *(2) How does the design iteration (initial vs. revised) affect the feedback generated by the different crowds?* Answers to the questions are critical for designers to better allocate their financial resources, social capital, and time for acquiring feedback that best suits their individual needs.

In [10], twenty-two professional designers used the CRAFT site to collect feedback on their own project from three genres of crowd platforms. They were asked to rate the perceived quality of each piece of feedback, and then revised the initial design based on the feedback they received. We repeated the same process for the revised design so that we can compare the feedback received at different iterations.

Among many findings, we found that a paid task market provided feedback that contains more design suggestions, is longer, and has more positive valence. A Web forum provides more process oriented feedback and the most responses without payment, while social networks provide more design suggestions. Surprisingly, all three crowds produced feedback of similar quality according to the designers' ratings. During the post-study interviews, designers reported that they appreciated the crowd-sourced feedback because it was more open and honest than face-to-face discussion, and they could make evidence-based arguments from a large volume of feedback.

However, prior work has shown that feedback recipients may not always act on the feedback even when the feedback had high quality [7]. This motivated my second study, where I designed and tested a lightweight intervention to help designers better incorporate the feedback into the ongoing design.

Study 2: Using Reflection as a Strategy to Promote Feedback Interpretation

In the study, I tested how including and ordering a reflection activity in a feedback loop affects the design performance and the perceptions of performance [9]. The reflection activity was designed based on Schön' theory of reflection-on-action [8]. I hypothesized that by engaging in a reflection activity, designers would establish a deeper understanding of the current design situation and could better transform crowd feedback into coherent actions for improving that design.

Each designer (N=90) created a design and revised it after experiencing one of the four scenarios: reviewing feedback only, reflecting only, reflecting before reviewing feedback, and reflecting after reviewing feedback. We controlled the feedback generation in a way that designers across all the conditions rated the feedback as reasonably useful.

We found that when coupling reflection with feedback review, the resulting designs had the most extensive revision compared to those from the reflecting only or reviewing feedback only scenarios. In addition, performing reflection *after* reviewing feedback yielded a higher quality design according to the experts' ratings. Designers reported that the reflection activity helped them recall their design goals, question their choices, and plan and prioritize their revisions.

However, we noted that the degree of change between the interactions was low across all the conditions (i.e. below three on a seven-point Likert item). Self-reflection may not be able to resolve feedback that contains conflicting or vague viewpoints. An illustrative quote from a designer was: "*Everything was almost conflicting, so I just decided to go with my gut as a designer.*" Additionally, we found that designers tended to only address objective critique, and ignored feedback seemed to be subjective: "*I found the critiques that were objective to be useful and I disregarded critiques I thought to be purely subjective.*"

Study 3: Using Collaborative Interpretation as Approach to Enhance Feedback Interpretation

My next attempt to enhance the usage of feedback is to investigate the effects of collaborative feedback interpretation on iterative design. Collaborative sense-making processes have been used to enhance information-sharing tasks [1, 4]. I speculate that attending to such practices could also help increase the effectiveness of feedback.

I will follow a mix-methods approach by first surveying designers' current strategies for seeking people for interpreting feedback together. Second, I will perform a series of factorial experiments to investigate the beneficial effects of different pairing mechanisms for feedback interpretation. Third, I will implement a lightweight collaborative activity into the CRAFT system and test it in a design-oriented class where the students are required to produce a design project.

For the survey, I plan to ask two questions: *(1) Think of a time you received feedback but could not interpret it properly. Please describe the situation*, and *(2) Think of one person that you would like to discuss that feedback with. Outside of personal relationship with the person, how would you describe his or her characteristics?* Survey responses will be analyzed using open coding method [5]. The goal of the survey is to identify the features of a person designers take into account when deciding whether to share the feedback with.

Following the survey, I will perform a factorial experiment to investigate the benefits of performing collaborative interpretation over self-interpretation. Participants will be categorized into two groups: *self* and *with-helper.* Each participant will be given a sample design and six pieces of feedback that are of high quality yet conflict with each other. In the *self* condition, participant will be asked to read the feedback and write down an action plan for improving the design. In the *with-helper* condition, participants will be paired together to work on the same feedback interpretation task. I will perform quantitative analysis on the behavioral data and qualitative analysis on the content of the generated action plan. I will then conduct another factorial experiment comparing different pairing mechanisms for feedback interpretation. The outcome of the experiments will serve as the empirical knowledge about how to pair people to best improve the performance of feedback interpretation. I will interview the participants to gain insights about how to develop such collaborative interpretation practice into the CRAFT system.

Finally, I will develop a lightweight activity in the CRAFT system supporting collaborative interpretation. I plan to test the platform in the User Interface Design class offered at the University of Illinois, as the students will have design projects to work on during the semester.

Dissertation Status and Future Plans

So far, I have explored two approaches for enhancing the usage of crowd feedback [9, 10]. I am currently working on the third component of my dissertation which is to investigate how to leverage pairing technique to promote deeper feedback interpretation. I have completed a pilot survey within my institution (N=12) and found interesting patterns about how people chose a peer to interpret feedback with. I will complete the survey study and factorial experiment by June 2017. For the platform development, I will build on the CRAFT system which already supports individual interpretation. I plan to incorporate the collaborative activity into the system from July to August 2017, and deploy the system in the UI Design class offered in Fall 2017.

References

1. Donald Cox and Saul Greenberg. Supporting collaborative interpretation in distributed Groupware. In *Proceedings of the 2000 ACM conference on Computer supported cooperative work*. ACM. Philadelphia, Pennsylvania, USA. 2000. 289-298. http://dx.doi.org/10.1145/358916.359000.
2. Richard Higgins, Peter Hartley, and Alan Skelton, 2001. Getting the Message Across: The problem of communicating assessment feedback. *Teaching in Higher Education*, *6 (2)*, 269-274. 10.1080/13562510120045230.
3. Julie S. Hui, Elizabeth M. Gerber, and Steven P. Dow. Crowd-based design activities: helping students connect with users online. In

Proceedings of the 2014 conference on Designing interactive systems. ACM. Vancouver, BC, Canada. 2014. 875-884. http://dx.doi.org/10.1145/2598510.2598538.

4. Ruogu Kang, Aimee Kane, and Sara Kiesler. Teammate inaccuracy blindness: when information sharing tools hinder collaborative analysis. In *Proceedings of the 17th ACM conference on Computer supported cooperative work & social computing*. ACM. Baltimore, Maryland, USA. 2014. 797-806. http://dx.doi.org/10.1145/2531602.2531681.
5. Matthew Miles and Michael Huberman, 1984. *Qualitative Data Analysis*. Sage, Newbury Park, CA.
6. David Nicol. From monologue to dialogue: improving written feedback processes in mass higher education.
7. Margaret Price, Karen Handley, Jill Millar, and Berry O'donovan, 2010. Feedback : all that effort, but what is the effect? *Assessment & Evaluation in Higher Education*, *35 (3)*, 277-289. http://dx.doi.org/10.1080/02602930903541007.
8. Donald A. Schon, 1992. Designing as reflective conversation with the materials of a design situation. *Research in Engineering Design*, *3 (3)*, 131-147. http://dx.doi.org/10.1007/bf01580516.
9. Yu-Chun (Grace) Yen, Steven P. Dow, Elizabeth Gerber, and Brian P. Bailey, 2017. Listen to Others, Listen to Yourself: Combining Feedback Review and Reflection to Improve Iterative Design. In *ACM Conference on Creativity and Cognition* ACM.
10. Yu-Chun Yen, Steven P. Dow, Elizabeth Gerber, and Brian P. Bailey. Social Network, Web Forum, or Task Market?: Comparing Different Crowd Genres for Design Feedback Exchange. In *Proceedings of the ACM Conference on Designing Interactive Systems*. ACM. Brisbane, QLD, Australia. 2016. 773-784. http://dx.doi.org/10.1145/2901790.2901820.

Notational Communication with Co-creative Systems: Studying Improvements to Musical Coordination

Prashanth Thattai Ravikumar
National University of Singapore
Lower Kent Ridge Rd, 119077,
Singapore
prashanth.thattai@u.nus.edu

CC '17, June 27-30, 2017, Singapore, Singapore
ACM 978-1-4503-4403-6/17/06.
http://dx.doi.org/10.1145/3059454.3078702

Abstract
This research examines the impact of differences in extra-musical notational communication on a musician's co-creative experience with a music improvisation system. The method involves the development of musical improvisation agent technologies that support mixed-initiative communication and the use of mixed methods for studying the musician's co-creative engagement. The expected contributions are the findings about the impact of differences in extra-musical communication on the co-creative engagement with co-improvisation systems.

Author Keywords
coordination; musical co-improvisation; extra-musical communication; computational co-creativity; engagement

ACM Classification Keywords
H.5.m [Information interfaces and presentation (e.g., HCI)]: Miscellaneous

Introduction
Computational co-creativity is an emerging domain within the intersection of computational creativity and interaction design. Co-creativity involves multiple parties contributing to the creative process in a blended manner [4]. In computational co-creativity, one of the co-creators is a computational system (e.g., an AI program). Co-creative systems

have been developed in artistic domains such as painting partners [7], procedural game level generation [20], and joke generation [10]. Within computational co-creativity, the study of user's experiences of co-creation with artificial partners is a challenging problem that the research community is currently addressing. This work addresses the problem in the context of collaborative music improvisation (co-improvisation).

While co-improvising, musicians are engaged in coordination, i.e., maintaining certain musical relationships between each other's playing. While coordinating, musicians perform several actions such as managing shared responsibility, covering up for the group's mistakes, sharing blame etc. that affect their experience of co-improvisation. One approach to study the experiences of co-improvisation is to study the musician's experience of coordination during musical co-improvisation.

Research studies on coordination have identified several ways in which extra-musical communication such as eye contact [11, 18], bodily motion [6, 3] and non-verbal gesturing (e.g., touching the head) impact the musician's experience of coordination. The larger question of interest involves the study of the impact of extra-musical communication on the experience of coordination with co-improvisation system. Let us turn to related work that has focused on this problem.

Related work

Related work has focused on improving human-AI musical coordination through meta-musical communication, and studying first experiences with co-improvisational systems.

Meta-musical communication for improving coordination
Related work on improving human-AI musical coordination through meta-musical communication has focused on improving coordination via offline notational communication, real-time non-verbal communication, and hybrid notational communication.

Offline notational communication is facilitated through shared performance structure that specifies an improvisation plan through sparse musical information (e.g., chord charts, lead sheets). [15]. However, shared structures account for limited aspects of real-time communication and coordination that occur during improvised coordination. Real-time non-verbal communication has been facilitated with several robotic musician systems. This includes systems that use visual contact for temporal coordination [5], nodding and gazing [17, 12], for role changes. However, such communication has been available only for robotic musicians. Hybrid notational communication has been used for enabling new coordination strategies with software music systems [16]. The notational communication is hybrid as the system visualizes real-time information about future musical content through the musical notation [8]. However, in such interactions, the communication about musical future is one-way communication from the system's side.

Studying first experience with co-improvisational systems
Related work on first experiences with co-improvisational systems have adopted a qualitative approaches and controlled studies for evaluating the first person experiences.

In qualitative approaches to evaluation, musicians report their subjective experiences of performing along with the system [2]. However, privileging the improviser's experiences for evaluation makes it difficult to separate an individual musician's values and expectations of their partners from an evaluation of what the system did. In controlled experiments, several aspects of musician's interaction with the system have been experimentally varied to study changes in the musician's experience. This includes changes in the

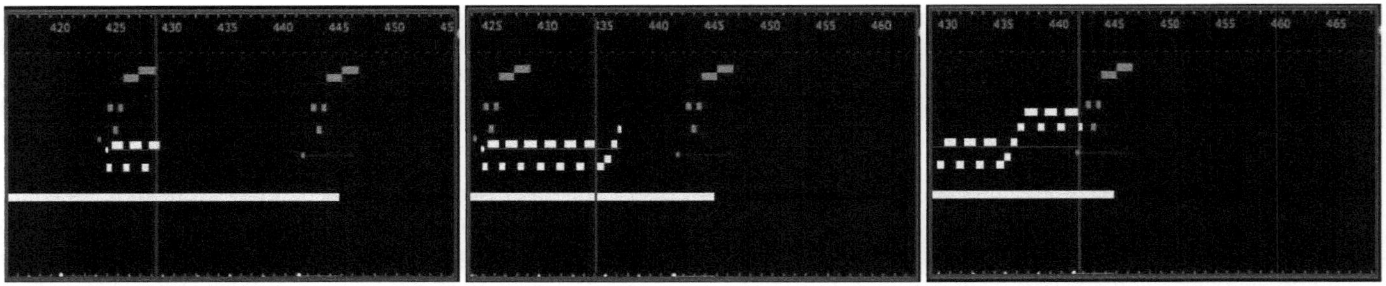

Figure 1: Coordinating musical transitions in the Anticipatory score system.

Protocol for coordinating musical transitions with notational communication (Figure 1.)

(1) Player1 (Red) communicates upcoming transition, beginning of coordination

(2) Player2 (Yellow) transitions by playing alternating notes, player1 is silent at this time

(3) Player2 increases the pitch to reach the destination point, both of them complete the transition

grouping of the participants and system [1], altered social perceptions of system [13], and varying behavioral components in the system design [9]. However, related research does not seem to have studied the impact of varying communication on the experience of co-improvisation.

Research question

Related work indicates that there is a research gap in terms of studying the impact of extra-musical notational communication on the experience of coordinating musical transitions with a co-improvisation system. The central question that guides this research is: *will the addition of two-way extra-musical notational communication enhance the human's experience of coordinating musical transitions with AI music partners?*

Musical transitions are quintessential places where musicians communicate in order to coordinate their actions. This communication is often extra-musical (e.g., facial gestures, eye contact), and conveys information about an upcoming transition (e.g., when it starts and ends, what changes should happen). The central claim is this extra-musical communication creates a sense of anticipation that enhances the musicians' engagement with AI partners.

Extra-musical communication is enabled by the Anticipatory score system, a software music gesture interface for human-human musical collaborations [19]. Notations placed in the future portion of the interface are played at a later point in time and form the extra-musical signaling in this setup. Figure 1 illustrates the use of notational communication for coordinating musical transitions in the Anticipatory score system.

The musician's engagement during transition coordination is measured through the quality of coordination. The quality of coordination is measured through the musician's experiences of co-creation. A few relevant dimensions for measuring co-creative experience are taking up roles and responsibility, elaborating on other performer's contributions, and supporting other performers. For the rest of this document, the musician's co-creative experiences while coordinating transitions are referred to as *co-creative engagement.*

Experimental controls in research studies

RQ1: RQ1 tests whether differences in human and AI communication initiative about the upcoming transition will impact co-creative engagement? transition.

RQ2: RQ2 tests whether differences in notational detail and representation will impact co-creative engagement. Parameters such as how much information about the future is visualized and how the notation is represented (musical notes/gestures) will be varied.

The main contributions from this research are the findings about the impact of extra-musical communication on co-creative engagement with music co-improvisation systems. This involves answering two research questions: 1) How do the specific mixes of communication initiatives affect co-creative engagement? 2) How do different communication protocols and notational strategies affect co-creative engagement?.

Method - work in progress

The method for conducting this research is currently under development. It has three parts (1) Derive abstractions of good transition coordination behaviors (2) develop improvisational agents using derived abstractions (3) evaluate co-creative engagement with developed prototypes. The remaining part of the section outlines the developments in the different stages of the method.

Abstracting rules of good transition coordination

In order to carefully separate the experience of co-improvising with the system from the quality of the musical output, a restricted musical environment is used. The musical environment allows musicians to play improvised duet using scores that provide a controlled balance between structure and freedom (e.g., the "in C" score). In this environment, transitions are restricted to changes in three musical dimensions (e.g., pitch, loudness, and note density) for three types of transitions, namely, "go to next section", "take it up" and "take it down". Qualitative studies are performed with human musicians to find patterns of good transition coordination.

Agents in Anticipatory score

The second part of the method involves the development of improvisational agents for transition coordination on the Anticipatory score platform. These agents receive notational information from a shared workspace as input, and algorithmically generates musical notation, that is visualized back in the shared workspace. For interactive algorithmic generation, the agent makes decisions using multiple sources, namely, its musical state (e.g, pitch, note density, sequence in score), information from a recency window, the musical score, and signals about arriving transitions. In the next phase of development, patterns derived from human-human improvised performances will be used to refine the AI's decision-making module.

Evaluation

The developed system will be evaluated in multiple study conditions that vary in communication initiatives and notational strategies. A mixed method is proposed for data collection and analysis. The data collection will involve a mix of observations, data logs, and semi-structured interviews from the performance session. For the analysis, statistical tests will be used to determine differences between co-creative engagement ratings under different study conditions. The next phase of development will identify relevant communicative action categories (e.g, initiating, maintaining, extending, support, interrupted etc) [14] and quantitative metrics from performance logs for rating co-creative engagement.

Conclusion

This research addresses a gap in the study of musician's experience with co-improvisation systems. The proposal to evaluate the musician's experience involves a study of co-creative engagement while coordinating musical transitions with an AI under study conditions that vary in extra-musical communication. This main contributions involve the findings about the impact of extra-musical communication on the musician's experience. Other contributions include patterns for good transition coordination behaviors.

Acknowledgements

I thank Dr. Lonce Wyse, and Dr. Kevin McGee for their extensive support and helpful comments on previous versions of this document. I thank Dr, Jude Yew, Dr. Micheal Spicer, Dr. Alex Mitchell, Dennis Ang, and Benjamin Loh for their constructive feedback and inspiring thoughts.

REFERENCES

1. Anna Rita Addessi, Francois Pachet, and Roberto Caterina. 2004. Children Confronting an Interactive Musical System. In *Proceedings of 8th International Conference on Music Perception & Cognition (ICMPC8), Adelaide.*
2. Ritwik Banerji. 2012. Maxine's Turing test–a player-program as co-ethnographer of socio-aesthetic interaction in improvised music. In *Proceedings of the Artificial Intelligence and Interactive Digital Entertainment (AIIDE'12) Conference.*
3. Michele Biasutti, Eleonora Concina, David Wasley, and Aaron Williamon. 2016. Music Regulators in Two String Quartets: A Comparison of Communicative Behaviors Between Low-And High-Stress Performance Conditions. *Frontiers in Psychology* 7 (2016).
4. Linda Candy and Ernest Edmonds. 2002. Modeling co-creativity in art and technology. In *Proceedings of the 4th conference on Creativity & cognition.* ACM, 134–141.
5. Marcelo Cicconet, Mason Bretan, and Gil Weinberg. 2012. Visual cues-based anticipation for percussionist-robot interaction. In *Proceedings of the seventh annual ACM/IEEE international conference on Human-Robot Interaction (HRI'12).* ACM, Boston, Massachusetts, USA, 117–118.
6. Jane W. Davidson. 2012. Bodily Movement and Facial Actions in Expressive Musical Performance By Solo and Duo Instrumentalists: Two Distinctive Case Studies. *Psychology of Music* 40, 5 (2012), 595–633.
7. Nicholas Davis. 2013. Human-computer co-creativity: blending human and computational creativity. In *Ninth Artificial Intelligence and Interactive Digital Entertainment Conference.*
8. Alexandre RJ François, Elaine Chew, and Dennis Thurmond. 2007. *Mimi-A Musical Improvisation System That Provides Visual Feedback To the Performer.* Technical Report 07-889. University of Southern California Computer Science Department.
9. William T Hsu and Marc H Sosnick. 2009. Evaluating Interactive Music Systems: An HCI Approach.. In *Proceedings of the International Conference on New Interfaces for Musical Expression.* 25–28.
10. Anna Aurora Kantosalo, Jukka Mikael Toivanen, Hannu Tauno Tapani Toivonen, and others. 2015. Interaction Evaluation for Human-Computer Co-Creativity. In *Proceedings of the Sixth International Conference on Computational Creativity.*
11. Satoshi Kawase. 2014. Gazing Behavior and Coordination During Piano Duo Performance. *Attention, Perception, & Psychophysics* 76, 2 (2014), 527–540.
12. Angelica Lim, Takeshi Mizumoto, Tetsuya Ogata, and Hiroshi G Okuno. 2012. A Musical Robot That Synchronizes With a Coplayer Using Non-Verbal Cues. *Advanced Robotics* 26, 3-4 (2012), 363–381.

13. Louis McCallum and Peter W McOwan. 2014. Shut up and play: A musical approach to engagement and social presence in Human-Robot Interaction. In *The 23rd IEEE International Symposium on Robot and Human Interactive Communication.* IEEE, 949–954.

14. Dave Murray-Rust and Alan Smaill. 2011. Towards a Model of Musical Interaction and Communication. *Artificial Intelligence* 175, 9 (2011), 1697–1721.

15. Jérôme Nika and Marc Chemillier. 2012. Improtek: integrating harmonic controls into improvisation in the filiation of OMax. In *Proceedings of the International Computer Music Conference (ICMC'12).* Ljubljana, Slovenia, 180–187.

16. Isaac Schankler, Alexandre Francois, and Elaine Chew. 2011. Preparing for the Unpredictable: Identifying Successful Performance Strategies in Human-Machine Improvisation. In *Proceedings of the International Symposium on Performance Science.* Toronto, Canada, 157–162.

17. Gil Weinberg, Brian Blosser, Trishul Mallikarjuna, and Aparna Raman. 2009. The Creation of a Multi-Human, Multi-Robot Interactive Jam Session.. In *Proceedings of 10th International Conference on New Interfaces for Musical Expression (NIME).* Pittsburgh, PA, USA, 70–73.

18. Aaron Williamon and Jane W. Davidson. 2002. Exploring Co-Performer Communication. *Musicae Scientiae* 6, 1 (2002), 53–72.

19. Lonce Wyse and Jude Yew. 2014. A Real-Time Score for Collaborative Just-In-Time Composition. *Organised Sound* 19, 03 (2014), 260–267.

20. Georgios N Yannakakis, Antonios Liapis, and Constantine Alexopoulos. 2014. Mixed-initiative co-creativity. In *Proceedings of the 9th Conference on the Foundations of Digital Games.* Society for the Advancement of the Science of Digital Games, Liberty of the Seas, Caribbean.

DrumBall: Design and Implementation of a Digital Orality Hypermedia System

Pierre Tchetgen
University of California at Berkeley
Berkeley, CA 97602, USA
akwerius@berkeley.edu

C&C '17, June 27-30, 2017, Singapore, Singapore

ACM ISBN 978-1-4503-4403-6/17/06.
http://dx.doi.org/10.1145/3059454.3078703

Abstract
This paper describes the concept and design plan of DrumBall, a device that allows for rhythmic input to be turned into and used as letters, words and phrases. Thinking beyond the computer screen and keyboard as traditional interface models, and their reliance on numeric and alphabetic language representations, we propose to explore drum language as a mode of HCI, whereby hand-played rhythms are input methods to the system, which generates speech, text and visualization output. Based largely on the talking drum model of communicating messages, with some influence from Morse code, this digital talking drum project could set the foundation for a new way to think about learning, as well as provide a fresh (and fun) perspective on the role of rhythm in the 21st century information society.

Author Keywords
Tangible user interfaces; beyond computer screen and keyboard; haptic I/O; translation of rhythm to letters; learning, and literacy development in marginalized learners; "talking drum" model of communicating; collaborative design; and storytelling. A prototype interactive system is described, Drumball.

ACM Classification Keywords
H5.2. Haptic I/O

1. Introduction

The changes in the conditions surrounding schooling brought about by the information technology revolution are such that we need to reconsider the epistemological bias towards 'literacy' – as opposed to 'orality' and its related practices – which has predominantly informed what and how we teach. As Gunther Kress reminds educators in *Literacy in the New Media Age*, "we can no longer treat literacy (or 'language') as the sole, the main, let alone the major means for representation and communication", as "communication, whatever the mode, always happens as text." (Kress, 2003).

Rhythm is a fundamental force in children's lives, which plays an important role in their early language development, whether it is through clapping along to songs or beating out the syllables in words. Yet, when literacy-supporting technology is found in the classroom, it typically resides in a desktop computer where an individual child is placed in front of a computer monitor and a keyboard, which makes it difficult both for children to collaborate, and for them to involve their bodies in play. Despite the diffusion of technological innovations for today's digital youth, there persists a lack of computer-mediated systems that supports and connects children's early awareness of rhythm and ability to drum with their communication needs. In particular, at the pre-literate and early learning stages of language acquisition, moving, listening and speaking rather than sitting, reading and writing serve as the bedrock foundation for literacy.

The purpose for my research is to support children's emergent literacy development via a collaborative and interactive rhythmic communication tool that departs from the typical keypad-screen computing paradigm. I build upon the premise that the talking drum is an extension of the mouth, and thus serves the same social function as language to communicate at a distance. My dissertation investigates the potential of applying technology design innovation to extend the drum-oral tradition as a model of communication and language learning for children in U.S urban schools.

2. Conceptual Framework

Learning today is taking place in a context where "the possibilities of choice are increasing," which constitutes an important reason for my focus on leveraging rhythm (a universal human faculty) as a communication mode. As the aim of schooling has also shifted to reflect a new focus on the "awareness of the affordances of modes" (Kress) and the gaining of competency across different modalities, my choice of drumming as a pedagogical approach to literacy learning is pointing to a focus, not on rhythm as music, but rather as drum language text.

The principle of drum language is a paradigmatic and epistemic phenomenon of African oral traditional cultures, with relevant pedagogical implications, in the same way that the pen (as the preferred instrument for communication) is a paradigmatic tool of literate (or visual) cultures. Since "knowledge changes its shape when it is realized in the different modal material" (Kress), not only could these shifts in modal uses in school culture have an impact on the forms of imagination, they can also have significant affective and cognitive consequences, notably in relationship to social behavior and identity development in children.

3. Pilot Studies

To explore these objectives of the research, I already conducted a series of pilot studies. These focus groups, modeled after a media salon and design workshop, were first held at United Roots Oakland, a green youth arts & media center in Oakland, CA (2014) and subsequently in other sites including the UC Berkeley Upward Bound Trio summer program (2015) and the

Figure 1: Mother and Child participants interacting via DrumBall at the Urban Griots Media Salon (2014).

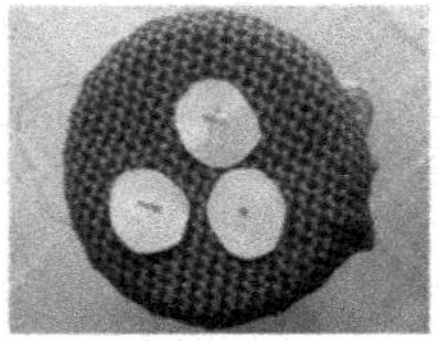

Figure 2: DrumBall custom fabric cover with force-resistive sensors

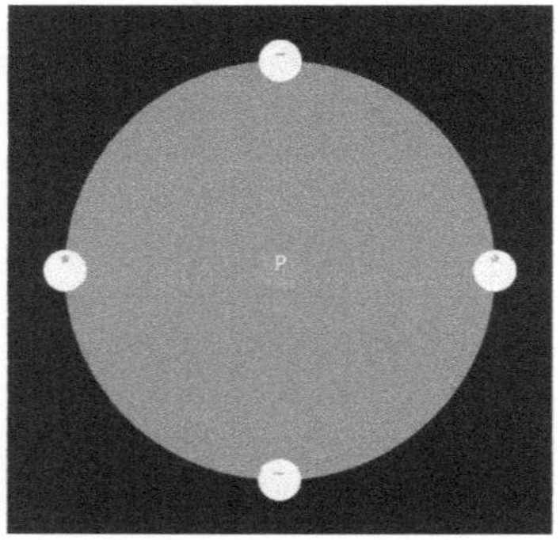

Figure 3: Alpharhythm code for the letter "P" (-*-*, slap-tone-slap-tone) set on a time cycle

Business Of Success in Sports camp (BOSS) in Hayward (2016).

3.1 Community Media Salon (PreK-8)

The community media salon - presented by the Urban Griots Collaborative (www.urbangriot.org) - is a space for youth, creative thinkers, artists and educators of all walks (as well as parents and children) to engage in critical discussions on or interactive experiences mediated by arts, digital media and technology. Sessions are complemented by focus group discussions, one-on-one interviews and questionnaire with questions probing the participants' perception and understanding of the use of drums as a communicative instrument.

The main method of data collection was via participatory observation of participants' interaction while immersed in a digital rhythm-based language play activity. In the analysis, I was interested in the nature of participants' digitally mediated talk. At this early stage, the tangible user interface is introduced to transduce rhythmic input patterns into sound output (letter names based on alpha-rhythmic patterns similar to Morse code - see figure 3). Sample cards with each letter of the alphabet mapped □to a 4-beat permutation of 3 drum sounds (•: tone; - slap; x: bass) were provided to the users as a guide for interacting with the system. Participants interacted individually and collaboratively, taking turns playing and talking.

2.2 Design Workshop (9-12)

Several focus groups, modeled after a STEAM media design workshop session were offered at the Upward Bound (2015) Trio summer program at UC Berkeley and the Bay Area BOSS camp in Hayward (2016). Students were led through a series of STEAM sessions probing their embodied and intuitive understanding of rhythm to design a new digital tool or technology that leverages people's ability to move or communicate via rhythm/movement, or a combination of both.

Students were asked to apply their skills in science, technology, engineering and mathematics in reimagining new possibilities for communication, especially as related to the employ of rhythm in computers use. They participated in critical discussions with designers and researchers, and engaged in collaborative design work through collaborative experiences mediated by arts, digital media and technology. I also collected audio, image and video data of their experiences in the context of collaborative design thinking process activities.

2.3 Digital Drum Language Corpus

Through archival research on the poetic and speech function of drum language, I am in the process of producing a synthesis of drum text data (proverbs, poems) collected through audio, video and literature sources in the form of a multi-modal corpus that will serve as a database for DrumBall users to interact. Audio recordings of drum language texts from archival sources are systematically transcribed and translated. Using the Praat phonetic analysis software, multimodal representations of the information contained within each recorded drum phrases (tonal pattern or sequence, syllabic contour, word fragments) are also generated and incorporated into the multi-lingual, multi-modal (text, audio, images) digital corpus to be used as metadata in the online learning environment.

3. Research Design

For the dissertation, my design research work is centered on the following research questions:

1. What is the connection between drumming and speech as modes of communication? How

do drummers function as *messengers* within the community to transmit social knowledge and information via drums?

2. What are the cultural roots of the talking drum as a technology born of an oral society/tradition? How do attitudes, perceptions and cognition towards the use of drum rhythms as a mode of communication differ across age cohort and cultural background?

3. What if we invented a digital talking drum? What would be the social and literacy learning outcomes for marginalized digital youth who could benefit from culturally relevant pedagogy and curriculum? How would such a system impact the preservation/revitalization of drum language?

While discourse analysis of interviews and generational analysis of drum circle focus group observations will help to answer the first two questions, participatory youth action research and design-based research will constitute the primary methods for answering the third.

6. Deliverables

At the end of my thesis work, I expect to deliver:

1. one or more interactive prototypes that have been designed in collaboration with youth
2. a web-based drum language corpus for facilitating the collection and annotation of drum vocabularies
3. a model and principles of collaborative drum talk
4. a set of culturally responsive design principles for learning technology research and development.

7. Timeline

May 2017. Finish collecting and translating drum texts from print/oral sources in different languages. Group them into a multimodal corpus (nouns, verbs, actions). Prepare for and complete oral qualifying examination.

June 2017 Finish conducting drummer interviews. Finish recruiting children and mentors for summer intervention. Travel to Creativity & Cognition 2017.

July-August 2017 Begin implementation of summer drum language vocabulary intervention (Oakland, CA; Boulder, CO; and Boston, MA). Ongoing analysis of results. Evaluate interactive prototype with researchers.

September 2017 Festival/Competition. Assemble panel of judges to evaluate the efficacy of students' drum talk. Judge final DrumBall competition using it.

October-May 2018 Research data analysis. Post-evaluation and analysis. Final dissertation write-up.

Conclusion

The purpose of the *DrumBall* invention is to explore drum language as a learning mode for composition and communication. In school contexts, learners can use this hypermedia system as a communal repertoire to communicate. Teachers, in turn, can use the system to access a record of students' talk and interactions over time. For marginalized students struggling academically and disciplinarily who are in need of interventions to address cognitive and emotional problems linked to chronic stress, digital innovations aimed at shifting the ways schools approach literacy instruction and socialization in such ways could open up new pathways of learning and social transformation in urban schools.

Acknowledgements
We thank all the drummers, scholars, researchers, graduate students, and authors who wrote and provided inspiration and helpful comments on previous versions of this document, notably CK Ladzekpo, Kwaku Manu, Angela Chang, Jabari Mahiri, Erin Murphy-Graham, Laura Sterponi, Marti Hearst Grace Kim, Jennifer Higgs, Arvind Thyagarajan, Jetesh Hariramani.

References
1. Akwerius. Drum Language Audio Research. 2016. Retrieved March 9, 2017 from https://soundcloud.com/akwerius/sets/drum-language-audio-research
2. Allen, B. A., & Butler, L. (1996). The effects of music and movement opportunity on the analogical reasoning performance of African American and White school children: Preliminary study. Journal of Black Psychology, 22, 316-328.
3. Bakhtin, M. M., & Holquist, M. (1981). *The dialogic imagination: Four essays*. Austin: University of Texas Press.
4. Banks, A. J. (2006). *Race, rhetoric, and technology: Searching for higher ground*. Mahwah, NJ: Lawrence Erlbaum.
5. Bastian, J. A. (2003). *Owning memory: How a Caribbean community lost its archives and found its history*. Westport, Conn: Libraries Unlimited.
6. Belgrave, Faye Z.; Allison, Kevin W. (2006). *African American psychology: From Africa to America.* Thousand Oaks, CA, US: Sage Publications, Inc
7. Bilby, K. M. (1992). Drums of defiance: Maroon music from the earliest free black communities of Jamaica. Washington, DC: Smithsonian/Folkways.
8. Blommaert, J. 2005. *Discourse.* Cambridge: Cambridge University Press.
9. Blumer, H. (1969). Symbolic interactionism: Perspective and method.Englewood Cliffs, NJ: Prentice Hall
10. Briggs C. L. and Bauman, R. (1992) "Genre, Intertextuality, and Social Power." *Journal of Linguistic Anthropology*. 2(2):131-72
11. Carrington, J. F. (1949). *Talking drums of Africa*. London: Carey Kingsgate press.
12. Cassell, J. (2004). Towards a model of technology and literacy development: Story listening systems, Applied Developmental Psychology, vol. 25, pp 75-105.
13. Clarke, Roger T. (1934) *The Drum language of the Tumba people*. American Journal of Sociology 40:34-38.
14. Clottey, K. (2004). *Mindful Drumming – Ancient Wisdom for Unleashing the Human Spirit and Building Community,* Sankofa.
15. Coe, C. (2005). *Dilemmas of culture in African schools: Youth, nationalism, and the transformation of knowledge*. Chicago: University of Chicago Press.

16. Cole, J. M., & Boykin, A. W. (2008 August) *Examining Culturally Structured Learning Environments With Different Types of Music-Linked Movement Opportunity. 34 (3)*, 331-355. *Computing Research*, 25(1), 17-34.

17. Croson, M. (2009, January 08). *When Drums Were Outlawed*. Retrieved April 07, 2016, from http://www.croson.net/new_page_33.htm

18. Darling-Hammond, L., Bransford, J., LePage, P., Hammerness,

19. K., & Duffy, H. (2005). *Preparing teachers for a changing world: What teachers should learn and be able to do.* New York, NY: Jossey-Bass.

20. Diouf, M., Nwankwo, I.K. *Rhythms of the Afro-Atlantic World : Rituals and Remembrances*. Ann Arbor :University of Michigan Press, 2010. Print.

21. Few, S. "Dyslexics Could be Our Most Talented Data Visualizers." Perceptual Edge. 22 August 2011. Web: https://www.perceptualedge.com/blog/?p=1071

22. Finnegan, R. (2014). Communicating: The Multiple Modes of Human Interconnection. (2nd Edition, Routledge). Chapters 1-2

23. Finnegan, R. (1971). *Oral Literature in Africa*. Oxford University Press

24. Foray, D. and J. Raffo (2009), "A small explosion: patent in educational and instructional technologies and methods; What do they tell us?", 4th EPIP Conference, Bologna.

25. Foucault, M. 1980. *Power/Knowledge.* Ed. By Colin Gordon. Trsl. C.Gordon, L.Marshall, J.Mepham, K.Soper. New York: Pantheon.

26. Gee, J P. (2003). *What Video Games Have to Teach Us About Learning and Literacy* (New York: Palgrave Macmillan, 2003);

27. Gutiérrez, K. D., & Rogoff, B. (2003). Cultural ways of learning: Individual traits or repertoires of practice. *Educational Researcher*, 32(5), 19-25.

28. Hatano, Giyoo; James V. Wertsch (March 2001). "Sociocultural Approaches to Cognitive Development: The Constitutions of Culture in Mind". *Human Development* 2 (3): 78.

29. Havelock, Eric Alfred. *The Muse Learns to Write: Reflections on Orality and Literacy from Antiquity to the Present*. New Haven: Yale UP, 1986. Print.

30. Hood, M., *Atumpan*. Los Angeles: Institute of Ethnomusicology, University of California Los Angeles.

31. Kramsch, C. and A. Whiteside. Language ecology in multilingual settings. In *Applied Linguistics 29/4: 654-671*. Oxford University Press 2008.

32. Kress, G. (2003). *Literacy and multimodality: A theoretical framework.* In Literacy in the new media age. London: Routledge.

33. Kristeva, Julia. *Desire in Language: A Semiotic Approach to Literature and Art*. New York: Columbia UP, 1980. Print.

34. Kumi, E., Manu, J. (1996). Talking Drum: Rhythms of Life, Songs of Wisdom: Akan Music from Ghana. Washington, DC: Smithsonian/Folkways.

35. Ladson-Billings, G. (1994). *The dreamkeepers: Successful teachers of African American children*. San Francisco: Jossey-Bass.

36. Lam, E. (2013). Multilingual Practices in Transnational Digital Contexts. Tesol Quarterly. Doi: 10.1002/tesq.132

37. Lee, C. D. (2001). Is October brown Chinese? A cultural modeling activity system for underachieving students. *American Educational Research Journal*, 38, 97-141.

38. Lemke, J. 1995. Discourse and social theory. In *Textual Politics: Discourse and social dynamics.* London: Taylor & Francis. 19-36.

39. Lesaux, N.K. & Kieffer, M.J. (2010). Exploring sources of reading comprehension difficulties among language minority learners and their classmates in early adolescence. *American Educational Research Journal,* 47(3), 596-632.

40. Mahiri, J. (2011). Digital Tools in Urban Schools: Mediating a Remix of Learning. UMich Press

41. McHoul, A., & Luke, A. (1989). Discourse as language and politics: An introduction to the philology of political culture in Australia. Journal of Pragmatics, 13(3), 323–332.

42. Moje, & P.P. Afflerbach (Eds.), Handbook of reading research (Volume IV, pp. 107-135). New York, NY: Routledge

43. Mizuko, I. (2009). Hanging Out, Messing Around and Geeking Out. MIT Press.

44. Niangoran-Bouah, G. (1981). *Introduction à la drummologie*. Abidjan: Université Nationale de Côte d'Ivoire, Institut d'Ethno-sociologie.

45. Nketia, K. *Our Drums and Drummers*. Ghana Publishing House; First Edition edition (1968).

46. Noguera, P., & Wing, J. Y. (2006). *Unfinished business: Closing the racial achievement gap in our schools*. San Francisco: Jossey-Bass, a Wiley imprint.

47. Nora, P. 1997. *Les lieux de memoire.* Paris: Gallimard.

48. Ogbu, J. U. (2008). *Minority status, oppositional culture, and schooling*. New York: Routledge.

49. Ong, W. (1977). African Talking Drums and Oral Noetics *New Literary History*, Vol. 8, No. 3. (1977), pp. 411-429

50. Ong, Walter. Orality and Literacy: The Technologizing of the Word. London: Methuen, 1982.

51. Orr, J., McCleery A. (2012). Intangible Cultural Heritage in Scotland: Developing Appropriate Methodologies. In Gauthier, A. *Les Mesures de Soutien au Patrimoine Immateriel.* Conseil Quebecois du Patrimoine Vivant.

52. Paratore, J. R., Cassano, C. M., & Schickedanz, J. A. (2011). *Supporting early (and later) literacy development at home and at school: The long view.* In M. L. Kamil, P. D. Pearson, E. B.

53. Pennycook, A. (1994). Incommensurable discourses? Applied Linguistics 15.2, 115–138.

54. Phillpotts, Bertha S. *Edda and Saga*. London: T. Butterworth, Limited, 1931. Print.

55. Pinkard, N. (2001). Rappin' reader and say say oh playmate: Using children's songs as literacy scaffolds in computer-based learning environments. *Journal of Educational*

56. Resnick, M., Rusk, N., and Cooke, S. (1998). The Computer Clubhouse: Technological Fluency in the Inner City. In Schon, D., Sanyal, B., and Mitchell, W. (eds.), High Technology and Low-Income Communities, pp. 266-286. Cambridge: MIT Press.

57. Resnick, M. (2001). Closing the Fluency Gap. Communications of the ACM, vol. 44, no. 3.

58. Schegloff, E.A. (2007). *Sequence Organization in Interaction: A Primer in Conversation Analysis,* vol. 1. Cambridge: Cambridge University Press.

59. Scribner, S., & Cole, M. (1981). *The psychology of literacy*. Cambridge, Mass: Harvard University Press.

60. Stein, P. (2004). Representation, rights, and resources: Multimodal pedagogies in the language and literacy classroom. In B. Norton & K. Toohey (Eds.), Critical pedagogies and language learning (pp. 95-115). Cambridge, England: Cambridge University Press.

61. Stern, T. (1957). Drum and whistle languages: an analysis of speech surrogates. Amer Anthropol 59: 487-506.

62. Stevens, T., Sharp, J. & Nelson, B. (2001). *The intersection of two unlikely worlds: Ratios & Drums.* Teaching Children Mathematics, 7(6), 376-383.

63. Tang, P. (2007). Masters of the Sabar: Wolof griot percussionists of Senegal. Temple University Press.

64. UNESCO, Information Society Division (2003). Guidelines for the Preservation of Digital Heritage.

65. UNESCO, Intangible Cultural Heritage, (2009). Kit of the 2003 Convention. http://www.unesco.org/culture/ich/en/kit

66. Vasudevan, L., Schultz, K., & Bateman, J. (2010). Rethinking composing in a digital age: Authoring literate identities through multimodal storytelling. *Written Communication, 27*(4), 442- 468. doi: 10.1177/0741088310378217

67. Villepastour, A. (2010). Ancient Text Messages of the Yoruba Bata Drum – Cracking the Code, Ashgate Publishing

68. Warschauer, M. (2002). Reconceptualizing the digital divide. First Monday, vol. 7, no. 7.

69. Winter, Y. "On the grammar of a Senegalese drum language." *Language*, vol. 90 no. 3, 2014, pp. 644-668. *Project MUSE*, doi:10.1353/lan.2014.0061

70. J. Zimmerman, J. Forlizzi, S. Evenson - Research Through Design as a Method for Interaction Design Research in HCI, Carnegie Mellon University

Exploring the Effects of Physical Embodiment in a Puzzle-Based Educational Programming Game

Edward F. Melcer
New York University
Brooklyn, NY 11201, USA
eddie.melcer@nyu.edu

C&C '17, June 27-30, 2017, Singapore, Singapore

ACM ISBN 978-1-4503-4403-6/17/06.
http://dx.doi.org/10.1145/3059454.3078704.

Abstract
One prominent aspect of programming skills/expertise is that it requires the use of many creative processes such as problem-solving, visualization, reflection, motivation and handling failure. While there have been a variety of puzzle-based educational programming games created to help teach learners these skills, few have been evaluated to assess their efficacy in developing programming and problem-solving skills or improving learners' positive emotional responses. Furthermore, most games are designed for a single player touchpad/mouse experience. This is problematic when trying to understand the validity of these designs, and whether there are alternative physically embodied design approaches that may prove more effective. My dissertation work helps address this problem. After creating a framework based on a meta-review that carefully dissects embodiment strategies in learning games, I am creating and evaluating tangible and augmented reality versions of a programming game. I plan to examine how these different forms of physical interaction help to facilitate and enhance meaning-making, problem-solving, and positive emotions.

Author Keywords
Physical Embodiment; Embodied Cognition; Enactment; Embodied Interaction; Tangibles; Computational Thinking; Educational Programming Game.

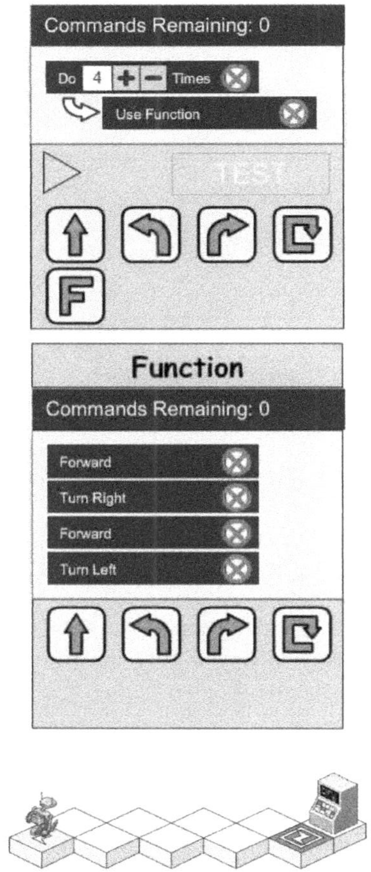

Figure 1: The Bots & (Main)Frames game. The UI is identical for all versions of the game and only differs on physical embodiment and interaction using 1) the mouse; 2) tangible programming blocks; and 3) AR enactment of code execution.

ACM Classification Keywords

H.5.m. Information interfaces and presentation (e.g., HCI): Miscellaneous.

Introduction

One prominent aspect of computational thinking (CT) and programming skills/expertise is that they require the use of creative processes such as problem-solving, idea generation, reflection, and understanding failure [9, 34, 48]. Much like the cyclic process of ideation and evaluation that underlies creativity [27], programming can be seen as a search through different problem spaces that requires the iterative generation and testing of hypotheses [23]. Programmers must identify a problem, generate ideas/solutions, evaluate and reflect upon the effectiveness of said ideas, and be motivated enough to cope with and understand failure in order to generate new ideas. However, the radical novelty [10] of these processes and the subject matter in general can evoke strong negative feelings towards programming [18, 24, 41], presenting challenges to learners' self-beliefs, and creating barriers to learning [44]. Conversely, video games are promising tools for improving students' motivation and practicing the ideation/evaluation cycle of creativity since playing video games involves guessing, thinking, testing, and repeated opportunities for failure or success [1, 12].

In programming education, there have been numerous educational programming games created that are puzzle-based and focus on learning through problem-solving and reflection (e.g., Mazzy [21], BOTS [15, 16], Blockly [8], and Machineers [26]). However, little is understood about the effects of these programming-focused puzzle games and design choices made within them [31]. Do they actually improve problem-solving ability, performance, and positive emotional responses needed for STEM learning and creativity, or do they simply function as chocolate-covered broccoli?

Furthermore, the similar design choices of most programming puzzle games—which focus on single player touchpad/mouse and keyboard experiences [14, 31]—may be neglecting recent research highlighting the efficacy of alternative body-centric, physically embodied theories and approaches (i.e., embodied cognition, embodied interaction, and enactment) in helping learners make meaning, problem-solve, and improve positive emotional responses [22, 30, 31, 36, 38]. Two robust and common physical embodiment approaches within HCI and Learning Science communities are tangibles/manipulatives [33, 36] and augmented reality (AR) [6, 22]. The principal advantage of tangibles is that they allow for learning concepts to be embedded directly into the physical material and design of an object, as well as through the embodied interactions learners have by manipulating these objects [36, 39]. AR's primary advantage is utilizing embodied cognition to help learners develop understanding through mirroring or enacting learning concepts with their body [22]. Both tangibles and AR have been found to result in benefits for a wide range of factors in non-programming domains such as engagement [11], interest [2], and collaboration [46].

The goal of my research is to explore how the diverse affordances of various forms of physical embodiment differentially impact meaning-making processes, enhance positive emotional responses for learners, and improve performance in problem-solving tasks [28–31]. This will be done through controlled comparison of

Figure 2: The tangible programming blocks version of Bots & (Main)Frames.

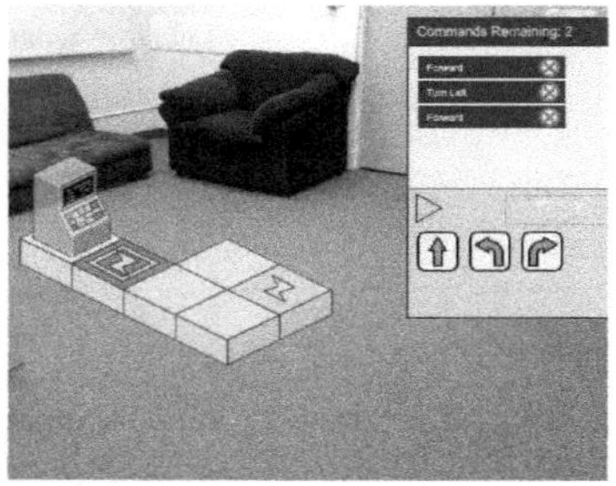

Figure 3: The proposed AR version of Bots & (Main)Frames.

different versions of an educational programming game I created called Bots & (Main)Frames (see Figure 1).

Bots & (Main)Frames

Bots & (Main)Frames is designed to incorporate common design characteristics of many educational programming games (i.e., players program a virtual robot to solve puzzles [14]), and provides a comparison point for differing forms of physical embodiment and interaction (e.g., mouse vs. tangible programming blocks vs. AR enactment). The game objective is to program a virtual robot to reach all red tiles in a maze from a given starting point, using a limited number of commands in each level. Players are able to program the robot to move forward, rotate 90 degrees left or right, use a loop (repeat one command a specified number of times), or use a function. In the mouse version of Bots & (Main)Frames, players click UI buttons to program (see Figure 1). In the tangibles version, players instead physically connect wooden blocks to program (see Figure 2). In the AR version, players use a tablet to program and then physically walk through space to enact the code execution. For all versions, the graphics and gameplay are identical; differing only in the way players program/execute code.

Related Work

Physical Embodiment

My research takes a broad perspective towards embodiment: centering it around the notion that human reasoning and behavior is connected to and influenced by our bodies and their physical/social experience and interaction with the world [40]. Applying this perspective in a meta-review comparing and taxonomizing embodiment strategies [29], I identified five different forms of physical embodiment: 1) ***Direct Embodied*** focuses on gestural congruency and how the body can physically represent learning concepts [20]; 2) ***Enacted*** focuses on acting out/enacting knowledge through physical action (i.e., knowledge-as-action) [17]; 3) ***Manipulated*** focuses on utilization of embodied metaphors and interactions with physical objects [3], and the objects' physical embodiment of learning concepts [19, 37]; 4) ***Surrogate*** focuses on learners manipulating a physical agent or "surrogate" representative of themselves to enact learning concepts [7]; and 5) ***Augmented*** focuses on combined use of a representational system and augmented feedback system to embed the learner within an augmented reality system [7].

Computational Thinking

CT is a complex construct with a wide variety of definitions. However, [4, 5] have identified a core set of CT skills commonly utilized in the literature as: 1) *Conditional Logic* - the use of an "if-then-else" construct; 2) *Algorithm Building* - a data "recipe" or set of instructions; 3) *Simulation* - modeling or testing of algorithms or logic; 4) *Debugging* - the act of determining problems in order to fix rules that are malfunctioning; and 5) *Abstraction* - use of procedures to encapsulate a set of often repeated commands.

Tangibles and Computational Concepts

There has been some work in the tangible and embodied interaction community on the creation of tangibles to teach computing concepts such as roBlocks [43], Note Code [25], Thingy Oriented Programming [13], TanProRobot 2.0 [47], and Electronic Blocks [49]. However, concepts covered by these tools are focused on physical computing, electronics, and music rather than explicitly addressing programming or games.

Completed and Ongoing Work

Completed Work

The goal of this research is to explore if applying physically embodied designs results in improved learning outcomes for core CT skills, increased problem-solving performance and ability, and positive emotional responses that are desirable for learning and creativity (e.g., enjoyment, motivation, situational interest, etc.). I have already laid the theoretical basis for this examination through creation of a design framework [29] and categorization of existing designs [30] for embodied learning games and simulations. Additionally, I conducted a preliminary study comparing tangible programming blocks to mouse input, looking at impacts upon players' programming self-beliefs and enjoyment [31]. While both mouse and tangible blocks similarly improved self-beliefs, use of the tangible blocks proved to be significantly more enjoyable.

Ongoing Work

Currently, I am conducting a larger 2x2 study comparing individual and collaborative play with the tangible blocks and mouse versions of Bots & (Main)Frames. The study will examine problem-solving performance on puzzle-based tasks (i.e., completion speed and number of mistakes made), usage of computational thinking concepts, influences from collaboration, and changes in emotional responses (i.e., situational interest, programming self-beliefs, and enjoyment). My hypothesis is that while the blocks may prove slower for manipulation and problem-solving, players will make fewer mistakes, have more positive emotional responses, and demonstrate improved usage of algorithm building and simulation CT skills since the blocks will aid in externalizing cognition. Furthermore, based on the beneficial notion of pair programming [32], I also believe the positive effects will be further enhanced in the collaborative condition.

Research Trajectory and Future Work

My aim is to create different versions of a puzzle-based educational programming game called Bots & (Main)Frames that utilize common forms of physical embodiment—i.e., *manipulated embodiment* through tangible programming blocks and *enacted embodiment* through augmented reality. The versions will be evaluated, compared, and refined across two major studies with novice programmers. The first study is described in Ongoing Work. For the second study, I will compare the tangible programming blocks and mouse versions of Bots & (Main)Frames to an AR version where programming is touch-based on a tablet and players enact execution of their code by walking through physical space (see Figure 3). I plan to analyze learning outcomes for these studies between-subjects designs with video recording and qualitative analysis [42] to identify occurrences of CT, collaboration, and physical embodiment during play. This will be done in conjunction with assessments of programming self-beliefs [45], situational interest [35], and enjoyment to compare increases in positive emotional responses.

Through this dissertation work, I expect to make the following contributions: 1) empirical and artifact-based contributions towards understanding the design space of physically embodied educational games, in the form of a design framework [29, 30] and CT games with strategically varied interactional properties that have been evaluated in between-subjects comparison studies; and 2) new understanding concerning how physical embodiment can impact meaning-making and problem-solving during the learning process.

References

1. Amory, A. et al. 1999. The use of computer games as an educational tool: identification of appropriate game types and game elements. *British Journal of Educational Technology*. 30, 4 (1999), 311–321.
2. Antle, A.N. et al. 2008. Playing with The Sound Maker: Do Embodied Metaphors Help Children Learn? *Proceedings of the 7th international conference on Interaction design and children - IDC '08* (2008), 178.
3. Bakker, S. et al. 2012. Embodied metaphors in tangible interaction design. *Personal and Ubiquitous Computing* (2012).
4. Barr, V. and Stephenson, C. 2011. Bringing computational thinking to K-12: what is Involved and what is the role of the computer science education community? *ACM Inroads*.
5. Berland, M. and Lee, V.R. 2011. Collaborative Strategic Board Games as a Site for Distributed Computational Thinking. *International Journal of Game-Based Learning*. 1, 2 (2011), 65–81.
6. Birchfield, D. et al. 2008. Embodiment, Multimodality, and Composition: Convergent Themes across HCI and Education for Mixed-Reality Learning Environments. *Advances in Human-Computer Interaction*. 2008, (2008), 1–19.
7. Black, J.B. et al. 2012. Embodied cognition and learning environment design. *Theoretical foundations of learning environments*. 198–223.
8. Blockly: A visual programming editor: *https://developers.google.com/blockly/*. Accessed: 2016-10-09.
9. Burleson, W. 2005. Developing creativity, motivation, and self-actualization with learning systems. *International Journal of Human Computer Studies*. 63, 4–5 (2005), 436–451.
10. Dijkstra, E.W. and others 1989. On the cruelty of really teaching computing science. *Communications of the ACM*. 32, 12 (1989), 1398–1404.
11. Gnoli, A. et al. 2014. Back to the future: Embodied Classroom Simulations of Animal Foraging. *Proceedings of the 8th International Conference on Tangible, Embedded and Embodied Interaction - TEI '14* (2014), 275–282.
12. Green, G. and Kaufman, J.C. 2015. *Video Games and Creativity*. Academic Press.
13. Güldenpfennig, F. et al. 2016. Toward Thingy Oriented Programming: Recording Marcos With Tangibles. *Proceedings of the TEI'16: Tenth International Conference on Tangible, Embedded, and Embodied Interaction* (2016), 455–461.
14. Harteveld, C. et al. 2014. A Design-Focused Analysis of Games Teaching Computer Science. *Proceedings of Games+ Learning+ Society 10* (2014).
15. Hicks, A. et al. 2014. Building Games to Learn from Their Players: Generating Hints in a Serious Game. *Intelligent Tutoring Systems: 12th International Conference, ITS 2014, Honolulu, HI, USA, June 5-9, 2014. Proceedings*. S. Trausan-Matu et al., eds. Springer International Publishing. 312–317.
16. Hicks, A. 2012. Creation, evaluation, and presentation of user-generated content in community game-based tutors. *Proceedings of the International Conference on the Foundations of Digital Games - FDG '12* (2012).
17. Holton, D.L. 2010. Constructivism + embodied cognition = enactivism: theoretical and practical implications for conceptual change. *AERA 2010 Conference* (2010).
18. Huggard, M. 2004. Programming trauma: Can it be avoided. *Proceedings of the BCS Grand Challenges in Computing: Education*. (2004), 50–51.
19. Ishii, H. 2008. Tangible bits: beyond pixels. *Proceedings of the 2nd international conference on Tangible and Embedded Intreaction (TEI '08)* (2008).
20. Johnson-Glenberg, M.C. et al. 2014. Collaborative embodied learning in mixed reality motion-capture environments: Two science studies. *Journal of Educational Psychology*. 106, 1 (2014), 86–104.
21. Kao, D. and Harrell, D.F. 2015. Mazzy: A STEM Learning Game. *Foundations of Digital Games* (2015).

22. Kelliher, A. et al. 2009. SMALLab: A mixed-reality environment for embodied and mediated learning. *MM'09 - Proceedings of the 2009 ACM Multimedia Conference, with Co-located Workshops and Symposiums* (2009), 1029–1031.
23. Kim, J. and Lerch, F.J. 1997. Why is programming (sometimes) so difficult? Programming as scientific discovery in multiple problem spaces. *Information Systems Research*. 8, 1 (1997), 25–50.
24. Kinnunen, P. and Simon, B. 2010. Experiencing programming assignments in CS1: the emotional toll. *Proceedings of the Sixth international workshop on Computing education research* (2010), 77–86.
25. Kumar, V. et al. 2015. Note Code – A Tangible Music Programming Puzzle Tool. *Proceedings of the 10th International Conference on Tangible, Embedded, and Embodied Interaction - TEI '15* (2015), 625–629.
26. Lode, H. et al. 2013. Machineers: playfully introducing programming to children. *CHI '13 Human Factors in Computing Systems* (2013), 2639–2642.
27. Lubart, T.I. 2001. Models of the creative process: Past, present and future. *Creativity Research Journal*. 13, 3–4 (2001), 295–308.
28. Melcer, E. 2017. Moving to Learn: Exploring the Impact of Physical Embodiment in Educational Programming Games. *CHI'17 Extended Abstracts* (Denver, CO, USA, 2017).
29. Melcer, E. and Isbister, K. 2016. Bridging the Physical Divide: A Design Framework for Embodied Learning Games and Simulations. *CHI'16 Extended Abstracts* (2016), 2225–2233.
30. Melcer, E. and Isbister, K. 2016. Bridging the Physical Learning Divides: A Design Framework for Embodied Learning Games and Simulations. *Proceedings of the 1st International Joint Conference of DiGRA and FDG* (2016).
31. Melcer, E.F. et al. 2017. Tangibles vs . Mouse in Educational Programming Games: Influences on Enjoyment and Self-Beliefs. *CHI'17 Extended Abstracts* (Denver, CO, USA, 2017).
32. Nagappan, N. et al. 2003. Improving the CS1 experience with pair programming. *ACM SIGCSE Bulletin*. 35, 1 (2003), 359–362.
33. O'Malley, C. and Fraser, S. 2004. *Literature review in learning with tangible technologies*.
34. Pea, R.D. 1983. *Logo Programming and Problem Solving.[Technical Report No. 12.]*. ERIC.
35. Plass, J.L. et al. 2013. The impact of individual, competitive, and collaborative mathematics game play on learning, performance, and motivation. *Journal of Educational Psychology*. 105, 4 (2013), 1050–1066.
36. Pouw, W.T.J.L. et al. 2014. An Embedded and Embodied Cognition Review of Instructional Manipulatives. *Educational Psychology Review*. 26, 1 (2014), 51–72.
37. Price, S. 2008. A representation approach to conceptualizing tangible learning environments. *Proceedings of the 2nd international conference on Tangible and embedded interaction TEI 08* (2008).
38. Price, S. et al. 2010. Action and representation in tangible systems: implications for design of learning interactions. *Proceedings of the fourth international conference on Tangible, embedded, and embodied interaction - TEI '10* (2010), 145–152.
39. Price, S. et al. 2008. Towards a framework for investigating tangible environments for learning. *International Journal of Arts and Technology*. 1, 3/4 (2008), 351–368.
40. Price, S. and Jewitt, C. 2013. A multimodal approach to examining "embodiment" in tangible learning environments. *Proceedings of TEI '13* (2013), 43–50.
41. Rogerson, C. and Scott, E. 2010. The fear factor: How it affects students learning to program in a tertiary environment. *Journal of Information Technology Education*. 9, 1 (2010), 147–171.
42. Saldaña, J. 2015. *The coding manual for qualitative researchers*. Sage.
43. Schweikardt, E. and Gross, M. 2008. The robot is the program: interacting with roBlocks. *Proceedings of the*

second international conference on Tangible, embedded, and embodied interaction - TEI '08 (2008).

44. Scott, M.J. and Ghinea, G. 2013. Educating programmers: A reflection on barriers to deliberate practice. *Proceedings of the 2nd Annual HEA STEM Conference* (2013).
45. Scott, M.J. and Ghinea, G. 2014. Measuring enrichment: the assembly and validation of an instrument to assess student self-beliefs in CS1. *Proceedings of the tenth annual conference on International computing education research* (2014).
46. Shelley, T. et al. 2011. Evaluating the Embodiment Benefits of a paper-based TUI for Spatially Sensitive Simulations. *Extended Abstracts of the 2011 Conference on Human Factors in Computing Systems* (2011).
47. Wang, D. et al. 2016. A Tangible Embedded Programming System to Convey Event-Handling Concept. *Proceedings of the TEI'16: Tenth International Conference on Tangible, Embedded, and Embodied Interaction* (2016), 133–140.
48. Webb, A.M. et al. 2013. Promoting reflection and interpretation in education. *Proceedings of the 9th ACM Conference on Creativity & Cognition - C&C '13* (2013), 53–62.
49. Wyeth, P. 2008. How Young Children Learn to Program With Sensor, Action, and Logic Blocks. *Journal of the Learning Sciences*. 17, 4 (2008), 517–550.

Designers' Experience on the Cloud

Julija Naskova
The Hong Kong Polytechnic University
School of Design
Hung Hom, Kowloon
Hong Kong, SAR
naskova_productions@hotmail.com

C&C '17, June 27-30, 2017, Singapore, Singapore

ACM ISBN 978-1-4503-4403-6/17/06.
http://dx.doi.org/10.1145/3059454.3078705

Abstract
This research started with a case study of Adobe DW. Based on it, a questionnaire was devised and distributed to thousand designers featured on Bēhance. Following were semi-structured interviews with subjects from different fields of design.
Their experiences depend on the manner of use or 'strip of activity' of various Cloud based tools. Accordingly, the 'active agents' were segregated into three groups: designers, developers and artists. Goffman's frame analysis offered the solution to present each groups' experience as a distinctive frame. While evaluating designers' experiences on the Cloud, three distinctive frames were created: creative, technical and experimental.
By the end of the research, the results will be compared to contemporary experience theories such as flow experience and technology acceptance theory. The final goal of this research is to evaluate how existing experience theories apply to Cloud based non-hedonistic systems.

Author Keywords
UX; dramaturgy; Erving Goffman; Cloud; frame analysis; digital tools.

ACM Classification Keywords

C.5.3. Portable devices (e.g., laptops, personal digital assistants): H.5.2 User-centered design: H.5.3. Web-based interaction.

Introduction of the research area

The field of Experience Design evolved from human factors studies focusing primarily on how physical products affect human emotions. It grew as a cross disciplinary practice combining theatre, sociology, psychology, product design and service design [9]. When computers came about, they added a new dimension to experience design and academics tried to define it.

The introduction of Cloud based tools and services created yet another shift in user experience. This shift has greatly affected web and mobile designers and developers, graphic designers, architects, industrial designers, digital artist etc. Since they've been using different digital tools, once those tools transitioned to the Cloud their experiences changed as well.

While symbolic interactionism is used to analyze human computer interaction, it doesn't offer a solution to organizing data coming from various sources. In this research, Goffman's frame analysis is applied to organize the data in a complex structure.

At its base is the 'primary frame' representing designers' experience with computer based digital tools. Their move to the Cloud initiated by businesses creates 'fabrications'. The fabrications are then 'keyed' during their application in a 'strip of activity' by designers or 'active agents'. Their experiences form the creative, technical and experimental frame. In the final phase of this research, those experiences will be compared to existing experience theories.

Summary of completed and ongoing work

The research question for the thesis *Designers' Experience on the Cloud* is how designers' experience changed with the introduction of Cloud based tools and functions in their daily work. The research design employed grounded theory methods [10] for data collection and applied symbolic interactionist principles for its analysis [11].

The first method applied was a case study of Adobe Dreamweaver Creative Cloud – how does this tool changed in comparison to Adobe Dreamweaver Creative Suite 4 [8]. Based on this research, an eleven questions questionnaire was devised to obtain information relevant to designers' perception of the Cloud, changes in their workflow and experience with the use of Cloud based tools and functions.

Netnographic method [5] was employed through randomly distributing the questionnaire to thousand designers featured on Bēhance, receiving back around fifty responses. Out of those ten designers were interviewed through Skype, FacebookIM or in-person.

Group observation and informal interviews were conducted through participation in design related networking events in Hong Kong, some of which were advertised on meetup.com. These events also presented an opportunity to recruit designers for in-person semi-structured interviews, completing ten more interviews.

In July and August of 2016, another five interviews were conducted in Macedonia with designers, developers and professors in the field of design and human computer interaction. Three European artists/designers working on a cross cultural project at a local design center were also interviewed.

Participation in a one week hacking workshop called PIF_camp in Trente, Slovenia offered an opportunity to observe how digital artists apply Cloud technology in their artwork.

Consequently, a journal paper proposal was presented at SSSI Topola under the name *Symbolic Interactionism and Human-Centered Design; Blumer's principles in user experience studies* [6]. The following month at SSSI Seattle a paper proposal on *Symbolic Interactionism and Acting Techniques; From Blumer to Stanislavski* was presented [7]. During both conferences, the researcher was exposed to various research methods applied in sociology, most notably Goffman's frame theory and discourse analysis [3] [4].

That same summer, the researcher attended a one day UX camp in Los Angeles where she reconnected with old contacts and accomplished few more interviews, in addition to meeting few new UX experts. While in Seattle she attended meetups with UXPA and WordPress designers.

The WordPress group proved to be very interesting, comprised mostly of web designers and developers with private practices. The researcher interviewed people with decades of experience in the field. Some were traditional graphic designers who switched to computer design in the late 80's. As computers became commercially available and the WWW was expanding, they gradually ventured into web design.

In December of 2016, the researcher presented at SKIMA conference in Chengdu, Sichuan Province, China the paper *Dreamweaver on the Cloud; Web designers' perspectives* [8]. She used this opportunity to interview local designers and developers for comparative cultural study purposes.

The learning process was gradual during this research. It started with Grounded theory and triangulating data collection methods in mind. After reading work that applies this theory in the field of design, the data collection process was re-classified as iterative.

When interviewing mostly young visual designers did not yield much information, a decision was made to add new knowledge by widening the research group. There is a disparity in the way designers define and use the Cloud depending on their educational background, years in the field and type of practice.

Therefore, the interviewees were segmented into three groups. First group are the visual designers that come from art and design schools. The second group are the more technically savvy designers and developers. They either come from the field of computer technology or have attained significant technical knowledge through practice. The third group are the designer/artist type, those who are experimenting with open source technology while using the Cloud as their stage.

Upon reflecting on the data, the researcher found different answers to the research questions. Therefore, she needed to analyze how each group of participants uses and defines Cloud based technology. In this case, Goffman's frame analysis [4] came in handy, because it is built around the notion that people frame their experience in different ways. Goffman's frame analysis provided the structure to organize the data and to create a coherent story. As far as this researcher is informed, this theory hasn't been applied to design research before.

Preliminary results

Most young designer are not aware of their use of Cloud based tools and services, especially if living in countries with effective WiFi coverage. When made aware of Cloud based functions, such as file sharing and transfer, they claim those are useful, but they

don't feel dependent on them. Some said they can always use a memory stick in case of an emergency.
Security concerns differ depending on the designers' origin, but those dissipate once their favorite tool is mentioned. Most designers feel that their artwork is not that important to protect, unless it is a project done for a client. They believe that online presence is more important than worrying about the possibility of somebody copying or misappropriating their work.

In the case of mobile prototyping tools, interaction designers think that there are so many options on the market, each doing one thing better than the other. The issue is that most of them are not for free, and the costs add up quickly. Another obstacle is that for some browser based tools, such as InVision, all collaboration and file exchange need to be done within the application.

Visual designers expressed a wish to see all Cloud based applications and functions put into 'one place'. Adobe attempts to meet this demand by creating prototyping tools that integrate well with their staple design tools such as Illustrator and Photoshop. But some designers are concerned with how much power certain companies have over their tools.

Certain browser based tools such as WordPress have a large following. At its early stages, it helped many graphic designers transition into web design. Even some web developers like the tool because it offers an easy interface for their clients to edit content.

Automattic, the company that maintains this web design tool, is constantly in touch with its user base and each tool update is a design collaboration.

But for this to happen, the users need to be well informed and interested in influencing their tool development. This is typical of the developers group whose tools exist primarily to promote collaboration. They work within developers' suites, offered for free from companies such as Microsoft in exchange for their work made public. Github, the social coding browser based tool, is the place to be for any developer interested in honing their skills.

The artists group on the other hand, uses open source tools to move between the physical and digital world. They collect data on wind speeds and plug it into a browser based tool that transforms it into sound. The elaborate shapes that growing fungus creates are exhibited in a petri dish, demonstrating nature's way of creating intricate designs. In many cases, this type of research is not aimed at producing specific results but as a philosophical treatise. Most interviewed artists have day jobs as designers. This is their way of maintaining creativity through artistic exploration.

Trajectory of research toward completion

Currently, specific theories of experience are being researched, such as Technology Acceptance Model [2] and flow experience [1]. In the next few months, additional literature review will be done to inform the findings. Once the research develops few theories those will be tested by conducting industry expert interviews.

In June, a workshop on technology acceptance theories as applied to non-hedonistic systems is planned. The purpose is to find out how the newly found theories fit the existing concepts. The participants will come from the field of design, so this will be an opportunity for member validation.

By the end of August, the thesis should be finalized and submitted to the research office. The thesis will present the current situation and will offer solutions to improve designers experience with Cloud based tools. Hopefully, it will contribute new knowledge to the field of experience design.

References

1. Mihaly, Csikszentmihalyi. 2014. Applications of Flow in Human Development and Education: The Collected Works of Mihaly Csikszentmihalyi. Springer Netherlands.
2. Fred D. Davis, Richard P. Bagozzi & Paul R. Warshaw. 1989. "User acceptance of information technology: a comparison of two theoretical models." *Management Science* 35(8), 982–1003. http://dx.doi.org/10.1287/mnsc.35.8.982
3. Erving Goffman. 1959. The Presentation of Self in Everyday Life. New York: Anchor Books.
4. Erving Goffman. 1986. Frame Analysis: An Essay on the Organization of Experience. Boston: Northeastern University Press.
5. Robert V. Kozinets. 2010. Netnography: Doing Ethnographic Research Online. Los Angeles: SAGE Publications.
6. Julija Naskova. 2016a. "Symbolic Interactionism and Human-Centered Design; Blumer's principles in user experience studies." ResearchGate.net. Retrieved February 14, 2017 from https://www.researchgate.net/publication/313651035_Symbolic_Interactionism_and_Human-Centered_Design_Blumer%27s_principles_in_user_experience_studies doi:10.13140/RG.2.2.32952.55041
7. Julija, Naskova. 2016b. "Symbolic Interactionism and Acting Techniques; From Blumer to Stanislavsky." *ResearchGate.net.* Retrieved February 14, 2017 from https://www.researchgate.net/publication/313650973_Symbolic_Interactionism_and_Acting_Techniques_From_Blumer_to_Stanislavsky. doi:10.13140/RG.2.2.36307.99360
8. Julija, Naskova. 2016c. "Dreamweaver on the Cloud; Web designers' perspectives." *ResearchGate.net.* Retrieved February 14, 2017 from https://www.researchgate.net/publication/313651232_Dreamweaver_on_the_Cloud_Web_designers%27_perspectives
9. Nathan, Shedroff. (2001). Experience Design. Upper Sadle River, NJ, USA: Pearson Education.
10. Stephen L. Schensul, Jean J. Schensul, and Margaret D. LeCompte, *Initiating Ethnographic Research: A Mixed Methods Approach*: AltaMira Press, 2013.
11. Society for the Study of Symbolic Interaction. 2016. "Welcome to SSSI." Retrieved June 27, 2016 from https://sites.google.com/site/sssinteraction/

Difficulty in Video Games: Understanding the Effects of Dynamic Difficulty Adjustment in Video Games on Player Experience

Dennis Ang
Department of
Communications and New Media
National University of Singapore
Blk AS6, #03-41
11 Computing Drive
dennis@u.nus.edu

C&C '17, June 27-30, 2017, Singapore, Singapore

ACM ISBN 978-1-4503-4403-6/17/06.
http://dx.doi.org/10.1145/3059454.3078706

Abstract
This thesis investigates the impact of difficulty in the context of Dynamic Difficulty Adjustment (DDA) in video games on the player experience (PX). A series of quantitative and qualitative studies were employed to compare the effects of DDA systems on the PX and to gain an understanding of the lived PX of players engaging with such systems. This research contributes to game design knowledge and the current limited understanding of the impact of DDA systems on the PX. The findings are of relevance to practitioners and researchers in the domain of entertainment games as well as other related domains such as games for education and health care.

Author Keywords
Dynamic difficulty adjustment; video games; challenge; player experience; player skill; computational systems;

ACM Classification Keywords
H.5.m. Information interfaces and presentation (e.g., HCI): Miscellaneous;

Study #1 (Experiment)

Aim: Test if the mere presence of DDA mechanics result in an improved player experience; if so, does it matter what DDA mechanic is employed?

Hypothesis 1 (Simplified): PXs of video games with DDA mechanics are significantly better than PXs of video games with no DDA mechanics

Hypothesis 2 (Simplified): PXs of video games with Player-Oriented DDA mechanics are significantly better than PXs of video games with System-Oriented (Ramping) DDA mechanics with the exception of Concentration on Task at Hand.

Introduction

Not all games provide motivation for the player to want to continue playing. The designers for games that allow for such motivation usually go through an iterative process called playtesting in order to tune the overall game experience [11,30]. This playtesting process allows designers to fine-tune different aspects of the game, including the challenge or difficulty, which should result in a better game experience for players. However, playtesting is tedious, painstaking and time consuming.

Some game designers employ additional mechanisms that delegates the task of fine tune game challenge to the game system. The dynamic difficulty adjustment (DDA) mechanic allows for the game difficulty to be fine-tuned to the player's skills even after games have left the hands of the developer. The process of fine-tuning can be done with lesser time and at a greater accuracy if the implementation of such a mechanism is done appropriately [16]. This thesis examines the impact of different DDA implementations in video games on the player experience (PX) as a means to explore the role of DDA in the enhancement of PX.

Related Work

The related literature mainly focuses on the exploration of DDA systems through a variety of implementations, the assessment and measurement of video game experiences, and theories of player experience.

Difficulty Adjustment in Video Games

According to Missura and Gärtner [26], an "ideal game should be able to adjust its difficulty dynamically governed by the player's performance". In the pursuit of this ideal game and the resulting optimal game experience, several scholars have investigated the use of artificial intelligence (AI) in game systems [13,15,31,33] that enable the automatic adjustment of game challenge to the skill of a player.

Of significance to this investigation, Hunicke [16] observes that even rudimentary algorithms can lead to improved player performance without adversely impacting the player's sense of accomplishment and agency. This suggests that mere presence of a DDA mechanism, without any sophisticated AI system, can in general lead to a superior PX of games.

Video Game Experience

It is difficult to measure video game experiences. The difficulty of measuring these experiences stems from the multifaceted nature of PX. Many have attempted to chip away at this problem in their work by developing definitions, scales and frameworks that allow for a more objective measurement of these PXs.

Scholars have conceptualized portions of the player experience such as that of fun [10,22,24], engagement [2,3,27], immersion [1,4,12,21], presence [23,25,28], involvement and incorporation [6], enjoyment [14,17] and Flow [7,8,19,32]. However, there is no clear acceptance or adoption of any particular concept or definition by the community, and the community remains fragmented over this particular conundrum of what constitutes a PX of games.

Others have tried to make sense of the multitude of concepts by theorizing how the concepts are part of a holistic overarching concept such as Flow or immersion. Cairns, Cox and Nordin [5] argue conceptually that Flow is a "all-or-nothing" experience while immersion is

Study #2 (Interview)

Aim: Understand the PX of games with DDA mechanics through players' lived experiences.

Research Question 1: What are the lived game experience of players in games that implement DDA mechanics?

Research Question 2: What does it mean for players to have, or not have agency over the challenge of the game?

Research Question 3: Does Flow theory sufficiently explain the lived experiences of these players, or are there aspects of PX that are specific to DDA mechanics not explained by Flow theory?

"more of a graded experience", suggesting that perhaps Flow is an extreme state while immersion is easier to get into. Procci and Bowers [29] empirically tested the operational constructs pertaining to immersion and Flow focusing on popular measuring apparatuses - Immersive Tendencies Questionnaire (ITQ) [35], Dispositional Flow State Scale (DFS-2) and Flow State Scale (FSS-2) [18,20]. They found that despite having items that seem to be asking about related concepts such as that of "Do you ever become so involved in doing something that you lose all track of time?" and "I lose my normal awareness of time" from the ITQ and DFS-2 respectively, there was not overlap in variance between ITQ and DFS-2.

It is still unclear whether immersion and Flow are exclusive concepts or related concepts of different intensities. It seems that the ITQ item describes a higher intensity of time dilation compared that of the DFS-2 item but one would intuitively expect Flow as an "all-or-nothing" experience, to be the one with a more intense experience.

Flow in Video Games

Csikszentmihalyi, in his theory of intrinsic motivation of Flow [8,9], posits that one enters Flow when the experience of doing the task itself is autotelic - so rewarding that a person is willing to put themselves through the experience of doing the task for the sake of going through that optimal experience again as if the task was an excuse to do so.

Research Problem

The focus on the PX for this investigation is guided by the motivation to inform the design of video games that allow for optimal experiences which motivate players to want to continue addressing challenges and difficult tasks. While scholars frequently discuss Flow theory and note its compatibility and usefulness in understanding video game experiences, few have empirically tested the theory in the context of games. As such, this investigation begins with a comparison of the impact of the presence or non-presence of DDA mechanics on the PX conceptualized as Flow.

Method

Study #1 (Completed)

The aim of the first study is to test if the mere presence of DDA mechanics improve the PX through a controlled experiment in which participants play Tetris with different or no DDA mechanics. Furthermore, it aims to extend the limited understanding of the effect of DDA mechanics should such improvements be significant through the comparison of two implementations of DDA, namely Ramping (rDDA; fall rate of Tetris pieces increase automatically based on player performance) and Player-Oriented DDA (pDDA; player chooses when to increase/decrease difficulty throughout the game).

The results indicate that the presence of both DDA mechanics employed resulted in significantly better PX in the dimensions of *Challenge-skill balance*, *Action-awareness merging*, *Concentration on Task at Hand* and *Transformation of Time*, demonstrating that DDA helps players enter the state of Flow. Also, pDDA was shown to support better *Sense of Control* but resulted in significantly poorer of *Loss of self-consciousness* and *Transformation of time* compared to rDDA.

Study #2 (Ongoing)

The aim of Study #2 is to supplement the first phase of the investigation with rich descriptions that allow for

Study #3 (Experiment)

Aim: Study the effects of where the player makes a choice (direct control or through game mechanics) and when the choice can be made (once, a few times or at any time during the game) on PX in the context of Player-Oriented DDA.

Hypothesis 1 (Simplified): PXs of video games with difficulty choices presented through Game Mechanics are significantly better than PXs of video games with difficulty choices presented through Direct Control.

Hypothesis 2 (Simplified): PXs of video games with difficulty choices presented a few times during a game are significantly better than PXs of video games with difficulty choices presented once or at any time during the game.

better understanding of what DDA mechanics mean to players and to rigorously test if Flow theory sufficiently explains the experiences from the player's perspective. This study employs semi-structured interviews and participant observation where interviewees are invited to play the same Tetris games used in the first study and talk about both their experience with the Tetris games as well as their life experiences with other games as means to understand the PX of games with DDA mechanics through their lived experiences.

Study #3 (Ongoing)
Study #3 aims to expand the understanding of pDDA as a viable alternative to be considered against System-Oriented DDA such as the traditional rDDA and Adaptive DDA in the context of PX. A 2x3 within subjects factorial design with modified versions of the game *Snake* is employed to investigate different control modalities of pDDA in video games, namely *where* the difficulty choice is made (via direct controls or through the game mechanics) and *when* the choice is made (once, sometimes or at any time during the game). The difficulty of the game (speed of the snake) can be altered using keyboard buttons or by eating special food (with +/- symbols) and this choice can be made once, sometimes or at any time during the game in the respective conditions.

Discussion
Preliminary results from Study #2 indicate several interesting directions for further research. The results also reflect the results of Study #1, where players reported boredom. However, they highlighted potential scenarios where no DDA would be useful. Other preliminary findings indicate certain problems in each DDA mechanics covered so far. Players described adaptive DDA as being "too smooth" even when the challenge presented is a notch higher than their skill. Skilled players indicated frustration and boredom in having to go up the ramp towards the zone of appropriate challenge-skill balance for Ramping DDA. Some players recounted instances of Player-oriented DDA in relation to the notion of cheating where they felt guilt after choosing to tone down the difficulty in several different games.

Participants seem to personify the game as a living being that presents to them challenges. They expect respect from the game – for example, to make a game easier means to disrespect or look down on the player. This indicates that player awareness of the presence DDA mechanics may impact the resulting PX. These observations indicate the need for deeper and wider investigation of the impact of difficulty in the context of DDA in video games on the PX.

Planned Trajectory
The broader planned trajectory for this investigation would be to collate a body of design knowledge based on the collective contributions of each study conducted, design a hybrid DDA mechanic that incorporates the advantages of some DDA mechanics studied, and evaluate the hybrid DDA mechanic through a study.

Contributions
The findings will contribute domain knowledge that aid game and system designers in their quest to design artefacts that help motivate people to take on challenging tasks or difficult problems, particularly those whom address design problems that tackle a user base with a wide spectrum or high volatility of skill levels.

References

1. Ernest Adams. 2009. *Fundamentals of Game Design*. New Riders Publishing, Thousand Oaks, CA, USA.

2. David Altimira, Florian 'Floyd Mueller, Jenny Clarke, Gun Lee, Mark Billinghurst, and Christoph Bartneck. 2017. Enhancing Player Engagement Through Game Balancing in Digitally Augmented Physical Games. *International Journal of Human-Computer Studies*.

3. Jeanne H Brockmyer, Christine M Fox, Kathleen A Curtiss, Evan McBroom, Kimberly M Burkhart, and Jacquelyn N Pidruzny. 2009. The development of the Game Engagement Questionnaire: A measure of engagement in video game-playing. *Journal of Experimental Social Psychology* 45, 4: 624–634.

4. Emily Brown and Paul Cairns. 2004. A Grounded Investigation of Game Immersion. *CHI '04 Extended Abstracts on Human Factors in Computing Systems*, ACM, 1297–1300.

5. Paul Cairns, Anna Cox, and A Imran Nordin. 2014. Immersion in digital games: review of gaming experience research. *Handbook of digital games*: 337–361.

6. Gordon Calleja. 2010. Digital games and escapism. *Games and Culture* 5, 4: 335–353.

7. Jenova Chen. 2007. Flow in Games (and Everything else). *Commun. ACM* 50, 4: 31–34.

8. Mihaly Csikszentmihalyi and Isabella Selega Csikszentmihalyi. 1992. *Optimal experience: Psychological studies of flow in consciousness*. Cambridge university press.

9. Mihaly Csikszentmihalyi. 2014. Toward a psychology of optimal experience. In *Flow and the foundations of positive psychology*. Springer, 209–226.

10. Dénes Eglesz, Istvan Fekete, Orhidea Edith Kiss, and Lajos Izso. 2005. Computer games are fun? On professional games and players' motivations. *Educational Media International* 42, 2: 117–124.

11. Tracy Fullerton, Chris Swain, and Steven Hoffman. 2004. *Game design workshop: Designing, prototyping, & playtesting games*. CRC Press.

12. Yiannis Georgiou and Eleni A Kyza. 2017. The development and validation of the ARI questionnaire: An instrument for measuring immersion in location-based augmented reality settings. *International Journal of Human-Computer Studies* 98: 24–37.

13. Arend Hintze, Randal S Olson, and Joel Lehman. 2016. Orthogonally Evolved AI to Improve Difficulty Adjustment in Video Games. *European Conference on the Applications of Evolutionary Computation*, Springer, 525–540.

14. Shirley S Ho, May O Lwin, Jeremy RH Sng, and Andrew ZH Yee. 2017. Escaping through exergames: Presence, enjoyment, and mood experience in predicting children's attitude toward exergames. *Computers in Human Behavior* 72: 381–389.

15. Robin Hunicke and Vernell Chapman. 2004. AI for dynamic difficulty adjustment in games. *International conference on advances in computer*, Northwestern University, 91–96.

16. Robin Hunicke. 2005. The Case for Dynamic Difficulty Adjustment in Games. *Proceedings of the*

2005 ACM SIGCHI International Conference on Advances in Computer Entertainment Technology, ACM, 429–433.

17. Wijnand IJsselsteijn, Wouter Van Den Hoogen, Christoph Klimmt, et al. 2008. Measuring the experience of digital game enjoyment. *Proceedings of Measuring Behavior*, Noldus Information Tecnology Wageningen, Netherlands, 88–89.

18. Susan A Jackson and Robert Charles Eklund. 2004. *The flow scales manual*. Fitness Information Technology.

19. Susan A Jackson and Herbert W Marsh. 1996. Development and validation of a scale to measure optimal experience: The Flow State Scale. *Journal of Sport and Exercise Psychology* 18: 17–35.

20. Susan A Jackson, Andrew J Martin, and Robert C Eklund. 2008. Long and short measures of flow: The construct validity of the FSS-2, DFS-2, and new brief counterparts. *Journal of Sport and Exercise Psychology* 30, 5: 561–587.

21. Charlene Jennett, Anna L Cox, Paul Cairns, et al. 2008. Measuring and defining the experience of immersion in games. *International journal of human-computer studies* 66, 9: 641–661.

22. R Koster. 2005. *Theory of Fun for Game Designers*. Paraglyph Press, Scottsdale, Arizona.

23. Matthew Lombard and Theresa Ditton. 1997. At the heart of it all: The concept of presence. *Journal of Computer-Mediated Communication* 3, 2.

24. Thomas W Malone. 1981. What makes things fun to learn? A study of intrinsically motivating computer games. *Pipeline* 6, 2: 50.

25. Alison McMahan. 2003. Immersion, engagement and presence. *The video game theory reader* 67: 86.

26. Olana Missura and Thomas Gärtner. 2009. Player modeling for intelligent difficulty adjustment. *International Conference on Discovery Science*, Springer, 197–211.

27. Heather L O'Brien and Elaine G Toms. 2008. What is user engagement? A conceptual framework for defining user engagement with technology. *Journal of the American Society for Information Science and Technology* 59, 6: 938–955.

28. Jorge Peña and Meng Chen. 2017. Playing with power: Power poses affect enjoyment, presence, controller responsiveness, and arousal when playing natural motion-controlled video games. *Computers in Human Behavior* 71: 428–435.

29. Katelyn Procci and Clint Bowers. 2011. An Examination of Flow and Immersion in Games. *Proceedings of the Human Factors and Ergonomics Society Annual Meeting* 55, 1: 2183–2187.

30. Andrew Rollings and Ernest Adams. 2003. *Andrew Rollings and Ernest Adams on game design*. New Riders.

31. Pieter Spronck, Marc Ponsen, Ida Sprinkhuizen-Kuyper, and Eric Postma. 2006. Adaptive game AI with dynamic scripting. *Machine Learning* 63, 3: 217–248.

32. Penelope Sweetser and Peta Wyeth. 2005. GameFlow: A Model for Evaluating Player Enjoyment in Games. *Comput. Entertain.* 3, 3: 3–3.

33. Chin Hiong Tan, Kay Chen Tan, and Arthur Tay. 2011. Dynamic game difficulty scaling using adaptive behavior-based AI. *IEEE Transactions on Computational Intelligence and AI in Games* 3, 4: 289–301.

34. Robert W White. 1959. Motivation reconsidered: The concept of competence. *Psychological review* 66, 5: 297.

35. Bob G Witmer and Michael J Singer. 1998. Measuring presence in virtual environments: A presence questionnaire. *Presence: Teleoperators and virtual environments* 7, 3: 225–240.

Creative Coding for the Raspberry Pi using the HappyBrackets Platform

Sam Ferguson
Creativity and Cognition Studios
University of Technology Sydney
NSW, Australia
samuel.ferguson@uts.edu.au

Oliver Bown
UNSW Art & Design
Paddington Campus, Oxford St, Paddington
NSW, Australia
o.bown@unsw.edu.au

C&C'17, June 27–30, 2017, Singapore.

ACM ISBN978-1-4503-4403-6/17/06 ...$15.00.
http://dx.doi.org/10.1145/3059454.3059482

Abstract
This workshop will introduce creative coding audio for the Raspberry Pi, using the *beads* platform for audio programming, and the *HappyBrackets* platform for inter-device communication and sensor data acquisition. We will demonstrate methods to allow each self-contained battery-powered device to acquire sensor data about its surroundings and the way it is being interacted with, as well as methods for designing systems where groups of these devices wirelessly communicate their state, allowing new interaction possibilities and approaches.

Author Keywords
interaction, physical computing

ACM Classification Keywords
H.5.5 [Information Interfaces and Presentation]: Sound and Music Computing; H.5.2 [Information Interfaces and Presentation]: User Interfaces—Haptic I/O

Introduction and Call for Participation
This workshop will introduce creative coding audio for the Raspberry Pi, using the *beads* platform for audio programming, and the *HappyBrackets* platform for inter-device communication and sensor data acquisition. We will demonstrate methods to allow each self-contained battery-powered device to acquire sensor data about its

surroundings and the way it is being interacted with, as well as methods for designing systems where groups of these devices wirelessly communicate their state, allowing new interaction possibilities and approaches.

The Raspberry Pi is an ultra-cheap, ultra-small Linux microcomputer. Introduced in 2012, it is a flagship device lighting the path towards generally available ubiquitous computing technology. The creative potential of cheap, tiny network-connected general purpose linux computers that are the size of credit cards is immense. Similarly, Java is one of the world's most popular general purpose programming language, and underlies the creative coding environment *Processing*, itself one of the most popular environments for creative coding. Java opens up a world of infinite possibilities, and the coding examples in this course have been designed to be incredibly easy to learn, allowing you to get stuck into your creative goals from the get-go.

In this course you will learn the essentials of programming real-time audio software and apply these skills to the exciting world of the Internet of Things. You will use the Raspberry Pi as a rapid prototyping platform, exploring the creative potential of real-time sensor and network interaction, combined with real-time sound generation, creating systems that respond to user input, communicate with other devices and play sound. Make your own musical instruments, develop devices for sonic artworks, and create new sound design concepts for sonifying everyday objects. Through this course you will develop a basic understanding of audio programming and the core concepts behind programming for the Internet of Things. You will be able to conceptualize and design your own innovative interactive devices.

Topics

This course will include the following topics:

Morning Session:

- Introduction to Beads and IntelliJ, Continuous and Event-Based Control in Beads
- Sampling and Synthesis, Introduction to Audio on the Pi
- Live Coding the Pi, Network Communication with the Pi
- Responding to Sensor Data

Afternoon Session:

- Collaborative Exercises.
- Composition Tasks

Logistics

This workshop will be a **full-day** session framed as a pedagogical workshop which will introduce the platform in an interactive hands-on manner.

To undertake this workshop effectively, we would need the following resources to be supplied:

- a room with sufficient desks for participants
- a projector
- power sources for each participant (extension cables and power boards).

All other equipment we will provide. Participants in this workshop will require a raspberry pi, sensor system, battery system and access to a wifi or wired network which we will provide. Some participants may wish to purchase these devices in advance of the workshop, so that they learn on equipment they can take with them, and for these participants we will provide a description of the equipment we use and suggestions for how to buy them and set them up in advance of the workshop. For participants who do not bring their own equipment we will provide a device for the day. If there are a large number of participants sharing may be necessary.

Participants will benefit from some experience in programming Java. No electronics knowledge will be necessary but familiarity with linux and/or raspberry pis would be advantageous also. This course will not introduce Java from first principles, although the coding examples will start off being very simple and easy to pick up. Specific programming examples and techniques will be explained as a central part of the workshop.

Partner Online Course

This workshop will benefit from an online MOOC course we have recorded and which we will make available to participants in advance of the course. Kadenze provide best of breed online resources for teaching creative topics. We will expect participants to have enough time to review the course materials and videos in advance of the workshop, but not to have completed the assignments. The workshop itself will focus on reviewing the material, running through and clarifying any unclear content, and then on completing collaborative composition asssignments in the second half of the workshop.

Previous Workshop Iteration

This workshop was run at the 2016 edition of the International **New Interfaces for Musical Expression** confernece. It was highly subscribed, and also won the **Best Workshop** award for this conference. Given its focus on technical skills of a leading-edge nature, we have found demand is generally quite high.

Biographies

Sam Ferguson (Workshop Presenter) is a musician and a researcher in audio technology. He is currently a lecturer at the University of Technology, Sydney associated with the Creativity and Cognition Studios in the Faculty of Engineering and IT, but in the past he has also worked at the University of Sydney (where he gained his PhD) and at the University of NSW. He has worked in a number of fields, from designing audio alerts for air traffic controllers, to developing methods for understanding data through listening to sound, to investigations of the relationship between emotion and music, to the quantitative analysis of singing and contemporary dance. He is also an enthusiastic educator, designing and teaching audio, acoustics, human computer interaction and programming courses at both postgraduate and undergraduate levels.

Ollie Bown is a researcher and maker working with creative technologies. He comes from a highly diverse academic background spanning social anthropology, evolutionary and adaptive systems, music informatics and interaction design, with a parallel career in electronic music and digital art spanning over 15 years. He is interested in how artists, designers and musicians can use advanced computing technologies to produce complex creative works. His current active research areas include media multiplicites, musical metacreation, the theories and methodologies of computational creativity, new interfaces for musical expression, and multi-agent models of social creativity.

How can Computers Support, Enrich, and Transform Collaborative Creativity?

Peter Dalsgaard
Digital Creativity Lab
Center for Advanced Visualisation and Interaction
Aarhus University
Helsingforsgade 14, 8200 Aarhus
dalsgaard@cavi.au.dk

Nanna Inie
Center for Advanced Visualisation and Interaction
Aarhus University
Helsingforsgade 14, 8200 Aarhus
inie@cavi.au.dk

Nicolai Brodersen Hansen
Center for Advanced Visualisation and Interaction
Aarhus University
Helsingforsgade 14, 8200 Aarhus
nbhansen@cavi.au.dk

C&C '17, June 27-30, 2017, Singapore, Singapore
ACM 978-1-4503-4403-6/17/06.
http://dx.doi.org/10.1145/3059454.3059483

Abstract
The aim of the workshop is to examine and discuss how computers can support, enrich, and transform collaborative creative processes. By exploring and combining methodological, theoretical, and design-oriented perspectives, we wish to examine the implications, potentials, and limitations of different approaches to providing digital support for collaborative creativity. Participation in the workshop requires participants to actively document and identify salient themes in one or more examples of computer-supported collaborative creativity, and the resulting material will serve as the empirical grounding for workshop discussions.

Author Keywords
Creativity Studies; Computer-Supported Creativity; Collaborative Creativity; Ideation; Design.

ACM Classification Keywords
H.5.m. Information interfaces and presentation (e.g., HCI): Miscellaneous.

Introduction
How do digital tools influence and transform collaborative creativity?

Many work practices in the creative industries are

Workshop format

We propose a highly participatory workshop with short and concise presentations and several group work sessions.

We will begin with short cycles of case/methods presentation (10-15 minutes each), focusing on insights and findings from the obligatory documentation and study of salient themes in one or more examples of computer-supported collaborative creativity. This is followed by joint discussions in which we identify and articulate key themes, challenges, and potentials. After this, a rapid explorative design exercise, in which groups of participants develop a concept for a novel tool or system based on the discussions. We will end with a dialogue on how to establish a community around the topic of collaborative creativity support, and on the potentials of editing a special issue on the topic.

collaborative, as professionals with different competences and roles work towards a shared goal. Digital tools play an increasingly central role in this domain, in which they have transformed many practices of collaborative creative work in disciplines such as design, fashion, and architecture. As digital tools evolve, so do creative practices, and the two become increasingly intertwined. For instance, many designers now use digital sketching, 3D modelling software, hardware prototyping, and 3D printing as an integral part of their creative work processes. In spite this, we have limited knowledge of how and why collaborative creativity, for better or worse, is influenced and transformed by digital tools.

We tend to focus on the new opportunities afforded by digital tools, but they also bring new challenges, especially because they often offer poor support for collaborative creative work. Firstly, many of these tools have been developed with insufficient understanding of the creative processes in which they are employed; secondly, they have predominantly been designed to support individual use, rather than collaboration. For instance, very few digital tools directly support collaborative creative sessions such as joint concept development, and most of the software that designers use for sketching, modelling, and prototyping only allows one person using one computer to work on a file at a time; sharing it with others implies a string of tasks that break the creative flow. Although the creative industries are a major driver of growth [7], research into the role and nature of digital tools in collaborative creativity in professional practices is scarce and scattered. In short, *we know little about how, when, and why digital tools hinder and/or benefit collaborative creativity*, and as a result, digital tools employed in practice are seldom well-suited to support collaborative creativity. While this is clearly problematic, it also represents a highly relevant research challenge with potential for major impact.

In this workshop, we will therefore explore and combine methodological, theoretical, and design-oriented perspectives in order to examine the implications, potentials, and limitations of different approaches to providing digital support for collaborative creativity.

Related Work

Guilford's address to the American Psychological Association [10] is widely regarded as the beginning of modern creativity studies. It resulted in a series of studies that predominantly examined creativity as an individual, cognitive capability - an "intramental" perspective, in the terminology of Gedenryd [9]. The primary research approach was to study these capabilities through problem-solving tests in controlled lab experiments. In the 1980s and 1990s, a new wave of research emerged, looking beyond the individual in isolation and towards cultural and social aspects of creativity [1;3]. Along these lines of research, studies into collaborative ideation shows the potential of joint ideation and demonstrates that creative processes shift between individual and collaborative phases [4;11]. Related studies have demonstrated that team-based creativity holds great, yet underexplored, potential [23], and that individual and social creativity can be beneficially combined [8]. A prominent theoretical influence in this work has been the development of the *distributed cognition* perspective [14], which posits that cognition can be studied as a phenomenon distributed across people, environment, and tools, rather than as a solely individual and intramental property.

Much research in IT-supported creativity focuses on the properties of specific products and systems, rather than on how use of these tools unfolds in practice, but there are notable exceptions, including work from prominent figures in the *Creativity and Cognition* community [e.g. 6;15;24]. In terms of studying collaborative IT in practice, the field of Computer-Supported Cooperative Work (CSCW) specifically examines how IT can support joint work. This includes creative aspects of collaborative work, e.g. joint sketching [12] and design meetings [13]. While this field has yielded many insights into the interplay between IT and collaboration, the fact remains that in practice the vast majority of IT systems have been developed as single-user interfaces on individual devices. Even the most widely known collaborative tool, Google Docs, is in essence a single-user interface akin to Microsoft Word overlaid with functions for collaboration.

However, recent pioneering work on *Blended Interaction* [17] shows the potentials of supporting more dynamic flows between individual and collaborative interfaces. Similarly, *Shareable Dynamic Media* [19], demonstrates the feasibility of creating web-based tools, in which collaboration is the norm rather than the exception. These approaches are initially aimed at supporting team collaboration, whereas other studies have explored the potential of systems and processes that in various ways enable and exploit crowd-sourcing in creative processes. One such example, which combines individual and collaborative efforts, is found in *Ensemble* [18], a web-based collaborative writing system that employs crowd-sourcing input based on a lead authors prompts. Chan et al. [2] have similarly examined how facilitators can improve crowd-based creative processes, and Luther et al. [21] have demonstrated the benefits of crowd-sourcing design critique to improve designers' work.

In our own work, we have among other things developed digital ideation support systems such as *iCard*, a multi surface collaborative ideation system, the *Process Reflection Tool* [5], an online system for documenting and collaborating on creative design projects, and explored and developed novel formats and setups to support collaborative design and involvement of end users, e.g. via *Dialogue Labs* [20].

Key themes and questions of the workshop

Based on the themes identified in related work, and on our findings from previous and ongoing research projects, we propose to explore the following four themes pertaining to methodological, theoretical, use-oriented, and design-oriented challenges. We remain open to incorporating further themes from participants based on their position papers.

1) *Studying computer-supported collaborative creativity*. Studying computer-supported collaborative creativity entails *methodological challenges*. Which study approaches are apt for capturing and analysing collaborative creativity? How can we identify the particular role that a digital system or tool plays in the process? How can we study creative processes of different time spans, e.g. a single ideation event vs an entire creative project? How do we examine the use and impact of tools in collaborative and distributed processes, as opposed to an individual's use of a tool? Which questions do we ask when studying such tools,

Participants and selection criteria

Maximum number of participants: 25. Participants will be selected on the basis of the position papers (2- 4 pages) described in the *How to Participate* section.

Duration: 1 full day.

Announcement and recruitment: The workshop will be announced on a dedicated website providing a more thorough description potential tools for documenting design processes, and on mailing lists (CHI Announcements, PhD Design List, etc.). Furthermore, the organisers will actively recruit participants through their networks in the HCI community.

Required facilities: The workshop requires no special facilities beyond a standard room for joint work, and adjacent facilities for break-out groups.

and how do we pose them? How do we study the potential effects of a novel system at a prototype level, as opposed to studying existing systems that are well incorporated into use situations? How can we productively combine methods to study collaborative creativity in controlled settings (in vitro) and in real-life situations (in vivo) [26]?

2) *Understanding the role and nature of digital tools in collaborative creativity*. Understanding the role and nature of digital tools in collaborative creativity entails *theoretical challenges*. Which theories can we build on when we seek to understand such tools? To which extent can we lean on existing frameworks in HCI - many of which are arguably oriented towards functional aspects [22] and may have little to say about creative processes - and to which extent is there a need to import or develop novel perspectives? Are there well-developed strands of theory outside of the normal scope of HCI research that are particularly apt for these purposes?

3) *Transitions and dynamics between individual and collaborative work*.

Co-located collaboration in creative industries is often mixed-focus collaboration [25] and transition between phases of tightly coupled collaboration between team members and loosely coupled parallel work during which individuals pursue own approaches or prepare their personal contributions to the joint effort [16]. This entails a number of use-oriented challenges when it comes to the transitions and dynamics between individual and collaborative work. How can we support the interplay between these different modes of activity, and how can we help creatives transition between them? In many real-world practices, creative collaboration is a distributed, concurrent, and sometimes seemingly chaotic activity that eludes predefined sequences or rigid application structures. Is it possible to accomodate messy and unpredictable processes, and how? What is the role of spatial cognition and physical movement in space for individual and collaborative interaction? Also, which novel modes of collaboration do digital tools enable, e.g. crowd-sourcing, and how can we (re)design creative processes to accomodate them?

4) *Mimicking existing tools and approaches and/or developing novel ones*.

Creative work is often built around well-established processes and routines, and novel tools and approaches must build on a thorough understanding of how and why existing processes and structures work, and how they are embedded into the spatial and social structures of the studio. This presents us with a series of *design challenges*. When and how is it feasible and desirable to replace existing tools with novel digital ones, and when is it preferable to provide novel tools as supplements to existing practices? How can we - and when should we - create hybrids of existing and new tools? How do we involve creative professionals and domain experts in the design of new systems? Many existing collaborative creative work practices to a large extent relies on analogue tools, such as pen, paper, sticky notes, and whiteboards. What makes these tools so well suited for these processes, and what are the good strategies for finding the proper mix of analogue and digital tools?

Organizers

Peter Dalsgaard

Nanna Inie

Nicilai Brodersen Hansen

How to participate

The workshop requires participants to commit to capturing and documenting one or more cases in which digital tools have been employed to support collaborative creativity. This documentation forms the basis for the presentations during the workshop and grounds the subsequent discussions. In order to participate, interested parties must therefore do the following:

1) Submit a proposal (2-4 pages SIGCHI Extended Abstracts Format) describing the case to be documented, the project or institutional/organizational frame (e.g. at which institution or company is it carried out and what partners are involved), the focus of the case (for instance, how a novel multi-surface tool can support collaborative ideation; how skilled practitioners have adapted a tool to fit specific needs in a work practice; how an online system has opened up new opportunities for crowd-sourced concept development, etc.), and the method and strategy for documenting the project.

2) Participants must then document the case as outlined in their proposals. This work forms the empirical data for the workshop.

Organizers

Peter Dalsgaard is an Associate Professor at Aarhus University. His work combines practice-based experimental interaction design projects and theoretical developments aimed at understanding and developing digitally enhanced tools and spaces that help people create and innovate. He is the PI and director of three major research projects that explore the role of digital tools in creative processes: *CoCreate, Creative Tools,* and *PLACED*. He has published a series of conference and journal articles on creativity and design, and has extensive experience in organising research workshops, and has been the organiser of workshops at e.g. *Creativity and Cognition*, *CHI*, and DIS.

Nanna Inie is a PhD student on the project *Creativity in Blended Interaction Spaces*. Her work focuses on understanding the emergence and transformation of design ideas. This includes studies and surveys of real-life creative work practices as well as controlled studies of particular forms of ideation and concept development techniques.

Nicolai Brodersen Hansen is a Postdoc in the project *Creativity in Blended Interaction Spaces*. His research focuses on design materials and their role and nature in design processes, particularly in Participatory Design. His research is published in venues such as DIS, NordiCHI, CoDesign, Communities & Technologies, and the International Journal of Human-Computer Studies.

Acknowledgements

This work is sponsored by the grants *CIBIS* (Creativity in Blended Interaction Spaces) from Innovation Fund Denmark, *CoCreate* from the Velux Foundations, and *Creative Tools* from the Aarhus University Research Foundation.

References

1. Amabile, T. (1983). *The social psychology of creativity.* New York: Springer-Verlag.
2. Chan, J., Dang, S., & Dow, S. P. (2016). Improving crowd innovation with expert facilitation. In *Proceedings of the 19th ACM Conference on Computer-Supported Cooperative Work & Social Computing* (pp. 1223-1235). ACM.

3. Csikszentmihalyi, M. (1988). Society, culture, and person: A systems view of creativity. In R. J. Sternberg (Ed.), *The nature of creativity* (pp. 325–339). New York: Cambridge University Press.
4. Dalsgaard, P., Halskov, K., & Nielsen, R. (2008). Maps for design reflection. *Artifact*, 2(3-4), 176-189.
5. Dalsgaard, P., & Halskov, K. (2012, June). Reflective design documentation. In *Proceedings of the Designing Interactive Systems Conference* (pp. 428-437). ACM.
6. Edmonds, E.A. and Candy, L. (1996) Computer support for concept engineering design: Enabling interaction with design knowledge. Journal of Systems Engineering and Electronics 7, 2 (1996), 55--71.
7. EY (2014): *Creating growth: Measuring cultural and creative markets in the EU.* Accessed online 2016-10-15 at http://www.creatingeurope.eu/
8. Fischer, G., Giaccardi, E., Eden, H., Sugimoto, M., & Ye, Y. (2005). Beyond binary choices: Integrating individual and social creativity. *International Journal of Human-Computer Studies*, 63(4), 482-512.
9. Gedenryd, H. (1998). *How Designers Work*, Sverige, Lund University Cognitive Studies.
10. Guilford, J. P. (1950). Creativity. *The American Psychologist, 5,* 444–454.
11. Halskov, K., Dalsgaard, P. 2007, "The Emergence of Ideas", CoDesign – International Journal of CoCreation in Design and the Arts, vol. 3 no. 4, pp. 185 – 211.
12. Harrison, S. (Ed.). (2009). *Media space: 20+ years of mediated life*. Springer Science & Business Media.
13. Herrmann, T. (2010). Support of collaborative creativity for Co-located Meetings. In *From CSCW to Web 2.0: European Developments in Collaborative Design* (pp. 65-95). Springer London.
14. Hutchins, E. (1995). *Cognition in the Wild*. MIT Press.
15. Jacucci, G., & Wagner, I. (2007). Performative roles of materiality for collective creativity. In Proceedings of 6th ACM SIGCHI conference on Creativity & cognition, ACM, 73-82.
16. Jetter, H. C., Gerken, J., Zöllner, M., Reiterer, H., & Milic-Frayling, N. (2011, May). Materializing the query with facet-streams: a hybrid surface for collaborative search on tabletops. In *Proceedings of the SIGCHI Conference on Human Factors in Computing Systems* (pp. 3013-3022). ACM.
17. Jetter, H. C., Reiterer, H., & Geyer, F. (2014). Blended Interaction: understanding natural human–computer interaction in post-WIMP interactive spaces. *Personal and Ubiquitous Computing*, 18(5), 1139-1158.
18. Kim, J., Cheng, J., & Bernstein, M. S. (2014). Ensemble: exploring complementary strengths of leaders and crowds in creative collaboration. In *Proceedings of the 17th ACM conference on Computer supported cooperative work & social computing* (pp. 745-755). ACM.
19. Klokmose, C. N., Eagan, J. R., Baader, S., Mackay, W., and Beaudouin-Lafon, M. (2015). Webstrates: Shareable Dynamic Media. Proceedings of ACM User Interface Software and Technology 2015.
20. Lucero, A., Vaajakallio, K., & Dalsgaard, P. (2012). The dialogue-labs method: process, space and materials as structuring elements to spark dialogue in co-design events. *CoDesign*, *8*(1), 1-23.
21. Luther, K., Tolentino, J. L., Wu, W., Pavel, A., Bailey, B. P., Agrawala, M., & Dow, S. P. (2015). Structuring, aggregating, and evaluating crowdsourced design critique. In *Proceedings of the 18th ACM Conference on Computer Supported*

Cooperative Work & Social Computing (pp. 473-485). ACM.

22. Rogers, Y. (2004). New theoretical approaches for HCI. *Annual review of information science and technology*, *38*(1), 87-143.
23. Sawyer, R. K. (2008). *Group genius*: The creative power of collaboration. Basic Books.
24. Smith, S.M., Linsey, J.S., Kerne, A. (2010). "Using Evolved Analogies to Overcome Creative Design Fixation." Proceedings of Design Creativity 2010, 35-39.
25. Tang, A., Tory, M., Po, B., Neumann, P., & Carpendale, S. (2006, April). Collaborative coupling over tabletop displays. In *Proceedings of the SIGCHI conference on Human Factors in computing systems* (pp. 1181-1190). ACM.
26. Wiltschnig, S., & Onarheim, B. (2010). Insights into insight-How do in-vitro studies of creative insight match the real-world complexity of in-vivo design processes. In *Design Research Society International Conference*.

Creative Artefacts and Digital Technology: Enriching Urban Societies through Interactive Experiences

Cynthia C. S. Liem
Multimedia Computing Group
Delft University of Technology
Delft, The Netherlands
c.c.s.liem@tudelft.nl

Andrew Quitmeyer
Communications and New Media
Department
National University of Singapore
cnmqaj@nus.edu.sg

C&C '17, June 27-30, 2017, Singapore, Singapore
ACM 978-1-4503-4403-6/17/06.
http://dx.doi.org/10.1145/3059454.3059484

Abstract
In this workshop, we will interactively and jointly investigate with the community how intrinsic creative and artistic values, technology and society are critical to one another, and how our present-day urban and digital societies can demonstrably be enriched and advanced by effective connections between these all. The workshop will include interactive discussions, as well as a hands-on outdoors making session.

Author Keywords
Cultural artefacts; digital technology; consumption; engagement; audiences

ACM Classification Keywords
J.5 Arts and Humanities; H.5.1 Multimedia Information Systems; H1.2 User/Machine Systems; H5.2 User Interfaces; J.4 Social and Behavioral Sciences; J.3 Life and Medical Sciences

Motivation
Amidst fast economic growth and digital globalization, our urban societies are confronted with increasing information overload, a strong focus on immediate fulfilment, and full-time productivity and availability demands. In such environments, creative

and artistic expressions may be considered 'irrelevant' or even 'useless' to society.

However, intrinsic values connected to creative and artistic expressions (e.g. being triggered to think 'outside the box', being able to consider material from different perspectives) may actually play a critical role in keeping our urban and digital societies healthy, happy, informed and connected. Novel technology will often play a major role here, both as supporting enabler to realize enrichments, but also as a consequence of implementing intrinsic creative values.

In this workshop, in an interdisciplinary setting, we therefore want to initiate discussions on how we can bring such points forward better. In an integrated making session, for these discussions, we will both have ourselves be inspired by the natural urban environment, and try to inspire the other people for whom this environment is part of their daily lives.

Foreseen discussion topics

The artist and audience perspective

As artists, we are good at creating creative artefacts. As technologists, we are good at representing and enriching the creative artefact digitally. Digital technology opens opportunities for artists to express themselves in richer ways, and for audiences to engage with the resulting artefacts in more versatile ways as well. Doing this in the right way requires solving considerable challenges though. What do our audiences need? Is technology already capable of handling our creative requirements? How can audiences be properly reached and engaged in a world of digital abundance?

The societal utility perspective

This is not the end of the story. Creative artefacts are more than mere library items, but also more than mere entertainment. They can help people detaching from everyday routines, stimulate people to be more effective at completing such routines, and help creating atmosphere and setting scenes in everyday non-cultural settings. Are we already sufficiently aware of this broader societal utility of the creative artefact, and do we sufficiently act on this?

The information consumption perspective

Finally, creative artefacts fundamentally are meant to engage people deeply and longitudinally, to broaden their horizons, maybe slightly get them out of their comfort zones, and make them experience the world in new ways. Considering how we interact, consume information, and organize our lives digitally amidst information overload, these intrinsic values have become increasingly non-trivial. Can we find ways to reintegrate them, and thus counteract current concerns on polarization and superficiality in digital consumption?

Making session

To make the discussed ideas more concrete, we will connect the discussions to an outdoors making session in Singapore's Fort Canning Park. Considering the topics mentioned above, what could be appropriate interactive interfaces that would enrich the urban citizen's environment? How can such interfaces be integrated into the natural environments these citizens will pass through and appreciate? How can they help in impacting a citizens' world perspectives and daily life experiences in positive ways?

Organizer bio

Dr. Cynthia C. S. Liem MMus is an assistant professor at the Multimedia Computing Group of Delft University of Technology. She holds degrees in both Computer Science and Classical Piano Performance, and gained industrial experience interning at Bell Labs Europe Netherlands, Philips Research, Google UK and Google Research, Mountain View, USA. Her research interests involve pushing a multimedia paradigm to digital music analysis, exploiting multiple sources of music information to quantify consumption-relevant information beyond 'objective description' (e.g. affective, subjective, artistic, and utility-oriented aspects), and employing recommendation techniques for stimulating taste broadening towards serendipitous new interests.

She co-acquired and co-coordinated the European FP7 PHENICX project, focusing on digital enrichment of classical symphonic concert performances. Besides, she was the leader of the Social Zap subproject of the Dutch national FES COMMIT SEALINCMedia project (Socially Enriched Access to Linked Cultural Media). Currently, she leads the Delft Data Science 'Smart Culture' focus area, connecting data science expertise to smart technological approaches to cultural resources.

As a computer scientist, she is recipient of several prestigious awards, including the Lucent Global Science (2005) and Google Anita Borg Europe Memorial (2008) scholarships and the Google European Doctoral Fellowship 2010 in Multimedia. Besides, in 2016 she was elected as Teacher of the Year in Computer Science by the Delft University of Technology students. As a performing musician, her Magma Duo (with Emmy Storms, violin) has been award-winning both nationally and internationally. The debut CD of the Magma Duo has been released internationally in Summer 2016.

Dr. Andrew Quitmeyer is a digital adventurer studying intersections between wild animals and computational devices. His PhD research in "Digital Naturalism" from Georgia Tech blends biological fieldwork and DIY digital crafting. This work has taken him through the wilds of Panama, Madagascar, and Southeast Asia where he's run workshops with diverse groups of scientists, artists, designers, and engineers. Much of his current work involves running series of "Hiking Hacks" around the world where participants build technology entirely in the wild for interacting with nature. This work has even spun off into an international television series he hosted for Discovery Networks. Andy is the winner of several design awards and his trans-disciplinary, multimedia projects have been featured in Wired, PBS, NPR, Cartoon Network, Make Magazine, Fast Company, Gizmodo, along with other print and digital internet news and educational sources. He currently serves as an Assistant Professor in the Communications and New Media Department of the National University of Singapore.

Author Index

NOTES

www.ingramcontent.com/pod-product-compliance
Ingram Content Group UK Ltd.
Pitfield, Milton Keynes, MK11 3LW, UK
UKHW051417290926
15471UKWH00009B/1642

9 781450 356077